THE FEDERAL INCOME TAXATION OF CORPORATIONS, PARTNERSHIPS, LIMITED LIABILITY COMPANIES, AND THEIR OWNERS

FOURTH EDITION

by

JEFFREY L. KWALL
Kathleen and Bernard Beazley Professor of Law
Loyola University Chicago School of Law

FOUNDATION PRESS
2012

THOMSON REUTERS™

© 1995, 2000, 2005 FOUNDATION PRESS
© 2012 By THOMSON REUTERS/FOUNDATION PRESS

      1 New York Plaza, 34th Floor
      New York, NY 10004
      Phone Toll Free 1–877–888–1330
      Fax 646–424–5201
      foundation–press.com

Printed in the United States of America

ISBN 978–1–59941–400–3

Mat #40642836

To my sister,
Donna Kwall Smith,

and to the memory of our parents,
Saul A. Kwall and Clara Sigal Kwall

PREFACE TO THE FOURTH EDITION

Much has occurred during the seventeen years since this casebook was originally published. Many Internal Revenue Code provisions have been amended. New regulations, court decisions and Internal Revenue Service rulings have modified and clarified many of the rules governing the three business tax regimes: the C Corporation, the S Corporation and the partnership. In addition, the novel tax issues presented by limited liability companies and other relatively new unincorporated business forms have begun to be addressed.

Notwithstanding the many changes that have occurred during the past seventeen years, the original structure of this casebook continues to reflect the current landscape. Although the fourth edition incorporates all relevant changes in the law and several new cases and rulings, the overall structure of the book remains intact. Moreover, the philosophy that guided the creation of this book continues to guide the fourth edition. The Preface to the First Edition delineates this philosophy and follows in its entirety. Readers are encouraged to examine the Preface to the First Edition carefully and to return to it frequently throughout their course of study.

The fourth edition has profited from many helpful comments and suggestions received from colleagues including Evelyn Brody, Mary Ferrari, Cliff Fleming, Christian Johnson, Lloyd Mayer, Denise Roy, and Chris Sanchirico. Thanks to Dean David Yellen and Associate Deans Michael Kaufman and James Faught for their continued support and to Loyola University Chicago School of Law for research support. I have had valuable student assistance on this edition from Jacqueline Helmrick, Jonathan Motto, Nicholas Novak, Janet Soave, Yelena Vayner, Katherine Wilbur, and Sam Wieczorek.

The fourth edition was prepared with knowledge of events reported through September 30, 2011.

JEFFREY L. KWALL
Chicago, Illinois

September 2011

PREFACE TO THE FIRST EDITION

Most students using this casebook recently completed a basic law school course in personal income tax. These students probably expect the study of business taxation to differ dramatically from the study of personal income tax. After all, the basic course focused on the taxation of individuals, whereas this casebook addresses the taxation of corporations, partnerships and limited liability companies. In spite of its appearance, however, this casebook draws upon and further develops much of what was learned in the basic income tax course.

The basic tax course introduced the fundamental concepts on which the United States system for taxing income is based. These concepts were explored in contexts to which the uninitiated student could most easily relate; namely, the personal and business activities of an individual. This casebook is designed to deepen the student's understanding of the same fundamental concepts introduced in the basic course. It explores these concepts in the context of issues that arise when a business takes on a legal identity of its own; specifically, when the business is conducted by a corporation, a partnership or a limited liability company.

Three alternative tax regimes ("C Corporation", "S Corporation", and "partnership") apply to businesses that are accorded a legal identity separate from their individual owners. The tax regime that applies to a given business depends largely on the legal form in which that business is conducted. Every corporation is taxed as a "C Corporation" or as an "S Corporation". Most state law partnerships and limited liability companies are governed by the "partnership" tax regime.

This casebook deviates from most business tax casebooks by examining the three different tax regimes in an integrated fashion, rather than treating each tax regime as a discrete subject. Several of the major topics explored in this casebook are divided into separate chapters on each tax regime. This approach is intended to encourage a comparison of the three regimes on an ongoing basis. This end may be achieved by studying the chapters in the order presented or, in the alternative, by examining all the chapters that apply to each regime separately and deferring a comparison until later in the course. In either case, a primary goal of the casebook is to foster the ability to compare the tax consequences of all three tax regimes, an ability that has become increasingly important in recent years in light of fundamental reforms that dramatically changed the relative tax costs associated with each of the three tax regimes.

This casebook is divided into six parts. Parts One through Four are designed to accommodate a basic business taxation course that examines the fundamentals of the three different tax regimes that apply to business enterprise. Part One (Chapter 1) provides an overview of the different legal forms in which a business may be conducted and the Federal income tax treatment of these different forms. After this overview, Part Two (Chapters 2 through 4) explores how the income of a business is defined and taxed under each of the three alternative tax regimes: C Corporation, S Corporation and partnership. Part Two focuses on the operational stage of the business, rather than adhering to the more traditional approach of beginning with the tax issues that arise when a new business is formed. The casebook begins at the operational stage so that the study of business taxation will parallel the basic personal income tax course which focused on how the income of an individual is defined and taxed. Part Three (Chapters 5 through 7) focuses on the consequences that follow when business profits are physically transferred by the business to its owners. Part Three examines the tax consequences to the business and its owners under each of the three tax regimes when business profits are distributed. After distributions are examined, Part Four (Chapters 8 through 10) explores the tax consequences that result under each of the three tax regimes when value is transferred in the opposite direction; namely, from the owner to the business.

Parts Five and Six of the casebook examine a series of more advanced corporate transactional issues. Part Five (Chapters 11 through 14) focuses on the tax consequences that result when a corporate business is disposed of (or acquired) in a taxable sale or a nontaxable reorganization. Part Six (Chapters 15 and 16) addresses the tax consequences that occur when a corporation divests itself of a business or when a corporation's capital structure or operating entity is modified. While some students may be introduced to the materials in Parts Five and Six in a basic business taxation course, an in-depth examination of these topics normally must be reserved for a more advanced course. The organization of this casebook reflects the fact that choices must be made in terms of how much can be covered in a basic business taxation course. This organization also reflects the judgment that a business lawyer who used this book in law school is more likely to seek the assistance of a tax expert when dealing with an out of the ordinary corporate disposition, acquisition, division or rearrangement, than when counseling a client with respect to the choice of business form, day-to-day operating activities, and transfers of value to and from the business.

This casebook is not intended to serve as a comprehensive source of all of the income tax rules that currently apply to business enterprises and their owners. Nor is it intended to analyze in great detail every rule it identifies. Instead, its goal is to examine existing law as a means of furthering the student's understanding of the underlying fundamental concepts and of refining the student's ability to master technically complex rules. This approach is taken for two reasons. First, in light of the frequency with which tax legislation has been enacted in recent years, many of the current rules are likely to be changed or refined by the time that students taking this course graduate from law school. In addition, even if the rules do not change, it is unlikely that students will remember in detail many of the technical rules explored in this course after the final exam ends! Consequently, a principal goal of the casebook is to cause the student to raise the right question, rather than to think that he or she knows the right answer.

A great deal of care has gone into the selection of cases for inclusion in this casebook. Aside from selecting cases on the basis of each court's substantive analysis, many cases were chosen to expose students to practical problems that arise in the conduct of a business. Taxation is a highly practical endeavor and those students who have not been exposed to real world business decisions can learn from the events described in these cases. Other cases demonstrate how a lawyer who counsels a client in connection with a business transaction can create serious tax problems for the client if the lawyer is inadequately versed in the tax law. Hopefully, these cases will alert those students who do not specialize in taxation of the importance of knowing when to seek the assistance of a more knowledgeable professional.

Most of the explanatory materials in this casebook are developed in the notes that follow the cases and rulings, rather than provided in advance of the cases and rulings. This approach is intended to enable the student to think independently about the particular issues explored in the case or ruling before editorial discussion is provided to help channel the student's thinking. Examples and problems are included where appropriate, though an effort has been made not to stress mechanics to the point that the inevitable uncertainties of the law become obscured. Most of the cases and rulings reproduced in this casebook have been heavily edited with the deletions indicated by asterisks. Many of the original footnotes in the cases have been deleted and those that remain are numbered consecutively, rather than preserving the original numbering from the case. Editorial additions are designated as such.

I owe gratitude to many individuals. I thank Stuart Duhl for teaching me how to put the tax law into perspective. I thank Alan Gunn for continuously offering thoughtful insights and suggestions over the entire course of this project. I thank Loretta Argrett, Evelyn Body, Patricia Bryan, Glenn Coven, Mary Ferrari, Stuart Filler, Christine Manolakas, William Popkin, Philip Postlewaite, George Yin and Lawrence Zelenak for many helpful comments and suggestions. I thank Dean Nina Appel, Associate Dean Thomas Haney and my colleagues and friends at Loyola University Chicago School of Law and at Schwartz & Freeman for their interest and encouragement. Gratitude is also expressed to Loyola University Chicago for research support. For invaluable research and editorial assistance, I thank Sally Joyce, Tom Thesing, Sara Fiedler, Jamie Goldman, Linda Hanes, Ginger Heyman, Eileen Rosen, Candyce Wilson, David Buckley, William Hahn, Lauri Aldrich, Jim Montague, and Matt Bryant. Appreciation is also expressed to all of the students who were taught from earlier drafts of this work. Thanks to Patricia Hallen for secretarial assistance. I also wish to lovingly thank my wife, Bobbi, and my daughters Shanna, Rachel and Nisa for tolerating my obsession with this project.

Finally, I encourage students not to view the road ahead as a dry and dusty one. Many students probably approached the personal income tax course with dread, yet found the experience to be quite stimulating. Most (all?) students should find the taxation of business enterprise to be at least as satisfying. With this expectation, let us begin.

JEFFREY L. KWALL
Chicago, Illinois

September, 1994

SUMMARY OF CONTENTS

PART ONE. INTRODUCTION

Chapter

PART TWO. OPERATIONS

TABLE OF CONTENTS

PART ONE. INTRODUCTION

Chapter

PART TWO. OPERATIONS

TABLE OF INTERNAL REVENUE CODE SECTIONS

TABLE OF TREASURY REGULATIONS

TABLE OF INTERNAL REVENUE RULINGS

TABLE OF MISCELLANEOUS RULINGS

TABLE OF CASES

Principal cases are in bold type. Non-principal cases are in roman type. References are to Pages.

TABLE OF AUTHORITIES

THE FEDERAL INCOME TAXATION OF CORPORATIONS, PARTNERSHIPS, LIMITED LIABILITY COMPANIES, AND THEIR OWNERS

PART ONE

INTRODUCTION

The law of the United States takes two fundamentally different approaches to taxing business income. The income of many corporations is taxed to the corporation when earned and again to the shareholders when corporate profits are distributed to them. In contrast, the income of most corporations, partnerships and limited liability companies is taxed only once, directly to the owners of the enterprise when the income is earned. Part One of this casebook provides an historical overview of the dramatically different effects of these alternative approaches to taxing business income. Part One also considers a proposal for taxing all enterprises in a uniform manner, regardless of their legal form. Though unlikely to be adopted in the foreseeable future, the proposal provides a useful perspective for examining and contrasting the multiple approaches to taxing business income that now exist.

*

CHAPTER 1

PERSPECTIVE

The basic personal income tax course normally explores the principle that the owner of property is taxed on any income generated by that property.[1] Accordingly, if a collection of assets owned by an individual comprises a business (a "sole proprietorship"), all income generated by the business is taxed to that individual. State law does not treat the sole proprietorship as an entity that owns property separately from the individual entrepreneur. Similarly, Federal law does not treat the sole proprietorship as a separate entity for income tax purposes. If state law did treat the business as a separate entity, Federal tax law might also treat it as a separate entity, in which case income of the business might be taxed to the business entity, rather than to the individual proprietor.

In contrast to a sole proprietorship, when individuals create a business by pooling their resources (a state law partnership) or by utilizing a business form of statutory creation (a corporation or a limited liability company), the business, rather than its individual owners, is normally viewed by state law as the owner of the property. Who does Federal tax law treat as the taxpayer under these circumstances? Does the tax law also regard the business as separate from its owners and tax the business, itself, or is income generated by the business still taxed directly to the individual owners of the business? The answers to these questions depend on the legal form in which the business is conducted and on how that legal form is treated under the Federal tax law.

A. THE BUSINESS AS AN ENTITY UNDER STATE LAW

For purposes of state law, a partnership exists when two or more individuals engage collectively in an activity with the expectation of generating profits. Under these circumstances, state law recognizes the partnership as the owner of the enterprise's assets. A partnership is a very flexible business form because it is a purely consensual arrangement. Any of the individual owners of the partnership (any "partner") may dissolve the partnership at any time and depart with her share of the assets of the

---

1. See, e.g., Helvering v. Horst, 311 U.S. 112, 61 S.Ct. 144 (1940)(holding that interest paid on a coupon bond owned by parent was included in the parent's gross income, notwithstanding that the parent gratuitously transferred the coupon to child who collected the interest from the issuer).

enterprise (though generally not the specific assets that she contributed). Moreover, each partner is personally responsible for any partnership obligations that arise during the existence of the partnership.[2]

A corporation is a more rigid arrangement than a partnership. Collective business activity alone does not create a corporation. Indeed, the presence of a corporation is not contingent upon a pooling of resources by more than one individual; a single individual can create a corporation. To have a corporation, the owner or owners of an enterprise must follow the specific state law requirements for creating that entity. Once the entity is created, the assets of the enterprise must be transferred (by assignment or deed) to the corporation. The corporation is recognized by state law as a legal entity, separate from its owners ("shareholders"). State law provides that the corporation owns the assets of the enterprise and is solely responsible for any obligations of the enterprise. Absent a contractual agreement to the contrary, the shareholders are not personally responsible for obligations of the corporation. Thus, the shareholders of the corporation are exposed to corporate obligations only to the extent of their investment in the corporation. The shareholders merely own stock in the corporation which represents legal ownership of the corporation and a stake in the corporation's assets and any future profits.[3]

The limited liability company is an alternative business form of relatively recent origin now authorized by all states. Though a limited liability company resembles a corporation in many respects, it accommodates more flexible business arrangements. Like a corporation, a limited liability company can be created only by following the requirements of state law. The limited liability company is treated as a legal entity, separate from its individual owners ("members") and is recognized as the owner of the enterprise's property. The members of a limited liability company, like the shareholders of a corporation, are exposed to obligations of the enterprise only to the extent of their investment in the limited liability company.[4]

The fact that state law treats the partnership, the corporation and the limited liability company as the owner of the enterprise does not dictate that any party other than the individual partners, shareholders or members

---

2. Limited partners are not personally responsible for the obligations of a limited partnership, a statutory creation that is examined in Chapter 4. For additional information on the state law implications of a partnership, see Alan R. Bromberg and Larry E. Ribstein, *Bromberg and Ribstein on Partnership* (2008); J. William Callison & Maureen A. Sullivan, *Partnership Law and Practice, General and Limited Partnerships* (2002 and Supp. 2011).

3. For additional information on the state law implications of a corporation, see Harry G. Henn & John R. Alexander, *Laws of Corporations* (3d ed. 1983 & Supp. 1986); William M. Fletcher, *Fletcher Cyclopedia of the Law of Corporations* (2010); F. Hodge O'Neal & Robert B. Thompson, *O'Neal's and Thompson's Close Corporations and LLCs* (rev. 3d ed. 2004 & Supp. 2011).

4. For additional information on the state law implications of a limited liability company, see Larry E. Ribstein & Robert R. Keatinge, *Ribstein and Keatinge on Limited Liability Companies* (2d ed. 2010). The limited liability company is examined in greater detail in Chapter 4.

be taxed on the income of the enterprise. No partnership, corporation or limited liability company can exist by itself. Rather, the existence of every enterprise conducted in these forms, irrespective of its magnitude, ultimately can be traced to individual partners, shareholders or members. Thus, all business income presumably could be taxed to the individual owners of the enterprise irrespective of the legal form in which the business is conducted.

If, at the end of each year, all business income was divided and distributed among the individual owners of the enterprise, it would be a relatively simple matter to tax that income to the individuals to whom it is attributable. Quite often, however, the enterprise retains the income it generates and reinvests this income to maintain or expand the enterprise. Under these circumstances, it is appealing, if not necessary, to accord some tax significance to the enterprise. At the very least, it is convenient to treat the enterprise as an accounting entity for tax purposes where income can be calculated and then be allocated among the individual owners. Alternatively, it may be desirable not only to calculate income at the enterprise level, but also to tax the enterprise on that income.

The Federal tax treatment of a business enterprise depends largely on the legal form in which the business is conducted. As a general rule, corporations are treated as taxpaying entities. In other words, the corporation pays tax on the enterprise's income. (The shareholders are also taxed, but not until the corporation's income is distributed to them.) Corporations treated as taxpaying entities are identified by the tax law as "C Corporations" because the taxation of these corporations is governed by Subchapter C (I.R.C. §§ 301–385) of Chapter 1 of Subtitle A of the Internal Revenue Code.

In contrast to corporations, most state law partnerships and limited liability companies are treated simply as accounting entities. These enterprises are identified as "partnerships" by the tax law and are governed by Subchapter K (I.R.C. §§ 701–777) of Chapter 1 of Subtitle A of the Internal Revenue Code. The income of an enterprise taxed as a partnership is computed by the enterprise but such income is taxed directly to the individual owners of the enterprise. Certain corporations also may elect to be treated as accounting entities. Eligible corporations that so elect are identified by the tax law as "S Corporations" because the taxation of these corporations is governed by Subchapter S (I.R.C. §§ 1361–1378) of Chapter 1 of Subtitle A of the Internal Revenue Code. In recent years, S Corporations have significantly outnumbered C Corporations.[5]

---

5. The following is a rough estimate of the number of enterprises reporting to the Internal Revenue Service in 2010 as:

C Corporations	2,000,000	(20%)
S Corporations	4,400,000	(45%)
Partnerships	3,400,000	(35%)

Internal Revenue Service, *Statistics of Income Bulletin* (Spring 2011), Table 22.

B.   THE BUSINESS AS A TAXPAYING ENTITY— THE C CORPORATION

Since 1913, C Corporations have been taxed on their income.   In addition to this corporate tax, the individual income tax is imposed on C Corporation income, but not until the corporation distributes its earnings to its shareholders (pays dividends).   Therefore, the income of a C Corporation is taxed twice.

The fact that the income of C Corporations is taxed twice does not mean that twice as much tax is imposed on corporate income as on individual income derived from other sources.   The total tax burden on corporate income depends largely upon the design of the corporate tax.   The corporate tax could be designed to *substitute* for part or all of the tax that the individual owners would otherwise pay on the business's income, in which case the corporate tax merely serves as a mechanism for collecting the individual income tax on business profits that are not immediately distributed to the owners.   Alternatively, the corporate tax could be designed to *supplement* the individual income tax on the owners' profits, in which case some independent justification should exist for taxing corporate income more heavily than other forms of income.

Exhibit I compares the tax burden on corporate income distributed as dividends to the tax burden on individual income from other sources.   Columns A and B list the maximum corporate tax rate and the maximum individual tax rate, respectively, over time. Column C shows the effective rate of the double tax on corporate income distributed as dividends.   Column D compares the double tax on dividends to the single tax that applies to an individual's income from other sources.

EXHIBIT I[6]

Comparison of Double Tax on Dividends
With Single Tax on Other Income

Years	(A) Maximum Corporate Tax Rate	(B) Maximum Individual Tax Rate	(C) Double Tax on Dividends	(D) Column C As a % of Column B
1913–1915	1.00%	7.0%	6.94%	99%
1916	2.00%	15.0%	14.74%	98%
1917	6.00%	54.0%	53.00%	98%
1918	12.00%	77.0%	69.20%	90%
1919–1921	10.00%	73.0%	68.50%	94%
1922–1923	12.50%	58.0%	56.25%	97%
1924	12.50%	46.0%	47.50%	103%

---

6.   Derived from Jeffrey L. Kwall, "Subchapter G of the Internal Revenue Code: Crusade Without a Cause?," 5 Virginia Tax Review 223 (1985).

Years	(A) Maximum Corporate Tax Rate	(B) Maximum Individual Tax Rate	(C) Double Tax on Dividends	(D) Column C As a % of Column B
1925	13.00%	25.0%	30.40%	122%
1926–1927	13.50%	25.0%	30.80%	123%
1928	12.00%	25.0%	29.60%	118%
1929	11.00%	24.0%	28.80%	120%
1930–1931	12.00%	25.0%	29.60%	118%
1932–1933	13.75%	63.0%	61.19%	97%
1934–1935	13.75%	63.0%	64.64%	103%
1936–1937	15.00%	79.0%	82.15%	104%
1938–1939	19.00%	79.0%	82.46%	104%
1940	22.10%	79.0%	83.64%	106%
1941	31.00%	81.0%	86.89%	107%
1942–1943	40.00%	88.0%	92.90%	106%
1944–1945	40.00%	94.0%	96.40%	103%
1946–1947	38.00%	86.4%	91.57%	106%
1948–1949	38.00%	82.1%	88.90%	108%
1950	42.00%	84.4%	90.95%	108%
1951	50.75%	91.0%	95.57%	105%
1952–1953	52.00%	92.0%	96.16%	105%
1954–1963	52.00%	91.0%	93.76%	103%
1964	50.00%	77.0%	87.50%	114%
1965–1978	48.00%	70.0%	84.40%	121%
1979–1980	46.00%	70.0%	83.80%	120%
1981–1986	46.00%	50.0%	73.00%	146%
1987	40.00%	38.5%	63.10%	164%
1988–1990	34.00%	28.0%	52.48%	187%
1991–1992	34.00%	31.0%	54.46%	176%
1993–2000	35.00%	39.6%	60.74%	153%
2001	35.00%	39.1%	60.42%	155%
2002	35.00%	38.6%	60.09%	156%
2003–	35.00%	35.0%	44.75%[7]	128%

As Exhibit I demonstrates, prior to the 1980's, the two taxes imposed on corporate income distributed as dividends (column (C)) did not cause corporate income to bear a significantly greater burden than other forms of individual income that were taxed only once (column (B)). The burden of the double tax on corporate income was moderated by the fact that corporate tax rates (column (A)) were significantly lower than individual tax rates (column (B)).[8] Moreover, to the extent that corporate income was accumulated rather than immediately distributed, deferral of the high-rate

---

7. If $100 of corporate income is taxed at 35% (column (A)), a $35 corporate tax results. If the remaining $65 is paid out as a dividend, a 15% individual income tax is normally imposed ($65 x 15% = $9.75) because dividends received by individuals are now generally taxed at capital gains rates. I.R.C. §§ 1(h)(1), (11). Total taxes are $44.75 ($35 + $9.75 = $44.75).

8. During much of this period, dividends were also taxed less heavily than other forms of individual income. Indeed, from 1913–1923 and 1932–1933, the favorable treatment accorded dividends caused corporate income distributed as dividends to bear a lighter burden than other forms of individual income that were only taxed once. See Exhibit I, rows 1–6, 13.

individual income tax further reduced the overall tax burden on corporate income due to the time value of money.[9]   Finally, when shareholders sold their stock before accumulated earnings were distributed (in which case the accumulated earnings augmented the value of the stock), their gains were generally taxed at low capital gains rates, rather than at the higher individual tax rates that applied to dividends.[10]   Consequently, before the 1980's, the corporate tax did little more than neutralize the tax savings derived from the *deferral* of the individual income tax on accumulated corporate earnings and the *conversion* of potential dividends to capital gains.

From 1981 until 2002, corporate income distributed as dividends bore a significantly greater tax burden than other forms of individual income.[11] That result stemmed principally from the dramatically lower individual tax rates that prevailed during this period. By virtue of these lower rates, the tax burden on individual income other than dividends was much lower than in the past. Dividends, by contrast, continued to bear a large corporate tax in addition to the individual income tax. Congress offered no justification for taxing corporate income more heavily than other forms of income during this period.

In 2003, Congress drastically reduced the tax burden on dividends by causing dividends received by individuals to be taxed at the lower tax rates that apply to capital gains (generally 15%) while continuing to tax other individual income at rates as high as 35%. This favorable treatment of dividends is scheduled to expire at the end of 2012. Thus, the double taxation of corporate income has been temporarily reduced, but not eliminated.[12] Unfortunately, the relationship between the corporate tax and the individual income tax continues to evolve in a largely haphazard fashion, rather than from a clear Congressional policy.

C.   THE BUSINESS AS A TAX ACCOUNTING ENTITY—THE S CORPORATION AND THE PARTNERSHIP

The income of enterprises taxed as partnerships [13] and S Corporations (collectively referred to as "pass-through entities") is not normally subject

---

9. For a review of the time value of money, see pp. 468–470. For an explanation of how the time value of money reduces the tax burden on undistributed corporate income when individual tax rates exceed corporate rates, see Alvin C. Warren, Jr., "The Timing of Taxes," 39 National Tax Journal 499 (1986). Exhibit I does not reflect the impact of deferral on the tax burden on corporate income.

10. Exhibit I does not reflect the impact of capital gains rates on the tax burden on corporate income during this period.

11. See Exhibit I, compare columns (C) and (B). During this period, the tax burden on corporate income was greatly reduced when shareholders sold their stock before corporate earnings were distributed. When a sale occurred, individual shareholders were taxed at lower capital gains rates, rather than the higher ordinary income rates that then applied to dividends.

12. See Exhibit I, bottom row, column (D).

13. Some enterprises that are treated as partnerships under state law are not taxed as partnerships, but instead are taxed as C Corporations. See pp. 197–198. On the other hand, some enterprises that are not treated as partnerships under state law are taxed as partner-to the corporate tax or any other entity-level tax. Instead, the income of a pass-through entity is taxed immediately to the owners of the enterprise. Although the pass-through entity, itself, does not pay taxes, the owners must often withdraw a sufficient amount of the business's earnings to satisfy their personal income tax liabilities attributable to the income of the pass-through entity.

Prior to the 1980's, when corporate tax rates were significantly lower than individual tax rates, pass-through entities were generally disfavored tax regimes for profitable enterprises. Although the pass-through entity did not pay the corporate tax, its income was taxed to the owners of the enterprise, generally at much higher individual tax rates.[14] If the owners withdrew funds from the business to pay their personal income tax liabilities, the amount of earnings available to reinvest in the business was smaller than the amount of earnings available to a C Corporation with the same amount of income because the C Corporation could reinvest its earnings after paying the lower corporate tax.

Example 1–A (Amount of earnings available to reinvest in pass-through entity versus C Corporation): If the individual tax rate is 70% and the corporate tax rate is 40%, $100 of income earned by a pass-through entity generates $70 of tax liability to the owners. If the owners withdraw $70 to pay the tax they owe, only $30 remains for reinvestment in the business. In contrast, if the $100 is earned by a C Corporation, the corporation pays a tax of $40 and $60 remains to finance expansion of the business. While it is true that this $60 will someday be subjected to a second tax at the owner level, that future tax burden may not be important to the owners of a growing enterprise with a great need for capital.

Before the 1980's, when the maximum individual tax rate greatly exceeded the maximum corporate tax rate, pass-through entities generally appealed only to those income producing enterprises at the extreme ends of the business life-cycle continuum. The pass-through entity often was desired by the owners of the fledgling enterprise that generated small amounts of income. If the owners of these businesses had little income from outside sources, the income of the pass-through entity was subject to tax at individual tax rates far below the maximum individual rate and even lower than the corporate rate that applied to a C Corporation. At the other extreme, the pass-through entity was preferred over the C Corporation by the mature enterprise that was past its heyday and was winding down, perhaps because the original owners were advancing in age and unable to find successors. Although an enterprise at this stage often generates substantial amounts of income, the earnings are likely to be withdrawn by the owners (as dividends in the case of a C Corporation), rather than retained by the enterprise, because no interest exists in expanding the business. Consequently, as long as the individual income

---

ships. For example, most limited liability companies are taxed as partnerships. See pp. 192–197.

14. See pp. 6–7, Exhibit I, compare columns (A) and (B).

tax would be incurred immediately in any case, it made little sense to incur the corporate tax as well.[15]

In more recent years, individual tax rates have declined considerably. Now, the maximum individual tax rate is identical to the maximum corporate rate. Thus, the owners of a pass-through entity can satisfy their total tax burden by paying an individual tax that often approximates the corporate tax imposed on a C Corporation[16] and need not contend with a second tax when business profits are distributed. As a result, the pass-through entity is now generally favored over the C Corporation at all stages of the business life cycle.

D.   PROPOSAL FOR UNIFORM TAXATION OF ALL BUSINESSES— PREVIEW OF THE FUTURE?

The tax system that now exists generally imposes heavier burdens on the income of C Corporations than on the income of pass-through entities. In earlier years, the income of pass-through entities was often taxed more heavily than the income of C Corporations. When the income of a business subjected to one tax regime is taxed more heavily than the same amount of income generated by a business subjected to another tax regime, tax considerations are likely to influence the choice of business form decision. When the tax law influences a business decision, economic inefficiencies may result.

To eliminate the distortions created by the different tax regimes that now exist, many analysts advocate the adoption of a tax system that imposes the same tax burden on the income of a business, irrespective of the legal form in which the business is conducted. The process for achieving this goal is referred to as "integration". In its purest form, integration entails repealing the corporate tax and taxing corporate income directly to the corporation's shareholders when it is earned. In effect, every business, regardless of its legal form, is treated as a pass-through entity. Less extreme versions of integration involve retaining the corporate tax but reducing or eliminating the shareholder tax on dividends.

In 1992, the Treasury Department issued a comprehensive report intended to serve as "a source document to begin the debate on the desirability of integration." That report concludes that integration is desirable and explores several alternative techniques for accomplishing

---

15. Professionals, such as physicians and attorneys, generally conducted business in partnership form even when individual tax rates were much higher than corporate tax rates because they were originally barred by state law from using the corporate form of business. States did not allow the professional to incorporate his practice because the traditional corporation insulated the individual professional from malpractice claims. Many states subsequently enacted professional corporation laws that permitted the professional to utilize the corporate form but preserved the individual's exposure to malpractice claims even when the corporate form was utilized.

16. The two taxes generally differ to some extent because not all income is taxed at the maximum rate. See I.R.C. §§ 1(a), 11(b)(1).

integration. Although integration has not been adopted to date and is not currently on the legislative agenda, the following excerpts from the Treasury report provide a useful point of departure from which to begin the study of existing law.

Treasury Department Report
Integration of the Individual and
Corporate Tax Systems

January 6, 1992.

PART I: THE CASE FOR INTEGRATION

Current U.S. tax law treats corporations and their investors as separate taxable entities. Under this classical system of corporate income taxation, two levels of income tax are generally imposed on earnings from investments in corporate equity. First, corporate earnings are taxed at the corporate level. Second, if the corporation distributes earnings to shareholders, the earnings are taxed again at the shareholder level. In contrast, investors in business activities conducted in non-corporate form, such as sole proprietorships or partnerships, are generally taxed only once on the earnings, and this tax is imposed at the individual level. Corporate earnings distributed as interest to suppliers of debt capital also are taxed only once because interest is deductible by the corporation and generally taxed to lenders as ordinary income.

Despite its long history, considerable debate surrounds the role of the corporate income tax in the Federal tax structure. The central issue is whether corporate earnings should be taxed once rather than taxed both when earned and when distributed to shareholders. Integration of the individual and corporate income tax refers to the taxation of corporate income once. This Report discusses and evaluates several integration alternatives.

Despite their differences, the methods of integration studied in this Report reflect a common goal: where practical, fundamental economic considerations, rather than tax considerations, should guide business investment, organization and financial decisions. * * * Corporate integration can thus be regarded as a phase of tax reform in the United States, extending the goal of neutral taxation to the choice of business organization and financial policy.

The current two-tier system of corporate taxation discourages the use of the corporate form * * *. The two-tier tax also discourages new equity financing of corporate investment, encourages debt financing of such investment, distorts decisions with respect to the payment of dividends, and encourages corporations to distribute earnings in a manner designed to avoid the double-level tax.

These distortions have economic costs. The classical corporate tax system reduces the level of investment and interferes with the efficient allocation of resources. In addition, the tax bias against corporate equity can encourage corporations to increase debt financing beyond levels supported by nontax considerations, thereby increasing risks of financial distress and bankruptcy.

Historically, the corporation has been an important vehicle for economic growth in the United States, but the classical corporate tax system often perversely penalizes the corporate form of organization. With the increasing integration of international markets for products and capital, one must consider effects of the corporate tax system on the competitiveness of U.S. firms. Most of the major trading partners of the United States have revised their tax systems to provide for some integration of the corporate and individual tax systems.

*　*　*

The classical system of corporate taxation is inefficient because it creates differences in the taxation of alternative sources of income from capital. Under the classical system, a taxpayer conducting business in corporate form faces a different tax burden on equity financing than a taxpayer conducting the same business in noncorporate form. A corporation that raises capital in the form of equity faces a different tax burden than a corporation that raises the same amount of capital from debt. A similar disparity exists in the treatment of corporations that finance with retained earnings and those that pay dividends and finance with new equity. This Report provides evidence that these distortions impose significant economic costs, including reduced financial flexibility of corporations and an inefficient allocation of capital.

A traditional goal of integration proposals has been to tax corporate income only once at the tax rate of the shareholder to whom the income is attributed or distributed. Under the traditional approach, corporate income ideally would be taken into account when earned in determining each individual's economic income and would be taxed at each individual's marginal tax rate. *　*　*

Assuring that corporate income is taxed once *　*　* does not require that corporate income be taxed at individual rates, however. Attaining a single level of tax—with the most significant efficiency gains we project from any system of integration—can be achieved with a schedular system in which all corporate income is taxed at a uniform rate at the corporate level without regard to the tax rate of the corporate shareholder. *　*　*

Neutral taxation of capital income will reduce the distortions under the current system. Economic efficiency suggests that all capital income should be taxed at the same rate. Accordingly, we place less emphasis than some advocates of integration on either trying to tax corporate income at shareholder tax rates or on simply trying to eliminate one level of tax on distributed corporate income.

The prototypes advanced in this Report use the corporation not as a withholding agent for individual shareholders (which implies ultimate taxation at shareholder rates), but rather as a means of collecting a single level of tax on capital income at a uniform rate. *　*　*

We approach integration primarily as a means of reducing the distortions of the classical system and improving economic efficiency. This Report's emphasis on enhancing neutrality in the taxation of capital income can be summarized in four goals for the design of an integrated tax system:

Integration should make more uniform the taxation of investment across sectors of the economy. The U.S. corporate system discourages investment in the corporate sector relative to investment in the noncorporate sector and owner-occupied housing. That is, current law results in too little capital in the corporate sector relative to that elsewhere in the economy. Integration seeks to reduce this distortion.

Integration should make more uniform the taxation of returns earned on alternative financial instruments particularly debt and equity. The U.S. corporate tax system discourages corporations from financing investments with equity as opposed to debt. Such a system violates the goal of neutral taxation. Although equalizing the tax treatment of debt and equity need not be the overriding goal of integration, equal treatment follows from the goal of attaining neutral taxation of capital income.

Integration should distort as little as possible the choice between retaining and distributing earnings. The U.S. corporate system discourages the payment of dividends and encourages corporations to retain earnings * * *.

Integration should create a system that taxes capital income once. Imposing double or triple taxation on some forms of capital income while not taxing others violates the objective of achieving neutrality between corporate and noncorporate forms of investment.

* * *

Revenue concerns * * * may prevent integration from fully equalizing the taxation of alternative investments. Some integration proposals would reduce government revenue from income taxes. Lost tax revenue must be made up either by increasing other taxes or by reducing government spending. Replacement taxes may create distortions and alter the distribution of tax burdens.

* * *

PART II: PROTOTYPES

This Part presents three prototypes for implementing integration in the United States: (1) a dividend exclusion prototype, (2) a shareholder allocation prototype, and (3) the Comprehensive Business Income Tax (CBIT) prototype. * * *

DIVIDEND EXCLUSION PROTOTYPE

The dividend exclusion prototype * * * would, with few changes in current law, implement many of this Report's key policy recommendations.

The principal advantage of the dividend exclusion prototype is its simplicity and relative ease of implementation. * * *

Under the dividend exclusion prototype, corporations would continue to calculate their income under current law rules and pay tax at a 34 percent rate. Shareholders receiving corporate distributions treated as dividends under current law, however, generally would exclude the dividends from gross income. * * *

SHAREHOLDER ALLOCATION PROTOTYPE

The dividend exclusion prototype * * * provides relief from double taxation only for distributed income. As a consequence, [it] may create an incentive for corporations to distribute, rather than retain, earnings * * *. In contrast, the shareholder allocation prototype would extend integration to retained earnings by allocating a corporation's income among its shareholders as the income is earned. Shareholders would include allocated amounts in income, with a credit for corporate taxes paid * * *. [Distributions of corporate earnings would normally be tax-free to the recipient shareholders.]

Thus, the shareholder allocation prototype treats retained and distributed earnings equally. We do not favor adopting the shareholder allocation prototype, however, because of the policy results and administrative complexities it produces. * * *

COMPREHENSIVE BUSINESS INCOME TAX PROTOTYPE

The Comprehensive Business Income Tax (CBIT) is the most comprehensive of the integration prototypes developed in this Report. * * *

CBIT would equate the treatment of debt and equity, would tax corporate and noncorporate businesses alike, and would significantly reduce the tax distortions between retained and distributed earnings. CBIT would accomplish these results by not allowing deductions for dividends or interest paid by the corporation, while excluding from income any dividends or interest received by shareholders and debtholders. To ensure consistent treatment of corporate and noncorporate entities, CBIT would apply to all but the smallest businesses, whether conducted in corporate form or as partnerships or sole proprietorships. The result is that one—but only one—level of tax would be collected on capital income earned by businesses. * * *

Under current law, income distributed on corporate equity generally bears two levels of tax, while interest paid to suppliers of debt capital bears * * * [only] one level of tax. CBIT not only eliminates the double taxation of corporate equity income, but also provides equal treatment for debt income. By denying a deduction for interest, the CBIT prototype subjects interest income, like dividend income, to a single level of U.S. tax equal to the top individual rate * * *, regardless of the lender's actual marginal tax rate * * *.

* * *

PART V: ECONOMIC ANALYSIS OF INTEGRATION
DISTRIBUTIONAL EFFECTS OF
INTEGRATION

Incidence of the Corporate Tax: Theoretical Predictions

* * *

A basic principle underlying proposals for integration is that because corporations are owned by shareholders, corporations have no taxpaying ability independent of their shareholders. Corporations pay taxes out of the incomes of their shareholders. The economic burden of a tax, however, frequently does not rest with the person or business who has the statutory liability for paying the tax to the government. This burden, or incidence, of a tax refers to the change in real incomes that results from the imposition of a change in a tax. Importantly, the burden of the corporate tax may not fall on shareholders. A corporate tax change could induce responses that would alter other forms of income as well. For example, some of the burden may be shifted to workers through lower wages, to consumers of corporate products through higher prices, to owners of noncorporate capital through lower rates of return on their investments, or to landowners through lower rents. This shifting might not happen quickly, so the short-run incidence could well differ from the long-run incidence.

Tax policy analysts have long been concerned with the incidence of the corporate tax. Although there is no unanimous view, the most frequent finding is that, while shareholders are likely to bear the burden of the tax in the short run, much of the tax is probably shifted to owners of all capital in the long run. Some further shifting onto labor or consumers also may be possible, however, under certain circumstances.

* * *

Assessing Distributional Impacts of Integration Prototypes

* * *

The preceding discussion highlights the importance of assumptions about incidence for analyzing long-run distributional effects of corporate tax integration. Effects of integration on the distribution of the tax burden also depend on how integration would be financed (discussed below). * * *

[In light of existing revenue needs, we adhered to] the requirement that revenues lost as a result of integration be compensated by offsetting tax increases. [W]e considered as replacement taxes * * * uniform increases in taxes on capital income. [W]e present * * * information * * * assuming that tax rates on capital income are increased to finance integration.

Dividend Exclusion

The dividend exclusion prototype would reduce total revenues when fully phased in. [Individuals at all income levels] would receive a slight reduction in effective tax rates. With the capital tax replacement, there would be very small differences in the effective tax rates under current law and the dividend exclusion prototype (including a slight increase in the effective tax rate for the highest income group). Hence, the efficiency gains made possible by this integration prototype could be obtained with no loss in revenue and with only slight changes in the distribution of tax burdens across income groups. * * *

Shareholder Allocation

[T]here would be a significant annual revenue loss under shareholder allocation when fully phased in, leading to reductions in effective tax rates larger than under the [dividend exclusion proposal], particularly for the top two income groups (with [economic income] of at least $100,000 per year). With an offsetting uniform increase in tax rates on capital income to finance the revenue loss, tax reductions for upper-income taxpayers are attenuated, with slight overall increases in tax burdens for middle-income groups.

CBIT

Unlike the other integration prototypes considered in this Report, CBIT would not lose revenue. When fully phased in, the CBIT prototype would raise * * * revenue * * *. [This prototype entails only slight changes in the distribution of tax burdens across income groups.] * * *

NOTES

1. *Taxing undistributed corporate profits.* Undistributed corporate profits normally increase the value of the stock of a corporation and thereby accrue to the benefit of the shareholders even before these earnings are distributed. Is the requirement that gains be realized before they are taxed an impediment to implementing the "shareholder allocation prototype" where corporate profits are included in the gross income of individual shareholders before the profits are distributed? See I.R.C. § 1001(a). What arguments can be advanced for or against changing the tax law to include corporate income in the tax base of shareholders when that income is earned, regardless of whether it is distributed?

2. *Recent developments.* In 2003, President Bush recommended the enactment of a system of integration similar to the "dividend exclusion prototype" discussed in the Treasury Department Report. Instead, Congress chose to tax dividends received by individual shareholders at the lower tax rates that apply to an individual's capital gains. See I.R.C. § 1(h)(11). This favorable treatment of dividends is scheduled to expire at the end of 2012. Whether Congress extends this treatment remains to be seen.

PART TWO

OPERATIONS

Part Two examines the consequences that result when a business operates under the C Corporation, S Corporation or partnership tax regimes. In all three cases, the enterprise computes its gross income and deductions on an annual basis in much the same way that an individual computes gross income and deductions. Whether these items are taxed to the business itself or, instead, are allocated and taxed to the owners of the business depends upon the tax regime that governs the enterprise.

When a business is taxed as a C Corporation, the business is taxed on its profits and the owners are also taxed, but not until the profits are actually divided among the owners. In contrast, when a business is taxed as an S Corporation or a partnership, the business itself is normally not taxed. The profits of an S Corporation or a partnership are immediately taxed to the owners, regardless of when these profits are ultimately divided among the owners.

Chapter 2 focuses principally on the computation of a C Corporation's gross income and deductions and the corporate level taxes imposed on these items. Chapters 3 and 4 focus principally on the allocation of the income and deductions of the S Corporation and the partnership among the owners of the enterprise and on the dividing line between the C Corporation and each of these alternative tax regimes.

*

CHAPTER 2

C CORPORATION OPERATIONS

The tax law treats the C Corporation as a taxpaying entity separate and distinct from its individual shareholders. A C Corporation, like an individual, must compute its gross income and deductions on an annual basis. If gross income exceeds deductions, a C Corporation pays the higher of the regular corporate tax under I.R.C. § 11 or the corporate alternative minimum tax under I.R.C. § 55. A C Corporation files an annual tax return (Form 1120—see Exhibit II, p. 20).

If a C Corporation distributes its earnings by paying dividends to shareholders, the dividends are taxed to the shareholders upon receipt. See I.R.C. § 61(a)(7). Although no shareholder level tax is imposed as long as a C Corporation accumulates its earnings, certain penalty taxes may be imposed on the C Corporation under these circumstances. These penalty taxes are in addition to the regular corporate tax and the corporate alternative minimum tax.

When a C Corporation has deductions in excess of gross income, no corporate tax liability normally results. Because a C Corporation is treated as an entity separate from its shareholders, the excess deductions are "trapped" in the corporation and cannot be used by the shareholders to offset personal income from other sources.

EXHIBIT II

Form **1120**	**U.S. Corporation Income Tax Return**	OMB No. 1545-0123
Department of the Treasury Internal Revenue Service	For calendar year 2010 or tax year beginning _____ , 2010, ending _____ , 20 ____ ▶ See separate instructions.	**2010**

A Check if:		Name		B Employer Identification number
1a Consolidated return (attach Form 851)	☐			
b Life/nonlife consolidated return	☐	Number, street, and room or suite no. If a P.O. box, see instructions.		C Date incorporated
2 Personal holding co. (attach Sch. PH)	☐			
3 Personal service corp. (see instructions)	☐	City or town, state, and ZIP code		D Total assets (see instructions)
4 Schedule M-3 attached	☐			$

E Check if: (1) ☐ Initial return (2) ☐ Final return (3) ☐ Name change (4) ☐ Address change

Income	1a	Gross receipts or sales	b Less returns and allowances	c Bal ▶	1c	
	2	Cost of goods sold (Schedule A, line 8)		2	
	3	Gross profit. Subtract line 2 from line 1c		3	
	4	Dividends (Schedule C, line 19)		4	
	5	Interest		5	
	6	Gross rents		6	
	7	Gross royalties		7	
	8	Capital gain net income (attach Schedule D (Form 1120))		8	
	9	Net gain or (loss) from Form 4797, Part II, line 17 (attach Form 4797)		9	
	10	Other income (see instructions—attach schedule)		10	
	11	**Total income.** Add lines 3 through 10 ▶		11	
Deductions (See instructions for limitations on deductions.)	12	Compensation of officers (Schedule E, line 4) ▶		12	
	13	Salaries and wages (less employment credits)		13	
	14	Repairs and maintenance		14	
	15	Bad debts		15	
	16	Rents		16	
	17	Taxes and licenses		17	
	18	Interest		18	
	19	Charitable contributions		19	
	20	Depreciation from Form 4562 not claimed on Schedule A or elsewhere on return (attach Form 4562)		20	
	21	Depletion		21	
	22	Advertising		22	
	23	Pension, profit-sharing, etc., plans		23	
	24	Employee benefit programs		24	
	25	Domestic production activities deduction (attach Form 8903)		25	
	26	Other deductions (attach schedule)		26	
	27	**Total deductions.** Add lines 12 through 26 ▶		27	
	28	Taxable income before net operating loss deduction and special deductions. Subtract line 27 from line 11.		28	
	29	Less: a Net operating loss deduction (see instructions)	29a		
		b Special deductions (Schedule C, line 20)	29b	29c	
Tax, Refundable Credits, and Payments	30	**Taxable income.** Subtract line 29c from line 28 (see instructions)		30	
	31	**Total tax** (Schedule J, line 10)		31	
	32a	2009 overpayment credited to 2010	32a		
	b	2010 estimated tax payments	32b		
	c	2010 refund applied for on Form 4466	32c ( )	d Bal ▶	32d	
	e	Tax deposited with Form 7004		32e	
	f	Credits: (1) Form 2439 (2) Form 4136		32f	
	g	Refundable credits from Form 3800, line 19c, and Form 8827, line 8c	32g	32h	
	33	Estimated tax penalty (see instructions). Check if Form 2220 is attached ▶ ☐		33	
	34	**Amount owed.** If line 32h is smaller than the total of lines 31 and 33, enter amount owed		34	
	35	**Overpayment.** If line 32h is larger than the total of lines 31 and 33, enter amount overpaid		35	
	36	Enter amount from line 35 you want: **Credited to 2011 estimated tax** ▶	Refunded ▶	36	

Sign Here ▶

Under penalties of perjury, I declare that I have examined this return, including accompanying schedules and statements, and to the best of my knowledge and belief, it is true, correct, and complete. Declaration of preparer (other than taxpayer) is based on all information of which preparer has any knowledge.

			May the IRS discuss this return with the preparer shown below (see instructions)? ☐ Yes ☐ No
Signature of officer	Date	Title	

Paid Preparer Use Only	Print/Type preparer's name	Preparer's signature	Date	Check ☐ if self-employed	PTIN
	Firm's name ▶			Firm's EIN ▶	
	Firm's address ▶			Phone no.	

For Paperwork Reduction Act Notice, see separate instructions.   Cat. No. 11450Q   Form **1120** (2010)

A.   CORPORATE INCOME TAX

To determine the annual income tax liability of a corporation, the corporate tax base must be defined and corporate tax rates must be established. "Taxable income" is the base on which the corporate tax is imposed. I.R.C. § 11(a). Taxable income is the difference between gross income and allowable deductions. See I.R.C. § 63(a). Before considering the scope of corporate gross income and deductions, corporate tax rates are addressed.

1.   TAX RATES

I.R.C. §§ 1, 11(b), 1211(a), 1212(a)

A graduated rate structure applies to corporate taxable income. The first $50,000 of taxable income is taxed at a rate of 15% and the next $25,000 is taxed at 25%. Corporate taxable income in excess of $75,000 is taxed at a rate of 34% and amounts in excess of $10,000,000 are taxed at 35%. See I.R.C. § 11(b).

A corporation pays tax at lower rates on the first $75,000 of taxable income regardless of whether the corporation's shareholders derive vast amounts of income from other sources. Consequently, the lower corporate rates cannot be justified by the subsistence needs of the individual shareholders. Moreover, the lower corporate rates deprive the government of significant revenue.[1] Somewhat surprisingly, however, little interest appears to exist in eliminating the graduated corporate rate structure, notwithstanding its weak conceptual foundation and Congress's never ending search for tax revenue.

NOTES

1. *Restriction on multiple low-rate corporations.* In the absence of a statutory restriction, the low tax rates that apply to the first $75,000 of corporate income might induce taxpayers to fragment their business activities among multiple corporations to increase the amount of corporate income subjected to the lower rates. For example, if all business activities conducted by a single C Corporation would generate annual taxable income of $500,000, why not divide the activities among ten separate corporations with each generating $50,000 of taxable income (assuming this is feasible from a business standpoint) and, thereby reduce the rate of tax on all corporate income from 34% to 15%? I.R.C. § 1561(a) bars this result by, in effect, aggregating the taxable income of all members of a "controlled

---

1. The reduced rates on the first $10,000,000 of corporate taxable income have been estimated to cost the government between three and four billion dollars per year. See Joint Committee on Taxation, Estimates of Federal Tax Expenditures for Fiscal Years 2010–2014 (December 15, 2010).

group of corporations." A "controlled group of corporations" includes all corporations in which any five or fewer people (and certain related persons) own more than 50% of the stock of each corporation taking into account each person's interest only to the extent of the smallest interest owned by that person in any of the corporations. See I.R.C. § 1563(a)(2). Hence, the amount of income subjected to the lower corporate rates cannot be increased by dividing business activities among multiple corporations unless little overlapping ownership exists.

2. *Phase-out of lower corporate rates.* The second sentence of I.R.C. § 11(b) eliminates the benefit of the lower marginal rates that apply to the first $75,000 of taxable income by taxing corporate income ranging from $100,000 to $335,000 at a marginal rate of 39%. As a result, a corporation with taxable income ranging from $335,000 to $10,000,000 pays tax at a flat rate of 34% on all of its income. The third sentence of I.R.C. § 11(b) eliminates the benefit of the 34% rate on the first $10,000,000 of taxable income by taxing corporate income ranging from $15,000,000 to $18,333,333 at a marginal rate of 38%. Thus, a corporation with taxable income exceeding $18,333,333 pays tax at a flat rate of 35% on all of its income.

3. *Capital gains and losses.* What tax rate applies to corporate income characterized as capital gains? See I.R.C. §§ 1(h), 11. Does a corporate taxpayer ever prefer deriving capital gains to deriving a like amount of ordinary income? See I.R.C. § 1211(a). What happens in a tax year in which a corporation's capital losses exceed its capital gains? See I.R.C. § 1212(a)(1).

2. SCOPE OF CORPORATE GROSS INCOME

The definition of "gross income" in I.R.C. § 61 does not only apply to individuals. The gross income of a corporation is also governed by I.R.C. § 61. Certain unique problems are presented, however, when applying the concept of gross income to a corporation.

a. INCLUSIONARY ASPECTS—INCOME FROM SERVICES

I.R.C. §§ 61(a)(1), (2), 269A, 482

Haag v. Commissioner

United States Tax Court, 1987.
88 T.C. 604, aff'd, 855 F.2d 855 (8th Cir.1988).

■ WILLIAMS, JUDGE: The Commissioner determined deficiencies in petitioner's Federal income tax as follows:

Year	Deficiency
1979	$94,060.30
1980	72,057.91
1981	84,240.17

The issues we must decide are (1) whether certain income reported by petitioner's closely-held corporation during the years in issue is taxable to petitioner pursuant to section 61 and the assignment of income doctrine; and (2) whether such income is allocable to petitioner pursuant to section 482.

FINDINGS OF FACT

* * *

Petitioner is a physician licensed to practice medicine in the state of Iowa. Prior to March 16, 1976, petitioner was a general partner in the Hilltop Medical Clinic ("Hilltop"), a partnership organized * * * under the laws of the state of Iowa * * *.

On March 16, 1976 petitioner organized Stanley W. Haag, M.D., P.C. (the "P.C."), under the Iowa Professional Corporation Act. The P.C. subsequently adopted by-laws, opened bank accounts in its name, caused a board of directors to be elected, elected officers and held shareholders' and directors' meetings. Petitioner was the sole director of the P.C. Petitioner and John L. Henss were the officers of the P.C., and petitioner * * * [was] the sole shareholder. The P.C. at all times has been a validly organized and operated professional corporation under Iowa law. The P.C. is not a sham or dummy corporation and is an entity taxable apart from its owners and employees * * *.

On or about March 16, 1976, petitioner assigned his interest in Hilltop to the P.C * * *.

[T]he P.C.'s * * * share of Hilltop income * * * [for the tax years at issue is] as follows:

Year	[Share of Hilltop Income]
1979	$205,383.00
1980	204,716.00
1981	228,802.00

Petitioner entered into an employment agreement with the P.C. on March 16, 1976 * * *. Compensation for petitioner's services was left to the discretion of the board of directors * * *.

* * *

The P.C. reported its * * * share of Hilltop income on its corporate tax returns. Petitioner reported only his salary from the P.C. on his individual tax returns. * * *

The nature of the medical services that petitioner provided to patients at Hilltop was not changed by the existence of the P.C. Neither petitioner nor the P.C. made any effort to notify patients treated at Hilltop before or after March 16, 1976 that the P.C. existed and had assumed petitioner's medical practice.

* * *

In his notice of deficiency * * *, respondent allocated the P.C.'s Hilltop income to petitioner.

OPINION

The first issue we must decide is whether petitioner or the P.C. earned the income from the Hilltop Medical Center Partnership during the taxable years 1979, 1980 and 1981 and thus whether such income is taxable to petitioner pursuant to section 61 and the assignment of income doctrine. The principle that income is taxed to the one who earns it is basic to our system of income taxation. Lucas v. Earl, 281 U.S. 111 (1930). The generally accepted test for resolving who is to be taxed requires us to determine who actually earned the income. In the corporate context, however, the actual earner test may be inadequate because a corporation can earn income only through the personal services of its employees and agents. Johnson v. Commissioner, 78 T.C. 882, 890–891 (1982), affd. without published opinion 734 F.2d 20 (9th Cir.1984), cert. denied 469 U.S. 857 (1984). This Court, therefore, has applied a more refined test which looks to who controls the earning of income. In Johnson v. Commissioner, we set out the two requirements that must be met before a corporation, rather than its service-performer employee, will be considered the controller of the income and taxable thereon:

> *First*, the service-performer employee must be just that—an employee of the corporation who the corporation has the right to direct or control in some meaningful sense. *Second*, there must exist between the corporation and the person or entity using the services a contract or similar indicium recognizing the corporation's controlling position. 78 T.C. at 890–91. (Emphasis added.)

* * *

[T]he first element of the control test is satisfied if petitioner was an employee over whom the P.C. could exercise control in a meaningful sense. The employment agreement that petitioner and the P.C. entered into on March 16, 1976 provides in relevant part:

1. EMPLOYMENT

   (a) The Corporation hereby employs the Employee to perform professional services on behalf of the Corporation and to render such services as are necessary for the Corporation to operate and maintain an establishment for * * * the practice of medicine.

      * * *

   (d) The Employee agrees to devote his entire time, attention, knowledge and skill to such employment and shall at all times maintain and enhance the reputation of the Corporation, its shareholders and employees and the profession, generally.

Respondent contends that this agreement did not give the P.C. any real control over petitioner's services because, as the P.C.'s sole director and * * * only * * * shareholder * * *, petitioner could modify or rescind the agreement or could, and did, ignore it. We find respondent's argument to be without merit. There is nothing in the record to indicate that petitioner ignored the employment agreement. The ability of a majority or sole shareholder to ignore, rescind or modify an agreement entered into with his corporation exists in every closely-held corporation. A holding that such ability precludes a corporation from exercising control over its employee's earning of income, and thus being taxable on that income, would violate the long-standing recognition of corporations as entities independent of their shareholders. We find that the employment agreement effectively gave the P.C. the right to control petitioner's medical practice.

The second element of the control test requires that there exist a contract or similar indicium recognizing the corporation's controlling position entered into between the corporation and the entity to whom it provides services. There was no written agreement between Hilltop and the P.C. Petitioner assigned his interest in Hilltop to the P.C., but Hilltop did not amend its partnership agreement to reflect the assignment. It is nonetheless evident that Hilltop recognized the P.C. as a partner because it listed the P.C., and not petitioner, as the partner on [the information return it filed with the Internal Revenue Service] for each of the years in issue. * * * Although there was no formal contract between Hilltop and the P.C., Hilltop recognized the P.C. as the entity who controlled the provision of medical services by petitioner, and therefore the earning of income.

   * * *

In the present case, * * * an effective employment agreement existed between petitioner and the P.C.; Hilltop recognized the P.C. as the entity through whom petitioner provided medical services; and the medical partnership interest could be transferred to a corporation under Iowa law. We, therefore, hold that the P.C., and not petitioner, earned the income from Hilltop in 1979, 1980 and 1981.

Our determination that the P.C. earned the income from Hilltop does not, however, end our inquiry. Next we must decide whether respondent properly allocated the Hilltop income for the taxable years 1979, 1980 and 1981 from the P.C. to petitioner pursuant to section 482. Section 482 permits respondent to reallocate income actually earned by one member of a controlled group to other members of that group if (1) there are two or more trades, businesses or organizations, (2) the enterprises are owned or controlled by the same interest, and (3) reallocation of income among the enterprises is necessary to clearly reflect income or to prevent the evasion of taxes. Respondent's section 482 allocation will be sustained unless petitioner establishes that it is arbitrary, capricious and unreasonable.

This Court has held that section 482 applies in the one-man personal service corporation context. The purpose of section 482 is to place a controlled taxpayer in the same position as an uncontrolled taxpayer by determining the true taxable income of the controlled taxpayer in accordance with the standard of an uncontrolled taxpayer dealing at arm's length.

The requirement that there be two or more trades, businesses or organizations for a section 482 allocation is to be construed broadly. Petitioner and the P.C. satisfy the dual business requirement. Petitioner is in the business of providing medical services as an employee of the P.C., and the P.C., as a partner in Hilltop, is in the business of providing medical services through petitioner. Petitioner's business and the P.C.'s business are also under common control. At issue is whether a reallocation of income is necessary to clearly reflect income or to prevent the evasion of taxes. * * *

* * *

* * * The chief inquiry is whether petitioner's total compensation * * * after incorporation approximated what he would have received absent incorporation. * * *

* * * If petitioner had not incorporated he would have received his * * * share of income as a partner in Hilltop [as well as the other income and deductions of the P.C.]. * * *

The following schedule * * * approximates the taxable income that petitioner would have received absent incorporation:

	1979	1980	1981
Hilltop income	$205,383	$204,716	$228,802
Other income	44,238	35,633	33,146
Total income	249,621	240,349	261,948
Less: deductions [2]	135,136	154,682	173,086
Adjusted income	$114,485	$ 85,667	$ 88,862

Petitioner's compensation from the P.C. during the years in issue, including [contributions by the corporation on petitioner's behalf to a tax deferred pension plan] * * *, was as follows:

	1979	1980	1981
Total compensation	$51,159	$8,686	$85,648

Petitioner thus received 45 percent of the income that he would have received absent incorporation in 1979, 10 percent in 1980 and 96 percent in 1981.

In previous cases involving physicians who incorporated their medical practices, we found that it would be reasonable for a high bracket taxpayer to accept employment with an uncontrolled corporation at a lower salary because of the benefits available through a corporation, such as a tax deferred pension plan. To a high bracket taxpayer, pension plan contributions may be worth more than the equivalent amount as an outright payment. The existence of pension plans was a significant factor in our holdings that respondent's section 482 allocations were unreasonable in [two other] cases. In [those cases, however,] the taxpayers' average earn-

---

2. Editor's note. In addition to the partnership interest in Hilltop, the P.C. owned certain farm, kennel and breeding operations that generated substantial deductions during the years in issue.

ings in each year after they incorporated their medical practices [including contributions to corporate pension plans] were approximately 86 percent and 87 percent, respectively, of what they would have earned absent incorporation. * * *

In the present case, after petitioner incorporated his medical practice * * * he received 45 percent and 10 percent in 1979 and 1980, respectively, of the income that he would have received absent incorporation. A taxpayer dealing at arm's length would not have accepted employment at a salary so significantly lower than he could otherwise earn. In 1981, in contrast, petitioner received 96 percent of the income he would have received absent incorporation * * *. We find that petitioner's compensation from the P.C. in 1981 was comparable to the amount he would have received absent incorporation.

Section 1.482–2(b)(1), Income Tax Regs., provides that when one member of a group of controlled entities performs services on behalf of another member of the group for less than an arm's-length charge, respondent may make allocations to reflect an arm's-length charge for such services. An arm's-length charge for services is the amount that would have been charged for the same or similar services in a transaction between unrelated parties. Section 1.482–2(b)(3), Income Tax Regs. Petitioner would not have accepted employment in 1979 and 1980 for so much less than he otherwise could have earned if he had been dealing at arm's length with an unrelated party. We, therefore, uphold respondent's section 482 allocation to the extent of $63,326 in 1979 and $76,981 in 1980, the difference between the amount of compensation petitioner would have received in each year absent incorporation and the amount he actually received.

NOTES

1. *Reconciling assignment of income doctrine with personal service corporation.* In Johnson v. Commissioner, 78 T.C. 882 (1982), aff'd without published opinion 734 F.2d 20 (9th Cir.1984), the taxpayer, a professional basketball player, entered into a contract with the San Francisco Warriors and assigned his rights under the contract to a personal service corporation. The Warriors remitted the contract payments to the personal service corporation but refused to sign an agreement with any person or entity other than the taxpayer. The court held that the amounts remitted to the personal service corporation represented gross income of the taxpayer because the Warriors did not recognize the personal service corporation's controlling position.

The following excerpt from Johnson, 78 T.C. at 890–91, vividly describes the problem of reconciling the assignment of income doctrine with the personal service corporation:

> [T]he realities of the business world prevent an overly simplistic application of the Lucas v. Earl rule whereby the true earner may be identified by merely pointing to the one actually turning the spade or dribbling the ball. Recognition must be given to corporations as taxable

entities which, to a great extent, rely upon the personal services of their employees to produce corporate income. When a corporate employee performs labors which give rise to income, it solves little merely to identify the actual laborer. Thus, a tension has evolved between the basic tenets of Lucas v. Earl and recognition of the nature of the corporate business form.

While the generally accepted test for resolving the "who is taxed" tension is who actually earns the income, that test may easily become sheer sophistry when the "who" choices are a corporation or its employee. Whether a one-person professional service corporation or a multi-faceted corporation is presented, there are many cases in which, in a practical sense, the key employee is responsible for the influx of moneys. Nor may a workable test be couched in terms of for whose services the payor of the income intends to pay. In numerous instances, a corporation is hired solely * * * to obtain the services of a specific corporate employee. (Such instances are commonplace in personal service businesses such as law, medicine, accounting, and entertainment * * *.)

Given the inherent impossibility of logical application of a per se actual earner test, a more refined inquiry has arisen in the form of who controls the earning of the income. * * *

Even when a professional sports team enters into an agreement with a player's professional corporation, the Tax Court has twice held that amounts paid to the corporation represent gross income to the player. In both cases, however, the player also entered into a separate agreement with the sports team in which the player personally agreed to perform the services called for in the agreement between the sports team and the player's professional corporation. See Sargent v. Commissioner, 93 T.C. 572 (1989), rev'd, 929 F.2d 1252 (8th Cir.1991); Leavell v. Commissioner, 104 T.C. 140 (1995).

2. *Nature of income.* Is the income of a personal service corporation described in I.R.C. § 61(a)(1) or § 61(a)(2)?

3. *Impact of form.* How significant was the form of the transaction to the Haag court's resolution of whether the P.C. or Haag earned the income in question? What additional steps might the taxpayers have taken to improve the form of the transaction?

4. *Pension plans.* One of the principal historical reasons for utilizing a C Corporation to conduct a personal service business was to enable owner-employees to take advantage of the tax-deferred retirement plan provisions of the Internal Revenue Code. Subsequent changes in the tax law have extended most aspects of these tax-favored plans to all business forms. Thus, it is no longer necessary to incorporate a personal service business to gain access to these plans.

5. *I.R.C. § 269A.* In 1982, a new reallocation provision was enacted that applies specifically to personal service corporations. I.R.C. § 269A delegates the same reallocation powers to the Internal Revenue Service as I.R.C.

§ 482, but I.R.C. § 269A only applies when substantially all the services of a personal service corporation are performed for one entity and the principal purpose of the personal service corporation is the avoidance of Federal income tax by reducing the income or securing a tax benefit that would not otherwise be available to an owner-employee. See I.R.C. § 269A(a). After the enactment of I.R.C. § 269A, income could be reallocated from a personal service corporation to an owner-employee even in jurisdictions that would not sanction such a reallocation under I.R.C. § 482. See, e.g., Foglesong v. Commissioner, 691 F.2d 848 (7th Cir.1982), rev'g 77 T.C. 1102 (1981) (in contrast to the Haag court, the Seventh Circuit held that I.R.C. § 482 did not apply to a one-person personal service corporation because the dual trade, business or organization requirement is not met).

6. *Tax rates.* Read I.R.C. § 11(b)(2). Are personal service corporations less deserving of lower tax rates on the first $10,000,000 of corporate income than other corporations? How does this rule impact on the desirability of utilizing a C Corporation to conduct a personal service business?

b. INCLUSIONARY ASPECTS—GAINS FROM PROPERTY

I.R.C. §§ 61(a)(3), 311, 1001

If a corporation buys a painting for $2,000 and later sells the painting for $1,002,000, the tax consequences of the sale to the corporation are as follows:

Realization Event?	Yes, the sale.	(I.R.C. § 1001(a))
Amount Realized	$1,002,000	(I.R.C. § 1001(b))
Less: Adjusted Basis	2,000	(I.R.C. § 1012)
Realized Gain	$1,000,000	(I.R.C. § 1001(a))
Recognition?	Yes.	(I.R.C. § 1001(c))
Characterization?	Capital gain, unless inventory.	(I.R.C. § 1221)

Are the tax consequences to the corporation any different if the corporation sells the painting to its sole shareholder? What if the corporation merely transfers ownership of the painting to the shareholder for no cash payment?

General Utilities & Operating Co. v. Helvering

Supreme Court of the United States, 1935.
296 U.S. 200, 56 S.Ct. 185.

■ MR. JUSTICE MCREYNOLDS delivered the opinion of the Court.

January 1st, 1927, petitioner—General Utilities, a Delaware corporation—acquired 20,000 shares * * * [of the] common stock of Islands Edison Company, for which it paid $2,000 * * *.

During January, 1928, Whetstone, President of Southern Cities Utilities Company, contemplated acquisition by his company of all Islands Edison common stock. He discussed the matter with Lucas, petitioner's president * * *. Lucas pointed out that the shares which his company held could only be purchased after distribution of them among stockholders, since a sale by it would subject the realized profit to taxation, and when the proceeds passed to the stockholders there would be further exaction. Lucas had no power to sell, but he * * * and Whetstone were in accord concerning the terms and conditions under which purchase of * * * the stock might become possible—"it being understood and agreed between them that petitioner would make distribution of the stock of the Islands Edison Company to its stockholders and that counsel would prepare a written agreement embodying the terms and conditions of the said sale, agreement to be submitted for approval to the stockholders of the Islands Edison Company after the distribution of said stock by the petitioner."

Petitioner's directors, March 22, 1928, considered the disposition of the Islands Edison shares. Officers reported they were worth $1,122,500 * * *. Thereupon a resolution directed * * * "that a dividend * * * be and it is hereby declared on the Common Stock of this Company payable in Common Stock of The Islands Edison Company at a valuation of $56.12-½ a share, * * * viz, $1,120,500, the payment of the dividend to be made by the delivery to the stockholders of this Company, pro rata, of certificates for the Common Stock of The Islands Edison Company held by this Company at the rate of two shares of such stock for each share of Company Stock of this Corporation."

Accordingly, 19,090 shares were distributed amongst petitioner's thirty-three stockholders and proper transfers to them were made upon the issuing corporation's books. It retained 910 shares.

After this transfer, all holders of Islands Edison stock, sold to Southern Cities Utilities Company at $56.12-½ per share. Petitioner realized $46,346.30 net profit on 910 shares and this was duly returned for taxation. There was no report of gain upon the 19,090 shares distributed to stockholders.

The Commissioner of Internal Revenue declared a taxable gain upon distribution of the stock in payment of the dividend declared March 22nd, and made the questioned deficiency assessment. Seeking redetermination by the Board of Tax Appeals, petitioner alleged, "The Commissioner of Internal Revenue has erroneously held that the petitioner corporation made a profit of $1,069,517.25 by distributing to its own stockholders certain capital stock of another corporation which it had theretofore owned." And it asked a ruling that no taxable gain resulted from the appreciation upon its books and subsequent distribution of the shares. * * * [T]he Board heard the cause.

It found " * * * The only question presented in this proceeding for redetermination is whether petitioner realized taxable gain in declaring a dividend and paying it in the stock of another company at an agreed value per share, which value was in excess of the cost of the stock to petitioner."

Also, "On March 26, 1928, the stockholders of the Islands Edison Company (one of which was petitioner, owning 910 shares) and the Southern Cities Utilities Company, entered into a written contract of sale of the Islands Edison Company stock. At no time did petitioner agree with Whetstone or the Southern Cities Utilities Company, verbally or in writing, to make sale to him or to the Southern Cities Utilities Company of any of said stock except the aforesaid 910 shares of the Islands Edison Company."

The opinion recites—The Commissioner's "theory is that upon the declaration of the dividend on March 22, 1928, petitioner became indebted to its stockholders in the amount of $1,071,426.25, and that the discharge of that liability by the delivery of property costing less than the amount of the debt constituted income, citing United States v. Kirby Lumber Co., 284 U.S. 1." "The intent of the directors of petitioner was to declare a dividend payable in Islands Edison stock; their intent was expressed in that way in the resolution formally adopted; and the dividend was paid in the way intended and declared. We so construe the transaction, and * * * we hold that the declaration and payment of the dividend resulted in no taxable income."

The Commissioner asked the Circuit Court of Appeals, 4th Circuit, to review the Board's determination. He alleged, "The only question to be decided is whether the petitioner [taxpayer] realized taxable income in declaring a dividend and paying it in stock of another company at an agreed value per share, which value was in excess of the cost of the stock."

The court stated: "There are two grounds upon which the petitioner urges that the action of the Board of Tax Appeals was wrong: First, that the dividend declared was in effect a cash dividend and that the respondent realized taxable income by the distribution of the Islands Edison Company stock to its stockholders equal to the difference between the amount of the dividend declared and the cost of the stock. Second, that the sale made of the Islands Edison Company stock was in reality a sale by the respondent (with all the terms agreed upon before the declaration of the dividend), through its stockholders who were virtually acting as agents of the respondent, the real vendor."

Upon the first ground, it sustained the Board. Concerning the second, it held that, although not raised before the Board, the point should be ruled upon. "When we come to consider the sale of the stock of the Islands Edison Company, we cannot escape the conclusion that the transaction was deliberately planned and carried out for the sole purpose of escaping taxation. The purchaser was found by the officers of the respondent; the exact terms of the sale as finally consummated were agreed to by the same officers; the purchaser of the stock stated that the delivery of all the stock was essential and that the delivery of a part thereof would not suffice; the details were worked out for the express and admitted purpose of avoiding the payment of the tax and for the reason that the attorneys for the respondent had advised that, unless some such plan was adopted, the tax would have to be paid; and a written agreement was to be prepared by counsel for the respondent which was to be submitted to the stockholders—

all this without the stockholders, or any of them, who were ostensibly making the sale, being informed, advised, or consulted. Such admitted facts plainly constituted a plan, not to use the harsher terms of scheme, artifice or conspiracy, to evade the payment of the tax * * *.

"The sale of the stock in question was, in substance, made by the respondent company, through the stockholders as agents or conduits through whom the transfer of the title was effected. The stockholders, even in their character as agents, had little or no option in the matter and in no sense exercised any independent judgment. They automatically ratified the agreement prepared and submitted to them."

A judgment of reversal followed.

Both tribunals below rightly decided that petitioner derived no taxable gain from the distribution among its stockholders of the Islands Edison shares as a dividend. This was no sale; assets were not used to discharge indebtedness.

The second ground of objection, although sustained by the court, was not presented to or ruled upon by the Board. The petition for review relied wholly upon the first point; and, in the circumstances, we think the court should have considered no other. Always a taxpayer is entitled to know with fair certainty the basis of the claim against him. Stipulations concerning facts and any other evidence properly are accommodated to issues adequately raised.

Recently (April, 1935) this court pointed out: "The Court of Appeals is without power on review of proceedings of the Board of Tax Appeals to make any findings of fact. The function of the court is to decide whether the correct rule of law was applied to the facts found; and whether there was substantial evidence before the Board to support the findings made." * * *

Here the court undertook to decide a question not properly raised. Also it made an inference of fact directly in conflict with the stipulation of the parties and the findings, for which we think the record affords no support whatever * * *.

The judgment of the court below must be reversed. The action of the Board of Tax Appeals is approved.

NOTES

1. *Issue.* Which element in the analysis of the tax consequences of a transfer of property (see p. 29) was at issue in the General Utilities case?

2. *Repeal of General Utilities rule.* The rule that a distribution of appreciated property by a corporation to a shareholder does not trigger gain to the corporation (commonly referred to as the "General Utilities rule") was gradually eroded until the Tax Reform Act of 1986 repealed the rule in its entirety. How did Congress deal with the difficult question of whether a realization event occurs when a corporation distributes appreciated property to a shareholder? See I.R.C. § 311(b)(1).

3. *Shareholder level tax.* This chapter focuses on the corporation as a taxpaying entity and, therefore, on the first tax on corporate income. Property transferred by a corporation to a shareholder, however, is also taxed to the shareholder upon receipt. (The shareholder then takes a fair market value basis in the property.) The shareholder level tax is the second of the two taxes on corporate income and is examined in detail in Chapter 5.

4. *Significance of repeal of General Utilities rule.* Do not underestimate the significance of the repeal of the General Utilities rule. While the General Utilities rule was in place, only the operating income of a corporation was subject to two levels of tax; first to the corporation when earned and then to the shareholders when distributed to them. When property owned by a corporation increased in value, that property could be distributed to shareholders without triggering a corporate level tax on the appreciation; only a shareholder level tax was imposed. After the repeal of the General Utilities rule, however, both corporate operating income and unrealized appreciation in corporate assets are generally subject to double taxation. Moreover, although appreciation in corporate assets, when recognized, is often characterized as capital gains, the capital gains of a C Corporation are taxed at the same rates as its ordinary income (up to 35%). See I.R.C. § 11. Thus, the repeal of the General Utilities rule has made the C Corporation a much more costly form in which to operate a business.

5. *Nonrecognition of loss.* The General Utilities rule was repealed only with respect to distributions of appreciated property. When a corporation distributes property with a basis in excess of value, a loss is not normally recognized by the corporation. See I.R.C. § 311(a)(2). Can a corporation avoid this restriction on loss recognition by selling the property to,

> (a) an unrelated party?
>
> (b) a shareholder? See I.R.C. §§ 267(a)(1), (b)(2), (c).

c.   EXCLUSIONARY ASPECTS—GENERAL

All income derived by a taxpayer is included in gross income, unless it is specifically excluded by statute. See I.R.C. § 61(a). For the most part, the same statutory exclusions that apply to individuals also apply to corporations. See I.R.C. §§ 101–139. The unique nature of the corporate entity, however, sometimes leads to controversy.

Castner Garage, Limited v. Commissioner
Universal Motor Company v. Commissioner
Island Securities, Limited, A Dissolved Corporation v. Commissioner

Board of Tax Appeals, 1940.
43 B.T.A. 1, acq. 1941–1 Cum.Bull. 2.

■ MURDOCK, JUDGE: * * *

The issue for decision by the Board is whether and to what extent the petitioners are taxable upon amounts received by them in 1935 and 1936 from the Prudential Insurance Co. of America as disability payments under policies of combined life, health, and accident insurance upon their president, Charles C. Pittam * * *.

The Castner Garage, Ltd., and Universal Motor Co., hereinafter referred to as Castner and Universal, are corporations organized under the laws of the Territory of Hawaii. Island Securities, hereinafter referred to as Island, formerly a Hawaiian corporation, was dissolved on August 26, 1936 * * *. Charles C. Pittam owned a majority of the outstanding capital stock of Island, which in turn owned a majority of the stock of both Castner and Universal. Most of the remaining stock of the three companies was owned by Pittam's brother-in-law and by officers or employees.

Four policies of combined life, health, and accident insurance in the Prudential Insurance Co. of America were taken out upon Charles C. Pittam prior to 1930 * * *. [E]ach of the petitioners, prior to the taxable years, acquired for valuable consideration certain beneficial rights in one or more of the policies and was thereby entitled to receive and did receive during the taxable years certain payments on account of the fact that Pittam became disabled from ill health. He had been regularly engaged in the business of these petitioners at salaries prior to his disability. The rights and interests in the four policies held by the petitioners during the taxable years were acquired by the petitioners for the purpose of strengthening their credit and for their use as collateral for bank loans. That purpose had been accomplished and all of the policies were assigned to the insured on May 23, 1936.

The petitioners, while the policies were assigned to them, paid all of the premiums due * * *.

The petitioners contend that the amounts received by them during the taxable years by reason of the disability of the insured are exempt from taxation under the express provisions of sections 22(b)(5) of the Revenue Acts of 1934 and 1936 [the predecessors to I.R.C. § 104(a)(3)], which exempt from taxation:

> (5) COMPENSATION FOR INJURIES OR SICKNESS. Amounts received, through accident or health insurance * * *, as compensation for personal injuries or sickness, * * *.

* * * The respondent's only reply to the contention of the petitioners is that section 22(b)(5) does not apply in the case of a corporation. He argues at considerable length that the exemption applies only to individuals, and goes even further, as his logic forces him, to say "Congress intended the exemption to be personal to the insured."

Section 22, entitled "GROSS INCOME", applies generally to both individual taxpayers and corporate taxpayers. [N]one of its provisions are expressly limited in their application to one or the other class of taxpayers * * *. [I]t is necessary to examine the particular provision here in question to see whether, by natural implication, it might be limited in its application to the insured or, at least, to individual taxpayers.

All revenue acts beginning with that of 1928 have contained, in section 22(b)(5), a provision identical with the one above quoted. Prior to that time and beginning with the Revenue Act of 1918, the same provision appeared as section 213(b)(6) * * *. Thus, the possibility of the present question has been present under all prior acts, beginning with the Revenue Act of 1918. Yet, apparently, it has never arisen until now.

Section 22(b)(5) deals with amounts received as compensation for personal injury or sickness. It contains no express statement that it relates to such amounts when received by any particular limited class of taxpayers. The Commissioner contends that the provision is limited in its application to amounts received by the insured, but that argument is contrary to his own regulations and, apparently, his practice. The regulations have held consistently that the exemption was not limited to amounts received by the insured * * *. [They] contain a provision substantially like * * * [the following]:

> Whether he be alive or dead, the amounts received by an insured or his estate or other beneficiaries through accident or health insurance or under workmen's compensation acts as compensation for personal injuries or sickness are excluded from the gross income of the insured, his estate and other beneficiaries.

> Amounts received by one member of a family as compensation for personal injuries or sickness of another member of the family would thus be exempt. We conclude that the exemption is not limited to the person who suffers the personal injuries or sickness.

Since section 22(b)(5) would apply in the case of a father who received compensation because of the illness of his insured son, even though the son happened to be his employee, what is there to indicate that the provision would not apply to amounts received by any taxpayer who had an insurable interest[3] in the health of an insured? It is futile to argue that a corporation can not suffer personal injury or sickness and can be compensated only for the loss of services of its employees. The same argument could be made in the case of an individual employer. In fact none but the insured actually suffers the injury or sickness. Yet we have concluded that the exemption is not limited to the insured * * *.

[I]t is interesting to note the conclusion which the Supreme Court reached in the case of United States v. Supplee–Biddle Hardware Co. * * *. The Court was there interpreting section 213(b)(1) of the Revenue Act of 1918 [the predecessor to I.R.C. § 101(a)], which, like (b)(6) supra, exempted certain items from taxation. The exemption was in this language: "The

---

3. Editor's note. "Insurable interest" is an insurance law term that requires the owner of insurance to have something to gain from the nonoccurrence of the insured risk. In the case of disability insurance, the owner of the policy should have something to gain from the continued health of the insured. The doctrine deters the purchase of insurance to speculate on a risk about which the purchaser of the policy would normally not be concerned.

proceeds of life insurance policies paid upon the death of the insured to individual beneficiaries or to the estate of the insured." The Court said:

> We think the Treasury Department erred in assuming that Congress intended * * * to distinguish between individual beneficiaries and corporate beneficiaries in including the proceeds of life insurance policies as within gross income. We think the two sections have no such purpose. * * *

[I]t is reasonable that the purpose of section 213 to exclude entirely the proceeds of life insurance policies from taxation in the case of individuals should be given the same effect in adapting its application to corporations, and that such proceeds should be so excluded whether by the direction of the insured they were to go to specially named beneficiaries or were to inure to the estate of the insured.

The language of section 22(b)(5) is certainly no less favorable to the contention of the respondent than was the language of section 213(b)(1). There is no sound reason for differentiating here between corporations and individuals other than the insured. We conclude that section 22(b)(5) is general in its application and is not limited so as to exclude corporations, such as these, which have insurable interests.

NOTES

1. *Rationale.* Is it sensible to allow a corporation to exclude from its gross income the proceeds of insurance covering the death or disability of a shareholder-employee? Do the same considerations apply to life insurance and disability insurance?

2. *No deduction for premium payments.* Premiums paid by a corporation for life insurance or disability insurance are not allowed as a deduction if the corporation is a beneficiary of the policy. See I.R.C. § 264(a)(1) (life insurance); Rev. Rul. 66–262, 1966–1 C.B. 105 (disability insurance).

d. EXCLUSIONARY ASPECTS—CORPORATE SPECIFIC

I.R.C. §§ 118, 362(a)(2), 1032

A corporation can derive certain benefits for which no individual analogue exists. For example, when a shareholder transfers property to a corporation, the corporation is enriched by the value of that property. In most cases, however, the corporation is treated in much the same way as the recipient of a gift. Specifically, the value of the property is excluded from the corporation's gross income and the corporation takes a transferred basis in the property. See I.R.C. §§ 118, 362(a)(2).

If a corporation issues stock in exchange for money, I.R.C. § 118 (an exclusion) does not apply to the issuing corporation, if the newly issued corporate stock is regarded as "property". Why does I.R.C. § 118 not apply? See I.R.C. §§ 61(a)(3), 1001(c). Although the corporation's amount realized can easily be determined in these circumstances, a corporation's basis in its own stock is indeterminable. Consequently, it is impossible to quantify the gain or loss realized by a corporation when it sells or exchanges its own stock. This problem can be sidestepped, however, because I.R.C. § 1032 (a nonrecognition provision) insulates the issuing corporation from recognizing gain or loss when it receives money or other property in exchange for its own stock.

NOTES

1. *Treasury stock.* "Treasury stock" is previously issued stock which the issuing corporation buys back from its shareholders. If the issuing corporation subsequently resells the treasury stock, no gain or loss is recognized by the corporation. See I.R.C. § 1032(a). Was it sensible for Congress to include treasury stock in the scope of I.R.C. § 1032?

2. *Stock of a different corporation.* Does I.R.C. § 1032 apply to a corporation that receives money from a shareholder in exchange for stock of a different corporation? See I.R.C. § 1032(a).

3. *Non-stock consideration.* Does I.R.C. § 118 or I.R.C. § 1032 apply to a corporation that receives money from a shareholder in exchange for property other than stock?

4. *Shareholder level tax effects.* This Chapter focuses on the corporation as a taxpaying entity and not on shareholder level tax consequences. When a person transfers property to a corporation, tax consequences may also occur at the shareholder level. A mere contribution of property to the corporation is normally not a taxable event to the contributing shareholder, just as a gift is not a taxable event to a donor. When a person transfers property to a corporation in exchange for stock, a realization event occurs at the shareholder level. Any gain or loss realized by the transferor is not recognized, however, if certain conditions are satisfied. See I.R.C. § 351(a). If nonrecognition treatment is granted, the transferor takes an exchanged basis in the substituted stock and the corporation takes a transferred basis in the contributed property. See I.R.C. §§ 358(a)(1), 362(a)(1). The shareholder level tax effects of a transfer of property to a corporation are examined in Chapter 8.

5. *Shareholder level economic effects.* From an economic standpoint, does it make any difference whether a shareholder who transfers property to a corporation receives additional stock from the corporation if the contributing shareholder,

    (a) is the sole shareholder of the corporation?

    (b) is *not* the sole shareholder of the corporation?

3.   SCOPE OF CORPORATE DEDUCTIONS

In contrast to I.R.C. § 61, which includes all receipts in a taxpayer's gross income unless specifically excluded, I.R.C. § 161 bars a deduction for any disbursement unless specifically allowed. In many cases, the deduction provisions that apply to individuals also apply to corporations. For example, I.R.C. § 162(a) applies to individuals and to corporations because both types of taxpayers can incur ordinary and necessary business expenses. Other deduction provisions apply differently to corporations from how they apply to individuals. Deduction provisions that apply differently to corporations include the following:

(a) *Interest expense deduction.* Note the scope of I.R.C. §§ 163(d), (h).

(b) *Loss deduction.* Note the scope of I.R.C. § 165(c). But see I.R.C. §§ 165(f), 1211(a), 469(a)(2)(B), (C).

(c) *Bad debt deduction.* Note the scope of I.R.C. § 166(d).

(d) *Charitable contribution deduction.* See I.R.C. § 170(b)(2).

(e) *Deductions allowed only to individuals.* See I.R.C. §§ 212–223.

Unlike individuals, corporations need not distinguish between deductions to and from adjusted gross income. See I.R.C. § 62. Thus, the general limitation on certain deductions from adjusted gross income does not apply to corporations. See I.R.C. § 67. Moreover, corporations are not allowed a standard deduction or any exemptions. I.R.C. §§ 63(b), 151.

a. REDUCING DOUBLE TAXATION

I.R.C. §§ 162(a), 163(a), 385

As discussed in Chapter 1, corporate income is subject to the individual income tax when a corporation distributes earnings to its shareholders (pays dividends). From the corporation's perspective, the logical inquiry is whether a deduction is allowed for these distributions when computing the corporation's taxable income. The answer, quite simply, is no. **A corporation may not deduct the dividends it pays.** Indeed, the nondeductibility of dividends is the source of the double taxation of corporate income. If dividends were deductible, no corporate tax would be imposed on corporate income distributed as dividends. Under these circumstances, distributed corporate income, like all other forms of individual income, would be subject only to the individual income tax.

Although no deduction is allowed for dividends, payments made by the corporation to compensate a shareholder for acting in a non-shareholder capacity are often deductible to the corporation. As a result, corporate income used to compensate shareholders for acting in a non-shareholder capacity generally is only taxed once, at the shareholder level through the individual income tax. Shareholders often relate to the corporation in one or more capacities other than that of a shareholder, particularly when the corporation is closely-held. Under these circumstances, it is common for shareholders to serve as key-employees, officers and directors of the corporation. At times, shareholders lend money to the corporation or lease property to the corporation. When the corporation compensates its shareholders for the services they perform (via salary) and the money or property they make available to the corporation (via interest or rent), the corporation is allowed a deduction, to the extent that the payment represents an ordinary and necessary business expense. See I.R.C. § 162(a). As the cases that follow demonstrate, it is often difficult to determine whether payments to a shareholder represent deductible business expenses or non-deductible dividends.

Elliotts, Inc. v. Commissioner

United States Court of Appeals, Ninth Circuit, 1983.
716 F.2d 1241.

■ HUG, CIRCUIT JUDGE: * * *

I. Background

Taxpayer is an Idaho corporation that sells equipment manufactured by John Deere Co. and services equipment made by Deere and several other manufacturers * * *.

Taxpayer was incorporated in 1952. During its first year, it grossed $500,000 in agricultural equipment sales in the Burley area. It employed about eight people at that time. By 1975, Taxpayer was employing 40 people, selling both agricultural and industrial equipment throughout southeast Idaho, and achieving gross annual sales in excess of $5 million.

Edward G. Elliott has been Taxpayer's chief executive officer since its incorporation and he has also been its sole shareholder since 1954. He has always had total managerial responsibility for Taxpayer's business. In addition to being Taxpayer's ultimate decision and policy maker, he has performed the functions usually delegated to sales and credit managers. It is undisputed that he works about 80 hours each week.

For several years, Taxpayer has paid Elliott a fixed salary of $2000 per month plus a bonus at year's end. Since Taxpayer's incorporation, Elliott's bonus has been fixed at 50% of net profits (before subtraction of taxes and management bonuses).

On its return for the fiscal year ending February 28, 1975, Taxpayer claimed a $181,074 deduction for total compensation paid Elliott. It claimed a similar $191,663 deduction on its return for the fiscal year ending February 28, 1976. The Commissioner of Internal Revenue ("Commissioner") found these deductions to be in excess of the amounts Taxpayer properly could deduct as reasonable salary under section 162(a)(1). On June 16, 1978, the Commissioner issued Taxpayer a notice of deficiency which limited deductions for Elliott's salary to $65,000 for each fiscal year.

Taxpayer petitioned the Tax Court for a redetermination of liability. The court * * * concluded that the payments to Elliott, in addition to providing compensation for personal services, were intended in part to distribute profits. Although the Tax Court acknowledged that it could not determine what amounts paid Elliott actually were dividends, it found that the total amounts paid him were in excess of reasonable compensation. It determined that $120,000 was reasonable compensation for the year 1975 and that $125,000 was reasonable for 1976. The deficiencies assessed to

Taxpayer by the Commissioner were reduced accordingly. Taxpayer appeals the Tax Court's determination of reasonable compensation.

II. The Shareholder–Employee Problem

The issue presented by this case concerns the deductibility by a corporation of payments ostensibly made as compensation for services to an employee who is also a shareholder. If the payments are reasonable compensation for services rendered, the corporation may deduct them. 26 U.S.C. § 162(a)(1). If, however, they are actually dividends, they are not deductible. Thus, it will normally be in a corporation's interest to characterize such payments as compensation rather than dividends.

The general problem is that of distinguishing between dividends and compensation for services received by a shareholder-employee of a closely held corporation. What makes this situation troublesome is that the shareholder-employee and the corporation are not dealing with each other at arm's length. It is likely to be in the interests of both the corporation and the shareholder-employee to characterize any payments to the shareholder-employee as compensation rather than dividends. For this reason, a taxpayer's characterization of such payments may warrant close scrutiny to ensure that a portion of the purported compensation payments is not a disguised dividend.

The problem of determining whether compensation payments contain an element of disguised dividend is exacerbated in a case such as this one where the shareholder-employee is the corporation's sole shareholder. Not only is a sole shareholder likely to have complete control over the corporation's operations, he will also be the only recipient of its dividends. If a corporation has multiple shareholders, the existence of a plan which compensates shareholder-employees in proportion to their ownership interests may be evidence that compensation payments contain disguised dividends. In the case of a sole shareholder, such evidence is meaningless.

Section 162(a)(1) of the Internal Revenue Code permits a corporation to deduct "a reasonable allowance for salaries or other compensation for personal services actually rendered." There is a two-prong test for deductibility under section 162(a)(1): (1) the amount of the compensation must be reasonable and (2) the payments must in fact be purely for services.

Proof of the second prong, which requires a "compensatory purpose," can be difficult to establish because of its subjective nature * * *. By and large, the inquiry under section 162(a)(1) has turned on whether the amounts of the purported compensation payments were reasonable.

One court has departed from this practice of restricting the inquiry in most cases to the reasonableness of the payments. In Charles McCandless Tile Serv. v. United States, 422 F.2d 1336 (Ct.Cl.1970), the Court of Claims held that ostensible compensation payments paid to two shareholder-employees, even though reasonable in amount, "necessarily" contained disguised dividends because the closely held corporation had been profitable and had not paid out any dividends since its formation. This has become known as the "automatic dividend rule," and has been subjected to much criticism.

We reject the automatic dividend rule of McCandless for several reasons. First, there is no statute requiring profitable corporations to pay dividends. Congress has chosen to handle abuses in this area through the accumulated earnings tax. 26 U.S.C. §§ 531–537 * * *. Beyond the penalties contained in the accumulated earnings tax, Congress has not indicated that it wants the Commissioner or the courts to require the payment of dividends as a matter of federal tax policy.

Second, the automatic dividend rule is based on the faulty premise that shareholders of a profitable corporation will demand dividends. Shareholders are generally concerned with the return on their investment. While some shareholders may prefer to see their return in the form of dividends, others will prefer to have the corporation reinvest its profits so that their return will be in the form of appreciation and the potential of greater future return. If the shareholders prefer to have their return in the form of appreciation rather than dividends, there is nothing in the law precluding the corporation from reinvesting its profits * * *.

For these reasons, we will not presume an element of disguised dividend from the bare fact that a profitable corporation does not pay dividends * * *.

In evaluating the reasonableness of compensation paid to a shareholder-employee, particularly a sole shareholder it is helpful to consider the matter from the perspective of a hypothetical independent investor. A relevant inquiry is whether an inactive, independent investor would be willing to compensate the employee as he was compensated. The nature and quality of the services should be considered, as well as the effect of those services on the return the investor is seeing on his investment. The corporation's rate of return on equity would be relevant to the independent investor in assessing the reasonableness of compensation in a small corporation where excessive compensation would noticeably decrease the rate of return * * *.

III.   Reasonableness Determination

Section 162(a)(1) provides that a taxpayer may deduct "all the ordinary and necessary expenses paid or incurred during the taxable year in carrying on any trade or business," including "a reasonable allowance for salaries or other compensation for personal services actually rendered." That Elliott actually rendered services as an employee of Taxpayer is not disputed. At issue is whether the payments made to Elliott are attributable to that employment relationship or to his role as Taxpayer's sole shareholder. Our inquiry focuses on whether the Tax Court, in finding that a part of the payments made to Elliott could not be attributed to his employment status, correctly defined and applied the factors that determine what is "reasonable compensation" under section 162(a)(1).

Although we accord deference to the Tax Court's special expertise, definition of the appropriate factors is reviewable by this court as a question of law. The Tax Court's findings of fact, derived from application of the appropriate factors, must be affirmed unless clearly erroneous.

Our cases have defined a number of factors that are relevant to this attribution determination, "with no single factor being decisive of the question." For analytical purposes, these factors may be divided into five broad categories.

A.   Role in Company

The first category of factors concerns the employee's role in the taxpaying company. Relevant considerations include the position held by the employee, hours worked, and duties performed, as well as the general importance of the employee to the success of the company. If the employee has received a large salary increase, comparing past duties and salary with current responsibilities and compensation also may provide significant insights into the reasonableness of the compensation scheme.

The Tax Court found that Elliott worked 80 hours per week, performed the functions of general manager, sales manager, and credit manager, and made all policy decisions concerning the parts and service department. These are all appropriate considerations. The Tax Court also considered Elliott's qualifications and found that although he was a "capable executive" he had no "special expertise." The Tax Court did not seem, however, to consider Elliott's extreme personal dedication and devotion to his work. To the extent that this benefited the corporation, it is surely something for which an independent shareholder would have been willing to compensate Elliott * * *.

B.   External Comparison

The second set of relevant factors is a comparison of the employee's salary with those paid by similar companies for similar services.

The Tax Court did compare Elliott's compensation to that of managers at other John Deere dealers. In making these comparisons, it appears that the Tax Court considered that Elliott was performing the functions that two or three people performed at other dealers. This was correct. Such comparisons should be made on the basis of services performed. If Elliott was performing the work of three people, the relevant comparison would be the combined salaries of those three people at another dealer.

C.   Character and Condition of Company

The third general category of factors concerns the character and condition of the company. The focus under this category may be on the company's size as indicated by its sales, net income, or capital value. Also relevant are the complexities of the business and general economic conditions. To the extent that they are relevant to this case, the Tax Court did adequately consider these factors.

D. Conflict of Interest

The fourth category focuses on those factors that may indicate a conflict of interest. The primary issue within this category is whether some relationship exists between the taxpaying company and its employee which might permit the company to disguise nondeductible corporate distributions of income as salary expenditures deductible under section 162(a)(1). Such a potentially exploitable relationship may exist where, as in this case, the employee is the taxpaying company's sole or controlling shareholder, or where the existence of a family relationship indicates that the terms of the compensation plan may not have been the result of a free bargain. Other factors also may point toward an attempt to distribute income through "compensation," including the existence of a bonus system that distributes all or nearly all of the company's pre-tax earnings, that amounts to a disproportionately large percentage of gross income when combined with salary, or that provides large bonuses to owner-executives, but none to non-owner management.

In this case, where Elliott was the sole shareholder, the sort of relationship existed that warrants scrutiny. The mere existence of such a relationship, however, when coupled with an absence of dividend payments, does not necessarily lead to the conclusion that the amount of compensation is unreasonably high. Further exploration of the situation is necessary.

In such a situation, as discussed earlier, it is appropriate to evaluate the compensation payments from the perspective of a hypothetical independent shareholder. If the bulk of the corporation's earnings are being paid out in the form of compensation, so that the corporate profits, after payment of the compensation, do not represent a reasonable return on the shareholder's equity in the corporation, then an independent shareholder would probably not approve of the compensation arrangement. If, however, that is not the case and the company's earnings on equity remain at a level that would satisfy an independent investor, there is a strong indication that management is providing compensable services and that profits are not being siphoned out of the company disguised as salary.

During the fiscal year ending February 28, 1975, Taxpayer reported equity of $415,133 and net profits (profits less taxes and compensation paid Elliott) of $88,969—a return of 21%. For fiscal year 1976, Taxpayer reported equity of $513,429 and net profits of $98,297—a return of 19%. Thus, the average rate of return on equity during these years was 20%. The Tax Court failed to consider the significance of this data. It seems clear, however, that this rate of return on equity would satisfy an independent investor and would indicate that Taxpayer and Elliott were not exploiting their relationship.

The Tax Court erred by limiting its analysis in this area to the facts that Elliott was Taxpayer's sole shareholder and Taxpayer paid no dividends. These are relevant factors, but they cannot be viewed in isolation
* * *

E.   Internal Consistency

Finally, evidence of an internal inconsistency in a company's treatment of payments to employees may indicate that the payments go beyond reasonable compensation. Bonuses that have not been awarded under a structured, formal, consistently applied program generally are suspect, as are bonuses consistently designated in amounts tracking either the percentage of the recipient's stock holdings, or some type of tax benefit. Similarly, salaries paid to controlling shareholders are open to question if, when compared to salaries paid non-owner management, they indicate that the level of compensation is a function of ownership, not corporate management responsibility. On the other hand, evidence of a reasonable, longstanding, consistently applied compensation plan is evidence that the compensation paid in the years in question was reasonable.

There was evidence in this case of a longstanding, consistently applied compensation plan. Since Taxpayer's incorporation, it had paid to Elliott an annual bonus equal to 50% of its net profits. Taxpayer contended before the Tax Court that because the yearly bonuses paid Elliott were derived from a predetermined formula that had been in use for over 20 years, it could be inferred that the bonuses constituted compensation for services rather than a dividend distribution. It noted that under the bonus formula Elliott's salary in some prior years had been too low to compensate him for the services he had rendered to Taxpayer, so that the higher salaries in the years in issue "resulted in average reasonable compensation during the 10–year period * * * 1968 through 1978."

In considering the significance of this longstanding bonus formula, the Tax Court erred in several respects.

The Tax Court failed to consider the reasonableness of the contingent formula itself; it concentrated instead on the amounts paid under the formula in two particular years. Such a formula may overcompensate in good years and undercompensate in bad years. This feature, however, does not necessarily make the formula unreasonable. It is permissible to pay and deduct compensation for services performed in prior years.

Whether payments under such a formula are reasonable will depend on whether the formula is reasonable. The reasonableness of a longstanding formula should not be determined on the basis of just one or two years. Taxpayer persuasively argues that, accepting the Tax Court's determination of reasonable compensation for 1974 and 1975, Elliott was severely undercompensated in terms of constant dollars in six of the seven preceding years.

Also relevant to the reasonableness of the formula used in this case is the return on equity an independent investor would have achieved. A formula which would not allow a reasonable return on equity is likely to be unreasonable. In this case, however, as discussed earlier, the return on equity in the years at issue was about 20%.

Over the long run, such a formula should reasonably compensate for the work done, the performance achieved, the responsibility assumed, and the experience and dedication of the employee. At the same time, it should not stand in the way of a satisfactory return on equity.

The Tax Court also discounted the significance of the bonus formula on the ground that "[n]o special incentive is necessary to insure [Elliott's] best efforts since he would 'receive the fruits of success through his status as the majority shareholder.' " To the extent that this implied that incentive payment plans for shareholder-employees are unreasonable, it was error.

Incentive payment plans are designed to encourage and compensate that extra effort and dedication which can be so valuable to a corporation. There is no reason a shareholder-employee should not also be entitled to such compensation if his dedication and efforts are instrumental to the corporation's success. In this case, there is no doubt that Elliott's extreme dedication and hard work were valuable to Taxpayer. If an outside investor would approve of such a compensation plan, that plan is probably reasonable. The fact that the recipient is a shareholder-employee does not make the plan unreasonable.

IV.   Conclusion

We reverse and remand to the Tax Court for reconsideration in light of this opinion * * *.

NOTES

1. *Elevation of independent investor test in determining reasonableness.* Courts continue to use various multi-factor tests to determine whether the amount of compensation paid to shareholder-employees is reasonable. See, e.g., Normandie Metal Fabricators v. Commissioner, 79 TCM 1738 (2000), aff'd per curiam, 2001–2 USTC ¶ 50,467 (2d Cir.2001) (employing the five factors delineated in Elliotts); Alpha Medical v. Commissioner, 172 F.3d 942 (6th Cir.1999) (employing a more elaborate nine factor test). The "independent investor" standard identified by the Elliotts' court (see pp. 43–44) has taken on increased significance in certain jurisdictions. Although the Second Circuit continues to apply a multi-factor test, it has stated that "the independent investor test is not a separate autonomous factor; rather, it provides a lens through which the entire analysis should be viewed." Dexsil Corp. v. Commissioner, 147 F.3d 96, 100–01 (2d Cir. 1998). The Seventh Circuit has gone even further by announcing that the independent investor test supplants the multi-factor test. See Exacto Spring Corp. v. Commissioner, 196 F.3d 833 (7th Cir.1999); Menard, Inc. and John R. Menard, Jr. v. Commissioner, 560 F.3d 620 (7th Cir. 2009). Not all courts, however, are moving in this direction. See Haffner's Service Stations v. Commissioner, 326 F.3d 1 (1st Cir.2003) (opting not to adopt independent investor test as the "exclusive answer" because "multiple factors may often be relevant"); Eberl's Claim Service v. Commissioner, 249 F.3d 994 (10th Cir.2001) (declining taxpayer's invitation to adopt independent investor test and adhering to traditional multi-factor test);

E.J. Harrison & Sons v. Commissioner, 270 F. Appx. 667 (9th Cir. 2008) (affirming the lower court's application of the factors delineated in Elliotts and rejecting a test based solely on a hypothetical independent investor).

2. *Compensatory purpose requirement.* In addition to the reasonableness requirement, purported compensation is deductible only if the payments are "purely for services" (see pp. 40–41). Although the requisite compensatory purpose is generally inferred if the amount paid to the employee-shareholder is reasonable, a court may consider corporate intent as a separate issue if it suspects a disguised dividend. For example, the Ninth Circuit ruled that an incentive compensation plan granting a large percentage of the company's profits to shareholder-employees was merely a vehicle for distributing profits that bore no relationship to the value of the services provided and disallowed the entire compensation deduction without regard to the purported reasonableness of the payments. OSC & Associates v. Commissioner, 187 F.3d 1116 (9th Cir.1999).

3. *Statutory authority.* What is the basis for concluding that a corporation may not deduct the dividends it pays? See I.R.C. § 161.

4. *$1,000,000 limitation.* No deduction is allowed for annual compensation in excess of $1,000,000 paid by a publicly-held corporation to its chief executive officer and its four other highest paid officer-employees. I.R.C. § 162(m). This limit applies regardless of whether the compensation would otherwise be "reasonable" under I.R.C. § 162(a)(1). The limitation does not apply to remuneration payable on a commission basis and to certain other performance-based compensation. For the Treasury Department's interpretation of this statutory limitation, see Treas. Reg. § 1.162–27.

5. *Shareholder level consequences.* Prior to 2003, dividends and compensation were taxed alike at the shareholder level. Now, dividends received by individuals are generally taxed at a maximum rate of 15%. I.R.C. § 1(h)(11). By contrast, compensation received by a shareholder-employee is taxed at a maximum rate of 35%. I.R.C. § 1(a). In addition, certain employment taxes are imposed on compensation. The double tax on corporate income paid out as nondeductible dividends (e.g., a 34% corporate tax and a 15% shareholder tax) still generally exceeds the individual taxes imposed on deductible compensation (e.g., a 35% shareholder tax and employment taxes). Nevertheless, the magnitude of the difference has declined considerably.

Thoni Service Corporation v. United States

United States Court of Appeals, Eleventh Circuit, 1997.
119 F.3d 10, 97–2 U.S. Tax Cas. (CCH) ¶ 50,548.

■ O'NEILL, SENIOR DISTRICT JUDGE:

* * *

I.

On March 3, 1987 Thoni Service Corporation ["TSC"] sold a parcel of improved real property worth $1,600,000 to its president and sole shareholder Richard Thoni for $75,000, thus transferring $1,525,000 of value to Mr. Thoni as the bargain element of the sale. [The purpose of the sale was to remove assets from the corporation in anticipation of civil judgments against the corporation.] On September 15, 1987, Mr. Thoni sold the property to a third party for $1,600,000.

TSC reported the transfer to Mr. Thoni as a capital gain [of $20,000] by subtracting its basis [of $55,000] from the actual transfer price of $75,000. On the same return TSC reported paying Mr. Thoni $116,666.66 in compensation and no dividends. Richard Thoni reported a $1,525,000 capital gain realized upon his sale of the property to a third party. Neither TSC's nor Mr. Thoni's tax return recorded the bargain element of the sale and neither characterized it either as a dividend or as a payment of compensation. Both returns were prepared by Dorothy Thoni, a TSC officer married to Richard Thoni.

[T]he IRS audited both TSC's and Mr. Thoni's tax returns and concluded that the March, 1987 bargain sale resulted in a dividend to Mr. Thoni, generating ordinary income upon his receipt of the property rather than capital gains upon its sale. The IRS adjusted TSC's tax return to reflect additional income of $1,525,000 from the disposition of appreciated property in the bargain sale. * * *

TSC paid the assessed deficiency then filed a claim for a refund. It asserted that the assessment resulted in an overpayment because the $1,525,000 in value transferred to Richard Thoni in 1987 was deductible as compensation for Mr. Thoni's services from 1983 to 1986, years in which he received no wages. The IRS disallowed the deduction and TSC filed this suit. * * * The district court granted summary judgment in favor of the IRS.

II.

In proceedings before the district court TSC contended that "the question of whether there is a sale is not the issue in this case. What we have is a factual question as to whether the $1,525,000 which exceeded the price actually paid by Richard Thoni was intended to be compensation." The district court, however, relying on the government's contention that "if there was a sale, the case ends" held that because "the government's theory of the case requires no factual proof other than that a sales transaction occurred, the Government is entitled to summary judgment after demonstrating the lack of genuine issue regarding the material fact of the sale."

Contrary to the position it successfully urged below, the government now concedes that "taxpayer is correct that the bargain element of a sale *can,* in theory, be compensation." Under applicable Treasury Regulations a bargain sale to a shareholder-employee can give rise to either non-deductible dividends or deductible compensation depending on whether the transaction is intended as a distribution to a shareholder "in his capacity as such," Treas. Reg. § 1.301–1(c), or as compensation to an employee through "a transfer of property in connection with the performance of services." Treas. Reg. § 1.83–6(a).

[W]e must decide whether there is a genuine issue of material fact as to whether TSC's bargain sale to its employee-shareholder Richard Thoni was intended, when it was made, to be a compensatory "transfer of property in connection with the performance of services."

III.

* * *

In its opposition to summary judgment TSC submitted the affidavit of Dorothy Thoni, a TSC officer knowledgeable about the transaction at issue when it was made. She attested that TSC made the bargain transfer "due to Richard's hard work and efforts as an employee" so he could be "compensated in small part for the years during which he did not take pay." Mrs. Thoni explained that despite this compensatory purpose she initially failed to claim the compensation deduction because having "not included the $1,525,000 as income, a deduction in that amount did not seem proper because it would cause a large loss on the corporate return." From this evidence a reasonable trier of fact could conclude that TSC intended the bargain sale as compensation rather than as a dividend.

While a taxpayer may not restructure a prior non-compensatory transaction once the taxpayer has structured a transaction as something *other than* the payment of compensation, in this case the original bargain sale structure of the transfer is not inconsistent with a payment of compensation. None of the record evidence demonstrated a contemporaneous intent to treat the transfer as a dividend. This case is therefore distinguishable from cases forbidding taxpayers from recharacterizing past transactions.

Given the lack of any prior inconsistent characterization in this case nothing precludes TSC from proving by competent evidence its contemporaneous intent that the transfer, when made, was intended to be compensatory.

Viewed in the light most favorable to TSC, as it must be on summary judgment, the evidence in the record could allow a reasonable finder of fact to conclude that TSC intended the transfer of valuable property to compensate Mr. Thoni for his services as an employee. This genuine issue of material fact as to whether the March 1987 bargain sale resulted in deductible compensation precludes entry of summary judgment. We therefore reverse and remand for further proceedings.

NOTES

1. *Sale vs. compensation for services.* Rather than selling the real estate to Mr. Thoni, the corporation presumably could have simply transferred the property to Mr. Thoni as compensation for his services. Why might the parties have been counseled to structure the transaction as a sale?

2. *Impact of taxing dividends at capital gains rates.* If the events in the Thoni case transpired today, would you still expect the taxpayers to argue that the bargain element of the sale represented compensation, rather than a dividend, now that dividends received by individuals are generally taxed at capital gains rates? See I.R.C. § 1(h)(11).

3. *Compensating for past services.* In the early stages of a corporate business, shareholder-employees may be paid artificially low salaries to enable the corporation to preserve cash to meet more immediate needs. After the business matures, the corporation may be in a position to pay additional amounts to compensate the shareholder-employees for any underpayment for past services. Payments for past services are regarded as reasonable only if both of the following are demonstrated:

(a) the employee was undercompensated in prior years, and

(b) the corporation intended to catch-up in the later year.

For instances where corporations were permitted to deduct compensation paid for past services, see Comtec Systems, Inc. v. Commissioner, 69 T.C.M. 1581 (1995); Acme Construction Co. v. Commissioner, 69 T.C.M. 1596 (1995); Pulsar Components International, Inc. v. Commissioner, 71 T.C.M. 2436 (1996).

Fin Hay Realty Co. v. United States

United States Court of Appeals, Third Circuit, 1968.
398 F.2d 694.

■ FREEDMAN, CIRCUIT JUDGE: We are presented in this case with the recurrent problem whether funds paid to a close corporation [a corporation with few shareholders] by its shareholders were additional contributions to capital or loans on which the corporation's payment of interest was deductible under § 163 of the Internal Revenue Code * * *.

Fin Hay Realty Co., the taxpayer, was organized on February 14, 1934, by Frank L. Finlaw and J. Louis Hay. Each of them contributed $10,000 for which he received one-half of the corporation's stock and at the same time each advanced an additional $15,000 for which the corporation issued to him its unsecured promissory note payable on demand and bearing interest at the rate of six per cent per annum. The corporation immediately purchased an apartment house in Newark, New Jersey, for $39,000 in cash. About a month later the two shareholders each advanced an additional $35,000 to the corporation in return for six per cent demand promissory notes and the next day the corporation purchased two apartment buildings in East Orange, New Jersey, for which it paid $75,000 in cash and gave the seller a six per cent * * * purchase money mortgage for the balance of $100,000.

[E]ach of the shareholders advanced an additional $3,000 to the corporation, bringing the total advanced by each shareholder to $53,000, in addition to their acknowledged stock subscriptions of $10,000 each.

Finlaw died in 1941 and his stock and notes passed to his two daughters in equal shares * * *. In 1949 Hay died * * *. [The corporation bought his stock and retired his notes.] Finlaw's daughters then became and still remain the sole shareholders of the corporation.

Thereafter the corporation continued to pay and deduct interest on Finlaw's notes, now held by his two daughters. In 1962 the Internal Revenue Service for the first time declared the payments on the notes not allowable as interest deductions and disallowed them for the tax years 1959 and 1960. The corporation thereupon repaid a total of $6,000 on account of the outstanding notes and in the following year after refinancing the mortgage on its real estate repaid the balance of $47,000. A short time later the Internal Revenue Service disallowed the interest deductions for the years 1961 and 1962. When the corporation failed to obtain refunds it brought this refund action in the district court. After a nonjury trial, the court denied the claims and entered judgment for the United States. From this judgment the corporation appeals.

This case arose in a factual setting where it is the corporation which is the party concerned that its obligations be deemed to represent a debt and not a stock interest * * *. [The] advantages in having the funds entrusted to a corporation treated as corporate obligations instead of contributions to capital have required the courts to look beyond the literal terms in which the parties have cast the transaction in order to determine its substantive nature.

In attempting to deal with this problem courts and commentators have isolated a number of criteria by which to judge the true nature of an investment which is in form a debt: (1) the intent of the parties; (2) the identity between creditors and shareholders; (3) the extent of participation in management by the holder of the instrument; (4) the ability of the corporation to obtain funds from outside sources; (5) the "thinness" of the capital structure in relation to debt; (6) the risk involved; (7) the formal indicia of the arrangement; (8) the relative position of the obligees as to other creditors regarding the payment of interest and principal; (9) the voting power of the holder of the instrument; (10) the provision of a fixed rate of interest; (11) a contingency on the obligation to repay; (12) the source of the interest payments; (13) the presence or absence of a fixed maturity date; (14) a provision for redemption by the corporation; (15) a provision for redemption at the option of the holder; and (16) the timing of the advance with reference to the organization of the corporation.

While the Internal Revenue Code of 1954 was under consideration, and after its adoption, Congress sought to identify the criteria which would determine whether an investment represents a debt or equity, but these and similar efforts have not found acceptance. It still remains true that neither any single criterion nor any series of criteria can provide a conclusive answer in the kaleidoscopic circumstances which individual cases present.

The various factors which have been identified in the cases are only aids in answering the ultimate question whether the investment, analyzed in terms of its economic reality, constitutes risk capital entirely subject to the fortunes of the corporate venture or represents a strict debtor-creditor relationship. Since there is often an element of risk in a loan, just as there is an element of risk in an equity interest, the conflicting elements do not end at a clear line in all cases.

In a corporation which has numerous shareholders with varying interests, the arm's-length relationship between the corporation and a shareholder who supplies funds to it inevitably results in a transaction whose form mirrors its substance. Where the corporation is closely held, however, and the same persons occupy both sides of the bargaining table, form does not necessarily correspond to the intrinsic economic nature of the transaction, for the parties may mold it at their will with no countervailing pull. This is particularly so where a shareholder can have the funds he advances to a corporation treated as corporate obligations instead of contributions to capital without affecting his proportionate equity interest. Labels, which are perhaps the best expression of the subjective intention of parties to a transaction, thus lose their meaningfulness.

[U]nder an objective test of economic reality it is useful to compare the form which a similar transaction would have taken had it been between the corporation and an outside lender, and if the shareholder's advance is far more speculative than what an outsider would make, it is obviously a loan in name only.

In the present case all the formal indicia of an obligation were meticulously made to appear. The corporation, however, was the complete creature of the two shareholders who had the power to create whatever appearance would be of tax benefit to them despite the economic reality of the transaction. Each shareholder owned an equal proportion of stock and was making an equal additional contribution, so that whether Finlaw and Hay designated any part of their additional contributions as debt or as stock would not dilute their proportionate equity interests. There was no restriction because of the possible excessive debt structure, for the corporation had been created to acquire real estate and had no outside creditors except mortgagees who, of course, would have no concern for general creditors because they had priority in the security of the real estate * * *.

The shareholders here, moreover, lacked one of the principal advantages of creditors. Although the corporation issued demand notes for the advances, nevertheless, as the court below found, it could not have repaid them for a number of years. The economic reality was that the corporation used the proceeds of the notes to purchase its original assets, and the advances represented a long term commitment dependent on the future value of the real estate and the ability of the corporation to sell or refinance it. Only because such an entwining of interest existed between the two shareholders and the corporation, so different from the arm's-length relationship between a corporation and an outside creditor, were they willing to invest in the notes and allow them to go unpaid for so many years while the corporation continued to enjoy the advantages of uninterrupted ownership of its real estate.

It is true that real estate values rose steadily with a consequent improvement in the mortgage market, so that looking back the investment now appears to have been a good one. As events unfolded, the corporation reached a point at which it could have repaid the notes through refinancing, but this does not obliterate the uncontradicted testimony that in 1934 it was impossible to obtain any outside mortgage financing for real estate of this kind except through the device of a purchase money mortgage taken back by the seller.

It is argued that the rate of interest at six per cent per annum was far more than the shareholders could have obtained from other investments. This argument, however, is self-defeating, for it implies that the shareholders would damage their own corporation by an overcharge for interest. There was, moreover, enough objective evidence to neutralize this contention. The outside mortgage obtained at the time the corporation purchased the East Orange property bore interest at the rate of six per cent even though the mortgagee was protected by an equity in excess of forty per cent of the value of the property. In any event, to compare the six per cent interest rate of the notes with other 1934 rates ignores the most salient feature of the notes—their risk. It is difficult to escape the inference that a prudent outside businessman would not have risked his capital in six per cent unsecured demand notes in Fin Hay Realty Co. in 1934. The evidence therefore amply justifies the conclusion of the district court that the form which the parties gave to their transaction did not match its economic reality * * *.

The burden was on the taxpayer to prove that the determination by the Internal Revenue Service that the advances represented capital contributions was incorrect. The district court was justified in holding that the taxpayer had not met this burden.

■ VAN DUSEN, CIRCUIT JUDGE, dissenting.

I respectfully dissent on the ground that the "entire evidence," in light of appellate court decisions discussing the often-presented problem of corporate debt versus equity, does not permit the conclusion reached by the District Court.

When the parties holding debt of the taxpayer corporation have a formal debt obligation and it is clear that all parties intended the investment to take the form of debt, a series of considerations such as those mentioned by the District Court should be used to determine whether the form and intent should be disregarded for federal tax purposes. As I read the District Court's opinion, the focus was entirely on inferring "the intent of the taxpayer's only two stockholders" at the time the debt was created. To that end, the District Court drew certain inferences which are largely immaterial to the proper decision, and which are clearly erroneous in light of the stipulated facts and uncontroverted evidence.

Whether or not the corporate taxpayer is entitled to an interest deduction turns in this case on the "real nature of the transaction in question" or on whether "the degree of risk may be said to be reasonably equivalent to that which equity capital would bear had an investor, under similar circumstances, made the advances * * *." When this test is used, the entire history of the corporate taxpayer becomes relevant and a focus solely on the year of incorporation or investment of the debt is not sufficient.

Turning within this framework to the facts, the record does not justify the conclusion that the form of the debt should be disregarded for purposes of federal taxation. The debt was evidenced by written notes, carried 6% interest which was paid every year, and was not subordinated in any way to similar debt of general creditors. It was carried on the corporate books and tax returns as debt, being payable on demand, it was always listed as a debt maturing in less than one year * * *. The parties clearly intended the advances as debt and unfailingly treated them as such * * *.

[T]he District Court placed heavy reliance on the fact that the stockholder's debt was in the same proportion as their equity holdings. This fact, without more, is not controlling since there is no doubt that investors can have a dual status. The inferences that "more" was involved in this case are not justified by this record. The fact that the loans were used to begin the corporate life and buy the income-producing assets must be placed in proper perspective. Without any basis in the record, the District Court assumed that the loans were advanced to prevent a sudden corporate deficit that was created by the Wainwright Street property investment's unexpectedly requiring more funds than the corporation had. Real estate cases, however, and uncontroverted testimony in this case show that corporations owning and operating buildings frequently and traditionally borrow the substantial part of money needed to secure their principal assets and that this was contemplated by a corporate resolution passed in the month of organization at the original directors' meeting. Cases denying the validity of debt because it is contemporaneously advanced with the start of corporate life generally involve other industries or a partnership * * *.

The loans were denied debt status because there was no intent to seek repayment within a "reasonable time," because the corporation had no retirement provision (or fund) for the principal and because the debt had no maturity date. To the contrary, demand notes have a maturity date at the discretion of the holder (or of his transferee when the notes are freely negotiable, as were the Fin Hay notes). And failure to transfer the notes or demand payment is irrelevant when, as here, the evidence shows that the 6% rate made the debt a good investment * * *. There was no evidence and no discussion of what constitutes a "reasonable time" for refraining from making a demand on such a promissory note.

Although appellate decisions on the debt-equity problem constantly reiterate the maxim that each instance of definition turns on the particular facts of each case, a reading of many of these cases * * * indicates * * * distinct conclusions concerning the assessment of the severity of the "risk" attached to alleged debt transactions * * *. [F]ew cases (and particularly few where taxpayers holding formal debt lose) deny debt status or even raise the question where the enterprise risk, as in this case, involves the mere holding and operation of real estate. As the risks increase, involving, in addition, construction of the real estate, or non-real estate operations subject to more immediate risk-creating problems or marketing, labor, advertisement, supplies, etc., the frequency of cases challenging debt and of decisions finding equity increase. The uncontradicted testimony * * * of the universal practice in the Newark area in conformity to the course followed by taxpayer is entitled to consideration. Also, the subsequent successful history of this corporate taxpayer cannot be disregarded and militates strongly against denying an interest deduction on this record. The Fin Hay Realty Co. did not go bankrupt, was not unable to refinance or extend its purchase money mortgage due in 1939, and has never failed to meet a demanded purchase of the notes * * *.

In J. S. Biritz Construction Co. v. C.I.R., the court said:

There is actually no evidence that this was not a loan, was not intended to be a loan, or that Biritz actually intended to make a capital investment rather than a loan.

We think the Tax Court has painted with too broad a brush in limiting the permissible activities of an entrepreneur in personally financing his business. Financing embraces both equity and debt transactions and we do not think the courts should enunciate a rule of law that a sole stockholder may not loan money or transfer assets to a corporation in a loan transaction. If this is to be the law, Congress should so declare it. We feel the controlling principle should be that any transaction which is intrinsically clear upon its face should be accorded its legal due unless the transaction is a mere sham or subterfuge set up solely or principally for tax-avoidance purposes.

I would reverse and enter judgment for the corporate taxpayer.

NOTES

1. *Illustration of deductible interest.* Courts continue to resolve the question of whether payments by a corporation with respect to money provided by a shareholder represent deductible interest or nondeductible dividends on a case-by-case basis by considering the factors delineated in Fin Hay, as well as any other factors relevant to the case at hand. See, e.g., Delta Plastics, Inc. v. Commissioner, 85 T.C.M. 940 (2003) (illustrating use of this approach where a court concluded that the payments in question constituted deductible interest). For an appellate opinion rejecting the Tax Court's disallowance of a corporation's interest deduction, see Indmar Prods. Co. v. Commissioner, 444 F.3d 771 (6th Cir. 2006).

2. *I.R.C. § 385.* In 1969, Congress delegated to the Treasury the task of developing rules for determining whether an interest in a corporation is stock or debt. See I.R.C. § 385(a), (b). After more than 40 years, the Treasury has yet to complete this task. In 1992, Congress enacted I.R.C. § 385(c) which requires the holder of an interest in a corporation to treat the interest in the same manner as the corporation or to disclose an inconsistent position on the holder's tax return. For further discussion of the problem of distinguishing debt from equity, see William T. Plumb, Jr., "The Federal Income Tax Significance of Corporate Debt: A Critical Analysis and a Proposal," 26 Tax Law Review 369 (1971).

3. *Eliminating both levels of tax.* Is it ever possible to eliminate both layers of tax on corporate income disbursed to shareholders? See the Maxwell case that follows.

Maxwell v. Commissioner
Hi Life Products, Inc. v. Commissioner

United States Tax Court, 1990.
95 T.C. 107.

■ RUWE, JUDGE: Respondent determined a deficiency of $64,185 in Peter E. Maxwell's and Helen E. Maxwell's Federal income tax for taxable year ending December 31, 1977. In a separate notice of deficiency, respondent determined a deficiency of $58,800 in the Federal corporate income tax of Hi Life Products, Inc., for its taxable year ending October 31, 1977. * * *

Unless otherwise stated, "petitioner" shall hereinafter refer only to Mr. Maxwell, and "petitioners" shall hereinafter collectively refer to Mr. Maxwell and Hi Life.

Hi Life was organized * * * by petitioner and Mrs. Maxwell, and engages in the manufacturing of urethane foam carpet padding. At all relevant times, the shareholders of Hi Life and their respective percentage of shares of stock owned were as follows:

Shareholder	Percentage of Stock Owned
Peter E. Maxwell	47.5 percent
Helen E. Maxwell	47.5 percent
Alan Sadler	2.5 percent
Marlene Sadler	2.5 percent

Petitioner was president of Hi Life and acted as the general manager of Hi Life's operations. In this capacity petitioner was responsible for sales, purchase of major materials, and engineering of plant equipment. Mrs. Maxwell was the executive vice president, secretary, and treasurer of Hi Life * * *. Mr. Sadler was vice president of Hi Life and was also the plant manager * * *. Mrs. Sadler was the assistant secretary/treasurer * * *. During 1977, Hi Life's board of directors was comprised of petitioner, Mrs. Maxwell, and Mr. Sadler.

At the time Hi Life was incorporated, petitioner had approximately 19 years' experience working in the urethane foam industry * * *.

On or about September 24, 1976, all four officers of Hi Life (the Maxwells and the Sadlers) signed a State of California compensation fund statement to exclude all executive officers of Hi Life from coverage under Hi Life's workers' compensation policy. The officers excluded themselves from coverage in order to reduce the insurance premiums.

One of the pieces of equipment used at Hi Life is a mixing machine that was designed by petitioner and assembled at Hi Life's plant during February 1977 * * *.

During the operation of the machine, a cylinder rotates at approximately 3600 revolutions per minute * * *.

On March 9, 1977, petitioner was injured while operating the mixing machine. The mixing machine had been operated on only one prior occasion, approximately one week before. At the time of the injury, petitioner had been training plant personnel to operate the mixing machine. He failed to notice, however, that a bolt was protruding from the rotating cylinder in place of the flush setscrew. As petitioner was attempting to turn off the machine, his sweater sleeve caught on the protruding bolt, and he was pulled into the mixing machine. As a result, petitioner suffered serious injury including a fractured forearm, soft tissue lacerations, and second and third degree burns. The injury required surgery and the installation of a metal plate in his forearm. Petitioner experienced some loss of use of his forearm * * *.

Petitioner did not return to work at Hi Life for approximately six to eight weeks after he was injured by the mixing machine * * *.

Approximately two months after he was injured, petitioner read * * * in the Wall Street Journal about an employee's claim against an employer corporation which was partly owned by the employee. Following up on this, petitioner consulted Hi Life's corporate attorney, Floyd R. Brown * * *. Attorney Brown informed petitioner that he might have a claim against Hi Life, but recommended that he seek outside counsel and referred petitioner to several other attorneys. Petitioner subsequently retained attorney Tristan Pico to handle his claim against Hi Life. For services rendered, Mr. Maxwell paid attorney Pico a flat fee retainer of $4,000, no part of which was reimbursed by Hi Life. Attorney Brown provided professional services to Hi Life with regard to the personal injury claim of petitioner and billed Hi Life for those services.

On October 18, 1977, attorney Pico sent a demand letter to attorney Brown which proposed that Hi Life pay the sum of $125,000 in settlement of petitioner's claim * * *. The demand letter contained an analysis of the aforementioned facts * * *. The demand letter also analyzed the law upon which the claim was based * * *. The demand letter finally provided that the offer would be withdrawn and a lawsuit filed if the demand was not met by October 24, 1977. No lawsuit was ever filed against Hi Life on petitioner's behalf.

Attorney Brown performed research into the legal issues raised by the demand letter, and concluded that Hi Life was liable for petitioner's injuries. His conclusion was based on Hi Life's failure to obtain workers' compensation coverage for petitioner. Attorney Brown also performed research into the tax consequences of petitioner's claim. He subsequently contacted Mrs. Maxwell and recommended to her that Hi Life settle petitioner's claim.

On or about October 28, 1977, approximately 10 days after attorney Pico sent the demand letter to attorney Brown, petitioner called a special meeting of the board of directors for the purpose of considering his settlement offer. Present at the meeting were petitioner, Mrs. Maxwell, Mr. Sadler, and attorney Brown. Attorney Pico was not present. Although petitioner was a member of the board of directors, he excused himself from consideration of the matter. Attorney Brown recommended to the board of directors that Hi Life settle petitioner's claim for the total sum of $122,500. The board of directors, consisting of Mrs. Maxwell and Mr. Sadler, unanimously decided to settle petitioner's claim for the sum of $122,500.

The parties have stipulated, and we find, that the reasonable monetary value of the injuries suffered by petitioner was $122,500.

On the same day as the meeting of the board of directors, petitioner signed a "General Release of all Claims," in which petitioner agreed to release his claim against Hi Life in consideration for $122,500 * * *. Pursuant to this settlement, Hi Life issued two checks to petitioner * * * in the amount of $72,500 [and] * * * $50,000 * * *.

On its corporate Federal income tax return for the taxable year ending October 31, 1977, Hi Life deducted $122,500 as a "miscellaneous office expense" under section 162(a) * * *.

[O]n their individual tax return for the calendar year ending December 31, 1977, petitioner and Mrs. Maxwell did not report the $122,500 as part of their gross income.

Respondent determined that the $122,500 payment by Hi Life to petitioner was a dividend. He, therefore, determined that petitioner's 1977 taxable income should be increased by $122,500, and disallowed Hi Life's claimed deduction of the same $122,500.

OPINION

Resolution of both issues in these consolidated cases depends upon our characterization of the $122,500 that Hi Life paid to petitioner during 1977. Petitioners argue that the $122,500 that Hi Life paid to petitioner is: (1) properly deductible by Hi Life under section 162(a), as a payment in settlement of petitioner's personal injury claim against Hi Life; and (2) excludable from petitioner's gross income under section 104(a)(2) as a payment for damages received on account of personal injuries.

Respondent argues that petitioners have failed to prove that the $122,500 that Hi Life paid to petitioner was paid on account of petitioner's personal injuries. Respondent determined that the payment from Hi Life to petitioner was a disguised dividend to petitioner and, therefore, not deductible by Hi Life, and not excludable from petitioner's gross income. Respondent's determination is presumed correct and petitioners bear the burden of proving otherwise * * *.

Section 162(a) allows as a deduction all the ordinary and necessary expenses paid or incurred during the taxable year in carrying on any trade or business. Amounts paid or accrued by a taxpayer on account of injuries received by employees and lump-sum amounts paid or accrued as compensation for injuries are proper deductions as ordinary and necessary expenses * * *. Thus, Hi Life is entitled to a deduction for the $122,500 that it paid to petitioner, if such payment was paid to petitioner as compensation for his personal injuries.

Section 61(a) defines gross income as "all income from whatever source derived." Under section 104(a)(2), however, gross income does not include "the amount of any damages received (whether by suit or agreement) on account of personal injuries or sickness." * * *. Thus, if it is determined that the payment from Hi Life to petitioner was to compensate petitioner for his physical injuries and to settle his claim for damages, then petitioner is entitled to exclude that amount from his gross income * * *.

In rendering our decision, we are mindful that the settlement transaction between Hi Life and petitioner was a transaction between a closely held corporation and its president who, along with his wife, were the controlling shareholders. Under the facts of these consolidated cases, petitioner and Hi Life could not be said to have been dealing at arm's length. We must, therefore, carefully scrutinize the settlement transaction between petitioner and Hi Life * * *.

In determining whether the form of a transaction between closely related parties has substance, we should compare their actions with what would have occurred if the transaction had occurred between parties who were dealing at arm's length * * *. One would normally expect unrelated parties who were involved in a claim for damages resulting from serious personal injuries to consult legal counsel * * * to get an informed opinion regarding their respective rights and liabilities. Petitioner and Hi Life each retained independent legal counsel. Petitioner's attorney advised him that he had a legal claim against Hi Life and that based upon Hi Life's failure to secure workers' compensation, the traditional defenses of contributory negligence, assumption of risk, and fellow servant rule were abrogated. Hi Life's board of directors was advised by its own attorney that payment of damages was reasonable in light of the circumstances and applicable California law. There is nothing in the record to show that this legal advice was given in bad faith or that petitioners were not entitled to rely upon it in good faith * * *.

It appears to us that the contemporaneous legal advice given to petitioners was reasonable. More importantly, we find that petitioners' reliance on their attorneys was reasonable under the circumstances * * *. We find that the $122,500 payment from Hi Life to petitioner was in substance a payment in settlement of the injuries petitioner sustained from operation of the mixing machine. Thus, petitioner is entitled to exclude this amount from his gross income under section 104(a)(2), and Hi Life is entitled to a deduction in this amount under section 162(a).

We recognize that tax considerations played a part in petitioner's claim against Hi Life and in the ultimate settlement of that claim. In that respect, these cases are no different [from] cases in which we must determine whether corporate payments to an employee-stockholder are compensation for personal services or nondeductible dividends. The question in both instances is whether there was a reasonable basis, independent of tax considerations, for the taxpayer's characterization of the payment. The fact that settlement of petitioner's claim entitled Hi Life to a deduction and petitioner to exclude the $122,500 payment, does not vitiate the reasonableness of the underlying transaction. The fact that after petitioner sustained serious personal injuries, he consulted counsel and eventually entered into a settlement that had tax advantages, does not detract from the reasonableness of the settlement under the circumstances in these cases. Taxpayers have the legal right to decrease taxes, or avoid them altogether, by means which the law permits. The question is whether what was done, apart from the tax motive, was the thing which the law intended * * *. In light of the facts in these cases, we hold that the law intended a deduction under section 162(a) for Hi Life and an exclusion for petitioner under section 104(a)(2).

NOTES

1. *Importance of form*. Identify the specific actions taken by the taxpayers and their counsel that led the court to find in favor of the taxpayers. Would the court have reached the same result in the absence of such careful adherence to proper form?

2. *Stipulation of damages*. How did the Internal Revenue Service's stipulation to the monetary value of the damages suffered by Maxwell affect the outcome of the case?

b.   INHIBITING TRIPLE TAXATION

I.R.C. §§ 243, 246(c), 1059(a)–(c)

One corporation may be a shareholder of another corporation. In this situation, three or more layers of tax can potentially be imposed on corporate income because dividends cannot be deducted by the distributing corporation and are included in the gross income of the corporate shareholder.

> *Example 2–A (Potential for triple taxation when corporate shareholder exists):* Alan owns all of the stock of Parent Corporation ("P") which, in turn, owns all of the stock of Subsidiary Corporation ("S"). Earnings of S that are distributed as dividends to P and, in turn, distributed by P as dividends to Alan can potentially be taxed three times because these earnings represent gross income,
>
> (1) to S when earned,
>
> (2) to P when distributed by S, and
>
> (3) to Alan when distributed by P.
>
> If lower tier subsidiaries exist (e.g., S owns all the stock of T), the earnings of each lower tier subsidiary could be taxed more than three times. An additional layer of tax could be imposed as income earned by

the lowest tier subsidiary moves up each link in the corporate chain until the final tax is imposed when the corporate income reaches the individual shareholder (Alan).

Congress has enacted a variety of relief measures to mitigate the imposition of multiple layers of *corporate* tax. One of these mechanisms is I.R.C. § 243, which allows a corporation *receiving* dividends a deduction equivalent to at least 70% of the dividends received. Although this dividend received deduction might be seen as an appropriate mechanism for limiting multiple layers of corporate tax, it also renders dividend income more desirable to corporations than other forms of gross income. As a result, I.R.C. § 243 is sometimes utilized as an affirmative planning tool.

Litton Industries, Inc. v. Commissioner

United States Tax Court, 1987.
89 T.C. 1086.

■ CLAPP, JUDGE: Respondent determined a deficiency in petitioner's Federal corporate income tax for the year ended July 29, 1973, in the amount of $11,583,054. After concessions, the issue for decision is whether Litton Industries received a $30,000,000 dividend from Stouffer Corporation, its wholly owned subsidiary, or whether that sum represented proceeds from the sale of Stouffer stock to Nestle Corporation.

FINDINGS OF FACT

[L]itton Industries, Inc. (petitioner) and its subsidiaries manufactured and sold business systems and equipment, defense and marine systems, industrial systems and equipment, and microwave cooking equipment * * *.

On October 4, 1967, petitioner acquired all the outstanding stock of Stouffer Corporation (Stouffer), a corporation whose common stock was listed and traded on the New York stock exchange. Stouffer manufactured and sold frozen prepared food and operated hotels and food management services and restaurants * * *.

In early 1972, Charles B. Thornton (Thornton), the chairman of Litton's board of directors; Joseph Imirie, president of Stouffer; and James Biggar, an executive of Stouffer, discussed project "T.I.B.," i.e., the sale of Stouffer. In July 1972, Litton's board of directors discussed the mechanics and problems of selling Stouffer. As of August 1, 1972, Stouffer's accumulated earnings and profits exceeded $30 million. On August 23, 1972, Stouffer declared a $30 million dividend which it paid to Litton in the form of a $30 million negotiable promissory note, and at that time, Thornton believed that Litton would have no difficulty receiving an adequate offer for Stouffer. Two weeks later, on September 7, 1972, petitioner announced publicly its interest in disposing of Stouffer. Subsequent to said announcement, Litton received inquiries from a number of interested sources * * * about the possible purchase of * * * Stouffer's business.

On March 1, 1973, Nestle Alimentana S.A. Corporation (Nestle), a Swiss corporation, offered to buy all of Stouffer's stock for $105,000,000. On March 5, 1973, Nestle paid Litton $74,962,518 in cash for all the outstanding stock of Stouffer and $30,000,000 in cash for the promissory note * * *.

OPINION

The issue for decision is whether the $30,000,000 dividend declared by Stouffer on August 23, 1972, and paid to its parent, Litton, by means of a negotiable promissory note was truly a dividend for tax purposes or whether it should be considered part of the proceeds received by Litton from the sale of all of Stouffer's stock on March 1, 1973. If, as petitioner contends, the $30,000,000 constitutes a dividend, petitioner may deduct [100] percent of that amount * * * pursuant to section 243 * * *. However, if the $30,000,000 represents part of the selling price of the Stouffer stock, as contended by respondent, the entire amount will be added to the proceeds of the sale and taxed to Litton as additional capital gain * * *.

The instant case is substantially governed by Waterman Steamship Corp. v. Commissioner, 50 T.C. 650 (1968), rev'd. 430 F.2d 1185 (5th Cir.1970), cert. denied 401 U.S. 939 (1971) * * *.

In many respects, the facts of this case and those of Waterman Steamship are parallel. The principal difference, and the one which we find to be most significant, is the timing of the dividend action. In Waterman Steamship, the taxpayer corporation received an offer to purchase the stock of two of its wholly-owned subsidiary corporations, Pan–Atlantic and Gulf Florida, for $3,500,000 cash. The board of directors of Waterman Steamship rejected that offer but countered with an offer to sell the two subsidiaries for $700,000 after the subsidiaries declared and arranged for payments of dividends to Waterman Steamship amounting in the aggregate to $2,800,000. Negotiations between the parties ensued, and the agreements which resulted therefrom included, in specific detail, provisions for the declaration of a dividend by Pan–Atlantic to Waterman Steamship prior to the signing of the sales agreement and the closing of that transaction. Furthermore, the agreements called for the purchaser to loan * * * funds to Pan–Atlantic promptly in order to pay off the promissory note by which the dividend had been paid. Once the agreement was reached, the entire transaction was carried out by a series of meetings commencing at 12 noon on January 21, 1955, and ending at 1:30 p.m. the same day. At the first meeting the board of directors of Pan–Atlantic met and declared a dividend in the form of a promissory note in the amount of $2,799,820. The dividend was paid by execution and delivery of the promissory note. At 12:30 p.m., the board of directors of the purchaser * * * met and authorized the purchase and financing of Pan–Atlantic and Gulf Florida. At 1 p.m., the directors of Waterman authorized the sale of all outstanding stock of Pan–Atlantic and Gulf Florida to [the purchaser]. Immediately following that meeting, the sales agreement was executed by the parties. The agreement provided that the purchaser guaranteed prompt payment of the liabilities of

Pan–Atlantic and Gulf Florida including payment of any notes given by either corporation as a dividend.

Finally at 1:30 p.m., the new board of directors of Pan–Atlantic authorized the borrowing of sufficient funds from the purchaser * * * to pay off the promissory note to Waterman Steamship, which was done forthwith. As the Fifth Circuit pointed out, "By the end of the day and within a ninety minute period, the financial cycle had been completed. Waterman had $3,500,000, hopefully tax-free, all of which came from * * * the buyers of the stock." This Court concluded that the distribution from Pan–Atlantic to Waterman was a dividend. The Fifth Circuit reversed, concluding that the dividend and sale were one transaction.

The timing in the instant case was markedly different. The dividend was declared by Stouffer on August 23, 1972, at which time the promissory note in payment of the dividend was issued to Litton. There had been some general preliminary discussions about the sale of Stouffer, and it was expected that Stouffer would be a very marketable company which would sell quickly. However, at the time the dividend was declared, no formal action had been taken to initiate the sale of Stouffer. It was not until 2 weeks later that Litton publicly announced that Stouffer was for sale. There ensued over the next 6 months many discussions with various corporations * * * regarding Litton's disposition of Stouffer through sale of all or part of the business to a particular buyer * * *. All of this culminated on March 1, 1973, over 6 months after the dividend was declared, with the purchase by Nestle of all of Stouffer's stock. Nestle also purchased the outstanding promissory note for $30,000,000 in cash.

In the instant case, the declaration of the dividend and the sale of the stock were substantially separated in time in contrast to Waterman Steamship where the different transactions occurred essentially simultaneously. In Waterman Steamship, it seems quite clear that no dividend would have been declared if all of the remaining steps in the transaction had not been lined up in order on the closing table and did not in fact take place. Here, however, Stouffer declared the dividend, issued the promissory note and definitely committed itself to the dividend before even making a public announcement that Stouffer was for sale. Respondent argues that the only way petitioner could ever receive the dividend was by raising revenue through a sale of Stouffer. Therefore, respondent asserts the two events (the declaration of the dividend and then the sale of the company) were inextricably tied together and should be treated as one transaction for tax purposes. In our view, respondent ignores the fact that Stouffer could have raised sufficient revenue for the dividend from other avenues, such as a partial public offering or borrowing. Admittedly, there had been discussions at Litton about the sale of Stouffer which was considered to be a very saleable company. However, there are many slips between the cup and the lip, and it does not take much of a stretch of the imagination to picture a variety of circumstances under which Stouffer might have been taken off the market and no sale consummated. Under these circumstances it is

unlikely that respondent would have considered the dividend to be a nullity
* * *.

The term "dividend" is defined in section 316(a) as a distribution by a corporation to its shareholders out of earnings and profits. The parties have stipulated that Stouffer had earnings and profits exceeding $30,000,000 at the time the dividend was declared. This Court has recognized that a dividend may be paid by a note. Based on these criteria, the $30,000,000 distribution by Stouffer would clearly constitute a dividend if the sale of Stouffer had not occurred. We are not persuaded that the subsequent sale of Stouffer to Nestle changes that result merely because it was more advantageous to Litton from a tax perspective.

It is well established that a taxpayer is entitled to structure his affairs and transactions in order to minimize his taxes. This proposition does not give a taxpayer carte blanche to set up a transaction in any form which will avoid tax consequences regardless of whether the transaction has substance. Gregory v. Helvering, 293 U.S. 465 (1935). A variety of factors present here preclude a finding of sham or subterfuge. Although the record in this case clearly shows that Litton intended at the time the dividend was declared to sell Stouffer, no formal action had been taken and no announcement had been made. There was no definite purchaser waiting in the wings with the terms and conditions of sale already agreed upon * * *. Nothing in the record here suggests that there was any prearranged sale agreement, formal or informal, at the time the dividend was declared * * *.

On this record, we hold that for Federal tax purposes Stouffer declared a dividend to petitioner on August 23, 1972, and, subsequently, petitioner sold all of its stock in Stouffer to Nestle for $75,000,000.

NOTES

1. *I.R.C. § 243.* If Y Corporation paid a $100,000 dividend to X corporation, how much taxable income would the dividend create for X corporation if,

> (a) X Corporation owned 1% of the stock of Y Corporation? See I.R.C. § 243(a)(1).
>
> (b) X Corporation owned 25% of the stock of Y Corporation? See I.R.C. § 243(c).
>
> (c) X Corporation owned 90% of the stock of Y Corporation? See I.R.C. §§ 243(a)(3), (b).

Why might Congress have decided to provide a different degree of relief in each of the above situations?

2. *Dividend stripping.* In contrast to the strategy employed by Litton Industries, some corporations have endeavored to exploit the dividend received deduction by buying corporate stock in advance of a dividend, receiving the dividend and then selling the stock to recognize a capital loss.

Example 2–B (Combining dividend received deduction with capital loss): If X Corporation buys $10,000,000 of Y Corporation stock shortly before Y Corporation is to pay a $2,000,000 dividend on that stock, X Corporation takes a $10,000,000 basis in the Y stock. When X receives the $2,000,000 dividend from Y, X incurs a tax liability of approximately $200,000.[4] The value of the Y stock should decline roughly to $8,000,000 after the dividend is paid. Why? If X then sells the Y stock for $8,000,000, X recognizes a $2,000,000 capital loss. If X has a $2,000,000 capital gain from some other transaction, X would normally pay a tax of $680,000 on that gain.[5] The capital loss from the sale of the Y stock, however, offsets X's $2,000,000 capital gain. Hence, the purchase and sale of the Y stock enables X to substitute $2,000,000 of dividend income (on which it pays a tax of $200,000) for $2,000,000 of capital gain (on which X would have paid a tax of $680,000).

Congress has impeded the result in Example 2–B with the following mechanisms:

(a) *I.R.C. § 246(c):* The dividends received deduction is not allowed with respect to dividends received on stock held for 45 days or less during the 90–day period beginning on the date which is 45 days before the date on which such shares become ex-dividend and in certain other circumstances. See I.R.C. § 246(c)(1). In certain cases, a dividend received deduction is not allowed even if the stock is held for more than 45 days. See I.R.C. §§ 246(c)(2), (4). What are the tax consequences to X, in Example 2–B, if X held the Y stock for exactly 45 days during the period specified in § 246(c)(1)(A)?

(b) *I.R.C. § 1059:* A corporate shareholder that receives an "extraordinary dividend" must reduce its basis in the stock of the dividend paying corporation by the amount of any dividend received deduction allowed for the extraordinary dividend, unless the recipient held the stock for more than two years before the dividend announcement date. See I.R.C. §§ 1059(a), (b). Generally, an "extraordinary dividend" is defined as a dividend that equals or exceeds 10% of the recipient's basis in the stock of the dividend paying corporation. (The threshold is reduced to 5% of basis in the case of preferred stock.) See I.R.C. § 1059(c). What are the tax

---

4.

$2,000,000
−1,400,000   (70% dividend received deduction)
$600,000
×   34%   (tax rate)
$200,000.

5.

$2,000,000
×   34%   (tax rate)
$680,000.

consequences to X, in Example 2–B, if X had held the Y stock for exactly two years before the announcement date of the $2,000,000 dividend?

4.   CORPORATE ALTERNATIVE MINIMUM TAX

I.R.C. §§ 55–59

C Corporations that generate substantial gross receipts are subject to an alternative tax regime that can increase their annual tax liability.[6] The regular corporate tax is imposed, for the most part, at rates of 34% or 35% on a base of "taxable income." See I.R.C. § 11. The corporate alternative minimum tax is imposed at a rate of 20% on a broader base; namely, "alternative minimum taxable income" ("AMTI"). See I.R.C. § 55(b). The corporation pays its regular tax plus any amount by which its alternative minimum tax exceeds the regular tax. See I.R.C. § 55(a). In effect, the corporation pays the higher of the two taxes.

In 1986, Congress dramatically expanded the scope of AMTI. Prior to that time, some analysts believed that economically profitable corporations were exploiting statutory exclusions and deductions to minimize taxable income under the regular corporate tax. Rather than repealing these exclusions and deductions, Congress strengthened the corporate alternative tax regime by expanding the scope of AMTI to reflect more closely the economic profitability of the corporation. In this way, it was thought that all economically profitable corporations would at least pay the alternative minimum tax.

AMTI is derived from taxable income, the base on which the regular corporate tax is imposed. See I.R.C. §§ 11(a), 55(b)(2). In the course of computing AMTI, certain regular tax exclusions are eliminated, certain regular tax deductions are scaled-down or disallowed and certain regular tax deferrals are accelerated (yielding an amount referred to later in this paragraph as "tentative AMTI"). See generally, I.R.C. §§ 56(a), 57. Most importantly, a blanket adjustment is made to insure that AMTI is not less than 75% of the corporation's "adjusted current earnings" ("ACE"). See I.R.C. § 56(g). The ACE computation is highly technical. Basically, ACE represents tentative AMTI augmented by virtually all remaining regular tax exclusions (e.g., life insurance proceeds and tax-exempt interest) and by certain remaining regular tax deductions (e.g., the 70% dividend received deduction of I.R.C. § 243(a)).

After a corporation incurs an alternative minimum tax liability, it may be able to offset its regular tax liability in future years by part or all of the alternative minimum tax it paid. See generally, I.R.C. § 53. The possibility of a future credit, however, often fails to diminish significantly the sting of the alternative minimum tax due to the time value of money.[7]

---

6. Corporations with average gross receipts below a ceiling amount ranging from $5,000,000 to $7,500,000 are not subject to the corporate alternative minimum tax. See I.R.C. § 55(e).

7. For a review of the time value of money, see pp. 468–470.

When calculating a corporation's tax liability, it is critical to determine whether a potential alternative minimum tax liability exists.[8] (The same can be said when quantifying the tax liability of an individual.) Many large corporations that would otherwise pay little, if any, tax due to "regular" tax exclusions, deferrals, deductions and credits face substantial alternative minimum tax liabilities.

B.   CORPORATE PENALTY TAXES

Corporations are potentially subject to taxes other than the regular corporate tax and the corporate alternative minimum tax. In addition, corporations that accumulate their earnings can be subject to one of two penalty taxes; namely, the accumulated earnings tax or the personal holding company tax.

1.   ACCUMULATED EARNINGS TAX

I.R.C. §§ 531–537

In addition to the regular corporate tax and the corporate alternative minimum tax, a penalty tax known as the "accumulated earnings tax" is imposed on certain corporations. Unlike the regular corporate tax and the alternative minimum tax, the accumulated earnings tax is not self-assessed. Rather, the Internal Revenue Service assesses this penalty tax when it audits a corporation's tax return.

The accumulated earnings tax applies to corporations "formed or availed of" to avoid the shareholder income tax imposed when corporate earnings are distributed as dividends. I.R.C. § 532. This penalty tax was enacted when individual tax rates were much higher than corporate tax rates, a condition that existed during most of the twentieth century. See Exhibit I, pp. 6–7. When this condition prevails, a strong incentive exists to accumulate corporate income and thereby avoid the high individual taxes imposed when corporate earnings are distributed to shareholders as dividends. Corporations that yield to this temptation run the risk of being subjected to the accumulated earnings tax. The threat of the penalty tax is intended to induce corporations that would otherwise accumulate their earnings to pay dividends to shareholders. At present, the maximum individual tax rate is identical to the maximum corporate tax rate. See Exhibit I, p. 7 (bottom row). Nevertheless, Congress has not seen fit to repeal the accumulated earnings tax and its presence may still induce corporations potentially within its scope to pay dividends.

---

8. This section merely highlights the highly technical corporate alternative minimum tax regime. A detailed analysis of the statute and the regulations is necessary to determine whether, and to what extent, a corporate alternative minimum tax liability exists in any particular case. For a detailed analysis of this subject, see Tax Management Portfolio 752–2nd, Corporate Alternative Minimum Tax (Bureau of National Affairs, 2007).

When a corporation accumulates earnings in excess of reasonable business needs, the proscribed intent to avoid the shareholder income tax is deemed to exist, unless the taxpayer can prove that it did not accumulate earnings for the purpose of avoiding the shareholder tax. I.R.C. § 533(a). Due to the difficulty of proving a negative, the factual question of whether the corporation accumulated earnings in excess of reasonable business needs is the focus of most accumulated earnings tax cases.

United States v. Donruss Co.

Supreme Court of the United States, 1969.
393 U.S. 297, 89 S.Ct. 501.

■ MR. JUSTICE MARSHALL delivered the opinion of the Court.

* * *

Respondent is a corporation engaged in the manufacture and sale of bubble gum and candy * * *. Since 1954, all of respondent's outstanding stock has been owned by Don B. Wiener. In each of the tax years from 1955 to 1961, respondent operated profitably, increasing its undistributed earnings from $1,021,288.58 to $1,679,315.37. [N]o dividends were declared during the entire period.

Wiener gave several reasons for respondent's accumulation policy; among them were capital and inventory requirements, increasing costs, and the risks inherent in the particular business and in the general economy. Wiener also expressed a general desire to expand * * *.

The Commissioner of Internal Revenue assessed accumulated earnings taxes against respondent for the years 1960 and 1961. Respondent paid the tax and brought this refund suit. At the conclusion of the trial, the Government specifically requested that the jury be instructed that:

> It is not necessary that avoidance of shareholder's tax be the sole purpose for the unreasonable accumulation of earnings; it is sufficient if it is one of the purposes for the company's accumulation policy.

The instruction was refused and the court instructed the jury in the terms of the statute that tax avoidance had to be "the purpose" of the accumulations. The jury, in response to interrogatories, found that respondent had accumulated earnings beyond the reasonable needs of its business, but that it had not retained its earnings for the purpose of avoiding income tax on Wiener. Judgment was entered for respondent and the Government appealed.

The Court of Appeals * * * rejected the Government's proposed instruction and held that the tax applied only if tax avoidance was the "dominant * * * motive" for the accumulation. We granted the Government's petition for certiorari to resolve a conflict among the circuits over the degree of "purpose" necessary for the application of the accumulated earnings tax * * *.

I.

The accumulated earnings tax is established by §§ 531–537 of the Internal Revenue Code of 1954. Section 531 imposes the tax. Section 532 defines the corporations to which the tax shall apply. That section provides:

> The accumulated earnings tax imposed by section 531 shall apply to every corporation * * * formed or availed of for the purpose of avoiding the income tax with respect to its shareholders * * *, by permitting earnings and profits to accumulate instead of being divided or distributed.

Section 533(a) provides that:

> For purposes of section 532, the fact that the earnings and profits of a corporation are permitted to accumulate beyond the reasonable needs of the business shall be determinative of the purpose to avoid the income tax with respect to shareholders, unless the corporation by the preponderance of the evidence shall prove to the contrary.

> * * *

The dispute before us is a narrow one. The Government contends that in order to rebut the presumption contained in § 533(a), the taxpayer must establish by the preponderance of the evidence that tax avoidance with respect to shareholders was not "one of the purposes" for the accumulation of earnings beyond the reasonable needs of the business. Respondent argues that it may rebut that presumption by demonstrating that tax avoidance was not the "dominant, controlling, or impelling" reason for the accumulation. [R]espondent does not challenge the jury's finding that its accumulation was indeed unreasonable. We intimate no opinion about the standards governing reasonableness of corporate accumulations.

We conclude from an examination of the * * * purpose and the legislative history of the statute that the Government's construction of the statute is the correct one. Accordingly, we reverse the judgment of the court below and remand the case for a new trial on the issue of whether avoidance of shareholder tax was one of the purposes of respondent's accumulations.

> * * *

III.

The accumulated earnings tax is one congressional attempt to deter use of a corporate entity to avoid personal income taxes. The purpose of the tax "is to compel the company to distribute any profits not needed for the conduct of its business so that, when so distributed, individual stockholders will become liable" for taxes on the dividends received, Helvering v. Chicago Stock Yards Co., 318 U.S. 693, 699 (1943). The tax originated in the Tariff Act of 1913, the first personal income tax statute following ratification of the Sixteenth Amendment. * * *

> * * *

[T]he legislative history of the accumulated earnings tax demonstrates a continuing concern with the use of the corporate form to avoid income tax on a corporation's shareholders. Numerous methods were employed to prevent this practice, all of which proved unsatisfactory in one way or another. Two conclusions can be drawn from Congress' efforts. First, Congress recognized the tremendous difficulty of ascertaining the purpose of corporate accumulations. Second, it saw that accumulation was often necessary for legitimate and reasonable business purposes. It appears clear to us that the congressional response to these facts has been to emphasize unreasonable accumulation as the most significant factor in the incidence of the tax. The reasonableness of an accumulation, while subject to honest difference of opinion, is a much more objective inquiry, and is susceptible of more effective scrutiny, than are the vagaries of corporate motive.

Respondent would have us adopt a test that requires that tax avoidance purpose need be dominant, impelling, or controlling. It seems to us that such a test would exacerbate the problems that Congress was trying to avoid. Rarely is there one motive, or even one dominant motive, for corporate decisions. Numerous factors contribute to the action ultimately decided upon. Respondent's test would allow taxpayers to escape the tax when it is proved that at least one other motive was equal to tax avoidance. We doubt that such a determination can be made with any accuracy, and it is certainly one which will depend almost exclusively on the interested testimony of corporate management. Respondent's test would thus go a long way toward destroying the presumption that Congress created to meet this very problem. * * *.

* * *

Finally, we cannot subscribe to respondent's suggestion that our holding would make purpose totally irrelevant. It still serves to isolate those cases in which tax avoidance motives did not contribute to the decision to accumulate. Obviously in such a case imposition of the tax would be futile. In addition, "purpose" means more than mere knowledge, undoubtedly present in nearly every case. It is still open to the taxpayer to show that even though knowledge of the tax consequences was present, that knowledge did not contribute to the decision to accumulate earnings.

Reversed and remanded.

■ Mr. Justice Harlan, whom Mr. Justice Douglas and Mr. Justice Stewart join, concurring in part and dissenting in part.

[Omitted]

Snow Manufacturing Company v. Commissioner

United States Tax Court, 1986.
86 T.C. 260.

■ Gerber, Judge: Respondent determined deficiencies in petitioner's income tax for petitioner's taxable years ended June 30, 1979, and June 30, 1980, in the respective amounts of $109,816 and $70,968. [T]he issue before us is whether petitioner is liable for the accumulated-earnings tax imposed by section 531.

FINDINGS OF FACT

   * * *

Background

   Petitioner [was] a California corporation * * *.

   * * *

   Petitioner's business consisted of reconditioning and rebuilding small automobile parts, such as pumps, generators, brakes, starters, and distributors. * * *.

   Petitioner's manufacturing activities were conducted in a 20,000–square-foot [rented] building * * *.

Business Operations

A.   Growth and Shortage of Space

   Between 1974 and 1979 new antipollution laws led to an increase in the number of models of parts remanufactured by petitioner presumably because of the public's tendency to attempt to retain "pre-antipollution" vehicles. During this period petitioner experienced a growth in its total sales, from approximately $1.9 million in 1974 to approximately $3.1 million in 1979. Between 1974 and 1979 petitioner added new remanufacturing equipment to meet the growing demand for its products.

   Petitioner required operating space for the machinery used in the remanufacturing process, and storage space for new and used parts, finished goods, and materials. As early as 1973 (and perhaps before) and continuing through the taxable years at issue, petitioner stored some of these items on its property outside its building.

   * * *

   Storage problems affected petitioner's choice of present and future product lines. [Lowell Lewis (Lewis), petitioner's general manager,] wanted to add additional product lines and generate more business, work, and profit. Lewis met with a management consultant in 1978 or 1979 * * * [who] suggested that petitioner would need to acquire additional space before much could be done.

B.   Expansion

   * * *

   Prior to and during 1979 and 1980, Lewis contacted or received correspondence from a number of real estate brokers regarding the location of additional property for petitioner. Lewis visited several proposed sites but found each of them unacceptable.

   * * *

On December 15, 1979, petitioner's board of directors held a special meeting * * *. The minutes of the meeting in part provide:

The increasing necessity of an additional 30,000 square foot building and the purchase of sufficient land for the building * * * was discussed. The Board approved [an offer to purchase] the adjoining property or other land as continuing to operate in the present small facility with outside storage for expensive parts and cores was becoming a heavy burden in inclement weather.

The latest cost figures for the required additional space is:
Land and 30,000 foot building. $765,000
Machinery acquisition, moving,
   installation and wiring.   150,000
                                                  $915,000

At the time of the meeting petitioner did not own property on which to build a 30,000–square-foot building * * * and was not negotiating for the purchase of * * * property.

* * *

Financial Data

The following table presents petitioner's accumulated earnings and profits, and additions thereto:

Taxable Year Ended	Accumulated Earnings and Profits	Increase in Earnings and Profits Over Prior Years
June 30, 1978	$2,088,321	—
June 30, 1979	2,402,774	$314,453
June 30, 1980	2,613,898	211,124

The next table summarizes petitioner's net liquid assets (excess of current assets over current liabilities[9]) for the same taxable years:

Taxable Year Ended	Net Liquid Assets	Increase Over Prior Year
June 30, 1978	$2,397,661	—
June 30, 1979	2,693,944	$296,283
June 30, 1980	2,903,546	209,602

* * *

Throughout its existence as a corporation, petitioner paid no dividends.

On May 3, 1979, petitioner purchased a tax-exempt Michigan Housing bond for $904,239. * * *

OPINION

The disparity during the years in question between corporate and individual tax rates may have encouraged the use of corporations to reduce

---

9. Editor's note. "Current assets" represent money and rights expected to be converted to money within a short time period (e.g., accounts receivable and inventory). "Current liabilities" represent obligations expected to be paid within a relatively short time period.

shareholders' overall tax liabilities through the accumulation of earnings in excess of reasonable business needs. The accumulated-earnings tax is a means of discouraging the accumulation of corporate earnings not needed in the conduct of a business. * * *. The tax is considered to be a penalty and therefore is to be strictly construed.

Where a corporation accumulates earnings and profits, the most significant factor in determining whether the accumulated-earnings tax applies is the reasonableness of the corporate accumulation. Section 533(a) establishes the presumption that a corporation that accumulates earnings and profits beyond its reasonable business needs does so for the proscribed purpose of tax avoidance. The section 533(a) presumption, however, is rebuttable by a preponderance of evidence to the contrary. Therefore, the accumulated-earnings tax is not imposed where a corporation has made an unreasonable accumulation but lacks the proscribed purpose. * * *.

Whether a corporation has permitted its earnings and profits to accumulate beyond its reasonable business needs and whether the corporation was availed of for tax-avoidance purposes are both questions of fact. The reasonable needs of a business should be determined by the officers and directors of the corporation. We are reluctant to substitute our business judgment for theirs unless the facts and circumstances, buttressed by the presumptive correctness of respondent's determination, require us to do so.

* * *

Very generally, both parties in comparing petitioner's resources to its needs follow the approach adopted by this Court in Bardahl Manufacturing Corp. v. Commissioner, T.C. Memo. 1965–200, and since used in many cases. In Bardahl Manufacturing Corp. v. Commissioner, we determined the reasonableness of a corporate accumulation by numerically comparing the corporate taxpayer's resources with its total business needs. Petitioner and respondent disagree on [two] critical points that relate to the Bardahl comparison: * * * [1] whether petitioner was justified in retaining funds for expansion; and [2] whether to compare petitioner's total business needs to its accumulated earnings and profits or its net liquid assets.

* * *

Expansion

A business may need funds to expand. To provide for the bona fide expansion of its business, a corporation may accumulate earnings and profits. See sec. 1.537–2(b)(1), Income Tax Regs. * * *. Section 537(a) provides that the term ''reasonable needs of the business,'' a concept critical to a determination of whether the accumulated-earnings tax applies, includes the ''reasonably anticipated needs of the business.'' As section 1.537–1(b), Income Tax Regs., indicates, ''reasonably anticipated needs of the business'' do not include the vague or uncertain plan of a corporate taxpayer to acquire new property * * *.

* * * The requirement [imposed by the regulations] of a ''specific, definite, and feasible'' plan does not demand that the taxpayer produce

meticulously drawn, formal blueprints for action. A corporation, however, cannot immunize itself from the accumulated-earnings tax merely by referring to expansion in its corporate minutes. Definiteness of plan coupled with action taken towards its consummation are essential to justify an accumulation as reasonable. * * *. The test is a practical one, namely, that the projected need appears to have been a real consideration during the taxable year, and not simply an afterthought to justify a challenged accumulation.

Petitioner presently maintains that its reasonable business needs for fiscal 1979 and 1980 included the need to accumulate $1,500,000 to acquire adequate space for its operation * * *. Respondent argues that petitioner lacked "specific, definite, and feasible" expansion plans during the 1979 and 1980 taxable years, and accordingly cannot justify accumulating any corporate earnings for expansion. Determining whether petitioner had "specific, definite, and feasible" expansion plans requires that we carefully review petitioner's stated efforts to acquire additional property.

By 1973, petitioner lacked adequate space for storage and operations. The problem did not ameliorate in succeeding years, which were marked by growth in petitioner's business. We accordingly are convinced that petitioner needed additional space during the taxable years at issue.

* * *

Petitioner at various times explored the availability of * * * several nearby industrial sites, and maintained contact with real estate agents. None of this activity resulted in negotiations to acquire specific properties. We accordingly regard these initiatives as merely preliminary efforts.

In petitioner's consideration of various properties, Lewis played an important role. Lewis, however, lacked authority to purchase property and, consequently, we do not regard his interest in various sites as tantamount to a plan by petitioner to purchase additional land. * * *.

Petitioner contends that the minutes of the board meeting of December 15, 1979, indicate the board's willingness to finance petitioner's expansion. The minutes, as petitioner notes, contain estimates of both the cost and square footage of additional property. They reflect, however, that as of late 1979 petitioner's board had not selected a specific site for a new building. * * *.

* * *

[T]he demand of the statute is not met merely by proof that a need for accumulation exists. [T]he need must be coupled with a determination on the part of the taxpayer to meet that need. * * *. The record indicates that during [1978 and 1979] petitioner gave no more than preliminary consideration to purchasing property * * *. Discussions of possible options and incipient investigations are not a substitute for a clear plan coupled with action. We accordingly conclude that petitioner lacked a "specific, definite, and feasible" plan for expansion during the taxable years at issue.

Application of Section 533

* * * The parties disagree on how to apply section 533(a) to this case. * * *

Since the parties agree that petitioner accumulated earnings and profits during the taxable years at issue, the dispute here may be stated quite simply: should we compare petitioner's reasonable business needs with its accumulated earnings and profits ($2,402,774 as of June 30, 1979, and $2,613,898 as of June 30, 1980) [as the taxpayer contends] or with its net liquid assets ($2,693,944 as of June 30, 1979, and $2,903,546 as of June 30, 1980) [as the Internal Revenue Service contends]? We conclude that the proper measure is a comparison of reasonable business needs with accumulated earnings and profits, since net liquid assets exceeded accumulated earnings and profits.

Accumulated earnings and profits and net liquid assets are distinct concepts in tax law. Accumulated earnings and profits is the historical net increase in a corporation's assets above stockholders' contributions to capital. Net liquid assets or working capital is the excess of current assets over current liabilities.

As stated in Smoot Sand & Gavel Corp. v. Commissioner, 274 F.2d 495, 500–501 (4th Cir.1960), the nature of the surplus a corporation accumulates determines whether the accumulated earnings tax applies:

> [T]he size of the accumulated earnings and profits or surplus is not the crucial factor; rather, it is the reasonableness and nature of the surplus. Part of the surplus may be justifiably earmarked in the form of reserves, for specific, necessary business needs. Again, to the extent the surplus has been translated into plant expansion, increased receivables, enlarged inventories, or other assets related to its business, the corporation may accumulate surplus with impunity. Where, on the other hand, the accumulation of surplus is reflected in liquid assets in excess of the immediate or reasonably foreseeable business needs of the corporation, there is a strong indication that the purpose of the accumulation is to prevent the imposition of income taxes upon dividends which would have been distributed to the shareholders.
>
> * * *

Respondent's position in essence renders the amount of accumulated earnings and profits irrelevant under section 533(a) where it is lesser in amount than net liquid assets. The Code provides no support for this position. The case law, although utilizing net liquid assets as a quantitative measure of accumulated earnings and profits within the meaning of section 533, has not breathed life into net liquid assets by establishing it as a substitute for the statutorily mandated standard of accumulated earnings and profits.

Where net liquid assets exceed accumulated earnings and profits, net liquid assets are reflected in the full amount of accumulated earnings and profits. Reasonable business needs may be met from this amount, and dividends may be distributed from any excess. We conclude that where net liquid assets exceed accumulated earnings and profits, reasonable business needs should be compared against the latter amount.

Conclusion

We can now compare petitioner's accumulated earnings and profits reflected in net liquid assets with its reasonable business needs and determine whether petitioner had a proscribed accumulation of earnings and profits. During each of the taxable years at issue, petitioner's accumulated earnings and profits reflected in net liquid assets exceeded its reasonable business needs, as the following chart indicates:

	Year Ending June 30, 1979		Year Ending June 30, 1980	
Accumulated Earnings and Profits Reflected in Net Liquid Assets		$2,402,774		$2,613,898
Reserve for Tax Deficiencies	$256,544		$256,544	
Working Capital [Needs]	1,239,572		1,721,406	
Reserve for Acquiring Additional Space	0		0	
[Total] Needs of Business		$1,496,116		$1,977,950
Excess of Accumulated Earnings and Profits Over Business Needs		$906,658		$635,948

During the taxable year ended June 30, 1979, petitioner's earnings and profits increased by $314,453, while during the following taxable year its earnings and profits increased by $211,124. We, accordingly, conclude that during fiscal 1979 and fiscal 1980 petitioner permitted its earnings and profits to accumulate beyond its reasonable business needs.

As we have observed, under section 533(a) the fact that a corporation has permitted its earnings and profits to accumulate beyond the reasonable needs of its business is determinative of the purpose to avoid the income tax with respect to its shareholders, unless the corporation by the preponderance of evidence proves to the contrary. In the alternative to its argument that it did not so accumulate earnings and profits, petitioner maintains that if it permitted its earnings and profits to accumulate beyond its reasonable business needs, tax avoidance was not one of its purposes. We find that the evidence not only fails to overcome the presumptions but additionally corroborates a purposeful avoidance of income tax.

A poor dividend history is an indicium of the purpose to avoid income tax with respect to a corporation's shareholders. Sec. 1.533–1(a)(2), Income Tax Regs. During its entire corporate existence, petitioner paid no dividends. Another indicium is investment by the corporation in assets having no reasonable connection with the business. Sec. 1.533–1(a)(2), Income Tax Regs. Petitioner, a California corporation engaged in the remanufacture of auto parts, in 1979 purchased a tax-exempt Michigan Housing bond for $904,239. Petitioner does not explain why this asset was acquired, and we see no reasonable relationship between its acquisition and petitioner's business.

We conclude that petitioner has not rebutted the statutory presumption and hold that during the taxable years in issue petitioner was availed of for the proscribed purpose of section 532, and is thus liable for the section 531 tax.

* * *

NOTES

1. *Purpose of avoiding shareholder tax.* Although it is normally difficult to prove that avoidance of shareholder tax is not one of the purposes for an accumulation of earnings in excess of business needs, certain factors can strengthen an argument to this effect.

(a) *Pattern of paying dividends.* The fact that a corporation establishes a consistent pattern of distributing part of its earnings as dividends bolsters the position that the corporation did not intend to avoid the shareholder tax on dividends. See, e.g., Bremerton Sun Publishing Co. v. Commissioner, 44 T.C. 566 (1965) (fact that petitioner paid dividends for six consecutive years, the last two of which were the years in issue, ranging from 27.8% to 30.4% of after-tax earnings contributed to finding that proscribed purpose did not exist, notwithstanding that petitioner, in fact, accumulated more earnings than it needed). Thus, the threat of the penalty tax may cause some corporations to pay dividends to provide evidence that the corporation was not being utilized to avoid the shareholder tax on dividends.

(b) *Publicly traded stock.* An absence of highly concentrated stock ownership is normally inconsistent with the intent to avoid shareholder tax, unless a small group of shareholders effectively control the company. See Trico Products Corp. v. Commissioner, 46 B.T.A. 346 (1942), aff'd 137 F.2d 424 (2d Cir.1943) (holding that intent to avoid shareholder tax existed in case of widely-held corporation where six shareholders owned 74% of the stock during the years in issue). Consequently, the penalty tax is normally applied to closely-held corporations, although no statutory limitation on the number of shareholders exists. See I.R.C. § 532(c); Technalysis Corporation v. Commissioner, 101 T.C. 397 (1993) (confirming that I.R.C. § 531 can apply to a publicly held corporation in case where a small group of shareholders owned less than 40% of the stock, but court held that intent to avoid shareholder tax did not exist and that the accumulated earnings tax did not apply, despite finding that the corporation had accumulated earnings in excess of business needs).

2. *Penalty tax base.* If a corporation with accumulated earnings in excess of business needs cannot rebut the presumption of I.R.C. § 533(a), it is subject to the accumulated earnings tax. The accumulated earnings tax is imposed on "accumulated taxable income." I.R.C. § 531. Accumulated taxable income is derived from taxable income, the base on which the regular corporate tax is imposed. I.R.C. § 535(a). Taxable income, however, is reduced by the regular corporate tax (I.R.C. § 535(b)(1)) and any dividends paid to shareholders (I.R.C. § 535(a)) since these disbursements reduce the amount of earnings available for distribution to shareholders, notwithstanding that these amounts are not deductible for regular tax purposes. (Several other additions to and subtractions from taxable income must also be made. See I.R.C. §§ 535(b), (c).) Thus, accumulated earnings tax liability can often be avoided for any tax year in which a corporation distributes all of its after-tax income as dividends to shareholders.

It is important to understand that the accumulated earnings tax is generally not imposed on the entire difference between accumulated earnings and reasonable business needs. Rather, the tax is only imposed on that part of the excess accumulation created by undistributed earnings from the tax year for which the penalty tax is assessed.

Example 2–C (Undistributed earnings for year at issue caps penalty tax base): At the end of Year 10, Willco had accumulated earnings of $10,000,000 and reasonable business needs of $8,000,000. During Year 10, Willco had taxable income of $140,000 and paid a regular corporate tax of $40,000. If the Internal Revenue Service audited Willco's Year 10 tax return and assessed an accumulated earnings tax for that year, Willco's accumulated taxable income is $100,000 (taxable income of $140,000 less regular corporate tax of $40,000), assuming that Willco paid no dividends during Year 10 and that no other adjustments under I.R.C. § 535 need to be made. Thus, the accumulated earnings tax for Year 10 can only be assessed on $100,000, notwithstanding that Willco's accumulated earnings exceeded its reasonable business needs by $2,000,000 at the end of Year 10.

3. *Penalty tax rate.* The rate of the accumulated earnings tax is the same as the maximum individual tax rate that applies to dividends, currently 15%. I.R.C. §§ 1(h), 531. In effect, the corporation pays a tax equal to the tax that the shareholders would have paid had the corporation distributed all unneeded earnings accumulated during the tax year as dividends. The corporate penalty tax, however, does not substitute for the shareholder tax imposed when corporate earnings are actually distributed. The shareholders will still be taxed when the corporation ultimately distributes the earnings that were subject to the accumulated earnings tax. Thus, corporate earnings subjected to the accumulated earnings tax are effectively taxed three times: first by the regular corporate tax, then by the accumulated earnings tax, and finally by the shareholder income tax when the earnings are actually distributed as dividends.

Example 2–D (Accumulated earnings tax does not substitute for shareholder tax): With regard to Example 2–C, if Willco's accumulated taxable income in Year 10 is $100,000, its accumulated earnings tax liability for that year is $15,000.[10] This is the same amount of tax Willco's shareholders would have paid if Willco had distributed a

---

10. $100,000 x 15% = $15,000.

$100,000 dividend during Year 10, assuming that all the shareholders are subject to the maximum individual tax rate applicable to dividends. (If Willco had distributed the $100,000 as a dividend during Year 10, Willco would not be subject to the accumulated earnings tax because the dividend would reduce Willco's accumulated taxable income to zero.) Notwithstanding that Willco's Year 10 earnings have been subjected to the accumulated earnings tax, Willco's shareholders will still be taxed when those earnings are actually distributed as dividends.

4. *Timing of dividends.* For purposes of computing accumulated taxable income, dividends paid within two and one-half months after the close of the taxable year are treated as paid during the prior tax year. I.R.C. § 563(a). This rule allows a corporation that desires to eliminate its exposure to the accumulated earnings tax sufficient time to calculate the amount of the dividend that must be paid to achieve this end.

> *Example 2–E (Deduction for dividends paid after year-end)*: Willco cannot compile all the income and expense data to calculate accumulated taxable income for Year 10 until early in Year 11. Once Willco compiles its Year 10 tax data, it determines that its Year 10 accumulated taxable income is $100,000. Willco has until March 15 of Year 11 to pay dividends that will reduce its Year 10 accumulated taxable income. Note, however, that a dividend paid on or before March 15 of Year 11 only reduces Year 10 accumulated taxable income. That dividend does *not* reduce Year 11 accumulated taxable income. See Treas. Reg. § 1.563–1 ("[A] dividend paid after the close of any tax year and on or before the 15th day of the third month following the close of such taxable year * * * shall not be included in the computation of the dividends paid deduction for the year of payment.").

2.   Personal Holding Company Tax

I.R.C. §§ 541–547

The personal holding company tax is another corporate penalty tax. It applies to those corporations that satisfy the statutory definition of a "personal holding company." Personal holding companies are *not* subject to the accumulated earnings tax, so the two penalty taxes cannot apply simultaneously. I.R.C. § 532(b)(1). The personal holding company tax is designed to be self-assessed.

The personal holding company tax was enacted in 1934, "to prevent the avoidance of income tax on individuals by means of the formation of closely-held corporations to which were transferred the individuals' investments and services or talents."[11] Like the accumulated earnings tax, the personal holding company tax was enacted when individual tax rates were much higher than corporate rates. That condition created a significant incentive for high-income individuals to transfer stocks, bonds and certain other income producing properties to a corporation so that their investment

---

11.   S. Rep. No. 1041, 86th Cong. 2d Sess., 1960–1 Cum.Bull. 817, 820.

income would only be subjected to the low corporate tax as long as the corporate earnings were not distributed as dividends. At present, the maximum individual tax rate is identical to the maximum corporate tax rate. See Exhibit I, p. 7 (bottom row). Nevertheless, Congress has not seen fit to repeal the personal holding company tax.

In marked contrast to the ambiguous standard that controls the application of the accumulated earnings tax, the conditions that must be satisfied for a corporation to be a personal holding company are statutorily defined in technical detail. A corporation is a personal holding company in any tax year in which both of the following conditions are satisfied.

1. At least 60% of the corporation's gross income (after certain adjustments) is "personal holding company income" (e.g., interest, dividends, certain rents, and certain royalties).

2. More than 50% of the corporation's stock is owned by five or fewer individuals (and certain related parties) at any time during the last half of the tax year.

See generally, I.R.C. §§ 542(a), 543. Much to the chagrin of taxpayers, the technical personal holding company rules are strictly construed.

Irving Berlin Music Corporation v. United States

United States Court of Claims, 1973.
487 F.2d 540.

■ KASHIWA, JUDGE, delivered the opinion of the court:

Plaintiff filed this suit for the refund of federal personal holding company income taxes * * * for the fiscal years ended January 31, 1965, and January 31, 1966, in the respective amounts of $137,524 and $160,851, plus interest.

The case comes before us on defendant's motion for summary judgment and plaintiff's cross-motion for summary judgment. The facts are stipulated and there are no material issues of fact. We hold for the defendant for the reasons hereinafter stated.

The essential facts are as follows. Irving Berlin has composed about 1,000 musical compositions, of which about 650 continued to be published and offered for sale to the general public and to professional users of music during the tax years in question. In 1946 he incorporated Irving Berlin Music Corporation (hereinafter Berlin Music) * * *. Irving Berlin has been the sole owner of all of the authorized and issued capital stock of Berlin Music since its formation. In 1946 Irving Berlin entered into an agreement with Berlin Music establishing their working relationship * * *.

On January 31, 1960, Irving Berlin and Berlin Music entered into a new agreement superseding the earlier 1946 agreement. Under the 1960 agreement, Berlin Music continued as exclusive licensee to publish * * * the music compositions of Irving Berlin; however, Irving Berlin [also] engaged Berlin Music to act as his "exclusive agent" to * * * issue licenses with regard to all performing rights to his music. * * *.

* * *

The major revenues obtained from the exploitation and promotion of musical compositions by music publishers are derived from royalties paid by music users for grand performing rights licenses. It is with respect to grand performing rights that the controversy in this case arises. [G]rand performing rights encompass dramatic performances of music, including legitimate stage productions, electrical transcriptions, phonograph records, motion picture sound synchronization, stock and amateur theater rights, and dramatic uses on radio and television. * * *. Berlin Music collects royalties from music users under licenses issued solely for the use of or the right to use Irving Berlin's musical compositions. * * *. During the life span of a particular song, these licenses number many hundreds, requiring specialized business expertise to achieve the highest possible royalties without pricing the musical composition out of the market.

It has been stipulated that all of the services performed by Berlin Music were performed in a manner similar to other established music publishers typical of the music industry. Under both the 1946 and 1960 agreements between Irving Berlin and his corporation, Berlin Music was empowered to deduct and retain as compensation for its music publisher services 50 per cent of the gross royalties paid by music users to Berlin Music under the performing rights licenses it issued. * * *.

During the fiscal years ended January 31, 1965, and January 31, 1966, Berlin Music deducted and retained $233,877 and $230,565, respectively, as the 50 per cent portions of the gross royalties paid by music users under the performing rights licenses it issued for the use of or the right to use Irving Berlin's songs. In a statutory notice of deficiency dated June 9, 1967, the Government determined that these amounts constituted copyright royalties under section 543(a)(4) of the Internal Revenue Code of 1954, and, therefore, that Berlin Music was a personal holding company under section 542(a) of the Code.

The case was ably briefed and argued by the respective counsel for plaintiff and defendant, and the parties have succeeded in narrowing the issue before us to one of statutory construction. We are called upon to determine whether the shares of copyright royalties received and retained by taxpayer Berlin Music under performing rights licenses issued to music users for the right to use the musical compositions of taxpayer's sole stockholder, Irving Berlin, constitute copyright royalties to it within the meaning of section 543(a)(4) and hence are subject to the tax on personal holding company income; or whether such amounts are merely compensation for services rendered.

* * *

Section 543 * * * defines exactly what income is to be classified as "personal holding company income." Section 543(a)(4) is a long, intricate, but not altogether lucid paragraph which includes copyright royalties within the definition of personal holding company income; excepts from this broad inclusion certain types of copyright royalties; and seeks to define exactly what is meant by the term "copyright royalties." * * *.

Essentially, the taxpayer argues that for the definition of copyright royalties, included as one form of personal holding company income, we need look no further than the law of copyrights. It is asserted that section 543(a)(4) effectively adopts the copyright law definition, the latter of which requires that the party receiving "royalties" must hold a proprietary interest in the copyright. Since Berlin Music never had a proprietary interest in Irving Berlin's copyrights, plaintiff would halt our inquiry at the definitional level. Thus, according to plaintiff, Berlin Music never received "copyright royalties" but only mere compensation for services rendered. We cannot agree.

    * * *

While Congress could have merely adopted the definition of royalties contained in the copyright laws, this procedure was not followed. Rather, copyright royalties, for personal holding company income purposes, was broadly and specially defined [in I.R.C. § 543(a)(4)] as:

> * * * *compensation, however designated,* for the use of, or the right to use, copyrights in works protected by copyright * * * and includes payments from any person for performing rights in any such copyrighted work * * *. (Emphasis supplied.)

The focus is thus not upon any proprietary interest in the copyright but rather that "compensation, however designated" be classified as copyright royalties (and, ultimately, as personal holding company income) when it is paid "for use of, or the right to use, copyrights." We find that paragraph 10 of the 1960 agreement brings the income within the statutory definition when it was provided that—

> 10. As full compensation for Publisher's services, Writer agrees that Publisher may deduct and retain 50% of the gross license fees received by Publisher as Writer's agent from licenses granted by Publisher on Writer's behalf * * *.

The crucial point is that, although designated as compensation for "services," the payment is solely * * * a percentage of the royalties received. Berlin Music was far more than a mere collection agent. It had the exclusive right throughout the term of the copyrights to issue licenses * * * and, in general, to exploit those copyrights in return for which it received 50 per cent of the royalties derived from the copyrights. It is precisely the same arrangement, in fact if not in words, which would have existed had a standard publishing agreement to an outside firm been negotiated.

Irving Berlin was the sole shareholder of Berlin Music and could, in his unfettered discretion, choose to call the amounts retained by Berlin Music agency fees. However, whatever the consequences of this decision are in other tax and non-tax areas, with respect to personal holding companies, such a unilateral classification cannot alter what are, otherwise, copyright royalties in the hands of Berlin Music. The detailed and specific definition of copyright royalties for purposes of personal holding company income leaves no room for plaintiff's argument that royalties cannot exist in the hands of a taxpayer not having a proprietary interest in the copyright.

* * *

In enacting section 543(a)(4)(A), (B), and (C), Congress undoubtedly intended to exclude certain qualifying music publishers from the burden of the personal holding company tax. Berlin Music, however, simply does not fall within this exceptional class. Congress evidently determined that the relationship between an author and his own publishing company, regardless of the formal arrangements (dictated by the shareholder) governing that relationship and regardless of the similarities the company might bear to any other active publishing company, gave rise to the potential for use of that company as an "incorporated pocketbook" against which the personal holding company tax is aimed.

[W]e cannot ascribe to Congress an intent to open a loophole to a taxpayer when its sole shareholder simply relabels the amounts received as compensation for the work of an agent. * * *. [W]hen compensation is "operationally" identical to that of the classic royalty scheme, such payments cannot be converted to something other than copyright royalties for the purpose of that definition.

We hold that section 543(a)(4) simply does not define copyright royalties in a manner which requires a finding of a "proprietary interest" in the underlying copyright. The definition does not spring from a finding of proprietary interest but rather from the situation in which compensation is to be measured in terms of a percentage of the royalties paid for the use or right to use copyrights.

* * *

Darrow v. Commissioner

United States Tax Court, 1975.
64 T.C. 217.

■ Forrester, Judge:

FINDINGS OF FACT

* * *

Kenneth Farmer Darrow (hereinafter referred to as "petitioner") was trustee for the shareholders and creditors of Rendar Enterprises, Ltd. (Rendar), at the time the petition herein was filed * * *. Rendar filed a corporate income tax return for its fiscal year ending July 31, 1968 * * *.

On March 27, 1968, the board of directors of Rendar voted to pay a dividend of * * * $2,000, on September 30, 1968 * * *. Such declaration was made by the directors in an attempt to avoid personal holding company classification for the corporation's [July 31,] 1968 fiscal year. Payment of the dividend was delayed until September, however, on the advice of Rendar's firm of certified public accountants, experienced in tax matters. * * *. It was the opinion of such firm, communicated to Rendar's board prior to the close of its 1968 fiscal year that payment of the dividend, if accomplished at any time up to 2–½ months after the close of Rendar's fiscal year on July 31, 1968, would prevent the imposition on Rendar of the personal holding company tax for such fiscal year.

* * * Pursuant to such advice, Rendar, while financially capable of paying the $2,000 dividend on March 27, actually paid the dividend on September 27, 1968. No dividends were actually paid by Rendar during its fiscal year ending July 31, 1968. The $2,000 dividend was divided in equal amounts between Rendar's two 50–percent shareholders, petitioner and Renee Liddle, each of whom included the $1,000 dividend received on their respective 1968 calendar year Federal income tax returns.

Over [60%] of Rendar's gross income in fiscal 1969 was composed of rents, and the parties do not dispute that, if we hold that less than $1,548.52 of the above-described dividend can be deemed as having been paid during its 1968 fiscal year, Rendar was a personal holding company during 1968 and subject to the section 541 imposition as determined by respondent.

* * *

In his statutory notice of deficiency respondent determined that Rendar, during its 1968 fiscal year, was a personal holding company ["PHC"] described in section 542(a) of the Code. He further determined that Rendar had undistributed personal holding company income during such year (undisputed as to amount) which was subject to the * * * imposition of [the personal holding company tax of] section 541.

OPINION

* * *

The actual issue upon which Rendar's tax liability rests is a very narrow one: whether or not, under section 563, at least $1,548.52 of the dividend paid to Rendar's two 50–percent shareholders on September 27, 1968, may be deemed as having been paid on the last day of Rendar's 1968 fiscal year, July 31, 1968.

Under section 543(a)(2) of the Code, personal holding company income includes the adjusted income from rents unless certain conditions are met. In the instant case, the parties do not dispute that the condition specified in section 543(a)(2)(B) cannot be met unless we find that at least $1,548.52 of the above-mentioned dividend was paid on the last day of Rendar's 1968 fiscal year. If such condition is not met, the parties again do not dispute that Rendar would have been a PHC because of section 542(a), and liable for the * * * imposition of [the personal holding company tax of] section 541.

Petitioner did not even attempt, on brief, to argue that any statutory language supports his position that any part of the $2,000 dividend, paid on

September 27, 1968, should be deemed as having been paid on the last day of Rendar's 1968 fiscal year. Indeed, the statute clearly points to the contrary conclusion. Section 563(c) provides, in substance, that for PHC tax purposes, a dividend paid within 2–½ months after the close of the taxpayer's taxable year will be considered as having been paid "on the last day of such taxable year." While the $2,000 dividend declared by Rendar's board on March 28 was actually paid within such period, section 543(a)(2)(B)(ii) further provides that the amount to be considered as paid on the last day of the fiscal year is subject to the limitation posited in the second sentence of section 563(b). Such limitation is as follows:

> The amount allowed as a dividend by reason of the application of this subsection with respect to any taxable year shall not exceed * * * [20] percent of the sum of the dividends paid during the taxable year, computed without regard to this subsection.

Petitioner paid no dividends during its 1968 fiscal year and thus is not entitled to claim that any part of the dividend paid subsequent to the close of its fiscal year is eligible for the special treatment provided for by section 563(d).

Petitioner makes basically two arguments against such an apparently straightforward reading of the statute. He first contends that, because the dividends paid on September 27 were included by Rendar's two 50–percent shareholders in their own personal income tax returns for the calendar year 1968, the abuses which Congress attempted to remedy by the PHC provisions are simply not present in the instant case. Hence, petitioner asserts it is appropriate, in the instant case, to allow the subsequently paid dividend to be considered as having been paid during Rendar's 1968 fiscal year in order to prevent the imposition of the [penalty] tax. Congress, however, has given us virtually no leeway to consider such a position. The clear import of the second sentence of section 563(b) is that if a company fails to actually pay any dividends during its fiscal year, then it is not entitled to rely on section 563(d) in having dividends paid subsequent to the fiscal year considered as having been paid during such fiscal year. When the congressional language is so clear, arguments such as petitioner's are in effect requesting us to rewrite a section of the Code, an action we simply cannot take in the instant situation.

Petitioner finally argues that because the [personal holding company] tax * * * has been described as a penalty-type imposition, its assessment should not be permitted when as here the taxpayer can show that its failure to escape the clutches of the statute was due to reasonable cause. The PHC provisions, however, contain no mention of a reasonable cause standard for determining a taxpayer's PHC status and liability, and we must again reject petitioner's efforts to have us legislate in these matters.

In enacting the PHC surcharge in the Revenue Act of 1934, it was the congressional intent to set forth specific standards for the determination of whether or not a company should be deemed a PHC and taxed accordingly. If a company meets the criteria set down by Congress in the statute, the imposition of the tax is to follow without further question * * *.

Relying upon this language in the legislative history, we and other courts have been consistent in holding that the PHC provisions must be applied strictly in order to fulfill this expression of congressional intent. Despite any harshness or other subjective factors which may be present, if a company fits the literal description of a PHC contained in the Code, and if it has undistributed PHC income as defined in the statute, imposition of the [penalty] tax is a matter of course.

In light of the above long-standing authority, we can accord very little attention to petitioner's request that we allow a taxpayer to escape PHC characterization if he can show "reasonable cause" for having failed to avoid the grasp of the statute. Such a rewriting of the statute would clearly impinge upon the automatic quality of the PHC provisions which Congress intended, an intent which has caused the courts, as described above, to consistently refuse to take into account subjective factors in determining the applicability of the PHC provisions to individual cases.

* * *

We are very sympathetic toward petitioner's position, but on the facts of the instant case we must hold that the PHC provisions, strictly read, do not allow any dividends paid after the close of Rendar's 1968 fiscal year to be deemed as having been paid on the last day of such fiscal year pursuant to section 563(d).

Decision will be entered for the respondent.

NOTES

1. *Penalty tax base*. The personal holding company tax is imposed on undistributed personal holding company income ("UPHCI"). I.R.C. § 541. UPHCI closely resembles accumulated taxable income, the base on which the accumulated earnings tax is imposed. (See p. 76, Note 2). UPHCI is derived by reducing taxable income (I.R.C. § 545(a)) by the regular corporate tax (I.R.C. § 545(b)(1)) and any dividends paid by the corporation (I.R.C. § 545(a)). (Certain other adjustments are also made. See generally, I.R.C. § 545(b).) Thus, no exposure to the personal holding company tax normally exists for any tax year in which a corporation distributes all of its after-tax earnings as dividends.

2. *Penalty tax rate*. Like the accumulated earnings tax rate, the personal holding company tax rate is the same as the maximum individual tax rate that applies to dividends, currently 15%. I.R.C. §§ 1(h), 541. In effect, the corporation pays a tax equal to the tax that the shareholders would have paid had the corporation distributed all of its after-tax earnings as dividends. The corporate penalty tax, however, does not substitute for the shareholder tax imposed when corporate earnings are actually distributed. The shareholders will still be taxed when the corporation ultimately distributes the earnings that were subject to the personal holding company tax. Thus, corporate earnings subjected to the personal holding company tax are taxed three times: first by the regular corporate tax, then by the personal holding company tax, and finally by the shareholder income tax when distributed as dividends.

3. *Timing of dividends*. In contrast to the dividend timing rule that applies to the accumulated earnings tax (See p. 78, Note 4), dividends paid within two and one-half months after the close of the taxable year *may* (at the election of the corporation) be treated as paid during the prior tax year for personal holding company tax purposes. The amount of the dividend that may be treated as paid during the prior tax year is limited to 20% of the dividends actually paid during the prior tax year. See I.R.C. § 563(b). Thus, a personal holding company that wishes to eliminate its undistributed personal holding company income cannot achieve this goal if it does not pay any dividends until after year-end. Rather, at least five-sixths of the necessary dividends must be paid by year-end.

> *Example 2–F (Limited deduction for dividends paid after year-end)*: Voss Co. cannot avoid personal holding company status in Year 6. Near the end of Year 6, Voss Co. estimates its undistributed personal holding company income ("UPHCI") to be $200,000 and pays a dividend of this amount on December 31 of Year 6. Paying a $200,000 dividend before the end of Year 6 creates the opportunity for Voss Co. to pay up to $40,000[12] of additional dividends by March 15 of Year 7 to reduce the UPHCI for Year 6. Early in Year 7, Voss Co. determines that its actual UPHCI for Year 6, before taking into account the $200,000 dividend, is $230,000. Voss Co. can eliminate any Year 6 personal holding company tax liability by paying an additional dividend of $30,000 by March 15 of Year 7 and electing to treat that dividend as paid in Year 6.

4. *Deficiency dividend*. Once the accumulated earnings tax is assessed, it is too late to pay dividends to avoid the tax. In contrast, an opportunity often exists to reduce personal holding company tax exposure by paying a "deficiency dividend" even after liability for the personal holding company tax is established. I.R.C. § 547. The deficiency dividend procedure is governed by complicated rules that create potential pitfalls for the uninitiated. See, e.g., Leck Co. v. United States, 73–2 U.S. Tax Cases ¶ 9694 (D.Minn.1973) (denying I.R.C. § 547 relief to a corporation that declared a dividend before an agreement with the Commissioner became final under I.R.C. § 547(c), notwithstanding that the corporation's action was an, "apparently unwitting, good faith, harmless departure from a highly technical statutory scheme"); Fletcher v. United States, 674 F.2d 1308 (9th Cir.1982)(denying § 547 relief to the shareholder of a corporation that liquidated prior to a determination that the corporation was a personal holding company).

C. CONSEQUENCES OF OPERATING LOSS

I.R.C. §§ 172(a), (b)(1)(A), (2), (3), (c)

When the amount of deductions allowed to a C Corporation in a taxable year exceed the corporation's gross income for that year, the

---

12. $200,000 x 20% = $40,000.

corporation has no taxable income and, accordingly, no regular corporate tax is imposed. In addition, the difference between the corporation's deductions and its gross income represents a "net operating loss." I.R.C. § 172(c). A net operating loss is a deduction allowed to the corporation that may be applied against taxable income generated in certain past or future years. I.R.C. § 172(a).

I.R.C. § 172 is intended to allow cyclical businesses to average "lean" years against "fat" years for purposes of computing tax liability. Because economic cycles generally exceed one year, relaxing the rigidity of the taxable year is necessary to achieve the goal of taxing businesses on their net income.

When a net operating loss arises, it is first applied against any taxable income reported *two* years before the year in which the loss occurs and a refund is claimed to the extent the additional deduction reduces the tax liability in the earlier year.[13] If the net operating loss exceeds taxable income reported two years before the loss occurred, the excess is applied against taxable income reported in the year immediately preceding the loss year. If the entire net operating loss is still not absorbed, the remainder is applied against any taxable income generated in the year after the loss was incurred and then to taxable income generated in each subsequent tax year. If the entire net operating loss is not absorbed after *twenty* tax years following the year in which the loss arose, the remainder simply expires without yielding any tax savings. I.R.C. §§ 172(b)(1)(A), (2). A net operating loss applied to income in a tax year *before* the net operating loss was incurred is referred to as a "net operating loss carryback." I.R.C. § 172(b)(1)(A)(i). A net operating loss applied to income in a tax year *after* the net operating loss was incurred is referred to as a "net operating loss carryover." I.R.C. § 172(b)(1)(A)(ii).[14]

Example 2–G (Ordering rules for applying net operating loss): In Years 1 and 2, Ute Corporation reported the following taxable income and tax liability:

Year	Taxable Income	Tax Liability
1	$100,000	$20,000
2	$200,000	$50,000

In Year 3, Ute incurs a net operating loss ("NOL") of $1,000,000. Ute first applies the $1,000,000 NOL as a carryback to Year 1, reduces Year 1 taxable income to zero and claims a $20,000 tax refund. Ute then applies the remaining NOL of $900,000 as a carryback to Year 2,

---

13. Interest is not normally paid by the government on a tax refund that arises when a net operating loss is applied against taxable income reported in an earlier tax year. I.R.C. § 6611(f)(1)("[I]f any overpayment of tax * * * results from a carryback of a net operating loss * * *, such overpayment shall be deemed not to have been made prior to the filing date for the taxable year in which such net operating loss * * * arises.").

14. The ability to use a net operating loss carryover may be severely curtailed if more than half the stock of the corporation is sold or exchanged. See generally, I.R.C. § 382 (examined in Chapter 13).

reduces taxable income to zero and claims a $50,000 tax refund. In Year 4, Ute has taxable income of $50,000 before applying the remaining Year 3 NOL. Ute, however, applies the remaining NOL of $700,000 as a carryover to Year 4, reduces taxable income to zero and has no tax liability in Year 4. Ute has until Year 23 to utilize the remaining NOL carryover of $650,000.

Because the tax law treats a C Corporation as a taxpaying entity separate from its individual shareholders, a corporation's net operating loss can only be applied against past or future income *of that corporation*. The shareholders cannot apply the corporation's loss against their individual income. Consequently, if the corporation does not generate sufficient income during the period before the loss expires, the loss will be wasted because it is "trapped" in the corporation.

> *Example 2–H (Net operating loss trapped in C Corporation)*: In Year 3, Tanda Corporation is allowed deductions that exceed gross income by $1,000,000. From Year 1 through Year 2 and from Year 4 through Year 23, Tanda's aggregate gross income exceeds its aggregate deductions by $400,000. During this period, Tanda's shareholders have taxable income which greatly exceeds $600,000. Nevertheless, Tanda's unused net operating loss of $600,000 cannot be applied against any taxable income of Tanda's shareholders and, therefore, is wasted.

The fact that net operating losses are trapped in a C Corporation often renders the C Corporation an unattractive tax regime. New businesses often reject the C Corporation regime because these businesses frequently generate net operating losses in their early years. In addition, more established businesses that tend to generate tax losses due to the nature of their assets (e.g., businesses with real estate holdings that generate tax losses due to substantial depreciation deductions) also shy away from the C Corporation because net operating losses are trapped in the corporation.

NOTES

1. *Choice of year*. How much discretion does a corporation have with regard to the first tax year to which it may apply a net operating loss? See I.R.C. §§ 172(b)(1), (3). Why would a corporation ever make an election under I.R.C. § 172(b)(3)?

2. *Net operating loss of individual*. Do not assume that a net operating loss can only be incurred by a corporation. An individual who conducts business as a sole proprietor can incur a net operating loss if deductions attributable to the business exceed income from the business. In computing the net operating loss of an individual, however, nonbusiness deductions are not allowed to the extent that they exceed nonbusiness income. See I.R.C. § 172(d)(4); Weinstein v. Commissioner, 29 T.C. 142 (1957). Consequently, an individual who is not engaged in a trade or business and who has itemized deductions in excess of gross income is not permitted to apply the excess deductions against income generated in other tax years.

D.   DISTINGUISHING CORPORATION FROM SHAREHOLDERS

Commissioner v. Bollinger

Supreme Court of the United States, 1988.
485 U.S. 340, 108 S.Ct. 1173.

■ JUSTICE SCALIA delivered the opinion of the Court.

Petitioner, the Commissioner of Internal Revenue challenges a decision by the United States Court of Appeals for the Sixth Circuit holding that a corporation which held record title to real property as agent for the corporation's shareholders was not the owner of the property for purposes of federal income taxation. We granted certiorari * * * to resolve a conflict in the courts of appeals over the tax treatment of corporations purporting to be agents for their shareholders.

I

Respondent Jesse C. Bollinger, Jr., developed, either individually or in partnership with some or all of the other respondents, eight apartment complexes in Lexington, Kentucky. (For convenience we will refer to all the ventures as "partnerships.") Bollinger initiated development of the first apartment complex, Creekside North Apartments, in 1968. The Massachusetts Mutual Life Insurance Company agreed to provide permanent financing by lending $1,075,000 to "the corporate nominee of Jesse C. Bollinger, Jr." at an annual interest rate of eight percent, secured by a mortgage on the property and a personal guaranty from Bollinger. The loan commitment was structured in this fashion because Kentucky's usury law at the time limited the annual interest rate for noncorporate borrowers to seven percent. Lenders willing to provide money only at higher rates required the nominal debtor and record title holder of mortgaged property to be a corporate nominee of the true owner and borrower. On October 14, 1968, Bollinger incorporated Creekside, Inc., under the laws of Kentucky; he was the only stockholder. The next day, Bollinger and Creekside, Inc., entered into a written agreement which provided that the corporation would hold title to the apartment complex as Bollinger's agent for the sole purpose of securing financing, and would convey, assign, or encumber the property and disburse the proceeds thereof only as directed by Bollinger; that Creekside, Inc., had no obligation to maintain the property or assume any liability by reason of the execution of promissory notes or otherwise; and that Bollinger would indemnify and hold the corporation harmless from any liability it might sustain as his agent and nominee.

Having secured the commitment for permanent financing, Bollinger, acting through Creekside, Inc., borrowed the construction funds for the apartment complex from Citizens Fidelity Bank and Trust Company. Creekside, Inc., executed all necessary loan documents including the promissory note and mortgage, and transferred all loan proceeds to Bollinger's individual construction account. Bollinger acted as general contractor for the construction, hired the necessary employees, and paid the expenses out of the construction account. When construction was completed, Bollinger obtained, again through Creekside, Inc., permanent financing from Massachusetts Mutual Life in accordance with the earlier loan commitment. These loan proceeds were used to pay off the Citizens Fidelity construction loan. Bollinger hired a resident manager to rent the apartments, execute leases with tenants, collect and deposit the rents, and maintain operating records. The manager deposited all rental receipts into, and paid all operating expenses from, an operating account, which was first opened in the name of Creekside, Inc., but was later changed to "Creekside Apartments, a partnership." The operation of Creekside North Apartments generated losses for the taxable years 1969, 1971, 1972, 1973, and 1974, and ordinary income for the years 1970, 1975, 1976, and 1977. Throughout, the income and losses were reported by Bollinger on his individual income tax returns.

Following a substantially identical pattern, seven other apartment complexes were developed by respondents through seven separate partnerships. * * *.

The Commissioner of Internal Revenue disallowed the losses reported by respondents,[15] on the ground that the standards set out in National Carbide Corp. v. Commissioner, 336 U.S. 422 (1949), were not met. The Commissioner contended that National Carbide required a corporation to have an arm's-length relationship with its shareholders before it could be recognized as their agent. * * *. Since, in the Commissioner's view, the corporation rather than its shareholders owned the real estate, any losses sustained by the ventures were attributable to the corporation and not respondents. Respondents sought a redetermination in the United States Tax Court. The Tax Court held that the corporations were the agents of the partnerships and should be disregarded for tax purposes. On appeal, the United States Court of Appeals for the Sixth Circuit affirmed. We granted the Commissioner's petition for certiorari.

II

For federal income tax purposes, gain or loss from the sale or use of property is attributable to the owner of the property. The problem we face here is that two different taxpayers can plausibly be regarded as the owner. Neither the Internal Revenue Code nor the regulations promulgated by the Secretary of the Treasury provide significant guidance as to which should be selected. It is common ground between the parties, however, that if a corporation holds title to property as agent for a partnership, then for tax

---

15. Editor's note. The income and deductions of a partnership are allocated among the partners and reported on their individual tax returns. When partnership deductions exceed income, each partner may generally apply her share of the partnership loss against any other income on her personal tax income. In contrast, when a C Corporation incurs a net operating loss, the loss is "trapped" in the corporation and cannot be applied by the shareholders against their personal income. See pp. 86–88. (The tax consequences of operating a business under the partnership tax regime are examined in Chapter 4.)

purposes the partnership and not the corporation is the owner. Given agreement on that premise, one would suppose that there would be agreement upon the conclusion as well. For each of respondents' apartment complexes, an agency agreement expressly provided that the corporation would "hold such property as nominee and agent for" the partnership and that the partnership would have sole control of and responsibility for the apartment complex. The partnership in each instance was identified as the principal and owner of the property during financing, construction, and operation. The lenders, contractors, managers, employees, and tenants—all who had contact with the development—knew that the corporation was merely the agent of the partnership, if they knew of the existence of the corporation at all. In each instance the relationship between the corporation and the partnership was, in both form and substance, an agency with the partnership as principal.

The Commissioner contends, however, that the normal indicia of agency cannot suffice for tax purposes when, as here, the alleged principals are the controlling shareholders of the alleged agent corporation. That, it asserts, would undermine the principle of Moline Properties v. Commissioner, 319 U.S. 436 (1943), which held that a corporation is a separate taxable entity even if it has only one shareholder who exercises total control over its affairs. Obviously, Moline's separate-entity principle would be significantly compromised if shareholders of closely held corporations could, by clothing the corporation with some attributes of agency with respect to particular assets, leave themselves free at the end of the tax year to make a claim—perhaps even a good-faith claim—of either agent or owner status, depending upon which choice turns out to minimize their tax liability. The Commissioner does not have the resources to audit and litigate the many cases in which agency status could be thought debatable. Hence, the Commissioner argues, in this shareholder context he can reasonably demand that the taxpayer meet a prophylactically clear test of agency.

We agree with that principle, but the question remains whether the test the Commissioner proposes is appropriate. The parties have debated at length the significance of our opinion in National Carbide Corp. v. Commissioner, supra. In that case, three corporations that were wholly owned subsidiaries of another corporation agreed to operate their production plants as "agents" for the parent, transferring to it all profits except for a nominal sum. The subsidiaries reported as gross income only this sum, but the Commissioner concluded that they should be taxed on the entirety of the profits because they were not really agents. We agreed, reasoning first, that the mere fact of the parent's control over the subsidiaries did not establish the existence of an agency, since such control is typical of all shareholder-corporation relationships; and second, that the agreements to pay the parent all profits above a nominal amount were not determinative since income must be taxed to those who actually earn it without regard to anticipatory assignment. We acknowledged, however, that there was such a thing as "a true corporate agent * * * of [an] owner-principal," and proceeded to set forth four indicia and two requirements of such status, the sum of which has become known in the lore of federal income tax law as the "six National Carbide factors": "[1] Whether the corporation operates in the name and for the account of the principal, [2] binds the principal by its actions, [3] transmits money received to the principal, and [4] whether receipt of income is attributable to the services of employees of the principal and to assets belonging to the principal are some of the relevant considerations in determining whether a true agency exists. [5] If the corporation is a true agent, its relations with its principal must not be dependent upon the fact that it is owned by the principal, if such is the case. [6] Its business purpose must be the carrying on of the normal duties of an agent."

We readily discerned that these factors led to a conclusion of nonagency in National Carbide itself. There each subsidiary had represented to its customers that it (not the parent) was the company manufacturing and selling its products; each had sought to shield the parent from service of legal process; and the operations had used thousands of the subsidiaries' employees and nearly $20 million worth of property and equipment listed as assets on the subsidiaries' books.

The Commissioner contends that the last two National Carbide factors are not satisfied in the present case. To take the last first: The Commissioner argues that here the corporation's business purpose with respect to the property at issue was not "the carrying on of the normal duties of an agent," since it was acting not as the agent but rather as the owner of the property for purposes of Kentucky's usury laws. We do not agree. It assuredly was not acting as the owner in fact, since respondents represented themselves as the principals to all parties concerned with the loans. Indeed, it was the lenders themselves who required the use of a corporate nominee. Nor does it make any sense to adopt a contrary-to-fact legal presumption that the corporation was the principal, imposing a federal tax sanction for the apparent evasion of Kentucky's usury law. To begin with, the Commissioner has not established that these transactions were an evasion. Respondents assert without contradiction that use of agency arrangements in order to permit higher interest was common practice, and it is by no means clear that the practice violated the spirit of the Kentucky law, much less its letter. * * *. In any event, even if the transaction did run afoul of the usury law, Kentucky, like most States, regards only the lender as the usurer, and the borrower as the victim. Since the Kentucky statute imposed no penalties upon the borrower for allowing himself to be victimized * * *, the United States would hardly be vindicating Kentucky law by depriving the usury victim of tax advantages he would otherwise enjoy. In sum, we see no basis in either fact or policy for holding that the corporation was the principal because of the nature of its participation in the loans.

Of more general importance is the Commissioner's contention that the arrangements here violate the fifth National Carbide factor—that the corporate agent's "relations with its principal must not be dependent upon the fact that it is owned by the principal." The Commissioner asserts that this cannot be satisfied unless the corporate agent and its shareholder principal have an "arm's-length relationship" that includes the payment of a fee for agency services. The meaning of National Carbide's fifth factor is, at the risk of understatement, not entirely clear. Ultimately, the relations between a corporate agent and its owner-principal are always dependent upon the fact of ownership, in that the owner can cause the relations to be altered or terminated at any time. Plainly that is not what was meant, since on that interpretation all subsidiary-parent agencies would be invalid for tax purposes, a position which the National Carbide opinion specifically disavowed. We think the fifth National Carbide factor—so much more abstract than the others—was no more and no less than a generalized statement of the concern, expressed earlier in our own discussion, that the separate-entity doctrine of Moline not be subverted.

In any case, we decline to parse the text of National Carbide as though that were itself the governing statute. As noted earlier, it is uncontested that the law attributes tax consequences of property held by a genuine agent to the principal; and we agree that it is reasonable for the Commissioner to demand unequivocal evidence of genuineness in the corporation-shareholder context, in order to prevent evasion of Moline. We see no basis, however, for holding that unequivocal evidence can only consist of the rigid requirements (arm's-length dealing plus agency fee) that the Commissioner suggests. Neither of those is demanded by the law of agency, which permits agents to be unpaid family members, friends, or associates. It seems to us that the genuineness of the agency relationship is adequately assured, and tax-avoiding manipulation adequately avoided, when the fact that the corporation is acting as agent for its shareholders with respect to a particular asset is set forth in a written agreement at the time the asset is acquired, the corporation functions as agent and not principal with respect to the asset for all purposes, and the corporation is held out as the agent and not principal in all dealings with third parties relating to the asset. Since these requirements were met here, the judgment of the Court of Appeals is Affirmed.

NOTE

Corporation as alter-ego of shareholder. In contrast to the situation in Bollinger, the government, rather than the taxpayer, may challenge the separate entity status of a corporation particularly when the shareholders of a closely-held corporation interact with the corporation in too casual a manner. As a general matter, a corporation is treated as a separate entity under the tax law if it is formed for a valid purpose, regardless of how informally the shareholders relate to the corporation. Moline Properties, Inc. v. Commissioner, 319 U.S. 436, 63 S.Ct. 1132 (1943). If the corporation is sufficiently dominated by its owners, however, the government may treat the corporation as the alter-ego of the shareholders and hold the shareholders responsible for the tax liabilities of the corporation. See, e.g., Wolfe v. United States, 798 F.2d 1241 (9th Cir.1986) (government prevailed in its effort to treat corporation as viable for purposes of assessing tax, yet held the controlling shareholder liable for the corporation's taxes where the corporation had no bank account, corporate expenses were paid from the bank account of the shareholder's proprietorship and corporate receipts were deposited into the proprietorship's bank account). Consequently, it is critical that the shareholders of a closely-held corporation treat the corporation as a separate economic unit by adhering to formalities, notwithstanding the temptation to interact with the corporation in a more casual fashion.

CHAPTER 3

S CORPORATION OPERATIONS

A business conducted in corporate form that satisfies certain eligibility requirements may elect to be taxed as an S Corporation.[1] An S Corporation is governed by the rules of Subchapter S (I.R.C. §§ 1361–1378). In contrast to a C Corporation, an S Corporation is not normally treated as a taxpaying entity. The income and deductions of the business are still computed at the corporate level, but these items are then allocated to the individual shareholders and reported on their personal tax returns. Although Subchapter S often enables a corporate business to avoid a corporate level tax, its rigid rules severely constrain the economic relations that may be established among the owners of an enterprise. Chapter 3 first focuses on the tax treatment of S Corporations, then explores the eligibility requirements for S Corporation status, and finally examines the limited circumstances in which an S Corporation pays tax.

A. COMPUTATION OF GROSS INCOME AND DEDUCTIONS

I.R.C. §§ 1363(a)–(b), 1371(a)(1)

An S Corporation normally does not pay tax. I.R.C. § 1363(a). Nevertheless, an S Corporation is treated as a tax accounting entity. Accordingly, it must compute its gross income and deductions, and file an annual information return (Form 1120S—see Exhibit III, p. 96) reporting these items to the Internal Revenue Service. I.R.C. § 6037(a). The Form 1120S includes a separate schedule for each shareholder (Schedule K–1—see Exhibit IV, p. 97) where the S Corporation reports the amount of each item of the corporation's income and deductions allocated to that shareholder. The corporation must provide each shareholder with a copy of her Schedule K–1. I.R.C. § 6037(b). The items reflected on the shareholder's Schedule K–1 must be included on her personal tax return.

---

1. A corporation is eligible for S Corporation status only if it satisfies all of the following requirements:

1. The corporation is a domestic corporation (other than certain ineligible corporations).

2. The corporation has no more than one hundred shareholders.

3. All of the corporation's shareholders are individuals (none of whom are nonresident-aliens), estates or certain trusts.

4. The corporation issues only one class of stock.

I.R.C. § 1361. These requirements are explored in detail at pp. 121–131.

EXHIBIT III

Form **1120S**	**U.S. Income Tax Return for an S Corporation**	OMB No. 1545-0130
Department of the Treasury Internal Revenue Service	▶ Do not file this form unless the corporation has filed or is attaching Form 2553 to elect to be an S corporation. ▶ See separate instructions.	2010

For calendar year 2010 or tax year beginning _____, 2010, ending _____, 20____

A S election effective date		Name	D Employer Identification number
B Business activity code number (see instructions)	**TYPE OR PRINT**	Number, street, and room or suite no. If a P.O. box, see instructions.	E Date Incorporated
		City or town, state, and ZIP code	F Total assets (see instructions) $
C Check if Sch. M-3 attached ☐			

G Is the corporation electing to be an S corporation beginning with this tax year? ☐ Yes ☐ No   If "Yes," attach Form 2553 if not already filed
H Check if: (1) ☐ Final return   (2) ☐ Name change   (3) ☐ Address change
(4) ☐ Amended return   (5) ☐ S election termination or revocation
I   Enter the number of shareholders who were shareholders during any part of the tax year . . . . ▶

Caution. *Include only trade or business income and expenses on lines 1a through 21. See the instructions for more information.*

Income	1a	Gross receipts or sales	b Less returns and allowances	c Bal ▶	**1c**	
	2	Cost of goods sold (Schedule A, line 8)	**2**	
	3	Gross profit. Subtract line 2 from line 1c	**3**	
	4	Net gain (loss) from Form 4797, Part II, line 17 *(attach Form 4797)*	**4**	
	5	Other income (loss) *(see instructions—attach statement)*	**5**	
	6	**Total income (loss).** Add lines 3 through 5 . . . . ▶	**6**	
Deductions (see instructions for limitations)	7	Compensation of officers	**7**	
	8	Salaries and wages (less employment credits)	**8**	
	9	Repairs and maintenance	**9**	
	10	Bad debts	**10**	
	11	Rents	**11**	
	12	Taxes and licenses	**12**	
	13	Interest	**13**	
	14	Depreciation not claimed on Schedule A or elsewhere on return (attach Form 4562)	**14**	
	15	Depletion **(Do not deduct oil and gas depletion.)**	**15**	
	16	Advertising	**16**	
	17	Pension, profit-sharing, etc., plans	**17**	
	18	Employee benefit programs	**18**	
	19	Other deductions *(attach statement)*	**19**	
	20	**Total deductions.** Add lines 7 through 19 . . . . ▶	**20**	
	21	**Ordinary business income (loss).** Subtract line 20 from line 6	**21**	
Tax and Payments	22a	Excess net passive income or LIFO recapture tax (see *instructions*) . .	22a		
	b	Tax from Schedule D (Form 1120S)	22b		
	c	Add lines 22a and 22b (see *instructions for additional taxes*)	**22c**	
	23a	2010 estimated tax payments and 2009 overpayment credited to 2010	23a		
	b	Tax deposited with Form 7004	23b		
	c	Credit for federal tax paid on fuels (attach Form 4136)	23c		
	d	Add lines 23a through 23c	**23d**	
	24	Estimated tax penalty (see *instructions*). Check if Form 2220 is attached . . . . . ▶ ☐	**24**	
	25	**Amount owed.** If line 23d is smaller than the total of lines 22c and 24, enter amount owed . .	**25**	
	26	**Overpayment.** If line 23d is larger than the total of lines 22c and 24, enter amount overpaid . .	**26**	
	27	Enter amount from line 26 **Credited to 2011 estimated tax** ▶	Refunded ▶	**27**	

Sign Here	Under penalties of perjury, I declare that I have examined this return, including accompanying schedules and statements, and to the best of my knowledge and belief, it is true, correct, and complete. Declaration of preparer (other than taxpayer) is based on all information of which preparer has any knowledge.	May the IRS discuss this return with the preparer shown below (see instructions)? ☐ Yes ☐ No
	▶ Signature of officer Date Title	

Paid Preparer Use Only	Print/Type preparer's name	Preparer's signature	Date	Check ☐ if self-employed	PTIN
	Firm's name ▶			Firm's EIN ▶	
	Firm's address ▶			Phone no.	

For Paperwork Reduction Act Notice, see separate instructions.   Cat. No. 11510H   Form **1120S** (2010)

EXHIBIT IV

```
                                                                    671110
                                         ☐ Final K-1    ☐ Amended K-1    OMB No. 1545-0130
Schedule K-1                    2010     Part III  Shareholder's Share of Current Year Income,
(Form 1120S)                                        Deductions, Credits, and Other Items
Department of the Treasury               1  Ordinary business income (loss)   13  Credits
Internal Revenue Service    For calendar year 2010, or tax
                            year beginning _____, 2010
                                   ending _____, 20 ____   2  Net rental real estate income (loss)

Shareholder's Share of Income, Deductions,            3  Other net rental income (loss)
Credits, etc.      ▶ See back of form and separate Instructions.
                                                      4  Interest income
  Part I   Information About the Corporation
                                                      5a Ordinary dividends
A   Corporation's employer identification number
                                                      5b Qualified dividends          14  Foreign transactions
B   Corporation's name, address, city, state, and ZIP code
                                                      6  Royalties

                                                      7  Net short-term capital gain (loss)

                                                      8a Net long-term capital gain (loss)
C   IRS Center where corporation filed return
                                                      8b Collectibles (28%) gain (loss)
  Part II   Information About the Shareholder
                                                      8c Unrecaptured section 1250 gain
D   Shareholder's identifying number
                                                      9  Net section 1231 gain (loss)
E   Shareholder's name, address, city, state, and ZIP code
                                                      10 Other income (loss)           15  Alternative minimum tax (AMT) items




F   Shareholder's percentage of stock
    ownership for tax year . . . . . . _____ %


                                                      11 Section 179 deduction         16  Items affecting shareholder basis

                                                      12 Other deductions




For IRS Use Only
                                                                                      17  Other information




                                         * See attached statement for additional information.

For Paperwork Reduction Act Notice, see Instructions for Form 1120S.   Cat. No. 11520D   Schedule K-1 (Form 1120S) 2010
```

As a general rule, the gross income and deductions of an S Corporation are computed in the same manner as these items are computed for an individual. I.R.C. § 1363(b). Many exceptions to the general rule exist, however, and the precise scope of the general rule remains unclear. The general rule is applied in Revenue Ruling 93–36 and its limitations are discussed in the notes that follow the ruling.

Revenue Ruling 93–36

1993–1 Cum.Bull. 187.

ISSUE

If an S corporation has a nonbusiness bad debt under section 166 of the Internal Revenue Code, does the S Corporation compute its taxable income by deducting the debt as an ordinary loss under section 166(a) or does the S corporation separately state the debt as a short-term capital loss under section 166(d)?

FACTS

X is an S Corporation as defined by section 1361 of the Code that reports its income on a calendar year basis. In 1990, X makes a $100x loan to Y which constitutes a nonbusiness debt. X's loan to Y becomes partially worthless in 1993 to the extent of $20x, and X charges off this amount on its books. The balance of the loan, $80x, becomes worthless in 1994, and X charges off the balance in that year.

LAW AND ANALYSIS

Section 166(a)(1) of the Code allows a deduction for any debt that becomes worthless within the tax year. Section 166(a)(2) provides that when satisfied that a debt is recoverable only in part, the Secretary may allow the debt as a deduction in an amount not in excess of the part charged off within the tax year.

Under section 166(d)(1) of the Code, concerning a taxpayer other than a corporation, (A) section 166(a) does not apply to any nonbusiness debt, and (B) when any nonbusiness debt becomes worthless within the tax year, the resulting loss is considered a loss from the sale or exchange, during the tax year, of a capital asset held for not more than 1 year.

Section 166(d)(2) of the Code provides that for purposes of section 166(d)(1), the term "nonbusiness debt" means a debt other than (A) a debt created or acquired in connection with a trade or business of the taxpayer, or (B) a debt the loss from the worthlessness of which is incurred in the taxpayer's trade or business.

* * *

Under section 1363(b) of the Code, an S Corporation's taxable income is generally computed in the same manner as an individual's, except that (A) the items described in section 1366(a)(1)(A) are separately stated, (B) the deductions listed in section 703(a)(2) are not allowed to the corporation, (C) section 248 (relating to organizational expenditures) applies, and (D) section 291 (relating to corporate preference items) applies if the S corporation (or any predecessor) was a C corporation for any of the three immediately preceding tax years. * * *

Section 166 of the Code is not specifically enumerated as an exception to the general rule of section 1363(b); therefore, section 166 applies in the same manner as it does for an individual when computing an S corporation's taxable income. Thus, an S corporation must (1) include in its separately stated short-term capital loss any wholly worthless nonbusiness debt, and (2) deduct as an ordinary loss any partially or wholly worthless business debt.

In the present situations, X's $100x loan to Y is a nonbusiness debt within the meaning of section 166(d)(2) of the Code. Accordingly, X is not allowed a $20x ordinary loss deduction in its 1993 tax year under section 166(a)(2) when the loan becomes partially worthless. X also is not allowed an $80x ordinary loss deduction in its 1994 tax year under section 166(a)(1) when the loan becomes wholly worthless. Under section 166(d)(1)(B), X includes the $100x nonbusiness bad debt as a short-term capital loss in its 1994 tax year when the loan becomes wholly worthless.

HOLDING

An S corporation that has a nonbusiness bad debt under section 166 of the Code must separately state the debt as a short-term capital loss under section 166(d).

NOTES

1. *S Corporation denied certain deductions allowed to individuals.* An S Corporation is denied a variety of deductions that are allowed to individuals including the deduction for personal exemptions, the deduction for charitable contributions and the itemized deductions allowed under I.R.C. §§ 212–223. See I.R.C. §§ 1363(b)(2), 703(a)(2). Why are these deductions denied to an S Corporation?

2. *Subchapter C rules apply to S Corporation.* Subject to certain exceptions, the rules of Subchapter C (I.R.C. §§ 301–385) also apply to an S Corporation. See I.R.C. § 1371(a). For example, when a corporation distributes property with a value in excess of its basis to a shareholder, a corporate level gain is normally triggered, regardless of whether the distributing corporation is a C Corporation or an S Corporation. See, e.g., I.R.C. § 311(b); pp. 29–33. When the distributing corporation is an S Corporation, the gain represents an item of the S Corporation's gross income that is allocated among the shareholders of the S Corporation and reported on their personal tax returns.

3. *S Corporation treated as corporation under certain rules outside of Subchapter C.* A contribution to the capital of a corporation is excluded from the corporation's gross income, regardless of whether the recipient is a C Corporation or an S Corporation. See I.R.C. § 118, pp. 36–37. In addition, neither a C Corporation nor an S Corporation recognizes gain or loss when it issues its stock in exchange for money or property. See I.R.C. § 1032, pp. 36–37. In contrast to a C Corporation, however, an S Corporation is not allowed a dividends received deduction. See I.R.C. § 243, pp. 59–64. Why not?

4. *Further departure from treating S Corporation as an individual.* Subsequent to the issuance of Revenue Ruling 93–36, the Tax Court concluded that an S Corporation is not treated as an individual for purposes of I.R.C. § 1244, a Code provision that converts certain capital losses of an individual to ordinary losses. The Tax Court based its conclusion on the fact that I.R.C. § 1244 does not explicitly treat S Corporations as individuals. In response to the taxpayers' contention that Revenue Ruling 93–36 suggests a different result, the Tax Court stated:

> Petitioners' reliance on Rev. Rul. 93–36 * * * is misplaced. Absent special circumstances, revenue rulings merely represent respondent's position with respect to a specific factual situation * * * and are not treated as precedent in this Court. Consequently, we express no opinion regarding the revenue ruling.

Rath v. Commissioner, 101 T.C. 196, 205 n. 10 (1993). Thus, the scope of the general rule that the income of an S Corporation is computed like that of an individual remains far from clear.

B. ALLOCATION TO SHAREHOLDERS

1. SHAREHOLDERS TAXED WHEN INCOME EARNED

I.R.C. §§ 1366(a)–(c), 1367(a)

After the income of an S Corporation is computed, it must be allocated among the shareholders and included on their individual tax returns. I.R.C. § 1366(a). **The income of an S Corporation is taxed to the shareholders at the time it is earned, regardless of whether the S Corporation distributes its earnings to the shareholders.** Generally, the shareholders are not taxed again when the S Corporation actually distributes its earnings to them.[2]

Knott v. Commissioner

United States Tax Court, 1991.
62 T.C.M. 287.

■ DINAN, SPECIAL TRIAL JUDGE: * * *

The issue for decision is whether petitioners were required to report a proportionate share of undistributed income from a subchapter S corporation of which they were shareholders.

The facts indicate that Mr. Knott was a 24.5 percent shareholder of West Augusta Company (West Augusta), a subchapter S corporation, during 1986. Further, the 1986 tax return (Form 1120S) for West Augusta indicated that the company had $43,730 in taxable income. * * *

The taxable income of West Augusta was attributed to the company's shareholders according to their percentage of ownership by way of the preparation of a Schedule K–1 for each shareholder. Both Mr. Knott and

---

2. The tax consequences of S Corporation distributions are explored in Chapter 6.

the Internal Revenue Service were issued a Schedule K–1 with regard to Mr. Knott's share of West Augusta's income. The Schedule K–1 as issued to Mr. Knott allocated to him 24.5 percent of the income of West Augusta as shown on West Augusta's 1986 tax return. None of the shareholders of West Augusta actually received any distribution of income. Petitioners did not report any income from West Augusta on their 1986 Federal income tax return.

Petitioners claim that they do not have any taxable income as shareholders of West Augusta because they never actually received any income from the company. Further, they contend that the Schedule K–1 as prepared for them is fraudulent because it attributes income to them which they never possessed. * * *

Generally, S corporations are not subject to income taxes. Sec. 1363(a). Nonetheless, S corporations must compute their taxable income in a manner similar to individuals. Sec. 1363(b). This computation facilitates the process of passing-through items of income, loss, deduction, and credit * * * from the S corporation to its shareholders. Sec. 1366(a). In particular, section 1366(c) requires that the gross income of a shareholder of an S corporation shall include his proportionate share of the gross income of the corporation.

The facts of the present case show that for the year 1986 Mr. Knott owned 24.5 percent of West Augusta in his capacity as a shareholder. As a result, Mr. Knott was under an obligation to report 24.5 percent of the gross income of West Augusta for 1986 on his 1986 tax return. Sec. 1366(c). Petitioners' contention that a pro rata share of an S corporation's income is not taxable income until it is actually distributed is clearly wrong. This argument is contrary to the plain language of the statute and the overall purpose of the subchapter S framework.

[I]ncome of the subchapter S corporation need not be distributed in order to be included in the taxable income of the shareholders. Accordingly, we reject petitioners' argument * * *.

NOTES

1. *Payment of tax on undistributed income.* How can a shareholder of an S Corporation afford to pay the tax on his share of the corporation's income if the corporation does not distribute any of its earnings? Why did the magnitude of Mr. Knott's ownership interest in West Augusta render him particularly vulnerable to this problem?

2. *Segregation of certain items.* The income (or loss) of an S Corporation is not always reported to its shareholders as a single net amount. Instead, items of gross income and deduction are segregated if the nature of the item could affect the determination of an individual shareholder's tax liability. I.R.C. §§ 1363(b)(1), 1366(a)(1)(A). The unique nature of these segregated items flows through to the personal tax return of each shareholder. I.R.C. § 1366(b). All other items of income and deduction are simply reported as a single net amount (the "nonseparately computed income or loss"). I.R.C. §§ 1366(a)(1)(B), (2).

Example 3–A (Segregating items from nonseparately computed income or loss): Candice and Dale each own 50% of the stock of Squawk, Inc., an S Corporation. In Year 1, Squawk earns $50,000 of business income, incurs $10,000 of business expenses, receives $5,000 of tax-exempt interest (see I.R.C. § 103(a)) and recognizes $20,000 of long-term capital gain. For reporting purposes, Squawk's $5,000 of tax-exempt interest and $20,000 of capital gain are segregated from its other income and deductions, which are netted to $40,000 (the nonseparately computed income). Candice and Dale each add $20,000 of Squawk's nonseparately computed income and $10,000 of Squawk's long-term capital gain to the other items reported on their Year 1 personal tax returns and each excludes $2,500 of Squawk's tax-exempt interest. If Candice (or Dale) has a capital loss from other activities, this capital loss can offset her share of Squawk's capital gain. I.R.C. § 1211(b).

3. *Adjustments to stock basis*. As the Knott Case illustrates, the income of an S Corporation is taxed to its shareholders when it is earned, regardless of whether the corporation actually distributes any of those earnings to its shareholders. In addition, each shareholder is awarded an increase in the basis of her stock to reflect any corporate income allocated to her that she has not yet received. I.R.C. § 1367(a)(1). Note that basis is increased to reflect both nonseparately computed income and all segregated items of corporate income, including tax-exempt items. I.R.C. §§ 1366(a)(1)(A), 1367(a)(1)(A). Correspondingly, basis is reduced by both deductible expenses and nondeductible expenses (e.g., a fine or penalty, see I.R.C. § 162(f)). I.R.C. §§ 1367(a)(2)(B)–(D).

How do the items described in Example 3–A affect the stock basis of each shareholder?

2.   RIGID ALLOCATION RULE

I.R.C. §§ 1366(a), 1377(a)

Treas. Reg. § 1.1377–1

A rigid, mechanical rule controls the allocation of S Corporation income among the corporation's shareholders. Each shareholder is required to include his "pro rata share" of the corporation's income on his individual tax return. I.R.C. § 1366(a). In effect, the pro rata share computation assumes that the corporation earns the same amount of income on each day of the year ($\frac{1}{365}$ of the annual income, or $\frac{1}{366}$ of the annual income in the event of a leap year). Each day's income is then allocated evenly among the shares outstanding on that day. I.R.C. § 1377(a)(1).

Example 3–B (Per-share/per-day rule): Standard Co., an S Corporation, has 1,000 shares of stock outstanding during Year 8 (a leap year with 366 days), 500 of which are owned by Ellen and 500 of which are owned by Floyd. Standard earns $360,000 during the first half of Year

8 and only $6,000 during the second half of Year 8. Standard's Year 8 income is allocated between its shareholders as follows:

(a) $1,000 of income is allocated to each day of Year 8.[3] I.R.C. § 1377(a)(1)(A).

(b) $1 of income is allocated to each outstanding share on each day of Year 8.[4] I.R.C. § 1377(a)(1)(B).

(c) Ellen's pro rata share of the Year 8 income is $183,000.[5]

(d) Floyd's pro rata share of the Year 8 income is $183,000.[6]

Example 3–B demonstrates that the mechanical "per-share/per-day" rule leads to logical results when a fixed number of shares are outstanding during the entire year and no shares are transferred during the year. If additional shares of an S Corporation are issued during the year or if outstanding shares are transferred, the mechanical rule often misallocates the S Corporation's income among its shareholders.

Example 3–C (Misallocation of income): Standard Co., an S Corporation, has 1,000 shares of stock outstanding during Year 8 (a leap year with 366 days), 500 of which are owned by Ellen and 500 of which are owned by Floyd. Standard earns $360,000 during the first half of Year 8 and only $6,000 during the second half of Year 8. Floyd sells all 500 of his Standard Co. shares to Grant in the middle of Year 8. The "per-share/per-day" rule causes Standard's income to be allocated among its shareholders as follows:

(a) $1,000 of income is allocated to each day of Year 8.[7] I.R.C. § 1377(a)(1)(A).

(b) $1 of income is allocated to each outstanding share on each day of Year 8.[8] I.R.C. § 1377(a)(1)(B).

(c) Ellen's pro rata share of the Year 8 income is $183,000.[9]

(d) Floyd's pro rata share of the Year 8 income is $91,500.[10]

(e) Grant's pro rata share of the Year 8 income is $91,500.[11]

Although Standard earned $360,000 during the period that Floyd was a 50% shareholder (the first half of Year 8), Floyd is taxed on less than 50% of that amount. The per-share/per-day rule causes Floyd to be taxed on only $91,500 of the Year 8 income. In contrast, although Standard earned only $6,000 during the period that Grant was a 50%

---

3. $366,000 ÷ 366 days = $1,000 per-day.

4. $1,000 of income per-day ÷ 1,000 outstanding shares = $1 per-share/per-day.

5. $1 per-share/per-day × 500 shares × 366 days = $183,000.

6. $1 per-share/per-day × 500 shares × 366 days = $183,000.

7. $366,000 ÷ 366 days = $1,000 per-day.

8. $1,000 of income per-day ÷ 1,000 outstanding shares = $1 per-share/per-day.

9. $1 per-share/per-day × 500 shares × 366 days = $183,000.

10. $1 per-share/per-day × 500 shares × 183 days = $91,500.

11. $1 per-share/per-day × 500 shares × 183 days = $91,500.

shareholder, Grant is taxed on more than 50% of that amount. The per-share/per-day rule causes Grant to be taxed on $91,500 of the Year 8 income. Under these circumstances, the per-share/per-day rule causes Floyd to be undertaxed and Grant to be overtaxed.

In certain circumstances, a "closing of the books" election may be made to remedy the misallocation of income that otherwise occurs when outstanding shares are transferred or additional shares are issued during the tax year. When a shareholder of an S Corporation "terminates" her interest during the taxable year, an election may be made to allocate a share of the income actually earned through the date the interest terminates to the terminating shareholder. Correspondingly, a share of the income actually earned during the remainder of the taxable year is allocated to the person to whom the terminating shareholder transferred shares. The election requires the consent of both the terminating shareholder and the person to whom she transferred shares (the "affected shareholders"). See I.R.C. § 1377(a)(2). The election does not apply to any shareholder who is not an affected shareholder.

> *Example 3–D (Closing of the books election):* Same as Example 3–C (p. 103), except that Floyd and Grant consent to a "closing of the books" election under I.R.C. § 1377(a)(2). Pursuant to the election, Year 8 is divided into two tax years for purposes of allocating income to Floyd and Grant, the first of which covers the period that Floyd was a shareholder during which Standard earned $360,000. The second tax year covers the period that Grant was a shareholder during which Standard earned $6,000. As a result of the closing of the books election, Standard's Year 8 income is allocated among its shareholders as follows:

Ellen:	$183,000[12]
Floyd:	$180,000[13]
Grant:	$3,000[14]

---

[12].

  $366,000 ÷ 366 days=$1,000 per-day
  $1,000 ÷ 1,000 shares=$1.00 per-share/per-day
  $1.00 × 500 shares × 366 days=$183,000

[13].

  $360,000 ÷ 183 days=$1967.21 per-day
  $1967.21 ÷ 1,000 shares=$1.96721 per-share/per-day
  $1.96721 × 500 shares × 183 days=$180,000

[14].

  $6,000 ÷ 183 days=$32.79 per-day
  $32.79 ÷ 1,000 shares=$.03279 per-share/per-day
  $.03279 × 500 shares × 183 days=$3,000

A closing of the books election may also be made when a single shareholder disposes of 20% or more of the issued stock of an S Corporation during any thirty day period. Treas. Reg. § 1.1368–1(g)(2)(i)(A). In addition, the regulations permit a closing of the books election when the S Corporation issues an amount of stock equal to at least 25% of its previously outstanding stock to one or more new shareholders during any thirty day period. Treas. Reg. § 1.1368–1(g)(2)(i)(C). In both of these cases, the election requires the consent of all persons who were shareholders at any time during the taxable year. Treas. Reg. § 1.1368–1(g)(2)(iii).

NOTES

1. *Prudence of closing of books election.* In Example 3–D, was it prudent for each of Floyd and Grant to consent to the I.R.C. § 1377(a)(2) election? Which shareholder might have improved his position by not consenting to the election? Why might that shareholder have consented to the election?

2. *Mechanics of closing of books election.* When is the "closing of the books" election made? See Treas. Reg. §§ 1.1368–1(g)(2)(iii), 1.1377–1(b)(5). At what point in time are the parties most likely to be amenable to the election?

3. *Sale of some but not all shares.* In Example 3–C (p. 103), could a closing of the books election be made if, rather than selling all 500 of his Standard shares to Grant, Floyd sold,

   (a) 100 shares to Grant?

   (b) 200 shares to Grant?

   (c) 200 shares to Ellen?

See Treas. Reg. § 1.1368–1(g)(2)(i)(A).

4. *Issuance of new shares.* In Example 3–C (p. 103), could a closing of the books election be made if Floyd did not sell any of his Standard shares but instead, Standard issued,

   (a) 200 shares to Grant?

   (b) 250 shares to Grant?

   (c) 250 shares to Ellen?

See Treas. Reg. § 1.1368–1(g)(2)(i)(C).

5. *Neutralizing a misallocation.* The basis of each shareholder's stock of an S Corporation is increased by the amount of income allocated to that shareholder. See I.R.C. § 1367(a)(1). Thus, any misallocation of income resulting from the absence of a "closing of the books" election may be neutralized by the corresponding increase in the shareholder's stock basis.

For example, if too much income is allocated to one shareholder (e.g., to Grant in Example 3–C, p. 103), a corresponding amount of extra basis is created that will reduce gain (or create a loss) on a later sale of that shareholder's stock. In most cases, however, the additional basis does not neutralize the misallocation of income due to differences in timing and characterization. This problem is further explored in Chapters 6 and 14.

Problem 3–1 (Impact of closing of books election): Stench, Inc., an S Corporation, has 100 outstanding shares of stock during Year 4 (a leap year with 366 days). At the beginning of Year 4, 75 Stench shares are owned by Henry and 25 Stench shares are owned by Ilsa. On the 122nd day of Year 4, Ilsa sells all of her Stench shares to Judy. Stench earns $122,000 during the first 122 days of Year 4 and $610,000 during the last 244 days of Year 4.

(a) What is each shareholder's pro rata share of Stench's Year 4 income if Ilsa or Judy does not consent to a closing of the books election?

(b) What is each shareholder's pro rata share of Stench's Year 4 income if Ilsa and Judy consent to a closing of the books election?

(c) Would you advise each of Ilsa and Judy to consent to a closing of the books election if you were rendering advice,

  (i) at the time Ilsa sold her shares to Judy?

  (ii) after the end of Year 4?

C. Consequences of Operating Loss

I.R.C. §§ 1366(d)(1), (2), 1367(a)(2), (b)(2)

When a C Corporation incurs a net operating loss that it cannot use, its shareholders may not apply the loss against their personal income. In effect, the loss is "trapped" in the corporation. See pp. 86–88. This problem is avoided if the business is conducted by an S Corporation. When an S Corporation has deductions in excess of gross income, the individual shareholders may apply the excess deductions against income they derive from other sources. I.R.C. § 1366(a)(1). Indeed, owner access to an S Corporation's operating losses has long been one of the principal attractions of the S Corporation tax regime.

Example 3–E (Shareholder access to corporate operating loss): Linda is the sole shareholder of Sallo Corporation, an S Corporation. Linda's Year 1 gross income exceeds her deductions by $1,000,000, before taking into account her pro rata share of Sallo's income and deductions. Sallo's Year 1 deductions exceed its gross income by $1,000,000. Linda's excess gross income can be offset by Sallo's excess deductions, provided that Linda's ability to use Sallo's excess deductions is not limited by the rules discussed below. If Linda may claim all of Sallo's deductions, her Year 1 taxable income is zero.

Certain hurdles must be overcome before the shareholders of an S Corporation may deduct operating losses of the business. First, the operating loss must be allocated among the shareholders. The same allocation rule applies regardless of whether an S Corporation generates taxable income or an operating loss; each shareholder is required to include her "pro rata share" on her individual tax return. I.R.C. § 1366(a). Under the pro rata share approach, an equivalent amount of the corporation's loss is allocated to each day of the tax year and each day's loss is allocated evenly among the shares outstanding on that day.[15] Thus, each shareholder's share of an S Corporation's operating loss is based solely on the percentage of the corporation's stock owned by that shareholder.

After the S Corporation's loss is allocated among the shareholders, it must be determined whether each shareholder may deduct his or her share of the operating loss. In other words, notwithstanding that deductions were allowed at the corporate level before being allocated to the individual shareholders, each individual to whom these deductions are allocated must satisfy certain additional requirements before the deductions may be claimed on that individual's tax return.

Each shareholder may immediately deduct her pro rata share of the S Corporation's operating loss only to the extent that it does not exceed the sum of the shareholder's basis in,

(a) her stock of the corporation,[16] *and*

(b) any indebtedness of the corporation to her.

I.R.C. § 1366(d)(1). The shareholder's pro rata share of the S Corporation's operating loss first reduces the basis in her stock and then reduces the basis in any indebtedness of the corporation to her, but not below zero. I.R.C. §§ 1367(a)(2)(B), (C), (b)(2)(A). If the shareholder's pro rata share of the S Corporation's operating loss exceeds her basis in such stock and debt, she may not deduct the excess operating loss until she establishes additional basis. I.R.C. § 1366(d)(2).

> *Problem 3–2 (Limitation on deductibility of pro rata share of loss):* Ben and Carol each own half of the outstanding stock of an S Corporation. At the beginning of Year 1, each shareholder contributed $100,000 to the corporation and had a basis of $100,000 in his/her stock. Determine each shareholder's pro rata share of the S Corporation's Year 1 loss and the amount that may be deducted on each shareholder's Year 1 tax return under each of the following alternative scenarios.
>
> (a) *No borrowing.* During Year 1, the S Corporation derives no gross income and incurs deductible expenses of $150,000.

---

15. Under certain circumstances, a closing of the books election may be made with the consent of certain shareholders. See I.R.C. § 1377(a)(2); Treas. Reg. § 1.1368–1(g); pp. 102–105.

16. A shareholder establishes basis in her stock when she acquires the stock and subsequent to acquisition if she contributes additional capital to the corporation or if the corporation generates income. See I.R.C. § 1367(a)(1).

(b) *Borrowing from shareholder.* The S Corporation borrows $200,000 from Ben at the beginning of Year 1. During Year 1, the S Corporation derives no gross income and incurs $300,000 of deductible expenses.

(i) Are the tax consequences of this scenario sensible? Is the source of the problem the allocation rule or the allowance rule?

(ii) What are the tax consequences to Ben if the S Corporation repays its debt to Ben after the close of Year 1? See I.R.C. § 1367(b)(2).

(c) *Borrowing from Bank.* The S Corporation borrows $200,000 from the Bank at the beginning of Year 1. During Year 1, the S Corporation derives no gross income and incurs $300,000 of deductible expenses.

(i) What are the tax consequences if the S Corporation only incurs $200,000 of deductible expenses during Year 1 but it pays those expenses with the money it borrowed from the Bank, rather than the money contributed by its shareholders?

(ii) What justification exists for denying a current deduction to a shareholder whose pro rata share of an S Corporation's operating loss exceeds the basis of the shareholder's stock and the basis of any indebtedness of the corporation to that shareholder?

(d) *Borrowing from Bank with shareholder guarantee.* Same as (c), but Ben and Carol each agree to satisfy the S Corporation's obligation to the Bank if the S Corporation defaults on the loan (i.e., the shareholders guarantee the corporation's debt). See the Selfe and Leavitt cases that follow.

Selfe v. United States

United States Court of Appeals, Eleventh Circuit, 1985.
778 F.2d 769.

■ KRAVITCH, CIRCUIT JUDGE:

* * *

Taxpayer, Jane B. Selfe, formerly Jane Simon, entered into a retail clothing business in 1977 under the name of Jane Simon, Inc. She applied to the First National Bank of Birmingham for financing. In consideration of her pledge of 4500 shares of stock in Avondale Mills owned by her and close family members, the bank agreed to extend a line of credit to her in the amount of $120,000 for use in the business. Shortly thereafter, the business was incorporated. Taxpayer and her former husband were issued all of the stock, which was subsequently conveyed to Jane upon their divorce. The * * * corporation elected * * * [S Corporation status]. At the request of the bank, all loans made to the taxpayer individually pursuant to the line of credit * * * were converted to corporate loans. Taxpayer executed an agreement guaranteeing the corporation's indebtedness to the bank. The loan officer testified that the bank wanted the assurance of having the corporation primarily liable to repay the loan, but that the conversion did not abridge the stock pledged as collateral, or the bank's rights against the taxpayer as guarantor, in the event of the corporation's default. Subsequently, the corporation granted the bank a security interest in its receivables, inventory and contract rights in order to obtain a renewal of its loans. The business began operations on August 4, 1977 and suffered losses for each year through 1980. It never, however, defaulted on its loan payments and the bank never was required to proceed against either the Avondale Mills stock or the taxpayer. On June 30, 1980, the outstanding balance of the corporation's indebtedness to the bank exceeded $130,000.

The * * * loss of Jane Simon, Inc. for the fiscal year ending June 30, 1980 was $33,824. Taxpayer and her new husband, Edward Selfe, deducted the entire loss from gross income on their joint income tax return for the year 1980. The government, however, determined that the allowable portion of the loss was limited to $4,946, the amount it determined was the taxpayer's adjusted basis in the corporation, and accordingly disallowed $28,878 of the claimed deduction * * *. Taxpayer paid the [deficiency] and then filed a claim for refund of the tax * * *. The government disallowed the claim and the taxpayer instituted a refund suit in the district court. The district court judge denied the taxpayer's motion for summary judgment, but granted summary judgment to the government.

I.R.C. Section [1366(a)] permits a shareholder in a Subchapter S Corporation to deduct his portion of the corporation's * * * loss from his personal income. Section [1366(d)] limits the amount of the deduction, however, to the sum of the adjusted basis of the shareholder's stock in the corporation, plus the adjusted basis of any indebtedness of the corporation to the shareholder. Relying upon the principles of Plantation Patterns, Inc. v. Commissioner, 462 F.2d 712 (5th Cir.1972), the appellant argues that the bank is deemed to have made the loan directly to her and that she then contributed the loan proceeds to Jane Simon, Inc., thereby increasing her basis in the stock of the corporation. In Plantation Patterns, the Fifth Circuit held that a loan is deemed to be made to a stockholder who has guaranteed a corporate note when the facts indicate that the lender is looking primarily to the stockholder for repayment. Plantation Patterns, however, did not involve section [1366] as the corporation in that case was not a Subchapter S Corporation. Rather, in Plantation Patterns, the former Fifth Circuit affirmed as not clearly erroneous, a Tax Court finding that a transaction structured as a loan by an independent third party to a corporation, and guaranteed by a shareholder, was in substance a loan to the shareholder followed by his contribution of the loan proceeds to the capital of the corporation, and that as a result, the corporation's payments of * * * interest on the debt * * * [were not deductible]. The taxpayer here does not argue that the cases are identical; rather, she argues that the principles announced in Plantation Patterns should apply here and points to the testimony of her bank officer that the loan to Jane Simon, Inc. was secured by the taxpayer's Avondale stock and that the bank was primarily looking to the taxpayer and her pledged stock for repayment of the loan.[17]

* * *

---

17. It is not clear from the bank officer's deposition testimony that the bank was primarily looking to the taxpayer for repayment. Mr. Anthony, the bank officer, testified that

The district court, primarily relying upon Brown v. Commissioner, 706 F.2d 755 (6th Cir.1983), held that an economic outlay resulting in an increase in a shareholder's basis in a Subchapter S corporation occurs only when the shareholder-guarantor is called upon to pay the corporation's debt. Here, although the corporation each year had suffered losses, it did not default on the payments due the bank on the loan. Furthermore, the bank had renewed the loan to the corporation upon assignment of its accounts receivable. The government points out that taxpayer has cited no decision in which a court has held that a shareholder's guarantee of a loan made to a Subchapter S corporation increased his basis in the corporation * * *.

We find the Sixth Circuit's reasoning in Brown only partially persuasive. We agree with Brown inasmuch as that court reaffirms that economic outlay is required before a stockholder in a Subchapter S corporation may increase her basis. We disagree, however, with the proposition that a stockholder/taxpayer must, in all cases, absolve a corporation's debt before she may recognize an increased basis as a guarantor of a loan to a corporation.[18] Instead, we conclude that under the principles of Plantation Patterns, a shareholder who has guaranteed a loan to a Subchapter S corporation may increase her basis where the facts demonstrate that, in substance, the shareholder has borrowed funds and subsequently advanced them to her corporation.

The government correctly argues that generally taxpayers are liable for the tax consequences of the transaction they actually execute and may not reap the benefit of some other transaction that they might have made. In other words, taxpayers ordinarily are bound by the "form" of their transaction and may not argue that the "substance" of their transaction triggers different tax consequences. * * *.

It is equally well settled that the Commissioner need not always determine the tax effect of transactions based on the form of the transaction. This principle is particularly evident where characterization of capital as debt or equity will have different tax consequences. Thus, in Plantation Patterns, the court * * * recharacterized debt as equity at the insistence of the Commissioner. These principles, however, are not solely for the government's benefit. I.R.C. section 385(b) sets forth five factors which are available to determine "whether a debtor-creditor relationship exists or a corporation-shareholder relationship exists." Similarly this circuit applies a thirteen factor analysis to characterize a taxpayer's interest in a corporation. In re Lane, 742 F.2d 1311 (11th Cir.1984).

---

the loans originally advanced to the taxpayer were converted to corporate loans because "it just made more sense to have the company primarily liable and then the individuals would be just as liable as they were when the loans were direct to them." Mr. Anthony also testified, however, that the taxpayer's collateral and personal guaranty were "primarily" why the bank renewed the corporation's loans. On remand, the court will have to determine what the bank's intentions were.

18. For example, a guarantor who has pledged stock to secure a loan has experienced an economic outlay to the extent that the pledged stock is not available as collateral for other investments. The guarantor in this example has lost the time value or use of its collateral.

Although the question of whether a stockholder's advances to a corporation constitute debt or capital contributions is usually raised by the government, nothing in the Internal Revenue Code or our decisions suggests that the factors used to determine the substantive character of a taxpayer's interest in a corporation are available only to the government. Accordingly, where the nature of a taxpayer's interest in a corporation is in issue, courts may look beyond the form of the interest and investigate the substance of the transaction. These situations present an exception to the general proposition that a shareholder/taxpayer is bound by the form of her transaction.

At issue here, however, is not whether the taxpayer's contribution was either a loan to or an equity investment in Jane Simon, Inc. The issue is whether the taxpayer's guarantee of the corporate loan was in itself a contribution to the corporation sufficient to increase the taxpayer's basis in the corporation. In most cases, a mere guarantee of a corporate loan is insufficient, absent subrogation, to increase a taxpayer's basis. Thus arguments similar to Selfe's—that the taxpayer's guarantee is in reality a loan made to the shareholder/taxpayer that is subsequently advanced to the corporation—usually meet with little success because the taxpayer is unable to demonstrate that the substance of his transaction is different than its form. * * *. That taxpayers rarely, if ever, have demonstrated that a guarantee was in reality a loan to the corporation from the shareholder/taxpayer does not mean that this argument is legally inadequate per se. * * *.

Under the principles of Plantation Patterns, a shareholder guarantee of a loan may be treated for tax purposes as an equity investment in the corporation where the lender looks to the shareholder as the primary obligor. Essential to the Plantation Patterns court's analysis was that the notes guaranteed by the shareholder were issued by a thinly capitalized corporation and had more equity characteristics than debt. The Plantation Patterns court stressed that its inquiry focused on highly complex issues of fact and that similar inquiries must be carefully evaluated on their own facts. Here, the taxpayer has presented the deposition testimony of her loan officer stating that the bank primarily looked to the taxpayer and not the corporation for repayment of the loan. Moreover, the taxpayer also has elicited testimony indicating that Jane Simon, Inc. was thinly capitalized. The taxpayer argues that it is highly unlikely that the bank would have advanced funds directly to Jane Simon, Inc.—a fledgling enterprise operated by a novice in a highly competitive field. This argument is further supported by the fact that the bank previously had approved a line of credit consistent with the credit enjoyed by Jane Simon, Inc. to Jane Selfe, nee Simon, based upon her pledge of Avondale stock. The government, however, notes that it was at the bank's insistence that the line of credit originally approved for the taxpayer was converted to loans to the corporation guaranteed by the taxpayer.

Accordingly, we conclude that there are material facts still in issue and therefore summary judgment was inappropriate. We remand for a determination of whether or not the bank primarily looked to Jane Selfe for repayment and for the court to apply the factors set out in In re Lane and I.R.C. section 385 to determine if the taxpayer's guarantee amounted to either an equity investment in or shareholder loan to Jane Simon, Inc. In short, we remand for the district court to apply Plantation Patterns and determine if the bank loan to Jane Simon, Inc. was in reality a loan to the taxpayer.

* * *

Estate of Leavitt v. Commissioner

United States Court of Appeals, Fourth Circuit, 1989.
875 F.2d 420.

■ Murnaghan, Circuit Judge.

The appellants, Anthony D. and Marjorie F. Cuzzocrea and the Estate of Daniel Leavitt, Deceased, et al., appeal the Tax Court's decision holding them liable for tax deficiencies for the tax years 1979, 1980 and 1981 * * *.

I

As shareholders of VAFLA Corporation, a subchapter S corporation during the years at issue, the appellants claimed deductions under [§ 1366] of the Internal Revenue Code of 1954 to reflect the corporation's operating losses during the three years in question. The Commissioner disallowed deductions above the $10,000 bases each appellant had from their original investments.

The appellants contend, however, that the adjusted bases in their stock should be increased to reflect a $300,000 loan which VAFLA obtained from the Bank of Virginia ("Bank") on September 12, 1979, after the appellants, along with five other shareholders ("Shareholders–Guarantors"), had signed guarantee agreements whereby each agreed to be jointly and severally liable for all indebtedness of the corporation to the Bank. At the time of the loan, VAFLA's liability exceeded its assets, it could not meet its cash flow requirements and it had virtually no assets to use as collateral. The appellants assert that the Bank would not have lent the $300,000 without their personal guarantees.

VAFLA's financial statements and tax returns indicated that the bank loan was a loan from the Shareholders–Guarantors. Despite the representation to that effect, VAFLA made all of the loan payments, principal and interest, to the Bank. The appellants made no such payments. In addition, neither VAFLA nor the Shareholders–Guarantors treated the corporate payments on the loan as constructive income taxable to the Shareholders–Guarantors.

The appellants present the question whether the $300,000 bank loan is really, despite its form as a borrowing from the Bank, a capital contribution from the appellants to VAFLA. They contend that if the bank loan is characterized as equity, they are entitled to add a pro rata share of the $300,000 bank loan to their adjusted bases, thereby increasing the size of their operating loss deductions. Implicit in the appellants' characterization of the bank loan as equity in VAFLA is a determination that the Bank lent the $300,000 to the Shareholders–Guarantors who then contributed the funds to the corporation. The appellants' approach fails to realize that the $300,000 transaction, regardless of whether it is equity or debt, would permit them to adjust the bases in their stock if, indeed, the appellants, and not the Bank, had advanced VAFLA the money. The more precise question, which the appellants fail initially to ask, is whether the guaranteed loan from the Bank to VAFLA is an economic outlay of any kind by the Shareholders–Guarantors. To decide this question, we must determine whether the transaction involving the $300,000 was a loan from the Bank to VAFLA or was it instead a loan to the Shareholders–Guarantors who then gave it to VAFLA, as either a loan or a capital contribution * * *.

II

To increase the basis in the stock of a subchapter S corporation, there must be an economic outlay on the part of the shareholder * * *. A guarantee, in and of itself, cannot fulfill that requirement. The guarantee is merely a promise to pay in the future if certain unfortunate events should occur. At the present time, the appellants have experienced no such call as guarantors, have engaged in no economic outlay, and have suffered no cost.

The situation would be different if VAFLA had defaulted on the loan payments and the Shareholders–Guarantors had made actual disbursements on the corporate indebtedness. Those payments would represent corporate indebtedness to the shareholders which would increase their bases for the purpose of deducting * * * losses under [§ 1366(d)(1)(B)] * * *.

The appellants accuse the Tax Court of not recognizing the critical distinction between [§ 1366(d)(1)(A)] (adjusted basis in stock) and [§ 1366(d)(1)(B)] (adjusted basis in indebtedness of corporation to shareholder). They argue that the "loan" is not really a loan, but is a capital contribution (equity). Therefore, they conclude, [§ 1366(d)(1)(A)] applies and [§ 1366(d)(1)(B)] is irrelevant. However, the appellants once again fail to distinguish between the initial question of economic outlay and the secondary issue of debt or equity. Only if the first question had an affirmative answer, would the second arise * * *.

The Tax Court correctly determined that the appellants' guarantees, unaccompanied by further acts, in and of themselves, have not constituted contributions of cash or other property which might increase the bases of the appellants' stock in the corporation.

The appellants, while they do not disagree with the Tax Court that the guarantees, standing alone, cannot adjust their bases in the stock, nevertheless argue that the "loan" to VAFLA was in its "true sense" a loan to the Shareholders–Guarantors who then theoretically advanced the $300,000 to the corporation as a capital contribution. The Tax Court declined the invitation to treat a loan and its uncalled-on security, the guarantee, as identical and to adopt the appellants' view of the "substance" of the transaction over the "form" of the transaction they took. The Tax Court did not err in doing so.

Generally, taxpayers are liable for the tax consequences of the transaction they actually execute and may not reap the benefit of recasting the transaction into another one substantially different in economic effect that they might have made. They are bound by the "form" of their transaction and may not argue that the "substance" of their transaction triggers different tax consequences * * *. In the situation of guaranteed corporate debt, where the form of the transaction may not be so clear, courts have permitted the taxpayer to argue that the substance of the transaction was in actuality a loan to the shareholder. However, the burden is on the taxpayer and it has been a difficult one to meet. That is especially so where, as here, the transaction is cast in sufficiently ambiguous terms to permit an argument either way depending on which is subsequently advantageous from a tax point of view.

In the case before us, the Tax Court found that the "form" and "substance" of the transaction was a loan from the Bank to VAFLA and not to the appellants:

> The Bank of Virginia loaned the money to the corporation and not to petitioners. The proceeds of the loan were to be used in the operation of the corporation's business. Petitioners submitted no evidence that they were free to dispose of the proceeds of the loan as they wished. * * *. Accordingly, we find that the transaction was in fact a loan by the bank to the corporation guaranteed by the shareholders.

Whether the $300,000 was lent to the corporation or to the Shareholders/Guarantors is a factual issue which should not be disturbed unless clearly erroneous. Finding no error, we affirm.

It must be borne in mind that we do not merely encounter naive taxpayers caught in a complex trap for the unwary. They sought to claim deductions because the corporation lost money. If, however, VAFLA had been profitable, they would be arguing that the loan was in reality from the Bank to the corporation, and not to them, for that would then lessen their taxes. Under that description of the transaction, the loan repayments made by VAFLA would not be on the appellants' behalf, and, consequently, would not be taxed as constructive income to them. See Old Colony Trust Co. v. Commissioner, 279 U.S. 716, 49 S.Ct. 499 (1929) (payment by a corporation of a personal expense or debt of a shareholder is considered as the receipt of a taxable benefit). It came down in effect to an ambiguity as to which way the appellants would jump, an effort to play both ends against the middle, until it should be determined whether VAFLA was a profitable or money-losing proposition. At that point, the appellants attempted to treat the transaction as cloaked in the guise having the more beneficial tax consequences for them.

Finally, the appellants complain that the Tax Court erred by failing to apply debt-equity principles to determine the "form" of the loan. We believe that the Tax Court correctly refused to apply debt-equity principles here, a methodology which is only relevant, if at all, to resolution of the second inquiry—what is the nature of the economic outlay. Of course, the second inquiry cannot be reached unless the first question concerning whether an economic outlay exists is answered affirmatively. Here it is not.

The appellants, in effect, attempt to collapse a two-step analysis into a one-step inquiry which would eliminate the initial determination of economic outlay by first concluding that the proceeds were a capital contribution (equity). Obviously, a capital contribution is an economic outlay so the basis in the stock would be adjusted accordingly. But such an approach simply ignores the factual determination by the Tax Court that the Bank lent the $300,000 to the corporation and not to the Shareholders–Guarantors.

The appellants rely on * * * Selfe v. United States, 778 F.2d 769 (11th Cir.1985), to support their position * * *.

With regard to Selfe, the Tax Court [in Leavitt] stated:

the Eleventh Circuit applied a debt-equity analysis and held that a shareholder's guarantee of a loan made to a subchapter S corporation may be treated for tax purposes as an equity investment in the corporation where the lender looks to the shareholder as the primary obligor. We respectfully disagree with the Eleventh Circuit and hold that a shareholder's guarantee of a loan to a subchapter S corporation may not be treated as an equity investment in the corporation absent an economic outlay by the shareholder.

The Tax Court then distinguished Plantation Patterns, 462 F.2d 712 (5th Cir.1972), relied on by Selfe, because that case involved a C corporation, reasoning that the application of debt-equity principles to subchapter S corporations would defeat Congress' intent to limit a shareholder's pass-through deduction to the amount he or she has actually invested in the corporation * * *.

Although Selfe does refer to debt-equity principles, the specific issue before it was whether any material facts existed making summary judgment inappropriate. The Eleventh Circuit said:

At issue here, however, is not whether the taxpayer's contribution was either a loan to or an equity investment in Jane Simon, Inc. The issue is whether the taxpayer's guarantee of the corporate loan was in itself a contribution to the corporation [as opposed to a loan from the bank] sufficient to increase the taxpayer's basis in the corporation.

The Selfe court found that there was evidence that the bank primarily looked to the taxpayer and not the corporation for repayment of the loan.[19]

---

19. * * * The Eleventh Circuit noted that "a guarantor who has pledged stock to secure a loan has experienced an economic outlay to the extent that that pledged stock is not available as collateral for other investments. [The guarantor in this example has lost the time value or use of its collateral.]" * * *.

This particular situation is not before us and we decline to address the question of whether a guarantee can be an economic outlay when accompanied by pledged collateral.

Therefore, it remanded for "a determination of whether or not the bank primarily looked to Jane Selfe [taxpayer] for repayment [the first inquiry] and for the court to apply the factors * * * to determine if the taxpayer's guarantee amounted to either an equity investment in or shareholder loan to Jane Simon, Inc. [the second inquiry]." The implications are that there is still a two-step analysis and that the debt-equity principles apply only to the determination of the characterization of the economic outlay, once one is found.

Granted, that conclusion is clouded by the next and final statement of the Selfe court: "In short, we remand for the district court to apply Plantation Patterns and determine if the bank loan to Jane Simon, Inc. was in reality a loan to the taxpayer." To the degree that the Selfe court agreed * * * that an economic outlay is required before a shareholder may increase her basis in a subchapter S corporation, Selfe does not contradict current law or our resolution of the case before us. Furthermore, to the extent that the Selfe court remanded because material facts existed by which the taxpayer could show that the bank actually lent the money to her rather than the corporation, we are still able to agree. It is because of the Selfe court's suggestion that debt-equity principles must be applied to resolve the question of whether the bank actually lent the money to the taxpayer/shareholder or the corporation, that we must part company with the Eleventh Circuit for the reasons stated above.

In conclusion, the Tax Court correctly focused on the initial inquiry of whether an economic outlay existed. Finding none, the issue of whether debt-equity principles ought to apply to determine the nature of the economic outlay was not before the Tax Court. The Tax Court is affirmed.

NOTES

1. *Plantation Patterns.* The Plantation Patterns case, on which the taxpayers in Selfe and Leavitt relied, also involved a loan to a corporation that was guaranteed by its shareholders. In that case, however, the corporation was a C Corporation. The Internal Revenue Service disallowed the corporation's interest deduction by arguing that, in substance, the bank had lent funds to the shareholders who then contributed the funds to the corporation. To deny the interest deduction to Plantation Patterns, the Internal Revenue Service had to establish two points: first, that the bank lent the funds to the shareholders; and second, that the shareholders *contributed* the funds to the C Corporation. (If the shareholders lent the funds to the C Corporation, the corporation still would have been allowed an interest deduction.) In contrast, the taxpayers in Selfe and Leavitt merely needed to establish the first point. They would have achieved the necessary basis for deducting the allocated loss regardless of whether the transfer of funds by the shareholders to the corporation was treated as a contribution or a loan. I.R.C. § 1366(d)(1).

2. *Other courts deny basis for guarantee.* Notwithstanding the Eleventh Circuit's opinion in Selfe, the courts uniformly continue to reject efforts by

S Corporation shareholders to increase basis for shareholder guarantees of corporate obligations. See, e.g., Goatcher v. United States, 944 F.2d 747 (10th Cir.1991); Reser v. Commissioner, 112 F.3d 1258 (5th Cir.1997); Estate of Bean v. Commissioner, 268 F.3d 553 (8th Cir. 2001); Maloof v. Commissioner, 456 F.3d 645 (6th Cir. 2006). Even the Eleventh Circuit has acknowledged that Selfe is limited to a narrow fact pattern. See Sleiman v. Commissioner, 187 F.3d 1352 (11th Cir.1999) (holding that appellants "have not presented one of the unusual sets of facts that would lead us to conclude that the substance of the loans did not equal their form.")

3. *Economic outlay.* The Selfe and Leavitt opinions express the prevailing view that an "economic outlay" must occur before an S Corporation shareholder may increase his basis. Quite clearly, an "economic outlay" occurs when a shareholder contributes or lends money to an S Corporation. I.R.C. § 1366(d)(1). What differences exist between lending money to a corporation and promising to satisfy a corporate obligation if the corporation is unable to do so (i.e., guaranteeing the obligation)? Do these differences still exist when a shareholder's guarantee is accompanied by pledged collateral? Does an "economic outlay" occur when a shareholder's guarantee is accompanied by pledged collateral? See p. 115, fn. 19. Can it be argued that an "economic outlay" occurs even if the guarantee is not accompanied by pledged collateral?

In terms of what is regarded as an "economic outlay", consider whether, in Problem 3–2(c) (p. 108), Ben and Carol could deduct their entire pro rata shares of the S Corporation's loss if,

(a) Ben and Carol had executed the original note to the Bank along with the S Corporation? Nigh v. Commissioner, 60 T.C.M. 91 (1990) (holding that shareholder may not increase basis when shareholder is co-maker with S Corporation on promissory note).

(b) Ben and Carol each gave the S Corporation a note promising to contribute $100,000 to the corporation at a future time? Rev. Rul. 81–187, 1981–2 C.B. 167 (ruling that shareholder may not increase basis by issuing a promissory note to the S Corporation).

(c) Ben and Carol each gave the Bank a personal promissory note for $100,000 in exchange for the S Corporation's note? Rev. Rul. 75–144, 1975–1 C.B. 277 (ruling that shareholder may increase basis by substituting his note to bank for corporation's note to bank).

4. *Avoiding the problem.* If an S Corporation needs additional money and a bank loan is necessary to satisfy that need, how should the shareholders be advised to structure the loan? Should the advice differ depending on whether the bank would demand the shareholders to guarantee a loan made directly to the corporation? What determines whether a bank will demand that shareholders guarantee a loan made to the corporation?

5. *Deferral of loss.* A shareholder with insufficient basis to claim her pro rata share of an S Corporation's loss is allowed to claim the loss as soon as she establishes additional basis. The loss does not expire after a fixed period of years. See I.R.C. § 1366(d)(2). In light of this rule, is the presence of basis at the time the loss is incurred really that important? What happens if a shareholder without sufficient basis to absorb her pro rata share of an S Corporation loss sells her stock before establishing additional basis to deduct the loss? See Treas. Reg. § 1.1366–2(a)(5).

6. *Characterization of loss.* The characterization of a shareholder's pro rata share of each item of S Corporation loss or deduction is determined at the corporate level. I.R.C. § 1366(b). When a shareholder has insufficient basis to deduct his entire pro rata share of an S Corporation's capital losses and ordinary losses, what is the character of the losses he may deduct? For example, if an S Corporation has $20,000 of capital losses and $40,000 of ordinary losses and the basis of its sole shareholder is $30,000, the shareholder may claim $30,000 of losses. How much of the permitted loss is capital and how much is ordinary? See Treas. Reg. § 1.1366–2(a)(4).

7. *Other restrictions.* Even if a shareholder has sufficient basis to deduct her entire pro rata share of an S Corporation's losses, other loss limitation rules may cause the losses to be deferred or even disallowed. See, e.g., I.R.C. §§ 465 (at-risk rules), 469 (passive activity loss rules).

Hitchins v. Commissioner

United States Tax Court, 1994.
103 T.C. 711.

■ Tannenwald, Judge: * * *

Petitioners are husband and wife (hereinafter references to petitioner in the singular are to [Mr.] Hitchins). * * *

Petitioner was the founder and president of Champaign Computer Company (CCC) * * *. During the relevant years, CCC was engaged in the business of computer hardware and software sales, service and development * * *. [Petitioners owned the majority of the stock of CCC.] * * *

On August 24, 1985, petitioner and Scot Miller and his wife, Barbara, (the Millers) entered into an agreement to develop and market a chemical database * * *. The agreement provided that development of the database structure and software would be undertaken by CCC and that the ownership of the database would be transferred to a company to be formed upon obtaining venture capital or the occurrence of sales. The agreement also provided that CCC would be reimbursed for its expenses in developing the database system. Pursuant to the agreement, ChemMultiBase Company, Inc. (CMB), a subchapter S corporation, was incorporated on September 30, 1986. Petitioners, collectively, were 50–percent shareholders in CMB. The remaining 50–percent interest was owned, collectively, by the Millers. * * * Petitioners' basis in their CMB stock was $10,158.46.

In 1985 and 1986, CCC undertook development of the chemical database. In 1986, petitioner personally loaned a total of $34,000 to CCC, to pay the operating expenses of CCC relating to the database project. * * * CCC "booked" the $34,000 loan as a "loan from shareholder" in its corporate books and records. No portion of the amounts constituting the $34,000 loan to CCC were paid to or deposited in any account of CMB. Nor were the amounts treated as loans from petitioner to CMB by petitioner, CCC, or CMB.

On October 1, 1986, CCC invoiced CMB in the amount of $65,645.39 for expenses incurred by CCC relating to the development of the chemical database. * * *

CMB paid the invoice by * * * a combination of currency and CMB's agreement to pay the $34,000 liability owed by CCC to petitioner. * * * CCC was not relieved of its liability to petitioner, nor was any note executed between petitioner and CMB with respect to the $34,000 loan.

In their returns for the years at issue, petitioners deducted their share of CMB's losses. In applying the basis limitation under section 1366(d), they included in their basis in CMB stock the $34,000 as "Loan from Hitchins to CCC transferred to CMB." Respondent disallowed the inclusion of this amount.

Section 1366(a) requires a taxpayer to take into account the pro rata share of income, losses, and deductions of an S corporation of which the taxpayer is a shareholder. The losses and deductions taken into account are limited [under § 1366(d)(1)] * * *.

The decided cases have established certain principles in respect of the application of the indebtedness limitation under section 1366(d)(1)(B). First and foremost is the requirement that there be an actual economic outlay by the taxpayer. The second principle is that the indebtedness of the S corporation must run directly to the shareholders: an indebtedness to an entity with passthrough characteristics which advanced the funds and is closely related to the taxpayer does not satisfy the statutory requirements.

There is no question that there was an economic outlay by petitioner. Nor is there any question that, by virtue of the assumption, CMB became obligated to pay to petitioner the amount owed him on the note from CCC representing his loan to it. * * * We are * * * left with the question whether CMB's assumption of CCC's obligation to petitioner created "any indebtedness of the S corporation to the shareholder" within the meaning of section 1366(d)(1)(B).

Petitioners argue that, because section 1366(d)(1)(B) refers to "*any* indebtedness" (emphasis added), without qualifying language, the debt assumed by CMB should be considered an indebtedness to petitioners.

Respondent counters that, because of the words "of" and "to" in section 1366(d)(1)(B) (emphasis added), the indebtedness must represent an outlay from the taxpayer directly to the S corporation incurring the loss and that CMB's assumption of CCC's liability does not constitute such an outlay.

The issue before us has not been specifically addressed by any of the decided cases. In arriving at our decision, we have taken into account two general principles: (1) The word "indebtedness" can have different meanings in different provisions of the Internal Revenue Code; and (2) the courts have strictly construed the term "indebtedness" in the context of determining the extent to which a taxpayer can deduct S corporation losses. * * *

In the absence of any evidence of a direct obligation from CMB to him, petitioner was simply a creditor beneficiary of CMB whose rights against it were derivative through CCC, albeit that he could probably sue CMB without joining CCC. We think it significant that, as between CCC and CMB, CCC remained liable as a surety of the obligation of CMB to petitioner; there was no novation relieving CCC of its liability to petitioner as a primary obligor. Thus, if CMB failed to pay its obligation, petitioner would have had recourse against CCC. The continued obligation of CCC to petitioner would, if CMB defaulted, provide a remedy to petitioner which would in effect produce a reimbursement of his initial outlay by way of his loan to CCC. Thus, petitioner's position ultimately depended upon his status as a creditor and shareholder of CCC, and not as an investor in CMB. We are satisfied that, under these circumstances, there was no "investment" by petitioner in CMB * * *.

The continued existence of petitioner's rights against CCC distinguishes Gilday v. Commissioner, T.C. Memo. 1982–242, and Rev. Rul. 75–144, 1975–1 C.B. 277, upon which petitioners rely. In Gilday, a bank held the note of an S corporation. The taxpayer and other shareholders of the S corporation issued their note to the bank, and the bank canceled the note of the S corporation. In exchange, the S corporation then gave its note, in the same amount, to the shareholders. The result was that the shareholders became the sole obligors to the bank, and the S corporation was directly indebted to the shareholders. We held the shareholders had a basis in the debt for purposes of * * * section 1366(d). The same situation existed in Rev. Rul. 75–144. We recognize that in neither instance did the shareholder of the S corporation make an actual outlay of funds, but it is clear that the basis of Gilday and Rev. Rul. 75–144 is that the substitution of the shareholders as the sole unconditional obligors to the bank and of the S corporation as the sole unconditional debtor to the shareholders constituted a constructive furnishing by the shareholder of the funds previously loaned by the third party bank.

We are not unaware of the fact that petitioner might well have succeeded had he adopted another form of the transaction in question, e.g., by way of a novation releasing CCC from liability and obtaining a replacement note from CMB. Alternatively, petitioner could have lent $34,000 to CMB, and then CMB could have paid its debt to CCC, and CCC could have paid its debt to petitioner. The result would have been that CMB would be directly and solely indebted to petitioner in the amount of $34,000. Under Gilday and other precedent, the form of such a transaction would have been upheld, and petitioner would have had a basis in CMB's indebtedness. But, in the area of indebtedness for the purpose of applying section 1366(d), form coupled with adequate substance or reality is not to be disregarded.

In sum, we hold that the $34,000 loan from petitioner to CCC cannot be included, under section 1366(d)(1)(B), in his basis in determining the amount of CMB's losses which petitioners can deduct.

NOTES

1. *Economics before taxes*. Are there any economic reasons why the Hitchins' might have been reluctant to utilize the alternative forms suggested by the Tax Court that would have established a basis in CMB's indebtedness?

2. *Election to treat family as one shareholder*. Any member of a family may elect to treat the entire family as one shareholder for purposes of the 100 shareholder limitation. See I.R.C. § 1361(c)(1).

D. DISTINGUISHING S CORPORATION FROM C CORPORATION

Subchapter S was enacted in 1958. It was intended to minimize the influence of the tax law when the owners of a "small business" selected the legal form for conducting their business. The eligibility requirements for S Corporation status were designed with simplicity in mind.

To qualify as an S Corporation under Federal tax law, a corporation must satisfy all of the following eligibility requirements:

(a) The corporation must be a domestic corporation, other than certain ineligible corporations.

(b) The corporation must not have more than one hundred shareholders.

(c) All shareholders of the corporation must be individuals (none of whom are nonresident-aliens), estates, certain trusts, or certain tax-exempt organizations.

(d) The corporation must issue only one class of stock.

See I.R.C. § 1361(b). In addition to satisfying these eligibility requirements, the corporation must make the requisite "S" election. See I.R.C. § 1362.

When Subchapter S was enacted, Congress was not very concerned with confining the elective tax regime to small enterprises. The only eligibility requirement that relates to the size of the enterprise is the limit on the number of shareholders. The shareholder limit was originally set at 10. That limit has since been increased to 100. I.R.C. § 1361(b)(1)(A). Subchapter S imposes no limit on the amount of assets that the corporation may own or on the amount of income that the corporation may generate. Even if Congress had wanted to preclude high income businesses from utilizing Subchapter S, little need existed for a statutory prohibition because individual tax rates were historically much higher than corporate tax rates. As a result of this rate structure, C Corporation status was generally more desirable than S Corporation status. See pp. 5–8.

The outer limits of the Subchapter S eligibility requirements were tested for the first time in the late 1980's when individual tax rates fell below corporate tax rates. See pp. 8–10. The number of S Corporations has risen steadily since that time. In fact, more than half of the corporations reporting to the Internal Revenue Service are now S Corporations and that number may continue to grow.

1. SMALL BUSINESS CORPORATION

a. NOT MORE THAN 100 SHAREHOLDERS

I.R.C. § 1361(b)(1)(A)

Revenue Ruling 94–43

1994–2 Cum.Bull. 198.

In Rev. Rul. 77–220, 1977–1 C.B. 263, thirty unrelated individuals entered into the joint operation of a single business. The individuals divided into three equal groups of ten individuals and each group formed a separate corporation. The three corporations then organized a partnership for the joint operation of the business. The principal purpose for forming three separate corporations instead of one corporation was to avoid the 10 shareholder limitation of Section 1371 of the Internal Revenue Code of 1954 (the predecessor of Section 1361) and thereby allow the corporations to elect to be treated as S corporations under Subchapter S.

Rev. Rul. 77–220 concluded that the three corporations should be considered to be a single corporation, solely for purposes of making the election, because the principal purpose for organizing the separate corporations was to make the election. Under this approach, there would be 30 shareholders in one corporation and the election made by this corporation would not be valid because the 10 shareholder limitation would be violated.

The Service has reconsidered Rev. Rul. 77–220 and concluded that the election of the separate corporations should be respected. The purpose of the number of shareholders requirement is to restrict S corporation status to corporations with a limited number of shareholders so as to obtain administrative simplicity in the administration of the corporation's tax affairs. In this context, administrative simplicity is not affected by the corporation's participation in a partnership with other S corporation partners; nor should a shareholder of one S corporation be considered a shareholder of another S corporation because the S corporations are partners in a partnership. Thus, the fact that several S corporations are partners in a single partnership does not increase the administrative complexity at the S corporation level. As a result, the purpose of the number of shareholders requirement is not avoided by the structure in Rev. Rul. 77–220 and, therefore, the election of the corporations should be respected.

NOTES

1. *Stringency of shareholder limitation.* How does Rev. Rul. 94–43 impact on the 100 shareholder limitation?

2. *Election to treat family as one shareholder.* Any member of a family may elect to treat the entire family as one shareholder for purposes of the 100 shareholder limitation. See I.R.C. § 1361(c)(1).

b. NO INELIGIBLE SHAREHOLDERS

I.R.C. §§ 1361(b)(1)(B), (C)

IRS Letter Ruling 9138025

9/20/91.

* * *

X, formerly a corporation taxed under subchapter C of the Internal Revenue Code, elected S corporation status for its tax year beginning December 1, 1989.

X represents that prior to December 1, 1989, A, a stockholder in X, pledged his shares in X to B to secure a personal loan from B. X further represents that on May 1, 1990, B purchased A's X stock pursuant to a foreclosure sale of that stock. On October 10, 1990, X successfully negotiated the repurchase of its stock from B and retired that stock. B is an ineligible shareholder of X under section 1361(b)(1) of the Code.

* * *

Section 1362(d)(2)(A) of the Code provides that an election under section 1362(a) shall be terminated whenever * * * the corporation ceases to be a small business corporation.

* * *

Section 1362(f) of the Code provides that if (1) an election under section 1362(a) by any corporation was terminated * * *, (2) the Secretary determines that the termination was inadvertent, (3) no later than a reasonable period of time after discovery of the event resulting in such termination, steps were taken so that the corporation is once more a small business corporation, and (4) the corporation, and each person who was a shareholder of the corporation at any time during the period specified pursuant to this subsection, agrees to make such adjustments (consistent with the treatment of the corporation as an S corporation) as may be required by the Secretary with respect to the period, then, notwithstanding the terminating event, the corporation shall be treated as continuing to be an S corporation during the period specified by the Secretary.

S. Rep. No. 640, 97th Cong., 2d Sess. 12–13 (1982), 1982–2 C.B. 718, 723–24, in discussing section 1362(f) of the Code, states in part as follows:

If the Internal Revenue Service determines that a corporation's subchapter S election is inadvertently terminated, the Service can waive the effect of the terminating event for any period if the corporation timely corrects the event and if the corporation and the shareholders agree to be treated as if the election had been in effect for such period.

The committee intends that the Internal Revenue Service be reasonable in granting waivers, so that corporations whose subchapter S eligibility requirements have been inadvertently violated do not suffer the tax consequences of a termination if no tax avoidance would result from the continued subchapter S treatment. In granting a waiver, it is hoped that taxpayers and the government will work out agreements that protect the revenues without undue hardship to taxpayers. * * * It is expected that the waiver may be made retroactive for all years, or retroactive for the period in which the corporation again became eligible for subchapter S treatment, depending on the facts.

Based upon the information submitted, it is held (i) that a termination of X's S corporation status occurred on May 1, 1990, the date that X's stock was purchased by B, and (ii) that such termination was an inadvertent termination within the meaning of section 1362(f) of the Code.

It is further held that, pursuant to the provisions of section 1362(f) of the Code, X will be treated as continuing to be an S corporation during the period May 1, 1990, to October 10, 1990, and for subsequent periods, unless X's S corporation election is otherwise terminated under the provisions of section 1362(d). During the period May 1, 1990, to October 10, 1990, B will be treated as a shareholder of X. Therefore, B must, in determining its federal income tax liability, include its pro rata share of the separately and nonseparately computed items of X as provided in section 1366 [and] make adjustments to stock basis as provided in section 1367 * * *. This ruling shall be null and void should B fail to comply with the above-described adjustments.

NOTES

1. *Inadvertent versus intentional terminations.* In light of the relief available under I.R.C. § 1362(f), how concerned should the shareholders of an S Corporation be about a transfer of shares to an ineligible shareholder? See Treas. Reg. § 1.1362–4. How can the shareholders of an S Corporation preclude a renegade shareholder from transferring shares to an ineligible shareholder?

2. *Restriction on partnership shareholders.* Revenue Ruling 94–43 (p. 122) demonstrates that an S Corporation may be a partner in a partnership. May a partnership ever be a shareholder of an S Corporation? See I.R.C. § 1361(b)(1)(B).

3. *Restriction on corporate shareholders.* If 99% of the stock of Z Corporation is owned by A, an individual, and the other 1% of the stock of Z is owned by Y Corporation, is Z eligible for S Corporation status? See I.R.C.

§ 1361(b)(1)(B). If 100% of the stock of Z Corporation is owned by Y Corporation and Y is an S Corporation, Y may elect to treat Z as a "qualified subchapter S subsidiary." I.R.C. § 1361(b)(3). If Y makes that election, Z's separate corporate existence is ignored for tax purposes and all Z's assets, liabilities, income, deductions and credits are attributed to Y. From a state law standpoint, however, Z remains a separate corporate entity and Y would normally be insulated from any claims against Z.

4. *Restriction on nonresident alien shareholders.* If foreign law allows a U.S. corporation to conduct business in a foreign country but also requires a resident of the foreign country to own at least one share of the stock of the U.S. corporation, can the U.S. corporation qualify for S Corporation status? See I.R.C. § 1361(b)(1)(C).

5. *Trusts, estates, and tax-exempt organizations as shareholders.* Several exceptions exist to the general rule that all shareholders of an S Corporation must be individuals. I.R.C. § 1361(b)(1)(B) (parenthetical language).

(a) *Estates and testamentary trusts.* When a shareholder of an S Corporation dies, the stock is transferred to the decedent's estate by operation of law unless the decedent's will causes the stock to be transferred to a trust. A decedent's estate is a permissible S Corporation shareholder. I.R.C. § 1361(b)(1)(B). (The bankruptcy estate of an individual is also a permissible S Corporation shareholder. I.R.C. § 1361(c)(3).) A trust to which stock is transferred pursuant to the terms of a will is also a permissible S Corporation shareholder, but only for a two year period beginning on the day the stock is transferred to the trust. See I.R.C. § 1361(c)(2)(A)(iii).

(b) *Grantor and section 678 trusts.* An inter vivos trust is a permissible S Corporation shareholder if the terms of the trust cause all trust property to be treated, for Federal income tax purposes, as owned by an individual who is eligible to be an S Corporation shareholder. I.R.C. § 1361(c)(2)(A)(i). If the individual treated as owning the property of the trust dies and the trust continues in existence after the individual's death, the trust remains a permissible S Corporation shareholder, but only for the two year period beginning on the date of the individual's death. I.R.C. § 1361(c)(2)(A)(ii).

(c) *Qualified subchapter S trusts.* A trust that fails to meet the standard of I.R.C. § 1361(c)(2)(A)(i) but satisfies the statutory definition of a "qualified subchapter S trust" is also a permissible S Corporation shareholder, if the beneficiary of the trust makes a special election. I.R.C. § 1361(d)(1). To satisfy the statutory definition of a qualified subchapter S trust, certain specific provisions must be included in the trust instrument and all the trust's income must be distributed (or be required to be distributed) to a single individual who is eligible to be an S Corporation shareholder. I.R.C. § 1361(d)(3). If a qualified subchapter S trust owns stock of more than one S Corporation, a separate election must be made for each corporation. I.R.C. § 1361(d)(2).

(d) *Voting trust.* A trust created primarily to exercise the voting power of stock transferred to it is also a permissible S Corporation shareholder. I.R.C. § 1361(c)(2)(A)(iv).

(e) *Electing small business trust.* An "electing small business trust" is also a permissible S Corporation shareholder. I.R.C. § 1361(c)(2)(A)(v). To qualify for this treatment, all beneficiaries of the trust must generally be individuals or estates eligible to be S Corporation shareholders, all interests in the trust must generally be acquired by gift or bequest and the trustee must make a special election. I.R.C. § 1361(e). Any person who may receive a distribution from the trust is counted as a shareholder for purposes of the 100 shareholder limitation. I.R.C. § 1361(c)(2)(B)(v).

(f) *Tax-exempt organization.* Certain tax-exempt organizations, such as pension plans and charitable organizations, are also permissible S Corporation shareholders. I.R.C. §§ 1361(b)(1)(B), (c)(6).

c. NOT MORE THAN ONE CLASS OF STOCK

I.R.C. § 1361(b)(1)(D)

Treas. Reg. § 1.1361–1(*l*)

Paige v. United States

United States Court of Appeals, Ninth Circuit, 1978.
580 F.2d 960.

■ Skopil, District Judge: * * *

Tackmer is a small California company that was first incorporated in 1965. When Tackmer first issued stock, it received two different kinds of consideration. Plaintiffs [husband and wife] and another party assigned their rights to an exclusive license agreement in exchange for Tackmer stock ("property shareholders"). Eight other parties paid cash ("cash shareholders").

The Articles of Incorporation state that "No distinction shall exist between the shares of the corporation [or] the holders thereof." The applicable California Corporation Code stated that there could be no distinction between shares unless specified in the Articles.

Before Tackmer could issue any stock, it was required to obtain a permit from the California Department of Corporations. The California Corporation Code gave the Department authority to impose conditions on corporations for the protection of the public. Pursuant to this authority the Department had a policy of imposing certain conditions on small corporations such as Tackmer which were capitalized with both cash and property that had an indeterminate value. The purpose of the conditions was to protect the shareholders who paid with cash from having their interests diluted by overissue of stock to the shareholders who paid with property.

The conditions imposed by the Department of Corporations were as follows:

(a) The stock had to be deposited in escrow and could not be sold without the Department's consent;

(b) If the company defaulted on dividend payments for two years, the cash shareholders would have irrevocable power of attorney to vote the property shareholders' shares for the board of directors;

(c) On dissolution, the property shareholders had to waive their rights to the distribution of assets until the cash shareholders had received the full amount of their purchase price plus any unpaid accumulated dividends at 5% per year;

(d) The property shareholders had to waive their rights to any dividends until the cash shareholders annually received cumulative dividends equal to 5% of the purchase price per share;

(e) The conditions were to remain in effect until the shares were released from escrow. The conditions were in effect from 1965 to 1970.

The property shareholders signed an agreement with the company stating that they would abide by the conditions. * * *. Notwithstanding the conditions, the differences between the two kinds of shareholders were never taken into account and all dividends were distributed on a pro rata basis.

* * *

The taxpayers filed a timely joint tax return in 1970. The return claimed their proportionate share of * * * Tackmer's income and losses for the years before 1970. On January 14, 1973, the Commissioner of Internal Revenue disallowed these claims and assessed additional taxes * * *. The reason stated for the disallowance was that the conditions imposed by the California Department of Corporations created more than one class of stock, disqualifying Tackmer for subchapter S treatment.

On October 25, 1973, the taxpayers prepaid the tax and filed a timely claim for refund. On December 7, 1973, the government sent taxpayers a Notice of Disallowance of the claim. On December 12 the taxpayer filed this action.

The issue was submitted to the District Court for the Central District of California * * * [which] entered judgment for the United States.

The taxpayers contend that because the Articles and state law authorized only one class of stock, there can be only one class for subchapter S purposes. We hold, however, that the interpretation of subchapter S qualifications is a federal question.

[Former] Treas. Reg. § 1.1371–1(g) provide[d] that:

If the outstanding shares of stock of the corporation are not identical with respect to the *rights* and interests which they convey in the control, profits, and assets of the corporation, then the corporation is considered to have more than one class of stock [emphasis added].

The cash shareholders had preferred rights over property shareholders, notwithstanding that the cash shareholders chose not to exercise those rights. The possibility of the exercise of differing rights is enough to disqualify a corporation for subchapter S tax treatment.

Taxpayers' assertion that Tackmer in fact made all distributions on a pro rata basis is irrelevant. A corporation's qualifications for subchapter S status is judged at the date of election. The court may not consider Tackmer's actual distributions after its election. The language in the statute is clear. Tax planners must be able to assume that the court will give it its plain meaning.

* * *

There is a strong policy behind the requirement that subchapter S corporations have only one class of stock. The corporations themselves pay no corporate income tax. The shareholders pay individual income tax on a pro rata share of all corporate income, regardless of whether any money or property has actually been distributed to the shareholder. If the statute allowed more than one class of stock, complicated allocation problems could arise.

* * *

We agree with the taxpayers that the purpose of subchapter S is to benefit small corporations such as the one here. It is unfortunate that a requirement of state law has caused a result that no one intended. However, the taxpayers' subjective intent to create one class of stock cannot be allowed to override statutory requirements. Congress has set forth specific objective requirements for subchapter S qualification, and we must follow the mandate of the statute.

We affirm.

NOTES

1. *Differences in voting rights.* Differences in voting rights among shares of stock of a corporation are now disregarded in determining whether a corporation has more than one class of stock. I.R.C. § 1361(c)(4). Thus, an S Corporation may have voting and nonvoting common stock, a class of stock that may vote only on certain issues, irrevocable proxy agreements, or groups of shares that differ with respect to rights to elect members of the board of directors. Treas. Reg. § 1.1361–1(l)(1).

2. *Differences in economic rights.* Under the current regulations, a corporation is treated as having only one class of stock if all outstanding shares of stock confer identical rights to distribution and liquidation proceeds. Treas. Reg. § 1.1361–1(l)(1). The determination of whether all outstanding shares of stock confer identical rights to distribution and liquidation proceeds is based on the corporate charter, articles of incorporation, by-laws, applicable state law, and binding agreements relating to distribution and liquidation proceeds. Treas. Reg. § 1.1361–1(l)(2)(i). If the current regulations applied to the fact pattern in Paige, would a second class of stock exist? See Treas. Reg. § 1.1361–1(*l*)(2)(vi) Example 1.

3. *Commercial agreements between corporation and shareholder.* A "commercial contractual agreement" between a corporation and a shareholder operating in a non-shareholder capacity (e.g., a lease, an employment agreement or a loan agreement) is not a binding agreement relating to distribution and liquidation proceeds. Such an agreement will not create a second class of stock unless a principal purpose of the agreement is to circumvent the one class of stock requirement. Treas. Reg. § 1.1361–1(*l*)(2)(i). Is this principal purpose standard problematic from,

(a) the taxpayer's perspective?

(b) the government's perspective?

The fact that a "commercial contractual agreement" between a corporation and a shareholder operating in a non-shareholder capacity is not designed to circumvent the one class of stock requirement does not prevent the government from reclassifying the arrangement under other provisions of the Internal Revenue Code.

> *Example 3–F (Reclassification under another Code provision):* Standard Corporation, an S Corporation, has two equal shareholders, Carol and David, who each have binding employment agreements with Standard. The compensation paid by Standard to Carol under Carol's employment agreement is reasonable. The compensation paid by Standard to David under David's employment agreement is excessive. The facts and circumstances do not indicate that a principal purpose of David's employment agreement is to circumvent the one class of stock requirement of section 1361(b)(1)(D). Under the regulations, the employment agreements are not "binding agreements relating to distribution and liquidation proceeds." Accordingly, Standard is not treated as having more than one class of stock by reason of the employment agreements. However, Standard is not allowed a deduction under I.R.C. § 162(a) for the excessive compensation paid to David.

Treas. Reg. § 1.1361–1(*l*)(2)(vi) Example 3. See also Treas. Reg. § 1.1361–1(*l*)(2)(vi) Examples 4 and 5.

4. *Agreements restricting the transfer of shares.* When the stock of a corporation is controlled by only a few shareholders, it is common for the shareholders to agree that any departing shareholder must sell his shares back to the corporation or to the remaining shareholders. Under the current regulations, a bona fide agreement of this type that is triggered at the time of a shareholder's death, divorce, disability, or termination of employment is disregarded in determining whether an S Corporation has more than one class of stock. Agreements restricting the transfer of shares that are activated by other events are disregarded unless,

(a) a principal purpose of the agreement is to circumvent the one class of stock requirement, and

(b) the agreement establishes a purchase price that deviates significantly from the market value of the stock at the time of the agreement.

Treas. Reg. § 1.1361–1(*l*)(2)(iii). See Treas. Reg. § 1.1361–1(*l*)(2)(v) Examples 8 and 9.

Shareholder agreements restricting the transfer of shares often address the receipt of an offer from a third party to buy a shareholder's shares. A shareholder receiving such an offer must normally offer to sell the shares to the corporation (or to the other shareholders) at the price offered by the third party before accepting the outsider's offer. Could such an agreement involving stock of an S Corporation create a second class of stock?

5. *Debt reclassified as equity.* Amounts advanced to a corporation that are treated as debt by the parties may be reclassified as equity for Federal income tax purposes. See pp. 49–54. Debt of an S Corporation that is reclassified as equity is treated as a second class of stock only if a principal purpose of the arrangement is,

(a) to circumvent the rights to distribution or liquidation proceeds conferred by the outstanding shares of stock, or

(b) to circumvent the limitation on eligible shareholders. Treas. Reg. § 1.1361–1(*l*)(4)(ii)(A).

Moreover, an arrangement that satisfies any one of the following conditions is ignored when determining whether a second class of stock exists, regardless of the motivation for the arrangement.

(a) *Small, short-term advances.* Undocumented advances by a shareholder to the corporation are not treated as a second class of stock even if the advances are considered equity under general principles of Federal tax law if the shareholder's advances,

(i) do not exceed $10,000 in the aggregate at any time during the taxable year of the corporation,

(ii) are treated as debt by the parties, and

(iii) are expected to be repaid within a reasonable time.

Treas. Reg. § 1.1361–1(*l*)(4)(ii)(B)(1).

(b) *Proportionately held obligations.* Obligations of a corporation that are considered equity under general principles of Federal tax law are not treated as a second class of stock if,

(i) the obligations are owned solely by the shareholders, and

(ii) each shareholder's proportionate share of the obligations is identical to that shareholder's proportionate share of the outstanding stock.

Furthermore, corporate obligations owned by the sole shareholder of a corporation are never treated as a second class of stock. Treas. Reg. § 1.1361–1(*l*)(4)(ii)(B)(2). What justification exists for these exceptions?

(c) *Straight debt.* Obligations that satisfy the statutory definition of "straight debt" are not treated as a second class of stock. I.R.C. § 1361(c)(5). The term straight debt means a written unconditional obligation to pay a sum certain either on demand or on a specified due date, regardless of whether embodied in a formal note, that,

> (i) does not provide for an interest rate or payment date that is contingent on profits, the borrower's discretion, the payment of dividends with respect to common stock, or similar factors;

> (ii) is not convertible into stock or any other equity interest in the S Corporation; and

> (iii) is held by an eligible S Corporation shareholder or by a person in the business of lending money.

An obligation that is subordinated to other debt of the corporation may qualify as straight debt. Treas. Reg. § 1.1361–1(*l*)(5).

2. THE ELECTION

I.R.C. § 1362

Treas. Reg. § 1.1362–6

Leather v. Commissioner

United States Tax Court, 1991.
62 T.C.M. 1087.

■ COHEN, JUDGE: * * *

FINDINGS OF FACT

    * * *

Articles of Incorporation for Flexible Ink, Inc. (the corporation) were filed on June 19, 1986. Petitioner was the president and sole shareholder of the corporation. At the suggestion of petitioner's daughter, Leslee Hippert (Hippert), a practicing attorney, petitioner decided that the corporation should elect S status.

On July 19, 1986, Hippert prepared a Form 2553, Election by a Small Business Corporation, for the corporation. Petitioner and Hippert met for lunch, at which time petitioner signed the Form 2553 in her capacity as president and sole shareholder. * * *

On July 23, 1986, after making a copy of the signed Form 2553 for her records, Hippert placed the original form in an envelope with a typewritten address to the Internal Revenue Service, Ogden, Utah. She weighed the envelope and placed postage on the envelope containing the Form 2553 using a postage meter in her law office. She placed a yellow adhesive notepaper on the retained copy and wrote "mailed 7/23/86" on the adhesive notepaper. Hippert then put the envelope containing the original Form 2553 on a built-in shelf in the back office next to the postage meter.

If outgoing mail from Hippert's law firm was ready before the usual time that the United States Postal Service employee delivered mail to the office, it was placed at the office's receptionist desk * * * to be taken by the postal employee when the mail was delivered. Outgoing mail that was prepared after the postal employee had visited the office was collected on the built-in shelf in the back office and taken to the mailbox on the corner of Church and Alameda Streets in Tucson by 5:30 each night by one of the secretaries in the office.

When a Form 2553 is received by the Internal Revenue Service Ogden Service Center, the Receipt and Control Branch runs the envelope through a composite mail processing machine that opens the envelope. The envelopes are then sorted into different trays and taken into an extracting unit, where employees manually extract the contents at a "tingle" table. The "tingle" table contains a light to "candle" the envelope to ensure that there are no other documents left in the envelope.

Once the envelopes have been completely searched and the documents retrieved, the Forms 2553 are * * * taken to the Entity Section at the Service Center. At the Entity Section, a tax examiner reviews the Forms 2553 for completeness and timeliness. * * * Once the Service Center has accepted a Form 2553 as a valid election, a Form 385–C letter is sent to the taxpayer. The Form 2553 is retained by the Service Center for 6 weeks and then shipped to the Federal Records Center in Denver, Colorado, where it is retained for 75 years.

* * *

On May 5, 1987, the corporation filed a Form 1120S [the annual information return that must be filed by an S Corporation] for the calendar year 1986. The Form 1120S reflected a loss of $33,583. Because the Internal Revenue Service Center records did not reflect an election on file, on July 16, 1987, a letter was sent to the taxpayer asking for a Form 2553. [N]o response was received from the corporation * * *.

Forms 1120S were filed by the corporation on April 13, 1988, and April 6, 1989, for the calendar years 1987 and 1988, respectively. Each of these returns reported a loss. * * *

Petitioner filed individual income tax returns for 1986, 1987, and 1988. On each of these returns, she claimed a loss passed through from the corporation. Separate statutory notices [of a tax deficiency] for 1986, 1987, and 1988 were sent to petitioner on April 13, 1990 * * *. Each notice adjusted petitioner's taxable income by disallowing the loss claimed with respect to the corporation. * * *

On or about July 3, 1989, petitioner received a letter from the Internal Revenue Service Center. The letter informed the corporation that the Form 1120S for the calendar year 1988 could not be processed because there was no record of a Form 2553. In July 1989, petitioner completed and filed a new Form 2553. On August 9, 1989, the Service Center sent a letter accepting the corporation's S election effective January 1, 1990. * * *

A search of the Internal Revenue Service Center files disclosed no Form 2553 for the corporation prior to the Form 2553 sent by petitioner in July 1989.

OPINION

The parties each point to lapses in the other's procedures and speculate as to how the Form 2553 prepared and signed by petitioner in July 1986 could have been lost. The controlling circumstance in this case, however, is that there is no evidence that the envelope containing the Form 2553 was actually deposited in the United States mail. As petitioner acknowledges, she cannot supply the Court "with any precedent in which a taxpayer has successfully used habit evidence to prove delivery of a S Election to the Service." * * *

We recognize that the result may seem unfair to petitioner and that documents are lost at the Internal Revenue Service Center. Petitioner, however, is seeking the benefit of special statutory provisions that are dependent on timely filing of a Form 2553. The burden of proving that the S election was made by the corporation must fall on her. She has failed to satisfy that burden. She may not deduct the losses claimed in 1986, 1987, or 1988 with respect to the corporation.

NOTES

1. *Avoiding the problem.* What steps should have been taken to avoid the problem that arose in Leather?

2. *Relief for late election or no election.* Subsequent to Leather, Congress enacted I.R.C. § 1362(b)(5). In light of that relief provision, how concerned should the shareholders of an S Corporation be about avoiding the problem that arose in Leather?

3. *Election by 15th day of third month of tax year.* A calendar year corporation that, except as indicated below, is a "small business corporation" files an S election on March 10 of Year 3. See I.R.C. §§ 1362(b)(1), (2); Treas. Reg. § 1.1362–6(a)(2).

(a) When is the election generally effective?

(b) When is the election effective if the corporation had 101 shareholders until January 3 of Year 3?

(c) When is the election effective if the corporation had 101 shareholders until March 13 of Year 3?

(d) When is the election effective if the corporation was a small business corporation since January 1 of Year 3 but Shareholder A sold her shares to B on February 11 of Year 3?

(e) I.R.C. § 1362(f) permits the Internal Revenue Service to validate certain S elections that were not effective by reason of failing to meet an eligibility requirement or to obtain shareholder consents. How does that relief provision impact on the answers to the preceding questions?

4. *Election after 15th day of third month of tax year.* A calendar year corporation that, except as indicated below, is a "small business corporation" files an S election on April 10 of Year 3. See I.R.C. § 1362(b)(3); Treas. Reg. § 1.1362–6(a)(2).

(a) When is the election generally effective?

(b) When is the election effective if the corporation is not a small business corporation on April 10 of Year 3 but is a small business corporation on January 1 of Year 4?

(c) When is the election effective if the corporation is a small business corporation on April 10 of Year 3, but is not a small business corporation on January 1 of Year 4?

(d) When is the election effective if the corporation is a small business corporation on April 10 of Year 3 and on January 1 of Year 4, but is not a small business corporation on June 1 of Year 3?

(e) How does I.R.C. § 1362(f) impact on the answers to the preceding questions?

5. *New corporation.* If a new corporation that uses the calendar year as its tax year begins its first taxable year on November 17 of Year 1, can that corporation make an S election effective from November 17 of Year 1? By when must that election be made? See I.R.C. § 1362(b)(4); Treas. Reg. § 1.1362–6(a)(2).

6. *One election.* Must a new S election be made every year? I.R.C. § 1362(c).

7. *Termination of election.* How can an S election be terminated? What is the earliest termination date that can be achieved by the shareholders of a calendar year S Corporation who decide on April 15 of Year 5 that they wish to convert the corporation to a C Corporation? How would such a termination be achieved? See I.R.C. § 1362(d); Treas. Reg. §§ 1.1362–2, – 6(a)(3).

8. *In and out of Subchapter S.* Can a corporation be taxed as a C Corporation in even number years and an S Corporation in odd number years? See I.R.C. § 1362(g); Treas. Reg. § 1.1362–5.

E. TRANSITIONAL PROBLEMS

Any corporation that operates as an S Corporation from its inception is unaffected by the double tax regime that applies to C Corporations. For such an enterprise, all operating income and all gains from the disposition of appreciated property (§ 61(a)(3) income) are subject only to a single layer of tax, the individual income tax. In addition, operating losses (deductions in excess of gross income) flow through to the shareholders and have no tax impact at the corporate level.

A corporation need not operate as an S Corporation from its inception to qualify for S Corporation status. Many corporations operate as a C

Corporation for some period of time and then convert to S Corporation status. When a C Corporation elects S Corporation status, all operating income and gains that accrue *after* the conversion are subject only to the individual income tax. Similarly, all operating losses that occur *after* the conversion to S Corporation status simply flow through to the shareholders.

Transitional rules are needed to deal with certain corporate level items that may exist at the time a C Corporation converts to S Corporation status; specifically, unrealized gains in corporate assets, accumulated earnings, and net operating loss carryovers. Unrealized gains and accumulated earnings are addressed by highly technical provisions that require certain S Corporations that were formerly C Corporations to pay corporate level taxes even after converting to S Corporation status. Net operating loss carryovers from C Corporation years generally cannot be utilized after S Corporation status commences.

1. BUILT-IN GAINS

I.R.C. § 1374

Treas. Reg. §§ 1.1374–1, –2(a)–(c), –3, –4(a)–(b)

When a C Corporation sells assets with a value in excess of basis, the gain is recognized and taxed at the corporate level. The gain is also taxed to the C Corporation if it distributes the appreciated assets to its shareholders. See I.R.C. § 311(b)(1); pp. 29–33. A C Corporation that is eligible for S Corporation status need not sell its assets or transfer its assets to its shareholders to convert; it must merely make a tax election. Consequently, an opportunity to avoid the corporate level tax on asset appreciation appears to exist simply by converting to S Corporation status before selling or distributing the appreciated assets.

Congress could have eliminated the opportunity to avoid a corporate level tax on asset appreciation by creating a fictional realization event immediately preceding the effective date of an S election. Though simple, such a rule would make the S election extremely costly in many cases. Instead, Congress chose to impose a corporate level tax on appreciation existing in the assets of a C Corporation if that appreciation is recognized within ten years after S Corporation status becomes effective. I.R.C. § 1374.

The I.R.C. § 1374 tax is imposed on the "net recognized built-in gain" of an S Corporation at the highest corporate tax rate. I.R.C. § 1374(b)(1). To understand the meaning of "net recognized built-in gain," certain other statutory terms must first be examined. These terms will be explored in the context of the following fact pattern:

> Wheel Corp. operated as a C Corporation until its S election became effective on January 1 of Year 2. On that date, Wheel Corp. owned the following assets:

Asset	Adjusted Basis	Value
A	$ 300,000	$ 600,000
B	200,000	600,000
C	300,000	100,000
D	200,000	200,000
Total	$1,000,000	$1,500,000

Net Unrealized Built–In Gain ("NUBG")—NUBG is the *net* appreciation in the corporation's assets at the time the S election becomes effective. NUBG is calculated by subtracting the aggregate adjusted basis of the assets from the aggregate market value of the assets. I.R.C. § 1374(d)(1). Wheel Corp.'s NUBG is $500,000.

NUBG is a fixed amount that never changes. It represents the maximum amount that can be subject to a corporate level tax after the S election becomes effective. It is critical that the assets of the corporation be appraised as of the effective date of the S election so that this ceiling amount can be calculated.

Recognized Built–In Gain ("RBG")—RBG is that part of the NUBG that is recognized each year during the first ten years after the S election becomes effective. Any gain recognized within the ten year period is presumed to be attributable to NUBG, unless the taxpayer can prove to the contrary. See I.R.C. §§ 1374(d)(3), (7). Thus, it is critical that the asset appraisal as of the effective date of the S election identifies and values each asset owned by the corporation at that time.

> *Example 3–G (Import of asset-by-asset appraisal):* If Wheel Corp. sells Asset D for $300,000 in Year 3 (and the basis in D remains at $200,000), the $100,000 gain is treated as attributable to NUBG unless the taxpayer can prove that a lesser gain (or in this case, no gain at all) existed in that asset on the effective date of the S election. An appraisal that identifies the value and basis of each asset held by the corporation on the effective date of the S election should enable the taxpayer to demonstrate that none of the Asset D gain is attributable to NUBG.

Recognized Built–In Losses ("RBL")—RBL is any loss recognized with respect to any asset during the first ten years after the effective date of the S election to the extent that the loss was "built-in" (i.e., the basis of the asset exceeded its fair market value on the effective date of the S election). Any loss recognized within the ten year period is presumed *not* to be an RBL, unless the taxpayer can prove to the contrary. I.R.C. § 1374(d)(4). Thus, built-in losses can normally be demonstrated only if an asset appraisal identifies and values each asset owned by the corporation on the effective date of the S election.

Net Recognized Built–In Gain ("NRBG")—NRBG is the base on which the I.R.C. § 1374 tax is imposed. Generally, it represents the difference between RBG and RBL in a given year. I.R.C. § 1374(d)(2)(A)(i).[20] Aggregate NRBG, however, may never exceed the NUBG. I.R.C. § 1374(c)(2).

---

20. If RBL exceeds RBG in a given year, the excess has no tax effect. The excess RBL is *not* carried over to subsequent tax years.

Example 3–H (Computation of NRBG): Consider the following alternative scenarios:

(a) If, in Year 4, Wheel Corp. sells Asset A for $600,000 and Asset C for $100,000 (and the basis in each asset remains at $300,000), the NRBG for that year is only $100,000 ($300,000 RBG from Asset A less $200,000 RBL from Asset C).

(b) If Asset A is sold in Year 4 for $600,000 and Asset C is sold in Year 3 or Year 5 for $100,000 (and the basis in each asset remains at $300,000), the NRBG for Year 4 is $300,000 (the RBG from Asset A).

(c) If Asset A is sold in Year 4 for $600,000, Asset C is sold in Year 5 for $100,000 and Asset B is sold in Year 6 for $600,000 (and the basis in each asset remains the same as it was on January 1 of Year 2), the NRBG for Year 4 is $300,000, but the NRBG for Year 6 is only $200,000. Although the RBG in Year 6 is $400,000, the $500,000 NUBG caps the aggregate NRBG. Since the NRBG for Year 4 was $300,000, only $200,000 of the Year 6 RBG represents NRBG.

If, in a given year, the taxable income of an S Corporation is less than the difference between RBG and RBL, the § 1374 tax is imposed on the lesser amount and the excess is treated as RBG in the following year. I.R.C. § 1374(d)(2)(A)(ii).

Example 3–I (Taxable income ceiling on NRBG): If, in Year 4, Wheel Corp. sells Asset B for $600,000 and Asset D for $100,000 (and each asset's basis remains at $200,000) and no other items of gross income or deduction exist in Year 4, the $400,000 gain from Asset B less the $100,000 loss from Asset D results in $300,000 of taxable income (characterization permitting). The $100,000 loss from Asset D is *not* RBL because it was not built into Asset D when the S election became effective. I.R.C. § 1374(d)(4)(B). Thus, in Year 4, the difference between RBG and RBL ($400,000) exceeds taxable income ($300,000) so NRBG is only $300,000. The $100,000 excess, however, is treated as RBG in Year 5.

Problem 3–3 (Treatment of appreciated corporate assets before and after S election): Y Corp. was incorporated in Year 1 as a C Corporation. Y Corp. made an S election that became effective on January 1 of Year 3. At that time, Y Corp. owned some land with a value of $1,400,000 and an adjusted basis of $200,000. The aggregate value of all the other assets of Y Corp. was $1,200,000 and their aggregate adjusted basis was $700,000 on January 1 of Year 3.

(a) If Y Corp. had sold the land for $1,400,000 on December 31 of Year 2, what would have been the tax consequences to Y?

(b) If Y Corp. sells the land for $1,400,000 on January 1 of Year 3, what are the tax consequences to Y? How much of Y's gain is allocated to Y's shareholders? See I.R.C. § 1366(f)(2).

(c) If Y Corp. transfers the land to its shareholders on January 1 of Year 3, what are the tax consequences to Y? See I.R.C. § 311(b).

(d) If Y Corp. sells the land for $2,000,000 on January 1 of Year 4, what are the tax consequences to Y? How does this answer change if the value of the land on January 1 of Year 3 cannot be demonstrated?

(e) If Y Corp. sells the land for $1,400,000 on January 1 of Year 13, what are the tax consequences to Y?

Problem 3–4 (Impact of § 1374 on new corporation): Client forms a new corporation on December 30 of Year 1. On that date, the corporation owns land with a value of $1,001,000 and a basis of $1,000. The corporation uses the calendar year as its tax year and generates no income during the last two days of Year 1. Client suggests that the corporation become an S Corporation as of January 1 of Year 2. How should Client be advised? See I.R.C. § 1374(c)(1).

2.   ACCUMULATED C EARNINGS

I.R.C. § 1375

Treas. Reg. § 1.1375–1

The problem presented by earnings accumulated by a C Corporation that converts to S Corporation status is different from the problem presented by built-in gains. In contrast to built-in gains, accumulated earnings have already been subjected to the corporate tax. It is the shareholder level tax that has not yet been imposed on earnings that were accumulated during C Corporation years, because the earnings of a C Corporation are not taxed to the shareholders until the earnings are distributed to them.

Generally, the shareholder level tax on accumulated C Corporation earnings cannot be deferred indefinitely because corporate level penalty taxes apply to corporations that accumulate earnings in excess of business needs and to personal holding companies. See pp. 66–86. These penalty taxes do not apply to S Corporations. I.R.C. § 1363(a). Moreover, a C Corporation is not required to distribute its accumulated earnings before converting to S Corporation status. Consequently, in the absence of a special rule, the shareholder tax on accumulated C Corporation earnings could be deferred indefinitely by converting to S Corporation status.

Congress could have dealt with this problem by treating the S election as causing a fictional distribution of all accumulated C Corporation earnings immediately prior to the effective date of the S election. Though simple, such treatment would often make the S election extremely costly. Instead, Congress chose to impose a corporate tax on those S Corporations with accumulated C earnings that generate certain types of passive income (e.g., interest and dividends) in excess of a threshold amount. See I.R.C. § 1375.

I.R.C. § 1375 imposes a corporate tax on an S Corporation in any year in which *both* of the following conditions are satisfied:

1.   The corporation has accumulated C Corporation earnings at year-end.

2.   The corporation's "passive investment income" exceeds 25% of its gross receipts.

I.R.C. § 1375(a). Passive investment income ("PII") is defined as gross receipts from royalties, rents, dividends, interest and annuities. I.R.C. §§ 1375(b)(3), 1362(d)(3)(C).[21] Gross receipts ("GR") are not defined by statute but include virtually all revenue received, unreduced by the cost of goods sold or deductions.[22] In contrast, gross income represents the difference between the amount of revenue received and the cost of goods sold.[23] Thus, well over 25% of an S Corporation's gross income or taxable income may consist of PII without subjecting the corporation to the § 1375 tax.

> *Example 3–J (Exposure to § 1375 tax):* Zebra Co., an S Corporation that operated as a C Corporation before Year 3, has accumulated C Corporation earnings at the end of Year 3. Zebra Co. buys widgets from a wholesaler and sells them to retail customers. During Year 3, Zebra Co. derives $90,000 of revenue from the sale of widgets that cost $80,000, resulting in $10,000 of § 61(a)(2) income. In addition, Zebra Co. receives $10,000 of interest income in Year 3. Although PII (the interest income) represents 50% of Zebra Co.'s Year 3 gross income,[24] no § 1375 tax is imposed because PII represents only 10% of Zebra Co.'s gross receipts.[25]

In any tax year in which an S Corporation with accumulated C earnings has PII in excess of 25% of gross receipts, a tax is imposed under I.R.C. § 1375 at the highest corporate tax rate. This tax is imposed on the "excess net passive income" ("ENPI") of the corporation. I.R.C. § 1375(a). ENPI is computed by utilizing the following formula:

$$\text{ENPI} = \text{Net Passive Income} \times \frac{\text{PII} - (.25 \times \text{GR})}{\text{PII}}$$

See I.R.C. § 1375(b)(1); Treas. Reg. § 1.1375–1(b). Net passive income is PII reduced by deductions attributable to the production of such income. I.R.C. § 1375(b)(2).

> *Example 3–K (Computation of § 1375 tax):* Jetstar Co., an S Corporation that operated as a C Corporation before Year 5, has accumulated C Corporation earnings at the end of Year 5. During Year 5, Jetstar Co. derives $25,000 of revenue from the sale of doorknobs. In addition, Jetstar Co. receives $75,000 of dividend income in Year 5. Jetstar Co. incurs $15,000 of deductible expenses in connection with producing the dividend income.

---

21.   The regulations refine the meaning of these terms. Treas. Reg. § 1.1362–2(c)(5)(ii). For example, rents derived from the active trade or business of renting property are not treated as PII. Treas. Reg. § 1.1362–2(c)(5)(ii)(B)(2). See, e.g., IRS Letter Ruling 201118011 (ruling that rents derived by an S Corporation from real estate were not passive investment income because the S Corporation provided a variety of services to the tenants).

22.   Treas. Reg. § 1.1362–2(c)(4).

23.   Treas. Reg. § 1.61–3(a).

24. $10,000 PII ÷ ($10,000 § 61(a)(2) + $10,000 § 61(a)(4)) = 50%.

25. $10,000 PII ÷ ($90,000 Widget revenue + $10,000 interest) = 10%.

(a) Jetstar Co. is subject to the § 1375 tax in Year 5 because,

    (i) accumulated C earnings exist at the end of Year 5, and

    (ii) PII exceeds 25% of gross receipts.[26]

(b) Jetstar Co.'s ENPI is $40,000.

$$\text{ENPI} = \text{Net Passive Income} \times \frac{\text{PII} - (.25 \times \text{GR})}{\text{PII}}$$

$$\text{ENPI} = (\$75,000 - \$15,000) \times \frac{\$75,000 - \$25,000}{\$75,000}$$

$$\text{ENPI} = \$40,000.$$

(c) Jetstar Co.'s § 1375 tax liability is $14,000.

    § 1375 tax = ENPI × highest corporate rate

    § 1375 tax = $40,000 × 35% = $14,000.

If the taxable income of an S Corporation is less than ENPI, the § 1375 tax is imposed on the lesser amount. The excess amount has no tax effect (e.g., it is *not* treated as ENPI in the following year). I.R.C. § 1375(b).

> *Example 3–L (Taxable income ceiling):* If, in Example 3–K, Jetstar Co.'s Year 5 taxable income was only $10,000, Jetstar Co.'s ENPI would be limited to $10,000. In this event, the § 1375 tax liability would be $3,500.[27]

The threat of the § 1375 tax creates an incentive for a narrow class of S Corporations with accumulated C earnings to distribute those earnings to its shareholders. If the earnings are not distributed and a § 1375 tax is imposed, little, if any, tax savings will be derived from the S election in that year. Moreover, an S Corporation that is subjected to the § 1375 tax must distribute all of its accumulated C earnings (or reduce the percentage of PII that it generates) before being subjected to the tax in three consecutive years. Otherwise, the S election will terminate at the beginning of the fourth year. I.R.C. § 1362(d)(3).

> *Problem 3–5 (Tax liability under § 1375):* Special Co. was incorporated in Year 1 as a C Corporation. Special Co. operates a wholesale clothing business. On January 1 of Year 5, Special Co. became an S Corporation. At that time, it had $5,000,000 of accumulated C Corporation earnings. During Year 5, Special Co. derives $1,000,000 of revenue from the sale of clothing and incurs $900,000 of expenses with respect to those sales. In addition, Special Co. earns $400,000 of interest income and $200,000 of dividend income. Special Co. does not incur any deductible expenses in connection with producing the interest and dividend income.

---

26. $75,000 (PII) > 25% × $100,000 (gross receipts).

27. $10,000 × 35% = $3,500.

(a) What is the amount of Special Co.'s § 1375 tax liability for Year 5? How much of Special Co.'s Year 5 income is allocated to its shareholders? See I.R.C. § 1366(f)(3).

(b) If Special Co. distributed $4,999,999 of its accumulated C Corporation earnings on December 31 of Year 5, what is the amount of Special Co.'s § 1375 tax liability for Year 5? See I.R.C. § 1375(d).

(c) How would the answers to (a) and (b) change if, instead of earning $400,000 of taxable interest income and $200,000 of dividend income in Year 5, Special Co. earned $600,000 of tax-exempt interest (I.R.C. § 103(a))? See Treas. Reg. §§ 1.1362–2(c)(5)(i), (ii)(D)(1).

Problem 3–6 (Impact of § 1375 on new corporation): If the corporation formed by Client in Problem 3–4 (p. 138) did not have any appreciated assets, how should Client be advised?

NOTES

1. *Election to eliminate C earnings.* Mechanisms exist to cleanse an S Corporation of its accumulated C Corporation earnings. When these mechanisms are utilized, the shareholders must include all the accumulated C Corporation earnings in their gross income as dividends. See I.R.C. § 1368(e)(3); Treas. Reg. § 1.1368–1(f). These cleansing mechanisms will be examined in Chapter 6.

2. *Overlap question.* Can the § 1374 tax and the § 1375 tax ever apply to the same item of income? See I.R.C. § 1375(b)(4).

3. *Conversion to S status triggers corporate tax on LIFO reserve.* I.R.C. §§ 1374 and 1375 do not impose corporate level taxes until after S Corporation status becomes effective. In contrast, an additional corporate tax may be imposed immediately before S Corporation status becomes effective when a C Corporation that uses the "last-in, first-out" (LIFO) inventory method elects S Corporation status. See I.R.C. § 1363(d).

3.   NET OPERATING LOSS

I.R.C. § 1371(b)(1)

When a C Corporation incurs a net operating loss, the loss may only be applied against past or future income of the corporation. The shareholders cannot apply the C Corporation's loss against their personal income. See pp. 86–88. In contrast, when an S Corporation incurs an operating loss, that loss is allocated to the shareholders who may apply it against income they derive from other sources. See pp. 106–108. Can a C Corporation with insufficient income to absorb a net operating loss pass that loss to its shareholders by electing S Corporation status? See I.R.C. § 1371(b)(1).

Rosenberg v. Commissioner

United States Tax Court, 1991.
96 T.C. 451.

■ FEATHERSTON, JUDGE: Respondent determined a deficiency in petitioners' Federal income tax for 1984 in the amount of $151,238. The issue for decision is whether a net operating loss carryover generated by a subchapter C corporation in earlier years may offset income in a later year, at which time a subchapter S election is in effect for the same corporation * * *.

Prince David Inc. (hereinafter, the corporation) was incorporated in April 1979 and engaged in real estate development. The only business that the corporation conducted before the end of 1984 was the construction of a 15–unit condominium building, the sale of one of the units in 1981, the rental of some of the units, and the sale of * * * the remaining units in 1984.

The corporation reported its income as a subchapter C corporation, with a fiscal year ending November 30, until an election of subchapter S status became effective on December 1, 1982. Thereafter, at least through 1984, the corporation reported its income on a calendar year basis as an S corporation. At the time of the election, petitioners owned a total of 50 percent of the stock. During 1984, petitioners were the sole shareholders of the corporation.

As of November 30, 1982, the corporation had a net operating loss carryover of $353,773, accumulated over four taxable years:

Fiscal year ended	Amount
November 30, 1979	$6,738
November 30, 1980	66,938
November 30, 1981	110,696
November 30, 1982	169,401

The parties stipulated that "construction carrying charges" amounted to $303,513 of the total $353,773 carryover. Under subchapter S, the corporation had a loss of $5,645 for the remainder of 1982, a loss of $46,974 in 1983, and reported income of $46,268 in 1984.

In May 1981 the corporation sold one condominium unit. It rented other units until 1984, when it sold [them] * * *.

On its 1984 U.S. Income Tax Return for an S Corporation (Form 1120S), the corporation excluded $303,513 from gross sales, as follows:

Gross Sales:	
Rental	$22,782
Sale of condominiums	1,268,923
Subtotal	1,291,705
Excluded from income per Statement 2	303,513
	988,192

Statement 2 attached to the return explains:

Costs of $303,513 for interest, taxes and certain other costs for construction and carrying the condominium units sold in 1984 that were incurred and deducted in periods ending prior to December 1, 1982, but provided no tax benefit to the Corporation, have been excluded from the sales revenues under the tax benefit rule of Internal Revenue Code [section] 111 * * *.

Respondent contends that the statutory scheme for the taxation of the income of subchapter S corporations forbids the exclusion petitioners seek and that the tax benefit rule does not apply to the facts here presented.

We hold for respondent. Although petitioners cast their argument in terms of an exclusion from income, they are in fact seeking to carry forward to the S corporation's 1984 year a deduction of the net operating losses, to the extent of $303,513, incurred while the corporation was in subchapter C status. [S]ection 1371(b)(1) * * * states:

* * *

(b) NO CARRYOVER BETWEEN C YEAR AND S YEAR.—

(1) FROM C YEAR TO S YEAR.—No carryforward, and no carryback, arising for a taxable year for which a corporation is a C corporation may be carried to a taxable year for which such corporation is an S corporation * * *.

The language of section 1371(b)(1) could hardly be more clear. It expressly forbids the carryforward of a net operating loss incurred by a subchapter C corporation to a later year for which the corporation is in subchapter S status * * *.

Petitioners, however, invoke the longstanding equitable doctrine known as the tax benefit rule. Under that rule, partially codified in section 111, a taxpayer may exclude from income a "recovery during the taxable year of any amount deducted in any prior taxable year to the extent such amount did not reduce the amount of tax imposed by this chapter," i.e., under the income tax provisions. This is known as the exclusionary aspect of the tax benefit rule. The corollary, emphasizing the inclusionary aspect, is that when an item previously deducted by the taxpayer is restored, it must be included in income to the extent that the earlier loss (deduction) generated a tax benefit * * *. Notwithstanding section 1371(b)(1), petitioners claim the right to invoke the tax benefit rule * * *.

[P]etitioners' corporation does not qualify for a coveted exclusion under the tax benefit rule for [various] reasons. First, petitioners have not shown that the taxes and interest portion of the net operating losses incurred when the corporation was a C corporation did not produce a tax benefit. The net operating loss carryovers would have been available as deductions in future years if petitioners had decided to rent the condominium units indefinitely through the C corporation. * * *

Recognizing that net operating loss carryovers have valuable attributes, section 111(c) provides the following principle which is to be observed in the application of the tax benefit rule:

(c) TREATMENT OF CARRYOVERS.—For purposes of this section, an increase in a carryover which has not expired before the beginning of the taxable year in which the recovery or adjustment takes place shall be treated as reducing tax imposed by this chapter.

In other words, a net operating loss addition is to be treated as a tax benefit. Because the corporation here received such a benefit from each increase in its net operating losses for its fiscal years ending in 1979 through 1982, the foundation for the application of the tax benefit rule does not exist.

Second, the sale of the condominium units in 1984 did not effectuate, within the meaning of section 111(a), a recovery of the interest and taxes paid by the corporation when it was in subchapter C status * * *. In Hillsboro National Bank v. Commissioner and United States v. Bliss Dairy, Inc., 460 U.S. 370, 383 (1983), the Supreme Court explained the controlling principle:

The basic purpose of the tax benefit rule is to achieve rough transactional parity in tax * * * and to protect the Government and the taxpayer from the adverse effects of reporting a transaction on the basis of assumptions that an event in a subsequent year proves to have been erroneous. Such an event, unforeseen at the time of an earlier deduction, may in many cases require the application of the tax benefit rule. * * * [T]he tax benefit rule will "cancel out" an earlier deduction only when a careful examination shows that the later event is indeed fundamentally inconsistent with the premise on which the deduction was initially based. * * *

Petitioners seek to distance themselves from this "fundamentally inconsistent" standard, formulated by the Supreme Court in the context of the inclusionary part of the tax benefit rule, by arguing that the standard does not apply to the exclusionary part. However, the Court of Appeals for the Ninth Circuit, to which this case is appealable, recently stated that the exclusionary part of the tax benefit rule is "limited to cases in which a later event turns out to be fundamentally inconsistent with the premise on which the deduction was initially based." * * *

In this case, there is nothing "fundamentally inconsistent" about the corporation's deductions of taxes and interest followed by the inclusion of the proceeds of the condominium sales in its gross sales for the years in which the sales are made. Indeed, the record clearly establishes that those sales were contemplated, and strived for, from the beginning of the corporate existence * * *.

NOTES

1. *Opposite result.* What would have been the tax consequences if the taxpayer had prevailed in the Rosenberg case?

2. *Impact of I.R.C. § 263A*. Under current law, Prince David probably would have been required to add the interest and taxes to its basis in the condominiums, rather than deducting those expenses. See I.R.C. § 263A. If § 263A had applied to Prince David, would the petitioners have been in a better position or a worse position? Why?

3. *Impact of I.R.C. § 1374*. The Rosenberg case focuses on the tax liability of the individual shareholders. Did a potential corporate tax liability exist when the condos were sold? See I.R.C. § 1374. What impact, if any, would the corporation's net operating loss carryover have had on that potential liability? See I.R.C. § 1374(b)(2). Is this result sensible?

4. *Impact of conversion on inclusionary aspect of tax benefit rule*. If deductions accrued by Prince David while a C Corporation had sheltered gross income and not created a net operating loss, what consequences would follow if, after becoming an S Corporation, Prince David was released from its obligation to pay the accrued items? See Frederick v. Commissioner, 101 T.C. 35 (1993) (holding that the shareholders of an S Corporation must include an item of accrued interest recovered by the corporation in income because that item had been deducted by the corporation in a prior year when it was a C Corporation).

*

CHAPTER 4

PARTNERSHIP OPERATIONS

Every state law corporation is taxed either as a C Corporation or as an S Corporation. In contrast, state law partnerships and limited liability companies are usually taxed as partnerships, but may elect to be taxed as C Corporations. See I.R.C. § 761(a); Treas. Reg. § 301.7701–3.[1] A business taxed as a partnership is governed by the rules of Subchapter K (I.R.C. §§ 701–777). Chapter 4 focuses first on the consequences of partnership tax treatment and then explores the range of enterprises that qualifies for partnership tax treatment.

The hallmark of partnership tax treatment is flexibility. Like an S Corporation, an enterprise taxed as a partnership is treated as a mere accounting entity by the tax law. The business itself does not pay tax. Rather, income and deductions are allocated among the partners and reported on their personal tax returns. In contrast to Subchapter S, Subchapter K does not constrain the economic relations that may be established among the owners of an enterprise. Instead, the partnership tax regime is designed to accommodate almost any business arrangement by causing tax consequences to follow from the economic relationship established by the owners of the enterprise.

A. COMPUTATION OF GROSS INCOME AND DEDUCTIONS

I.R.C. §§ 701, 703, 721(a), 731(b), 761(a)

Treas. Reg. §§ 1.701–1, 1.703–1, 301.7701–3

An enterprise that satisfies the Internal Revenue Code's definition of a partnership does not pay tax. I.R.C. §§ 701, 761(a). Like an S Corporation, a partnership is treated as an accounting entity for purposes of computing its gross income and deductions and files an annual information return (Form 1065—see Exhibit V, p. 148) reporting these items to the Internal Revenue Service. I.R.C. § 6031(a). The Form 1065 includes a separate schedule for each partner (Schedule K–1—see Exhibit VI, p. 149) where the partnership reports the amount of each item of partnership income and deduction that is allocated to that partner. The partnership must provide each partner with a copy of her Schedule K–1. I.R.C. § 6031(b). The items reflected on the partner's Schedule K–1 must be included on her personal tax return.

---

1. Publicly traded partnerships and publicly traded limited liability companies are automatically taxed as C Corporations. See I.R.C. § 7704.

EXHIBIT V

Form **1065**	U.S. Return of Partnership Income	OMB No. 1545-0099
Department of the Treasury Internal Revenue Service	For calendar year 2010, or tax year beginning _____ , 2010, ending _____ , 20 _____ ▶ See separate instructions.	2010

A Principal business activity		Name of partnership	D Employer identification number
B Principal product or service	Print or type.	Number, street, and room or suite no. If a P.O. box, see the instructions.	E Date business started
C Business code number		City or town, state, and ZIP code	F Total assets (see the instructions) $

G Check applicable boxes: (1) ☐ Initial return (2) ☐ Final return (3) ☐ Name change (4) ☐ Address change (5) ☐ Amended return
(6) ☐ Technical termination - also check (1) or (2)

H Check accounting method: (1) ☐ Cash (2) ☐ Accrual (3) ☐ Other (specify) ▶ _____

I Number of Schedules K-1. Attach one for each person who was a partner at any time during the tax year ▶ _____

J Check if Schedules C and M-3 are attached . . . . ☐

Caution. *Include only trade or business income and expenses on lines 1a through 22 below. See the instructions for more information.*

Income	1a	Gross receipts or sales	1a		
	b	Less returns and allowances	1b		1c
	2	Cost of goods sold (Schedule A, line 8)			2
	3	Gross profit. Subtract line 2 from line 1c			3
	4	Ordinary income (loss) from other partnerships, estates, and trusts *(attach statement)* . .			4
	5	Net farm profit (loss) *(attach Schedule F (Form 1040))*			5
	6	Net gain (loss) from Form 4797, Part II, line 17 *(attach Form 4797)*			6
	7	Other income (loss) *(attach statement)*			7
	8	**Total income (loss).** Combine lines 3 through 7			8
Deductions (see the instructions for limitations)	9	Salaries and wages (other than to partners) (less employment credits)			9
	10	Guaranteed payments to partners			10
	11	Repairs and maintenance			11
	12	Bad debts			12
	13	Rent			13
	14	Taxes and licenses			14
	15	Interest			15
	16a	Depreciation *(if required, attach Form 4562)*	16a		
	b	Less depreciation reported on Schedule A and elsewhere on return	16b		16c
	17	Depletion (**Do not deduct oil and gas depletion.**)			17
	18	Retirement plans, etc.			18
	19	Employee benefit programs			19
	20	Other deductions *(attach statement)*			20
	21	**Total deductions.** Add the amounts shown in the far right column for lines 9 through 20 .			21
	22	**Ordinary business income (loss).** Subtract line 21 from line 8			22

Sign Here

Under penalties of perjury, I declare that I have examined this return, including accompanying schedules and statements, and to the best of my knowledge and belief, it is true, correct, and complete. Declaration of preparer (other than general partner or limited liability company manager) is based on all information of which preparer has any knowledge.

May the IRS discuss this return with the preparer shown below (see instructions)? ☐ Yes ☐ No

▶ _____ Signature of general partner or limited liability company member manager
▶ _____ Date

Paid Preparer Use Only	Print/Type preparer's name	Preparer's signature	Date	Check ☐ if self- employed	PTIN
	Firm's name ▶			Firm's EIN ▶	
	Firm's address ▶			Phone no.	

For Paperwork Reduction Act Notice, see separate instructions.   Cat. No. 11390Z   Form **1065** (2010)

EXHIBIT VI

651110

Schedule K-1 (Form 1065)	2010	Part III Partner's Share of Current Year Income, Deductions, Credits, and Other Items

☐ Final K-1   ☐ Amended K-1   OMB No. 1545-0099

Schedule K-1 (Form 1065)

2010

Department of the Treasury
Internal Revenue Service

For calendar year 2010, or tax
year beginning _____, 2010
ending _____, 20 ____

Partner's Share of Income, Deductions, Credits, etc. ▶ See back of form and separate instructions.

Part I   Information About the Partnership

A   Partnership's employer identification number

B   Partnership's name, address, city, state, and ZIP code

C   IRS Center where partnership filed return

D   ☐ Check if this is a publicly traded partnership (PTP)

Part II   Information About the Partner

E   Partner's identifying number

F   Partner's name, address, city, state, and ZIP code

G   ☐ General partner or LLC member-manager   ☐ Limited partner or other LLC member

H   ☐ Domestic partner   ☐ Foreign partner

I   What type of entity is this partner? _____

J   Partner's share of profit, loss, and capital (see instructions):

	Beginning	Ending
Profit	%	%
Loss	%	%
Capital	%	%

K   Partner's share of liabilities at year end:

Nonrecourse . . . . . . $ _____
Qualified nonrecourse financing $ _____
Recourse . . . . $ _____

L   Partner's capital account analysis:

Beginning capital account . . . $ _____
Capital contributed during the year $ _____
Current year increase (decrease) . $ _____
Withdrawals & distributions . . $ (_____)
Ending capital account . . . . $ _____

☐ Tax basis   ☐ GAAP   ☐ Section 704(b) book
☐ Other (explain)

M   Did the partner contribute property with a built-in gain or loss?
☐ Yes   ☐ No
If "Yes", attach statement (see instructions)

Part III Partner's Share of Current Year Income, Deductions, Credits, and Other Items

1 Ordinary business income (loss)	15 Credits
2 Net rental real estate income (loss)	
3 Other net rental income (loss)	16 Foreign transactions
4 Guaranteed payments	
5 Interest income	
6a Ordinary dividends	
6b Qualified dividends	
7 Royalties	
8 Net short-term capital gain (loss)	
9a Net long-term capital gain (loss)	17 Alternative minimum tax (AMT) items
9b Collectibles (28%) gain (loss)	
9c Unrecaptured section 1250 gain	
10 Net section 1231 gain (loss)	18 Tax-exempt income and nondeductible expenses
11 Other income (loss)	
12 Section 179 deduction	19 Distributions
13 Other deductions	
	20 Other information
14 Self-employment earnings (loss)	

*See attached statement for additional information.

For IRS Use Only

For Paperwork Reduction Act Notice, see Instructions for Form 1065.   Cat. No. 11394R   Schedule K-1 (Form 1065) 2010

As a general rule, the gross income and deductions of a partnership are computed by utilizing the same rules that apply to an individual. I.R.C. § 703(a). A partnership, however, is denied a variety of deductions that are allowed to individuals, including the deduction for personal exemptions, the deduction for charitable contributions and the itemized deductions allowed under I.R.C. §§ 212–223. I.R.C. § 703(a)(2). Why are these deductions denied to a partnership?

> *Problem 4–1 (Partnership gross income)*: How do each of the following transactions impact on the gross income of the AB Partnership?
>
> (a) Al and Bonnie form the AB Partnership. Al and Bonnie each transfer $1,000 to AB in exchange for a 50% interest in the partnership.[2] See I.R.C. § 721(a). Compare I.R.C. § 1032.
>
> (b) Al and Bonnie each contribute an additional $1,000 to AB and each retains a 50% interest in the partnership. See I.R.C. § 721(a). Compare I.R.C. § 118.
>
> (c) AB sells a parcel of land used in its business for $1,001,000. AB's basis in the land is $1,000. See I.R.C. §§ 61(a)(3), 1231.
>
> (d) Rather than selling the parcel of land described in (c), AB distributes the parcel of land to Al and Bonnie. See I.R.C. § 731(b). Compare I.R.C. § 311(b).

B. ALLOCATION TO PARTNERS

1. PARTNERS TAXED WHEN INCOME EARNED

I.R.C. §§ 702, 705, 706(a), (b)

Treas. Reg. § 1.702–1

After the income of a partnership is computed, it must be allocated among the partners and included on their individual tax returns. I.R.C. § 702. **The income of a partnership is taxed to the partners at the time it is earned, regardless of whether the partnership distributes its earnings to the partners.** Generally, the partners are not taxed again when the partnership actually distributes its earnings to them.[3]

Burke v. Commissioner

United States Court of Appeals, First Circuit, 2007
485 F.3d 171.

■ TORRUELLA, CIRCUIT JUDGE: * * *

I. Background

On October 13, 1993, Timothy Burke formed a partnership with Jeffrey Cohen named "Cohen & Burke," agreeing to split the proceeds of the enterprise evenly * * *. In 1998, a dispute arose between the two partners * * * . when Cohen allegedly * * * stole money received by the

---

2. A partnership interest is difficult to conceptualize. At this point, it is best to think of a partnership interest as analogous to corporate stock (i.e., as an investment asset that has a basis and is independent from the assets of the partnership).

3. The tax consequences of partnership distributions are explored in Chapter 7.

partnership. As a result of the dispute, Burke filed suit against Cohen in Massachusetts state court on October 4, 1999 * * *. Cohen and Burke agreed to keep the partnership receipts in an escrow account pending the outcome of the litigation.

Meanwhile, Cohen filed the partnership tax return for 1998 reporting $242,000 in ordinary income, with $121,000 as each partner's * * * share. Burke reported zero as his * * * share of partnership income and filed a notice of inconsistent determination stating that Cohen's partnership tax filing was * * * inaccurate.

The Commissioner of Internal Revenue issued Burke a notice of deficiency alleging that Burke had improperly failed to report his * * * share of partnership income on his individual return. Burke timely petitioned the tax court for redetermination of the deficiency, claiming that his [share] of partnership income from 1998 should not have been taxed that year because the money was being held in escrow and he therefore did not have access to it. The IRS filed a motion for summary judgment arguing that, as a matter of law, a partner's [share] of partnership income was taxable in the year the partnership received the income, regardless of whether the partner actually received [a] distribution. * * * The tax court granted summary judgment in favor of the IRS, holding that Burke was required to include his * * * share of partnership income for the 1998 taxable year even though he had not yet received [it].

II. Discussion

    * * *

Burke argues that his [share] of partnership income for 1998 should not have been taxed that year because that income was (and remains) "frozen" in an escrow account, such that neither he, nor his partner, has access to the income. In support of his argument, Burke cites several cases (none of which deal with partnership or partner taxation) that hold that an individual taxpayer must only include income to which he has a claim of right. * * * Citing § 703's language that "[t]he taxable income of a partnership shall be computed in the same manner as in the case of an individual," Burke contends that under these cases, the partnership did not earn taxable income in 1998 because "the restriction of funds ... defers the recognition of income at the partnership level, as it does for individuals, until the restriction is removed."

But § 703 does not help Burke. A self-imposed restriction on the availability of income cannot legally defer recognition of that income. The partnership received the money free and clear in 1998. It was the individual partners, Burke and Cohen, who chose to place the funds in escrow—not the partnership's clients or other persons owing the partnership money. Thus, Burke's contentions have only to do with the individual partners' access to the funds after they were placed in escrow and not the partnership's access to them.

It is well settled that [each partner is taxed on his or her share of a partnership's earnings] in the year the partnership receives its earnings, regardless of whether [those earnings are distributed to the partners]: "Few principles of partnership taxation are more firmly established than that, no matter the reason for nondistribution, each partner must pay taxes on his distributive share." United States v. Basye, 410 U.S. 441, 454 (1973); see also 26 C.F.R. § 1.702–1 (providing that a partner must separately account for his distributive share of partnership income "whether or not distributed"). Consistent with this long-standing principle, courts have uniformly held that partners must currently recognize in their individual incomes their proportionate shares of partnership income, even if the partnership income was not actually distributed to them for any reason, including disputes, consensual arrangements, ignorance, concealment, or force of law. Thus, Burke was required to report his distributive share of the partnership's income in 1998, even if he had not yet received it.

NOTES

1. *Segregation of certain items.* The income (or loss) of a partnership is not generally reported to the partners as a single net amount. Instead, each item of gross income and deduction that, due to its nature, could affect the determination of an individual partner's tax liability is segregated. I.R.C. §§ 702(a)(1)–(7); Treas. Reg. § 1.702–1(a)(8)(ii). The unique nature of these segregated items flows through to each partner's personal tax return. I.R.C. § 702(b). All other items of partnership income and deduction are simply reported as a single net amount. I.R.C. § 702(a)(8).

> *Example 4–A (Segregating items from net income or loss)*: Chuck and Damon form the CD Partnership and agree that all income and deductions of the partnership will be allocated 50% to Chuck and 50% to Damon. In Year 1, CD earns $50,000 of business income, incurs $10,000 of business expenses, receives $5,000 of tax-exempt interest (I.R.C. § 103(a)) and recognizes $20,000 of long-term capital gain. For reporting purposes, CD's tax-exempt interest and capital gain are segregated from its other income and deductions, which are netted to $40,000. Chuck and Damon each reports half ($20,000) of CD's net income and half ($10,000) of CD's long-term capital gain on his Year 1 personal tax return and each excludes half ($2,500) of CD's tax-exempt interest. If Chuck or Damon has a capital loss from other activities, that capital loss can offset his share of CD's capital gain. I.R.C. § 1211(b).

2. *Adjustments to basis in partnership interest.* Each partner is awarded an increase in the basis of his partnership interest to reflect any partnership income allocated to him that he has not yet received. I.R.C. § 705(a)(1). Basis is increased to reflect both net partnership income and all segregated items of partnership income, including tax-exempt items. I.R.C. §§ 705(a)(1)(A), (B). Moreover, basis is reduced by both deductible expenses and nondeductible expenses (e.g., a fine or penalty, see I.R.C.

§ 162(f)). I.R.C. § 705(a)(2). How do the items described in Example 4–A affect the basis of each partner in his partnership interest?

3. *Partnership tax year*. The adoption of a partnership tax year other than the calendar year historically created an opportunity for the partners to defer income. See I.R.C. § 706(a). For example, if a partnership's tax year ends on January 31 of Year 3, partnership income from February 1 of Year 2 through January 31 of Year 3 is reported on the Year 3 tax returns of the partners. Thus, the tax on eleven months of Year 2 partnership income is deferred until Year 3. Under current law, however, few partnerships may use a tax year other than the calendar year. See I.R.C. § 706(b).

4. *Simplified flow-through for electing large partnerships*. Certain partnerships with at least 100 partners can elect to reduce significantly the number of partnership items that must be segregated and allocated separately to the partners. See I.R.C. §§ 771–777.

2.   FLEXIBLE ALLOCATION RULE

I.R.C. § 704

A flexible rule controls the allocation of partnership income (or loss) among the partners. Each partner is required to include her "distributive share" of the partnership's income (or loss) on her individual tax return. I.R.C. § 702(a). In contrast to the rigid statutory rule that governs the allocation of S Corporation income (or loss) among shareholders,[4] partners may allocate partnership income (or loss) among themselves by agreement. I.R.C. § 704(a). Moreover, the partners may allocate specific items of partnership gross income and deduction differently from other items. An agreed upon allocation will be respected, however, only if the allocation has "substantial economic effect". I.R.C. § 704(b)(2).

> *Example 4–B (Special allocations)*: Ernie and Fran form the EF Partnership. The parties contribute equal amounts of money to the partnership and, as a general matter, view themselves as equal partners. Consequently, they agree to allocate most items of partnership income and deduction 50% to Ernie and 50% to Fran. They agree to "special" allocations of the following items:

	Ernie	Fran
Rental Income from Property A	80%	20%
Salary Paid to Employee B	40%	60%
Depreciation Deduction on Property C	30%	70%

> In Year 1, EF's gross income consists of $300,000 of rental income, including $100,000 from Property A. EF's deductions consist of $200,000 of business expenses, including $10,000 of salary paid to Employee B and $10,000 of depreciation allowed on Property C. If each of the allocations agreed to by the partners has "substantial economic effect," EF's Year 1 income is allocated as follows:

---

4.   See I.R.C. §§ 1366(a), 1377(a); pp. 102–106.

	Ernie	Fran
Rent from Property A	$ 80,000	$ 20,000
Salary Paid to Employee B	(4,000)	(6,000)
Depreciation on Property C	(3,000)	(7,000)
Other Ordinary Items (Net) [5]	10,000	10,000
Distributive Share of Partnership Income	$ 83,000	$ 17,000

The substantial economic effect standard is intended to ensure that items of partnership gross income and deduction are allocated among the partners for tax purposes in a manner that accurately reflects the actual economic arrangement of the partners. In contrast to the rigid allocation rules that govern S Corporations,[6] the partnership tax regime does not restrain the economic relationship that partners may establish among themselves. The economic relationship established by the partners, however, effectively controls the allocation of partnership gross income and deductions among the partners for tax purposes.

The Treasury Department has promulgated voluminous regulations interpreting the substantial economic effect standard. These regulations divide the standard into two discrete elements, economic effect and substantiality. Both elements must be satisfied before an allocation will be respected by the tax law.[7]

a. INTRODUCTION TO ECONOMIC EFFECT

The rules for achieving economic effect for an allocation of partnership income or deduction are most easily understood by thinking in relatively simplistic terms about the most fundamental economic decisions that partners make. When Ernie and Fran form the EF Partnership in Example 4–B (p. 153), they must decide how to share any economic profits resulting from their collective activity. Since they contribute equal amounts of money and view themselves as equal partners, it is likely that they would agree to share the economic profits of their venture equally. It is also likely that they would expect to report equal amounts of each item of partnership gross income and deduction on their personal tax returns.

5.

Total Year 1 Gross Income	$300,000	
Specially Allocated Rental Income	(100,000)	
Gross Income Subject to General Allocation		$200,000
Total Year 1 Deductions	200,000	
Specially Allocated Salary and Depreciation	(20,000)	
Deductions Subject to General Allocation		180,000
Other Ordinary Items (Net)		$ 20,000

6.   I.R.C. §§ 1361(b)(1)(D), 1366(a).

7.   See Treas. Reg. § 1.704–1(b)(2)(i).

Of course, Ernie and Fran could agree to share economic profits or some specific partnership receipt unequally. For example, they might agree that Ernie should receive 80% of the rents derived from a particular piece of partnership property (e.g., Property A in Example 4–B). In this event, it is also likely that the partners would agree that 80% of the rental income from Property A should be reported on Ernie's tax return and only 20% should be reported on Fran's tax return. An 80/20 allocation of rental income for tax purposes deviates from the general 50/50 allocation of all other items of partnership gross income and deduction. Nevertheless, the special allocation of rental income has "economic effect" because the tax allocation is consistent with the economic arrangement between the partners (i.e., the way that Ernie and Fran agreed to share the revenue received from Property A).

In contrast, if Ernie and Fran had agreed to share the revenue from Property A in the same manner as they agreed to share all other partnership revenue (50/50), an 80/20 allocation of the Property A rental income for tax purposes would not have economic effect. If an agreed to allocation does not have economic effect, the item of income or deduction is allocated in accordance with each partner's "interest" in the partnership. I.R.C. § 704(b). Had Ernie and Fran agreed to a 50/50 division of the revenue from Property A, they would be compelled to report the rental income from Property A on their personal tax returns in accordance with each partner's overall interest in the partnership (probably 50/50).

When a tax allocation lacks economic effect, the amounts reported on the partners' tax returns are modified to conform with the economic arrangement. I.R.C. § 704(b) does *not* modify the partners' economic arrangement to conform with the tax allocation. In other words, if the partners agree that each partner should receive $50,000 of the actual rents derived from Property A but Ernie reports $80,000 of rental income and Fran reports $20,000, the tax law causes each partner instead to report $50,000 of rental income. The tax law does not mandate (nor could it mandate) that Ernie receive $80,000 of the actual rents derived from Property A.

In addition to deciding how to share economic profits, Ernie and Fran must decide how to share the burden of any economic losses. In other words, if the partnership loses money (expenses exceed revenues), will Ernie's dollars or Fran's dollars be lost? Since Ernie and Fran contributed equal amounts of money and view themselves as equal partners, they would likely agree to bear the burden of economic losses equally. It is possible, however, that Ernie and Fran might agree to share economic losses or some specific partnership expense unequally. For example, they might agree that Fran should bear the cost of 60% of the salary paid to a particular partnership employee (e.g., Employee B in Example 4–B). In this event, a tax allocation of 60% of the partnership deduction for Employee B's salary to Fran has "economic effect" because it is consistent with how Ernie and Fran agreed to share the economic burden of the disbursement made to Employee B.

If Ernie and Fran agreed to bear the burden of B's salary in the same manner as they agreed to share all other partnership expenses (50/50), a 40/60 allocation of the deduction would not have economic effect. In this situation, Ernie and Fran would be required to report the deduction in accordance with each partner's overall interest in the partnership (probably 50/50). Here again, I.R.C. § 704(b) does *not* modify the economic arrangement between the partners to conform with the tax allocation. In other words, if the partners agree that each should bear $5,000 of B's salary but Ernie deducts $4,000 and Fran deducts $6,000, the statute compels each partner instead to deduct $5,000. The statute does not mandate (nor could it mandate) that Fran bear $6,000 of the salary actually paid to B.

Matters become more complicated when a partnership is allowed a tax deduction before it incurs a corresponding economic cost. For example, the EF Partnership in Example 4–B is allowed a $10,000 depreciation deduction with respect to Property C in Year 1 even if the value of Property C does not decline. The deduction must be allocated among the partners in Year 1 even if no partner suffers a corresponding economic burden at that time. How is economic effect established with respect to the allocation of a partnership deduction that does not impose an immediate economic burden on the partners?

Orrisch v. Commissioner

United States Tax Court, 1970.
55 T.C. 395.

■ Featherston, Judge: * * *.

FINDINGS OF FACT

[Petitioners] Stanley C. Orrisch (hereinafter sometimes referred to as Orrisch) and Gerta E. Orrisch were husband and wife until a judgment of divorce was entered * * * on May 22, 1969. * * *

In May of 1963, Domonick J. and Elaine J. Crisafi (hereinafter the Crisafis) and petitioners formed a partnership to purchase and operate two apartment houses * * *. The cost of [one] property was $229,011.08, and of the [other] was $155,974.90. The purchase of each property was financed principally by a secured loan. Petitioners and the Crisafis initially contributed to the partnership cash in the amounts of $26,500 and $12,500, respectively. During 1964 and 1965 petitioners and the Crisafis each contributed additional cash in the amounts of $8,800. Under the partnership agreement, which was not in writing, they agreed to share equally the profits and losses from the venture.

During each of the years 1963, 1964, and 1965, the partnership suffered losses, attributable in part to * * * depreciation * * *. The amounts of the depreciation deductions, the reported loss for each of the 3 years as reflected in the partnership returns, and the amounts of each partner's share of the losses are as follows:

			Each partner's share of the losses—50 per-cent of the total loss
Year	Depreciation deducted	Total loss	
1963	$ 9,886.20	$ 9,716.14	$4,858.07
1964	21,051.95	17,812.33	8,906.17
1965	19,894.24	18,952.59	9,476.30

Petitioners and the Crisafis respectively reported in their individual income tax returns for these years the partnership losses allocated to them.

Petitioners enjoyed substantial amounts of income from several sources * * *. In their joint income tax returns for 1963, 1964, and 1965, petitioners reported taxable income in the respective amounts of $10,462.70, $5,898.85, and $50,332 * * *.

The Crisafis were also engaged in other business endeavors * * *. They owned other real property, however, from which they realized losses, attributable largely to substantial depreciation deductions. In their joint income tax returns for 1963, 1964, and 1965, they reported no net taxable income.

Early in 1966, petitioners and the Crisafis orally agreed that, for 1966 and subsequent years, the entire amount of the partnership's depreciation deductions would be specially allocated to petitioners, and that the gain or loss from the partnership's business, computed without regard to any deduction for depreciation, would be divided equally. They further agreed that, in the event the partnership property was sold at a gain, the specially allocated depreciation would be "charged back" to petitioner's capital account and petitioners would pay the tax on the gain attributable thereto.

The operating results of the partnership for 1966 and 1967 as reflected in the partnership returns were as follows:

Year	Depreciation deducted	Loss (including depreciation)	Gain (or loss) without regard to depreciation
1966	$18,412.00	$19,396.00	($984.00)
1967	17,180.75	16,560.78	619.97

The partnership returns for these years show that, taking into account the special arrangement as to depreciation, losses in the amounts of $18,904 and $16,870.76 were allocated to petitioners for 1966 and 1967, respectively, and petitioners claimed these amounts as deductions in their joint income tax returns for those years. * * *

The net capital contributions, allocations of profits, losses and depreciation, and ending balances of the capital accounts, of the Orrisch–Crisafi partnership from May 1963 through December 31, 1967, were as follows:

	Petitioners'	Crisafis'
Excess of capital contributions over withdrawals during 1963	$26,655.55	$12,655.54
Allocation of 1963 loss	(4,858.07)	(4,858.07)
Balance 12/31/63	21,797.48	7,797.47
Excess of capital contributions over withdrawals during 1964	4,537.50	3,537.50
Allocation of 1964 loss	(8,906.17)	(8,906.16)
Balance 12/31/64	17,428.81	2,428.81
Excess of capital contributions over withdrawals during 1965	4,337.50	5,337.50
Allocation of 1965 loss	(9,476.30)	(9,476.29)
Balance 12/31/65	12,290.01	(1,709.98)
Excess of capital contributions over withdrawals during 1966	2,610.00	6,018.00
Allocation of 1966 loss before depreciation	(492.00)	(492.00)
Allocation of depreciation	(18,412.00)	0
Balance 12/31/66	(4,003.99)	3,816.02
Excess of withdrawals over capital contributions during 1967	(4,312.36)	(3,720.35)
Allocation of 1967 profit before depreciation	309.99	309.98
Allocation of depreciation	(17,180.75)	0
Balance 12/31/67	(25,187.11)	405.65

In May of 1968, before petitioners Stanley C. Orrisch and Greta E. Orrisch were divorced, they entered into a marital property settlement agreement which, as part of paragraph 8, contained the following:

(c) The parties recognize that each of said parcels of real property is encumbered by loans and requires certain maintenance, upkeep and repair and certain other expenses for the operation thereof. The parties further understand that at the present time neither of said parcels of real property produces sufficient cash flow to meet loan payments and the other expenses above referred to. For this reason, husband agrees that from the date of this agreement forward * * *, he * * * shall be responsible for providing * * * any money required to meet said loan payments or expenses. * * * Upon the sale or disposition of either or both of said parcels of real property, the parties hereto will equally divide the profits or proceeds of such sale or disposition, provided that from such profits or proceeds husband shall be first reimbursed for such moneys as he may have advanced for the parties' joint benefit * * *.

(d) In consideration of the foregoing, wife agrees that she will not deduct on her Federal and State income tax returns any depreciation allowable by reason of the ownership of the said 2 parcels of real property. * * * Upon the sale or other disposition of either or both of said parcels of real property, each party hereto shall be responsible for reporting on his or her respective income tax returns one-half of the capital gain or loss, if any, realized from such sale or disposition. * * *

In the notice of deficiency, respondent determined that the special allocation of the depreciation deduction provided by the amendment to the partnership agreement "was made with the principal purpose of avoidance of income taxes" and should, therefore, be disregarded. Partnership losses for 1966 and 1967 * * * were allocated equally between the partners. * * *

OPINION

The only issue presented for decision is whether tax effect can be given the agreement between petitioners and the Crisafis that, beginning with 1966, all the partnership's depreciation deductions were to be allocated to petitioners for their use in computing their individual income tax liabilities. In our view, the answer must be in the negative, and the amounts of each of the partners' deductions for the depreciation of partnership property must be determined in accordance with the ratio used generally in computing their distributive shares of the partnership's profits and losses.

Among the important innovations of the 1954 Code are limited provisions for flexibility in arrangements for the sharing of income, losses, and deductions arising from business activities conducted through partnerships. The authority for special allocations of such items appears in section 704(a), which provides that a partner's share of any item of income, gain, loss, deduction, or credit shall be determined by the partnership agreement. That rule is coupled with a limitation in section 704(b), however, which states that a special allocation of an item will be disregarded if its "principal purpose" is the avoidance or evasion of Federal income tax. In case a special allocation is disregarded, the partner's share of the item is to be determined in accordance with the ratio by which the partners divide the general profits or losses of the partnership.

The report of the Senate Committee on Finance accompanying the bill finally enacted as the 1954 Code explained the tax-avoidance restriction prescribed by section 704(b) as follows:

> Subsection (b) * * * provides that if the principal purpose of any provision in the partnership agreement dealing with a partner's distributive share of a particular item is to avoid or evade the Federal income tax, the partner's distributive share of that item shall be redetermined in accordance with * * * the ratio used by the partners for dividing general profits or losses. * * *

> Where, however, a provision in a partnership agreement for a special allocation of certain items has substantial economic effect and is not merely a device for reducing the taxes of certain partners without actually affecting their shares of partnership income, then such a provision will be recognized for tax purposes. * * *

This reference to "substantial economic effect" did not appear in the House Ways and Means Committee report discussing section 704(b), and was apparently added in the Senate Finance Committee to allay fears that special allocations of income or deductions would be denied effect in every case where the allocation resulted in a reduction in the income tax liabilities of one or more of the partners. The statement is an affirmation that special allocations are ordinarily to be recognized if they have business validity apart from their tax consequences.

* * *

Petitioners rely primarily on the argument that the allocation has "substantial economic effect" in that it is reflected in the capital accounts of the partners. * * *

According to the regulations, an allocation has economic effect if it "may actually affect the dollar amount of the partners' shares of the total partnership income or loss independently of tax consequences." The agreement in this case provided not only for the allocation of depreciation to petitioners but also for gain on the sale of the partnership property to be "charged back" to them. The charge back would cause the gain, for tax purposes, to be allocated on the books entirely to petitioners to the extent of the special allocation of depreciation, and their capital account would be correspondingly increased. The remainder of the gain, if any, would be shared equally by the partners. If the gain on the sale were to equal or exceed the depreciation specially allocated to petitioners, the increase in their capital account caused by the charge back would exactly equal the depreciation deductions previously allowed to them and the proceeds of the sale of the property would be divided equally. In such circumstances, the only effect of the allocation would be a trade of tax consequences, i.e., the Crisafis would relinquish a current depreciation deduction in exchange for exoneration from all or part of the capital gains tax when the property is sold, and petitioners would enjoy a larger current depreciation deduction but would assume a larger ultimate capital gains tax liability. Quite clearly, if the property is sold at a gain, the special allocation will affect only the tax liabilities of the partners and will have no other economic effect.

To find any economic effect of the special allocation agreement aside from its tax consequences, we must, therefore, look to see who is to bear the economic burden of the depreciation if the buildings should be sold for a sum less than their original cost. There is not one syllable of evidence bearing directly on this crucial point. We have noted, however, that when the buildings are fully depreciated, petitioners' capital account will have a deficit, or there will be a disparity in the capital accounts, approximately equal to the undepreciated basis of the buildings as of the beginning of 1966. Under normal accounting procedures, if the building were sold at a gain less than the amount of such disparity petitioners would either be required to contribute to the partnership a sum equal to the remaining deficit in their capital account after the gain on the sale had been added back or would be entitled to receive a proportionately smaller share of the partnership assets on liquidation. Based on the record as a whole, we do not think the partners ever agreed to such an arrangement. On dissolution, we think the partners contemplated an equal division of the partnership assets which would be adjusted only for disparities in cash contributions or withdrawals. Certainly there is no evidence to show otherwise. That being true, the special allocation does not "actually affect the dollar amount of the partners' share of the total partnership income or loss independently of tax consequences" within the meaning of the regulation referred to above.

Our interpretation of the partnership agreement is supported by an analysis of a somewhat similar agreement, quoted in material part in our Findings, which petitioners made as part of a marital property settlement agreement in 1968. Under this agreement, Orrisch was entitled to deduct all the depreciation for 1968 in computing his income tax liability, and his wife was to deduct none; but on the sale of the property they were to first reimburse Orrisch for "such moneys as he may have advanced," and then divide the balance of the "profits or proceeds" of the sale equally, each party to report one-half of the capital gain or loss on his income tax return. * * * Significantly, in both this agreement and the partnership agreement, as we interpret it, each party's share of the sales proceeds was determined independently from his share of the depreciation deduction.

In the light of all the evidence we have found as an ultimate fact that the "principal purpose" of the special allocation agreement was tax avoidance within the meaning of section 704(b). Accordingly, the deduction for depreciation for 1966 and 1967 must be allocated between the parties in the same manner as other deductions.

NOTES

1. *Impact of personal matters on business taxation*. In light of the court's discussion of the Orrischs' marital property settlement, should a lawyer who represents a client in business and investment affairs review a proposed settlement of a personal matter, such as the client's divorce?

2. *Post-Orrisch amendments*. I.R.C. § 704(b)(2) was amended in 1975 at which time the substantial economic effect standard replaced the "principal purpose" language referred to in the Orrisch case. The 1975 amendment also modified the default rule in the first clause of I.R.C. § 704(b) that applies when an agreed upon allocation is not respected or when the agreement fails to provide for allocations of gross income and deduction. In these circumstances, each partner's distributive share is now determined "in accordance with the partner's interest in the partnership (determined by taking into account all facts and circumstances)."

b. INTRODUCTION TO CAPITAL ACCOUNTS

The Orrisch court looked to the capital accounts of the Orrischs and the Crisafis to determine whether the special allocation of depreciation deductions had economic effect. Current tax law continues to rely on the partners' capital accounts to determine whether an agreed upon allocation of partnership income or deduction has economic effect.[8] To understand the technical requirements for economic effect under current law, it is necessary to explore the concept of a partner's capital account.

---

8. Regulations promulgated under I.R.C. § 704(b) provide elaborate rules for calculating each partner's capital account for tax purposes. Treas. Reg. § 1.704–1(b)(2)(iv).

As a matter of state law, a partner is normally entitled to the return of her investment in the partnership when she departs from the partnership.[9] Her investment includes amounts she contributes to the partnership, less any amounts she withdraws. Her investment is augmented by her share of partnership profits and reduced by her share of partnership losses.

The capital account is a financial accounting mechanism used to keep track of each partner's investment in the partnership. Although capital accounts are governed by the partnership agreement, certain general rules are normally followed. A separate capital account is maintained for each partner. When a partner contributes money to the partnership, her capital account is increased by the amount of money she contributes. If a partner contributes property to the partnership, her capital account is increased by the market value of the property at the time of the contribution. The capital account is increased by the value of the contributed property, not its adjusted basis, because the capital account is designed to measure the partner's economic investment in the partnership, not her tax investment. When a partner withdraws amounts from the partnership, the amount to which she is entitled declines and her capital account is reduced accordingly. A partner's capital account is reduced by the amount of any money distributed to the partner. If a partner receives a distribution of property, her capital account is reduced by the market value of the distributed property.

Partnership operations also impact on the partners' capital accounts. Each partner's capital account is increased by her share of the partnership's income, including items excluded from gross income. Regardless of whether a partnership receipt is taxable, the receipt accrues to the benefit of the partners and, accordingly, causes their capital accounts to increase. Conversely, each partner's capital account is normally reduced by her share of the partnership's expenses, regardless of whether the expense is deductible. Even if a disbursement is not deductible, capital accounts are normally reduced because the amount disbursed is no longer available for distribution to the partners.

Amounts borrowed by a partnership do not increase the partners' capital accounts. Borrowed amounts do not accrue to the benefit of the partners because creditors, rather than the partners, hold the primary claims against the borrowed amounts. Even if a partner lends money to the partnership, his capital account is not increased because his legal rights with respect to the loan stem from his capacity as a creditor, not his capacity as a partner. Correspondingly, the partners' capital accounts are not reduced when a partnership repays borrowed amounts.

It is possible for a partner to have a deficit balance in her capital account. For example, a deficit balance can result if a partner withdraws more value from the partnership than she contributes to it. The partnership agreement may obligate a partner with a deficit capital account

---

9. For a discussion of a partner's financial rights under state law, see Alan R. Bromberg & Larry E. Ribstein, *Bromberg & Ribstein on Partnership* § 6.02 (2008).

balance to contribute sufficient money to eliminate that deficit, but this is not always the case.

The capital account is a useful device for keeping track of each partner's investment in the partnership.[10] The economic effect regulations rely on capital accounts to serve as a proxy for the economic arrangement of the partners.

NOTE

Source of deficit capital account. In the Orrisch case (p. 156), the petitioners had a deficit capital account in 1966 and 1967. What caused this deficit? How else could a deficit capital account arise? Is it possible for all the partners in a partnership to have deficit capital accounts at the same time?

c. GENERAL TEST FOR ECONOMIC EFFECT

Treas. Reg. § 1.704–1(b)(2)(ii)(b).

For an allocation of partnership income or deduction to have economic effect, the regulations under I.R.C. § 704(b) generally require that three conditions be satisfied. Specifically, the partnership agreement must provide,

(a) for the maintenance of a capital account for each partner pursuant to the rules set forth in the regulations,[11]

(b) that liquidating distributions will be made in accordance with the positive capital account balances of the partners, and

(c) that any partner with a deficit capital account is unconditionally obligated to restore the deficit upon the liquidation of the partnership (or when the partner leaves the partnership).

---

10. One shortcoming is that capital account balances normally do not reflect changes in the value of the partnership's assets. Under certain circumstances, however, the partnership agreement may provide for adjusting the partners' capital accounts to reflect the current value of the partnership's assets.

11. The regulations provide elaborate rules for calculating each partner's capital account. Treas. Reg. § 1.704–1(b)(2)(iv). The most fundamental elements in the computation of a partner's capital account under the regulations are listed below.

The capital account is increased by,

(a) the amount of money contributed by the partner to the partnership,

(b) the market value of property contributed by the partner to the partnership, and

(c) the amount of partnership gross income (and tax-exempt income) allocated to the partner.

The capital account is decreased by,

(a) the amount of money distributed to the partner by the partnership,

(b) the market value of property distributed to the partner by the partnership, and

(c) the amount of partnership deductions (and non-deductible disbursements) allocated to the partner.

Treas. Reg. § 1.704–1(b)(2)(ii)(b). These rules recognize that tax deductions are sometimes allowed before, or even without, a corresponding economic burden. The rules basically allow the partners free rein to allocate the tax deductions among themselves in any manner provided that *if* a corresponding economic burden ultimately results, that burden is borne by the partners in the same manner that the tax deductions were allocated.

Example 4–C (Illustration of economic effect). Gil and Harriet form the GH Partnership and their partnership agreement incorporates the three requirements for economic effect in Treas. Reg. § 1.704–1(b)(2)(ii)(b). Each partner contributes $500,000 and each partner's initial capital account balance is therefore $500,000. GH uses the $1,000,000 received from the partners to acquire an apartment building. The partnership agreement allocates all items of partnership gross income and deduction, except for the depreciation deduction, 50% to Gil and 50% to Harriet. The depreciation deduction is allocated 100% to Gil. During its initial years of operation, GH is allowed $100,000 of depreciation deductions but has no other items of gross income or deduction. Pursuant to the agreement, all $100,000 of depreciation deductions are allocated to Gil and his capital account is correspondingly reduced from $500,000 to $400,000. GH then sells the building and liquidates.

(a) *Building declines in value.* If the partnership sells the building for $900,000, the partnership realizes no gain or loss.[12] When GH liquidates, the proceeds from the sale of the building ($900,000) must be distributed in accordance with each partner's capital account, $400,000 to Gil and $500,000 to Harriet. In these circumstances, the $100,000 of tax depreciation manifests a $100,000 economic loss. The allocation of all depreciation deductions to Gil has economic effect because Gil suffers the corresponding economic loss (he contributed $500,000 to the partnership but only receives $400,000 on liquidation).

(b) *Building does not decline in value.* If GH sells the building for $1,000,000, the partnership recognizes a $100,000 gain.[13] If the gain on

---

[12].

Partnership's Amount Realized		$900,000
Partnership's Original Basis	$1,000,000	
Less: Depreciation Deductions	100,000	
Less: Partnership's Adjusted Basis		900,000
Realized Gain		$ 0

[13].

Partnership's Amount Realized		$1,000,000
Partnership's Original Basis	$1,000,000	
Less: Depreciation Deductions	100,000	
Less: Partnership's Adjusted Basis		900,000
Realized Gain		$ 100,000

the sale of the building is allocated like all other items of partnership gross income (50% to each partner), $50,000 would be allocated to each partner. As a result, Gil's capital account is increased to $450,000 and Harriet's capital account is increased to $550,000. Because the partnership agreement provides that liquidation proceeds are to be distributed in accordance with capital accounts, the liquidation proceeds must be distributed $450,000 to Gil and $550,000 to Harriet. The special allocation of depreciation deductions to Gil has economic effect but Gil loses $50,000, notwithstanding the absence of any decline in the value of the building. Correspondingly, Harriet gains $50,000, notwithstanding the absence of any appreciation in the building.

Problem 4–2 (No decline in value but gain charge back provision is used): If, in Example 4–C(b), the partnership agreement provides that all gain attributable to depreciation deductions is allocated to Gil (a "gain charge back" provision like that utilized in the Orrisch case), does the special allocation of all depreciation deductions to Gil still have economic effect? If the building is ultimately sold for $1,000,000, how much of the proceeds from the sale of the building should each partner receive under these circumstances? Is the use of the gain charge back provision beneficial to Gil or detrimental to him?

d. ALTERNATE TEST FOR ECONOMIC EFFECT

Treas. Reg. § 1.704–1(b)(2)(ii)(d)

As a general rule, allocations of partnership gross income and deduction have economic effect only if the partnership agreement unconditionally obligates any partner with a deficit capital account to pay to the partnership an amount equal to that deficit upon the liquidation of the partnership or upon the partner's departure from the partnership (commonly referred to as a "deficit restoration obligation"). See Treas. Reg. § 1.704–1(b)(2)(ii)(b)(3). Partners are often reluctant to agree to a deficit restoration obligation because it could make them liable for amounts that they would not otherwise be liable for as a matter of law (e.g., a nonrecourse partnership debt). If partners do not wish to use a deficit restoration obligation, economic effect can often still be established under an alternate test set forth in the regulations. Treas. Reg. § 1.704–1(b)(2)(ii)(d).

Under the alternate test, a tax allocation can have economic effect to the extent that it does not cause or increase a deficit in a partner's capital account if the partnership agreement includes a "qualified income offset". The qualified income offset causes future partnership income to be allocated to eliminate, as quickly as possible, any deficit capital account that results from certain unanticipated events. Regardless of whether a qualified income offset or a deficit restoration obligation is utilized, a tax allocation will have economic effect only if the partnership agreement also provides,

(a) that capital accounts will be maintained in accordance with the regulations, and

(b) that liquidating distributions will be made in accordance with positive capital account balances.

See Treas. Reg. §§ 1.704–1(b)(2)(ii)(b), (d).

Problem 4–3 (Application of general and alternate tests for economic effect): Andy and Bobbi each contribute $40,000 to the AB Partnership. AB buys depreciable property for $80,000. The partnership agreement allocates all items of AB's gross income and deduction 50% to Andy and 50% to Bobbi, except for depreciation deductions which are allocated 100% to Andy. Does the allocation of all depreciation deductions to Andy have economic effect under each of the following alternatives?

(a) The partnership agreement provides that capital accounts will be maintained for each partner in accordance with the regulations, that distributions upon liquidation will be made equally to the partners, and that *no* partner is required to restore a deficit capital account. See Treas. Reg. § 1.704–1(b)(5) Example 1(i).

(b) The partnership agreement provides that capital accounts will be maintained for each partner in accordance with the regulations. The partnership agreement also provides that distributions upon liquidation will be made in accordance with positive capital account balances if AB is liquidated within five years of formation, but will be made equally if the liquidation occurs after that time. In addition, the agreement contains a deficit restoration obligation. Compare Treas. Reg. § 1.704–1(b)(5) Example (1)(ii).

(c) The partnership agreement provides that capital accounts will be maintained for each partner in accordance with the regulations and that distributions upon liquidation will be made in accordance with positive capital account balances. The agreement also contains a qualified income offset, but does not contain a deficit restoration obligation. See Treas. Reg. §§ 1.704–1(b)(5) Example (1)(iii), (iv).

(d) The partnership agreement provides that capital accounts will be maintained for each partner in accordance with the regulations and that distributions upon liquidation will be made in accordance with positive capital account balances. The agreement also contains a deficit restoration obligation. See Treas. Reg. § 1.704–1(b)(5) Example (1)(vii).

e. SUBSTANTIALITY

Treas. Reg. § 1.704–1(b)(2)(iii)

A special allocation of partnership income or deduction that has economic effect will be respected only if the economic effect is "substantial". Economic effect is an objective test that evaluates each special allocation discretely. To satisfy the economic effect test, a tax allocation of a particular item of gross income or deduction must be consistent with how the partners agreed to share the economic benefit of the corresponding receipt or the economic burden of the corresponding disbursement. In contrast, the substantiality requirement is a subjective test that acts as a backstop to the economic effect requirement. The substantiality requirement is intended to insure that multiple tax allocations that satisfy the economic effect requirement when viewed discretely do not violate the spirit of that requirement when their aggregate effect is considered. The substantiality requirement focuses on whether the economic effect of one special allocation is neutralized by another special allocation. If multiple special allocations, when viewed in the aggregate, reduce the total amount of tax paid by the partners without changing the relative economic positions of the partners, the economic effect of the allocations is generally not substantial.

(1) TRANSITORY ALLOCATIONS AND SHIFTING TAX CONSEQUENCES

The regulations do not delineate the contours of the substantiality requirement in an affirmative fashion. They simply describe circumstances in which the economic effect of a special allocation is not substantial because one special allocation is neutralized by another special allocation. Some of these descriptions focus on the impact of the allocations on the capital accounts of the partners. Specifically, the substantiality requirement is violated if the special allocations reduce the total amount of taxes paid by the partners, but do not cause the balance of each partner's capital account to differ significantly from the balance that would exist in the absence of the special allocations. In these circumstances, the neutralizing allocation might impact on a partnership year subsequent to the year affected by the original allocation ("transitory allocations"[14]) or both special allocations might affect the same partnership year ("shifting tax consequences"[15]).

> *Example 4–D (Illustration of transitory allocations)*: Jay contributes $200,000 and Kaye contributes $800,000 to the JK Partnership. The partnership agreement allocates profits and losses 20% to Jay and 80% to Kaye. The partnership agreement incorporates the three requirements for economic effect delineated in Treas. Reg. § 1.704–1(b)(2)(ii)(b). The partners anticipate that JK will generate $100,000 of income in Year 3 and $400,000 of income in Year 4. Jay has a $100,000 net operating loss carryover ("NOL") that will expire at the end of Year 3. Kaye expects to pay tax at the maximum rate in Years 3 and 4, regardless of how much partnership income she reports in each year.
>
> (a) *Absence of special allocations*. If the anticipated partnership income materializes, JK's income is allocated as follows:

---

14.   Treas. Reg. § 1.704–1(b)(2)(iii)(c).

15.   Treas. Reg. § 1.704–1(b)(2)(iii)(b).

	Jay	Kaye
Year 3	$ 20,000	$ 80,000
Year 4	80,000	320,000
Total	$100,000	$400,000

Jay's capital account is increased by $100,000 and Kaye's capital account is increased by $400,000. Because of his NOL, Jay pays no tax on his distributive share of JK's Year 3 income. Jay pays tax on his distributive share of JK's Year 4 income because his NOL expired at the end of Year 3.

(b) Presence of special allocations. If, during Year 3, the partners agree to allocate all Year 3 income to Jay and all future partnership income to Kaye until the amount of Year 3 income she sacrifices is restored to her, JK's income is allocated as follows:

	Jay	Kaye
Year 3	$100,000	$ 0
Year 4	0	400,000
Total	$100,000	$400,000

Jay's capital account is still increased by $100,000 and Kaye's capital account is still increased by $400,000. Thus, the amount of economic profits to which each partner is entitled has not changed. From an economic standpoint, therefore, the Year 4 special allocation neutralizes the Year 3 special allocation. Because of his NOL, Jay pays no tax on his entire distributive share of JK's Year 3 income. Thus, the special allocation of Year 3 income to Jay enables him to avoid paying tax on $80,000 of income that otherwise would have been taxed to him in Year 4. As a result, the total tax liability of the partners is less than what it would have been if the special allocations had not been utilized. The allocation of Year 3 income to Jay has economic effect.[16] The economic effect is not substantial, however, because the allocation is "transitory".[17]

Example 4–E (Illustration of shifting tax consequences): Maurice and Nisa each contribute $100,000 to the MN Partnership. The partnership agreement allocates profits and losses 50% to Maurice and 50% to Nisa. The partnership agreement incorporates the three requirements for economic effect delineated in Treas. Reg. § 1.704–1(b)(2)(ii)(b). The partners anticipate that, during Year 1, MN will earn more than $10,000 of tax-exempt interest on municipal bonds and more than $10,000 of dividends on corporate stock. During Year 1, Maurice's income is expected to be taxed at a higher rate than Nisa's income.

(a) *Absence of special allocations.* If MN generates $10,000 of tax-exempt interest and $10,000 of dividends in Year 1, $5,000 of tax-

---

16. Under the partnership agreement, Jay's capital account is increased by $100,000 at the end of Year 3. If JK were liquidated at that time, Jay would receive a distribution of the $100,000. See Treas. Reg. §§ 1.704–1(b)(2)(ii)(b)(1), (2). Thus, if JK were liquidated at the end of Year 3, the Year 3 income sacrificed by Kaye would never be restored to her.

17. See Treas. Reg. § 1.704–1(b)(2)(iii)(c).

exempt interest and $5,000 of dividends is allocated to each of Maurice and Nisa. Each partner's capital account is increased by $10,000. Neither partner is taxed on the distributive share of exempt interest (I.R.C. § 103(a)). Maurice pays more tax on his distributive share of the dividend income than Nisa pays on her distributive share because he is subject to a higher marginal tax rate.

(b) *Presence of special allocations.* The parties agree that Maurice is to be allocated the first $10,000 of tax-exempt interest generated during Year 1 on MN's municipal bonds, and that Nisa is to be allocated the first $10,000 of dividends generated during Year 1 on MN's corporate stock. If MN generates $10,000 of tax-exempt interest and $10,000 of dividends in Year 1, each partner's capital account is still increased by $10,000. Thus, the special allocations do not change the amount of economic profits to which each partner is entitled. The special allocations nevertheless reduce the collective tax liability of the partners because Nisa pays less tax on the additional $5,000 of dividend income allocated to her than Maurice would have paid on that income. Thus, the total tax liability of the partners is less because the special allocations were utilized. The special allocations have economic effect.[18] The economic effect is not substantial, however, because the allocations have "shifting tax consequences."[19]

NOTES

1. *Strong likelihood standard.* When partners agree to multiple allocations which are designed to offset one another, a degree of uncertainty normally exists as to whether all items of income or deduction that are involved in the allocations will ultimately materialize. If one or more of these items do not materialize, the allocations may cause the partners' capital account balances to differ from the balances that would have existed in the absence of the special allocations, despite the partners' intention that one allocation would neutralize the other. Substantiality is lacking if, at the time the allocations are agreed to, a "strong likelihood" exists that the offsetting allocation will occur. Moreover, if an offsetting allocation does, in fact, occur, it is presumed that a strong likelihood existed at the time the allocations were agreed to that the offsetting allocation would occur. This presumption may be overcome by a showing of facts and circumstances that prove otherwise. See Treas. Reg. §§ 1.704–1(b)(2)(iii)(b), (c).

2. *Decline in value presumption.* As illustrated by the Orrisch case (p. 156), a special allocation of depreciation deductions accompanied by a "gain charge back" provision has economic effect if the partner to whom the deduction is allocated suffers any corresponding economic loss. See Example 4–C(a), p. 164. If the likelihood of an economic loss is remote, the economic effect of the allocation appears not to be substantial because the

---

18. See Treas. Reg. § 1.704–1(b)(2)(ii)(b).

19. See Treas. Reg. §§ 1.704–1(b)(2)(iii)(b), –1(b)(5) Example (7)(ii).

allocation of depreciation deductions in the early years is likely to be neutralized by the allocation of the gain on disposition. See Problem 4–2, p. 165. In determining whether the substantiality requirement is satisfied, however, the regulations presume that depreciation deductions are matched by an actual decline in the value of the underlying property. This presumption eliminates any "strong likelihood" at the time of the allocation that an offsetting allocation will occur. See Treas. Reg. §§ 1.704–1(b)(2)(iii)(c), 1.704–1(b)(5) Example (1)(xi). Thus, special allocations of depreciation deductions accompanied by a gain charge back provision do not violate the substantiality requirement.

3. *Five-year limitation.* As explained in Note 1, the substantiality requirement may be violated even if it is not certain when the special allocations are agreed to that the items to which they relate will materialize. The substantiality requirement is presumed to be satisfied, however, when a strong likelihood exists that the offsetting allocation will not, in large part, be made within five years after the original allocation. Thus, the regulations implicitly adopt the view that predictions made by the partners regarding events that are to occur more than five years in the future are merely speculative. See Treas. Reg. §§ 1.704–1(b)(2)(iii)(c), –1(b)(5) Example 2.

> *Problem 4–4 (Determining whether the substantiality requirement is satisfied)*: Kara and Lars are equal partners in the KL Partnership. Their partnership agreement incorporates the three requirements for economic effect in Treas. Reg. § 1.704–1(b)(2)(ii)(b). KL expects to incur a loss on the sale of a capital asset in Year 1. Lars expects to derive capital gains from other activities in Year 1. Kara expects to derive no capital gains in Year 1 or at any time thereafter.
>
> (a) If the partnership agreement is amended to allocate all the capital losses recognized by KL in Year 1 to Lars and an equivalent amount of KL's Year 1 ordinary deductions to Kara, will the allocations have substantial economic effect? See Treas. Reg. §§ 1.704–1(b)(2)(iii)(b), –1(b)(5) Example (6).
>
> (b) If the partnership agreement is amended to allocate all the capital losses recognized by KL in Year 1 to Lars and an equivalent amount of KL's *Year 2* ordinary deductions to Kara, will the Year 1 allocation have substantial economic effect? See Treas. Reg. § 1.704–1(b)(2)(iii)(c).
>
> (c) If the partnership agreement is amended to allocate all the capital losses recognized by KL in Year 1 to Lars and an equivalent amount of KL's *Year 6* ordinary deductions to Kara, will the Year 1 allocation have substantial economic effect? See Treas. Reg. § 1.704–1(b)(2)(iii)(c).

(2) GENERAL RESTRICTION

The "transitory allocation" and "shifting tax consequences" restrictions focus on special allocations that, when viewed in the aggregate, do not cause the capital accounts of the partners to differ significantly from what the capital accounts would have been without the allocations. If a material change in capital accounts were the only prerequisite to satisfying the substantiality requirement, economically sophisticated taxpayers could devise multiple allocations that would cause capital accounts to differ without causing the taxpayers to feel that their relative economic positions had changed. This result is possible because sophisticated taxpayers evaluate their economic position by considering the effects of taxes and the time value of money.[20] Capital accounts do not normally reflect either of these factors.

The regulations implicitly acknowledge the deficiency of utilizing capital accounts as a proxy for determining the relative economic position of the partners by providing that, as a general matter, the economic effect of an allocation is not substantial when,

(a) the after-tax economic consequences of at least one partner may, in present value terms, be enhanced by the allocation, and

(b) a strong likelihood exists that the after-tax economic consequences of no partner will, in present value terms, be substantially diminished as a result of the allocation.[21]

Thus, even if partners can demonstrate that multiple special allocations will cause the partners' capital accounts to deviate significantly from what their capital accounts would be without the allocations, the substantiality requirement still might be violated.

Example 4–F (Illustration of general restriction on substantiality): Ivan and Julia are equal partners in the IJ Partnership that owns tax-exempt debt instruments and taxable debt instruments. The partnership agreement incorporates the three requirements for economic effect in Treas. Reg. § 1.704–1(b)(2)(ii)(b). For the foreseeable future, Ivan expects to be in a 30% marginal tax bracket and Julia expects to be in a 15% marginal tax bracket. In addition, the partners anticipate that the partnership will generate annually $500 of tax-exempt interest and $500 of taxable interest. Ivan and Julia agree to allocate the partnership's tax-exempt interest 85% to Ivan and 15% to Julia. Ivan and Julia also agree to allocate 100% of the partnership's taxable interest to Julia.

(a) The allocations are neither transitory nor entail shifting tax consequences because they cause the partners' capital accounts to differ significantly from what they would have been without the allocations. In the absence of the special allocations, the annual increase in each equal partner's capital account is $500.[22] With the special allocations, the annual increase in Ivan's capital account is $425[23] and the annual increase in Julia's capital account is $575.[24]

---

20. For a review of the time value of money, see pp. 468–470.

21. Treas. Reg. § 1.704–1(b)(2)(iii)(a).

22. (50% × $500 tax-exempt interest) + (50% × $500 taxable interest) = $500.

23. 85% × $500 tax-exempt interest = $425.

24. (15% × $500 tax-exempt interest) + $500 taxable interest = $575.

(b) The economic effect of the allocations is still not substantial, however, because of the general restriction. In the absence of the allocations, Ivan derives $425 annually after-tax[25] and Julia derives $462.50 annually after-tax.[26] As a result of the allocations, Ivan still derives $425 annually after-tax ($425 tax-free) but Julia derives $500 annually after-tax.[27] Hence, the after-tax economic consequences to Julia are enhanced by the allocations without diminishing the after-tax economic consequences to Ivan. See Treas. Reg. § 1.704–1(b)(5) Example (5).

NOTE

Uncertain scope. From a planning standpoint, the general restriction is far more difficult to deal with than the transitory allocation and shifting tax consequences restrictions. The general restriction could invalidate many allocations because of its broad terms. Until further guidance is provided, the actual scope of the general restriction will remain ambiguous.

f. PARTNER'S INTEREST IN PARTNERSHIP

Treas. Reg. § 1.704–1(b)(3)

If an agreed upon allocation does not have substantial economic effect (or if the partnership agreement does not provide for tax allocations), partnership gross income and deductions are allocated in accordance with the interests of the partners in the partnership. I.R.C. § 704(b). Under the regulations, the determination of a partner's interest in a partnership shall be made by taking into account all facts and circumstances relating to the economic arrangement of the parties. Among the factors to be considered are,

(a) the relative contributions of the partners to the partnership,

(b) the interests of the partners in economic profits and losses,

(c) the interests of the partners in cash flow, and

(d) the distribution rights of the partners upon liquidation.

Treas. Reg. § 1.704–1(b)(3). Little guidance exists with respect to the meaning of a partner's interest in the partnership, notwithstanding that many allocations of partnership income and loss are based on this standard.

NOTE

Allocation of deductions for nonrecourse debt. Deductions attributable to partnership "nonrecourse debt" (indebtedness secured by partnership

---

25. $500 received − (30% × $250 taxable interest) = $425.

26. $500 received −(15% × $250 taxable interest) = $462.50.

27. $575 received −(15% × $500 taxable interest) = $500.

property for which no partner bears personal risk)[28] cannot have economic effect to the partners. Rather, it is the lender who bears the economic risk of the investment. See Treas. Reg. § 1.704–2(b)(1). For example, assume that Roberto and Shana each own a 50% interest in the RS Partnership. The partnership borrows $800,000 and uses the money to buy a building. The loan is secured by the building but the partners are not personally liable for the debt. The partnership claims $500,000 of depreciation deductions and the value of the property falls from $800,000 to $300,000. The partnership defaults on the loan and the lender forecloses on the property, the only remedy available to the lender. In this situation, the lender, not the partners, bears the $500,000 economic loss incurred with respect to the building.

Because allocations attributable to nonrecourse debt cannot have economic effect to the partners, deductions funded by nonrecourse debt must be allocated based on the interests of the partners in the partnership. The regulations provide a test under which an allocation of nonrecourse deductions is deemed to be in accordance with the partners' interests in the partnership. See Treas. Reg. § 1.704–2(e). To satisfy this test, deductions attributable to nonrecourse debt must be allocated among the partners, "in a manner that is reasonably consistent with allocations that have substantial economic effect of some other significant partnership item attributable to the property securing nonrecourse liabilities." Treas. Reg. § 1.704–2(e)(2). Thus, an allocation of deductions attributable to nonrecourse debt may be respected if it "piggybacks" a related allocation that has economic effect. In addition, the following requirements must be satisfied:

(a) capital accounts must be maintained in accordance with the regulations,

(b) distributions upon liquidation must be made in accordance with positive capital account balances,

(c) income attributable to nonrecourse deductions must be allocated pursuant to a highly technical "minimum gain chargeback" requirement, and

(d) all other material allocations must be recognized under the conventional economic effect rules.

See Treas. Reg. §§ 1.704–2(e)(1), (3), (4).

C. ALLOWANCE OF ALLOCATED DEDUCTION/LOSS

I.R.C. §§ 704(d), 752(a)

Treas. Reg. §§ 1.752–1(a), (b), (c), –2(a), (b)

Even when the allocation of a particular partnership deduction or a bottom-line partnership loss[29] has substantial economic effect, each partner

---

28. Treas. Reg. §§ 1.704–2(b)(3); 1.752–1(a)(2).

29. See I.R.C. § 702(a)(8).

may immediately deduct her distributive share only to the extent of the basis in her partnership interest. I.R.C. § 704(d). The basis in her partnership interest is then reduced, but not below zero, by her distributive share of the deduction or loss. I.R.C. § 705(a)(2)(A). If the partner does not have sufficient basis to deduct the entire distributive share, the excess may be deducted as soon as additional basis is established in her partnership interest. I.R.C. § 704(d).

A partner's basis in her partnership interest ("outside basis")[30] often differs from the partner's capital account.[31] A partner's outside basis, like a partner's capital account, is increased by any money contributed to the partnership by the partner. See I.R.C. § 722.[32] Both outside basis and capital accounts are also increased by the partner's distributive share of partnership income. See I.R.C. § 705(a)(1).[33] Unlike a partner's capital account, however, a partner receives additional outside basis for her share of all amounts borrowed by the partnership.[34] The tax law, in effect, treats each partner as though she borrowed a portion of the funds and then contributed the money to the partnership, thereby increasing the basis of her partnership interest. See I.R.C. § 752(a).[35]

When a partnership incurs liabilities, each partner's outside basis is increased only to the extent of that partner's share of the liabilities. Each partner's share is normally determined by the "economic risk of loss" borne by the partner, i.e., the amount that the partner would be compelled to pay in the event that the partnership defaulted on all of its debts. The regulations delineate a fictional series of events to establish the economic risk of loss borne by each partner in these circumstances. Specifically, to determine the amount by which each partner may increase her outside basis to reflect her share of the partnership's liabilities, all of the following *fictional* events are assumed to occur:

(a) All of the partnership's liabilities become payable in full.

---

30. Each partner in a partnership has a basis in her partnership interest. A partner's basis in her interest is commonly referred to as "outside basis." In addition, the partnership, itself, has a basis in each of its assets. The partnership's basis in its assets is commonly referred to as "inside basis."

31. For a general discussion of the partner's capital account, see pp. 161–163.

32. Outside basis is also increased by the partner's adjusted basis in any contributed property. I.R.C. § 722. In contrast, the partner's capital account is increased by the value of the contributed property. Treas. Reg. § 1.704–1(b)(2)(iv)(b). The tax issues raised by a contribution of property with a value that differs from the contributing partner's basis are explored in Chapter 10.

33. See Treas. Reg. § 1.704–1(b)(2)(iv)(b) (capital account).

34. Partners get outside basis for all partnership debts, regardless of whether the monies are advanced by a partner or by an unrelated lender. In contrast, shareholders of an S Corporation do not get basis against which S Corporation losses may be deducted for monies advanced by non-shareholder lenders. See pp. 106–108.

35. Reductions in outside basis occur when the partnership distributes money or other property, or when a partnership liability is reduced (an event which is treated as a distribution of money). See I.R.C. §§ 705(a)(2), 752(b). The tax effects of partnership distributions (including their impact on outside basis) are examined in Chapter 7.

(b) All of the partnership's assets have a value of zero.

(c) The partnership disposes of all of its property in a fully taxable transaction for no consideration.

(d) All items of income, gain, loss, or deduction are allocated among the partners and their capital accounts are adjusted accordingly.

(e) The partnership liquidates.

Treas. Reg. § 1.752–2(b)(1). Each partner increases the basis of her partnership interest to the extent that the partner would be compelled to pay the debts with her own funds if all the fictional events had actually occurred.

> *Example 4–G (Identifying the economic risk of loss borne by each partner):* At the beginning of Year 1, Randy and Sally each contribute $50,000 to the RS Partnership. The partnership agreement allocates profits and losses 40% to Randy and 60% to Sally. Assume that the allocations have substantial economic effect and that the partnership agreement unconditionally obligates any partner with a deficit capital account at the time of liquidation to pay the deficit amount to the partnership (a "deficit restoration obligation").
>
> Immediately after RS is formed, RS purchases land for $1,000,000 by delivering the $100,000 contributed by the partners and a $900,000 promissory note to the seller. To allocate outside basis for the $900,000 partnership liability between Randy and Sally, the following series of events is deemed to occur:
>
> (a) The $900,000 debt is treated as due and payable.
>
> (b) The land is treated as having a value of zero.
>
> (c) The partnership is deemed to sell the land in a taxable transaction resulting in a $1,000,000 tax loss.[36]
>
> (d) The deemed loss is allocated in accordance with the partnership agreement, $400,000 to Randy and $600,000 to Sally, causing the partners' capital accounts to be adjusted as follows:
>
> | | Randy | Sally |
> |---|---|---|
> | Contribution | $ 50,000 | $ 50,000 |
> | Loss on hypothetical sale | (400,000) | (600,000) |
> | Ending balance | (350,000) | (550,000) |
>
> (e) The partnership liquidates (but has nothing to distribute) and the deficit restoration obligation is activated. The deficit restoration obligation causes Randy to contribute $350,000 and Sally to contribute $550,000 to enable the partnership to pay the lender.

36.

Amount Realized (sale of land with value of zero)	$	0
Less: Adjusted Basis (original purchase price)		1,000,000
Realized Loss		$1,000,000

Due to the outcome of the fictional events, Randy increases the basis of his partnership interest by $350,000 and Sally increases the basis of her partnership interest by $550,000 to reflect each partner's share of the partnership liability. Therefore, at the beginning of Year 1, Randy's outside basis is $400,000 and Sally's outside basis is $600,000.[37] See Treas. Reg. § 1.752–2(f) Example 2.

Example 4–G illustrates that obligations to the partnership that are imposed by the partnership agreement, including the obligation to restore a deficit capital account upon liquidation, are taken into account when determining the extent to which a partner bears the economic risk of loss for partnership liabilities. In addition to obligations created by the partnership agreement, state law normally renders partners liable for the obligations of the partnership. Payment obligations imposed by state law are also taken into account when determining the extent to which a partner bears the economic risk of loss. See Treas. Reg. § 1.752–2(b)(3).

When a partnership defaults on a debt, state law allows the lender to collect from any or all of the general partners of the partnership.[38] In a general partnership, all partners are general partners. A limited partnership must have at least one general partner.[39] The remaining partners in a limited partnership are limited partners. State law does not expose the personal assets of a limited partner to claims against the partnership.[40] Only the limited partner's contributions are exposed to the claims of the partnership's creditors.

The state law rules that govern the liability of partners for partnership debts can be modified by contract.[41] For example, a limited partner may

---

37. Each partner's outside basis at the beginning of Year 1 is as follows:

	Randy	Sally
Actual contribution of money	$ 50,000	$ 50,000
Share of partnership liability	350,000	550,000
Total	$400,000	$600,000

38. The total amount that the lender may recover from the general partners is limited to the amount of the partnership's debt. The lender may collect the entire amount from any general partner; it need not collect a proportionate amount from each general partner. Any partner who pays more than his proportionate share of the debt, however, normally has a right under state law to be reimbursed by his partners for the amount paid in excess of his proportionate share. See Alan R. Bromberg & Larry E. Ribstein, *Bromberg & Ribstein on Partnership* § 5.08 (2008).

39. See Uniform Limited Partnership Act of 2001, § 102(11).

40. See Uniform Limited Partnership Act of 2001, § 303.

41. A lender may advance funds to the partnership and agree to limit its remedy in the event of a default to collecting only from assets of the partnership. In this event, no partner is personally liable under state law for the partnership debt. Nevertheless, the outside basis of the partners is still increased by the amount of the debt. See Crane v. Commissioner, 331 U.S. 1, 67 S.Ct. 1047 (1947) (holding that basis is established in property acquired with a nonrecourse loan, notwithstanding that the lender cannot reach the borrower's personal assets agree to become personally liable for a particular partnership obligation. Contractual obligations outside the partnership agreement (such as guarantees, indemnifications and reimbursement agreements) running directly to creditors, partners, or the partnership are also taken into account when determining each partner's economic risk of loss for a partnership liability.[42] See Treas. Reg. § 1.752–2(b)(3). To determine the economic risk of loss, it is assumed that all partners who have obligations to make payments on partnership debts will actually perform those obligations, irrespective of their actual net worth, unless the facts and circumstances indicate a plan to circumvent or avoid the obligation. Treas. Reg. § 1.752–2(b)(6).

> *Example 4–H (General partner's legal obligation and limited partner's contractual obligation):* At the beginning of Year 1, Terry and Ursula form the TU limited partnership. Terry, the general partner, contributes $2,000 and Ursula, the limited partner, contributes $8,000. The partnership agreement allocates losses 20% to Terry and 80% to Ursula until Ursula's capital account is reduced to zero, then all losses are allocated to Terry. Assume that the allocations have substantial economic effect but the agreement does not include a deficit restoration obligation.[43]

> Immediately after TU is formed, TU borrows $15,000 from a bank and, with the $10,000 contributed by the partners, purchases land for $25,000. If TU defaults on the loan, Terry (the general partner) is liable for the partnership's debt under state law. In addition, to induce the bank to make the loan to TU, Ursula contractually agrees to pay the bank up to $5,000 of any amount of the debt that remains unpaid after the bank has exhausted all of its state law remedies.

> To allocate basis for the partnership liability between Terry and Ursula, the following series of events is deemed to occur:

> (a) The $15,000 debt is treated as due and payable.

> (b) The land is treated as having a value of zero.

> (c) The partnership is deemed to sell the land in a taxable transaction resulting in a $25,000 tax loss.[44]

---

in the event of a default). The economic risk of loss standard does not apply to the allocation of basis for a partnership liability when no partner is personally liable for the debt, i.e., a nonrecourse debt. The special rules that apply to the allocation of basis for nonrecourse debts are noted later in Chapter 4. See p. 179, Note 4.

42. In contrast, the tax law ignores contractual modifications that render a shareholder liable for the debts of an S Corporation. See pp. 108–118.

43. Normally, a limited partner will not agree to a deficit restoration obligation because that contractual obligation could expose him to claims that he would otherwise be insulated from under state law. Even without a deficit restoration obligation, an allocation can still have economic effect if a qualified income offset is utilized. See pp. 165–166.

44.

Amount Realized (sale of land with value of zero)	$ 0
Less: Adjusted Basis (original purchase price)	25,000
Realized Loss	$25,000

(d) The deemed loss is allocated in accordance with the partnership agreement, $17,000 to Terry and $8,000 to Ursula[45] causing capital accounts to be adjusted as follows:

	Terry	Ursula
Contribution	$ 2,000	$ 8,000
Loss on hypothetical sale	(17,000)	(8,000)
Ending balance	$(15,000)	$ 0

(e) The partnership liquidates (but has nothing to distribute). When the hypothetical liquidation occurs, Terry, the general partner, is obligated by operation of law to contribute $15,000 to the partnership. Because it is assumed that Terry will satisfy his legal obligation,[46] Ursula's guarantee is not activated.

As a result of these fictional events, Terry's economic risk of loss is $15,000 and, therefore, his outside basis is increased by $15,000. Thus, at the beginning of Year 1, Terry's outside basis is $17,000 and Ursula's outside basis is $8,000.[47] See Treas. Reg. § 1.752–2(f) Example 3.

Problem 4–5 (Limitation on deductibility of distributive share of loss): At the beginning of Year 1, Fran and Gary each contribute $100,000 to the FG Partnership, a general partnership. Assume that all allocations have substantial economic effect. Unless otherwise indicated, assume that the partnership agreement unconditionally obligates any partner with a deficit capital account upon liquidation to restore the deficit amount to the partnership (a "deficit restoration obligation"). Complete the grid for each of the following alternative scenarios:

	Fran	Gary
Outside Basis at Beginning of Year 1	?	?
Distributive Share of Year 1 Loss	?	?
Deductible Amount of Year 1 Loss	?	?
Outside Basis at End of Year 1	?	?

(a) *No borrowing.* During Year 1, FG derives no gross income and incurs deductible expenses of $150,000. The partners agree to allocate losses,

---

45. Pursuant to the partnership agreement, the first $10,000 of loss is allocated $2,000 to Terry and $8,000 to Ursula (which reduces her capital account to zero) and the remaining $15,000 of loss is allocated entirely to Terry.

46. Treas. Reg. § 1.752–2(b)(6).

$40,000 ordinary loss/$60,000 total losses = 2/3.

47. Each partner's outside basis at the beginning of Year 1 is as follows:

	Terry	Ursula
Actual contribution of money	$ 2,000	$8,000
Share of partnership liability	15,000	0
Total	$17,000	$8,000

    (i) 50% to Fran and 50% to Gary.

    (ii) 80% to Fran and 20% to Gary.

(b) *Borrowing from Bank.* FG borrows $200,000 from the Bank at the beginning of Year 1. The liability is a general obligation of the partnership (i.e., no partner has been relieved from personal liability). FG derives no gross income and incurs $300,000 of deductible expenses during Year 1. The partners agree to allocate losses,

    (i) 50% to Fran and 50% to Gary.

    (ii) 66⅔% to Fran and 33⅓% to Gary.

(c) *Borrowing from partner.* FG borrows $200,000 from Fran at the beginning of Year 1. The liability is a general obligation of the partnership (i.e., no partner has been relieved from personal liability). FG derives no gross income and incurs $300,000 of deductible expenses during Year 1. The partners agree to allocate the losses 50% to Fran and 50% to Gary.

(d) *Borrowing from Bank with partner guarantee.* FG borrows $200,000 from the Bank at the beginning of Year 1 but the Bank contractually agrees to waive its state law right to collect from the general partners in the event of a default. Fran, however, contractually agrees to pay any unpaid portion of the loan after the Bank has exhausted its rights against the partnership. FG derives no gross income and incurs $300,000 of deductible expenses during Year 1. The partners agree to allocate the losses 66⅔% to Fran and 33⅓% to Gary. Assume that the allocations have substantial economic effect but that the partnership agreement does not have a deficit restoration obligation. See Treas. Reg. § 1.752–2(f) Example 5.

NOTES

1. *Economic effect versus economic risk of loss.* What relationship, if any, exists between the economic effect test (see pp. 163–165) and the economic risk of loss standard?

2. *Liability equated to contribution of money.* Partnership liabilities are treated as a contribution of money solely for purposes of determining the outside basis of the partners. Partnership liabilities do not increase the capital accounts of the partners. Why not?

3. *Anti-abuse rule.* The regulations under I.R.C. § 752 include an anti-abuse rule that permits the obligation of a partner to make a payment to be disregarded or treated as an obligation of another person. This anti-abuse rule is triggered if the facts and circumstances indicate that a principal purpose of the arrangement is to eliminate a partner's economic risk of loss or to create the appearance of a partner bearing the economic risk of loss when, in fact, the substance of the arrangement is otherwise. Treas. Reg. § 1.752–2(j).

4. *Nonrecourse debt.* The economic risk of loss rules cannot be utilized to allocate basis to the partners for nonrecourse partnership debt because, by definition, no partner bears the economic risk of loss for these obligations.

Treas. Reg. § 1.752–1(a). Partners are still awarded outside basis for nonrecourse partnership liabilities but special rules are utilized for this purpose. Treas. Reg. § 1.752–3.

As a general rule, nonrecourse liabilities are allocated among the partners in accordance with each partner's relative interest in partnership profits. See Treas. Reg. § 1.752–3(a)(3). This rule is based on the theory that a nonrecourse liability will only be satisfied if the partnership generates future profits. As a result, even a limited partner, who is insulated from *all* partnership liabilities, is awarded basis for the partnership's nonrecourse liabilities to the extent of the limited partner's share of profits. The partnership agreement may specify the partners' interests in the partnership for purposes of allocating nonrecourse liabilities provided that the interests specified are consistent with the allocation of some other item of partnership income or gain that has substantial economic effect. Alternatively, nonrecourse partnership debt may be allocated in the same manner that deductions attributable to that debt are reasonably expected to be allocated. See Treas. Reg. § 1.752–3(c) Example 2. A third, even more complex allocation method also exists. See Treas. Reg. § 1.752–3(a)(3) (fifth sentence). Special rules apply when the amount of the nonrecourse liability exceeds the basis in property securing the liability, either at the time the property is acquired by the partnership or thereafter. See Treas. Reg. §§ 1.752–3(a)(1), (2), (c) Example 1.

5. *Partnership versus S Corporation.* Compare the allowance rules that govern a partner's distributive share of partnership loss to the allowance rules that govern a shareholder's pro rata share of S Corporation loss (pp. 106–108). What are the strengths and weaknesses of each set of rules? Can the fact that partners receive basis for a partnership liability, regardless of whether any partner is personally liable for the debt, be reconciled with the fact that S Corporation shareholders are denied basis for a corporate liability, even if the debt is personally guaranteed by the shareholders?

6. *Characterization of loss.* The characterization of a partner's distributive share of each item of partnership loss or deduction is determined at the partnership level. I.R.C. § 702(b). When a partner has insufficient basis to deduct her entire distributive share of partnership capital loss and partnership ordinary loss, she must allocate her basis between each item of loss in proportion to the amount of the total loss represented by that item. Treas. Reg. § 1.704–1(d)(2). For example, if a partner with an outside basis of $45,000 has a $20,000 distributive share of partnership capital loss and a $40,000 distributive share of partnership ordinary loss, one-third ($15,000) of the outside basis is allocated to the capital loss and two-thirds ($30,000) of the outside basis is allocated to the ordinary loss.[48] Thus, she can deduct $15,000 of the capital loss and $30,000 of the ordinary loss. Her remaining $5,000 distributive share of the capital loss and $10,000 distributive share

---

48. $20,000 capital loss/$60,000 total losses = 1/3. $40,000 ordinary loss/$60,000 total losses = 2/3.

of the ordinary loss can be deducted if and when she establishes additional basis in her partnership interest.

7. *Other loss limitation rules.* Even if a partner in a partnership has sufficient outside basis to allow him to deduct his distributive share of partnership loss, other loss limitation rules may cause the loss to be deferred or even disallowed. See, e.g., I.R.C. §§ 465 (at-risk rules), 469 (passive activity loss rules).

8. *Partner level treatment.* As you read the next case, consider which of the following statements is more accurate:

(a) A deduction allowed at the partnership level may be disallowed at the partner level.

(b) All deductions attributable to partnership activity must be allowed at the partner level.

Garcia v. Commissioner

United States Tax Court, 1991.
96 T.C. 792.

■ CLAPP, JUDGE: * * *

FINDINGS OF FACT

    * * *

In January 1985, petitioner [Garcia] entered into a partnership agreement as one of four general partners in Banana U.S.A. and made a capital contribution of $137,000 to the partnership. The other three general partners in Banana U.S.A. on January 31, 1985, were Daniel Caamano, Bruno Caamano and Ramiro Lluis. The terms of the partnership agreement provided that each general partner was entitled to 25 percent of the partnership's profits and losses. In March 1985, petitioner sent a letter to Daniel Caamano in which petitioner demanded the return of his investment in Banana U.S.A., "Based on common principals [sic] of gross mismanagement." On January 21, 1986, petitioner filed a complaint against the other three partners and the partnership for rescission, damages, dissolution of partnership and an accounting in United States District Court for the Central District of California.

The partnership issued a Schedule K–1 to petitioner for tax year 1985 and allocated to him as a distributive share item an ordinary loss in the amount of $101,920. On petitioners' [Garcia and spouse] timely filed joint Federal income tax return for 1985, they claimed a $101,920 loss attributable to their 25–percent interest in the Banana U.S.A. partnership. Respondent has disallowed this loss pursuant to section 165, contending that petitioners have not sustained a loss in 1985 as a result of their investment in Banana U.S.A.

OPINION

The issue for decision is whether petitioners are entitled to claim a "bottom line" partnership loss attributable to Banana U.S.A. partnership in tax year 1985.

The fundamental concept of partnership taxation is that a partnership is not a separate taxpaying entity. Partnerships are not subject to and are not responsible for payment of Federal income tax. Sec. 701. Partnerships are entities for purposes of calculating and filing information returns, but they are conduits through which the taxpaying obligation passes to the individual partners in accord with their distributive shares * * *. Section 703(a) requires that partnership taxable income be separately computed, and section 6031(a) requires this income to be reported by the partnership on an information return. However, section 702(a) requires each partner to take into account his distributive share of partnership gain or loss in determining his income tax liability. Section 702(a), in conjunction with section 702(b), preserves the character of certain items of partnership income, gain, loss, deduction, or credit in the hands of partners. Under this statutory scheme, the tax characteristics of partnership activities are preserved and the tax incidence of such activities is passed through to the partners.

Section 703(a) provides that the taxable income of a partnership shall be computed in the same manner as in the case of an individual, with some exceptions. The exceptions require that the items described in section 702(a) be separately stated and that certain deductions be disallowed to the partnership. Such deductions include, among other things, charitable contributions under section 170 and personal exemptions under section 151. These deductions are disallowed at the partnership level because they are allowed directly to individual partners.

Section 702(a)(1) through (a)(7) requires that specific items of partnership gain, loss, deduction, and credit be segregated by the partnership and separately stated on the returns of the individual partners. Section 702(a)(8) includes all those remaining partnership items that are not separately stated and is referred to as partnership net or bottom line taxable income or loss. In determining his personal income tax, a partner combines his distributive share of each separately stated partnership item with similar items realized by him from other sources and includes his distributive share of partnership net bottom line income or loss. Respondent's determination of a deficiency in petitioners' 1985 income tax is based upon his disallowance of petitioners' distributive share bottom line partnership loss.

Section 165(a) deals comprehensively with the income tax treatment of losses. Section 165(a) provides that there shall be allowed as a deduction any loss sustained during a taxable year unless compensated for by insurance or otherwise * * *.

To be allowable as a deduction under section 165(a), a loss must be evidenced by closed and completed transactions, fixed by identifiable events and, with exceptions not relevant in this case, actually sustained during the taxable year. Sec. 1.165–1(b), Income Tax Regs. Further, no loss will be allowed if in the year of the loss there exists a claim for reimbursement for which there is a reasonable prospect of recovery. Sec. 1.165–1(d), Income Tax Regs. The issue presented by respondent is whether section 165(a) limitations on losses apply to an individual partner's distributive share bottom line partnership loss.

The parties have stipulated that petitioner made a capital contribution to the Banana U.S.A. partnership in 1985 of $137,000 and that, pursuant to the terms of the partnership agreement, petitioner was entitled to 25 percent of all gain or loss incurred by the partnership. Respondent does not contest that petitioner entered Banana U.S.A. for profit, that the partnership actually incurred a loss in 1985, or that petitioners' share of that loss was $101,920 as shown on Schedule K–1. Respondent disallowed petitioners' distributive share of partnership loss solely because of a lawsuit filed by petitioner in 1986, in which petitioner demanded rescission of the partnership agreement and return of his capital investment. Respondent asserts that, as a result of this lawsuit, petitioners have not sustained a loss in 1985, pursuant to section 165.

Petitioners argue that the limitation on losses under section 165 is not applicable to their share of bottom line partnership loss. Section 165, they contend * * * does not have any reference to or impose limits on losses relating to a partner's distributive share of bottom line loss from a partnership's operations. They argue that this evidences a statutory intent to impose section 165 limitations at the partnership level and not at the partner level * * *.

Petitioners' final contention is that their claimed loss was generated by the partnership's operations, and it must not be confused with the loss of petitioner's capital investment. They agree that section 165 would apply to disallow any deduction claimed for loss of their initial $137,000 capital investment, at least during the period for which they had a reasonable prospect of recovery. In such instance, respondent would be correct in asserting that, at least during litigation, there was no loss which could be evidenced by closed and completed transactions. However, petitioners are not claiming a loss deduction for their capital investment in the Banana U.S.A. partnership. They are claiming a deduction for their distributive share bottom line partnership loss. Such loss was actually sustained during the partnership's operations from January through March 1985, and the partnership was never compensated for this loss by insurance. Therefore, they argue, the partnership sustained a loss under section 165. As their basis in the partnership exceeded their distributive share of this loss, petitioners claim that they are entitled to a deduction for their distributive share of the loss.

We think that respondent is in error in applying section 165 to disallow petitioners' distributive share of partnership operating loss. The overall statutory scheme requires that the determination of whether section 165 is applicable to a partner's distributive share of bottom line partnership loss be made at the partnership level and not at the partner level. Under the statute, partnership activities are taxed to partners in the following manner: First, separately stated items of partnership income and expenses and bottom line partnership taxable income or loss are computed under section 702, and next, pursuant to section 704, each partner determines his distributive share of each separately stated item and of net partnership income or loss to determine his income tax. It is not until after the partnership's taxable income has been determined that the partners' distributive shares can be ascertained * * *. A partner's distributive share consists of partnership profits and losses already calculated with consideration of the tax law. Therefore, in asserting a disallowance for partnership loss under section 165, respondent's focus should have been on ascertaining whether the Banana U.S.A. partnership incurred a loss in 1985. Finally, we note that under section 704(d), a partner's distributive share of partnership loss is allowed only to the extent of his adjusted basis in the partnership at the end of the year in which the loss occurred. This section, which imposes limitations on a partner's distributive share of partnership loss, makes no reference to section 165 * * *.

We find that the bottom line loss incurred by the Banana U.S.A. partnership in 1985 is an ordinary loss under the provisions of section 165(a). Each general partner, by virtue of sections 702(a) and 704, has a distributive share of such loss to the extent of his adjusted basis in the partnership at the end of 1985. The fact that petitioner initiated a lawsuit against the partnership subsequent to 1985 for rescission of the partnership agreement and return of his original capital investment cannot serve to deny petitioners a deduction for such loss * * *.

NOTE

Impact of suit for rescission. If Garcia prevails in his suit for rescission of the partnership agreement, what tax consequences will result?

D.   Modifying an Allocation

I.R.C. §§ 706(d), 761(c)

The allocation issues on which this chapter has focused generally arise when a partnership is initially capitalized. Often, an existing partnership will sell additional interests to new or existing partners after its operating activities are underway. Consider the allocation issues that arise when additional interests in an existing partnership are sold.

Lipke v. Commissioner

United States Tax Court, 1983.
81 T.C. 689.

■ Fay, Judge: * * *

In 1972 petitioner[s] * * * Reger, * * * Rautenstrauch, and * * * Luksch, formed Marc Equity Partners I, a limited partnership. The partnership was organized for the purpose of acquiring and operating apartment buildings in the suburbs of Buffalo, New York. Reger, Rautenstrauch, and Luksch were the general partners * * *. The general partners made a capital contribution in the total amount of $100. Shortly after formation of the partnership, limited partnership interests were sold to 14 investors for a total amount of $1,175,000 * * *. [T]he partnership agreement allocated all profits and losses to the limited partners. At all relevant times, the partnership computed its taxable income on a calendar year basis using the accrual method of accounting.

In 1972 and 1973 the partnership acquired several apartment buildings. At all relevant times, these apartment buildings were subject to mortgages. In 1974 and 1975, the partnership experienced severe financial problems and defaulted on the mortgages. After the mortgagee foreclosed on one of the apartment buildings, the partnership obtained additional capital of $300,000 in order to avoid losing its remaining apartment buildings. Of the $300,000, $84,000 was contributed by six of the fourteen original limited partners who together held interests in the partnership totaling 28 percent. The remaining $216,000 was contributed by petitioners * * * James, * * * Francis, * * * Lipke, (herein sometimes collectively referred to as the new partners), and Reger (one of the general partners), in return for new limited partnership interests. All of these capital contributions were made on October 1, 1975 * * *.

In connection with these additional capital contributions, effective October 1, 1975, the general and limited partners executed an amendment to the partnership agreement (herein the Amendment). The Amendment created two classes of limited partners. All of the original limited partners * * * were designated as Class A limited partners. Together with Reger and the new partners, the six original partners who made new capital contributions also became Class B partners. Reger, Rautenstrauch, and Luksch continued as the general partners.

The Amendment also provided that the partnership was to be owned 49 percent by the Class A limited partners, 49 percent by the Class B limited partners, and 2 percent by the general partners * * *.

[T]he Amendment reallocated 98 percent of all the partnership's 1975 losses to the Class B limited partners. This reallocation was made expressly in consideration of the new capital contributions made to the partnership. The Amendment also reallocated 2 percent of all the partnership's 1975 losses to the general partners.

On its 1975 return, the partnership reported losses of $933,825 * * *. On their 1975 returns, petitioners (Lipke, [James], [Francis] * * *, Rautenstrauch, and Reger) reported their distributive shares of these losses. In his notices of deficiency, respondent disallowed that portion of the reported losses attributable to losses accrued by the partnership prior to October 1, 1975. [The IRS did not challenge the partnership's allocation of losses accrued from October 1, 1975 through December 31, 1975.]

The primary issue is whether the partnership properly allocated its 1975 losses among its partners. Respondent contends that section 706[(d)] prevents the partnership from reallocating losses accrued before October 1, 1975, to either the Class B limited partners or to the general partners. Petitioners * * * argue that * * * section 706[(d)] * * * does not prevent the retroactive reallocation of losses to those petitioners who were already partners when the reallocation was made. [W]e hold that the partnership's retroactive reallocation of losses to the Class B limited partners was not permitted by section 706[(d)] because it was made as a result of additional capital contributions. It makes no difference that the additional capital was contributed by, and the resulting retroactive reallocation was made to, both new and existing partners. However, we also hold that the partnership's retroactive reallocation of losses to the general partners was permissible since it did not result from additional capital contributions and therefore constituted nothing more than a readjustment of partnership items among existing partners.

Section 702(a) requires a partner to report his distributive share of the partnership's income or loss. With certain exceptions, section 704(a) provides that a partner's distributive share is to be determined by the partnership agreement. A partnership agreement includes any amendments made before the time for filing the partnership return. Sec. 761(c). However, section 706(c)(2) provides for certain tax consequences to a partner whose partnership interest changes during the partnership's taxable year * * *.

In Richardson v. Commissioner, 76 T.C. 512 (1981), affd. 693 F.2d 1189 (5th Cir.1982), * * * we held that the reduction in the capital interests of the original partners resulting from the admission of the new partners constituted a reduction of interests within the meaning of section 706[(d)]. The fact that the original partners' equity interests in the partnership remained the same was deemed to be irrelevant. Accordingly, under section 706[(d)] the original partners and the new partners were required to determine their distributive shares of partnership items by taking into account their varying interests in the partnership during the taxable year. Thus, a retroactive reallocation of partnership items to the new partners was not allocable * * *.

[A]ccordingly, since petitioners James, Francis, and Lipke were newly admitted as partners on October 1, 1975, they are not entitled to report losses accrued by the partnership prior to that date.

We also hold that section 706[(d)] prevents the retroactive reallocation of losses to petitioner Reger as a limited partner even though he was already a partner when he made his additional capital contribution. Together with the new capital contributions made by the new partners and by six of the original limited partners, Reger's additional capital contribution reduced the capital interests of the non-contributing partners. For purposes of section 706[(d)], we find no difference between a reduction in partners' interests resulting from the admission of new partners, as in Richardson, and, as here, the reduction in partners' interests resulting from additional capital contributions made by existing partners. In both situations partners' interests were reduced and retroactive reallocations were made as a result of the additional capital contributions. We are unwilling to sustain, for example, the retroactive reallocations of losses made to petitioner Reger merely because he had previously contributed $34 to the partnership, and yet deny petitioners Lipke, James, and Francis that same benefit because they were new partners. That would create an illusory distinction which the language of section 706[(d)] simply does not require us to make.

With respect to the partnership's retroactive reallocation of losses to the general partners, however, we find that it did not result from additional capital contributions and therefore did not contravene the varying interest rules of section 706[(d)]. Prior to October 1, 1975, the general partners held only a residual interest in gains arising from "major capital events." Pursuant to the October 1, 1975, amendment to the partnership agreement, however, the general partners were granted a 2 percent interest in the partnership's 1975 profits and losses including the losses accrued by the partnership during the preceding nine months. In contrast to the retroactive reallocation of losses to the Class B limited partners, this reallocation to the general partners was not made in consideration for additional capital contributions. General partners Rautenstrauch and Luksch made no additional capital contributions and Reger's contribution was made in exchange for a limited partnership interest, not for an increase in his interest as a general partner. Accordingly, this reallocation of losses to the general partners was not directly accompanied by a reduction in any other partner's capital interest within the meaning of section 706[(d)]. It constituted nothing more than a readjustment of partnership items among existing partners which, by itself, is permissible * * *.

Finally, we must determine how much of the partnership's 1975 losses can be allocated to the period after September 30, 1975. In his notice of deficiency, respondent allocated losses of $125,770 to that period. This determination was based on the partnership's interim closing of its books as of September 30, 1975, whereby it determined how much of its losses were allocable to the withdrawing partner. Significantly, petitioners do not dispute that respondent's determination in this respect accurately reflects the amount of losses incurred by the partnership during the relevant period. Rather, they simply argue that the partnership should be allowed to use the "year-end totals" method of accounting and thereby allocate losses of $212,431 to the period October 1, 1975, through December 31, 1975.

We summarily reject petitioner's argument. The amount of losses accrued by the partnership after September 30, 1975, is clearly shown by the partnership's interim closing of its books and allocation of losses to the withdrawing partner. There is simply no justification for now allowing the partnership to use the relatively less accurate "year-end totals" method of accounting for purposes of allocating losses to petitioners. Accordingly, we sustain respondent's determination in this respect.

NOTES

1. *Permissible retroactive allocations.* What is the latest date that the partners in Lipke could have agreed on the allocation of the partnership's 1975 losses among themselves, if no new partners had entered the partnership and no existing partners had made additional capital contributions during 1975? See I.R.C. §§ 761(c), 6031(a), 6072(a).

2. *Three groups of partners.* The Lipke court addresses the tax consequences to three different groups of individuals. Identify each group and consider how each group was treated by the Lipke court. Was it sensible for the Lipke court to treat the old partners who made additional contributions on October 1, 1975, in the same manner as the new partners?

3. *Substantial economic effect.* What impact, if any, does the substantial economic effect test have on the allocation of the losses in Lipke?

4. *Partnership versus S Corporation.* Which, if any, of the issues confronted by the Lipke court could have arisen if Marc Equity Partners I had been an S Corporation? See I.R.C. §§ 1366(a)(1), 1377(a)(1).

5. *Closing of books versus year-end total methods.* Why did the taxpayers in Lipke wish to allocate the loss between the two segments of the partnership's year by using the "year-end total" method of accounting? Under what circumstances would the taxpayers have preferred to allocate the loss between the two segments of the partnership's year by using the "closing of the books" method of accounting? Which of the two methods could have been utilized if Marc Equity Partners I had been an S Corporation? See I.R.C. § 1377(a); Treas. Reg. § 1.1368–1(g)(2).

E.   Distinguishing Partnership From Proprietorship

Now that the consequences of partnership tax treatment have been explored, it is important to define the range of enterprises that qualifies for partnership tax treatment. An individual conducting an unincorporated business by herself will not be treated as a partnership for tax purposes. Rather, partnership tax treatment requires some degree of collective business activity. See I.R.C. § 761(a); Treas. Reg. § 301.7701–3. The point at which collective business activity reaches the threshold of a partnership for tax purposes is not always clear.

Revenue Ruling 75–374

1975–2 Cum.Bull. 261.

Advice has been requested whether, under the circumstance described below, the co-owners of an apartment project would be treated as a partnership for Federal income tax purposes.

X * * * and Y * * * each own an undivided one-half interest in an apartment project. X and Y entered into a management agreement with Z * * * and retained it to manage, operate, maintain, and service the project.

Generally, under the management agreement Z negotiates and executes leases for apartment units in the project; collects rents and other payments from tenants; pays taxes, assessments, and insurance premiums payable with respect to the project; performs all other services customarily performed in connection with the maintenance and repair of an apartment project; and performs certain additional services for the tenants beyond those customarily associated with maintenance and repair. Z is responsible for determining the time and manner of performing its obligations under the agreement and for the supervision of all persons performing services in connection with the carrying out of such obligations.

Customary tenant services, such as heat, air conditioning, hot and cold water, unattended parking, normal repairs, trash removal, and cleaning of public areas are furnished at no additional charge above the basic rental payments. All costs incurred by Z in rendering these customary services are paid for by X and Y. As compensation for the customary services rendered by Z under the agreement, X and Y each pay Z a percentage of one-half of the gross rental receipts derived from the operation of the project.

Additional services, such as attendant parking * * * and gas, electricity, and other utilities are provided by Z to tenants for a separate charge. Z pays the costs incurred in providing the additional services, and retains the charges paid by tenants for its own use. These charges provide Z with adequate compensation for the rendition of these additional services.

Section 761(a) of the Internal Revenue Code of 1954 provides that the term "partnership" includes a syndicate, group, pool, joint venture or other unincorporated organization through or by means of which any business, financial operation, or venture is carried on, and which is not a corporation or a trust or estate.

[Section 301.7701–1(a)(2)] of the Regulations provides that mere coownership of property that is maintained, kept in repair, and rented or leased does not constitute a partnership. Tenants in common may be partners if they actively carry on a trade, business, financial operation, or venture and divide the profits thereof. For example, a partnership exists if co-owners of an apartment building lease space and in addition provide services to the occupants either directly or through an agent.

The furnishing of customary services in connection with the maintenance and repair of the apartment project will not render a coownership a partnership. However, the furnishing of additional services will render a coownership a partnership if the additional services are furnished directly by the co-owners or through their agent. In the instant case by reason of the contractual arrangement with Z, X and Y are not furnishing the additional services either directly or through an agent. Z is solely responsible for determining the time and manner of furnishing the services, bears all the expenses of providing these services, and retains for its own use all the income from these services. None of the profits arising from the rendition of these additional services are divided between X and Y.

Accordingly, X and Y will be treated as co-owners and not as partners for purposes of section 761 of the Code.

Barron v. Commissioner

United States Tax Court, 1992.
64 T.C.M. 1034.

■ NAMEROFF, SPECIAL TRIAL JUDGE: * * *

FINDINGS OF FACT

* * *

In late 1980, Barron entered into an oral agreement with Sanders, * * * Herrman and * * * LeClerc to conduct business activities, such as the bagging and shipping of various wood products and potting soil, under the name of B & B. Barron contributed [two trucks] to B & B * * *. Sanders contributed three * * * trailers * * *.

On October 16, 1980, Barron applied to the City of Torrance for a business license under the name of B & B, indicating B & B would be owned and operated as his sole proprietorship. Additionally, Barron acquired a workers' compensation liability policy in his own name [doing business as] B & B Forest Products. However, on October 17, 1980, * * * [Barron, Sanders,] Herrman, and LeClerc each * * * deposited [$500] into a [single] bank account in the name of B & B, and each of the four men signed the signature card allowing them each access to the account.

To conduct its activities, B & B needed substantial additional equipment. Thus, from time to time, Barron, usually accompanied by LeClerc, traveled to several auctions in northern California to purchase such equipment. The equipment was purchased with cash obtained prior to each trip from Barron, Herrman, Sanders and LeClerc. At trial, Barron was unable to present any receipts, bills of sale, or certificates of title to substantiate these purchases. * * *

B & B did not file a partnership return for the 1981 tax year. * * *. Barron explained that his accountant had advised him it was unnecessary to file an information return for the 1981 tax year because B & B had a very small loss, and such loss could be accounted for in the subsequent year. Neither Barron nor any of the alleged partners claimed their distributive share of B & B's alleged loss on their 1981 individual tax returns. * * * [The Commissioner determined that the business, in fact, generated $25,486 of taxable income in 1981.]

OPINION

The first issue for resolution is whether B & B constituted a partnership. Respondent, in the notice of deficiency, determined that B & B was Barron's sole proprietorship. Respondent also determined that Barron had

* * * income of $25,486 from the operation of B & B in 1981 * * *. Barron contends that B & B was a partnership in which he was one of four equal partners, and therefore, is only responsible for reporting one-fourth of the income * * * of B & B. * * *

For Federal income tax purposes, the term "partnership" includes:

> Sec. 761(a). Partnership.—* * * a syndicate, group, pool, joint venture, or other unincorporated organization through or by means of which any business, financial operation, or venture is carried on, and which is not, within the meaning of this title, a corporation * * *.

The test of whether a partnership exists is primarily one of intent, the key inquiry being whether "the parties in good faith and acting with a business purpose intended to join together in the present conduct of an enterprise." Commissioner v. Culbertson, 337 U.S. 733, 742 (1949). In determining whether persons have formed a partnership which is to be afforded recognition for tax purposes, the court looks at the following factors, none of which is conclusive:

> The agreement of the parties and their conduct in executing its terms; the contributions, if any, which each party has made to the venture; the parties' control over income and capital and the right of each to make withdrawals; whether each party was a principal and coproprietor, sharing a mutual proprietary interest in the net profits and having an obligation to share losses, or whether one party was the agent or employee of the other, receiving for his services contingent compensation in the form of a percentage of income; whether business was conducted in the joint names of the parties; whether the parties filed Federal partnership returns or otherwise represented to respondent or to persons with whom they dealt that they were joint venturers; whether separate books of account were maintained for the venture; and whether the parties exercised mutual control over and assumed mutual responsibilities for the enterprise. [Luna v. Commissioner, 42 T.C. 1067, 1077–1078 (1964).]

Moreover, a partnership agreement may be oral, as in the instant case. * * *

We are persuaded from the record that [Barron, Sanders,] Hermann and LeClerc, intended to conduct an enterprise jointly for profit. The initial creation of a bank account with all four signatures, the contribution by Barron and Sanders of the trucks and trailers to the venture, and the cash contributions of the men for the purchase of additional assets indicate B & B was created and operated as a partnership. Although there are various documents to the contrary, such documents were explained by Barron as prepared either based upon the exigency of the moment or by others without his consultation and, we think, are not controlling. Accordingly, we hold that B & B was a partnership for Federal income tax purposes.

* * *

NOTES

1. *Impact of partnership tax treatment.* What difference did it make to Barron whether B & B was taxed as a proprietorship or a partnership?

2. *Impact of state law treatment.* The fact that an enterprise is treated as a partnership for state law purposes does not insure that the enterprise will be treated as a partnership for Federal tax purposes. Moreover, an enterprise that is not treated as a partnership by state law may still qualify as a partnership for Federal tax purposes. See, e.g., Rev. Rul. 58–243, 1958–1 Cum.Bull. 255 (ruling that (a) the fact that an asserted husband and wife partnership would be valid under state law does not necessarily require recognition of such partnership for Federal income tax purposes; and (b) the fact that a husband and wife could not legally become partners under state law does not necessarily prevent the recognition of the partnership for federal income tax purposes); Rev. Proc. 2002–22, 2002–14 I.R.B. 733 (delineating when the Internal Revenue Service will consider ruling that a common law tenancy-in-common in rental real property is not a partnership for federal tax purposes); I.R.C. § 761(f) (providing that a husband and a wife who operate a qualified joint venture may elect not to treat the joint venture as a partnership for tax purposes).

F. DISTINGUISHING PARTNERSHIP FROM TAXPAYING ENTITY

A threshold level of collective activity must exist for an unincorporated enterprise to be treated as a partnership for Federal tax purposes. When this level of activity is achieved, the enterprise will normally be taxed as a partnership, unless it elects to be taxed as a corporation. See Treas. Reg. § 301.7701–3. If ownership interests of an unincorporated enterprise are sufficiently marketable, however, the enterprise will be deemed a "publicly-traded partnership." See I.R.C. § 7704. A publicly-traded partnership is taxed as a C Corporation, notwithstanding that the enterprise is not a corporation under state law.

1. NON-PUBLICLY TRADED PARTNERSHIPS

I.R.C. §§ 7701(a)(2), (3)

Treas. Reg. §§ 301.7701–1(a), (b), –2(a), (b)(1),(2), (c), –3(a), (b)(1).

Prior to 1996, an unincorporated enterprise could be deemed an "association" and taxed as a C Corporation if it possessed certain characteristics historically attributed to corporations. See I.R.C. § 7701(a)(3); Larson v. Commissioner, 66 T.C. 159 (1976), acq. 1979–1 C.B. 1. The regulations implementing this corporate resemblance system never significantly constrained partnership tax status. As a result, partnership tax treatment could normally be achieved even when an unincorporated enterprise was imbued with corporate characteristics to the maximum extent permitted by state law.

Although the threat of "association" treatment under the tax law rarely deterred unincorporated enterprises from adopting corporate features, state law did not historically sanction an unincorporated enterprise with all the characteristics of a corporation. For example, only the corporate form enabled each owner to limit liability to her investment in the enterprise, even if the owner participated in the control of the business. In recent years, however, state legislatures have created new non-corporate legal forms, such as the limited liability company ("LLC"), that possess all the significant characteristics of corporations.

By 1996, every state had enacted a statute that allows a business to be conducted as an LLC.[49] Although LLC statutes vary from state to state, certain common ground exists. An LLC may own property, may sue or be sued, and generally may carry on any lawful business. In most cases, the owners of an LLC (called "members") are liable for obligations of the business only to the extent of their investment in the enterprise. Hence, a member is generally not exposed to the risks and liabilities of a business conducted by an LLC any more than a shareholder is exposed to the obligations of a corporation or a limited partner is exposed to the obligations of a limited partnership.

With the advent of LLCs and other new business forms, the Internal Revenue Service recognized that it was not sensible to distinguish partnerships from associations based on characteristics no longer unique to the corporate form. In 1996, regulations were promulgated that automatically tax most non-publicly traded, unincorporated enterprises with at least two owners as partnerships, unless the enterprise elects to be taxed as an association.[50] Treas. Reg. § 301.7701–3(a), (b)(1)(i). Excerpts from the Treasury's explanation of these regulations follow.

Simplification of Entity Classification Rules

Department of the Treasury
December 17, 1996.

Explanation of Provisions

Section 7701(a)(2) of the Code defines a partnership to include a syndicate, group, pool, joint venture, or other unincorporated organization, through or by means of which any business, financial operation, or venture is carried on, and that is not a trust or estate or a corporation. Section 7701(a)(3) defines a corporation to include associations, joint-stock companies, and insurance companies.

---

49. See Larry E. Ribstein & Robert R. Keatinge, *Ribstein and Keatinge on Limited Liability Companies*, § 1.2 "The Emergence and History of LLCs" (2d ed. 2010); Susan P. Hamill, "The Origins Behind the Limited Liability Company," 59 Ohio State Law Journal 1459 (1998). 1.9 million limited liability companies filed partnership tax returns in 2008. Internal Revenue Service, *Statistics of Income Bulletin* (Spring 2011), Table 11.

50. An enterprise that elects to be taxed as an association may elect to be taxed as an S Corporation if it satisfies all the eligibility requirements for S Corporation status. See I.R.C. § 1361(b); Treas. Reg. § 1.1361–1(c).

The existing regulations for classifying business organizations as associations (which are taxable as corporations under section 7701(a)(3)) or as partnerships under section 7701(a)(2) are based on the historical differences under local law between partnerships and corporations.

[Editor's note: The parenthetical material that follows appeared in the preamble to the proposed entity classification regulations.] (However, many states have revised their statutes to provide that partnerships and other unincorporated organizations may possess characteristics that traditionally have been associated with corporations, thereby narrowing considerably the traditional distinctions between corporations and partnerships under local law. For example, all states have enacted statutes allowing the formation of limited liability companies. These entities provide protection from liability to all members but may qualify as partnerships for federal tax purposes under the existing regulations.

One consequence of the increased flexibility under local law in forming a partnership or other unincorporated business organization is that taxpayers generally can achieve partnership tax classification for a nonpublicly traded organization that, in all meaningful respects, is virtually indistinguishable from a corporation. To accomplish this, however, taxpayers and the IRS must expend considerable resources on classification issues. Small business organizations may lack the resources and expertise to achieve the tax classification they want under the current classification regulations.

In light of these developments, Treasury and the IRS believe that it is appropriate to replace the increasingly formalistic rules under the current regulations with a much simpler approach that generally is elective.)

* * *

Summary of Regulations

Section 301.7701–1 provides an overview of the rules applicable in determining an organization's classification for federal tax purposes. * * *

Section 301.7701–2 clarifies that business entities that are classified as corporations for federal tax purposes include corporations denominated as such under applicable law, as well as associations [and] joint-stock companies * * *.

Any business entity that is not required to be treated as a corporation for federal tax purposes (referred to in the regulation as an "eligible entity") may choose its classification under the rules of § 301.7701–3. Those rules provide that an eligible entity with at least two members can be classified as either a partnership or an association, and that an eligible entity with a single owner can be classified as an association or can be disregarded as an entity separate from its owner.

In order to provide most eligible entities with the classification they would choose without requiring them to file an election, the regulations provide default classification rules that aim to match taxpayers' expectations (and thus reduce the number of elections that will be needed). The regulations adopt a passthrough default for domestic entities, under which a newly formed eligible entity will be classified as a partnership if it has at least two members, or will be disregarded as an entity separate from its owner if it has a single owner. * * * An entity's default classification continues until the entity elects to change its classification by means of an affirmative election.

An eligible entity may affirmatively elect its classification on Form 8832, Entity Classification Election. * * *

NOTES

1. *Proposed treatment of certain corporations as partnerships for tax purposes.* Under current law, partnership tax treatment is confined to certain non-corporate enterprises. See I.R.C. § 7701(a)(2). Whether Congress will ever allow some corporations to be taxed as partnerships remains to be seen.

2. *S Corporation versus LLC.* Both a corporation and an LLC offer limited liability to all owners of the enterprise. Moreover, many of the tax advantages that result because an LLC is taxed as a partnership can also be obtained when a corporation is taxed as an S Corporation. An LLC offers far greater flexibility, however, than a corporation subject to the constraints of Subchapter S.

An LLC may have more than 100 members, and may have members that would otherwise be ineligible shareholders for an S Corporation. An LLC may also issue a wider variety of ownership interests than an S Corporation which is subject to the one-class of stock rule (I.R.C. § 1361(b)(1)(D)). In addition, the members of an LLC have much greater flexibility when allocating the enterprise's income and loss among themselves than the shareholders of an S Corporation who are bound by the rigid pro rata share allocation rule (I.R.C. § 1377(a)(1)).

3. *Benefit of partnership tax treatment may not always outweigh cost.* Circumstances can exist where it will be desirable for an unincorporated enterprise to be taxed as a corporation. For example, IRS Letter Ruling 9740011 (6/30/97) involved an LLC governed by a state law that exempted manufacturing corporations (but not partnerships) from the state's personal property tax. The treatment of the LLC under state law was determined by its Federal tax classification. Thus, the LLC elected to be taxed as a corporation for Federal income tax purposes to qualify for the exemption from the state's personal property tax.

4. *Single member LLC.* Every state now permits single member LLCs. Under the entity classification regulations, an LLC owned by a single member is not treated as an entity separate from its owner unless an election is made to classify the LLC as an association taxable as a corporation. In no event is a single member LLC taxed as a partnership. What are the consequences when a single member LLC becomes an entity with more than one owner? See Revenue Ruling 99–5 which follows.

Revenue Ruling 99–5

1999–1 Cum.Bull. 434.

ISSUE

What are the federal income tax consequences when a single member limited liability company (LLC) that is disregarded for federal tax purposes as an entity separate from its owner under § 301.7701–3 of the Regulations becomes an entity with more than one owner that is classified as a partnership for federal tax purposes?

FACTS

In each of the following two situations, an LLC is formed and operates in a state which permits an LLC to have a single owner. Each LLC has a single owner, A, and is disregarded as an entity separate from its owner for federal tax purposes under § 301.7701–3. * * * For the sake of simplicity, it is assumed that neither LLC is liable for any indebtedness, nor are the assets of the LLCs subject to any indebtedness.

Situation 1. B, who is not related to A, purchases 50% of A's ownership interest in the LLC for $5,000. A does not contribute any portion of the $5,000 to the LLC. A and B continue to operate the business of the LLC as co-owners of the LLC.

Situation 2. B, who is not related to A, contributes $10,000 to the LLC in exchange for a 50% ownership interest in the LLC. The LLC uses all of the contributed cash in its business. A and B continue to operate the business of the LLC as co-owners of the LLC.

After the sale, in both situations, no entity classification election is made under § 301.7701–3(c) to treat the LLC as an association for federal tax purposes.

* * *

HOLDING(S)

Situation 1. In this situation, the LLC, which, for federal tax purposes, is disregarded as an entity separate from its owner, is converted to a partnership when the new member, B, purchases an interest in the disregarded entity from the owner, A. B's purchase of 50% of A's ownership interest in the LLC is treated as the purchase of a 50% interest in each of the LLC's assets, which are treated as held directly by A for federal tax purposes. Immediately thereafter, A and B are treated as contributing their respective interests in those assets to a partnership in exchange for ownership interests in the partnership.

Under § 1001, A recognizes gain or loss from the deemed sale of the 50% interest in each asset of the LLC to B.

Under § 721(a), no gain or loss is recognized by A or B as a result of the conversion of the disregarded entity to a partnership.

* * *

Situation 2. In this situation, the LLC is converted from an entity that is disregarded as an entity separate from its owner to a partnership when a new member, B, contributes cash to the LLC. B's contribution is treated as a contribution to a partnership in exchange for an ownership interest in the partnership. A is treated as contributing all of the assets of the LLC to the partnership in exchange for a partnership interest.

Under § 721(a), no gain or loss is recognized by A or B as a result of the conversion of the disregarded entity to a partnership.

* * *

NOTE

Limited liability partnerships. Every state has enacted legislation that enables a general partnership to become a limited liability partnership ("LLP"). In contrast to LLC legislation, which creates an entirely new legal form, LLP legislation generally amends state partnership law to enable general partners to insulate themselves from tort liabilities of the partnership, including malpractice claims against other partners. Thus, the LLP appeals to professionals wishing to protect their personal assets from malpractice claims against their partners. Many LLP statutes also insulate the partners from contract claims against the partnership.

2. PUBLICLY TRADED PARTNERSHIPS

I.R.C. § 7704

Treas. Reg. § 1.7704–1(a)–(e), (h), (j)

Prior to the 1980's, few analysts envisioned the possibility of utilizing the partnership form for the profitable, widely-held enterprise. Historically, the partnership form was confined to enterprises whose proprietary interests were held indefinitely by a small number of participating owners or investors, rather than frequently traded among members of the public. During the 1980's, the relative tax burdens imposed on C Corporations increased dramatically. See pp. 6–8. As a result, tax savings could often be achieved by using the partnership form. These circumstances motivated creative advisors to explore the viability of utilizing the partnership form for the publicly traded enterprise. Although certain practical problems existed, several publicly traded partnerships were operating by the mid–1980's. In response to concerns that use of the partnership form by publicly traded enterprises would undermine the revenue generating potential of the corporate tax, Congress enacted I.R.C. § 7704 in 1987.

Under I.R.C. § 7704(a), a "publicly traded" partnership is taxed as a corporation. The statute defines "publicly traded" as "traded on an established securities market, or * * * readily tradable on a secondary market (or the substantial equivalent thereof)." I.R.C. § 7704(b). Partnership interests are tradable on a secondary market or the substantial equivalent thereof if, based on all the facts and circumstances, the partners are readily able to buy, sell, or exchange their partnership interests in a manner that is comparable, economically, to trading on an established securities market. Treas. Reg. § 1.7704–1(c)(1). The regulations delineate several sets of circumstances where partnership interests are tradable on a secondary market or the substantial equivalent thereof. See Treas. Reg. § 1.7704–1(c)(2). Publicly traded status generally cannot occur, however, unless the partnership participates in the establishment of the market or recognizes transfers made on the market. See Treas. Reg. § 1.7704–1(d).

The regulations provide certain safe harbors that insure against publicly traded partnership status. Publicly traded partnership status will not be imposed on any partnership with as many as 100 partners if all interests in the partnership are issued in transactions not required to be registered under the Securities Act of 1933. See Treas. Reg. § 1.7704–1(h). Alternatively, publicly traded partnership status will be averted when the aggregate interests transferred during the taxable year do not exceed 2% of the total interests in partnership capital and profits. See Treas. Reg. § 1.7704–1(j). Certain private transfers, including the following, are excluded from the determination of whether the 2% threshold is met:

(a) transfers where the basis of the transferee's interest is determined with reference to the basis of the transferor;

(b) transfers at death;

(c) transfers between family members (as defined in I.R.C. § 267(c)(4));

(d) transfers involving the issuance of interests by the partnership;

(e) certain "block" transfers (i.e., transfers by a partner and any related persons within a 30 day period of interests representing more than 2% of partnership capital or profits);

(f) certain transfers pursuant to redemption or repurchase agreements;

(g) transfers by one or more partners of interests representing 50% or more of total partnership capital and profits in one or a series of related transactions.

See Treas. Reg. § 1.7704–1(e).

NOTES

1. *Opportunity versus trap.* Did attorneys who counseled their clients to form publicly traded partnerships perform a valuable service in light of the subsequent enactment of I.R.C. § 7704? (Note that I.R.C. § 7704 did not apply until 1998 to publicly traded partnerships in existence when the provision was enacted. Moreover, § 7704 still does not apply to a partnership that existed when § 7704 was enacted if the partnership elected to pay an annual tax of 3.5% of the partnership's gross income from all actively conducted trades and businesses beginning in 1998. See I.R.C. § 7704(g).)

2. *Passive income.* Why does § 7704 not cover certain partnerships that generate passive income? See I.R.C. § 7704(c).

3. *Evaluation of public trading standard.* Is "public trading" of interests in an enterprise a prudent standard for distinguishing between C Corporation and partnership tax treatment? What are the advantages and disadvantages of using this standard?

PART THREE

DISTRIBUTIONS

Part Two examined the tax consequences to a business and its owners when a business earns income or incurs losses. Part Three explores the tax consequences when a business physically transfers money or other property to its owners. The tax consequences of these transfers differ depending upon whether the business making the distribution is taxed as a C Corporation, an S Corporation, or a partnership.

Chapter 5 focuses on distributions by C Corporations. As a general rule, the distribution of profits by a C Corporation to its shareholders creates income to the shareholders (and no deduction to the corporation). Indeed, the tax paid by the shareholders on distributed corporate profits represents the second of the two taxes on C Corporation income. Chapters 6 and 7 focus on distributions by S Corporations and partnerships. In contrast to C Corporation distributions, the distribution of profits by an S Corporation or a partnership is generally tax-free to the owners because the owners were taxed when the business earned these profits.

It is convenient to approach the tax rules that govern distributions by distinguishing between a return *on* an individual's capital and the return *of* that person's capital. Most students were introduced to this perspective in the personal income tax course. For example, if Harry transfers possession of land he owns to Jill, a question might arise as to whether payments Jill makes to Harry represent rent (a return on property Harry still owns) or purchase price (a return of Harry's investment, and perhaps a profit, in exchange for all ownership rights). The answer to this question is likely to affect both the amount of Harry's income and the characterization of that income. If Harry originally bought the land for $100,000 and now receives payments from Jill totaling $180,000, what is the amount and character of Harry's income if the payments represent rent? See I.R.C. § 61(a)(5). What is the amount and character of Harry's income if the payments represent the purchase price of the land? See I.R.C. §§ 61(a)(3), 1001(a), 1221, 1231.

*

CHAPTER 5

C CORPORATION DISTRIBUTIONS

A "distribution" is a transfer of property made by a corporation to a shareholder in her capacity as an owner. Some distributions are treated as a return on the shareholder's investment (taxable in full as a dividend) while others are treated as a return of the shareholder's investment (taxable only to the extent the distribution exceeds the recipient's basis in her stock and as capital gain). The tax treatment of a corporate distribution is determined by how the distribution is classified. Every distribution falls into one of three classes: "one-side distribution", "redemption", or "liquidation".

A. ONE-SIDE DISTRIBUTION

The term "one-side distribution" describes the transfer of some (but not all) of a corporation's property to its shareholders in their capacity as owners where the shareholders do not surrender any of their stock to the distributing corporation. See I.R.C. § 301(a). A one-side distribution requires a transfer of "property". What is the meaning of the term "property" for this purpose? See I.R.C. § 317(a). In addition, the property must be transferred to each shareholder in her capacity as an owner, in contrast to some other capacity, such as that of an employee or a borrower.

The term "one-side distribution" is not found in the Internal Revenue Code. The term is used in this casebook as a matter of convenience to distinguish a distribution where some corporate property is transferred to shareholders who retain all of their stock from,

(a) a distribution where some of the corporation's property is transferred in exchange for some of the corporation's outstanding stock (a "redemption"), and

(b) a distribution where all of the corporation's property is transferred to its shareholders (a "liquidation").

1. DIVIDEND TO THE EXTENT OF EARNINGS & PROFITS

I.R.C. § 301

Treas. Reg. § 1.301–1(a)–(c)

A one-side distribution is generally treated as a return on the shareholder's investment (i.e., her stock in the distributing corporation). By definition, the shareholder receives property from the corporation in her capacity as a shareholder and she retains all of her shares. Because the shareholder does not transfer any of her shares to the distributing corporation, it is difficult to envision how a one-side distribution could ever represent the return *of* a shareholder's investment. If, however, the corporation never generated income (or previously distributed all of its profits), a one-side distribution will represent a return of the shareholder's original investment in the corporation.

The tax law distinguishes between one-side distributions that represent a return *on* a shareholder's capital from those that represent a return *of* the shareholder's capital by using a corporate level account referred to as "earnings and profits" ("E & P"). If the one-side distribution does not exceed the corporation's E & P, the distribution is designated a "dividend" and is taxed in full, generally at capital gains rates. See I.R.C. §§ 1(h)(11), 301(c)(1), 316(a).[1] To the extent that a one-side distribution exceeds the corporation's E & P, it is taxed as a return of the shareholder's investment (i.e., taxable only to the extent it exceeds the recipient's stock basis and as capital gain). See I.R.C. § 301(c)(2), (3).[2]

One-side distributions and dividends are not synonymous. You now know that not all one-side distributions are treated as dividends. Later in this chapter, you will learn that not all dividends result from one-side distributions.

a.   CONCEPTUALIZING EARNINGS & PROFITS

Notwithstanding the substantive significance of "earnings & profits," the term is not defined in the Internal Revenue Code. E & P is not equivalent to taxable income. The scope of E & P is broader than taxable income, in the sense that it includes receipts excluded from gross income (e.g., tax-exempt interest). The scope of E & P is also narrower than taxable income, in the sense that it is offset by disbursements not allowed as deductions in the computation of taxable income (e.g., payments of Federal income tax). A rough approximation of E & P is as follows:

	Taxable Income
Plus:	Excluded Receipts
Minus:	Nondeductible Disbursements

NOTES

1. *Asset appreciation.* Any difference between the value of a corporate asset and the corporation's adjusted basis in that asset is not included in "earnings & profits" until the gain is realized and recognized. See I.R.C. § 312(f)(1). Is this rule defensible? See I.R.C. § 1001.

---

1. The scope of a dividend for Federal income tax purposes often deviates from the scope of a dividend for corporate law purposes. For a discussion of dividends for corporate law purposes, see Harry G. Henn & John R. Alexander, *Laws of Corporations* Chap. 12 (3d ed. 1983 & Supp. 1986).

2. For persuasive critiques of the earnings & profits concept, see William Andrews, " 'Out of Its Earnings and Profits': Some Reflections on the Taxation of Dividends," 69 Harvard Law Review 1403 (1956); Walter Blum, "The Earnings and Profits Limitation on Dividend Income: A Reappraisal," 53 Taxes 68 (1975).

2. *Borrowed funds.* Borrowed funds are not normally included in E & P. Why not?

3. *Cash versus E & P.* Acme Corporation has $2,000,000 of cash. Is it possible that Acme has,

    (a) less than $2,000,000 of E & P?

    (b) more than $2,000,000 of E & P?

Can a corporation with no cash have E & P?

4. *Assets versus E & P.* Beta Corporation has cash of $2,000,000, inventory worth $2,000,000, plant and equipment worth $2,000,000, and E & P of $2,000,000. Beta owns nothing of value aside from the foregoing items. What is the total value of Beta's assets?

b.   QUANTIFYING EARNINGS & PROFITS

I.R.C. §§ 312(a)–(c), 316(a)

Treas. Reg. §§ 1.312–6(a), (b), 1.316–1(a)(1), (e), –2(a), (b), (c)

A corporation's E & P must be calculated to determine the amount of a one-side distribution that represents a dividend. The statute treats distributions as first made from current year E & P, then from E & P accumulated prior to the current year. See I.R.C. § 316(a) (second sentence). Current year E & P is calculated at the end of the tax year, not when the distribution is made. I.R.C. § 316(a)(2) (parenthetical language).

Determining the amount of a distribution that represents a dividend is a relatively simple matter when a corporation has both current year E & P and accumulated E & P from prior years (see Rev. Rul. 74–164, Situation 1). Matters often become more complicated when the distributing corporation enters the year of the distribution with a deficit in its E & P account (see Rev. Rul. 74–164, Situation 2) or has an E & P deficit for the year of the distribution (see Rev. Rul. 74–164, Situation 3).

Revenue Ruling 74–164

1974–1 Cum.Bull. 74.

X corporation and Y corporation each using the calendar year for Federal income tax purposes made distributions of $15,000 to their respective shareholders on July 1, 1971, and made no other distributions to their shareholders during the taxable year. The distributions were taxable as provided by section 301(c) of the Internal Revenue Code of 1954.

Situation 1

At the beginning of its taxable year 1971, X corporation had earnings and profits accumulated after February 28, 1913, of $40,000. It had an operating loss for the period January 1, 1971 through June 30, 1971, of $50,000 but had earnings and profits for the entire year 1971 of $5,000.

Situation 2

At the beginning of its taxable year 1971, Y corporation had a deficit in earnings and profits accumulated after February 28, 1913, of $60,000. Its net profits for the period January 1, 1971 through June 30, 1971, were $75,000 but its earnings and profits for the entire taxable year 1971 were only $5,000.

Situation [3]

Assume the same facts as in Situation 1 except that X had a deficit in earnings and profits of $55,000 for the entire taxable year 1971.

* * *

Section 316(a) of the Code provides that the term "dividend" means any distribution of property made by a corporation to its shareholders out of its earnings and profits accumulated after February 28, 1913, or out of its earnings and profits of the taxable year computed as of the close of the taxable year without diminution by reason of any distribution made during the year, and *without regard to the amount of earnings and profits at the time the distribution was made.*

Section 1.316–2(a) of the Income Tax Regulations provides, in part, that in determining the source of a distribution, consideration should be given first, to the earnings and profits of the taxable year; and second, to the earnings and profits accumulated since February 28, 1913, only in the case where, and to the extent that, the distributions made during the taxable year are not regarded as out of the earnings and profits of that year.

Applying the foregoing principles, in Situation 1, the earnings and profits of X corporation for the taxable year 1971 of $5,000 and the earnings and profits accumulated since February 28, 1913, and prior to the taxable year 1971, of $40,000 were applicable to the distribution paid by it on July 1, 1971. Thus, $5,000 of the distribution of $15,000 was paid from the earnings and profits of the taxable year 1971 and the balance of $10,000 was paid from the earnings and profits accumulated since February 28, 1913. Therefore, the entire distribution of $15,000 was a dividend within the meaning of section 316 of the Code.

In Situation 2 the earnings and profits of Y corporation for the taxable year 1971 of $5,000 were applicable to the distribution paid by Y corporation on July 1, 1971. Y corporation had no earnings and profits accumulated after February 28, 1913, available at the time of the distribution. Thus, only $5,000 of the distribution by Y corporation of $15,000 was a dividend within the meaning of section 316 of the Code. The balance of such distribution, $10,000 which was not a dividend, applied against and reduced the adjusted basis of the stock in the hands of the shareholders, and to the extent that it exceeded the adjusted basis of the stock was gain from the sale or exchange of property.

In the case of a deficit in earnings and profits for the taxable year in which distributions are made, the taxable status of distributions is dependent upon the amount of earnings and profits accumulated since February 28, 1913, and available at the dates of distribution. In determining the amount of such earnings and profits, section 1.316–2(b) of the regulations provides, in effect, that the deficit in earnings and profits of the taxable year will be prorated to the dates of distribution.

Applying the foregoing to Situation [3], * * * the distribution paid by X corporation on July 1, 1971, * * * was a dividend within the meaning of section 316 of the Code to the extent indicated as follows:

* * *

Situation [#3]

Accumulated E & P 1/1	$40,000
E & P deficit for entire taxable year ($55,000). Prorate to date of distribution 7/1 (½ of $55,000)	(27,500)
E & P available 7/1	12,500
Distribution 7/1 ($15,000)	(12,500) taxable as a dividend
E & P deficit from 7/1–12/31	(27,500)
Accumulated E & P balance 12/31	(27,500)

NOTES

1. *Conflict with regulation.* In Situation 3, Rev. Rul. 74–164 cites Treas. Reg. § 1.316–2(b) as authority for prorating earnings and profits to the date of the distribution. That regulation provides, in relevant part, as follows:

> In any case in which it is necessary to determine the amount of earnings and profits accumulated since February 28, 1913, *and the actual earnings and profits to the date of a distribution within any taxable year * * * cannot be shown,* the earnings and profits for the year * * * in which the distribution was made shall be prorated to the date of the distribution * * *. [Emphasis added.]

In light of the emphasized language of the regulation, what should be the tax consequences of Situation 3?

2. *Deficit in E & P.* Can a one-side distribution create a deficit in E & P? Can a corporate operating loss create a deficit in E & P? Consider the following excerpt from DeNiro v. Commissioner, 60 T.C.M. 300, 306–307 (1990):

> [P]etitioners admit that they did not know what [the corporation's] accumulated E & P balance was from 1955 through [1967]. Therefore, Mr. Rogan [the corporation's accountant] *presumed* the retained earnings account was representative of the accumulated E & P account and treated it accordingly.

> The term "earnings and profits" is not defined in the Internal Revenue Code, and does not correspond exactly to taxable income or any corporate accounting concepts, i.e., retained earnings. Thus, a corpora-

tion's retained earnings does not necessarily reflect its "earnings and profits".

The most flagrant mistake Mr. Rogan made, when computing accumulated E & P as of January 1, 1969, was using [the corporation's] December 31, 1967, retained earnings account as a starting point, i.e., a deficit $105,500. That deficit resulted from a 1967 [distribution], not an operating loss. A distribution cannot reduce E & P below zero. Sec. 312(a). Even if we assume [the corporation's] retained earnings account, as of January 1, 1967, properly reflected accumulated E & P, accumulated E & P as of January 1, 1968, would be zero, not a deficit of $105,500 * * *.

3. *One-side distribution of money.* What impact does a one-side distribution of money have on E & P? See I.R.C. § 312(a)(1).

4. *One-side distribution of property, other than money.* When a corporation distributes property with a value in excess of basis, the distributing corporation's E & P is increased by the amount of the gain in the property. I.R.C. § 312(b)(1). Why is E & P increased by the gain? See I.R.C. § 311(b); pp. 29–33. In addition to increasing E & P by the gain in the distributed property, E & P is reduced by the value of the property (to the extent the distribution is treated as a dividend). I.R.C. §§ 312(a)(3), (b)(2). By contrast, when a corporation distributes property with a value that does not exceed its basis, E & P is reduced by the adjusted basis of the distributed property. I.R.C. § 312(a)(3).

> *Problem 5–1 (One-side distribution of money).* Jacob is the sole shareholder of Benedum, Inc. Jacob has a basis of $10,000 in his Benedum stock. Benedum commenced operations on January 1 of Year 1. Benedum's E & P for each of its first four years of operations is as follows:
>
> | | |
> |---|---|
> | Year 1 | ($100,000) |
> | Year 2 | 60,000 |
> | Year 3 | 70,000 |
> | Year 4 | (30,000) |

(a) Benedum distributed $50,000 to Jacob on May 1 of Year 1. What are the tax consequences of the distribution to Jacob? What is the amount of Benedum's accumulated E & P at the end of Year 1, Year 2, Year 3, and Year 4?

(b) Rather than distributing $50,000 to Jacob in Year 1, Benedum distributed $50,000 to Jacob on May 1 of Year 2. What are the tax consequences of the distribution to Jacob? What is the amount of Benedum's accumulated E & P at the end of Year 1, Year 2, Year 3, and Year 4?

(c) Rather than distributing $50,000 to Jacob in Year 2, Benedum distributed $50,000 to Jacob on May 1 of Year 3. What are the tax consequences of the distribution to Jacob? What is the amount of Benedum's accumulated E & P at the end of Year 2, Year 3, and Year 4?

(d) Rather than distributing $50,000 to Jacob in Year 3, Benedum distributed $50,000 to Jacob on May 1 of Year 4. What are the tax consequences of the distribution to Jacob? What is the amount of Benedum's accumulated E & P at the end of Year 3 and Year 4?

Problem 5–2 (One-side distribution of property other than money). Kerry purchased all the stock of Catalina Corporation for $90,000 during Year 4. At the end of Year 4, Catalina has accumulated E & P of zero. During Year 5, Catalina does not engage in any operating activity but Catalina distributes one of the items described below to Kerry. What are the tax consequences to Catalina and Kerry and what is Catalina's accumulated E & P at the end of Year 5 if the item that Catalina distributes is,

(a) a parcel of land with a market value of $500,000 in which Catalina has a basis of $100,000? See I.R.C. §§ 301, 311(b), 312(a), (b).

(b) 2,000 shares of XYZ stock with a market value of $130,000 in which Catalina has a basis of $300,000? See I.R.C. §§ 301, 311(a)(2), 312(a)(3).

(c) 2,000 shares of stock of Catalina Corporation? See I.R.C. §§ 317(a), 301(a), 305(a), 311(a)(1).

c. QUALIFIED DIVIDEND INCOME

I.R.C. § 1(h)(11)

Prior to 2003, dividends received by individuals were taxed in full as ordinary income. By contrast, one-side distributions in excess of earnings & profits were taxed only in part (to the extent the amount of the distribution exceeded the distributee's stock basis) and as capital gain. I.R.C. §§ 301(c)(2), (3). Thus, before 2003, a one-side distribution constituting a dividend normally resulted in:

    1. a larger amount of income,

    2. taxed at a higher rate,

than a one-side distribution in excess of earnings & profits.

A one-side distribution constituting a dividend still generally results in a greater amount of shareholder income than a one-side distribution in excess of earnings & profits because dividends may not be offset by the recipient's stock basis. Until the end of 2012, however, dividends received by an individual are generally taxed at the preferential rates that apply to an individual's capital gains. I.R.C. § 1(h)(11).[3] Thus, both dividends and capital gains are now generally taxed at a 15% rate. I.R.C. §§ 1(h)(1), (11)(A).

Although dividends are now generally taxed at preferential capital gains rates, **dividends are not characterized as capital gains.** See

---

3. Taxing dividends at capital gains rates has been estimated to cost the government between $66 billion and $90 billion per year. See Joint Committee on Taxation, Estimates of Federal Tax Expenditures for Fiscal Years 2010–2014 (December 15, 2010).

I.R.C. § 1(h)(11)(A). This distinction is important in the case of an individual shareholder with capital losses. An individual with capital losses may not apply those losses against dividend income. I.R.C. §§ 1(h)(11), 1211(b). By contrast, an individual's capital losses can be applied against the capital gains that result when a distribution exceeds the distributing corporation's earnings & profits and the shareholder's stock basis. I.R.C. §§ 301(c)(3), 1211(b).

Normally, for an individual to be eligible for the 15% capital gains rate, the gain must be derived from property held for more than one year. I.R.C. §§ 1(h)(1)(C), 1222. Yet, dividends received with respect to stock held less than a year qualify for the 15% capital gains rate. I.R.C. § 1(h)(11)(A). To qualify for the 15% tax rate, however, the dividend must constitute "qualified dividend income." I.R.C. § 1(h)(11)(B). To receive "qualified dividend income," the shareholder must have held the underlying stock for at least 61 days during the 121 day period beginning 60 days before the shares become "ex-dividend" (the date on which the shares no longer trade with the right to receive the most recently declared dividend). I.R.C. §§ 1(h)(11)(B)(iii)(I), 246(c).

Problem 5–3 (Stock holding requirement): Iz receives a dividend from Rodef Corporation. Assuming the dividend represents "qualified dividend income" if the stock holding requirement is met, will the dividend be taxed at capital gains rates if:

(a) Iz bought the stock on March 15 of Year 1, the ex-dividend date is March 16 of Year 1, and Iz sold the stock on May 14 of Year 1? I.R.C. §§ 1(h)(11)(B)(iii)(I), 246(c)(1), (3)(A).

(b) Iz bought the stock on March 15 of Year 1, the ex-dividend date is March 16 of Year 1, and Iz sold the stock on May 15 of Year 1? I.R.C. §§ 1(h)(11)(B)(iii)(I), 246(c)(1), (3)(A).

(c) Iz bought the stock on March 15 of Year 1, the ex-dividend date is May 14 of Year 1, and Iz sold the stock on May 15 of Year 1? I.R.C. §§ 1(h)(11)(B)(iii)(I), 246(c)(1), (3)(A).

NOTE

Importance of earnings & profits. Prior to 2003, the tax consequences of a one-side distribution constituting a dividend were dramatically different from the consequences of a one-side distribution in excess of earnings & profits. Now that dividends are normally taxed at capital gains rates, does the level of a corporation's earnings & profits still matter?

2. CAMOUFLAGED ONE–SIDE DISTRIBUTION

A shareholder might receive money or other property from a corporation for acting in a capacity other than that of an owner. A transfer of this type is not a distribution. Instead, the tax consequences are determined by the nature of the economic relationship that governs the transfer. For example, if a shareholder borrows money from the corporation, the borrowed funds are excluded from the shareholder's gross income. If a shareholder receives money for performing services on behalf of the corporation, the compensation is included in the shareholder's gross income, but can generally be deducted by the corporation. See pp. 38–46.

The tax consequences of a one-side distribution are generally more burdensome than the tax consequences of a transfer made in a non-shareholder capacity. The magnitude of the difference, however, has diminished considerably now that dividends received by individuals are generally taxed at capital gains rates. See I.R.C. § 1(h)(11)(A). If a shareholder receives a one-side distribution treated as a dividend, the dividend is included in the shareholder's gross income and taxed at capital gains rates, but cannot be deducted by the corporation. In contrast, a transfer in a non-shareholder capacity is generally either excluded from the shareholder's gross income (e.g., amounts borrowed from the corporation), or taxed to the shareholder as ordinary income but deducted by the corporation (e.g., compensation paid by the corporation). Thus, dividends bear both a corporate level tax (because they are not deductible) and a shareholder level tax (albeit at capital gains rates). By contrast, transfers in a non-shareholder capacity generally bear only one tax; either a corporate tax (e.g., nondeductible amounts borrowed from the corporation) or a shareholder tax at ordinary income rates (e.g., deductible compensation paid by the corporation).

Due to the greater tax burden imposed on one-side distributions, an incentive exists for shareholders to receive payments for acting in non-shareholder capacities, rather than to receive one-side distributions. In response to this incentive, the government often claims that transfers to shareholders purportedly made in non-shareholder capacities actually represent disguised one-side distributions that should be taxed as dividends.

a.   LOAN OR DISTRIBUTION

Jaques v. Commissioner

United States Court of Appeals, Sixth Circuit, 1991.
935 F.2d 104.

■ MARTIN, CIRCUIT JUDGE. * * *

[L]eonard C. Jaques is an attorney specializing in the practice of plaintiffs' class action law. In 1971, Jaques formed a professional corporation, Leonard C. Jaques, P.C. From the time of incorporation, Jaques has always been the sole shareholder of the corporation. Jaques' basis in the stock of the corporation was $20,000 * * *. Beginning in 1977 and continuing throughout the years in issue, Jaques began making withdrawals from the corporation. Jaques used the amounts withdrawn from the corporation during the years at issue to pay day-to-day personal living expenses. The following amounts were withdrawn:

Year Ended October 31	Amount
1983	$ 14,687
1984	275,682
1985	803,398

These withdrawals were reflected as "Accounts Receivable–Officer" by bookkeeping entries made on the books and records of the corporation. Jaques did not execute notes for these withdrawals nor was there a maturity date set for repayment. There was no collateral pledged as security for the repayment of the amounts withdrawn by Jaques. On its income tax returns, the corporation reflected the loans to stockholders as assets as follows:

Year Ended October 31	Amount
1983	$ 764,166.72
1984	1,007,119.02
1985	1,820,837.25

[D]uring each of the years in issue, the corporation paid Jaques a salary of $150,000. During 1984 and 1985, the corporation also reported on its W–2 Forms $37,093 and $131,416, respectively, as other compensation paid to Jaques for imputed interest on the withdrawals.

Jaques' personal financial statement prepared as of December 17, 1987, noted that "Leonard C. Jaques owes his law firm $2,645,000, but since the professional corporation stock is wholly owned by Leonard C. Jaques, the 'loan' is a wash." Jaques' personal financial statement prepared as of November 30, 1988, reflected loans payable to the corporation in the amount of $3,042,000. In the note to the financial statement, petitioner disclosed that, "The $3,042,000 represents monies I have borrowed over the years from the P.C. to be repaid whenever convenience may focus."

This case illustrates the tension which arises when individual professional practitioners are permitted to create separate corporate identities * * *. The taxpayer in this case, a lawyer by trade, like many accountants, physicians, architects, and other professionals, found it to be financially beneficial to incorporate his legal practice as a professional corporation. There is Leonard Jaques the private citizen and Leonard Jaques the professional corporation. In the eyes of the federal tax law, these are two separate taxable entities; in reality, they are a single individual. Not surprisingly, problems frequently arise when the two entities engage in transactions which have federal tax implications.

In the typical business context, business persons engage in business transactions with one another at arms-length. Therefore, it is usually safe to assume that a particular transaction is entered into because each party concludes that it is in his own self-interest to do so. This assumption breaks down, however, when the parties engaging in the transaction are in reality the same individual; the self-interest test usually employed to judge a contemplated transaction ceases to be applied by each party to the transaction. In this case, Leonard Jaques the professional corporation "loaned" Leonard Jaques the private citizen large amounts of money. Because in reality these transactions resulted in nothing more than Jaques lending himself his own money, it is very difficult to characterize the relationship between Jaques and his corporation as one of debtor and creditor. The potential for tax evasion is clear. A sole shareholder of a professional corporation could withdraw large sums from the corporation without incurring any tax liability simply by characterizing the withdrawals as loans, repayment of which could be postponed indefinitely.

The Tax Court determined that the amounts withdrawn by Jaques were not intended to be loans, but were taxable distributions under Section 316 of the Internal Revenue Code. The court found that Jaques failed to prove that the withdrawals were intended to be loans because he did not offer any "objective manifestations of contemporaneous intent to repay" other than his "own unsupported testimony." Other factors which the Tax Court relied upon in reaching its conclusion were: (1) the withdrawals were not represented by interest-bearing notes; (2) Jaques did not periodically repay the principal or interest; (3) the withdrawals were unsecured and were not subject to a fixed repayment schedule; (4) the withdrawals were in proportion to his holdings as the sole shareholder; and (5) the corporation had substantial current earnings but did not pay any dividends during this period.

Jaques argues that the Tax Court erred in finding that the withdrawals in question were constructive dividends and not loans * * *.

Whether the withdrawals made by Jaques from his professional corporation are treated for tax purposes as loans or dividends turns on the intention of the parties at the time the withdrawals were made. To determine whether the taxpayer intended to repay the withdrawals, courts have looked to a number of objective factors. The taxpayer's testimony that he intended to repay is one factor which is considered, but such self-serving testimony "can appropriately be viewed with some diffidence unless supported by other facts which bring the transaction much closer to a normal arms-length loan." * * *

Jaques * * * argues the Tax Court erred in holding that without a written loan agreement the advances he received from his corporation were presumptively dividends. However, the Tax Court's decision did not presume the advances were dividends and not loans merely because of the absence of a written loan agreement. The Tax Court simply cited the absence of a written loan agreement as one factor which helped illuminate the true intent of the parties. This was entirely proper.

To support his argument, Jaques cites Faitoute v. Commissioner, 38 B.T.A. 32 (1938). In that case, the Tax Court held that a sole stockholder's withdrawal of money from his corporation was a loan even though there was no written loan agreement, no security interest given, and no interest charged. The court held that the absence of these arrangements did not make the loan a dividend "if the money advanced was in good faith loaned by the corporation to the petitioner * * * ''. Jaques argues that Faitoute stands for the proposition that such factors as no written loan agreement, no repayment agreement, and no charged interest are irrelevant as a matter of law in determining the taxpayer's intent when repayments are made on the loans. Faitoute, however, seems to hold that the absence of these arrangements is not dispositive of the issue; it does not make them irrelevant.

Jaques next argues that the Tax Court erred in not according adequate consideration to his partial repayment of the loan proceeds in determining whether his withdrawals were legitimate loans. Jaques did repay approximately $48,000 of the $1,220,000 withdrawn during the years at issue. This repayment was addressed by the Tax Court and found to be "small" and "sporadic." The case which Jaques relies upon to support this argument * * * considered total repayment within a reasonable time as more indicative of the true arrangement than the absence of notes evidencing the corporation's indebtedness or maturity date for the repayment. There is no total repayment within a reasonable time in this case.

* * *

There is no doubt that a withdrawal by a controlling stockholder from his corporation can be considered a loan for federal income tax purposes. Something more is required, however, than the mere representations of the parties that the withdrawals were considered to be loans. There must be at least some evidence of the corporate formalities which usually accompany such transactions. Otherwise, a sole owner of a corporation could have his personal expenses paid by the corporation as a loan and postpone repayment indefinitely, thus escaping the double taxation which is normally incident to the corporate form. Because cases of this type are unique on their facts, we do not attempt to establish the line between those withdrawals that will be considered loans and those that will not. We simply note that the present case exceeds that line. We have little difficulty with the facts before us in affirming the decision of the Tax Court.

NOTES

1. *Factors for distinguishing loan from distribution.* A transfer of money to a shareholder will be treated as a loan, rather than as a distribution, if, at the time of the transfer, the shareholder intends to repay the amount received and the corporation intends to require repayment. The mere declaration by a shareholder that a withdrawal is intended to constitute a loan is not sufficient without more reliable indicia of a debt. Courts have considered various factors when deciding whether a withdrawal is a distribution or a loan; however, no single factor is determinative. The factors that courts have considered include the following:

(1) the extent to which the shareholder participates in the management of, and controls, the corporation;

(2) whether the corporation has a history of paying dividends;

(3) the existence of earnings and profits;

(4) the magnitude of the advances and whether a ceiling existed to limit the amount the corporation advanced;

(5) how the parties recorded the advances on their books and records;

(6) whether the parties executed notes;

(7) whether security was provided for the advances;

(8) whether there was a set maturity date;

(9) whether there was a fixed schedule of repayment;

(10) whether interest was paid or accrued;

(11) whether the shareholder made any repayments;

(12) whether the shareholder was in a position to repay the advances;

(13) whether the corporation ever attempted to force repayment; and

(14) whether the advances to the shareholder were made in proportion to his stock holdings.

See Piggy Bank Stations, Inc. v. Commissioner, 755 F.2d 450, 453 (5th Cir.1985); Alterman Foods, Inc. v. United States, 505 F.2d 873, 875–877 (5th Cir.1974); Cepeda v. Commissioner, 66 T.C.M. 1032 (1993), aff'd, 56 F.3d 1384 (5th Cir. 1995).

2. *Illustration of bona fide loan to shareholder.* While recognizing that "the question was close," the Tax Court held that a corporation's advances to a 50% shareholder were bona fide loans where: (1) the petitioner testified that he expected to repay all amounts advanced; (2) the advances were recorded on the company's books as accounts receivable and some were evidenced by notes; (3) the petitioner made substantial repayments to the company; (4) the amount of the loans to petitioner far exceeded the loans made to the other 50% shareholder of the company; and (5) the company had a deficit in E & P for all years in issue. Pierce v. Commissioner, 61 T.C. 424 (1974).

3. *Imputed interest.* In addition to paying Jaques an annual salary of $150,000, the professional corporation reported "other compensation paid to Jaques for imputed interest on the withdrawals." What was the purpose of reporting this item? See I.R.C. § 7872. How would you expect this item to have been reflected on the tax returns of Jaques and the corporation? What impact does the court's holding have on the tax reporting of this item?

4. *Corporate-level effect.* Did it make any difference to the corporation whether the transfers to Jaques were treated as loans or distributions? Are there any non-shareholder capacities in which a shareholder might receive value from a corporation where corporate level tax consequences would be affected if the transfers were treated as distributions? See pp. 38–59.

5. *Relevance of document prepared for non-tax purpose.* The court makes reference to a personal financial statement prepared for Jaques. Why is that statement relevant to the income tax issue addressed by the court?

How should a lawyer advise a client when a personal financial statement is prepared for a non-tax purpose (e.g., to secure a loan from a bank)? In light of the result in the Jaques case, should a plaintiffs' class action lawyer ever implement unreviewed income tax planning?

6. *Constructive dividends.* Camouflaged one-side distributions are often referred to as "constructive dividends". Is every camouflaged one-side distribution a "dividend?" See I.R.C. §§ 301(c), 316(a). Was the camouflaged distribution in Jaques really "constructive"? Keep this last question in mind when comparing the camouflaged distribution in Jaques to the camouflaged distributions in the cases that follow.

b. BUSINESS OR PERSONAL USE OF CORPORATE PROPERTY

Resenhoeft v. Commissioner

United States Tax Court, 1971.
56 T.C. 1225.

■ Withey, Judge: * * *

FINDINGS OF FACT

* * *

Nicholls, North, Buse Co., a Wisconsin corporation, hereinafter referred to as Nicholls, had its principal place of business in Milwaukee, Wis. * * *.

Petitioners Herbert A. Resenhoeft ["Resenhoeft"] and Charlotte Resenhoeft [are] husband and wife * * *.

Nicholls was engaged as a broker of foodstuffs * * *.

In 1964 the common-stock ownership, officers, and directors of Nicholls were as follows:

	Number of Common Shares			
Shareholders	Class A	Class B	Officer	Director
Herbert A. Resenhoeft	577	3,057	X	X
Charlotte Resenhoeft	264	1,088	X	X
Robert R. Resenhoeft		2,212	X	X
James Resenhoeft		2,212		X
Totals	841	8,569		

[T]he shares of class A common and class B common were identical in all respects except that the latter had no voting rights.

Nicholls has paid no dividends from its inception through the years in question.

Shareholders Robert R. Resenhoeft and James Resenhoeft * * * are the sons of petitioner Herbert Resenhoeft. In 1964, James was 25 years old and * * * was Nicholls' sales manager * * *. Robert and James received their stock through periodic gifts from Resenhoeft as well as by purchase.

Resenhoeft has been a principal stockholder since the company's beginning in 1921. During 1963 and 1964 in his capacity as president of Nicholls, Resenhoeft was required to meet customers, suppliers, and business associates.

* * *

Pea Picker III, the yacht at the center of this controversy, was a Chris Craft Constellation, a 52–foot wood-hulled cruiser with teak decks. It contained sleeping accommodations for passengers (two staterooms), and crew's quarters, as well as a bathroom and galley * * *.

Prior to the time of purchase of Pea Picker III, Resenhoeft was the owner of boats Pea Picker I and Pea Picker II. [P]ea Picker II was sold on August 24, 1964, the day following the date of final payment for Pea Picker III, to the distributor from whom Pea Picker III was purchased. The proceeds from the sale of Pea Picker II, $20,000, were paid by the purchaser to Resenhoeft who, by prior arrangement, loaned the same amount to Nicholls to aid in the purchase of Pea Picker III. This loan was to be repaid at a rate of $4,000 per year, beginning July 1, 1965. The payment due in 1965 was made on a timely basis.

[E]ach of Resenhoeft's sons was free to operate each of the crafts, including Pea Picker III, without special permission. Resenhoeft himself was unable to operate any of the three crafts and had little if any technical knowledge of their capacity or characteristics. James appears to have been the principal operator of all three boats, and was a boating enthusiast during 1964 and for several previous years.

Because of his experience with Pea Picker I and II and because of Resenhoeft's total unfamiliarity with such craft, it was James rather than Resenhoeft who negotiated the purchase of Pea Picker III * * *. The invoice was prepared in Nicholls' name for the total purchase price * * *.

Subsequent to the initial $3,000 deposit, paid by check drawn on Nicholls' account, but prior to the final payment of $57,000, also paid by check drawn on Nicholls' account, the Nicholls board of directors, in a special meeting, unanimously approved the purchase, stating in the resolution "any expenses incurred in the personal use of the boat are to be borne by H. A. Resenhoeft and an accurate log is to be kept of all business use." * * *

* * *

Following * * * a "shakedown" cruise * * * to acquaint the new operator with the handling characteristics of [the] boat and to disclose any possible deficiencies in its structure, engines, and equipment * * *, Pea Picker III was operated or used on no less than 9 days [in 1964] * * *. Of the 8 days remaining after excluding the [one-day] journey for storage, Pea Picker III was used as follows: The boat was admittedly limited to personal use by James on 2 of the 8 days; on 6 days, there was some use for business purposes * * *.

The use of the boat on dates in 1964 for business purpose ranged from having her tied to the dock but with guests aboard for drinks to using the boat for drinks and conversation on board in conjunction with local area cruises.

* * * On only one occasion was an entry made [in the log register] regarding business actually transacted * * *.

James' primary purpose for recording events in the log was to preserve what he believed to be an adequate record of actual operation of the boat and of the occasions on which business guests were on board * * *. For 1965, the log of the Pea Picker III indicates an increased effort to indicate the nature of the business transaction as well as the titles or employers of business guests.

Besides the events recorded in the official log, there were an unidentified number of days in 1964 during which James was aboard in the company of nonbusiness friends for periods of 1 to 3 hours. For the most part, these occasions took place not by design or advance planning but as a result of spur-of-the-moment invitations extended to friends present at the yacht club at times when James was on board for purposes of maintenance and upkeep.

The cost of Pea Picker III * * * was $68,290. Depreciation was taken for Federal income tax purposes in 1964 in the amount of $2,845. Operating expenses were incurred in the amount of $1,734 * * *. 25 percent of the combined depreciation and operating expense [($1,145) was attributed to personal use of the boat by Resenhoeft and reported as income on his personal tax return.] * * *

* * *

In the notice of deficiency * * * mailed to Resenhoeft, the respondent determined * * * that in 1964 Nicholls had "expended $68,879 on your behalf consisting of $68,290 to acquire a yacht and $589 as yacht expenses [$1,734 of total operating expenses less the $1,145 that Resenhoeft had already reported on his personal return] * * *."

* * *

OPINION

[T]he issues with regard to individual petitioner Resenhoeft resolve themselves down to the following: (a) Was there a constructive dividend; (b) may the use of the yacht by James, a stockholder in his own right, be imputed to his father who was in control of the corporation to make the father the recipient of the constructive dividend; and (c) is the measure of the dividend the purchase price of the craft plus actual operating expenses or is the fair rental value of the use of the yacht during the period in question the appropriate measure?

(a) It is well established that any expenditure made by a corporation for the personal benefit of its stockholders, or the making available of corporate-owned facilities to stockholders for their personal benefit, may result in the receipt by the stockholders of a constructive dividend * * *.

Upon consideration of all the evidence, including the possible instances of unrecorded personal use, we conclude that Pea Picker III was used for business purposes 25 percent and for personal purposes 75 percent of the time in 1964.

(b) Since we have found that there was personal use constituting under some circumstances a dividend, the next question is, to whom was the benefit directed? Resenhoeft has established by convincing evidence that he was not interested in the yacht for his own personal pleasure as a boating enthusiast. He had little knowledge of the workings of such craft, could not operate them himself, and played no direct part in the purchase of Pea Picker III or the sale of her predecessor. However, to the extent that he was present on an occasion of personal use, he received a benefit and an argument that others benefited as well is of no avail here. He shared in the friendships and joined in the social activity on board on those occasions.

The question remains, however, whether James' personal use of Pea Picker III on occasions when Resenhoeft was not present may nevertheless be attributed to Resenhoeft. The essential elements underlying the taxation of assigned income to the assignor were set down in Helvering v. Horst, 311 U.S. 112 (1940). The Court stated in that case that: "The power to dispose of income is the equivalent of 'ownership' of it and the exercise of that power to procure the payment of income to another is the 'enjoyment' and hence the 'realization' of the income by him who exercises it." In this case Resenhoeft personally owned well over 50 percent of all voting stock and together with his wife owned all of it, and in addition was the president of the company and on the board of directors. It is manifestly clear that it was Resenhoeft's decision that the corporation acquire Pea Picker III. Resenhoeft's decision to allow the use of the boat by his sons as they desired and without direct control over either the circumstances of use or the maintenance of appropriate supportive documentation must be given particular emphasis. There is no indication here that information regarding the actual use of the boat, or the type of records maintained, was being kept from Resenhoeft or that he had no way of learning the truth.

[W]e remain unpersuaded that Resenhoeft's purpose in agreeing to the acquisition of a large pleasure craft was only to benefit the corporation. This is particularly so in light of his prior personal ownership of Pea Pickers I and II which were available for the use and benefit of his sons. Once it is understood that Resenhoeft was in complete control of the events, the fact that James, the principal user of the boat for noncorporate purposes, was a mature adult and a shareholder in his own right becomes irrelevant.

(c) Although we have determined that there was a dividend, and that the dividend must be attributed to Resenhoeft, we have yet to ascertain the amount of the dividend. Two standards have been used on different occasions, the first being the initial cost of the facility and the second, the approximate rental value for the period at issue * * *. In Louis Greenspon, the Court held that continued corporate ownership of farm equipment used by the petitioner shareholder prevented the assessment of a constructive dividend based on the purchase price of the equipment. No determination of a dividend was made based on the rental value since respondent failed to raise that issue. Our holding in Greenspon that ownership of the asset is a principal factor has not been altered by subsequent cases involving the year an asset was acquired. Although in some cases subsequent to Greenspon we have determined the amount of the dividend to be the acquisition cost, in those cases the evidence clearly pointed to shareholder ownership * * *, or the location of title could not be determined and therefore was presumptively in the shareholder * * *. These cases have not been followed when the title was clearly with the corporation * * *.

In this case, ownership continued to rest with Nicholls. The bill of sale was made in Nicholls' name, Nicholls' principal creditor was informed of the purchase and the yacht's intended devotion to corporate purposes, a license to operate short-wave radio equipment installed on Pea Picker III was acquired in the corporate name, registration by U.S. Customs was attempted in the corporate name, registration and licensing was received from the State of Wisconsin in the corporate name, and sales tax was paid by the corporation although a significant savings would have resulted by treating this as a purchase by Resenhoeft. Although a listing in the Lake Michigan Yachting Association catalogue showed James as the owner of the Pea Picker III, the association provided no means for noting corporate ownership, and registration in whatever name offered values significant to the corporation as well as to James. Therefore we hold that petitioner has not received a constructive dividend equivalent to the cost of acquisition of Pea Picker III.

* * *

Respondent's alternative theory is that the fair rental value of Pea Picker III for the period of use in 1964 is the measure of the dividend received * * *. The amended answer alleged that the fair value was not less than Nicholls' combined depreciation and operating expenses, $4,579, of which $1,145 concededly was included as income by Resenhoeft at the time he filed his 1964 return. Since we have already determined that Resenhoeft should be charged with 75 percent of the total value of the use of the yacht rather than 100 percent as argued by respondent, the remaining amount actually in dispute is $2,289 * * *.

[U]pon considering all evidence, including the rental value of similar craft * * *, we hold that the full rental value of Pea Picker III for the period following the shakedown cruise and ending with the final storage of the boat was $4,000. Resenhoeft gained personal benefit and therefore received a constructive dividend from his own use and the use of the craft by his sons equaling 75 percent of the above rental value; of that amount he has voluntarily recognized income to the extent of $1,145. We have no reason to believe Nicholls' earnings and profits were insufficient for the payment of a taxable dividend of the amount determined above.

NOTES

1. *Amount of income.* How much additional income did the Internal Revenue Service claim should have been reported by the taxpayer? As a result of the court's holding, how much additional income did the taxpayer have to report?

2. *Pivotal issue.* What was the most important factual question in the Resenhoeft case? Which side prevailed on that issue? Why?

3. *Absence of earnings & profits.* If the corporation in Resenhoeft had no earnings & profits, would it have mattered whether the court had determined that the corporate funds used to purchase the yacht had been expended for the shareholders' benefit? See Boulware v. United States, which follows.

Boulware v. United States

Supreme Court of the United States, 2008.
552 U.S. 421, 128 S.Ct. 1168.

■ JUSTICE SOUTER delivered the opinion of the Court.

Sections 301 and 316(a) of the Internal Revenue Code set the conditions for treating certain corporate distributions as returns of capital, nontaxable to the recipient. The question here is whether a distributee accused of criminal tax evasion may claim return-of-capital treatment without producing evidence that either he or the corporation intended a capital return when the distribution occurred. We hold that no such showing is required.

I

"[T]he capstone of [the] system of sanctions . . . calculated to induce . . . fulfillment of every duty under the income tax law," is 26 U.S.C. § 7201, making it a felony willfully to "attemp[t] in any manner to evade or defeat any tax imposed by" the Code. One element of tax evasion under § 7201 is "the existence of a tax deficiency," which the Government must prove beyond a reasonable doubt. * * *

II

In this criminal tax proceeding, petitioner Michael Boulware was charged with several counts of tax evasion and filing a false income tax return, stemming from his diversion of funds from Hawaiian Isles Enterprises (HIE), a closely held corporation of which he was the president, founder, and controlling (though not sole) shareholder. At trial, the United States sought to establish that Boulware had received taxable income by "systematically divert[ing] funds from HIE in order to support a lavish lifestyle." The Government's evidence showed that:

> [Boulware] gave millions of dollars of HIE money to his girlfriend . . . and millions of dollars to his wife . . . without reporting any of this money on his personal income tax returns. . . . [H]e siphoned off this money primarily by writing checks to employees and friends and having them return the cash to him, by diverting payments by HIE customers, by submitting fraudulent invoices to HIE, and by launder-

ing HIE money through companies in the Kingdom of Tonga and Hong Kong.

In defense, Boulware sought to introduce evidence that HIE had no retained or current earnings and profits in the relevant taxable years, with the consequence (he argued) that he in effect received distributions of property that must have been returns of capital, up to his basis in his stock. See § 301(c)(2). Because the return of capital was nontaxable, the argument went, the Government could not establish the tax deficiency required to convict him.

The Government moved to bar evidence in support of Boulware's return-of-capital theory, on the grounds of "irrelevan[ce] in [this] criminal tax case." The Government relied on the Ninth Circuit's decision in *United States* v. *Miller*, 545 F.2d 1204 (1976), in which that court held that in a criminal tax evasion case, a diversion of funds may be deemed a return of capital only after "some demonstration on the part of the taxpayer and/or the corporation that such [a distribution was] intended to be such a return." Boulware, the Government argued, had offered to make no such demonstration.

The District Court granted the Government's motion. * * * The jury * * * found him guilty of tax evasion and of filing a false return. The Ninth Circuit affirmed. * * * Judge Thomas concurred because the panel was bound by *Miller*, but noted that "*Miller*—and now the majority opinion—hold that a defendant may be criminally sanctioned for tax evasion without owing a penny in taxes to the government." That, he said, not only "indicate[s] a logical fallacy, but is in flat contradiction with the tax evasion statute's requirement * * * of a tax deficiency."

We granted certiorari to resolve a split among the Courts of Appeals over the application of §§ 301 and 316(a) to informally transferred or diverted corporate funds in criminal tax proceedings. We now vacate and remand.

III

A

The colorful behavior described in the allegations requires a reminder that tax classifications like "dividend" and "return of capital" turn on "the objective economic realities of a transaction rather than . . . the particular form the parties employed." As for distributions with respect to stock, in economic reality a shareholder's informal receipt of corporate property "may be as effective a means of distributing profits among stockholders as the formal declaration of a dividend," or as effective a means of returning a shareholder's capital. * * *

There is no reason to doubt that economic substance remains the right touchstone for characterizing funds received when a shareholder diverts them before they can be recorded on the corporation's books. [E]ven diverted funds may be seen as dividends or capital distributions for purposes of §§ 301 and 316(a).

B

Miller's view that a criminal defendant may not treat a distribution as a return of capital without evidence of a corresponding contemporaneous intent sits uncomfortably not only with the tax law's economic realism, but with the particular wording of §§ 301 and 316(a), as well. As those sections are written, the tax consequences of a "distribution by a corporation with respect to its stock" depend, not on anyone's purpose to return capital or to get it back, but on facts wholly independent of intent: whether the corporation had earnings and profits, and the amount of the taxpayer's basis for his stock. * * *

[T]here is no criminal tax evasion without a tax deficiency, and there is no deficiency owing to a distribution (received with respect to a corporation's stock) if a corporation has no earnings and profits and the value distributed does not exceed the taxpayer-shareholder's basis for his stock. Thus the fact that a shareholder distributee of a successful corporation may have different tax liability from a shareholder of a corporation without earnings and profits merely follows from the way §§ 301 and 316(a) are written (to distinguish dividend from capital return), and from the requirement of tax deficiency for a § 7201 crime. Without the deficiency there is nothing but some act expressing the will to evade, and, under § 7201, acting on "bad intentions, alone, [is] not punishable."

It is neither here nor there whether the *Miller* court was justified in thinking it would improve things to convict more of the evasively inclined by dropping the deficiency requirement and finding some other device to exempt returns of capital. Even if there were compelling reasons to extend § 7201 to cases in which no taxes are owed, it bears repeating that "[t]he spirit of the doctrine which denies to the federal judiciary power to create crimes forthrightly admonishes that we should not enlarge the reach of enacted crimes by constituting them from anything less than the incriminating components contemplated by the words used in the statute." If § 301, § 316(a), or § 7201 could stand amending, Congress will have to do the rewriting.

C

Not only is *Miller* devoid of the support claimed for it, but it suffers [an anomaly] of its own. [Sections] 301 and 316 are odd stalks for grafting a contemporaneous intent requirement, given the fact that the correct application of their rules will often become known only at the end of the corporation's tax year, regardless of the shareholder's or corporation's understanding months earlier when a particular distribution may have been made. Section 316(a)(2) conditions treating a distribution as a constructive dividend by reference to earnings and profits, and earnings and profits are to be "computed as of the close of the taxable year ... without regard to the amount of the earnings and profits at the time the distribution was made." A corporation may make a deliberate distribution to a shareholder, with everyone expecting a profitable year and considering the distribution to be a dividend, only to have the shareholder end up liable for no tax if the company closes out its tax year in the red (so long as the shareholder's basis covers the distribution); when such facts are clear at the time the reporting forms and returns are filed, the shareholder does not violate § 7201 by paying no tax on the moneys received, intent being beside the point. And since intent to make a distribution a taxable one cannot control, it would be odd to condition nontaxable return-of-capital treatment on contemporaneous intent, when the statute says nothing about intent at all.

* * *

IV

The Government has raised nothing that calls for affirmance in the face of the Court of Appeals' reliance on *Miller*. * * * The Government's argument, instead, is that we should affirm under the rule that before any distribution may be treated as a return of capital (or, by a parity of reasoning, a dividend), it must first be distributed to the shareholder "with respect to ... stock." The taxpayer's intent, the Government says, may be relevant to this limiting condition, and Boulware never expressly claimed any such intent.

The Government is of course correct that "with respect to ... stock" is a limiting condition in § 301(a). As the Government variously says, it requires that "the distribution of property by the corporation be made to a shareholder because of his ownership of its stock," and that " 'an amount paid by a corporation to a shareholder [be] paid to the shareholder in his capacity as such.' "

This, however, is not the time or place to hone in on the "with respect to ... stock" condition. Facts with a bearing on it may range from the distribution of stock ownership to conditions of corporate employment (whether, for example, a shareholder's efforts on behalf of a corporation amount to a good reason to treat a payment of property as salary). The facts in this case have yet to be raked over with the stock ownership condition in mind and if consideration is to be given to that condition now, the canvas of evidence and Boulware's proffer should be made by a court familiar with the whole evidentiary record.

* * *

But we decline to take up the question whether an unlawful diversion may ever be deemed a "distribution ... with respect to [a corporation's] stock," a question which was not considered by the Ninth Circuit. We do, however, reject the Government's current characterization of the jury verdict in Boulware's case. True, the jurors were not moved by Boulware's suggestion that the diversions were corporate advances or loans, or that he was using the funds for corporate purposes. But the jury was not asked, and cannot be said to have answered, whether Boulware breached any fiduciary duty as a controlling shareholder, unlawfully diverted corporate funds to defraud his wife, or embezzled HIE's funds outright.

V

[Sections] 301 and 316(a) govern the tax consequences of constructive distributions made by a corporation to a shareholder with respect to its stock. A defendant in a criminal tax case does not need to show a contemporaneous intent to treat diversions as returns of capital before relying on those sections to demonstrate no taxes are owed. The judgment of the Court of Appeals is vacated, and the case is remanded for further proceedings consistent with this opinion.

NOTES

1. *Shareholder's stock basis.* Of what relevance is the basis of Boulware's stock to his potential liability? See I.R.C. § 301(c)(2), (3).

2. *Capacity in which funds were withdrawn.* Of what relevance is the "with respect to stock" language of § 301(a) to the ultimate resolution of this controversy?

3. *The conviction stands.* On remand, the Ninth Circuit affirmed the conviction. United States v. Boulware, 558 F.3d 971 (9th Cir. 2009). Because Boulware had failed to provide evidence demonstrating a connection between the corporate distribution and his stock ownership, the District Court did not err by denying Boulware the opportunity to present a return of capital theory at trial.

c.   DISCHARGE OF CORPORATE OR PERSONAL OBLIGATION

Sullivan v. United States

United States Court of Appeals, Eighth Circuit, 1966.
363 F.2d 724.

■ STEPHENSON, DISTRICT JUDGE: * * *

[T]he taxpayer Sullivan purchased the assets of an automobile dealership in Blytheville, Arkansas in 1941. He then formed a corporation to operate the dealership * * *. [I]n September, 1948, Frank Nelson became the resident manager of the dealership under an arrangement which included an agreement permitting Nelson to acquire up to forty per cent of the stock and further providing for taxpayer's repurchase of said stock upon Nelson's termination of his employment. After acquiring approximately 38% of the corporation's outstanding stock, Nelson announced his intention to depart from his position in 1956 and offered to sell his stock to taxpayer Sullivan. The corporation's Board of Directors then authorized the [purchase of] Nelson's stock by the corporation. [The purchase by a corporation of its own stock is called a "redemption". See I.R.C. § 317(b).]

The ultimate question before the District Court involved a determination of whether the payment by the corporation in redemption of Nelson's stock constituted a taxable distribution to taxpayer Sullivan, the sole remaining stockholder of the corporation. The District Court found that taxpayer Sullivan was unconditionally and primarily obligated to purchase

Nelson's stock in 1956 and that said stock was purchased by the Corporation out of profits distributable as a dividend and therefore held that the taxpayer constructively received income equivalent to a dividend in the amount paid by the Corporation for said stock, ($198,334.58) * * *.

* * *

[T]he District Court was justified in concluding that Sullivan was unconditionally obligated to purchase Nelson's stock.

At this juncture, the payment by the corporation to Nelson presents [the following question]: Was that payment in actuality a dividend and therefore includable in Sullivan's gross income under §§ 61(a)(7), 316(a) and 301(c)(1) of the Internal Revenue Code? * * *

When an individual shareholder receives an economic benefit through a diversion of corporate earnings and profits, such a receipt may be taxed as a constructive dividend. This court set forth a criteria for determining whether a payment constitutes a constructive dividend in Sachs v. Commissioner of Internal Revenue, 277 F.2d 879, 882–883 (8th Cir.1960):

> The motive, or expressed intent of the corporation is not determinative, and constructive dividends have been found contrary to the expressed intent of the corporation. The courts, as arbiters of the true nature of corporate payments, have consistently used as a standard the measure of receipt of economic benefit as the proper occasion for taxation.
>
> * * *

The general net effect and the purpose of and circumstances surrounding the transaction involved herein must be carefully scrutinized to ascertain whether Sullivan received a taxable dividend. Prior to the transaction, Sullivan held approximately 62% of the shares outstanding while Nelson owned the remaining shares. As previously discussed, Sullivan was unconditionally obligated to purchase Nelson's stock if it was offered to him for sale. After the transaction was completed, the relevant facts were essentially as follows: (1) Sullivan's personal obligation had been discharged; (2) Sullivan owned all of the outstanding shares of stock of the corporation; (3) the corporation's assets were decreased by the amount paid to Nelson for his stock; and (4) Nelson's stock was held by the corporation as treasury stock. It is true that in terms of the financial worth of Sullivan's interest in the corporation, it was the same after the transaction as it was before. The transaction still resulted in an economic benefit to Sullivan, however, because he was relieved of his personal obligation to purchase Nelson's stock * * *. On the facts of this case, Sullivan received a taxable dividend as the result of the corporation's purchase of Nelson's stock.

This court is aware that it is often difficult to distinguish true substance from mere form. Tax law places some weight and significance on form and the choice of one alternative rather than another for achieving a desired end is often critical and may be determinative of the tax effect of a transaction. [The lower court's] opinion comprehensively deals with the evidence and the applicable law of this case. The taxpayer has failed to establish grounds for reversal * * *.

NOTE

Relation of wealth to income. What did the court mean when it concluded that Sullivan's "financial worth" was not increased by the corporation's purchase of Nelson's shares? Is this consideration relevant to whether Sullivan received income or was the court right to ignore it?

Revenue Ruling 69–608

1969–2 Cum.Bull. 43.

[W]here the stock of a corporation is held by a small group of people, it is often considered necessary to the continuity of the corporation to have the individuals enter into agreements among themselves to provide for the disposition of the stock of the corporation in the event of the resignation, death, or incapacity of one of them. Such agreements are generally recipro-cal among the shareholders and usually provide that on the resignation, death, or incapacity of one of the principal shareholders, the remaining shareholders will purchase his stock. Frequently such agreements are assigned to the corporation by the remaining shareholder and the corpora-tion actually redeems its stock from the retiring shareholder.

Where a corporation redeems stock from a retiring shareholder, the fact that the corporation in purchasing the shares satisfies the continuing shareholder's executory contractual obligation to purchase the redeemed shares does not result in a distribution to the continuing shareholder provided that the continuing shareholder is not subject to an existing primary and unconditional obligation to perform the contract and that the corporation pays no more than fair market value for the stock redeemed.

On the other hand, if the continuing shareholder, at the time of the assignment to the corporation of his contract to purchase the retiring shareholder's stock, is subject to an unconditional obligation to purchase the retiring shareholder's stock, the satisfaction by the corporation of his obligation results in a constructive distribution to him. The constructive distribution is taxable as a distribution under section 301 of the Internal Revenue Code of 1954.

If the continuing shareholder assigns his stock purchase contract to the redeeming corporation prior to the time when he incurs a primary and unconditional obligation to pay for the shares of stock, no distribution to him will result. If, on the other hand, the assignment takes place after the time when the continuing shareholder is so obligated, a distribution to him will result. While a pre-existing obligation to perform in the future is a necessary element in establishing a distribution in this type of case, it is not until the obligor's duty to perform becomes unconditional that it can be said a primary and unconditional obligation arises.

The application of the above principles may be illustrated by the situations described below.

Situation 1

A and B are unrelated individuals who own all of the outstanding stock of corporation X. A and B enter into an agreement that provides in the event B leaves the employ of X, he will sell his X stock to A at a price fixed by the agreement. The agreement provides that within a specified number of days of B's offer to sell, A will purchase at the price fixed by the agreement all of the X stock owned by B. B terminates his employment and tenders the X stock to A. Instead of purchasing the stock himself in accordance with the terms of the agreement, A causes X to assume the contract and to redeem its stock held by B. In this case, A had a primary and unconditional obligation to perform his contract with B at the time the contract was assigned to X. Therefore, the redemption by X of its stock held by B will result in a constructive distribution to A.

Situation 2

A and B are unrelated individuals who own all of the outstanding stock of corporation X. An agreement between them provides unconditionally that within ninety days of the death of either A or B, the survivor will purchase the decedent's stock of X from his estate. Following the death of B, A causes X to assume the contract and redeem the stock from B's estate.

The assignment of the contract to X followed by the redemption by X of the stock owned by B's estate will result in a constructive distribution to A because immediately on the death of B, A had a primary and unconditional obligation to perform the contract.

* * *

Situation 4

A and B owned all of the outstanding stock of X corporation. A and B entered into a contract under which, if B desired to sell his X stock, A agreed to purchase the stock or to cause such stock to be purchased. If B chose to sell his X stock to any person other than A, he could do so at any time. In accordance with the terms of the contract, A caused X to redeem all of B's stock in X.

At the time of the redemption, B was free to sell his stock to A or to any other person, and A had no unconditional obligation to purchase the stock and no fixed liability to pay for the stock. Accordingly, the redemption by X did not result in a constructive distribution to A.

Situation 5

A and B owned all of the outstanding stock of X corporation. An agreement between A and B provided that upon the death of either, X will redeem all of the X stock owned by the decedent at the time of his death. In the event that X does not redeem the shares from the estate, the agreement provided that the surviving shareholder would purchase the unredeemed shares from the decedent's estate. B died and, in accordance with the agreement, X redeemed all of the shares owned by his estate.

In this case A was only secondarily liable under the agreement between A and B. Since A was not primarily obligated to purchase the X stock from the estate of B, he received no constructive distribution when X redeemed the stock.

* * *

Situation 7

A and B owned all of the outstanding stock of X corporation. An agreement between the shareholders provided that upon the death of either, the survivor would purchase the decedent's shares from his estate at a price provided in the agreement. Subsequently, the agreement was rescinded and a new agreement entered into which provided that upon the death of either A or B, X would redeem all of the decedent's shares of X stock from his estate.

The cancellation of the original contract between the parties in favor of the new contract did not result in a constructive distribution to either A or B. At the time X agreed to purchase the stock pursuant to the terms of the new agreement, neither A nor B had an unconditional obligation to purchase shares of X stock. The subsequent redemption of the stock from the estate of either pursuant to the terms of the new agreement will not constitute a constructive distribution to the surviving shareholder.

NOTES

1. *Cross-purchase agreement versus redemption agreement.* As Revenue Ruling 69–608 indicates, it is common for the shareholders of a closely held corporation to enter into an agreement that provides for the purchase of a shareholder's stock in the event of death, disability, termination of employment, and other designated triggering events involving a shareholder. An agreement of this type is often referred to as a "buy-sell agreement". Buy-sell agreements can be structured in two different ways. Either the corporation can purchase the stock of the departing shareholder when a triggering event occurs (a "redemption agreement") or the continuing shareholders can purchase the departing shareholder's stock (a "cross-purchase agreement"). Moreover, a combination agreement can be utilized whereby certain triggering events cause the corporation to buy the stock and other events cause the continuing shareholders to purchase the stock.

Life insurance and lump-sum disability insurance are often used to provide the money to purchase a deceased or disabled shareholder's stock under a buy-sell agreement. When a buy-out is to be funded with insurance proceeds, a cross-purchase agreement may be preferable to a redemption agreement. When a cross purchase arrangement is used, the insurance proceeds are paid to the continuing shareholders who generally receive the proceeds tax-free. See I.R.C. §§ 101, 104–106. In contrast, if a redemption arrangement is utilized, the insurance proceeds are received by the corporation and may be taxed. Insurance proceeds add to the base on which the corporate alternative minimum tax is imposed. Thus, the receipt of insurance proceeds by a C Corporation can trigger a tax liability if the corporation is subject to the corporate alternative minimum tax. See pp. 65–66.

When a buy-out is triggered by an event that is not covered by insurance (e.g., termination of employment), a mandatory cross-purchase arrangement generally should not be utilized. See Rev. Rul. 69–608, Situation 1. How should the buy-out be structured under these circumstances?

2. *Continuing shareholder versus departing shareholder.* The Sullivan case and Rev. Rul. 69–608 address the tax consequences to the continuing shareholders when the corporation purchases shares of a departing shareholder. The next section addresses the tax consequences to the departing shareholder.

B. Redemption

In contrast to the term "one-side distribution," the term "redemption" is used by, and defined in, the Internal Revenue Code. A redemption occurs when a corporation acquires *its* stock from a shareholder in exchange for property. I.R.C. § 317(b).

Is a shareholder who receives a distribution in redemption of some (or all) of his shares treated as receiving a return *on* his investment or a return *of* his investment? Because the shareholder actually transfers shares to the distributing corporation, one might think that a redemption should always be treated as a return of the shareholder's investment (i.e., a sale of the transferred shares). In many cases, however, the surrender of shares does not significantly reduce the shareholder's ownership interest in the distributing corporation. In these circumstances, it is logical to equate the redemption to a one-side distribution and treat the shareholder as receiving a return on his investment (i.e., a dividend to the extent of the distributing corporation's E & P).

For example, assume that Paul, who owns all 100,000 of the outstanding shares of Paul's Chevrolet, Inc. ("PCI"), transfers 100 PCI shares to PCI in exchange for $1,000. The transaction is a redemption. See I.R.C. § 317(b). Yet, Paul's ownership interest in the corporation has not declined; he owns 100% of PCI both before and after the redemption. In these circumstances, the surrender of some of Paul's PCI shares is a meaningless gesture because he owns the entire company after the distribution, despite his surrender of the 100 shares. Consequently, the surrender of shares is ignored for tax purposes and the redemption is treated as a one-side distribution (i.e., the entire $1,000 is taxed as a dividend to the extent of PCI's E & P). See I.R.C. § 302(d).

By contrast, assume Nisa owns 100 shares of General Motors Corporation ("GM") that she wishes to sell. She instructs her broker to sell the shares and, by coincidence, GM happens to buy those shares. This transaction is also a redemption. See I.R.C. § 317(b). This redemption, however, entails the surrender of Nisa's entire ownership interest in GM and, not surprisingly, the tax law treats this redemption as a sale. As a result, the redemption proceeds are offset by Nisa's basis in the shares she surrenders and the resulting gain or loss is characterized as capital gain or capital loss. See I.R.C. §§ 302(a), (b)(3).

Although dividends received by individuals are now generally taxed at capital gains rates (see I.R.C. § 1(h)(11)), it often remains important to distinguish between a redemption treated as a sale and a redemption treated as a one-side distribution. When determining the amount of the redeemed shareholder's income, the redemption proceeds are offset by the basis in the redeemed shares if the redemption is treated as a sale, but not if the redemption results in a dividend. With regard to the character of the redeemed shareholder's income, if the shareholder has capital losses from other transactions, those capital losses can offset a capital gain resulting from a redemption treated as a sale but cannot offset a dividend. See I.R.C. § 1211(b). Finally, with regard to the timing of the redeemed shareholder's income, if payment of part or all of the redemption price is deferred until a later tax year, the shareholder can use the installment method to defer reporting taxable gain until the payments are received only if the redemption is treated as a sale. See I.R.C. § 453. Therefore, it often remains important to distinguish between a redemption treated as a sale and a redemption treated as a one-side distribution.

1.   DISTINGUISHING SALE FROM ONE–SIDE DISTRIBUTION

A redemption is treated as a sale if it reduces the shareholder's relative interest in the corporation to an extent that satisfies *any* of three alternative standards. I.R.C. § 302(a). Sale treatment results only if the redemption: (1) is "not essentially equivalent to a dividend," (2) is "substantially disproportionate," or (3) is "in complete redemption of all of the stock of the corporation owned by the shareholder." I.R.C. §§ 302(b)(1)–(3).[4] If the redemption does not satisfy any of these three standards, the surrender of shares is ignored and the redemption is treated as a one-side distribution. I.R.C. § 302(d).

a.   NOT ESSENTIALLY EQUIVALENT TO A DIVIDEND

I.R.C. § 302(b)(1)

Treas. Reg. § 1.302–2

The first standard for establishing sale treatment requires proof of a negative. The taxpayer must prove that the redemption is "not essentially equivalent to a dividend." I.R.C. § 302(b)(1). In contrast to the other two standards, the first standard is not an objective mechanism that enables the planner to know with certainty whether sale treatment will be achieved. Consequently, the first standard is rarely relied on when planning a redemption that is intended to qualify for sale treatment.

---

4. Sale treatment also results when the transaction represents a "partial liquidation" of the redeeming corporation. See I.R.C. § 302(b)(4). See p. 267, Note 3.

How much of a reduction in proportionate interest is necessary for a redemption to be "not essentially equivalent to a dividend?"

United States v. Davis

Supreme Court of the United States, 1970.
397 U.S. 301, 90 S.Ct. 1041.

■ Mr. Justice Marshall delivered the opinion of the Court.

In 1945, taxpayer and E.B. Bradley organized a corporation. In exchange for property transferred to the new company, Bradley received 500 shares of common stock, and taxpayer and his wife similarly each received 250 such shares. Shortly thereafter, taxpayer made an additional contribution to the corporation, purchasing 1,000 shares of preferred stock at a par value of $25 per share.

The purpose of this latter transaction was to increase the company's working capital and thereby to qualify for a loan previously negotiated through the Reconstruction Finance Corporation. It was understood that the corporation would redeem the preferred stock when the RFC loan had been repaid. Although in the interim taxpayer bought Bradley's 500 shares and divided them between his son and daughter, the total capitalization of the company remained the same until 1963. That year, after the loan was fully repaid and in accordance with the original understanding, the company redeemed taxpayer's preferred stock.

In his 1963 personal income tax return taxpayer did not report the $25,000 received by him upon the redemption of his preferred stock as income. Rather, taxpayer considered the redemption as a sale of his preferred stock to the company * * * under § 302 of the Internal Revenue Code of 1954 resulting in no tax since taxpayer's basis in the stock equaled the amount he received for it. The Commissioner of Internal Revenue, however, did not approve this tax treatment. According to the Commissioner, the redemption of taxpayer's stock was essentially equivalent to a dividend and was thus taxable [in its entirety] under §§ 301 and 316 of the Code. Taxpayer paid the resulting deficiency and brought this suit for a refund. The District Court ruled in his favor * * * and on appeal the Court of Appeals affirmed.

The Court of Appeals held that the $25,000 received by taxpayer was "not essentially equivalent to a dividend" within the meaning of that phrase in § 302(b)(1) of the Code because the redemption was the final step in a course of action that had a legitimate business (as opposed to a tax avoidance) purpose * * *.

I

The Internal Revenue Code of 1954 provides generally in §§ 301 and 316 for the tax treatment of distributions by a corporation to its shareholders; under those provisions, a distribution is includable in a taxpayer's gross income as a dividend out of earnings and profits to the extent such earnings exist. There are exceptions to the application of these general provisions, however, and among them are those found in § 302 involving certain distributions for redeemed stock. The basic question in this case is whether the $25,000 distribution by the corporation to taxpayer falls under that section—more specifically, whether its legitimate business motivation qualifies the distribution under § 302(b)(1) of the Code. Preliminarily, however, we must consider the relationship between § 302(b)(1) and the rules regarding the attribution of stock ownership found in § 318(a) of the Code.

Under subsection (a) of § 302, a distribution is treated as "payment in exchange for the stock," thus qualifying for [sale treatment] rather than [dividend] treatment, if the conditions contained in any one of the four paragraphs of subsection (b) are met. In addition to paragraph (1)'s "not essentially equivalent to a dividend" test, [sale] treatment is available where (2) the taxpayer's voting strength is substantially diminished [or] (3) his interest in the company is completely terminated * * *. [T]axpayer agrees that for the purposes of §§ 302(b)(2) and (3) the attribution rules of § 318(a) apply and he is considered to own the 750 outstanding shares of common stock held by his wife and children in addition to the 250 shares in his own name.

Taxpayer, however, argues that the attribution rules do not apply in considering whether a distribution is essentially equivalent to a dividend under § 302(b)(1). According to taxpayer, he should thus be considered to own only 25 percent of the corporation's common stock, and the distribution would then qualify under § 302(b)(1) since it was not pro rata or proportionate to his stock interest, the fundamental test of dividend equivalency. See Treas. Reg. § 1.302–2(b). However, the plain language of the statute compels rejection of the argument. In subsection (c) of § 302, the attribution rules are made specifically applicable "in determining the ownership of stock for purposes of this section." Applying this language, both courts below held that § 318(a) applies to all of § 302, including § 302(b)(1) * * *.

Against this weight of authority, taxpayer argues that the result under paragraph (1) should be different because there is no explicit reference to stock ownership as there is in paragraphs (2) and (3). Neither that fact, however, nor the purpose and history of § 302(b)(1) support taxpayer's argument. The attribution rules—designed to provide a clear answer to what would otherwise be a difficult tax question—formed part of the tax bill that was subsequently enacted as the 1954 Code. [T]he bill as passed by the House of Representatives contained no provision comparable to § 302(b)(1). When that provision was added in the Senate, no purpose was evidenced to restrict the applicability of § 318(a). Rather, the attribution rules continued to be made specifically applicable to the entire section, and we believe that Congress intended that they be taken into account wherever ownership of stock was relevant.

[W]e conclude, therefore, that the attribution rules of § 318(a) do apply; and, for the purposes of deciding whether a distribution is "not essentially equivalent to a dividend" under § 302(b)(1), taxpayer must be deemed the owner of all 1,000 shares of the company's common stock.

II

After application of the stock ownership attribution rules, this case viewed most simply involves a sole stockholder who causes part of his shares to be redeemed by the corporation. We conclude that such a redemption is always "essentially equivalent to a dividend" within the meaning of that phrase in § 302(b)(1) * * *.

[I]n an effort to eliminate "the considerable confusion which exists in this area" and thereby to facilitate tax planning, * * * the authors of the [1954] Code sought to provide objective tests to govern the tax consequences of stock redemptions. Thus, the tax bill passed by the House of Representatives contained no "essentially equivalent" language. Rather, it provided for "safe harbors" where capital gains treatment would be accorded to corporate redemptions that met the conditions now found in §§ 302(b)(2) and (3) of the Code.

It was in the Senate Finance Committee's consideration of the tax bill that § 302(b)(1) was added, and Congress thereby provided that [sale] treatment should be available "if the redemption is not essentially equivalent to a dividend." Taxpayer argues that the purpose was to continue "existing law" * * *. According to the Government, even under the old law it would have been improper for the Court of Appeals to rely on "a business purpose for the redemption" and "an absence of the proscribed tax avoidance purpose to bail out dividends at favorable tax rates." * * *

[W]e agree with the Government that by making the sole inquiry relevant for the future the narrow one whether the redemption could be characterized as a sale, Congress was apparently rejecting past court decisions that had also considered factors indicating the presence or absence of a tax-avoidance motive * * *. Congress clearly mandated that pro rata distributions be treated under the general rules laid down in §§ 301 and 316 rather than under § 302, and nothing suggests that there should be a different result if there were a "business purpose" for the redemption * * *. We conclude that the Court of Appeals was therefore wrong in looking for a business purpose and considering it in deciding whether the redemption was equivalent to a dividend * * *.

Taxpayer strongly argues that to treat the redemption involved here as essentially equivalent to a dividend is to elevate form over substance. Thus, taxpayer argues, had he not bought Bradley's shares or had he made a subordinated loan to the company instead of buying preferred stock, he could have gotten back his $25,000 with favorable tax treatment. However, the difference between form and substance in the tax law is largely problematical, and taxpayer's complaints have little to do with whether a business purpose is relevant under § 302(b)(1). It was clearly proper for Congress to treat distributions generally as taxable dividends when made out of earnings and profits and then to prevent avoidance of that result without regard to motivation where the distribution is in exchange for redeemed stock.

We conclude that that is what Congress did when enacting § 302(b)(1). If a corporation distributes property as a simple dividend, the effect is to transfer the property from the company to its shareholders without a change in the relative economic interests or rights of the stockholders. Where a redemption has that same effect, it cannot be said to have satisfied the "not essentially equivalent to a dividend" requirement of § 302(b)(1). Rather, to qualify for preferred treatment under that section, a redemption must result in a meaningful reduction of the shareholder's proportionate interest in the corporation. Clearly, taxpayer here, who (after application of the attribution rules) was the sole shareholder of the corporation both before and after the redemption, did not qualify under this test. The decision of the Court of Appeals must therefore be reversed * * *.

[Dissenting opinion omitted.]

NOTES

1. *Illustrations.* The following Revenue Rulings illustrate how the Internal Revenue Service has interpreted the "not essentially equivalent to a dividend" standard:

Rev. Rul. 78–401, 1978–2 C.B. 127 (ruling that reduction of interest from 90% to 60% was essentially equivalent to a dividend).

Rev. Rul. 77–218, 1977–1 C.B. 81 (ruling that reduction of interest by 8% was essentially equivalent to a dividend where the redeemed shareholder continued to control more than 50% of the voting power of the outstanding shares).

Rev. Rul. 75–502, 1975–2 C.B. 111 (ruling that reduction of interest from 57% to 50% was *not* essentially equivalent to a dividend where the other 50% was owned by an unrelated party).

Rev. Rul. 76–364, 1976–2 C.B. 91 (ruling that reduction of interest from 27% to 22% was *not* essentially equivalent to a dividend where unrelated parties owned the remainder of the stock).

Rev. Rul. 56–183, 1956–1 C.B. 161 (ruling that reduction of interest from 11% to 9% was *not* essentially equivalent to a dividend where unrelated parties owned the remainder of the stock).

2. *No reduction in interest.* Can a redemption that does not reduce the redeemed shareholder's relative interest in the corporation ever be "not essentially equivalent to a dividend?" See Rev. Rul. 81–289, which follows.

Revenue Ruling 81–289

1981–2 Cum.Bull. 82.

ISSUE

Whether a redemption of stock pursuant to an isolated tender offer is taxable as an exchange under sections 302(a) and (b)(1) of the Internal Revenue Code.

FACTS

X corporation has outstanding 1,000,000x shares of voting common stock which are widely held and publicly traded. X has approximately 1,000x shareholders, none of whom owns a significant amount of the X common stock. In an isolated transaction and not as part of a periodic redemption plan, X offered to purchase from its shareholders 25,000x shares of its common stock at the rate of $20x per share. Approximately 10 percent of X's shareholders tendered stock for redemption. X redeemed a total of 20,000x shares of its stock pursuant to the tender offer. Individual A, who owned 2,000x shares of X stock at the time of the tender offer, surrendered 40x shares for redemption. Accordingly, A's proportionate interest in X was .2 percent (2,000x shares divided by 1,000,000x shares) before the tender offer and remained .2 percent (1,960x shares divided by 980,000x shares) after the tender offer * * *.

LAW AND ANALYSIS

Section 302(a) of the Code provides, in part, that a redemption of stock will be treated as a distribution in part or full payment in exchange for the stock redeemed if section 302(b)(1), (2), or (3) applies. Section 302(b)(1) will apply if the redemption is "not essentially equivalent to a dividend" * * *.

Section 1.302–2(b) of the Income Tax Regulations provides, with respect to section 302(b)(1) of the Code, that the question of whether a distribution in redemption of stock of a shareholder is not essentially equivalent to a dividend depends on the facts and circumstances of each case, and that all distributions in pro rata redemptions generally will be treated as distributions under section 301 if the corporation has only one class of stock outstanding.

[I]n Himmel, the Second Circuit emphasized that stock ownership involves these important rights: (1) the right to vote and thereby exercise control; (2) the right to participate in current earnings and accumulated surplus; and (3) the right to share in net assets on liquidation * * *.

HOLDING

In the present situation the redemption did not result in any reduction of A's right to vote, to participate in current earnings and accumulated surplus, or to share in the corporation's net assets on liquidation. Thus, this redemption with regard to A * * * does not qualify as an exchange within the meaning of sections 302(a) and (b)(1) of the Code.

NOTES

1. *Avoiding the problem.* If you owned 100 shares of stock of a publicly traded corporation that solicited the purchase of 20% of all of its outstanding stock, how could you dispose of 20 shares and still be certain that the disposition would be treated as a sale?

2. *Basis in redeemed shares.* In Revenue Ruling 81–289, what happened to A's basis in the 40x shares she surrendered to X? See Treas. Reg. § 1.302–2(c).

> *Problem 5–4 (Redemption or sale to third party).* Rachel purchased all 100 of the outstanding shares of Atlas Corporation for $100,000. Her Atlas stock is now worth $1,000,000. Atlas has no E & P. Rachel is considering selling 10 Atlas shares for $100,000. What are the tax consequences to Rachel if,
>
> (a) she sells 10 shares to Atlas? See I.R.C. §§ 301(c), 302(d).
>
> (b) she sells 10 shares to a third party? See I.R.C. § 1001.

b. ATTRIBUTION RULES

I.R.C. § 318

Treas. Reg. § 1.318

Measuring the change in the relative interest of a shareholder who participates in a redemption is a relatively simple matter when the participating shareholder is not "related" (as defined in I.R.C. § 318(a)) to any other shareholder and the rights of all outstanding shares are identical. In these circumstances, the focus is exclusively on the shareholder who is surrendering shares. That shareholder's relative interest before the redemption is calculated as follows:

$$\frac{\text{total number of shares owned by the shareholder } \textit{before} \text{ the redemption}}{\text{total number of shares outstanding } \textit{before} \text{ the redemption}}$$

The resulting quotient is then compared to the redeemed shareholder's relative interest after the redemption. That relative interest is calculated as follows:

$$\frac{\text{total number of shares owned by the shareholder } \textit{after} \text{ the redemption}}{\text{total number of shares outstanding } \textit{after} \text{ the redemption}}$$

When calculating the redeemed shareholder's relative interest after the redemption, both the numerator and the denominator of the fraction are reduced by the number of shares redeemed. Why?

> *Example 5–A (Reducing numerator and denominator by redeemed shares).* X Corporation has 1,000 identical shares of common stock outstanding that are held by the following unrelated individuals:

Shareholder	Number of Shares
A	400
B	300
C	200
D	100
Total	1,000

X redeems 200 shares from A. A's relative interest before the redemption is 40% (400 ÷ 1,000). A's relative interest after the redemption is 25% (200 ÷ 800). Note that both the numerator and the denominator were reduced by the 200 redeemed shares.

As the Davis case (p. 230) illustrates, a shareholder participating in a redemption is treated as owning shares held by certain related parties in addition to the shares she actually owns. See I.R.C. §§ 302(c)(1), 318(a). If the redeemed shareholder is "related" (as defined in I.R.C. § 318(a)) to one or more of the corporation's other shareholders, the redeemed shareholder's relative interest before and after the redemption is measured by including the shares held by the related party or parties. Thus, the attribution rules can cause the redeemed shareholder to be treated as owning more shares than she actually owns. The attribution rules can never cause the redeemed shareholder to be treated as owning fewer shares than she actually owns.

When related shareholders exist, the surrendering shareholder's relative interest before the redemption is calculated as follows:

$$\frac{\text{(number of shares actually owned before the redemption + number of shares owned by "related" shareholders before the redemption)}}{\text{total number of shares outstanding before the redemption}}$$

The resulting quotient is compared to the redeemed shareholder's relative interest after the redemption. That relative interest is calculated as follows:

$$\frac{\text{(number of shares actually owned after the redemption + number of shares owned by "related" shareholders after the redemption)}}{\text{total number of shares outstanding after the redemption}}$$

Again, when calculating the shareholder's relative interest after the redemption, both the numerator and the denominator of the fraction must be reduced by the redeemed shares.

Example 5–B (Impact of attribution rules). X Corporation has 1,000 outstanding shares of common stock held by the following individuals:

Shareholder	Number of Shares
A	400
B	300
C	200
D	100
Total	1,000

A is B's daughter. C and D are not related to each other or to A and B. X redeems 200 shares from A. A's relative interest before the redemption is 70%.[5] A's relative interest after the redemption is 62.5%.[6] When calculating A's relative interest after the redemption, both the numerator and the denominator of the fraction are reduced by the 200 redeemed shares.

---

5. (400 shares of A + 300 shares of B) ÷ 1,000 outstanding shares = 70%.

6. (200 shares of A + 300 shares of B) ÷ 800 outstanding shares = 62.5%.

Problem 5–5 (Measuring relative interest). X Corporation has 1,200 outstanding shares of common stock. Each of A, B, C, and D own 300 shares. If X redeems 200 of A's shares, what is A's relative interest before and after the redemption under each of the following alternatives?

(a) B is A's grandfather, C is A's granddaughter, and D is C's husband. See I.R.C. §§ 318(a)(1), (5)(B).

(b) B is A's brother, C is A's sister, and D is the estate of A's father. D's beneficiaries are A, B, and C. See I.R.C. §§ 318(a)(1), (2)(A).

(c) A is a corporation with 200 outstanding shares, 100 of which are owned by B and 100 of which are owned by B's sister, C. D is not related to A, B, or C. See I.R.C. § 318(a)(3)(C).

(d) Same as (c), but assume that X is redeeming 200 of *B's* shares, rather than 200 of *A's* shares. Is B treated as owning any of C's X shares under § 318? See I.R.C. §§ 318(a)(3)(C), (2)(C), (5)(C).

c. SUBSTANTIALLY DISPROPORTIONATE REDEMPTION

I.R.C. § 302(b)(2)

Treas. Reg. § 1.302–3

Unlike the "not essentially equivalent to a dividend" standard of I.R.C. § 302(b)(1), the "substantially disproportionate" standard of I.R.C. § 302(b)(2) provides an objective, mechanical test for determining if a redemption will be treated as a sale. For a redemption to meet the substantially disproportionate standard, all three conditions set forth in I.R.C. § 302(b)(2) must be satisfied. What are those three conditions?

Revenue Ruling 87–88

1987–2 Cum.Bull. 81.

ISSUE

If shares of both voting and nonvoting common stock are redeemed from a shareholder in one transaction, are the two classes aggregated for purposes of applying the substantially disproportionate requirement in section 302(b)(2)(C) of the Internal Revenue Code?

FACTS

X corporation had outstanding 10 shares of voting common stock and 30 shares of nonvoting common stock. The fair market values of a share of voting common stock and a share of nonvoting common stock are approximately equal. A owned 6 shares of X voting common stock and all the nonvoting common stock. The remaining 4 shares of the X voting common stock were held by persons unrelated to A within the meaning of section 318(a) of the Code.

X redeemed 3 shares of voting common stock and 27 shares of nonvoting common stock from A in a single transaction. Thereafter, A owned 3 shares of X voting common stock and 3 shares of nonvoting common stock. The ownership of the remaining 4 shares of X voting common stock was unchanged.

LAW AND ANALYSIS

If a distribution in redemption of stock qualifies under section 302(b)(2) of the Code as substantially disproportionate, the distribution is treated under section 302(a) as a payment in exchange for the stock redeemed.

Under sections 302(b)(2)(B) and (C) of the Code, a distribution is substantially disproportionate if (i) the shareholder owns less than 50 percent of the total combined voting power of the corporation immediately after the redemption, (ii) immediately after the redemption the ratio of voting stock owned by the shareholder to all the voting stock of the corporation is less than 80 percent of the same ratio immediately before the redemption, and (iii) immediately after the redemption the ratio of common stock owned by the shareholder to all of the common stock of the corporation (whether voting or nonvoting) is less than 80 percent of the same ratio immediately before the redemption.

Under section 302(b)(2)(C) of the Code, if more than one class of common stock is outstanding, the determination in (iii) above is made by reference to fair market value. Section 302(b)(2) applies to a redemption of both voting stock and other stock (although not to the redemption solely of nonvoting stock). Section 1.302–3(a) of the Income Tax Regulations.

With regard to requirements (i) and (ii) described above, after the redemption, A owned less than 50 percent of the voting power of X (43 percent), and A's voting power was reduced to less than 80 percent of the percentage of voting power in X that A owned before the redemption (from 60 percent to 43 percent for a reduction to 72 percent of the pre-redemption level).

With regard to requirement (iii) above, section 302(b)(2)(C) of the Code provides that, if there is more than one class of common stock outstanding, the fair market value of all of the common stock (voting and nonvoting) will govern the determination of whether there has been the requisite reduction in common stock ownership. The fact that this test is based on fair market value and is applied by reference to all of the common stock of the corporation suggests that the requirement concerning reduction in common stock ownership is to be applied on an aggregate basis rather than on a class-by-class basis. Thus, the fact that A has no reduction in interest with regard to the nonvoting common stock and continues to own 100 percent of this stock does not prevent the redemption of this class of stock from qualifying under section 302(b)(2) when the whole transaction meets the section 302(b)(2) requirements. To conclude otherwise would require that, notwithstanding a redemption of one class of common stock in an amount sufficient to reduce the shareholder's aggregate common stock ownership by more than 20 percent in value, every other class of common stock owned by the shareholder must be subject to a redemption.

Prior to the redemption, A owned 90 percent of the total fair market value of all the outstanding X common stock (36 out of the 40 shares of voting and nonvoting common stock). After the redemption, A owned 60 percent of the total fair market value of all the X common stock (6 out of 10 shares). The reduction in ownership (from 90 percent to 60 percent) was a reduction to less than 80 percent of the fraction that A previously owned of the total fair market value of all the X common stock.

HOLDING

If more than one class of common stock is outstanding, the provisions of section 302(b)(2)(C) of the Code are applied in an aggregate and not a class-by-class manner. Accordingly, the redemption by X of 3 shares of voting common stock and 27 shares of nonvoting common stock qualifies as substantially disproportionate within the meaning of section 302(b)(2), even though A continues to own 100 percent of the outstanding nonvoting common stock.

Glacier State Electric Supply Company v. Commissioner

United States Tax Court, 1983.
80 T.C. 1047.

■ Dawson, Judge: * * *

FINDINGS OF FACT

[G]lacier State Electric Supply Company (hereinafter referred to as "Glacier State" or "petitioner") is a corporation * * *.

Petitioner was incorporated in 1946 by Donald P. Rearden (hereinafter "Rearden") and J. Kenneth Parsons (hereinafter "Parsons"). One hundred ninety shares of common stock were issued by Glacier State at its incorporation: 94 each to Rearden and Parsons, and 1 each to their wives. Parsons was president of Glacier State and Rearden was vice-president.

Business was good. Wishing to expand, Parsons and Rearden, through petitioner, joined with Arthur E. Pyle (hereinafter "Pyle") to establish the Glacier State Electric Supply Company of Billings (hereinafter "GSB"). GSB was organized and incorporated in 1953. Upon incorporation, GSB issued 339 shares of stock * * *. [T]he stock of GSB was held as follows: Rearden and Parsons, 1 share [each]; Pyle 113 shares; petitioner 224 shares.

In September 1954, Rearden and Parsons entered into an agreement with Glacier State which provided that in the event of either of their deaths, the shares of Glacier State owned by the deceased would be redeemed by that corporation.

In November 1954, Pyle and petitioner [also] entered into * * * agreements regarding the sale and purchase of the GSB stock * * *.

The November 1954 agreements were amended by an addendum agreement on January 20, 1969 (the amendment). The amendment provided that upon the death of Pyle, his interest in GSB would be purchased by GSB. The amendment also stated that in the event of either Parsons' or Rearden's death, GSB would redeem the one share held in the name of the deceased along with one-half of the stock in GSB owned by petitioner * * *.

Parsons died on April 10, 1976 * * *. [A] Memorandum of Agreement was entered into between petitioner and the Parsons estate in July 1976 which provided a method for the required disposition of the stock in petitioner that was held by the estate * * *.

On August 30, 1977 petitioner, GSB, and the Parsons estate entered into an agreement for the disposition of 112 shares in GSB owned by petitioner along with the one share owned by the Parsons estate. Petitioner was required under the terms of the agreement to assign to the Parsons estate the redemption payments it received from GSB. Thereafter, two redemptions took place: [(1) one-half of the stock of GSB held by petitioner along with the one GSB share owned by the Parsons estate was redeemed, and (2) the stock of petitioner owned by the Parsons estate and Parsons' widow was redeemed.]

In part payment for the value of the GSB stock, the Parsons estate was assigned a promissory note in the principal amount of $56,576.99 which had been issued by GSB to petitioner on August 30, 1977 * * *. The balance due the estate for the value of the GSB shares was also paid by endorsing to the estate a $56,519.24 check issued to petitioner by GSB.

In the interim period between the incorporations and Parsons' death, [William Hogan, an unrelated party, had acquired 35 newly issued shares of GSB from GSB.] * * *.

Immediately prior to the disposition agreement arranged between the Parsons estate, petitioner, and GSB on August 30, 1977, the stock ownership of GSB was as follows:

Glacier State	224 shares
Rearden	1 share
Parsons estate	1 share
Pyle	113 shares
William Hogan	35 shares

After that disposition, the ownership of GSB was as follows:

Glacier State	112 shares
Rearden	1 share
Pyle	113 shares
William Hogan	35 shares

[G]SB had current or accumulated earnings and profits of at least $109,257.08 in 1977 * * *.

OPINION

Issue 1: The Step Transaction Doctrine

As a result of the GSB redemption, respondent contends that petitioner recognized long term capital gain. Petitioner argues that although the appreciated stock of GSB was technically owned approximately one-third by Pyle and two-thirds by itself; Parsons, Rearden, and Pyle (hereinafter referred to as the "officers") treated the stock for all intents and purposes as being owned by them individually. Therefore, petitioner claims that the substance of the transactions was that the GSB stock had been transferred to the Parsons estate as part payment for the redemption of petitioner's stock, followed by a redemption of that GSB stock directly from the estate.

Respondent's answer to this contention is that in this case the substance of the transactions was its form: that Glacier State satisfied its obligation under the buy/sell agreements to redeem its stock from the Parsons estate by selling one of its assets, i.e., one-half of the GSB shares it held. We hold for respondent as to issue one.

We agree with petitioner that it is the substance of a transaction rather than mere form which should determine the resultant tax consequences when the form does not coincide with economic reality. The taxpayer as well as the Commissioner is entitled to assert the substance-over-form argument although in such situations taxpayers may face a higher than usual burden of proof.

To assure that the substance of transactions will be determinative, courts have employed the "step transaction" doctrine. The essence of the doctrine is that an integrated transaction will not be broken down into independent steps; or, viewed from the other side, separate steps must be taken together in attaching tax consequences if that combination is the substance of the transaction.

To justify its invoking the doctrine to find the true substance, petitioner points to numerous facts and claimed facts. At the center of its argument is its claim that "the (officers) treated the GSB stock as being owned by the three of them as individuals." * * * In short, petitioner claims it was merely a conduit through which the proceeds passed. We disagree.

To accept petitioner's argument that it was merely a conduit would require us to determine that the real owners of the GSB stock were the officers. This we cannot do. Such a determination necessarily requires that we ignore petitioner's existence as a taxable entity. Despite petitioner's strong urging, the facts are clear that not only was Glacier State in substance the "real" owner of the stock for over 20 years, but also that Parsons and Rearden did in fact accept it as such. Rearden testified at trial that he and Parsons had discussed holding the GSB shares in their individual capacity many times, yet did not do so for tax reasons. Such a statement necessarily implies that they believed that they were not the owners. Also, if Parsons and Rearden thought that they owned the stock, why did they observe all the technical formalities during the execution of the buy/sell agreements, the amendment to those agreements, and the later redemptions? The answer must be that Parsons and Rearden thought that petitioner was the true owner.

[I]n sum, the fact that Rearden and Parsons may have deemed themselves the owners of the GSB shares because of their control over Glacier State is insufficient to establish that they were the actual or true owners of such shares.

Although we agree with petitioner that where appropriate, under the step transaction doctrine, separate steps must be taken together in attaching tax consequences, this is not a correct case in which to apply that doctrine. Petitioner is not asking us to skip, collapse, or rearrange the steps he employed. He is instead asking that we accept an entirely new series of steps or events that did not take place. The step transaction doctrine cannot be stretched so far.

Despite petitioner's present objections, in essence it is merely arguing that since the transaction would have been nontaxable if cast in another form, we should grant similar treatment to the form it utilized. This we cannot do.

The cornerstone of tax planning is that the same economic or business result may be validly achieved through a variety of routes, each with differing tax consequences. The step transaction doctrine may be argued by taxpayers in cases where the form chosen does not reflect that transaction's true substance (which is reflected in the combining of the individual steps). This is to be distinguished, however, from situations where, as in the instant case, the substance of the transaction coincides with the form employed * * *.

Accordingly, we conclude that in both form and substance, the two redemptions occurred here as they were originally cast, and that the step transaction doctrine is of no aid to petitioner.

Issue 2: Series of Redemptions

In the alternative, petitioner asserts that the payments it received from GSB should be treated as dividend income. If characterized as a dividend, [80] percent of the distribution qualifies for a deduction from petitioner's gross income under section 243(a).

Petitioner claims that because there was a planned later redemption of Pyle's GSB shares upon his death, pursuant to the agreements, this constitutes a series of redemptions under section 302(b)(2)(D). It contends that by taking this later redemption into account the present distribution fails the substantially disproportionate tests of section 302(b)(2), or is essentially equivalent to a dividend and hence does not qualify under section 302(b)(1).

[Respondent disagrees with petitioner.] * * *

The proper tax treatment to be afforded to the distribution from a corporation in redemption of its stock depends upon whether section 302(a) applies. If the distribution does not qualify under section 302(a), section 302(d) directs that section 301 will apply.

Under section 302(a), a redemption is treated as an exchange if any of the numbered paragraphs of section 302(b) are met. The parties apparently agree that, viewed separately, the GSB redemption satisfies both the 50 and 80 percent tests of section 302(b)(2).

The main question then is whether we should view the "redemption" of Pyle's shares along with the GSB redemption as part of a single plan under section 302(b)(2)(D).

* * *

We agree that the GSB redemption was made pursuant to a plan. However, we think it plain that the plan's purpose was not a series of redemptions that eventually would result in a distribution which in the aggregate is not substantially disproportionate with respect to the shareholder.

The regulations state that whether a plan with the requisite purpose or effect exists is to be determined from all the facts and circumstances. Section 1.302–2(a), Income Tax Regs. Little authority is available that directs us as to which facts should be weighted more than others in resolving this issue. There is no clear indication of how close in time the redemptions must occur in order to constitute a series, or whether a plan to make a series of distributions might exist without a contractual requirement that it be carried through.

The purpose for enacting section 302(b)(2)(D) was to prevent an obvious abuse of the 50–percent and 80–percent tests of section 302(b)(2). We do not think the facts of the instant case show that the buy-out plan's "purpose or effect" was to result in a substantially proportionate distribution. Clearly the plan's purpose was merely to prevent unapproved parties from acquiring an interest in GSB and also to provide a market for the shares upon the death of the deceased. This plan, as with most buy/sell agreements concerning closely-held corporations, represents legitimate business purposes. Obviously, this was not a vehicle in which to bail out earnings of the corporation at capital gain rates.

Moreover, we cannot agree that the overall effect of this plan would not be a substantially disproportionate distribution. The second redemption required to establish the series has not and may never occur. In the interim period the corporation could dissolve, Pyle could sell his shares to qualified third parties, the parties may rescind the agreements, or sufficient additional shares may be issued to other shareholders, thereby diluting Pyle's holding to an insignificant amount. We conclude, then, that petitioner's redemption of one-half of the GSB shares satisfies the substantially disproportionate tests of section 302(b)(2)(B) and (C).

Petitioner also claims that the GSB redemption is essentially equivalent to a dividend and hence fails to qualify for exchange treatment under section 302(b)(1). Because that redemption vastly altered the control rights in GSB, the distribution obviously does not qualify as a dividend.

Accordingly, since the requirements of sections 302(b)(2) and 302(b)(1), were met, the transaction is afforded exchange treatment. The GSB redemption therefore results in capital gain to petitioner.

NOTES

1. *Tax Court's view of transaction.* The Tax Court analyzed the transaction in accordance with the form chosen by the taxpayer. Specifically, the following steps were taken in the following order:

(a) GSB distributed money and a promissory note to Glacier State in redemption of half (112 shares) of the GSB stock owned by Glacier State.

(b) Glacier State distributed money and GSB's promissory note (received from GSB in step (a)) to Parsons' estate in redemption of all the Glacier State stock owned by Parsons' estate.

The case focused on the tax consequences of step (a) to Glacier State. The taxpayer was arguing for one-side distribution treatment and the government was arguing for sale treatment. Thus, the parties took positions contrary to the position that each party normally takes. Why did the taxpayer seek one-side distribution treatment? See I.R.C. § 243. Would one-side distribution treatment benefit the taxpayer under current law? See I.R.C. §§ 1059(a), (b), (e)(1)(A)(ii).

2. *Application of I.R.C. § 302(b)(2).* Demonstrate that the redemption of half of the GSB shares held by Glacier State satisfied all three conditions imposed by the substantially disproportionate standard of I.R.C. § 302(b)(2). How would the analysis change if Pyle were Reardon's father? See I.R.C. §§ 318(a)(1)(A), (a)(3)(C).

3. *Relationship of tests in I.R.C. § 302(b).* Why did the court consider whether the redemption satisfied the I.R.C. § 302(b)(1) standard after it concluded that the redemption satisfied the I.R.C. § 302(b)(2) standard?

4. *Taxpayer's view of transaction.* In contrast to the steps that were actually taken (see Note 1), the taxpayer argued that the transaction should have been analyzed as though the following steps were taken in the following order:

(a) Glacier State distributed GSB stock to Parsons' estate in redemption of all the Glacier State stock owned by Parsons' estate.

(b) GSB distributed money and a promissory note to Parsons' estate in redemption of all the GSB stock received by the estate in step (a).

If the court had adopted this view of the transaction, what would have been the tax consequences of step (a) to,

(1) Parsons' estate? See I.R.C. §§ 302(b)(3), 1014.

(2) Glacier State? Nonrecognition of gain because of the existence of the General Utilities rule (see pp. 29–33). What would be the tax consequences to Glacier State under current law? See I.R.C. § 311(b).

If the court had adopted the taxpayer's view of the transaction, what would have been the tax consequences of step (b) to,

(1) Parsons' estate? See I.R.C. § 302(b)(3).

(2) GSB? See I.R.C. § 311.

5. *Substance-over-form.* The taxpayer's view of the transaction did not prevail because the Glacier State court rejected the taxpayer's substance-over-form argument. As indicated in the opinion, a substance-over-form argument may be advanced in appropriate cases either by the taxpayer or by the Internal Revenue Service. Why should a taxpayer that asserts a substance-over-form argument "face a higher than usual burden of proof?" How can a taxpayer avoid the situation where it must advance a substance-over-form argument?

Glacier State's substance-over-form argument was based on the "step transaction" doctrine, a doctrine that is frequently invoked in the corporate tax area. As the court suggests, the step transaction doctrine normally causes a series of related transactions to be collapsed into a single event for purposes of assessing tax consequences. Several cases involving the application of the step-transaction doctrine are included in this casebook. You should be attuned to the circumstances in which the doctrine has been invoked and attempt to refine your understanding of the doctrine each time it appears.

> *Example 5–C (Series of redemptions):* X Corporation has 300 shares outstanding, 100 of which are owned by each of A, B and C, who are unrelated. X has a substantial amount of E & P. A, B and C would like to withdraw half of the value of their shares from X. They devise the following plan: on Day 1, X will redeem 50 of A's shares; on Day 2, X will redeem 50 of B's shares; and on Day 3, X will redeem 50 of C's shares.
>
> If each redemption is treated as independent from the others, each redemption satisfies the substantially disproportionate standard. See I.R.C. § 302(b)(2). As illustrated below, each of A, B and C owns less than 50% of the voting stock of X immediately after that shareholder is redeemed and the percentage of voting stock (and common stock) owned by each shareholder after that shareholder is redeemed is less than 80% of the percentage of voting stock (and common stock) owned by that shareholder immediately before the redemption.

Shareholder	After Redemption		Before Redemption
A	50 ÷ 250 20%	<80% ×	100 ÷ 300 33.33%
B	50 ÷ 200 25%	<80% ×	100 ÷ 250 40%
C	50 ÷ 150 33.33%	<80% ×	100 ÷ 200 50%

Because the three redemptions are part of a single plan, however, the reduction in each shareholder's proportionate interest will be measured by comparing each shareholder's interest before any of the redemptions to each shareholder's interest after *all* of the redemptions have occurred. See I.R.C. § 302(b)(2)(D). When the shareholders' interests are measured in this fashion, the percentage of voting stock (and common stock) of each shareholder does not decline as a result of the redemptions, as illustrated below.

Shareholder	After Redemption	Before Redemption
A	50 ÷ 150 33.33%	100 ÷ 300 33.33%
B	50 ÷ 150 33.33%	100 ÷ 300 33.33%
C	50 ÷ 150 33.33%	100 ÷ 300 33.33%

Because the redemptions do not reduce any shareholder's relative interest in X, the redemptions are treated as one-side distributions. I.R.C. § 302(d).

Problem 5–6 (Redemption of Parsons and Pyle as series of redemptions): With regard to the Glacier State case, explain why the redemption of the GSB shares held by Glacier State would not have satisfied the substantially disproportionate standard if the court had treated that redemption and the future redemption of Pyle's 113 GSB shares as a series of redemptions under I.R.C. § 302(b)(2)(D).

d. COMPLETE TERMINATION OF INTEREST

I.R.C. § 302(b)(3)

A redemption is also treated as a sale when the redemption represents a "complete termination of interest". I.R.C. § 302(b)(3). A complete termination of interest occurs when all shares owned by a shareholder are redeemed, unless the redeemed shareholder is treated as owning the shares of another shareholder under the attribution rules.

(1) SALE AND/OR REDEMPTION

Zenz v. Quinlivan

United States Court of Appeals, Sixth Circuit, 1954.
213 F.2d 914.

■ GOURLEY, DISTRICT JUDGE.

* * *

Appellant is the widow of the person who was the motivating spirit behind the [closely-held] corporation which engaged in the business of excavating and laying of sewers. Through death of her husband she became the owner of all [108] shares of stock issued by the corporation. She operated the business until remarriage, when her second husband assumed the management. As a result of a marital rift, separation, and final divorce, taxpayer sought to dispose of her company to a competitor who was anxious to eliminate competition.

Prospective buyer did not want to assume the tax liabilities which it was believed were inherent in the accumulated earnings and profits of the corporation. To avoid said profits and earnings as a source of future taxable dividends, buyer purchased [47 shares] of taxpayer's stock for cash. Three weeks later, * * * the corporation redeemed the balance [(61 shares)] of taxpayer's stock * * *.

Taxpayer, in her tax return, invoked [the predecessor to Section 302(b)(3) of the Internal Revenue Code] * * * as constituting a * * * redemption by a corporation of all the stock of a particular shareholder, and therefore was not subject to being treated as a distribution of a taxable dividend.

The District Court sustained the deficiency assessment of the Commissioner that the amount received from accumulated earnings and profits was [dividend] income since the stock redeemed by the corporation was "at such time and in such manner as to make the redemption thereof essentially equivalent to the distribution of a taxable dividend" * * *.

The District Court's findings were premised upon the view that taxpayer employed a circuitous approach in an attempt to avoid the tax consequences which would have attended the outright distribution of the surplus to the taxpayer by the declaration of a taxable dividend.

The rationale of the District Court is dedicated to piercing the external manifestations of the taxpayer's transactions in order to establish a subterfuge or sham.

Nevertheless, the general principle is well settled that a taxpayer has the legal right to decrease the amount of what otherwise would be his taxes or altogether avoid them, by means which the law permits. The taxpayer's motive to avoid taxation will not establish liability if the transaction does not do so without it.

The question accordingly presented is not whether the overall transaction, admittedly carried out for the purpose of avoiding taxes, actually avoided taxes which would have been incurred if the transaction had taken a different form, but whether the sale constituted a taxable dividend or the sale of a capital asset.

It is a salutary fact that [the predecessor to Section 302(b)(3)] is an exception to [the predecessor to Section 301] that all distributions of earning and profits are taxable as a dividend.

* * *

We cannot concur with the legal proposition enunciated by the District Court that a corporate distribution can be essentially equivalent to a taxable dividend even though that distribution extinguishes the shareholder's interest in the corporation. To the contrary, we are satisfied that where the taxpayer effects a redemption which completely extinguishes the taxpayer's interest in the corporation, and does not retain any beneficial interest whatever, that such transaction is not the equivalent of the distribution of a taxable dividend as to him.

[T]he use of corporate earnings or profits to purchase and make payment for all the shares of a taxpayer's holdings in a corporation is not controlling, and the question as to whether the distribution in connection with the cancellation or the redemption of said stock is essentially equivalent to the distribution of a taxable dividend under the Internal Revenue Code and Treasury Regulation must depend upon the circumstances of each case.

Since the intent of the taxpayer was to bring about a complete liquidation of her holdings and to become separated from all interest in the corporation, the conclusion is inevitable that the distribution of the earnings and profits by the corporation in payment for said stock was not made at such time and in such manner as to make the distribution and cancellation or redemption thereof essentially equivalent to the distribution of a taxable dividend.

In view of the fact that the [the predecessor to § 301] of the Internal Revenue Code contemplates that the shareholder receiving the distribution will remain in the corporation, the circumstances of this proceeding militate against treating taxpayer's sale as a distribution of a taxable dividend.

We do not feel that a taxpayer should be penalized for exercising legal means to secure a tax advantage. The conduct of this taxpayer does not appear to contravene the purpose or congressional intent of the provisions of the Internal Revenue Act which taxpayer invoked.

We conclude that under the facts and circumstances of the present case the District Court was in error, and the taxpayer is not liable as a distributee of a taxable dividend * * *.

NOTE

Importance of form. Subsequent to the decision in Zenz, the courts and the Internal Revenue Service sanctioned sale treatment for certain redemptions that led to a complete termination of interest notwithstanding that the redemption of some of the shareholder's shares occurred before the sale of the remaining shares to a third party. See United States v. Carey, 289 F.2d 531 (8th Cir.1961); Rev. Rul. 75–447, 1975–2 C.B. 113 (ruling that the order of the steps does not matter if both steps are "clearly part of an overall plan"). Is it likely that the taxpayer in Zenz would have prevailed if the sale and redemption had been reversed in that case (i.e., the bulk of the widow's shares were redeemed first and then the balance of the shares were sold to the buyer)?

Arnes v. United States

United States Court of Appeals, Ninth Circuit, 1992.
981 F.2d 456.

■ HUG, CIRCUIT JUDGE:

* * *

Joann Arnes, the Taxpayer–Appellee, married John Arnes in 1970. In 1980, they formed a corporation, "Moriah", to operate a McDonald's franchise in Ellensburg, Washington. That corporation issued 5,000 shares of stock in the joint names of John Arnes and Joann Arnes. In 1987, the couple agreed to divorce. McDonald's Corporation required 100% ownership of the equity and profits by the owner/operator, and informed John Arnes that there should be no joint ownership of the restaurant after the divorce.

Joann and John Arnes entered into an agreement to have their corporation redeem Joann Arnes' 50 percent interest in the outstanding stock for $450,000. The corporation would pay that money to Joann Arnes by * * * [paying $178,042] to her during 1988 and by paying the remainder * * * in monthly installments over ten years * * *. The agreement was incorporated into the decree of dissolution of the marriage, dated January 7, 1988. Joann Arnes surrendered her 2,500 shares to the corporation on December 31, 1987, and the corporation cancelled her stock certificate on May 4, 1988, then issuing another 2,500 shares to John Arnes.

On her federal income tax return for 1988, Joann Arnes reported that she sold her stock in Moriah on January 2, 1988, for a price of $450,000, and that her basis was $2,500, resulting in a profit of $447,500. She received $178,042 in 1988 as part of the sales price. Using an installment method, she treated $177,045 as long-term capital gain and the remainder as recovery of a portion of her basis.

On December 27, 1989, she filed a timely claim for refund of $53,053 for 1988 on the ground that she was not required to recognize any gain on the transfer of her stock because the transfer was made pursuant to a divorce instrument. The IRS did not allow the claim for refund, and Joann Arnes initiated this suit.

The district court found that the redemption of Joann Arnes' stock in Moriah was required by a divorce instrument, and that John Arnes had benefitted from the transaction because it was part of the marital property settlement, which limited future * * * claims that Joann Arnes might have brought against him. The court * * * found that, although Joann transferred her stock directly to Moriah, the transfer was made on behalf of John and should have been treated as having been made to John. Therefore, the transfer qualified for nonrecognition of gain pursuant to the I.R.C. exemption for transfers made to spouses or former spouses incident to a divorce settlement. See I.R.C. § 1041. Summary judgment was granted in favor of Joann Arnes.

The Government appeals. Meanwhile, * * * to insure that * * * [someone] will be taxed, the Government has asserted a protective income tax deficiency against John Arnes, who has contested the deficiency by filing a petition with the Tax Court. His case is pending but not before this court. The Government maintains that, although Joann Arnes is the appropriate party to be taxed for the gain, John Arnes should be taxed if the district court's ruling is upheld. If neither John nor Joann is taxed, the $450,000 used to redeem Joann's appreciated stock apparently will be taken out of the corporation tax-free.

* * *

The Government contends that the gain resulting from Moriah's redemption of Joann Arnes' stock does not qualify for exemption under section 1041, which is limited to transfers made directly to one's spouse or former spouse * * *. Joann Arnes' transfer to Moriah, the Government contends, is outside the scope of the exemption.

Joann Arnes contends that her transfer of stock to Moriah should be considered a transfer to John, resulting in a benefit to John, and absolving her of the obligation to bear the burden of any resulting tax.

* * *

John Arnes had an obligation to Joann Arnes that was relieved by Moriah's payment to Joann. That obligation was based in their divorce property settlement, which called for the redemption of Joann's stock. Although John and Joann were the sole stockholders in Moriah, the obligation to purchase Joann's stock was John's, not Moriah's. Furthermore, John personally guaranteed Moriah's note to Joann. Under Washington law, Joann could sue John for payment without suing Moriah. Thus, John was liable, with Moriah, for the payments due Joann.

We hold that Joann's transfer to Moriah did relieve John of an obligation, and therefore constituted a benefit to John. Joann's transfer of stock should be treated as a constructive transfer to John, who then transferred the stock to Moriah. The $450,000 was paid to Joann by Moriah on behalf of John. The transfer of $450,000 from the corporate treasury need not escape taxation, if we hold, as we do, that Joann is not required to recognize any gain on the transfer of her stock, because it is subject to section 1041. The tax result for Joann is the same as if she had conveyed the property directly to John.

The Government argues that because Joann transferred her stock to the corporation, rather than to John, the exception in section 1041 should not apply. * * *

We reject the Government's application of the statute. * * *

The judgment of the district court is AFFIRMED.

NOTES

1. *Guarantee of corporation's obligation.* Might the Ninth Circuit have reached a different result if John had not guaranteed the corporation's payment obligation? Putting aside the tax issue, is it likely that Joann would have consented to the transaction without John's guarantee?

2. *Effect on continuing shareholder.* Why did the government assert a "protective income tax deficiency" against John? Why did John contest that deficiency in the Tax Court, rather than in the Federal District Court? The Tax Court's decision in John's case follows.

Arnes v. Commissioner

United States Tax Court, 1994.
102 T.C. 522.

■ FAY, JUDGE: This case is before the Court on the parties' cross-motions for summary judgment * * *.

    * * *

FINDINGS OF FACT

[Omitted. See Arnes v. United States, p. 249.]

OPINION

Respondent argues that the [Ninth Circuit's decision in Arnes v. United States] controls our decision here. Petitioner [John Arnes] contends to the contrary * * *. We agree with petitioner * * *.

    * * *

The issue before us is whether Moriah's redemption of Joann [Arnes's] stock resulted in a constructive dividend to petitioner. If a corporation redeems stock that its remaining shareholder was obligated to buy, a constructive dividend results to the remaining shareholder. However, this rule is limited to those circumstances where the obligation of the remaining shareholder is both primary and unconditional.

    * * *

[P]etitioner did not have a primary and unconditional obligation to acquire Joann's stock. From the inception, Moriah was obligated to redeem Joann's stock * * *.

[Petitioner] is * * * supported by respondent's own published position in Rev. Rul. 69–608 [p. 225]. Situation 5 states:

> A and B owned all of the outstanding stock of X corporation. An agreement between A and B provided that upon the death of either, X will redeem all of the X stock owned by the decedent at the time of his death. In the event that X does not redeem the shares from the estate, the agreement provided that the surviving shareholder would purchase the unredeemed shares from the decedent's estate. B died and, in accordance with the agreement, X redeemed all of the shares owned by his estate.
>
> In this case A was only secondarily liable under the agreement between A and B. Since A was not primarily obligated to purchase the X stock from the estate of B, he received no constructive distribution when X redeemed the stock.

This scenario is directly analogous to the case before us. Indeed, petitioner argues on brief that, in structuring the redemption of Joann's Moriah stock, he had the right to rely on Rev. Rul. 69–608, situation 5. Petitioner and Joann owned all of the stock of Moriah. Their property settlement agreement provided that Moriah would redeem Joann's shares with Moriah's obligation guaranteed by petitioner. Under applicable Washington State law, the property settlement agreement created at most a secondary obligation, which could only mature on Moriah's default on its primary obligation. * * * Because petitioner was not primarily obligated to purchase Joann's shares, he received no constructive distribution when Moriah redeemed the stock.

> * * *

Respondent contends * * * that the following statement by the Court of Appeals for the Ninth Circuit in Arnes v. United States controls our decision in the instant case:

> John Arnes had an obligation to Joann Arnes that was relieved by Moriah's payment to Joann. That obligation was based in their divorce property settlement, which called for the redemption of Joann's stock. Although John and Joann were the sole stockholders in Moriah, the obligation to purchase Joann's stock was John's, not Moriah's. Furthermore, John personally guaranteed Moriah's note to Joann. Under Washington law, Joann could sue John for payment without suing Moriah. Thus, John was liable with Moriah, for the payments due Joann.

* * * Arnes v. United States does not address the legal issue here: whether there is a constructive dividend to petitioner. That case concerned the tax consequences to Joann under section 1041. We note that petitioner was not a party in Arnes, and Joann had a possibly adverse position to petitioner in that case.

Moreover, petitioner's guarantee did not create a primary and unconditional obligation. Under [Washington law], any obligation of petitioner would arise only after Moriah failed to make payments to Joann. Any obligation of petitioner implied in the property settlement agreement would be the same as would exist in any situation involving a divorce and a division of property * * *. [W]e conclude that the obligation is not primary and unconditional and [that any suggestion to the contrary by the Court of Appeals for the Ninth Circuit in Arnes v. United States] constitutes dictum.

Applying these standards to the record as a whole, and the undisputed facts therein, we conclude that petitioner demonstrated that there is no genuine issue of material fact that could establish that payments made by Moriah to Joann in redemption of her stock were constructive distributions by Moriah to petitioner that could properly be treated as dividends to him.

In hindsight, tactically, it might have been preferable if respondent had taken action to facilitate simultaneous consideration of petitioner's and Joann's cases by the Court of Appeals for the Ninth Circuit, instead of the course that was taken.

Petitioner's motion for partial summary judgment will be granted. In view of our above conclusions, respondent's motion for summary judgment will be denied in full.

* * *

■ BEGHE, J., concurring:

* * *

* * * In the absence of any showing that Congress, in enacting section 1041 * * * intended to displace the tax common law on redemptions of closely held corporations, that law should remain in place. The way to accomplish this result is to interpret section 1041 * * * so that no redemption of one spouse will be considered to be "on behalf of" the remaining spouse unless it discharges that spouse's primary and unconditional obligation to purchase the subject stock, as summarized and set forth in the examples in Rev. Rul. 69–608 and the case law on which it relies.

Although the tax treatment of continuing shareholders is not specifically set forth in the Code, the bright line is well established by court decisions and by administrative rulings, such as Rev. Rul. 69–608. A nonredeeming shareholder realizes no gain or loss or dividend income solely because all or a portion of the stock of another shareholder was redeemed, even though the effect of the redemption is to increase his percentage ownership in the corporation. The line has been drawn in terms of whether the remaining shareholder blundered into incurring a direct and primary obligation to purchase the stock, which he belatedly attempts to shift to the corporation.

These longstanding rules amount to a "social compact" that contemplates a pattern in which, when one shareholder * * * withdraws from the corporation, wholly or partly, with a resulting increase in the percentage ownership of the remaining shareholder, the remaining shareholder will not be taxed. The withdrawing shareholder is treated as having sold or exchanged a capital asset, while the remaining shareholder is considered to have realized nothing that can be viewed as a taxable gain or dividend.

Although the withdrawal and shift in interest is financed out of the corporate treasury rather than individual bank accounts, and may be viewed as conferring an indirect benefit on the remaining shareholder, the transaction is considered no more than a sale to the corporation by the holder whose stock interest is terminated or substantially reduced.

* * *

It is obvious that John and his counsel and Joann and her counsel negotiated the separation agreement to have Joann's stock redeemed against the background of and in reliance on these rules. Joann originally reported the redemption transaction as resulting in capital gains to her, in accordance with the advice of the attorney who represented her in the negotiation of the separation agreement. She then changed her mind and claimed a refund in repudiation of the original agreement. John's counsel demonstrated on brief, and respondent did not disagree, that the separation agreement was based on the assumption that the community property and liabilities would be equally divided between John and Joann. In agreeing on that equal division, the parties assumed that Joann would bear capital gains taxes on the Moriah distributions that she would receive as payment in exchange for her stock, and that there would be no tax on John. The net effect of taxing John and exonerating Joann is that she would receive and retain more than twice as much of the community property as John.

One of the benefits of having these bright line rules apply to redemptions by family corporations is that they reduce the opportunities for tax game playing between private parties. It is game playing, and engaging in second thoughts, that Joann, with the assistance of counsel, indulged in when she sandbagged John by reneging on their original deal.

* * *

Hewing to the bright line rules of Rev. Rul. 69–608 in the marital dissolution context will reduce the tax costs of divorce for the owners of small businesses held and operated in corporate form. If the shareholder spouses can negotiate their separation agreement with the assurance that the redemption will be tax free to the remaining shareholder and a capital gain transaction to the terminating shareholder, the overall tax costs will ordinarily be less than if the terminating spouse qualifies for nonrecognition under section 1041, but the remaining spouse suffers a dividend tax. This will leave a bigger pie to be divided in setting the consideration for the shares to be redeemed.

* * *

[Additional concurring and dissenting opinions are omitted.]

NOTES

1. *Common practice.* When both spouses own stock in a closely held corporation at the time of divorce, it is quite common for one spouse to surrender his or her stock. Prior to the Arnes cases, the prevailing view was that the parties could control which spouse bore the resulting tax liability by utilizing the appropriate form. If one spouse's shares were redeemed and the remaining spouse did not have a "primary and unconditional" obligation to buy the redeemed shares, the redemption proceeds were taxable to the departing spouse but not to the spouse who remained a shareholder. By contrast, if one spouse was obligated to purchase the other spouse's shares and corporate funds were utilized to satisfy the purchase obligation, the spouse obligated to purchase the shares was deemed to receive a one-side distribution governed by I.R.C. § 301 and the departing spouse enjoyed non-recognition treatment under I.R.C. § 1041. The Arnes cases and subsequent decisions made the tax consequences unpredictable when a redemption occurred pursuant to a divorce.

2. *Regulations restore predictability.* In 2003, regulations were promulgated that restore predictability to this area. See Treas. Reg. § 1.1041–2. Pursuant to the regulations, if the shares of one spouse are redeemed and a valid written agreement between the parties expressly provides that both spouses intend for the transaction to be treated as a redemption of the departing spouse, the redeemed shareholder will recognize any gain and cannot invoke I.R.C. § 1041 to avert that result. By contrast, if the parties enter into a valid written agreement providing that both spouses intend that the redemption be treated as resulting in a constructive distribution to the continuing spouse, the continuing spouse will be treated as receiving a constructive one-side distribution and the departing spouse can invoke I.R.C. § 1041. Thus, the tax consequences to both parties are now predictable when their intent is reflected in an agreement drafted in accordance with the regulations.

3. *Import now that dividends taxed at capital gains rates.* Now that dividends are generally taxed at capital gains rates, does it matter whether the redemption of a divorced shareholder's shares is taxed as a redemption of the departing shareholder or as a constructive dividend to the shareholder who remains?

(2) ATTRIBUTION ISSUES

I.R.C. §§ 302(c)(2), 318

Treas. Reg. § 1.302–4

When the family attribution rules of I.R.C. § 318(a)(1) impede a shareholder who surrenders all of her shares from achieving a complete termination of interest, the redemption is still treated as a sale if all of the following conditions are satisfied:

(a) The redeemed shareholder does not retain any interest in the corporation (including an interest as officer, director, or employee), other than an interest as a creditor.

(b) The redeemed shareholder does not acquire any interest in the corporation (other than by bequest or inheritance) within the ten year period following the date of the redemption.

(c) The redeemed shareholder agrees to notify the Internal Revenue Service if a proscribed interest is acquired within the ten year period following the redemption.

See I.R.C. § 302(c)(2)(A). In effect, the family attribution rules do not apply if the redeemed shareholder agrees to distance herself from the corporation for a ten year period following the redemption. Can a shareholder who utilizes this attribution waiver mechanism maintain any relationship with the corporation after she surrenders all of her shares?

Lynch v. Commissioner

United States Court of Appeals, Ninth Circuit, 1986.
801 F.2d 1176.

■ HALL, CIRCUIT JUDGE: * * *

I

Taxpayers, William and Mima Lynch, formed the W.M. Lynch Co. on April 1, 1960. The corporation issued all of its outstanding stock to William Lynch (taxpayer). The taxpayer specialized in leasing cast-in-place concrete pipe machines * * *.

On December 17, 1975 the taxpayer sold 50 shares of the corporation's stock to his son, Gilbert Lynch (Gilbert), for $17,170. Gilbert paid for the stock with a $16,000 check given to him by the taxpayer and $1,170 from his own savings. The taxpayer and his wife also resigned as directors and officers of the corporation on the same day.

On December 31, 1975 the corporation redeemed all 2300 shares of the taxpayer's stock. In exchange for his stock, the taxpayer received $17,900 of property and a promissory note for $771,920 * * *.

In the years immediately preceding the redemption, Gilbert had assumed greater managerial responsibility in the corporation. He wished, however, to retain the taxpayer's technical expertise with cast-in-place concrete pipe machines. On the date of the redemption, the taxpayer also entered into a consulting agreement with the corporation. The consulting agreement provided the taxpayer with payments of $500 per month for five years, plus reimbursement for business related travel, entertainment, and automobile expenses * * *.

After the redemption, the taxpayer shared his former office with Gilbert. The taxpayer came to the office daily for approximately one year; thereafter his appearances dwindled to about once or twice per week * * *.

II

We must decide whether the redemption of the taxpayer's stock in this case is taxable as a dividend distribution * * * or as long-term capital gain * * *.

Section 302(b)(3) provides that a shareholder is entitled to sale or exchange treatment if the corporation redeems all of the shareholder's stock. In order to determine whether there is a complete redemption for purposes of section 302(b)(3), the family attribution rules of section 318(a) must be applied unless the requirements of section 302(c)(2) are satisfied. Here, if the family attribution rules apply, the taxpayer will be deemed to own constructively the 50 shares held by Gilbert (100% of the corporation's stock) and the transaction would not qualify as a complete redemption within the meaning of section 302(b)(3).

* * *

[T]he Commissioner argues that in every case the performance of post-redemption services is a prohibited interest under section 302(c)(2)(A)(i), regardless of whether the taxpayer is an officer, director, employee, or independent contractor.

The Tax Court rejected the Commissioner's argument, finding that the services rendered by the taxpayer did not amount to a prohibited interest in the corporation. In reaching this conclusion, the Tax Court relied on a test derived from Lewis v. Commissioner * * *:

> Immediately after the enactment of the 1954 Code, it was recognized that section 302(c)(2)(A)(i) did not prohibit office holding per se, but was concerned with a retained financial stake in the corporation, such as a profit-sharing plan, or in the creation of an ostensible sale that really changed nothing so far as corporate management was concerned. Thus, in determining whether a prohibited interest has been retained under section 302(c)(2)(A)(i), we must look to whether the former stockholder has either retained a financial stake in the corporation or continued to control the corporation and benefit by its operations. In particular, where the interest retained is not that of an officer, director, or employee, we must examine the facts and circumstances to determine whether a prohibited interest has been retained under section 302(c)(2)(A)(i).

After citing the "control or financial stake" standard, the Tax Court engaged in a two-step analysis. First, the court concluded that the taxpayer was an independent contractor rather than an employee because the corporation had no right under the consulting agreement to control his actions. Second, the court undertook a "facts and circumstances" analysis to determine whether the taxpayer had a financial stake in the corporation or managerial control after the redemption. Because the consulting agreement was not linked to the future profitability of the corporation, the court found that the taxpayer had no financial stake. The court also found no evidence that the taxpayer exerted control over the corporation. Thus, the Tax Court determined that the taxpayer held no interest prohibited by section 302(c)(2)(A)(i).

III

* * *

We reject the Tax Court's interpretation of section 302(c)(2)(A)(i). An individualized determination of whether a taxpayer has retained a financial stake or continued to control the corporation after the redemption is inconsistent with Congress' desire to bring a measure of certainty to the tax consequences of a corporate redemption. We hold that a taxpayer who provides post-redemption services, either as an employee or an independent contractor, holds a prohibited interest in the corporation because he is not a creditor.

The legislative history of section 302 states that Congress intended to provide "definite standards in order to provide certainty in specific instances." * * * The facts and circumstances approach created by the Tax Court undermines the ability of taxpayers to execute a redemption and know the tax consequences with certainty.

The taxpayer's claim that the Senate rejected the mechanical operation of the House's version of section 302 is misleading. The Senate did reject the House bill because the "definitive conditions" were "unnecessarily restrictive." However, the Senate's response was to add paragraph (b)(1) to section 302, which reestablished the flexible, but notoriously vague, "not essentially equivalent to a dividend" test * * *. The confusion that stemmed from a case-by-case inquiry into "dividend equivalence" prompted the Congress to enact definite standards for the safe harbors in section 302(b)(2) and (b)(3). The Tax Court's refusal to recognize that section 302(c)(2)(A)(i) prohibits all non-creditor interests in the corporation creates the same uncertainty as the "dividend equivalence" test.

The problem with the Tax Court's approach is apparent when this case is compared with Seda v. Commissioner, 82 T.C. 484 (1984). In Seda, a former shareholder, at his son's insistence, continued working for the corporation for two years after the redemption. He received a salary of $1,000 per month. The Tax Court refused to hold that section 302(c)(2)(A)(i) prohibits the retention of employment relations per se, despite the unequivocal language in the statute. Instead, the court applied the facts and circumstances approach to determine whether the former shareholder retained a financial stake or continued to control the corporation. The Tax Court found that the monthly payments of $1,000 constituted a financial stake in the corporation. This result is at odds with the holding in Lynch that payments of $500 per month do not constitute a financial stake in the corporation. The court also found in Seda no evidence that the former shareholder had ceased to manage the corporation. Again, this finding is contrary to the holding in Lynch that the taxpayer exercised no control over the corporation after the redemption, even though he worked daily for a year and shared his old office with his son. Seda and Lynch thus vividly demonstrate the perils of making an ad hoc determination of "control" or "financial stake."

A recent Tax Court opinion further illustrates the imprecision of the facts and circumstances approach. In Cerone v. Commissioner, 87 T.C. 1 (1986), a father and son owned all the shares of a corporation formed to operate their restaurant. The corporation agreed to redeem all of the father's shares in order to resolve certain disagreements between the father and son concerning the management of the business. However, the father remained an employee of the corporation for at least five years after the redemption, drawing a salary of $14,400 for the first three years and less thereafter. The father claimed that he was entitled to capital gains treatment on the redemption because he had terminated his interest in the corporation within the meaning of section 302(b)(3).

Even on the facts of Cerone, the Tax Court refused to find that the father held a prohibited employment interest per se. Instead, the Tax Court engaged in a lengthy analysis, citing both Seda and Lynch. The court proclaimed that Lynch reaffirmed the rationale of Seda, even though Lynch involved an independent contractor rather than an employee. After comparing the facts of Seda and Cerone, the Tax Court eventually concluded that the father in Cerone held a financial stake in the corporation because he had drawn a salary that was $2,400 per year more than the taxpayer in Seda and had been employed by the corporation for a longer period after the redemption * * *. Thus, the Tax Court found that the father in Cerone held a prohibited interest because he had a financial stake as defined by Seda.

Although the Tax Court reached the correct result in Cerone, its approach undermines the definite contours of the safe harbor Congress intended to create with sections 302(b)(3) and 302(c)(2)(A)(i). Whether a taxpayer has a financial stake according to the Tax Court seems to depend on two factors, length of employment and the amount of salary. Length of employment after the redemption is irrelevant because Congress wanted taxpayers to know whether they were entitled to capital gains treatment on the date their shares were redeemed. As for the amount of annual salary, the Tax Court's present benchmark appears to be the $12,000 figure in Seda. Salary at or above this level will be deemed to be a financial stake in the enterprise, though the $6,000 annual payments in this case were held not to be a financial stake. There is no support in the legislative history of section 302 for the idea that Congress meant only to prohibit service contracts of a certain worth, and taxpayers should not be left to speculate as to what income level will give rise to a financial stake.

In this case, the taxpayer points to the fact that the taxpayers in Seda and Cerone were employees, while he was an independent contractor. On appeal, the Commissioner concedes the taxpayer's independent contractor status. We fail to see, however, any meaningful way to distinguish Seda and Cerone from Lynch by differentiating between employees and independent contractors. All of the taxpayers performed services for their corporations following the redemption. To hold that only the employee taxpayers held a prohibited interest would elevate form over substance * * *.

Our holding today that taxpayers who provide post-redemption services have a prohibited interest under section 302(c)(2)(A)(i) is inconsistent with the Tax Court's decision in Estate of Lennard v. Commissioner, 61 T.C. 554 (1974). That case held that a former shareholder who, as an independent contractor, provided post-redemption accounting services for a corporation did not have a prohibited interest. The Tax Court found that "Congress did not intend to include independent contractors possessing no financial stake in the corporation among those who are considered as retaining an interest in the corporation for purposes of the attribution waiver rules." We disagree. In the context of Lennard, the Tax Court appears to be using financial stake in the sense of having an equity interest or some other claim linked to the future profit of the corporation. Yet, in cases such as Seda and Cerone, the Tax Court has found that fixed salaries of $12,000 and $14,400, respectively, constitute a financial stake. Fees for accounting services could easily exceed these amounts, and it would be irrational to argue that the definition of financial stake varies depending on whether the taxpayer is an employee or an independent contractor. In order to avoid these inconsistencies, we conclude that those who provide post-redemption services, whether as independent contractors or employees, hold an interest prohibited by section 302(c)(2)(A)(i) because they are more than merely creditors.

* * *

IV

Our decision today comports with the plain language of section 302 and its legislative history. Taxpayers who wish to receive capital gains treatment upon the redemption of their shares must completely sever all non-creditor interests in the corporation. We hold that the taxpayer, as an independent contractor, held such a non-creditor interest, and so cannot find shelter in the safe harbor of section 302(c)(2)(A)(i). Accordingly, the family attribution rules of section 318 apply and the taxpayer fails to qualify for a complete redemption under section 302(b)(3). The payments from the corporation in redemption of the taxpayer's shares must be characterized as a dividend distribution taxable as ordinary income under section 301.

NOTES

1. *Acquisition of interest within ten years after redemption.* Assume that Lynch did not serve as a consultant to the corporation after the redemption. How would the tax treatment of the redemption be affected by each of the following alternatives?

(a) Lynch's son died five years after the redemption and, under his will, left the shares he owned to Lynch.

(b) Lynch's son gave Lynch 10 shares of stock as a birthday present five years after the redemption.

See I.R.C. § 302(c)(2)(A)(ii).

2. *Permissible retained interests.* A shareholder who surrendered all of her shares to the corporation was permitted to waive the family attribution rules, notwithstanding her retention of the right to receive payments under an unfunded pension plan. Rev. Rul. 84–135, 1984–2 C.B. 80. Similarly, a shareholder who surrendered all shares but continued to lease certain property to the corporation at a fixed monthly rental was permitted to waive the family attribution rules. Rev. Rul. 77–467, 1977–2 C.B. 92. The pension plan payments and the rents were neither dependent on the future earnings of the corporation nor subordinate to the claims of the corporation's general creditors.

3. *Notifying Internal Revenue Service of proscribed acquisition.* To achieve a complete termination of interest when the family attribution rules would otherwise bar that result, the redeeming shareholder must agree to notify the Internal Revenue Service if she reacquires stock or any other proscribed interest in the corporation within ten years after the redemption. See I.R.C. § 302(c)(2)(A)(iii). What is the purpose of this requirement? See I.R.C. § 302(c)(2)(A) (second sentence). What incentive exists for a taxpayer who acquires a proscribed interest to comply with this notification requirement?

4. *Acquisition of shares within ten years before redemption.* A shareholder who surrenders his entire interest in the distributing corporation cannot waive the family attribution rules if he acquired any shares in that corporation from certain related persons during the ten year period before the redemption, unless he can demonstrate that the avoidance of Federal income tax was not one of the principal purposes of that acquisition. See I.R.C. § 302(c)(2)(B)(i). When sale treatment is contingent on demonstrating the absence of a tax avoidance purpose, one can no longer be certain, in most cases, that a contemplated redemption will qualify for sale treatment. Sale treatment is certain under these circumstances only if the fact pattern closely resembles a fact pattern on which the Internal Revenue Service has issued a published ruling. See, e.g., Rev. Rul. 56–584, 1956–2 C.B. 179 (ruling that a gift of shares to child from parent to encourage child's interest in the business did not manifest tax avoidance motive, and the child was permitted to waive the family attribution rules when the child's shares were subsequently redeemed because the earlier gift was made for bona fide business reasons and no plan existed when the gift was made to effect a redemption of the shares); Rev. Rul. 79–67, 1979–1 C.B. 128 (ruling that a transfer of shares to mother from father's estate did not manifest a tax avoidance motive, and mother was permitted to waive the family attribution rules when her shares were subsequently redeemed because neither the estate nor the mother retained any control and/or economic interest in the corporation, and the distribution of the stock by the estate and the subsequent redemption of the stock from the mother were intended to give a child who was active in the business sole ownership of the corporation).

5. *Disposition of shares within ten years before redemption.* A shareholder who surrenders her entire interest in the distributing corporation cannot waive the family attribution rules if she transferred any shares in that corporation to certain related persons during the ten year period before the redemption, unless (1) she can demonstrate that the avoidance of Federal income tax was not one of the principal purposes of the earlier transfer *or* (2) the transferred shares are also redeemed. See I.R.C. § 302(c)(2)(B)(ii).

The Internal Revenue Service has issued published rulings illustrating situations where a transfer of shares to a related person within ten years of a redemption does not manifest a tax avoidance motive. See, e.g., Rev. Rul. 77–293, 1977–2 C.B. 91 (ruling that a gift of shares to a child, who was active and knowledgeable in the affairs of the business, that was intended solely for the purpose of enabling the parent to retire while leaving the business to the child, did not manifest a tax avoidance motive, and the retiring parent was permitted to waive the family attribution rules when he subsequently surrendered his remaining shares to the corporation); Rev. Rul. 77–455, 1977–2 C.B. 93 (ruling that a sale of shares to a child did not manifest a tax avoidance motive, and the retiring parent was permitted to waive the family attribution rules when he subsequently surrendered his remaining shares to the corporation); Rev. Rul. 85–19, 1985–1 C.B. 94 (ruling that a sale of shares by a child to a parent that were previously given by the parent to the child did not manifest a tax avoidance motive, and the child was permitted to waive the family attribution rules when the child's remaining shares were subsequently redeemed because the facts did not indicate any attempt by the child to retain either control of, or an economic interest in, the corporation).

> *Problem 5–7 (Acquisition or transfer of shares within ten years before redemption):* Southco, Inc. has 100 outstanding shares. Hal initially owns 20 of the Southco shares and his daughter Inge owns the other 80 shares. During Year 5, Inge gives 30 shares to Hal. Will the redemption of Hal's 50 shares in Year 11 or the redemption of Inge's 50 shares in Year 11 qualify as a complete termination of interest? See I.R.C. § 302(c)(2)(B).

6. *Waiver by entity.* What happens when the shareholder that surrenders all of its shares and attempts to waive the attribution rules is an entity (corporation, partnership, trust or estate)? See I.R.C. § 302(c)(2)(C). The Rickey case that follows was decided shortly *before* the enactment of I.R.C. § 302(c)(2)(C).

Rickey v. United States

United States Court of Appeals, Fifth Circuit, 1979.
592 F.2d 1251.

■ Fay, Circuit Judge: * * *

Horace B. Rickey, Sr. (the decedent), the President and principal stockholder of Horace B. Rickey, Inc. (the Company) died in May of 1967. At the time of his death, the decedent owned 1,292 of the 2,255 shares of common stock of the company. The decedent was survived by his second wife, Flora Womack, and three children: Horace B. Rickey, Jr., the child of his first marriage, and Robert H. Rickey and Elizabeth Ann Rickey, minor children of his second marriage to Flora Womack. At the time of the decedent's death, Horace Rickey, Jr. was 42 years of age, Robert Rickey was 14 years of age and Elizabeth was 12 years of age. The three children are the plaintiffs in these consolidated actions.[7] Horace Rickey, Jr. at the time of the decedent's death was an officer, director and an active employee of the Company and had founded the business with his father in the late 1940's. Elizabeth and Robert * * * had no active participation in the business. Robert and Elizabeth had acquired their relatively insignificant interest in the Company through a gift from their father.

* * *

Immediately prior to the decedent's death, the stock ownership in the Company was as follows:

Stockholders	Number of Shares	Percentage
Horace B. Rickey, Sr.	1,292	57.295%
Horace B. Rickey, Jr.	708	31.396%
Robert H. Rickey	40	1.774%
Elizabeth Ann Rickey	40	1.774%
	2,080	92.239%
Others	175	7.761%
	2,255	100%

The will of the decedent named as residuary universal legatees his three surviving children and his second wife was named as executrix of his estate. The will directed that the executrix was to tender the stock owned by the decedent in the Company to the Company * * *.

In accordance with the directions of the decedent, the executrix offered the 1,292 shares owned by Horace B. Rickey, Sr. at the time of his death to the Company * * *. The price was determined in September of 1967 and on October 23, 1967, $383,194 was paid to the estate.

After the redemption, the percentage ownership interest of the Company shareholders was as follows:

Stockholders	Number of Shares	Percentage
Horace B. Rickey, Jr.	708	73.520%
Robert Rickey	40	4.154%
Elizabeth Rickey	40	4.154%
	788	81.828%
Others	175	18.172
	963	100%

* * *

For federal income tax purposes, the taxpayers treated the redemption of the decedent's 1,292 shares as a distribution in full payment in exchange for the stock and since their basis in the shares had been stepped-up to fair market value at the time of the decedent's death pursuant to Section 1014

---

7. Editor's note. This case focuses on the income tax liability of the Estate of Rickey, Sr. that arose when shares were redeemed from the Estate. The beneficiaries of the Estate were parties to the litigation (rather than the Estate itself) because the Estate had distributed its assets to the beneficiaries prior to the litigation.

of the Code, they reported no income from the redemption. Upon audit of the estate and the individuals' returns for 1968, the Commissioner determined that the redemption was essentially equivalent to a dividend and the 1967 redemption proceeds (to the extent they exceeded the amounts used to pay death taxes under Code Section 303) were dividends to the estate, taxable as ordinary income to the taxpayers as distributees of the estate. Accordingly, each of the taxpayers [as successor to the estate of the decedent] was treated as having received approximately $51,400 additional income in 1968.

In April of 1973, the taxpayers waived their right to receive statutory notices of deficiencies, and consented to immediate assessment of the tax as determined by the Commissioner. In June of 1973 all of the assessed amounts were paid * * *.

The taxpayers subsequently filed timely claims for refunds which were denied by the Commissioner and the instant suit was instituted in District Court. The District Court found in favor of the taxpayers holding that the redemption from the estate was a complete termination of the estate's interest under Section 302(b)(3) and that the waiver agreement filed in 1973 was effective to waive the entity-beneficiary attribution rules * * *.

[S]ection 302(d) provides that unless a redemption meets one of several exceptions spelled out in the Code, a redemption shall be treated as a distribution of property to which Code Section 301 applies. Thus, unless one of the exceptions is applicable, property distributed by a corporation in redemption of its shares will constitute a dividend, to the extent of post–1913 earnings and profits. I.R.C. § 301(c)(1) * * *.

Section 302 of the Code provides a set of exceptions to the general rule outlined above * * *.

One of these exceptions to the general rule of 302(d) is set forth in Section 302(b)(3) which applies "if the redemption is in complete redemption of all of the stock of the corporation owned by the shareholder." At first blush, Section 302(b)(3) would appear to mandate [sale] treatment in the case at bar. Here the estate, which owns 57.295% of Rickey, Inc., sells all of the stock which it owns to Rickey, Inc. But life, particularly tax life, is not so simple.

Section 318 of the Code provides that in certain situations, a shareholder will, for tax purposes, be deemed to own shares of stock which that shareholder does not actually own. One of the situations where this so-called constructive ownership applies, is the area of complete terminations * * *. I.R.C. § 302(c)(1). Thus, a shareholder who completely terminates his interest in a corporation by allowing all the shares which he actually owns to be redeemed, may not qualify under 302(b)(3) if he is deemed to constructively own additional shares of that corporation.

The attribution rules of Section 318 contain four horror stories for taxpayers, only one of which is here relevant. Section 318(a)(3) provides that stock owned, directly or indirectly, by a beneficiary of an estate shall be considered as owned by the estate. Thus, in our case, the estate, owner of Horace B. Rickey, Sr.'s 57.295% of the Company shares, is also deemed by Section 302(c)(1) to own, for purpose of applying Section 302(b)(3), those shares owned by the estate beneficiaries. And so, the argument goes, when the estate sold its 57.295% of Horace B. Rickey, Inc., that redemption did not qualify as a 302(b)(3) complete termination exception to the general rule of 302(d) because 302(c)(1) mandates application of 318(a)(3) and the estate still constructively owns the 788 shares actually owned by the children. Accordingly, the government urges, the redemption is treated as a distribution of property, taxable as per the directives of 301(c) * * *.

* * *

The theory behind the attribution rules is that certain relationships bespeak an economic identity of interest and common control. Thus, partners will act to the betterment of other partners, sons and daughters will so act with respect to their parents and children, estates to their beneficiaries. The Code does, however, recognize that there will be situations where a family may be estranged, or where family members legitimately seek to completely terminate all meaningful contact with a business. This recognition takes the form of Section 302(c)(2) which provides that for purposes of complete termination type redemptions, the attribution rules of 318(a)(1) shall not apply if certain conditions are met. In other words, 302(c)(2) provides an exception to the rule of attribution of 318(a)(1) which is normally applied in determining whether a taxpayer qualifies for the 302(b)(3) (and hence 302(a)) exception to the general rule of 302(d).

Note however that the Code merely provides for the waiver of 318(a)(1) attribution—family attribution * * *. [U]nder a literal reading of the Code, the Rickey estate, regardless of the relationships amongst the estate and the heirs, could not effectively waive the entity attribution rules of 318(a)(3).

Nevertheless, we are asked by appellee to uphold the District Court finding in this case that an estate may file a waiver of the entity attribution rules * * *.

The harsh results which are obtained from mechanical application of the attribution rules, coupled with a vigilant eye on the Congressional purpose in enacting the attribution rules, has led some courts to the conclusion that a slavish application of the attribution rules is improper.

In Estate of Squier v. Commissioner, 35 T.C. 950 (1961), the Tax Court embraced the principle that family discord could belie the community of interest rationale of the attribution rules and was thus a relevant circumstance in determining dividend equivalency under Section 302(b)(1):

> the record herein reveals a sharp cleavage between the executor and members of the Squier family, and in spite of the attribution rules as to stock "ownership", the redemptions herein in fact resulted in a crucial reduction of the estate's control over the corporation. Accordingly, notwithstanding the attribution rules, the redemptions in this case did result in a substantial dislocation of relative stockholdings in

the corporation and also in fact brought about a significant change in control.

Estate of Squier v. Commissioner, 35 T.C. 950, 955–56 (1961).

* * *

In this case, the District Court relied heavily upon the Tax Court opinion in Estate of Crawford, 59 T.C. 830 (1973), when it concluded that the Rickey estate could effectively waive the entity attribution rules of 318(a)(3). Although we agree with the Tax Court's rationale in Crawford, we cannot agree with the District Court's conclusion here that "the (Crawford) court was faced with this identical issue." Crawford involved a redeemed estate whose sole beneficiary was Lillian Crawford mother of Jack and Don Crawford. Jack, Don and the estate owned all the stock of the redeeming corporations. By application of the attribution rules, however, Lillian Crawford was deemed to constructively own all of her children's shares and the estate, in turn, was deemed to own all of her shares. Therefore, the estate owned, actually and constructively, 100% of the subject corporations. Thus, when the redemption of stock by the estate occurred, the Service argued that the estate still owned 100% of the corporation by family attribution to the mother and entity attribution to the estate. The Crawford court held that the estate could properly waive family attribution. Since Mrs. Crawford did not actually own any stock, her son's shares were not attributed to her and then reattributed to the estate. Accordingly, when the estate sold its shares back to the corporation, it had no ownership, actual or constructive, in the companies.

This case is different. Here we have no family attribution problem. There is no attribution among brothers and sisters. See I.R.C. § 318(a)(1). Here the estate is not waiving family attribution of 318(a)(1) but rather the estate attribution rules of 318(a)(3).

* * *

[We nevertheless] hold that an estate may file a waiver of the attribution rules of 318(a)(3) in order to qualify for a 302(b)(3) termination.

NOTES

1. *Impact of I.R.C. § 302(c)(2)(C).* I.R.C. § 302(c)(2)(C) was enacted in response to the Rickey decision. What impact does I.R.C. § 302(c)(2)(C) have on the result in,

(a) the Rickey case?

(b) the Crawford case (discussed by the Rickey court)?

Problem 5–8 (Redemption planning in connection with anticipated death of a shareholder). Father, son, and daughter each own 100 of the 300 outstanding shares of the Atlas Corporation. The stock of each shareholder has a value of $600,000 and a basis of $100,000. Atlas has $1,500,000 of E & P. Father's shares can be redeemed now or after his death which is imminent. When father dies, son and daughter will each receive half of father's property under his will. To minimize income tax costs to all parties, should father's shares be redeemed from,

(a) father before he dies?

(b) father's estate after father dies?

(c) son and daughter after father's estate distributes half of father's shares to each of them?

(d) son after the estate distributes half of father's shares to him, if daughter wishes to retain the shares that father's estate distributes to her?

How does the answer change if mother is the sole beneficiary of father's estate (i.e., son and daughter are not beneficiaries of father's estate)?

2. *Impact of hostility on attribution rules.* Few courts have been willing to follow the Estate of Squier case (discussed by the Rickey court) which refused to apply the attribution rules where hostility existed between the redeemed shareholder and the related shareholders. But see Haft Trust v. Commissioner, 510 F.2d 43 (1st Cir.1975) (holding that family discord is a relevant factor to consider when determining whether the attribution rules should be applied in a case that involved the redemption of the stock of certain children by a corporation that was controlled by their father subsequent to a bitter divorce that effectively severed the father's relationship with his children).

3. *Partial liquidation.* Even if a distribution in redemption of shares does not reduce a shareholder's relative interest in the corporation, the redemption will qualify for sale treatment if the distribution represents a "partial liquidation" of the distributing corporation. I.R.C. § 302(b)(4). In contrast to the standards of I.R.C. §§ 302(b)(1), (2), and (3), the partial liquidation standard focuses on shrinkage at the corporate level, rather than at the shareholder level. I.R.C. § 302(e)(1)(A) ("not essentially equivalent to a dividend (determined at the corporate level, rather than at the shareholder level)"). For example, a partial liquidation can often be achieved if a corporation distributes the assets of a business with an operating history of at least five years (or sells those assets and distributes the proceeds of sale) if, after the distribution, the corporation continues to own assets of another business with an operating history of at least five years. See I.R.C. §§ 302(e)(2), (3). A distribution in partial liquidation can qualify for sale treatment even if no shareholder's relative interest in the corporation changes (e.g., the distribution is pro rata). See I.R.C. § 302(e)(4). Partial liquidations are rarely attractive from an income tax standpoint because of the corporate tax that is triggered when a corporation distributes or sells appreciated assets. See I.R.C. § 311(b). Partial liquidations are examined in greater detail at pp. 683–689.

4. *Post-death redemptions.* Under certain circumstances, a limited amount of a decedent's shares may be redeemed in a transaction that automatically qualifies for sale treatment, regardless of whether any of the standards set forth in I.R.C. § 302(b) are satisfied. See I.R.C. § 303. I.R.C. § 303 was intended to help the family of a closely held corporation's principal owner to meet certain costs triggered by the death of the owner without having to sell the business. The provision, however, is drafted somewhat more broadly than necessary to achieve this goal.

In general terms, if stock of a single corporation represents more than 35% of the value of the decedent's estate, a portion of that stock may be redeemed by the corporation in a transaction that automatically qualifies for sale treatment. I.R.C. § 303(b)(2)(A). Alternatively, if the decedent owns at least 20% of the stock of more than one corporation, automatic sale treatment is available if the aggregate value of the decedent's stock in these corporations exceeds 35% of the value of the decedent's estate. I.R.C. § 303(b)(2)(B). In either case, the amount of stock that may be redeemed under I.R.C. § 303 cannot exceed the amount of funeral and administration expenses and certain taxes triggered by death. I.R.C. § 303(a). Even when the decedent's estate has sufficient cash to pay these death related expenses, taxpayers are often advised to allow the corporation to redeem the maximum amount of shares permitted by I.R.C. § 303. Why is it often desirable to engage in a § 303 redemption when the opportunity exists? See I.R.C. § 1014.

5. *No deduction for redemption expenses.* Regardless of whether a redemption qualifies for sale treatment, the distributing corporation may not deduct any expenses incurred "in connection with" the redemption of its stock. I.R.C. § 162(k). Interest paid on funds borrowed to finance a redemption is excepted from this prohibition. I.R.C. § 162(k)(2)(A)(i).

6. *Exploitation of attribution rules.* Taxpayers may sometimes design transactions that intentionally cause the attribution rules to apply. See IRS Notice 2001–45, below.

IRS Notice 2001–45

2001–33 I.R.B. 129.

The Internal Revenue Service and the Treasury Department have become aware of a type of transaction, described below, that is being used by taxpayers for the purpose of generating losses or reducing income or gains. This Notice alerts taxpayers and their representatives that the tax benefits purportedly generated by such transactions are not properly allowable for Federal income tax purposes. This Notice also alerts taxpayers, their representatives, and promoters of such transactions of certain responsibilities that may arise from participating in such transactions.

FACTS

The transaction involves the use of the attribution rules of § 318 of the Internal Revenue Code and § 1.302–2(c) of the Income Tax Regulations to increase the basis of stock owned by a taxpayer (the "Taxpayer") that claims a loss upon disposition of that stock. In the transaction, there is a redemption of stock that is owned by a person (other than the Taxpayer) that is not subject to U.S. tax or is otherwise indifferent to the Federal income tax consequences of the redemption. Purportedly as a result of the application of the attribution rules of § 318, the redemption of stock is claimed to be a dividend under § 301 rather than a payment in exchange for stock under § 302(a). A variety of devices, often including options, is employed to treat the redeemed shareholder as owning stock in the redeeming corporation owned or treated as owned by the Taxpayer under the attribution rules of § 318. The attribution of ownership of such shares purportedly prevents the redemption of stock from reducing the redeemed shareholder's ownership interest in the redeeming corporation, thereby causing the redemption to be treated as a dividend.

As a result of the redemption, the Taxpayer takes the position that under § 1.302–2(c) all or a portion of the basis of the redeemed stock is added to the basis of stock in the redeeming corporation that the Taxpayer owns. The Taxpayer then sells the stock and claims a loss.

* * *

ANALYSIS

Section 302(a) provides that if a corporation redeems its stock and § 302(b)(1), (2), (3), or (4) applies, such redemption shall be treated as a distribution in part or full payment in exchange for the redeemed stock. * * * Section 302(d) provides that if § 302(a) does not apply, the distribution will be treated as a distribution subject to § 301. Section 302(c)(1) provides that, in determining whether the provisions of § 302(b) are satisfied, the attribution rules of § 318 shall apply. Section 301(c)(1) provides that the portion of the distribution that is a dividend shall be included in the redeemed shareholder's gross income.

Section 1.302–2(c) provides that when an amount received in a redemption of stock is treated as a distribution of a dividend, "proper adjustment" of the basis of the remaining stock will be made with respect to the stock redeemed. Example 2 of § 1.302–2(c) illustrates a proper adjustment where the entire amount received in redemption of the stock held by one spouse is treated as a dividend because the redeemed spouse is treated as owning stock held by the other spouse. In that example, the basis of the stock of the non-redeemed spouse is properly increased by the basis of the stock of the redeemed spouse.

It is the position of the Service and the Treasury that such an adjustment is not proper in every case in which the redeemed shareholder retains no stock in the redeeming corporation. The example in the regulations is premised on the concept that an adjustment is appropriate where the redeemed spouse is required to include the full redemption proceeds as a dividend in gross income that is subject to U.S. tax and such spouse retains no stock to which the basis of the redeemed stock could attach.

The Service intends to disallow losses claimed (or to increase taxable income or gains) in the transactions described in this Notice to the extent a taxpayer derives a tax benefit that is attributable to stock basis purportedly shifted from the redeemed shares. Depending on the facts of the particular case, reasons for disallowance may include, but are not limited to, the following: (1) the redemption does not result in a dividend (and consequently there is no basis shift) because, viewing the transaction as a whole, the redemption results in a reduction of interest in the redeeming corporation to which § 302(b) applies; (2) the basis shift is not a "proper adjustment" as contemplated by § 1.302–2(c); and (3) there is no attribution of stock ownership or basis shift because the steps taken to achieve those results are transitory and serve no purpose other than tax avoidance.

In addition, the Service may impose penalties on participants in these transactions, or, as applicable, on persons who participate in the promotion or reporting of these transactions, including the accuracy-related penalty under § 6662, the return preparer penalty under § 6694, the promoter penalty under § 6700, and the aiding and abetting penalty under § 6701.

* * *

The Service and Treasury recognize that some taxpayers may have filed tax returns taking the position that they were entitled to the purported tax benefits of the type of transaction described in this Notice. We advise these taxpayers to take prompt action to file amended returns.

NOTES

1. *Impact on redeemed shareholder.* Why was the redeemed shareholder in Notice 2001–45 willing to forego sale treatment?

2. *Right or wrong?* If the fact pattern delineated in the Notice were litigated, would you expect the Taxpayer or the Internal Revenue Service to prevail?

e.   IMPACT ON EARNINGS & PROFITS

I.R.C. §§ 312(a), (b), (n)(7)

A redemption that fails to satisfy any of the tests set forth in I.R.C. § 302(b) or § 303 is treated as a one-side distribution. I.R.C. § 302(d). The effect of a one-side distribution on the distributing corporation's earnings & profits was previously examined. See I.R.C. §§ 312(a), (b); pp. 203–207.

When a redemption satisfies one of the tests set forth in I.R.C. § 302(b) or § 303, the redeemed shareholder is treated as selling her shares to the distributing corporation. I.R.C. § 302(a). When a redemption is treated as a sale, the distributing corporation's earnings & profits are reduced according to the rules of I.R.C. § 312(n)(7). Under that provision, the distributing corporation's E & P are reduced by the "ratable share of the earnings & profits * * * attributable to the stock redeemed" but this reduction may not exceed the actual amount of the distribution. The ratable share of E & P attributable to the redeemed stock often may be computed as follows:[8]

---

8. The computation is more complicated when the redeeming corporation has more than one class of outstanding stock. See Staff of the Joint Committee on Taxation, General Explanation of the Revenue Provisions of the Tax Reform Act of 1984, 181 (1984).

E&P × Number of shares redeemed
        Number of shares outstanding
        before redemption

In effect, a redemption that qualifies as a sale generally reduces the distributing corporation's E & P by a percentage equal to the percentage of the corporation's stock surrendered by the redeemed shareholder.

> *Example 5–D (Reduction in E & P when redemption treated as sale):* Distributing Corporation has $100,000 of E & P. Jill owns 20 of the 100 outstanding shares of Distributing. Lewis, who is unrelated to Jill, owns the other 80 shares of Distributing. Distributing redeems all of Jill's shares for $150,000. Jill surrenders a 20% interest in Distributing and, accordingly, Distributing's E & P is reduced by 20%. Thus, the redemption reduces Distributing's E & P by $20,000.[9]

> *Problem 5–9 (Distribution of less than ratable share of E & P).* In Example 5–D, by how much would Distributing's E & P be reduced if Jill's shares were redeemed for $15,000? See I.R.C. § 312(n)(7).

> *Problem 5–10 (Redemption treated as one-side distribution).* In Example 5–D, by how much would Distributing's E & P be reduced if Jill's shares were redeemed for $150,000, Lewis was Jill's father and Jill continued to serve as a director of Distributing after the redemption? See I.R.C. §§ 302, 312(a).

NOTES

1. *Impact on continuing shareholder.* Of what relevance is I.R.C. § 312(n)(7) to the continuing shareholders? Why should a redemption that is treated as a sale to the departing shareholder cause any reduction in the distributing corporation's E & P account?

2. *Redemptions effectuated with property other than money.* When a corporation distributes property other than money to a shareholder in a redemption, does the distributing corporation recognize gain or loss? See I.R.C. § 311. Are the tax consequences to the distributing corporation affected by whether the redemption is treated as a sale or a one-side distribution to the redeemed shareholder? What impact does the distribution have on the distributing corporation's E & P? See I.R.C. §§ 312(a), (b), (n)(7).

> *Problem 5–11 (Distribution of property other than money):* The Benton Corporation has 1,000 outstanding shares and E & P of $100,000. Marta owns 100 Benton shares and she has a basis of $30,000 in these shares. Benton redeems Marta's 100 shares by distributing a parcel of land to her. For each of the following alternatives, determine the tax consequences of the redemption to Benton and Marta, and the amount of Benton's E & P after the redemption.

---

9. $100,000 × (20 ÷ 100) = $20,000.

(a) The land has a value of $100,000, Benton has a basis in the land of $10,000, and the redemption is treated as,

    (i) a one-side distribution. See I.R.C. §§ 311(b), 312(a), (b).

    (ii) a sale. See I.R.C. §§ 311(b), 312(b), (n)(7).

(b) The land has a value of $10,000, Benton has a basis in the land of $100,000, and the redemption is treated as,

    (i) a one-side distribution. See I.R.C. §§ 311(a), 312(a).

    (ii) a sale. See I.R.C. §§ 311(a), 312(n)(7).

2.   SALE TO RELATED CORPORATION

I.R.C. §§ 304(a), (b)(1), (2), (c)

Treas. Reg. § 1.304–2[10]

I.R.C. § 304 subjects certain sales of stock that do not meet the statutory definition of a redemption to the standards set forth in I.R.C. § 302. I.R.C. § 304 is designed to prevent sale treatment when a shareholder who owns a substantial interest in each of two corporations sells stock of one corporation (the "issuing corporation") to the other corporation (the "acquiring corporation").[11] Because the transferring shareholder owns a substantial interest in the acquiring corporation, he can be viewed as indirectly continuing to own part or all of the transferred shares. I.R.C. § 304 adopts this view and limits sale treatment to transfers that result in a meaningful reduction in the transferring shareholder's interest in the issuing corporation. Unless the requisite reduction in interest is achieved, the transaction is treated as a one-side distribution, rather than as a sale.

The evil that I.R.C. § 304 is designed to combat is illustrated by the following example:

Example 5–E (Acquisition by one corporation of stock of a sibling corporation): Alex owns all of the outstanding stock of both X Corporation and Y Corporation. Each corporation has substantial E & P. Alex wishes to receive a distribution from X or Y that qualifies for sale treatment, rather than one-side distribution treatment. If Alex sells half of his X shares to X, a redemption that will be taxed as a one-side distribution occurs because Alex's ownership interest in X is not diminished by the redemption (i.e., Alex owns 100% of X both before and after the redemption). See I.R.C. § 302. The same result occurs if Alex sells half of his Y shares to Y. If, however, Alex sells half of his X shares to Y, the transaction does not satisfy the statutory definition of a "redemption". See I.R.C. § 317(b). Consequently, without § 304, the transaction would be treated as a sale, notwithstanding that Alex still

---

10. Omit Treas. Reg. § 1.304–2(c) Example 2 because, under current law, that example is no longer correct.

11. Technically, this transaction is not a redemption because the acquiring corporation is not the issuer of the acquired stock. See I.R.C. § 317(b).

effectively owns 100% of X (i.e., 50% directly and 50% indirectly through his ownership of Y).

When a person sells stock in one corporation to another corporation, I.R.C. § 304 applies if the seller controls both corporations. I.R.C. § 304(a)(1). The seller is deemed to control both corporations if the seller and/or certain related parties own at least 50% of the stock of each corporation. See I.R.C. § 304(c). When I.R.C. § 304 applies to a transaction, a determination must be made as to whether the consideration received is treated as the proceeds of a sale (which would be offset by basis with any resulting gain or loss characterized as capital gain or loss) or as a one-side distribution (which would be taxed as a dividend to the extent of E & P). See I.R.C. § 304(b). Although dividends are now generally taxed at capital gains rates, dividend treatment still normally results in greater income than sale treatment because dividends cannot be offset by the recipient's stock basis. Also, an individual with capital losses may not apply those capital losses against dividend income. I.R.C. § 1211(b). Finally, dividend treatment will accelerate the income of a shareholder who receives deferred payments that would qualify for the installment method of reporting gain if sale treatment were conferred. See I.R.C. § 453.

I.R.C. § 304 is a masterpiece of complexity and can best be understood by studying the statutory provision in the context of a concrete fact pattern. Follow the Coyle court's analysis of each aspect of the provision and study the notes that follow the case.

Coyle v. United States

United States Court of Appeals, Fourth Circuit, 1968.
415 F.2d 488.

■ SOBELOFF, CIRCUIT JUDGE: * * *

In 1958, taxpayer George L. Coyle, Sr. (now deceased) transferred 66 shares of Coyle & Richardson, Inc. [hereinafter referred to as C & R] to Coyle Realty Company [hereinafter referred to as Realty] for $19,800. Reporting a long term capital gain on this "sale", Coyle paid a tax computed at that rate on $9,900, which is the difference between the sale price and his basis in the stock. The Internal Revenue Service was of the view that the proceeds should be treated as a dividend and assessed the taxpayer an additional $7,181.90 plus interest. Having fully paid the assessment, taxpayer made timely claim for refund. The District Court granted the refund, but we conclude that it should be denied.

Before the transaction, the 688 outstanding shares of C & R were distributed in the following manner: taxpayer, 369; taxpayer's three sons, an aggregate of 288; taxpayer's wife, 1; O. M. Buck, 25; Julia Farley, 5. Thus, taxpayer and his immediate family owned more than 95.6% of the corporation whose shares were sold. Realty, the acquiring corporation, was owned in equal parts by taxpayer's three sons, each holding 125 of the 375 outstanding shares * * *.

The initial point of controversy is whether the purchase by Realty is to be treated as a sale or as a redemption. Section 304 of the Internal Revenue Code of 1954 provides in pertinent part:

(a) Treatment of certain stock purchases.—

(1) Acquisition by related corporation * * *.—If

(A) one or more persons are in control of each of two corporations, and

(B) in return for property, one of the corporations acquires stock in the other corporation from the person (or persons) so in control,

then * * * such property *shall be treated as a distribution in redemption* of the stock of the corporation acquiring such stock. * * * (Emphasis added.)

Control is defined in § 304(c)(1) as at least 50% of the combined voting power of all voting stock or at least 50% of the total value of all classes of stock. For purposes of determining control, § 304(c)(2) specifically makes applicable the constructive ownership provisions of § 318. Under that section, "[an] individual shall be considered as owning the stock owned, directly or indirectly, by or for * * * his children * * *."

Thus, applying the statute literally, taxpayer was in control of both corporations and the acquisition from him by Realty of the C & R stock must be treated as a redemption. His control of C & R results from his actual ownership of 54% of its outstanding stock, not to mention the attribution to him of his sons' 40%. He had 100% control of Realty by virtue of the fact that all of his sons' stock is attributable to him. The District Court recognized and the taxpayer concedes, as he must, that a plain meaning application of sections 304 and 318 requires this conclusion.

However, the District Court eschewed this direct approach. The court reasoned that since the taxpayer actually owned no shares in Realty, there should be no attribution to him and thus the transaction here was not one between related corporations. Its conclusion then was that the transfer should not be deemed a redemption but a simple sale entitled to long term capital gain treatment.

This interpretation of the constructive ownership rules is at war with both the language of the statute and legislative purpose of Congress. The family attribution rules, which are specifically prescribed by the statute, were designed to create predictability for the tax planner and to obviate the necessity of a court's scrutinizing family arrangements to determine whether every family member is in fact a completely independent financial entity * * *. Yet despite the clear congressional judgment and mandate that the shares of a son are to be treated as his father's for certain limited purposes, the court below read the explicit language as no more than a presumption and then disregarded it.

The statute does not require that a person be an actual shareholder in a corporation before shares in that corporation may be attributed to him

* * *. Indeed, any other construction would be untenable. Under the District Court's reading, if the taxpayer had [owned] at the time of the transfer [an] otherwise insignificant single share in Realty, then 100% of the stock of that corporation could be attributed to him. Clearly such a distinction could not have been intended by Congress.

* * *

Since the District Court held redemption treatment unwarranted, it did not reach the second question to which we now turn: Is the redemption here to be treated as an exchange of stock * * * or is it to be treated as a dividend * * *?

Section 302(b) enumerates those categories of redemptions which are to be treated as exchanges. Both sides agree that the only pertinent category in this case is the most general one, (b)(1), which provides that a redemption shall be treated as an exchange if it "is not essentially equivalent to a dividend."

* * *

[A]ppellee's sole contention is that a payment by a corporation to a non-shareholder may not be characterized as a dividend. With this we agree, for § 316 defines a "dividend" as "any distribution of property made by a corporation to its shareholders" out of earnings and profits. The rub is that § 304(b)(1) specifically states:

> * * * determinations as to whether the acquisition is, by reason of section 302(b), to be treated as a distribution in part or full payment in exchange for the stock shall be made by reference to the stock of the *issuing corporation*. (Emphasis added.)

Thus, in determining whether this redemption was essentially equivalent to a dividend, we must focus attention upon C & R, of which taxpayer was not only a shareholder but by far the major one.

Although several tests have been devised and several factors exalted in determining whether a redemption is not in essence a dividend, we think there is one overriding objective criterion—significant modification of shareholder interests * * *. If the taxpayer's control or ownership of the corporation is basically unaltered by the transaction, then the proceeds he has received as a result of manipulating his corporate stock must be taxed as a dividend.

In examining the respective shareholder interests of C & R before and after the transfer of stock we must bear in mind that § 302(c)(1) explicitly makes applicable to this inquiry the constructive stock ownership rules of § 318. Thus, before the transfer, taxpayer is deemed to have owned not only the 369 shares of C & R actually in his name but also the 288 shares owned by his sons and the one share held by his wife. In all, for purposes of § 302, taxpayer before the transaction owned 658 of C & R's 688 outstanding shares. After the transaction, he held only 303 shares in his own name, but in addition, of course, he also is deemed to have owned the 289 shares of his wife and sons. Moreover, the 66 shares now held by Realty must likewise be attributed to him. Section 318(a)(2)(C) provides that stock owned by a corporation will be attributed proportionately to any person owning 50% or more of the corporation. Section 304(b)(1) directs that in applying the constructive ownership rules for testing whether a redemption is an exchange or a dividend, the 50% requirement of § 318(a)(2)(C) shall not be applicable. In the instant case, this means that the 66 shares held by Realty shall be attributed equally to its owners, taxpayer's sons, and under § 318(a)(1)(A)(ii), these shares are attributed from the sons to the taxpayer. Consequently, after the transaction taxpayer owned 658 shares of C & R, precisely the number with which he started.

As noted in Wiseman v. United States, 371 F.2d 816, 818 (1st Cir. 1967), "the real question here is what was accomplished by this transaction." The answer here is that while corporate ownership and control remained the same, taxpayer, the major shareholder, had come into possession of $19,800. This was essentially nothing but a dividend and was properly taxed as such.

One tangential difficulty arising from this disposition of the case is the proper allocation of taxpayer's basis in the 66 transferred shares. This potential problem is not before us at this time, but we note in passing that there are at least two reasonable solutions. Ordinarily, when there is an acquisition by a related corporation the controlling person is a shareholder in both, and the basis of his stock in the acquiring corporation is increased by his basis in the stock transferred by him. See Treas. Reg. § 1.304–2. In this case, since taxpayer held no shares in Realty, such an approach is not feasible. However, it would be consonant with the underlying rationale of this approach to increase pro rata the basis of the sons' shares in Realty * * *. As an alternative to increasing the basis of taxpayer's sons in Realty, taxpayer's own basis in his remaining 303 shares of C & R could be augmented by his basis in the 66 transferred shares. In any event, it is clear that taxpayer's basis will not disappear.

To sum up, we construe this transaction as a redemption under § 304(a) and find that this redemption was essentially equivalent to a dividend under § 302(b). Therefore, we reverse the judgment of the District Court and enter judgment in favor of the Government.

NOTES

1. *Determining when § 304 applies.* The most dangerous aspect of I.R.C. § 304 is that it can easily be overlooked. When corporate stock is sold and the buyer is a corporation (other than the issuing corporation), an alarm should sound as a reminder to determine whether the transaction is within the scope of I.R.C. § 304. An analysis of whether the selling shareholder is in "control" of both corporations should be undertaken if any shares of the acquiring corporation are owned by: (1) the selling shareholder, (2) an individual related to the selling shareholder, or (3) an entity in which the selling shareholder or any of her relatives owns an interest.

(a) *Low "control" threshold.* "Control" entails a relatively low threshold for I.R.C. § 304 purposes, actual or constructive ownership of stock representing at least 50% of the voting power *or* the value of all classes of stock. See I.R.C. § 304(c). A much higher ownership threshold is required to establish "control" of a corporation for other purposes. See, e.g., I.R.C. § 368(c) (defining control as actual ownership of 80% of the voting stock *and* 80% of the nonvoting stock). Transactions to which the 80% control requirement applies are examined in Chapters 8 and 12.

(b) *Liberal attribution rules for "control".* The attribution rules of I.R.C. § 318 apply when determining "control" under I.R.C. § 304. I.R.C. § 304(c)(3)(A). The attribution net for the purpose of determining "control" under § 304 is larger than the net used when measuring a shareholder's proportionate interest in a conventional redemption. When determining "control" under § 304, the threshold level of ownership for stock to be attributed to or from a corporation is reduced from 50% to 5%. See I.R.C. § 304(c)(3)(B).

Problem 5–12 (Applicability of § 304 to modified facts of Coyle case): Would I.R.C. § 304 have applied to Coyle if only 75 of the 375 outstanding shares of Realty were owned by Coyle's sons and the remaining 300 shares were owned by Z Corporation? For purposes of this problem, assume that Z Corporation had 1,000 outstanding shares, 400 owned by Coyle's daughter and the remaining 600 owned by parties unrelated to the Coyle family.

2. *Mechanics for distinguishing sale from one-side distribution.* The fact that I.R.C. § 304 applies to a transaction does not automatically cause the transaction to be treated as a one-side distribution. If I.R.C. § 304 applies, the transaction is merely subjected to the same tests as a redemption. Thus, the transaction will still be taxed as a sale if any one of the tests set forth in I.R.C. § 302(b) is satisfied.

(a) *Focus is on issuing corporation.* The tests of I.R.C. § 302(b) are applied to the selling shareholder's interest in the *issuing* corporation, not the *acquiring* corporation. See I.R.C. § 304(b)(1)(first sentence). Why?

(b) *More liberal attribution rules for classifying distribution.* When I.R.C. § 304 applies to a transaction, the attribution rules of I.R.C. § 318 apply to measure the selling shareholder's interest in the issuing corporation before and after the transaction. See I.R.C. §§ 304(b)(1) (first sentence), 302(c). The attribution net for measuring the selling shareholder's interest in an I.R.C. § 304 transaction is larger than the net that is used in a conventional redemption. When I.R.C. § 304 applies to a transaction, no minimum threshold level of ownership is required for stock to be attributed to or from a corporation. See I.R.C. § 304(b)(1) (second sentence). The attribution net used to determine whether a transaction within the scope of I.R.C. § 304 is treated as a sale or a one-side distribution is also larger than the attribution net used to determine whether I.R.C. § 304 applies to the transaction (see Note 1(b)).

(c) *E & P of both corporations considered.* If an I.R.C. § 304 transaction is treated as a one-side distribution, the amount of the distribution that constitutes a dividend is determined by first looking at the E & P of the *acquiring* corporation and then at the E & P of the *issuing* corporation. See I.R.C. § 304(b)(2). Prior to 1982, the amount of the dividend was limited to the E & P of the acquiring corporation. Before the law was changed, how could I.R.C. § 304 have been circumvented in Example 5–E (p. 272) if Y Corporation had substantial E & P and X Corporation had no E & P? Can I.R.C. § 304 still be circumvented in these circumstances?

(d) *Shareholder's basis.* If an I.R.C. § 304 transaction is treated as a one-side distribution, the shareholder's basis in the surrendered shares is added to the basis in his shares of the *acquiring* corporation. See Treas. Reg. § 1.304–2(a). What happens to the basis in the surrendered shares if, in a situation like that of the Coyle case, the surrendering shareholder does not actually own any shares of the acquiring corporation? See Rev. Rul. 71–563, 1971–2 C.B. 175 (ruling that the basis in the surrendered shares adds to the basis in the stock actually owned by the surrendering shareholder in the *issuing* corporation). If an I.R.C. § 304 transaction is treated as a sale, what happens to the shareholder's basis in the surrendered shares? See I.R.C. § 1001(a).

(e) *Acquiring corporation's basis.* What is the acquiring corporation's basis in the shares acquired in an I.R.C. § 304 transaction if,

> (i) the transaction is treated as a one-side distribution? See I.R.C. §§ 304(a)(1) (second sentence), 362(a).

> (ii) the transaction is treated as a sale? See I.R.C. § 1012.

Why is the acquiring corporation's basis in the acquired shares not an issue in a conventional redemption? See I.R.C. § 1032.

For illustrations of the methodology for determining whether an I.R.C. § 304 transaction is to be treated as a sale or a one-side distribution and the consequences that follow, see Treas. Reg. § 1.304–2(c) Examples 1, 3.

Problem 5–13 (Waiver of attribution in a § 304 transaction): If Coyle had sold all of his 369 C & R shares to Realty and he satisfied the three requirements set forth in I.R.C. § 302(c)(2)(A), would the transaction have been treated as a sale? What if Coyle actually owned a few shares of Realty?

3. *Subsidiary acquisition of parent's stock.* I.R.C. § 304 applies not only to the acquisition of one corporation's stock by a "sibling" corporation (a "sibling acquisition" governed by I.R.C. § 304(a)(1)). It also applies to the acquisition of stock by a corporation controlled by the issuing corporation (a "subsidiary acquisition"). See I.R.C. § 304(a)(2); Treas. Reg. § 1.304–3.

(a) *Issuing corporation must "control" acquiring corporation.* For I.R.C. § 304(a)(2) to apply, the issuing corporation must "control" the acquiring corporation. For this purpose, the same definition of "control" applies as in the case of a sibling acquisition (i.e., actual or constructive ownership of stock representing at least 50% of the voting power *or* the value of all classes of stock). See I.R.C. § 304(c). The liberal attribution rules also apply in measuring stock ownership. See Note 1(b). Thus, an I.R.C. § 304 subsidiary acquisition can occur even when the issuing corporation actually owns little, if any, of the acquiring corporation's outstanding shares.

(b) *Mechanics for distinguishing sale from one-side distribution.* Whether a subsidiary acquisition is treated as a sale or a one-side distribution depends upon whether any test set forth in I.R.C. § 302(b) is satisfied.

> (i) *Focus is on issuing corporation.* Like a sibling acquisition, the tests of I.R.C. § 302(b) are applied to the selling shareholder's interest in the *issuing* corporation. See I.R.C. § 304(b)(1) (first sentence). Why?

> (ii) *Attribution rules.* Like a sibling acquisition, the attribution rules of I.R.C. § 318 apply (see I.R.C. §§ 304(b)(1) (first sentence), 302(c)) and the attribution net for measuring the selling shareholder's interest is larger than the net that is used in a conventional redemption because no threshold level of ownership is required for stock to be attributed to or from a corporation. See I.R.C. § 304(b)(1) (second sentence).

> (iii) *E & P of both corporations considered.* Like a sibling acquisition, if an I.R.C. § 304(a)(2) transaction is treated as a one-side distribution, the amount of the distribution that is a dividend is determined by first looking at the E & P of the *acquiring* corporation and then at the E & P of the *issuing* corporation. See I.R.C. § 304(b)(2).

> (iv) *Shareholder's basis.* In contrast to a sibling acquisition, if an I.R.C. § 304(a)(2) transaction is treated as a one-side distribution, the shareholder's basis in the surrendered shares is added to his basis in his remaining shares of the *issuing* corporation. See Treas. Reg. § 1.304–3. If the surrendering shareholder does not retain any shares of the issuing corporation, it is unclear what happens to the basis in the surrendered shares. If an I.R.C. § 304(a)(2) transaction is treated as a sale, what happens to the shareholder's basis in the surrendered shares? See I.R.C. § 1001(a).

> (v) *Acquiring corporation's basis.* The statute does not address the acquiring corporation's basis in the shares it acquires in an I.R.C. § 304(a)(2) transaction. Presumably, the acquiring corporation takes a cost basis in the acquired shares. See Broadview Lumber Co. v. United States, 561 F.2d 698 (7th Cir.1977) (finding

that an acquiring corporation takes a cost basis in the stock acquired in an I.R.C. § 304(a)(2) transaction).

C.   LIQUIDATION

A "liquidation" occurs when a corporation transfers all of its assets to its shareholders. In contrast to the statutory provisions governing one-side distributions and redemptions, the liquidation provisions do not include a mechanism for distinguishing a return *on* a shareholder's investment from the return *of* the shareholder's investment. Instead, liquidating distributions are always treated as a return *of* the shareholder's investment (i.e., offset by the shareholder's stock basis with any resulting gain or loss characterized as capital gain or capital loss). See I.R.C. § 331. The corporation's earnings & profits do not affect the tax consequences of a liquidating distribution.

NOTE

Reconciliation of distribution rules. Is it possible to reconcile the shareholder level tax rules that apply to one-side distributions, redemptions and liquidations? Is it sensible to determine the shareholder level tax consequences of liquidations and certain redemptions without regard to the E & P of the distributing corporation when E & P plays such a critical role in determining the shareholder level tax consequences of other redemptions and one-side distributions?

1.   TAXABLE LIQUIDATION

I.R.C. §§ 331, 334(a), 336

Treas. Reg. § 1.331–1

A liquidating distribution generally triggers both a corporate level tax and a shareholder level tax, regardless of whether the corporation sells its assets before it liquidates.[12] If the corporation sells its assets and then distributes the proceeds in liquidation, the corporation is taxed on any difference between the selling price and its basis in each of the transferred assets. I.R.C. § 1001. If, instead, the corporation liquidates by simply distributing all of its assets, the corporation is still treated as selling its assets at fair market value and, accordingly, is taxed on any difference between the market value and the basis of each corporate asset. I.R.C. § 336.[13] When a corporation liquidates, each shareholder is also taxed on

---

12.   Nonrecognition of gain or loss at both the corporate and shareholder levels is provided for certain liquidations of a subsidiary into its corporate parent. See I.R.C. §§ 332, 337; pp. 292–299.

13.   I.R.C. § 336(a) normally permits the distributing corporation to recognize both gains (for those assets with a value in excess of basis) and losses (for those assets with a basis in excess of value). But see I.R.C. § 336(d). I.R.C. § 336 is in marked contrast to I.R.C. § 311

the value of the assets distributed to him to the extent that value exceeds: (1) his share of the corporation's liabilities (including any corporate tax liability triggered by the liquidation)[14] and (2) the basis in his stock. I.R.C. § 331. In addition, each shareholder takes a market value basis in any property received in a liquidating distribution. I.R.C. § 334(a).

Example 5–F (Tax consequences of liquidation). Umbo Corp. owns a single parcel of land with a value of $1,340,000 in which Umbo has a basis of $340,000. Umbo's sole shareholder, Bill, has a basis of $200,000 in his stock. Umbo liquidates by distributing its sole asset to Bill.

Tax consequences to Umbo Corp.
Realization Event (I.R.C. § 336(a))

Amount Realized		$1,340,000
Less: Adjusted Basis in Land		340,000
Realized Gain		$1,000,000
Recognized		
Characterized		
Corporate Tax Liability		$ 340,000 [15]

Tax consequences to Bill
Realization Event (I.R.C. § 331(a))

Amount Realized		
Value of Land	$1,340,000	
Less: Corporate Tax Liability	340,000	
		$1,000,000
Less: Adjusted Basis in Stock		200,000
Realized Gain		$ 800,000
Recognized		
Characterized as Capital Gain		
Shareholder Tax Liability		$ 120,000 [16]
Bill's Basis in Land (I.R.C. § 334(a))		$1,340,000

---

which does not permit a corporation to recognize loss when it distributes property with a basis in excess of value in a non-liquidating distribution (i.e., a one-side distribution or a redemption).

14. A shareholder who receives a distribution in liquidation can be liable for the corporation's obligations to the extent of the liquidation proceeds received by that shareholder. See Harry G. Henn & John R. Alexander, *Laws of Corporations* § 382 (3d Ed. 1983 & Supp. 1986). Any corporate tax triggered by a liquidation normally cannot be collected from the corporation because the liquidation usually coincides with the end of the corporation's existence. Even if the corporation is not dissolved under state law, the corporation normally does not have any assets with which to pay a tax after the liquidation occurs. Thus, any corporate tax triggered by a liquidation is normally collected from the shareholders. The liability of a distributee-shareholder for corporate taxes is known as "transferee liability". See I.R.C. § 6901. Transferee liability is a secondary and derivative liability for unpaid taxes that gives the Internal Revenue Service a secondary method for collecting a transferor's unpaid tax, but only to the extent of the amount transferred to the distributee-shareholder.

15. $1,000,000 × 34% tax rate (I.R.C. § 11(b)(1)(C)) = $340,000. The corporate tax rate is the same regardless of whether the corporation's gain is characterized as capital gain or ordinary income.

16. $800,000 × 15% tax rate (I.R.C. § 1(h)) = $120,000.

Rendina v. Commissioner

United States Tax Court, 1996.
72 T.C.M. 474.

■ Beghe, Judge: * * *

FINDINGS OF FACT

* * *

In 1986, petitioner, an accountant, and Ackerman, a construction contractor, formed WSAI as a general business corporation under Ohio law, for the purposes of constructing and selling 18 condominium units. WSAI was operated as a C corporation. Petitioner and Ackerman each paid WSAI approximately $250 for an equal number of common shares of WSAI.

In 1987 and 1988, WSAI constructed the 18 condominium units, known as South Wood * * *.

WSAI financed the construction of South Wood primarily with borrowed funds. The funds used by WSAI consisted of a loan from Security Federal Savings & Loan of approximately $740,000, approximately $68,000 in loans from three of petitioner's accounting clients, and [a loan from petitioner of approximately $40,000].

* * *

Toward the end of 1988, two of the 18 units remained unsold. [By this time, the Corporation had repaid the Security Federal Savings loan.] Petitioner and Ackerman orally agreed that WSAI would transfer title to the two remaining condominium units to petitioner in consideration of petitioner's assumption of [the $68,000 of loans from petitioner's accounting clients] and petitioner's discharge of WSAI's [$40,000] debt owed to him.

In December 1988, WSAI transferred South Wood's two remaining condominium units to petitioner. Petitioner did not report any income or gain from the receipt of the two condominium units on his 1988 Federal income tax return * * *.

With the transfer of the last two condominium units to petitioner in 1988, WSAI no longer held business assets, and ceased to be a going concern. Upon transfer of all 18 condominium units in 1988, WSAI ceased doing business, but did not formally dissolve. Its charter was revoked in 1990 for nonpayment and nonfiling of Ohio franchise tax returns.[17]

* * *

OPINION

* * *

The substantive tax question before us is whether petitioner's receipt of two condominium units, during the taxable year 1988, was a taxable

---

17. Editor's note. Dissolution is a corporate law concept that entails the voluntary filing of proper documents with the state to terminate the corporation's existence. An involuntary dissolution can occur when the corporation fails to pay periodic fees imposed by the state.

distribution from WSAI. Respondent determined that petitioner's receipt of the last two units was a dividend in the amount of $135,800 during the taxable year 1988. Petitioner contended that * * * he received the condominium units in de facto liquidation of WSAI, which would entitle him to use the basis of his WSAI stock to compute his gain on the distribution.

* * *

Applying the three-pronged test of Estate of Maguire v. Commissioner, 50 T.C. 130 (1968): (1) Whether there is a manifest intention to liquidate; (2) whether there is a continuing purpose to terminate corporate affairs; and (3) whether the activities of the corporation and its shareholders are directed toward that objective, we are convinced that WSAI and its shareholders displayed a manifest intention to liquidate and continuing purpose to terminate corporate affairs, and that the activities of WSAI and its shareholders were directed to that end.

Neither the Code nor the regulations to section 331 define the term "complete liquidation." However, the regulations under section 332 (governing subsidiary liquidations) contain a definition of "complete liquidation" under section 332 that applies equally to section 331:

> A status of liquidation exists when the corporation ceases to be a going concern and its activities are merely for the purpose of winding up its affairs, paying its debts and distributing any remaining balance to its shareholders. A liquidation may be completed prior to the actual dissolution of the liquidating corporation. However, legal dissolution of the corporation is not required. Nor will the mere retention of a nominal amount of assets for the sole purpose of preserving the corporation's legal existence disqualify the transaction. [Sec. 1.332–2(c), Income Tax Regs.]

Respondent maintains that petitioner never liquidated WSAI. In support of her position, respondent relies on Haley Bros. Constr. Corp. v. Commissioner, 87 T.C. 498 (1986). In Haley Bros. Constr. Corp., the corporation at issue, Marywood Corp., was not dissolved formally in accordance with State law, and continued to maintain a checking account. We held that there was no liquidation because there was a business purpose for the continued existence of Marywood, which continued to be operated in accordance with that business purpose, holding and selling real property, maintaining a checking account, paying expenses, and filing tax returns. Moreover, the continued corporate existence of Marywood served the purpose of insulating its parent corporation from liabilities on a mortgage and in pending litigation.

In the case at hand, there was no business purpose for WSAI to continue operating. [W]ith the sale or distribution of all of the condominium units, WSAI had no further assets of any consequence.

We are unpersuaded by respondent's assertion that, because WSAI continued some activities through the beginning of 1989, it did not liquidate. Complete liquidation can occur despite an extended liquidation process, and several earlier opinions of this court have upheld liquidations despite protracted time frames. In order for complete liquidation treatment to apply, it is not essential that a formal plan of liquidation be adopted or that the corporation dissolve, as long as there is a manifest intention to liquidate that is carried out.

[T]he intentions of petitioner and Ackerman to liquidate WSAI at the end of 1988 were apparent from the sales of WSAI's assets, its cessation of business, and the agreement of petitioner and Ackerman that WSAI would distribute the last two condominium units to petitioner, in consideration of petitioner's assumption of the corporation's liabilities to its lenders and his recovery of his investment out of the balance. With that final distribution, WSAI held title to no further assets of any substantial consequence.

Finally, respondent argues that petitioner made no disclosure of any kind on his 1988 individual income tax return regarding the receipt of the two condominium units as a liquidating distribution, as required by section 1.331–1(d), Income Tax Regs. * * *.

Section 1.331–1(d), Income Tax Regs., does not impair our ultimate conclusion that a de facto liquidation did occur during the taxable year 1988 in the case at hand. Although section 1.331–1(d), Income Tax Regs., appears to complement section 6043 and section 1.6043–1, Income Tax Regs., thereunder, providing for the filing of Form 966 (Corporate Dissolution or Liquidation) by a corporation that adopts any resolution or plan of liquidation, the filing of Form 966 is not a condition of liquidation treatment under any provision of the Internal Revenue Code. We are satisfied that section 1.331–1(d), Income Tax Regs., like the regulation under section 6043, is directory only. While compliance with these regulations serves the evidentiary function of supporting the conclusion that a distribution was received in a corporate liquidation, and helps to avoid controversies of the sort we now deal with, we regard them as playing only a facilitating role. Petitioner's compliance with section 1.331–1(d), Income Tax Regs., is not a condition precedent to our treating the distribution of the condominium units to petitioner as a liquidating distribution.

We are convinced that the agreement of the WSAI shareholders, petitioner and Ackerman, for the distribution of the last two condominium units to petitioner, in consideration of his taking care of the corporate liabilities and recovering his own investment, manifested WSAI's intention to liquidate, and that that intention was carried out in the informal winding-up of WSAI's affairs that followed.

> * * *

NOTES

1. *Proper form.* What additional steps might the taxpayer in Rendina have taken to avoid the litigation?

2. *Continued importance?* Now that dividends are normally taxed at capital gains rates, is the issue in the Rendina case still significant?

Ethel M. Schmidt v. Commissioner

United States Tax Court, 1970.
55 T.C. 335.

■ BRUCE, JUDGE: * * *

FINDINGS OF FACT

   * * *

The Highland Co. was organized in 1949, under the laws of Kentucky, to engage in the construction business as a contractor or subcontractor. During the year 1965, the petitioner [Ethel M. Schmidt] owned 812 of the total 1,353 shares of common stock of the Highland Co. issued and outstanding * * *. Petitioner's total tax basis in the 812 shares was $62,440.

On January 4, 1965, the stockholders of the Highland Co. unanimously adopted a resolution providing for the dissolution and liquidation of the assets of the Highland Co. A statement of intent to dissolve was prepared and filed * * * in January 1965. All of the outstanding shares of the company were delivered by the stockholders to the secretary-treasurer of the company in 1965. The stock had not been formally canceled, however, nor had the company been finally and completely dissolved in 1965 or at the date of the trial herein.

By the end of the year 1965, the Highland Co. had substantially liquidated its assets, including all of its machinery and equipment, inventories, and other tangible personal property. The remaining assets of the Highland Co. on December 31, 1965, consisted of cash in the amount of $2,551.68 and [bonds] in the amount of $18,531.06 and other claims receivable from customers in the amount of $26,067.11 * * *. Outstanding liabilities were $4,281 * * *. None of the remaining assets were of a type normally subject to appreciation in value.

Petitioner was the owner of the land and buildings at 644 Baxter Avenue on which the Highland Co. had conducted its business operations. She sold this property and relinquished possession to the purchaser on April 15, 1965. Petitioner realized a long-term capital gain in the amount of $24,059.50 upon the sale of the Baxter Avenue property.

   * * *

The proceeds of the liquidation received by the Highland Co. during 1965 were applied in part to the payment of debts, and distributions aggregating $44,000 were made, pro rata, to the stockholders. The petitioner received $26,406.51 in liquidating dividends from the Highland Co. in 1965 * * *.

On her income tax return for the year 1965, petitioner claimed a long-term capital loss on her Highland Co. stock in the amount of $10,440.36, which was applied as an offset in part against the long-term capital gain ($24,059.50) realized by her upon the sale of the Baxter Avenue property. The amount of the long-term capital loss claimed on her Highland Co. stock represented the difference between her unrecovered basis ($36,033.49) and her proportionate interest ($25,593.13) in the remaining unliquidated assets of the corporation as of December 31, 1965, the computation of which took the [bonds] at face value and the accounts receivable at book value * * *.

OPINION

The ultimate issue to be determined herein is whether petitioner is entitled to a capital loss deduction in 1965 on the shares of stock which she owned in the Highland Co.

It was abundantly clear at the end of 1965, that had all the remaining assets of the company been liquidated and the amounts thereof distributed to its stockholders in 1965, petitioner would have sustained a loss on her stock in the Highland Co. Since she had realized a substantial capital gain on the sale of the Baxter Avenue property, it is to her advantage, taxwise, to have the potential loss on her Highland Co. stock recognized in 1965 and offset against her capital gain.

Respondent disallowed the deduction claimed by petitioner on her tax return for 1965 as a loss resulting from the liquidation of the Highland Co. on the ground that "it has not been established that any loss was sustained within the taxable year."

* * *

At the trial, neither of the parties mentioned the statutes deemed applicable by them. On the basis of the pleadings and the facts presented, it might reasonably be assumed that petitioner was claiming a loss deduction on the shares of stock which she owned in the Highland Co. in 1965, on the ground that at the end of 1965 it was apparent that the most she could possibly receive from the liquidation of the Highland Co., in addition to the cash distribution, was $25,593.13, representing the maximum value of her interest in the remaining assets of the corporation, and accordingly that her loss was "identifiable and determinable with reasonable certainty at December 31, 1965," and therefore deductible under section 165 of the Internal Revenue Code of 1954. Respondent so treated the case on his opening brief. On brief, however, petitioner appears to have taken a position different from that referred to above. Her principal contention, as stated on opening brief, is that the loss claimed by her "is unquestionably authorized by * * * section 331(a) of the Internal Revenue Code." * * *

Initially petitioner argues that she should be allowed the loss claimed on her Highland Co. stock in 1965 for the reason that: "It is the general policy of the Code and of sound principles of accounting to offset income by the expenses incurred in producing it, and to offset gains by any losses which may have been incurred in connection with the same transaction." Pointing out that the property sold in April 1965 on which the large gain was realized, was the same property previously used by the Highland Co. in its construction business, petitioner argues: "Since this gain was made in the sale of property in the process of liquidating the business conducted by the Highland Company, that gain should be reducible by all the losses which were sustained in connection with the liquidation of that business." The obvious answer to this argument is that the Baxter Avenue property was owned by petitioner individually. She was not required to sell it because of the liquidation of the Highland Co., but could have leased it to another tenant had she chosen to do so. The sale of the Baxter Avenue property and the liquidation of the Highland Co. were entirely separate transactions.

* * *

Petitioner's contention that she is entitled to a capital loss deduction on her Highland Co. stock in 1965, under the provisions of section 331(a), is likewise without merit.

* * *

As a general rule, losses resulting from a complete liquidation will be recognized only after the corporation has made its final distribution * * *.

In Dresser v. United States, (55 F.2d 499 (Ct.Cl.1932), cert. denied 287 U.S. 635 (1932)), which involved facts substantially similar to those in the present case, the court stated:

> When it appears, as here, that it is reasonably certain that the stockholders will receive a further liquidating dividend, a loss may not be allowed under the taxing act until there is a distribution of such dividend in property or money.

The reason for this rule was explained by the court as follows:

> Until this is done the stock has a value to its owner, and the mere fact that because the corporation is in process of liquidation its value has declined in a particular taxable year to a figure which is less than cost does not entitle the stockholder to elect in which year he will take his loss. It often happens, as here, that the liquidation of a corporation extends over a period of years and a decision that a loss may be taken upon the basis of a valuation of the unliquidated assets and an estimate of the remaining liabilities and expenses would enable the taxing authorities to place the loss in a taxable year in which the taxpayer might have a very small income and would enable the taxpayer to select a taxable year in which to take the loss in which he might have a large income and thereby obtain a greater benefit from the loss.

Certain exceptions to the general rule have been recognized by the courts where the stock is shown to have been worthless prior to complete liquidation, such as, for example, where the corporation's liabilities exceeded its assets * * *; or where the losses are so reasonably certain in fact and ascertainable in amount as to justify their deductions before they were absolutely realized * * *.

Commissioner v. Winthrop, (98 F.2d 74 (2d Cir.1938)), relied upon by petitioner is clearly distinguishable. In that case, a corporation, pursuant to a plan of liquidation, distributed to each of its stockholders certain bonds and a "liquidation certificate" representing an interest in cash, the only remaining asset retained by it. The bonds had a definite market value and, the value of those received by the taxpayer was several thousand dollars less than the cost basis of his stock. The disbursement to be made against the retained cash for payment of taxes, expenses, and cost of dissolution were known with sufficient certainty to enable determination of the amount to be distributed in final liquidation. Based on such valuation the liquidation certificate received by the taxpayer in 1932 had an estimated value of $900 and that was the amount actually received by him in 1934. It was held that the fact and amount of the taxpayer's loss on his stock was determinable with reasonable certainty in 1932.

* * *

In the present case, the Highland Co. was in the process of liquidation but had not been finally and completely liquidated or dissolved as of the end of 1965. It still retained substantial assets, no final liquidating distribution in cash or property had been made as of the end of 1965, and the amount that would eventually be distributed was indefinite and uncertain. The petitioner does not come within any of the recognizable exceptions to the general rule discussed above. We hold that petitioner is not entitled to a capital loss deduction on her Highland Co. stock in 1965, under the provisions of section 331(a).

The fact that petitioner is claiming only the minimum loss which she would sustain on her Highland Co. stock even if the maximum (face) value of the assets retained by the corporation were realized and distributed, does not justify a different conclusion. The fact remains that the precise amount of the loss which petitioner would sustain on her Highland Co. stock was indefinite and uncertain at the end of 1965, and she is not entitled thus to split her anticipated losses. Petitioner has not called our attention to any authorities holding otherwise. As was held by the Supreme Court in Weiss v. Wiener, 279 U.S. 333 (1929), in order to be deductible a loss "must be actual and present, not merely contemplated as more or less sure to occur in the future."

* * *

For the reasons hereinabove discussed, we hold that petitioner is not entitled to a capital loss deduction for the taxable year 1965 on the stock which she owned in the Highland Co.

NOTES

1. *Timing of loss.* In light of the court's holding, would Mrs. Schmidt ever recognize a loss with respect to her Highland Co. stock? Why was it so important to her to recognize the loss in 1965, instead of in a later year? See I.R.C. §§ 1211(b), 1212(b).

2. *Multiple distribution liquidation.* Highland Co. distributed $44,000 pro rata to its shareholders in 1965 of which Mrs. Schmidt received $26,407. What were the tax consequences of this distribution to Mrs. Schmidt? If the parties had not decided to liquidate Highland Co. until January 1, 1966, what would have been the tax consequences of the 1965 distribution to Mrs. Schmidt?

3. *Distribution of difficult to value rights.* If the Highland Co. had distributed all of its assets during 1965, including the right to collect the corporation's remaining claims against customers, Mrs. Schmidt might have been allowed a loss in 1965. The loss would have been allowed if the liquidation were treated as a "closed transaction," causing the value of the contingent rights to be estimated when they were distributed and Mrs. Schmidt to include that value in her amount realized at that time. Any resulting loss would then be allowed. In contrast, if the liquidation were treated as an "open transaction," the rights would not be valued in 1965, but instead would be dealt with when the claims were collected or treated as uncollectible. Open transaction treatment would have left Mrs. Schmidt in the same position she found herself in in the case. See Burnet v. Logan, 283 U.S. 404, 51 S.Ct. 550 (1931).

When closed transaction treatment will cause the taxpayer to realize a gain, the Internal Revenue Service normally insists on closed transaction treatment in all but the most extreme cases. See Rev. Rul. 58–402, 1958–2 C.B. 15 (requiring the "valuation of contracts and claims to receive indefinite amounts of income, such as those acquired with respect to stock in liquidation of a corporation, except in rare and extraordinary cases"). The Internal Revenue Service is likely to resist closed transaction treatment, however, when such treatment results in a loss, as in Mrs. Schmidt's case.

4. *Distribution of installment obligation.* When a corporation sells its assets in a deferred payment transaction that qualifies as an installment sale, the corporation's gain is normally recognized as each payment is received. See I.R.C. § 453. If the corporation liquidates before receiving all the deferred payments, the corporation normally must recognize the remaining gain when it distributes the installment obligation. See I.R.C. § 453B(a). Under certain circumstances, however, the shareholders receiving the installment obligation in a liquidating distribution may defer the recognition of gain realized with respect to their stock until they receive payments under the installment obligation. See I.R.C. § 453(h)(1).

Ford v. United States

United States Court of Claims, 1963.
311 F.2d 951.

OPINION OF COMMISSIONER

[T]he plaintiffs * * * were stockholders in the W. F. Taylor Company, Inc., which owned the Free State Plantation (hereinafter referred to as the plantation) * * *.

On December 30, 1936, the corporation was liquidated and thereupon * * * the [plantation was] distributed to the plaintiffs * * *. The liabilities of the corporation aggregating [$150,000] were assumed * * * by the plaintiffs * * *.

As a result of the liquidation, the shareholders paid a capital gains tax in accordance with [the predecessor to I.R.C. § 331]. The tax was computed on the difference between the shareholders' basis of their stock in the corporation [$25,000] and the market value of the assets received [$250,-000], less the assumed liabilities of [$150,000] * * *. Thus, the amount of the corporate liabilities assumed by the plaintiffs * * * served * * * to decrease the amount of gain they realized on the liquidation and therefore the amount of their individual income tax liabilities.

* * *

On March 1, 1955, plaintiffs sold the plantation * * * for [$750,000] * * *. Prior to the sale, the liabilities of the corporation which plaintiffs * * * had assumed upon its liquidation were discharged.

In reporting the capital gains realized from the sale of the plantation in their income tax returns for 1955 and 1956, plaintiffs used the figure of [$400,000] as the basis of the plantation. This amount was arrived at by adding to their claimed cost for the plantation * * * the indebtedness assumed at the time of liquidation of the corporation. The Commissioner asserted deficiencies against the plaintiffs upon his determination that their total adjusted basis for the plantation was [$250,000] * * * the market value of the * * * plantation that was distributed to plaintiffs when the corporation was liquidated * * *. Plaintiffs' timely claims for refund of taxes paid for the years 1955 and 1956 were disallowed and these actions were instituted.

* * *

[T]he sole issue is whether the basis of the plantation, which was distributed to plaintiffs upon the complete liquidation of the Taylor Company and upon which a gain was recognized at the time they received such property, should be computed by adding to the fair market value of the plantation on the date of liquidation * * * the corporate liabilities which they then assumed and discharged prior to their sale of the property in 1955.

The Internal Revenue Code of 1954 states that the gain from the sale of properties shall be the excess of the amount realized from the sale over the adjusted basis of the property sold, I.R.C. § 1001. Generally, cost is the basis but corporate distributions are an exception. I.R.C. § 1012.

The exception to the basis-shall-be-the-cost rule with respect to corporate distributions of the type involved here is I.R.C. § 334(a) * * *.

* * *

It is defendant's position that * * * plaintiffs' basis for the sale of the plantation in 1955 was the market value of that property at the time it was distributed to plaintiffs.

Plaintiffs agree that * * * when the property was distributed to them, its basis in their hands was its fair market value. Plaintiffs, however, insist that their receipt of the plantation upon liquidation should be viewed as a purchase of the property and that the amount of obligations which they assumed at liquidation but discharged in subsequent years should be added to its fair market value as of the date of liquidation in order to arrive at the proper basis at the time they sold it in 1955. Plaintiffs point to the first sentence of I.R.C. § 1016(a) * * *.

The fallacy in plaintiffs' contention is that the basis of identical property in the hands of a purchaser or stockholder-distributee is to be computed in the same manner. Under current concepts of our law of taxation, a purchase is not considered an appropriate time to measure gain or loss and is not a taxable transaction. It is quite true that a purchaser of property is generally entitled to include in his cost basis, immediately upon purchase, the amount of any mortgages or any other liabilities assumed. On the other hand, a corporate liquidation is a taxable transaction in which the gain or loss is then measured to the shareholders and the amount of gain or loss becomes a factor in fixing the basis of distributed corporate property in the hands of the stockholder-distributees * * *. When known liabilities are assumed by the stockholders upon the liquidation of a corporation * * * [the amount received is reduced by the shareholder's portion of the amount of the liability which he agrees to pay, even though it is paid in a year subsequent to the distribution].

Exactly that procedure was followed by the Commissioner in computing plaintiffs' capital gains upon the liquidation of the Taylor Company in 1936.

Read in its entirety, section 1016 contains no provision which authorizes or requires a double deduction such as plaintiffs now seek * * *.

* * *

It follows that plaintiffs are not entitled to add any portion of the liabilities assumed upon the liquidation of the Taylor Company to the fair market value of the plantation at that time for the purpose of computing capital gains upon the sale in 1955. The total adjusted basis of the plantation at the time of the sale in 1955 was [$250,000] * * *.

NOTE

Right or wrong. Did the Ford court correctly resolve the issue before it? Why or why not?

Problem 5–14 (Impact of corporate liabilities on liquidating distribution). Briles Corp. owns a parcel of land with a market value of $250,000 in which it has a basis of $100,000. Briles Corp. liquidates by distributing all of its assets (the parcel of land) to its sole shareholder, Nelson, who has a basis of $25,000 in his stock. What are the corporate level and shareholder level tax consequences when Briles Corp. liquidates if,

(a) Briles Corp. has no liabilities other than the corporate tax liability triggered by the liquidating distribution?

(b) in addition to the corporate tax liability triggered by the liquidating distribution, Briles Corp. has $150,000 of liabilities that Nelson effectively assumes when Briles Corp. liquidates?

2.   SUBSIDIARY LIQUIDATION

I.R.C. §§ 332, 334(b), 337

Treas. Reg. §§ 1.332–1, –2, –5, –7

Although liquidations are always treated as a sale at the shareholder level, the gain or loss realized by a shareholder receiving a liquidating distribution is not recognized in certain cases. See I.R.C. § 332. To qualify for nonrecognition treatment, the shareholder receiving the distribution must be a corporation (the "Parent") which owns stock representing at least 80% of the voting power *and* at least 80% of the value of the outstanding stock of the liquidating corporation (the "Subsidiary"). See I.R.C. §§ 332(b)(1), 1504(a)(2). In addition, the liquidating distributions must be made within a specified time frame. See I.R.C. §§ 332(b)(2), (3). Does I.R.C. § 332 apply if the Parent reaches the 80% threshold in anticipation of the liquidation?

George L. Riggs, Inc. v. Commissioner

United States Tax Court, 1975.
64 T.C. 474.

■ DRENNEN, JUDGE: * * *

FINDINGS OF FACT

[T]he petitioner, George L. Riggs, Inc. (hereinafter Riggs), is a corporation * * *.

* * *

The Standard Electric Time Co. (hereinafter Standard) is a liquidated Connecticut corporation * * *.

* * *

Standard * * * had 11,156 shares of common stock issued and outstanding. Petitioner owned 8,047 shares of Standard's common stock (approximately 72.13 percent) * * *.

Frances Riggs–Young was president and a member of the board of directors of both Standard and petitioner * * *.

The corporate charter or by-laws of * * * Standard * * * required a vote of at least two-thirds of the [voting] shares * * * to authorize a liquidation of these corporations.

By * * * letter dated December 13, 1967, Frances Riggs–Young, in her capacity as president of Standard, notified the * * * shareholders of Standard of * * * a special meeting to be held on December 27, 1967, * * *:

called for the purpose of authorizing the sale of substantially all of the Company's assets to a subsidiary of Johnson Service Company for $3,475,000 * * *. [T]o permit Johnson's subsidiary to carry on the business under the name "The Standard Electric Time Company", it is proposed to change the name of your Company to Riggs–Young Corporation.

The [letter] also indicated that an affirmative vote of two-thirds of the outstanding shares of common stock * * * would be necessary to approve the sale. In addition, the letter * * * stated:

> If the sale of assets is approved and carried out, it is contemplated that during the year 1968 your Company will make an offer to purchase the shares of Common Stock held by all shareholders other than George L. Riggs, Inc.

[On December 27, 1967, the shareholders of Standard held a special meeting and approved the sale of assets. On December 29, 1967, substantially all of the assets of Standard were sold to a wholly owned subsidiary of Johnson Service Co. In connection with this transaction, the name of Standard was changed to Riggs–Young Corp. (hereinafter Riggs–Young).]

* * *

On April 17, 1968, the board of directors of Riggs–Young held a special meeting and * * * authorized Riggs–Young to make an offer to all of its common shareholders with the exception of George L. Riggs, Inc. * * * to purchase such shareholder's common stock for $279 per share * * *.

* * *

On April 26, 1968, Frances Riggs–Young, in her capacity as president of Riggs–Young, sent a letter to the common shareholders of Riggs–Young, stating an offer by Riggs–Young to purchase all of its outstanding common stock, except those shares held by petitioner * * *. This letter also stated:

> If this offer is accepted by substantially all of the stockholders to whom it is directed, the Directors will consider liquidation and final dissolution of the Corporation.

* * *

The tender offer was motivated in part at least by the following: (1) A desire to eliminate minority shareholders who might have different investment objectives or needs from those of the majority shareholder; and (2) a desire to provide the minority shareholders, many of whom were former employees of Standard, the opportunity to receive cash for their shares so they could avoid being locked into a personal holding company. Counsel for petitioner and Riggs–Young also recognized the desirability of petitioner's owning 80 percent of the common stock of Riggs–Young * * * to permit the possible further liquidation of Riggs–Young under section 332 of the Code to simplify the corporate structure.

[The] redemption of sufficient shares of common stock to give the petitioner at least 80 percent of the Riggs–Young common stock occurred on May 9, 1968.

* * *

On June 20, 1968, the board of directors and shareholders of Riggs–Young held separate meetings and voted to adopt a plan of complete liquidation and dissolution of the corporation with the liquidating distribution to be completed no later than December 31, 1970.

On or about July 10, 1968, Riggs–Young Corp. filed a Form 966, an information return noting the adoption of the plan of liquidation and dissolution, with the district director of internal revenue, Boston, Mass. The form was accompanied by a certified copy of the resolution of liquidation.

Between June 20, 1968, and December 31, 1968, pursuant to the liquidation of Riggs–Young, the petitioner received liquidating distributions in the total amount of $2,211,440 * * *.

* * *

Liquidation and dissolution of Riggs–Young were completed by the end of its 1968 taxable year * * *.

Petitioner realized a gain of $2,168,975 from the liquidation of Riggs–Young, the difference between liquidating distributions in the total amount of $2,211,440 and petitioner's basis in the stock of Riggs–Young of $42,465. This gain was reported on the petitioner's Federal income tax return for the taxable year ended March 31, 1969, but not recognized under the provisions of section 332(a), I.R.C. 1954.

* * *

OPINION

The only question for decision is whether petitioner owned at least 80 percent of the outstanding stock of its subsidiary, Riggs–Young Corp., at the time Riggs–Young Corp. adopted a plan of liquidation within the meaning of section 332, I.R.C. 1954, so that the gain realized by petitioner on the liquidation of Riggs–Young is not to be recognized by virtue of that section. The vital question is when did Riggs–Young adopt a plan of liquidation within the meaning of section 332.

Respondent argues that the plan of liquidation was adopted on December 27, 1967, when about 90 percent of the stock of Riggs–Young (then Standard) was voted in favor of selling substantially all of the assets of Riggs–Young * * *; or not later than about April 17, 1968, when the board of directors of Riggs–Young voted to * * * make an offer to purchase all of the common stock of Riggs–Young then outstanding with the exception of the stock owned by petitioner * * *.

On the other hand petitioner contends that the plan of liquidation of Riggs–Young was first adopted when it was formally adopted by vote of the stockholders on June 20, 1968, or at the earliest when counsel for petitioner recommended to petitioner in the early days of June 1968 that it liquidate Riggs–Young. Petitioner also contends that section 332, is an elective section and a taxpayer, by taking appropriate steps, can render that section applicable or inapplicable.

* * *

Nowhere in the pertinent statute is the phrase "the date of the adoption of the plan of liquidation" defined * * *. The date of the shareholder resolution [authorizing the distribution of all the assets of the corporation] should ordinarily be considered the date of the adoption of the plan of liquidation for purposes of section 332 * * *.

This Court has noted, in interpreting section 112(b)(6), I.R.C. 1939 (the predecessor of section 332, I.R.C. 1954), that although the adoption of the plan of liquidation "need not be evidenced by formal action of the corporation or the stockholders * * * even an informal adoption of the plan to liquidate presupposes some kind of definitive determination to achieve dissolution * * *." Distributors Finance Corporation, 20 T.C. 768 (1953). The mere general intention to liquidate is not the adoption of a plan of liquidation * * *.

* * *

Respondent, in an effort to show that the plan of liquidation of Riggs–Young was informally adopted on December 27, 1967, or no later than April 1968, alludes to actions and statements made in connection therewith taken between December 1967 and June 1968. Petitioner offered the testimony of persons involved in those actions to explain what the parties had in mind in taking those actions and making the statements which cast a quite different light on the reasons therefor. This testimony was credible and not shaken by cross-examination. In light of such evidence, we cannot agree with respondent's inference that these actions constituted an informal adoption of a plan of liquidation of Riggs–Young prior to May 9, 1968.

Respondent argues that the letter dated December 13, 1967, sent to the common shareholders of Standard (Riggs–Young) notifying them of the proposed sale of its assets and that the corporation was contemplating an offer to purchase the common shares held by all shareholders other than petitioner if the sale was approved, clearly indicates that the shareholders at the meeting on December 27, 1967, intended to approve not only the sale of the assets, but also the liquidation of Standard (Riggs–Young).

We believe this infers too much. As petitioner points out, the use of the word "contemplated" shows the acquisition of the common stock of the minority shareholders was merely a possibility about which a final decision had not been made. In any event, from the possibility of a tender offer to the minority shareholders, we cannot conclude ipso facto, that a plan for the liquidation had been adopted. Petitioner explained that the possibility of this tender offer was made known to the shareholders in order to avoid any possible disclosure problem with the securities law and to apprise the shareholders, from a fairness standpoint, of eventual possibilities resulting from the sale. This explanation is reasonable.

* * *

[R]espondent views the letter dated April 26, 1968, drafted by Frances Riggs–Young as president of Riggs–Young, which contained the tender offer to the common shareholders, other than petitioner * * *, as an additional indication of a prior adoption of a plan to liquidate. In this letter, Frances Riggs–Young did state that if substantially all of the shareholders accepted the offer, the directors of the corporation would consider liquidation and final dissolution of Riggs–Young.

[Petitioner's attorney] candidly admitted that he had undoubtedly discussed the possibility of liquidation of Riggs–Young at some prior point with Frances Riggs–Young, but hastened to add that he neither recommended liquidation at this time nor did she direct steps be taken to liquidate. Further, [he] testified that he would never have recommended liquidation of Riggs–Young if petitioner had failed to achieve the 80–percent ownership.

* * *

The very most that can be gleaned from the evidence favorable to respondent's contention is that there may have been a general intent on the part of petitioner's advisors somewhere along the line prior to May 9, 1968, to liquidate Riggs–Young when and if petitioner achieved 80–percent ownership of Riggs–Young stock as a result of the tender offer. However, the formation of a conditional general intention to liquidate in the future is not the adoption of a plan of liquidation.

A mere intent by a taxpayer-corporation to liquidate a subsidiary prior to meeting the 80–percent requirement of section 332 should not be tantamount to the adoption of a plan of liquidation for the subsidiary at the point in time when that intent is formulated or manifested. Such a result would thwart the congressional intent of section 332 and prior judicial interpretations of this section and its predecessor.

The predecessor of section 332, I.R.C. 1954, was section 112(b)(6), first enacted in 1935. The purpose of section 112(b)(6) was to encourage the simplification of corporation structures and allow the tax-free liquidation of a subsidiary.

* * *

The [Senate Finance Committee Report to the 1954 Code] seems inescapably to reflect a legislative understanding * * * that taxpayers can, by taking appropriate steps, render the subsection applicable or inapplicable as they choose, rather than be at the mercy of the Commissioner on an "end-result" theory. Nowhere in the subsection is there any express reference to an "election" or an "option" * * *.

Based on legislative history of this section and prior judicial decisions, we conclude that section 332 is elective in the sense that with advance planning and properly structured transactions, a corporation should be able to render section 332 applicable or inapplicable * * *.

Such power of planning presupposes some right to forethought and the accompanying intent to achieve the desired goal. It would be a logical inconsistency equivalent to a "Catch–22" to say that a corporation has the power to control the application of this section, but that once the corporation formulates the intent to do so (assuming that at or subsequent to the time the intent was formed, it owned less than the required 80 percent but enough stock to cause the liquidation of the subsidiary), it has adopted a plan of liquidation and has precluded itself from the section.

A basic tenet of our tax laws is that a taxpayer has the legal right to decrease or altogether avoid his taxes by means which the law permits. At most, petitioner did no more than follow this prerogative.

The shareholders of Riggs–Young formally adopted the plan of liquidation of the corporation on June 20, 1968 * * *. We recognize that the adoption of a plan of liquidation need not be evidenced by formal action of the corporation or shareholders. In this case, however, we find on the evidence that the plan of liquidation was adopted when the formal action was taken on June 20, 1968 * * *.

Respondent has cited and relied on Rev. Rul. 70–106, 1970–1 C.B. 70 as supportive of his position. This Court is not bound by a revenue ruling. In addition, we find the facts of this case are greatly dissimilar to those contained in the ruling * * *.

Revenue Ruling 70–106

1970–1 Cum.Bull. 70.

The liquidation of a subsidiary fails to meet the 80 percent control requirement under section 332(b)(1) of the Code where a corporate shareholder owning 75 percent of the subsidiary's stock causes the subsidiary to redeem the minority shareholders' 25 percent interest before adopting a liquidation plan.

Minority shareholders owned twenty-five percent of the capital stock of corporation X. The remaining seventy-five percent of the capital stock of X was owned by Corporation Y. Y desired to liquidate X in a transaction to which section 332 of the Internal Revenue Code of 1954 would apply in order that Y would recognize no gain on the transaction. The minority shareholders agreed to have their stock of X redeemed. Following the distribution to the minority shareholders, Y owned all the stock of X. Y then adopted a formal plan of complete liquidation of X and all of the remaining assets of X were distributed to Y.

Held, all of the shareholders of X received a distribution in liquidation under the provisions of section 331 of the Code, and the gain is recognized to Y and gain or loss is recognized to the minority shareholders under section 331 of the Code. The liquidation fails to meet the eighty percent stock ownership requirements of section 332(b)(1) of the Code since the plan of liquidation was adopted at the time Y reached the agreement with the minority shareholders and at such time, Y owned seventy-five percent of the stock of X.

NOTES

1. *Distinguishing case from ruling.* The Riggs court stated that the facts in that case, "are greatly dissimilar to those contained in [Rev. Rul. 70–106]." Can you describe the factual differences? Why did the taxpayer prevail in Riggs? How would you advise a corporation that owned 70% of the stock of Xerxes Corporation and wished to cause Xerxes to liquidate without triggering any current taxes? See Rev. Rul. 75–521, 1975–2 C.B. 180 (ruling that § 332 applies when a corporate shareholder owning 50% of a corporation's stock purchased the remaining shares and, immediately thereafter, adopted a plan of complete liquidation of the subsidiary).

2. *Reconciling I.R.C. § 332 with double taxation.* When Parent Corporation ("Parent") owns at least 80% of the stock of Subsidiary Corporation ("Subsidiary") and Subsidiary liquidates, is the gain or loss realized by Parent with respect to its stock in Subsidiary lost or preserved? See I.R.C. § 334(b). Can I.R.C. § 332 be reconciled with the general rule of taxing C Corporation income twice? What relationship exists between I.R.C. § 332 and § 243 (see pp. 59–65)?

3. *Corporate level tax consequences.* When Parent Corporation ("Parent") owns at least 80% of the stock of Subsidiary Corporation ("Subsidiary") and Subsidiary liquidates, I.R.C. § 332 impacts on the realization event that occurs with respect to Parent's stock in Subsidiary. Does a realization event also occur with respect to Subsidiary's assets when it liquidates? See I.R.C. § 336(a). Does Subsidiary recognize its gains or losses when it liquidates? See I.R.C. § 337. Are the gains and losses realized by Subsidiary when it liquidates lost or preserved? See I.R.C. § 334(b). Does I.R.C. § 337 have the same effect as I.R.C. § 332? Can I.R.C. § 337 be reconciled with the general rule of taxing C Corporation income twice?

> *Problem 5–15 (Impact of minority shareholder):* Parent owns 90% of the stock of Subsidiary and has a basis of $500,000 in its stock. Minority owns the remaining 10% of the stock of Subsidiary and has a basis of $80,000 in its stock. Subsidiary's assets consist of two parcels of land; Parcel A with a value of $900,000 in which Subsidiary has a basis of $100,000 and Parcel B with a value of $100,000 in which Subsidiary has a basis of $10,000. If Subsidiary distributes Parcel A to Parent and Parcel B to Minority, what are the tax consequences to all parties?

> *Problem 5–16 (Impact of indebtedness to parent):* Parent owns 100% of the stock of Subsidiary and has a basis of $600,000 in its stock. In addition, Parent lent Subsidiary $300,000. Subsidiary has assets with a value of $1,800,000 in which Subsidiary has a nominal basis. If Subsidiary liquidates, what are the tax consequences to Parent and to Subsidiary? See I.R.C. § 337(b)(1). How does the answer change if

Subsidiary's assets have a value of only $180,000 (rather than $1,800,000)?

D.   Special Characterization Rules

I.R.C. §§ 1202, 1244

When shareholders sell their stock or receive distributions that are treated as sales, any gain or loss recognized by each shareholder is normally characterized as capital gain or capital loss. I.R.C. §§ 1221, 1222. In the case of an individual, capital gains are taxed at a maximum rate of 15%. I.R.C. § 1(h). An individual's capital losses may only offset capital gains and up to $3,000 of ordinary income in any tax year, but unabsorbed capital losses may be carried forward indefinitely. I.R.C. §§ 1211(b), 1212(b). The notes that follow summarize special characterization rules that apply to certain stock sales and certain distributions treated as sales.

NOTES

1. *Shareholder may exclude 50% of gain for certain sales of stock (I.R.C. § 1202).* I.R.C. § 1202 permits a non-corporate taxpayer who holds "qualified small business stock" for more than five years to exclude 50% of any gain recognized on the sale or exchange of the stock. I.R.C. § 1202(a). The 50% of the gain included in gross income is taxed at a maximum capital gains rate of 28%, not 15%. See I.R.C. § 1(h)(4)(A)(ii). (In addition, 7% of the excluded gain is subject to the alternative minimum tax. See I.R.C. § 57(a)(7).) A shareholder may apply the exclusion to as much as $10 million of recognized gain for each qualifying corporation in which the shareholder owns stock. The exclusion may be applied to even greater amounts of gain in any qualifying corporation in which the taxpayer has invested more than $1 million. See I.R.C. § 1202(b). The exclusion only applies to newly issued stock acquired from the issuing corporation. In other words, the exclusion does not apply to outstanding stock acquired from another shareholder. See I.R.C. § 1202(c)(1).

Only a C Corporation may issue "qualified small business stock." The issuing corporation cannot have more than $50 million in assets either before or immediately after the issuance. (Assets are measured by their adjusted basis. In determining the adjusted basis of property contributed to the corporation, however, such property is treated as having a basis equal to its market value at the time of the contribution.) See I.R.C. § 1202(d). In addition, at least 80% of the corporation's assets must be used in the conduct of a trade or business other than many specifically excluded businesses. Among the excluded businesses are banking, leasing, farming, the operation of a hotel or restaurant and any business where the principal asset is the reputation or skill of one or more of its employees (e.g., a medical practice, a law firm, or a consulting firm). See I.R.C. §§ 1202(c)(2), (e).

The exclusion applies only to stock that is held for more than five years. In addition to applying to gains recognized when qualifying stock is sold, the provision will presumably apply to gains recognized when the issuing corporation liquidates or redeems shares in a transaction that is treated as a sale.

If qualified small business stock held by a noncorporate taxpayer for more than six months is sold, the seller may elect not to recognize gain to the extent that other qualified small business stock is purchased within sixty days of the sale. See I.R.C. § 1045.

2. *Shareholder loss characterized as ordinary loss if corporation is small business corporation (I.R.C. § 1244).* Pursuant to I.R.C. § 1244, certain losses recognized on the sale of corporate stock are characterized as ordinary losses, rather than capital losses. The following three conditions must be satisfied for stock to qualify for § 1244 treatment (see I.R.C. § 1244(c)(1)):

(a) the issuing corporation must satisfy the definition of a "small business corporation" when the stock is issued,

(b) the stock must be issued by the corporation (and not acquired from another shareholder) in exchange for money or property, and

(c) the corporation must have derived less than 50% of its gross receipts from dividends, interest and other designated types of passive income during the five taxable years ending before the loss was sustained.

A "small business corporation" under I.R.C. § 1244 is a corporation with no more than $1,000,000 of capital (when the stock is issued). See I.R.C. § 1244(c)(3). This definition is entirely unrelated to the definition of "small business corporation" for S Corporation eligibility. See I.R.C. § 1361(b). In fact, § 1244 stock may be issued by either a C Corporation or an S Corporation. The amount of loss to which a taxpayer may apply § 1244 in any tax year is limited to $50,000 ($100,000 in the case of a husband and wife who file a joint return). See I.R.C. § 1244(b). In addition to applying to losses allowed when qualifying stock is actually sold, the provision also apparently applies to losses allowed when the issuing corporation liquidates or redeems the shares in a transaction treated as a sale.

CHAPTER 6

S CORPORATION DISTRIBUTIONS

The income of an S Corporation is generally taxed only once. In contrast to a C Corporation, the income of an S Corporation is not normally taxed at the corporate level. I.R.C. § 1363(a). Instead, the income is taxed to the shareholders when the S Corporation earns it and the basis in each shareholder's stock is increased to reflect the income allocated to that shareholder. I.R.C. §§ 1366, 1367. When the S Corporation subsequently makes distributions to its shareholders, each shareholder is treated as receiving a return *of* her investment (taxable only to the extent it exceeds the basis in her stock and as a capital gain), rather than a return *on* her investment (taxable in full as dividend income).

The term "distribution" describes a transfer of property by a corporation to a shareholder in the capacity of an owner, regardless of whether the distributing corporation is a C Corporation or an S Corporation. I.R.C. §§ 301, 1368. All corporate distributions are classified according to the same three-pronged scheme. Thus, regardless of whether the distributing corporation is a C Corporation or an S Corporation, the same criteria are used to classify a distribution as a one-side distribution, a redemption or a liquidation. After a distribution by an S Corporation is classified, the tax consequences to the corporation and its shareholders are governed by the same rules that apply to C Corporations, unless Congress has specifically mandated a different treatment. See I.R.C. § 1371(a). The only type of S Corporation distribution that is treated in a unique manner is the one-side distribution. See I.R.C. § 1368.

A. ONE-SIDE DISTRIBUTION

A "one-side distribution" is any distribution where some (but not all) of the corporation's property is transferred to its shareholders and the shareholders do not surrender any of their stock to the distributing corporation.[1] A one-side distribution from a C Corporation is treated as a return *on* the shareholder's investment (i.e., as a dividend) to the extent that the distribution does not exceed the distributing corporation's E & P. I.R.C. §§ 301, 316. E & P is a measure of corporate earnings not yet taxed to the shareholders. See pp. 201–207.

---

1. "One-side distribution" is not a statutory term. The term is used in this casebook as a matter of convenience to distinguish this type of distribution from distributions in redemption and liquidation.

Because S Corporation income is taxed to the shareholders when it is earned, an S Corporation does not generate E & P. Thus, a one-side distribution by a corporation that has operated as an S Corporation since its inception is treated as a return *of* the owner's investment (i.e., taxable only to the extent it exceeds stock basis and as a capital gain). See I.R.C. § 1368(b). Although an S Corporation does not generate E & P, an S Corporation can have accumulated E & P if the corporation previously operated as a C Corporation. A hybrid scheme of taxation governs a one-side distribution by an S Corporation that has accumulated E & P. I.R.C. § 1368(c).

1.   NO ACCUMULATED EARNINGS & PROFITS

I.R.C. §§ 301, 311, 1368(a), (b), (d)

Treas. Reg. §§ 1.1368–1(a), (c), (e)(2)

The tax consequences to a shareholder of an S Corporation who receives a one-side distribution of money are relatively simple when the distributing corporation has no E & P. In such a case, the distribution is tax-free to the extent of the shareholder's basis in his stock and any excess is taxed as a capital gain. I.R.C. § 1368(b). Before determining the tax consequences of the distribution, the basis of the shareholder's stock must be adjusted upward to reflect the shareholder's pro rata share of the S Corporation's income for the year of the distribution, regardless of when the distribution occurs. I.R.C. § 1367; Treas. Reg. § 1.1368–1(e)(2). After determining the tax consequences of the distribution, the basis of the shareholder's stock is reduced by the tax-free amount of the distribution. I.R.C. § 1367(a)(2)(A).

Example 6–A (One-side distribution of money): Shanna and Tom each own half of the stock of Yellowstone, Inc., an S Corporation with no E & P. On January 1 of Year 6, Shanna has a basis of $97,000 in her stock and Tom has a basis of $7,000 in his stock. On March 1 of Year 6, Yellowstone distributes $25,000 in cash to each of Shanna and Tom. Yellowstone has $6,000 of income in Year 6.

(a) Half ($3,000) of Yellowstone's Year 6 income is taxed to each of Shanna and Tom. I.R.C. § 1366(a).

(b) The basis of each shareholder's stock is increased by his or her share of Yellowstone's Year 6 income. I.R.C. § 1367(a)(1); Treas. Reg. § 1.1368–1(e)(2). Thus, Shanna's basis increases to $100,000 and Tom's basis increases to $10,000.

(c) Shanna receives her entire $25,000 distribution tax-free because the distribution does not exceed the basis of her stock. I.R.C. § 1368(b)(1). Her stock basis is then reduced to $75,000. I.R.C. § 1367(a)(2)(A).

(d) Tom receives only $10,000 of his distribution tax-free (I.R.C. § 1368(b)(1)) and his stock basis is reduced to zero (I.R.C. § 1367(a)(2)(A)). The remaining $15,000 of Tom's distribution is included in his gross income as a capital gain (I.R.C. § 1368(b)(2)) and does not affect his stock basis.

Distributions of property other than money are governed by the same rules that apply to distributions of money. I.R.C. § 1368(b). If the value of the distributed property exceeds the S Corporation's basis, however, the distribution triggers a taxable gain at the corporate level. I.R.C. § 311(b). The gain triggered by a distribution of appreciated property increases the S Corporation's income for the year of the distribution and is taxed to the shareholders. I.R.C. § 1366(a). Each shareholder's stock basis is adjusted upward to reflect her pro rata share of the gain before the tax consequences of the distribution are determined. See Treas. Reg. § 1.1368–1(e)(1).

Example 6–B (One-side distribution of property, other than money): Same as Example 6–A, except that instead of distributing $25,000 of cash to each of Shanna and Tom, Yellowstone distributes: (1) inventory with a value of $25,000 and a basis of $15,000 to Shanna, and (2) XYZ stock with a value of $25,000 and a basis of $50,000 to Tom.

(a) Yellowstone recognizes a $10,000 ordinary gain on the inventory but does not recognize a loss on the XYZ stock. I.R.C. §§ 311, 1221(1).

(b) Half ($5,000) of Yellowstone's ordinary gain (as well as half ($3,000) of Yellowstone's other Year 6 income) is taxed to each of Shanna and Tom. I.R.C. §§ 1366(a), (b).

(c) The basis of each shareholder's stock is increased by his or her share of Yellowstone's Year 6 income (including the gain triggered by the distribution). I.R.C. § 1367(a)(1); Treas. Reg. § 1.1368–1(e)(2). Thus, Shanna's basis increases to $105,000 and Tom's basis increases to $15,000.

(d) Shanna receives her $25,000 distribution tax-free because the value of the property distributed to her does not exceed the basis of her stock. I.R.C. §§ 301(b), 1368(b)(1). Her stock basis is then reduced to $80,000. I.R.C. § 1367(a)(2)(A).

(e) Tom receives only $15,000 of his property distribution tax-free (I.R.C. § 1368(b)(1)) and his stock basis is reduced to zero (I.R.C. § 1367(a)(2)(A)). The remaining $10,000 property distribution is included in Tom's gross income as a capital gain (I.R.C. § 1368(b)(2)) and does not affect his stock basis.

(f) Shanna's basis in the inventory is $25,000 and Tom's basis in the XYZ stock is also $25,000. I.R.C. § 301(d).

NOTES

1. *Relevance of stock basis to form of distribution.* In light of the results in Examples 6–A and 6–B, should a low basis shareholder (like Tom) in an S Corporation without E & P prefer that the corporation make distributions in the form of money or appreciated property, or should he be indifferent about the form of the distribution? What about a high basis taxpayer like Shanna?

2. *Preserving loss.* In Example 6–B, is Yellowstone's unrecognized loss in the XYZ stock preserved after the stock is distributed to Tom? See I.R.C. § 301(d). How could the transaction be restructured to enable the parties to derive some tax benefit from that loss?

3. *Characterization.* If Shanna later sells the property that Yellowstone distributed to her in Example 6–B for $35,000, what is the character of her gain?

4. *Distribution in loss year.* When a one-side distribution occurs in a year in which the S Corporation has income, the basis of each shareholder's stock is adjusted upward before the tax consequences of the distribution are determined. Treas. Reg. § 1.1368–1(e)(2). When an S Corporation makes a one-side distribution in a loss year, however, the distribution reduces the shareholder's stock basis before the corporation's loss is allocated to the shareholders. I.R.C. §§ 1366(d)(1)(A), 1368(d). In Example 6–A (p. 302), if Yellowstone had a $20,000 operating loss in Year 6 (rather than $6,000 of income), what are the tax consequences to Tom of his $10,000 share of the loss and his $25,000 distribution?

2.   ACCUMULATED EARNINGS & PROFITS

I.R.C. §§ 1368(c), (d), (e)

Treas. Reg. §§ 1.1368–1(d)(1), (e), –2(a)

The tax consequences are more complex in the case of a one-side distribution by an S Corporation with accumulated E & P. I.R.C. § 1368(c). The complexity results from the requirement that an S Corporation with E & P must maintain an "accumulated adjustments account" ("AAA"). See I.R.C. § 1368(e).

The AAA is analogous to the E & P account in that it (roughly) measures the amount of earnings accumulated over a given period of time. The E & P account measures the amount of earnings accumulated during C Corporation years that has not yet been taxed to the shareholders. See pp. 201–207. By contrast, the AAA measures the amount of earnings accumulated during S Corporation years that has already been taxed to the shareholders. As might be expected, distributions attributable to the E & P account continue to be taxed as dividends to the recipient shareholders even after an S election has become effective. In contrast, distributions by an S Corporation attributable to the AAA are generally received tax-free by the recipient shareholders. Moreover, just as distributions attributable to the E & P account reduce E & P, distributions attributable to the AAA reduce the AAA.

The distribution rules that apply to an S Corporation with E & P are designed to allow the shareholders to withdraw all post S election earnings before withdrawing accumulated E & P. This result is achieved by treating any one-side distribution that does not exceed the AAA like a one-side distribution by an S Corporation with no E & P. I.R.C. § 1368(c)(1). Before determining the tax consequences of the distribution, however, the AAA must be adjusted upward to reflect the S Corporation's income for the year of the distribution, regardless of when the distribution occurs. Treas. Reg. § 1.1368–1(e)(2). Any one-side distribution in excess of the AAA is attributed to E & P and treated as a dividend to the recipient shareholders. I.R.C. § 1368(c)(2). Any one-side distribution in excess of both AAA and E & P is treated simply as a return of the shareholder's investment (taxable only to the extent it exceeds the basis of the shareholder's stock and as a capital gain). I.R.C. § 1368(c)(3).

Example 6–C (Ordering rules for one-side distribution by S Corporation with accumulated E & P): On January 1 of Year 5, Stray Corp., an S Corporation that was formerly a C Corporation, has an accumulated E & P account of $500,000 and an AAA of $80,000. Stray's sole shareholder, William, has a basis of $100,000 in his stock on January 1 of Year 5. On May 1 of Year 5, Stray distributes $150,000 to William. Stray has $120,000 of income in Year 5.

(a) All $120,000 of Stray's Year 5 income is taxed to William. I.R.C. § 1366(a).

(b) The basis of William's stock increases to $220,000. I.R.C. § 1367(a)(1); Treas. Reg. § 1.1368–1(e)(2).

(c) Stray's AAA is increased by Stray's Year 5 income. I.R.C. § 1368(e)(1)(A); Treas. Reg. § 1.1368–1(e)(2). Thus, Stray's AAA increases to $200,000.

(d) The entire $150,000 distribution is attributable to Stray's AAA and the AAA is reduced to $50,000. I.R.C. §§ 1368(c)(1), (e)(1)(A).

(e) William receives the entire $150,000 distribution tax-free. I.R.C. §§ 1368(c)(1), (b)(1). He then reduces his stock basis to $70,000. I.R.C. § 1367(a)(2)(A).

Problem 6–1 (One-side distribution of money by S Corporation with accumulated E & P). Shanna and Tom each own half of the stock of Yellowstone, Inc., an S Corporation that previously operated as a C Corporation. On January 1 of Year 6, Shanna has a basis of $97,000 in her stock and Tom has a basis of $7,000 in his stock. On January 1 of Year 6, Yellowstone has an E & P account of $50,000 and an AAA of $24,000. Yellowstone has $6,000 of income in Year 6. What are the tax consequences to Shanna and Tom if, on March 1 of Year 6, Yellowstone distributed $25,000 to each of them? Compare Example 6–A, p. 302. What is the balance of Yellowstone's E & P account and AAA on January 1 of Year 7?

Problem 6–2 (One-side distribution of property other than money by S Corporation with accumulated E & P). Same as Problem 6–1, except that instead of distributing $25,000 of cash to each shareholder, Yellowstone distributes: (1) inventory with a value of $25,000 and a basis of $15,000 to Shanna, and (2) XYZ stock with a value of $25,000 and a basis of $50,000 to Tom. What are the tax consequences of these distributions to Yellowstone, Shanna and Tom? Compare Example 6–B, p. 303. What is the balance of Yellowstone's E & P account and AAA on January 1 of Year 7?

NOTES

1. *Relevance of stock basis to form of distribution.* In light of the results in Problems 6–1 and 6–2, should a low basis shareholder (like Tom) in an S Corporation with E & P prefer that the corporation make distributions in the form of money or appreciated property, or should he be indifferent about the form of the distribution? What about a high basis taxpayer like Shanna?

2. *Elections to reverse distribution rules.* An S Corporation with E & P may elect to reverse the distribution rules of I.R.C. § 1368(c) and apply one-side distributions against the E & P account first and then to the AAA. See I.R.C. § 1368(e)(3); Treas. Reg. § 1.1368–1(f)(2)(i). An S Corporation can even elect to be treated as distributing part or all of its E & P without actually distributing any money or other property. See Treas. Reg. § 1.1368–1(f)(3). These elections can only be made if all of the corporation's shareholders consent, in which case the shareholders are treated as receiving taxable dividend income. Why would shareholders ever consent to these elections? See I.R.C. §§ 1362(d)(3), 1375. Could the dividend received deduction (I.R.C. § 243) ever motivate a shareholder to consent to these elections? See I.R.C. § 1361(b)(1)(B). How do the solutions to Problems 6–1 and 6–2 change if Yellowstone makes an election under I.R.C. § 1368(e)(3) for the year in which the distributions were made?

3. *Purpose of the AAA.* Undistributed S Corporation earnings increase the basis of each shareholder's stock. I.R.C. § 1367(a)(1). Why, then, did Congress not simply allow the shareholders of an S Corporation with E & P to receive distributions tax-free to the extent of their stock basis, rather than creating the complex AAA concept?

4. *Impact of exempt income.* What consequences follow from not increasing the AAA by "income * * * which is exempt from tax"? See I.R.C. § 1368(e)(1)(A).

5. *Cash versus AAA.* Xerxes Corporation, an S Corporation, has cash of $2,000,000 and an E & P account of $500,000. Can you determine the balance of Xerxes' AAA?

6. *Assets versus AAA.* Zorro Corporation, an S Corporation, has cash of $2,000,000, inventory worth $2,000,000, an E & P account of $1,000,000, and an AAA of $1,000,000. Zorro owns nothing of value aside from the foregoing items. What is the total value of Zorro's assets?

7. *Impact of corporate tax.* Recall that a one-side distribution of appreciated property by an S Corporation may trigger a corporate level tax. See I.R.C. §§ 311, 1374; pp. 135–138. Must the S Corporation have E & P for this to occur? When a corporate tax is triggered to an S Corporation, do the shareholders receive any sort of credit against their individual income taxes? See I.R.C. § 1366(f)(2).

8. *Inheriting E & P.* Do not assume that a corporation that operates as an S Corporation from its inception can never have E & P. An S Corporation can inherit the E & P account of a corporation it acquires by a merger or a similar transaction. See I.R.C. § 381(c)(2). The tax consequences of mergers and similar transactions are explored in Chapter 12.

3. CAMOUFLAGED ONE–SIDE DISTRIBUTION

C Corporations and their shareholders are often motivated to treat a distribution as a transfer made in a capacity other than as a shareholder. See pp. 38–59, 214–219. In contrast, S Corporations and their shareholders sometimes desire to treat a transfer made in a non-shareholder capacity as a distribution. The Radtke case, which follows, illustrates an incentive for an S Corporation to transfer value to a shareholder-employee as a distribution, rather than as compensation.

Joseph Radtke, S.C. v. United States

United States District Court, Eastern District of Wisconsin, 1989.
712 F.Supp. 143, aff'd 895 F.2d 1196 (7th Cir.1990).

■ TERENCE T. EVANS, DISTRICT JUDGE:

* * *

FACTS

Joseph Radtke received his law degree from Marquette University in 1978. The Radtke corporation was incorporated in 1979 to provide legal services in Milwaukee. Mr. Radtke is the firm's sole incorporator, director, and shareholder. In 1982, he also served as the unpaid president and treasurer of the corporation, while his wife Joyce was the unpaid and nominal vice-president and secretary. The corporation is a * * * subchapter S corporation. This means that it is not taxed at the corporate level. All corporate income is taxed to the shareholder, whether or not the income is distributed.

In 1982, Mr. Radtke was the only full-time employee of the corporation * * *. Under an employment contract executed between Mr. Radtke and his corporation in 1980, he received,

> an annual base salary, to be determined by its board of directors, but in no event shall such annual salary be less than $0 per year. * * * Employee's original annual base salary shall be $0.

This base salary of $0 continued through 1982, a year in which Mr. Radtke devoted all of his working time to representing the corporation's clients.

Mr. Radtke received $18,225 in dividends from the corporation in 1982. Whenever he needed money, and whenever the corporation was showing a profit—that is, when there was money in its bank account—he would do what was necessary under Wisconsin corporate law to have the board declare a dividend, and he would write a corporate check to himself.

Mr. Radtke paid personal income tax on the dividends in 1982. The Radtke corporation also declared the $18,225 on its Form 1120S, the small business corporation income tax return. But the corporation did not file a federal employment tax form (Form 941) or a federal unemployment tax form (Form 940). In other words, it did not [pay] * * * Social Security (FICA) and unemployment compensation (FUTA).[2] The IRS subsequently assessed deficiencies as well as interest and penalties. The Radtke corporation paid the full amount that IRS demanded under FUTA—$366.44—and it also paid $593.75 toward the assessed FICA taxes, interest, and penalties. Then the corporation sued here after a fruitless claim for refunds.

DISCUSSION

* * *

The Radtke corporation acknowledges that wages are subject to FICA and FUTA taxes, but it argues that the Internal Revenue Code nowhere treats a shareholder-employee's dividends as wages for the purpose of employment taxes. The government, on the other hand, contends that "since Joseph Radtke performed substantial services for Joseph Radtke, S.C., and did not receive reasonable compensation for such services other than 'dividends', the 'dividends' constitute 'wages' subject to federal employment taxes." * * *

The Federal Insurance Contributions Act defines "wages" as "all remuneration for employment," with various exceptions that are not relevant to this dispute. 26 U.S.C. § 3121(a). Similarly, the Federal Unemployment Tax Act defines "wages" as "all remuneration for employment," with certain exceptions that are not relevant. 26 U.S.C. § 3306(b) * * *. Mr. Radtke was clearly an "employee" of the Radtke corporation, as the plaintiff concedes. Likewise, his work for the enterprise was obviously "employment."

* * *

[I] am not moved by the Radtke corporation's * * * argument that "dividends" cannot be "wages." Courts reviewing tax questions are obligated to look at the substance, not the form, of the transactions at issue. Transactions between a closely held corporation and its principals, who may have multiple relationships with the corporation, are subject to particularly careful scrutiny. Whether dividends represent a distribution of profits or instead are compensation for employment is a matter to be determined in view of all the evidence. Cf. Logan Lumber Co. v. Commis-

---

2. Editor's note. FICA and FUTA are employment taxes (not income taxes) paid with respect to compensation disbursed to employees. FUTA is imposed on the employer as is half of FICA (the other half of FICA is collected by the employer through withholding on the employee's wages). No FICA or FUTA is imposed on payments made to a shareholder in his capacity as an owner (i.e., distributions).

sioner, 365 F.2d 846, 851 (5th Cir.1966) (examining whether dividends were paid in guise of salaries).

In the circumstances of this case—where the corporation's only director had the corporation pay himself, the only significant employee, no salary for substantial services—I believe that Mr. Radtke's "dividends" were in fact "wages" subject to FICA and FUTA taxation. His "dividends" functioned as remuneration for employment.

* * *

An employer should not be permitted to evade FICA and FUTA by characterizing all of an employee's remuneration as something other than "wages." * * *. This is simply the flip side of those instances in which corporations attempt to disguise profit distributions as salaries for whatever tax benefits that may produce * * *.

Accordingly, * * * the defendant's motion for summary judgment is GRANTED * * *.

NOTE

1. *Payment of base salary.* Purported S Corporation distributions may be recast as compensation even when a base salary is also paid. See, e.g., Watson v. U.S., 714 F.Supp.2d 954 (S.D. Iowa 2010) (denying taxpayer-CPA's summary judgment motion in case where Internal Revenue Service recharacterized more than $130,000 of purported S Corporation distributions as wages, notwithstanding that taxpayer received an annual base salary of $24,000).

2. *Impact on C Corporations.* Now that dividends paid by C Corporations are generally taxed at capital gains rates, might a C Corporation and its shareholders also be motivated to camouflage compensation as dividends?

B. REDEMPTION

I.R.C. §§ 302, 311, 1368

Treas. Reg. § 1.1368–2(d)(1)

A redemption occurs when a corporation transfers property to a shareholder in exchange for part or all of the shareholder's stock in the distributing corporation. I.R.C. § 317(b). A redemption by an S Corporation is governed by the same rules that apply to a redemption by a C Corporation. I.R.C. §§ 302, 311. Thus, if the redemption satisfies any of the tests set forth in I.R.C. § 302(b), the redeemed shareholder is treated as receiving a return of her investment (i.e., she may offset the amount received by the basis in the surrendered shares and the resulting gain or loss is taxed as a capital gain or a capital loss). I.R.C. § 302(a). By contrast, if the redemption does not satisfy any of the tests set forth in I.R.C. § 302(b), the shareholder is treated as receiving a one-side distribution governed by the rules of I.R.C. § 1368. I.R.C. § 302(d).

When an S Corporation uses appreciated property to fund a redemption, a taxable gain is triggered to the corporation regardless of whether the redemption is treated as a sale or a one-side distribution to the recipient shareholder. I.R.C. § 311(b). The S Corporation's gain is allocated among *all* of the shareholders and increases the basis of each shareholder's stock (and increases the AAA if the S Corporation has accumulated E & P). I.R.C. §§ 1366(a)(1)(A), 1367(a)(1)(A), 1368(e)(1)(A).

If an S Corporation with an AAA makes a distribution in redemption of shares, the AAA is reduced to reflect the distribution. If the redemption is treated as a sale, the AAA is reduced by the percentage of outstanding shares that were redeemed. I.R.C. § 1368(e)(1)(B); Treas. Reg. § 1.1368–2(d)(1)(i). For example, if Alan and Bobbi each own 50% of the outstanding shares of an S Corporation (Xtra Corp.), Xtra redeems all of Alan's shares and the redemption is treated as a sale, then Xtra's AAA would be reduced by 50%. Xtra's E & P account is adjusted under I.R.C. § 312 independently of any adjustments made to the AAA. I.R.C. § 1371(c)(2); Treas. Reg. § 1.1368–2(d)(1)(iii). Thus, Xtra's E & P account would be reduced either by 50% or by the amount of the distribution, whichever is less. I.R.C. § 312(n)(7); pp. 270–272. In contrast, if the redemption is treated as a one-side distribution, adjustments to the AAA and the E & P account are governed by the rules discussed at pp. 304–307.

Revenue Ruling 95–14

1995–1 Cum.Bull. 169.

ISSUE

If an S corporation shareholder receives proceeds in a redemption that is characterized as a distribution under § 301 of the Internal Revenue Code, is the redemption treated as a distribution for purposes of § 1368 that reduces the corporation's accumulated adjustments account?

FACTS

A, and A's child B, together own all of the stock of X, a corporation that files returns for a calendar year. X has a valid S election in effect. X redeems for cash a portion of A's stock at fair market value. There are no facts present that cause the redemption to be treated as a sale or exchange under § 302(a) or § 303(a). X makes no other distributions during the taxable year.

At the end of the year, A has a basis in X stock in excess of the amount of the distribution made by X during the year. In addition, X has an accumulated adjustments account (AAA) in excess of that distribution. X also has subchapter C earnings and profits.

LAW AND ANALYSIS

Section 1371(a)(1) provides that except as otherwise provided in the Code, and except to the extent inconsistent with subchapter S, subchapter C applies to an S corporation and its shareholders.

Under the rules of subchapter C, a redemption is treated either as a sale or exchange under § 302(a) or § 303(a), or as a distribution of property to which § 301 applies. See § 302(d). Because the redemption of A's stock is not treated as a sale or exchange under § 302(a) or § 303(a), the redemption is treated, under § 302(d), as a distribution of property to which § 301 applies.

* * *

An S corporation's AAA tracks the amount of undistributed income that has been taxed to the shareholders, similar to the manner in which earnings and profits generally track a C corporation's undistributed income * * *. AAA is the mechanism that allows previously taxed but undistributed income to be distributed tax-free to S corporation shareholders. It is an account of the S corporation and is not apportioned among shareholders. Reg. § 1.1368–2(a).

Section 1368(e)(1)(B) provides a special rule to determine the adjustment to AAA in the case of a redemption that is treated as an exchange. In the case of any redemption that is treated as an exchange under § 302(a) or § 303(a), the adjustment to AAA is an amount that bears the same ratio to the balance in the account as the number of shares redeemed bears to the number of shares of stock in the corporation immediately before the redemption. Section 1368(e) does not provide a specific rule for adjusting AAA in the case of a redemption treated as a § 301 distribution.

Because X has subchapter C earnings and profits, distributions are treated in the manner provided in § 1368(c). A has an adjusted basis in X stock in excess of the amount of the distribution made by X during the year and X has AAA in excess of the amount of that distribution. Thus, under § 1368(c)(1), the distribution is not included in A's income.

Section 1368(e)(1)(A) provides that AAA is adjusted in a manner similar to the adjustments under § 1367. Section 1367(a)(2)(A) requires an S corporation shareholder to decrease basis in S stock for distributions by the corporation that were not includible in the shareholder's income because of § 1368. Reg. § 1.1368–2(a)(3)(iii) provides that AAA is decreased (but not below zero) by any portion of a distribution to which § 1368(b) or § 1368(c)(1) applies. Because, under these facts, § 1368(b) and § 1368(c)(1) apply to the entire distribution, X's AAA is reduced by the full amount of X's distribution in redemption of A's stock. The provision of § 1368(e)(1) that refers to redemptions does not apply on these facts because this is not a redemption that is treated as an exchange under § 302(a) or § 303(a).

HOLDING

When an S corporation shareholder receives proceeds in a redemption that is characterized as a distribution under § 301, the entire redemption is treated as a distribution for purposes of § 1368 that reduces the corporation's AAA.

Example 6–D (Redemption treated as sale): Zebulon Corporation was incorporated on January 1 of Year 1. On that date, Alex contributed $100,000 for 100 shares of stock, Bill contributed $60,000 for 60 shares of stock and Clara contributed $40,000 for 40 shares of stock. By the end of Year 4, Zebulon had an E & P account of $600,000. Zebulon made an S election effective January 1 of Year 5. Zebulon has taxable income of $300,000 in Year 5. Zebulon redeems all of Bill's shares on December 31 of Year 5 for $320,000 in a transaction that is treated as a sale under I.R.C. § 302(a). The tax consequences are as follows:

(a) Alex, Bill and Clara each reports his or her pro rata share of Zebulon's Year 5 income and the stock basis of each shareholder is increased accordingly. I.R.C. §§ 1366(a)(1), 1367(a)(1).

Shareholder	Pro rata share	Stock basis
Alex (50%)	$150,000	Increased to $250,000
Bill (30%)	$ 90,000	Increased to $150,000
Clara (20%)	$ 60,000	Increased to $100,000

(b) Effect of redemption on Bill

> Realization Event (I.R.C. §§ 302(a), 1001)
>
> | | |
> |---|---|
> | Amount Realized | $320,000 |
> | Less: Adjusted Basis | 150,000 |
> | Realized Gain | $170,000 |
> | Recognized | |
>
> Characterized as capital gain (I.R.C. § 1221)

(c) Effect of redemption on Zebulon

	Before redemption	After redemption
AAA	$300,000	$210,000 [3]
E & P	$600,000	$420,000 [4]

---

3. The reduction in the AAA is computed as follows:

$$\text{AAA (pre-redemption)} \times \frac{\text{Number of shares redeemed}}{\text{Number of shares outstanding pre-redemption}}$$

$$\$300,000 \times \frac{60}{200} = \$90,000$$

The AAA is apparently reduced by the amount that the above formula yields even if that amount exceeds the total amount of the distribution. I.R.C. § 1368(e)(1)(B); Treas. Reg. § 1.1368–2(d)(1)(i).

4. Pursuant to I.R.C. § 312(n)(7), E & P is reduced by the lesser of the amount of the distribution ($320,000) or the ratable share of E & P attributable to the redeemed stock which is determined as follows:

$$\text{E\&P (pre-redemption)} \times \frac{\text{Number of shares redeemed}}{\text{Number of shares outstanding pre-redemption}}$$

$$\$600,000 \times \frac{60}{200} = \$180,000$$

I.R.C. § 1371(c)(2); Treas. Reg. § 1.1368–2(d)(1)(iii).

Problem 6–3: Same facts as Example 6–D, but instead of redeeming Bill's shares in a transaction treated as a sale under I.R.C. § 302(a), what are the tax effects of each of the following alternatives on Zebulon, its shareholders, its AAA and its E & P account?

(a) *Redemption treated as one-side distribution.* Zebulon redeems all of Bill's shares on December 31 of Year 5 for $320,000 in a transaction that is treated as a one-side distribution under I.R.C. § 302(d).

(b) *Sale of shares.* Bill sells all of his shares to Dayna on December 31 of Year 5 for $320,000, and, later that day, Zebulon makes a $200,000 distribution pro rata to its shareholders ($100,000 to Alex, $60,000 to Dayna, and $40,000 to Clara).

Problem 6–4 (Redemption using appreciated property). How does Example 6–D change if Zebulon distributes a capital asset with a value of $320,000 and a basis of $220,000 to Bill, instead of distributing money to him? See I.R.C. §§ 311, 1374. How does the solution to Problem 6–3(a) change if Zebulon distributes the capital asset to Bill, rather than money?

Problem 6–5 (Redemption during the tax year): Ethel and Francine each own half of the stock of Westcott, Inc., an S Corporation since its inception. Each shareholder has $100,000 of basis in her Westcott stock on December 31 of Year 5. For the period from January 1 of Year 6 through May 1 of Year 6, Westcott has taxable income of $40,000. (Assume that May 1 of Year 6 is the 122nd day of a 366 day year.) On May 1 of Year 6, Westcott redeems all of Ethel's stock for $120,000 in a transaction that qualifies as a sale under I.R.C. § 302. For the period from May 2 through December 31 of Year 6, Westcott has taxable income of $260,000. What are the tax consequences of these events to Ethel and Francine if,

(a) Westcott does not elect to close its tax year on May 1 of Year 6? See I.R.C. § 1377(a)(1); pp. 102–104.

(b) Westcott elects under I.R.C. § 1377(a)(2) to close its tax year on May 1 of Year 6? See I.R.C. § 1377(a)(2); pp. 104–105.

NOTE

Closing of the books election for certain redemptions. An S Corporation may make a closing of the books election with the consent of all shareholders when a redeeming shareholder surrenders all of her shares in the distributing corporation. See I.R.C. § 1377(a)(2). A closing of the books election may also be made with the consent of all shareholders when a redeeming shareholder who owns more than 20% of the corporation's outstanding stock retains some shares, provided that: (1) the number of shares surrendered by the redeeming shareholder represents at least 20%

of the outstanding shares of the corporation, (2) the redemption is treated as a sale, and (3) the shares are surrendered in one or more transactions during any thirty-day period during the corporation's taxable year. Treas. Reg. § 1.1368–1(g)(2)(i)(B). For other instances when an S Corporation can make a closing of the books election, see Treas. Reg. § 1.1368–1(g)(2); p. 105.

C. LIQUIDATION

I.R.C. §§ 331, 334(a), 336

A "liquidation" occurs when a corporation transfers all of its assets to its shareholders. When an S Corporation liquidates, the corporation and its shareholders are governed by the same tax rules that apply to the liquidation of a C Corporation. I.R.C. §§ 336, 331, 334(a). The presence of an E & P account and an AAA does not affect the tax consequences of an S Corporation liquidation because the transaction is always treated as a sale at the shareholder level. I.R.C. § 331. The fact that corporate level gains (and usually losses) are recognized when an S Corporation liquidates, however, may dramatically affect the character and the amount of the shareholders' income.

> *Problem 6–6 (Liquidation of S Corporation with E & P):* Zebulon Corporation was incorporated on January 1 of Year 1. On that date, Alex contributed $100,000 for 100 shares of stock, Bill contributed $60,000 for 60 shares of stock and Clara contributed $40,000 for 40 shares of stock. By the end of Year 4, Zebulon had an E & P account of $600,000. Zebulon made an S election effective January 1 of Year 5. For the period from January 1 through June 14 of Year 5, Zebulon has taxable income of $300,000. On June 15 of Year 5, Zebulon owns assets with a value of $1,300,000 and a basis of $1,200,000. Zebulon has no liabilities. What are the tax consequences to Zebulon and its shareholders if Zebulon liquidates on June 15 of Year 5?

> *Problem 6–7 (Liquidation of S Corporation with ordinary income assets):* Yabadoo Co., an S Corporation since its inception, owns an asset with a market value of $400,000 and a basis of $100,000. Yabadoo has no other assets and no liabilities. Barney, Yabadoo's sole shareholder, has a basis of $100,000 in his stock.

> (a) If Yabadoo's asset is a capital asset and Yabadoo liquidates, what are the tax consequences to Yabadoo and Barney?

> (b) If Yabadoo's asset is inventory and Yabadoo liquidates, what are the tax consequences to Yabadoo and Barney?

> (c) If Barney dies immediately before Yabadoo liquidates, what are the tax consequences to Yabadoo and the successor shareholder (see I.R.C. § 1014) if,

>> (i) Yabadoo's asset is a capital asset?
>> (ii) Yabadoo's asset is inventory?

NOTE

Distribution of installment obligation. When an S Corporation sells its assets in a deferred payment transaction that qualifies as an installment sale, the S Corporation's gain is normally recognized and allocated to the shareholders as each payment is received. See I.R.C. § 453. If the S Corporation liquidates before receiving all the deferred payments, the S Corporation recognizes the remaining gain for purposes of determining any tax liability of the S Corporation under I.R.C. § 1374 or I.R.C. § 1375. However, if certain conditions are satisfied, the remaining gain will not be taxed to the S Corporation's shareholders when the installment obligation is distributed in the liquidation. See I.R.C. §§ 453(h)(1), 453B(h). Instead, the shareholders to whom the installment obligation is distributed will recognize gain when they receive payments under the installment obligation. See I.R.C. § 453(h)(1).

*

CHAPTER 7

PARTNERSHIP DISTRIBUTIONS

The income of a business that is taxed as a partnership is only taxed once. No partnership level tax is imposed. I.R.C. § 701. Instead, partnership income is taxed to the partners when it is earned. In addition, each partner's basis in his partnership interest ("outside basis") is increased to reflect amounts that were taxed to the partner but not yet distributed to him. I.R.C. §§ 702, 705(a)(1). When partnership earnings are ultimately distributed, each partner is generally treated as receiving a return *of* his investment (taxable only to the extent that the amount of money received exceeds his outside basis and as capital gain), rather than a return *on* his investment (taxable in full as ordinary income).

A transfer of property by a corporation to a shareholder in her capacity as an owner is referred to as a "distribution". See Chapters 5 and 6. The term "distribution" also describes the transfer of property by a partnership to a partner in his capacity as an owner. I.R.C. § 731. In contrast to the three-pronged scheme that is used to classify corporate distributions (i.e., one-side distribution, redemption, liquidation), only two categories of partnership distributions exist. A partnership distribution is classified as either a "current distribution" or as a "distribution in liquidation of a partner's interest."

A. CURRENT DISTRIBUTION

A "current distribution" describes any partnership distribution to a partner who does not surrender his entire interest in the partnership.[1] Thus, a current distribution is analogous both to a corporate one-side distribution and to a corporate redemption in which the distributee-shareholder retains some stock. The tax consequences of current distributions differ depending upon whether money or property other than money is distributed.

---

1. See Treas. Reg. § 1.731–1(a)(1)(i); I.R.C. § 761(d).

1.   DISTRIBUTION OF MONEY

a.   ACTUAL DISTRIBUTION

I.R.C. §§ 731(a)(1), 733(1)

Treas. Reg. §§ 1.731–1(a)(1), (3)

A current distribution of money is treated as a return of the partner's investment in the partnership. As such, the distribution is received tax-free to the extent that it does not exceed the recipient partner's "outside basis" (the basis in his partnership interest). In addition, the partner's outside basis is reduced by the amount received. If the amount distributed exceeds the recipient's outside basis, the excess is included in the partner's gross income, generally as capital gain. The partner's outside basis is not affected by the taxable portion of a current distribution. See I.R.C. §§ 731(a)(1), 733(1).[2]

When a partner receives a current distribution of money, the amount of the distribution is compared to the recipient's outside basis immediately *before* the distribution. I.R.C. § 731(a)(1). If a current distribution of money is made during a year in which the partnership has income, the tax consequences of the distribution are normally determined before the recipient's outside basis is adjusted upward to reflect his share of the partnership's income. It is possible, however, to delay determining the tax consequences of the distribution until after the recipient's outside basis is adjusted upward to reflect partnership income for the year of the distribution. This result can be accomplished if the partnership transfers the money to the partner as an "advance" against the partner's distributive share of income, rather than as an unconditional distribution. If the partnership merely advances the money, a distribution is not deemed to occur until the end of the partnership year, after the partner's outside basis has been adjusted upward to reflect his distributive share of the partnership's income for the year. See Treas. Reg. § 1.731–1(a)(1)(ii).

> *Example 7–A:* Rachel owns a 50% interest in the RS Partnership. On January 1 of Year 6, Rachel has an outside basis of $10,000. On March 1 of Year 6, RS transfers $25,000 to Rachel. Rachel's distributive share of RS's Year 6 income is $30,000.
>
> (a) *Current distribution:* If RS unconditionally transfers the $25,000 to Rachel on March 1 of Year 6, a distribution occurs on that date and Rachel's tax consequences are as follows:
>
> > (i) Rachel receives only $10,000 of the distribution tax-free and her outside basis is reduced from $10,000 to zero. The remaining $15,000 of Rachel's distribution is included in her gross income (probably as a capital gain) and does not affect her outside basis. I.R.C. §§ 731(a)(1), 733(1).

---

2. Special rules that may affect the amount and characterization of partner income resulting from a distribution are examined later in this chapter. See I.R.C. § 751(b); pp. 353–358.

(ii) Then, Rachel is taxed on her $30,000 distributive share of RS's Year 6 income and her outside basis is increased from zero to $30,000. I.R.C. §§ 702(a)(8), 705(a)(1)(A).

(b) *Advance against distributive share:* If, instead of unconditionally transferring the $25,000 to Rachel on March 1 of Year 6, RS advances the money to Rachel on that date against her distributive share of RS's Year 6 income, Rachel is not treated as receiving a distribution until December 31 of Year 6 and Rachel's tax consequences are as follows:

(i) Rachel is taxed on her $30,000 distributive share of RS's Year 6 income and her outside basis is increased from $10,000 to $40,000. I.R.C. §§ 702(a)(8), 705(a)(1)(A).

(ii) Then, Rachel receives the entire $25,000 distribution tax-free because the distribution does not exceed her outside basis. I.R.C. § 731(a)(1). Finally, her outside basis is reduced from $40,000 to $15,000. I.R.C. § 733(1).

When a partnership makes a current distribution of money in a loss year, the distribution is applied against the recipient partner's outside basis *before* the tax consequences of the recipient's distributive share of the partnership loss are determined. See I.R.C. § 704(d); Treas. Reg. § 1.704–1(d)(2). Revenue Ruling 66–94 illustrates the consequences of this rule.

Revenue Ruling 66–94

1966–1 Cum.Bull. 166.

Advice has been requested as to the manner in which a partner should compute the basis of his partnership interest under section 705(a) of the Internal Revenue Code of 1954 for purposes of determining the extent to which his distributive share of partnership losses will be allowed as a deduction, and the extent to which gain will be [recognized] by a partner upon the distribution of cash to him by the partnership.

During the taxable year, A, a member of the partnership, contributed 50x dollars to the partnership as his initial capital contribution, and received 30x dollars as a cash distribution from the partnership. A's distributive share of partnership losses at the end of its taxable year was 60x dollars.

Section 705(a) of the Code provides, in part, that the adjusted basis of a partner's interest in a partnership shall be the basis of such interest determined under section 722 of the Code (relating to contributions to a partnership)—(1) increased by the sum of his distributive share for the taxable year and prior taxable years of taxable income of the partnership [and] tax exempt income of the partnership * * *, and (2) decreased, but not below zero, by distributions by the partnership as provided in section 733 and by the sum of his distributive share of partnership losses [and by certain nondeductible expenditures].

Section 1.704–1(d)(1) of the Income Tax Regulations provides, in part, that a partner's distributive share of partnership loss will be allowed only to the extent of the adjusted basis (before reduction by current year's losses) of such partner's interest in the partnership at the end of the partnership taxable year in which such loss occurred.

Section 1.704–1(d)(2) of the regulations provides, in part, that in computing the adjusted basis of a partner's interest for the purpose of ascertaining the extent to which a partner's distributive share of partnership loss shall be allowed as a deduction for the taxable year, the basis shall first be increased under section 705(a)(1) of the Code and decreased under section 705(a)(2) of the Code, except for losses of the taxable year and losses previously disallowed.

Section 1.731–1(a) of the regulations provides, in part, that where money is distributed by a partnership to a partner, no gain or loss shall be recognized to the partner except to the extent that the amount of money distributed exceeds the adjusted basis of the partner's interest in the partnership immediately before the distribution. For purposes of sections 731 and 705 of the Code, advances or drawings of money or property against a partner's distributive share of income shall be treated as current distributions made on the last day of the partnership taxable year with respect to such partner.

Based on the foregoing, it is concluded that:

(1) * * *

(2) In order to determine the extent to which A's distributive share of partnership losses will be allowed as a deduction, A's basis for his interest in the partnership computed in accordance with section 705(a) of the Code, should be determined without taking into account his distributive share of partnership losses for the taxable year. Thus:

A's contribution to the partnership	50x dollars
Deduct cash distribution made to A by the partnership	−30x dollars
	20x dollars
A's distributive share of partnership losses for the taxable year are not taken into account	0
A's basis for determining the amount of his allowable partnership losses	20x dollars

(3) In order to determine the extent to which gain will be [recognized] by A upon the distribution of cash to him by the partnership, A's basis for his interest in the partnership computed in accordance with section 705(a) of the Code, should be determined without taking into account cash distributions made to him by the partnership during its current taxable year. Thus:

A's contribution to the partnership . . . .   50x dollars
Cash distributions made by the partnership
   to A during the taxable year are not
   taken into account . . . .   −0
                                                                        50x dollars
Deduct A's distributive share of partnership losses
   to the extent allowed by section 704(d) of
   the Code. [See (2) above.] . . . .   − 20x dollars
A's basis for determining the amount of gain
   he [recognized] upon the distribution of
   cash to him by the partnership . . . .   30x dollars

A may deduct his distributive share of the partnership loss to the extent of 20x dollars [see (2), above] and he [recognizes] no gain from the cash distribution of 30x dollars because his basis for determining the amount of gain upon such distribution is 30x dollars [see (3), above].

b. REDUCTION IN PARTNERSHIP LIABILITIES

I.R.C. § 752(b)

When a partnership borrows money, each partner is treated as contributing money to the partnership in an amount equal to that partner's share of the liability, thereby resulting in an increase in the partner's outside basis. See I.R.C. §§ 752(a), 722; pp. 173–179. In contrast, when a partnership repays a debt, each partner is treated as receiving a distribution of money equal to the partner's share of the extinguished liability. See I.R.C. § 752(b). Thus, the distribution rules that apply to an actual distribution of money also apply when a partnership liability is reduced. See I.R.C. §§ 731(a), 733(1).

Example 7–B (Reduction in partnership liability treated as distribution of money): Waldo and Vernon each own a 50% interest in the WV Partnership. On January 1 of Year 3, the WV Partnership borrowed $100,000 from the First National Bank and each partner increased his outside basis by $50,000 to reflect his share of the liability. I.R.C. §§ 752(a), 722. On December 31 of Year 5, Waldo has an outside basis of $70,000 and Vernon has an outside basis of $30,000. On December 31 of Year 5, the WV Partnership repays $80,000 of its debt to the Bank. The consequences of the repayment are as follows:

(a) Each partner's share of the partnership liability is reduced by $40,000.

(b) Waldo is treated as receiving a $40,000 distribution of money, all of which is tax-free, and Waldo's outside basis is reduced from $70,000 to $30,000. I.R.C. §§ 752(b), 731(a)(1), 733(1).

(c) Vernon is also treated as receiving a $40,000 distribution of money. $30,000 of the deemed distribution is tax-free and the remaining $10,000 is taxed, probably as capital gain. Vernon's outside basis is reduced from $30,000 to zero. I.R.C. §§ 752(b), 731(a)(1), 733(1).

(1) Change in Form of Partnership

Revenue Ruling 84–52

1984–1 Cum.Bull. 157.

ISSUE

What are the federal income tax consequences of the conversion of a general partnership interest into a limited partnership interest in the same partnership?

FACTS

In 1975, X was formed as a general partnership under the Uniform Partnership Act of state M. X is engaged in the business of farming. The partners of X are A, B, C, and D. The partners have equal interests in the partnership.

The partners propose to amend the partnership agreement to convert the general partnership into a limited partnership under the Uniform Limited Partnership Act of State M. Under the certificate of limited partnership, A and B will be limited partners, and both C and D will be general partners and limited partners. Each partner's total percent interest in the partnership's profits, losses, and capital will remain the same when the general partnership is converted into a limited partnership. The business of the general partnership will continue to be carried on after the conversion.

LAW AND ANALYSIS

* * *

Under the facts of this revenue ruling, A, B, C, and D, will remain partners in X after X is converted to a limited partnership. Although the partners have exchanged their interests in the general partnership X for interests in the limited partnership X, under section 721 of the Code, gain or loss will not be recognized by any of the partners of X except as provided in section 731 of the Code.

HOLDINGS

Except as provided below, under section 721 of the Code, no gain or loss will be recognized by A, B, C, or D as a result of the conversion of a general partnership interest in X into a limited partnership in X.

* * *

If, as a result of the conversion, there is a change in the partners' shares of X's liabilities under section 1.752 of the regulations, and such change causes a deemed contribution of money to X by a partner under section 752(a) of the Code, then the adjusted basis of that partner's interest shall, under section 722 of the Code, be increased by the amount of such deemed contribution. If the change in the partners' shares of X's liabilities causes a deemed distribution of money by X to a partner under section 752(b) of the Code, then the basis of that partner's interest shall, under section 733 of the Code, be reduced (but not below zero) by the amount of such deemed distribution, and gain will be recognized by that partner under section 731 of the Code to the extent the deemed distribution exceeds the adjusted basis of that partner's interest in X.

* * *

The holdings contained herein would apply with equal force if the conversion had been of a limited partnership to a general partnership.

NOTE

Conversion to limited liability company. The tax consequences described in Revenue Ruling 84–52 also apply when a general partnership or limited partnership converts to a limited liability company taxed as a partnership. These consequences apply regardless of whether the limited liability company is formed in the same state or in a different state from the converting partnership. Rev. Rul. 95–37, 1995–1 C.B. 130.

(2) CANCELLATION OF PARTNERSHIP INDEBTEDNESS

When a borrower cannot repay a debt, the lender might cancel part or all of the debt. When part or all of a debt is canceled, the borrower normally must report income from the discharge of indebtedness. I.R.C. § 61(a)(12). When a partnership's debt is canceled, the partnership's discharge of indebtedness income, like all other partnership income, is allocated among and taxed to the partners. See I.R.C. § 702.[3] Each partner's outside basis is increased to reflect that partner's share of the partnership's income. See I.R.C. § 705(a)(1)(A). In addition to triggering discharge of indebtedness income, the cancellation of a partnership debt reduces the amount of a partnership liability. As a result, each partner is also treated as receiving a current distribution of money equal to that partner's share of the canceled debt. I.R.C. § 752(b). The tax consequences resulting from the cancellation of a partnership liability have been analyzed by the Tax Court as follows:

> In general, gross income includes income from the discharge of indebtedness. Sec. 61(a)(12); United States v. Kirby Lumber Co., 284 U.S. 1 (1931). Income realized by a partnership on the discharge of indebtedness is passed through to each partner under section 702, and the

---

3. Discharge of indebtedness income may be excluded from gross income in the event of insolvency or bankruptcy, or if the canceled debt represents qualified farm indebtedness or qualified real property indebtedness. See I.R.C. § 108(a)(1). When a partnership's debt is canceled, the tests for excluding discharge of indebtedness income are applied at the partner level. I.R.C. § 108(d)(6). For example, if Al and Bea are equal partners in the AB Partnership and $50,000 of partnership debt is canceled, $25,000 of discharge of indebtedness income is allocated to each partner, even if the partnership is insolvent. If Al is insolvent, however, he may exclude his distributive share of the discharge of indebtedness income to the extent of his insolvency, even if the partnership is solvent. See I.R.C. § 108(a)(3).

partner's basis in his partnership interest is increased by his distributive share of such income. Sec. 705(a)(1) * * *.

[A]ny decrease in the partner's share of the partnership liabilities is treated as a distribution of money by the partnership to the partner under section 752(b) and results in the recognition of gain by the partner to the extent that such a distribution exceeds his adjusted basis in his partnership interest. Sec. 731(a)(1). The gain recognized is characterized as gain from the sale or exchange by the partner of his partnership interest, and is taken into income under section 61(a)(3)(gains derived from dealings in property).

* * *

[E]ach [partner] must recognize ordinary income with respect to his share of the partnership's [discharge of indebtedness] income under section 702(a)(8). This income will provide each partner with an increase in basis under section 705(a)(1)(A). At the same time, each partner will receive a distribution from the partnership in an amount equal to his share of the partnership indebtedness. Sec. 752(b). This distribution will offset each partner's basis under section 733(1). Thus, the increase in basis under section 705, coupled with the distribution and decrease in basis under sections 752 and 733 result in a net change of zero in each partner's basis * * *.

Gershkowitz v. Commissioner, 88 T.C. 984, 1005–1008 (1987).

Problem 7–1 (Cancellation of Partnership Debt): Same facts as Example 7–B (p. 321) but the Bank cancels $80,000 of the WV Partnership's debt on December 31 of Year 5, instead of WV repaying $80,000 to the Bank. What are the tax consequences to the WV Partnership, Waldo, and Vernon? Might the tax consequences be different if the partnership's debt is canceled on a day other than December 31? See Rev. Rul. 94–4.

Revenue Ruling 94–4

1994–1 Cum.Bull. 196.

ISSUE

If a deemed distribution of money under § 752(b) of the Internal Revenue Code occurs as a result of a decrease in a partner's share of the liabilities of a partnership, is the deemed distribution taken into account at the time of the distribution or at the end of the partnership taxable year?

LAW

Under § 752(b), a decrease in a partner's share of partnership liabilities is considered a distribution of money to the partner by the partnership. The partner will recognize gain under § 731(a)(1) if the distribution of money exceeds the adjusted basis of the partner's interest immediately before the distribution.

Section 1.731–1(a)(1)(ii) of the Income Tax Regulations provides that for purposes of §§ 731 and 705, advances or drawings of money or property against a partner's distributive share of income are treated as current distributions made on the last day of the partnership taxable year with respect to that partner.

* * *

HOLDING

A deemed distribution of money under § 752(b) resulting from a decrease in a partner's share of the liabilities of a partnership is treated as an advance or drawing of money under § 1.731–1(a)(1)(ii) to the extent of the partner's distributive share of income for the partnership taxable year. An amount treated as an advance or drawing of money is taken into account at the end of the partnership taxable year. A deemed distribution of money resulting from a cancellation of debt may qualify for advance or drawing treatment under this revenue ruling * * *.

NOTE

Timing of deemed distribution. When a partnership's debt is canceled, what difference does it make whether the deemed distribution that results is treated as occurring: (a) when the debt is canceled, or (b) at the end of the partnership tax year? When a partnership repays a debt, does it make any difference whether the deemed distribution that results is treated as occurring: (a) when the debt is repaid, or (b) at the end of the partnership tax year?

IRS Technical Advice Memorandum 9739002[4]

5/19/97.

ISSUE

Whether Taxpayer properly increased his basis in his partnership interest under section 705(a)(1)(A) of the Internal Revenue Code for discharge of indebtedness income that was excluded from Taxpayer's gross income under the insolvency exclusion under section 108(a)(1)(B)?

FACTS

The Taxpayer owned a 50 percent interest in a partnership, Partnership, which was involved in the development of real property. Partnership had an outstanding debt owed to A in the principal amount of *a*. * * *

---

4. A technical advice memorandum is a response by the National Office of the Internal Revenue Service to a request made either by an examining agent or the taxpayer during the course of an audit with respect to issues of law. A technical advice memorandum, like a private letter ruling, applies only to the taxpayer involved in the audit and may not be cited as precedent. See I.R.C. § 6110(j)(3).

[P]artnership's liability was discharged, resulting in [cancellation] of indebtedness income ("COD income") to Partnership. This COD income was allocated to each of the partners of Partnership, including Taxpayer. Taxpayer increased his basis in Partnership interest by this amount pursuant to section 705(a)(1)(A). However, Taxpayer excluded the COD income from gross income on his individual return pursuant to the insolvency exclusion under section 108(a)(1)(B).

LAW AND ANALYSIS

Section 61(a)(12) provides that * * * gross income means all income from whatever source derived, including (but not limited to) income from the discharge of indebtedness.

Section 108(a)(1)(B) provides that gross income does not include any amount which would be includible in gross income by reason of the discharge of indebtedness of the taxpayer if the discharge occurs when the taxpayer is insolvent. * * *

Section 108(d)(6) provides that in the case of a partnership, sections 108(a)(the exclusion from gross income) * * * shall be applied at the partner level.

* * *

Section 752(b) provides that any decrease in a partner's share of the liabilities of a partnership * * * shall be considered as a distribution of money to the partner by the partnership.

Section 733(1) provides that in the case of a distribution by a partnership to a partner * * *, the adjusted basis to the partner of his interest in the partnership shall be reduced (but not below zero) by the amount of money distributed to the partner.

* * *

[W]e note that the Committee Reports to the Bankruptcy Tax Act of 1980 ("1980 Act") specifically address the basis increase issue:

> The bill provides that the rules of exclusion from gross income * * * in section 108 of the Code are to be applied at the partner level and not at the partnership level. Accordingly, income from discharge of a partnership debt is not excludable at the partnership level under amended section 108. Instead, such income is treated as an item of income which is allocated separately to each partner pursuant to section 702(a) of the Code.

> This allocation of an amount of debt discharge income to a partner *results in that partner's basis in the partnership being increased by such amount (§ 705).* At the same time, the reduction in the partner's share of partnership liabilities caused by the debt discharge results in a deemed distribution (under § 752), in turn resulting in a reduction (under § 733) of the partner's basis in the partnership. The section 733 basis reduction offsets the section 705 basis increase * * *. [Emphasis added.]

See S. Rep. 96–1035, 96th Cong., 2d Sess. 21 (1980). Accordingly, * * * the amount of COD income allocated to a partner, whether solvent or insolvent, will result in an increase in that partner's partnership basis.

* * *

Under the facts in this case, COD income from the discharge of Partnership's indebtedness was not excludable at the partnership level pursuant to section 108(d)(6). Instead, the COD income was treated as an item of income that was allocated separately to each partner, including Taxpayer, pursuant to section 702(a). This allocation of an amount of COD income to each partner, including Taxpayer, resulted in that partner's basis in the partnership being increased by the amount under section 705(a)(1)(A). At the same time, the reduction in any partner's share of partnership liabilities caused by the debt discharge resulted in a deemed distribution under section 752, which in turn resulted in a reduction of that partner's basis in the partnership under section 733. The tax treatment of the COD income allocated to each partner, including Taxpayer, depended on that partner's own circumstances, such as insolvency, and should not affect the basis increase under section 705(a)(1)(A).

CONCLUSION

The Taxpayer properly increased his basis in his partnership interest under section 705(a)(1)(A) for COD income that was excluded from Taxpayer's gross income under the insolvency exclusion under section 108(a)(1)(B).

NOTE

Right or wrong? Do the statutory provisions identified in the Technical Advice Memorandum mandate the result the IRS reached? Is the result sensible?

2. DISTRIBUTION OF PROPERTY, OTHER THAN MONEY

I.R.C. §§ 731, 732(a), (c), 733

Treas. Reg. §§ 1.731–1(b), 1.732–1(a), 1.733–1

When a partnership makes a current distribution of property other than money, the tax law views the partnership as a mere extension of the partners, rather than as a separate entity. Consequently, a current distribution of property other than money is not a taxable event at either the partner level or the partnership level. Thus, a partner who receives a current distribution of property other than money does not recognize gain, regardless of whether the value of the distributed property exceeds the recipient's outside basis. I.R.C. § 731(a)(1). Moreover, if the value of the distributed property is less than the recipient's outside basis, the recipient partner is barred from recognizing a loss. I.R.C. § 731(a)(2). In addition, the partnership does not recognize gain or loss with respect to the distributed property, regardless of whether the value of the distributed property deviates from the partnership's basis in the property. I.R.C. § 731(b).[5]

The partner receiving a current distribution of property takes a transferred basis in the property (the "inside basis" that the partnership had in the asset) and reduces his outside basis by the amount of basis he takes in the distributed property. I.R.C. §§ 732(a)(1), 733(2), 7701(a)(43). The basis a partner takes in distributed property, however, may not exceed the amount of his outside basis immediately before the distribution. I.R.C. § 732(a)(2). Consequently, if a partner with an outside basis of $10 receives a current distribution of property in which the partnership had an inside basis of $30, the distributee takes a basis of only $10 in the distributed property. If the current distribution consists of more than one property, the $10 of basis is allocated among the various properties pursuant to the rules of I.R.C. § 732(c). In either case, the distributee-partner's outside basis is reduced to zero. I.R.C. § 733(2).

> *Problem 7–2 (Current distributions):* Determine the tax consequences to Jeff in each of the following alternative scenarios:
>
> (a) Jeff receives a current distribution of $5,000 from the JKL Limited Liability Company (LLC). The LLC is classified as a partnership under Treas. Reg. § 301.7701–3. Jeff's outside basis before the distribution is $7,000. See I.R.C. §§ 731(a)(1), 733(1).
>
> (b) Same as (a), except that Jeff's outside basis before the distribution is $3,000. See I.R.C. §§ 731(a)(1), 733(1).
>
> (c) Same as (a), except that, instead of money, a parcel of land with a value of $5,000 and an inside basis of $4,000 is distributed to Jeff. See I.R.C. §§ 731(a)(1), 732(a)(1), 733(2).
>
> (d) Same as (a), except that, instead of money, a parcel of land with a value of $5,000 and an inside basis of $9,000 is distributed to Jeff. See I.R.C. §§ 731(a)(1), 732(a)(2), 733(2).
>
> (e) Same as (a), except that both $5,000 of money and a parcel of land with a value of $5,000 and an inside basis of $4,000 are distributed to Jeff. See Treas. Reg. § 1.732–1(a).
>
> (f) Same as (e), except that the land is distributed to Jeff in a separate transaction before the money is distributed to him.

NOTES

1. *Nonrecognition provision or exclusion.* I.R.C. § 731(a) is a nonrecognition provision. Nonrecognition provisions normally apply only to gain (or loss) that is realized when a taxpayer transfers property. See I.R.C. §§ 61(a)(3), 1001. What property is transferred by a partner who receives a current distribution? If Kaye and Lynne each own a 50% interest in the KL Partnership before and after the partnership distributes property with a

---

5. Exceptions to these general nonrecognition rules are examined later in this chapter and in Chapter 10. See I.R.C. § 731(c).

value of $1,000 to each of them, has either partner transferred any property (i.e., has a realization event occurred for either partner)? If not, does I.R.C. § 731(a) enable each partner to *exclude* from gross income the value of the property she receives from the partnership?

2. *Preserving gain or loss.* When a partner receives a current distribution of property other than money, any potential gain or loss in her partnership interest is not recognized. What happens to the gain or loss that previously existed in her partnership interest? See I.R.C. §§ 732(a), 733. Why does the general non-recognition rule not apply when a partner receives a current distribution of money in excess of outside basis? See I.R.C. § 731(a)(1). Why does the Code not allow a loss to be recognized when a partner receives a current distribution of money that is less than her outside basis? See I.R.C. § 731(a)(2).

3. *Preserving characterization.* If a partnership distributes an "unrealized receivable" (as defined in I.R.C. § 751(c)), any gain or loss recognized when the distributee-partner subsequently disposes of that property is character- ized as ordinary income or ordinary loss, even if the distributee-partner holds the item as a capital asset. See I.R.C. § 735(a)(1). Similarly, when a partnership distributes an "inventory item" (as defined in I.R.C. § 751(d)), any gain or loss recognized if the distributee-partner disposes of the property *within five years* of the distribution is characterized as ordinary income or ordinary loss, even if the distributee-partner holds the item as a capital asset. See I.R.C. § 735(a)(2). The impact of unrealized receivables and inventory items on partnership distributions is examined later in this chapter. See pp. 353–358.

4. *Partnership level treatment versus S Corporation treatment.* A distribu- tion of appreciated property by a C Corporation triggers gain to the distributing corporation. I.R.C. § 311(b); pp. 29–33. In contrast, I.R.C. § 731(b) insulates a partnership from recognizing gain when it distributes property with a value in excess of inside basis. This different treatment can be explained by the fact that the tax law often views the partnership as a mere extension of its partners. In contrast, the tax law generally views the C Corporation as an entity separate from its shareholders. When an S Corporation distributes appreciated property, gain is triggered at the corpo- rate level. See I.R.C. § 311(b); p. 303. Thus, with regard to distributions of appreciated property, the tax law views an S Corporation more like a C Corporation than a partnership. Is this view sensible?

3.   DISTRIBUTION OF MARKETABLE SECURITIES

I.R.C. § 731(c)

Prior to 1995, the distribution of a marketable security by a partner- ship was treated as a distribution of property, other than money. I.R.C. § 731(c) now treats the distribution of a "marketable security" like a distribution of money for gain recognition purposes. A "marketable securi- ty" is an actively traded financial instrument (including stocks and other equity interests, evidences of indebtedness, and options) or foreign currency. I.R.C. § 731(c)(2).

When a partner receives a marketable security as a current distribution, the partner generally recognizes gain to the extent that the value of the distributed security exceeds the partner's basis in her partnership interest. I.R.C. § 731(a)(1). The partner's basis in the distributed security is governed by I.R.C. § 732(a) but is also increased by any gain recognized on the distribution. I.R.C. § 731(c)(4). The partner's outside basis after the distribution is governed by I.R.C. § 733(2) as if no adjustment were made under § 731(c)(4) to the basis of the distributed security. I.R.C. § 731(c)(5). Thus, the distributee partner's outside basis is reduced by the lesser of the partnership's inside basis in the distributed security (I.R.C. § 732(a)(1)) or the partner's outside basis before the distribution (I.R.C. § 732(a)(2)).

The general rule of I.R.C. § 731(c) is subject to certain exceptions. See I.R.C. § 731(c)(3). The Committee Report that follows summarizes these exceptions.

Partnership Distributions of Marketable Securities

H.Rep. No. 826(I), 103d Cong., 2d Sess. (1994).

* * *

*Explanation of provision.—In general.—*The bill generally provides that, for purposes of determining the amount of gain that a partner recognizes upon the distribution of marketable securities by a partnership, the fair market value of the securities is treated as money. Thus, a partner generally recognizes gain under the provision to the extent that the sum of the fair market value of marketable securities and money received exceeds the partner's basis in its partnership interest. The value of the marketable securities is their fair market value as of the date of the distribution.

* * *

*Exceptions.—*The bill provides four exceptions to the general rule that gain is recognized upon a partnership distribution of marketable securities to the extent the sum of the value of the marketable securities and money distributed exceeds the partner's basis in its partnership interest.

*Securities contributed by the distributee.—*The provision generally does not apply to the distribution of a marketable security to a partner if the security was contributed to the partnership by the partner. * * *

*Securities not marketable when acquired.—*To the extent provided in regulations, the provision does not apply to a distribution of a marketable security that was not a marketable security when the partnership acquired it. * * *

*Distributions by investment partnerships.—*The provision does not apply to [certain] distributions of marketable securities by an investment partnership * * *. An investment partnership is a partnership that (1) has never been engaged in a trade or business and (2) substantially all of whose assets consist of specified investment-type assets. * * *

Limitation on gain recognized.—The bill permits a partner to receive a distribution of marketable securities without recognizing the gain that is attributable to his share of the partnership's net appreciation with respect to securities of the type distributed. For this purpose, a type of securities means a class of securities (for example, residual common stock) of a single issuer.

The bill provides that the amount of marketable securities treated as money is reduced by the excess of (1) the partner's distributive share of any net gain that he would take into account if all the securities (of the type distributed) held by the partnership immediately before the transaction were sold for their fair market value, over (2) the partner's distributive share of any net gain that he would take into account if all the securities (of that type) held by the partnership immediately after the transaction had been sold. * * *

For example, assume that partnership ABC holds 300 shares of the common stock of X corporation, a marketable security, and other assets. A holds a 1/3 interest in the capital and profits of the partnership. Each share of stock held by the partnership has a basis of $10 and a value of $100. A's adjusted basis in its partnership interest is $5,000. Assume that the partnership distributed all the shares of X corporation to A * * *. Under the general rule of new section 731(c), the $30,000 value of the X stock would be treated as money for purposes of determining A's gain. Under this gain limitation rule, however, the $30,000 amount is reduced by $9,000, the amount of gain that A would have taken into account if the partnership had sold all 300 shares of X stock for a total of $30,000. Thus, A recognizes a gain of $16,000 ($30,000 reduced by $9,000 (or $21,000) further reduced by A's $5,000 basis in his partnership interest).

* * *

Problem 7–3 (Current distribution of marketable security): Lauren and Max each own a 50% interest in the LM Partnership. Lauren has an outside basis of $7,000. Determine the tax consequences to Lauren in each of the following alternative scenarios:

(a) The LM Partnership owns a single marketable security with a value of $5,000 and an inside basis of $5,000. The LM Partnership makes a current distribution of the security to Lauren. See I.R.C. §§ 731(c)(1), (4), (5), 732(a)(1), 733(2).

(b) Same as (a), except that the security has a value of $10,000 and an inside basis of $10,000. See I.R.C. §§ 731(c)(1), (4), (5), 732(a)(2), 733(2).

(c) Same as (a), except that the security has a value of $20,000 and an inside basis of $2,000. See I.R.C. §§ 731(c)(1), (3)(B), (4), (5), 732(a)(1), 733(2).

(d) The LM Partnership owns two marketable securities of the same class and issuer each of which has a value of $20,000. One of the marketable securities has an inside basis of $2,000 and other has an inside basis of $14,000. The LM Partnership makes a current distribution to Lauren of the marketable security with an inside basis of:

(i) $2,000. See I.R.C. §§ 731(c)(1), (3)(B), (4), (5), 732(a)(1), 733(2).

(ii) $14,000. See I.R.C. §§ 731(c)(1), (3)(B), (4), (5), 732(a)(2), 733(2).

B.   Distribution in Liquidation of Partner's Interest

The phrase "distribution in liquidation of a partner's interest" describes one or more transfers of value by a partnership to a partner that terminates the partner's interest in the partnership. See I.R.C. § 761(d). Thus, a distribution in liquidation of a partner's interest is analogous to a corporate redemption where the redeemed shareholder surrenders all of his stock.

1.   General Rules

I.R.C. §§ 731(a)(2), 732(b), (c)

Treas. Reg. §§ 1.731–1(a)(2), 1.732–1(b), (c)

Subject to certain exceptions, distributions in liquidation of a partner's interest are governed by the same rules that apply to current distributions. See I.R.C. §§ 731–733. In effect, the partnership is viewed as an extension of the partners; thus, distributions of property other than money are generally received tax-free by the departing partner. When property other than money is distributed in liquidation of a partner's interest, the departing partner takes a basis in the distributed property in an amount equal to her outside basis immediately before the distribution. See I.R.C. § 732(b).[6] If the partner whose interest is liquidated receives more than one piece of property from the partnership, her outside basis is allocated among the properties pursuant to the rules of I.R.C. § 732(c). See Treas. Reg. § 1.732–1(c).

A distribution of money or marketable securities that exceeds the departing partner's outside basis may cause the departing partner to recognize a gain, regardless of whether the distribution is in liquidation of the partner's interest or a current distribution. See I.R.C. §§ 731(a)(1), (c). In contrast, a partner may recognize a loss only when a distribution is in liquidation of the partner's interest. When a partner's interest is liquidated, a loss is recognized if the departing partner's outside basis exceeds

---

6. In the case of a current distribution, the distributee-partner's outside basis determines the basis of the distributed property only if her outside basis is less than the partnership's inside basis. I.R.C. § 732(a)(2). Otherwise, the distributee-partner takes the partnership's inside basis in the distributed property (I.R.C. § 732(a)(1)) and her outside basis is reduced by a like amount (I.R.C. § 733(2)).

the sum of: (1) the money received and (2) the basis received in any unrealized receivables or inventory items distributed by the partnership, but only if the distributee receives no assets other than money, unrealized receivables and inventory items. See I.R.C. § 731(a)(2); Treas. Reg. § 1.731–1(a)(2).

> *Problem 7–4 (Distributions in liquidation of partner's interest):* Determine the tax consequences to Yael in each of the following alternative scenarios:
>
> > (a) Yael receives a distribution of $5,000 in liquidation of her interest in the XYZ Limited Liability Company (LLC). The LLC is classified as a partnership under Treas. Reg. § 301.7701–3. Yael's outside basis before the distribution is $7,000. See I.R.C. § 731(a)(2).
> >
> > (b) Same as (a), except that Yael's outside basis before the distribution is $3,000. See I.R.C. § 731(a)(1).
> >
> > (c) Same as (a), except that a parcel of land (that is not inventory) with a value of $5,000 and an inside basis of $4,000 is distributed to Yael. See I.R.C. §§ 731(a), 732(b).
> >
> > (d) Same as (a), except that a parcel of land (that is not inventory) with a value of $5,000 and an inside basis of $9,000 is distributed to Yael. See I.R.C. §§ 731(a), 732(b).
> >
> > (e) Same as (a), except that both $5,000 of money and a parcel of land (that is not inventory) with a value of $5,000 and an inside basis of $4,000 are distributed to Yael. See Treas. Reg. § 1.732–1(b).

2.   IDENTIFYING THE TAXABLE EVENT

I.R.C. §§ 752, 1001

Weiss v. Commissioner

United States Court of Appeals, Eleventh Circuit, 1992.
956 F.2d 242.

■ EDMONDSON, CIRCUIT JUDGE:

> * * *

Robert Weiss was * * * a real estate developer * * * and the * * * president of * * * a motel operation and management business. Sometime in late 1977 or early 1978, Weiss became aware that the Hawaiian Village Motel (Motel) in Tampa was for sale. [Following negotiations, Weiss and] * * * David Hillman, a Washington accountant who invested in real estate * * *, agreed to form a partnership in which Hillman would provide limited working capital and obtain financing to purchase the Motel and in which Weiss would manage the Motel.

Weiss and Hillman signed a letter of intent confirming their partnership in November 1978. In December, Weiss, Hillman and two Hillman associates, Martin Thaler and Melvin Lenkin, formed a general partnership, the Hawaiian Village Partnership (Partnership), to purchase and operate the Motel. The partnership agreement stated that the profits and losses of the Partnership would be divided in the following manner: fifty percent allocated to Weiss and fifty percent allocated collectively to Hillman, Thaler and Lenkin (Hillman Group).

The Partnership then entered into an agreement with Weiss to manage the Motel * * *. This separate management agreement called for Weiss * * * to receive five percent of the Motel's gross income, with a monthly draw of $10,000 to be applied against the five percent fee. The management agreement could be terminated at the option of the Partnership if the Motel failed to show an annual net cash flow of at least $250,000.

[T]he partnership agreement stated that Weiss would forfeit his partnership interest if Weiss failed to advance capital to the Partnership if requested to do so or if the management agreement between the Partnership and Weiss * * * was terminated.

Immediately before forming the Partnership in December 1978, the Hillman Group arranged to borrow $1,000,000 from Union First National Bank of Washington (Union First). The loan was jointly and severally guaranteed by Hillman, Thaler and Lenkin. In February, 1979, the Partnership renewed the loan, at which time Union First successfully requested to have Flagship Bank of Tampa (Flagship) participate in $300,000 of the $1,000,000 loan. To participate, Flagship required Weiss personally to guarantee Flagship's $300,000 participation.

By late-summer 1979, the day-to-day operations of the Motel were in disarray under Weiss' management. At Weiss' request, Hillman hired two accounting firms to determine the extent of the financial difficulties. One firm determined that an immediate infusion of $300,000 was necessary to bring accounts current, while the other firm determined that a $450,000 infusion was necessary * * *.

Based on these independent studies and on his own review of the Motel's financial affairs, Hillman acted. On October 4, 1979, Hillman, on behalf of the Partnership, terminated the management agreement with Weiss * * *. On October 5, he made a capital call to the partners, requesting $400,000 in capital to boost the Motel's finances. Weiss' fifty percent share of this capital infusion would have been $200,000.

The Hillman Group satisfied their portion of the capital call by establishing a $200,000 line of credit with Flagship. Weiss, though, failed to remit his portion of the capital call. As a result, Hillman notified Weiss on November 19 that Weiss' partnership interest had been acquired on November 15 pursuant to the partnership agreement that allowed the Partnership to acquire the interests of a partner who failed to satisfy a capital call * * *.

Despite the termination of the Partnership, Weiss' tax return for 1979 took partnership * * * loss deductions. Upon later review of Weiss' return, the IRS issued a Notice of Deficiency, stating that, because Weiss' partnership interest was terminated and because he was relieved of partnership liabilities before November 15, 1979, the IRS disallowed * * * Weiss' tax loss * * * accruing after November 15 * * *. The IRS also claimed that, because Weiss was relieved of partnership liability, Weiss realized a short-term capital gain on his share of the partnership liabilities for which he was no longer responsible.

After receiving the IRS Notice of Deficiency, Weiss filed a petition in the Tax Court for a redetermination of the deficiency. The Tax Court sustained the deficiency, and this appeal followed.

* * *

Weiss appeals two Tax Court conclusions that determined the outcome of his case: first, that Weiss' partnership interest was terminated on or before November 15, 1979; and second, that Weiss was relieved of partnership liability on or before November 15, 1979. Because we readily conclude from the facts that the Tax Court correctly determined, for tax purposes, Weiss' partnership interest was terminated in November 1979, we address only whether Weiss was also relieved of partnership liability at that time.

* * *

Weiss' $300,000 personal guarantee on Flagship's participation in the loan to the Partnership disposes of the issue before us. Weiss could only have realized a taxable gain if he was relieved of partnership liability. See I.R.C. § 752(b). After reviewing the record, we have found nothing to indicate that, between November 15, 1979 and December 31, 1979, Weiss was relieved of his personal guarantee on Flagship's $300,000 participation in the partnership loan.

In concluding that Weiss continued to be liable on his guarantee of the Flagship's participation loan, we reject the Tax Court's interpretation of Florida partnership law. The Tax Court relied on two Florida statutes to decide that Weiss had been relieved of partnership liability. The Tax Court looked first at Fla.Stat. § 620.76(6), which states:

> When a partner is expelled and the remaining partners continue the business, either alone or with others without liquidation of the partnership affairs, creditors of the dissolved partnership are also creditors of the person or partnership continuing the business.

While this statute protects partnership creditors, it does not divest them of their legal right to go after an ex-partner to whom they extended credit or an ex-partner who personally guaranteed a loan to the partnership. In fact, another Florida statute * * * expressly states that "the dissolution of the partnership of itself does not discharge the existing liability of any partner." Fla.Stat. § 620.735(1).

The Tax Court, though, overlooked section 620.735(1) and went straight to Fla.Stat. § 620.735(2):

> A partner is discharged from any existing liability upon dissolution of the partnership by an agreement to that effect between himself, the

partnership creditor and the person or partner continuing the business. The agreement may be inferred from the course of dealing between the creditor having knowledge of the dissolution and the person or partnership continuing the business.

No express or inferred [sic] agreement existed here. There was no express agreement between Weiss and the Hillman Group partners relieving Weiss of liability; Flagship did not expressly release Weiss from his personal guarantee; and nothing in the course of dealings between the Hillman Group and Flagship permits the inference that Flagship released Weiss from his personal guarantee.

Because the Tax Court did not indicate what course of dealings showed that Weiss was relieved of liability, we suppose that Flagship's extension of a $200,000 line of credit to the Hillman Group somehow influenced the Tax Court. But this credit extension is in no way inconsistent with the fact that Flagship still considered Weiss personally liable on his guarantee of the loan participation. Without a clear inconsistency between the written guarantee and later conduct by Flagship, we see no reason to infer that Weiss had been discharged from his obligation pursuant to the guarantee. For example, we *might* decide that Weiss was relieved from liability by the course of dealings if, without expressly releasing Weiss, Flagship had substituted a new written guarantee from the Hillman Group or one of its members after Weiss' partnership interest was terminated. Or, for another example, we *might* also have decided that Weiss was released if, in the course of dealings, Flagship had been forced to recover on their loan participation and sought recovery only from the Hillman Group and not from Weiss. But here nothing in the record shows that Flagship had released Weiss from his personal guarantee.

The Tax Court also erred in focusing on whether Weiss ultimately was held accountable for partnership liabilities. The issue does not turn on ultimate accountability; instead, the question is whether, in the forty-six days between November 15 and December 31, Weiss remained liable for partnership liabilities. We conclude that he remained liable: first, for the reasons stated above in the discussion of Florida partnership statutes, Weiss remained liable for partnership debt despite the dissolution of the partnership; and second, the personal guarantee to Flagship evidenced ongoing liability.

[W]hether Weiss was ever held accountable for partnership liability does not change the fact that he remained liable for partnership liabilities in 1979. The Tax Court, therefore, erred in holding that Weiss was relieved of partnership liability. We vacate the Tax Court's judgment and remand this case to the Tax Court to determine the consequences of this opinion.

NOTES

1. *Position of Internal Revenue Service.* What was the foundation for the Internal Revenue Service's claim that Weiss recognized a short-term capital gain on November 15, 1979? See I.R.C. §§ 731(a), 752(b).

2. *Release of guarantee.* What would have been the tax consequences to Weiss if the bank had in fact released Weiss from his guarantee on November 15, 1979? How would the release of Weiss from his guarantee have affected the outside basis of the continuing partners? See I.R.C. § 752(a); pp. 321–325.

3. *Trigger for deemed distribution.* The court concluded that Weiss did not realize a taxable gain because he was not relieved of a partnership liability under I.R.C. § 752(b). Might the court have reached a different conclusion regarding the liability if it had equated Weiss's departure from the partnership to a sale of his partnership interest? See I.R.C. §§ 752(d), 1001(b); Treas. Reg. §§ 1.1001–2(a)(1), (4)(ii), 1.1001–2(c) Example (1).

3. DISTINGUISHING LIQUIDATION OF INTEREST FROM SALE

I.R.C. § 741

Treas. Reg. §§ 1.741–1(a), (b)

Rather than transferring her interest to the partnership for money or other property (a distribution in liquidation of the interest), a departing partner might transfer her interest to the continuing partners for money (a sale) or other property (an exchange). In the absence of taxes, the departing partner would be indifferent between transferring her interest to the partnership or to her partners, as long as she received the same amount of consideration. From an income tax standpoint, however, the form of the transaction is important because any gain realized by a departing partner who transfers her partnership interest to the continuing partners is recognized, regardless of whether the consideration received is money or other property. See I.R.C. § 1001(c). In contrast, the departing partner's gain can generally be deferred if her interest is acquired by the partnership for property other than money. See I.R.C. § 731(a).

Crenshaw v. United States

United States Court of Appeals, Fifth Circuit, 1971.
450 F.2d 472.

■ BROWN, CHIEF JUDGE: In this hotly contested suit for refund of Federal income taxes an ingenious taxpayer and a skeptical tax collector vigorously dispute the legal characterization of an imaginative financial maneuver. If the elaborate multi-stage transaction in question amounted to no more than a "sale or exchange" of a partnership interest under § 741 of the Internal Revenue Code of 1954, the Commissioner properly assessed and collected a $47,128.92 deficiency. On the other hand, if it was merely a "liquidating distribution" of a partnership interest * * *, the District Court correctly granted Taxpayer's motion for summary judgment * * *.

Like most sophisticated schemes for minimizing taxes, the plan was an intricate one. It originated in 1962 while Taxpayer (Mrs. Frances Wood

Wilson)[7] was the owner of an undivided $^{50}\!/_{225}$ interest in the Pine Forest Associates partnership, the remaining interests belonging to Mr. and Mrs. Leon Blair. Mr. Blair approached Taxpayer's attorney with an offer to purchase her partnership interest for cash, and * * * the attorney responded by pointing out that Taxpayer's general financial position suggested the most appropriate course would be the exchange of her interest for other income-producing property, rather than for cash. Mr. Blair did not then own such property, but subsequent investigation revealed that it could be obtained from the estate of Taxpayer's husband. The stage was then set for the following planned, integrated sequence of steps:

(i) Taxpayer withdrew completely from the partnership in exchange for an undivided $^{50}\!/_{225}$ interest in a parcel of real estate (the Pine Forest Apartments) owned by the partnership.

(ii) Acting individually and as executrix of her husband's estate, Taxpayer then exchanged her interest in the Pine Forest Apartments for other real property (the Oglethorpe Shopping Center) belonging to the estate.

(iii) Acting solely in her capacity as executrix, Taxpayer transferred the estate's interest in the Pine Forest Apartments for $200,000 cash to the Blairs' newly erected closely held corporation (the Blair Investment Company).

(iv) Finally, the Blair Investment Company transferred its $^{50}\!/_{225}$ interest in the Pine Forest Apartments to the partnership in exchange for the partnership interest formerly owned by Taxpayer.

The Government argues that the ultimate consequence of these steps was in every material respect equivalent to that which would have resulted from a taxable sale. The partnership continued to own the same interest in the Pine Forest Apartments that it had purported to distribute in liquidation of Taxpayer's partnership interest, while the Blairs acquired Taxpayer's partnership interest in return for a $200,000 cash outlay. On the other hand, Taxpayer contends that the entire transaction was nothing more than a perfectly legitimate tax-free liquidation followed by an equally legitimate tax-free exchange of like-kind property under § 1031, and that it must therefore be governed by the long-established rule that a taxpayer may properly take advantage of any method allowed by law to avoid taxes.

The critical significance of step (iv) grows out of the two parallel assertions implicit in the Government's theory of the case. First, * * * the substance rather than the form of a transaction determines its tax consequences, particularly if the form is merely a convenient device for accomplishing indirectly what could not have been achieved by the selection of a more straightforward route * * *. Transparent devices totally devoid of any non-tax significance to the parties cannot pass muster even though a literal reading of the statutory language might suggest otherwise * * *.

---

7. Editor's note. Mrs. Wilson later died and Crenshaw (the named party to the case) became the executor of her estate.

A corollary proposition, equally well established, is that the tax consequences of an interrelated series of transactions are not to be determined by viewing each of them in isolation but by considering them together as component parts of an overall plan. Taken individually * * * each step in the sequence may very well fit neatly into an untaxed transactional compartment. But the individual tax significance of each step is irrelevant when, considered as a whole, they all amount to no more than a single transaction which in purpose and effect is subject to the given tax consequence.

Here the successful application of these principles depends upon a showing by the Government that, while in form these transfers may appear to be no more than a liquidation of a partnership interest followed by a tax-free § 1031 exchange, in substance they are really nothing more than a camouflaged sale of a partnership interest masquerading as a liquidation. But in order to reach this conclusion it must be shown that the character of the transaction is in every respect, other than the superficial and irrelevant one of form, a sale, resulting in precisely those consequences that would have occurred had Taxpayer simply sold her interest in the partnership to the partnership or to the surviving partners for $200,000 cash and then purchased with that money her income producing property * * *.

Obviously what happened here was not equivalent to a sale unless the final step (iv) was consummated—that is, unless Mrs. Wilson's undivided $^{50}/_{225}$ interest in the Pine Forest Apartments ultimately found its way back into the partnership now owned by the two Blairs. If it had not, Taxpayer's partnership interest would have been "liquidated", in every conceivable sense of that term, and the complete obliteration of it simply could not have been characterized as a "sale" if none of it had survived to be "sold".

However, the partnership interest did survive because it was transferred to the Blair Investment Company in return for its undivided interest in the Pine Forest Apartments. In return for its $200,000 cash payment the corporation (Blair Investment) received exactly the partnership interest it would have obtained by way of a direct purchase from Taxpayer. A sale, not a "liquidation", occurred because what had formerly been Taxpayer's partnership interest was acquired by the Blairs' corporate alter ego and the relative economic positions of the parties were the same as they ultimately would have been had a direct sale taken place.

* * *

What does * * * make the transaction in question a sale is the fact that while theoretically a matter of indifference to Taxpayer, consummation of the step (iv) was practically essential to its success, since without it there might have been no deal. Mr. Blair wanted Taxpayer's partnership interest, and to get it he was willing to go along with a suggested alternative plan which he thought amounted to practically the same thing as a direct sale. The key was to keep Pine Forest Apartments in the partnership. From the partnership's standpoint, this goal would have been frustrated by transferring (and keeping) $^{50}/_{225}$ of it in the separate corporate entity, a result which might have brought about substantial tax disadvantages. From Taxpayer's standpoint, she needed (or desired) income-producing properties which she could not get from the partnership in a liquidating distribution. To acquire such property (Oglethorpe Shopping Center) she needed cash to pay the seller. But it was disadvantageous for her to get the cash on distribution from the partnership. This cash came through the payment of $200,000 by the corporation for the Pine Forest Apartments interest, which soon got back to the partnership exactly as it all began. And her partnership interest was then owned by the Blairs. Taxwise, taking two to tango, the transaction had to have the equivalent of step (iv) as an indispensable ingredient * * *.

Our conclusion is not affected by the undisputed fact that Taxpayer disposed of her entire partnership interest rather than a portion of it * * *.

Nor do we overlook Taxpayer's clearly correct contention that Congress, in enacting these provisions, has provided an individual with alternative methods for divesting himself of a partnership interest. Taxpayers have a choice between selling and liquidating. But they cannot compel a court to characterize the transaction solely upon the basis of a concentration on one facet of it when the totality of circumstances determines its tax status. The most obvious answer to Taxpayer's argument that the parties' characterization is conclusive is that such a result would completely thwart the Congressional policy to tax transactional realities rather than verbal labels. The tax is realized on the sale of a partnership interest, and it cannot be avoided by the simple expedient of constructing an admittedly clever series of successive transfers, each nontaxable in itself, that together work the same result. Otherwise, form, rather than substance, would invariably prevail.

The judgment of the District Court is reversed * * *.

NOTES

1. *Tax consequences of each step.* According to the taxpayer, what were the tax consequences of each of the four steps outlined in the Crenshaw opinion (p. 338)?

2. *Identity of partnership interests.* The court states that the Blair Investment Company acquired "the" partnership interest formerly owned by Mrs. Wilson. Is this really the case? When a partner's interest is liquidated, does that interest exist in the partnership or does it disappear? Could the court have reached the same result by finding that the Blair Investment Company acquired an interest equivalent to Mrs. Wilson's interest, but not the same interest? Could the court have reached the same result if the Blair Investment Company had not transferred the undivided interest in the real estate back to the partnership (i.e., if step (iv) did not occur)? What if the Blair Investment Company had leased the property back to the partnership?

3. *Impact of death.* If the taxpayer had prevailed and Mrs. Wilson still owned the Oglethorpe Shopping Center at her death (see step (ii), p. 338), would the tax impact of her death have made the lawyer who planned this transaction look like a genius or an idiot? See I.R.C. §§ 1031(d), 1014.

4. *Form normally controls.* Notwithstanding the Crenshaw decision, the form used by the taxpayers normally controls whether the acquisition of a departing partner's interest is treated as a liquidation of the interest or as a sale of the interest. If the acquisition agreement imposes the primary obligation to acquire the departing partner's interest on the partnership, the transaction is normally treated as a liquidation of the interest. Alternatively, if the agreement primarily obligates the continuing partners to acquire the departing partner's interest, the transaction is normally treated as a sale. When the purchase obligation rests with the continuing partners, sale treatment is normally achieved even if partnership property is used as the consideration for the acquisition. What are the tax consequences to the continuing partners when partnership property is used to satisfy their obligation to acquire the departing partner's interest? See I.R.C. § 731(a).

4. SERVICE PARTNERSHIP

I.R.C. § 736

Treas. Reg. § 1.736–1

When a partner retires or dies, the departing partner (or the decedent's successor) and the continuing partners are, in certain circumstances, afforded a great deal of flexibility in establishing the tax consequences of a buy-out of the departing partner's interest. This flexible treatment is available only if the buy-out is structured as a liquidation of the departing partner's interest and not as a sale of that interest to the continuing partners. See I.R.C. § 736. In addition, this flexible treatment is now limited to the retirement or death of a "general partner" in a partnership where "capital is not a material income-producing factor." See I.R.C. § 736(b)(3).[8]

I.R.C. § 736 divides payments made by a service partnership to acquire the interest of a retiring or a deceased general partner into two categories; I.R.C. § 736(a) payments and I.R.C. § 736(b) payments. See I.R.C. § 736.[9]

---

8. The House Committee Report to the Revenue Reconciliation Act of 1993 elaborates on the meaning of "capital is not a material income-producing factor" as follows:

> * * * For purposes of [§ 736], capital is not a material income-producing factor where substantially all the gross income of the business consists of fees, commissions, or other compensation for personal services performed by an individual. The practice of his or her profession by a doctor, dentist, lawyer, architect, or accountant will not, as such, be treated as a trade or business in which capital is a material income-producing factor even though the practitioner may have a substantial capital investment in professional equipment or in the physical plant constituting the office from which such individual conducts his or her practice so long as such capital investment is merely incidental to such professional practice. * * *.

Ways and Means Budget Reconciliation Act of 1993 (H.R. 2141), Explanation of Title XIV—Revenue Provisions, 345.

9. Even if the distributing partnership is not a service partnership (i.e., if capital is a material income-producing factor), payments made in liquidation of the interest of a retiring

The structure of I.R.C. § 736 requires that the amount of the § 736(b) payments be determined before attempting to determine the amount of the § 736(a) payments.

Amounts paid to the departing partner are § 736(b) payments to the extent that the payments are made, "in exchange for the interest of such partner in partnership property." I.R.C. § 736(b)(1). Notwithstanding this general rule, payments made for the departing partner's interest in any "unrealized receivables" of the partnership are not § 736(b) payments. I.R.C. § 736(b)(2)(A). In addition, payments made for the departing partner's interest in partnership "goodwill" (i.e., an intangible asset that encompasses the reputation of the business) are not § 736(b) payments, unless payments for goodwill are specifically provided for in the partnership agreement. I.R.C. § 736(b)(2)(B). Section 736(b) payments may take the form of money or other property.

Section 736(b) payments are governed by the general rules that apply to distributions in liquidation of a partner's interest. See pp. 332–333. Specifically, § 736(b) payments are generally received tax-free or as capital gain by the departing partner. See I.R.C. § 731(a). Moreover, § 736(b) payments do not reduce the amount of partnership income taxed to the continuing partners (e.g., the partnership is not allowed a deduction for § 736(b) payments).

In contrast to § 736(b) payments, amounts paid for the departing partner's share of any "unrealized receivables" of the partnership are § 736(a) payments. See I.R.C. §§ 736(b)(2)(A), 751(c). More significantly, any premium paid to compensate the departing partner for his share of certain intangible partnership assets like goodwill is a § 736(a) payment, except to the extent that the partnership agreement explicitly provides for a payment for goodwill. I.R.C. § 736(b)(2)(B). Section 736(a) payments may take the form of money or other property.

In contrast to § 736(b) payments, § 736(a) payments are not governed by the rules that apply to partnership distributions. Rather, a § 736(a) payment is treated as either a "distributive share" or a "guaranteed payment". If the amount of the payment is conditioned on future partnership income, the payment is treated as a distributive share; otherwise, it is treated as a guaranteed payment. See I.R.C. § 736(a). In effect, payments governed by § 736(a) are treated as if the former partner continues to share in partnership profits (distributive share) or receives compensation-like payments from the partnership (guaranteed payments), rather than as a return of the departing partner's investment. In most cases, § 736(a) payments create ordinary income to the departing partner.[10] In addition,

---

or a deceased partner are technically to be divided into section 736(a) payments and section 736(b) payments. See I.R.C. § 736. As a practical matter, however, virtually all payments to a departing partner in a partnership in which capital is a material income-producing factor are taxed under the general distribution rules.

10. If § 736(a) payments are tied to the income of the partnership and thereby treated as a distributive share of partnership income under I.R.C. § 736(a)(1), the character of the partnership's income controls the character of the departing partner's distributive share. If these payments reduce the amount of partnership income taxed to the continuing partners, either by deflecting a portion of future partnership income to the departing partner (distributive share) or by creating a future deduction for the partnership (guaranteed payment). See I.R.C. §§ 702(a),(b), 707(c).

The departing partner and the continuing partners of a service partnership generally have adverse interests with respect to how payments are classified under I.R.C. § 736. The departing partner generally desires to maximize the I.R.C. § 736(b) payments. In contrast, the continuing partners normally desire to maximize the I.R.C. § 736(a) payments. Why?

Congress has accorded the partners of a service partnership a great deal of flexibility by allowing them to control whether payments for a departing general partner's share of the partnership's goodwill are treated under I.R.C. § 736(a) or I.R.C. § 736(b). See I.R.C. § 736(b)(2)(B). Specifically, if the partnership agreement is silent as to goodwill, all payments for goodwill are treated as § 736(a) payments. In contrast, if the partnership agreement provides for a specific payment for goodwill, that payment is a § 736(b) payment.

Example 7–C: Nisa, Rachel and Shanna are architects and each owns a one-third interest in the NRS Architecture Partnership, a general partnership. Although NRS's tangible assets are only worth $75,000, NRS's business was recently valued at $375,000, the difference due largely to the reputation of the business (goodwill). Nisa has an outside basis of $10,000. She is to receive a cash payment of $125,000 in liquidation of her interest. No part of this payment is contingent on the future income of NRS. For the sake of simplicity, assume that NRS has no unrealized receivables.

(a) *(Maximizing § 736(a) payments):* If the partnership agreement is silent with respect to goodwill, Nisa is treated as receiving a $25,000 distribution (I.R.C. § 736(b) payment)[11] and a $100,000 guaranteed payment (I.R.C. § 736(a) payment).[12] Consequently, Nisa reports

---

the partnership generates capital gains income, the departing partner's distributive share will retain its capital gains character. See I.R.C. § 702(a).

11.

Partnership property and specified goodwill	$75,000
Nisa's interest	× .3333
	$25,000

12.

Total payments received	$125,000
Less: § 736(b) payments	25,000
§ 736(a) payments	$100,000

$15,000 of capital gain[13] and $100,000 of ordinary income. I.R.C. § 707(c). The partnership (now comprised of Rachel and Shanna) is allowed a $100,000 deduction for the guaranteed payment (I.R.C. § 707(c)) which reduces the amount of partnership income that otherwise would be reported by the continuing partners.

(b) *(Maximizing § 736(b) payments):* If the partnership agreement provides that the $100,000 premium represents a payment for goodwill, Nisa is treated as receiving a $125,000 distribution (I.R.C. § 736(b) payment).[14] In this case, Nisa reports a $115,000 capital gain (I.R.C. § 731(a)) and the amount of partnership income taxed to the continuing partners is not reduced by any part of the amount paid by the partnership for Nisa's interest.

Tolmach v. Commissioner

United States Tax Court, 1991.
62 T.C.M. 1102.

■ HALPERN, JUDGE: * * *

FINDINGS OF FACT

* * *

[P]etitioner [Milton Tolmach] was one of two senior partners in the law firm of Hayt, Hayt, Tolmach, & Landau (the Tolmach firm). [References to "petitioners" in the plural are to Tolmach and his wife.] The other senior partner was Bernard Landau (Landau). The firm specialized in collection work for the health care industry and enjoyed a national reputation. [T]here was no written agreement of partnership. [P]etitioner was in his mid-sixties and 17 years older than Landau. [D]iscussions between petitioner and Landau concerning petitioner's retirement had proceeded for some time without the two being able to reach agreement * * *. On April 26, 1976, Landau convened all of the partners of the firm except for petitioner and they voted to dissolve the firm. Landau and the partners voting with him notified petitioner, the firm's employees, and its clients * * *. They (the continuing partners) announced that a new firm, Hayt, Hayt & Landau (the Landau firm), would continue the practice formerly conducted by the Tolmach firm. The Landau firm took over the offices, personnel, equipment, bank accounts, leases, books, papers, records, files,

---

13.

Distribution of money	$25,000
Less: Outside basis	10,000
Recognized gain	$15,000

14.

Partnership property and specified goodwill	$375,000
Nisa's interest	× .3333
Amount of distribution	$125,000

and all other assets of the Tolmach firm. The continuing partners were the initial partners of the Landau firm. Petitioner was excluded from the offices of the Landau firm.[15]

Legal action followed the dissolution * * *. A judgment was rendered for petitioner on his * * * claim for damages resulting from his expulsion from the firm * * *. The referee was directed to ascertain and report on the amount of damages that should be paid. The referee subsequently issued a report that valued the partnership at $11,410,000. He summarized the components of that value as follows:

1.	Equity	$ 660,000
2.	Work in progress	2,000,000
3.	Goodwill	8,750,000
	Total	$11,410,000

Applying petitioner's partnership percentage as determined by the court (23.5 percent), the referee determined that petitioner's share of that value equaled $2,681,350 * * *. The findings of the referee were confirmed by the court.

Plaintiffs (the continuing partners) filed a notice of appeal * * *. Because the parties agreed to a settlement, no appeal was ever prosecuted. Petitioner agreed to receive payments in an amount less than recommended by the referee. The parties to the agreement (the Agreement) included petitioner, the (dissolved) Tolmach firm, * * * the continuing partners (in their individual capacities), and the Landau firm. Two pertinent recitals in the Agreement are as follows:

> WHEREAS, [the Landau firm] as successor to the [Tolmach firm] is willing to pay Tolmach the sum of $1.7 million in payment for his share of the unrealized receivables of the [Tolmach firm] at the time of dissolution, and to pay in addition the sum of $155,000 as and for Tolmach's interest in the fixed assets and goodwill of the [Tolmach firm], and to guarantee the payment of said sums regardless of the income received by the Partnership; and

> WHEREAS, Tolmach is willing to accept said sums as full payment for his interest in the partnership.

The Agreement goes on to provide that the sum of $1.7 million shall be paid in various monthly installments * * *. [A]ll installments of the $1.7 million are described as being intended to qualify as guaranteed payments under section 736(a)(2). The Agreement provides that the $155,000 pay-

---

15. Editor's note. The departure of a partner from a partnership generally triggers a "dissolution" under state law. A state law dissolution does not cause the dissolved partnership to be treated for tax purposes as distributing all of its assets to its partners with the continuing partners recontributing the assets to a new partnership. Instead, the tax law simply views the new partnership as a continuation of the dissolved partnership if the owners of a majority of the interests in the dissolved partnership form a reconstituted partnership, as in the Tolmach case. A dissolved partnership is treated as distributing all of its assets for tax purposes only if the dissolution results in a "termination" of the partnership. See I.R.C. § 708; pp. 366–371.

ment for petitioner's interest in the fixed assets and goodwill of the Tolmach firm is to be paid in one lump sum. That payment is described as being intended to qualify as a payment under section 736(b) * * *.

* * *

In 1983 and 1984 (the years here in issue), in discharge of its obligation to pay to petitioner $1.7 million pursuant to the Agreement, the Landau firm made payments to petitioner of $135,417 and $170,833, respectively. The Landau firm provided to petitioner for each such year a Schedule K–1, Partner's Share of Income, Credits, Deductions, etc., showing such payments as guaranteed payments. Petitioner took a position inconsistent with such characterization in his individual Federal income tax returns. He reported the payments as resulting from a sale of his partnership interest in the Tolmach firm. Petitioner treated the payments as giving rise to long-term capital gains * * *.

OPINION

Introduction

The principal issue before us concerns the nature of the payments of $135,417 and $170,833 received by petitioner pursuant to the Agreement in 1983 and 1984 (the payments). Petitioners argue that the payments were received on account of the sale of petitioner's interest in the Tolmach firm to his former partners in that firm. [P]etitioners argue, section 741 governs the taxation of such payments. Under section 741, gain recognized on the sale of an interest in a partnership generally is considered gain from the sale or exchange of a capital asset * * *. Respondent argues that the payments were received in liquidation of petitioner's interest in the Tolmach firm and, thus, taxation of the payments is governed by section 736. Respondent further argues that the payments cannot be considered as received in exchange for an interest in partnership property under section 736(b) but rather must be considered as guaranteed payments under section 736(a)(2). Guaranteed payments give rise to ordinary income. See sec. 707(c) * * *.

Tax Consequences of a Sale Versus a Liquidation

The tax consequences of the sale of a partnership interest may differ significantly from those of a liquidation of that interest. That is so even though the economic consequences of those alternatives may be indistinguishable under certain circumstances. For example, when a partner retires, it generally makes little or no economic difference to either him or the continuing partners whether his interest is purchased pro rata by the continuing partners or liquidated in exchange for payments from the partnership. In either case, the continuing partners ultimately bear the cost of acquiring the interest and their interests in the partnership are increased proportionately. When faced with such a situation, it is clear that the partners have complete flexibility to structure the transaction as either a section 741 sale of the withdrawing partner's interest to the other partners or a section 736 liquidation of the retiring partner's interest by the partnership. It must be kept in mind, however, that the flexibility that is permitted is not a license to determine the tax result simply by checking a box on the tax return. The permitted flexibility is the flexibility to structure the transaction as either a sale or a liquidation. A transaction properly structured as a sale or liquidation will be taxed accordingly.

* * *

Payments to Petitioner: Sale or Liquidation

* * *

As we stated in Cooney v. Commissioner:

> The critical distinction between a sale of a partnership interest under section 741 and a liquidation of such an interest under section 736 is that a sale is a transaction between a third party or the continuing partners individually and the withdrawing partner, whereas a liquidation is a transaction between the partnership as such and the withdrawing partner. * * * [65 T.C. at 109.]

The payments here in question were made by the Landau firm to petitioner pursuant to its obligation under the Agreement to make such payments. Although the Agreement is not unambiguous, we think that the terms thereof better indicate a transaction between the Landau Firm as such and petitioner than they do a transaction between the continuing partners individually and petitioner.

Indications consistent with a transaction between the partnership as such and petitioner are as follows: Both the Tolmach firm and the Landau firm are parties to the Agreement. The Agreement recites that the Landau firm, ''as successor to the [Tolmach firm],'' is willing to make payments to petitioner and to guarantee such payments regardless of the income received by the partnership. The Agreement binds not only the Landau firm but ''its successor firm or entity.'' * * * The above are all factors consistent with a transaction between the partnership as such and petitioner.

There are, however, inconsistencies in the Agreement * * *. [P]etitioners argue that the Agreement was a contract of purchase and sale entered into by the continuing partners and petitioner. Petitioners rely heavily on the fact that the continuing partners were parties to the Agreement * * *. It is true that, in their individual capacities, the continuing partners were parties to the Agreement * * *. Nevertheless, the Agreement further provides that petitioner ''shall not obtain judgment against the [continuing partners] or any of them on account of a breach of the Agreement until execution shall first have been returned unsatisfied against [the Landau firm] or its successor firm or entity.'' * * * We view the obligation of the continuing partners in their own right as being secondary to the obligation of the Landau firm. Their obligation provided additional security to the primary obligation of the Landau firm. That obligation did not change the basic character of the Agreement, which was an agreement by the partnership to make payments in liquidation of petitioner's interest in the continuing Tolmach firm.

Finally, the Agreement not only is more consistent with a liquidation of petitioner's interest than it is with a sale of that interest but its references to section 736 expressly describe the intended tax treatment of the payments called for under the Agreement as being that of payments in liquidation of a partner's interest * * *. Petitioner was a party to the Agreement and we will not separate him from that expression of intent.

We conclude * * * that the transaction at bar was a transaction between the partnership as such and petitioner rather than a transaction between the continuing partners in their own rights and petitioner * * *.

Application of Section 736

Pursuant to the Agreement, petitioner was to receive payments of $1,855,000, $1.7 million in payment for his share of the unrealized receivables of the Tolmach firm, and $155,000 for his interest in the fixed assets and goodwill of the firm. At issue here are installments of the $1.7 million received in 1983 and 1984. [P]ayments made pursuant to the Agreement were made in liquidation of petitioner's interest in the Tolmach firm and are to be taxed pursuant to section 736. The Agreement provides that the payments are to be made to petitioner without regard to the income of the Landau firm. Accordingly, the payments appear to be guaranteed payments made in liquidation of petitioner's partnership interest, the tax treatment of which is governed by section 736(a)(2). Petitioners, however, would recharacterize some portion of the payments. Based on the finding of the referee appointed by the New York Supreme Court that goodwill accounted for approximately 77 percent of the value of the Tolmach firm, petitioners argue that the allocation in the Agreement of approximately 10 percent of the total payments to goodwill should be ignored and 77 percent of the total payments received by him under the Agreement should be treated as for goodwill. That we cannot do.

Section 736(b) is specific with regard to payments for goodwill. Except to the extent provided for in the partnership agreement, payments for goodwill are considered as either a distributive share or a guaranteed payment under section 736(a). Sec. 736(b). The term "partnership agreement" is defined in section 761(c). A partnership agreement includes modifications made up to the time (determined without extensions) for filing the partnership return for the taxable year, which are agreed to by all of the partners, or otherwise adopted as provided for in the partnership agreement. The agreement may be oral. Sec. 1.761–(1)(c), Income Tax Regs. On April 26, 1976, at the time of dissolution of the Tolmach firm, there was no written partnership agreement. Petitioners argue that there was an agreement among the partners providing for a payment in exchange for a withdrawing partner's interest in goodwill * * *.

[After reviewing the facts, the court concluded that there was no agreement among the partners providing for a payment in exchange for a withdrawing partner's goodwill.] * * *

[W]e admit that it is likely that, on April 26, 1976, the Tolmach firm did enjoy goodwill and that such goodwill constituted a substantial portion of the value of the firm * * *. Nevertheless, * * * there was no agreement among the partners of the Tolmach firm providing that any portion of the payments to be made to petitioner pursuant to the Agreement was to be attributed to petitioner's interest in the goodwill of the firm in excess of the $155,000 payment for goodwill there provided for. Moreover, petitioners have not argued that any portion of the $1.7 million described as being for petitioner's share of unrealized receivables is for partnership property other than goodwill (or unrealized receivables) so that taxation under section 736(b) would otherwise be appropriate. Accordingly, even were we to agree with petitioners that partnership goodwill constituted a substantial portion of the value of the Tolmach firm, we would be unable to hold that any portion of the $1.7 million described in the Agreement as being for petitioner's share of unrealized receivables was other than a payment subject to ordinary income treatment under section 736(a).

Finally, petitioners disavow the allocation of payments found in the Agreement, claiming that by the subtle threat of an expensive appeal petitioner had no choice but to accept the Agreement on a "take-it-or-leave-it" basis. They argue that, therefore, the payments should be reallocated, with 77 percent going to goodwill * * *. Petitioners must show a mistake, overreaching, duress, or other reason that, in an action between the parties to the transaction, would be sufficient to alter the contested construction or set it aside. Petitioners have not done so. In essence, petitioners are claiming only that petitioner did not receive sufficient after-tax dollars for his interest in the partnership. Had petitioner received a larger guaranteed payment, he would have been in the same after-tax position as if a greater portion of the payments he did receive were attributed to his interest in goodwill. There is no economic difference between a liquidating payment for a withdrawing partner's interest in the goodwill of the partnership that is attributed to goodwill and one that is in liquidation of his interest in goodwill but that is not so attributed. It is clear, however, * * * that Congress has allowed the withdrawing and continuing partners to allocate the resulting tax benefits and burdens as they see fit, by attributing or not attributing such payments to goodwill. See sec. 736(b)(2)(B). Petitioners have not demonstrated to us that, given the permitted flexibility to bargain over tax consequences and the underlying nature of petitioners' complaint (that petitioner did not get enough money), a court in an action between the parties would reform the Agreement by reattributing to goodwill payments previously attributed as guaranteed payments. Thus, we will not disregard the allocation of payments found in the Agreement. The payments to petitioner designated in the Agreement as in payment for his share of unrealized receivables must be treated under section 736(a)(2) as guaranteed payments made in liquidation of the interest of a retiring partner.

For the reasons stated, we sustain the deficiencies determined by respondent.

NOTES

1. *Complexity of Subchapter K, in general, and § 736, in particular.* I.R.C. § 736 was enacted in 1954 as part of the "first comprehensive statutory treatment of partners and partnerships in the history of the income tax laws" when "simplicity" was one of Congress's principal objectives. H. Rep. No. 1337, 83d Cong., 2d Sess., 65. When considering this history, the Tax Court remarked that, "there can be little doubt that the attempt to achieve 'simplicity' has resulted in utter failure." Foxman v. Commissioner, 41 T.C. 535, 551 (1964). The Foxman court elaborated on this statement as follows:

> The distressingly complex and confusing nature of the provisions of subchapter K present a formidable obstacle to the comprehension of these provisions without the expenditure of a disproportionate amount of time and effort even by one who is sophisticated in tax matters with many years of experience in the tax field. If there is any lingering doubt on this matter one has only to reread section 736 in its entirety and give an honest answer to the question whether it is reasonably comprehensible to the average lawyer or even to the average tax expert who has not given special attention and extended study to the tax problems of partners. Surely a statute has not achieved "simplicity" when its complex provisions can confidently be dealt with by at most only a comparatively small number of specialists who have been initiated into its mysteries.

Foxman, 41 T.C. at 551, fn 9.

2. *Partner forced-out.* I.R.C. § 736 applies only to a "retiring or deceased partner." A partner is deemed to retire when he ceases to be a partner under local law. Treas. Reg. § 1.736–1(a)(1)(ii). Thus, I.R.C. § 736 applies regardless of whether a partner voluntarily departs or is forced out of the partnership.

3. *Value of interest in partnership property.* In theory, partners in a service partnership can only control the tax treatment of amounts that compensate the departing partner for his share of the partnership's goodwill. Payments for the departing partner's interest in partnership property, other than unrealized receivables, are automatically treated as § 736(b) payments and payments for unrealized receivables are automatically treated as § 736(a) payments. The regulations, however, provide as follows:

> Generally, the valuation placed by the partners upon a partner's interest in partnership property in an arm's length agreement will be regarded as correct.

Treas. Reg. § 1.736–1(b)(1). In the Tolmach case, the $155,000 amount allocated by the Settlement Agreement to Tolmach's interest in the fixed assets of the partnership was apparently arrived at by applying Tolmach's percentage interest (23.5%) to the referee's value of the partnership equity ($660,000). Would the Tolmach court have respected an allocation of only $100,000 to Tolmach's interest in the fixed assets? How small an amount could have been allocated to Tolmach's interest in the fixed assets?

4. *Motive for identifying goodwill.* One might infer from the facts of the Tolmach case that the continuing partners drafted the Settlement Agreement and controlled the negotiation of its terms. The Agreement identified "the sum of $155,000 as and for Tolmach's interest in the fixed assets *and* *goodwill* of the [Tolmach firm]." (Emphasis added.) Assuming that the continuing partners desired to maximize the amount of § 736(a) payments, what possible benefit could they derive by providing for goodwill in the Settlement Agreement?

5. *Section 736(a) versus section 736(b) payments.* If the retiring partner and the continuing partners of a service partnership pay tax at the highest rates and have equal bargaining power, would you expect the liquidation of the retiring partner's interest to be structured to maximize the amount of § 736(a) payments or the amount of § 736(b) payments? See I.R.C. §§ 1(a), (h). How can the desired result be accomplished?

6. *Sale versus liquidation of interest.* When the partnership interest of a retiring partner is sold to the continuing partners, no flexibility exists with respect to the tax consequences of that part of the purchase price, if any, which represents compensation for the departing partner's share of the partnership's goodwill. See I.R.C. § 741. In the case of a sale, any payment for goodwill is automatically taxed in the same fashion as an I.R.C. § 736(b) payment (tax-free or as capital gain to the departing partner with no reduction in the amount of partnership income taxed to the continuing partners). See I.R.C. § 741. If the retiring partner and the continuing partners of a service partnership pay tax at the highest rates and have equal bargaining power, would you expect the acquisition of the retiring partner's interest in a service partnership to be structured as a sale to the continuing partners or as a liquidation of the retiring partner's interest?

7. *Unrealized receivables and inventory items.* Regardless of whether the interest of a partner in a service partnership is liquidated or sold, that portion of the purchase price attributable to the departing partner's share of partnership "unrealized receivables" triggers ordinary income to the departing partner. In addition, the portion of the purchase price attributable to the departing partner's share of "inventory items" may trigger ordinary income to the departing partner. If the partner's interest is liquidated, any payments for "unrealized receivables" are treated as § 736(a) payments and taxed as ordinary income. See I.R.C. §§ 736(b)(2)(A), 751(c)(first sentence). In addition, payments attributable to certain other partnership assets defined as "unrealized receivables" (see I.R.C. § 751(c)(second and third sentences)) and/or "inventory items which have appreciated substantially in value" (see I.R.C. §§ 751(d), (b)(1)(A)(ii)) create ordinary income to the departing partner. See §§ 736(b), 731, 751(b). When a partnership interest is sold, that portion of the purchase price attributable to the selling partner's share of partnership assets that are "unrealized receivables" (see I.R.C. § 751(c)) and "inventory items" (see I.R.C. § 751(d)) triggers ordinary income to the selling partner. See I.R.C. §§ 741, 751(a). Regardless of whether the departing partner's interest is liquidated or sold, the continuing partners are not taxed on the departing partner's share of the partnership's unrealized receivables and inventory items if the partnership makes an election under I.R.C. § 754. See I.R.C. §§ 734, 743, 754.

8. *Payments for a departing member's share of the goodwill of a limited liability company.* An LLC will generally be taxed as a partnership. See pp. 192–197. If an LLC in which capital is not a material income-producing factor makes a distribution in liquidation of the interest of a retiring or a deceased member, can payments attributable to goodwill be treated as I.R.C. § 736(a) payments by not providing for goodwill in the agreement? See I.R.C. § 736(b)(2)(B). Is the fact that a member of an LLC is normally not personally liable for obligations of the LLC dispositive of whether payments for goodwill can be treated as I.R.C. § 736(a) payments? See I.R.C. § 736(b)(3)(B).

5.   Impact of § 751 Assets

As a general matter, any gain or loss recognized by a partner whose interest is liquidated or sold is characterized as capital gain or capital loss. See I.R.C. §§ 731(a), 741. An exception to this rule is designed to insure that the departing partner reports the ordinary income inherent in her share of certain partnership assets ("unrealized receivables"[16] and certain "inventory items"). See I.R.C. § 751. Section 751 effectively treats the departing partner as owning a proportionate part of certain partnership assets that would create ordinary income if they were sold by the partnership. Like the general distribution rules, I.R.C. § 751 views the partnership as a mere extension of its partners.

a.   SALE OF INTEREST

I.R.C. §§ 741, 751(a), (c), (d)

Treas. Reg. §§ 1.751–1(a), (g) Example (1)

When a partner sells part or all of her partnership interest to the continuing partners or to an outsider, she must normally report as ordinary income her share of the unrealized gain in any "unrealized receivables" and/or "inventory items" of the partnership. See I.R.C. §§ 751(a), (c), (d). Any remaining gain or loss recognized on the sale of her partnership interest is characterized as capital gain or capital loss. I.R.C. § 741(a).

> *Example 7–D (Illustration of I.R.C. § 751(a)):* Francine, Gwen and Harold each own a one-third interest in the FGH Partnership. Each partner has an outside basis of $200,000. Francine sells her partnership interest to Ivan for $300,000. At the time of the sale, FGH has no liabilities and the following assets:
>
> | | Basis | Value |
> |---|---|---|
> | Money | $300,000 | $300,000 |
> | Inventory | 60,000 | 390,000 |
> | Equipment | 240,000 | 210,000 |
> | Total | $600,000 | $900,000 |

---

16. The term "unrealized receivables" is defined more broadly for purposes of I.R.C. § 731 and I.R.C. § 741 than for purposes of I.R.C. § 736. See I.R.C. § 751(c) (second and third sentences).

In the absence of § 751(a), Francine would recognize a $100,000 capital gain on the sale of her partnership interest. Section 751(a) applies to the sale of Francine's interest, however, because of FGH's inventory. See I.R.C. § 751(a)(2). Francine's share of FGH's unrealized gain in the inventory is $110,000.[17] Therefore, Francine recognizes $110,000 of ordinary income on the sale of her partnership interest. In addition, Francine recognizes a $10,000 capital loss, the difference between the $100,000 gain she would have recognized in the absence of § 751(a) and the $110,000 of ordinary income resulting from the application of § 751(a). See Treas. Reg. §§ 1.751–1(a)(2), (g) Example 1.

b.   LIQUIDATION OF INTEREST

I.R.C. §§ 731, 751(b), (c), (d)

Treas. Reg. §§ 1.751–1(b), (g) Examples (2)–(3)

If a partner receives payments in liquidation of her interest from a partnership that owns "unrealized receivables" and/or "substantially appreciated inventory," a portion of the consideration she receives for her interest may be taxed as ordinary income on receipt. See I.R.C. §§ 751(b), (c), (d).[18] Specifically, ordinary income is triggered to the departing partner if she receives *less* than her share of the partnership's assets that represent unrealized receivables or substantially appreciated inventory. In contrast, I.R.C. § 751(b) triggers ordinary income to the continuing partners if the departing partner receives *more* than her share of the partnership's unrealized receivables or substantially appreciated inventory.

In the case of a sale, I.R.C. § 751(a) operates simply as a recharacterization device with respect to the selling partner. In the case of a distribution, I.R.C. § 751(b) can likewise operate as a recharacterization device with respect to the selling partner. However, I.R.C. § 751(b) also *accelerates* the income inherent in certain partnership assets by triggering that income when the departing partner leaves the partnership, rather than when the future sale of those assets occurs.

The mechanics of I.R.C. § 751(b) are exceedingly complex. Example 7–E represents a rough illustration of how the provision operates.

Example 7–E (Illustration of I.R.C. § 751(b)): Francine, Gwen and Harold each own a one-third interest in the FGH Partnership. Each partner has an outside basis of $200,000. FGH distributes assets with a value of $300,000 to Francine in liquidation of her interest. Before the distribution, FGH has no liabilities and the following assets:

---

17. If the partnership had sold the inventory for $390,000 prior to Francine's sale of her interest, the partnership would recognize $330,000 of ordinary income, 1/3 of which ($110,000) would be Francine's distributive share.

18. This casebook examines I.R.C. § 751(b) only in connection with distributions in liquidation of a partner's interest. Section 751(b) also applies to any current distribution that results in a reduction (or increase) in a partner's share of § 751 property in exchange for an increase (or reduction) in her interest in other partnership property.

	Basis	Value
Money	$300,000	$300,000
Inventory	60,000	390,000
Equipment	240,000	210,000
Total	$600,000	$900,000

FGH's inventory represents "substantially appreciated inventory." See I.R.C. § 751(b)(1)(A)(ii), (b)(3).

Alternative 1—Proportionate Distribution: If FGH liquidates Francine's interest by distributing $100,000 of money, inventory with a value of $130,000 and an inside basis of $20,000, and equipment with a value of $70,000 and an inside basis of $80,000, the following consequences result:

(a) No gain or loss is recognized by the partnership (§ 731(b)).

(b) Francine receives the money, inventory, and equipment tax-free (§ 731(a)) and takes a basis of $20,000 in the inventory and a basis of $80,000 in the equipment (§§ 732(b), (c)).

If Francine sells the distributed inventory for $130,000 within five years of the distribution, she has $110,000 of ordinary income. See I.R.C. § 735(a)(2).[19] If the partnership sells the retained inventory for $260,000, it derives $220,000 of ordinary income,[20] and Gwen and Harold each reports half ($110,000) of FGH's ordinary income as a distributive share. See I.R.C. § 702.

Alternative 2—Distribution of Less than Partner's Share of § 751 Assets: FGH distributes $300,000 of money to Francine in liquidation of her interest. Section 751(b) recasts the transaction as if FGH distributed Francine's share of the inventory to her which she sold back to FGH for the additional money she actually received. See Treas. Reg. § 1.751–1(b)(3).

Fictional current distribution: Francine is treated as receiving a current distribution of inventory with a value of $130,000 and an inside basis of $20,000, and a liquidating distribution of $170,000 of money. The consequences of these distributions are as follows:

(a) No gain or loss is recognized by FGH (§ 731(b)).

19.

Money Received	$130,000
Less: Adjusted Basis	20,000
Ordinary Income	$110,000

20.

Money Received	$260,000
Less: Inside Basis	40,000
Ordinary Income	$220,000

(b) Francine receives the inventory tax-free (§ 731(a)), takes a basis of $20,000 in the inventory (§ 732(a)(1)) and reduces her outside basis to $180,000 (§ 733(2)).

(c) Francine recognizes a $10,000 capital loss with respect to the $170,000 of money (§ 731(a)(2)).[21]

Fictional sale back to partnership: Francine is treated as selling the inventory received in the fictional distribution back to the partnership for $130,000. The consequences of the fictional sale are as follows:

(a) Francine recognizes $110,000 of ordinary income (§§ 1001, 1221).[22]

(b) FGH takes a basis of $170,000 in its inventory.[23]

If FGH later sells its entire inventory for $390,000, it derives $220,000 of ordinary income,[24] and Gwen and Harold each reports half ($110,000) of FGH's ordinary income as a distributive share. As a result of the fictional transactions, each of the three partners reports his/her share of the ordinary income stemming from the inventory, notwithstanding that the partnership did not actually distribute any inventory to Francine and that all the inventory was sold after Francine departed from the partnership.

Alternative 3—Distribution of More than Partner's Share of § 751 Assets: FGH distributes inventory with a value of $300,000 and an inside basis of

---

21.

Money Received	$170,000
Less: Outside Basis	180,000
Gain (Loss)	($10,000)

22.

Money Received	$130,000
Less: Adjusted Basis	20,000
Ordinary Income	$110,000

23.

Inside Basis of Retained Inventory	$ 40,000
Inside Basis of "Purchased" Inventory	130,000
Total Inside Basis	$170,000

24.

Money Received	$390,000
Less: Inside Basis	170,000
Ordinary Income	$220,000

$46,154[25] to Francine in liquidation of her interest. Section 751(b) recasts the transaction as if the partnership distributed Francine's share of the inventory ($130,000) and, in addition, distributed her share of the other partnership assets, which she then transferred back to the partnership in exchange for the additional inventory she actually received. See Treas. Reg. § 1.751–1(b)(2).

Fictional current distribution: Francine is treated as receiving a current distribution of her share of the non–§ 751 property of the partnership ($100,000 of money and equipment with a value of $70,000 and an inside basis of $80,000)[26] and a liquidating distribution of her share of the inventory ($130,000). The consequences of these distributions are as follows:

(a) No gain or loss is recognized by FGH (§ 731(b)).

(b) Francine receives the money and equipment tax-free (§ 731(a)).

(c) Francine takes a basis of $80,000 in the equipment (§ 732(a)(1)) and reduces her outside basis to $20,000 (§ 733(2)).[27]

(d) Francine receives her share of the inventory tax-free (§ 731(a)) and takes a basis of $20,000 in her share of the inventory (§ 732(b)).

Fictional sale back to partnership: Francine is treated as transferring the money and equipment back to the partnership in exchange for an additional $170,000 of inventory. The consequences of the fictional sale are as follows:

(a) Francine recognizes a $10,000 capital loss with respect to the equipment (§§ 1001, 1221).[28]

---

25. The actual inside basis of the distributed inventory must be known to perform the necessary calculations under I.R.C. § 751(b). As a matter of convenience, it is assumed that FGH has 390 identical items of inventory, each of which has a value of $1,000 and an inside basis of $153.846. FGH distributes 300 of these items to Francine with an inside basis of $46,154.

Inside basis per item of inventory	$ 153.846
Number of items distributed	× 300
Inside basis of distributed inventory	$ 46,154

26. The fictional distribution consists of a proportionate amount of each of the non–§ 751 assets of the partnership in the absence of a specific agreement among the partners as to the properties exchanged. See Treas. Reg. § 1.751–1(g) Example 4.

27.

Original outside basis	$200,000
Less: Amount of money deemed received	100,000
Less: Basis in equipment deemed received	80,000
Outside basis after deemed distribution	$20,000

28.

Amount Realized	$70,000
Less: Adjusted Basis	80,000
Realized Gain (Loss)	($10,000)

(b) Francine takes a basis of $170,000 in the purchased inventory (§ 1012).

(c) FGH recognizes $143,846 of ordinary income with respect to the $170,000 of inventory it is treated as selling to Francine.[29] Gwen and Harold each reports half ($71,923) of FGH's ordinary income as a distributive share.

(d) The partnership retains $90,000 of inventory in which it has a basis of $13,846.[30]

If Francine sells all the inventory that was actually distributed to her within five years of the distribution for $300,000, she derives $110,000 of ordinary income.[31] See I.R.C. § 735(a)(2). If FGH later sells the inventory it

---

29.

Money and Property Received	$170,000
Less: Inside Basis (see below)	26,154
Ordinary Income	$143,846

Inside Basis:

$$\frac{\text{amount of inventory deemed sold}}{\text{amount of inventory actually distributed}} \times \text{inside basis of distributed inventory (fn 25)} =$$

$$\frac{\$170,000}{\$300,000} \times \$46,154 = \$26,154$$

30. As a matter of convenience, it was assumed that FGH had 390 identical items of inventory, each of which had an inside basis of $153.846. See fn 25. FGH retained 90 of these items with an inside basis of $13,846.

Inside basis per item of inventory	$ 153.846
Number of items retained	×90
Inside basis of retained inventory	$13,846

31.

Money Received	$300,000
Less: Adjusted Basis (see below)	190,000
Ordinary Income	$110,000

Adjusted Basis:	
From liquidating distribution	$ 20,000
From fictional purchase	170,000
Total	$190,000

retained for $90,000, it derives $76,154 of ordinary income,[32] and Gwen and Harold each reports half ($38,077) of FGH's ordinary income as a distributive share. Gwen and Harold, therefore, each reported a total of $110,000 of ordinary income, $71,923 at the time of the distribution to Francine and $38,077 when the partnership sold its remaining inventory. As a result of the fictional transactions, each of the three partners reports his/her share of the ordinary income stemming from the inventory, notwithstanding that FGH distributed more than Francine's share of the inventory to her and that all the inventory was sold after Francine departed from the partnership.

NOTE

Problematic nature of § 751(b). Despite the intricate mechanics of I.R.C. § 751(b), partners can often shift ordinary income among themselves by carefully selecting the partnership assets to be distributed to the departing partner. See William Lyons & James Repetti, *Partnership Income Taxation, 5th ed.* at 164 (2011). Due to the complexity of I.R.C. § 751(b) and the fact that the provision can often be circumvented, analysts have recommended its repeal. See, e.g., American Law Institute, *Federal Income Tax Project, Subchapter K* at 54 (1984).

c.   DISPOSITION OF DISTRIBUTED PROPERTY

I.R.C. §§ 735, 751(c), (d)
Treas. Reg. § 1.735–1(a)

When a partnership distributes certain property in a current distribution or in liquidation of a partner's interest, the character of the property to the partnership is preserved in the distributee's hands. Specifically, when a partnership distributes an "unrealized receivable", any gain or loss recognized when the distributee subsequently disposes of the property is characterized as ordinary income or ordinary loss, regardless of whether the property would otherwise be a capital asset in the distributee's hands. See I.R.C. §§ 735(a)(1), 751(c). Similarly, when a partnership distributes an "inventory item", any gain or loss recognized when the distributee subsequently disposes of the property is characterized as ordinary income or ordinary loss *if the subsequent disposition occurs within five years of the*

32.

Money Received	$90,000
Less: Inside Basis (see fn 30)	13,846
Ordinary Income	$76,154

distribution, regardless of whether the distributee continued to hold the property as inventory. See I.R.C. § 735(a)(2).

Problem 7–5 (Characterization on subsequent disposition of distributed property). Charlotte owns an interest in the ABC Limited Liability Company (LLC), a jewelry retailer. The LLC is classified as a partnership under Treas. Reg. § 301.7701–3. On January 1 of Year 2, ABC distributes to Charlotte her proportionate share of the unrealized receivables, inventory, and other assets of the partnership in liquidation of her interest. Among the assets distributed to Charlotte is a ruby ring with a value of $4,000 that ABC purchased for $3,000. Assume that Charlotte takes a basis of $3,000 in the ruby ring. What are the tax consequences to Charlotte if:

(a) she sells the ring in Year 3 for $4,000?

(b) she sells the ring in Year 3 for $10,000?

(c) she sells the ring in Year 3 for $1,000?

(d) she sells the ring in Year 8 for $10,000?

(e) same as (d) except that she opens her own jewelry store and sells the ruby ring to a customer?

(f) she dies while holding the ring? See I.R.C. § 1014.

6.   PARTNERSHIP LEVEL ADJUSTMENTS

I.R.C. §§ 734, 743, 754, 755

Treas. Reg. §§ 1.734–1, 1.743–1(a), (b), 1.754–1, 1.755–1(a)(1), (b)(1), (2)

When a partner sells his partnership interest, any gain (or loss) recognized by the departing partner does not, as a general rule, affect the partnership's basis in its assets. I.R.C. § 743(a). Similarly, any gain or loss recognized by a partner who receives a distribution (whether current or in liquidation of her interest) does not affect the partnership's basis in its assets. I.R.C. § 734(a). If the partnership makes an election under I.R.C. § 754, however, inside basis will be stepped-up or stepped-down to reflect any gain or loss recognized by the selling partner or the distributee partner. I.R.C. §§ 743(b), 734(b). The allocation of the step-up or step-down among the partnership's assets is controlled by I.R.C. § 755.

Example 7–F (Illustration of I.R.C. § 743 and § 734): Al, Bobbi, Clara and Don each own a 25% interest in the ABCD Partnership. Each partner has an outside basis of $700,000. ABCD's assets consist of $1,000,000 of money and a building with a value of $3,000,000 and an inside basis of $1,800,000. ABCD has no liabilities.

Sale of Interest: Al sells his partnership interest to Evan for $1,000,000. As a result, Al recognizes a $300,000 capital gain. I.R.C. § 741. Evan's outside basis is $1,000,000. I.R.C. § 742. If Evan immediately resells the acquired interest for $1,000,000, he realizes no gain on the sale. In contrast, if ABCD sells the building for $3,000,000 immediately after Evan acquires Al's interest, the tax consequences to

Evan differ depending on whether the partnership makes a § 754 election.

No § 754 Election: If a § 754 election is not made, the sale of the building for $3,000,000 causes the partnership to recognize a $1,200,000 gain. Each 25% partner (including Evan) has a $300,000 distributive share of that gain. In effect, Evan is taxed on the same gain that Al was taxed on when Al sold his interest to Evan. Does the tax law compensate Evan for being taxed on a gain that accrued before Evan acquired his interest? See I.R.C. § 705(a)(1)(A).

§ 754 Election: If the partnership makes a § 754 election, ABCD steps-up its basis in the building by $300,000. See I.R.C. § 743(b).[33] This additional $300,000 of inside basis is reserved exclusively for Evan's benefit. See I.R.C. § 743(b) (second sentence). If the building is subsequently sold for $3,000,000, the partnership's amount realized is offset first by the $1,800,000 of "common" inside basis in the building resulting in a $1,200,000 gain. Then, Evan's $300,000 distributive share of the partnership's gain is offset by the additional $300,000 of inside basis resulting from the § 754 election. Hence, Evan's distributive share of the partnership's gain is zero. The other three partners each have a $300,000 distributive share of the gain, the same amount of gain each partner would have had if Al had not sold his interest.

Liquidation of Interest: Instead of Al selling his interest to Evan, the partnership distributes $1,000,000 to Al in liquidation of his interest. As a result, Al recognizes a $300,000 capital gain. I.R.C. § 731(a)(1). If, immediately after the liquidation of Al's interest, the partnership sells the building for $3,000,000, the tax consequences to the three continuing partners differ depending on whether the partnership makes a § 754 election.

No § 754 Election: If a § 754 election is not made, the sale of the building for $3,000,000 causes the partnership to recognize a $1,200,000 gain. The three remaining partners each have a $400,000 distributive share of that gain. In effect, $100,000 of the gain allocated to each of the three remaining partners represents the same gain that was taxed to Al when his interest was liqui-

---

33.

Evan's outside basis		$1,000,000
Less: Evan's share of inside basis (see below)		700,000
Step-up in inside basis		$300,000

Evan's share of inside basis:		
Total inside basis	$2,800,000	
Evan's interest	× .25	
	$700,000	

dated. Does the tax law compensate the three remaining partners for being taxed on gain that accrued to Al? See I.R.C. § 705(a)(1)(A).

§ 754 Election: If the partnership makes a § 754 election, the partnership's basis in the building is stepped-up by the amount of gain recognized by Al when his interest was liquidated ($300,000). See I.R.C. § 734(b). Thus, the partnership's inside basis increases from $1,800,000 to $2,100,000. If the building is subsequently sold for $3,000,000, the partnership recognizes a $900,000 gain. The three remaining partners each have a $300,000 distributive share of the partnership gain, the same amount of gain each partner would have had if Al's interest had not been liquidated.

Jones v. United States

United States Court of Claims, 1977.
553 F.2d 667.

■ KASHIWA, JUDGE: * * *

Decedent, Carl T. Jones, died on October 7, 1967. At the time of his death, decedent was a partner in three firms located in Huntsville, Alabama * * *.

At the time of decedent's death, no election under § 754 to adjust the basis of partnership property under §§ 734(b) or 743(b) was in effect for any of the partnerships.[34]

The three partnerships, each on a calendar year basis, timely filed income tax returns for the calendar years 1967 and 1968. These returns did not contain an election under § 754, nor was there on or attached to these returns a special depreciation schedule attributable to decedent's interests in the partnerships. All partnership depreciation schedules were regular continuations of original cost amounts with no reference to the death of Carl T. Jones.

The Estate of Carl T. Jones succeeded to decedent's partnership interests. The estate retained a member of the Appraisal Institute to appraise the real property of the three partnerships. The appraisals, dated August, September, October and December 1968, valued the total real estate holdings, about 63 parcels, at $3,508,745.55. The appraised values of the real property were used in the estate tax return for the Estate of Carl T. Jones, which was filed on January 6, 1969. * * *

---

34. The basis of partnership assets is not affected by the death of a partner. [I.R.C. § 743(a).] To be consistent with the concept that property owned by a decedent receives a stepped-up basis equal to its fair market value at the date of death * * * (§ 1014(a)), § 754 permits the partnership under § 743 an elective adjustment to the basis of the partnership property. This adjustment will affect the basis of the partnership assets only for the heir of the deceased partner and not for the other partners. However, if the partnership does not make the election, an heir's basis for partnership assets remains the same as the partnership's and is not increased to reflect * * * the inherited partnership interest.

On August 20, 1969, a § 754 election to adjust the basis of partnership property under §§ 734(b) and 743(b) was filed by the * * * partnerships * * *. The election, which did not accompany either a partnership return or an amended return, indicated it was to apply to the calendar year 1967 and each subsequent year. Between October 7, 1967, decedent's date of death, and August 20, 1969, the date on which the elections were filed, no extension of time to file an election under § 754 was ever requested by or granted to the partnerships or the estate.

The Estate of Carl T. Jones timely filed fiduciary income tax returns for the fiscal years October 31, 1968; October 31, 1969; and October 31, 1970. By schedule attached to each return, the estate claimed additional depreciation deductions on assets held by the partnerships * * *; it also claimed additional deductions for inherited basis in partnership assets—cattle—that were sold * * *. These additional deductions were attributable to the estate taking a stepped-up basis in the partnership property.

The Internal Revenue Service, upon audit of the estate's fiduciary income tax returns, disallowed the additional deductions attributable to the adjustments to basis of the partnership property. The Service determined that the § 754 elections were not timely filed based upon Treas. Reg. § 1.754–1(b) and assessed income tax deficiencies totaling $43,363.86 for fiscal years ended October 31, 1968, 1969 and 1970. The plaintiff made payments of the assessed deficiencies * * * to the Internal Revenue Service. The estate filed timely claims for refund; after such claims were not acted upon by the Internal Revenue Service for more than six months after the date of filing, the estate filed the instant suit.

* * *

The optional adjustment to basis of partnership property on transfer of a partnership interest is specifically conditioned on the filing of an election under § 754. The election applies both to § 734(b), on distribution of partnership property, and to § 743(b), on transfer of a partnership interest. Unless the election is revoked, the § 754 election applies to all distributions and to all transfers of partnership interests made during the year for which the election is made and in all subsequent years.

Congress by § 754 has delegated to the Secretary specific authority to "legislate" in this area. Pursuant to this express grant of authority, in 1956 the Secretary promulgated Treas. Reg. § 1.754–1(b) which provided that the § 754 election to adjust basis had to be filed with the partnership return for the first taxable year to which the election applies. * * *. [F]rom 1956 to the present, the position of the Internal Revenue Service consistently has been that in order for the optional basis adjustment election to be effective as to a transferee partner who acquired a partnership interest on the death of a partner, the election must be filed by the partnership with a timely return for the taxable year in which the transfer occurs.

The regulatory requirement that the election to adjust basis of partnership property, to be effective, must be filed for the taxable year of the partnership in which a transfer of an interest in the partnership occurs, finds support in the legislative history of § 754. * * *. Therefore, we do not find that the regulation in issue is plainly inconsistent with the statute.

Nevertheless, the plaintiff asserts that the regulation is unreasonable by requiring that the election be made in the year the transfer upon death occurs, since the value of the partnership interest is not likely to be finally determined in the year of death. In the instant case, plaintiff alleges that the partnerships had insufficient time in which to gather the facts essential for them to make the determination as to whether an election should be made; "as soon as the partnerships had sufficient information to make an informed and intelligent decision that the election was necessary," plaintiff contends that the elections were filed. However, the facts do not fully support plaintiff's contentions.

In the instant case, Carl T. Jones died on October 7, 1967. The partnerships involved herein filed federal income tax returns on a calendar year basis. Their returns for 1967 were due to be filed on or before April 15, 1968, and were timely filed without extension. Thus, the partnerships had over six months to determine whether they wished to file elections under § 754, even without requesting any extension of time.[35] However, it should be noted that the stipulated facts indicate that no requests for extensions of time to file the partnership returns or to make the elections were ever made. In addition, the deductions claimed on the plaintiff's fiduciary income tax returns for the years in suit are of two types— additional basis in cattle sold and additional depreciation deductions on real estate. With respect to the cattle, the plaintiff was able to secure an appraisal within one week of decedent's death. Concerning the additional depreciation deductions, copies of the partnerships' 1967 returns show that the bulk of depreciable assets held by the partnerships had substantially reduced adjusted bases in the hands of the partnerships due to previous depreciation deductions. This should have indicated that a § 754 election might have been beneficial with respect to such depreciable assets. * * *. Finally, plaintiff's statement that the elections were filed "as soon as the partnerships had sufficient information to make an informed and intelligent decision that the election was necessary" seems erroneous. The initial fiduciary income tax return for decedent's estate was filed on February 10, 1969, and claimed the additional deductions for depreciation and for increased basis in cattle which are here in dispute. Thus, by February 10, 1969, plaintiff clearly had all necessary information and yet, inexplicably, the partnerships did not file elections under § 754 until August 20, 1969. This lapse of six additional months, coupled with the fact that no extension of time to file the partnership returns was ever requested, gives plaintiff's arguments in this case the distinct appearance of afterthought explanations.

---

35. [T]he initial period for making a § 754 election may be increased not only if the partnership requests and is granted an extension of time to file its return, Treas. Reg. § 1.754–1(b)(1), but also if the partnership requests and is granted an extension of time to file the election.

On these facts, we do not find appealing plaintiff's argument that the partnerships had insufficient time in which to gather the facts essential to determine whether to elect the optional basis adjustment. * * *. [W]e agree with the Government that the elections filed on August 20, 1969, were too late to be effective for the year 1967. For the partnerships to have made a valid § 754 election for the year 1967, the election should have been timely made in the original return or by an amended return filed within the statutory time for filing the original return.

We now turn to plaintiff's alternative argument. Plaintiff intimates that it is entitled to use a stepped-up basis in the partnership assets for the year 1970 and all subsequent years because the elections filed on August 20, 1969, were effective as to partnership year 1970 and years thereafter. We also find no merit in this contention.

Section 754 provides that a valid § 754 election shall apply to all distributions of partnership property and to all transfers of partnership interests during the taxable year with respect to which the election was filed and all subsequent years. As applied to the instant case, the written statements filed by the partnerships on August 20, 1969, if valid § 754 elections, would apply for the year 1970 and all years thereafter, unless properly revoked. However, a valid § 754 election for the taxable year 1970 does not permit any adjustments to basis resulting from a 1967 transfer of partnership interests occasioned by the death of the decedent partner. As a result, plaintiff is not entitled to use a stepped-up basis in the partnership assets.

* * *

NOTES

1. *Impact of § 754 election.* A § 754 election can trigger adjustments to inside basis when any of the following events occurs: (a) a partner sells part or all of a partnership interest, (b) a partnership makes a current distribution or a distribution in liquidation of a partner's interest, or (c) a partner dies. See I.R.C. §§ 734, 743. The adjustments to inside basis are intended to eliminate the disparity between outside basis and inside basis that is caused by the triggering event.

(a) *Sale of interest.* The purchasing partner's outside cost basis will likely deviate from her share of the inside basis, particularly if the selling partner recognized gain or loss on the sale. In this situation, the § 754 election results in an upward or downward adjustment to the purchasing partner's share of inside basis thereby matching her share of the inside basis to her outside basis.

(b) *Partnership distribution.* A § 754 election leads to adjustments to inside basis when the distributee-partner recognizes gain or loss. See I.R.C. §§ 731(a), 734(b)(1)(A), (b)(2)(A). Even if gain or loss is not recognized by the distributee-partner, the § 754 election causes inside basis to be adjusted when a partner takes a basis in distributed property which is different from the partnership's basis in the property. See I.R.C. §§ 732(a)(2), (b), 734(b)(1)(B), (2)(B). In both situations, the adjustments are necessary to prevent the partnership's inside basis from declining by a greater or lesser amount than the distributee-partner's outside basis.

(c) *Death of a partner.* In the case of a partner's death, the outside basis of the decedent's successor will likely deviate from his share of the inside basis because of the step-up or step-down in the decedent's outside basis under I.R.C. § 1014. In this situation, the § 754 election leads to an upward or downward adjustment to the successor's share of the inside basis thereby matching his share of the inside basis to his outside basis.

2. *Beneficiary of § 754 election.* When a partnership interest is sold, any inside basis adjustment that results from a § 754 election is reserved exclusively for the benefit of the purchasing partner. See I.R.C. § 743(b). In contrast, when a distribution leads to an inside basis adjustment pursuant to a § 754 election, all partners share the adjustment. See I.R.C. § 734(b). Can this difference be justified? When a partner dies, is the inside basis adjustment that results from a § 754 election reserved exclusively for one partner or shared by all partners? See I.R.C. § 743(b). Why?

3. *Mandatory step-down of inside basis.* Under certain circumstances, a partnership's inside basis must be adjusted downward even in the absence of a § 754 election. Specifically, when a partner in a partnership with a "substantial built-in loss" sells her interest or dies, inside basis must be adjusted downward regardless of whether a § 754 election is made. See I.R.C. §§ 743(a), (b). A partnership has a substantial built-in loss when aggregate inside basis exceeds the fair market value of the partnership's assets by more than $250,000. See I.R.C. § 743(d). Similarly, when a partnership makes a distribution that would lead to a "substantial basis reduction," inside basis must be adjusted downward even in the absence of a § 754 election. See I.R.C. §§ 734(a), (b). A substantial basis reduction occurs when the basis reductions resulting from a § 754 election exceed $250,000. See I.R.C. § 734(d).

How would the results of Example 7–F (pp. 359–361) change if, before Al's interest was sold (or liquidated), each partner had had an outside basis of $1,450,000 and the inside basis of the building had been $4,800,000?

4. *Strategy of § 754 election.* Should a § 754 election routinely be filed with the first tax return of any new partnership to eliminate the risk that the election will not be in place when a triggering event occurs?

5. *Effect of inside basis adjustments before sale of partnership assets.* Example 7–F (p. 359) illustrates how inside basis adjustments affect the partners in the event of a subsequent sale of partnership assets. Can inside basis adjustments impact on the partners even if the partnership does not sell any of its assets? See I.R.C. §§ 167, 168.

Problem 7–6 (Impact of § 754 election on sale of interest): Francine, Gwen and Harold each own a one-third interest in the FGH Partnership. Each partner has an outside basis of $200,000. FGH has no liabilities and the following assets:

	Basis	Value
Money	$300,000	$300,000
Inventory	60,000	390,000
Equipment	240,000	210,000
Total	$600,000	$900,000

Francine sells her partnership interest to Ivan for $300,000.[36] How does the sale of Francine's interest affect FGH's inside basis if FGH makes a § 754 election? See I.R.C. §§ 743(b), 755; Treas. Reg. §§ 1.755–1(a)(1), (b)(2).

C.   Termination of Partnership

I.R.C. § 708

Treas. Reg. §§ 1.708–1(a), (b)(1)

When a partnership distributes all of its assets, the partnership analogue of a corporate liquidation occurs. The same distribution rules that apply to a distribution in liquidation of a partner's interest (other than I.R.C. § 736) also apply when a partnership distributes all of its assets.

Crawford v. Commissioner

United States Board of Tax Appeals, 1939.
39 B.T.A. 521.

■ Hill: * * *

The petitioners are executors of the will of George W. Crawford, deceased. During his lifetime the decedent was a one-fourth co-owner of the Venempa Investment Co., a partnership, formed December 26, 1928, in Pittsburgh, Pennsylvania, to engage in buying, selling, and dealing in stocks, bonds, and other commercial securities. Including contributions made at the time of the partnership's organization, each of the four partners paid in to its capital cash in the amount of $262,815.96 * * *.

In and during the years 1928 to 1932, inclusive, the partnership had net earnings which, for the whole period, exceeded its losses. It distributed no part of its earnings to members and, at the end of 1932, had on hand undistributed earnings, represented principally by investments in securities, of which the value of decedent's partnership interest amounted to $128,250.65. On December 31 of the latter year the partnership was dissolved by mutual consent and its assets were distributed. The decedent received in this distribution $83.69 in cash and securities of a total market value amounting to $233,500.

---

36.   The tax consequences to Francine are illustrated in Example 7–D. See p. 352.

In decedent's income tax return for 1932 no deduction from gross income was claimed for any loss sustained in liquidating his interest, as aforesaid, in the partnership. The petitioners claim, and ask us to find in this proceeding, that a loss was sustained in that transaction, and that failure to take a deduction for it in decedent's income tax return for 1932 resulted in an overpayment of taxes * * *. The issue is governed by the Revenue Act of 1932, and the pertinent provisions of Treasury Regulation No. 77.

* * * Regulation 77, among other things, provides that * * * if in a dissolution the partnership assets are distributed to the members in kind and not in cash, the partner realizes no gain or loss until he disposes of the property received in liquidation.

The petitioners contend that * * * a loss to the decedent through liquidation of his partnership interest is established. That this loss is the amount by which the cost of his partnership interest exceeds the cash ($83.69) and the market value ($233,500) of the assets distributed to him.

The parties are in accord on the cost of decedent's partnership interest. They also agree what the "market value" of all assets distributed to decedent was when the partnership was dissolved. However, at the time the return here involved was filed, the assets distributed to decedent had not been disposed of, and the respondent contends that, under the provision of the regulation last above mentioned, no gain or loss may be recognized until a sale or disposition of them has been made. The petitioners counter this contention with the argument that application of the provision is logical and proper, only when applied to cases where the assets distributed in a partnership liquidation have no determinable value. They argue that where basic values are agreed upon, as in the case at bar, the actual gain or loss is ipso facto established and must be recognized under the provisions of such regulations, as well as under the provisions of section 111 of the Revenue Act of 1932, reading as follows:

(a) COMPUTATION OF GAIN OR LOSS.—Except as hereinafter provided in this section, the gain from the sale or other disposition of property shall be the excess of the amount realized therefrom over the adjusted basis provided in section 113(b), and the loss shall be the excess of such basis over the amount realized.

* * *

In our opinion the portion of the regulation objected to by the petitioners is reasonable in its application to the facts before us and must be sustained. Obviously, the petitioners misconstrue the exact character of the transactions which, they conclude, resulted in a loss to the decedent. The net effect of petitioners' reasoning is that, when a partnership dissolves and distributes its capital assets among members, each member disposes of his partnership interest for a price, or that he receives such distribution in cancellation or redemption of an interest in the partnership. The fact is that such distribution does not confer title to the assets upon the members, but is merely an apportioning among them of what they already owned jointly. Petitioners' decedent and others contributed securities and cash to a fund to be used in the partnership business. The partnership operated this fund over a period of years. The net profits from such operation were taxable distributively to the members of the partnership and likewise the net losses of the operation were deductible proportionately by the members in determining their income tax liability. What remained of the fund at the dissolution of the partnership was the property of the members and was the residuum of what they had contributed to the fund. The partnership fund was at all times the property of the members and neither the dissolution of the partnership nor the distribution of the fund affected such ownership in any way.

* * *

* * * What the decedent received in the distribution was not a consideration in exchange for his investment in the partnership fund, but his aliquot part, in kind, of the assets comprising such fund which theretofore he and his partners owned and held at risk in the business. Obviously, there was no disposition of partnership interest or of the interest of decedent in the partnership fund in this case and the provision of the regulation aptly applied to the transaction.

* * *

[W]hen the assets are distributed "in kind", rather than being liquidated through sale and the cash disbursed, the partner receives, individually, his interest or part of that property which he therefore already owned, although collectively or jointly with his co-partners. If the corpus of the partnership is first reduced to cash, and the cash distributed to the member, then of course, gain or loss may be realized as provided for in like cases of sales of property * * *.

In view of our findings, we hold that the decedent suffered no loss * * *.

NOTES

1. *Issue.* What fundamental tax question was in dispute in the Crawford case? See I.R.C. § 1001(a). How is that issue resolved under current law? See I.R.C. § 731(a).

2. *Timing of loss.* When the loss in a departing partner's partnership interest is not recognized because the partner receives a distribution of partnership property (see I.R.C. § 731(a)(2)), does the transfer of the recipient's outside basis to the distributed property (see I.R.C. § 732(b)) insure that the loss is merely deferred? If current law applied to the distribution to George Crawford, would his loss ever have been recognized? See I.R.C. § 1014.

Revenue Ruling 99–6

1999–1 Cum.Bull. 432.

ISSUE

What are the federal income tax consequences if one person purchases all of the ownership interests in a domestic limited liability company (LLC) that is classified as a partnership under § 301.7701–3 of the Regulations, causing the LLC's status as a partnership to terminate under § 708(b)(1)(A) of the Internal Revenue Code?

FACTS

In each of the following situations, an LLC is formed and operates in a state which permits an LLC to have a single owner. Each LLC is classified as a partnership under § 301.7701–3. Neither of the LLCs holds any unrealized receivables or substantially appreciated inventory for purposes of § 751(b). For the sake of simplicity, it is assumed that neither LLC is liable for any indebtedness, nor are the assets of the LLCs subject to any indebtedness.

Situation 1. A and B are equal partners in AB, an LLC. A sells A's entire interest in AB to B for $10,000. After the sale, the business is continued by the LLC, which is owned solely by B.

Situation 2. C and D are equal partners in CD, an LLC. C and D sell their entire interests in CD to E, an unrelated person, in exchange for $10,000 each. After the sale, the business is continued by the LLC, which is owned solely by E.

After the sale, in both situations, no entity classification election is made under § 301.7701–3(c) to treat the LLC as an association for federal tax purposes.

LAW

Section 708(b)(1)(A) and § 1.708–1(b)(1) of the Regulations provide that a partnership shall terminate when the operations of the partnership are discontinued and no part of any business, financial operation, or venture of the partnership continues to be carried on by any of its partners in a partnership.

* * *

Section 735(b) provides that, in determining the period for which a partner has held property received in a distribution from a partnership, there shall be included the holding period of the partnership, as determined under § 1223, with respect to the property.

Section 741 provides that gain or loss resulting from the sale or exchange of an interest in a partnership shall be recognized by the transferor partner, and that the gain or loss shall be considered as gain or loss from a capital asset, except as provided in § 751 (relating to unrealized receivables and inventory items).

Section 1.741–1(b) provides that § 741 applies to the transferor partner in a two-person partnership when one partner sells a partnership interest to the other partner, and to all the members of a partnership when they sell their interests to one or more persons outside the partnership.

Section 301.7701–2(c)(1) provides that, for federal tax purposes, the term "partnership" means a business entity that is not a corporation and that has at least two members.

In Edwin E. McCauslen v. Commissioner, 45 T.C. 588 (1966), one partner in an equal, two-person partnership died, and his partnership interest was purchased from his estate by the remaining partner. The purchase caused a termination of the partnership under § 708(b)(1)(A). The Tax Court held that the surviving partner did not purchase the deceased partner's interest in the partnership, but that the surviving partner purchased the partnership assets attributable to the interest. As a result, the surviving partner was not permitted to succeed to the partnership's holding period with respect to these assets.

* * *

ANALYSIS AND HOLDINGS

Situation 1. The AB partnership terminates under § 708(b)(1)(A) when B purchases A's entire interest in AB. Accordingly, A must treat the transaction as the sale of a partnership interest. Reg. § 1.741–1(b). A must report gain or loss, if any, resulting from the sale of A's partnership interest in accordance with § 741.

Under the analysis of McCauslen, for purposes of determining the tax treatment of B, the AB partnership is deemed to make a liquidating distribution of all of its assets to A and B, and following this distribution, B is treated as acquiring the assets deemed to have been distributed to A in liquidation of A's partnership interest.

B's basis in the assets attributable to A's one-half interest in the partnership is $10,000, the purchase price for A's partnership interest. Section 1012. Section 735(b) does not apply with respect to the assets B is deemed to have purchased from A. Therefore, B's holding period for these assets begins on the day immediately following the date of the sale. * * *

Upon the termination of AB, B is considered to receive a distribution of those assets attributable to B's former interest in AB. B must recognize gain or loss, if any, on the deemed distribution of the assets to the extent required by § 731(a). B's basis in the assets received in the deemed liquidation of B's partnership interest is determined under § 732(b). Under § 735(b), B's holding period for the assets attributable to B's one-half interest in AB includes the partnership's holding period for such assets.

Situation 2. The CD partnership terminates under § 708(b)(1)(A) when E purchases the entire interests of C and D in CD. C and D must report gain or loss, if any, resulting from the sale of their partnership interests in accordance with § 741.

For purposes of classifying the acquisition by E, the CD partnership is deemed to make a liquidating distribution of its assets to C and D. Immediately following this distribution, E is deemed to acquire, by purchase, all of the former partnership's assets. * * *

E's basis in the assets is $20,000 under § 1012. E's holding period for the assets begins on the day immediately following the date of sale.

NOTES

1. *Holding period of assets.* In Rev. Rul. 99–6, of what significance is each party's holding period for the assets? See I.R.C. §§ 1(h), 1222.

2. *Two types of partnership termination.* A partnership terminates when no part of the partnership's business continues to be carried on by any of its partners in a partnership. See I.R.C. § 708(b)(1)(A). A partnership also terminates when 50% or more of the total interests in partnership capital and profits are sold or exchanged within a twelve-month period. I.R.C. § 708(b)(1)(B). When the latter type of termination occurs, how do the distribution rules impact on the partners? See Treas. Reg. § 1.708–1(b)(4). A termination precipitated by a sale or exchange of more than 50% of the partnership interests within a twelve-month period has a variety of other tax effects, including the nullification of any I.R.C. § 754 election.

Problem 7–7 (Partnership distribution of all assets): Ruth and Saul each own a 50% interest in the RS Partnership. Each partner has an outside basis of $50,000. RS's assets consist of two pieces of property (property #1 and property #2). Each property has a value of $200,000 and an inside basis of $50,000. RS has no other assets and no liabilities. RS distributes property #1 to Ruth and property #2 to Saul. What are the tax consequences to RS, Ruth and Saul under each of the following alternatives?

(a) Both properties are capital assets. See I.R.C. §§ 731, 732(b).

(b) Both properties are inventory. See I.R.C. §§ 731, 732(b), 735.

(c) Same as (a), but Ruth and Saul die in an accident shortly before the properties are distributed to each partner's successor. See I.R.C. §§ 731, 732(b), 743, 1014. Does it matter whether RS makes a § 754 election?

*

PART FOUR

CONTRIBUTIONS

Part Three explored the tax consequences when business owners receive distributions of property. Part Four examines transfers of value in the opposite direction; namely, from the owner to the business. Chapter 8 focuses on contributions to C Corporations, Chapter 9 focuses on contributions to S Corporations and Chapter 10 focuses on contributions to businesses that are taxed as partnerships.

When a person transfers property to a business in exchange for an ownership interest, a realization event occurs and the transferor realizes gain to the extent that the value of the interest received exceeds the basis of the transferred property. See I.R.C. § 1001. Alternatively, a loss is realized if the value of the ownership interest received is less than the transferor's basis in the transferred property. Any gain is taxed when it is realized, unless a nonrecognition provision applies. See I.R.C. § 1001(c). Any realized loss *that otherwise would be allowed as a deduction* is deductible when the loss is realized, unless a nonrecognition provision applies. See I.R.C. §§ 165, 1001(c). Nonrecognition treatment is often granted to a person who transfers property to a business in exchange for an ownership interest. See I.R.C. §§ 351, 721.

Certain nonrecognition provisions are generally examined in the personal income tax course. See, e.g., I.R.C. §§ 1031, 1033, 1041. The following excerpt from a Treasury Regulation promulgated under the predecessor to I.R.C. § 1001(c) provides a useful perspective for exploring the nonrecognition rules that apply when property is transferred to a business in exchange for an ownership interest.

Former Regulation on Exchanges

Treas. Reg. § 1.1002–1.
Deleted by Treas. Dec. 7665 (1/25/80).

(a) *General rule.* The general rule with respect to gain or loss realized upon the sale or exchange of property as determined under section 1001 is that the entire amount of such gain or loss is recognized except in cases where specific provisions * * * of the Code provide otherwise.

(b) *Strict construction of exceptions from general rule.* The exceptions from the general rule requiring the recognition of all gains and losses, like other exceptions from a rule of taxation of general and uniform application, are strictly construed and do not extend either beyond the words or the underlying assumptions and purposes of the exception. Nonrecognition is accorded by the Code only if the exchange is one which satisfies both (1) the specific description in the Code of an excepted exchange, and (2) the underlying purpose for which such exchange is excepted from the general rule. The exchange must be germane to, and a necessary incident of, the investment or enterprise in hand. The relationship of the exchange to the venture or enterprise is always material, and the surrounding facts and circumstances must be shown. As elsewhere, the taxpayer claiming the benefit of the exception must show himself within the exception.

(c) *Certain exceptions to general rule.* Exceptions to the general rule are made, for example, by sections 351(a), * * * 721 [and] 1031 * * *. These sections describe certain specific exchanges of property in which at the time of the exchange particular differences exist between the property parted with and the property acquired, but such differences are more formal than substantial. As to these, the Code provides that such differences shall not be deemed controlling, and that gain or loss shall not be recognized at the time of the exchange. The underlying assumption of these exceptions is that the new property is substantially a continuation of the old investment still unliquidated * * *.

(d) *Exchange.* Ordinarily, to constitute an exchange, the transaction must be a reciprocal transfer of property, as distinguished from a transfer of property for a money consideration only.

NOTES

1. *Nonrecognition versus exclusion.* With respect to potential income, what is the difference between a nonrecognition provision and an exclusion?

2. *Nonrecognition versus allowance.* In the case of a realized loss, what is the relationship between a nonrecognition provision and an allowance provision? See I.R.C. §§ 165, 1001(c).

3. *Consequences to transferee.* Part Four focuses on tax consequences to the transferor when property is transferred to a business. Regardless of whether the transferee is a C Corporation, an S Corporation or a partnership, property received from an owner normally does not create income for the transferee. See I.R.C. §§ 118, 721, 1032.

CHAPTER 8

C CORPORATION CONTRIBUTIONS

A person who transfers property to a corporation in exchange for stock of the corporation is often accorded nonrecognition treatment. See I.R.C. § 351(a). This treatment is based on the theory that the stock issued to the transferor represents a continuation of the transferor's investment in the property. If the transferor receives both stock and "boot" (i.e., money or other property) from the corporation, any gain realized by the transferor is recognized to the extent of the boot. Chapter 8 examines the tax consequences when a person transfers property to a corporation: (a) in exchange for stock, (b) in exchange for a combination of stock and "boot", or (c) as a contribution to the capital of the corporation.

A. TRANSFER OF PROPERTY FOR STOCK

When a person transfers property to a corporation in exchange for stock of the corporation, any gain or loss realized with respect to the transferred property is not recognized if the transaction satisfies the requirements of I.R.C. § 351(a). When I.R.C. § 351(a) is satisfied, the person who transferred the property takes an "exchanged basis" in the stock received. See I.R.C. §§ 358(a), 7701(a)(44). The corporation takes a "transferred basis" in the property. See I.R.C. §§ 362(a)(1), 7701(a)(43). As a result, any gain or loss that existed when the property was in the transferor's hands is preserved at both the shareholder level (in the stock received) and the corporate level (in the property).

Example 8–A (Transfer of appreciated property to controlled corporation): Alan forms the Access Corporation and transfers a building with a value of $1,000,000 and a basis of $100,000 to Access. In exchange, Alan receives all of the Access stock. The tax consequences of the exchange to Alan are as follows:

Realization Event (I.R.C. § 1001)

Amount Realized	$1,000,000	(value of Access stock)
Less: Adjusted Basis	100,000	(in building)
Realized Gain	$900,000	
Recognition?	No. I.R.C. § 351(a).	
Alan's Basis in Access Stock:	$100,000	(I.R.C. § 358(a)(1))
Access's Basis in Building:	$100,000	(I.R.C. § 362(a)(1))

If Alan sells the Access stock for $1,000,000, he realizes and recognizes a gain of $900,000. If Access sells the building for $1,000,000, it realizes and recognizes a gain of $900,000. Thus, although Alan's gain is deferred by I.R.C. § 351, two potential gains exist after the property is transferred to Access.

1. DEFERRAL OF GAIN OR LOSS

I.R.C. §§ 351(a), (d)

Treas. Reg. §§ 1.351–1(a), (b)

To qualify for nonrecognition treatment under I.R.C. § 351(a), all of the following conditions must be satisfied:

(1) "property" must be transferred to the corporation,

(2) in exchange for stock,

(3) by one or more persons ("transferors"), and

(4) the transferors must be in "control" of the corporation "immediately after the exchange."

"Control" is defined as ownership of at least 80% of the voting stock and at least 80% of all other classes of stock. I.R.C. § 368(c).

The cases that follow examine the various conditions imposed by I.R.C. § 351(a). As you read these cases, consider whether each condition can be reconciled with the goal of insuring that the interest received by the transferor is sufficiently similar to the transferred property to justify nonrecognition treatment.

Kamborian v. Commissioner

United States Tax Court, 1971.
56 T.C. 847.

FINDINGS OF FACT

■ RAUM, JUDGE: * * *

International Shoe Machine Corp. (International) was incorporated in * * * 1938 and * * * was engaged in the business of manufacturing and leasing shoe machinery * * *.

On September 1, 1965, prior to the transaction here in question, International's capital stock was held as follows:

| | Shares of International | |
Name	Class A common	Class B common
Jacob Kamborian Revocable Trust	20,324	82,916
Jacob Kamborian, Jr.	4,220	37,980
Lisbeth (Kamborian) Godley	3,620	32,580
Michael Becka	60	540
Elizabeth Kamborian Trust	5,000	45,000
Others	3,916	35,244
	37,140	234,260

Jacob S. Kamborian (Jacob) founded International and served as its president at all times relevant herein. Jacob S. Kamborian, Jr., and Lisbeth Kamborian Godley are the children of Jacob and his wife, Elizabeth. Michael Becka (Becka) is not related to the members of the Kamborian family. [H]e * * * had served as International's executive vice president and general manager since approximately 1960 * * *.

The Elizabeth Kamborian Trust (Elizabeth's trust) was established by Jacob in 1949. At about that time Jacob and Elizabeth experienced domestic difficulties; they separated for a time; and the trust was established on their reconciliation in order to provide financial security for Mrs. Kamborian * * *.

* * * As of September 1, 1965, Becka and Lisbeth K. Godley were the trustees * * *. At all times relevant herein, Becka served as the managing trustee * * *.

Campex Research & Trading Corp. (Campex) * * * was a patent holding and licensing company. It held primarily foreign shoe machine patents (i.e., patents not issued by the United States) and granted and administered licenses under them * * *. On September 1, 1965, and prior to the transaction here in question, the outstanding stock of Campex was held as follows:

Name	Shares of Campex
Jacob Kamborian Revocable Trust	39
Jacob Kamborian, Jr.	4
Lisbeth (Kamborian) Godley	4
Michael Becka	3

On September 1, 1965, the board of directors of International authorized Jacob to enter into an agreement under which (a) the owners of all of the issued and outstanding shares of Campex would exchange their stock for common stock of International and (b) "certain stockholders" of International would purchase for cash additional shares of International's common stock * * *. As part of the transaction it was contemplated that the Elizabeth Kamborian Trust would purchase additional shares of theretofore unissued International stock for about $5,000, so that the former owners of the Campex stock and the Elizabeth Kamborian Trust, when considered collectively and treated as transferors under section 351(a), I.R.C. 1954, would own at least 80 percent of International's stock immediately after the transaction in an attempt to comply with the requirements of section 368(c), I.R.C. 1954. If the Elizabeth Kamborian Trust were not taken into account, the International stock held by the former owners of Campex immediately after the transaction amounted to 77.3 percent of each class of outstanding stock of International—an amount that was insufficient to satisfy the requirements of section 368(c).

* * *

As vice president and general manager of International, Becka participated from the beginning in the planning of the acquisition of the Campex stock. Moreover, during 1964 and 1965, Jacob was seriously ill for an extended period of time * * *. For approximately 9 months he was on his back and for a year thereafter he was "very limited" in what he could do. During this period Becka was in charge of International's affairs, and it was at about this time that International acquired the Campex stock. During the course of planning for the transaction, International received legal advice with regard to qualifying the acquisition as a tax-free exchange * * *.

As trustee of Elizabeth's trust, Becka borrowed approximately $5,000 * * * to finance the trust's purchase of the total of 418 shares of International stock on September 1, 1965. The corpus of the trust consisted exclusively of International stock, and Becka anticipated that the loan would be repaid out of dividends paid on the stock * * *.

Prior to the purchase of the International stock on behalf of the trust, Becka discussed his plans with both Jacob and Elizabeth. Jacob, personally and as grantor of the Jacob S. Kamborian Revocable Trust, held a sufficient number of International shares to control the corporation and thus to determine whether it would issue additional shares. In his discussions with Elizabeth, Becka explained that because the $5,000 loan would have to be repaid out of dividends paid on the International stock held by the trust, her income from the trust would be diminished until the loan was repaid. Elizabeth told Becka to go ahead with the transaction.

* * *

On their respective Federal income tax returns for 1965, petitioners [Jacob Kamborian, Jacob Kamborian, Jr., Lisbeth Godley and Michael Becka] reported no gain or loss stemming from the exchange of their Campex stock for International stock. In his deficiency notices to petitioners, the Commissioner determined that they realized long-term capital gains * * *.

OPINION

* * * Petitioners contend that the gain they realized on their transfer of Campex stock to International in return for International's common stock qualifies for nonrecognition under section 351(a), I.R.C. 1954. That section provides for nonrecognition of gain or loss on the transfer of property to a corporation in exchange for the corporation's stock * * * if immediately after the exchange the transferor or transferors are "in control" of the corporation. Section 351(a) makes reference to section 368(c), I.R.C. 1954, for the definition of "control" * * *.

Immediately after the exchange here in issue the stock of International was held as follows:

Shares of –

	Class A (voting common)	Class B (nonvoting common)	Percent total of each class
Jacob S. Kamborian Revocable Trust	22,108	198,971	56.01
Jacob S. Kamborian, Jr.	4,403	39,627	11.16
Lisbeth (Kamborian) Godley	3,803	34,227	9.64
Michael Becka	197	1,775	0.50
Elizabeth Kamborian Trust	5,042	45,376	12.77
Others	3,916	35,244	9.92
Total	39,469	355,220	100.00

Petitioners contend that the transferors of property for purposes of section 351(a) were the five named stockholders listed above and that their percentage stockholdings after the transfer satisfy the 80–percent control requirement imposed by sections 351(a) and 368(c).

The Commissioner's position is that only the first four stockholders listed above—i.e., the former owners of Campex—may be considered as transferors of property here, that the fifth (the Elizabeth Kamborian Trust) may not be taken into account in this connection, and that since there would thus be a failure to satisfy the control requirement, all gain realized on the exchange must be recognized. In particular, he urges that International stock issued to the Elizabeth Kamborian Trust in return for $5,016 does not qualify as stock issued for property within the meaning of section 351(a) and that consequently the persons making qualified transfers of property to International in return for its stock held only 77.3 percent of its stock after the exchange. The Commissioner relies on regulations section 1.351–1(a)(1)(ii):

Sec. 1.351–1 Transfer to corporation controlled by transferor.

(a)(1) Section 351(a) provides, in general, for the nonrecognition of gain or loss upon the transfer by one or more persons of property to a corporation solely in exchange for stock * * * in such corporation, if immediately after the exchange, such person or persons are in control of the corporation to which the property was transferred * * *. The phrase "immediately after the exchange" does not necessarily require simultaneous exchanges by two or more persons, but comprehends a situation where the rights of the parties have been previously defined and the execution of the agreement proceeds with an expedition consistent with orderly procedure. For purposes of this section—

* * *

(ii) Stock * * * *issued for property which is of relatively small value in comparison to the value of the stock and securities already owned* (or to be received for services) by the person who transferred such property, *shall not be treated as having been issued in return for property if the primary purpose of the transfer is to qualify under this section* the exchanges of property by other persons transferring property * * *.

[Emphasis supplied.]

The Commissioner contends that since the Elizabeth Kamborian Trust purchased only 42 shares of class A common and 376 shares of class B common, the securities issued were "of relatively small value" in relation to the 5,000 shares of class A common and 45,000 shares of class B common which it already held and that the primary purpose of the transfer was to qualify the exchange of Campex stock by the other stockholders for nonrecognition treatment under section 351(a).

Petitioners * * * urge (a) that regulations section 1.351–1(a)(1)(ii) is invalid; [and] (b) that even if valid it is inapplicable to the transaction in issue * * *.

(a) *Validity of the regulation.*—Initially we note the well-settled principle that "Treasury regulations must be sustained unless unreasonable and plainly inconsistent with the revenue statutes and that they constitute contemporaneous constructions by those charged with administration of these statutes which should not be overruled except for weighty reasons." * * *

    * * *

Petitioners * * * contend that the regulation's reference to "property which is of relatively small value in comparison to the value of stock or securities already owned" and its reliance upon the taxpayer's motive find support nowhere in the language of section 351 and that the regulation is for that reason invalid as beyond the scope of the statute. [W]e must disagree. By disqualifying certain token exchanges, the regulation is reasonably designed to exclude from the scope of section 351 transactions which comply with its requirements in form but not in substance. Far from being unreasonable or inconsistent with the statute, the regulation promotes its purpose by helping to ensure substantial compliance with the control requirement before the nonrecognition provisions become operative. In this light the absence of direct support for the regulation in the language of the statute is of minimal significance * * *.

(b) *Applicability of the regulation.*—Petitioners contend that even if it is valid, the regulation is inapplicable to the transaction here in issue. They argue first that even if Elizabeth's trust had not purchased shares of International stock, the control requirement would have been satisfied, that therefore the purchase was not necessary to meet the control requirement, and that consequently the regulation is by its own terms inapplicable. Petitioners reach this conclusion by asserting that the shares held by Becka and Lisbeth Godley as trustees of Elizabeth's trust should be attributed to them as individuals and added to the shares they held personally in nonfiduciary capacities. On the basis of this premise, petitioners conclude that the 80–percent-control requirement would have been satisfied even if Elizabeth's trust had not participated in the September 1, 1965, transaction. Petitioners' argument is ingenious but unacceptable, for it falters on petitioners' premise that the trust's shares may be attributed to the individual trustees. While legal title to the shares may have been in the names of the trustees, they had no beneficial interest in such shares. The distinction is not one of form but of plain economic reality. In these circumstances we think the trustees' interests in the trust's shares were far too remote to justify attributing the shares to them for purposes of section 351.

Petitioners also contend that the primary purpose for the trust's acquisition of International's stock was not to qualify the other stockholders' exchanges under section 351 and that for this reason the regulation is inapplicable. We note at the outset that the regulation does not make it entirely clear whose purpose is to be taken into account. However, both parties have assumed that the purpose of the transferor of property is critical. The language of the regulation (which appears to distinguish between a "transfer" of property and the issuance of stock) supports their assumption, and we shall therefore proceed on this basis. Although Elizabeth's trust was technically the transferor herein, the parties have also assumed that Becka's purpose is critical in this respect—apparently on the ground that as the managing trustee he was primarily responsible for the decision to make the purchase of International stock. We shall proceed on the basis of this assumption as well.

The question of Becka's primary purpose is one of fact and after a review of all the evidence we conclude that his primary purpose was to qualify the other stockholders' exchanges under section 351. We note * * * that * * * Becka was in charge of International's affairs, that * * * Becka participated in lengthy discussions with regard to planning the transaction as a tax-free exchange, and that * * * the agreement of September 1, 1965, treated the purchase by Elizabeth's trust and the exchange of Campex stock by the other stockholders as component parts of an integrated transaction avowedly designed to meet the 80–percent-control requirement and thereby qualify for nonrecognition under section 351.

At trial herein, Becka testified that if the trust had not participated in the transaction, the issue of International stock to the other major stockholders would have diluted the trust's percentage interest in International and that he authorized the purchase of International stock * * * to minimize such dilution * * *. We do not give his testimony very much weight * * *.

Becka also testified that he authorized the purchase of the stock because it was a "good investment." While he may have taken this into account in making his decision, the record leaves us convinced that the purchase was made primarily to qualify the exchanges by the other stockholders (one of whom was Becka himself) under section 351. We conclude that section 1.351–1(a)(1)(ii) is applicable.

NOTES

1. *Actual ownership of Campex stock.* Would the Kamborian court have reached a different result if:

(a) Elizabeth's trust had owned $5,000 worth of Campex stock for several years before the September 1, 1965 transaction, and the trust transferred those shares (rather than money) to International in exchange for the same number of additional International shares that were issued to the trust?

(b) Elizabeth's trust had purchased $5,000 of Campex stock in August, 1965, and the trust transferred those shares (rather than money) to International on September 1, 1965, in exchange for the same number of additional International shares that were issued to the trust?

2. *Constructive ownership of International stock.* The court rejected the argument that the International shares held by Elizabeth's trust could be attributed to the trustees (Becka and Lisbeth) and added to the shares they held personally for purposes of determining whether the transferors satisfied the "control" requirement of I.R.C. § 351(a). Why did the taxpayers not argue that the "control" requirement was satisfied because the beneficiaries of Elizabeth's trust (presumably Elizabeth and/or her children, Jacob, Jr. and Lisbeth) constructively owned the trust's shares under I.R.C. § 318(a)(2)(B)? See I.R.C. §§ 318(a) (first clause), 351.

3. *Transferor of money.* In the case, Elizabeth's trust transferred money to International. The Internal Revenue Service has ruled that money is within the scope of "property" in I.R.C. § 351(a). Rev. Rul. 69–357, 1969–2 C.B. 256. Is a person who transfers money to a corporation concerned about whether money is treated as property under I.R.C. § 351(a)? If not, who would care whether money is treated as property under I.R.C. § 351? Why is I.R.C. § 317(a) not dispositive of the question of whether money is within the scope of "property" in I.R.C. § 351(a)?

4. *Purpose of "control" requirement.* Can the "control" requirement of I.R.C. § 351(a) be reconciled with the theory that the stock received by the transferor(s), "is substantially a continuation of the old investment still unliquidated"? See former Treas. Reg. § 1.1002–1(c), p. ___. Is the "control" requirement of § 351(a) directed at insuring,

(a) collective activity?

(b) substantial similarity between the property surrendered by each transferor and the proprietary interest received?

(c) both (a) and (b)?

5. *Transfer to existing corporation.* Do not assume that I.R.C. § 351(a) only applies when a new corporation is initially capitalized. The Kamborian case illustrates that this provision can also apply when additional property is transferred to an ongoing corporation in exchange for stock, provided that the "control" requirement is satisfied.

Intermountain Lumber Company v. Commissioner

United States Tax Court, 1976.
65 T.C. 1025.

■ WILES, JUDGE: * * *

FINDINGS OF FACT

Petitioners are the Intermountain Co. * * * and its affiliates (hereinafter collectively referred to as Intermountain or petitioner) * * *.

From 1948 until March of 1964, Mr. Dee Shook (hereinafter Shook) individually owned a saw mill at Conner, Montana. During that time Mr. Milo Wilson (hereinafter Wilson) had logs processed there into rough lumber for a fee. Shook owned the remaining logs processed at the sawmill, which constituted about half of all the logs processed there * * *.

In March of 1964, fire damaged the sawmill. Shook and Wilson wanted to replace it with a larger one * * *. Shook was financially unable, however, to do so. He accordingly induced Wilson to personally co-guarantee a $200,000 loan to provide financing. In return, Wilson insisted upon an equal voice in rebuilding the sawmill and upon an opportunity to become an equal shareholder with Shook in the new sawmill.

On May 28, 1964, Shook [and] Wilson * * * executed Articles of Incorporation for S & W Sawmill, Inc. (hereinafter S & W). The corporate name, S & W, was derived from the names Shook and Wilson.

* * *

Shook executed a bill of sale for his sawmill equipment and deeded his sawmill site to S & W on July 15 and 16, 1964, respectively. In exchange, Shook received 364 S & W shares on July 15, 1964 * * *.

Also on that date, minutes of a special meeting stated in part that "[the] President, Dee Shook, announced that he and Milo E. Wilson had entered into an agreement whereby Mr. Wilson was to purchase 182 shares of Mr. Shook's stock." That agreement, dated July 15, 1964, and entitled "Agreement for Sale and Purchase of Stock" (hereinafter Agreement for Sale) provided in part as follows:

[It] is the intention * * * that Shook and Wilson are to be the owners of * * * the stock of said corporation;

* * *

AND WHEREAS, it is the desire and plan of both parties hereto that a sufficient number of shares of stock be sold by Shook to Wilson so that eventually the stock ownership would be equal; * * *

IT IS THEREFORE AGREED, that * * *

1. Dee Shook is to sell to Milo E. Wilson 182 shares of stock in S & W * * * for the agreed price of $500 per share.

2. Wilson is to pay Shook for said stock * * * [interest only until 1969 at which time principal payments of $15,000 per year are to commence].

3. As each principal payment is made the proportionate number of shares of stock are to be transferred on the corporate records and delivered to Wilson.

4. * * *

5. For the period of one year from the date hereof Wilson is to have the full power to vote all of the stock herein agreed to be sold to him by Shook * * *.

On July 15, 1964, Shook also executed an irrevocable proxy granting to Wilson voting rights in 182 shares until September 10, 1965.

* * *

In connection with the agreement for sale, Shook deposited stock certificates representing 182 shares with an escrow agent on July 17, 1964.

* * *

On July 1, 1967, before principal payments were required by the agreement for sale, petitioner [Intermountain] purchased all outstanding S & W stock. [A] letter to petitioner dated May 3, 1967, and signed by Shook and Wilson stated as follows:

[W]ilson owes * * * Shook $91,000 for 182 shares of S & W * * * stock in escrow at Citizens State Bank * * *. On the purchase contract, Intermountain * * * would pay * * * Shook $91,000 more * * * than * * * Wilson.

OPINION

* * *

In this case, respondent is in the unusual posture of arguing that a transfer to a corporation in return for stock was nontaxable under section 351, and Intermountain is in the equally unusual posture of arguing that the transfer was taxable because section 351 was inapplicable. The explanation is simply that Intermountain purchased all stock of the corporation, S & W, from its incorporators, and that Intermountain and S & W have filed consolidated income tax returns for years in issue.[1] Accordingly, if section 351 was applicable to the incorporators when S & W was formed, S & W * * * must depreciate the assets * * * on the incorporators' basis. Sec. 362(a). If section 351 was inapplicable, and the transfer of assets to S & W was accordingly to be treated as a sale, S & W * * * could base depreciation * * * on the fair market value of those assets at the time of incorporation, which was higher than the incorporators' cost and which would accordingly provide larger depreciation deductions.

Petitioner thus maintains that the transfer to S & W of all of S & W's property at the time of incorporation by the primary incorporator, one Dee Shook, was a taxable sale. It asserts that section 351 was inapplicable because an Agreement for Sale required Shook, as part of the incorporation transaction, to sell almost half of the S & W shares outstanding to one Milo

---

1. Editor's note. Intermountain and S & W were members of an "affiliated group". See I.R.C. § 1504(a). When affiliated group status exists, the members of the group may elect to file a single tax return that reflects the collective taxable income of the group (a "consolidated return"), in lieu of each corporation filing a separate tax return. See I.R.C. § 1501. The rules governing consolidated returns are delineated in an elaborate set of regulations promulgated under I.R.C. § 1502.

Wilson over a period of time, thereby depriving Shook of the requisite percentage of stock necessary for "control" of S & W immediately after the exchange.

Respondent, on the other hand, maintains that the agreement between Shook and Wilson did not deprive Shook of ownership of the shares immediately after the exchange, as the stock purchase agreement merely gave Wilson an option to purchase the shares. Shook accordingly was in "control" of the corporation and the exchange was thus nontaxable under section 351.

Respondent has abandoned on brief his contention that Wilson was a transferor of property and therefore a person to also be counted for purposes of control under section 351. Respondent is correct in doing so, since Wilson did not transfer any property to S & W upon its initial formation in July of 1964 * * *.

Since Wilson was not a transferor of property and therefore cannot be counted for control under section 351 * * *, we must determine if Shook alone owned the requisite percentage of shares for control. This determination depends upon whether, under all facts and circumstances surrounding the Agreement for Sale of 182 shares between Shook and Wilson, ownership of those shares was in Shook or Wilson.

A determination of "ownership," as that term is used in section 368(c) and for purposes of control under section 351, depends upon the obligations and freedom of action of the [recipient] with respect to the stock when he acquired it from the corporation. Such traditional ownership attributes as legal title, voting rights, and possession of stock certificates are not conclusive. If the [recipient], as part of the transaction by which the shares were acquired, has irrevocably foregone or relinquished at that time the legal right to determine whether to keep the shares, ownership in such shares is lacking for purposes of section 351. By contrast, if there are no restrictions upon freedom of action at the time he acquires the shares, it is immaterial how soon thereafter the [recipient] elects to dispose of his stock or whether such disposition is in accord with a preconceived plan not amounting to a binding obligation.

After considering the entire record, we have concluded that Shook and Wilson intended to consummate a sale of the S & W stock, that they never doubted that the sale would be completed, that the sale was an integral part of the incorporation transaction, and that they considered themselves to be co-owners of S & W upon execution of the stock purchase agreement in 1964 * * *.

We accordingly cannot accept respondent's contention that the substance varied from the form of this transaction, which was, of course, labeled a "Sale." * * *

We thus believe that Shook, as part of the same transaction by which the shares were acquired (indeed, the Agreement for Sale was executed before the sawmill was deeded to S & W), had relinquished when he acquired those shares the legal right to determine whether to keep them

* * *. Shook therefore did not own, within the meaning of section 368(c), the requisite percentage of stock immediately after the exchange to control the corporation as required for nontaxable treatment under section 351.

We note also that the basic premise of section 351 is to avoid recognition of gain or loss resulting from transfer of property to a corporation which works a change of form only. Accordingly, if the transferor sells his stock as part of the same transaction, the transaction is taxable because there has been more than a mere change in form. In this case, the transferor agreed to sell and did sell 50 percent of the stock to be received, placed the certificates in the possession of an escrow agent, and granted a binding proxy to the purchaser to vote the stock being sold. Far more than a mere change in form was effected * * *.

NOTES

1. *Reversal of normal positions.* Why was the Internal Revenue Service arguing that I.R.C. § 351 applied and the taxpayer arguing that it did not apply? Should the Internal Revenue Service have been reluctant to litigate this case?

2. *Identity of transferor.* I.R.C. § 351 applies to the transferor, not to the transferee-corporation. If the Internal Revenue Service had prevailed in the Intermountain Lumber case, who was the transferor to which I.R.C. § 351 would have applied? How would that taxpayer have been affected by an Internal Revenue Service victory in the Intermountain Lumber case?

James v. Commissioner
Talbot v. Commissioner

Tax Court of the United States, 1969.
53 T.C. 63.

■ SIMPSON, JUDGE: * * *

FINDINGS OF FACT

* * *

On January 12, 1963, Mr. and Mrs. Talbot entered into an agreement with Mr. James for the promotion and construction of a rental apartment project, consisting of not less than 50 apartments, the project to conform to Federal Housing Administration (FHA) standards. The agreement provided that on completion of the project the parties would form a corporation to take title to the project. The voting stock in such corporation was to be distributed one-half to the Talbots and one-half to Mr. James * * *. The Talbots agreed to transfer to the corporation the land on which the apartment project was to be built * * *. Mr. James agreed "to promote the project * * * and * * * [to] be responsible for the planning, architectural work, construction, landscaping, legal fees, and loan processing of the entire project." * * *

After the execution of the January 12 agreement, Mr. James began negotiations to fulfill his part of the contract. He made arrangements with an attorney and an architectural firm to perform the work necessary to meet FHA requirements—development of legal documents, preparation of architectural plans, and the like; and he obtained from United Mortgagee Service Corp. (United Mortgagee), a lender, its agreement to finance the project and a commitment by FHA to insure the financing * * *.

* * *

On November 5, 1963, Chicora Apartments, Inc. (Chicora), was granted, upon application of Messrs. Talbot and James, a corporate charter, stating its authorized capital stock to consist of 20 no-par common shares. On the same date, the land on which the apartment project was to be constructed was conveyed to Chicora by Mrs. Talbot in consideration for 10 shares of stock * * *. Chicora's board of directors determined that on the date of this conveyance the value of the real property so transferred was $44,000. Also on November 5, 1963, 10 shares of stock were issued to Mr. James * * *.

On November 6, 1963, the FHA issued to Chicora its commitment * * * in the amount of $850,700. Under FHA regulations, this commitment could not be issued to an individual, but was required to be issued to a corporation * * *.

The apartment project was built by W. A. James Construction Co. Construction was begun in late 1963 or early 1964, and the buildings were completed and occupancy begun on or about July 28, 1964.

* * *

Both Mr. and Mrs. James and Mr. and Mrs. Talbot deemed their receipt of Chicora common stock to be in return for a transfer of property to a controlled corporation under section 351. Accordingly, neither family reported any income from such receipt on their respective income tax returns for 1963. In his statutory notice of deficiency, the respondent determined that Mr. James received such stock, with a value of $22,000, for services rendered and not in exchange for property, and thus received taxable income in that amount. He further determined that the Talbot's transfer of property to Chicora did not meet the requirements of section 351, with the result that they should have recognized a long-term capital gain of $14,675—the difference between $7,325, the basis of the land transferred, and $22,000, the value of the stock received.

OPINION

The first, and critical, issue for our determination is whether Mr. James received his Chicora stock in exchange for the transfer of property or as compensation for services. The petitioners argue that he received such stock in consideration of his transfer to Chicora of the FHA and United Mortgagee commitments and that such commitments constituted "property" within the meaning of section 351 * * *. [T]he sole question * * * is whether Mr. James' personal services, which the petitioners freely admit were rendered, resulted in the development of a property right which was transferred to Chicora, within the meaning of section 351.

* * *

According to the petitioners' argument, Mr. James, as a result of the services performed by him, acquired certain contract rights which constituted property and which he transferred to Chicora. The fact that such rights resulted from the performance of personal service does not, in their view, disqualify them from being treated as property for purposes of section 351. In support of this position, the petitioners refer to situations involving the transfer of patents and secret processes.

It is altogether clear that for purposes of section 351, not every right is to be treated as property. [Section 351(d)(1)] indicates that, whatever may be considered as property for purposes of local law, the performance of services, or the agreement to perform services, is not to be treated as a transfer of property for purposes of section 351. Thus, if in this case we have merely an agreement to perform services in exchange for stock of the corporation to be created, the performance of such services does not constitute the transfer of property within the meaning of section 351.

Although patents and secret processes—the product of services—are treated as property for purposes of section 351, we have carefully analyzed the arrangement in this case and have concluded that Mr. James did not transfer any property essentially like a patent or secret process; he merely performed services for Chicora. In January of 1963, he entered into an agreement to perform services for the corporation to be created. He was to secure the necessary legal and architectural work and to arrange for the financing of the project, and these were the services performed by him * * *. He put in motion the wheels that led to the FHA commitment, but it was not a commitment to him—it was a commitment to United Mortgagee to insure a loan to Chicora, a project sponsored by Mr. James. It was stipulated that under the FHA regulations, a commitment would not be issued to an individual, but only to a corporation. Throughout these arrangements, it was contemplated that a corporation would be created and that the commitment would run to the corporation. The petitioners rely heavily on the claim that Mr. James had a right to the commitment, that such right constituted property, and that such right was transferred to the corporation in return for his stock. However, the commitment was not his to transfer; he never acquired ownership of the commitment—he could not and did not undertake to acquire such ownership * * *. Thus, throughout these arrangements, Mr. James never undertook to acquire anything for himself * * *. The enterprise would be operated, once the initial steps were completed by a corporation * * * and everything that was done by him was done on behalf of the contemplated corporation. In these circumstances, it seems clear that Mr. James received his share of the stock in the corporation in return for the services performed by him and that he did not transfer any property, within the meaning of section 351, to the corporation.

* * *

The next question is whether the Talbots are taxable on the gain realized from the exchange of their land for Chicora stock. Section 351(a) applies only if immediately after the transfer those who transferred property in exchange for stock owned at least 80 percent of Chicora's stock. Sec. 368(c). Since Mr. James is not to be treated as a transferor of property, he cannot be included among those in control for purposes of this test. The transferors of property, the Talbots, did not have the required 80–percent control of Chicora immediately after the transfer, and therefore, their gain must be recognized * * *.

In their petition, the Jameses alleged that the respondent erred in valuing the 10 shares Mr. James received at $22,000. However, they have failed to offer any evidence to establish a different value, and they appear to have dropped this allegation. Accordingly, we sustain the respondent's determination of value.

NOTES

1. *Services versus property.* Why does § 351 not apply to a person who transfers services in exchange for stock? See I.R.C. §§ 61(a)(1), (3), 1001. Is it always easy to distinguish services from "property"? Why or why not?

2. *Relevance to transferor of property.* The Talbots clearly transferred "property" to Chicora. Why, then, were the Talbots a party to this case?

3. *Alternative transaction.* What would the tax consequences have been if: (a) Mrs. Talbot had transferred half of her land to Mr. James as compensation for his services, then (b) Mrs. Talbot and Mr. James each transferred half of the land to the corporation in exchange for half of the stock? If the transaction had been structured in this manner, would the parties have been better off from an income tax standpoint?

4. *Investment company limitation.* Section 351 does not apply to certain transfers of property to an "investment company." I.R.C. § 351(e). A corporation is an investment company if more than 80% of its assets are held for investment in the form of stock, securities, money or certain other investment assets. See I.R.C. § 351(e)(1); Treas. Reg. § 1.351–1(c)(1)(ii). If property is transferred to an investment company *and* the transfer results in diversification of the transferors' interests, § 351 does not apply. See Treas. Reg. § 1.351–1(c)(1)(i). A transfer normally results in diversification when two or more persons transfer nonidentical assets to a corporation. See Treas. Reg. § 1.351–1(c)(5). The investment company limitation was originally directed at individuals who transferred portfolios of publicly-traded stock to a corporation to diversify their investments. The investment company definition has been expanded in recent years. As a result, a narrower array of transactions qualifies for non-recognition treatment under I.R.C. § 351(a).

2.   BASIS AS GAIN/LOSS PRESERVATION MECHANISM

I.R.C. §§ 358(a)(1), 362(a)(1), (e)(2)

Nonrecognition rules are generally designed to *defer*, rather than eliminate, any gain or loss. Deferral is accomplished by perpetuating the historical basis associated with the transferred property. When a person transfers appreciated property to a corporation in a transaction that satisfies I.R.C. § 351(a), the single unrealized gain that exists before the transfer is transformed into two potential gains. After the transfer, the gain is preserved at the shareholder level because the transferor takes an "exchanged basis" in the stock received (i.e., the transferor's basis in the property attaches to the stock). I.R.C. §§ 358(a)(1), 7701(a)(44). In addition, the gain is preserved at the corporate level because the corporation takes a "transferred basis" in the property it receives (i.e., the transferor's basis in the property remains attached to the property now held by the corporation). I.R.C. §§ 362(a)(1), 7701(a)(43).

> *Example 8–B (Gain preserved at both shareholder level and corporate level)*: Aaron and Brenda form a corporation. Aaron transfers operating assets with a value of $500,000 and a basis of $200,000 in exchange for 100 shares of stock. Brenda transfers $500,000 of money in exchange for 100 shares of stock.
>
> (a) Aaron realizes a $300,000 gain on the exchange of the operating assets for the stock but does not recognize the gain. I.R.C. § 351(a).
>
> (b) Aaron takes a $200,000 basis in his stock. I.R.C. § 358(a)(1).
>
> (c) The corporation takes a $200,000 basis in the operating assets transferred by Aaron. I.R.C. § 362(a).
>
> (d) A $300,000 unrealized gain now exists in both Aaron's stock[2] and the corporation's operating assets.[3]

The fact that a transfer of appreciated property to a corporation qualifies for nonrecognition treatment presents both "good news" and "bad news" to the transferor. The good news is that a realized gain is not currently taxed. Why is this beneficial? The bad news is that, after the transfer, two potential gains exist instead of the single gain that existed before the transfer.

> *Problem 8–1 (Double taxation of gain)*: In Example 8–B, assume that Aaron and Brenda form the corporation and transfer the property and money on January 1 of Year 5. Also assume that the corporation is a C Corporation. What are the tax consequences to all the parties if, on January 2 of Year 5, the corporation transfers the operating assets back to Aaron in exchange for all of his stock in the corporation? See I.R.C. §§ 311(b)(1), 302(b)(3).

Problem 8–1 illustrates that **a tax-free transfer of appreciated property to a C Corporation normally converts a single potential gain into two potential gains**. Conversely, a tax-free transfer of property with a basis in excess of its value does *not* convert a single potential tax loss into two potential losses. Rather, the basis of the transferee-corporation is limited to the fair market value of the contributed property. See I.R.C.

---

2. The stock received by Aaron has a value of $500,000 (50% interest in corporation with assets worth $1,000,000) and a basis of $200,000.

3. The operating assets have a value of $500,000 and a basis of $200,000.

§ 362(e)(2)(A). This limit on the corporation's basis can be avoided, however, if the parties elect to limit the shareholder's basis in the stock to the fair market value of the loss property. See I.R.C. § 362(e)(2)(C).

> *Problem 8–2 (Transfer of loss property):* Same facts as Example 8–B, but, rather than transferring $500,000 of money to the corporation, Brenda transfers a building with a value of $500,000 and a basis of $600,000 in exchange for 100 shares of stock.
>
> (a) What are the tax consequences of the transfer to Brenda and the corporation? See I.R.C. §§ 351(a), 358(a)(1), 362(e)(2).
>
> (b) What are the tax consequences to all parties if, on January 2 of Year 5, the corporation transfers the building back to Brenda in exchange for all of her stock in the corporation? See I.R.C. §§ 311, 302(b)(3), 165.
>
> (c) Rather than transferring the building back to Brenda, what are the tax consequences to all parties if, on January 2 of Year 5, the corporation sells the building to an unrelated party for $500,000 and transfers the money to Brenda in exchange for all of her stock in the corporation? See I.R.C. §§ 1001, 302(b)(3), 165.

3.   ASSIGNMENT OF INCOME

When appreciated property is transferred to a C Corporation, any income that results from a subsequent sale of the property is taxed to the corporation (see I.R.C. § 362(a)(1)), rather than to the individual who transferred the property. Section 351 sanctions this result with respect to gains from dealings in property (potential I.R.C. § 61(a)(3) income). Did Congress also intend to permit a shifting of tax burdens by an individual who earns business income (I.R.C. § 61(a)(2)) and incorporates the business before that income has been reported under the cash method of accounting?

Revenue Ruling 80–198

1980–2 Cum.Bull. 113.

ISSUE

Under the circumstances described below, do the nonrecognition of gain or loss provisions of section 351 of the Internal Revenue Code apply to a transfer of the operating assets of an ongoing sole proprietorship (including unrealized accounts receivable) to a corporation in exchange solely for the common stock of a corporation and the assumption by the corporation of the proprietorship liabilities?

FACTS

Individual A conducted a medical practice as a sole proprietorship, the income of which was reported on the cash receipts and disbursements method of accounting. A transferred to a newly organized corporation all of the operating assets of the sole proprietorship in exchange for all of the stock of the corporation, plus the assumption by the corporation of all of the liabilities of the sole proprietorship. The purpose of the incorporation was to provide a form of business organization that would be more conducive to the planned expansion of the medical services to be made available by the business enterprise.

The assets transferred were tangible assets having a fair market value of $40,000 and an adjusted basis of $30,000 and unrealized trade accounts receivable having a face amount of $20,000 and an adjusted basis of zero. The liabilities assumed by the corporation consisted of trade accounts payable in the face amount of $10,000 * * *. A had neither accumulated the accounts receivable nor prepaid any of the liabilities of the sole proprietorship in a manner inconsistent with normal business practices in anticipation of the incorporation. If A had paid the trade accounts payable liabilities, the amounts paid would have been deductible by A as ordinary and necessary business expenses under section 162 of the Code. The new corporation continued to utilize the cash receipts and disbursements method of accounting.

LAW AND ANALYSIS

The applicable section of the Code is section 351(a) * * *.

In Hempt Bros., Inc. v. United States, 490 F.2d 1172 (3d Cir.1974), cert. denied, 419 U.S. 826 (1974), the United States Court of Appeals for the Third Circuit held, as the Internal Revenue Service contended, that a cash basis transferee corporation was taxable on the monies it collected on accounts receivable that had been transferred to it by a cash basis partnership in a transaction described in section 351(a) of the Code. The corporate taxpayer contended that it was not obligated to include the accounts receivable in income; rather the transferor partnership should have been taxed on the stock the partnership received under the assignment of income doctrine which is predicated on the well-established general principle that income be taxed to the party that earned it.

The court in Hempt Bros. solved the conflict between the assignment of income doctrine and the statutory non-recognition provisions of section 351 of the Code by reasoning that if the cash basis transferor were taxed on the transfer of the accounts receivable, the specific congressional intent reflected in section 351(a) that the incorporation of an ongoing business should be facilitated by making the incorporation tax free would be frustrated.

The facts of the instant case are similar to those in Hempt Bros. in that there was a valid business purpose for the transfer of the accounts receivable along with all of the assets and liabilities of A's proprietorship to a corporate transferee that would continue the business of the transferor. Further, A had neither accumulated the accounts receivable nor prepaid any of the account payable liabilities of the sole proprietorship in anticipation of the incorporation, which is an indication that, under the facts and circumstances of the case, the transaction was not designed for tax avoidance.

HOLDING

The transfer by A of the operating assets of the sole proprietorship (including unrealized accounts receivable) to the corporation in exchange solely for the common stock of the corporation and the assumption by the corporation of the proprietorship * * * accounts payable * * * is an exchange within the meaning of section 351(a) of the Code. Therefore, no gain or loss is recognized to A with respect to the property transferred, including the accounts receivable * * *. The corporation, under the cash receipts and disbursements method of accounting, will report in its income the account receivables as collected, and will be allowed deductions under section 162 for the payments it makes to satisfy the assumed trade accounts payable when such payments are made.

A's basis in the stock received * * * under section 358(a)(1) of the Code is [$30,000] * * *.

LIMITATIONS

Section 351 of the Code does not apply to a transfer of accounts receivable which constitute an assignment of an income right in a case such as Brown v. Commissioner, 40 B.T.A. 565 (1939), aff'd 115 F.2d 337 (2d Cir.1940). In Brown, an attorney transferred to a corporation, in which he was the sole owner, a one-half interest in a claim for legal services performed by the attorney and his law partner. In exchange, the attorney received additional stock of the corporation. The claim represented the corporation's only asset. Subsequent to the receipt by the corporation of the proceeds of the claim, the attorney gave all of the stock of the corporation to his wife. The United States Court of Appeals for the Second Circuit found that the transfer of the claim for the fee to the corporation had no purpose other than to avoid taxes and held that in such a case the intervention of the corporation would not prevent the attorney from being liable for the tax on the income which resulted from services under the assignment of income rule of Lucas v. Earl, 281 U.S. 111 (1930). Accordingly, in a case of a transfer to a controlled corporation of an account receivable in respect of services rendered where there is a tax avoidance purpose for the transaction (which might be evidenced by the corporation not conducting an ongoing business), the Internal Revenue Service will continue to apply assignment of income principles and require that the transferor of such a receivable include it in income when received by the transferee corporation.

* * *

NOTES

1. *Preservation of income in substituted stock.* Does I.R.C. § 351(a) really *shift* the tax burden with respect to appreciated property from the individual transferor to the corporation? See I.R.C. § 358(a)(1). If the tax burden is not shifted, why should Congress be concerned about the situation addressed in Revenue Ruling 80–198?

2. *Accrual method of accounting.* Does the problem addressed in Revenue Ruling 80–198 occur if,

(a) the transferor uses the accrual method of accounting?

(b) the transferee corporation uses the accrual method of accounting?

3. *Restrictions on cash method.* With regard to the ability of a C Corporation to use the cash method of accounting, see I.R.C. § 448.

4. *Characterization.* When the assignment of income doctrine does not override nonrecognition treatment, I.R.C. § 351 facilitates a shifting of the unrealized gain in property transferred to a C Corporation from the transferor to the corporation. Under these same circumstances, I.R.C. § 351 can also facilitate a change in the characterization of the potential gain existing in the transferred property.

> *Problem 8–3 (Impact of transfer on characterization)*: Ginger and Sara each own 50% of the stock of a C Corporation that owns and operates an automobile dealership. Ginger also owns and operates an art gallery as a sole proprietorship. On January 1 of Year 3, Ginger takes a painting from the stock of the art gallery with a value of $5,000 that she purchased for $3,000 and transfers it to the corporation. Also on January 1 of Year 3, Sara transfers $5,000 to the corporation. In exchange, the corporation issues 100 additional shares of stock to each shareholder. For four years, the painting is displayed in an auto showroom for aesthetic purposes during which time it is not held for sale. What are the tax consequences if, on January 1 of Year 7, the corporation sells the painting for $12,000? See I.R.C. § 1221.

B. TRANSFER OF PROPERTY FOR OTHER CONSIDERATION

When a person transfers property to a corporation in exchange for stock, nonrecognition treatment can be justified by viewing the stock received in the exchange as representing a continuing investment in the transferred property. This justification for nonrecognition treatment is weakened when part of the consideration received by the transferor is "boot" (i.e., money or other property).

1. RECEIPT OF PROPERTY IN ADDITION TO STOCK

I.R.C. §§ 351(b), (f), 358(a), 362(a)

Treas. Reg. § 1.351–2

When a person who transfers property to a corporation in exchange for stock and boot realizes a gain in a transaction that otherwise satisfies the requirements of I.R.C. § 351(a), the transferor recognizes the lesser of,

(a) the entire realized gain, or

(b) the amount of money and the value of any other property received. See I.R.C. § 351(b)(1).

If, instead of realizing a gain, the transferor realizes a loss in such an exchange, none of the loss is recognized. I.R.C. § 351(b)(2).

When boot is received in an exchange that otherwise satisfies the requirements of I.R.C. § 351(a), the transferor's basis in the stock is reduced by the amount of money and the value of any other property received. I.R.C. §§ 358(a)(1)(A)(i), (ii). In addition, the transferor's stock basis is increased by any gain recognized by the transferor. I.R.C. § 358(a)(1)(B)(ii). The transferee-corporation's basis in the property is also increased to reflect any gain recognized by the transferor. I.R.C. § 362(a).

> *Problem 8–4 (Impact of boot):* Gary and Heidi form the Zanzibar Corporation. Gary transfers $100,000 to the corporation in exchange for 100 shares of stock. Heidi transfers property worth $160,000 to the corporation in exchange for 100 shares of stock and $60,000.

(a) Heidi has a basis of $20,000 in the transferred property.
  (i) How much gain does she recognize? I.R.C. § 351(b).
  (ii) What is her basis in the Zanzibar stock? I.R.C. §§ 358(a)(1)(A)(ii), (B)(ii).
  (iii) What is Zanzibar's basis in the property it receives from Heidi? See I.R.C. § 362(a).
  (iv) Can the operation of the basis rules in these circumstances be reconciled with their operation in instances where the transferor does not receive boot?

(b) Heidi has a basis of $120,000 in the transferred property.
  (i) How much gain does she recognize? I.R.C. § 351(b).
  (ii) What is her basis in the Zanzibar stock? See I.R.C. §§ 358(a)(1)(A)(ii), (B)(ii).
  (iii) What is Zanzibar's basis in the property it receives from Heidi? See I.R.C. § 362(a).
  (iv) Can the operation of the basis rules in these circumstances be reconciled with their operation in instances where the transferor does not receive boot?

(c) Should Gary or Heidi feel that he or she is contributing more than the other in either situation (a) or situation (b)?

The ruling that follows illustrates the application of I.R.C. § 351(b) in situations where a person transfers more than one asset to a corporation in exchange for stock and boot.

Revenue Ruling 68–55

1968–1 Cum.Bull. 140.

Advice has been requested as to the correct method of determining the amount and character of the gain to be recognized by Corporation X under section 351(b) of the Internal Revenue Code of 1954 under the circumstances described below.

Corporation Y was organized by [Corporation X] and A, an individual who owned no stock in X. A transferred 20x dollars to Y in exchange for stock of Y having a fair market value of 20x dollars and X transferred to Y three separate assets and received in exchange stock of Y having a fair market value of 100x dollars plus cash of 10x dollars.

In accordance with the facts set forth in the table below if X had sold at fair market value each of the three assets it transferred to Y, the result would have been as follows:

	Asset I	Asset II	Asset III
* * *			
Fair market value	$22x	$33x	$55x
Adjusted basis	40x	20x	25x
Gain (loss)	($18x)	$13x	$30x
Character of gain or loss	Long-term Capital loss.	Short-term capital gain.	Ordinary income.

* * *

Under section 351(a) of the Code, no gain or loss is recognized if property is transferred to a corporation solely in exchange for its stock and immediately after the exchange the transferor is in control of the corporation. If section 351(a) of the Code would apply to an exchange but for the fact that there is received, in addition to the property permitted to be received without recognition of gain, other property or money, then under section 351(b) of the Code gain (if any) to the recipient will be recognized, but in an amount not in excess of the sum of such money and the fair market value of such other property received, and no loss to the recipient will be recognized.

The first question presented is how to determine the amount of gain to be recognized under section 351(b) of the Code. The general rule is that each asset transferred must be considered to have been separately exchanged. Thus, for purposes of making computations under section 351(b) of the Code, it is not proper to total the bases of the various assets transferred and to subtract this total from the fair market value of the total consideration received in the exchange. Moreover, any treatment other than an asset-by-asset approach would have the effect of allowing losses that are specifically disallowed by section 351(b)(2) of the Code.

The second question presented is how, for purposes of making computations under section 351(b) of the Code, to allocate the cash and stock received to the amount realized as to each asset transferred in the exchange. The asset-by-asset approach for computing the amount of gain realized in the exchange requires that for this purpose the fair market value of each category of consideration received must be separately allocated to the transferred assets in proportion to the relative fair market values of the transferred assets * * *.

Accordingly, the amount and character of the gain recognized in the exchange should be computed as follows:

	Total	Asset I	Asset II	Asset III
Fair market value of asset transferred	$110x	$22x	$33x	$55x
Percent of total fair market value		20%	30%	50%
Fair market value of Y stock received in exchange	$100x	$20x	$30x	$50x
Cash received in exchange	10x	2x	3x	5x
Amount realized	$110x	$22x	$33x	$55x
Adjusted basis		40x	20x	25x
Gain (loss) realized		($18x)	$13x	$30x

Under section 351(b)(2) of the Code the loss of 18x dollars realized on the exchange of Asset Number I is not recognized. Such loss may not be used to offset the gains realized on the exchanges of the other assets. Under section 351(b)(1) of the Code, the gain of 13x dollars realized on the exchange of Asset Number II will be recognized as short-term capital gain in the amount of 3x dollars, the amount of cash received. Under section 351(b)(1) * * * of the Code, the gain of 30x dollars realized on the exchange of Asset Number III will be recognized as ordinary income in the amount of 5x dollars, the amount of cash received.

NOTE

Treatment of certain preferred stock as property. When a person who transfers property to a corporation in a transaction that otherwise satisfies the requirements of I.R.C. § 351(a) receives "nonqualified preferred stock," the nonqualified preferred stock is treated as boot. I.R.C. § 351(g)(1). "Nonqualified preferred stock" includes preferred stock that requires the issuer to purchase the stock, confers on the holder the right to require the issuer to purchase the stock, or permits the issuer to purchase the stock pursuant to terms that make it more likely than not that the issuer will purchase the stock. See I.R.C. § 351(g)(2). Boot treatment does not result, however, when the issuer's obligation or right to purchase the preferred stock is contingent upon the death or disability of the holder or, in certain cases, the termination of the holder's employment with the issuer. See I.R.C. § 351(g)(2)(C). "Nonqualified preferred stock" also includes preferred stock with a dividend rate that varies with reference to interest rates, commodity prices, or a similar indices. See I.R.C. § 351(g)(2)(A)(iv).

2. RELIEF FROM LIABILITIES

I.R.C. §§ 357, 358(d)

Treas. Reg. §§ 1.357–1, –2, 1.358–3

A person who transfers property to a corporation in exchange for stock receives additional consideration when liabilities are transferred to the corporation along with the property. The transfer of a liability to a corporation is economically equivalent to receiving money from the corporation. When a liability is transferred to a corporation in a transaction that otherwise qualifies under I.R.C. § 351, however, the tax consequences are generally different from when the transferor receives money in such a transaction.

> *Example 8–C (Receipt of money versus transfer of liability)*: Janine owns property with a value of $100,000 and a basis of $40,000. She also owes Leonard $30,000. Janine wishes to transfer the property to a corporation and is considering the following alternative approaches:
>
> (a) Transfer the property to the corporation in exchange for stock worth $70,000 and $30,000 of money and use the money to satisfy her debt to Leonard.
>
> (b) Transfer the property to the corporation in exchange for stock worth $70,000 and have the corporation assume her debt to Leonard.

From an economic standpoint, Janine should be indifferent toward the two options (at least if option (b) entails a "novation" from Leonard releasing Janine from any personal responsibility for the debt). Yet, if the exchange otherwise qualifies for nonrecognition treatment under I.R.C. § 351(a), the tax consequences of the two options are very different. Option (a) causes Janine to recognize a gain of $30,000. See I.R.C. § 351(b)(1). In contrast, Janine recognizes no gain under option (b) because the transfer of liabilities to a corporation in a § 351 transaction is generally not treated as the receipt of money by the transferor for gain recognition purposes. See I.R.C. § 357(a).[6] Hence, Janine can choose option (b) without incurring any tax liability.[7]

This liberal treatment of the transfer of liabilities to a controlled corporation reflects Congress's intention to facilitate the incorporation of an ongoing business. Because most ongoing businesses have some liabilities, treating the transfer of liabilities as the receipt of boot would make it virtually impossible to avoid triggering a tax liability when incorporating an ongoing business.

In two situations, however, the transfer of liabilities in a § 351 transaction can trigger a taxable gain to the transferor. The first situation is when the transferor's principal purpose for the transfer of liabilities is to avoid Federal income tax or is not a bona fide business purpose. In these

---

6. Although the transferred liabilities are not generally treated as the receipt of money for gain recognition purposes, the transferred liabilities are usually treated as money received by the transferor for purposes of determining the transferor's basis in the stock received. See I.R.C. § 358(d). Thus, under option (b), Janine takes a $10,000 basis in the stock received from the corporation. See I.R.C. §§ 358(d), (a)(1)(A)(ii). In contrast, under option (a), Janine takes a $40,000 basis in the stock received. See I.R.C. §§ 358(a)(1)(A)(ii), (B)(ii).

7. Janine's ability to execute option (b) in a tax-free fashion assumes that I.R.C. § 357(b) does not apply to the transaction.

circumstances, the transferor is treated as receiving money equal to the amount of the transferred liabilities (i.e., treated as receiving boot). See I.R.C. § 357(b). Thus, if Janine's liability to Leonard in Example 8–C was unrelated to the transferred property and unrelated to the business of the corporation, Janine could be compelled to recognize the $30,000 gain even if she chose option (b).

A second situation exists in which the transfer of liabilities in a § 351 transaction triggers income to the transferor. If the amount of the transferred liabilities exceeds the transferor's basis in the transferred property, the difference is treated as taxable gain. See I.R.C. § 357(c)(1). Taxable gain is triggered in this situation regardless of the taxpayer's motive for the transfer. Is the rule of I.R.C. § 357(c)(1) sensible? Can it be avoided? See the Lessinger and Peracchi cases that follow.

Lessinger v. Commissioner

United States Court of Appeals, Second Circuit, 1989.
872 F.2d 519.

■ OAKES, CHIEF JUDGE: * * *

Sol Lessinger operated a proprietorship under the name "Universal Screw and Bolt Co." for over twenty-five years prior to 1977 * * *. [The business] engaged in the wholesale distribution of metal fasteners * * *.

In 1976, the factor that had provided working capital to the proprietorship refused to continue lending funds to it as a noncorporate entity because under New York law one can charge higher interest rates to a corporation. The taxpayer instructed the individual who was his attorney and accountant to do whatever was necessary to make the proprietorship a corporation. The Universal proprietorship was then consolidated into [an existing corporation all of the stock of which was owned by the taxpayer,] the Universal corporation * * *. The Tax Court found that the taxpayer was not informed of the details of the transaction.

The proprietorship's unaudited balance sheet dated December 31, 1976, shows that the business had [liabilities that exceeded the basis of its assets by approximately $259,000.] * * *

The consolidation of the proprietorship into the corporation was conducted in a most casual manner, the transfer transaction being naked in its simplicity. The taxpayer already owned all of the corporation's stock, and no new stock was issued. There were no written agreements documenting the transfer. On January 1, 1977, the proprietorship's bank account was closed, and the corporation took over the proprietorship's operating assets * * *.

The corporation expressly assumed the * * * proprietorship liabilities * * *. All notes payable were changed to show that the corporation was the maker of the notes, and the debt to the factor was expressly assumed * * *.

On June 1, 1977, journal entries were made to the corporation's books to reflect the consolidation * * *. Total proprietorship liabilities exceeded total proprietorship assets by [$259,000], and that amount was debited to a corporate asset account in an entry entitled "Loan Receivable—[Sol Lessinger]." * * *

[I]n January 1977, the taxpayer [disbursed] * * * $62,210 to pay the corporation part of his $259,000 debt to it. Thus, at the end of 1977, he owed $196,790 to the corporation. In 1981, Marine Midland Bank, a principal creditor of the corporation, requested that the taxpayer execute a promissory note for the debt, and he did so, the note being used as collateral for the bank's loan to the corporation. No interest was ever paid on the debt, however, and the debt had risen to $237,044 by the end of 1982, by which point the corporation was insolvent * * *.

DISCUSSION

The first question is whether section 351 applies when no new shares are issued to the shareholder, having in mind the statutory language that a transfer must be made "solely in exchange for stock * * *." See § 351(a) * * *. [T]he exchange requirements of section 351 are met where a sole stockholder transfers property to a wholly-owned corporation even though no stock * * * is issued therefor. Issuance of new stock in this situation would be a meaningless gesture * * *.

The taxpayer's principal argument, broadly stated, is that section 357 is inapplicable to him because in neither an accounting nor an economic sense did he realize a gain. He "merely exchanged creditors" from trade creditors to Universal, and his gain, therefore, was a "phantom" which Congress did not intend to tax.

[Taxpayer argues that] * * * there was no taxable gain since he contributed "property," that is, the account receivable from him in the approximate amount of [$259,000], which * * * should be deemed to have a basis equal to its face value.

The Commissioner responds with the general, unchallenged proposition that discharge of indebtedness may be income. The Commissioner argues that the taxpayer had a negative net worth with liabilities "tantamount to personal debts" which he was "essentially relieved from meeting" by virtue of the incorporation.[8]

* * *

[W]e must determine whether the taxpayer's purported debt to his corporation would offset [the assumed] liabilities and prevent a net excess of liabilities over assets. The obligation which the taxpayer owed to his

---

8. Nowhere is there the slightest hint or innuendo that the taxpayer had a tax avoidance purpose so as to fall under § 357(b). Rather it can be said—if the Commissioner were to prevail—that the factor's demand for higher interest led Lessinger into a § 351 "trap."

wholly-owned corporation, it must quickly be conceded, was not as well documented as a debt to a third party would be.

* * *

The Tax Court refused to count the debt as "property" transferred in the transaction, although its reasoning is not explicit. First, the opinion says that the corporate accounting entry entitled "Loan receivable—[Sol Lessinger]" "merely represents the excess of the liabilities over the adjusted basis," noting that the debt was not at first represented by a promissory note and that Lessinger paid no interest on it. The Tax Court then cites a decision in which it had ignored an entry that the taxpayer had characterized as an "artificial receivable." The Tax Court opinion concludes that "even if [Lessinger] had executed a note, it would have a zero basis in the hands of the corporation." The Tax Court thus apparently believed there were two independently sufficient reasons to ignore the debt: first, that it was artificial, and, second, that it would have had a zero basis.

We are unpersuaded by the argument that the obligation was artificial. The Commissioner argues:

> This open account was not so much a debt as it was an accommodation by the corporation to its president and sole shareholder, who was having liquidity problems. In effect, he caused the corporation to apply its assets to satisfy his personal obligations, including those owed to trade creditors which were shortly to fall due, intending to pay the money back only as and when he found it convenient to do so.

The Commissioner points out that the receivable lacked a due date, interest, security, or "other accepted features of true debt," but this analysis begs the question we have before us * * *.

We believe * * * that a due date, interest, and security are not necessary to characterize Lessinger's obligation to his corporation as debt, and that his obligation was binding. The promissory note he signed in 1981, which the corporation endorsed to Marine Midland as collateral for a loan, is significant because it shows that Marine Midland depended on his personal responsibility. And, in general, it is obvious that the creditors of the corporation continued to do business with it on the strength of the taxpayer's personal credit * * *. Lessinger received consideration when he gave his promise to the corporation, and we have no doubt that any court would enforce that promise to protect the corporate creditors if the corporation failed, even in the absence of alter ego liability. We conclude that the taxpayer's obligation to the corporation was real, not artificial.

We now turn to the Tax Court's second reason for ignoring the debt. The Tax Court quoted [its Alderman decision], which, like our case, involved the incorporation of an accrual basis proprietorship with a negative net worth. In Alderman, the Tax Court disregarded the taxpayers' personal promissory note to their corporation because,

> the Aldermans incurred no cost in making the note, so its basis to them was zero. The basis to the corporation was the same as in the hands of the transferor, i.e., zero. Consequently, the application of

section 357(c) is undisturbed by the creation and transfer of the personal note to the corporation.

Alderman purported to follow the literal language of the Tax Code. Section 357(c) does support the Alderman court's reliance on the concept of basis, but the statutory language is not addressed to a transaction such as Lessinger's, where the transferor's obligation has a value to the transferee corporation. The Alderman court did not consider the value of the obligation to the transferee.

[Section 357(c)(1) provides in relevant part:]

if the sum of the amount of the liabilities assumed * * * exceeds the total of the *adjusted basis* of the property transferred pursuant to such exchange, then such excess shall be considered as a gain * * *.

(emphasis added). In general, then, the "adjusted basis" of the property transferred is crucial to the calculation.

"Basis", as used in tax law, refers to assets, not liabilities. Section 1012 provides that "the basis of property shall be the cost of such property, except as otherwise provided." Liabilities by definition have no "basis" in tax law generally or in section 1012 terms specifically * * *. The taxpayer could, of course, have no "basis" in his own promise to pay the corporation [$259,000], because that item is a liability for him * * *. But the corporation should have a basis in its obligation from Lessinger, because it incurred a cost in the transaction involving the transfer of the obligation by taking on the liabilities of the proprietorship that exceeded its assets, and because it would have to recognize income upon Lessinger's payment of the debt if it had no basis in the obligation.[9] Assets transferred under section 351 are taken by the corporation at the transferor's basis, to which is added any gain recognized in the transfer. § 362(a). Consideration of "adjusted basis" in section 357(c) therefore normally does not require determining whether the section refers to the "adjusted basis" in the hands of the transferor-shareholder or the transferee-corporation, because the basis does not change. But here, the "basis" in the hands of the corporation should be the face amount of the taxpayer's obligation. We now hold that in the situation presented here, where the transferor undertakes genuine personal liability to the transferee, "adjusted basis" in section 357(c) refers to the transferee's basis in the obligation, which is its face amount.

Yet, the Commissioner says that to reverse the Tax Court would * * * "effectively eliminate section 357(c) from the Internal Revenue Code." Would it? The question of substance is whether the taxpayer in fact realized a gain from the transaction. He certainly did not do so by a cancellation of his indebtedness. If there was any cancellation, it was illusory: While his trade creditors at the time of the incorporation may have been paid off (or their accounts rolled over as a result of sales and payments by the corporation and further advances of credit by the trade

---

9. Our approach requires acceptance of the fact that section 362(a), which requires a carryover basis for "property" transferred in nonrecognition transactions under section 351, cannot be applied to the corporation's valuation of its receivable from the taxpayer * * *.

creditors), the taxpayer's indebtedness to the corporation itself continued (except to the extent he paid it off). If Lessinger had a "gain" from the incorporation, it did not show up in his personal balance sheet, let alone by way of economic benefit in his pocket.

The purpose of section 357(c) is to provide a limited exception to section 351's nonrecognition treatment that operates, as the Commissioner reminds us here, "where the transferor realized economic benefit which, if not recognized, would otherwise go untaxed." Section 351 was intended to allow changes in business form without requiring the recognition of income * * *. In 1938, the Supreme Court held that under the predecessor of section 351, * * * any assumption of liability by the transferee would be considered a payment of money or property to the transferor, causing the transferor to recognize income. Congress reacted immediately by enacting * * * the predecessor of section 357(a), which provided that the assumption of a liability should not be considered the payment of property or money and should not provoke the recognition of gain.

Congress did not add section 357(c), which requires the recognition of gain when liabilities exceed assets, until 1954, when a House committee referred to the section as an "additional safeguard against tax avoidance not found in existing law." * * *. The House and Senate committees that approved section 357(c) both cited a single example of a transaction that the section was intended to govern: If a taxpayer transfers property with an adjusted basis of $20,000 subject to a $50,000 mortgage, he should recognize $30,000 gain. [C]ongress's example is * * * quite reasonable. The transferor, who has already benefited by depreciating the property or holding it while its value appreciates, has income because he will never have to pay the mortgage. Forcing the taxpayer in our case to recognize a gain, however, would be contrary to Congress's intent because it would tax a truly phantom gain, because his liability to the corporation, as we have said, was real, continuing, and indirectly, at least, enforceable by the corporation's creditors.

     * * *

We conclude that our holding will not "effectively eliminate section 357(c)." Lessinger experienced no enrichment and had no unrecognized gains whose recognition was appropriate at the time of the consolidation. Any logic that would tax him would certainly represent a "trap for the unwary." Lessinger could have achieved incorporation without taxation under the Commissioner's theory by borrowing $260,000 cash, transferring the cash to the corporation (or paying some of the trade accounts payable personally), and later causing the corporation to buy his promissory note from the lender (or pay it off in consideration of his new promise to pay the corporation). If taxpayers who transfer liabilities exceeding assets to controlled corporations are willing to undertake genuine personal liability for the excess, we see no reason to require recognition of a gain, and we do not believe that Congress intended for any gain to be recognized.

     * * *

Peracchi v. Commissioner

United States Court of Appeals, Ninth Circuit, 1998.
143 F.3d 487.

■ KOZINSKI, CIRCUIT JUDGE:

* * *

The taxpayer, Donald Peracchi, needed to contribute additional capital to his closely-held corporation (NAC) to comply with Nevada's minimum premium-to-asset ratio for insurance companies. Peracchi contributed two parcels of real estate. The parcels were encumbered with liabilities which together exceeded Peracchi's total basis in the properties by more than half a million dollars. [U]nder section 357(c), contributing property with liabilities in excess of basis can trigger immediate recognition of gain in the amount of the excess. In an effort to avoid this, Peracchi also executed a promissory note, promising to pay NAC $1,060,000 over a term of ten years at 11% interest. Peracchi maintains that the note has a basis equal to its face amount, thereby making his total basis in the property contributed greater than the total liabilities. If this is so, he will have extracted himself from the quicksand of section 357(c) and owe no immediate tax on the transfer of property to NAC. The IRS, though, maintains that the note * * * does not increase Peracchi's basis in the property contributed.

The parties are not splitting hairs: Peracchi claims the basis of the note is $1,060,000, its face value, while the IRS argues that the note has a basis of zero. If Peracchi is right, he pays no immediate tax on the half a million dollars by which the debts on the land he contributed exceed his basis in the land; if the IRS is right, the note becomes irrelevant for tax purposes and Peracchi must recognize an immediate gain on the half million. * * *

[D]oes Peracchi's note have a basis in Peracchi's hands for purposes of section 357(c)? The language of the Code gives us little to work with. The logical place to start is with the definition of basis. Section 1012 provides that "the basis of property shall be the cost of such property * * *." But "cost" is nowhere defined. What does it cost Peracchi to write the note and contribute it to his corporation? The IRS argues tersely that the "taxpayers in the instant case incurred no cost in issuing their own note to NAC, so their basis in the note was zero." Building on this premise, the IRS makes Peracchi out to be a grifter: He holds an unenforceable promise to pay himself money, since the corporation will not collect on it unless he says so.

It's true that all Peracchi did was make out a promise to pay on a piece of paper, mark it in the corporate minutes and enter it on the corporate books. It is also true that nothing will cause the corporation to enforce the note against Peracchi so long as Peracchi remains in control. But the IRS ignores the possibility that NAC may go bankrupt, an event that would suddenly make the note highly significant. Peracchi and NAC are separated by the corporate form, and this gossamer curtain makes a difference in the shell game of C Corp organization and reorganization. Contributing the note puts a million dollar nut within the corporate shell, exposing Peracchi to the cruel nutcracker of corporate creditors in the event NAC goes bankrupt. And it does so to the tune of $1,060,000, the full face amount of the note. Without the note, no matter how deeply the corporation went into debt, creditors could not reach Peracchi's personal assets. With the note on the books, however, creditors can reach into Peracchi's pocket by enforcing the note as an unliquidated asset of the corporation.

The key to solving this puzzle, then, is to ask whether bankruptcy is significant enough a contingency to confer substantial economic effect on this transaction. If the risk of bankruptcy is important enough to be recognized, Peracchi should get basis in the note: He will have increased his exposure to the risks of the business—and thus his economic investment in NAC—by $1,060,000. If bankruptcy is so remote that there is no realistic possibility it will ever occur, we can ignore the potential economic effect of the note as speculative and treat it as merely an unenforceable promise to contribute capital in the future.

When the question is posed this way, the answer is clear. Peracchi's obligation on the note was not conditioned on NAC's remaining solvent. It represents a new and substantial increase in Peracchi's investment in the corporation.[10] The Code seems to recognize that economic exposure of the shareholder is the ultimate measuring rod of a shareholder's investment. Peracchi therefore is entitled to a step-up in basis to the extent he will be subjected to economic loss if the underlying investment turns unprofitable.

* * *

We find further support for Peracchi's view by looking at the alternative: What would happen if the note had a zero basis? The IRS points out that the basis of the note in the hands of the corporation is the same as it was in the hands of the taxpayer. Accordingly, if the note has a zero basis for Peracchi, so too for NAC. See I.R.C. § 362(a).[11] But what happens if NAC—perhaps facing the threat of an involuntary petition for bankruptcy—turns around and sells Peracchi's note to a third party for its fair market value? According to the IRS's theory, NAC would take a carryover basis of zero in the note and would have to recognize $1,060,000 in

---

10. We confine our holding to a case such as this where the note is contributed to an operating business which is subject to a non-trivial risk of bankruptcy or receivership. NAC is not, for example, a shell corporation or a passive investment company; Peracchi got into this mess in the first place because NAC was in financial trouble and needed more assets to meet Nevada's minimum premium-to-asset ratio for insurance companies.

11. But see Lessinger v. Commissioner, 872 F.2d 519 (2d Cir.1989). In Lessinger, the Second Circuit analyzed a similar transaction. It agreed with the IRS's (faulty) premise that the note had a zero basis in the taxpayer's hands. But then, brushing aside the language of section 362(a), the court concluded that the note had a basis in the corporation's hands equal to its face value. The court held that this was enough to dispel any section 357(c) gain to the taxpayer, proving that two wrongs sometimes do add up to a right.

We agree with the IRS that Lessinger's approach is untenable. Section 357(c) contemplates measuring basis of the property contributed in the hands of the taxpayer, not the corporation. * * * Because we hold that the note has a face value basis to the shareholder for purposes of section 357(c), however, we reach the same result as Lessinger.

phantom gain on the subsequent exchange, even though the note did not appreciate in value one bit. That can't be the right result.

Accordingly, we hold that Peracchi has a basis of $1,060,000 in the note he wrote to NAC. The aggregate basis exceeds the liabilities of the properties transferred to NAC under section 351, and Peracchi need not recognize any section 357(c) gain.

* * *

■ FERNANDEZ, CIRCUIT JUDGE, Dissenting:

Is there something that a taxpayer, who has borrowed hundreds of thousands of dollars more than his basis in his property, can do to avoid taxation when he transfers the property? Yes, says Peracchi, because by using a very clever argument he can avoid the strictures of § 357(c). He need only make a promise to pay by giving a "good," though unsecured, promissory note to his corporation when he transfers the property to it. That is true even though the property remains subject to the encumbrances. How can that be? Well, by preparing a promissory note the taxpayer simply creates basis without cost to himself. Thus he can extract a large part of the value of the property, pocket the funds, use them, divest himself of the property, and pay the tax another day, if ever at all.

But as with all magical solutions, the taxpayer must know the proper incantations and make the correct movements. He cannot just transfer the property to the corporation and promise, or be obligated, to pay off the encumbrances. That would not change the fact that the property was still subject to those encumbrances. According to Peracchi, the thaumaturgy that will save him from taxes proceeds in two simple steps. He must first prepare a ritualistic writing—an unsecured promissory note in an amount equal to or more than the excess of the encumbrances over the basis. He must then give that writing to his corporation. That is all. * * * I understand the temptation to embrace that argument, but I see no real support for it in the law.

* * *

NOTES

1. *Conceptual sensibility.* Do the results reached by the Lessinger and Peracchi courts make sense conceptually? Why or why not?

2. *Technical analysis.* How defensible is the Lessinger court's holding that "where the transferor undertakes genuine personal liability to the transferee, 'adjusted basis' in section 357(c) refers to the transferee's basis in the obligation, which is its face amount" (p. 402)? Does the Peracchi court agree with the Lessinger court's technical analysis? How defensible is the Peracchi court's finding that "if the risk of bankruptcy is important enough to be recognized, Peracchi should get basis in the note?"

3. *Portrayal of taxpayer.* Consider the following statements by the Lessinger court:

(a) "[T]he taxpayer was not informed of the details of the transaction."

(b) "The consolidation of the proprietorship into the corporation was conducted in a most casual manner, the transfer transaction being naked in its simplicity."

(c) "Nowhere is there the slightest hint or innuendo that the taxpayer had a tax avoidance purpose so as to fall under § 357(b). Rather it can be said—if the Commissioner were to prevail—that the factor's demand for higher interest led Lessinger into a § 351 'trap'."

(d) "Any logic that would tax [the taxpayer] would certainly represent a 'trap for the unwary'."

How relevant were these statements to the outcome of the case? Was the Ninth Circuit as enamored of Peracchi as the Second Circuit was of Lessinger?

4. *Transfer of liability under § 357.* What is required to "transfer" a liability for purposes of I.R.C. § 357(c)? Must the corporation agree to satisfy the liability *and* the lender give the transferor a "novation" (i.e., release the transferor from any personal responsibility for the debt)? Is the mere agreement by the corporation to satisfy the liability sufficient? Can a liability ever be transferred in the absence of an agreement by the corporation to satisfy the liability? See I.R.C. § 357(d).

Problem 8–5 (Transfer of liabilities in excess of basis): Gary and Heidi form the Zanzibar Corporation. Gary transfers $100,000 to the corporation in exchange for 100 shares of stock. Heidi transfers property worth $160,000 to the corporation in exchange for 100 shares of stock and Zanzibar agrees to satisfy $60,000 of Heidi's liabilities.

(a) Heidi has a basis of $20,000 in the transferred property.

  (i) How much gain does she recognize? I.R.C. § 357(c)(1).

  (ii) What is her basis in the Zanzibar stock? See I.R.C. §§ 358(d), (a)(1)(A)(ii), (B)(ii).

  (iii) What is Zanzibar's basis in the property it receives from Heidi? I.R.C. § 362(a).

  (iv) Can the operation of the basis rules in these circumstances be reconciled with their operation in instances where the transferor does not transfer any liabilities to the corporation?

(b) Heidi has a basis of $120,000 in the transferred property.

  (i) How much gain does she recognize? I.R.C. § 357(c)(1).

  (ii) What is her basis in the Zanzibar stock? I.R.C. §§ 358(d), (a)(1)(A)(ii), (B)(ii).

  (iii) What is Zanzibar's basis in the property it receives from Heidi? I.R.C. § 362(a).

(iv) Can the operation of the basis rules in these circumstances be reconciled with their operation in instances where the transferor does not transfer any liabilities to the corporation?

(c) Should Gary or Heidi feel that he or she is contributing more than the other in either situation (a) or situation (b)?

(d) How do the answers to situation (a) change if the $60,000 of liabilities transferred to Zanzibar would have created a deduction for Heidi if she had paid them (e.g., if the liabilities were the accounts payable of a cash method proprietor)? See I.R.C. §§ 357(c)(3), 358(d)(2). Is I.R.C. § 357(c)(3) a sensible exception to the general rule of I.R.C. § 357(c)(1)?

Revenue Ruling 95–74

1995–2 Cum.Bull. 36.

ISSUES

(1) Are the liabilities assumed by S in the § 351 exchange described below liabilities for purposes of §§ 357(c)(1) and 358(d)?

(2) Once assumed by S, how will the liabilities in the § 351 exchange described below be treated?

FACTS

Corporation P is an accrual basis, calendar-year corporation engaged in various ongoing businesses, one of which includes the operation of a manufacturing plant (the Manufacturing Business). The plant is located on land purchased by P many years before. The land was not contaminated by any hazardous waste when P purchased it. However, as a result of plant operations, certain environmental liabilities, such as potential soil and groundwater remediation, are now associated with the land.

In Year 1, for bona fide business purposes, P engages in an exchange to which § 351 of the Internal Revenue Code applies by transferring substantially all of the assets associated with the Manufacturing Business, including the manufacturing plant and the land on which the plant is located, to a newly formed corporation, S, in exchange for all of the stock of S and for S's assumption of the liabilities associated with the Manufacturing Business, including the environmental liabilities associated with the land. P has no plan or intention to dispose of (or have S issue) any S stock. S is an accrual basis, calendar-year taxpayer.

P did not undertake any environmental remediation efforts in connection with the land transferred to S before the transfer and did not deduct or capitalize any amount with respect to the contingent environmental liabilities associated with the transferred land.

In Year 3, S undertakes soil and groundwater remediation efforts relating to the land transferred in the § 351 exchange and incurs costs * * * as a result of those remediation efforts. Of the total amount of costs incurred, a portion would have constituted ordinary and necessary business expenses that are deductible under § 162 and the remaining portion would have constituted capital expenditures under § 263 if there had not been a § 351 exchange and the costs for remediation efforts had been incurred by P.

LAW AND ANALYSIS

Issue 1: Section 351(a) provides that no gain or loss shall be recognized if property is transferred to a corporation solely in exchange for stock and immediately after the exchange the transferor is in control of the corporation.

* * *

The legislative history of § 351 indicates that Congress viewed an incorporation as a mere change in the form of the underlying business and enacted § 351 to facilitate such business adjustments generally by allowing taxpayers to incorporate businesses without recognizing gain. Section 357(c)(1), however, provides that the transferor recognizes gain to the extent that the amount of liabilities transferred exceeds the aggregate basis of the assets transferred.

* * *

Congress [determined] that including in the § 357(c)(1) determination liabilities that have not yet been taken into account by the transferor results in an overstatement of liabilities of, and potential inappropriate gain recognition to, the transferor because the transferor has not received the corresponding deduction or other corresponding tax benefit. To prevent this result, Congress enacted § 357(c)(3)(A) to exclude certain deductible liabilities from the scope of § 357(c), as long as the liabilities had not resulted in the creation of, or an increase in, the basis of any property (as provided in § 357(c)(3)(B)).

While § 357(c)(3) explicitly addresses liabilities that give rise to deductible items, the same principle applies to liabilities that give rise to capital expenditures as well. Including in the § 357(c)(1) determination those liabilities that have not yet given rise to capital expenditures (and thus have not yet created or increased basis) with respect to the property of the transferor prior to the transfer also would result in an overstatement of liabilities. Thus, such liabilities also appropriately are excluded in determining liabilities for purposes of § 357(c)(1).

In this case, the contingent environmental liabilities assumed by S had not yet been taken into account by P prior to the transfer (and therefore had neither given rise to deductions for P nor resulted in the creation of, or increase in, basis in any property of P). As a result, the contingent environmental liabilities are not included in determining whether the amount of the liabilities assumed by S exceeds the adjusted basis of the property transferred by P pursuant to § 357(c)(1).

Due to the parallel constructions and interrelated function and mechanics of §§ 357 and 358, liabilities that are not included in the determination under § 357(c)(1) also are not included in the § 358 determination of the transferor's basis in the stock received in the § 351 exchange. Therefore, the contingent environmental liabilities assumed by S are not treated as money received by P under § 358 for purposes of determining P's basis in the stock of S received in the exchange.

Issue 2: * * *

The present case is analogous to the situation in Rev. Rul. 80–198 [p. 391]. For business reasons, P transferred in a § 351 exchange substantially all of the assets and liabilities associated with the Manufacturing Business to S, in exchange for all of its stock, and P intends to remain in control of S. The costs S incurs to remediate the land would have been deductible in part and capitalized in part had P continued the Manufacturing Business and incurred those costs to remediate the land. The congressional intent to facilitate necessary business readjustments would be frustrated by not according to S the ability to deduct or capitalize the expenses of the ongoing business.

[A]ccordingly, the contingent environmental liabilities assumed from P are deductible as business expenses under § 162 or are capitalized under § 263, as appropriate, by S under S's method of accounting (determined as if S has owned the land for the period and in the same manner as it was owned by P).

HOLDINGS

(1) The liabilities assumed by S in the § 351 exchange described above are not liabilities for purposes of § 357(c)(1) and § 358(d) because the liabilities had not yet been taken into account by P prior to the transfer (and therefore had neither given rise to deductions for P nor resulted in the creation of, or increase in, basis in any property of P).

(2) The liabilities assumed by S in the § 351 exchange described above are deductible by S as business expenses under § 162 or are capital expenditures under § 263, as appropriate, under S's method of accounting (determined as if S has owned the land for the period and in the same manner as it was owned by P).

NOTE

Legislative limitation. In 2000, Congress amended I.R.C. § 358 to confine Rev. Rul. 95–74 to the transfer of an entire business. See I.R.C. § 358(h). Different treatment results when—

1. some, but not all, of the assets of a business are transferred in an I.R.C. § 351 exchange,

2. the transferee-corporation assumes certain liabilities of the transferor-shareholder that would not otherwise reduce the basis of the stock received by the shareholder, and

3. the basis of the stock received would, as a result of 2., exceed the fair market value of that stock.

When these events occur, the basis of the stock received is reduced by the assumed liabilities (but not below the fair market value of the stock). I.R.C. §§ 358(h)(1), (2). For purposes of determining fair market value, liabilities are defined to include contingent obligations. I.R.C. § 358(h)(3).

The amended provision operates as follows: Assume a taxpayer using the cash-method of accounting transfers assets with an adjusted basis and fair market value of $100 to its wholly-owned subsidiary that also uses the cash-method of accounting. In addition, the subsidiary assumes the taxpayer's liability to pay $40 of compensation to the taxpayer's employees. The taxpayer had not previously deducted the liability because no deduction is allowed until the liability is paid. The value of the stock received by the taxpayer is $60. Under prior law, the basis of the stock was $100 because the liability assumed by the corporation was not treated as money received by the taxpayer for purposes of adjusting the basis in the taxpayer's stock. See I.R.C. §§ 358(a)(1)(A)(ii), (d)(2). By virtue of the amendment, however, the basis of the stock is reduced to $60. I.R.C. § 358(h)(1).

C.   CONTRIBUTION TO CAPITAL

Commissioner v. Fink

Supreme Court of the United States, 1987.
483 U.S. 89, 107 S.Ct. 2729.

■ JUSTICE POWELL delivered the opinion of the Court.

The question in this case is whether a dominant shareholder who voluntarily surrenders a portion of his shares to the corporation, but retains control, may immediately deduct from taxable income his basis in the surrendered shares.

I

Respondents Peter and Karla Fink were the principal shareholders of Travco Corporation * * *. Travco had one class of common stock outstanding and no preferred stock. Mr. Fink owned 52.2 percent, and Mrs. Fink 20.3 percent, of the outstanding shares. Travco urgently needed new capital as a result of financial difficulties it encountered in the mid–1970's. The Finks voluntarily surrendered some of their shares to Travco in an effort to "increase the attractiveness of the corporation to outside investors." * * *. As a result, the Finks' combined percentage ownership of Travco was reduced from 72.5 percent to 68.5 percent. The Finks received no consideration for the surrendered shares, and no other shareholder surrendered any stock. The effort to attract new investors was unsuccessful, and the corporation eventually was liquidated.

On their 1976 and 1977 joint federal income tax returns, the Finks claimed ordinary loss deductions totaling $389,040, the full amount of their adjusted basis in the surrendered shares. The Commissioner of Internal Revenue disallowed the deductions. He concluded that the stock surrendered was a contribution to the corporation's capital. Accordingly, the Commissioner determined that the surrender resulted in no immediate tax consequences, and that the Finks' basis in the surrendered shares should be added to the basis of their remaining shares of Travco stock.

[T]he Tax Court sustained the Commissioner's determination for the reasons stated in Frantz v. Commissioner, 83 T.C. 162, 174–182 (1984), aff'd, 784 F.2d 119 (C.A.2 1986). In Frantz, the Tax Court held that a stockholder's non pro rata surrender of shares to the corporation does not produce an immediate loss. The court reasoned that—

> this conclusion * * * necessarily follows from a recognition of the purpose of the transfer, that is, to bolster the financial position of [the corporation] and, hence, to protect and make more valuable [the stockholder's] retained shares.

Because the purpose of the shareholder's surrender is "to decrease or avoid a loss on his overall investment," the Tax Court in Frantz was "unable to conclude that [he] sustained a loss at the time of the transaction." "Whether [the shareholder] would sustain a loss, and if so, the amount thereof, could only be determined when he subsequently disposed of the stock that the surrender was intended to protect and make more valuable." * * *

In this case, a divided panel of the Court of Appeals for the Sixth Circuit reversed the Tax Court. 789 F.2d 427 (1986). * * *

We granted certiorari to resolve a conflict among the Circuits and now reverse.

II

A

It is settled that a shareholder's voluntary contribution to the capital of the corporation has no immediate tax consequences. I.R.C. § 263; Treas. Reg. § 1.263(a)–2(f) (1986). Instead, the shareholder is entitled to increase the basis of his shares by the amount of his basis in the property transferred to the corporation. See I.R.C. § 1016(a)(1). When the shareholder later disposes of his shares, his contribution is reflected as a smaller taxable gain or a larger deductible loss. This rule applies not only to transfers of cash or tangible property, but also to a shareholder's forgiveness of a debt owed to him by the corporation. Treas. Reg. § 1.61–12(a) (1986). Such transfers are treated as contributions to capital even if the other shareholders make proportionately smaller contributions, or no contribution at all. The rules governing contributions to capital reflect the general principle that a shareholder may not claim an immediate loss for outlays made to benefit the corporation. We must decide whether this principle also applies to a controlling shareholder's non pro rata surrender of a portion of his shares.

B

The Finks contend that they sustained an immediate loss upon surrendering some of their shares to the corporation. By parting with the shares, they gave up an ownership interest entitling them to future dividends, future capital appreciation, assets in the event of liquidation, and voting rights.[12] Therefore, the Finks contend, they are entitled to an immediate deduction. * * *

III

A shareholder who surrenders a portion of his shares to the corporation has parted with an asset, but that alone does not entitle him to an immediate deduction. Indeed, if the shareholder owns less than 100 percent of the corporation's shares, any non pro rata contribution to the corporation's capital will reduce the net worth of the contributing shareholder.[13] A shareholder who surrenders stock thus is similar to one who forgives or surrenders a debt owed to him by the corporation; the latter gives up interest, principal, and also potential voting power in the event of insolvency or bankruptcy. But, as stated above, such forgiveness of corporate debt is treated as a contribution to capital rather than a current deduction. The Finks' voluntary surrender of shares, like a shareholder's voluntary forgiveness of debt owed by the corporation, closely resembles an investment or contribution to capital. * * * We find the similarity convincing in this case.

* * *

The Finks concede that the purpose of their stock surrender was to protect or increase the value of their investment in the corporation. They hoped to encourage new investors to provide needed capital and in the long run recover the value of the surrendered shares through increased dividends or appreciation in the value of their remaining shares. If the surrender had achieved its purpose, the Finks would not have suffered an economic loss. In this case, as in many cases involving closely held corporations whose shares are not traded on an open market, there is no reliable method of determining whether the surrender will result in a loss until the shareholder disposes of his remaining shares. Thus, the Finks' stock surrender does not meet the requirement that an immediately deductible loss must be "actually sustained during the taxable year." Treas. Reg. § 1.165–1(b) (1986).

Finally, treating stock surrenders as ordinary losses might encourage shareholders in failing corporations to convert potential capital losses to

---

12. As a practical matter, however, the Finks did not give up a great deal. Their percentage interest in the corporation declined by only 4 percent. Because the Finks retained a majority interest, this reduction in their voting power was inconsequential. Moreover, Travco, like many corporations in financial difficulties, was not paying dividends.

13. For example, assume that a shareholder holding an 80 percent interest in a corporation with a total liquidation value of $100,000 makes a non pro rata contribution to the corporation's capital of $20,000 in cash. Assume further that the shareholder has no other assets. Prior to the contribution, the shareholder's net worth was $100,000 ($20,000 plus 80 percent of $100,000). If the corporation were immediately liquidated following the contribution, the shareholder would receive only $96,000 (80 percent of $120,000). Of course such a non pro rata contribution is rare in practice. Typically a shareholder will simply purchase additional shares.

ordinary losses by voluntarily surrendering their shares before the corporation fails. In this way shareholders might avoid the consequences of I.R.C. § 165(g)(1), which provides for capital-loss treatment of stock that becomes worthless. Similarly, shareholders may be encouraged to transfer corporate stock rather than other property to the corporation in order to realize a current loss.

We therefore hold that a dominant shareholder who voluntarily surrenders a portion of his shares to the corporation, but retains control, does not sustain an immediate loss deductible from taxable income. Rather, the surrendering shareholder must reallocate his basis in the surrendered shares to the shares he retains.[14] The shareholder's loss, if any, will be recognized when he disposes of his remaining shares. A reallocation of basis is consistent with the general principle that "payments made by a stockholder of a corporation for the purpose of protecting his interest therein must be regarded as [an] additional cost of his stock," and so cannot be deducted immediately. Our holding today is not inconsistent with the settled rule that the gain or loss on the sale or disposition of shares of stock equals the difference between the amount realized in the sale or disposition and the shareholder's basis in the particular shares sold or exchanged. See I.R.C. § 1001(a); Treas. Reg. § 1.1012–1(c)(1) (1986). We conclude only that a controlling shareholder's voluntary surrender of shares, like contributions of other forms of property to the corporation, is not an appropriate occasion for the recognition of gain or loss.

IV

For the reasons we have stated, the judgment of the Court of Appeals for the Sixth Circuit is reversed.

[Concurring and dissenting opinions are omitted.]

NOTE

Contribution to capital of gain property. Does a taxable event occur when a shareholder contributes property with a value in excess of the shareholder's basis to the corporation without receiving stock in return? See I.R.C. § 1001; Lessinger, p. 399 ("[T]he exchange requirements are met where a sole stockholder transfers property to a wholly-owned corporation even though no stock * * * is issued therefor. Issuance of new stock in this situation would be a meaningless gesture.") If a taxable event occurs, is gain recognized? What is the tax effect of a contribution to capital on the contributing shareholder? See I.R.C. § 1016(a)(1).

---

14. The Finks remained the controlling shareholders after their surrender. We therefore have no occasion to decide in this case whether a surrender that causes the shareholder to lose control of the corporation is immediately deductible. * * *

CHAPTER 9

S CORPORATION CONTRIBUTIONS

When property is transferred to a corporation in a transaction that satisfies the requirements of I.R.C. § 351(a), nonrecognition treatment applies regardless of whether the transferee is a C Corporation or an S Corporation. A transfer of property to a corporation in exchange for stock, or in exchange for a combination of stock and "boot", often has dramatically different implications, however, when the transferee is subject to the single tax regime of Subchapter S, rather than the double tax regime of Subchapter C. Chapter 9 focuses on the consequences of transferring property to an S Corporation in exchange for stock or other consideration.

A. TRANSFER OF PROPERTY FOR STOCK

1. DEFERRAL OF GAIN OR LOSS

I.R.C. §§ 351(a), (d), 1361(b), 1362(d)(2), 1371(a)

I.R.C. § 351(a) provides nonrecognition treatment for certain persons who transfer property "to a corporation". This nonrecognition rule applies regardless of whether the transferee is a C Corporation or an S Corporation. See I.R.C. § 1371(a)(1). If a transfer to an S Corporation satisfies I.R.C. § 351(a), but results in a violation of any of the requirements for S Corporation status, that status will terminate. See I.R.C. §§ 1361(b), 1362(d)(2).

NOTES

1. *Kamborian case.* Would the tax consequences of the transaction in the Kamborian case (p. 376) be different if International Shoe Machine Corp. were an S Corporation, rather than a C Corporation? See I.R.C. § 351(a). Would the transaction affect International Shoe's S Corporation status?

2. *Intermountain Lumber case.* Would the tax consequences of the transaction in the Intermountain Lumber case (p. 382) be different if S & W Sawmill, Inc. were an S Corporation, rather than a C Corporation? See I.R.C. § 351(a). Would the transaction impact on S & W's S Corporation status? See I.R.C. § 1361(b)(3).

3. *James case.* Would the tax consequences of the transaction in the James case (p. 386) be different if Chicora were an S Corporation, rather than a C Corporation? See I.R.C. § 351(a). Would the transaction impact on Chicora's S Corporation status? See I.R.C. § 1361(b).

2.   BASIS AS GAIN/LOSS PRESERVATION MECHANISM

I.R.C. §§ 311, 358(a)(1), 362(a)(1), (e)(2), 1366, 1367

When a person transfers property to a corporation in a transaction that satisfies I.R.C. § 351(a), the same basis rules apply regardless of whether the transferee is a C Corporation or an S Corporation. In both cases, the potential gain that exists before the transfer is transformed into two potential gains. After the transfer, the gain is preserved at the shareholder level because the transferor takes an "exchanged basis" in the stock received (i.e., the transferor's basis in the property attaches to the stock). I.R.C. §§ 358(a)(1), 7701(a)(44). In addition, the gain is preserved at the corporate level because the corporation takes a "transferred basis" in the property it receives (i.e., the transferor's basis in the property remains attached to the property now held by the corporation). I.R.C. §§ 362(a)(1), 7701(a)(43).

> *Example 9–A (Gain preserved at both shareholder level and corporate level)*: Aaron and Brenda form a corporation whose first taxable year begins on December 30 of Year 5, and the corporation makes an S election effective on that date. Aaron transfers operating assets with a value of $500,000 and a basis of $200,000 in exchange for 100 shares of stock. Brenda transfers $500,000 of money in exchange for 100 shares of stock.
>
> (a) Aaron realizes a $300,000 gain on the exchange of the operating assets for the stock but does not recognize the gain. I.R.C. § 351(a).
>
> (b) Aaron takes a $200,000 basis in his stock. I.R.C. § 358(a)(1).
>
> (c) The corporation takes a $200,000 basis in the operating assets transferred by Aaron. I.R.C. § 362(a).
>
> (d) A $300,000 unrealized gain now exists both in Aaron's stock[1] and in the corporation's operating assets.[2]

Although the transfer of appreciated property to an S Corporation in a § 351 transaction creates the two potential gains, how likely is it that both potential gains will be taxed?

> *Problem 9–1 (Corporate gain triggered first)*: In Example 9–A, what are the tax consequences to all parties if, on December 31 of Year 5, the corporation transfers the operating assets back to Aaron in exchange for all of his stock in the corporation? See I.R.C. §§ 311(b)(1), 1366(a)(1)(A), 1367(a)(1)(A), 302(b)(3).
>
> *Problem 9–2 (Shareholder gain triggered first):* In Example 9–A, what are the tax consequences to all parties if: (a) on December 31 of Year 5, Aaron sells his S Corporation stock to Donna for $500,000, and (b) on January 1 of Year 6, the corporation transfers its operating assets to

---

1.   The stock received by Aaron has a value of $500,000 (50% interest in corporation with assets worth $1,000,000) and a basis of $200,000.

2.   The operating assets have a value of $500,000 and a basis of $200,000.

Donna in exchange for all of her stock in the corporation? See I.R.C. §§ 311(b)(1), 1366(a)(1)(A), 1367(a)(1)(A), 302(b)(3).

When property with a basis in excess of value is transferred to an S Corporation in a transaction that satisfies I.R.C. § 351(a), the potential loss cannot be duplicated. Under these circumstances, the shareholder takes an exchanged basis in the stock received (thereby preserving the loss at the shareholder level) but the transferee-corporation's basis is limited to the fair market value of the contributed property. See I.R.C. §§ 358(a)(1), 362(e)(2)(A). Alternatively, the limit imposed on the corporation's basis can be avoided (i.e., the corporation may take a transferred basis in the property) if the parties elect to limit the shareholder's basis in the stock to the fair market value of the loss property. See I.R.C. § 362(e)(2)(C). If the election is made, the loss is preserved at the corporate level, rather than at the shareholder level.

Problem 9–3 (Transfer of loss property to S Corporation): Same facts as Example 9–A, but, rather than transferring $500,000 of money to the corporation, Brenda transfers a building with a value of $500,000 and a basis of $600,000 in exchange for 100 shares of stock.

(a) What are the tax consequences of the transfer to Brenda and to the corporation? See I.R.C. §§ 351(a), 358(a)(1), 362(e)(2).

(b) What are the tax consequences to all parties if the corporation transfers the building back to Brenda on December 31 of Year 5 in exchange for all of her stock? See I.R.C. §§ 311, 302(b)(3), 165.

(c) Rather than transferring the building back to Brenda, what are the tax consequences to all parties if the corporation sells the building to an unrelated party on December 31 of Year 5 for $500,000 and transfers the money to Brenda in exchange for all of her stock? See I.R.C. §§ 1001, 1366(a)(1), 1367(a)(2), 302(b)(3), 165.

3.   ASSIGNMENT OF INCOME

The circumstances in which the assignment of income doctrine overrides I.R.C. § 351 are likely to be the same, regardless of whether the transferee is a C Corporation or an S Corporation. See Revenue Ruling 80–198, p. 391. When the assignment of income doctrine does not apply and the transferee is an S Corporation, the transferred basis rule of I.R.C. § 362(a) shifts potential gain in a manner that is very different from how the gain is shifted when the transferee is a C Corporation. When appreciated property is transferred to a C Corporation in a § 351 transaction, any gain recognized on a subsequent sale of the property is taxed to the corporation, rather than to the transferor. See I.R.C. § 11. In contrast, the subsequent sale of appreciated property transferred to an S Corporation in a § 351 transaction results in a shifting of *part* of the recognized gain to the other shareholders. The remainder of the gain is still taxed to the transferor, but in his capacity as a shareholder.

Problem 9–4 (Impact of transfer on the taxpayer): Clara owns and operates a jewelry store as a sole proprietorship. Durwood, her landlord, wishes to share Clara's business with her. The parties form an S Corporation on January 1 of Year 5, to which Clara transfers jewelry with a value of $400,000 and a basis of $300,000, and other assets with a value of $100,000 and a basis of $100,000. Durwood transfers to the corporation the building housing the business which has a value of $500,000 and a basis of $400,000. Clara and Durwood each receive 100 shares of stock from the corporation. What are the tax consequences to the parties if, during Year 5, the jewelry contributed by Clara is sold for $600,000? See I.R.C. § 1366(a)(1).

4.   CHARACTERIZATION ISSUES

When the assignment of income doctrine does not override nonrecognition treatment, I.R.C. § 351 facilitates a shifting of part of the unrealized gain in property transferred to an S Corporation from the transferor to the other shareholders. Under these same circumstances, I.R.C. § 351 can also facilitate a change in the characterization of the potential gain existing in the transferred property.

Problem 9–5 (Impact of transfer on characterization): Ginger and Sara each own 50% of the stock of an S Corporation that owns and operates an automobile dealership. Ginger also owns and operates an art gallery as a sole proprietorship. On January 1 of Year 3, Ginger takes a painting from the stock of the art gallery with a value of $5,000 that she purchased for $3,000 and transfers it to the corporation. Also on January 1 of Year 3, Sara transfers $5,000 to the corporation. In exchange, the corporation issues 100 additional shares of stock to each shareholder. For four years, the painting is displayed in an auto showroom for aesthetic purposes during which time it is not held for sale. What are the tax consequences if, on January 1 of Year 7, the corporation sells the painting for $12,000? See I.R.C. § 1221.

As a general rule, the character of any item of S Corporation income, deduction or loss is determined at the corporate level and the item retains that character when allocated to the shareholders. See I.R.C. § 1366(b). A different rule applies, however, when a shareholder who owns appreciated property that would be taxed as ordinary income if the shareholder sold the property utilizes an S Corporation for a principal purpose of converting that ordinary income to capital gain. Here, if the property is contributed to the S Corporation and the S Corporation sells the property, any gain recognized by the S Corporation will *not* be treated as capital gain. Treas. Reg. § 1.1366–1(b)(2). Likewise, when a shareholder of an S Corporation owns property with a basis in excess of value that would be taxed as capital loss if the shareholder sold the property, the S Corporation might be formed or availed of for a principal purpose of converting that capital loss to an ordinary loss. In theses circumstances, if the property is contributed to and sold by the S Corporation, the part of the loss recognized by the S Corporation that existed at the time the property was contributed to the S Corporation is still treated as a capital loss. Treas. Reg. § 1.1366–1(b)(3).

In Problem 9–5, if Ginger were deemed to have transferred the property to the corporation for a principal purpose of changing the character of the gain, what are the tax consequences of the subsequent sale? Note that the length of time between the contribution and sale are likely to influence the determination of whether the corporation was formed or availed of with a principal purpose of changing the character of the contributed property.

B. TRANSFER OF PROPERTY FOR OTHER CONSIDERATION

The consequences of receiving "boot" in a transaction that otherwise qualifies under I.R.C. § 351 are the same, regardless of whether the transferee is a C Corporation or an S Corporation. When a person who transfers property to an S Corporation in exchange for stock and "boot" realizes a gain in a § 351 transaction, the transferor recognizes the lesser of: (a) the realized gain, or (b) the amount of money and the value of any other property received. I.R.C. § 351(b)(1). If, instead of realizing a gain, the transferor realizes a loss, the loss is not recognized. I.R.C. § 351(b)(2). When boot is received in an exchange that otherwise satisfies I.R.C. § 351(a), the transferor's basis in the stock is reduced by the amount of money and the value of any other property received. See I.R.C. §§ 358(a)(1)(A)(i), (ii). In addition, the transferor's stock basis is increased by any gain recognized by the transferor. See § 358(a)(1)(B)(ii). The transferee's basis in the property is also increased by any gain recognized by the transferor. See I.R.C. § 362(a).

The transfer of liabilities to a corporation in a § 351 transaction is also governed by the same rules, regardless of whether the transferee is a C Corporation or an S Corporation. When, in connection with a § 351 transfer, an S Corporation assumes a liability of the transferor or receives property subject to a liability, the transferor is normally not treated as receiving money. I.R.C. § 357(a). If, however, the taxpayer's principal purpose for the transfer of liabilities is to avoid Federal income tax or is not a bona fide business purpose, the transferor is treated as receiving money equal to the amount of the transferred liabilities. See I.R.C. § 357(b). Moreover, if the amount of liabilities transferred to the corporation exceeds the transferor's basis in the transferred property, the difference is treated as taxable gain. See I.R.C. § 357(c).

*

CHAPTER 10

PARTNERSHIP CONTRIBUTIONS

A person who transfers property to an enterprise taxed as a partnership in exchange for a partnership interest generally receives nonrecognition treatment. See I.R.C. § 721(a). In contrast to I.R.C. § 351(a), the nonrecognition rule of I.R.C. § 721(a) applies regardless of whether the transferor "controls" the partnership. Chapter 10 examines the tax consequences of transfers of property to an enterprise taxed as a partnership in exchange for a partnership interest or other consideration.

A. TRANSFER OF PROPERTY FOR PARTNERSHIP INTEREST

When a person transfers property to a partnership in exchange for an interest in that partnership, any gain or loss realized with respect to the transferred property is generally not recognized. See I.R.C. § 721(a). When I.R.C. § 721(a) applies, the transferor takes an exchanged basis in the partnership interest received. See I.R.C. §§ 722, 7701(a)(44). The partnership takes a transferred basis in the property. See I.R.C. §§ 723, 7701(a)(43). As a result, any gain or loss that existed when the property was in the transferor's hands is preserved both at the partner level (in the partnership interest received) and at the partnership level (in the property).

Example 10–A (Transfer of appreciated property to partnership): Francine and Gregg form the FG Partnership. Francine transfers a building with a value of $1,000,000 and a basis of $100,000 in exchange for a 50% interest in the partnership. Gregg transfers $1,000,000 of money in exchange for a 50% interest in the partnership. The tax consequences of the exchange to Francine are as follows:

Realization Event (I.R.C. § 1001)

Amount Realized	$1,000,000	(value of partnership interest)
Adjusted Basis	100,000	(in building)
Realized Gain	$900,000	
Recognition?	No. I.R.C. § 721(a).	

Francine's Basis in Partnership Interest: $100,000 (I.R.C. § 722)

Partnership's Basis in Building: $100,000 (I.R.C. § 723)

1. DEFERRAL OF GAIN OR LOSS

I.R.C. § 721

Treas. Reg. § 1.721–1

For any realized gain or loss to qualify for nonrecognition treatment under I.R.C. § 721(a), the following conditions must be satisfied:

   (1) "property" must be transferred to the partnership,

   (2) in "exchange" for a partnership interest.

a. PROPERTY AND EXCHANGE REQUIREMENTS

United States v. Stafford

United States Court of Appeals, Eleventh Circuit, 1984.
727 F.2d 1043.

■ R. LANIER ANDERSON, III, CIRCUIT JUDGE: Taxpayers DeNean and Flora Stafford appeal the district court's summary judgment in favor of the government on their refund action for allegedly overpaid taxes. The refund action involves the Staffords' 1969 tax return, in which they did not account for their receipt of a limited partnership interest valued at $100,000. The taxpayers argue that the partnership share qualified for nonrecognition treatment under I.R.C. § 721(a) because it was received in "exchange" for "property" they contributed to the partnership. The district court held that nonrecognition was not available because the taxpayers' contribution of a letter of intent to the partnership did not meet the exchange and property requirements of the statute. We conclude that the district court applied an improper legal standard and under the proper legal test several issues should have been decided in favor of the taxpayers. With regard to additional issues, we conclude that genuine issues of fact remain such that summary judgment for the government was inappropriate. We therefore reverse and remand.

I. HISTORY OF THE CASE

    * * *

Throughout the 1960's, DeNean Stafford worked as a real estate developer, often in projects involving hotel property. * * *

In the early 1960's, [the Life Insurance Company of Georgia ("LOG")] * * * owned land adjacent to [its corporate] headquarters, which at the time was undeveloped. LOG officials * * * approached Stafford and began negotiations for construction of a hotel complex on the unused land. * * *

Negotiations between Stafford and LOG led to a July 2, 1968, letter * * * setting forth the numerous points of agreement as of that date and additional details in need of future resolution. In particular, the letter promised 6–¾% interest on the loan financing for the hotel and it specified lease terms; both the interest rate and lease terms were very favorable to Stafford given then existing market conditions. [LOG] sent additional correspondence to Stafford on July 3, 1968, indicating that the favorable conditions described in the July 2 letter would be open for Stafford's consideration for a period of 60 days.

Under the terms of the July 2 letter, Stafford or his designee were to provide 25% equity for the hotel development. With letter in hand, Stafford * * * investigated the formation of a limited partnership to provide that equity share. On August 30, 1968, he responded to the LOG letter of July 2, accepting the general terms set forth in the letter and proposing further negotiation on additional details.

* * *

In January of 1969, Stafford and a number of investors formed Center Investments, Ltd., a Georgia limited partnership, to pursue the development. Stafford was designated the sole general partner. He purchased two $100,000 shares and received a third limited partnership share [the "third partnership share"] for contributing to the partnership the letter of intent and the agreement with LOG contained therein. In all, the partnership sold 20 units for $100,000 each, which together with the unit Stafford received for his capital contribution made a total of 21 units. * * *

By mid–1970 the necessary capital had been raised and plans for the hotel development were set and approved. LOG and Center Investments executed formal lease and loan documents. * * * LOG * * * substantially abided by the terms set forth in the July 2, 1968, letter to DeNean Stafford. LOG maintained the 6–¾% interest rate on the [money] it loaned to Center Investments. * * * LOG and Center Investments also followed the formula set forth in the July 2 letter as the method for calculating lease payments. These terms had become even more favorable to Center Investments than when first proposed, owing to changed market conditions.

On their 1969 federal tax return, the Staffords did not report as income their receipt of the third partnership share. The Commissioner audited that return and determined that the Staffords should have treated the partnership share as compensation for services that Stafford rendered to the partnership in negotiating and developing the investment. The Commissioner thus concluded that the nonrecognition principles of § 721 did not apply to the third partnership share and assessed a deficiency of $64,000 plus interest. The Staffords paid the assessment and filed a claim for a refund.

After the Internal Revenue Service denied the refund claim, the taxpayers filed the present action in January of 1976. * * *

The district court * * * granted summary judgment in favor of the government. The taxpayers appealed to this court.

* * *

[II.] EXCHANGE AND PROPERTY REQUIREMENTS

To qualify for nonrecognition treatment on the receipt of a partnership share, the partner must establish that he made a contribution of "property" in "exchange" for that share. I.R.C. § 721(a). Contrary to the district court's holding that the exchange and property requirements were not met, we conclude that these issues should have been decided in the taxpayers' favor. * * *

A.   The Exchange Requirement

* * *

The district court held that Stafford's contribution of the letter of intent to the limited partnership was not an "exchange" for purposes of § 721. The court defined exchange as "a mutual or reciprocal transfer of one thing for another" and suggested that each side to the transaction must have a choice as to whether or not they desire the transfer. Because transfer of the letter of intent to the partnership was part of the partnership agreement as drafted by the taxpayers' attorneys, the court found that the limited partners never had a choice as to whether or not the transfer would take place.

The district court's opinion on this element lacks support in the language and principles of § 721. * * * That Stafford's contribution of the letter of intent was part of the partnership agreement at formation in no way undermines his argument that the contribution was part of an exchange with the partnership under § 721.

* * *

The district court opinion focused on the lack of agreement between Stafford and the limited partners. Viewed properly, the exchange that took place was between Stafford and the partnership, not the limited partners as individuals. * * * [T]hat this exchange occurred at the formation of the partnership and without a formal partnership vote does not alter our conclusion that an exchange took place.

* * *

B.   The Property Requirement

The district court alternatively held that Stafford had not received his third partnership share as the result of a contribution of "property." The court correctly stated that "the key to the benefit of nonrecognition afforded by I.R.C. § 721(a) is that *property must be exchanged for an interest in the partnership*." The district court then stated as its test for property under § 721:

> After having carefully considered the arguments of counsel * * *, it is the opinion of the court that both *value* and *enforceability* are necessary to a conclusion that a document is "property" for purposes of § 721.

Finding as a matter of law that the letter of intent was not enforceable, the court concluded that it was not property and the taxpayers were not eligible for nonrecognition under § 721.

We agree with the district court's conclusion that the letter of intent was not enforceable. Under Georgia law an agreement becomes enforceable when there is a meeting of the parties' minds "at the same time, upon the same subject matter, and in the same sense." In the present case, * * * the July 2, 1968 letter of intent acknowledged that "there were many details to be worked out" and stated only that "we [LOG] would like to continue our negotiations along the following general lines." The July 3 letter from LOG may have converted the proposal to negotiate to a firm proposal of major terms, but Stafford's response again made the execution of final lease and loan agreements expressly "subject to further negotiations" on several items. * * *

[W]here, as here, the parties' written documents clearly and definitely make final agreement subject to mutually satisfactory future negotiations, we must decide as a matter of Georgia law that "the parties did not intend the letter agreement to be a binding, enforceable contract."

Nevertheless, notwithstanding its lack of legal enforceability, we still must determine whether the letter of intent was "property" within the meaning of § 721. * * * An enforceable contract would perhaps be assured of property status; but the absence of enforceability does not necessarily preclude a finding that a document, substantially committing the parties to the major terms of a development project, is property.

Several nonenforceable obligations may rise to the level of property for purposes of § 721 or § 351. Unpatented know-how, which results from services and is not enforceable, nevertheless can be deemed property. * * *

The instant transfer of the letter of intent outlining the major terms of a proposed loan and lease agreement to which both parties felt morally bound is closely analogous to a transfer of goodwill, which although clearly unenforceable, nevertheless has been treated as property. * * *

Thus, we conclude that the district court's requirement of legal enforceability as an absolute prerequisite to finding property status under § 721 was improper.

For purposes of our discussion as to whether the instant letter of intent is "property", we will assume arguendo that the fact finder on remand determines that the letter had value. Under the appropriate legal standard and under the circumstances peculiar to this case, we conclude that the letter of intent encompassed a sufficient bundle of rights to constitute "property" within the meaning of § 721.

    * * *

A conclusion that the letter of intent is "property" under the instant circumstances comports with the purpose of § 721. Stafford exerted personal efforts on his own behalf in negotiating with LOG. When LOG and Stafford exchanged the letter of intent and acceptance in 1968, the government had not suggested that Stafford recognized taxable income. He could have completed the project as a sole proprietor without recognition of income based on his receipt of the letter. The purpose of §§ 721 and 351 is to permit the taxpayer to change his individual business into partnership or corporate form; the Code is designed to prevent the mere change in form from precipitating taxation. In keeping with this purpose, we can discern no reason to exclude Stafford's transfer of the letter of intent from the protective characterization as "property".

Stafford through his business reputation and work efforts was able to negotiate a very promising development project with LOG. He obtained from LOG officials a written document, morally, if not legally, committing LOG to the major terms of a proposed loan and lease. The transferability of the letter is undisputed and Stafford transferred his full interest in the project to the partnership. We conclude that the letter encompassed a sufficient bundle of rights and obligations to be deemed property for purposes of § 721.

* * *

[III.] THE QUID PRO QUO FOR STAFFORD'S RECEIPT OF THE PARTNERSHIP SHARE

[T]his dispute remains; from the record we cannot ascertain whether the partnership was compensating Stafford for services to be rendered or for contribution of the letter of intent, or partially for both.

On remand the fact finder could determine that Stafford received the partnership share wholly in exchange for the letter of intent he contributed to the partnership. If so, the nonrecognition principles of § 721 apply and Stafford is entitled to his refund. * * *

On the other hand, it might be determined on remand that Stafford received the partnership share wholly as compensation for services, in which case the government's tax assessment was proper. * * *

Finally, the fact finder might conclude that Stafford's receipt of the partnership share was partly in compensation for services and partly in exchange for property. If this is the case, the fact finder should determine the value of the property element (i.e., the letter of intent) and the value of the services element (i.e., the services to be rendered to the partnership by Stafford after formation of the partnership * * *), and allocate the $100,000 value of the third partnership share accordingly. * * *

NOTES

1. *Services versus property.* Did the letter of intent that Stafford contributed to the partnership result from the performance of services by Stafford? At what point do services mature into "property"?

2. *Relevance of service partner to transferor of property.* If two people form a partnership to which one person contributes property with a value in excess of basis for a 50% partnership interest and the other person performs services for a 50% partnership interest, what are the tax consequences to the person who contributes property? See I.R.C. § 721(a). Would the tax consequences to the property contributor be different if the two people formed a corporation and each person received 50% of the stock of the corporation for his contribution? See I.R.C. § 351(a); James v. Commissioner, Talbot v. Commissioner, p. 386.

3. *Nature of interest received.* The Stafford case focused on whether Stafford contributed property or services for his partnership interest. The parties apparently agreed that Stafford received a conventional partnership interest, in both *capital and profits*, with a readily ascertainable value. The next section explores the issues that arise when a person performs services for a partnership in exchange for an interest that is limited to a share of future partnership profits.

b.   RECEIPT OF A PROFITS INTEREST

Diamond v. Commissioner

United States Court of Appeals, Seventh Circuit, 1974.
492 F.2d 286.

■ FAIRCHILD, CIRCUIT JUDGE. This is an appeal from a decision of the Tax Court upholding the commissioner's assessment of deficiencies against Sol * * * Diamond * * *. The Tax Court concluded that Diamond realized ordinary income on the receipt of a right to a share of profit or loss to be derived from a real estate venture * * *.

During 1961, Diamond was a mortgage broker. Philip Kargman had acquired for $25,000 the buyer's rights in a contract for the sale of an office building. Kargman asked Diamond to obtain a mortgage loan for the full $1,100,000 purchase price of the building. Diamond and Kargman agreed that Diamond would receive a 60% share of profit or loss of the venture if he arranged the financing.

Diamond succeeded in obtaining a $1,100,000 mortgage loan from Marshall Savings and Loan. On December 15, 1961 Diamond and Kargman entered into an agreement which provided:

(1) The two were associated as joint venturers for 24 years (the life of the mortgage) unless earlier terminated by agreement or by sale;

(2) Kargman was to advance all cash needed for the purchase beyond the loan proceeds;

(3) Profits and losses would be divided, 40% to Kargman, 60% to Diamond;

(4) In event of sale, proceeds would be devoted first to repayment to Kargman of money supplied by him, and net profits thereafter would be divided 40% to Kargman, 60% to Diamond.

* * *

The purchase proceeded as planned and closing took place on February 18, 1962. Kargman made cash outlays totalling $78,195.33 in connection with the purchase. Thus, under the terms of the agreement, the property would have to appreciate at least $78,195.33 before Diamond would have any equity in it.

Shortly after closing, it was proposed that Diamond would sell his interest and one Liederman would be substituted, except on a 50–50 basis. Liederman persuaded Diamond to sell his interest for $40,000. This sale was effectuated on March 8, 1962 by Diamond assigning his interest to Kargman for $40,000. Kargman in turn then conveyed a similar interest, except for 50–50 sharing, to Liederman for the same amount.

[D]iamond reported the March 8, 1962 $40,000 sale proceeds as a short term capital gain. This gain was offset by an unrelated short term capital loss. [He] reported no tax consequences from the February 18 receipt of the interest in the venture. Diamond's position is that his receipt of this type of interest in partnership is not taxable income although received in return for services. He relies on § 721 and Reg. § 1.721–1(b)(1). He further argues that the subsequent sale of this interest produced a capital gain under § 741. The Tax Court held that the receipt of this type of interest in partnership in return for services is not within § 721 and is taxable under § 61 when received. The Tax Court valued the interest at $40,000 as of February 18, as evidenced by the sale for that amount three weeks later, on March 8.

Both the taxpayer and the Tax Court treated the venture as a partnership and purported to apply partnership income tax principles. It has been suggested that the record might have supported findings that there was in truth an employment or other relationship, other than partnership, and produced a similar result, but these findings were not made. It has also been suggested * * * that although on the face of the agreement Diamond appeared to receive only a right to share in profit (loss) to be derived, the value of the real estate may well have been substantially greater than the purchase price, so that Diamond may really have had an interest in capital, if the assets were properly valued. This finding was not made. * * *

Taking matters at face value, taxpayer received, on February 18, an interest in partnership, limited to a right to a share of profit (loss) to be derived. In discussion we shall refer to this interest either as his interest in partnership or a profit-share.

The Tax Court, with clearly adequate support, found that Diamond's interest in partnership had a market value of $40,000 on February 18. Taxpayer's analysis is that under the regulations the receipt of a profit-share February 18, albeit having a market value and being conferred in return for services, was not a taxable event, and that the entire proceeds of the March 8 sale were a capital gain. The Tax Court analysis was that the interest in partnership, albeit limited to a profit-share, was property worth $40,000, and taxpayer's acquisition, thereof on February 18 was compensation for services and ordinary income. Assuming that capital gain treatment at sale would have been appropriate, there was no gain because the sale was for the same amount.

There is no statute or regulation which expressly and particularly prescribes the income tax effect, or absence of one, at the moment a partner receives a profit-share in return for services. The Tax Court's holding rests upon the general principle that a valuable property interest received in return for services is compensation, and income. Taxpayer's argument is predicated upon an implication which his counsel, and others, have found in Reg. § 1.721–1(b)(1), but which need not, and the government argues should not, be found there.

I.R.C. § 721 is entitled "Nonrecognition of gain or loss on contribution," and provides: "No gain or loss shall be recognized to a partnership or to any of its partners in the case of a contribution of property to the partnership in exchange for an interest in the partnership." Only if, by a strained construction, "property" were said to include services, would § 721 say anything about the effect of furnishing services. It clearly deals with a contribution like Kargman's, of property, and prescribes that when he contributed his property, no gain or loss was recognized. It does not, of course, explicitly say that no income accrues to one who renders services and, in return, becomes a partner with a profit-share.

Reg. § 1.721–1 presumably explains and interprets § 721, perhaps to the extent of qualifying or limiting its meaning. Subsec. (b)(1), particularly relied on here, reads in part as follows:

> Normally, under local law, each partner is entitled to be repaid his contributions of money or other property to the partnership (at the value placed upon such property by the partnership at the time of the contribution) whether made at the formation of the partnership or subsequent thereto. To the extent that any of the partners gives up any part of his right to be repaid his contributions (as distinguished from a share in partnership profits) in favor of another partner as compensation for services (or in satisfaction of an obligation), section 721 does not apply. The value of an interest in such partnership capital so transferred to a partner as compensation for services constitutes income to the partner under section 61 * * *.

The quoted portion of the regulation may well be read, like § 721, as being directly addressed only to the consequences of a contribution of money or other property. It asserts that when a partner making such contributions transfers to another some part of the contributing partner's right to be repaid, in order to compensate the other for services or to satisfy an obligation to the other, § 721 does not apply, there is recognition of gain or loss to the contributing partner, and there is income to the partner who receives, as compensation for services, part of the right to be repaid.

The regulation does not specify that if a partner contributing property agrees that, in return for services, another shall be a partner with a profit-share only, the value of the profit-share is not income to the recipient. An implication to that effect, such as is relied on by taxpayer, would have to rest on the proposition that the regulation was meant to be all inclusive as to when gain or loss would be recognized or income would exist as a consequence of the contribution of property to a partnership and disposition of the partnership interests. It would have to appear, in order to sustain such implication, that the existence of income by reason of a creation of a profit-share, immediately having a determinable market value, in favor of a partner would be inconsistent with the result specified in the regulation.

We do not find this implication in our own reading of the regulation. It becomes necessary to consider the substantial consensus of commentators in favor of the principle claimed to be implied and to look to judicial interpretation, legislative history, administrative interpretation, and policy considerations to determine whether the implication is justified.

The Commentators: There is a startling degree of unanimity that the conferral of a profit-share as compensation for services is not income at the time of the conferral, although little by way of explanation of why this should be so, or analysis of statute or regulation to show that it is prescribed. * * *

* * *

Judicial Interpretation: [N]o decision cited by the parties or found by us appears squarely to reach the question * * *.

Legislative History: The legislative history is equivocal.

* * *

Administrative Interpretation: We are unaware of instances in which the Commissioner has asserted delinquencies where a taxpayer who received a profit-share with determinable market value in return for services failed to report the value as income, or has otherwise acted consistently with the Tax Court decision in Diamond. * * *

Consideration of partnership principles or practices: There must be wide variation in the degree to which a profit-share created in favor of a partner who has or will render service has determinable market value at the moment of creation. Surely in many if not the typical situations it will have only speculative value, if any.

In the present case, taxpayer's services had all been rendered, and the prospect of earnings from the real estate under Kargman's management was evidently very good. The profit-share had determinable market value.

If the present decision be sound, then the question will always arise, whenever a profit-share is created or augmented, whether it has a market value capable of determination. Will the existence of this question be unduly burdensome on those who choose to do business under the partnership form?

Each partner determines his income tax by taking into account his distributive share of the taxable income of the partnership. 26 U.S.C. § 702. Taxpayer's position here is that he was entitled to defer income taxation on the compensation for his services except as partnership earnings were realized. If a partner is taxed on the determinable market value of a profit-share at the time it is created in his favor, and is also taxed on his full share of earnings as realized, there will arguably be double taxation, avoidable by permitting him to amortize the value which was originally treated as income. Does the absence of a recognized procedure for amortization militate against the treatment of the creation of the profit-share as income?

Do the disadvantages of treating the creation of the profit-share as income in those instances where it has a determinable market value at that time outweigh the desirability of imposing a tax at the time the taxpayer has received an interest with determinable market value as compensation for services?

We think, of course, that the resolution of these practical questions makes clearly desirable the promulgation of appropriate regulations, to achieve a degree of certainty. But in the absence of regulation, we think it sound policy to defer to the expertise of the Commissioner and the Judges of the Tax Court, and to sustain their decision that the receipt of a profit-share with determinable market value is income.

* * *

The judgments of the Tax Court * * * are affirmed.

NOTE

For many years, the Diamond decision was perceived as an anomaly and the prevailing view was that the receipt of a profits interest does not trigger income. Then the Campbell decision, which follows, was rendered.

Campbell v. Commissioner

United States Tax Court, 1990.
59 T.C.M. 236, rev'd in part 943 F.2d 815 (8th Cir.1991).

■ SCOTT, JUDGE: * * *

FINDINGS OF FACT

* * *

During 1979 and 1980, * * * William G. Campbell (petitioner * * *) was employed by the Summa T. Group, a collection of affiliated entities which were primarily engaged in the formation and syndication of limited partnerships. Mr. Campbell performed most of his services for, and received compensation from, Summa T. Realty, Inc. (Summa T. Realty), a real estate brokerage and consulting firm which was a member of the Summa T. Group * * *. Mr. Campbell also served as vice president of Realty Properties Company (Realty Properties), a corporation organized under the laws of the State of Delaware which was also a member of the Summa T. Group. A man named David R. Kane served as the president of Realty Properties * * *.

* * *

[Mr. Campbell was] predominately responsible for locating suitable properties for Summa T. Realty, negotiating the acquisition of those properties, obtaining the financing necessary to acquire the properties, organizing the partnerships which would eventually acquire those properties, and assisting in the preparation of offering materials in connection with the syndication of those partnerships * * *.

Under [Mr. Campbell's compensation] arrangement, he was to receive 15 percent of the proceeds from each limited partnership syndication. In addition, for his services, Mr. Campbell was to obtain a "special limited partnership interest" in partnerships which he helped form and finance * * *.

* * *

Pursuant to this * * * compensation arrangement, Mr. Campbell received, in 1979, a 2–percent special limited partnership interest in Phillips House Associates, Ltd. (Phillips House * * *) in exchange for services he had rendered in the formation and syndication of the partnership. In 1980, petitioner received a 1–percent special limited partnership interest in The Grand, Ltd. (The Grand) and a 1–percent special limited partnership interest in Airport 1980, Ltd. (Airport) in exchange for services he had rendered in the formation and syndication of those partnerships. Realty Properties was the sole general partner of Phillips House, The Grand, and Airport. Mr. Kane also became a special limited partner in these three partnerships.

Phillips House

[Facts omitted]

The Grand

The Grand was organized * * * in November 1980 for the purpose of acquiring, improving, and operating a Howard Johnson's Motor Lodge (the Motel) which was located in Myrtle Beach, South Carolina with a view toward obtaining certain tax benefits. The Grand was to acquire the Motel, which was already in operation, * * * for approximately $11,125,000 * * *.

* * *

According to the original certificate of limited partnership, which had been filed on October 24, 1980, upon formation of The Grand, the sole general partner was Realty Properties and the sole limited partner was Mr. Campbell. * * * Mr. Campbell was required to contribute $150 in cash to The Grand in exchange for his interest * * *.

[Thirty-five] Class A limited partnership units in The Grand were offered for sale to investors [and all were sold] * * *. The purchase price of each partnership unit was $99,750 * * *.

Total capitalization of The Grand was projected to be $3,521,250, of which $3,491,250 was expected to be raised through sale of Class A limited partnership units in The Grand, $50,000 was to be contributed by Realty Properties, and $150 was to be contributed by each special limited partner * * *.

* * *

According to the offering memorandum, 97 percent of the profits and losses of The Grand were to be allocated to the Class A limited partners, 1 percent of the profits and losses were to be allocated to Realty Properties, and 1 percent of the profits and losses were to be allocated to each of the special limited partners, Mr. Campbell and Mr. Kane * * *.

* * *

According to projections contained within the offering memorandum, The Grand was expected to incur a taxable loss in each of the years 1980 through 1989. For example, in the taxable year ending December 31, 1980, The Grand was expected to incur a taxable loss in the amount of $1,173,072. This loss was, in large part, attributable to the deduction of consulting and management fees * * *. In addition, the projection reflects large deductions for interest expense and depreciation.

Each Class A limited partner's distributive share of The Grand's 1980 loss was projected to be $32,511 * * *. According to the figures contained in the offering memorandum, each of the remaining partners' (i.e., Mr. Campbell, Mr. Kane, and Realty Properties) distributive share of The Grand's 1980 loss would be approximately $11,737 * * *.

The offering memorandum for The Grand warned * * * that the partnership's positions with respect to certain deductions * * * were not based on settled interpretations of the tax laws and that the Internal Revenue Service might disallow any of the various deductions * * *. Nevertheless, the offering memorandum projected that each Class A limited partner would receive $246,259 in tax losses from his investment in The Grand and save approximately $123,128 in Federal income taxes (assuming his income from other sources was taxed at a rate of at least 50 percent) over the 10 taxable years for which projections were available (1980 through 1989) * * *. According to the figures contained in the offering memorandum, the remaining partners (i.e., Mr. Campbell, Mr. Kane, and Realty Properties) could each expect to receive tax losses totaling $88,902 * * *.

* * *

Airport

[Facts omitted]

[Mr. Campbell and his wife] did not report any income representing the value of the receipt of the special limited partnership interests in Phillips House, The Grand, or Airport * * *.

[R]espondent determined that petitioners should have included in income the value of the * * * interest[s] they received.

* * *

OPINION

Petitioners take the position that the interests Mr. Campbell received in Phillips House, The Grand, and Airport were merely interests in the profits of such partnerships and, as such, the value, if any, of these interests should not be included in petitioners' income in the year of receipt * * *.

Section 61(a) stated the general rule that:

Except as otherwise provided in this subtitle, gross income means all income from whatever source derived, including (but not limited to) the following items:

(1) Compensation for services, including fees, commissions, and similar items;

* * *

Thus, unless nonrecognition is provided for elsewhere, petitioners must include the value of the partnership interests which Mr. Campbell received in their income immediately upon receipt. Section 721(a) provides that no gain or loss is recognized to a partnership or the contributing partners, "in the case of a contribution of *property* to the partnership in exchange for an interest in the partnership." (Emphasis supplied.)

Despite the fact that section 721, by its own terms, applies only where the recipient of a partnership interest contributes property in exchange for such interest, petitioners argue that the regulations issued under section 721 have enlarged the scope of that section to also provide nonrecognition in situations where the contributing partner has contributed services, rather than property, in exchange for his partnership interest. Specifically, petitioners point to the language of section 1.721–1(b)(1), Income Tax Regs., which provides that:

Normally, under local law, each partner is entitled to be repaid his contributions of money or other property to the partnership * * *. To the extent that any of the partners gives up any part of his right to be repaid his contributions (*as distinguished from a share in partnership profits*) in favor of another partner as compensation for services (or in satisfaction of an obligation), section 721 does not apply. * * * [Emphasis supplied.]

Petitioners seize upon the language we have emphasized in the above-quoted regulation to support their argument that a distinction has been intentionally drawn in such regulation between situations in which a partner receives an interest in the capital of a partnership and situations in which a partner receives a mere profits interest. Petitioners argue that the former situation has been clearly excluded from nonrecognition treatment under section 721(a) while the latter situation has, by negative implication, been clearly singled out for nonrecognition treatment by the regulations.

We have previously addressed and rejected this same argument in Diamond v. Commissioner, [p. 427], a case with facts similar to those in the instant case. * * *

* * *

Petitioners state that our decision in the Diamond case * * * has been the subject of much criticism * * * and urge that * * * we reverse our holding in that case * * *.

We reject petitioners argument that we should no longer follow our decision in the Diamond case and reaffirm our holding that section 721(a) and the regulations thereunder are simply inapplicable where, as in the Diamond case and the instant case, a partner receives his partnership interest in exchange for services he has rendered to the partnership. In order to invoke the benefits of nonrecognition under section 721(a), the taxpayer must contribute "property" to the partnership in exchange for his partnership interest * * *.

The considerations which underlie section 721(a) nonrecognition treatment where a taxpayer receives a partnership interest in exchange for property are vastly different from those reasons advanced by petitioners in favor of section 721(a) nonrecognition treatment where a taxpayer receives a partnership interest in exchange for services. In the former situation, there has been no disposition of the contributed property. The partnership interest such partner receives represents a mere change in the form of an asset which the taxpayer already owns. In the latter situation, it represents compensation for services, the value of which has not previously been reported as income.

* * *

Putting aside for the moment the question of whether respondent could, by the issuance of regulations, significantly enlarge the scope of this clearly worded statute, we conclude that the language of section 1.721–1(b)(1), Income Tax Regs., does not lead to the result advanced by petitioners. As we noted in Diamond, section 1.721–1(b)(1), Income Tax Regs., is unartfully drafted, but this fact does not require an interpretation of the statute contrary to its clear words.

In the instant case, we conclude from the evidence that petitioner received his interests in Phillips House, The Grand, and Airport in exchange for prior services. Those services included locating suitable properties for his employer, negotiating the acquisition of those properties, organizing the limited partnerships which would eventually acquire those properties, and assisting in the preparation of offering materials in connection with the syndication of these limited partnerships. The records of the partnerships as shown in their respective returns of income show that Mr. Campbell acquired his interest in each partnership after the rendering of these services * * *. [T]he instant transaction is not within the scope of section 721(a).

In our view, the determination of when Mr. Campbell should be required to include in income the value of the partnership interests he received in Phillips House, The Grand, and Airport is governed by section 83. Under section 83, if property is transferred to any person in connection with the performance of services, the person who performed the services is required to include in income the fair market value of such property (less any amounts which were paid for such property) in the first taxable year in which such property becomes transferable or is not subject to a substantial risk of forfeiture, whichever occurs first. Thus, the operation of section 83 requires inclusion in income of the value of property transferred if three factors are present. [First, the thing transferred in connection with the performance of services must be "property" as that term is used in section

83. Second, such property must be transferred in connection with the performance of services. Third, either the property transferred must be transferable by the recipient or the property transferred must not be subject to a substantial risk of forfeiture. The court found that all three factors were present with respect to each of the three partnership interests.]

* * *

Since we conclude that the value of the special limited partnership interests which Mr. Campbell received in connection with his performance of services for his employer should have been included in petitioners' income under section 83, it is necessary to determine the fair market value of such interests. In his notice of deficiency, respondent valued Mr. Campbell's 2–percent special limited partnership interest in Phillips House at $42,084, his 1–percent special limited partnership interest in The Grand at $16,818, and his 1–percent special limited partnership interest in Airport at $20,683 * * *.

On brief, respondent * * * determined the value of each special limited partnership interest by discounting the future value of the tax benefits and cash distributions which, according to the projections contained in each partnership's offering memorandum, Mr. Campbell would be entitled to receive from the inception of the partnerships until liquidation. * * * On brief, respondent asks that we find as ultimate facts that, as of the time the interests which Mr. Campbell received had vested, his interest in Phillips House had a fair market value of approximately $67,000, his interest in The Grand had a fair market value of approximately $30,000, and his interest in Airport had a fair market value of approximately $19,000.

Petitioners object to respondent's valuations. Initially, petitioners claim that the value of each of the special limited partnership interests was so speculative that the interests should not be included in their income at all * * *.

Petitioners further contend that, even if the special limited partnership interests are capable of valuation, their value is far less than the values advanced by respondent in his notice of deficiency or on brief. In support of this contention, petitioners point to the testimony and appraisal reports of Mr. Steven Blumreich, an expert on valuation of intangible assets, who appraised each of Mr. Campbell's interests and testified on petitioners' behalf at trial * * *.

[M]r. Blumreich determined that the present value of the projected cash distributions of Phillips House, The Grand, and Airport were $8,407, $1,692, and $4,207, respectively. Although Mr. Blumreich acknowledged the existence of substantial tax benefits, he assigned no value to these tax benefits because, according to the partnership offering memorandums, there was a substantial risk that such benefits would be eliminated if the partnerships were audited by respondent.

[T]aking into account [various other] factors, Mr. Blumreich without further explanation determined that each of the special limited partnership units was worth no more than $1,000 upon its receipt.

According to section 83, a taxpayer must include in income the fair market value of property transferred in connection with services * * *.

The term "fair market value" generally refers to the price at which property would change hands between a willing buyer and a willing seller, neither being under any compulsion to buy or sell and both having reasonable knowledge of relevant facts. The determination of fair market value is an inherently imprecise process.

* * *

We * * * reject outright Mr. Blumreich's characterization of the value of each partnership interest as merely de minimis. Mr. Blumreich committed several errors in evaluating the benefits to which petitioners were entitled. For example, Mr. Blumreich erred in failing to assign any value at all to the tax benefits inherent in each special limited partnership interest, even though he clearly recognized that the tax benefits comprised a major portion of the benefits which Mr. Campbell, as well as the limited partners who purchased their interests, received. In 1979 and 1980 alone, petitioners utilized on their returns approximately $54,704 in tax losses * * * from the partnerships.

It is true that some of the items that generated these losses were questionable. However, the Class A limited partners were willing to pay substantial amounts for these very same tax losses despite the chance that some of them might be disallowed * * *.

* * *

On the other hand, we also find respondent's valuation of Mr. Campbell's special limited partnership interests to be flawed primarily by the discount rate he used * * *.

* * *

Respondent and petitioners' expert used the same method of valuing the interests petitioners received except for respondent's use of too low a discount rate and petitioners' failure to include in the value of the interests the tax benefits which petitioners anticipated receiving. We accept the method used by the parties. We conclude that the value of the tax benefits should be included in making the valuation but that the discount rate used by petitioners' expert should be applied since it is more realistic than the discount rate used by respondent.

[We conclude that the fair market value of the interest petitioner received in Phillips House was $25,000, in The Grand was $16,818 and in Airport was $15,000 and that these amounts should have been included in gross income in the year of receipt.]

NOTE

The Campbell decision shocked the legal community because of the prevailing view that the receipt of a profits interest does not trigger income. Rumor had it that the case even shocked high level Internal Revenue Service officials who may not have been aware of the litigation. Campbell was subsequently reversed on appeal. Campbell v. Commissioner, 943 F.2d 815 (8th Cir.1991). On appeal, the I.R.S. *conceded* "that the Tax Court erred in holding that the receipt of a profits interest in exchange for services to the partnership should be considered ordinary income to the service provider." Id. at 818. The Internal Revenue Service argued on appeal that Campbell in fact provided services to his corporate employer (rather than to the partnership) but the appellate court rejected that argument. After the Eighth Circuit's Campbell decision, the Internal Revenue Service further defused the controversy surrounding the receipt of a profits interest by issuing Revenue Procedure 93–27, which follows.

Revenue Procedure 93–27

1993–2 Cum.Bull. 343.

PURPOSE

This revenue procedure provides guidance on the treatment of the receipt of a partnership profits interest for services provided to or for the benefit of the partnership.

DEFINITIONS

The following definitions apply for purposes of this revenue procedure.

.01 A capital interest is an interest that would give the holder a share of the proceeds if the partnership's assets were sold at fair market value and then the proceeds were distributed in a complete liquidation of the partnership. This determination generally is made at the time of receipt of the partnership interest.

.02 A profits interest is a partnership interest other than a capital interest.

BACKGROUND

Under section 1.721–1(b)(1) of the Income Tax Regulations, the receipt of a partnership capital interest for services provided to or for the benefit of the partnership is taxable as compensation. On the other hand, the issue of whether the receipt of a partnership profits interest for services is taxable has been the subject of litigation. Most recently, in Campbell v. Commissioner, 943 F.2d 815 (8th Cir.1991), the Eighth Circuit in dictum suggested that the taxpayer's receipt of a partnership profits interest received for services was not taxable, but decided the case on valuation. Other courts have determined that in certain circumstances the receipt of a partnership profits interest for services is a taxable event under section 83 of the Internal Revenue Code. See, e.g., Campbell v. Commissioner, 59 T.C.M.

236, rev'd, 943 F.2d 815 (8th Cir.1991); St. John v. United States, No. 82–1134 (C.D.Ill. Nov.16, 1983). The courts have also found that typically the profits interest received has speculative or no determinable value at the time of receipt. See Campbell, 943 F.2d at 823; St. John. In Diamond v. Commissioner, 56 T.C. 530 (1971), aff'd, 492 F.2d 286 (7th Cir.1974), however, the court assumed that the interest received by the taxpayer was a partnership profits interest and found the value of the interest was readily determinable. In that case, the interest was sold soon after receipt.

APPLICATION

.01 Other than as provided below, if a person receives a profits interest for the provision of services to or for the benefit of a partnership in a partner capacity or in anticipation of being a partner, the Internal Revenue Service will not treat the receipt of such an interest as a taxable event for the partner or the partnership.

.02 This revenue procedure does not apply:

(1) If the profits interest relates to a substantially certain and predictable stream of income from partnership assets, such as income from high-quality debt securities or a high-quality net lease;

(2) If within two years of receipt, the partner disposes of the profits interest; or

(3) If the profits interest is a limited partnership interest in a "publicly traded partnership" within the meaning of section 7704(b) of the Internal Revenue Code.

NOTES

1. *Justification for exceptions.* What are the possible justifications for the three exceptions to tax-free treatment set forth in Revenue Procedure 93–27?

2. *Right answer.* What tax consequences should follow from the receipt of a profits interest in a partnership in exchange for the performance of services? Is nonrecognition a relevant concept? See I.R.C. §§ 61(a)(3), 1001(a). How can the value of a profits interest in a partnership be determined?

3. *Transfer to existing partnership.* Do not assume that I.R.C. § 721 applies only when a new partnership is formed. Treas. Reg. § 1.721–1(a) provides that I.R.C. § 721, "applies whether the contribution is made to a partnership in the process of formation or to a partnership which is already formed and operating."

4. *Investment company limitation.* Section 721(a) does not apply to gain realized on a transfer of property to a partnership which would be treated as an "investment company" if the partnership were a corporation. I.R.C. § 721(b). For a discussion of the "investment company" limitation, see p. 389, Note 4.

2. BASIS AS GAIN/LOSS PRESERVATION MECHANISM

I.R.C. §§ 722, 723

Treas. Reg. §§ 1.722–1, 1.723–1

Nonrecognition rules generally are designed to defer, rather than eliminate, any gain or loss. Deferral is accomplished by perpetuating the basis associated with the property immediately before the transfer occurred. When a person transfers property to a partnership in a transaction that qualifies for nonrecognition treatment, the potential gain (or loss) that exists before the transfer is transformed into two potential gains (or losses). After the transfer, the gain (or loss) is preserved at the partner level because the transferor takes an exchanged basis in the partnership interest received (i.e., the transferor's basis in the property attaches to the partnership interest). I.R.C. §§ 722, 7701(a)(44). In addition, the gain or loss is preserved at the partnership level because the partnership takes a transferred basis in the property it receives (i.e., the transferor's basis in the property remains attached to the property now held by the partnership). I.R.C. §§ 723, 7701(a)(43).

> *Example 10–B (Gain (or loss) preserved at both partner level and partnership level)*: Aaron, Brenda, and Calvin form the ABC Partnership and each receives a one-third interest in capital, profits, and losses. Aaron transfers operating assets with a value of $500,000 and a basis of $200,000 in exchange for his partnership interest. Brenda transfers a building with a value of $500,000 and a basis of $600,000 in exchange for her partnership interest. Calvin transfers $500,000 of money for his partnership interest.
>
> (a) Aaron realizes a $300,000 gain on the exchange of the operating assets for his partnership interest but does not recognize the gain. Brenda realizes a $100,000 loss on the exchange of the building for her partnership interest but does not recognize the loss. I.R.C. § 721(a).
>
> (b) Aaron takes a $200,000 basis in his partnership interest, Brenda takes a $600,000 basis in her partnership interest, and Calvin takes a $500,000 basis in his partnership interest. I.R.C. § 722.
>
> (c) The partnership takes a $200,000 basis in the operating assets transferred by Aaron and a $600,000 basis in the building transferred by Brenda. I.R.C. § 723.
>
> (d) A $300,000 unrealized gain now exists in both Aaron's partnership interest[1] and the partnership's operating assets.[2]
>
> (e) A $100,000 unrealized loss now exists in both Brenda's partnership interest[3] and the partnership's building.[4]

---

1. The partnership interest received by Aaron has a value of $500,000 (one-third interest in partnership with assets worth $1,500,000) and a basis of $200,000.

2. The operating assets have a value of $500,000 and a basis of $200,000.

3. The partnership interest received by Brenda has a value of $500,000 (one-third interest in partnership with assets worth $1,500,000) and a basis of $600,000.

4. The building has a value of $500,000 and a basis of $600,000.

Although the transfer of appreciated property to a partnership creates two potential gains, it is unlikely that both gains will be taxed.

Problem 10–1: In Example 10–B, assume that Aaron, Brenda and Calvin formed the partnership and transferred the properties on December 30 of Year 5. Also assume that the partnership has no "unrealized receivables" or "substantially appreciated inventory." What are the tax consequences to all parties of each of the following alternatives?

(a) *(No gain triggered)*: On December 31 of Year 5, the partnership transfers its operating assets back to Aaron in exchange for his partnership interest. See I.R.C. §§ 731(b), 731(a), 732(b).

(b) *(Partnership level gain triggered)*: On December 31 of Year 5, the partnership sells its operating assets for $500,000 and transfers the money to Aaron in exchange for his partnership interest. See I.R.C. §§ 1001, 704(c)(1)(A), 705(a)(1)(A), 731(a).

(c) *(Partner level gain triggered)*: On December 31 of Year 5, Aaron sells his partnership interest to Juliet for $500,000. See I.R.C. §§ 1001, 743, 754.

When property with a basis in excess of value is transferred to a partnership, two potential losses exist. The contributing partner takes an exchanged basis in the partnership interest (thereby preserving the loss at the partner level) and the partnership takes a transferred basis in the contributed property (thereby preserving the loss at the partnership level). See I.R.C. §§ 722, 723. The potential partnership level loss, however, can be allocated only to the partner who contributed the loss property. I.R.C. § 704(c)(1)(A). (For allocations to all the other partners, the partnership's basis in the loss property is limited to its fair market value at the time of the contribution. I.R.C.§ 704(c)(1)(C).) As Problem 10–2 will demonstrate, when either of the two potential losses is triggered, the other one is eliminated.

Problem 10–2: In Example 10–B, assume that Aaron, Brenda and Calvin formed the partnership and transferred the properties on December 30 of Year 5. Also assume that the partnership has no "unrealized receivables" or "substantially appreciated inventory." What are the tax consequences to all parties of each of the following alternatives?

(a) *(No loss triggered)*: On December 31 of Year 5, the partnership transfers the building back to Brenda in exchange for her partnership interest. See I.R.C. §§ 731(b), 731(a), 732(b).

(b) *(Partnership level loss triggered)*: On December 31 of Year 5, the partnership sells the building for $500,000 and transfers the money to Brenda in exchange for her partnership interest. See I.R.C. §§ 1001, 704(c)(1)(A), 705(a)(2)(A), 731(a). Does it make any difference if the partnership sells the building back to Brenda for $500,000? See I.R.C. § 707(b)(1)(A).

(c) *(Partner level loss triggered):* On December 31 of Year 5, Brenda sells her partnership interest to Denise for $500,000. See I.R.C. §§ 1001, 704(c)(1)(C), 743, 754.

3. Assignment of Income

Schneer v. Commissioner

United States Tax Court, 1991.
97 T.C. 643.

■ Gerber, Judge: * * *

FINDINGS OF FACT

* * *

Stephen B. Schneer (hereinafter petitioner * * *), was a practicing attorney * * *. Until February 25, 1983, petitioner was an associate with the law firm of Ballon, Stoll & Itzler (BSI). BSI was a partnership. * * *. Petitioner's financial arrangement with BSI consisted of a fixed * * * salary and a percentage of any fees which arose from clients petitioner brought or referred to the firm.

* * * When petitioner left BSI he had an understanding that he would continue to receive his percentage of fees which arose from clients he had referred when he was an associate with BSI. Petitioner was expected to consult regarding clients he referred to BSI and whose fees were to be shared by petitioner. Petitioner would have become entitled to his percentage of the fees even if he had not been called upon to consult.

After petitioner left BSI and while he was a partner of two other law partnerships * * * he consulted on numerous occasions concerning BSI clients. * * *

Late in February 1983, petitioner became a partner in the law firm of Bandler & Kass (B & K), and on August 1, 1985, petitioner became a partner in the law firm of Sylvor, Schneer, Gold & Morelli (SSG & M). BSI, B & K, SSG & M, and petitioner, at all pertinent times, kept their books and reported their income on the cash method of accounting. * * * The agreement between the partners of B & K was that each partner would receive a percentage of the partnership profits derived from all fees received beginning the date the partner joined the partnership. In addition, petitioner agreed to turn over to the partnership all legal fees received after joining the partnership, regardless of whether the fees were earned in the partnership's name * * *. The same agreement existed between the partners of SSG & M, including petitioner.

During 1984 and 1985, BSI remitted $21,329 and $10,585 to petitioner. The amounts represented petitioner's percentage of fees from BSI clients that he had referred to BSI at a time when he was an associate with BSI.

[A]ll of the fees received during 1984 and 1985 were for work performed after petitioner left BSI. Petitioner, pursuant to his agreements with B & K and SSG & M, turned those amounts over to the appropriate partnership. B & K and SSG & M, in turn, treated the amounts as partnership income which was distributed to each partner (including petitioner) according to the partner's percentage share of partnership profits.

* * *

OPINION

[T]here is agreement that the amounts paid to petitioner by his former employer-law firm are income in the year of receipt. The question is whether petitioner (individually) or the partners of petitioner's partnerships (including petitioner) should report the income in their respective shares.

The parties have couched the issue in terms of the anticipatory assignment-of-income principles. See Lucas v. Earl, 281 U.S. 111 (1930). Equally important to this case, however, is the viability of the principle that partners may pool their earnings and report partnership income in amounts different from their contribution to the pool. See sec. 704(a) and (b). The parties' arguments bring into focus potential conflict between these two principles and compel us to address both.

First, we examine the parties' arguments with respect to the assignment-of-income doctrine. Respondent argues that petitioner earned the income in question before leaving BSI, despite the fact that petitioner did not receive that income until he was a partner in B & K and, later, SSG & M. According to respondent, by entering into partnership agreements requiring payment of all legal fees to his new partnerships, petitioner anticipatorily assigned to those partnerships the income earned but not yet received from BSI.

* * *

Petitioner contends that the income in question was not earned until after he left BSI and joined B & K and SSG & M. He argues that the income received from BSI is reportable by the partners of the B & K and SSG & M partnerships (including petitioner) in their respective shares.
* * *

* * *

The transaction under consideration is one where petitioner had an agreement under which he would receive a percentage of fees received by BSI from clients who were referred by petitioner while he was an employee of BSI. Inherent in petitioner's unconditional right to payment is the condition precedent that billable services have been performed for the referred client. Additionally, petitioner's right to payment may also be subject to a second condition precedent that he may be required to consult and be involved in performing the services to be billed. Finally, there is the conditional aspect of payment. If the referred client does not pay for services rendered, then petitioner will not receive his percentage.

* * *

[W]e hold that petitioner had not earned the fees in question prior to leaving BSI * * *. More specifically, we hold that petitioner earned the income in question while a partner of a partnership to which he had agreed to pay such income. * * *

Two additional related questions remain for our consideration. First, respondent argues that irrespective of when petitioner earned the income from BSI, "there was no relationship * * * [between] the past activity of introducing a client to * * * [BSI], and the petitioner's work as a partner with * * * [B & K or SSG & M]." According to respondent, petitioner should not be allowed to characterize as partnership income fees that did not have a requisite or direct relationship to a partnership's business. * * * Second, while we generally hold that petitioner did not make an assignment of income already earned, the possibility that this was an assignment of unearned income was not foreclosed.

These final two questions bring into focus the true nature of the potential conflict in this case * * *. Both questions, in their own way, ask whether any partnership agreement—under which partners agree in advance to turn over to the partnership all income from their individual efforts—can survive scrutiny under the assignment-of-income principles.

Rev. Rul. 64–90, 1964–1 (Part 1) C.B. at 226–227, in pertinent part, contains the following:

* * *

In the instant case, several individuals formed a partnership for the purpose of engaging in the general practice of law. Aside from the partnership business, each of the partners has performed services from time to time in his individual capacity and not as a partner. The several partners have always regarded the fees received for such services as compensation to the recipient as an individual.

The partnership * * * uses the cash receipts and disbursements method of accounting * * *.

It is proposed to amend the partnership agreement * * * to provide that all compensation received by the partners be paid over to the partnership immediately upon receipt.

The question in the instant case is whether compensation remitted to the partnership pursuant to this provision will constitute partnership income.

* * *

In the instant case, the general practice of the partnership consists of rendering legal advice and services. Consequently, fees received by a partner for similar services performed in his individual capacity will be considered as partnership income if paid to the partnership in accor-

dance with the agreement. Those fees need not be reported separately by the partner on his individual return. However, the partner's distributive share of the partnership's taxable income which he must report on his individual return will include a portion of such fees.

[Emphasis supplied.]

A key requirement of this ruling is that the services for which fees are received by individual partners must be similar to those normally performed by the partnership. * * * Cases dealing with similar partnership agreement situations have also enforced this requirement. Respondent now attempts to add to this requirement by arguing that the fees here in question were earned through activity, which was admittedly legal work, but was not sufficiently related to the work of petitioner's new partnerships. In other words, respondent argues that the income here was earned in BSI's business activity and not B & K's or SSG & M's business activity.

* * *

[P]etitioner's * * * referral fee income was clearly earned through activities "within the ambit" of the business of his new partnerships. Their business was the practice of law as was petitioner's consulting activity for BSI. His work was incident to the conduct of the business of his partnerships. We decline to adopt respondent's more narrow characterization of the business of petitioner's new partnerships. Neither the case law nor respondent's rulings support such a characterization.

Thus, we arrive at the final question in this case. We have already held that petitioner had not yet earned * * * the income in question when he joined his new partnerships. Additionally, petitioner's fee income from his BSI clients qualifies, under the case law and respondent's rulings, as income generated by services sufficiently related to the business conducted by petitioner's new partnerships. If we decide that petitioner's partnerships should report the income in question, petitioner would be [taxed] only to the extent of his respective partnership share. This would allow petitioner, through his partnership agreements with B & K and SSG & M, to assign income not yet earned from BSI. Thus, the case law and respondent's rulings permit (without explanation), in a partnership setting, the type of assignment addressed by Lucas v. Earl, 281 U.S. 111 (1930).[5] We must reconcile the principle behind Rev. Rul. 64–90, 1964–1 C.B. (Part 1) 226, with Lucas v. Earl. The question is whether income not yet earned and anticipatorily assigned under certain partnership agreements are [beyond] the reach of the assignment-of-income principle.

The Internal Revenue Code of 1954 provided the first comprehensive statutory scheme for the tax treatment of partners and partnerships. No section of the 1954 Code, successive amendments or acts, nor the legislative

---

5. Editor's note. In Lucas v. Earl, the Supreme Court held that income from the taxpayer-husband's law practice was taxable to him, even though he and his wife had entered into a valid contract under State law to split all income not yet earned by each of them. Because the assignor could refuse to perform services, he had control over income yet to be earned.

history specifically addresses the treatment of income earned by partners in their individual capacity but which is pooled with other partnership income. It is implicit in subchapter K, however, that the pooling of income and losses of partners was intended by Congress. This question is more easily answered where the partnership contracts with the client for services which are then performed by the partner. The question becomes more complex where the partner contracts and performs the services when he is a partner.

* * *

The fundamental theme penned by Justice Holmes [in Lucas v. Earl] provides that the individual who earns income is liable for the tax. It is obvious that the partnership, as an abstract entity, does not provide the physical and mental activity that facilitates the process of ''earning'' income. Only a partner can do so. The income earned is turned over to the partnership due solely to a contractual agreement, i.e., an assignment, in advance, of income.

The pooling of income is essential to the meaningful existence of subchapter K. If partners were not able to share profits in an amount disproportionate to the ratio in which they earned the underlying income, the partnership provisions of the Code would, to some extent, be rendered unnecessary.

The provisions of subchapter K tacitly imply that the pooling of income is permissible. Said implication may provide sufficient reason to conclude that a partnership should be treated as an entity for the purpose of pooling the income of its partners. Under an entity approach, the income would be considered that of the partnership rather than the partner, even though the partner's individual efforts may have earned the income. If the partnership is treated as an entity earning the income, then assignment-of-income concepts would not come into play.

* * *

The theory concerning partnerships as entities is not easily defined. It is well established that the partnership form is a hybrid—part separate entity, part aggregate. The difficulty lies in deciding whether a particular set of circumstances relate to one end or the other of the partnership hybrid spectrum. * * *

* * *

The entity concept as it relates to partnerships is based, in part, on the concept that a partner may further the business of the partnership by performing services in the name of the partnership or individually. The name and reputation of a professional partnership plays a role in the financial success of the partnership business. If the partners perform services in the name of the partnership or individually they are, nonetheless, associated with the partnership as a partner. This is the very essence of a professional service partnership, because each partner, although acting individually, is furthering the business of the partnership. * * * The lack of structure inherent in the partnership form does not lend itself to easy

resolution of the assignment-of-income question. A partnership's characteristics do, however, militate in favor of treating a partner's income from
services performed in an individual capacity, which are contractually obligated to the partnership for allocation in accord with the pre-established
distributive shares, in the same manner as income earned through partnership engagement.

Accordingly, in circumstances where individuals are not joining in a
venture merely to avoid the effect of Lucas v. Earl, it is appropriate to treat
income earned by partners individually, as income earned by the partnership entity, i.e., partnership income, to be allocated to partners in their
respective shares. To provide the essential continuity necessary for the use
of an entity concept in the partnership setting, the income should be
earned from an activity which can reasonably be associated with the
partnership's business activity.

There is no apparent attempt to avoid the incidence of tax by the
formation or operation of the partnerships in this case. Petitioner, in
performing legal work for clients of another firm, was a partner with the
law firms of B & K and SSG & M. In view of the foregoing, we hold that
* * * the fee income from BSI was correctly returned by the two partnerships in accord with the respective partnership agreements.

    * * *

■ HALPERN, J., dissenting. The majority perceives a conflict between the
anticipatory assignment-of-income doctrine, see Lucas v. Earl, and the
principle that partners may pool their earnings and report partnership
income in amounts different from their contribution to the pool. With
respect, I believe the conflict to be illusory * * *.

According to the majority, the mere redistribution of income within a
partnership is inconsistent with the assignment-of-income doctrine. * * *

[The majority's] analysis wholly ignores the doctrine of agency. When a
partner, acting as agent for the partnership, performs services for a client,
the partnership is the earner of the income: the instrumentality (in this
case the partner) through which the partnership has earned its fee is of no
consequence. Therefore, the focus of the anticipatory assignment-of-income
analysis ought to be on whether the partner acted for himself individually
or as agent of the partnership. This is entirely consistent with the latitude
accorded partnerships to disproportionately distribute partnership income:
the pertinent requirement is merely that the partnership income so distributed have been earned by the partnership. In this case, it is quite clear that
petitioner earned the fees in question pursuant to an agreement he entered
into, on his own behalf, with Ballon, Stoll & Itzler—an agreement that was
consummated before petitioner's relationship with Bandler & Kass. Consequently, petitioner is the true earner of the income and should not escape
taxation by means of an anticipatory assignment.

The majority's "resolution" of the perceived conflict is unsatisfactory.
The majority considers the determinative question to be whether the
income is "of a type normally earned by the partnership. * * * " Thus, the

majority would allow a partner to assign fees to the partnership if the work performed for such fees is similar to that performed by the partnership, but not if the work is different.

The majority's distinction is unprincipled.[6] The majority observes that "The name and reputation of a professional partnership plays a role in the financial success of a partnership business" suggesting that partners, even acting individually, can further the business of the partnership by adding to its reputation. But, that may be so even if the partner acts individually, doing work entirely dissimilar to that normally performed by the partnership. In any event, the majority fails to explain why such an obviously incidental benefit to the partnership should permit us to frustrate the assignment-of-income doctrine. The majority asserts that: "The lack of structure inherent in the partnership form does not lend itself to easy resolution of the assignment-of-income question." * * * The lack of structure of the partnership form is irrelevant. All that matters is whether the partner has acted on his own behalf or on behalf, and as agent of, the partnership. Moreover, even if the lack of structure were relevant, the majority fails to explain why such would mandate the distinction between the type of income normally earned by the partnership and the type of income that is not. It would make far more sense to ask, with agency principles in mind, whether the income in question was earned by the partnership or by the partner acting as an individual.

  * * *

NOTE

Motivation for the litigation. If the Internal Revenue Service had prevailed in the Schneer case, is it likely that Schneer's underpayment of tax would have deviated significantly from his partners' overpayment?

a. ALLOCATION OF PRE–CONTRIBUTION GAIN OR LOSS

I.R.C. § 704(c)(1)(A)

The nonrecognition rule that applies to the transfer of property to a partnership defers any gain or loss that accrued before the property was contributed. See I.R.C. § 721(a). The transferred basis rule of I.R.C. § 723 generally preserves that gain or loss while the property is held by the partnership. Partners are normally permitted to allocate partnership gain or loss among themselves by agreement, provided that the allocation has substantial economic effect. I.R.C. § 704(b); see pp. 153–173. If the partners were permitted to allocate the gain or loss recognized when the partnership sells contributed property, the partners might agree to an allocation that would shift the gain or loss that accrued *before* the property

---

6. The majority fails to explain why the similarity of the work done by the partner to earn the fees to the work of the partnership is determinative. That failure not only casts doubt upon the correctness of this decision, but foreshadows the difficulty future courts will have in resolving the question: how similar is similar enough? Without any inkling of why similarity has been deemed important, future courts will lack any effective guidelines for answering that question.

was contributed away from the contributing partner. To avoid this result, I.R.C. § 704(c)(1)(A) mandates the allocation of any pre-contribution gain or loss to the contributing partner. Any additional gain or loss accruing after the property is contributed, however, may be allocated according to the partnership agreement, provided that the allocation has substantial economic effect. See I.R.C. § 704(b).

> *Problem 10–3 (Impact of transfer on the taxpayer)*: Clara owns and operates a jewelry store as a sole proprietorship. Durwood, her land-lord, wishes to share Clara's business with her. The parties form a limited liability company (LLC) on January 1 of Year 5. The LLC is classified as a partnership under Treas. Reg. § 301.7701–3. Clara transfers jewelry to the LLC with a value of $400,000 and a basis of $300,000, and other assets with a value of $100,000 and a basis of $200,000. Durwood transfers a building to the LLC which has a value of $500,000 and a basis of $400,000. Clara and Durwood agree to allocate all items of the LLC's gain or loss 50% to Clara and 50% to Durwood (other than items governed by I.R.C. § 704(c)(1)(A)). What are the tax consequences to Clara and Durwood if,
>
> (a) the jewelry contributed by Clara is eventually sold for $600,000?
>
> (b) the jewelry contributed by Clara is eventually sold for $200,000?
>
> (c) the other assets contributed by Clara are eventually sold for $50,000?
>
> (d) the other assets contributed by Clara are eventually sold for $300,000?

A sale of contributed property need not occur for I.R.C. § 704(c)(1)(A) to apply. For example, when depreciable property with a value in excess of basis is contributed to a partnership, I.R.C. § 704(c)(1)(A) normally causes a disproportionate amount of subsequent depreciation deductions to be allocated *away from* the contributing partner. The intention is to bestow a compensatory tax benefit on the other partners to neutralize the built-in tax burden associated with the contributed property. To the extent that I.R.C. § 704(c)(1)(A) shifts depreciation deductions away from the contrib-uting partner, the amount of gain to which that same section will apply on a subsequent sale of the property is correspondingly reduced.

> *Example 10–C (Impact of § 704(c)(1)(A) on depreciation deductions)*: Elizabeth contributes depreciable property with a value of $8,000 and an adjusted basis of $4,000 and Franco contributes $8,000 of money to the EF Partnership. The partnership agreement allocates all items of partnership gain or loss 50% to Elizabeth and 50% to Franco (other than items governed by I.R.C. § 704(c)(1)(A)). The partnership takes a $4,000 basis in the depreciable property contributed by Elizabeth. I.R.C. § 723. Therefore, Elizabeth appears to be transferring $4,000 of potential gain to the partnership. If the partnership immediately sells the property for $8,000, however, the $4,000 gain is allocated entirely to Elizabeth. See I.R.C. § 704(c)(1)(A).

Rather than selling the depreciable property contributed by Elizabeth, assume that the partnership holds the property and is allowed $4,000 of depreciation deductions. In these circumstances, I.R.C. § 704(c)(1)(A) may neutralize the $4,000 gain that Elizabeth transferred to the partnership by allocating the partnership's depreciation deductions entirely to Franco. After the $4,000 of depreciation deductions are allocated to Franco, I.R.C. § 704(c)(1)(A) no longer controls the allocation of any part of the gain recognized by the partnership on a subsequent sale of the property. Rather, any gain triggered by a sale of the property is allocated between the partners pursuant to the partnership agreement (50% to each partner), assuming that the allocation has substantial economic effect. See I.R.C. § 704(b).

The regulations permit a partnership to use any "reasonable method" that is consistent with the purpose of I.R.C. § 704(c) for allocating items under I.R.C. § 704(c)(1)(A). See Treas. Reg. § 1.704–3. The regulations also describe certain reasonable allocation methods. The least complicated allocation method described in the regulations often prevents I.R.C. § 704(c)(1)(A) from neutralizing the tax burdens in contributed property held by the partnership. For example, impediments often exist to allocating sufficient depreciation deductions away from a partner who contributes appreciated property. Other allocation methods better achieve the goals of I.R.C. § 704(c)(1)(A) but can be very complicated to apply.

NOTES

1. *Impact on Schneer.* What impact, if any, could I.R.C. § 704(c)(1)(A) have on the taxpayer in the Schneer case (p. 442)?

2. *Preservation of income in substituted partnership interest.* When I.R.C. § 721(a) applies to the transfer of property to a partnership, any gain or loss in the property is preserved at the partner level by the exchanged basis rule of I.R.C. § 722. Hence, a partner who transfers appreciated property to a partnership would not rid herself of the potential gain, even in the absence of I.R.C. § 704(c)(1)(A). Does I.R.C. § 704(c)(1)(A) achieve any goals that are not already accomplished by I.R.C. § 722?

b.   DISTRIBUTION OF CONTRIBUTED PROPERTY

I.R.C. § 704(c)(1)(B)

Treas. Reg. §§ 1.704–4(a)(1)–(4), (5) Ex. 1; –4(b), (e), (f)(1)

For I.R.C. § 704(c)(1)(A) to be effective, the property contributed to the partnership must either be disposed of in a taxable transaction or held by the partnership for a long enough period to make compensatory allocations. If, instead, the contributed property is distributed, a distribution is not normally treated as a taxable disposition (I.R.C. § 731(b)) and I.R.C. § 704(c)(1)(A) no longer applies to the property after the distribution occurs. Thus, in the absence of a special rule, I.R.C. § 704(c)(1)(A) could be avoided if the partnership distributed the contributed property.

To prevent distributions from serving as an escape route from I.R.C. § 704(c)(1)(A), Congress enacted I.R.C. § 704(c)(1)(B). That provision applies when contributed property is distributed, within seven years of the contribution, to a partner other than the contributing partner. When such a distribution is made, the contributing partner must recognize the same gain or loss that he would have recognized under I.R.C. § 704(c)(1)(A) if the contributed property had been sold for an amount equal to its fair market value at the time of the distribution. See I.R.C. § 704(c)(1)(B).

> *Problem 10–4 (Distribution to non-contributing partner)*: Clara operates a jewelry store as a sole proprietorship. Durwood, her landlord, wishes to share Clara's business with her. On January 1 of Year 5, the parties form a limited liability company (LLC). The LLC is classified as a partnership under Treas. Reg. § 301.7701–3. Clara transfers jewelry to the LLC with a value of $400,000 and a basis of $300,000, and other non-depreciable assets with a value of $100,000 and a basis of $200,000. Durwood transfers a building to the LLC which has a value of $500,000 and a basis of $400,000. Clara and Durwood agree to allocate all items of the LLC's gain or loss 50% to Clara and 50% to Durwood (other than items governed by I.R.C. § 704(c)(1)(A)). What are the tax consequences to Clara and Durwood if, on January 1 of Year 9,
>
> (a) the jewelry contributed by Clara is distributed to Durwood when its value is $600,000?
>
> (b) the jewelry contributed by Clara is distributed to Durwood when its value is $200,000?
>
> (c) the other assets contributed by Clara are distributed to Durwood when their value is $50,000?
>
> (d) the other assets contributed by Clara are distributed to Durwood when their value is $300,000?
>
> Do any of the answers change if the distribution does not occur until January 1 of Year 13?

4.   CHARACTERIZATION ISSUES

I.R.C. § 724

I.R.C. § 724 restricts the ability of a partner to change the characterization of certain property by contributing the property to a partnership. When a partner contributes an "unrealized receivable" to a partnership, any gain or loss recognized by the partnership on a disposition of the property is characterized as ordinary income or ordinary loss, even if the property is held by the partnership as a capital asset. See I.R.C. §§ 724(a), (d)(1). When a partner contributes an "inventory item" to a partnership, any gain or loss recognized by the partnership on a disposition of the property within five years of the contribution is characterized as ordinary income or ordinary loss, even if the property is held by the partnership as a capital asset. See I.R.C. §§ 724(b), (d)(2). When a partner contributes a capital asset with a basis in excess of value to the partnership, any loss recognized by the partnership on a disposition of the property within five years of the contribution is characterized as a capital loss, but only to the extent that the recognized loss does not exceed the difference between the basis of the property and its value at the time of the contribution. See I.R.C. § 724(c).

> *Problem 10–5 (Impact of transfer on characterization)*: Ginger and Sara each owns a 50% interest in a limited liability company (LLC) that owns and operates an automobile dealership. The LLC is classified as a partnership under Treas. Reg. § 301.7701–3. Ginger also owns and operates an art gallery as a sole proprietorship. On January 1 of Year 3, Ginger takes two $5,000 paintings from the stock of the art gallery. She bought each painting for $3,000. She sells one painting to Herma for a $5,000 promissory note and transfers Herma's promissory note to the LLC. She transfers the other painting to the LLC. The painting is displayed by the LLC in an auto showroom for aesthetic purposes and not held for sale. On January 1 of Year 3, Sara transfers her personal car to the LLC. Sara bought the car for $14,000, but, when she transfers the car to the LLC, its value is only $10,000. The car is held for sale by the LLC as a used car. What are the tax consequences to Ginger and Sara under each of the following alternatives? See I.R.C. §§ 704(c)(1)(A), 724.
>
> (a) The LLC sells the painting contributed by Ginger for $12,000.
>
> (b) The LLC sells the painting contributed by Ginger for $1,000.
>
> (c) The LLC sells Herma's promissory note for $5,500.
>
> (d) The LLC sells Herma's promissory note for $2,000.
>
> (e) The LLC sells the car contributed by Sara for $7,000. See Treas. Reg. § 1.165–9(b)(2).
>
> (f) The LLC sells the car contributed by Sara for $15,000.

B. TRANSFER OF PROPERTY FOR OTHER CONSIDERATION

I.R.C. §§ 707(a)(2)(B), 737

Treas. Reg. §§ 1.707–3, 1.737–1(a)–(c)(1), (d), –2(d)(1), –(3)(a)–(c)(1), –4(a)

When a person transfers property to a partnership in exchange for a partnership interest and other consideration (i.e., boot or relief from liabilities), I.R.C. § 721 does not address the tax consequences to the transferor of receiving the other consideration.[7] A transaction involving the transfer of property to a partnership and the receipt of both a partnership interest and other consideration can be viewed in two different ways. The transaction might be divided into a nontaxable exchange of part of the

---

7. The partnership tax provisions do not contain analogues to I.R.C. § 351(b) and § 357. See pp. 394–399.

property for a partnership interest (I.R.C. § 721(a)) and a taxable exchange of the rest of the property for the other consideration received from the partnership (I.R.C. § 1001(a)). Alternatively, the transaction might be viewed as a nontaxable exchange of the entire property for a partnership interest (I.R.C. § 721(a)) followed by a potentially nontaxable distribution of the other consideration (I.R.C. § 731(a)). The case that follows reveals the stakes associated with these alternative views and the difficulty of determining which view better reflects the substance of a given transaction.

Otey v. Commissioner

United States Tax Court, 1978.
70 T.C. 312, aff'd 634 F.2d 1046 (6th Cir.1980).

FINDINGS OF FACT

■ Hall, Judge: * * *

Petitioner is in the real estate business. In 1963 petitioner inherited from his uncle real property at 2612–14 Heiman Street in Nashville ("Heiman Street property"). At the time petitioner acquired the property, its fair market value was $18,500 * * *.

[S]ometime in 1971 petitioner and Marion Thurman ("Thurman"), a real estate developer, decided to develop the Heiman Street property into a moderate-income apartment complex, a type of complex for which there was then available FHA-insured financing. On October 19, 1971, petitioner and Thurman formed a partnership under the name of Court Villa Apartments for the purpose of building a 65–unit FHA-insured residential apartment on the Heiman Street property. Thurman, through his construction company, Marion Thurman Builders, was to build the rental units, and petitioner was to manage them.

On December 30, 1971, petitioner * * * transferred title to the Heiman Street property to the partnership. At the time of the transfer, petitioner's basis in the property was $18,500 and the fair market value of the property was $65,000. This transfer was pursuant to the partnership agreement, which provided:

> John H. Otey, Jr. has contributed the land to the Joint Venture and the parties agree that the said Otey shall draw the first Sixty Five Thousand ($65,000) Dollars of loan proceeds from the Joint Venture as soon as the loan closes * * *.

The agreement further provided that profits and losses would be shared equally. Similarly, withdrawals and distributions of cash were to be made equally, except that as previously noted the first $65,000 of the loan proceeds was to be paid to petitioner.

On January 11, 1972, the partnership obtained a construction loan of $870,300 from the Third National Bank. Both petitioner and Thurman were jointly and severally liable for the loan. Pursuant to the partnership agreement, petitioner was paid $64,750 from the loan proceeds * * *.

Marion Thurman Builders built the apartment units for the partnership and was paid by the partnership from the construction loan. Thurman contributed no cash or other assets to the partnership. His contribution was his ability to get financing for the partnership through his good credit * * *.

The partners intended that petitioner's transfer of the Heiman Street property to the partnership was a contribution to the capital of the partnership and not a sale of the property to the partnership. On receipt of the $64,750 cash from the partnership in 1972, petitioner reduced his basis in his * * * partnership [interest]. Since his basis, consisting of his $18,500 basis in the land contributed plus his liability for one-half of the borrowed construction money, exceeded the money distributed to him, he reported no income from this transaction on his 1972 return. Respondent, in his statutory notice, determined that petitioner realized gain from the "sale" of the Heiman Street property to the partnership in 1972 which should have been reported by petitioner on his 1972 return.

OPINION

Petitioner made a contribution of property worth $65,000 to a partnership of which he was a partner. Within a short period after such contribution, the partnership borrowed funds on which petitioner was jointly and severally liable, and pursuant to agreement distributed $64,750 of such borrowed funds to petitioner, retaining petitioner's property. The distribution of $64,750 did not exceed petitioner's basis in the partnership. The question presented is whether petitioner in reality "sold" his property to the partnership. Respondent, relying on section 707, contends that he did.

     * * *

Petitioner relies on section 721 * * * and section 731 * * *.

We are cautioned, however, by section 1.731–1(c)(3), Income Tax Regs. as follows:

(3) If there is a contribution of property to a partnership and within a short period:

(i) Before or after such contribution other property is distributed to the contributing partner and the contributed property is retained by the partnership, or

(ii) After such contribution the contributed property is distributed to another partner,

such distribution may not fall within the scope of section 731. Section 731 does not apply to a distribution of property, if, in fact, the distribution was made in order to effect an exchange of property between two or more of the partners or between the partnership and a partner. Such a transaction shall be treated as an exchange of property.

Thus we are faced with the question whether this transaction, which was in form a contribution of property to a partnership followed by a distribution of loan proceeds to the contributing partner, was in substance a sale of the property to the partnership by the partner.

* * *

Subchapter K provides two possible methods of analyzing the transfer by petitioner of his Heiman Street property to the partnership, with sharply divergent tax consequences depending upon which analysis applies. Using the contribution approach, sections 721 and 731 treat a partner's contribution of property to his partnership as a non-recognition transaction, producing neither gain nor loss, and withdrawals from the partnership are treated as reductions in basis rather than as taxable events. If these sections are applicable, we must sustain petitioner, because the immediate recourse borrowing by the partnership would (like most other borrowing) be a nontaxable event, increasing the basis of the parties in their partnership interest under sections 752(a) and 722. The distribution to a partner (petitioner) of part of the borrowed funds would not generate gain but would simply reduce pro tanto the distributee's basis under sections 731(a)(1) and 733. This approach treats petitioner in a manner rather similar to a proprietor. Had petitioner simply decided to use his Heiman Street property as a proprietor for an FHA housing project and had he been able to obtain an FHA construction loan in an amount exceeding the cost of building the proposed structure, and diverted to his personal use $64,750 of the loan, no gain or loss would have been realized. This would be the case even had he been able to borrow the money only by agreeing to pay half his profits over to Thurman for acting as the co-signer on the loan. Sections 721 and 731 parallel this treatment.

But the Code also recognizes that in some cases partners do not deal with a partnership in their capacity as partners. Even though they are personally on both sides of a transaction with the partnership to the extent of their partnership interest, partners may on occasion deal with the partnership in a capacity other than as a partner and must treat such dealings with the partnership accordingly under section 707. This section, among other things, prevents use of the partnership provisions to render nontaxable what would in substance have been a taxable exchange if it had not been "run through" the partnership * * *.

Neither the Code and regulations nor the case law offers a great deal of guidance for distinguishing whether transactions such as those before us are to be characterized as a contribution (nontaxable) under section 721, as petitioner contends, or as a sale to the partnership other than in the capacity of a partner (taxable) under section 707, as respondent urges. It is at least clear from the above-quoted regulation under section 731 that application or not of section 707 is not always merely elective with a taxpayer. Occasions exist on which he must be thrust unwillingly within it in order for it to serve its above-described prophylactic function * * *.

* * *

Turning to the facts before us, a number of circumstances militate in favor of a conclusion that section 721 rather than section 707 should govern. In the first place, the form of the transaction was a contribution to capital rather than a sale, and there are no elements of artificiality in the form selected which should induce us to be particularly astute to look behind it * * *. Second, and most importantly, the capital in question (borrowed funds aside) was emplaced in the partnership at its inception and as a part of the very raison d'etre of the partnership. Without this transfer, the partnership would have had no assets and no business. It is therefore most difficult for us to agree with respondent that the transaction was between petitioner and the partnership other than in petitioner's capacity as a partner. Third, the capital in question was the only contributed capital of the partnership. To treat this as an outside transaction would require us to hold in effect that no non-borrowed capital was contributed at all. While such partnerships can of course exist, they are unusual and it would seem very strained to contend that this is such a case. The property had to be in the partnership to make the borrowing possible. Fourth, petitioner enjoyed here no guarantee by the partnership that he would be paid (and get to keep) the $65,000 in all events. True, most of that sum was distributed to him almost at once out of borrowed funds, but he remained personally liable for the entire borrowing * * *. An important feature distinguishing transfers in the capacity of a partner from section 707 transactions is whether payment by the partnership to the partner is at the risk of the economic fortunes of the partnership. In the present case, whether partnership cash flow would ever suffice to repay the distributed $64,750 to the bank would depend on the partnership's subsequent economic fortunes. If they were adverse, petitioner could be called on to repay the loan himself. Fifth, the pattern here is a usual and customary partnership capitalization arrangement, under which the partner who put up a greater share of the capital than his share of partnership profits is to receive preferential distributions to equalize capital accounts. The only unusual feature here is the immediate availability of the equalizing distribution out of excess borrowed funds. The normality of this general pattern would make it most unsettling were we to accept respondent's invitation to recharacterize the capitalization of the partnership on account thereof * * *. For all the above reasons, we cannot sustain respondent in his attempted recharacterization of the transfer as a sale.

      * * *

We hold that the transfer constituted in substance what it was in form—the initial capitalization of the partnership. The early withdrawal of borrowed cash in an amount substantially equivalent to the agreed value of the contributed property reduced petitioner's basis in the partnership but did not create income to him.

NOTES

1. *Contribution/distribution treatment versus sale treatment.* Will a partner who transfers property to a partnership and receives consideration other than a partnership interest normally prefer contribution/distribution treatment or sale treatment if,

(a) the contributed property has a value in excess of its basis?

(b) the contributed property has a basis in excess of its value?

2. *I.R.C. § 707(a)(2)(B).* In response to Otey and similar cases, Congress attacked disguised sales to partnerships by enacting I.R.C. § 707(a)(2)(B), but delegated to the Treasury the task of promulgating regulations for determining whether a given transaction is a sale. Under the regulations, a transfer of property by a partner to a partnership and a transfer of money or other consideration by the partnership to the partner constitute a sale of property if, based on all the facts and circumstances,

(a) the transfer of money or other consideration would not have been made but for the transfer of property, *and*

(b) if the transfers are not made simultaneously, the subsequent transfer is not dependent on the entrepreneurial risks of partnership operations.

Treas. Reg. § 1.707–3(b)(1).

The regulations identify a variety of facts and circumstances that may tend to prove that a transaction is a sale. See Treas. Reg. § 1.707–3(b)(2). More significantly, the regulations provide that a transfer of property by a partner to a partnership and a transfer of money or other consideration by the partnership to the contributing partner are presumed to be a sale if the transfers are made within two years of each other, unless the facts and circumstances clearly establish that the transfers do not constitute a sale. See Treas. Reg. § 1.707–3(c). Conversely, such transfers are presumed not to be a sale if the transfers are separated by more than two years, unless the facts and circumstances clearly establish that the transfers constitute a sale. See Treas. Reg. § 1.707–3(d).

If these regulations had applied to the events in Otey, is it likely that the court would have reached a different result?

3. *I.R.C. § 737.* Even if sale treatment under I.R.C. § 707(a)(2)(B) is avoided, a partner who receives a distribution from a partnership within seven years of contributing appreciated property is now often compelled to recognize gain under I.R.C. § 737. Pursuant to I.R.C. § 737, a partner who,

(a) transfers appreciated property to the partnership and,

(b) within seven years of the contribution, receives other property from the partnership,

must recognize the pre-contribution gain in the contributed property to the extent that the distribution exceeds the partner's basis in her partnership interest.

If I.R.C. § 737 had applied to the events in Otey, is it likely that the court would have reached a different result?

Problem 10–6 (Sale versus contribution/distribution): Maria and Saul form the Zanzibar Partnership. Maria transfers a parcel of land with a value of $60,000 and a basis of $60,000 to the partnership in exchange for a 50% partnership interest. Saul transfers property with a value of $120,000 in exchange for 1) a 50% partnership interest, and 2) the parcel of land contributed by Maria.

(a) What are the tax consequences to Saul if the transaction is *not* treated as a sale of property under I.R.C. § 707(a)(2)(B) and Saul's basis in the transferred property is,

> (i) $20,000?
>
> (ii) $40,000?
>
> (iii) $140,000?

(b) What are the tax consequences to Saul if the transaction is treated as a sale of property under I.R.C. § 707(a)(2)(B) and Saul's basis in the transferred property is,

> (i) $20,000?
>
> (ii) $40,000?
>
> (iii) $140,000?

C. PARTNERSHIP ANTI-ABUSE RULE

Treas. Reg. § 1.701–2

Congress has responded to perceived abuses of the partnership tax rules by enacting a series of narrow provisions targeted at specific transactions. See, e.g., I.R.C. §§ 704(c)(1)(B), 707(a)(2)(B), 737; pp. 450–457. In 1995, the Treasury promulgated a more comprehensive anti-abuse rule designed to serve as a mechanism for attacking a wider variety of transactions involving enterprises taxed as partnerships under the Internal Revenue Code. See Treas. Reg. § 1.701–2. Both of the following conditions must normally be satisfied for the anti-abuse rule to apply to a transaction:

> (1) The transaction involves the use of a partnership with a principal purpose of reducing substantially the present value of the partners' aggregate Federal income tax liability.
>
> (2) The transaction achieves a tax result that is inconsistent with the intent of Subchapter K.

When a transaction satisfies these conditions, the I.R.S. is authorized to recast the transaction for Federal tax purposes to achieve tax results that are consistent with the intent of Subchapter K. Treas. Reg. § 1.701–2(b).

Instead of focusing directly on when a tax result is inconsistent with Subchapter K, the regulation delineates the intent of Subchapter K. "Subchapter K is intended to permit taxpayers to conduct joint business (including investment) activities through a flexible economic arrangement, without incurring an entity level tax." Treas. Reg. § 1.701–2(a). For a transaction to be consistent with the intent of Subchapter K, the following requirements must be satisfied:

(1) The partnership must be bona fide.

(2) Each partnership transaction or series of related transactions must be entered into for a substantial business purpose.

(3) The form of each partnership transaction must be respected under substance over form principles.

(4) The tax consequences under Subchapter K must accurately reflect the partners' economic agreement and clearly reflect the partner's income, unless the relevant provision clearly contemplates a different result.

Treas. Reg. § 1.701–2(a).

An analysis of all facts and circumstances is necessary to determine whether a transaction achieves a tax result that is consistent with the intent of Subchapter K. This analysis includes a comparison of the purported business purpose for a transaction and the claimed tax benefits resulting from the transaction. The regulation delineates a series of factors which may indicate that a partnership was used in an improper manner. See Treas. Reg. § 1.701–2(c). The regulation also provides a series of examples illustrating its operation. See Treas. Reg. § 1.701–2(d). Examples 1, 2, 8, and 9 involve topics within the scope of this casebook and should be carefully reviewed.

For an illustration of how the Internal Revenue Service has applied the anti-abuse regulation, see the Chief Counsel Advice Memorandum that follows.

IRS Chief Counsel Advice Memorandum 200650014[8]

2006 IRS CCA LEXIS 61.
9/7/06.

ISSUE

Whether a distribution purportedly in redemption of Taxpayer's interest in Partnership included the State Y house purchased by Partnership.

CONCLUSION

The non-recognition provision of § 731 and substituted basis rule of § 732(b) do not apply when a partnership acquires residential real estate that has no relation to a partnership's business activities, solely for purposes of immediately distributing the real estate to a partner in liquidation.

---

8. This Chief Counsel Advice Memorandum is a response by the Office of the Chief Counsel of the Internal Revenue Service to a request for assistance from IRS attorney-advisors. It may not be cited as precedent.

FACTS

Partnership owned a large parcel of [land] (parcel) in State X. Partnership was also an obligor on several promissory notes secured by deeds of trust encumbering certain portions of Partnership's parcel.

Taxpayer held a total of z percent interest in Partnership. The majority of the partnership interests were held by members of Taxpayer's family.

Due to ongoing disagreements among the partners, most of the partners (the exiting partners) in Partnership, including Taxpayer, liquidated their interests in Partnership leaving A and A's immediate family (the remaining partners) in control of Partnership. The remaining partners' interests in Partnership increased proportionately as a result of the liquidation of the exiting partners' interests.

The liquidation of Taxpayer's partnership interest was specifically outlined in a redemption agreement. [In addition to providing for a cash distribution,] the redemption agreement provided for the purchase and distribution to Taxpayer of a house in State Y. * * *

Taxpayer recognized $f in income on account of the money received in excess of Taxpayer's basis in Partnership. This amount consists of $g of I.R.C. § 752(b) of debt relief [resulting in a] deemed [cash] distribution and $h of cash * * *. Taxpayer claims that the total distribution of money does not include the fair market value of the State Y house because, under I.R.C. § 731(a)(1) and § 1.731–1(a)(1)(i), in the case of a distribution by a partnership to a partner, gain shall not be recognized to such partner, except to the extent that any money distributed exceeds the adjusted basis of such partner's interest in the partnership immediately before the distribution. * * *

LAW AND ANALYSIS

* * *

(a) Distribution not a distribution of partnership property

* * *

The facts in this case are consistent with a finding that the State Y house was acquired and held for the account of Taxpayer and became property of the Taxpayer at the time it was acquired for Taxpayer by the Partnership. See Rev. Rul. 55–39, 1955–1 C.B. 403 (investment by partnership of partner's contributed capital in securities of partner's choice and for partner's own account constituted a withdrawal of capital from the partnership and an investment by partner in securities purchased, resulting in reduction in partner's partnership interest). When Partnership purchased the State Y house for Taxpayer, it in effect distributed cash to Taxpayer in the amount of $a, the amount used by Partnership to acquire the State Y house. The subsequent purported distribution of the State Y house to Partner is not a distribution of partnership property under § 731.

We conclude that §§ 731 and 732 do not apply to the purported distribution of the State Y house to Taxpayer because the distribution was not a distribution of Partnership property.

(b) Partnership Anti–Abuse Rules

Alternatively, if the State Y house was properly considered to be property of Partnership, the transaction should be recast in accordance with the regulations under § 1.701–2 (the anti-abuse rules). The anti-abuse rules provide that if a partnership is formed or availed of in connection with a transaction a principal purpose of which is to reduce substantially the present value of the partners' aggregate federal tax liability in a manner that is inconsistent with the intent of subchapter K, the Commissioner can recast the transaction for federal tax purposes. § 1.701–2(b).

Section 1.701–2(a) provides that the following requirements are implicit in the intent of subchapter K: (1) The partnership must be bona fide and each partnership transaction or series of related transactions must be entered into for a substantial business purpose; (2) The form of each partnership transaction must be respected under substance over form principles; and (3) Except as otherwise provided in paragraph (a)(3), the tax consequences under subchapter K to each partner of partnership operations and of transactions between the partner and the partnership must accurately reflect the partners' economic agreement and clearly reflect the partner's income.

Section 1.701–2(c) describes certain factors that may be taken into account in determining whether a partnership was formed or availed of with a principal purpose to reduce substantially the present value of the partners' aggregate federal tax liability in a manner inconsistent with the intent of subchapter K. Three of those factors are: (i) the present value of the partners' aggregate federal tax liability is substantially less than had the partners owned the partnership's assets and conducted the partnership's activities directly, (ii) the present value of the partners' aggregate federal tax liability is substantially less than would be the case if purportedly separate transactions that are designed to achieve a particular end result are integrated and treated as steps in a single transaction, and (iii) substantially all of the partners are related to one another.

With respect to these three factors, if the Taxpayer purchased the State Y house directly, Taxpayer's tax liability would have been greater as Taxpayer would have to recognize an additional $a of income or gain. In addition, through the use of the subchapter K rules, Taxpayer's tax liability is substantially less than would have been the case if the steps of the transaction were integrated to treat Taxpayer as receiving a distribution of $a cash from Partnership, and then purchasing the State Y house. Furthermore, all of the partners in Partnership are related to one another.

To liquidate Taxpayer's interest in Partnership, Partnership made a purported distribution to Taxpayer of the fair market value of the State Y house (in addition to $g debt relief and $h cash) to Taxpayer for the value of Taxpayer's interests in Partnership. Because this exceeded Taxpayer's basis in Partnership, Taxpayer would have had to recognize an additional $a of income or gain if paid directly to Taxpayer. By attempting to characterize the distribution of the fair market value of the State Y house as a distribution of property other than money, Taxpayer and Partnership used the rules of subchapter K inappropriately in a manner that attempted to eliminate $a of income or gain with respect to Taxpayer.

We conclude that the transaction should be recast in accordance with the anti-abuse rules of § 1.701–2 as a distribution of $a in cash to Taxpayer, which Taxpayer then used * * * to acquire the State Y house.

PART FIVE

Corporate Dispositions and Acquisitions

Parts Three and Four of this casebook focused, for the most part, on transactions between a business and its current owners. Part Five explores the tax consequences that follow when a corporate business is transferred to new owners.[1] Chapter 11 examines transactions involving the transfer of assets by a corporation in exchange for money or the transfer of a corporation's stock by its shareholders in exchange for money. These transactions normally trigger immediate tax liability to the seller and are therefore referred to as "taxable transfers." In contrast, Chapter 12 focuses on certain statutorily defined transfers of corporate assets or stock to another corporation in exchange for stock of the acquiring corporation. When properly structured, these transactions allow the seller to defer tax liability and are therefore referred to as "nontaxable transfers." Chapter 13 addresses the effect of a taxable transfer or a nontaxable transfer on certain historical tax attributes of the seller and the buyer ("carryovers") and on certain tax attributes created by the combined enterprise ("carrybacks"). Finally, Chapter 14 explores the additional issues that arise when an S Corporation transfers its assets or the shareholders of an S Corporation transfer their stock.

---

1. The principal tax issues associated with the transfer of a business taxed as a partnership were examined in Chapter 7. See pp. 337–366. Other issues associated with the transfer of all businesses irrespective of form are noted in Chapter 11.

*

Taxable Transfers

Ownership of a business conducted in corporate form may be transferred in either of two ways. First, the corporation, itself, may transfer its assets to the buyer in exchange for money or other property which the selling corporation can then distribute to its shareholders. For example, Xerxes Corporation could sell all of its assets to Yandu Corporation for $1,000,000 and Xerxes, in turn, could distribute the money to its shareholders. After these steps occur, the original Xerxes shareholders still own the corporate shell that previously conducted the transferred business but the assets of the business are owned by Yandu. As an alternative to an asset transfer, the shareholders of Xerxes could simply sell their stock directly to Yandu for $1,000,000. In this event, the entire Xerxes corporation, with its business intact, migrates from the selling shareholders to Yandu and Xerxes continues to operate its historical business as a wholly-owned subsidiary of Yandu (Yandu owns all the stock of Xerxes). Although both transactions effectively transfer ownership of the business, the legal and tax implications of the two transactions may be dramatically different.

From a non-tax perspective, asset sales are normally preferred to stock sales because an asset transfer enables the buyer to be selective both with respect to the assets it acquires and, more importantly, with respect to the liabilities it assumes. Buyers are often reluctant to acquire stock because *all* liabilities (known and unknown) of the seller's business are transferred along with the business when stock is acquired. In contrast, when assets are acquired, only those liabilities that the buyer expressly assumes normally become the responsibility of the buyer.[1] A purchaser of stock may, of course, convince the selling shareholders to agree to reimburse the buyer for potential liabilities to which the buyer does not wish to be exposed by securing an indemnification agreement. Identifying all potential liabilities to be included in an indemnification agreement, however, is normally not an easy task. Moreover, a buyer generally prefers to avoid liability from the outset, rather than being limited to the remedy of chasing after the seller for reimbursement, perhaps many years after the acquisition occurred.

Liabilities are not the only non-tax consideration relevant to the structure of a corporate acquisition. An additional advantage of an asset sale is that it enables the buyer to negotiate exclusively with representatives of the selling corporation, rather than dealing with the idiosyncrasies

---

1. A purchaser of assets may be exposed to certain liabilities of the selling corporation, such as environmental clean-up liabilities and pension liabilities, regardless of whether the purchaser expressly assumes these liabilities. See William M. Fletcher, *Fletcher Cyclopedia of the Law of Corporations* § 7122 (2011).

of each individual shareholder. (State law normally requires the approval of at least a majority of the shareholders, however, before an asset acquisition can be effectuated.) Other considerations can favor a stock transfer. For example, the mechanics of a stock sale are often far simpler than those of an asset acquisition. When stock is transferred, title to each of the assets owned by the transferred business remains with the original corporation. In contrast, when assets are transferred, each individual asset of the selling corporation must be conveyed to the buyer. Moreover, if the business to be acquired owns a significant nontransferable asset (e.g., a copyright, franchise, lease, license or trademark), a stock transfer may be the only viable alternative.[2]

Tax considerations often markedly increase the appeal of a stock sale because an asset sale generally triggers two tax liabilities (one to the selling corporation and a second to its shareholders). In contrast, a stock sale normally triggers only a single tax liability (to the shareholders of the selling corporation).

> *Example 11–A (Comparing tax cost of asset sale to stock sale)*: Several years ago, Able contributed $100,000 to Xerxes Corporation for all of its stock. Xerxes Corporation used the $100,000 to acquire several parcels of land. The land is now worth $1,100,000.
>
> *Asset sale*: If Xerxes sells its land to Yandu for $1,100,000, Xerxes recognizes a gain of $1,000,000 on which a corporate tax of $340,000 is imposed.[3] If Xerxes distributes the remaining $760,000 to Able,[4] he recognizes a capital gain of $660,000 on which an individual income tax of roughly $99,000 (15%) is imposed.[5] Thus, Able retains $661,000 after all taxes are paid.[6]
>
> *Stock sale*: If Able sells all of his Xerxes stock to Yandu for $1,100,000, Able recognizes a capital gain of $1,000,000 on which a tax of roughly

---

2. For further discussion of the non-tax aspects of corporate acquisitions, see Harry G. Henn & John R. Alexander, *Laws of Corporations* § 341 (3d ed. 1983 & Supp. 1986).

3. See I.R.C. §§ 11, 1001. If the taxable income of Xerxes exceeds $10,000,000, a higher corporate tax rate applies.

4.

$1,100,000 (proceeds of sale)
− 340,000 (corporate tax)
$ 760,000

5. See I.R.C. §§ 331, 1221. The maximum individual capital gains rate is 15%. See I.R.C. § 1(h).

6.

$1,100,000 (proceeds of sale)
− 340,000 (corporate tax)
− 99,000 (individual tax)
$ 661,000

$150,000 (15%) is imposed.[7] Thus, Able retains $950,000 after the tax is paid.[8]

Example 11–A is somewhat misleading because it focuses exclusively on tax consequences on the seller's side of the transaction. If Yandu acquires the assets of Xerxes for $1,100,000, it takes a cost basis of $1,100,000 in the land. See I.R.C. § 1012. Thus, if Yandu subsequently resells the land for $1,100,000, Yandu realizes no gain on the second sale. In contrast, if Yandu acquires the stock of Xerxes, the basis in the land remains at $100,000. Hence, a subsequent sale of the land for $1,100,000 triggers a $1,000,000 gain that will be borne by Yandu because Yandu owns Xerxes when the gain is triggered. Thus, a stock sale that saves *current* taxes for the seller, generally results in the imposition of greater *future* taxes on the buyer. Notwithstanding this shift in tax burdens, stock sales generally remain less costly than asset sales due to the time value of money. Before examining the tax consequences of asset sales and stock sales in greater depth, it is useful to develop an analytical perspective from which to explore these transactions.

A. PERSPECTIVE

A taxable transfer of a business raises tax issues on both the seller's side and the buyer's side of the transaction. The seller is concerned with the *immediate* tax burdens that result from the realization event triggered by the sale. In contrast, the buyer is concerned with the *future* tax burdens associated with the newly acquired business if the value of its assets exceeds their basis. A dollar of current tax liability is more costly than a dollar of future tax liability because of the "time value of money." Consequently, collective tax savings are achieved when a transaction is structured to reduce the seller's current tax at the cost of a like-amount increase in the buyer's future tax. When this trade-off can be accomplished, a purchase price should be negotiated that enables the parties to share the tax savings (provided both parties are aware of this savings and have equal bargaining power).

> *Example 11–B (Creating and sharing collective tax savings)*: Buyer tentatively agrees to acquire a business from Seller for $1,000,000. The parties then discover that the acquisition can be restructured in a way that reduces the seller's *current* tax liability by $10,000 but, correspondingly, increases the buyer's *future* tax liability by $10,000.[9] Assume that $6,000 deposited in the bank by the buyer today will grow to

---

7. I.R.C. §§ 1(h), 1001, 1221.

8.

$1,100,000 (proceeds of sale)
− 150,000 (individual tax)
$ 950,000

9. Methods of restructuring a taxable acquisition to create collective tax savings are explored later in this chapter.

$10,000 by the time the buyer's future tax liability matures. In this event, $4,000 of collective tax savings is achieved by restructuring the transaction because the seller saves $10,000 at a present value cost to the buyer of only $6,000.

The $4,000 of collective savings can be shared by the parties ($2,000 apiece) if the purchase price is reduced to $992,000. In this event, the seller saves $10,000 of current tax (as a result of restructuring the transaction) but forgoes $8,000 of sales proceeds (by reducing the purchase price). The buyer saves $8,000 as a result of the reduced purchase price but must set aside $6,000 to finance its future tax liability. In effect, the parties have shared the $4,000 economic benefit that results from delaying the government's receipt of $10,000 in taxes.

In the personal income tax course, both the time value of money and the notion of collective tax savings were introduced. These topics will now be reviewed.

1. THE TIME VALUE OF MONEY

One thousand dollars received today is worth more than $1,000 received a year from now because the value of money in hand is enhanced by the mere passage of time. Specifically, the $1,000 received today may be deposited in an interest paying bank account (or otherwise invested) and the balance of the account will exceed $1,000 when a year has elapsed. The extent to which the balance will exceed $1,000 depends on the rate of return earned on the investment. If a 6% return is earned, the $1,000 received today will grow to $1,060 one year from now.

The time value of money is relevant to disbursements as well as receipts. It is less costly to pay $1,000 of tax one year from now than to pay $1,000 of tax today. This is because something less than $1,000 can be deposited in an interest paying bank account today for the account to grow to $1,000 when the tax is due next year. The actual amount that must be deposited today to accumulate $1,000 in a year depends on the rate of return earned by the depositor. If a 6% return can be earned, $943 set aside today will grow to $1,000 in one year.

The amount that must be set aside today to have a dollar available at a designated future time is referred to as the "present value" of a dollar and the assumed interest rate is referred to as the "discount rate." A present value factor may be derived by applying the following formula:

$$\$1 \div [(1+r)^n]$$

where "r" is the discount rate and "n" is the number of years that will pass before the dollar is to be paid. You may use the present value factors in Table 11–1 to solve the problems in this Chapter.

Table 11–1 highlights the economic significance of the time value of money. For example, $1,000 will be available in 20 years by setting aside only $311 today if a 6% annual return is earned on the deposit. If a 15%

annual return can be earned, only $61 must be set aside today to have $1,000 in 20 years!

Table 11–1

Present Value of $1 to Be Paid in a Specified Number of Years at a Specified Discount Rate

Number of Years	Discount Rate				
	4%	5%	6%	10%	15%
1	.962	.952	.943	.909	.870
2	.925	.907	.890	.826	.756
3	.889	.864	.840	.751	.658
4	.855	.823	.792	.683	.572
5	.822	.784	.747	.621	.497
10	.676	.614	.558	.386	.247
15	.555	.481	.417	.239	.123
20	.456	.377	.311	.149	.061
40	.208	.142	.097	.022	.004

In contrast to determining the present value of a lump sum paid at the end of a given period, it is sometimes necessary to determine the present value of a sum paid every year for a given number of years. For example, an opportunity may exist to pay $1,000 of tax each year for the next five years in lieu of paying $5,000 of tax today. Table 11–1 can be used to calculate the present value of a payment of $1,000 of tax in each of the next five years but the calculation would require five different factors from that Table. To make life easier, the factors in Table 11–2 may be used to solve problems that require the computation of the present value of a sum paid every year for a given number of years.[10]

Table 11–2

Present Value of $1 to Be Paid at the End of Each Year for a Specified Number of Years at a Specified Discount Rate

Number of Years	Discount Rate				
	4%	5%	6%	10%	15%
1	.96	.95	.94	.91	.87
2	1.89	1.86	1.83	1.74	1.63
3	2.78	2.72	2.67	2.49	2.28
4	3.63	3.55	3.47	3.17	2.85
5	4.45	4.33	4.21	3.79	3.35
10	8.11	7.72	7.36	6.14	5.02
15	11.12	10.38	9.71	7.61	5.85
20	13.59	12.46	11.47	8.51	6.26
40	19.79	17.16	15.05	9.78	6.64

10. For additional discussion of the time value of money, see Peter C. Canellos and Edward G. Kleinbard, "The Miracle of Compound Interest: Interest Deferral and Discount After 1982," 38 Tax Law Review 565 (1983).

Problem 11–1: What is the present value of $1,000 of tax to be paid every year for each of the next five years assuming you can earn 6% per year on your money?

Problem 11–2: How much money must be set aside today to accumulate $100,000 in fifteen years if a 10% annual return can be earned? Would you have to set aside more or less money today if the annual return you could earn was,

(a) higher than 10%?

(b) lower than 10%?

Problem 11–3: If you can earn 5% a year on your money, would you rather pay:

(a) $700 today, or

(b) $200 every year for each of the next four years, or

(c) $1,000 five years from now?

What if you can earn 6% a year on your money?

What if you can earn 10% a year on your money?

2. ACHIEVING COLLECTIVE TAX SAVINGS

Students are generally first exposed to the notion of structuring a transaction to achieve collective tax savings when studying the tax rules that apply to divorce in the personal income tax course. The following case should refresh your memory.

Davidson v. Davidson

United States Court of Appeals, Fifth Circuit, 1991.
947 F.2d 1294.

■ J. SMITH, CIRCUIT JUDGE.

I.

* * *

In 1983, the Davidsons signed a Marriage Settlement Agreement ("agreement"), which provided both for a division of marital property and periodic payments [by Mr. Davidson totaling $40,000 per year terminating after the sooner of ten years or the death of Mrs. Davidson]. * * *

* * *

The agreement further provided that the payments would be taxable as income to Mrs. Davidson and deductible as to Mr. Davidson * * * and that the intent of the parties was that the payments be in the nature of support, not property settlement.[11]

---

11. The provisions read as follows:

Mr. Davidson deducted all the payments he made * * * for the years 1983 through 1986. Mrs. Davidson reported them as income for the same years. After Mr. Davidson stopped making payments, Mrs. Davidson filed a state lawsuit to enforce the terms of their divorce, which she won on summary judgment. Mr. Davidson subsequently filed for Chapter 7 bankruptcy relief.

II.

The bankruptcy court determined that the parties had intended the periodic payments to be in the nature of a property settlement, rather than alimony. The court therefore held that all the periodic payment debt was dischargeable in bankruptcy. The district court upheld that decision on appeal, holding that these payments represented a division of marital property, which can be discharged.

The bankruptcy court further held that Mr. Davidson was not barred by the doctrine of equitable estoppel from asserting that the payments were not alimony. The district court agreed * * *.

III.

As a matter of law, we review de novo the district court's conclusion that Mr. Davidson is not estopped from claiming that the payments to Mrs. Davidson were not alimony. Title 11 U.S.C. § 523(a)(5) forbids the discharge in bankruptcy of debts to a spouse, former spouse or child for alimony to, maintenance for, or support of such spouse or child, in connection with a separation agreement, divorce decree, or property settlement agreement, but not to the extent that—

* * *

(B) such debt includes a liability designated as alimony, maintenance, or support, unless such liability is actually in the nature of alimony, maintenance, or support * * *.

A division of marital property in payments over time will not be declared nondischargeable in bankruptcy merely because the parties have labeled it "alimony." Rather, the bankruptcy court evaluates the intent of the parties at the time they established the alimony/division agreement.

[W]e reverse the district court and hold that Mr. Davidson is estopped from claiming that his payment obligations to Mrs. Davidson are not in the

---

8.02 Taxable Income to Wife. The parties here affirm their intention that the payments * * * shall be deductible by Husband and reportable as income by Wife for federal income tax purposes, such payments constituting periodic payments, taxable to Wife and deductible by Husband, under the income tax provisions of § 71 and § 215 of the Internal Revenue Code, as amended.

8.03 Wife Shall Report Income. Wife agrees to file timely a U.S. Individual Income Tax Return for the tax year 1983 and later calendar years reporting as income the periodic payments made to her by Husband * * * during each such calendar year; and, Wife further agrees to pay any federal income taxes attributable to such income.

* * *

nature of alimony when he has treated the payments as alimony for tax purposes.

* * *

One form of estoppel, "quasi estoppel," forbids a party from accepting the benefits of a transaction or statute and then subsequently taking an inconsistent position to avoid the corresponding obligations or effects. Mr. Davidson has accepted the benefits of his agreement: He has taken tax deductions for the payments to Mrs. Davidson. He now tries to escape the bankruptcy effects of his election to treat the payments as alimony.

* * *

To allow a spouse to set up an intricate and unambiguous divorce settlement, carefully distinguishing certain periodic payments, called alimony, from the division of marital property, and consistently taking advantage of this characterization for tax purposes, only then to declare that the payments truly represented a division of property, would be a legal affront to both the bankruptcy and tax codes. To uphold the discharge of those payments in bankruptcy would reward an admitted manipulation tantamount, at best, to deception. That Mr. Davidson did not know he would go broke when he agreed to the divorce settlement is not an uncommon scenario, but offers him no excuse for discharging the payments he chose to characterize as alimony.

NOTES

1. *Sharing collective tax savings in divorce.* Assume that when Mr. and Mrs. Davidson were negotiating their divorce settlement, Mr. Davidson paid tax at a marginal rate of 50% and Mrs. Davidson paid tax at a marginal rate of 30%. Also assume that Mrs. Davidson (who had no income from other sources) needed $25,000 a year on which to live and that Mr. Davidson was only willing to part with $23,000. Can you demonstrate that each party would exceed his/her respective goal by agreeing to treat the $40,000 annual payment under the marriage settlement agreement as alimony for tax purposes? See I.R.C. §§ 71, 215.

2. *Different sources of collective tax savings.* The potential for maximizing collective tax savings in a divorce is attributable to the possibility that a different tax rate applies to each party, not to a difference in the timing of each party's income. In Note 1, each dollar transferred by Mr. Davidson to Mrs. Davidson in the form of alimony saved Mr. Davidson 50 cents in tax, while costing Mrs. Davidson 30 cents in tax. As a result, an extra 20 cents was made available to the parties at the expense of the government.

In contrast to a divorce, the source of collective tax savings when a business is sold is often a difference in timing; the seller's *current* taxable income is reduced at the cost of *future* taxable income to the buyer. Even if the seller and the buyer pay tax at the same rate, the difference between a current tax to the seller and the present value of a future tax to the buyer creates a source of collective tax savings to the parties. This analysis is more fully developed later in this Chapter.

3. *Impact of non-tax considerations.* Should the attorneys representing Mr. and Mrs. Davidson at the time of the divorce have contemplated the prospect of Mr. Davidson's bankruptcy? How should that prospect have impacted on the advice rendered at the time of the divorce by,

(a) Mr. Davidson's counsel?

(b) Mrs. Davidson's counsel?

B.   ASSET TRANSFER

1.   TAX CONSEQUENCES TO SELLER

I.R.C. §§ 1001, 1221, 1231

Williams v. McGowan

United States Court of Appeals, Second Circuit, 1945.
152 F.2d 570.

■ L. HAND, CIRCUIT JUDGE.

* * *

Williams * * * had for many years been engaged [as a sole proprietor] in the hardware business * * *. On September 17, [1940], Williams sold the business as a whole to the Corning Building Company for $63,926.28— its agreed value as of February 1, 1940 * * *. This value was made up of cash of about $8,100, receivables of about $7,000, fixtures of about $800, and a merchandise inventory of about $49,000, less some $1,000 for bills payable * * *. Upon this sale, Williams suffered a loss * * * and in his income tax return he entered * * * [the loss as "ordinary,"] and not as transactions in "capital assets." [T]he Commissioner disallowed [this loss] and recomputed the tax accordingly; Williams paid the deficiency and sued to recover it in this action. The only question is whether the business was "capital assets" under [the predecessor to I.R.C. § 1221].

* * *

Our law has been sparing in the creation of juristic entities; * * * indeed for many years it fumbled uncertainly with the concept of a corporation * * *. Be that as it may, in this instance the [Code] section itself furnishes the answer. It starts in the broadest way by declaring that all "property" is "capital assets," and then makes three exceptions. The first is "stock in trade * * * or other property of a kind which would properly be included in the inventory"; next comes "property held * * * primarily for sale to customers"; and finally, property "used in the trade or business of a character which is subject to * * * allowance for depreciation." * * * Congress plainly did mean to comminute the elements of a business; plainly it did not regard the whole as "capital assets."

As has already appeared, Williams transferred to the Corning Company "cash," "receivables," "fixtures" and a "merchandise inventory." "Fixtures" are not capital because they are subject to a depreciation allowance;[12] the inventory, as we have just seen, is expressly excluded * * *. There can of course be no gain or loss in the transfer of cash; and, although Williams does appear to have made a gain of $1072.71 upon the "receivables," the point has not been argued that they are not subject to a depreciation allowance * * *.[13] The gain or loss upon every * * * item should be computed as an item in ordinary income.

Judgment reversed.

■ FRANK, CIRCUIT JUDGE (dissenting in part).

* * *

[I] do not agree that we should ignore what the parties to the sale, Williams and the Corning Company, actually did. They did not arrange for a transfer to the buyer, as if in separate bundles, of the several ingredients of the business. They contracted for the sale of the entire business as a going concern * * *.

To carve up this transaction into distinct sales—of cash, receivables, fixtures, trucks, [and] merchandise * * *—is to do violence to the realities. I do not think Congress intended any such artificial result * * *. Where a business is sold as a unit, the whole is greater than its parts * * *. Interpretation of our complicated tax statutes is seldom aided by saying that taxation is an eminently practical matter (or the like). But this is one instance where, it seems to me, the practical aspects of the matter should guide our guess as to what Congress meant * * *.

NOTES

1. *Benefit of loss to government.* Why might losing the Williams case have been a "blessing in disguise" for the government?

2. *Application to other forms of business.* The Williams holding applies to the sale of the assets of any business, regardless of whether the business is conducted as a proprietorship, partnership, limited liability company or corporation.

3. *Impact of characterization on seller.* In light of the tax rates that apply to corporate ordinary income and capital gains under current law, how significant is the holding of the Williams case to a corporation that sells its assets? See I.R.C. §§ 11, 1211(a), 1212(a). How significant is the Williams holding to a non-corporate seller of assets? See I.R.C. §§ 1(h), 702(b), 1211(b), 1212(b).

---

12. Editor's note. Under current law, the fixtures would be treated under I.R.C. §§ 1231 and 1221(a)(2).

13. Editor's note. Under current law, accounts receivable are explicitly excluded from the definition of capital asset and, of course, are not depreciable. See I.R.C. §§ 167(a), 1221(a)(4).

4. *Two levels of tax when corporation sells assets.* When a corporation sells its assets, a corporate tax is imposed on any recognized gain. I.R.C. § 1001. In addition, the selling corporation normally distributes the proceeds of sale to its shareholders in liquidation and a second tax is triggered at the shareholder level. I.R.C. § 331. See pp. 280–292. Thus, a taxable asset sale normally triggers two current taxes, thereby rendering the transaction very costly to the seller. Why does a corporation that sells its assets generally liquidate, rather than retain the proceeds of sale? See pp. 66–86.

5. *One level of tax when shareholder sells asset.* When an asset owned by a shareholder is sold, the shareholder is taxed on any gain but no corporate tax is imposed. It is sometimes difficult to distinguish shareholder assets from corporate assets. In this regard, consider the Martin Ice Cream Company case that follows.

Martin Ice Cream Company v. Commissioner

United States Tax Court, 1998.
110 T.C. 189.

■ BEGHE, JUDGE: * * *

FINDINGS OF FACT

[S]oon after World War II, Arnold [Strassberg], a high school mathematics teacher, began a part-time business after school hours, selling ice cream products wholesale to stores in Newark, New Jersey. * * * By 1960, Arnold had incorporated his own company, Arnold's Ice Cream, and was engaging full time in the wholesale distribution of ice cream. In the 1960's, Arnold began to develop relationships with the owners and managers of several supermarket chains when he conceived an innovative packaging and sales campaign that used bright colors and catchy slogans to market ice cream products to supermarkets for resale to consumers. * * * In the late 1960's, Arnold had a falling-out with his major supplier * * * which forced Arnold's Ice Cream into bankruptcy.

In 1971, Arnold organized [Martin Ice Cream Co. (MIC or petitioner)] as a part-time business, with one delivery truck, distributing ice cream to small grocery stores and food service accounts (restaurants, hotels, and clubs) in northern New Jersey. * * * At no time did Arnold * * * have an employment agreement with MIC.

In 1974, Ruben Mattus (Mr. Mattus), the founder of Haagen–Dazs, asked Arnold to use his ice cream marketing expertise and relationships with supermarket owners and managers to introduce Haagen–Dazs ice cream products into supermarkets. Haagen–Dazs manufactured an entirely new range of "super-premium" ice cream products that were differentiated from the competition by both higher quality and higher price. Haagen–Dazs had initially marketed its products to small stores and restaurants for single-serving on-premises consumption. Haagen–Dazs had made only minimal inroads into the supermarkets, and now Mr. Mattus wanted to intensify his marketing efforts in that sector. Mr. Mattus asked for Arnold's help because he had been unable to convince the supermarkets to carry his products * * *.

Arnold, as the first distributor of Haagen–Dazs ice cream to supermarkets, sparked a revolution in the retail sale of ice cream. Arnold and Haagen–Dazs tapped a hitherto hidden demand for a super-premium ice cream in supermarkets by consumers who were willing to pay higher prices for higher quality. By the late 1970's, MIC was distributing ice cream products, including Haagen–Dazs ice cream, to four major supermarket chains * * * (the supermarkets) and to smaller grocery stores. However, neither Arnold nor MIC ever entered into a written distribution agreement with Haagen–Dazs or Mr. Mattus.

* * *

In 1983, the Pillsbury Co. (Pillsbury) purchased Haagen–Dazs from Mr. Mattus. Pillsbury promptly initiated a business plan to consolidate the distribution of Haagen–Dazs ice cream products into its own distribution centers, with the goal of delivering directly to retail stores, especially large supermarket chains. Pillsbury believed it could deliver a uniformly higher quality product to supermarkets at lower cost than independent distributors whose refrigeration equipment was not as reliable. * * *

* * *

In late 1985 or early 1986, representatives of Haagen–Dazs first approached [Arnold] about acquiring direct access to Arnold's relationships with the supermarkets and removing him as a middleman in the chain of distribution. * * * Haagen–Dazs did not want to leave distributors like Arnold, who had been with Haagen–Dazs since the early days of Mr. Mattus, without adequate reward for the role they had played in bringing Haagen–Dazs to prominence. * * * Haagen–Dazs believed that these various relationships, personal to Arnold, had value for which it was willing to pay. At the same time, Haagen–Dazs wished to terminate any residual rights to distribute Haagen–Dazs ice cream that its distributors might have acquired over the years * * *. Haagen–Dazs was not interested in acquiring MIC as an ongoing distributor to either the supermarkets or the small grocery stores and food service accounts or in acquiring its physical assets.

* * *

On July 8, 1988, Arnold, individually, and as president of [MIC], and [Beth L. Bronner], on behalf of Haagen–Dazs, signed an "Agreement For Purchase and Sale of Assets" by Arnold and [MIC], as "Sellers," in which the parties agreed to the terms of the sale and related documents. * * * [T]he Arnold-[MIC]-Haagen–Dazs agreement * * * purported to provide * * * for the purchase of all rights [to distribute Haagen–Dazs product] including but not limited to supermarket rights. This agreement * * * allocated the stated $1.5 million price to be paid at the closing, $300,000 to "Records" and $1,200,000 to "Sellers' Rights." There is no evidence in the record of any negotiation over this allocation or of any of the considerations that led Haagen–Dazs to allocate the purchase price in this fashion.

* * *

On July 22, 1988, Arnold and representatives of Haagen–Dazs closed the sale to Haagen–Dazs. * * * The closing documents contained an amendment to the purchase agreement * * * [that reduced] the agreed sale price [from] $1.5 million to $1,430,340 * * *.

The bill of sale, signed by Arnold individually and as president of [MIC], listed the items acquired from [MIC] as all existing customer lists, price lists, historical sales records, promotional allowance and rebate records, "and other business records as requested by Buyer, and the goodwill associated therewith."

Arnold also signed an "Assignment of Rights," which referenced—and transferred to Haagen–Dazs—the rights described above, in two capacities: first, as president of [MIC], and second, as an individual; there was no allocation of the consideration paid for the rights as between Arnold and [MIC]. * * *

OPINION

[Petitioner (MIC) contends that the $1,430,340 paid by Haagen–Dazs was realized by Arnold, not by MIC. Respondent claims] that the $1,430,340 consideration [represents] gain realized and recognized by MIC. * * *

We disagree with respondent's overall position, insofar as it is predicated on the assumption or conclusion that petitioner owned assets with a value of $1,430,340 that were sold to Haagen–Dazs. Petitioner never owned all the assets sold to Haagen–Dazs. The record shows, and we have found as facts, that Arnold, acting on his own behalf and as agent for [MIC], of which he was the sole shareholder, entered into a contract to sell Haagen–Dazs two distinctly different types of assets: The first, and much more valuable, was the intangible assets of Arnold's rights under his oral agreement with Mr. Mattus and his relationships with the owners and managers of the supermarkets, which formed the basis of his ability to direct the wholesale distribution of super-premium ice cream to the supermarkets; the second, and much less valuable, was the business records that had been created by petitioner during Arnold's development of the supermarket business * * *.

* * *

Ownership of the intangible assets cannot be attributed to petitioner because Arnold never entered into a covenant not to compete with petitioner or any other agreement—not even an employment agreement—by which any of Arnold's distribution agreements with Mr. Mattus, Arnold's relationships with the supermarkets, and Arnold's ice cream distribution expertise became the property of petitioner. This Court has long recognized that personal relationships of a shareholder-employee are not corporate assets when the employee has no employment contract with the corporation. Those personal assets are entirely distinct from the intangible corporate asset of corporate goodwill.

In the case at hand, petitioner never obtained exclusive rights to either Arnold's future services or a continuing call on the business generated by Arnold's personal relationships with the supermarket owners and the rights under his agreement with Mr. Mattus; petitioner never had an agreement with Arnold that would have caused those relationships and rights to become petitioner's property. Even if there had been such an agreement, and the record shows that there was none, the value of these relationships and rights would not have become petitioner's property in toto. In 1974, Mr. Mattus sought Arnold as his agent to create a substantial presence for Haagen–Dazs ice cream in supermarkets after Mr. Mattus had been able to achieve only minimal market penetration through his own efforts. Mr. Mattus wanted what Arnold had already created in the 1960's when he operated Arnold's Ice Cream—the critical relationships with key supermarket owners and managers and the marketing know-how necessary to put ice cream products in supermarket freezers. The record shows that, at most, petitioner had only the benefit of the use of these assets while Arnold was associated with petitioner—which contributed heavily to the profitability of petitioner * * *.

[A]ccordingly, we find that the sale to Haagen–Dazs of Arnold's supermarket relationships and distribution rights cannot be attributed to petitioner. All that is at stake in this case is the value of [the property transferred by MIC to Haagen–Dazs], shorn of [Arnold's] supermarket relationships and distribution rights under his agreement with Mr. Mattus. [We find that the fair market value of the property transferred by MIC to Haagen–Dazs was only $141,000.]

NOTES

1. *Transfer of shareholder asset.* Compare the tax consequences to MIC and Arnold of the Internal Revenue Service's position with the tax consequences of the Tax Court's findings. When a corporation sells its assets and liquidates, why is it advantageous to the seller if part of the purchase price is allocable to intangible assets owned by the shareholders of the selling corporation?

2. *Importance of form.* The Martin Ice Cream Company court found, "sufficient evidence in the record to support a finding that [MIC] received the entire [$1,430,340] payment from Haagen–Dazs. However, * * *, initial receipt of payment by [MIC] instead of Arnold does not determine the Federal tax treatment to [MIC] of the transactions at issue." How should Arnold and MIC have instructed Haagen–Dazs to disburse the funds?

3. *Pre-sale shareholder services.* Of what relevance was the absence of any employment agreement between Arnold and MIC to the outcome of the case? Did the parties forego any potential tax benefits by not entering into an employment agreement? See I.R.C. § 162(a)(1).

4. *Post-sale shareholder services.* Shareholders of the selling corporation who served as key-employees are often retained by the buyer to perform future services (under an employment agreement or a consulting agreement) and/or restricted by the buyer from competing with the buyer (under a covenant not to compete). No corporate tax is imposed on payments allocated to an employment agreement or a covenant not to compete if the arrangement is entered into with a shareholder-employee of the selling corporation, rather than with the selling corporation. Payments received by the shareholder-employee, however, are taxed as ordinary income. I.R.C. § 61(a)(1). Serious legal questions exist concerning the enforceability of covenants not to compete. See generally, Harlan M. Blake, "Employee Agreements Not to Compete," 73 Harvard Law Review 625 (1960).

2. TAX CONSEQUENCES TO BUYER

When a corporation sells its assets, the character of the seller's gains and losses is determined by the allocation of the purchase price among the transferred assets. The buyer's basis in each of the assets it acquires is also established by the allocation of the purchase price among the assets. I.R.C. § 1012. Basis is valuable to the buyer because it can offset future income of the buyer and thereby reduce the buyer's taxes at that time.

Due to the time value of money, a buyer normally desires to allocate the purchase price among the acquired assets in a manner that enables the buyer to offset income as quickly as possible. Thus, it is desirable to establish basis in accounts receivable, which are likely to be collected within a relatively short time, in inventory, which is likely to be sold within a relatively short time, and in depreciable personalty (e.g., machinery and equipment) that is subject to a relatively short recovery period.[14] In contrast, basis established in buildings, which are subject to lengthy recovery periods,[15] and land, which is not depreciable, is of much less value to the buyer. Little of this basis will offset income within a short period of time unless the buyer quickly resells the acquired assets.

The purchase price of an ongoing business often exceeds the aggregate value of the tangible assets acquired by the buyer. The difference represents a "premium" that is generally attributable to the reputation of the business ("goodwill") and the ability of the business to continue to function as an operating unit notwithstanding the change in ownership ("going concern value"). Prior to 1993, any basis allocated to purchased goodwill and going concern value was not amortizable (i.e., could not offset income until the acquired business was sold). Hence, buyers attempted to minimize the allocation of basis to these intangible assets. Congress responded to these efforts by mandating "the residual method," an allocation method that endeavors to maximize the amount of the purchase price allocated to goodwill and going concern value. See I.R.C. § 1060.

In 1993, Congress enacted I.R.C. § 197 which authorizes the amortization of basis in purchased goodwill and going concern value over a fifteen

---

14. Basis in most depreciable personalty is recovered over periods ranging from three to seven years. See I.R.C. § 168(c).

15. Under current law, the recovery period for residential rental property is 27.5 years and for nonresidential real property is 39 years. I.R.C. § 168(c)(1).

year period. Hence, basis allocated to goodwill and going concern value in acquisitions governed by I.R.C. § 197 is far more valuable to asset purchasers than basis that was allocated to these intangible assets under prior law. Indeed, it is now more desirable to allocate basis to goodwill and going concern value than to buildings or land. This section examines I.R.C. §§ 1060 and 197.

a. RESIDUAL METHOD OF ALLOCATION

I.R.C. § 1060

Treas. Reg. § 1.1060–1

Congress has mandated that the residual method be used to allocate the purchase price among assets acquired in a taxable transaction. See I.R.C. § 1060. The following excerpt from the Senate Finance Committee Report addresses the residual method:

Allocation of Purchase Price in Certain Sales of Assets (* * * New Section 1060 of the Code)

S.Rep. No. 313, 99th Cong., 2d Sess. (1986).

Present Law

A sale of a going business for a lump-sum amount is viewed as a sale of each individual asset rather than of a single capital asset. Both the buyer and the seller must allocate the purchase price among the assets for tax purposes. An allocation by the seller is necessary to determine the amount and character of the gain or loss, if any, it will recognize on the sale. An allocation by the buyer is necessary to determine its basis in the assets purchased. This allocation of basis will affect the amount of allowable depreciation or amortization deductions * * * by the buyer * * *.

Although the parties may agree to a specific allocation of the purchase price among the assets and reflect this allocation in the sales contract, the Code does not require such agreement; thus the contract may simply state the total purchase price * * *.

In general, a seller will benefit if a larger portion of the purchase price is allocable to "pure" capital assets, such as goodwill or going concern value * * *.

A buyer, on the other hand, will benefit from an allocation that results in a higher basis for inventory or other assets that would generate ordinary income if resold [or] to depreciable tangible assets such as buildings and equipment * * *.

If the parties to the sale of a going business fail to make an allocation of the purchase price among the assets of the business that is respected for tax purposes, the purchase price * * * must still be allocated among the * * * assets in proportion to their respective fair market values * * *.

The valuation of goodwill and going concern value is generally recognized as more difficult than the valuation of tangible assets or certain other types of intangibles. [A] commonly used [method] to value goodwill and going concern value [is] the residual method * * *. Under the residual method, the value of the goodwill and going concern value is the excess of the purchase price of the business over the aggregate fair market values of the tangible assets and the identifiable intangible assets other than goodwill and going concern value * * *.

* * *

Reasons for Change

The committee is aware that the allocation of purchase price among the assets of a going business has been a troublesome area of the tax law. Purchase price allocations have been an endless source of controversy between the Internal Revenue Service and taxpayers, principally because of the difficulty of establishing the value of goodwill and going concern value. * * * The committee therefore is requiring taxpayers to apply the residual method in allocating basis to goodwill and going concern value in all purchases of a going business * * *.

* * *

The committee is also concerned about the potential for abuse inherent in the sale of a going business where there is no agreement between the parties as to the value of specific assets. In many instances the parties' allocations for tax reporting purposes are inconsistent, resulting in a whipsaw of the government. The committee expects that requiring both parties to use the residual method for allocating amounts to nonamortizable goodwill and going concern value may diminish some of this "whipsaw" potential * * *.

Explanation of Provision

The bill requires that, in the case of any "applicable asset acquisition," both the buyer and the seller must allocate purchase price * * * [by using] the residual method * * *. An applicable asset acquisition is any transfer of assets constituting a business in which the transferee's basis is determined wholly by reference to the purchase price paid for the assets * * *. A group of assets will constitute a business for this purpose if their character is such that goodwill or going concern value could under any circumstances attach to such assets * * *. In requiring use of the residual method, the committee does not intend to restrict in any way the ability of the Internal Revenue Service to challenge the taxpayer's determination of the fair market value of any asset by any appropriate method.

* * *

NOTES

1. *Implementation of residual method of allocation.* The mechanics for allocating purchase price among assets acquired in an applicable asset acquisition are delineated in the regulations. See Treas. Reg. §§ 1.1060–1(c)(2), 1.338–6(b). Under the regulations, purchase price is first allocated to any acquired cash or bank deposits (Class I assets), dollar for dollar. The remaining purchase price is then allocated to any acquired certificates of deposit and marketable stocks and bonds (Class II assets) based on the market value of these instruments, then to accounts receivable and mortgages (Class III assets) based on market value, and then to inventory and like assets (Class IV assets) based on market value. The purchase price that remains is then allocated to Class V assets which are all assets that do not fall into another class. Any remaining purchase price is allocated to Class VI assets which are intangible assets other than goodwill and going concern value. If the total market value of the Class VI assets is less than the purchase price that remains to be allocated, the excess is allocated to goodwill and going concern value (Class VII assets).

2. *Reporting requirements.* The regulations under I.R.C. § 1060 mandate that both buyer and seller disclose to the Internal Revenue Service the allocation of the purchase price among the transferred assets. Treas. Reg. § 1.1060–1(e). Severe penalty exposure exists for any taxpayer who disregards the disclosure requirement. See I.R.C. §§ 6721(e)(2)(A), 6724(d)(1)(B)(xvii). In addition, the parties are bound by any agreed upon written allocation. I.R.C. § 1060(a) (second sentence). The Internal Revenue Service, however, may still challenge an allocation of purchase price agreed to by both buyer and seller. Treas. Reg. § 1.1060–1(c)(4).

b. UNIFORM AMORTIZATION OF INTANGIBLE ASSETS

I.R.C. § 197

Section 197 authorizes the amortization of virtually all purchased intangible assets (including goodwill and going concern value) over fifteen years. The legislative history that follows explains § 197:

Amortization of Goodwill and Certain Other Intangibles (* * * New Section 197 of the Code)

H.Rep. No. 11, 103rd Cong., 1st Sess. (1993).

Present Law

In determining taxable income for Federal income tax purposes, a taxpayer is allowed depreciation or amortization deductions for the cost or other basis of intangible property that is used in a trade or business or held for the production of income if the property has a limited useful life that may be determined with reasonable accuracy. Treas. Reg. sec. 1.167(a)–(3). These Treasury Regulations also state that no depreciation deductions are allowed with respect to goodwill.

* * *

Reasons for Change

The Federal income tax treatment of the costs of acquiring intangible assets is a source of considerable controversy between taxpayers and the Internal Revenue Service. * * *

It is believed that much of the controversy that arises under present law with respect to acquired intangible assets could be eliminated by specifying a single method and period for recovering the cost of most acquired intangible assets and by treating acquired goodwill and going concern value as amortizable intangible assets. It is also believed that there is no need at this time to change the Federal income tax treatment of self-created intangible assets, such as goodwill that is created through advertising and other similar expenditures.

Accordingly, the bill requires the cost of most acquired intangible assets, including goodwill and going concern value, to be amortized ratably over a [15–year] period. It is recognized that the useful lives of certain acquired intangible assets to which the bill applies may be shorter than [15 years], while the useful lives of other acquired intangible assets to which the bill applies may be longer than [15 years].

Explanation of Provision

In general

The bill allows an amortization deduction with respect to the capitalized costs of certain intangible property (defined as a section 197 intangible) that is acquired by a taxpayer and that is held by the taxpayer in connection with the conduct of a trade or business or an activity engaged in for the production of income. The amount of the deduction is determined by amortizing the adjusted basis (for purposes of determining gain) of the intangible ratably over a [15–year] period that begins with the month that the intangible is acquired. No other depreciation or amortization deduction is allowed with respect to a section 197 intangible that is acquired by a taxpayer.

* * *

Definition of section 197 intangible

In general

The term "section 197 intangible" is defined as any property that is included in any one or more of the following categories: (1) goodwill and going concern value; (2) certain specified types of intangible property that generally relate to workforce, information base, know-how, customers, suppliers, or other similar items; (3) any license, permit, or other right granted by a governmental unit or an agency or instrumentality thereof; (4) any covenant not to compete (or other arrangement to the extent that the arrangement has substantially the same effect as a covenant not to compete) entered into in connection with the direct or indirect acquisition of an interest in a trade or business (or a substantial portion thereof); and (5) any franchise, trademark, or trade name.

* * *

Goodwill and going concern value

For purposes of the bill, goodwill is the value of a trade or business that is attributable to the expectancy of continued customer patronage, whether due to the name of a trade or business, the reputation of a trade or business, or any other factor.

In addition, for purposes of the bill, going concern value is the additional element of value of a trade or business that attaches to property by reason of its existence as an integral part of a going concern. Going concern value includes the value that is attributable to the ability of a trade or business to continue to function and generate income without interruption notwithstanding a change in ownership. * * *

* * *

Covenants not to compete and other similar arrangements

The term "section 197 intangible" also includes any covenant not to compete (or other arrangement to the extent that the arrangement has substantially the same effect as a covenant not to compete; hereafter "other similar arrangement") entered into in connection with the direct or indirect acquisition of an interest in a trade or business (or a substantial portion thereof). * * *

Any amount that is paid or incurred under a covenant not to compete (or other similar arrangement) entered into in connection with the direct or indirect acquisition of an interest in a trade or business (or a substantial portion thereof) is chargeable to capital account and is to be amortized ratably over the [15–year] period specified in the bill. * * *

For purposes of this provision, an arrangement that requires the former owner of an interest in a trade or business to continue to perform services (or to provide property or the use of property) that benefit the trade or business is considered to have substantially the same effect as a covenant not to compete to the extent that the amount paid to the former owner under the arrangement exceeds the amount that represents reasonable compensation for the services actually rendered (or for the property or use of property actually provided) by the former owner. * * *

Exception for certain self-created intangibles

The bill generally does not apply to any section 197 intangible that is created by the taxpayer * * *.

NOTES

1. *Impact of § 197 on goodwill and going concern value.* Now that I.R.C. § 197 permits the amortization of goodwill and going concern value, do circumstances exist when taxpayers will affirmatively desire to allocate purchase price to these intangible assets?

2. *Impact of § 197 on covenants not to compete and employment agreements.* Prior to the enactment of I.R.C. § 197, payments by the buyer for the performance (or nonperformance) of services normally were deductible over the term of the agreement. How does I.R.C. § 197 impact on the buyer's tax treatment of amounts allocated to an employment agreement or a covenant not to compete?

3. EVALUATING THE RELATIVE POSITIONS OF SELLER AND BUYER IN AN ASSET SALE

Every dollar of gain recognized by the seller in an asset sale translates into an additional dollar of asset basis for the buyer. The seller's dollar of gain is taxed currently. In contrast, the buyer's dollar of basis generates future tax savings. Normally, the tax the seller pays today on a dollar of gain is more costly than the present value of the tax the buyer will save when a dollar of basis offsets future income. It is important to be able to quantify the tax effects to both parties as taxes often impact on the terms of an acquisition.

Example 11–C, which follows, demonstrates how the tax effects of an asset acquisition can be quantified. Inevitably, a myriad of assumptions must be made that may or may not prove accurate. Moreover, a host of non-tax considerations usually enter into, and often control, the structure of an acquisition. Taxes, however, are generally a significant factor in the negotiations between seller and buyer.

Example 11–C (Quantifying the tax effects of an asset sale): Alex is the sole shareholder of Waldo Corporation and he has a basis of $100,000 in his Waldo stock. Waldo's tangible assets consist of inventory, a building and land. In addition, substantial goodwill is associated with Waldo's assets. The following table summarizes the value and basis of Waldo's tangible and intangible assets:

	Basis	Value
Inventory	$1,000,000	$2,000,000
Building	1,000,000	2,000,000
Land	1,000,000	2,000,000
Goodwill	0	2,000,000
Total	$3,000,000	$8,000,000

Waldo has $2,000,000 of liabilities. Veranda Corporation will acquire all of Waldo's assets by paying Waldo $6,000,000 and assuming all of Waldo's liabilities.

Tax Consequences to Seller

1. Corporate Level—Waldo

    a. Realization Event (I.R.C. § 1001)

Amount Realized	$8,000,000
Less: Adjusted Basis	3,000,000
Realized and Recognized Gain	$5,000,000

    b. Character of Gain

(1) Inventory	$1,000,000 ordinary income
(2) Building	$1,000,000 § 1231 gain
(3) Land	$1,000,000 § 1231 gain
(4) Goodwill	$2,000,000 capital gain

    c. Tax Liability: $1,700,000 [16]

2. Shareholder Level—Alex

    a. Realization Event (I.R.C. § 331)

Amount Realized	$4,300,000 [17]
Less: Adjusted Basis	100,000
Realized and Recognized Gain	$4,200,000

    b. Character of Gain: capital gain

    c. Tax Liability: $630,000[18]

3. Net After Both Taxes Paid: $3,670,000[19]

---

16. $5,000,000 × 34% = $1,700,000. See I.R.C. § 11(b). This calculation assumes that Waldo has no net operating loss carryovers and no capital loss carryovers. See I.R.C. §§ 172, 1212(a).

17.

$6,000,000	(proceeds from sale of Waldo's assets)
−1,700,000	(Waldo's tax liability)
$4,300,000	

18. $4,200,000 × 15% = $630,000. See I.R.C. §§ 1(h).

19.

$6,000,000	(proceeds from sale of Waldo's assets)
−1,700,000	(Waldo's tax liability)
−630,000	(Alex's tax liability)
$3,670,000	

Tax Consequences to Buyer (Veranda)

1. Allocation of $5,000,000 of Additional Basis Resulting from Waldo's Gain

   a. Inventory $1,000,000
   b. Building $1,000,000
   c. Land $1,000,000
   d. Goodwill $2,000,000

2. Nominal Tax Savings from Additional Basis

a.	Inventory	$1,000,000 × 34% =	$ 340,000
b.	Building	$1,000,000 × 34% =	340,000
c.	Land	$1,000,000 × 34% =	340,000
d.	Goodwill	$2,000,000 × 34% =	680,000
	Total		$1,700,000

3. Assumptions to Derive Present Value of Tax Savings

   a. Veranda will be taxed at a 34% marginal rate in all future years.
   b. Veranda can indefinitely earn an annual after-tax return of 6% on its investments (a 6% discount factor is appropriate).
   c. The inventory is sold one year after it is acquired.
   d. The recovery period for the building is forty years and Veranda will hold the building for forty years.
   e. Veranda will sell all of its assets at a gain after forty years.

4. Present Value of Tax Savings to Buyer [20]

a.	Inventory	$340,000 × .943	= $321,000
b.	Building	[$340,000 ÷ 40] × 15.05	= 128,000
c.	Land	$340,000 × .097	= 33,000
d.	Goodwill	[$680,000 ÷ 15] × 9.71	= 440,000
	Total		$922,000

Conclusion: $1,700,000 of Corporate Tax Paid by Seller Creates $922,000 of Savings for Buyer.

Problem 11–4 (Intangible asset owned by shareholder): How would the tax effects to Seller and Buyer in Example 11–C change if the value of Waldo's goodwill was only $1,000,000 and Veranda acquired all of Waldo's assets by paying $5,000,000 and assuming all of Waldo's liabilities? In addition, Veranda paid *Alex* $1,000,000 for an intangible asset that Alex created and owned. See I.R.C. § 197.

Problem 11–5 (Covenant not to compete): How would the tax effects to Seller and Buyer in Example 11–C change if the value of Waldo's goodwill was only $1,000,000 and Veranda acquired all of Waldo's assets by paying $5,000,000 and assuming all of Waldo's liabilities? In

---

20. See Tables 11–1 and 11–2, p. 469.

addition, Veranda paid *Alex* $1,000,000 to refrain from competing with Veranda for a period of one year. See I.R.C. § 197.

Problem 11–6 (Employment contract): How would the tax effects to Seller and Buyer in Example 11–C change if the value of Waldo's goodwill was only $1,000,000 and Veranda acquired all of Waldo's assets by paying $5,000,000 and assuming all of Waldo's liabilities? In addition, Veranda paid *Alex* $1,000,000 to perform services for Veranda for a period of one year. See I.R.C. § 162(a).

4. CONTINGENT LIABILITIES

IRS Technical Advice Memorandum 9721002

1/24/97.

* * *

FACTS

[Acquiring Corporation purchased the assets, assumed the liabilities and took over the employees of Target Corporation.] * * * [Shortly] after the purchase, [Acquiring Corporation] issued termination notices to 40 [individuals who had served as] senior executives of [Target Corporation] as part of a central office consolidation. * * * [T]he senior executives had previously entered into individual "termination protection agreements" with Target. These agreements guaranteed severance pay for two years if the executives were involuntarily terminated for any reason other than cause or disability. * * * [Acquiring Corporation made the severance payments to the terminated executives and] deducted these costs as ordinary and necessary business expenses * * *.

APPLICABLE LAW

Section 162(a) states that a deduction is allowed for all ordinary and necessary expenses paid or incurred during the taxable year in carrying on any trade or business. * * *

Section 263(a) denies a deduction for any amount paid out for new buildings or for permanent improvements or betterments made to increase the value of any property. * * *

Rev. Rul. 94–77, 1994–2 C.B. 19, holds that severance payments made by a taxpayer to its employees when down-sizing its business relate principally to previously rendered services, even though the payments may produce some future benefits. These payments are therefore generally deductible as business expenses under section 162. The ruling states, however, that no conclusion is reached on the tax treatment of severance payments made in connection with the acquisition of property.

* * *

DISCUSSION

Issue 1: Whether severance payments made by [Acquiring Corporation] resulted from [Target Corporation] liabilities, either fixed or contingent, [Acquiring Corporation] may be considered to have assumed.

A buyer who purchases business assets and assumes a seller's liabilities, fixed or contingent, in connection with the acquisition must capitalize payments made on such liabilities. A buyer's payment of the liabilities is not the discharge of a burden the law placed on the buyer; it is actually as well as theoretically a part of the purchase price. As a factual matter, however, it is sometimes difficult to distinguish between contingent liabilities assumed from the seller and expenses the buyer incurs while operating the ongoing acquired business.

In Pacific Transport Company v. Commissioner, 483 F.2d 209 (9th Cir.1973), the taxpayer purchased the [assets] of a corporation which, at the time of acquisition, was litigating an asserted tort liability for the loss of a cargo ship at sea. The taxpayer assumed the contingent tort liability * * * and then deducted the payment it made in discharging the liability. The court included the payment in the basis of the acquired assets, stating that:

> though the purchase price * * * was not discounted for the cargo loss liability, there is no question but that the parties were aware of the contingent liability and that * * * the assets were taken subject to that liability.

In Portland Gasoline Company v. Commissioner, 181 F.2d 538 (5th Cir.1950), the taxpayer purchased all the assets of a corporation in March of 1934 and agreed to pay a note the corporation had guaranteed in 1930. The court held that the taxpayer's payment of the note in 1943 to avoid a potential lawsuit was a capital expenditure because the threat of suit by the creditor derived from an obligation for which the selling corporation alone was liable.

In David R. Webb Company, Inc. v. Commissioner, 708 F.2d 1254 (7th Cir.1983), the taxpayer purchased the assets of a business in 1972. In 1950, the business had entered into an employment agreement with an employee-shareholder providing that, if he died while still an employee, his widow would be entitled to a lifetime pension. The shareholder died in 1952 and, from 1953 through 1966, the corporation made and deducted the annual pension payments. The assets of the corporation were sold in 1966, again in 1969, and finally sold to the taxpayer in 1972. In each sale, the pension liability was expressly assumed by the purchaser. The court disallowed the taxpayer's deduction of the pension payments and held that they should be capitalized and added to the basis of the acquired property.

In Rev. Rul. 76–520, 1976–2 C.B. 42, the Service considered the treatment of costs incurred by an acquiring corporation in fulfilling prepaid subscription contracts entered into by a target corporation before, and assumed by the acquiring corporation in, an [asset] acquisition * * *. The ruling holds that the payments must be capitalized and added to the basis of the assets acquired because they were made to satisfy a liability incurred not in the course of the acquiring corporation's operations, but in the course of the target's. As a result, the payments could not be deducted.

In contrast to the preceding precedent, the following cases treat the liabilities as those of the acquiring corporation.

In United States v. Minneapolis & St. Louis Railway Company, 260 F.2d 663 (8th Cir.1958), the court considered whether the taxpayer's payment of retroactive wage increases to employees of an acquired railroad were capital expenditures or deductible business expenses. In September 1942, labor unions with which the railroad had contracts demanded an increase in wages. In December 1943, the taxpayer acquired the railroad's assets and six weeks later agreed to a retroactive wage increase for February 1943 through November 1943. The court held that the taxpayer could deduct the retroactive wage payments as ordinary and necessary operating expenses. The trial court had noted, and the appellate court agreed, that the wages could not be characterized as capital expenditures unless the railroad was liable to pay them at the time of acquisition or the parties had agreed expressly or impliedly that the buyer would pay, as partial consideration for the assets, any retroactive wages resulting from a settlement of the wage dispute.

Similarly, in Albany Car Wheel Company v. Commissioner, 40 T.C. 831 (1963), aff'd per curiam 333 F.2d 653 (2d Cir.1964), the taxpayer corporation purchased a business and assumed its liabilities. The seller had been obligated, under a union contract, to compensate any covered employee who might be severed from employment. As part of the purchase, this contract was renegotiated so that the taxpayer need pay severance only if it failed to give adequate notice. The taxpayer argued that an estimate of this severance pay liability should be included in the basis of the acquired assets. The court concluded, however, that the obligation was not an assumed liability because the taxpayer had no obligation to pay if it gave the required notice. As this made the obligation speculative, it could not be considered a cost of acquiring the [Target Corporation's] assets.

In M. Buten & Sons, Inc. v. Commissioner, T.C. Memo. 1972–44, the taxpayer corporation, formed when a partnership of the same name was incorporated, assumed, upon formation, all liabilities of the partnership, including pension benefits paid under the partnership agreement to a partner's widow. At the time of incorporation, the partners-now-shareholders restated the pension obligation for then-living wives. Two years later, a shareholder died and pension payments were made to the post-incorporation widow as well as the pre-incorporation widow. The court allowed a deduction for payments to the post-incorporation widow but not the pre-incorporation widow, because the latter were made on an assumed liability, i.e., a cost of acquiring the assets.

To summarize, in the precedent requiring the buyer to capitalize, rather than deduct, the payment of an obligation, the events most crucial to creation of the obligation occur before the acquisition. Under these circumstances, the obligation is treated as a liability of the seller. By contrast, in cases allowing the buyer to take a deduction, the events most crucial to creation of the obligation occur after the acquisition. Under these circumstances, the obligation is a liability of the buyer. The difference in the cases is therefore the degree to which the obligation was fixed at the time of the acquisition.

In the instant case, a liability for severance payments to [the former employees of Target] could arise only if employees were involuntarily terminated. As no employee had been terminated by the date of acquisition, no liability existed for [Acquiring Corporation] to assume. * * * [Acquiring Corporation] was free to decide after the acquisition whether to terminate employees and become liable. * * *

Hence, this case more closely resembles cases in which the events most crucial to creation of the obligation occurred after the acquisition. Because no employee was terminated before the date of acquisition, no liability arose before the acquisition * * *. Thus, the severance payments did not result from liabilities of Target, either fixed or contingent, that [Acquiring Corporation] could be treated as assuming in the acquisition.

Issue 2: If the severance payments resulted from [Acquiring Corporation] liabilities (rather than [Target Corporation] liabilities), whether [Acquiring Corporation] may deduct the payments as ordinary and necessary business expenses or must capitalize them as a cost of acquiring [Target Corporation].

Whether an expenditure is capital or deductible is determined by carefully examining the facts and circumstances of each situation. An expenditure incurred in a taxpayer's business may qualify as ordinary and necessary under section 162 if it is appropriate and helpful in carrying on that business, is commonly and frequently incurred in the type of business conducted by the taxpayer, and is not a capital expenditure under section 263.

Generally, severance payments made in the ordinary course of a taxpayer's business are deductible as ordinary and necessary business expenses. However, courts have consistently held that costs incurred incident to a corporate reorganization, recapitalization, or acquisition by another entity should be capitalized.

A deductible expense, however, is not converted into a capital expenditure solely because the expense is incurred in a corporate acquisition. Rather, the nature of a payment should be determined under the "origin of the claim doctrine" established by the Supreme Court in United States v. Gilmore, 372 U.S. 39 (1963). This doctrine provides that the origin and character of a claim determine the deductibility of the related expense. The characterization of costs depends on the nature of the activities giving rise to the claim, not on consequence or result.

[A]lthough severance payments here were coincidental with [Acquiring Corporation's] acquisition of Target, the severance payments had their origin in [Acquiring Corporation's] termination of Target employees. While the acquisition may have been the catalyst for the employees' receipt of the severance payments, the acquisition was not itself the basis for the payments. Accordingly, the severance payments need not be capitalized and added to the basis of the stock purchased.

   * * *

CONCLUSIONS

The severance payments did not result from a liability of [Target Corporation], either fixed or contingent, that [Acquiring Corporation] could be treated as assuming. Because the severance payments were not made in connection with the acquisition of Target, [Acquiring Corporation] is not required to capitalize the cost of severance payments and is not precluded by section 263 from deducting severance payments as ordinary and necessary expenses under section 162.

* * *

NOTES

1. *Impact of capitalization on buyer.* Will the buyer derive any tax benefits if the buyer is required to capitalize payments made on an assumed liability? See I.R.C. §§ 197, 1060.

2. *Consequences to seller.* When a fixed liability of a corporation that sells its assets is assumed, the amount of the liability is included in the seller's amount realized at the time of sale. See Treas. Reg. §§ 1.1001–2(a)(1), (4)(ii). When a contingent liability of the seller is assumed, the tax consequences to the seller are less clear. The amount of the liability might be estimated at the time of sale and the estimated amount included in the seller's amount realized at that time. Alternatively, the actual amount of the liability might be added to the seller's income if and when the liability becomes fixed. If the contingent liability would have given rise to a deduction if paid by the seller, the seller may still be allowed a deduction, either at the time of sale or at the time the liability becomes fixed. Administrative guidance is sorely needed on these issues.

C.   STOCK TRANSFER

1.   TAX CONSEQUENCES TO SELLER

When all the stock of a corporation is sold, each selling shareholder recognizes as gain (or loss) the difference between the amount realized (the money received) and the seller's adjusted basis in the stock. I.R.C. § 1001. That gain (or loss) is normally characterized as capital gain (or loss). I.R.C. §§ 1221, 1222. But see I.R.C. § 1244 (p. 300, Note 2).

A stock sale normally results in only one tax to the seller (a shareholder level tax). In contrast, an asset sale normally results in two taxes to the seller (a corporate level tax and a shareholder level tax). No gain or loss is realized at the corporate level in a stock sale. Why not?

2.   TAX CONSEQUENCES TO BUYER

In a stock purchase, the buyer takes a cost basis in the acquired stock. I.R.C. § 1012. The basis of the assets of the acquired corporation (the "target"), however, is unaffected by the stock transfer. Why? When the target owns appreciated assets, the absence of any adjustment to the basis of those assets makes a stock purchase less attractive than an asset purchase from the buyer's perspective. Why? Both the courts and Congress have long been receptive to the desire of stock purchasers to step-up the basis of the target's appreciated assets to fair market value. The means to achieving this end, however, have changed dramatically over time.

a. HISTORICAL PERSPECTIVE

Kimbell–Diamond Milling Company v. Commissioner

Tax Court of the United States, 1950.
14 T.C. 74, aff'd. 187 F.2d 718 (5th Cir.1951).

■ BLACK, JUDGE: * * *

Petitioner is a Texas corporation, engaged primarily in the business of milling, processing, and selling grain products * * *.

[O]n December 26, 1942, petitioner's directors approved the transaction set forth in the minutes below:

1. That the proper officers of Kimbell–Diamond Milling Company be, and they are hereby, authorized, empowered and directed to purchase the entire authorized, issued and outstanding capital stock of Whaley Mill & Elevator Company, a Texas corporation * * *.

2. That as soon as practicable after the purchase of the Whaley Mill & Elevator Company stock hereby authorized has been consummated, all necessary steps be taken to completely liquidate the said corporation by transferring its entire assets * * * to Kimbell–Diamond Milling Company in cancellation and redemption of the entire issued and outstanding capital stock of Whaley Mill & Elevator Company * * *.

On December 26, 1942, petitioner acquired 100 per cent of the stock of Whaley Mill & Elevator Co. of Gainesville, Texas, paying therefor $210,000 in cash * * *.

On December 29, 1942, the stockholders of Whaley [i.e., Kimbell–Diamond] assented to the dissolution and distribution of assets thereof. On the same date an "Agreement and Program of Complete Liquidation" was entered into between petitioner and Whaley, which provided, inter alia:

THAT, WHEREAS, KIMBELL–DIAMOND owns the entire authorized issued and outstanding capital stock of WHALEY * * * which said stock was acquired by KIMBELL–DIAMOND primarily for the purpose of enabling it to secure possession and ownership of the flour mill and milling plant owned by WHALEY, the parties herewith agree that the said mill and milling plant shall forthwith be conveyed to KIMBELL–DIAMOND by WHALEY under the following program for the complete liquidation of WHALEY viz:

(1) KIMBELL–DIAMOND shall cause the * * * shares of the capital stock of WHALEY owned by it to be surrendered to WHALEY for cancellation and retirement, whereupon WHALEY shall forthwith convey, transfer and assign unto KIMBELL–DIAMOND all property of every kind and character owned or claimed by it * * * in full and complete liquidation of all of the outstanding stock of WHALEY. The

aforesaid distribution in complete liquidation shall be fully consummated by not later than midnight, December 31, 1942.

(2) When the entire assets of every kind and character, owned by WHALEY, have been transferred to KIMBELL–DIAMOND in full and complete liquidation of the capital stock of WHALEY, owned by KIMBELL–DIAMOND, WHALEY shall forthwith make application to the Secretary of State of the State of Texas for its dissolution as a corporation and surrender its corporate charter.

[Whaley was liquidated pursuant to the plan. Whaley's total adjusted basis in its assets at the time of liquidation was $328,736.59.]

[P]etitioner * * * proceeded under the theory that [Kimbell–Diamond] was entitled to Whaley's basis [in its assets]. Respondent takes the position that petitioner's cost [of the Whaley stock] is its basis in the assets acquired from Whaley * * *.

[P]etitioner argues that the acquisition of Whaley's assets and the subsequent liquidation of Whaley brings petitioner within the provisions of [the predecessor to I.R.C. § 332] and, therefore, by reason of [the predecessor to I.R.C. § 334(b)(1)], petitioner's basis in these assets is the same as the basis in Whaley's hands. In so contending petitioner asks that we treat the acquisition of Whaley's stock and the subsequent liquidation of Whaley as separate transactions. It is well settled that the incidence of taxation depends upon the substance of a transaction. Commissioner v. Court Holding Co., 324 U.S. 331. It is inescapable from petitioner's minutes set out above and from the "Agreement and Program of Complete Liquidation" entered into between petitioner and Whaley, that the only intention petitioner ever had was to acquire Whaley's assets.

* * *

We hold that the purchase of Whaley's stock and its subsequent liquidation must be considered as one transaction, namely, the purchase of Whaley's assets which was petitioner's sole intention. [P]etitioner's basis in these assets * * * is, therefore, its cost * * *. Since petitioner does not controvert respondent's allocation of cost to the individual assets acquired from Whaley, both depreciable and nondepreciable, respondent's allocation is sustained.

NOTES

1. *Principal beneficiary of decision.* Was the Kimbell–Diamond decision more likely to help the buyer or the government in most instances when a stock purchaser liquidated the target corporation immediately after the acquisition? Does the decision have any implications on transactions outside of the corporate acquisition area?

2. *Impact on seller.* What impact did the Kimbell–Diamond decision have on the sellers of the Whaley Stock?

3. *Mandatory regime of former I.R.C. § 334(b)(2).* After the Kimbell–Diamond decision was rendered, no clear guidelines existed as to when a stock purchase followed by a liquidation of the target would cause the acquiring corporation to be treated as though it bought the target's assets, rather than receiving those assets in a liquidating distribution from the target. Congress responded to the unpredictability created by the Kimbell–Diamond decision in the Internal Revenue Code of 1954. The 1954 Code treated the acquiring corporation as buying the target's assets when, pursuant to a plan, it bought target stock and liquidated the target within two years after the stock purchase. Under these circumstances, the basis in the target's assets would be "stepped-up" (or "stepped-down") to match the acquiring corporation's cost basis in the target stock. Former I.R.C. § 334(b)(2).

In 1982, Congress repealed the mandatory regime of former I.R.C. § 334(b)(2) and enacted a new and different elective regime. See I.R.C. § 338. Now, a mere election, rather than an actual liquidation, is necessary to establish a basis in the target's assets equivalent to the cost of its stock. Moreover, in light of Congress's intent to eliminate any remaining remnants of the Kimbell–Diamond doctrine from the stock purchase arena, the mere liquidation of a target should not affect the basis in the target's assets under any circumstances.

b.   THE I.R.C. § 338 GENERAL ELECTION

I.R.C. §§ 338(a), (b), (d), (g), (h)(1)–(3)

Under I.R.C. § 338, when a corporation that buys the stock of a target corporation makes the requisite election, the following events are deemed to occur with the corresponding tax consequences:

> 1.   The target corporation sells its assets at market value in a taxable transaction immediately *after* the stock purchase (the "deemed sale"); and,
>
> 2.   on the next day, a new corporation repurchases the target's assets at a price related to the cost of the target stock (the "deemed purchase").

See I.R.C. § 338(a).

Eligibility: A corporation need not purchase all of the target's stock to be eligible to make an election under I.R.C. § 338. Moreover, the buyer need not acquire the target's stock in a single transaction. Rather, eligibility to make the election exists whenever a "qualified stock purchase" occurs. See I.R.C. § 338(d)(3). Such a purchase occurs when stock representing at least 80% of the voting stock of target *and* at least 80% of the value of all the common stock (and certain preferred stock) of target is acquired by a corporation in one or more taxable transactions during a twelve month period (the "12–month acquisition period"). See I.R.C. §§ 338(h)(1), (3), 1504(a)(2). The election must be made on or before the fifteenth day of the ninth month beginning after the month that includes the day on which the 80% ownership threshold is crossed (the "acquisition date"). See I.R.C. §§ 338(g)(1), (h)(2).

Example 11–D (Identifying qualified stock purchase and time period for making election): Target Corporation has 1,000 shares of a single class of common stock outstanding on July 1, Year 3, and at all times thereafter. Acquiring Corporation purchased 950 shares of Target as follows:

Date of Purchase	Number of Shares
July 1, Year 3	100
October 1, Year 3	150
August 1, Year 4	600
September 1, Year 4	100

The first potential "12–month acquisition period" runs from July 1, Year 3 (the date of the first purchase of Target stock by Acquiring) until June 30, Year 4. No "qualified stock purchase" occurred during this period, however, because Acquiring only acquired 25% of the stock of Target during this period.[21] The next potential "12–month acquisition period" runs from October 1, Year 3 (the date of the second purchase of Target stock by Acquiring) until September 30, Year 4. A "qualified stock purchase" occurred during this period because Acquiring bought 85% of the stock of Target during this period.[22] The "acquisition date" was September 1, Year 4, the day during the "12–month acquisition period" that the 80% threshold was crossed. (Note that the 100 shares acquired on July 1, Year 3, are not counted for this purpose since they were acquired before the "12–month acquisition period" commenced.) The earliest date on which Acquiring may make a § 338 election is September 1, Year 4 (the "acquisition date"). The latest date on which Acquiring may make a § 338 election is June 15, Year 5 (the 15th day of the ninth month after the month in which the "acquisition date" occurred).

Deemed Sale and Deemed Repurchase: When a buyer makes an election under I.R.C. § 338, the price at which the target's assets are deemed to be sold is "market value" but the price at which the assets are deemed to be repurchased is tied to the basis of the target's stock, rather than the market value of the target's assets. Compare I.R.C. § 338(a)(1) to I.R.C. § 338(b). If the acquiring corporation purchases all of the target stock at a price equal to the value of target's assets less its liabilities, the election will lead to a market value basis in the target's assets.[23] To arrive at the basis

---

21. Acquiring acquired 250 of the 1,000 outstanding Target shares (25%) during the period from July 1, Year 3, through June 30, Year 4. Specifically, 100 shares of Target were acquired on July 1, Year 3, and an additional 150 shares of Target were acquired on October 1, Year 3.

22. Acquiring acquired 850 of the 1,000 outstanding Target shares (85%) during the period from October 1, Year 3, through September 30, Year 4. Specifically, 150 shares of Target were acquired on October 1, Year 3, 600 additional shares of Target were acquired on August 1, Year 4, and 100 additional shares of Target were acquired on September 1, Year 4.

23. If the buyer acquires less than 100% of target's stock or makes multiple purchases at different prices, the basis in the assets may deviate from the value of the assets. See I.R.C. § 338(b); Treas. Reg. § 1.338–5.

in the target's assets, the purchase price of the target stock is increased by all liabilities of the target, including the corporate tax liability triggered by the deemed sale. See Treas. Reg. § 1.338–5.

> *Example 11–E (Illustration of deemed sale and repurchase)*: Target Corporation has 1,000 shares of a single class of common stock outstanding on January 1, Year 5. Target has an adjusted basis in its assets of $340,000 and the assets have a fair market value of $1,340,000. On January 1, Year 5, Acquiring buys all of the stock of Target for $1,000,000 and makes an election under I.R.C. § 338. As a result, Target is deemed to sell its assets on January 1, Year 5 for their fair market value ($1,340,000) resulting in a gain of $1,000,000 and a tax liability of $340,000. Target also is deemed to repurchase its assets for $1,340,000 (an amount equal to the basis Acquiring took in the Target stock ($1,000,000) increased by the tax liability imposed on Target by the deemed sale ($340,000)).

When an election under I.R.C. § 338 is made, the "residual method of allocation" is utilized to allocate the basis among the target corporation's assets. See I.R.C. § 338(b)(5); Treas. Reg. § 1.338–6. This is the same method now mandated by I.R.C. § 1060 in the case of a taxable asset transfer.[24] In fact, because I.R.C. § 338 predates I.R.C. § 1060, Congress simply incorporated the allocation rules utilized by I.R.C. § 338 by reference when I.R.C. § 1060 was enacted. See I.R.C. § 1060(a) (end of first sentence).

NOTES

1. *Stock price less than value of assets.* In Example 11–E, why would the buyer only pay $1,000,000 for all the stock of a corporation that had assets with a fair market value of $1,340,000?

2. *Corporate versus individual purchaser.* Only a corporate purchaser is eligible to make an election under I.R.C. § 338. See I.R.C. §§ 338(a), (d)(1). How might an individual who purchases the stock of a target corporation establish a fair market value basis in the assets of the target? See I.R.C. §§ 331, 334(a), 336.

3. EVALUATING THE RELATIVE POSITIONS OF SELLER AND BUYER IN A STOCK SALE (WITH § 338 ELECTION)

Before the repeal of the General Utilities rule (pp. 29–33), an election under I.R.C. § 338 was routinely made when the target corporation owned

---

24. For a discussion of the residual method of allocation, see pp. 480–482.

appreciated assets and the election therefore resulted in a "step-up" in basis of the target's assets. Under these circumstances, the gain realized on the "deemed sale" generally was not recognized due to the General Utilities rule. Hence, an election under I.R.C. § 338 simply resulted in a "free" step-up in the basis of the target's assets as a result of the "deemed purchase."

Since the repeal of the General Utilities rule in 1986, however, gain is normally recognized by the target on the "deemed sale" that occurs when an election is made under I.R.C. § 338. Thus, the price of a step-up in basis in the target's assets under current law is a corporate tax on the appreciation in those assets. In effect, this is the same corporate tax imposed in an asset sale. The corporate tax is imposed on the buyer, however, in the case of a stock purchase followed by a § 338 election. Although the target technically incurs the tax liability, the buyer effectively bears the cost of the tax because the buyer owns the target when the tax is triggered.

A buyer that plans to make a § 338 election normally will pay less for target stock than for target assets. Specifically, the purchase price will be reduced by the corporate tax on the target's assets. The fact that the buyer will pay less for target stock than for target assets should not make a stock sale less appealing to the seller. The reduced purchase price simply reflects the shift to the buyer of a cost (the corporate tax liability) that would have been borne by the seller had the transaction been structured as an asset sale.

Example 11–F (Quantifying the tax effects of a stock sale with a § 338 election): In Example 11–C (p. 485), Veranda Corporation acquired all of Waldo Corporation's assets for $6,000,000 and the assumption by Veranda of all of Waldo's liabilities. The acquisition triggered a corporate tax liability to Waldo of $1,700,000.

If, instead of structuring the acquisition as an asset purchase, the transaction were structured as a stock purchase where Veranda intended to make a § 338 election, Veranda would bear Waldo's corporate tax liability. Thus, Veranda should only be willing to pay $4,300,000 for Waldo's stock.[25] How do Waldo's liabilities impact on the purchase price of its stock?

The analysis that follows demonstrates that the purchase of Waldo's stock for $4,300,000 leads to the same end points as the purchase of Waldo's assets and liabilities for $6,000,000 (compare pp. 485–487).

25.

$6,000,000 (value of Waldo's assets less its liabilities)
−1,700,000 (Waldo's tax liability if its assets are sold)
$4,300,000

Tax Consequences to Seller

1. Corporate Level—Waldo

   No Tax Liability

2. Shareholder Level—Alex

   a. Realization Event (I.R.C. § 1001)

Amount Realized	$4,300,000
Less: Adjusted Basis	100,000
Realized and Recognized Gain	$4,200,000

   b. Character of Gain: capital gain

   c. Tax Liability: $630,000 [26]

3. Net After Tax Paid: $3,670,000 [27]

Tax Consequences to Buyer (Veranda)

Impact of § 338 Election on Waldo

1. "Deemed Sale" (I.R.C. § 338(a)(1))

   a. Realization Event

Amount Realized	$8,000,000
Less: Adjusted Basis	3,000,000
Realized and Recognized Gain	$5,000,000

   b. Character of Gain

(1) Inventory	$1,000,000	ordinary income
(2) Building	$1,000,000	§ 1231 gain
(3) Land	$1,000,000	§ 1231 gain
(4) Goodwill	$2,000,000	capital gain

   c. Tax Liability: $1,700,000 [28]

---

26. $4,200,000 × 15% = $630,000. See I.R.C. § 1(h).

27.

$4,300,000 (proceeds from sale of Waldo's stock)
− 630,000 (Alex's tax liability)
$3,670,000

28. $5,000,000 × 34% = $1,700,000. See I.R.C. § 11(b). This calculation assumes that Waldo has no net operating loss carryovers and no capital loss carryovers. See I.R.C. §§ 172, 1212(a).

2. "Deemed Purchase" (I.R.C. §§ 338(a)(2), (b))

a. Grossed-up basis of recently purchased stock adjusted by target's liabilities (see Treas. Reg. § 1.338–5):

Stock Basis	$4,300,000
Liabilities of Target	2,000,000
Tax Liability of Target	1,700,000
Total	$8,000,000

b. Allocation of $5,000,000 of Additional Basis Resulting from Waldo's Gain (I.R.C. § 338(b)(5))
   (1) Inventory $1,000,000
   (2) Building $1,000,000
   (3) Land $1,000,000
   (4) Goodwill $2,000,000

c. Nominal Tax Savings from Additional Basis
   (1) Inventory $1,000,000 × 34% = $ 340,000
   (2) Building $1,000,000 × 34% = 340,000
   (3) Land $1,000,000 × 34% = 340,000
   (4) Goodwill $2,000,000 × 34% = 680,000
       Total $1,700,000

d. Assumptions To Derive Present Value of Tax Savings

   (1) Waldo will be taxed at a 34% marginal rate in all future years.
   (2) Waldo can indefinitely earn an annual after-tax return of 6% on its investments (a 6% discount factor is appropriate).
   (3) The inventory is sold one year after it is acquired.
   (4) The recovery period for the building is forty years and Waldo will hold the building for forty years.
   (5) Waldo will sell all of its assets at a gain after forty years.

e. Present Value of Tax Savings to Buyer [29]

   (1) Inventory $340,000 × .943 = $321,000
   (2) Building [$340,000 ÷ 40] × 15.05 = 128,000
   (3) Land $340,000 × .097 = 33,000
   (4) Goodwill [$680,000 ÷ 15] × 9.71 = 440,000
       Total $922,000

Conclusion: $1,700,000 of Corporate Tax Borne by Seller (due to reduction in purchase price of stock) Creates $922,000 of Savings for Buyer.

Example 11–F demonstrates that the tax law would not cause the parties to favor one acquisition technique over the other *if* the § 338 election were mandatory. Regardless of whether the transaction were

---

29. See Tables 11–1 and 11–2, p. 469.

structured as an asset sale or a stock sale, the government would collect the corporate tax on the target's assets in the year of sale and the step-up in the basis of the target's assets would generate tax savings in future years. Consequently, the collective tax cost would be the same whether the transaction was structured as an asset sale or as a stock sale.

4.   EVALUATING THE RELATIVE POSITIONS OF SELLER AND BUYER IN A STOCK SALE (WITHOUT § 338 ELECTION)

I.R.C. § 338 treatment is not mandatory; it is merely elective. An opportunity often exists, therefore, to effectuate a stock sale at a lower collective tax cost than an asset sale by having the buyer refrain from making an election under I.R.C. § 338. A stock sale without a § 338 election still shifts the burden of the corporate tax on the target's assets from the seller to the buyer. Foregoing the § 338 election, however, enables the buyer to bear that burden in the future (by foregoing additional basis in the target's assets that would offset future target income), rather than in the year of sale. The present value of the buyer's future tax burden is generally less than the cost of a current tax on the target's appreciated assets. The savings that result from deferring the corporate tax can be divided between the parties by establishing a purchase price that improves the position of the buyer and the position of the seller relative to each party's position in an asset sale or a stock sale with a § 338 election.

> *Problem 11–7 (Quantifying the tax effects of a stock sale without a § 338 election)*: In Example 11–F (p. 498), assume that Veranda purchases all of the stock of Waldo but refrains from making a § 338 election.
>
> (a) How much does foregoing the step-up in Waldo's assets cost Veranda from a present value standpoint? How does this cost compare to the cost of making a § 338 election? (The answers to these questions are in Example 11–F.)
>
> (b) What is the highest price that Veranda should be willing to pay for the Waldo stock if a § 338 election is *not* made?
>
> (c) What is the lowest price at which Alex should be willing to sell the Waldo stock if a § 338 election is *not* made?
>
> (d) If the seller and the buyer have equal bargaining power and each knows that Veranda need not make a § 338 election, at what price should the Waldo stock be transferred to Veranda?

NOTES

1.   *Impact of tax law on taxable transfer of incorporated business.* Focusing exclusively on tax considerations, would you expect most taxable acquisitions to be structured as asset transfers or stock transfers under current law? Can the way in which the tax law impacts on how taxable acquisitions are structured be justified? How might the tax law be changed to neutralize its impact on taxable acquisitions?

2.   *Identifying when a § 338 election is desirable.* Can you think of any circumstances in which an election under I.R.C. § 338 remains desirable after the repeal of the General Utilities rule? What if, in Example 11–F, Waldo had a $5,000,000 net operating loss? Is a stock sale preferable to an asset sale under these circumstances?

3. *Covenants not to compete and employment agreements.* When stock of a corporation is sold, does any tax incentive exist to allocate part of the purchase price to a covenant not to compete or an employment agreement between the selling shareholder and the buyer? See p. 478, Note 4. How is the seller affected by such an allocation? See I.R.C. §§ 61(a)(1), 1221. How is the buyer affected? See I.R.C. §§ 162, 167, 197. Is the buyer the taxpayer that is entitled to any deductions allowed with respect to amounts paid under these agreements? See Miller v. Commissioner, 65 T.C.M. 1912 (1993). The Miller court held that an individual who purchased the stock of a target corporation for $105,000 pursuant to an agreement that allocated $35,000 of the purchase price to the seller's promise not to compete was not the taxpayer entitled to deduct the $35,000 paid for the covenant. The individual was denied the deduction because the primary beneficiary of the covenant was the target corporation. Thus, the individual was treated as contributing $35,000 to the capital of the target corporation and the target corporation was presumably entitled to any deduction allowed for the payments under the covenant.

5. The I.R.C. § 338(h)(10) Election

As an alternative to the I.R.C. § 338 "general" election, an opportunity exists for the buyer and the seller to make a special *joint* election under I.R.C. § 338(h)(10) when the target corporation is a member of a "selling consolidated group". A "selling consolidated group" is any "affiliated group" of corporations that files a consolidated tax return and also includes certain affiliated groups that do not file consolidated returns.[30] To keep matters simple, this section of the casebook envisions the most basic "selling consolidated group" where a single corporate shareholder owns 100% of the stock of the target corporation.[31]

The § 338 general election allows for a step-up in asset basis at the cost of a current corporate level tax *in addition to* the shareholder level tax imposed on the target shareholders at the time of the stock sale. By contrast, the "(h)(10)" election allows for a step-up in asset basis at the

---

30. I.R.C. § 338(h)(10)(B); Treas. Reg. §§ 1.338(h)(10)–1(b)(3), (c)(1). For a target corporation to be a member of an "affiliated group", stock representing at least 80% of the total voting power of such corporation and at least 80% of the total value of such corporation must be owned by another corporation. See I.R.C. § 1504(a). When affiliated group status exists, the members of the group may elect to file a single tax return that reflects the collective taxable income of the group (a "consolidated return"), in lieu of each corporation filing a separate tax return. See I.R.C. § 1501. The rules governing consolidated returns are delineated in an elaborate set of regulations promulgated under I.R.C. § 1502.

Note that the regulations under I.R.C. § 338(h)(10) also allow the shareholders of a target S Corporation to join with the buyer of their stock in making an I.R.C. § 338(h)(10) election. Treas. Reg. §§ 1.338(h)(10)–1(b)(5), (c)(1).

31. A selling consolidated group may encompass far more attenuated relationships. All corporations in a lengthy chain may constitute an affiliated group as long as each corporation owns at least 80% of the next corporation in the chain. An affiliated group can even encompass multiple chains of corporations if the chains are connected through a common parent. See I.R.C. § 1504(a).

cost of a current corporate level tax *in lieu of* the shareholder level tax imposed on the target shareholder at the time of the stock sale. Thus, the "(h)(10)" election often remains beneficial even after the repeal of the General Utilities rule.

The following events are deemed to occur when an (h)(10) election is made:

1. The target corporation recognizes gain or loss as if it sold all of its assets in a taxable transaction at market value while still owned by the selling consolidated group.

2. The gain or loss actually realized by the corporation that sold the stock of the target corporation is not recognized.

3. The target corporation takes what generally amounts to a market value basis in its assets using rules similar to those that apply to the "deemed purchase" after a § 338 "general" election.

See Treas. Reg. § 1.338(h)(10)–1(d).

An "(h)(10)" election reduces the tax cost of a stock purchase when the amount of appreciation in the target corporation's assets is less than the amount of appreciation in the target shareholder's stock. Under these circumstances, an "(h)(10)" election causes the selling consolidated group to recognize the smaller gain in the target's assets, rather than the larger gain in the target's stock. Even if the asset gain triggered by the "(h)(10)" election exceeds the gain realized on the stock sale, the additional tax resulting from the "(h)(10)" election may be less than the present value of the future tax savings derived from stepping up the basis in the target's assets, in which case the "(h)(10)" election is still desirable. Consequently, the "(h)(10)" election often remains advantageous when stock of a target corporation is sold by a "selling consolidated group", in contrast to the general § 338 election which normally is undesirable under current law.

> *Problem 11–8 (Quantifying the tax effects of a stock sale with a § 338(h)(10) election)*: Using the facts in Example 11–F (p. 498), but assuming that all the stock of Waldo Corporation is owned by AAA Corporation (instead of Alex) and that Waldo and AAA constitute a "selling consolidated group", what are tax consequences if AAA sells the Waldo stock to Veranda for $4,300,000 and the parties make an "(h)(10)" election?

NOTES

1. *Joint consent.* It is the buyer's unilateral right to make a § 338 "general" election. See I.R.C. § 338(a). In contrast, both the buyer and the seller must consent to an "(h)(10)" election. See Treas. Reg. § 1.338(h)(10)–1(c)(2). Why must both parties consent to an "(h)(10)" election?

2. *I.R.C. § 336(e).* Congress has authorized the Treasury Department to allow for the consequences of an "(h)(10)" election in a wider variety of contexts. See I.R.C. § 336(e). In contrast to I.R.C. § 338(h)(10), I.R.C. § 336(e) imposes no apparent restrictions on the buyer of the target stock and applies to distributions, in addition to sales and exchanges of stock. For a more detailed discussion of I.R.C. § 336(e), see New York State Bar Association Tax Section Committee on Reorganizations, "Report on Section 336(e)," 55 Tax Notes 539 (1992).

CHAPTER 12

NONTAXABLE TRANSFERS

Chapter 11 focused on the sale of a corporate business. At least one tax is normally imposed when a corporation transfers its assets or its shareholders transfer their stock in exchange for money. By receiving money, the transferors sever their interest in the transferred assets or stock and, correspondingly, are taxed when the transfer occurs.

Chapter 12 examines transactions in which the assets or stock of a corporation are transferred to another corporation in exchange for stock of the acquiring corporation. It is often possible to structure these transactions without triggering even one current tax, an appealing prospect to both sellers and buyers. (Why would this result appeal to a buyer?) When a disposition satisfies both the statutory definition of a "corporate reorganization" (see I.R.C. § 368(a)(1)) and certain common law requirements, gains (or losses) realized by the corporation that transferred its assets or the shareholders who transferred their stock may not be recognized. Tax-free treatment is justified by the view that the stock received in the acquiring corporation represents a continuing ownership interest in the transferred business. Because the transferors did not sever their interest in the transferred business, gains and/or losses realized on the exchange may be deferred until the stock of the acquiring corporation received in the exchange is subsequently sold or exchanged.[1]

Like Chapter 11, Chapter 12 takes a transactional approach. Chapter 11 considered two alternative methods of transferring a corporate business, namely, an asset transfer or a stock transfer. Chapter 12 examines how an asset transfer or a stock transfer can be structured to qualify as a tax-free reorganization. Chapter 12 also addresses the statutory merger, a third method for transferring a corporate business. Before resuming the transactional approach, however, it is desirable to develop a perspective from which to explore nontaxable transfers by introducing certain relevant common law doctrines and the intricate statutory structure.

A. PERSPECTIVE

The statutory reorganization rules are technical and complex. See I.R.C. § 368. To make matters worse, these rules only partially codify a vast common law that retains continuing vitality. The most pervasive common law theme relates to whether the ownership interest received in

---

1. For a general discussion of the nonrecognition concept, see pp. 373–374.

the acquiring corporation is sufficiently similar to the surrendered interest in the transferor corporation to justify tax deferral. The Cottage Savings case that follows explores this theme in a different context but the Court relies on some of the earliest reorganization cases to reach its holding.

Cottage Savings Association v. Commissioner

Supreme Court of the United States, 1991.
499 U.S. 554, 111 S.Ct. 1503.

■ JUSTICE MARSHALL delivered the opinion of the Court.

* * *

I

Petitioner Cottage Savings Association (Cottage Savings) is a savings and loan association (S & L) formerly regulated by the Federal Home Loan Bank Board (FHLBB). Like many S & L's, Cottage Savings held numerous long-term, low-interest mortgages that declined in value when interest rates surged in the late 1970's. These institutions would have benefited from selling their devalued mortgages * * * to realize tax-deductible losses. However, they were deterred from doing so by FHLBB accounting regulations, which required them to record the losses on their books. Reporting these losses consistent with the then-effective FHLBB accounting regulations would have placed many S & L's at risk of closure by the FHLBB.

The FHLBB responded to this situation by relaxing its requirements for the reporting of losses. In a regulatory directive known as "Memorandum R–49," dated June 27, 1980, the FHLBB determined that S & L's need not report losses associated with mortgages that are exchanged for "substantially identical" mortgages held by other lenders. The FHLBB's acknowledged purpose for Memorandum R–49 was to facilitate transactions that would generate tax losses but that would not substantially affect the economic position of the transacting S & L's.

This case involves a typical Memorandum R–49 transaction. On December 31, 1980, Cottage Savings sold "90% participation interests" in 252 mortgages to four S & L's. It simultaneously purchased "90% participation interests" in 305 mortgages held by these S & L's. All of the loans involved in the transaction were secured by single-family homes, most in the Cincinnati area. The fair market value of the package of participation interests exchanged by each side was approximately $4.5 million. The face value of the participation interests Cottage Savings relinquished in the transaction was approximately $6.9 million.

On its 1980 federal income tax return, Cottage Savings claimed a deduction for $2,447,091, which represented the adjusted difference between the face value of the participation interests that it traded and the fair market value of the participation interests that it received. As permitted by Memorandum R–49, Cottage Savings did not report these losses to the FHLBB. [T]he Commissioner of Internal Revenue disallowed Cottage

Savings' claimed deduction * * *. The Tax Court held that the deduction was permissible.

[T]he Court of Appeals reversed * * *.

II

Rather than assessing tax liability on the basis of annual fluctuations in the value of a taxpayer's property, the Internal Revenue Code defers the tax consequences of a gain or loss in property value until the taxpayer "realizes" the gain or loss. The realization requirement is implicit in § 1001(a) of the Code which defines "the gain [or loss] from the sale or other disposition of property" * * *. As this Court has recognized, the concept of realization is "founded on administrative convenience." Under an appreciation-based system of taxation, taxpayers and the Commissioner would have to undertake the "cumbersome, abrasive, and unpredictable administrative task" of valuing assets on an annual basis to determine whether the assets had appreciated or depreciated in value. In contrast, "[a] change in the form or extent of an investment is easily detected by a taxpayer or an administrative officer."

Section 1001(a)'s language provides a straightforward test for realization: to realize a gain or loss in the value of property, the taxpayer must engage in a "sale or other disposition of property." The parties agree that the exchange of participation interests in this case cannot be characterized as a "sale" under § 1001(a); the issue before us is whether the transaction constitutes a "disposition of property." The Commissioner argues that an exchange of property can be treated as a "disposition" under § 1001(a) only if the properties exchanged are materially different. The Commissioner further submits that, because the underlying mortgages were essentially economic substitutes, the participation interests exchanged by Cottage Savings were not materially different from those received from the other S & L's. Cottage Savings, on the other hand, maintains that any exchange of property is a "disposition of property" under § 1001(a), regardless of whether the property exchanged is materially different. Alternatively, Cottage Savings contends that the participation interests exchanged were materially different because the underlying loans were secured by different properties.

We must therefore determine whether the realization principle in § 1001(a) incorporates a "material difference" requirement. If it does, we must further decide what that requirement amounts to and how it applies in this case. We consider these questions in turn.

A

Neither the language nor the history of the Code indicates whether and to what extent property exchanged must differ to count as a "disposition of property" under § 1001(a). Nonetheless, we readily agree with the Commissioner that an exchange of property gives rise to a realization event under § 1001(a) only if the properties exchanged are "materially different." The Commissioner himself has by regulation construed § 1001(a) to embody a material difference requirement * * *. Treas. Reg. § 1.1001–1. Because Congress has delegated to the Commissioner the power to promulgate "all needful rules and regulations for the enforcement of [the Internal Revenue Code]," [I.R.C.] § 7805(a), we must defer to his regulatory interpretations * * * so long as they are reasonable * * *.

We conclude that Treasury Regulation § 1.1001–1 is a reasonable interpretation of § 1001(a). Congress first employed the language that now comprises § 1001(a) of the Code in * * * the Revenue Act of 1924; that language has remained essentially unchanged through various reenactments. And since 1934, the Commissioner has construed the statutory term "disposition of property" to include a "material difference" requirement. As we have recognized, "Treasury regulations and interpretations long continued without substantial change, applying to unamended or substantially reenacted statutes, are deemed to have received congressional approval and have the effect of law."

Treasury Regulation § 1.1001–1 is also consistent with our landmark precedents on realization. In a series of early decisions involving the tax effects of property exchanges, this Court made clear that a taxpayer realizes taxable income only if the properties exchanged are "materially" or "essentially" different. Because these decisions were part of the "contemporary legal context" in which Congress enacted * * * the 1924 Act and because Congress has left undisturbed through subsequent reenactments of the Code the principles of realization established in these cases, we may presume that Congress intended to codify these principles in § 1001(a) * * *.

B

Precisely what constitutes a "material difference" for purposes of § 1001(a) of the Code is a more complicated question. The Commissioner argues that properties are "materially different" only if they differ in economic substance. To determine whether the participation interests exchanged in this case were "materially different" in this sense, the Commissioner argues, we should look to the attitudes of the parties, the evaluation of the interests by the secondary mortgage market, and the views of the FHLBB. We conclude that § 1001(a) embodies a much less demanding and less complex test.

[T]o give meaning to the material difference test, we must look to the case law from which the test derives and which we believe Congress intended to codify in enacting and reenacting the language that now comprises § 1001(a).

We start with the classic treatment of realization in Eisner v. Macomber. In Macomber, a taxpayer who owned 2,200 shares of stock in a company received another 1,100 shares from the company as part of a pro rata stock dividend * * *. At issue was whether the stock dividend constituted taxable income. We held that it did not, because no gain was realized. We reasoned that the stock dividend merely reflected the increased worth of the taxpayer's stock and that a taxpayer realizes increased worth of property only by receiving "something of exchangeable value proceeding from the property."

In three subsequent decisions—United States v. Phellis, Weiss v. Stearn, and Marr v. United States—we refined Macomber's conception of realization in the context of property exchanges. In each case, the taxpayer owned stock that had appreciated in value since its acquisition. And in each case, the corporation in which the taxpayer held stock had reorganized into a new corporation, with the new corporation assuming the business of the old corporation. While the corporations in Phellis and Marr both changed from New Jersey to Delaware corporations, the original and successor corporations in Weiss both were incorporated in Ohio. In each case, following the reorganization, the stockholders of the old corporation received shares in the new corporation equal to their proportional interest in the old corporation.

The question in these cases was whether the taxpayers realized the accumulated gain in their shares in the old corporation when they received in return for those shares stock representing an equivalent proportional interest in the new corporations. In Phellis and Marr, we held that the transactions were realization events. We reasoned that because a company incorporated in one State has "different rights and powers" from one incorporated in a different State, the taxpayers in Phellis and Marr acquired through the transactions property that was "materially different" from what they previously had. In contrast, we held that no realization occurred in Weiss. By exchanging stock in the predecessor corporation for stock in the newly reorganized corporation, the taxpayer did not receive "a thing really different from what he theretofore had." As we explained in Marr, our determination that the reorganized company in Weiss was not "really different" from its predecessor turned on the fact that both companies were incorporated in the same State.

Obviously, the distinction in Phellis and Marr that made the stock in the successor corporations materially different from the stock in the predecessors was minimal. Taken together, Phellis, Marr, and Weiss stand for the principle that properties are "different" in the sense that is "material" to the Internal Revenue Code so long as their respective possessors enjoy legal entitlements that are different in kind or extent. Thus, separate groups of stock are not materially different if they confer "the same proportional interest of the same character in the same corporation." However, they are materially different if they are issued by different corporations or if they confer "different rights and powers" in the same corporation. No more demanding a standard than this is necessary in order to satisfy the administrative purposes underlying the realization requirement in § 1001(a). For, as long as the property entitlements are not identical, their exchange will allow both the Commissioner and the transacting taxpayer easily to fix the appreciated or depreciated values of the property relative to their tax bases.

In contrast, we find no support for the Commissioner's "economic substitute" conception of material difference. According to the Commissioner, differences between properties are material for purposes of the Code only when it can be said that the parties, the relevant market (in this case the secondary mortgage market), and the relevant regulatory body (in this case the FHLBB) would consider them material. Nothing in Phellis, Weiss, and Marr suggests that exchanges of properties must satisfy such a subjective test to trigger realization of a gain or loss.

Moreover, the complexity of the Commissioner's approach ill serves the goal of administrative convenience that underlies the realization requirement. In order to apply the Commissioner's test in a principled fashion, the Commissioner and the taxpayer must identify the relevant market, establish whether there is a regulatory agency whose views should be taken into account, and then assess how the relevant market participants and the agency would view the transaction * * *.

Finally, the Commissioner's test is incompatible with the structure of the Code. Section 1001(c) provides that a gain or loss realized under § 1001(a) "shall be recognized" unless one of the Code's nonrecognition provisions applies. One such nonrecognition provision withholds recognition of a gain or loss realized from an exchange of properties that would appear to be economic substitutes under the Commissioner's material difference test. This provision, commonly known as the "like kind" exception, withholds recognition of a gain or loss realized "on the exchange of property held for productive use in a trade or business or for investment * * * for property of like kind which is to be held either for productive use in a trade or business or for investment." [I.R.C.] § 1031(a)(1). If Congress had expected that exchanges of similar properties would not count as realization events under § 1001(a), it would have had no reason to bar recognition of a gain or loss realized from these transactions.

C

Under our interpretation of § 1001(a), an exchange of property gives rise to a realization event so long as the exchanged properties are "materially different"—that is, so long as they embody legally distinct entitlements. Cottage Savings' transactions at issue here easily satisfy this test. Because the participation interests exchanged by Cottage Savings and the other S & L's derived from loans that were made to different obligors and secured by different homes, the exchanged interests did embody legally distinct entitlements. Consequently, we conclude that Cottage Savings realized its losses at the point of the exchange.

The Commissioner contends that it is anomalous to treat mortgages deemed to be "substantially identical" by the FHLBB as "materially different." The anomaly, however, is merely semantic; mortgages can be substantially identical for Memorandum R–49 purposes and still exhibit "differences" that are "material" for purposes of the Internal Revenue Code. Because Cottage Savings received entitlements different from those it gave up, the exchange put both Cottage Savings and the Commissioner in a position to determine the change in the value of Cottage Savings' mortgages relative to their tax bases. Thus, there is no reason not to treat the exchange of these interests as a realization event, regardless of the status of the mortgages under the criteria of Memorandum R–49.

* * *

■ JUSTICE BLACKMUN, with whom JUSTICE WHITE joins, dissenting.

* * *

It long has been established that gain or loss in the value of property is taken into account for income tax purposes only if and when the gain or loss is "realized" * * *. Mere variation in value—the routine ups and downs of the marketplace—do not in themselves have income tax consequences. This is fundamental in income tax law.

In applying the realization requirement to an exchange, the properties involved must be materially different in kind or in extent. Treas. Reg. § 1.1001–1(a) * * *.

That the mortgage participation interests exchanged * * * were "different" is not in dispute. The materiality prong is the focus. [A] material difference is one that has the capacity to influence a decision.

The application of this standard leads, it seems to me, to only one answer—that the mortgage participation partial interests released were not materially different from the mortgage participation partial interests received. Memorandum R–49 lists 10 factors that, when satisfied, as they were here, serve to classify the interests as "substantially identical." These factors assure practical identity; surely, they then also assure that any difference cannot be of consequence. Indeed, nonmateriality is the full purpose of the Memorandum's criteria. The "proof of the pudding" is in the fact of its complete accounting acceptability to the FHLBB. Indeed, as has been noted, it is difficult to reconcile substantial identity for financial accounting purposes with a material difference for tax accounting purposes. Common sense so dictates.

This should suffice and be the end of the analysis. Other facts, however, solidify the conclusion: The retention by the transferor of 10% interests, enabling it to keep on servicing its loans; the transferor's continuing to collect the payments due from the borrowers so that, so far as the latter were concerned, it was business as usual, exactly as it had been; the obvious lack of concern or dependence of the transferor with the "differences" upon which the Court relies (as transferees, the taxpayers made no credit checks and no appraisals of collateral); the selection of the loans by computer programmed to match mortgages in accordance with the Memorandum R–49 criteria; the absence of even the names of the borrowers in the closing schedules attached to the agreements; * * *; the restriction of the interests exchanged to the same State; the identity of the respective face and fair market values; and the application by the parties of common discount factors to each side of the transaction—all reveal that any differences that might exist made no difference whatsoever and were not material * * *.

We should be dealing here with realities and not with superficial distinctions. As has been said many times, * * * in income tax law we are to be concerned with substance and not with mere form. When we stray from that principle, the new precedent is likely to be a precarious beacon for the future.

NOTES

1. *Evaluating the opinions.* Which opinion is more compelling, the majority or the dissent? Why? The preceding chapters include several instances in which the non-tax effects of a transaction impact on income tax consequences. How does the Cottage Savings case affect your thinking about this relationship?

2. *Benefit of loss to government.* Why might losing the Cottage Savings case have been a "blessing in disguise" for the government?

3. *Exchange versus realization event.* Describe the relationship between an "exchange" and a "realization event." See I.R.C. § 1001(a). Is every exchange a realization event? Is every realization event an exchange?

4. *Early reorganization cases.* The Cottage Savings Court discusses the following decisions rendered in the 1920's regarding whether certain corporate transactions constituted realization events:

(a) *Eisner v. Macomber*, 252 U.S. 189, 40 S.Ct. 189 (1920). Macomber originally owned 2,200 common shares of a corporation. Assume that Macomber was the sole shareholder and that the corporation was worth $6,600. The corporation then distributed an additional 1,100 common shares to Macomber. Did the receipt of the additional shares represent a realization event for Macomber? What element of a sale or exchange was missing? Can a *fictional* exchange in which Macomber engaged be devised? Would that fictional exchange constitute a realization event after the Cottage Savings opinion? If Macomber is not viewed as engaging in an exchange, can Macomber be viewed as receiving a taxable dividend (assuming the distributing corporation had at least $2,200 of earnings & profits)? Would Macomber be treated as receiving a taxable dividend under current law? See I.R.C. §§ 61(a)(7), 301(a), 305(a), 317(a).

(b) *United States v. Phellis*, 257 U.S. 156, 42 S.Ct. 63 (1921). Oldco, a New Jersey corporation, transferred all of its assets to Newco, a Delaware corporation, in exchange for all of the stock and bonds of Newco. Oldco then distributed the Newco stock to its shareholders, but retained the Newco bonds. The Court held that the Oldco shareholders must include the value of the Newco shares in gross income. How can Phellis be distinguished from Macomber? Would the Phellis court have reached a different result if Oldco had liquidated, rather than retaining the Newco bonds? See Marr v. United States, below.

(c) *Marr v. United States*, 268 U.S. 536, 45 S.Ct. 575 (1925). The shareholders of Oldco, a New Jersey corporation, transferred their

Oldco stock to Newco, a Delaware corporation, in exchange for all of the stock of Newco. Oldco then liquidated into Newco. The Court held that the exchange of shares constituted a realization event for the Oldco shareholders and taxed them on the gain in their Oldco shares. Is it sensible to view stock in a Delaware corporation as "materially different" from stock in a New Jersey corporation? Is it sensible to tax the gain in the Oldco stock even though no change occurred in the relative stock ownership of the shareholders or in the assets comprising the corporate business?

(d) *Weiss v. Stearn*, 265 U.S. 242, 44 S.Ct. 490 (1924). The shareholders of Oldco, an Ohio corporation, transferred their Oldco stock to Newco, another Ohio corporation, in exchange for stock of Newco, representing half the consideration, and money, representing the other half of the consideration. (The money was transferred to Newco by an unrelated third party who also received stock in Newco.) The issue was whether the Oldco shareholders should be taxed on half or all of the gain in their Oldco stock. The Court held that the Oldco shareholders should be taxed on only half the gain because *no* realization event occurred with respect to the half of the Oldco stock exchanged for Newco stock. Is it sensible to view a 50% interest in the assets comprising a corporate business as *not* "materially different" from a 100% interest in those assets? From a theoretical standpoint, the transaction in Weiss could have been effectuated without utilizing Newco if the shareholders of Oldco simply sold 50% of their Oldco stock to the unrelated third party. Would this transaction have raised the same tax issues as the transaction actually utilized in Weiss?

5. *Realization event versus gross income.* Describe the relationship between a "realization event" and "gross income." See I.R.C. §§ 61(a), 1001(a). Does every realization event result in gross income? Is every item of gross income attributable to a realization event?

1.   COMMON LAW DOCTRINES

The early reorganization cases relied on by the Cottage Savings Court do not reflect the current state of the law. The Court struggled with the concept of realization in these cases. It is now generally accepted that any transfer of a corporate business in exchange for stock of the acquiring corporation triggers a realization event. Under current law, however, statutory nonrecognition rules may apply if the disposition is structured to comply with the statutory definition of a reorganization.

Although a transaction cannot qualify as a tax-free reorganization unless its form comports with the statute, mere adherence to the statutory pattern is not sufficient to effectuate a tax-free reorganization. In addition to the statutory requirements, the transaction must satisfy certain common law doctrines that still represent the essence of a reorganization. These common law doctrines are embraced by regulations as the following passage indicates:

Under the general rule, upon the exchange of property, gain or loss must be accounted for if the new property differs in a material particular, either in kind or in extent, from the old property. The purpose of the reorganization provisions of the Code is to except from the general rule certain specifically described exchanges incident to such readjustments of corporate structures made in one of the particular ways specified in the Code, *as are required by business exigencies and which effect only a readjustment of continuing interest in property under modified corporate forms*. Requisite to a reorganization under the Code are a *continuity of the business enterprise * * * under the modified corporate form*, and * * * a *continuity of [proprietary] interest * * *.* In order to exclude transactions not intended to be included, the specifications of the reorganization provisions of the law are precise. Both the terms of the specifications and their underlying assumptions and purposes must be satisfied in order to entitle the taxpayer to the benefit of the exception from the general rule * * *. (Emphasis added.)

Treas. Reg. § 1.368–1(b).

The following common law doctrines are introduced below: continuity of proprietary interest, continuity of business enterprise, business purpose and plan of reorganization. Each doctrine is multi-faceted and various relationships exist among these doctrines. The materials that follow are intended to provide a general background with respect to the common law requirements for a reorganization. The operation of these common law doctrines will become clearer when specific transactions are examined later in this Chapter.

a. CONTINUITY OF PROPRIETARY INTEREST

Treas. Reg. § 1.368–1(e)(1)

A corporate business can be transferred in a tax-free transaction only if the transferors maintain a continuing interest in the transferred enterprise by receiving a proprietary interest in the acquiring corporation. The cases that follow introduce this common law requirement.

John A. Nelson Co. v. Helvering

Supreme Court of the United States, 1935.
296 U.S. 374, 56 S.Ct. 273.

■ MR. JUSTICE MCREYNOLDS delivered the opinion of the Court.

* * *

In 1926, under an agreement with petitioner, the Elliott–Fisher Corporation organized a new corporation with 12,500 shares non-voting preferred stock and 30,000 shares of common stock. It purchased the [common stock] for $2,000,000 cash. This new corporation then acquired substantially all of petitioner's property * * * in return for $2,000,000 cash and the entire issue of preferred stock. [T]his cash * * * and the preferred stock of the new company went to [petitioner's] stockholders * * *. The preferred stock so distributed, except in case of default, had no voice in the control of the issuing corporation.

The Commissioner, Board of Tax Appeals and the court all concluded there was no reorganization. This, we think, was error.

The court below thought the facts showed:

that the transaction essentially constituted a sale of the greater part of petitioner's assets for cash and the preferred stock in the new corporation, leaving the Elliott–Fisher Company in entire control of the new corporation by virtue of its ownership of the common stock.

The controlling facts leading to this conclusion are that * * * there was no continuity of interest from the old corporation to the new; that the control of the property conveyed passed to a stranger, in the management of which petitioner retained no voice.

It follows that the transaction was not part of a strict merger or consolidation or part of something that * * * has a real semblance to a merger or consolidation involving a continuance of essentially the same interests through a new modified corporate structure. Mere acquisition by one corporation of a majority of the stock or all the assets of another corporation does not of itself constitute a reorganization, where such acquisition takes the form of a purchase and sale * * *.

True, the mere acquisition of the assets of one corporation by another does not amount to reorganization within the statutory definition. But where, as here, the seller acquires a definite and substantial interest in the affairs of the purchasing corporation, a wholly different situation arises. The owner of preferred stock is not without substantial interest in the affairs of the issuing corporation, although denied voting rights. The statute does not require participation in the management of the purchaser * * *.

The judgment below must be reversed.

Le Tulle v. Scofield

Supreme Court of the United States, 1940.
308 U.S. 415, 60 S.Ct. 313.

■ MR. JUSTICE ROBERTS delivered the opinion of the Court.

The Gulf Coast Irrigation Company was the owner of irrigation properties. Petitioner was its sole stockholder * * *. [On] November 4, 1931, the Irrigation Company, the Gulf Coast Water Company, and the petitioner, entered into an agreement * * *. The contract called for a conveyance of all the properties owned * * * by the Irrigation Company for $50,000 in cash and $750,000 in bonds of the Water Company, payable serially over the period January 1, 1933, to January 1, 1944 * * *. Three days later, at a special meeting of stockholders of the Irrigation Company, the proposed reorganization was approved * * *.

The contract between the two corporations was carried out November 18, with the result that the Water Company became owner of all the properties then owned by the Irrigation Company * * *. Subsequently all of [the Irrigation Company's] assets, including the bonds received from the Water Company, were distributed to the petitioner. The company was then dissolved. The petitioner * * * reported no gain as a result of the receipt of the liquidating dividend from the Irrigation Company. The latter reported no gain for the taxable year [by] virtue of its receipt of bonds and cash from the Water Company. The Commissioner of Internal Revenue assessed additional taxes against the [petitioner], by reason of the receipt of the liquidating dividend, and against the petitioner as transferee of the Irrigation Company's assets [by] virtue of the gain realized by the company on the sale of its property. The tax was paid and claims for refund were filed * * *. [Petitioner] alleged that the transaction constituted a tax-exempt reorganization as defined by the Revenue Act * * *. The respondent's contention that the transaction amounted merely to a sale of assets by the petitioner and the Irrigation Company and did not fall within the statutory definition of a tax-free reorganization was overruled by the District Court and judgment was entered for the petitioner.

The respondent appealed, * * * assigning as error the court's holding that the transaction constituted a nontaxable reorganization.

The Circuit Court of Appeals concluded that, as the Water Company acquired substantially all the properties of the Irrigation Company, there was a merger of the latter within the literal language of the statute, but held that, in the light of the construction this Court has put upon the statute, the transaction would not be a reorganization unless the transferor retained a definite and substantial interest in the affairs of the transferee. It thought this requirement was satisfied by the taking of the bonds of the Water Company, and, therefore, agreed with the District Court that a reorganization had been consummated * * *.

* * * [W]e are of opinion that the transaction did not amount to a reorganization * * *.

Section 112 (i) provides, so far as material:

"(1) The term 'reorganization' means (A) a merger or consolidation (including the acquisition by one corporation of at least a majority of the voting stock and at least a majority of the total number of shares of all other classes of stock of another corporation, or substantially all the properties of another corporation) * * *."

As the court below properly stated, the section is not to be read literally, as denominating the transfer of all the assets of one company for what amounts to a cash consideration given by the other a reorganization. We have held that where the consideration consists of cash and short term notes the transfer does not amount to a reorganization within the true meaning of the statute, but is a sale upon which gain or loss must be reckoned. We have said that the statute was not satisfied unless the transferor retained a substantial stake in the enterprise and such a stake was thought to be retained where a large proportion of the consideration was in common stock of the transferee, or where the transferor took cash and the entire issue of preferred stock of the transferee corporation. And, where the consideration is represented by a substantial proportion of stock, and the balance in bonds, the total consideration received is exempt from tax * * *.

[T]he courts have generally held that receipt of long term bonds as distinguished from short term notes constitutes the retention of an interest in the purchasing corporation * * *.

We are of the opinion that the term of the obligations is not material. Where the consideration is wholly in the transferee's bonds, or part cash and part such bonds, we think it cannot be said that the transferor retains any proprietary interest in the enterprise. On the contrary, he becomes a creditor of the transferee; and we do not think that the fact referred to by the Circuit Court of Appeals, that the bonds were secured solely by the assets transferred and that, upon default, the bondholder would retake only the property sold, changes his status from that of a creditor to one having a proprietary stake, within the purview of the statute.

We conclude that the Circuit Court of Appeals was in error in holding that, as respects any of the property transferred to the Water Company, the transaction was other than a sale or exchange upon which gain or loss must [be recognized] * * *.

NOTES

1. *"Good consideration" for continuity purposes.* Must stock of the acquiring corporation be entitled to vote to count as "good" consideration for purposes of the common law continuity of proprietary interest rule? See Nelson, above. Must such stock be common stock? See Nelson, above. Will debt of the acquiring corporation ever count as "good" consideration for continuity of interest purposes? See LeTulle, above.

2. *Essence of continuity.* Consider the following excerpt from a 1935 Supreme Court opinion:

> [The interest that the transferor must acquire in the acquiring corporation to achieve a continuity of proprietary interest] must be definite and material; it must represent a substantial part of the value of the thing transferred. * * *
>
> * * *
>
> True it is that the relationship of the taxpayer to the assets conveyed was substantially changed * * *. This, we think, is permissible so long as the taxpayer received an interest in the affairs of the transferee which represented a material part of the value of the transferred assets.

Helvering v. Minnesota Tea Company, 296 U.S. 378, 385–86, 56 S.Ct. 269, 272–73 (1935). In light of the Minnesota Tea standard, does the transfer of a $1,000,000 corporation to a $99,000,000 publicly traded corporation in exchange for $1,000,000 of newly issued stock in the acquiring corporation satisfy the continuity of proprietary interest requirement, notwithstanding that the transferors only own a 1% interest in the combined enterprise? Does the transfer of a $20,000,000 corporation to a $1,000,000 corporation in exchange for $17,000,000 in cash and $3,000,000 of newly issued stock in the acquiring corporation satisfy the continuity of proprietary interest requirement, given that the transferors own a 75% interest in the combined enterprise?

Which of the following describes the common law continuity of proprietary interest requirement?

(a) After the acquisition, the transferors must own a substantial equity interest in the acquiring corporation.

(b) A substantial part of the consideration received by the transferors must represent an equity interest in the acquiring corporation.

3. *Amount of "good consideration" necessary to achieve continuity.* It is not entirely clear what percentage of the consideration received by the transferors must consist of stock in the acquiring corporation to satisfy the common law continuity of proprietary interest requirement. The preferred stock received by the transferors in Nelson represented about 38% of the total consideration. The regulations reveal that the Internal Revenue Service regards continuity of proprietary interest to exist when stock of the acquiring corporation represents at least 40% of the consideration for the acquisition. See Treas. Reg. § 1.368–1T(e)(2)(v) Examples 1, 2(ii), 6, 8 and 12. In addition, the regulations reveal that the I.R.S. does not regard the continuity of proprietary interest requirement as being satisfied when stock of the acquiring corporation represents less than 30% of the consideration for the acquisition. See Treas. Reg. § 1.368–1T(e)(2)(v) Example 11 (40/140 or 28.57% is inadequate).

b.   CONTINUITY OF BUSINESS ENTERPRISE

Treas. Reg. § 1.368–1(d)

In addition to the requirement that the shareholders of the transferor corporation retain a continuing proprietary interest in the transferred business, the acquiring corporation must either continue to conduct the historical business of the transferor corporation or use a significant portion of the transferor's historical assets. Little judicial guidance exists with respect to this requirement but detailed regulations have been promulgated. See Treas. Reg. § 1.368–1(d).

Under the regulations, continuity of business enterprise requires that the acquiring corporation (P) either,

(a) continue the acquired corporation's (T's) historic business, or

(b) use a significant portion of T's historic business assets in a business.

A corporation's historic business is the business it has conducted most recently. A business entered into as part of a plan of reorganization, however, is not a corporation's historic business.

With regard to continuing T's historic business, the regulations provide that the fact that P is in the same line of business as T tends to establish the requisite continuity, but is not alone sufficient. If T has more than one line of business, continuity of business enterprise requires only that P continue a "significant" line of business. All facts and circumstances are considered in determining whether a line of business is "significant."

As an alternative to continuing T's historic business, the continuity of business enterprise requirement may be satisfied if P uses a significant portion of T's historic business assets in a business. A corporation's historic business assets are the assets used in its historic business. In general, the determination of the portion of a corporation's assets considered "significant" is based on the relative importance of the assets to the operation of the business. However, all other facts and circumstances, such as the net fair market value of those assets, are considered.

Problem 12–1 (Determining whether continuity of business enterprise is satisfied): Determine if the continuity of business enterprise requirement is satisfied in each of the following circumstances:

(a) T conducts three lines of business: manufacture of synthetic resins, manufacture of chemicals for the textile industry, and distribution of chemicals. The three lines of business are approximately equal in value. On July 1, Year 5, T sells the synthetic resin and chemicals distribution businesses to a third party for cash and marketable securities. On December 31, Year 5, T transfers all of its assets to P solely for P voting stock. P continues the chemical manufacturing business without interruption. See Treas. Reg. § 1.368–1(d)(5), Example 1.

(b) P manufactures computers and T manufactures components for computers. T sells all of its output to P. On January 1, Year 5, P decides to buy imported components only. On March 1, Year 5, T transfers all of its assets to P solely for P voting stock. P continues buying imported components but retains T's equipment as a backup source of supply. See Treas. Reg. § 1.368–1(d)(5), Example 2.

(c) T is a manufacturer of boys' and men's trousers. On January 1, Year 2, as part of a plan of reorganization, T sold all of its assets to a third party for cash and purchased a highly diversified portfolio of stocks and bonds. As part of the plan, T operates an investment business until July 1, Year 5. On that date, the plan of reorganization culminates in a transfer by T of all its assets to P solely in exchange for P voting stock. See Treas. Reg. § 1.368–1(d)(5), Example 3.

(d) T manufactures children's toys and P distributes steel and allied products. On January 1, Year 5, T sells all of its assets to a third party for $100,000 cash and $900,000 in notes. On March 1, Year 5, T transfers all of its assets to P solely for P voting stock. See Treas. Reg. § 1.368–1(d)(5), Example 4.

(e) T manufactures farm machinery and P operates a lumber mill. T transfers all of its assets to P solely for P voting stock. P disposes of T's assets immediately after the acquisition as part of the plan of reorganization. P does not continue T's farm machinery manufacturing business. See Treas. Reg. § 1.368–1(d)(5), Example 5.

c.   BUSINESS PURPOSE AND PLAN OF REORGANIZATION

In addition to satisfying the continuity of proprietary interest and the continuity of business enterprise requirements, a transfer must be effectuated for a valid business purpose for the transaction to qualify as a reorganization. At first blush, it may seem relatively easy to distinguish a transaction undertaken for legitimate business reasons from a transaction designed to avoid taxes. Quite often, however, a given transaction entails both business goals and tax reduction motives and it is not always so easy to determine the true motivation for the transaction. See, e.g., Gregory v. Helvering, at p. 692. As you examine each case in which a taxpayer desires reorganization treatment, think about the following questions: Who identifies the business purpose for a proposed transaction, the taxpayer or the attorney? Once the business purpose for a transaction is identified, what steps can the attorney take to cause that purpose to be associated with the transaction? What ethical issues does the business purpose requirement create for the attorney?

Somewhat related to the business purpose requirement is the mandate that a "plan of reorganization" exist. See Treas. Reg. § 1.368–2(g). In contrast to the continuity doctrines and the business purpose requirement, the need for a "plan of reorganization" is acknowledged by the statute. See I.R.C. §§ 354(a), 361(a). The plan of reorganization requirement does not focus on whether the taxpayer intends to accomplish a reorganization. (In fact, the Internal Revenue Service sometimes contends that a reorganization has occurred, notwithstanding the taxpayer's protests! See pp. 780–794.) Rather, the plan of reorganization requirement defines the scope of the transaction that must be considered in determining whether a reorganization has occurred.

A purported reorganization may violate certain statutory or common law requirements if events occurring before or after the acquisition are deemed a part of the transaction. For example, assume that the assets of Target Corporation are transferred to Acquiring Corporation for stock but that the acquired assets are sold by Acquiring shortly thereafter. If the "plan" encompasses both the transfer of Target assets to Acquiring and the sale of those assets by Acquiring, the transaction does not qualify as a reorganization. The continuity of business enterprise requirement is violated because Acquiring converted the Target assets to money rather than continuing Target's historic business or using Target's historic assets in another business. In contrast, if the sale of Target assets is not part of the "plan" and Acquiring continues Target's historic business during the period covered by the plan, the continuity of business enterprise requirement is satisfied. As this example illustrates, the scope of the transaction must be defined to determine whether a reorganization has occurred. As you study each case in which reorganization treatment is at issue, think about the steps that an attorney can take to establish the desired "plan of reorganization."

2.   THE STATUTORY SCHEME

Notwithstanding the continuing application of the common law doctrines, it is the statute that dictates the form that a corporate transfer must take to achieve reorganization status. Several different types of statutory provisions apply to reorganizations. These provisions are now summarized.

Definitional Provision (I.R.C. § 368): The statute describes seven classes of transactions that represent a "reorganization." See I.R.C. § 368(a)(1). Not all of these transactions involve the transfer of a corporate business to new owners. Rather, such a transfer can normally be structured only as an "A" reorganization (a transaction described in I.R.C. § 368(a)(1)(A)), a "B" reorganization (described in I.R.C. § 368(a)(1)(B)), a "C" reorganization (described in I.R.C. § 368(a)(1)(C)) or a "nondivisive D" reorganization (described in I.R.C. § 368(a)(1)(D) and § 354). These reorganizations are examined in this Chapter. In contrast, a "divisive D" reorganization (described in I.R.C. § 368(a)(1)(D) and § 355) involves the division of a single corporation into multiple corporations. Divisive D reorganizations are examined in Chapter 15. An "E" reorganization and an "F" reorganization describe transactions involving the rearrangement of a single corporation. E and F reorganizations are explored in Chapter 16. A "G" reorganization describes certain transfers or divisions of a corporate enterprise in bankruptcy, another topic addressed in this Chapter.

The definitional provision also addresses the term "party to a reorganization." See I.R.C. § 368(b). Identifying each party to a reorganization is important because the term serves as the link between the reorganization definition and the nonrecognition rules described below. See, e.g., I.R.C. §§ 354(a), 361(a).

Nonrecognition Rules (I.R.C. §§ 354, 355, 356, 361): When a transaction satisfies *both* the statutory definition of a reorganization *and* the common law requirements, certain nonrecognition rules apply to any gains or losses realized by the corporation that transfers its assets (I.R.C. § 361) and/or the shareholders who transfer their stock (I.R.C. §§ 354–356). When a corporate enterprise is transferred in an A, B, C or nondivisive D reorganization, I.R.C. § 354 or § 356 applies to the shareholders of the transferred enterprise. When a divisive D reorganization occurs, I.R.C. § 355 or § 356 applies to the shareholders of the divided enterprise.

Historical Basis Rules (I.R.C. §§ 358, 362(b)): As a general rule, any realized gains or losses are deferred, not eliminated, when a nonrecognition provision applies. Deferral is normally achieved by perpetuating historical basis. When a reorganization occurs, shareholders of the target corporation who exchange their stock for stock of the acquiring corporation take an "exchanged" basis (with certain adjustments) in the stock they receive. See I.R.C. §§ 358(a), 7701(a)(44). In addition, the acquiring corporation takes a "transferred" basis in the assets or stock that it acquires in a tax-free reorganization, increased by any gain recognized by the transferor. See I.R.C. §§ 362(b), 7701(a)(43).

Historical Tax Attribute Rules (I.R.C. § 381): Basis is not the only historical attribute that the acquiring corporation succeeds to in a reorganization. In addition, if the reorganization is accomplished by an asset transfer or a merger, the acquiring corporation inherits a lengthy list of historical tax attributes of the target corporation. See I.R.C. § 381(c). Included among these attributes is any net operating loss carryover of the target. See I.R.C. § 381(c)(1). The ability of the acquiring corporation to use a pre-acquisition net operating loss carryover, however, is often severely restricted by other statutory provisions.[2]

B. ASSET TRANSFER

I.R.C. §§ 368(a)(1)(C), (2)(G)

Treas. Reg. § 1.368–2(d)

The classic reorganization definition that applies to an asset transfer is located at I.R.C. §§ 368(a)(1)(C) (a "C" reorganization). To qualify an asset transfer as a C reorganization, the following statutory requirements must be satisfied:

(a) The transferor corporation must transfer "substantially all" of its assets to another corporation.

(b) The consideration received by the transferor corporation must be "solely voting stock" of the acquiring corporation.

(c) The transferor corporation must liquidate pursuant to the plan of reorganization.

I.R.C. §§ 368(a)(1)(C), (2)(G). In addition, the transaction must satisfy the common law doctrines introduced at pp. 513–521. The C reorganization and its corresponding tax consequences are illustrated by Example 12–A.

Example 12–A (Consequences of a non-taxable asset transfer): Alex is the sole shareholder of Waldo Corporation and has a basis of $100,000 in his Waldo stock. Waldo owns assets with a value of $8,000,000 in which Waldo has a basis of $3,000,000. Waldo has no liabilities. Waldo transfers all of its assets to Veranda Corporation in exchange for newly issued voting stock of Veranda worth $8,000,000 and Waldo then distributes the Veranda stock to Alex in liquidation.[3] Assume the

---

2. The restrictions imposed on pre-acquisition net operating loss carryovers are explored in Chapter 13.

3. This fact pattern resembles the fact pattern utilized in Chapter 11 to facilitate a comparison of the tax consequences of taxable and non-taxable transfers.

transaction satisfies all of the statutory and common law requirements for a C reorganization.

1. Tax Consequences to Waldo

    Exchange of Assets for Veranda Stock

    Realization Event (I.R.C. § 1001(a))
    Amount Realized $8,000,000 [4]
    Less: Adjusted Basis   3,000,000
    Realized Gain $5,000,000

    Not Recognized: I.R.C. §§ 361(a), 368(b)(2)

    Basis in Veranda Stock: $3,000,000—I.R.C. § 358(a)(1)

    Distribution of Veranda Stock

    Realization Event (I.R.C. § 336)
    Amount Realized $8,000,000 [5]
    Less: Adjusted Basis   3,000,000
    Realized Gain $5,000,000

    Not Recognized: I.R.C. §§ 361(c)(1), (2), (4)

2. Tax Consequences to Alex
    Exchange of Waldo Stock for Veranda Stock

    Realization Event (I.R.C. § 331)
    Amount Realized $8,000,000
    Less: Adjusted Basis   100,000
    Realized Gain $7,900,000

    Not Recognized: I.R.C. §§ 354(a)(1), 368(b)(2)

    Basis in Veranda Stock: $100,000—I.R.C. § 358(a)(1)

3. Tax Consequences to Veranda
    Exchange of Newly Issued Veranda Stock for Waldo Assets
    Nonrecognition of Gain or Loss: I.R.C. § 1032
    Basis in Waldo Assets: $3,000,000—I.R.C. § 362(b)

1.   TRANSFER OF "SUBSTANTIALLY ALL" THE ASSETS

Helvering v. Elkhorn Coal Co.

United States Court of Appeals, Fourth Circuit, 1937.
95 F.2d 732, cert. denied 305 U.S. 605, 59 S.Ct. 65 (1938).

■ Before PARKER and NORTHCOTT, CIRCUIT JUDGES, and WATKINS, DISTRICT JUDGE.

■ PARKER, CIRCUIT JUDGE.

This is a petition to review a decision of the Board of Tax Appeals holding profit realized by the Elkhorn Coal & Coke Company upon a transfer of certain mining properties to the Mill Creek * * * Company to

---

4. The value of the Veranda stock received in the exchange is $8,000,000.

5. The value of the Veranda stock distributed in liquidation is still assumed to be $8,000,000.

be nontaxable. The ground of the decision was that the transfer was made pursuant to a plan of reorganization within the meaning of [the predecessor to I.R.C. § 368(a)(1)(C)] * * *.

Prior to December 18, 1925, the Elkhorn Coal & Coke Company, to which we shall hereafter refer as the old company, owned certain coal mining properties in West Virginia and certain stocks in other mining companies engaged in business in that state. It was closely associated with the Mill Creek * * * Company, which owned neighboring property * * *. Early in December, 1925, a plan was formed whereby the old company was to transfer its mine, mining plant, and mining equipment at Maybeury, W.Va., to the Mill Creek Company in exchange for 1,000 shares of the capital stock of that company. This exchange was accomplished on December 31, 1925 * * *. [T]he argument of the taxpayer is that the transfer was of all the properties of one corporation for the stock of another * * *.

The contention that the transfer in question was of all the properties of the old company depends upon the legal conclusion to be drawn from * * * the prior organization of another corporation and the transfer to it of all the property of the old company which was not to be transferred to the Mill Creek Company. These facts * * * are as follows: At the time that the transfer to the Mill Creek Company was decided upon, the officers of the old company caused another corporation to be organized * * * which we shall refer to * * * as the new company, and on December 18, 1925, transferred to it, in exchange for 6,100 shares of its stock, all of the property of the old company which was not to be transferred to the Mill Creek Company * * *. The 6,100 shares of stock in the new company were promptly distributed by the old company as a dividend to its stockholders. This left the old company owning only the property which was to be transferred to the Mill Creek Company under the plan and which was transferred to that company on December 31st, as mentioned in the preceding paragraph * * *. [N]o reason appears for the organization of the new company except to provide a transferee to take over and hold the assets which were not to be transferred to the Mill Creek Company so that the transfer to that company when made would be a transfer of all the assets of the old company.

The Board was of [the] opinion that * * * these transactions were carried through pursuant to [a] prearranged plan * * *. The Board thought, however, with five members dissenting, that because the transfers from the old company to the new were genuine and were separate and distinct from the transfer to the Mill Creek Company, the latter must be treated as a transfer of substantially all of the properties of the corporation within the meaning of the reorganization statute, summing up its conclusions as follows: "In our opinion, the facts show affirmatively that the transfer to Mill Creek was completely separate and distinct from the earlier transfer by Elkhorn to the new corporation. The transfer made on December 18 was complete within itself, regardless of what Elkhorn planned to do later, or did subsequently do. It was not a sham or a device intended to obscure the character of the transaction of December 31. The stipulated facts do not suggest other than a bona fide business move. The transfer made on December 31 was also complete within itself, and was made for reasons germane to the business of both corporations * * *."

* * *

A careful consideration of the evidentiary facts discloses no purpose which could have been served by the creation of the new company and the transfer of the assets to it, except to strip the old company of all of its properties which were not to be transferred to the Mill Creek Company, in anticipation of that transfer. The creation of the new company and its acquisition of the assets of the old was not a corporate reorganization, therefore, within the meaning of the statute or within any fair meaning of the term "reorganization." It did not involve any real transfer of assets by the business enterprise or any rearranging of corporate structure, but at most a mere shifting of charters, having no apparent purpose except the avoidance of taxes on the transfer to the Mill Creek Company which was in contemplation * * *.

* * *

It is suggested in the opinion of the Board that the case before us is analogous to that which would have been presented if the old company, prior to the transfer to Mill Creek, had distributed to its stockholders all of the assets except those destined for such transfer; but the distinction is obvious. In the case supposed, the business enterprise would have definitely divested itself of the property distributed. Here it did not divest itself of the property at all, but merely made certain changes in the legal papers under which it enjoyed corporate existence. No rule is better settled than that in tax matters we must look to substance and not to form; and no one who looks to substance can see in the mere change of charters, which is all that we have here, any reason for permitting a transfer of a part of the corporate assets to escape the taxation to which it is subject under the statute.

Congress has seen fit to grant nonrecognition of profit in sale or exchange of assets only under certain conditions, one of which is that one corporation shall transfer "substantially all" of its properties for stock in another. If nonrecognition of profit can be secured by the plan adopted in this case, the exemption is broadened to cover all transfers of assets for stock, whether "substantially all" or not, if only the transferor will go to the slight trouble and expense of getting a new charter for his corporation and making the transfer of assets to the new corporation thus created in such way as to leave in the old only the assets to be transferred at the time the transfer is to be made. We do not think the statutory exemption may be thus broadened by such an artifice.

* * *

Reversed.

■ WATKINS, DISTRICT JUDGE (dissenting).

[T]he prevailing opinion recites the facts at some length but seems to lose sight of the emphasis that should be placed upon certain determinative and uncontradicted findings of the Board of Tax Appeals. Prior to December, 1925, when the transactions in question took place, Elkhorn Coal & Coke Company and Mill Creek * * * had been actively engaged in coal mining operations * * *. One of the Elkhorn Company's mines was located in McDowell county, W.Va.; the other at Maybeury in that state. Mill Creek's mines were located at Maybeury, adjacent to the property of Elkhorn. Owners of a controlling interest in the stock of Elkhorn likewise owned a controlling interest in Mill Creek, and the officers of the two companies were largely the same. In December, 1925, it was decided that it would be in the interest of economy to have all of the Maybeury properties owned by the two companies under one management, and for this purpose the reorganization plans outlined in the prevailing opinion were perfected. No claim is made that the transactions between Elkhorn Coal & Coke Company and [the new company] are taxable. The contention is that the transaction between Elkhorn Coal & Coke Company and Mill Creek * * * is taxable. Admittedly, if this transaction is isolated from the antecedent transactions, it was a transfer of all of the assets then owned by the one company to the other in exchange for stock. It is argued, however, that * * * the organization of the [new company], and the transfer to it by the original company of approximately 80 per cent of its properties in exchange for stock * * * showed that the whole transaction was a mere device to permit the sale of the Maybeury mines without incurring the liability for income * * * tax. In this connection we call attention to the fact that the very purpose of the statute in question was to permit, through corporate reorganization, an exchange of corporate stock without tax liability at the time, permitting the holder of the stock to await its sale before incurring such liability. Two facts should be borne in mind in determining the questions at issue; first, that the Elkhorn Coal & Coke Company received nothing but stock * * * in exchange for its properties; second, that the primary purpose of the plan of reorganization related to a more economical operation of the mining properties which had previously been carried on for many years, and which have since been carried on for approximately twelve years * * *. There was no sham or pretense about the whole matter * * *.

On Rehearing

■ PARKER, CIRCUIT JUDGE. The rehearing granted in this case * * * [has] served only to strengthen the majority of the court in the opinion heretofore expressed * * *. The question before the Board was whether the transfer to Mill Creek was of all the assets of the old company; and that question must necessarily have been answered * * * by a consideration of the real nature of the incorporation of the new company and the transfer made to it when reviewed in relation to the plan for the transfer of assets to Mill Creek.

It was not intended by what was said in the original opinion, to the effect that the transfer of assets from the old company to the new did not constitute a bona fide reorganization, to suggest that the transfer was a taxable transaction, but to point out that the creation of the new company and the transfer of the assets to it was a mere shifting of charters having no purpose other than to give to the later transfer to Mill Creek the appearance of a transfer of all the corporate assets so as to bring that transfer within [the predecessor to I.R.C. § 368(a)(1)(C)] * * *. The transfer to the new company was non-taxable whether it was a real reorganization or a mere shifting of charters * * *. It is only in relation to the subsequent transfer to Mill Creek that it becomes important to determine whether the organization of the new company and its taking over of the assets was a genuine reorganization. If there was no real reorganization and transfer, but a mere shifting of charters, the subsequent transfer to Mill Creek was not within the terms of the nonrecognition provision of the statute.

    * * *

In the case at bar, the "aim" of the incorporation of the new company and the transfer made to it, was that the transfer to Mill Creek should appear to be a transfer of all of the assets of the company; and this was the end accomplished, and the only end accomplished so far as the record shows, by the incorporation and transfer. The incorporation of the new company and the transfer to it was a "meaningless and unnecessary incident." * * * It is said that the transfer to Mill Creek had a real corporate purpose. This is true, but it was taxable unless constituting a transfer of all of the assets of the corporation. The incorporation of and transfer to the new company, which had no proper corporate purpose, were resorted to in order to give the transfer to Mill Creek the appearance of being a transfer of all the assets of the transferor and hence not taxable. All that was done by the complicated corporate maneuvering employed was the transfer of a part of the assets of the old company to Mill Creek in exchange for 1,000 shares of its stock, leaving the business of the old company in the hands of the old stockholders, with a new charter, but otherwise unaffected. This result is "not a different result because reached by following a devious path."

And we think it clear that the incorporation of the new company and the transfer made to it were but parts of a single plan under which the transfer was made to Mill Creek and that they should be treated as parts of one transaction. When this is done, there is no room for the contention that all of the assets of the corporation were transferred to Mill Creek. Even though there was no unifying contract, the unity of the plan [is dispositive] * * *.

■ WATKINS, DISTRICT JUDGE, dissents.

NOTES

1. *Divisive reorganization.* Two transactions occurred in the Elkhorn case. The first transaction entailed the transfer by Elkhorn of part of its assets to the "new company" in exchange for stock of the new company, followed by the distribution (by Elkhorn) of the new company stock to Elkhorn's shareholders. This transaction divided Elkhorn into two corporations, Elkhorn and the new company. After this transaction, both Elkhorn and the new company were owned by the same shareholders. The second transaction entailed the transfer by Elkhorn of all of its remaining assets to Mill Creek and was the focus of the court on rehearing.

With regard to the first transaction, a division of one corporation into two may qualify as a tax-free D reorganization but only if it satisfies I.R.C. § 355 (a "divisive" D reorganization). See I.R.C. § 368(a)(1)(D). For the time being, assume that the divisive transaction described in this Note does qualify as a tax-free reorganization. This assumption should be reevaluated after divisive reorganizations are examined in Chapter 15.

2. *Tax-free versus taxable disposition of extraneous assets.* The "substantially all" requirement of I.R.C. § 368(a)(1)(C) bars a divisive transaction from qualifying as a C reorganization. The principal "evil" historically associated with a tax-free divisive transaction is its resemblance to a dividend. For example, the distribution by Elkhorn of the new company stock to the Elkhorn shareholders (the first transaction described in Note 1) would be governed by I.R.C. § 301 and taxed as a dividend to the extent of earnings & profits, if it did not qualify as a tax-free reorganization. If Elkhorn had simply distributed its extraneous assets to its shareholders as a taxable dividend, rather than contributing those assets to the new company and distributing the new company stock in a tax-free transaction, the potential for tax avoidance would not exist. In this event, it is unlikely that the subsequent transfer of the remaining assets to Mill Creek would have been deemed to violate the substantially all requirement.

3. *Plan of reorganization.* The disposition of Elkhorn's extraneous assets preceded the transfer of Elkhorn's remaining assets to Mill Creek by less than two weeks. Would the Elkhorn court have reached a different result if the two transactions had been separated by,

(a) two months?

(b) two years?

(c) two decades?

The Elkhorn court found that the disposition of extraneous assets took place after the plan to transfer the assets to Mill Creek was formed. Would the Elkhorn court have reached a different result if the extraneous assets were disposed of before the plan to transfer the assets to Mill Creek was formed and the amount of time separating the two events was,

(a) one week?

(b) one day?

(c) one hour?

According to the taxpayer in the Elkhorn case, at what point did the "plan of reorganization" commence?

4. *Business purpose.* What was the business purpose for the reorganization in Elkhorn?

5. *Continuity of proprietary interest and business enterprise.* Can it be determined whether the transaction in Elkhorn satisfies,

(a) the continuity of proprietary interest doctrine?

(b) the continuity of business enterprise doctrine?

What additional information would be helpful to make these determinations?

6. *"Substantially all" thresholds.* The Internal Revenue Service will ordinarily rule that an asset transfer satisfies the "substantially all" requirement of I.R.C. § 368(a)(1)(C) if at least 90% of the value of the "net" assets and at least 70% of the value of the "gross" assets are transferred. Rev. Proc. 77–37, 1977–2 C.B. 568. For example, if the transferor corporation has $100 of assets and $40 of liabilities, it must transfer at least $70 of its assets for a favorable ruling.[6] In addition, the difference between the assets and liabilities it actually transfers must be at least $54.[7] Will transferor satisfy these thresholds if it transfers,

(a) $80 of assets and $20 of liabilities?

(b) $80 of assets and $30 of liabilities?

The thresholds specified in Revenue Procedure 77–37 merely represent standards created by the Internal Revenue Service for advance ruling purposes. These thresholds do not represent standards imposed by law. Thus, although the Internal Revenue Service will not normally issue a favorable ruling with respect to an asset transfer that fails to satisfy the Revenue Procedure, the transaction still may qualify as a C reorganization. As a practical matter, however, many taxpayers are unwilling to risk the hazards of litigation in this area and, therefore, transactions are often structured to conform with the Internal Revenue Service's ruling standards, even when the taxpayer does not seek an advance ruling.

7. *Reversing the transaction.* Would the "substantially all" requirement have been satisfied if, rather than transferring the assets its shareholders wanted *to retain* to the "new company," Elkhorn had transferred the assets its shareholders wanted *to dispose of*? In other words, what if the assets that were ultimately transferred to Mill Creek had been transferred by Elkhorn to the new company in exchange for stock of the new company that was then distributed to Elkhorn's shareholders, after which the new company (rather than Elkhorn) transferred all of its assets to Mill Creek? See Rev. Rul. 2003–79, 2003–29 I.R.B. 80 (ruling that the "substantially all" requirement is satisfied under these circumstances). Is this distinction sensible?

2.   RECEIPT OF SOLELY VOTING STOCK

The principal factor that distinguishes a nontaxable transfer of a corporation's assets from a taxable transfer of those assets is the nature of

---

6.   70% × "gross assets" of $100 = $70.

7.   90% × "net assets" of $60 [$100 – $40] = $54.

the consideration received. Nonrecognition treatment is contingent upon the transferor receiving a proprietary interest in the acquiring corporation. The receipt of that interest fosters the view that the transferor retains a continuing proprietary interest in the transferred enterprise. This is the essence of the common law continuity of proprietary interest doctrine. See pp. 514–518. In the case of a C reorganization, the continuity of interest principle is implemented by the statutory requirement that the assets be transferred "in exchange solely for * * * voting stock" of the acquiring corporation.

a. LIABILITIES OF THE TRANSFEROR

I.R.C. §§ 357, 361

United States v. Hendler

United States Court of Appeals, Fourth Circuit, 1937.
91 F.2d 680, rev'd 303 U.S. 564, 58 S.Ct. 655 (1938).

■ SOPER, CIRCUIT JUDGE.

* * *

[I]n conformity with a "reorganization agreement" of May 21, 1929, the Hendler Company transferred all of its assets to the Borden Company in exchange for 105,306 shares of the latter's stock * * * and the assumption by the Borden Company of * * * $501,000 first mortgage bonds * * *. As a result of the transaction, the Hendler Company made a total calculated profit of $6,608,713.65 based on the current market price of the Borden stock. After the transaction the Hendler Company discontinued business * * * and dissolved.

[T]he Borden Company, through the purchase of some of the bonds and the redemption of the rest, performed its promise to assume the payment of the bonds at a total cost to it of $534,297.40. This sum did not pass through the Hendler Company but was paid directly to the bondholders. The Hendler Company did not include it in its income tax return for 1929 nor any part of the profit realized in the reorganization. The Commissioner reached the determination that while the total profit on the exchange was not taxable, the item of $534,297.40 was taxable * * *. The District Court [found for the taxpayer] * * *.

Section 112 of the Revenue Act of 1928 [a predecessor to I.R.C. § 368(a)(1)(C)] * * * provides in part as follows:

> (b) Exchanges solely in kind—* * *
>> (4) [* * * Reorganization]—Gain of corporation. No gain or loss shall be recognized if a corporation a party to a reorganization exchanges property, in pursuance of the plan of reorganization, solely for stock * * * in another corporation a party to the reorganization. * * *
> (d) [Gain from Exchanges not Solely in Kind]—Gain of corporation. If an exchange would be within the provisions of subsection

(b)(4) of this section if it were not for the fact that the property received in exchange consists not only of stock * * * permitted by such paragraph to be received without the recognition of gain, but also of other property or money, then—

(1) If the corporation receiving such other property or money distributes it in pursuance of the plan of reorganization, no gain to the corporation shall be recognized from the exchange, but

(2) If the corporation receiving such other property or money does not distribute it in pursuance of the plan of reorganization, the gain, if any, to the corporation shall be recognized, but in an amount not in excess of the sum of such money and the fair market value of such other property so received, which is not so distributed.

[The government does not deny] that there was a "reorganization" * * *; but it is said that the taxpayer did not exchange its property in pursuance of a plan of reorganization solely for stock * * * in the Borden Company within the terms of section 112(b)(4), but also received * * * an assumption of the taxpayer's * * * bonded indebtedness discharged at a cost of $534,297.40; and it is contended that this assumption of indebtedness was not money or property within the true construction of section 112(d), or if it was money or property, it was not distributed in pursuance of the plan of reorganization within the terms of the section. Hence it is said that the item of $534,297.40 should be added to the taxable income.

At the outset we are * * * [surprised] by the failure of the government to press its argument to the conclusion which would seem to follow if its premises, based upon a literal interpretation of the language, are sound. If the assumption of the bonded indebtedness did not constitute money or property, but nevertheless represented taxable value received by the taxpayer, it would seem that the transaction was not covered by the literal terms of either section 112(b)(4) or section 112(d), and that therefore the entire profit of $6,608,713.85 was taxable * * *. [This omission by] the Government * * * is difficult to understand.

In our opinion, however, the decision of the District Court was correct. We do not question the rule that the payment of an obligation of a taxpayer by another person constitutes income to the taxpayer. Old Colony Trust Co. v. Commissioner, 279 U.S. 716. And of course the assumption * * * of all * * * forms of indebtedness owing by a taxpayer must necessarily be taken into account in computing the taxpayer's profit in a reorganization. However, it does not follow that the amount of indebtedness assumed is taxable as profit at the time that the reorganization is effected; and it is significant that the usual practice of the Commissioner has been quite to the contrary.

The sections of the act in question must be construed in view of the purposes which they were intended to effect. It is well known that the purpose was to provide for the exemption from taxation at the time of a business reorganization of the gains involved therein to the extent specified in the statute in order to remove impediments to corporate readjustments and also to prevent the recognition of fictitious gains or losses * * *. The result is to defer the taxation of such gains * * *.

So it was provided in effect that no gain should be recognized in the exchange of property solely for stock * * * in the transferee corporation; or if the property received in exchange should also include property or money other than stock * * *, the gain should be recognized only to the extent that such other property or money was not distributed in pursuance of the plan of reorganization. Now it seems to us * * * that it was not the intention of Congress to recognize for immediate taxation the gain derived in a corporate reorganization to the extent it should consist of an assumption of the debts of the corporate grantor. Such an assumption is undoubtedly an asset of value and may fairly be called property in the broad sense; but the money spent in the performance of the promise passes to creditors and does not come into the possession of the debtor corporation or its stockholders. It reduces the debts and therefore frees the assets from the claims of creditors so that they may be lawfully distributed amongst the stockholders * * *; but it does not increase in their hands the assets whose liquidation brings about the actual enjoyment of the realized profit. Therefore the recognition of the gain, to the extent of the amount of the debt assumed, would not serve the statutory purpose, but on the contrary would tend to defeat it. It is a matter of common knowledge that a promise by the grantee to assume the debts of the grantor corporation is a customary incident of reorganization agreements, and where the transaction yields a profit to the grantor, taxable gain up to the amount of the assumed debt would accrue in the current year if the present contention of the Commissioner is correct, whether or not at that time the corporation or its stockholders had actually realized the profit in the transaction.

It seems obvious that Congress in referring to the receipt of stock * * * in section 112(b)(4) and to the receipt of money and other property in section 112(d) had in mind the sort of property that is susceptible of distribution among stockholders. Indeed, this is part of the argument of the government which asserts that a distribution in reorganization generally contemplates a distribution among stockholders and that it would be a distortion of language to misconstrue the word "distribute" to mean the payment of creditors. But it does not follow, as the government contends, that when the taxpayer secures an assumption of its debts in addition to stock * * * or distributable property, it is not entitled to the exemption claimed. Congress has adopted the realistic conception that the substantial value which a corporation owns is the equity in its corporate property—that is, the value of its assets after provision has been made for the payment of its debts—that what the grantee acquires in a corporate reorganization is this equity, and that its assumption of liabilities is merely the means by which it is enabled to acquire a good title to the grantor's property. If this viewpoint is kept in mind, it is clear that the grantor in a reorganization agreement receives nothing from the assumption of its debts by the grantee that prevents it from claiming an exemption under either of the cited sections of the statute.

It must not be supposed that the gain derived by the corporate grantor from the assumption of its debts will entirely escape taxation through this construction of the act. Manifestly the price paid for the corporate assets by the grantee includes both the value which passes to the corporation or its stockholders and that which passes to its creditors; and the entire profit will be recognized, when upon the ultimate liquidation of the assets actually received by the corporation or its stockholders a comparison is made between that which was originally put into the venture and that which has been finally taken out.

* * *

United States v. Hendler

Supreme Court of the United States, 1938.
303 U.S. 564, 58 S.Ct. 655.

■ MR. JUSTICE BLACK delivered the opinion of the Court.

* * *

In this case, there was a * * * "reorganization" of the Borden Company and the Hendler Creamery Company, Inc., resulting in gains of more than six million dollars to the Hendler Company, Inc., a corporation of which respondent is transferee. The Court of Appeals * * * [held] all Hendler gains non-taxable.

This controversy between the government and respondent involves the assumption and payment—pursuant to the plan of reorganization—by the Borden Company of $534,297.40 bonded indebtedness of the Hendler Creamery Co., Inc. We are unable to agree with the conclusion reached by the courts below that the gain to the Hendler Company, realized by the Borden Company's payment, was exempt from taxation * * *.

It was contended below and it is urged here that since the Hendler Company did not actually receive the money with which the Borden Company discharged the former's indebtedness, the Hendler Company's gain of $534,297.40 is not taxable. The transaction, however, under which the Borden Company assumed and paid the debt and obligation of the Hendler Company is to be regarded in substance as though the $534,297.40 had been paid directly to the Hendler Company. The Hendler Company was the beneficiary of the discharge of its indebtedness. Its gain was as real and substantial as if the money had been paid it and then paid over by it to its creditors. The discharge of liability by the payment of the Hendler Company's indebtedness constituted income to the Hendler Company and is to be treated as such.

Section 112 provides no exemption for gains-resulting from "corporate reorganization"—either received as "stock * * *," nor received as "money or other property" and distributed to stockholders under the plan of reorganization * * *.

Since this gain or income of $534,297.40 of the Hendler Company was neither received as "stock * * * "nor distributed to its stockholders "in pursuance of the plan of reorganization" it * * * is taxable gain * * *. [T]he judgment of the court below is

Reversed.

NOTES

1. *Impact of liabilities on reorganization status.* In the Revenue Act of 1934, Congress restricted the statutory predecessor of a C reorganization to, "the acquisition by one corporation in exchange solely for all or part of its voting stock * * * of substantially all the properties of another corporation." Section 112(g)(1)(B). After the Supreme Court's decision in Hendler, it was unclear whether the statutory "solely for voting stock" requirement was satisfied when any liabilities of the transferor corporation were transferred to the acquiring corporation. Thus, the transfer of all of a corporation's assets in exchange for voting stock of the acquiring corporation might not have qualified as a reorganization if the acquiring corporation assumed *any* of the transferor's liabilities, in which case the transferor corporation would have been taxed on *all* of its gain. As a practical matter, it is virtually impossible to structure the transfer of a corporation's assets without transferring any of the corporation's liabilities. Consequently, the Code was subsequently amended to provide that liabilities of the transferor corporation that are assumed by the acquiring corporation are ignored for purposes of determining whether the "solely for voting stock" requirement is satisfied. See I.R.C. § 368(a)(1)(C) (last clause).

2. *Treatment of transferred liabilities as "boot."* Even if liabilities of the transferor corporation are ignored when determining whether an asset transfer qualifies as a C reorganization, an issue remains as to whether liabilities assumed by the acquiring corporation should be analogized to the receipt of money by the transferor corporation for gain recognition purposes. See I.R.C. § 361(b)(1). If the transfer of liabilities were equated to the receipt of money, the amount received presumably could not be distributed by the transferor corporation because it did not actually receive any money or property that it could transfer. Accordingly, any gain realized by the transferor would be recognized to the extent of the transferred liabilities. See I.R.C. § 361(b)(1)(B). As a general rule, however, the transfer of liabilities is not treated as the receipt of money or other property for gain recognition purposes under I.R.C. § 361. See I.R.C. §§ 357(a), (b). What are the tax consequences to the transferor corporation, however, if the acquiring corporation assumes liabilities that exceed the aggregate basis of the transferor corporation in the transferred assets? See I.R.C. § 357(c).

3. *Treatment of retained liabilities.* In lieu of causing the acquiring corporation to assume all of its liabilities, the transferor corporation might retain some of its liabilities. (The retention of liabilities also might aid in satisfying the "substantially all" requirement. Why? See p. 529, Note 6.) What are the tax consequences to the transferor corporation under each of the following alternatives?

(a) It pays off its creditors with stock received from the acquiring corporation. See I.R.C. § 361(c)(3); Problem 12–2(b).

(b) It sells some of the stock received from the acquiring corporation and uses the proceeds to pay its creditors. See I.R.C. § 361(c); Problem 12–2(c).

(c) It transfers the retained liabilities to its shareholders when it liquidates. See I.R.C. § 361(c)(2)(B)(i); Problem 12–2(d).

Problem 12–2 (Consequences of transferring or retaining liabilities in a C reorganization): Alex is the sole shareholder of Waldo Corporation and he has a basis of $100,000 in his Waldo stock. Waldo owns assets with a value of $8,000,000 in which Waldo has a basis of $3,000,000. Waldo has $2,000,000 of liabilities. Consider each of the following alternatives:

(a) Veranda Corporation acquires all of Waldo's assets for Veranda stock worth $6,000,000 and Veranda assumes all of Waldo's liabilities. Waldo distributes the Veranda stock to Alex in liquidation. What are the tax consequences to Waldo (I.R.C. §§ 368(a)(1)(C), 361(a), 357(a), 358(a)(1), 358(d), 361(c)), Alex (I.R.C. §§ 354(a), 358(a)(1)) and Veranda (I.R.C. §§ 1032, 362(b))?

(b) Veranda Corporation acquires all of Waldo's assets for Veranda stock worth $8,000,000. Waldo transfers $2,000,000 of Veranda stock to its creditors and distributes the remaining Veranda stock to Alex in liquidation. What are the tax consequences to Waldo (see I.R.C. § 361(c)(3)), Alex and Veranda?

(c) Veranda Corporation acquires all of Waldo's assets for Veranda stock worth $8,000,000. Waldo sells $2,000,000 of Veranda stock and uses the proceeds to pay its creditors. Waldo distributes the remaining Veranda stock to Alex in liquidation. What are the tax consequences to Waldo (see I.R.C. § 361(c)), Alex and Veranda?

(d) Veranda Corporation acquires all of Waldo's assets in exchange for Veranda stock worth $8,000,000 which Waldo distributes, along with Waldo's liabilities, to Alex in liquidation. What are the tax consequences to Waldo (see I.R.C. § 361(c)(2)(B)(i)), Alex and Veranda?

b. MONEY OR OTHER PROPERTY

I.R.C. § 368(a)(2)(B)

Treas. Reg. § 1.368–2(d)(2)

Revenue Ruling 73–102

1973–1 Cum.Bull. 186.

Advice has been requested whether, under the circumstances described below, the "solely for voting stock" requirement of section 368(a)(1)(C) of the Internal Revenue Code is satisfied.

For valid business reasons, X corporation entered into a plan of reorganization with unrelated Y corporation. Pursuant to the plan, X transferred all of its assets to Y in exchange for Y voting stock and the assumption by Y of the X liabilities, including liabilities to pay claims of dissenting shareholders.

Under the plan, Y paid 50x dollars to dissenting X shareholders in satisfaction of their claims, based on the fair market value of their X stock surrendered. The dissenting shareholders surrendered all their X stock for cash in the transaction. The fair market value of the gross assets transferred by X to Y was 2,000x dollars. The amount of the liabilities assumed by Y (other than the liability to pay dissenting shareholders) was 150x dollars.

Section 368(a)(1)(C) of the Code defines as a reorganization the acquisition by one corporation, in exchange solely for shares of its voting stock, of substantially all the properties of another corporation. Section 368(a)(1)(C) of the Code further provides that in determining whether the exchange is solely for stock the assumption by the acquiring corporation of a liability of the other will be disregarded.

Section 368(a)(2)(B) of the Code provides that if, in addition to voting stock, the acquiring corporation exchanges money or other property, and if the acquiring corporation acquires, solely for voting stock, property of the other corporation having a fair market value which is at least 80 percent of the fair market value of all the property of the other corporation, then such acquisition will be treated as qualifying under section 368(a)(1)(C) of the Code. For the purpose of the percentage computation of section 368(a)(2)(B) of the Code, liabilities assumed by the acquiring corporation are treated as money.

In Helvering v. Southwest Consolidated Corp., 315 U.S. 194 (1942), the Supreme Court of the United States held that the "solely for voting stock" requirement of the predecessor of section 368(a)(1)(C) of the Code was violated where the acquiring corporation directly or indirectly transferred to the acquired corporation or its shareholders property other than voting stock in exchange for the equity interest being acquired. The Court stated: " 'Solely' leaves no leeway."

The payment by Y of 50x dollars to dissenting shareholders of X in satisfaction of their claims was, in substance, the same as if Y had exchanged cash plus voting stock for the properties of X. Therefore, this cash payment is not a payment by Y of an assumed liability, but is additional consideration paid by Y in the exchange for the properties acquired by Y. Thus, the acquisition of the X property for the Y voting stock and cash cannot qualify under section 368(a)(1)(C) of the Code unless section 368(a)(2)(B) of the Code applies.

For purposes of section 368(a)(2)(B) of the Code, Y constructively paid a total of 200x dollars in money to X (liabilities assumed in the amount of 150x dollars, plus 50x dollars paid to the dissenting shareholders). Therefore, Y received property of X having a fair market value of 1,800x dollars (gross assets in the amount of 2,000x dollars, less 200x dollars in money constructively paid to X) solely for voting stock of Y, which represents 90 percent of the fair market value of all of the X property.

Accordingly, in the instant case, since at least 80 percent of all the property of X was acquired solely for voting stock of Y, it is held that the transaction qualifies as a reorganization under sections 368(a)(1)(C) and (a)(2)(B) of the Code. Under section 361(b)(1)(A) of the Code, no gain is recognized to X upon the constructive receipt and distribution of 50x dollars to the dissenting shareholders. Under section 361(b)(2) of the Code, no loss is recognized to X. The cash received by the dissenting shareholders will be treated as a constructive distribution to them by X in redemption of their X stock subject to the provisions and limitations of section 302 of the Code.

NOTES

1. *Solely for voting stock versus continuity of proprietary interest.* Identify the similarities and differences between the common law continuity of proprietary interest doctrine (pp. 514–518) and the statutory solely for voting stock requirement in a C reorganization. Which requirement is more stringent? Can you envision any circumstances in which the statutory requirement might be satisfied without satisfying the common law doctrine? See Treas. Reg. § 1.368–2(d)(1) (last three sentences).

2. *Boot relaxation rule.* In 1954, the "solely for voting stock" requirement of I.R.C. § 368(a)(1)(C) was liberalized dramatically by the enactment of a provision commonly referred to as the "boot relaxation rule." See I.R.C. § 368(a)(2)(B). When the acquiring corporation uses voting stock and an amount of boot within the parameters of the boot relaxation rule as consideration for an asset acquisition that qualifies as a C reorganization, does the transferor corporation recognize gain (or loss) when it receives the boot? See I.R.C. § 361(b). Does the transferor corporation recognize gain (or loss) when it subsequently distributes the boot to its shareholders in liquidation? See I.R.C. §§ 358(a)(2), 361(c). Are the shareholders of the transferor corporation taxed when they receive the boot? See I.R.C. §§ 354(a), 356(a). Does the use of boot create any adverse tax consequences to the acquiring corporation? See I.R.C. § 1001. These issues are explored in Problem 12–3(a) (p. 538).

3. *Treatment of certain preferred stock as boot.* When "nonqualified preferred stock" is received in a transaction that qualifies as a reorganization, the nonqualified preferred stock is treated as boot. See I.R.C. §§ 354(a)(2)(C)(i), 356(e). "Nonqualified preferred stock" includes preferred stock that requires the issuer to purchase the stock, confers on the holder the right to require the issuer to purchase the stock, or permits the issuer to purchase the stock pursuant to terms that make it more likely than not that the issuer will purchase the stock. See I.R.C. § 351(g)(2). Boot treatment does not result, however, when the issuer's obligation or right to purchase the preferred stock is contingent upon the death or disability of the holder or, in certain cases, the termination of the holder's employment with the issuer. See I.R.C. § 351(g)(2)(C). "Nonqualified preferred stock" also includes preferred stock with a dividend rate that varies with reference to interest rates, commodity prices, or similar indices. See I.R.C. § 351(g)(2)(A)(iv).

4. *Impact of liabilities.* The utility of the boot relaxation rule is diminished considerably by the manner in which liabilities of the transferor corporation that are assumed by the acquiring corporation are treated *for purposes of the boot relaxation rule.* Specifically, these liabilities are treated as money received by the transferor corporation for purposes of determining whether more than 20% of the consideration received by the transferor corporation represents boot. See I.R.C. § 368(a)(2)(B) (last sentence). Thus, if the transferor corporation's assets secure debt representing as little as 20% of the value of those assets, a transfer of all the transferor's assets subject to all of its liabilities will not qualify as a C reorganization if as little as $1 of money or other property is provided by the acquiring corporation. These relationships are explored in Problems 12–3(b) and (c).

> *Problem 12–3 (Consequences of boot in a C reorganization):* Alex is the sole shareholder of Waldo Corporation and he has a basis of $100,000 in his Waldo stock. Waldo owns assets with a value of $8,000,000 in which Waldo has a basis of $3,000,000. Consider each of the following alternatives:
>
> (a) Waldo has no liabilities. Veranda Corporation acquires all of Waldo's assets for newly issued voting stock worth $7,000,000 and $1,000,000 of other property (in which Veranda has a basis of $400,000) and Waldo distributes the Veranda stock and the boot to Alex in liquidation. What are the tax consequences to Waldo (see I.R.C. §§ 368(a)(1)(C), (a)(2)(B), 361(b), 358(a), 361(c)), Alex (see I.R.C. §§ 354(a), 356(a), 358(a)) and Veranda (see I.R.C. §§ 1032, 362(b))? How do the tax consequences to Alex change if Alex has a basis in his Waldo stock of $7,600,000 (rather than a basis of $100,000)? See I.R.C. § 356(a).
>
> (b) Waldo has $1,000,000 of liabilities. Veranda Corporation acquires all of Waldo's assets by issuing Veranda voting stock worth $6,990,000 to Waldo, paying Waldo $10,000, and assuming all of Waldo's liabilities. Waldo distributes the Veranda stock and the $10,000 to Alex in liquidation. What are the tax consequences to Waldo, Alex and Veranda? See I.R.C. § 368(a)(2)(B).
>
> (c) Waldo has $2,000,000 of liabilities. Veranda Corporation acquires all of Waldo's assets by issuing Veranda voting stock worth $5,990,000 to Waldo, paying Waldo $10,000, and assuming all of Waldo's liabilities. Waldo distributes the Veranda stock and the $10,000 to Alex in liquidation. What are the tax consequences to Waldo, Alex and Veranda? See I.R.C. § 368(a)(2)(B).

3.   Liquidation of the Transferor

I.R.C. § 368(a)(2)(G)

In addition to transferring "substantially all" of its assets and receiving "solely" voting stock, the transferor corporation must distribute the consideration received for its assets (as well as any assets it did not transfer to the acquiring corporation) for the transaction to qualify as a C reorganization. See I.R.C. § 368(a)(2)(G).

Revenue Procedure 89–50

1989–2 Cum.Bull. 631.

* * *

BACKGROUND

[R]ev. Proc. 77–37 * * * contains certain standard representations that ordinarily must be submitted as a prerequisite to the issuance of rulings on the tax consequences of reorganizations described in section 368(a) of the Internal Revenue Code. These representations ensure that specific statutory and judicial requirements and administrative ruling guidelines are satisfied and facilitate the timely processing of letter ruling requests.

The Service has received many requests for rulings under section 368(a)(1)(C) * * * of the Code with respect to transactions in which the target corporation does not dissolve under state law so that the value of its corporate charter can be realized. The retention of the corporate charter and those assets necessary to satisfy state law minimum capital requirements raises an issue of whether the distribution requirements applicable to reorganizations described in section 368(a)(1)(C) * * * have been satisfied. Section 368(a)(2)(G)(i) * * * requires as a prerequisite to qualifying as a reorganization under section 368(a)(1)(C) * * *, that the target corporation distribute all of the stock, securities, and property it receives from the acquiring corporation, as well as the target corporation's other properties, pursuant to the plan of reorganization.

Section 368(a)(2)(G)(ii) of the Code provides the Secretary with the authority to waive the distribution requirement in section 368(a)(1)(C) reorganizations subject to any conditions the Secretary may prescribe. The legislative history indicates that Congress anticipated that waivers would be granted in those cases where the distribution requirement would result in substantial hardship upon the condition that the target corporation and its shareholders are treated as if the retained assets are distributed and then contributed to the capital of a new corporation. The loss of a valuable nontransferable charter was considered to constitute a substantial hardship resulting from the distribution requirement.

* * *

Accordingly, the Service has established certain conditions under which it ordinarily will rule that the distribution requirement applicable to reorganizations under section 368(a)(1)(C) * * * of the Code has been satisfied. These conditions are contained in representations that must be submitted * * *.

PROCEDURE

Rev. Proc. 77–37 * * * is * * * amplified to include the following subsection under section 7:

.09 Additional representations for retention of corporate charters in section 368(a)(1)(C) * * * reorganization:

1. Target will retain only its corporate charter and those assets, if any, necessary to satisfy state law minimum capital requirements to maintain corporate existence (minimum capital).

2. For purposes of the representation that acquiring will acquire at least 90 percent of the fair market value of the net assets and at least 70 percent of the fair market value of the gross assets held by target immediately prior to the transactions, the corporate charter and minimum capital, if any, retained by target will be included as assets of target held immediately prior to the transaction.

3. The sole purpose for having target maintain its corporate existence under state law is to isolate target's charter for resale to an unrelated purchaser * * *.

4. As soon as practicable, but in no event later than 12 months following the date substantially all of the assets are transferred to acquiring, target will be sold to an unrelated purchaser or dissolved under state law. If target is sold, then immediately prior to the sale of target by its shareholders, the corporate charter and minimum capital, if any, retained by target will be treated for federal tax purposes as if they are distributed to target's shareholders in a distribution to which sections 356 and 361(c) of the Code apply and then contributed to the capital of a new corporation * * *. If target is dissolved, then in accordance with the plan of reorganization, the minimum capital will be received by target's shareholders in a distribution to which sections 356 and 361(c) of the Code apply or received by acquiring in a transfer to which section 361(a) applies.

* * *

NOTES

1. *Hidden rule.* The fact that all of the statutory requirements for each type of reorganization are not located in one place (and are not even cross-referenced) causes a trek through the reorganization rules by the uninitiated to be fraught with risk. As you can see, no distribution requirement exists in I.R.C. § 368(a)(1)(C). Rather, the distribution requirement for a C reorganization is in I.R.C. § 368(a)(2)(G).

2. *Retained assets.* If a corporation transfers "substantially all" of its assets to the acquiring corporation, but retains some of its assets, must the transferor distribute the assets it retained for the transaction to qualify as a C reorganization? See I.R.C. § 368(a)(2)(G). What are the tax consequences of the distribution of the retained assets to,

(a) the transferor corporation? See I.R.C. § 361(c)(2).

(b) the shareholders of the transferor corporation? See I.R.C. §§ 354(a)(1), 356(a), 358(a)(2).

Problem 12–4 (Consequences of distributing retained assets): Alex is the sole shareholder of Waldo Corporation and has a basis of $100,000 in his Waldo stock. Waldo owns assets with a value of $8,000,000 in which Waldo has a basis of $3,000,000. Waldo has no liabilities. Waldo transfers all of its assets, except for certain equipment with a value of $100,000 in which Waldo has a basis of $40,000, to Veranda in exchange for Veranda stock worth $7,900,000. Waldo then liquidates by distributing the Veranda stock and the equipment to Alex. What are the tax consequences to Waldo, Alex and Veranda?

4.   CREATIVE APPLICATION

IRS Letter Ruling 200709037

11/13/06.

Dear * * *:

This responds to your July 25, 2006 letter requesting rulings as to certain federal income tax consequences of a proposed transaction. The information provided in that request is summarized below.

SUMMARY OF FACTS

Target is a State A corporation that is engaged in Business A. Target has one class of voting common stock outstanding. Shareholder owns all of the outstanding voting common stock of Target. Acquiring is a publicly held corporation that has one class of common stock outstanding. Target owns approximately *a* percent of the common stock of Acquiring. The stock of Acquiring is Target's largest asset.

PROPOSED TRANSACTION

For what is represented to be a valid business purpose, Target and Acquiring will engage in the following transaction (the "Proposed Transaction"):

(i) To the extent practicable, Target will sell its assets other than the Acquiring shares to third parties and possibly Shareholder. The sales proceeds will be used to purchase additional shares of Acquiring common stock.

(ii) Target will transfer all of its Acquiring shares (the "Old Acquiring Shares") to Acquiring in exchange for a number of newly issued Acquiring common shares (the "New Acquiring Shares) equal to the number of Old Acquiring Shares owned by Target on the date of the exchange (the "Exchange"). In connection with the exchange, Acquiring will not assume any Target liabilities or receive any Target assets which are subject to liabilities.

(iii) Within one year of step (ii) above, Target will distribute its New Acquiring Shares to Shareholder. Target will then initiate the dissolution process.

REPRESENTATIONS

The following representations have been made regarding the Proposed Transaction:

(a) The fair market value of the New Acquiring Shares received by Shareholder will approximately equal the fair market value of the Target stock surrendered in the exchange.

* * *

(c) At least 40% of the proprietary interest in Target will be exchanged for Acquiring common stock and will be preserved (within the meaning of § 1.368–1(e)(1)(i)).

* * *

(e) Acquiring will acquire at least 90% of the fair market value of the net assets and at least 70% of the fair market value of the gross assets held by Target immediately before the transaction. * * *

(g) Target will distribute the stock, securities, and other property it receives in the transaction, and its other properties, in pursuance of the plan of reorganization.

* * *

(i) Following the transaction, Acquiring will continue the historic business of Target or use a significant portion of Target's business assets in a business.

* * *

RULINGS

Based solely on the information submitted and the representations set forth above, we rule as follows regarding the Proposed Transaction:

(1) The [acquisition by Acquiring of substantially all of Target's assets solely in exchange for New Acquiring Shares, as described above, followed by the distribution by Target of all of its assets, including the New Acquiring Shares, to Shareholder] will qualify as a reorganization under § 368(a)(1)(C). Acquiring and Target will each be a "party to a reorganization" under § 368(b).

(2) Target will recognize no gain or loss on the transfer of its Old Acquiring Shares to Acquiring solely in exchange for the New Acquiring Shares in the Exchange (§ 361(a)).

(3) Target will recognize no gain or loss on its distribution of the New Acquiring Shares to Shareholder (§ 361(c)(1)). Target will recognize gain on the distribution of other appreciated property, if any, to Shareholder as if such property had been sold by Target at its fair market value.

(4) Acquiring will recognize no gain or loss on its receipt of the Old Acquiring Shares solely in exchange for the New Acquiring Shares in the Exchange (§ 1032(a)).

(5) Shareholder will not recognize gain or loss on the exchange of its Target stock solely for the New Acquiring Shares (§ 354(a)(1)).

(6) Shareholder's basis in the New Acquiring Shares will equal the basis of the Target stock surrendered therefor (§ 358(a)).

* * *

CAVEATS

We express no opinion on the tax effect of the Proposed Transaction under any other provision of the Code and regulations, or the tax effect of any condition existing at the time of, or effect resulting from, the Proposed Transaction that is not specifically covered by the rulings set forth above.

PROCEDURAL STATEMENTS

This letter is directed only to the taxpayer who requested it. Section 6110(k)(3) of the Code provides that it may not be used or cited as precedent.

A copy of this letter should be attached to the federal income tax return of each taxpayer involved for the taxable year in which the Proposed Transaction covered by this ruling letter is completed.

* * *

NOTES

1. *Consequences if Target had liquidated.* If, rather than engaging in the transaction set forth in the ruling, Target had simply liquidated by distributing the Old Acquiring Shares to Shareholder, what would have been the tax consequences to Target? See I.R.C. § 336(a).

2. *Reorganization requirements.* Did the transaction set forth in the ruling satisfy all the statutory and common law requirements for a C reorganization?

3. *Consequences of reorganization.* What were the tax consequences of the transaction in the ruling—

(a) to Target, when Target transferred the Old Acquiring Shares to Acquiring? See I.R.C. § 361(a).

(b) to Target, when Target distributed the New Acquiring Shares to Shareholder? See I.R.C. § 361(c)(1).

(c) to Shareholder, on the receipt of the New Acquiring Shares? See I.R.C. § 354(a).

What tax benefit was achieved by the transaction described in the ruling that would not have resulted had Target merely liquidated?

5. The Nondivisive D Reorganization

I.R.C. §§ 368(a)(1)(D), 354(b)

Under certain circumstances, the transfer of a corporation's assets will satisfy the statutory definition of a "nondivisive D" reorganization. See I.R.C. § 368(a)(1)(D). (In fact, a single transaction can satisfy the definitional requirements of both a C reorganization and a nondivisive D reorganization in which case the transaction is treated as a D reorganization. See I.R.C. § 368(a)(2)(A).) Because the nondivisive D reorganization has not generally been utilized as an affirmative planning strategy (but instead has been utilized as a weapon by the government), a detailed examination of that type of reorganization is deferred until Chapter 16. At this point, however, it is useful to highlight the many definitional similarities between a C reorganization and a nondivisive D reorganization.

Transfer of "Substantially All the Assets": The requirement that a corporation must transfer "substantially all" of its assets is readily apparent in the definition of a C reorganization. See I.R.C. § 368(a)(1)(C). In contrast, the source of that requirement for a nondivisive D reorganization is somewhat elusive. See I.R.C. § 368(a)(1)(D). After I.R.C. § 355 is examined in Chapter 15, it will be apparent that an asset transfer can qualify as a nondivisive D reorganization only if it satisfies I.R.C. § 354. For a D reorganization to satisfy I.R.C. § 354, a corporation must transfer "substantially all" of its assets. See I.R.C. § 354(b)(1)(A). For advance ruling purposes, the same statutory thresholds must be met to satisfy the "substantially all" requirement in both a C reorganization and a nondivisive D reorganization. See Rev. Proc. 77–37, 1977–2 C.B. 568 (p. 529, Note 6).

No "Solely for Voting Stock" Requirement: No "solely for voting stock" requirement exists in the statutory definition of a nondivisive D reorganization. A different statutory mechanism, however, insures that the transferors retain a continuing ownership interest in the transferred business. Specifically, a "control" requirement exists.

"Control" Requirement: To accomplish a nondivisive D reorganization, one or more of the shareholders of the transferor corporation must be in "control" of the acquiring corporation immediately after the transfer. See I.R.C. § 368(a)(1)(D). The "control" standard that applies to a nondivisive D reorganization is a relatively easy standard to meet. "Control" for purposes of a nondivisive D reorganization is defined as the ownership of stock representing at least 50% of the vote *or* at least 50% of the value of all classes of stock. See I.R.C. §§ 368(a)(2)(H)(i) (another hidden rule!), 304(c).[8] Thus, the control requirement is normally satisfied when the

---

8. The "control" definition of I.R.C. § 304(c) was previously examined in Chapter 5. See pp. 276–277. In contrast, a much more stringent 80% standard for "control" exists under I.R.C. § 368(c), previously examined in Chapter 8. See pp. 375–376.

transferor corporation is larger than the acquiring corporation, if the entire consideration consists of stock of the acquiring corporation. In this situation, the former shareholders of the transferor corporation will own more than half of the stock of the acquiring corporation immediately after the transfer and, therefore, satisfy the control requirement. Even when the transferor corporation is smaller than the acquiring corporation, the control requirement may be satisfied if shareholders of the transferor corporation own some of the outstanding stock of the acquiring corporation before the acquisition. The control standard for a nondivisive D reorganization is made even easier to meet by broad attribution rules that apply when stock ownership is quantified under I.R.C. § 304(c). See I.R.C. § 304(c)(3). The events leading to the application of this liberal control standard to the nondivisive D reorganization are explored in Chapter 16.

Liquidation of Transferor Corporation: As in the case of a C reorganization, the transferor corporation must distribute the consideration received for its assets (as well as any assets it did not transfer to the acquiring corporation) for the transaction to qualify as a nondivisive D reorganization. The liquidation requirement for a nondivisive D reorganization is located at I.R.C. § 354(b)(1)(B). Rev. Proc. 89–50 (p. 539) applies in the same fashion to a nondivisive D reorganization as it applies to a C reorganization.

C. STOCK TRANSFER

I.R.C. § 368(a)(1)(B)

Treas. Reg. § 1.368–2(c)

The classic reorganization definition that applies to a stock transfer is located at I.R.C. § 368(a)(1)(B) (a "B" reorganization). To qualify a stock transfer as a B reorganization, the following statutory requirements must be satisfied:

(a) The acquiring corporation must be in "control" (as defined in I.R.C. § 368(c)) of the acquired ("target") corporation immediately after the acquisition.

(b) The consideration received by the target corporation's shareholders must be "solely voting stock" of the acquiring corporation.

In addition, the transaction must satisfy the common law doctrines that apply to reorganizations. See pp. 513–521. The B reorganization and its corresponding tax consequences are illustrated by Example 12–B.

Example 12–B (Consequences of a non-taxable stock transfer): Alex is the sole shareholder of Waldo Corporation and has a basis of $100,000 in his Waldo stock. Alex's Waldo stock has a value of $8,000,000. Alex transfers all of his Waldo stock to Veranda Corporation in exchange for newly issued voting stock of Veranda worth $8,000,000. Assume the transaction satisfies all of the statutory and common law requirements for a B reorganization.

1. Tax Consequences to Waldo

   None

2. Tax Consequences to Alex

   Exchange of Waldo Stock for Veranda Stock

   Realization Event (I.R.C. § 1001(a))

Amount Realized	$8,000,000 [9]
Less: Adjusted Basis	100,000
Realized Gain	$7,900,000

   Not Recognized: I.R.C. §§ 354(a)(1), 368(b)(2)

   Basis in Veranda Stock: $100,000—I.R.C. § 358(a)(1)

3. Tax Consequences to Veranda

   Exchange of Newly Issued Veranda Stock for Waldo Stock

   Nonrecognition of Gain or Loss: I.R.C. § 1032

   Basis in Waldo Stock: $100,000—I.R.C. § 362(b)

1.   "CONTROL" IMMEDIATELY AFTER THE ACQUISITION

Revenue Ruling 56–613

1956–2 Cum.Bull. 212.

* * *

X corporation's capital stock consists of shares of Class A and Class B common stock, evenly divided. These shares have equal voting and liquidation rights, the only distinction between them being in the payment of dividends. In the year 1949, X corporation sold all Class A stock to eight persons who continued to hold such stock until 1955. In that year, all of the Class A stock of the X corporation was acquired by Y corporation from the original shareholders in exchange for common stock of Y corporation. The Class B stock of X corporation was purchased in 1950 by Z corporation in an independent transaction in which Y had no interest. Thereafter, in 1951, all of the Z stock was acquired by Y. Thus, inasmuch as the Y corporation has now all of the Class A stock of X, and its subsidiary, Z, owns all of the Class B stock of X, the Y corporation has, for practical purposes, 100 percent voting control of X corporation.

The specific question presented is whether the exchange of Class A stock of the X corporation for Y's stock is a tax-free exchange to the shareholders participating in that exchange.

As a general rule, the entire amount of gain or loss on the exchange of property (which includes stock) is recognized for Federal income tax purposes. However, in the case of certain exchanges of stock pursuant to a plan of reorganization, no gain or loss is recognized. At issue in this case is whether the acquisition of stock by Y corporation constitutes a reorganization as defined in section 368(a)(1)(B) of the Internal Revenue Code of 1954.

---

9. The value of the Veranda stock received in the exchange is $8,000,000.

Section 368(a)(1) of such Code states, in part, that the term "reorganization" means—(B) the acquisition by one corporation, in exchange solely for all or a part of its voting stock, of stock of another corporation if, immediately after the acquisition, the acquiring corporation has control of such other corporation (whether or not such acquiring corporation had control immediately before the acquisition) * * *.

The term "control" under section 368(c) of the Code means ownership of stock possessing at least 80 percent of the total combined voting power of all classes of stock entitled to vote and at least 80 percent of the total number of shares of all other classes of stock of the corporation.

In the instant case, the acquisition by Y corporation does not qualify as a reorganization under section 368(a)(1)(B). Y corporation does not have control of X corporation immediately after the acquisition of the Class A stock, since it directly owns stock possessing only 50 percent of all of the voting power of the stock outstanding. Section 368(c) specifically defines control in terms of direct ownership of stock and not in terms of practical control. There is no basis for disregarding the separate legal entities of the parent and its subsidiary and for attributing the subsidiary's ownership of the X corporation stock to the parent.

In view of the foregoing considerations, the Service holds that gain or loss is recognized to the shareholders on the exchange of their Class A stock of the X corporation for common stock of Y corporation * * *.

NOTES

1. *Different definitions of "control."* Compare the definition of "control" for purposes of a B reorganization with the definition of "control" for purposes of a nondivisive D reorganization. See I.R.C. §§ 304(c), 368(a)(2)(H)(i), 368(c). The § 368(c) definition of control is more often invoked in the reorganization area than the § 304(c) definition of control. Why might this be the case?

2. *Attribution rules inapplicable.* Why could the X stock owned by Z not be attributed to Y under I.R.C. § 318(a)(2)(C)? See I.R.C. § 318(a)(1) (first clause).

3. *Analog to "substantially all" requirement.* Does any analog exist in the statutory definition of a B reorganization to the "substantially all" requirement that applies to a C reorganization? In the Elkhorn Coal case (p. 523), if the stock of Elkhorn Coal Co. (rather than its assets) had been transferred to Mill Creek after Elkhorn distributed its extraneous assets in a purportedly tax-free transaction, could the stock transfer have qualified as a reorganization? See Rev. Rul. 70–434, 1970–2 C.B. 83 (ruling that distribution of extraneous assets in advance of a stock transfer does not jeopardize the stock transfer from qualifying as a B reorganization).

2.   RECEIPT OF SOLELY VOTING STOCK

The principal factor that distinguishes a nontaxable transfer of a target corporation's stock from a taxable transfer of that stock is the nature of the

consideration received. Nonrecognition treatment is contingent upon the shareholders of the target receiving a proprietary interest in the acquiring corporation. The receipt of that interest fosters the view that the target shareholders retain a continuing proprietary interest in the transferred enterprise. This is the essence of the common law continuity of proprietary interest doctrine. See pp. 514–518. In the case of a B reorganization, the continuity of interest principle is implemented by the statutory requirement that the stock be transferred "in exchange solely for voting stock" of the acquiring corporation.

a. LIABILITIES OF THE TARGET

Revenue Ruling 79–89

1979–1 Cum.Bull. 152.

ISSUE

Is the "solely for * * * voting stock" requirement of section 368(a)(1)(B) * * * violated when the acquiring corporation, as part of a plan and in addition to the exchange of stock transaction, contributes cash to the acquired corporation to discharge an indebtedness to a third party guaranteed by a shareholder of the acquired corporation?

FACTS

Individuals A and B each owned 50 percent of the outstanding stock of corporation Y. A was a guarantor on a five-year unsecured note Y issued to Z, an unrelated third party, in exchange for a loan. Z, as a general practice, required a guarantee from a major shareholder as a condition for making loans to closely held corporations. The loan to Y represented a bona fide loan for federal income tax purposes.

In accordance with an agreement and plan of reorganization, X acquired all of the outstanding stock of Y from A and B in exchange for voting stock of X. A and B received X stock equal to the fair market value of their Y stock, measured prior to the contribution by X described below, in exchange for their Y stock. The fair market value of the Y stock was calculated with the Z loan being considered as an indebtedness of Y. Thereafter and pursuant to the plan, X contributed cash equal to Y's indebtedness to Z and Y upon receipt of the cash paid its indebtedness to Z. The contribution was not a condition for A exchanging A's Y stock for X stock. X's purpose in contributing the cash to Y was to strengthen Y's financial position so that Y could expand.

LAW AND ANALYSIS

* * *

Section 368(a)(1)(B) of the Code provides that a reorganization includes the acquisition by one corporation, in exchange solely for all or a part of its voting stock, of stock of another corporation if, immediately after

the acquisition, the acquiring corporation has control of such other corporation.

Section 1.368–2(c) of the regulations provides that in order to qualify as a reorganization under section 368(a)(1)(B) of the Code, the acquisition by the acquiring corporation of stock of another corporation must be in exchange solely for all or a part of the voting stock of the acquiring corporation, and the acquiring corporation must be in control of the other corporation immediately after the transaction. If, for example, corporation X, in one transaction, exchanges nonvoting preferred stock or bonds in addition to all or a part of its voting stock in the acquisition of stock of corporation Y, the transaction is not a reorganization under section 368(a)(1)(B).

Section 354(a)(1) of the Code provides no gain or loss will be recognized if stock or securities in a corporation a party to a reorganization are, in pursuance of the plan of reorganization, exchanged solely for stock or securities in another corporation a party to a reorganization.

In the present case, because: (1) the contribution of cash by X to Y to accelerate the payment of Y's indebtedness to Z was not a condition for the exchange of A's Y stock for X stock, and (2) the fair market values of the stocks exchanged, measured prior to the contribution by X, were equal in the cases of both A, the guarantor of the indebtedness, and B, the payment of the indebtedness and the incidental release of A from A's guarantee are considered to be separate from the acquisition of the Y stock even though both occurred as part of one overall plan. Since only X voting stock was utilized as consideration in the acquisition of the Y stock within the meaning of section 1.368–2(c) of the regulations, the "solely for * * * voting stock" requirement contained in section 368(a)(1)(B) of the Code is satisfied. Any benefit accruing to A by the repayment of the indebtedness to Z was only incidental to X's proposal of strengthening Y's financial position.

HOLDING

The "solely for * * * voting stock" requirement of section 368(a)(1)(B) of the Code is not violated when X, as part of a plan but separate from the exchange of stock transaction, contributes cash to Y to discharge an indebtedness to Z guaranteed by A. Any gain or loss realized by A as a result of the exchange of their stock is not recognized inasmuch as section 354(a)(1) of the Code is applicable * * *.

NOTES

1. *Target shareholder as guarantor of target corporation's debt.* In the case of a stock transfer, liabilities of the target corporation normally do not impact on the tax consequences to the target's shareholders. The liabilities simply remain with the target corporation when its stock is transferred. Why, then, did the liability involved in the Revenue Ruling create an issue when target stock was transferred?

2. *Existence of debt after transfer of target stock.* One fact on which the Internal Revenue Service based its ruling was that "the contribution of cash by X to Y to accelerate the payment of Y's indebtedness to Z was not a condition for the exchange of A's Y stock for X stock." If you were A, would you transfer the Y stock to X under these circumstances? Does this fact undermine the utility of the Revenue Ruling? Would a different result be reached if repayment of the debt by the acquiring corporation were a condition for the exchange? See Rev. Rul. 79–4, 1979–1 C.B. 150 (the solely for voting stock requirement of I.R.C. § 368(a)(1)(B) is violated when, as a condition to the exchange, the acquiring corporation satisfies a debt reflected on the target corporation's books that was treated for tax purposes as indebtedness of the shareholder-guarantor).

3. *Consideration received by other target shareholder.* Another fact on which the Internal Revenue Service based Revenue Ruling 79–89 was that "the fair market values of the stocks exchanged, measured prior to the contribution by X, were equal in the cases of both A, the guarantor of the indebtedness, and B." Of what significance was this fact to the outcome of the ruling?

b.   MONEY OR OTHER PROPERTY

Revenue Ruling 68–285

1968–1 Cum.Bull. 147.

Advice has been requested whether there can be a reorganization under section 368(a)(1)(B) * * * if the corporation to be acquired established an escrow account from its own funds to pay dissenting shareholders who elect to accept cash for their stock in the acquired corporation according to the provisions of a state banking law, rather than exchange their stock for stock in the acquiring corporation.

Corporation X and Corporation Y are banking corporations. X wanted to acquire all of the outstanding stock of Y in exchange for voting stock of X. In order to be assured 100 percent control of Y, X elected, pursuant to a plan, to acquire the Y stock in accordance with the state's banking law.

The state banking law allows dissenting shareholders of the acquired corporation to register their dissent and elect to be paid cash for their shares in the acquired corporation * * *. Shareholders of Y owning 25 percent of the outstanding stock of Y elected not to participate in the exchange and they all perfected their election to dissent under the state banking law.

Y established an escrow account and transferred from its funds to this account sufficient cash to pay all of the Y shareholders who desired to perfect their rights under the state banking law. All payments were made from the escrow account and no cash payments were made by X either to Y, the dissenting shareholders of Y, or to the escrow account. The balance remaining in the escrow account after the dissenting shareholders were paid was returned to Y. These payments were made both before and after the exchange of X stock for Y stock.

* * *

Establishment by Y of an escrow account to pay dissenting shareholders under the circumstances described above will not preclude a reorganization under section 368(a)(1)(B) of the Code. This is true even though Y had not redeemed all the dissenting shareholders' stock prior to the effective date of the exchange. Under the state banking law, each dissenting shareholder of Y ceased to have any shareholder rights except the right to demand payment for the fair market value of his shares. Therefore, immediately after the exchange, X owned all the outstanding Y stock.

Revenue Ruling 55–440, C.B. 1955–2, 226, involved the question of whether preferred shares that had been called for redemption but not yet surrendered at the time of the exchange should be counted as "stock" under section 368(c) of the Code for the purpose of determining whether the 80 percent control requirement of section 368(a)(1)(B) of the Code had been satisfied. Revenue Ruling 55–440 held that the rights of the owners of the preferred stock as stockholders had terminated upon the call of the preferred shares and they thereafter possessed only the right to demand the call price upon the presentation of such shares for redemption. Based on this determination, Revenue Ruling 55–440 concluded that the transaction is a reorganization within the meaning of section 368(a)(1)(B) of the Code, regardless of the number of shares of preferred stock of the acquired company that at the time of the consummation of the stock for stock exchange, had not been presented for redemption.

Similarly, the acquisition of the outstanding stock of Y in exchange for voting stock of X is a reorganization under section 368(a)(1)(B) of the Code even though, in accordance with state banking law, an escrow account was established in order to pay dissenting shareholders for their stock and even though the stock of some dissenting shareholders was not redeemed until after the consummation of the exchange. Thus, no gain or loss will be recognized to the shareholders of Y who exchanged their stock in Y solely for X voting stock, under section 354(a) of the Code.

However, it should be noted that section 368(a)(1)(B) of the Code does not treat as a reorganization any transaction in which the acquiring corporation pays the dissenting shareholders or reimburses the acquired corporation for its payment to the dissenting shareholders.

NOTES

1. *Statutory requirement at issue.* Is Rev. Rul. 68–285 about the "solely for voting stock" requirement, the "control immediately after the exchange" requirement, or both requirements?

2. *Relevance of which party sets up escrow.* Would a different result have been reached in Rev. Rul. 68–285 if the acquiring corporation set up the escrow?

3. *No analog to the "boot relaxation rule."* In contrast to the boot relaxation rule that applies to a C reorganization (see I.R.C. § 368(a)(2)(B)), "solely" means "solely" in case of a B reorganization. Thus, a few dollars transferred from the acquiring corporation to the target shareholders can theoretically convert a multi-million dollar transaction from non-taxable to fully taxable!

4. *Fractional shares.* The value of a share of stock of the acquiring corporation normally differs from the value of a share of stock of the target. Consequently, an acquiring corporation might be compelled to issue "fractional shares" to comply with the solely for voting stock requirement. For example, if a share of target stock is worth $100 and a share of acquiring stock is worth $30, acquiring might be compelled to issue 3⅓ acquiring shares to the owner of a single target share. The Internal Revenue Service has ruled, however, that the payment of cash by an acquiring corporation to the shareholders of a target corporation in lieu of issuing fractional shares does not violate the "solely for voting stock" requirement in a B reorganization. Rev. Rul. 66–365, 1966–2 C.B. 116. Returning to the example, acquiring can acquire the single target share for three shares of acquiring and $10 without violating the solely for voting stock requirement.

5. *Solely for voting stock versus continuity of proprietary interest.* Identify the similarities and differences between the common law continuity of proprietary interest doctrine (pp. 514–518) and the statutory solely for voting stock requirement in a B reorganization. Which requirement is more stringent? Can you envision any circumstances in which the statutory requirement might be satisfied without satisfying the common law doctrine?

6. *Continuity of business enterprise.* Although an early version of the continuity of business enterprise regulations created some uncertainty as to whether that rule applied to a B reorganization, the current regulations clarify that the requirement does apply to a stock transfer as well as an asset transfer. See pp. 518–520. Under what circumstances might a stock transfer violate the continuity of business enterprise requirement? See Treas. Reg. § 1.368–1(d)(5), Examples 3–5.

Chapman v. Commissioner

United States Court of Appeals, First Circuit, 1980.
618 F.2d 856.

■ Campbell, Circuit Judge.

Facts

Appellees were among the more than 17,000 shareholders of the Hartford Fire Insurance Company who exchanged their Hartford stock for shares of the voting stock of International Telephone and Telegraph Corporation * * *. [A]ppellees did not report any gain or loss from these exchanges. Subsequently, the Internal Revenue Service assessed deficiencies * * *. [In Chapman's case, the amount of the deficiency was

$15,452.93.] Appellees petitioned the Tax Court for redetermination of these deficiencies * * *. The Tax Court * * * granted appellees' motion for summary judgment, and the Commissioner of Internal Revenue filed this appeal.

The events giving rise to this dispute began in 1968, when the management of ITT, a large multinational corporation, became interested in acquiring Hartford as part of a program of diversification * * *. In November 1968, ITT learned that approximately * * * 6 percent of Hartford's voting stock [was] available for purchase from a mutual fund. [I]TT consummated the $63.7 million purchase from the mutual fund * * *. From November 13, 1968 to January 10, 1969, ITT also made a series of purchases on the open market * * * for approximately $24.4 million. A further purchase * * * from an ITT subsidiary in March 1969 brought ITT's holdings to about 8 percent of Hartford's outstanding stock, all of which had been bought for cash.

In the midst of this flurry of stock-buying, ITT submitted a written proposal to the Hartford Board of Directors for the [acquisition] of Hartford * * *, based on an exchange of Hartford stock for ITT * * * voting preferred stock * * *.

[O]n April 15, 1969, attorneys for the parties sought a ruling from the IRS that the proposed transaction would constitute a reorganization under Section 368(a)(1)(B) of the Internal Revenue Code of 1954, so that * * * gain realized on the exchange by Hartford shareholders would not be recognized. See I.R.C. § 354(a)(1). By private letter ruling, the Service notified the parties on October 13, 1969 that the proposed [acquisition] would constitute a nontaxable reorganization, provided ITT unconditionally sold its 8 percent interest in Hartford to a third party before Hartford's shareholders voted to approve or disapprove the proposal. On October 21, the Service ruled that a proposed sale of the stock to Mediobanca, an Italian bank, would satisfy this condition, and such a sale was made on November 9.

[In December, 1969] ITT proposed * * * a voluntary exchange offer to the shareholders of Hartford * * *. [T]he insurance commissioner approved the exchange offer on May 23, 1970, and three days later ITT submitted the exchange offer to all Hartford shareholders. More than 95 percent of Hartford's outstanding stock was exchanged for shares of ITT's * * * voting preferred stock. The Italian bank to which ITT had conveyed its original 8 percent interest was among those tendering shares, as were the taxpayers in this case.

In March 1974, the Internal Revenue Service retroactively revoked its ruling approving the sale of Hartford stock to Mediobanca, on the ground that the request on which the ruling was based had misrepresented the nature of the proposed sale. Concluding that the entire transaction no longer constituted a nontaxable reorganization, the Service assessed tax deficiencies against a number of former Hartford shareholders who had accepted the exchange offer. Appellees, along with other taxpayers, contested this action in the Tax Court, where the case was decided on appellees' motion for summary judgment. For purposes of this motion, the taxpayers conceded that questions of the merits of the revocation of the IRS rulings were not to be considered; the facts were to be viewed as though ITT had not sold the shares previously acquired for cash to Mediobanca. The taxpayers also conceded, solely for purposes of their motion for summary judgment, that the initial cash purchases of Hartford stock had been made for the purpose of furthering ITT's efforts to acquire Hartford.

Issue

Taxpayers advanced two arguments in support of their motion for summary judgment. Their first argument related to the severability of the cash purchases from the 1970 exchange offer. Because 14 months had elapsed between the last of the cash purchases and the effective date of the exchange offer, and because the cash purchases were not part of the formal plan of reorganization entered into by ITT and Hartford, the taxpayers argued that the 1970 exchange offer should be examined in isolation to determine whether it satisfied the terms of Section 368(a)(1)(B) of the 1954 Code. The Service countered that the two sets of transactions—the cash purchases and the exchange offer—were linked by a common acquisitive purpose, and that they should be considered together for the purpose of determining whether the arrangement met the statutory requirement that the stock of the acquired corporation be exchanged "solely for * * * voting stock" of the acquiring corporation. The Tax Court did not reach this argument; in granting summary judgment it relied entirely on the taxpayers' second argument.

For purposes of the second argument, the taxpayers conceded arguendo that the 1968 and 1969 cash purchases should be considered "parts of the 1970 exchange offer reorganization." Even so, they insisted * * * that the 1970 exchange of stock for stock satisfied the statutory requirements for a reorganization without regard to the presence of related cash purchases. The Tax Court agreed with the taxpayers, holding that the 1970 exchange in which ITT acquired more than 80 percent of Hartford's single class of stock for ITT voting stock satisfied the requirements of Section 368(a)(1)(B), so that no gain or loss need be recognized on the exchange under Section 354(a)(1). The sole issue on appeal is whether the Tax Court was correct in so holding.

I.

We turn first to the statutory scheme * * *. One exception to [the general rule of I.R.C. § 1001(c) that all realized gains and losses are recognized] appears in Section 354(a)(1), which provides that gain or loss shall not be recognized if stock or securities in a corporation are, in pursuance of the plan of reorganization, exchanged solely for stock or securities in another corporation which is a party to the reorganization. This exception does not grant a complete tax exemption for reorganizations, but rather defers the recognition of gain or loss until some later event such as a sale of stock acquired in the exchange. Section 354(a)(1) does not apply to an exchange unless the exchange falls within one of the six categories of "reorganization" defined in Section 368(a)(1). The category relevant to the transactions involved in this case is defined in Section 368(a)(1)(B) * * *. Subsection (B) * * * establishes two basic requirements for a valid, tax-free stock-for-stock reorganization. First, "the acquisition" of another's stock must be "solely for * * * voting stock." Second, the acquiring corporation must have control over the other corporation immediately after the acquisition.

The single issue raised on this appeal is whether "the acquisition" in this case complied with the requirement that it be "solely for * * * voting stock." It is well settled that the "solely" requirement is mandatory; if any part of "the acquisition" includes a form of consideration other than voting stock, the transaction will not qualify as a (B) reorganization. See Helvering v. Southwest Consolidated Corp., 315 U.S. 194, 198 (1942) (" 'Solely' leaves no leeway. Voting stock plus some other consideration does not meet the statutory requirement"). The precise issue before us is thus how broadly to read the term "acquisition." The Internal Revenue Service argues that "the acquisition * * * of stock of another corporation" must be understood to encompass the 1968–69 cash purchases as well as the 1970 exchange offer. If the IRS is correct, "the acquisition" here fails as a (B) reorganization. The taxpayers, on the other hand, would limit "the acquisition" to the part of a sequential transaction of this nature which meets the requirements of subsection (B). They argue that the 1970 exchange of stock for stock was itself an "acquisition" by ITT of stock in Hartford solely in exchange for ITT's voting stock, such that after the exchange took place ITT controlled Hartford. Taxpayers contend that the earlier cash purchases of 8 percent, even if conceded to be part of the same acquisitive plan, are essentially irrelevant to the tax-free reorganization otherwise effected.

The Tax Court accepted the taxpayers' reading of the statute * * *. The plurality opinion stated its "narrow" holding as follows:

> We hold that where, as is the case herein, 80 per cent or more of the stock of a corporation is acquired in one transaction, in exchange for which only voting stock is furnished as consideration, the 'solely for voting stock' requirement of section 368(a)(1)(B) is satisfied.

The plurality treated as irrelevant Hartford's stock purchased for cash * * *.

II.

For reasons set forth extensively in section III of this opinion, we do not accept the position adopted by the Tax Court. Instead we side with the Commissioner on the narrow issue presented in this appeal, that is, the correctness of taxpayers' so-called "second" argument premised on an assumed relationship between the cash and stock transactions * * *.

Our decision will not, unfortunately, end this case. The Tax Court has yet to rule on taxpayers' "first" argument * * *. The question of what factors should determine, for purposes of Section 368(a)(1)(B), whether a given cash purchase is truly "related" to a later exchange of stock requires further consideration by the Tax Court, as does the question of the application of those factors in the present case. We therefore will remand this case to the Tax Court for further proceedings on the question raised by the taxpayers' first argument in support of their motion for summary judgment.

We view the Tax Court's options on remand as threefold. It can hold that the cash and stock transactions here in question are related as a matter of law—the position urged by the Commissioner—in which case, under our present holding, there would not be a valid (B) reorganization. On the other hand, the Tax Court may find that the transactions are as a matter of law unrelated, so that the 1970 exchange offer was simply the final, nontaxable step in a permissible creeping acquisition. Finally, the court may decide that, under the legal standard it adopts, material factual issues remain to be decided, so that a grant of summary judgment would be inappropriate at this time.

III.

A.

Having summarized in advance our holding, and its intended scope, we shall now revert to the beginning of our analysis, and * * * describe the thinking by which we reached the result just announced. We begin with the words of the statute itself. The reorganization definitions contained in Section 368(a)(1) are precise, technical, and comprehensive. They were intended to define the exclusive means by which nontaxable corporate reorganizations could be effected. See Treas. Reg. § 1.368–1. In examining the language of the (B) provisions, we discern two possible meanings. On the one hand, the statute could be read to say that a successful reorganization occurs whenever Corporation X exchanges its own voting stock for stock in Corporation Y, and, immediately after the transaction, Corporation X controls more than 80 percent of Y's stock. On this reading, purchases of shares for which any part of the consideration takes the form of "boot" should be ignored, since the definition is only concerned with transactions which meet the statutory requirements as to consideration and control. To take an example, if Corporation X bought 50 percent of the shares of Y, and then almost immediately exchanged part of its voting stock for the remaining 50 percent of Y's stock, the question would arise whether the second transaction was a (B) reorganization. Arguably, the statute can be read to support such a finding. In the second transaction, X exchanged only stock for stock (meeting the "solely" requirement), and after the transaction was completed X owned Y (meeting the "control" requirement).

The alternative reading of the statute—the one which we are persuaded to adopt—treats the (B) definition as prescriptive, rather than merely descriptive. We read the statute to mean that the entire transaction which constitutes "the acquisition" must not contain any nonstock consideration if the transaction is to qualify as a (B) reorganization. In the example given above, where X acquired 100 percent of Y's stock, half for cash and half for voting stock, we would interpret "the acquisition" as referring to the entire transaction, so that the "solely for * * * voting stock" requirement would not be met. We believe if Congress had intended the statute to be read as merely descriptive, this intent would have been more clearly spelled out in the statutory language.

We recognize that the Tax Court adopted neither of these two readings. [T]he Tax Court purported to limit its holding to cases, such as this one, where more than 80 percent of the stock of Corporation Y passes to Corporation X in exchange solely for voting stock. The Tax Court presumably would assert that the 50/50 hypothetical posited above can be distinguished from this case, and that its holding implies no view as to the hypothetical. The plurality opinion recognized that the position it adopted creates no small problem with respect to the proper reading of "the acquisition" in the statutory definition. In order to distinguish the 80 percent case from the 50 percent case, it is necessary to read "the acquisition" as referring to at least the amount of stock constituting "control" (80 percent) where related cash purchases are present. Yet the Tax Court recognized that "the acquisition" cannot always refer to the conveyance of an 80 percent block of stock in one transaction, since to do so would frustrate the intent of the 1954 amendments to permit the so-called "creeping acquisition."

The Tax Court's interpretation of the statute suffers from a more fundamental defect, as well. In order to justify the limitation of its holding to transactions involving 80 percent or more of the acquiree's stock, the Tax Court focused on the passage of control as the primary requirement of the (B) provision. This focus is misplaced. Under the present version of the statute, the passage of control is entirely irrelevant; the only material requirement is that the acquiring corporation have control immediately after the acquisition. As the statute explicitly states, it does not matter if the acquiring corporation already has control before the transaction begins, so long as such control exists at the completion of the reorganization * * *. In our view, the statute should be read to mean that the related transactions that constitute "the acquisition," whatever percentage of stock they may represent, must meet both the "solely for voting stock" and the "control immediately after" requirements of Section 368(a)(1)(B). Neither the reading given the statute by the Tax Court, nor that proposed as the first alternative above, adequately corresponds to the careful language Congress employed in this section of the Code.

B.

* * *

[W]e can discern no clear Congressional mandate in the present structure of the (B) provision, either in terms of the abuses sought to be remedied or the beneficial transactions sought to be facilitated. At best, we think Congress has drawn some arbitrary lines separating those transactions that resemble mere changes in form of ownership and those that contain elements of a sale * * *. In such circumstances we believe it is more appropriate to examine the specific rules and requirements Congress enacted, rather than some questionably determined "purpose" or "policy," to determine whether a particular transaction qualifies for favorable tax treatment.

To the extent there is any indication in the legislative history of Congress' intent with respect to the meaning of "acquisition" in the (B) provision, we believe the intent plainly was to apply the "solely" requirement to all related transactions. In those statutes where Congress intended to permit cash or other property to be used as consideration, it made explicit provision therefor. See, e.g., I.R.C. § 368(a)(2)(B). It is argued that in a (B) reorganization the statute can be satisfied where only 80 percent of the acquiree's stock is obtained solely for voting stock, so that additional acquisitions are irrelevant and need not be considered. In light of Congress' repeated, and increasingly sophisticated, enactments in this area, we are unpersuaded that such an important question would have been left unaddressed had Congress intended to leave open such a possibility. We are not prepared to believe that Congress intended * * * to permit a corporation to exchange stock tax-free for 80 percent of the stock of another and in a related transaction to purchase the remaining 20 percent for cash. The only question we see clearly left open by the legislative history is the degree of separation required between the two transactions before they can qualify as a creeping acquisition under the 1954 amendments. This is precisely the issue the Tax Court chose not to address, and it is the issue we now remand to the Tax Court for consideration.

C.

Besides finding support for the IRS position both in the design of the statute and in the legislative history, we find support in the regulations adopted by the Treasury Department construing these statutory provisions * * *. The views of the Treasury on tax matters, while by no means definitive, undoubtedly reflect a familiarity with the intricacies of the tax code that surpasses our own.

* * *

When we turn to the regulations under the 1954 Act, the implication [is] that the entire transaction must be judged under the "solely" test * * *.

> In order to qualify as a 'reorganization' under section 368(a)(1)(B), the *acquisition* by the acquiring corporation of stock of another corporation must be in exchange solely for all or a part of the voting stock of the acquiring corporation * * * and the acquiring corporation must be in control of the other corporation immediately after *the transaction*. If, for example, Corporation X in one transaction exchanges nonvoting preferred stock or bonds *in addition to* all or a part of its voting stock in the acquisition of stock of Corporation Y, the transaction is not a reorganization under section 368(a)(1)(B). (Emphasis supplied.)

Treas. Reg. § 1.368–2(c)(1960). The equation of "transaction" and "acquisition" in the above-quoted passage is particularly significant, since it seems to imply a functional test of what constitutes "the acquisition" as opposed to a view of "the acquisition" as simply that part of a transaction which otherwise satisfies the statutory requisites. The regulation also goes on to say, in explaining the treatment of creeping acquisitions:

> The acquisition of stock of another corporation by the acquiring corporation solely for its voting stock * * * is permitted tax-free even though the acquiring corporation already owns some of the stock of the other corporation. Such an acquisition is permitted tax-free in a single transaction or in a series of transactions taking place over a relatively short period of time such as 12 months.

Treas. Reg. § 1.368–2(c). This regulation spells out the treatment afforded related acquisitions, some of which occur before and some after the acquiring corporation obtains the necessary 80 percent of stock in the acquiree. It would be incongruous, to say the least, if a series of stock-for-stock transactions could be combined so that the tax-free treatment of later acquisitions applied to earlier ones as well, yet a related cash purchase would be ignored as irrelevant. This section reinforces our view that all related transactions must be considered part of "the acquisition" for purposes of applying the statute.

D.

Finally, we turn to the body of case law that has developed concerning (B) reorganizations to determine how previous courts have dealt with this question. Of the seven prior cases in this area, all to a greater or lesser degree support the result we have reached, and none supports the result reached by the Tax Court * * *.

IV.

[I]n conclusion, we would like to respond briefly to the arguments raised by the Tax Court * * * and the taxpayers in this case against the rule we have reaffirmed today. The principal argument, repeated again and again, concerns the supposed lack of policy behind the rule forbidding cash in a (B) reorganization where the control requirement is met solely for voting stock. It is true that the Service has not pointed to tax loopholes that would be opened were the rule to be relaxed as appellees request. We also recognize * * * that the rule may produce results which some would view as anomalous. For example, if Corporation X acquires 80 percent of Corporation Y's stock solely for voting stock, and is content to leave the remaining 20 percent outstanding, no one would question that a valid (B) reorganization has taken place. If Corporation X then decides to purchase stock from the remaining shareholders, the * * * rule might result in loss of nontaxable treatment for the stock acquisition if the two transactions were found to be related. The Tax Court asserted that there is no conceivable Congressional policy that would justify such a result. Further, it argued, Congress could not have felt that prior cash purchases would forever ban a later successful (B) reorganization since the 1954 amendments, as the legislative history makes clear, specifically provided that prior cash purchases would not prevent a creeping acquisition.

While not without force, this line of argument does not in the end persuade us. [T]he language of the statute, and the longstanding interpretation given it by the courts, are persuasive reasons for our holding even in the absence of any clear policy behind Congress' expression of its will * * *.

Possibly, Congress' insertion of the "solely for * * * voting stock" requirement * * * was * * * an overreaction to a problem which could have been dealt with through more precise and discriminating measures. But we do not think it appropriate for a court to tell Congress how to do its job in an area such as this. If a more refined statutory scheme would be appropriate, such changes should be sought from the body empowered to make them. While we adhere to the general practice of construing statutes so as to further their demonstrated polices, we have no license to rework whole statutory schemes in pursuit of policy goals which Congress has nowhere articulated * * *.

A second major argument * * * is that the previous cases construing this statute are suspect because they did not give proper weight to the changes wrought by the 1954 amendments. In particular, the court argued the liberalization of the "boot" allowance in (C) reorganizations and the allowance of creeping (B) acquisitions showed that Congress had no intent or desire to forbid "boot" of up to 20 percent in a (B) reorganization. As we have discussed earlier, we draw the opposite conclusion from the legislative history. Liberalization of the (C) provision shows only that Congress, when it wished to do so, could grant explicit leeway in the reorganization rules. Nor do the creeping acquisition rules mark such a departure from a strict reading of the "solely" requirement as to persuade us that Congress intended to weaken it with respect to related transactions * * *.

* * *

Finally, we see no merit at all in the suggestion that we should permit "boot" in a (B) reorganization simply because "boot" is permitted in some instances in (A) and (C) reorganizations. Congress has never indicated that these three distinct categories of transactions are to be interpreted in *pari materia*. In fact, striking differences in the treatment of the three subsections have been evident in the history of the reorganization statutes. We see no reason to believe a difference in the treatment of "boot" in these transactions is impermissible or irrational.

Accordingly, we vacate the judgment of the Tax Court insofar as it rests on a holding that taxpayers were entitled to summary judgment irrespective of whether the cash purchases in this case were related by purpose or timing to the stock exchange offer of 1970. The case will be remanded to the Tax Court for further proceedings consistent with this opinion.

NOTES

1. *Problems with the ruling process.* Because the difference in cost between a taxable transaction and a nontaxable transaction is often quite high, it is fairly common for a taxpayer to request a letter ruling from the Internal Revenue Service in advance of effectuating an acquisition believed to qualify as a reorganization. A letter ruling delineates conclusions of law based upon facts stipulated by the taxpayer. What problems does the Chapman case reveal about the ruling process?

2. *Impact of preferred stock.* Did the fact that ITT used voting preferred stock as the consideration for the acquisition adversely affect qualification as a B reorganization? Would the use of nonvoting common stock have presented any problems? See I.R.C. § 368(a)(1)(B).

3. *Creeping acquisitions.* If ITT had acquired the initial 8% of Hartford for ITT voting stock, rather than cash, would a later acquisition of an additional 87% of Hartford for ITT voting stock have qualified as a B reorganization? What if the later acquisition was of an additional 77% of Hartford? What if the later acquisition was of an additional 67% of Hartford? In each of these situations, what are the tax consequences of the acquisition of the initial 8%? Are tax consequences affected by the time that lapses between the initial acquisition and the later acquisition? See Treas. Reg. § 1.368–2(c) ("[A]n acquisition is permitted tax-free in a single transaction or in a series of transactions taking place over a relatively short period of time such as 12 months.").

4. *Resolution of events in Chapman.* Before the courts could resolve the issue in Chapman, a settlement was reached. The following announcement details that settlement:

Miscellaneous Announcement 5425

5/8/81.

The Internal Revenue Service announced today that agreement has been reached with International Telephone and Telegraph Corporation with respect to the seven-year controversy over the tax status of International Telephone and Telegraph's 1970 acquisition of the Hartford Fire Insurance Company.

* * *

International Telephone and Telegraph will pay $18.5 million * * * to the United States Government, which will agree not to pursue tax claims against former Hartford shareholders who, in 1970 exchanged their shares for International Telephone and Telegraph shares, and who have treated and who continue to treat the exchange as nontaxable on their Federal income tax returns. The Government will continue litigation only in those instances where former Hartford shareholders who reported no gain in 1970 have sold or sell their International Telephone and Telegraph stock and claim a stepped-up basis rather than using the basis of the exchanged Hartford stock to report their taxable gain or loss.

A closing agreement * * * provides that International Telephone and Telegraph will not claim any part of the $18.5 million payment as an income tax deduction and that the payment will not result in taxable income to any International Telephone and Telegraph shareholder.

The settlement is expected to relieve International Telephone and Telegraph of any obligation for tax reimbursement to former Hartford shareholders, while Internal Revenue Service receives the value of its claims against those shareholders taking into account hazards of litigation and various administrative problems * * *.

More than 1,000 cases pending in the Tax Court and awaiting the outcome of the appellate cases now can be disposed of by stipulated decisions. In addition, more than 17,000 cases are still pending in various other stages of administrative appeal.

NOTES

1. *Continued litigation.* Why would the government continue to litigate in cases where "former Hartford shareholders who reported no gain in 1970 have sold or sell their International Telephone and Telegraph stock and claim a stepped-up basis rather than using the basis of the exchanged Hartford stock to report their taxable gain or loss"?

2. *Motivation of ITT.* Could the outcome of the Chapman litigation have affected the tax liability of ITT? Why would ITT pay $18,500,000 to make the Chapman case disappear?

3. *Tax consequences of settlement.* Could the settlement have exposed the shareholders of ITT to taxable income? See I.R.C. § 301. How was this issue handled in the settlement agreement?

3.   Substance Over Form

Revenue Ruling 67–274

1967–2 Cum.Bull. 141.

* * *

Pursuant to a plan of reorganization, corporation Y acquired all of the outstanding stock of corporation X from the X shareholders in exchange solely for voting stock of Y. Thereafter X was completely liquidated as part of the same plan and all of its assets were transferred to Y which assumed all of the liabilities of X. Y continued to conduct the business previously conducted by X. The former shareholders of X continued to hold 16 percent of the fair market value of all the outstanding stock of Y.

Section 368(a)(1)(B) of the Code provides in part that a reorganization is the acquisition by one corporation, in exchange solely for all or a part of its voting stock, of stock of another corporation if, immediately after the acquisition, the acquiring corporation has control * * * of such other corporation. Section 368(a)(1)(C) of the Code provides in part that a reorganization is the acquisition by one corporation, in exchange solely for all or a part of its voting stock, of substantially all of the properties of another corporation, but in determining whether the exchange is solely for stock the assumption by the acquiring corporation of a liability of the other, or the fact that property acquired is subject to a liability, is disregarded.

Under the circumstances of this case the acquisition of X stock by Y and the liquidation of X by Y are part of the overall plan of reorganization and the two steps may not be considered independently of each other for Federal income tax purposes. The substance of the transaction is an acquisition of assets to which section 368(a)(1)(B) of the Code does not apply.

Accordingly, the acquisition by Y of the outstanding stock of X will not constitute a reorganization within the meaning of section 368(a)(1)(B) of the Code but will be considered an acquisition of the assets of X which in this case is a reorganization described in section 368(a)(1)(C) of the Code * * *.

West Coast Marketing Corporation v. Commissioner

Tax Court of the United States, 1966.
46 T.C. 32.

FINDINGS OF FACT

* * *

Petitioner [is] a Florida corporation * * *.

Max B. Cohen is the sole stockholder and president of petitioner. His principal business was farming, but he has not farmed since 1955. He had formed petitioner in 1936 and transferred his farm lands to it * * *.

On January 4, 1956, Cohen entered into contractual arrangements to purchase about 12,000 acres of land in Hillsborough County, Fla., from C. W. Palmore and his wife. The total acreage involved was considered for convenience as comprising three parts, referred to respectively as the North Tract, the Middle Tract, and the South Tract * * *.

* * *

Subsequent to the execution of these agreements, Cohen assigned his interest in the Middle Tract to petitioner.

* * *

Sometime prior to September 1956, [petitioner and Cohen sold one-half of their interests in the three tracts to] George Coury, a banker and stockbroker * * *.

Coury's intention * * * was to resell the land for profit. He did not intend to farm the land with Cohen. The record contains no convincing evidence that Cohen ever intended to farm any of these lands, either individually, or through petitioner, or otherwise, or that they were acquired and held for any purpose other than to resell at a profit.

[T]itle to Coury's one-half interest in each of the three tracts was taken by each of three corporations, respectively, controlled by Coury * * *.

* * *

As previously noted, Coury was interested in selling the three tracts at a profit. He was acquainted with Louis E. Wolfson, who was the largest stockholder in Universal Marion Corp. (Universal), a publicly held corporation * * *. In February 1959 Coury suggested to Wolfson the possibility of Universal's acquiring and developing the three tracts * * *. [I]n early March of 1959, an oral agreement was reached as to the terms upon which Coury would be willing to sell. The price was $360 an acre, payable in preferred stock of Universal * * *.

Coury's negotiations with Wolfson and other representatives of Universal related to all the ownership interests in the three tracts and not merely to the undivided one-half interests held by his corporations * * *. Cohen was anxious to sell and he authorized Coury to "go ahead and negotiate" the proposed deal.

On April 16, 1959, in a letter addressed to Coury, James Mullaney, the president of Universal, made a formal offer to purchase the land comprising the three tracts at $360 an acre, payable in preferred stock of Universal * * *.

After receipt of the letter of April 16, 1959, Coury immediately secured the oral consent of Cohen [and] petitioner * * *.

* * *

The final sale of all three tracts of land to Universal was consummated in the fall of 1959, in accordance with the terms of the letter of April 16, 1959.

Meanwhile, however, Cohen caused to be organized on April 30, 1959, a Florida corporation named Manatee Land Co. (Manatee), and, on May 1, 1959, he and petitioner transferred to Manatee their * * * respective * * * interests in the three tracts—petitioner's in the Middle Tract and Cohen's in the North and South tracts.

Petitioner received 645 shares of the stock of Manatee for its * * * interest in the Middle Tract. Cohen received the remaining 769 shares of Manatee stock for his * * * interest in the North and South tracts.

* * *

In carrying out the terms of the agreement for the sale or exchange of the three tracts of land as proposed in the letter of April 16, 1959, the stockholders of Manatee, on October 27, 1959, transferred their stock in the corporation to Universal in exchange for 10,800 shares of Universal's * * * voting * * * preferred stock * * *.

Manatee was not engaged in the conduct of any business. It was used by petitioner and Cohen for no purpose other than to hold title to their respective undivided * * * interests in the three tracts of land, and to serve as a conduit for transferring title thereto to Universal.

On December 18, 1959, Manatee was liquidated by Universal.

In its income tax return for the year ended June 30, 1960, petitioner reported the transfer of all of the stock which it owned in Manatee in exchange for 4,913 shares of Universal "having an indeterminate market value" and did not report any taxable income from that transaction. Those shares in fact had a fair market value of $67 per share, as stipulated by the parties herein. The Commissioner determined that petitioner realized a long-term capital gain of $203,647.91 "on the exchange in form of stock of Manatee Land Co. for stock of Universal Marion Corporation" and increased the taxable income reported in its return by that amount.

OPINION

■ RAUM, JUDGE: If petitioner had transferred its * * * interest in the Middle Tract directly to Universal in exchange for the preferred shares of Universal, there is no dispute that the resulting gain would have been taxable * * *. Is a different result required by the use of Manatee, an intermediate agency that was employed to effectuate the transfer? On this record, we think the answer must be no.

Petitioner's position has been that Manatee was organized for a bona fide business purpose and that the transfer of its stock to Universal in exchange for stock of the latter constituted a tax-free "reorganization" under sections 354(a)(1) and 368(a)(1)(B) of the 1954 Code. To be sure, the transaction before us falls literally within those provisions. But if Manatee served no business purpose and the substance of the transaction was simply an exchange of land for stock of Universal, the tax consequences must turn upon the substance of the transaction rather than the form in which it was cast.

Cohen testified before us in an effort to show that there were bona fide business reasons for incorporating Manatee and transferring to it his and petitioner's respective undivided * * * interests in the three tracts. We found his testimony slippery and unconvincing. The burden was upon petitioner and it has not been carried. To the contrary, the record persuasively indicates that Manatee was incorporated for the purpose of being used as a conduit for passing title to petitioner's and Cohen's interests in the three tracts to Universal.

Manatee was brought into existence when the sale of the land was imminent. Petitioner's and Cohen's interests in the land were transferred to it. It engaged in no business and served no purpose other than to hold title pending the contemplated transfer to Universal. We reject as unworthy of belief any testimony that might be construed as suggesting that it had any other purpose.

All of the steps taken by petitioner and Cohen were but component parts of a single transaction the substance of which was a taxable disposition by them of their property interests to Universal. Accordingly, the Commissioner did not err in including in petitioner's taxable income, the long-term capital gain which it realized in that transaction.

NOTE

For a somewhat similar fact pattern where a court reached a contrary result, see Weikel v. Commissioner, 51 T.C.M. 432 (1986).

D. Statutory Merger

I.R.C. § 368(a)(1)(A)

Treas. Reg. § 1.368–2(b)(1)

This casebook has focused on two different methods of transferring a corporate enterprise; namely, the transfer of assets by the corporation and the transfer of stock by the corporation's shareholders. In addition to the physical transfer of assets or stock, every state and the District of Columbia has a merger law that facilitates the transfer of a corporate enterprise by operation of law. When one corporation ("target") is merged into another corporation ("acquiring"), the target is effectively swallowed by the acquiring corporation and the target's stock is transformed, by operation of law, into the consideration designated in the merger agreement. State merger laws generally allow the parties to agree to almost any form of consideration. Thus, the consideration may consist of stock of the acquiring corporation, a combination of stock and money, or only money. (An all cash merger is permissible in most jurisdictions.) A merger is effectuated when the directors and shareholders of both corporations approve the transaction and documents prescribed by state law are filed. No physical transfer of target assets or target stock is necessary. Dissenting shareholders are stripped of their proprietary interest in the target corporation but must be paid money for their shares.[10]

From a non-tax standpoint, the merger is a very desirable acquisition technique. A merger is generally preferable to an asset transfer because it eliminates the mechanical burden of transferring individual assets of the target. A merger is also often preferable to a stock transfer because the acquiring corporation need not negotiate with each of the individual stockholders of the target. Rather, the acquiring corporation deals exclusively with representatives of the target and each of the target's shareholders simply votes for or against the plan of merger.[11]

---

10.   See, e.g., Model Business Corporation Act Annotated, § 13.02(a)(1) (4th ed. Supp. 2010).

11.   For further discussion of the non-tax aspects of mergers, see Harry G. Henn & John R. Alexander, *Laws of Corporations* § 346 (3d ed. 1983 & Supp. 1986).

The tax consequences of a merger are more difficult to analyze than the tax consequences of an asset transfer or a stock transfer because a merger is achieved without a path of mechanical steps to which tax consequences can conveniently be attached. A merger may be envisioned as involving any series of steps that ends with the acquiring corporation holding the assets and liabilities of the target and the target's former shareholders holding the consideration provided by the acquiring corporation. Thus, a merger might be conceptualized as a transfer by the target of its assets to the acquiring corporation in exchange for the consideration designated in the merger agreement, followed by the distribution of this consideration to the target's shareholders in liquidation of the target. Alternatively, a merger might be viewed as a transfer by the target's shareholders of their target stock to the acquiring corporation in exchange for the consideration designated in the merger agreement, followed by the liquidation of the target into the acquiring corporation.

The question of whether a merger should be viewed as an asset transfer or a stock transfer for tax purposes has not been authoritatively resolved. The tendency, however, is to equate a merger to an asset transfer for reasons expressed by one court as follows:

> Although the plaintiffs vigorously assert that the transaction was a sale of stock directly from the [Target] shareholders to [the Acquiring Corporation], there is no basis for this assertion * * *. The merger had none of the usual features of a sale of stock. [The Acquiring Corporation] did not make tender offers to individual shareholders, and individual shareholders could not elect whether to sell or retain their stock but could only vote for or against the plan of merger * * *. Once two-thirds of the shareholders voted in favor of the plan, an individual shareholder only had a right to receive a liquidation distribution. After the transaction was completed, [the Acquiring Corporation] did not hold shares of [Target] but rather [Target] no longer existed as a separate corporate entity and its business was taken over by [Acquiring Corporation].
>
> The plan of merger * * *, rather than being a sale of stock, more closely resembled a sale of assets coupled with a liquidation, as a result of which [the Acquiring Corporation] became the sole owner and manager of [Target's] business, [Target] was dissolved, and [Target's] shareholders exchanged their shares for liquidation proceeds * * *.

West Shore Fuel, Inc. v. United States, 453 F.Supp. 956 (W.D.N.Y.1978), aff'd. 598 F.2d 1236 (2d Cir.1979) (case involving state law merger that did not qualify as a reorganization).[12]

---

12. See also Rev. Rul. 69–6, 1969–1 C.B. 104 (taxable merger equated to an asset transfer); Rev. Rul. 67–274, p. 562 (acquisition of stock of target immediately followed by liquidation of target treated as asset acquisition); Kimbell–Diamond Milling Company v. Commissioner, p. 493 (stock purchase followed by liquidation equated to asset purchase). But see pp. 609–610 (reverse triangular merger equated to stock transfer). For a detailed analysis of the alternative ways of conceptualizing a merger, see Jeffrey L. Kwall, "What Is A Merger?: The Case for Taxing Cash Mergers Like Stock Sales," 32 Journal of Corporation Law 1 (2006).

The transfer of a corporate enterprise in a transaction that qualifies as a merger under state law ("a statutory merger") satisfies the Internal Revenue Code's definition of an "A" reorganization. See I.R.C. § 368(a)(1)(A). Because no significant statutory restrictions are imposed by the Internal Revenue Code on an A reorganization, the common law doctrines act as the gatekeeper to A reorganization treatment. Before examining the impact of the common law doctrines on a merger, the transaction and its corresponding tax consequences are illustrated by Example 12–C.

> *Example 12–C (Consequences of non-taxable merger)*: Alex is the sole shareholder of Waldo Corporation and he owns stock with a value of $8,000,000 in which Alex has a basis of $100,000. Waldo owns assets with a value of $8,000,000 in which Waldo has a basis of $3,000,000. Veranda Corporation has 72,000 shares of a single class of common stock outstanding. Veranda's outstanding stock has a value of $72,000,000 ($1,000 per share). Waldo and Veranda agree that Waldo will be merged into Veranda and that Alex's stock in Waldo will be converted to 8,000 newly issued shares of Veranda common stock. If the transaction constitutes a merger under state law and satisfies all the common law requirements for an A reorganization, the transaction will likely be viewed as an asset transfer for tax purposes with consequences identical to those delineated in Example 12–A, p. 522.

1.   Continuity of Proprietary Interest

a.   NATURE OF CONSIDERATION

Roebling v. Commissioner

United States Court of Appeals, Third Circuit, 1944.
143 F.2d 810.

■ Before Jones and McLaughlin, Circuit Judges, and Kalodner, District Judge.

Kalodner, District Judge. * * *

Petitioner, an individual * * *, acquired * * * 166 shares of the stock of South Jersey Gas, Electric and Traction Co. (hereinafter referred to as South Jersey) * * * at a cost of $16,600.

South Jersey was a corporation organized * * * under the laws of the State of New Jersey, for the purpose of furnishing electricity and gas for public and private use * * *.

In June, 1903, South Jersey had leased all its franchises, plants and operating equipment to Public Service [Electric and Gas Company] for 900 years. The lessee was to pay rent which beginning December 1, 1908, amounted to $480,000 per annum. In addition the lessee agreed to pay * * * such sums as were necessary to maintain, repair, improve and extend the leased properties. All replacements and additions became the property of South Jersey subject to the terms of the lease.

The lease further provided that upon default of the terms of the lease for a period of 30 days, after notice, South Jersey could terminate the lease, reenter and reacquire the property and additions and extensions thereto.
* * *

From December 1, 1908, to June 1, 1937, the net rentals received by South Jersey, the lessor company, were distributed to its stockholders at the rate of 8% per annum on the par value of its stock. South Jersey had outstanding 60,000 shares of capital stock of $100 par value * * *.

Public Service Electric and Gas Company as a part of its unified electrical system held and operated under long-term leases the properties of many other utility companies. [P]ublic Service * * * had engaged in a systematic effort to acquire the fee to these properties * * *.

On May 10, 1937, the directors of South Jersey and of Public Service Electric and Gas Company adopted a "Plan of Reorganization" under which it was proposed that the former company be merged into the latter in accordance with the statutes of New Jersey. This plan provided that the stockholders of South Jersey * * * should exchange, dollar for dollar, their stock in South Jersey for 8% one hundred years first mortgage bonds of Public Service Electric and Gas Company. * * *. It was expressly provided in the "Agreement of Merger" executed on the same day: "The capital stock of the Public Service Electric and Gas Company * * * will not be changed by reason of this agreement." * * *

The "Agreement of Merger" was accepted by the stockholders of South Jersey and of Public Service Electric and Gas Company, and approved by the Board of Public Utilities Commissioners of the State of New Jersey * * *. The "Agreement of Merger" with the certificates of the secretaries of the constituent companies as to the confirmatory votes of the stockholders, and the certificate of approval of the Public Utility Commissioners of New Jersey * * * was filed with the Secretary of State of New Jersey on November 17, 1938.

The "Agreement of Merger" was consummated pursuant to its provisions. In accordance therewith the taxpayer received in exchange for his 166 shares of stock in South Jersey, $16,600, principal amount of 8% bonds which on November 25, 1938, had a fair market value of $34,777.

The Commissioner determined that the difference between the basis of the taxpayer's stock in South Jersey and the fair market value of the bonds received in exchange therefor must be recognized as taxable income in 1938 and * * * the Tax Court [agreed] * * *.

The issues presented here arise by reason of taxpayer's contention (1) that the merger of South Jersey into Public Service Electric and Gas Co. was a "true statutory merger" under the laws of the state of New Jersey and therefore the exchange of stock for bonds was not a taxable event under Sec. 112 of the Revenue Act of 1938; (2) that since there was a "true statutory merger" the "continuity of interest" doctrine in the Le Tulle v. Scofield case [p. 515] is inapplicable; and (3) that in any event a "continuity of interest" actually existed in the instant case.

As to the taxpayer's first two contentions, which may be considered together: The admitted fact that the merger of the two corporations was a "true statutory merger" under the New Jersey law is not dispositive of the question as to whether there was a "statutory merger" here within the meaning of Sec. 112(g)(1)(A). It is well-settled that a state law cannot alter the essential characteristics required to enable a taxpayer to obtain exemption under the provisions of a Federal Revenue Act.

* * *

[W]e cannot subscribe to the taxpayer's contention that under Sec. 112(g)(1)(A) of the Revenue Act of 1938 the requirements of New Jersey law supersede the "continuity of interest" test as applied in Le Tulle v. Scofield and * * * numerous other decisions.

The taxpayer's remaining contention that the requisite "continuity of interest" is present under the peculiar facts in this case is premised on a rather novel theory. He urges that "prior to the merger, the stockholders of South Jersey had no proprietary interest in its properties in any real sense", and that in sanctioning the merger "the decision of the New Jersey courts recognized that the stock in the lessor companies was substantially equivalent to a perpetual 8% bond."

This contention places the taxpayer in an anomalous position. Whereas the "continuity of interest" principle is predicated on the existence of the proprietary right which must be carried over into the reorganized corporation, the taxpayer at one and the same time asserts that a "continuity of interest" existed in the reorganized company, even though there was no proprietary interest by the stockholders in the merged corporation to be carried over into the reorganized corporation.

It is unnecessary, however, to further explore this contention because two things are clear * * *. First, the stockholders in South Jersey had a definite and clearly fixed proprietary interest in its property. The lease provided that all replacements and additions to the leased property were to be the property of South Jersey and subject to the terms and conditions of the lease. Further, on the expiration of the lease all the property subject to its terms was to be returned to South Jersey. South Jersey owned the property under lease even though that lease was for a 900–year term. * * *

In view of the incontrovertible facts the taxpayer's argument that the stockholders in South Jersey had no proprietary interest is without basis.

Finally, it is equally clear that when the stockholders of South Jersey exchanged their stock in that corporation for the long term bonds of Public Service Electric and Gas Company, they surrendered their proprietary interest and simply became creditors of Public Service. They no longer owned any of the former property of South Jersey and they had no proprietary interest in the property of Public Service. * * *

* * *

For the reasons stated the decision of the Tax Court of the United States is affirmed.

NOTES

1. *No statutory voting stock requirement for a reorganization.* The earliest continuity of proprietary interest cases involved asset acquisitions. See Nelson and Le Tulle, pp. 514–518. Roebling extends the continuity of proprietary interest doctrine to mergers. The statutory "solely for voting stock" requirement that now must be satisfied before a B reorganization or a C reorganization can be accomplished greatly reduces the significance of the common law continuity of interest doctrine in connection with asset and stock transfers. See I.R.C. §§ 368(a)(1)(B), (C). The common law doctrine remains of great significance in the case of a merger due to the absence of any constraints in the internal revenue code on the consideration that may be utilized to accomplish an A reorganization. See I.R.C. § 368(a)(1)(A). In addition, as indicated above, state merger laws rarely restrict the consideration that may be utilized to accomplish a merger (e.g., an all cash merger is normally permitted by state law).

2. *Amount of good consideration necessary to achieve continuity.* The regulations reveal that the common law continuity of proprietary interest requirement should be satisfied if at least 40% of the consideration received by the target shareholders consists of stock of the acquiring corporation. See Treas. Reg. § 1.368–1T(e)(2)(v) Examples 1, 2(ii), 6, 8 and 12. If Eileen and Jamie each own 40% of the outstanding shares of Target Corporation and Target is merged into Acquiring Corporation in exchange for $800,000 of Acquiring stock and $1,200,000 cash, will the continuity of proprietary interest doctrine be satisfied if Eileen gets all the Acquiring stock and Jamie and the other shareholders of Target get cash? See Rev. Rul. 66–224, 1966–2 C.B. 114 (ruling that continuity is measured in the aggregate and not on a shareholder-by-shareholder basis).

3. *Impact of "securities."* As Le Tulle (p. 515) and Roebling indicate, debt instruments issued in an acquisition never help to satisfy the continuity of proprietary interest requirement. Nevertheless, if a transaction in which debt instruments are issued otherwise qualifies as a reorganization, certain debt instruments of an acquiring corporation may receive favorable tax treatment. Specifically, "securities" issued in a reorganization may be received tax-free by a target shareholder who surrenders securities, but only if the principal amount of the securities received does not exceed the principal amount of the securities surrendered. See I.R.C. § 354(a). Otherwise, part or all of the securities received are treated as "boot." See I.R.C. § 356(d). The definition of a "security" for this purpose is not entirely clear, although debt instruments with a maturity of more than ten years are generally treated as securities, whereas debt instruments with a term of less than five years are generally not treated as securities.

4. *Warrants treated as "securities."* Rights to acquire stock issued by a corporation that is a party to a reorganization are treated as securities of the issuing corporation. Treas. Reg. § 1.354–1(e).

5. *Nonqualified preferred stock.* Nonqualified preferred stock (as defined in I.R.C. § 351(g)(2)) received in exchange for stock is generally not treated as stock or securities. Rather, the nonqualified preferred stock is treated as boot. See I.R.C. § 354(a)(2)(C)(i); p. 537, Note 3.

Paulsen v. Commissioner

Supreme Court of the United States, 1985.
469 U.S. 131, 105 S.Ct. 627.

■ Justice Rehnquist delivered the opinion of the Court.

Commerce Savings and Loan Association * * * merged into Citizens Federal Savings and Loan Association * * * in July 1976. Petitioners Harold and Marie Paulsen sought to treat their exchange of stock in Commerce for an interest in Citizens as a tax-free reorganization * * *. The Court of Appeals for the Ninth Circuit, disagreeing with the Court of Claims and other Courts of Appeals, reversed a decision of the Tax Court in favor of petitioners. We granted certiorari to resolve these conflicting interpretations * * *.

At the time of the merger, petitioner Harold T. Paulsen was president and a director of Commerce. He and his wife, petitioner Marie B. Paulsen, held as community property 17,459 shares of "guaranty stock" in Commerce. In exchange for this stock petitioners received passbook savings accounts and time certificates of deposit in Citizens. Relying on I.R.C. §§ 354(a)(1) and 368(a)(1)(A), they did not report the gain they realized on their 1976 federal income tax return because they considered the merger to be a tax-free reorganization.

Before it ceased to exist, Commerce was a state-chartered savings and loan association incorporated and operated under Washington State law. It was authorized to issue "guaranty stock," to offer various classes of savings accounts, and to make loans. Each stockholder, savings account holder, and borrower was a member of the association. Each share of stock and every $100, or fraction thereof, on deposit in a savings account carried with it one vote. Each borrower also had one vote.

The "guaranty stock" had all of the characteristics normally associated with common stock issued by a corporation * * *.

Citizens is a federally chartered mutual savings and loan association under the jurisdiction of the Federal Home Loan Bank Board. It offers savings accounts and makes loans, but has no capital stock. Its members are its depositors and borrowers. Each savings account holder has one vote for each $100, or fraction thereof, of the withdrawal value of his savings account up to a maximum of 400 votes. Each borrower has one vote.

Citizens is owned by its depositors. Twice each year its net earnings and any surplus are to be distributed to its savings account holders pro rata to the amounts on deposit. Its net assets would similarly be distributed if liquidation or dissolution should occur * * *.

The merger was effected pursuant to a "Plan of Merger," under which Commerce's stockholders exchanged all their stock for passbook savings accounts and certificates of deposit in Citizens. The plan was designed to conform to the requirements of Wash. Rev. Code § 33.40.010 (1983), which provides for mergers * * *, and to qualify as a tax-free reorganization under the terms of §§ 354(a)(1) and 368(a)(1)(A). Under the plan, Commerce stockholders received for each share a $12 deposit in a Citizens passbook savings account, subject only to the restriction that such deposits could not be withdrawn for one year. They also had the alternative of receiving time certificates of deposit in Citizens with maturities ranging from 1 to 10 years at the same $12–per-share exchange rate * * *. Following the exchange, the merged entity continued to operate under the Citizens name.

Petitioners had a cost basis in their Commerce stock of $56,802; in the exchange they received passbook accounts and certificates of deposit worth $209,508 * * *.

* * *

Section 368(a)(1)(A) defines a "reorganization" to include "a statutory merger or consolidation," and §§ 7701(a)(3), 7701(a)(7), and 7701(a)(8) further define the terms "corporation" to include "associations," "stock" to include "shares in an association," and "shareholder" to include a "member in an association." There is no dispute that at the time of the merger Commerce and Citizens qualified as associations, petitioners qualified as shareholders, Commerce's guaranty stock and Citizens' passbook accounts and certificates of deposit qualified as stock, and the merger qualified as a statutory merger within these provisions of the Code. Accordingly, under the literal terms of the Code the transaction would qualify as a tax-free "reorganization" * * *.

Satisfying the literal terms of the reorganization provisions, however, is not sufficient to qualify for nonrecognition of gain or loss. The purpose of these provisions is "to free from the imposition of an income tax purely 'paper profits or losses' wherein there is no realization of gain or loss in the business sense but merely the recasting of the same interests in a different form." In order to exclude sales structured to satisfy the literal terms of the reorganization provisions but not their purpose, this Court has construed the statute to also require that the taxpayer's ownership interest in the prior organization must continue in a meaningful fashion in the reorganized enterprise * * *. Known as the "continuity-of-interest" doctrine, this requirement has been codified in Treas. Regs. § 1.368–1(b).

The present case turns on whether petitioners' exchange of their guaranty stock in Commerce for their passbook savings accounts and certificates of deposit in Citizens satisfies this continuity-of-interest requirement * * *. [T]he Commissioner rejected petitioners' treatment of the Commerce–Citizens merger as a tax-free reorganization * * * and issued a statutory notice of deficiency finding petitioners liable for tax on their entire $152,706 gain.

Petitioners sought redetermination of the deficiency in the Tax Court, which * * * reasoned that the savings accounts and certificates of deposit were the only forms of equity in Citizens, and it held that the requisite continuity of interest existed.

The Commissioner appealed to the Court of Appeals for the Ninth Circuit, which * * * reversed. It reasoned that "despite certain formal equity characteristics" the passbook savings accounts and time certificates of deposit "are in reality indistinguishable from ordinary savings accounts and are essentially the equivalent of cash." * * *

Citizens * * * shares are hybrid instruments having both equity and debt characteristics. They combine in one instrument the separate characteristics of the guaranty stock and the savings accounts of stock associations like Commerce.

The Citizens shares have several equity characteristics. The most important is the fact that they are the only ownership instrument of the association. Each share carries in addition to its deposit value a part ownership interest in the bricks and mortar, the goodwill, and all the other assets of Citizens. Another equity characteristic is the right to vote on matters for which the association's management must obtain shareholder approval. The shareholders also receive dividends rather than interest on their accounts; the dividends are paid out of net earnings, and the shareholders have no legal right to have a dividend declared or to have a fixed return on their investment. The shareholders further have a right to a pro rata distribution of any remaining assets after a solvent dissolution.

These equity characteristics, however, are not as substantial as they appear on the surface. Unlike a stock association where the ownership of the assets is concentrated in the stockholders, the ownership interests here are spread over all of the depositors. The equity interest of each shareholder in relation to the total value of the share, therefore, is that much smaller than in a stock association. The right to vote is also not very significant. A shareholder is limited to 400 votes; thus any funds deposited in excess of $40,000 do not confer any additional votes. The vote is also diluted each time a loan is made, as each borrower is entitled to one vote. In addition * * *, when depositors open their accounts, they usually sign proxies giving management their votes.

The fact that dividends rather than interest are paid is by no means controlling. [I]n practice, Citizens pays a fixed, preannounced rate on all accounts. As the Court of Appeals observed, Citizens would not be able to compete with stock savings and loan associations and commercial banks if it did not follow this practice. Potential depositors are motivated only by the rate of return on their accounts and the security of their deposits * * *. The Code treats these dividends just like interest on bank accounts rather than like dividends on stock in a corporation * * *.

The right to participate in the net proceeds of a solvent liquidation is also not a significant part of the value of the shares. Referring to the possibility of a solvent liquidation of a mutual savings association, this Court observed: "It stretches the imagination very far to attribute any real value to such a remote contingency, and when coupled with the fact that it represents nothing which the depositor can readily transfer, any theoretical value reduces almost to the vanishing point."

In contrast, there are substantial debt characteristics to the Citizens shares that predominate. Petitioners' passbook accounts and certificates of deposit are not subordinated to the claims of creditors, and their deposits are not considered permanent contributions to capital. Shareholders have a right on 30 days' notice to withdraw their deposits, which right Citizens is obligated to respect * * *.

In our view, the debt characteristics of Citizens' shares greatly outweigh the equity characteristics. The face value of petitioners' passbook accounts and certificates of deposit was $210,000. Petitioners have stipulated that they had a right to withdraw the face amount of the deposits in cash, on demand after one year or at stated intervals thereafter. Their investment was virtually risk free and the dividends received were equivalent to prevailing interest rates for savings accounts in other types of savings institutions. The debt value of the shares was the same as the face value, $210,000; because no one would pay more than this for the shares, the incremental value attributable to the equity features was, practically, zero. Accordingly, we hold that petitioners' passbook accounts and certificates of deposit were cash equivalents.

Petitioners have failed to satisfy the continuity-of-interest requirement to qualify for a tax-free reorganization. In exchange for their guaranty stock in Commerce, they received essentially cash with an insubstantial equity interest. Under Minnesota Tea Co., their equity interest in Citizens would have to be "a substantial part of the value of the thing transferred." 296 U.S., at 385. Assuming an arm's-length transaction in which what petitioners gave up and what they received were of equivalent worth, their Commerce stock was worth $210,000 in withdrawable deposits and an unquantifiably small incremental equity interest. This retained equity interest in the reorganized enterprise, therefore, is not a "substantial" part of the value of the Commerce stock which was given up * * *.

　　* * *

Petitioners' real complaint seems to be our willingness to consider the equity and debt aspects of their shares separately. Clearly, if these interests were represented by separate pieces of paper—savings accounts on the one hand and equity instruments of some kind on the other—the value of the latter would be so small that we would not find a continuity of proprietary interest. In order not "to exalt artifice above reality and to deprive the statutory provision in question of all serious purpose," it is necessary in the present case to consider the debt and equity aspects of a single instrument separately * * *.

Petitioners also complain that the result reached by the court below is inconsistent with the Commissioner's position that a merger of one mutual savings and loan institution into another mutual association or into a stock association would still qualify as a tax-free reorganization. See Rev. Rul. 69–3, 1969–1 Cum. Bull. 103. If the continuity-of-interest test turns on the nature of the thing received, and not on the relative change in proprietary interest, argue petitioners, the interest received in the merger of two mutual associations is no different from the interest received in the instant case.

As already indicated, shares in a mutual association have a predominant cash-equivalent component and an insubstantial equity component. When two mutual associations merge, the shares received are essentially identical to the shares given up. As long as the cash value of the shares on each side of the exchange is the same, the equity interest represented by the shares received—though small—is equivalent to the equity interest represented by the shares given up * * *. In the case of a merger of a mutual association into a stock association, the continuity-of-interest requirement is even more clearly satisfied because the equity position of the exchanging shareholders is not only equivalent before and after the exchange, but it is enhanced.

* * *

The judgment of the Court of Appeals is Affirmed.

■ JUSTICE O'CONNOR, with whom CHIEF JUSTICE BURGER joins, dissenting.

Today the Court holds that the merger of a stock savings and loan association into a mutual savings and loan association does not qualify as a tax-deferred reorganization * * *. Although the merger meets all the statutory requirements, * * * the Court nevertheless concludes that such a merger fails to qualify under a refined interpretation of the judicially imposed "continuity-of-interest" doctrine. This holding introduces an unfortunate and unnecessary element of uncertainty into an area of our income tax laws where clear and consistent precedent is particularly helpful to both taxpayers and tax collectors. Because I find the Court's holding unwise as a matter of policy and unwarranted as a matter of law, I respectfully dissent.

* * *

[T]he basis of the Court's holding is a characterization of the mutual share accounts as "hybrid instruments" having both equity and debt characteristics. The Court finds that the debt characteristics outweigh the equity characteristics and concludes that the equity interest received does not represent "a substantial part of the value of the thing transferred."

I agree that a mutual share account is a hybrid security, and that it has substantial debt characteristics. The opportunity to withdraw from the account after one year cloaks the account holder with some of the attributes of a creditor, and the account with some of the attributes of debt. I nevertheless believe that the equity interest represented in a mutual share account is substantial, and thus satisfies the continuity-of-proprietary-interest requirement.

The taxpayers in this case received mutual share accounts and certificates of deposit from Citizens which gave them the same proprietary features of equity ownership which they previously had as stockholders in

Commerce, plus the right after a stated interval to withdraw their cash deposits. As the Court recognizes, the guaranty stockholders of Commerce were the equitable owners of the corporation and had a proportionate proprietary interest in the corporation's assets and net earnings. When they exchanged their shares for deposits in Citizens, they became the equitable owners of the mutual association. As equitable owners, the mutual share account holders retained all the relevant rights of corporate stockholders: the right to vote, the right to share in net assets on liquidation, and the right to share in the earnings and profits of the enterprise. Indeed, the proprietary interest obtained by petitioners here is more weighty than that obtained by the nonvoting, preferred shareholders in John A. Nelson Co. v. Helvering: The petitioners possess not only the primary voting interest in the continuing enterprise, but also the only interests in existence with proprietary and equity rights in the mutual association. To the extent there is any equity at all in a mutual association, it is represented by the share accounts obtained by the petitioners.

To find that the equity of a mutual association is insubstantial, the Court today looks to each equitable power or attribute of mutual share account ownership to determine its value and the extent to which it is actually exercised. The Court values the debt characteristics separately from the equity characteristics of the same instrument to determine whether the equity interest is a substantial part of the value of the property transferred. [A]pparently no court has ever relied on such a distinction with respect to a single instrument * * *.

The flaw in this approach is most clearly evident in the majority's attempt to explain why a merger between mutual associations qualifies as a tax-deferred reorganization whereas a merger of a stock savings and loan into a mutual association does not. When a more heavily capitalized mutual association is acquired by a thinly capitalized mutual association, the equity component of the value of share accounts will be reduced. Under the majority's separate valuation approach, at some point that value should be reduced so substantially as to defeat claims that a continuing proprietary interest is maintained. The Court avoids this result by noting that "the equity interest represented by the shares received—though small—is equivalent to the equity interest represented by the shares given up." But the same was true when Commerce merged into Citizens. The equity interest represented by the share accounts in Citizens is the sole and complete equity interest in that association, and it was obtained in exchange for shares in Commerce that represented the equivalent sole equity interest in the stock savings and loan association.

The Court's denigration of each of the equity attributes of a mutual share account is also troubling. The Court notes that the ownership interests in Citizens are "spread over all of the depositors" and that the right to vote "is * * * diluted each time a loan is made, as each borrower is entitled to one vote." But such characteristics are by no means confined to mutual share accounts. Dilution of voting power of shareholder equity in all corporations may and frequently does occur with each new stock issue or new class of stock. Yet the threat of dilution has never divested stock of its status as a substantial equity interest. Nor should the fact that mutual accounts are often voted by proxy affect the result: proxy voting, after all, is a common practice among holders of common stock in large corporations as well. Such factors should have no part in the determination of whether the continuing-proprietary-interest test is met. Indeed, this Court has found ownership of nonvoting preferred stock to provide a sufficient proprietary interest. John A. Nelson Co. v. Helvering, 296 U.S. at 377 [p. 514].

The Court also finds that the right to share in the profits of the association, through dividends and ownership of a share of the assets and undistributed profits of the association, is not controlling. The majority downplays the shareholders' interest in the assets and undistributed profits, a right that is solely one of ownership. It finds that the dividends paid to the shareholders are analogous to interest paid to bank depositors because the dividends are paid at a fixed, preannounced rate and are treated as interest for some other tax purposes. These dividends, however, cannot be properly equated with interest on bank deposits because shareholders have no enforceable legal right to compel the payment of dividends. That the amount of the dividend is preannounced at a suggested rate is not significantly different from preannounced dividends paid by many large corporations, particularly on preferred stock * * *.

Finally, the majority concludes that the right to participate in the proceeds of a solvent liquidation is "not a significant part of the value of the shares" because the possibility of a liquidation is remote. The task at hand is to classify the nature of the mutual share account; the market value of the share account on liquidation is a separate question. The remoteness of the contingency of liquidation cannot reasonably be dispositive of the equity character of the right of the shareholders * * *.

Having unpersuasively attempted to argue away the equity characteristics of the mutual share accounts, the Court then finds that the debt characteristics outweigh the equity characteristics, concluding that the equity value is "practically, zero." The Court's reasoning suggests that, no matter how much capital a mutual association possesses, the equity value of its shares is insubstantial because no one would pay more for the shares than their face value. This result is preordained by the Court's unsupported determination that the value of the "nonequity" features is equal to the face value of the account. By definition, nothing can be left to allocate to the equity features. A more realistic analysis would acknowledge that the equity aspects of a hybrid instrument are intertwined with the debt aspects and cannot be valued in isolation.

The result reached by the court today is inconsistent with the tax-deferred treatment accorded mergers between two mutual associations or between a stock association and a mutual association when the stock association is the survivor. Rev. Rul. 69-3, 1969-1 Cum. Bull. 103 (merger of two mutual associations qualifies as a tax free reorganization), and Rev. Rul. 69-646, 1969-2 Cum. Bull. 54 (merger of mutual association into stock association qualifies as a tax free reorganization). And because a transaction that is a sale rather than a tax-deferred exchange at the shareholder level cannot qualify as a tax-deferred reorganization at the corporate level, see I.R.C. §§ 361 and 381, the result of the Court's holding is to discourage an entire class of legitimate business transactions without regard to the desirability of such mergers from an economic standpoint. This result is directly contrary to the intent of Congress. "Congress * * * adopted the policy of exempting from tax the gain from exchanges made in connection with a reorganization, in order that ordinary business transactions [would] not be prevented on account of the provisions of the tax law." Senate Rep. No. 398, 68th Cong., 1st Sess., 14 (1924).

The Court's opinion also has ramifications beyond mutual associations. This case presents the first opportunity for the Court to consider the use of hybrid instruments in reorganizations. Previously, the Court has held that the receipt of stock, whether common, voting, or nonvoting preferred, satisfies the continuity-of-interest test. If the Court is to now examine the actual exercise of the proprietary rights conferred by ownership of a particular security, it will inevitably reach conflicting results in similar cases. Predicting the tax consequences of reorganizations undertaken for a valid business purpose will become increasingly difficult. I would adhere to precedent and to a clear test and hold that a hybrid instrument which has the principal characteristics of equity ownership should be treated as equity for purposes of the continuity-of-proprietary-interest requirement * * *.

NOTES

1. *Consequences of reversing the merger.* Would the transaction in Paulsen have qualified as a reorganization if, rather than merging Commerce into Citizens, Citizens had been merged into Commerce? See Rev. Rul. 69–646, 1969–2 C.B. 54 (approving reorganization treatment for merger of mutual association into stock association). Could terms have been devised that would have given the Paulsens the same relative interest in the combined enterprise regardless of which corporation survived the merger? Can the possibility that different tax consequences will result depending on whether X is merged into Y, or Y is merged into X, be justified?

2. *Statutory treatment versus continuity of interest treatment.* The Paulsen case indicates that the parties had agreed that "Citizens' passbook accounts and certificates of deposit qualified as 'stock' as defined in I.R.C. § 7701(a)(7)." Thus, these instruments were treated as "stock" for statutory purposes but not for continuity of interest purposes. What would the tax consequences be if the opposite approach were taken; the instruments were treated as "stock" for continuity of interest purposes but as "securities" or other property for statutory purposes? See I.R.C. §§ 354, 356, 361. How do these tax consequences differ from the consequences that followed from the Supreme Court's holding? Which approach is preferable from a policy standpoint? In light of the definition of "stock" in I.R.C. § 7701(a)(7), could either party have advanced the position that the instruments received by the Paulsens represented property other than stock?

b.   PRE–MERGER AND POST–MERGER CONTINUITY

Treas. Reg. § 1.368–1(e)

Kass v. Commissioner

United States Tax Court, 1973.
60 T.C. 218, aff'd 491 F.2d 749 (3d Cir.1974).

■ DAWSON, JUDGE.

Respondent determined a deficiency in petitioner's Federal income tax for the year 1966 in the amount of $10,134.67.

The only issue for decision is whether petitioner, a minority shareholder of an 84 percent-owned subsidiary, must recognize gain upon the receipt of the parent's stock pursuant to a statutory merger of the subsidiary into the parent.

* * *

For a period greater than six months prior to 1965, [May B. Kass (herein called petitioner)] had owned 2,000 shares of common stock of Atlantic City Racing Association (herein called ACRA). Her basis in the stock was $1,000 * * *.

ACRA was a New Jersey corporation which was formed in 1943 and which was engaged in the business of operating a racetrack. Its total authorized and outstanding stock consisted of 506,000 shares of common stock. It had approximately 500 stockholders.

Track Associates, Inc. (herein called TRACK) is a New Jersey corporation which was formed on November 19, 1965. [TRACK's] original capitalization consisted of 202,577 shares. Over 50 percent of the original issue was acquired by the Levy family and 8 percent was acquired by the Casey family. The remaining stock went to 18 other individuals. The Levys and the Caseys were also minority shareholders * * * in ACRA. [The Levys and Caseys transferred their ACRA shares to TRACK when TRACK was incorporated.] Their purpose in forming TRACK was to gain control over ACRA's racetrack business. They wanted to do away with ACRA's cumbersome capital structure and institute a new corporate policy with regard to capital improvements and higher purses for the races. Control was to be gained by establishing TRACK and then by (1) having TRACK purchase at least 80 percent of the stock of ACRA and (2) subsequently merging ACRA into TRACK.

* * *

On December 1, 1965, TRACK offered to purchase the stock of ACRA at $22 per share, subject to the condition that at least 405,000 shares (slightly more than 80 percent of ACRA's outstanding shares) be tendered. As a result of this tender offer * * * 424,764 shares of ACRA stock were received and paid for by TRACK. A total of 29,486 shares of ACRA stock were not tendered.

The board of directors of TRACK approved a Plan of Liquidation providing for the liquidation of ACRA by way of merger into TRACK. ACRA and TRACK, through their directors, entered into a Joint Agreement of Merger on February 11, 1966, which agreement provided that upon shareholder approval ACRA would "be merged with and into TRACK * * * pursuant to * * * the Revised Statutes of the State of New Jersey." At a special meeting of the shareholders of ACRA held on March 8, 1966, the aforementioned Plan of Liquidation and Joint Agreement were adopted. A copy of the notice of the meeting was sent to the petitioner, and it notified petitioner of the rights of a dissenting stockholder under New Jersey corporate law.

The merger having taken place, the remaining shares of ACRA that were not sold pursuant to the tender offer or the dissenting shareholder provisions were exchanged for TRACK stock, one for one. The petitioner exchanged 2,000 shares of ACRA stock, with a fair market value at the time of $22 per share, for 2,000 shares of TRACK stock. She did not report any capital gain in connection with this transaction.

Petitioner contends that the merger of ACRA into TRACK [is] * * * (1) a true statutory merger and (2) a section 368(a)(1)(A) reorganization, occasioning no recognition of gain on the ensuing exchange * * *. Respondent, on the other hand, argues that the purchase of stock by TRACK and the liquidation of ACRA into TRACK, which took the form of a merger, must be viewed at all levels as an integrated transaction; that the statutory merger does not qualify as a reorganization because it fails the continuity-of-interest test; and that, as a consequence, petitioner * * * must recognize gain.

    * * *

Respondent does not take the position that a statutory merger, such as the one we have here, can never qualify for reorganization-nonrecognition status * * *. Rather, his position is simply that the merger in question fails to meet the time-honored continuity-of-interest test. We agree with this and so hold.

[R]eorganization treatment is appropriate when [a subsidiary is merged into its parent if] the parent's stock ownership in the subsidiary was not acquired as a step in a plan to acquire assets of the subsidiary: the parent's stockholding can be counted as contributing to continuity-of-interest, so that since such holding represented more than 80 percent of the stock of the subsidiary, the continuity-of-interest test would be met. Reorganization treatment is inappropriate when the parent's stock-ownership in the subsidiary was purchased as the first step in a plan to acquire the subsidiary's assets * * *. The parent's stockholding could not be counted towards continuity-of-interest, so in the last example there would be a continuity-of-interest of less than 20 percent. (Less than 20 percent continuity would be significantly less continuity-of-interest than that allowed in

John A. Nelson Co. v. Helvering, 296 U.S. 374 (1935) [p. 514].) In short, where the parent's stock interest is "old and cold," it may contribute to continuity-of-interest. Where the parent's interest is not "old and cold," the sale of shares by the majority of shareholders actually detracts from continuity-of-interest.

In petitioner's case, TRACK's stock in ACRA was acquired as part of an integrated plan to obtain control over ACRA's business. The plan called for, first, the purchase of stock and, second, the subsidiary-into-parent merger. Accordingly, continuity-of-interest must be measured by looking to all the pre-tender offer stockholders rather than to the parent (TRACK) and the nontendering stockholders only; and by that measure the merger fails and petitioner must recognize her gain.

* * *

Faced with the general rule as to the applicability of the continuity-of-interest test, petitioner makes the following arguments, which we will deal with separately.

One, the continuity-of-interest doctrine should not be applied because TRACK was formed by a few stockholders in ACRA in order to purchase the business * * *. "In effect, the situation was the same as the sale of stock by some shareholders to other shareholders." The petitioner meets herself coming, so to speak, when making this argument. Confronted with the problem of how to characterize the second event in the present two-event transaction, she contends that the transaction was a true statutory merger in both form and substance, at least insofar as she, a minority shareholder, was concerned. Now, confronted with the continuity-of-interest problem, she would have us treat the transaction in a manner inconsistent with the characterization previously given to the transaction, that of a merger. Furthermore, the parties to these events (the selling-shareholders of ACRA, the organizers of TRACK, and the nontendering, nondissenting shareholders such as the petitioner) chose the steps that were followed. To allow one of them in a separate proceeding to characterize the facts as being in substance something else would lay the ground work for an enormous amount of "whipsawing" by and against both taxpayers and the Government.

Two, in applying the continuity-of-interest test, if it is applied, the purchase of stock by TRACK and the subsequent merger should not be viewed as steps in an integrated transaction because the choice of merger over liquidation as a second step had independent significance to the minority shareholders and either choice would have suited TRACK. By so arguing, the petitioner attempts in effect to avoid the step transaction doctrine and thus to limit the application of the continuity-of-interest test. If the merger can be separated from the stock purchase, the continuity-of-interest test might be applicable only with regard to ACRA's shareholders at the time of the statutory merger, namely, the parent corporation, TRACK, and the minority shareholders, including petitioner. We note at least one flaw: the choice—liquidation or merger—did make a difference to TRACK. If it had liquidated ACRA, TRACK would not have received all of

ACRA's assets. Some of the assets would have gone to the minority shareholders, and it would have had to have purchased them from those shareholders at an additional price. By choosing to merge ACRA into itself, it was able to avoid this and other problems.

Three, if the purchase and merger are to be viewed as parts of a single transaction for continuity and reorganization purposes, then the incorporation of TRACK should also be integrated into the transaction for section 351 purposes; thus the petitioner should be viewed as having participated in a tax-free section 351 transaction along with the Levys and Caseys. Briefly, the answer to this argument is that while the purchase and the merger were interdependent events, petitioner's exchange of ACRA stock for TRACK stock was not "mutually interdependent" with the incorporation transfers made by the Levys, Caseys, and 18 other individuals. This result merely illustrates the truism that the step transaction doctrine, even when worded consistently and applied to identical facts, may result in integration in one case and "separateness" in another case simply because the legal question to be answered has changed.

* * *

Finally, we emphasize that the petitioner is not any worse off than her fellow shareholders who sold their stock. She could have also received money instead of stock had she chosen to sell or to dissent from the merger * * *.

NOTES

1. *Critical facts.* Would Mrs. Kass have prevailed if more time had elapsed between the acquisition of the ACRA shares by TRACK and the merger of ACRA into TRACK? If so, how much more time? Would Mrs. Kass have prevailed if TRACK acquired fewer shares of ACRA prior to the merger than it actually acquired? See p. 518, Note 3. If so, how many fewer shares? In light of the Kass court's holding, what events were encompassed by the "plan of reorganization"?

2. *Impact on TRACK.* Did the fact that the transaction in Kass failed to qualify as an A reorganization cause TRACK to recognize gain when ACRA was merged into TRACK? See Reg. §§ 1.332–2(d), (e). Under current law, would ACRA recognize gain in the transaction? See I.R.C. § 337(a). At the time the transaction was executed, the liquidation of ACRA enabled TRACK to "step-up" the basis of the ACRA assets to reflect the price it paid for the ACRA stock. Under current law, would the liquidation result in a step-up in the basis of the ACRA assets? See I.R.C. § 334(b)(1). What mechanism now exists to achieve a step-up in the basis of the ACRA assets? See I.R.C. § 338. What is the cost of utilizing that mechanism?

J.E. Seagram Corp. v. Commissioner

United States Tax Court, 1995.
104 T.C. 75.

■ NIMS, JUDGE: * * *

[T]he only issue for decision is whether petitioner is entitled to a short-term capital loss in the amount of $530,410,896. * * *

BACKGROUND

[Conoco, Inc. (Conoco) was an integrated oil company. In 1981, Conoco had approximately 86 million shares of stock outstanding. In early August of 1981, petitioner purchased approximately 32 percent (28 million shares) of the Conoco stock for approximately $2.6 billion. At about the same time, DuPont purchased approximately 46 percent (40 million shares) of Conoco stock. The remaining 22 percent (18 million shares) of the Conoco stock was owned by the public.

On September 30, 1981, Conoco was merged into DuPont. Petitioner and the public shareholders of Conoco received DuPont stock for their Conoco shares. The value of the DuPont stock received by petitioner was approximately $2 billion.]

DuPont treated the * * * merger as a tax-free reorganization for Federal income tax purposes and filed its tax return for its 1981 taxable year accordingly. DuPont and Conoco advised former Conoco shareholders who had exchanged their stock for DuPont stock * * * that they had no taxable gain or loss.

* * *

Petitioner did not report a loss for financial accounting purposes as a result of its exchange of Conoco stock for DuPont stock. Petitioner ascribed its carrying cost for its Conoco stock to the DuPont stock which it received in exchange. [Petitioner did, however, report a tax loss on the exchange of approximately $600,000,000.]

DISCUSSION

The ultimate issue for decision is whether, for tax purposes, petitioner had a recognized loss upon the exchange of its Conoco stock for DuPont stock. Whether such a loss is to be recognized depends upon the effect to be given section 354(a)(1) under the above facts. * * *

[I]f DuPont and Conoco were parties to a reorganization, and if the statutory merger of Conoco into DuPont was in pursuance of a plan of reorganization, then no loss is to be recognized by petitioner upon the exchange of its Conoco stock for DuPont stock.

Petitioner challenges the validity of the putative reorganization * * * whereas respondent argues in support of the reorganization. * * *

There appears to be no dispute that the merger of Conoco into DuPont complied with the requirements of Delaware law, thus meeting the description of a "reorganization" in section 368(a)(1)(A) in that there was a "statutory merger or consolidation" * * *.

* * *

Petitioner argues that * * * the merger does not qualify as a reorganization because it fails the "continuity of interest" requirement.

* * *

[P]etitioner is essentially arguing that because it acquired approximately 32 percent of the [Conoco] shares for cash pursuant to its own tender offer, and DuPont acquired approximately 46 percent of these shares for cash pursuant to its tender offer, the combined 78 percent of Conoco shares acquired for cash * * * destroyed the continuity of interest requisite for a valid reorganization. We think petitioner's argument, and the logic that supports it, miss the mark.

Pursuant to its two-step tender offer/merger plan of reorganization, DuPont acquired approximately 54 percent of the * * * shares of Conoco stock in exchange for DuPont stock, which included petitioner's recently acquired Conoco shares that it tendered pursuant to DuPont's tender offer. If the 54 percent had been acquired by DuPont from Conoco shareholders in a "one-step" merger-type acquisition, there would be little argument that continuity of interest had been satisfied. Sec. 368(a)(1)(A).

* * *

Where sufficient continuity is lacking, the acquired corporation will not be a "party to a reorganization," thus causing the overall transaction to fail as a reorganization under section 368(a)(1)(A). * * * Thus the question petitioner raises is whether there is sufficient continuity of interest so as to qualify Conoco and DuPont as parties to a reorganization under this section.

The parties stipulated that petitioner and DuPont * * * were acting independently of one another and pursuant to competing tender offers. Furthermore, there is of course nothing in the record to suggest any prearranged understanding between petitioner and DuPont that petitioner would tender the Conoco stock purchased for cash if petitioner by means of its own tender offer failed to achieve control of Conoco. Consequently, it cannot be argued that petitioner, although not a party to the reorganization, was somehow acting in concert with DuPont, which was a party to the reorganization. If such had been the case, the reorganization would fail because petitioner's cash purchases of Conoco stock could be attributed to DuPont, thereby destroying continuity.

* * *

Respondent points out, correctly we believe, that the concept of continuity of interest advocated by petitioner would go far toward eliminating the possibility of a tax-free reorganization of any corporation whose stock is actively traded. Because it would be impossible to track the large volume of third party transactions in the target's stock, all completed transactions would be suspect. Sales of target stock for cash after the date of the announcement of an acquisition can neither be predicted nor controlled by publicly held parties to a reorganization. A requirement that the identity of the acquired corporation's shareholders be tracked to assume a sufficient number of "historic" shareholders to satisfy some arbitrary minimal percentage receiving the acquiring corporation's stock would be completely unrealistic.

* * *

In the "integrated" transaction before us petitioner, not DuPont, "stepped into the shoes" of 32 percent of the Conoco shareholders when petitioner acquired their stock for cash via [petitioner's] competing tender offer, held the 32 percent transitorily, and immediately tendered it in exchange for DuPont stock. For present purposes, there is no material distinction between petitioner's tender of the Conoco stock and a direct tender by the "old" Conoco shareholders themselves. Thus, the requirement of continuity of interest has been met.

[W]e also note that petitioner did not report a loss on the exchange of its Conoco stock for DuPont stock for financial accounting purposes. Instead, petitioner ascribed its carrying cost for its Conoco stock to the DuPont stock. [This act is not] consistent with the recognized loss petitioner claimed on its tax return.

[W]e hold that a loss cannot be recognized by petitioner on its exchange of Conoco stock for DuPont stock, made pursuant to the DuPont–Conoco plan of reorganization. * * *

Continuity of Interest—Final Regulations

Department of the Treasury, TD 8760
January 28, 1998.

* * *

Explanation of Provisions

* * *

The purpose of the continuity of interest [COI] requirement is to prevent transactions that resemble sales from qualifying for nonrecognition of gain or loss available to corporate reorganizations. The final regulations provide that the COI requirement is satisfied if in substance a substantial part of the value of the proprietary interest in the target corporation (T) is preserved in the reorganization. A proprietary interest in T is preserved if, in a potential reorganization, it is exchanged for a proprietary interest in the [acquiring] corporation (P) * * *. However, a proprietary interest in T is not preserved if, in connection with the potential reorganization, it is acquired by P for consideration other than P stock, or P stock furnished in exchange for a proprietary interest in T in the potential reorganization is redeemed. All facts and circumstances must be considered in determining whether, in substance, a proprietary interest in T is preserved.

Rationale for the COI Regulations

The COI requirement was applied first to reorganization provisions that did not specify that P exchange a proprietary interest in P for a proprietary interest in T. Supreme Court cases imposed the COI requirement to further Congressional intent that tax-free status be accorded only to transactions where P exchanges a substantial proprietary interest in P for a proprietary interest in T held by the T shareholders rather than to transactions resembling sales.

None of the Supreme Court cases establishing the COI requirement addressed the issue of whether sales by former T shareholders of P stock received in exchange for T stock in the potential reorganization cause the COI requirement to fail to be satisfied. * * * Therefore, consistent with Congressional intent and the Supreme Court precedent which distinguishes between sales and reorganizations, the final regulations focus the COI requirement generally on exchanges between the T shareholders and P. Under this approach, sales of P stock by former T shareholders generally are disregarded.

* * *

Dispositions of T Stock

[T]he IRS and Treasury Department believe that issues concerning the COI requirement raised by dispositions of T stock before a potential reorganization correspond to those raised by subsequent dispositions of P stock furnished in exchange for T stock in the potential reorganization. [T]he final regulations apply the rationale of the proposed COI regulations to transactions occurring both prior to and after a potential reorganization. The final regulations provide that, for COI purposes, a mere disposition of T stock prior to a potential reorganization to persons not related to P is disregarded and a mere disposition of P stock received in a potential reorganization to persons not related to P is disregarded.

* * *

Redemptions of T Stock or Extraordinary Distributions
   With Respect to T Stock

In addition to the final regulations, the IRS and Treasury Department are contemporaneously issuing temporary regulations * * * providing that a proprietary interest in T is not preserved if, in connection with a potential reorganization, it is redeemed or acquired by a person related to T, or to the extent that, prior to and in connection with a potential reorganization, an extraordinary distribution is made with respect to it.

NOTES

1. *Pre-merger stock sales.* The continuity of proprietary interest regulations adopt the finding of the Seagram court that sales of target corporation stock before the merger do not adversely affect continuity except to the extent the stock is sold to the acquiring corporation or certain related parties. See Treas. Reg. §§ 1.368–1(e)(1), (6) Examples 1(ii), 4(ii).

2. *Post-merger stock sales.* The continuity of proprietary interest regulations also permit target shareholders who receive stock in the acquiring corporation to sell that stock after the merger without adversely affecting continuity of interest unless the stock is sold to the acquiring corporation (see Note 3) or certain related parties. See Treas. Reg. §§ 1.368–1(e)(1), (6) Examples 1(i), 3, 4(iii).

3. *Redemptions.* If the target corporation redeems stock or makes a distribution in connection with a subsequent merger, the consideration for the redemption or distribution counts against continuity under certain circumstances; e.g., if the acquiring corporation furnishes the consideration. See Treas. Reg. §§ 1.368–1(e)(1)(ii), –1(e)(6) Example 9. In addition, if subsequent to but in connection with a merger, the acquiring corporation redeems shares issued in the merger, those shares are treated as purchased and count against continuity. See Treas. Reg. §§ 1.368–1(e)(1), –1(e)(6) Examples 4(i), 5.

> *Problem 12–5 (Pre–merger and post–merger continuity):* ABC Corporation purchases 75% of the outstanding stock of Target Corporation and DEF Corporation purchases 10% of the outstanding stock of Target Corporation. How is the continuity of proprietary interest requirement impacted if:
>
> (a) Target is merged into ABC?
>
> (b) Target is merged into DEF?
>
> (c) Target redeems ABC's stock shortly before the subsequent merger of Target into DEF?
>
> (d) Same as (b) but DEF redeems the DEF stock issued to ABC in the merger?
>
> (e) Same as (b) but ABC sells the DEF stock received in the merger to a party unrelated to DEF?

2.   Continuity of Business Enterprise

Honbarrier v. Commissioner

Tax Court of the United States, 2000.
115 T.C. 300.

■ Ruwe, J.

FINDINGS OF FACT

Colonial

Colonial Motor Freight Line, Inc. ("Colonial") was a trucking company that operated as a common carrier of packaged freight, principally furniture manufactured in North Carolina. * * * Colonial held an operating authority granted by the Interstate Commerce Commission (ICC) and an operating authority granted by the State of North Carolina. These authorities granted Colonial contract and common carrier status between specified points and places within the United States and North Carolina.

When the trucking industry was deregulated at the Federal level in the 1980's, Colonial was subjected to competition from small individual truckers, with low overhead costs. As a result, Colonial's ICC operating authority became worthless, and the company experienced significant business reversals.

Colonial operated at a loss in the late 1980's. In 1988, as a result of its financial losses, Colonial stopped hauling freight and began selling its operating assets. By December 31, 1990, Colonial had sold all of its operating assets, except for the ICC and North Carolina operating authorities, for cash and cash equivalents. On August 21, 1992, Colonial sold its North Carolina authority for $5,000 but retained its ICC authority. [Colonial operated as an S Corporation until the end of 1992, when its S election involuntarily terminated.]

Colonial invested the proceeds from the sale of its operating assets almost exclusively in tax-exempt bonds. * * *

Archie Honbarrier owned 100 percent of Colonial's issued and outstanding shares [and] was the sole director of Colonial. Mr. Honbarrier's Colonial stock had a tax basis of $291,506.

Central

Central Transport, Inc. ("Central") was a trucking company that operated as a bulk carrier of liquid and dry chemicals. * * * Central held operating authorities issued by the ICC, various States, and Canada. These authorities granted Central contract and common carrier status for the transportation of bulk chemicals, including liquid or dry toxic chemicals, in tanker trailers between points and places within the United States and Canada. Central faced minimal competition because of the expensive equipment required to engage in the tanker trucking business.

Central was an S corporation. Central was highly successful in its bulk chemical hauling business * * *.

On several occasions, Charles L. Odom, a certified public accountant and Mr. Honbarrier's tax and financial adviser, recommended that Central make distributions to shareholders if such funds were not needed in Central's business. In a memorandum to attorney Charles Lynch, dated November 5, 1993, Mr. Odom stated: "Central has $10 million in undistributed S Corp earnings and would like [to] make a significant distribution to shareholders, but needs its capital for expansion and replacement of aging equipment."

Unlike Colonial, Central did not invest in tax-exempt bonds. Central held passive investments in the form of short-term liquid investments, such as certificates of deposit, because it needed cash and cash equivalents to operate its business. * * *

[A]ll of Central's stock was owned by Mr. and Mrs. Honbarrier and their [two] children. Mr. and Mrs. Honbarrier and their children [also served as directors].

Merger of Colonial into Central

On December 31, 1993, Colonial merged into Central in accordance with the laws of North Carolina. Central was the surviving corporation. Prior to the merger, Mr. Odom requested that Mr. Lynch research the income tax implications of a merger. On November 5, 1993, 7 weeks before the merger, Mr. Odom made the following handwritten notes: "ALH Oks merger of Col. & Central, payout to Cen. shareholders—if tax free—need bus. purpose."

On November 11, 1993, Mr. Lynch sent Mr. Odom a memorandum identifying the following possible business reasons for the merger: (1) obtaining Colonial's ICC operating rights to expand Central's business; (2) reducing and simplifying operating procedures and expenses by utilizing Central's existing staff and facilities; (3) reducing administrative expenses due to projected increased revenue without increasing overhead expenses; and (4) use of Colonial's cash to permit Central to expand and capitalize on the operating rights acquired from Colonial.

In a letter dated November 12, 1993, Mr. Odom forwarded a copy of Mr. Lynch's memorandum to Mr. Honbarrier and stated the following:

> Since Colonial has no intention of returning to the transportation industry, its intangible assets (ICC Authority), which would be lost on liquidation, could benefit another company within that industry. It seems to me that a merger could benefit both Central and Colonial. Central would be acquiring valuable rights for current and future use, as well as a substantial addition to its working capital. Colonial would no longer be required to maintain records and manage its investments, file separate income tax returns and whatever other administrative duties are now required.

On December 22, 1993, Colonial and Central entered into an Agreement and Plan of Merger of Colonial with and into Central (Merger Agreement) providing for a merger of Colonial into Central to occur one-second before midnight on December 31, 1993. On December 22, 1993, the shareholders and directors of Central unanimously approved the merger.
* * *

For purposes of the merger, Mr. Odom determined that the pre-merger value of Central's stock was $417.45 per share. He then determined that the net asset value of Colonial, which was being acquired by Central, was $7,442,660 and that the number of Central shares necessary to compensate Mr. Honbarrier for his Colonial stock was 17,840 shares. Pursuant to the merger, Mr. Honbarrier's shares of Colonial stock were exchanged for 17,840 shares of Central stock.

On December 22, 1993, the board of directors of Central also declared a $7 million distribution payable to its shareholders on December 31, 1993. The shareholder distribution was allocated on a pro rata basis among the shareholders based on their stock ownership in Central on December 22, 1993. The amounts to be distributed to the various shareholders were as follows:

Mr. Honbarrier	$5,042,772
Mrs. Honbarrier	23,102
Gary Honbarrier	967,063
Linda Embler	967,063
Total	$7,000,000

With the exception of the amount allocable to Mr. Honbarrier, all of the declared distributions were paid by check on December 31, 1993. Central made the $5,042,772 distribution to Mr. Honbarrier in two parts. The first part was paid via a $493,626 check drawn on Central's account on December 31, 1993. * * * The second part of the distribution to Mr. Honbarrier was made on January 3, 1994, and consisted of $4,549,146 in tax-exempt bonds. The tax-exempt bonds distributed to Mr. Honbarrier on January 3, 1994, were the same bonds acquired by Central from Colonial in the merger.

For Federal income tax purposes, petitioners treated the merger as a tax-free reorganization within the meaning of section 368(a)(1)(A) and treated the $7 million distribution as a payment of previously taxed income reflected in Central's accumulated adjustments account.

OPINION

As a general rule, any gain recognized on the sale or exchange of property is taxable. However, the Internal Revenue Code provides that certain transactions may occur in such a way that ownership interests are exchanged, yet no taxable event is deemed to have taken place. One instance where nonrecognition is provided involves corporate reorganizations that come within the provisions of section 368. * * *

[S]ection 368(a)(1)(A) defines a reorganization as "a statutory merger or consolidation". A statutory merger or consolidation is one effected pursuant to the corporate laws of the United States, a State, a territory, or the District of Columbia. See Reg. § 1.368–2(b)(1). The merger of Colonial into Central meets this literal requirement.

It has long been held that qualification as a merger under State law is not, by itself, sufficient to qualify as a reorganization under section 368(a)(1)(A). Courts have interpreted section 368 as imposing three additional requirements for a merger to be treated as a reorganization under section 368(a)(1)(A). These are: (1) business purpose; (2) continuity of business enterprise; and (3) continuity of interest. Following judicial precedent, the regulations also [impose these requirements]. See Reg. § 1.368–1(b). Failure to comply with any one of these requirements will preclude treatment as a tax-free reorganization within the meaning of section 368(a)(1)(A).

Respondent argues that the merger failed to meet the continuity of business enterprise requirement necessary to qualify the merger as a tax-free reorganization within the meaning of section 368(a)(1)(A).[13] The conti-

---

13. Respondent also argues that the merger did not have any business purpose. Because we hold that the merger did not satisfy the continuity of business enterprise requirement, we need not address respondent's alternative argument.

nuity of business enterprise requirement * * * is now embodied in Reg. § 1.368–1(d). These regulations are based on an interpretation of judicial precedents which articulate the continuity of business enterprise doctrine. The basic concept behind the continuity of business enterprise requirement is that the receipt of a new ownership interest in an entity that retains none of the business attributes of the shareholder's former corporation is more closely akin to a sale or liquidation than to a mere adjustment in the form of ownership.

[C]ontinuity of business enterprise requires that the acquiring corporation either continue the acquired corporation's historic business or use a significant portion of the acquired corporation's historic business assets in a business. See Reg. § 1.368–1(d)(1). In essence, the acquiring corporation must retain a link to the business enterprise of the acquired corporation by continuing the acquired corporation's business or by using the acquired corporation's business assets in a business.

1. Continuation of Acquired Corporation's Historic Business

In general, a corporation's historic business is the business it has conducted most recently. See Reg. § 1.368–1(d)(2)(iii). Petitioners contend that there is a continuity of Colonial's trucking business because Central is also in the trucking business. We disagree.

Colonial terminated its business of hauling packaged freight in 1988. It then began selling its operating assets. From 1988 forward, Colonial had no customers. By the end of 1990, Colonial had essentially disposed of its trucking operation assets for cash and cash equivalents. The only trucking assets Colonial retained were its ICC and North Carolina operating authorities. The ICC operating authority had become worthless, and Colonial sold its North Carolina operating authority in 1992 for $5,000. For 3 years prior to the merger, Colonial's assets consisted principally of tax-exempt bonds. * * *

[W]e conclude that Colonial had abandoned its trucking business well before the merger. Colonial's most recent business type activity was acquiring and holding tax-exempt bonds. This was Colonial's historic business at the time of the merger for purposes of determining whether there was a continuity of business enterprise.[14]

As of October 31, 1993, Colonial held approximately $7.35 million in tax-exempt bonds and approximately $1,500 in cash. On December 31, 1993, Colonial liquidated some of those bonds for more than $2,550,000. As a result, Colonial's cash position increased significantly.

The fair market value of the tax-exempt bonds held directly by Colonial totaled $4,549,146 just before the merger on December 31, 1993. Three days after the merger, Central distributed these same tax-exempt bonds to Mr. Honbarrier. [U]nlike Colonial, Central did not invest in tax-exempt

---

14. We recognize that investment activity is not a trade or business for some purposes. However, investment activity has been recognized as a historic business for purposes of the continuity of business enterprise doctrine.

bonds. Central placed its money in short-term liquid investments, such as certificates of deposit because it needed cash and cash equivalents to operate its business. Thus, we conclude that Central did not continue Colonial's business of holding tax-exempt bonds.

2.   Significant Use of Acquired Corporation's Business Assets

Continuity of business enterprise can also be satisfied if the acquiring corporation uses a significant portion of the acquired corporation's historic business assets in a business. See Reg. § 1.368–1(d)(3)(i). A corporation's historic business assets are the assets used in its historic business. See Reg. § 1.368–1(d)(3)(ii). Business assets may include stock and securities. In general, the determination of the portion of the corporation's assets considered "significant" is based on the relative importance of the assets to the operation of the business. See Reg. § 1.368–1(d)(3)(iii). However, all other facts and circumstances, such as the net fair market value of those assets, will be considered.

Colonial's historic business assets were its tax-exempt bonds. It was never intended that Colonial's tax-exempt bonds be held by Central and, after the merger, Central did not use those assets in its business. On the day of the merger, Colonial liquidated some tax-exempt bonds for more than $2.5 million in cash. On the same day, Central made a cash distribution to Central's shareholders in the total amount of $2,450,854. Three days after the merger, tax-exempt bonds totaling $4,549,146 that had been held by Colonial were distributed to Mr. Honbarrier.

As a result of the transactions surrounding the merger, all of Colonial's investments in tax-exempt bonds were disposed of and Colonial ceased to exist. We find that Central did not use a significant portion of Colonial's historic business assets in a business.

3.   Conclusion

Central did not continue either Colonial's historic business or use a significant portion of Colonial's historic business assets in a business. As a result, Central did not satisfy the continuity of business enterprise requirement.

We hold that the merger of Colonial into Central was not a tax-free reorganization within the meaning of section 368(a)(1)(A). Because this merger did not qualify as a reorganization under section 368(a)(1)(A), Mr. Honbarrier's exchange of Colonial stock for valuable consideration was a taxable event. Colonial's assets had a net fair market value of $7,245,051 at the time Colonial was merged into Central. Petitioners acknowledge that Mr. Honbarrier received full fair market value for his stock in Colonial. Mr. Honbarrier must therefore recognize capital gain of $6,953,545, which is equal to the excess of the fair market value of assets he received for his Colonial stock ($7,245,051) over his basis ($291,506).

In the notice of deficiency to Colonial, respondent determined that Colonial had a gain on the sale or exchange of its assets in the merger transaction. However, respondent now agrees that Colonial did not realize any gain because the fair market value of its assets equaled its tax basis in those assets.

NOTES

1. *Timing of the distribution.* Would the court have reached a different result if Central had refrained from declaring the $7,000,000 distribution until after the merger of Colonial into Central? Under these circumstances, would it matter if Central had formulated an intent to declare the distribution before the merger? How soon after the merger could the distribution have been made without violating the continuity of business enterprise requirement? See Payne v. Commissioner, 85 T.C.M. 1073 (2003) (finding that the continuity of business enterprise requirement was satisfied where the target corporation's assets were sold by the acquiring corporation less than three months after being acquired where no direct evidence existed that the later sale was part of an overall plan existing when the assets were acquired).

2. *Reversing the transaction.* Would the continuity of business enterprise requirement have been satisfied if, rather than Colonial merging into Central, Central had merged into Colonial?

3. *Corporate level gain.* The final paragraph of the Honbarrier opinion indicates that the Internal Revenue Service also asserted a deficiency against Colonial. Why was Colonial potentially subject to tax?

3. PLAN OF REORGANIZATION

King Enterprises, Inc. v. United States

United States Court of Claims, 1969.
418 F.2d 511.

PER CURIAM: [The Court adopted the following opinion as the basis for its judgment.]

■ BERNHARDT, COMMISSIONER: * * * Petitioner, King Enterprises, Inc., is a Tennessee corporation * * *. It was one of 11 shareholders in Tenco, Inc., a corporation organized in 1951 to supply its shareholders with a reliable source of instant coffee for them to market under their own brand names. Tenco was financially successful over the years, and by 1959 had become the second largest producer of soluble coffee in the United States * * *.

Minute Maid Corporation had become by 1958 one of the nation's principal producers of frozen concentrated citrus juices. Because of financial reverses in 1957 Minute Maid decided to acquire other businesses in order to stabilize its income * * *. A * * * proposal [by Minute Maid to acquire the stock of Tenco] was approved by the respective boards on August 25, 1959, and on September 3, 1959, petitioner and other Tenco shareholders signed an agreement with Minute Maid entitled "Purchase and Sale Agreement".

Pursuant to the Agreement providing for the sale of their Tenco stock to Minute Maid, the Tenco shareholders received a total consideration consisting of $3,000,000 in cash, $2,550,000 in promissory notes, and 311,996 shares of Minute Maid stock valued at $5,771,926. Petitioner's share of the total consideration consisted of $281,564.25 in cash, $239,329.40 in promissory notes, and 29,282 shares of Minute Maid stock valued at $541,717. The Minute Maid stock received by Tenco stockholders represented 15.62 percent of the total outstanding Minute Maid shares, and constituted in excess of 50 percent of the total consideration received.

On December 10, 1959, the Minute Maid directors approved the November 24th recommendation of its general counsel to merge the company's four subsidiaries, including Tenco, into the parent company, and authorized that the merger be submitted to its stockholders for approval * * *. On April 30 and May 2, 1960, in accordance with the applicable state laws, Tenco and certain other subsidiaries were merged into Minute Maid.

On its income tax return for the fiscal year ended June 30, 1960, petitioner reported the cash and notes received as dividend income, subject to the 85 percent intercorporate dividends received deduction.[15] The value of the Minute Maid stock received by petitioner was not reported, it being petitioner's position that such stock was received in connection with a nontaxable corporate reorganization. The District Director of Internal Revenue assessed a deficiency on the ground that the gain portion of the total consideration received (cash, notes, and Minute Maid stock) constituted taxable capital gain from the sale of a capital asset. Petitioner paid the deficiency, then sued here.

Petitioner contends that the transfer by the Tenco stockholders of their Tenco stock to Minute Maid in exchange for Minute Maid stock, cash and notes, followed by the merger of Tenco into Minute Maid, were steps in a unified transaction qualifying as a reorganization under section 368(a)(1)(A) of the 1954 Code. Consequently, petitioner continues, the Minute Maid stock was received by it pursuant to the plan of reorganization and is nontaxable as such, while the cash and notes received constitute a dividend distribution to which the 85 percent intercorporate dividends received deduction is applicable. The Government asserts that the transfer of Tenco stock to Minute Maid was an independent sales transaction; therefore, the entire gain realized by petitioner on the payment to it of cash, notes and Minute Maid stock is taxable as gain from the sale of a capital asset.

I

The Reorganization Issue

The threshold issue is whether the transfer of Tenco stock to Minute Maid is to be treated for tax purposes as an independent transaction of

---

15.   Editor's note. The 85% dividend received deduction no longer exists. Under current law, a corporate recipient of dividends may normally deduct 70%, 80% or 100% of the dividends it receives. See I.R.C. § 243; pp. 59–63.

sale, or as a transitory step in a transaction qualifying as a corporate reorganization * * *.

The general rule is that when property is sold or otherwise disposed of, any gain realized must also be recognized, absent an appropriate nonrecognition provision in the Internal Revenue Code. One such nonrecognition provision [is] section 354(a)(1) * * *.

By its terms, this exception to the general rule of taxation depends * * * on the existence of a corporate reorganization * * *.

The premise of the corporate reorganization provisions is that certain transactions constitute corporate readjustments and are not the proper occasion for the incidence of taxation. Congressional policy is to free from tax consequences those corporate reorganizations involving a continuity of business enterprise under modified corporate form and a continuity of interest on the part of the owners before and after, where there is no basic change in relationships and not a sufficient "cashing in" of proprietary interests to justify contemporaneous taxation.

It is not disputed that there was a Type A reorganization in April 1960 when Tenco and Minute Maid were merged in accordance with state law. Nor does the Government dispute that Minute Maid continued the business of Tenco following the merger, or that the former Tenco shareholders had a continuity of interest in the enterprise by virtue of their ownership of stock in Minute Maid received in the exchange. The disagreement centers on whether the initial exchange of stock was a step in a unified transaction pursuant to a "plan of reorganization".

The underlying theory of the petitioner's claim is that the tax consequences of business transactions are properly determined by their substance and not by the form in which they are cast. Thus petitioner views the substance of the transaction under review to be an acquisition by Minute Maid of Tenco's assets in exchange for transferring Minute Maid stock, cash and notes to Tenco's stockholders. The value of the Minute Maid stock received, which exceeded 50 percent of the total consideration, constituted a sufficient continuity of interest to support a Type A reorganization. Petitioner concludes, therefore, that the net result of the entire transaction is a reorganization, not to be altered by splitting the entire transaction into its component transitory steps. Petitioner's conclusion is justified in fact and in law.

The problem of deciding whether to accord the separate steps of a complex transaction independent significance, or to treat them as related steps in a unified transaction, is a recurring problem in the field of tax law. The principle that even extended business transactions have determinate limits for tax purposes is based on a strong preference for "closed transactions" upon which to impose tax consequences. This preference is tempered, however, with respect for the integrity of an entire transaction. Accordingly, the essence of the step transaction doctrine is that an "integrated transaction must not be broken into independent steps or, conversely, that the separate steps must be taken together in attaching tax consequences''. The mere recitation of the doctrine, however, does not clarify the necessary relationship between the steps requisite to characterization as an integrated transaction.

[T]here is no universal test applicable to step transaction situations. It has been persuasively suggested that ''the aphorisms about 'closely related steps' and 'integrated transactions' may have different meanings in different contexts, and that there may be not one rule, but several, depending on the substantive provision of the Code to which they are being applied.''

[T]he courts have enunciated two basic tests. The ''interdependence test'' requires an inquiry as to ''whether on a reasonable interpretation of objective facts the steps were so interdependent that the legal relations created by one transaction would have been fruitless without a completion of the series''. The ''end result'' test, on the other hand, establishes a standard whereby:

> * * * purportedly separate transactions will be amalgamated into a single transaction when it appears that they were really component parts of a single transaction intended from the outset to be taken for the purpose of reaching the ultimate result.

In support of its position that the step transaction doctrine is inapplicable to the facts of this case the government correctly points out that there was no binding commitment for the merger of Tenco to follow the acquisition of its stock. Defendant erroneously concludes, however, that the absence of such a commitment here renders the step transaction doctrine inapplicable. The binding commitment requirement, relied upon by the Government, was enunciated by the Supreme Court in Commissioner v. Gordon wherein the Court said, ''if one transaction is to be characterized as a 'first step' there must be a binding commitment to take the later steps'' * * *.

* * *.

The opinion in Gordon contains not the slightest indication that the Supreme Court intended the binding commitment requirement as the touchstone of the step transaction doctrine in tax law * * *. Clearly, the step transaction doctrine would be a dead letter if restricted to situations where the parties were bound to take certain steps.

The doctrine derives vitality, rather, from its application where the form of a transaction *does not require* a particular further step be taken; but, once taken, the substance of the transaction reveals that the ultimate result was intended from the outset. In the majority of cases, it is the Government that relies on the step transaction doctrine for tax characterization. General application of the binding commitment requirement would effectively insure taxpayers of virtual exemption from the doctrine merely by refraining from such commitments. Such an untoward result cannot be intended by the Gordon opinion * * *.

In the alternative, the Government asserts that the step transaction doctrine has no application to this case because the merger of Tenco into Minute Maid was not the intended end result from the outset. Although the appropriate standard is invoked, defendant's assertion is inconsistent with the inferences to be drawn from the record.

The operative facts emerging from the record in this case suggest that Minute Maid, desirous of diversifying its operations in order to stabilize its income, was presented with the opportunity to acquire the entire stock of Tenco * * *. After the stock acquisition, moreover, Minute Maid was at liberty to operate Tenco as a wholly owned subsidiary, if it so desired. There is no persuasive evidence, however, that Minute Maid's appetite was limited to these goals * * *. On the contrary, the record reveals that, prior to the acquisition of Tenco stock, the officers of Minute Maid considered merging its existing subsidiaries into the parent in order to eliminate some of the general ledgers and extra taxes, and to bring about other savings. In fact, the merger of subsidiaries as a money-saving device was Mr. Speeler's (Minute Maid's vice president and general counsel) pet idea, which he discussed with Minute Maid's President Fox before the initial agreement with Tenco.

* * *

No express intention on the part of Minute Maid to effect a merger of Tenco surfaces in the record until after the initial agreement to exchange stock. It strains credulity, however, to believe other than that the plan to merge was something more than inchoate, if something less than announced, at the time of such exchange. One gains the impression that the record of intentions is edited, so in reconstruction we must lean heavily on the logic of tell-tale facts and lightly on chameleon words. It is difficult to believe that sophisticated businessmen arranging a multimillion dollar transaction fraught with tax potentials were so innocent of knowledge of the tax consequences as the testimony purports * * *.

The operative facts in this case clearly justify the inference that the merger of Tenco into Minute Maid was the intended result of the transaction in question from the outset, the initial exchange of stock constituting a mere transitory step. Accordingly, it is concluded that the initial exchange and subsequent merger were steps in a unified transaction qualifying as a Type A reorganization, and that petitioner received its Minute Maid stock pursuant to the plan of reorganization shown by the facts and circumstances above to have existed.

II

The Dividend Issue

Pursuant to the plan of reorganization, petitioner received $281,564.25 in cash, $239,329.40 in promissory notes, and Minute Maid stock valued at $541,717. Section 356(a)(1) provides that the amount of gain realized by petitioner must also be recognized, but not in excess of the cash and notes (i.e., "boot") received. With respect to the character of petitioner's recognizable gain, section 356(a)(2) provides:

If an exchange is described in paragraph (1) but has the effect of the distribution of a dividend [(determined with the application of section

318(a))], then there shall be treated as a dividend to each distributee such an amount of the gain recognized under paragraph (1) as is not in excess of his ratable share of the undistributed earnings and profits of the corporation * * *.

* * *

There can be little doubt, on the facts of the present case, that the receipt of boot by petitioner was essentially equivalent to a dividend. Defendant has conceded this by implication in declining to contest the issue in its brief * * *. Accordingly, the gain recognizable under section 356(a)(1) by petitioner upon its receipt of boot is characterized under section 356(a)(2) as (1) dividend income to the extent of petitioner's ratable share of Tenco's accumulated earnings and profits * * *.

III

The Deduction Issue

Section 243(a) provides, in parts pertinent to this suit, that:

In the case of a corporation, there shall be allowed as a deduction an amount equal to the following percentages of the amount received as dividends * * *:

(1) 85 percent, in the case of dividends other than dividends described in paragraph (2) or (3); * * *.

It has been decided above that the gain recognizable by petitioner upon its receipt of boot is characterized under section 356(a)(2) as dividend income to the extent of petitioner's ratable share of Tenco's accumulated earnings and profits. Thus, it is now concluded that petitioner is entitled under section 243(a)(1) to a dividends received deduction in the amount of 85 percent of the dividend portion of its recognizable gain * * *.

* * *

NOTES

1. *Magnitude of gain.* King Enterprises apparently treated the entire amount of the cash and notes as a dividend. In light of this position, what can be inferred about the relationship between the amount of gain King Enterprises realized and the amount of cash and notes it received? See I.R.C. § 356(a)(1).

2. *Characterization of boot gain.* When gain is recognized in a reorganization, it is characterized as capital gain unless it "has the effect of the distribution of a dividend." I.R.C. § 356(a)(2). Why was dividend treatment desirable to King Enterprises? See I.R.C. § 243. Some of the other shareholders of Tenco were individuals. Would an individual shareholder prefer capital gain treatment or dividend treatment? See I.R.C. § 1(h)(11). The Supreme Court has delineated an elaborate test for determining when a distribution of cash or other property in a reorganization has the effect of the distribution of a dividend. See Commissioner v. Clark, 489 U.S. 726, 109 S.Ct. 1455 (1989). Now that an individual's dividends and capital gains are generally taxed at the same rate, the importance of the Clark test has declined considerably.

3. *Alternative tests for step-transaction doctrine.* Courts have traditionally selected from among three different tests when determining whether to apply the step-transaction doctrine to a particular fact pattern; the end result test, the interdependence test, and the binding commitment test. The most commonly used tests are the end result test and the interdependence test. As the King Enterprises court notes, courts are often reluctant to adopt the third test, the binding commitment test, because of the ease with which taxpayers can avoid its application.

Which of the three tests did the King Enterprises court adopt? Would the court have reached the same result if it had adopted one of the other tests? The regulations now explicitly acknowledge that the step-transaction doctrine is to be applied when determining whether a transaction qualifies as a reorganization. Treas. Reg. § 1.368–1(a).

4. *Step-transaction doctrine and plan of reorganization.* What relationship exists between the step-transaction doctrine and the "plan of reorganization" requirement?

4.   Scope of a Merger

Revenue Ruling 2000–5

2000–5 I.R.B. 436.

ISSUES

Whether a transaction in which (1) a target corporation "merges" under state law with and into an acquiring corporation and the target corporation does not go out of existence, or (2) a target corporation "merges" under state law with and into two or more acquiring corporations and the target corporation goes out of existence, qualifies as a reorganization under § 368(a)(1)(A) of the Internal Revenue Code?

FACTS

Situation (1). A target corporation transfers some of its assets and liabilities to an acquiring corporation, retains the remainder of its assets and liabilities, and remains in existence following the transaction. The target corporation's shareholders receive stock in the acquiring corporation in exchange for part of their target corporation stock and they retain their remaining target corporation stock. The transaction qualifies as a merger under state X corporate law.

Situation (2). A target corporation transfers some of its assets and liabilities to each of two acquiring corporations. The target corporation liquidates and the target corporation's shareholders receive stock in each of the two acquiring corporations in exchange for their target corporation stock. The transaction qualifies as a merger under state X corporate law.

DISCUSSION

* * *

Historically, corporate law merger statutes have operated to ensure that "[a] merger ordinarily is an absorption by one corporation of the properties and franchises of another whose stock it has acquired. The merged corporation ceases to exist, and the merging corporation alone survives." Cortland Specialty Co. v. Commissioner, 60 F.2d 937, 939 (2d Cir.1932). Thus, unlike § 368(a)(1)(C), in which Congress included a "substantially all the properties" requirement, it was not necessary for Congress to explicitly include a similar requirement in § 368(a)(1)(A) because corporate law merger statutes contemplated an acquisition of the target corporation's assets by the surviving corporation by operation of law.

Compliance with a corporate law merger statute does not by itself qualify a transaction as a reorganization. See, e.g., Roebling v. Commissioner [p. 568]. In addition to satisfying the requirements of business purpose, continuity of business enterprise and continuity of interest, in order to qualify as a reorganization under § 368(a)(1)(A), a transaction effectuated under a corporate law merger statute must have the result that one corporation acquires the assets of the target corporation by operation of the corporate law merger statute and the target corporation ceases to exist. The transactions described in Situations (1) and (2) do not have the result that one corporation acquires the assets of the target corporation by operation of the corporate law merger statute and the target corporation ceases to exist. Therefore, these transactions do not qualify as reorganizations under § 368(a)(1)(A).

In contrast with the operation of corporate law merger statutes, a divisive transaction is one in which a corporation's assets are divided among two or more corporations. Section 355 provides tax-free treatment for certain divisive transactions, but only if a number of specific requirements are satisfied. [Section 355 is examined in Chapter 15.] Congress intended that § 355 be the sole means under which divisive transactions will be afforded tax-free status and, thus, specifically required the liquidation of the acquired corporation in reorganizations under both §§ 368(a)(1)(C) and 368(a)(1)(D) in order to prevent these reorganizations from being used in divisive transactions that did not satisfy § 355. No specific liquidation requirement was necessary for statutory mergers because corporate law merger statutes contemplated that only one corporation survived a merger. The transaction described in Situation (1) is divisive because, after the transaction, the target corporation's assets and liabilities are held by both the target corporation and acquiring corporation and the target corporation's shareholders hold stock in both the target corporation and acquiring corporation. The transaction described in Situation (2) is divisive because, after the transaction, the target corporation's assets and liabilities are held by each of the two acquiring corporations and the target corporation's shareholders hold stock in each of the two acquiring corporations.

HOLDING

The transactions described in Situations (1) and (2) do not qualify as reorganizations under § 368(a)(1)(A). However, the transactions described in Situations (1) and (2) possibly may qualify for tax-free treatment under other provisions of the Code.

NOTE

Regulations define a merger. Regulations clarifying the definition of a merger for reorganization purposes adopt the views advanced in Revenue Ruling 2000–5. See Treas. Reg. §§ 1.368–2(b)(1)(ii), (iii) Example 1.

E. Acquisition By Subsidiary For Parent Stock

The acquisition techniques explored in this chapter have thus far involved the acquisition by one corporation (the "parent") of the assets or stock of another corporation (the "target"). Quite often, however, it is desirable to utilize a new or existing corporation, all of the stock of which is owned by the parent (a "subsidiary"), to acquire the assets or stock of the target. Utilizing a subsidiary as the acquisition vehicle is particularly important when the parent owns other assets that it does not wish to expose to the liabilities of the target. If a subsidiary acquires the target's business, the parent's assets are not exposed to the liabilities of the target.

When a subsidiary acquires the assets or stock of the target in exchange for stock, stock of the parent is often utilized as the consideration for the acquisition. From the target shareholders' perspective, parent stock may be a more attractive commodity than subsidiary stock because it gives the target shareholders a proprietary interest in all the parent's businesses, not just the subsidiary's business. From the standpoint of the parent, utilizing parent stock enables the parent to retain 100% ownership of the subsidiary. In contrast, utilizing subsidiary stock to fund the acquisition would dilute the parent's ownership of the subsidiary. Although the Internal Revenue Code originally impeded the acquisition of target assets or stock by a subsidiary in exchange for parent stock, the impediments have, for the most part, been eliminated.

1. Acquisition of Assets or Stock by Subsidiary
I.R.C. §§ 368(a)(1)(B), (C), 368(b)

Groman v. Commissioner
Supreme Court of the United States, 1937.
302 U.S. 82, 58 S.Ct. 108.

■ Mr. Justice Roberts delivered the opinion of the Court.

This case involves the meaning and scope of the phrase "a party to a reorganization" as used in [the predecessor to I.R.C. § 368(b)].

January 29, 1929, the petitioner, and all other shareholders of Metals Refining Company, an Indiana corporation, hereinafter designated Indiana, entered into a contract with the Glidden Company, an Ohio corporation, reciting that the shareholders of Indiana [wanted to combine] * * * the properties of their company with Glidden and with a corporation Glidden was to organize under the laws of Ohio, which corporation we shall call Ohio. The shareholders [of Indiana] covenanted that they would assign their shares to Ohio * * * and Glidden covenanted that it would issue and deliver, or cause to be issued and delivered, to the shareholders a stated number of shares of its own [preferred] * * * stock * * *, a stated number of shares of the preferred stock of Ohio, * * * and * * * cash to equal the appraised value of Indiana's assets * * *, and that, after the exchange of stock, Glidden would cause Indiana to transfer its assets to Ohio.

Glidden organized Ohio and became the owner of all its common stock but none of its preferred stock. Pursuant to the contract the shareholders of Indiana transferred their stock to Ohio and received therefor a total consideration of $1,207,016 consisting of Glidden [preferred] * * * stock valued at $533,980, shares of the preferred stock of Ohio valued at $500,000, and $153,036 in cash. Indiana then transferred its assets to Ohio and was dissolved.

As a result of the reorganization petitioner received shares of Glidden stock, shares of Ohio stock, and $17,293 in cash. [H]e included the $17,293 as income received but ignored the shares of Glidden and of Ohio as stock received in exchange in a reorganization. The respondent ruled that Glidden was not a party to a reorganization within the meaning of the Revenue Act, treated the transaction as a taxable exchange to the extent of the cash and shares of Glidden, and determined a deficiency of $7,420. [T]he Board of Tax Appeals * * * reversed the Commissioner, holding that Glidden was a party to a reorganization. The Circuit Court of Appeals reversed the Board. We granted the writ of certiorari because of an alleged conflict of decision.

[The predecessor to I.R.C. § 354(a)] declares that "No gain or loss shall be recognized if stock or securities in a corporation a party to a reorganization are, in pursuance of the plan of reorganization, exchanged solely for stock or securities in such corporation or in another corporation a party to the reorganization." * * *

[The predecessor to I.R.C. § 368(b) provided]: "The term 'a party to a reorganization' includes a corporation resulting from a reorganization and includes both corporations in the case of an acquisition by one corporation of at least a majority of the voting stock and at least a majority of the total number of shares of all other classes of stock of another corporation."

It is agreed that under the plain terms of the statute the cash received by the petitioner was income, and that as the stock of Ohio was obtained in part payment for that of Indiana, the exchange, to that extent, did not give rise to income to be included in the computation of petitioner's tax.

The question is whether that portion of the consideration consisting of [preferred stock] of Glidden should be recognized in determining petitioner's taxable gain. The decision of this question depends upon whether Glidden's stock was that of a party to the reorganization for, if so, the statute declares gain or loss due to its receipt shall not be included in the taxpayer's computation of income for the year in which the exchange was made.

If [the predecessor to I.R.C. § 368(b) (quoted above)] is a definition of a party to a reorganization and excludes corporations not therein described, Glidden was not a party since its relation to the transaction is not within the terms of the definition. It was not a corporation resulting from the reorganization; and it did not acquire a majority of the shares of voting stock and a majority of the shares of all other classes of stock of any other corporation in the reorganization. The Circuit Court of Appeals thought the section was intended as a definition of the term party as used in the Act and excluded all corporations not specifically described. It therefore held Glidden could not be considered a party to the reorganization.

The petitioner contends, we think correctly, that the section is not a definition but rather is intended to enlarge the connotation of the term "a party to a reorganization" to embrace corporations whose relation to the transaction would not in common usage be so denominated or as to whose status doubt might otherwise arise. This conclusion is fortified by the fact that when an exclusive definition is intended the word "means" is employed * * *, whereas here the word used is "includes." * * *

* * *

[T]he crucial question is whether Glidden was a party to the reorganization thus effected. Glidden received nothing from the shareholders of Indiana. The exchange was between Indiana's shareholders and Ohio. Do the facts that Glidden contracted for the exchange and made it possible by subscribing and paying for Ohio's common stock in cash, so that Ohio could consummate the exchange, render Glidden a party to the reorganization? No * * *. Glidden was, in the transaction in question, no more than the efficient agent in bringing about a reorganization. It was not, in the natural meaning of the term, a party to the reorganization.

* * *

We hold that Glidden was not a party to the reorganization and the receipt of its stock by Indiana's shareholders in exchange, in part, for their stock was the basis for computation of taxable gain to them * * *.

NOTES

1. *Triangular B reorganization.* If Ohio had acquired all of the stock of Indiana solely for voting stock of Glidden, would the transaction qualify as a "reorganization" under current law? See I.R.C. § 368(a)(1)(B) (first parenthetical). Would Glidden be a "party to a reorganization" under current law? See I.R.C. § 368(b) (second sentence). Why is it important that Glidden be treated as a "party to a reorganization" under these circumstances? See I.R.C. § 354(a)(1).

2. *Triangular C reorganization.* If Ohio had acquired all of the assets of Indiana solely for voting stock of Glidden, would the transaction qualify as a "reorganization" under current law? See I.R.C. § 368(a)(1)(C) (first parenthetical). Would Glidden be a "party to a reorganization" under current law? See I.R.C. § 368(b) (second sentence). If Ohio acquired all of the assets of Indiana in exchange for voting stock of Glidden (representing 90% of the consideration) and voting stock of Ohio (representing 10% of the consideration), would the transaction qualify as a "reorganization" under current law? See I.R.C. § 368(a)(2)(B).

2. MERGER INTO SUBSIDIARY

I.R.C. §§ 368(a)(2)(D), (b)

Treas. Reg. § 1.368–2(b)(2)

Revenue Ruling 67–326

1967–2 Cum.Bull. 143.

Advice has been requested whether the nonrecognition provisions of section 361(a) * * * apply to a transaction qualifying as a merger under applicable State law where the acquiring corporation exchanged the stock of its parent for all of the assets of an unrelated corporation and whether section 354(a) * * * will apply to the exchange by the shareholders of the acquired corporation of all of their stock of the acquired corporation for stock of the parent of the acquiring corporation.

Corporation S is a wholly owned subsidiary of P corporation. In a transaction which qualified as a merger under the law of the State in which S and X are incorporated, S acquired from X, an unrelated corporation, all of its assets and assumed all of its liabilities in exchange for stock of P which had previously been contributed to S. Pursuant to the plan of reorganization, the shareholders of X exchanged their stock of X for stock of P.

[I]n order for [I.R.C. § 361(a)] to be applicable to the exchange of assets by X for stock of P, X and P must be parties to the reorganization.

[I]n order for [I.R.C. § 354(a)] to be applicable to the exchange of X stock by the shareholders of X for stock of P, X and P must be parties to the reorganization.

* * *

Section 368(b) of the Code provides that in the case of a reorganization qualifying under paragraph (1)(B) or (1)(C) of section 368(a) of the Code, if the stock exchanged for the stock or properties of another corporation is stock of a corporation which is in control of the acquiring corporation, the term "a party to a reorganization" includes the corporation so controlling the acquiring corporation. Section 368(b) of the Code does not include, however, as a party to a reorganization a corporation which is in control of the acquiring corporation in a reorganization qualifying under section 368(a)(1)(A) of the Code.

Accordingly, although the transaction described is a statutory merger of S and X under State law, the nontaxable provisions of section 361(a) of the Code will not apply to the exchange of the assets of X for stock of P and section 354(a) will not apply to the exchange by the shareholders of X of their stock of X for stock of P.

[S]ection 368(b) of the Code includes as a party to a reorganization described in section 368(a)(1)(C) of the Code a corporation which is in control of the acquiring corporation. Therefore, if the transaction otherwise qualifies as a reorganization as defined in section 368(a)(1)(C) of the Code, the nonrecognition provisions of sections 361(a) and 354(a) of the Code will apply to the exchanges described.

NOTES

1. *Forward triangular merger.* The transaction described in the ruling could qualify as an A reorganization under current law. See I.R.C. § 368(a)(2)(D). When a transaction qualifies as an A reorganization under I.R.C. § 368(a)(2)(D), is the parent treated as a "party to a reorganization?" See I.R.C. § 368(b) (fourth sentence). Why is this treatment important? See I.R.C. §§ 354(a)(1), 361(a). "Forward triangular merger" is a shorthand way of referring to the merger of a target corporation into a subsidiary when the target shareholders receive parent stock and the subsidiary is the surviving corporation.

2. *Forward triangular merger versus C reorganization.* Is it easier under current law to qualify a subsidiary acquisition as an A reorganization or a C reorganization? See I.R.C. §§ 368(a)(1)(C), (2)(B), (2)(D).

3. *Tax consequences to subsidiary in triangular acquisition.* When parent stock is used as the consideration in a triangular B reorganization, a triangular C reorganization, or a forward triangular merger, is any gain (or loss) in the parent stock recognized? See Treas. Reg. § 1.1032–2.

3. ACQUISITION BY PARENT FOLLOWED BY "DROP DOWN"

I.R.C. § 368(a)(2)(C)

In lieu of utilizing a subsidiary corporation as an acquisition vehicle, the same end result can be achieved if the parent acquires the assets or stock of the target (or the target is merged into the parent) and the acquired assets or stock are immediately transferred to a new or existing subsidiary of the parent (a "drop-down"). If the acquisition would qualify as an A reorganization, a B reorganization or a C reorganization in the absence of the drop-down, might the drop-down of target assets or stock spoil the reorganization? Note how the statute responds to this potential problem. See I.R.C. § 368(a)(2)(C).

When a corporation acquires target assets or stock which it immediately transfers to a subsidiary, the subsidiary will likely be treated as the "acquiring corporation". In this situation, can parent stock received by the target shareholders qualify for nonrecognition treatment under I.R.C. § 354(a)(1)? See I.R.C. § 368(b) (third sentence).

Although the tax consequences are normally the same regardless of whether a subsidiary acquires assets or stock of a target corporation in exchange for parent stock or the parent acquires target assets or stock which it immediately transfers to a subsidiary, the latter approach exposes the parent to the liabilities of the target (at least in the case of an asset acquisition or a merger). Hence, for non-tax reasons, it is often preferable to use the subsidiary as the acquisition vehicle.

Revenue Ruling 2002–85

2002–52 I.R.B. 986.

ISSUE

Whether an acquiring corporation's transfer of a target corporation's assets to a subsidiary controlled by the acquiring corporation as part of a plan of reorganization will prevent a transaction that otherwise qualifies as a reorganization under § 368(a)(1)(D) of the Internal Revenue Code from so qualifying.

FACTS

A, an individual, owns 100 percent of T, a state X corporation. A also owns 100 percent of P, a state Y corporation. For valid business reasons and pursuant to a plan of reorganization,

(i) T transfers all of its assets to P in exchange for consideration consisting of 70 percent P voting stock and 30 percent cash,

(ii) T then liquidates, distributing the P voting stock and cash to A, and

(iii) P subsequently transfers all of the T assets to S, a preexisting, wholly owned state X subsidiary of P, in exchange for stock of S.

S will continue T's historic business after the transfer and P will retain the S stock. Without regard to P's transfer of all the T assets to S, the transaction qualifies as a reorganization under § 368(a)(1)(D).

LAW

* * *

Section 368(a)(2)(C) provides that a transaction otherwise qualifying under §§ 368(a)(1)(A), (B), (C), or (G) shall not be disqualified by reason of the fact that part or all of the assets or stock which were acquired in the transaction are transferred to a corporation controlled by the corporation acquiring such assets or stock.

* * *

Congress enacted § 368(a)(2)(C) in response to the Supreme Court decisions in Groman v. Commissioner [p. 602], and Helvering v. Bashford, 302 U.S. 454 (1938). * * * As originally enacted, § 368(a)(2)(C) applied only to reorganizations under §§ 368(a)(1)(A) and 368(a)(1)(C), but Congress has since amended the statute to apply to * * * reorganizations under § 368(a)(1)(B) and § 368(a)(1)(G).

* * *

ANALYSIS

[Section 368(a)(2)(C) does not indicate] that an acquiring corporation's transfer of assets to a controlled subsidiary necessarily prevents a transaction that otherwise qualifies as a reorganization under § 368(a)(1)(D) from so qualifying. Because § 368(a)(2)(C) is permissive and not exclusive or restrictive, the absence of § 368(a)(1)(D) from § 368(a)(2)(C) does not indicate that such a transfer following a transaction that otherwise qualifies as a reorganization under § 368(a)(1)(D) will prevent the transaction from qualifying as such. * * *

Accordingly, an acquiring corporation's transfer of assets to a controlled subsidiary following a transaction that otherwise qualifies as a reorganization under § 368(a)(1)(D) will not cause a transaction to fail to qualify as such, provided that the original transferee is treated as acquiring substantially all of the assets of the target corporation, the transaction satisfies the [continuity of business enterprise ("COBE")] requirement and does not fail under the remote continuity principle of Groman and Bashford, and the transfer of assets to a controlled corporation does not prevent the original transferee from being a "party to the reorganization."

Section 354(b)(1)(A) requires that, in a reorganization under § 368(a)(1)(D), the corporation to which the assets are transferred acquire substantially all of the assets of the transferor of such assets. In this case, the requirement that P acquire substantially all of T's assets is satisfied because P retains the stock of S.

To qualify as a reorganization under § 368(a)(1)(D), a transaction must satisfy the COBE requirement of § 1.368–1(d). In the present transaction, P and S constitute a qualified group, and S will continue T's historic business after the transfer. Therefore, the transaction satisfies the COBE requirement.

* * *

Under the COBE regulations, stock or assets acquired in transactions that satisfy certain provisions of § 368(a)(1) may be transferred without limitation to successive lower-tier controlled subsidiaries within a qualified group. * * * Accordingly, a transfer of acquired stock or assets will not cause a transaction to fail for remote continuity if it satisfies the COBE requirement.

Under the facts described above, P's transfer of the T assets to S pursuant to the plan of reorganization satisfies the COBE requirement. Therefore, the transaction does not fail for remote continuity.

* * *

Reorganizations under § 368(a)(1)(D), like reorganizations under §§ 368(a)(1)(A) and 368(a)(1)(C), are asset reorganizations. In reorganizations under §§ 368(a)(1)(A) and 368(a)(1)(C), the original transferee is treated as a party to a reorganization, even if the acquired assets are transferred to a controlled subsidiary of the original transferee. The differences between reorganizations under § 368(a)(1)(D) on the one hand and reorganizations under §§ 368(a)(1)(A) and 368(a)(1)(C) on the other hand do not warrant treating the original transferee in a transaction that otherwise satisfies the requirements of a reorganization under § 368(a)(1)(D) differently from the original transferee in a reorganization under §§ 368(a)(1)(A) or 368(a)(1)(C). Therefore, the original transferee in a transaction that otherwise satisfies the requirements of a reorganization under § 368(a)(1)(D) is treated as a party to the reorganization, notwithstanding the original transferee's transfer of acquired assets to a controlled subsidiary of the original transferee.

For the reasons set forth above, P's transfer of the T assets to S will not prevent P's acquisition of those assets from T in exchange for P voting stock and cash from qualifying as a reorganization under § 368(a)(1)(D).

HOLDING

An acquiring corporation's transfer of the target corporation's assets to a subsidiary controlled by the acquiring corporation as part of a plan of reorganization will not prevent a transaction that otherwise qualifies as a reorganization under § 368(a)(1)(D) from so qualifying.

NOTE

1. *C reorganization treatment.* Could the transaction in Rev. Rul. 2002–85 have qualified as a C reorganization?

2. *Regulations expand permissible post-reorganization transfers of assets or stock.* The regulations now delineate a wide range of post-reorganization distributions, or other transfers, of assets or stock of the corporations participating in the acquisition that will not jeopardize reorganization treatment. See Treas. Reg. § 1.368–2(k).

F. REVERSE TRIANGULAR MERGER

I.R.C. § 368(a)(2)(E)

Treas. Reg. § 1.368–2(j)

"Reverse triangular merger" is a shorthand way of referring to the merger of a subsidiary into the target corporation where the *target* is the surviving corporation. In contrast, the *subsidiary* is the surviving corporation in a forward triangular merger. The substantive effects of the two transactions are very similar. In both transactions, the target shareholders receive parent stock (or boot) as consideration for their target stock and the parent emerges from the transaction owning the stock of the surviving corporation. In form, however, a forward triangular merger resembles an asset acquisition because the subsidiary acquires all of the target's assets and the target ceases to exist. In contrast, a reverse triangular merger resembles a stock acquisition because the assets of the target remain with the target and the stock of the target is owned by the parent after the acquisition. Thus, the reverse triangular merger is often analyzed as a potential B reorganization.

1. TREATMENT AS A "B" REORGANIZATION

Revenue Ruling 67–448

1967–2 Cum.Bull. 144.

Advice has been requested whether the transaction described below qualifies as a reorganization within the meaning of section 368(a)(1)(B) of the Internal Revenue Code * * *.

Corporation P and Corporation Y, incorporated in the same state, are publicly owned corporations. Corporation P wanted to acquire the business of Corporation Y but could do so with an effective result only if the corporate entity of Y were continued intact due to the necessity of preserving its status as a regulated public utility. P also desired to eliminate the possibility of minority shareholders in the event less than all of the shareholders of Y agreed to the transaction. Since an outright acquisition of stock pursuant to a reorganization as defined in section 368(a)(1)(B) of the Code would not achieve this result, the plan of reorganization was consummated as follows:

(a) P transferred shares of its voting stock to its newly formed subsidiary, S, in exchange for shares of S stock.

(b) S (whose only asset consisted of a block of the voting stock of P) merged into Y in a transaction which qualified as a statutory merger under the applicable state law.

(c) Pursuant to the plan of reorganization and by operation of state law, the S stock owned by P was converted into Y stock. At the same time the Y stock held by its shareholders was exchanged for the P stock received by Y on the merger of S into Y. The end result of these actions was that P acquired from the shareholders of Y in exchange for its own voting stock more than 95 percent of the stock of Y.

(d) Y shareholders owning less than five percent of the stock of Y dissented to the merger and had the right to receive the appraised value of their shares paid solely from the assets of Y. No funds, or other property, have been or will be provided by P for this purpose.

Thus, upon the consummation of the plan of reorganization Y became a wholly owned subsidiary of P.

* * *

The transaction described above does not constitute a reorganization within the meaning of either section 368(a)(1)(A) or section 368(a)(1)(C) of the Code because no assets of Y were transferred to nor acquired by another corporation in the transaction but rather all assets (except for amounts paid to dissenting shareholders) were retained in the same corporate entity.

Section 368(a)(1)(B) of the Code provides in part that the term "reorganization" means the acquisition by one corporation, in exchange solely for all or a part of its voting stock, of stock of another corporation if, immediately after the acquisition, the acquiring corporation has control of such other corporation (whether or not such acquiring corporation had control immediately before the acquisition).

It is evident that the shortest route to the end result described above would have been achieved by a transfer of P voting stock directly to the shareholders of Y in exchange for their stock. This result is not negated because the transaction was cast in the form of a series of interrelated steps. The transitory existence of the new subsidiary, S, will be disregarded. The effect of all the steps taken in the series is that Y became a wholly owned subsidiary of P, and P transferred solely its voting stock to the former shareholders of Y.

Accordingly, the transaction will be treated as an acquisition by P, in exchange solely for part of its voting stock, of stock of Y in an amount constituting control * * * of Y, which qualifies as a reorganization within the meaning of section 368(a)(1)(B) of the Code.

NOTES

1. *Non-tax goals.* Quite clearly, an acquisition of all of the Y stock by P solely in exchange for P voting stock would have qualified as a B reorganization. Why would that transaction have failed to achieve the non-tax goals of the parties?

2. *Source of funds.* Why would it matter if the dissenting Y shareholders had been paid with funds of P, rather than with funds of Y? See I.R.C. § 368(a)(1)(B).

3. *Current law.* The transaction described in the ruling could qualify as an A reorganization under current law. See I.R.C. § 368(a)(2)(E). When a transaction qualifies as an A reorganization under I.R.C. § 368(a)(2)(E), is the parent corporation (the corporation whose stock is utilized as the consideration for the acquisition) a "party to a reorganization"? See I.R.C. § 368(b) (fifth sentence). Why does this matter? See I.R.C. § 354(a)(1).

Revenue Ruling 74–564

1974–2 Cum.Bull. 124.

* * *

Corporation P is a publicly owned holding company which owns 100 percent of the stock of corporation S, an operating company. S has owned 98 percent of the stock of corporation R, also an operating company, for a number of years. The remaining stock of R was publicly held.

Under a plan to provide S with greater flexibility in the operation of R by owning all of the stock of R, the following steps were taken:

(a) P formed corporation Z and contributed cash, to satisfy capital requirements, and shares of P voting common stock equivalent in number to the outstanding shares of R stock publicly held in exchange for all of the Z stock.

(b) P contributed all of the Z stock to the capital of S.

(c) Pursuant to a joint merger agreement, Z was then merged into R under applicable state law, and R, the surviving corporation, acquired the P stock contributed to Z by P.

Each share of publicly held R common stock was exchanged for a share of P common stock, and the outstanding Z stock owned by S was converted into R stock. The cash transferred by P to Z was, upon the merger, transferred to R and from R to S and then back to P. R shareholders owning less than 5 percent of the publicly held R common stock dissented to the merger and had the right to receive the appraised value of their shares paid solely from assets of R. No funds, or other property, have been or will be provided by P for this purpose. After the consummation of the plan of reorganization described above, R continued its business but as a wholly owned subsidiary of S.

Section 368(a)(2)(E) of the Code, which is applicable to statutory mergers occurring after December 31, 1970, was enacted to permit, under certain circumstances, a tax-free statutory merger when stock of a parent corporation is used in a merger between a controlled subsidiary of the parent and another corporation, and the other corporation survives.

Section 368(a)(2)(E) of the Code provides that a transaction otherwise qualifying as a statutory merger under section 368(a)(1)(A) of the Code will not be disqualified by reason of the fact that stock of a corporation (controlling corporation) which before the merger was in control of the merged corporation is used in the transaction if (1) after the transaction, the corporation surviving the merger holds substantially all of its properties and of the properties of the merged corporation (other than stock of the controlling corporation distributed in the transaction), and (2) in the transaction, former shareholders of the surviving corporation exchanged, for an amount of voting stock of the controlling corporation, an amount of stock in the surviving corporation which constitutes control of such corporation.

In the instant case, the transaction does not qualify as a reorganization under section 368(a)(1)(A) and (a)(2)(E) of the Code, because (1) stock of P, rather than stock of the controlling corporation S, was transferred to the R shareholders, and (2) a sufficient amount of R stock to constitute control within the meaning of section 368(c) of the Code was not obtained by S in the transaction inasmuch as S already owned a controlling interest in R.

Section 368(a)(1)(B) of the Code provides, in part, that the term "reorganization" means the acquisition by one corporation, in exchange solely for all or a part of its voting stock, or in exchange solely for all or a part of the voting stock of a corporation which is in control of the acquiring corporation, of stock of another corporation if, immediately after the acquisition, the acquiring corporation has control of such other corporation (whether or not the acquiring corporation had control before the acquisition).

* * *

In the instant case, the net effect of the steps taken was that S acquired, solely for voting stock of P (which was in control of S), additional shares of stock of R, a corporation which S already controlled and continued to control.

Accordingly, the transaction in the instant case will be treated as an acquisition by S, in exchange solely for a part of P voting stock (P being in control of S), of stock of R (S being in control of R after the transaction), which qualifies as a reorganization within the meaning of section 368(a)(1)(B) of the Code.

Pursuant to section 354(a) of the Code the former shareholders of R will recognize no gain or loss on the exchange of their R stock for P stock. Furthermore, the cash transferred by P to Z and returned to P in the transaction is disregarded and has no tax consequences * * *.

NOTES

1. *Grandparent stock and pre-existing ownership.* If S did not own any R stock before the transaction described in Revenue Ruling 74–564 occurred, could the acquisition have qualified as an A reorganization pursuant to I.R.C. § 368(a)(2)(E) as long as P stock was used as consideration for the acquisition? See I.R.C. §§ 368(a)(2)(E) (first clause), 368(c). If S stock (rather than P stock) had been used as consideration for the acquisition, how much, if any, R stock could S have owned before the acquisition without barring the acquisition from qualifying as an A reorganization? See I.R.C. §§ 368(a)(2)(E)(ii), 368(c).

2. *Reverse triangular merger versus B reorganization.* Is it ever easier to qualify a reverse triangular merger as an A reorganization, pursuant to I.R.C. § 368(a)(2)(E), than as a B reorganization?

3. *Substance over form.* In Tribune Co. v. Commissioner, 125 T.C. 110 (2005), a corporation acquired Matthew Bender & Co., a subsidiary of Times Mirror Company, Inc. (the predecessor of Tribune Co.), in a reverse triangular merger where the sole consideration, in form, was voting stock of the acquiring corporation. Contemporaneously, Times Mirror received the managerial rights to a limited liability company capitalized by the acquiring corporation with $1.375 billion in cash pursuant to an agreement that gave Times Mirror effective control over the cash. Times Mirror claimed that the transaction qualified as a tax-deferred reorganization under I.R.C. § 368(a)(1)(B) and § 368(a)(2)(E). The Tax Court rejected Times Mirror's positions, holding as follows:

> From any perspective, the "true economic effect" of the Bender transaction was a sale. Because the consideration paid by the buyer, to wit, unfettered control over $1.375 billion in cash, passed to the seller from the buyer, the Bender transaction does not qualify as a reorganization under section 368(a)(1)(B), which requires that the exchange be solely for stock. Because the [stock issued to Times Mirror] lacked control over any assets, its value was negligible in comparison to the $1.1 billion value [80% of $1.375 billion] that would be required to qualify the Bender transaction as a tax-free reorganization under section 368(a)(2)(E).

2.   Multi–Step Acquisitions

Revenue Ruling 90–95

1990–2 Cum.Bull. 67.

ISSUES

(1) If a corporation organizes a subsidiary solely for the purpose of acquiring the stock of a target corporation in a reverse subsidiary cash merger, is the corporation treated on the occurrence of the merger as having acquired the stock of the target in a qualified stock purchase under section 338 of the Internal Revenue Code?

(2) If the corporation makes a qualified stock purchase of the target stock and immediately liquidates the target as part of a plan to acquire the assets of the target, is the corporation treated as having made an asset acquisition * * * or a section 338 qualified stock purchase followed by a liquidation of the target?

FACTS

Situation 1. P, a domestic corporation, formed a wholly-owned domestic subsidiary corporation, S, for the sole purpose of acquiring all of the stock of an unrelated domestic target corporation, T, by means of a reverse subsidiary cash merger. Prior to the merger, S conducted no activities other than those required for the merger.

Pursuant to the plan of merger, S merged into T with T surviving. The shareholders of T exchanged all of their T stock for cash from S. * * * Following the merger, P owned all of the outstanding T stock.

Situation 2. The facts are the same as in Situation 1, except that P planned to acquire T's assets through a prompt liquidation of T. State law prohibited P from owning the stock of T. Pursuant to the plan, T merged into P immediately following the merger of S into T. The merger of T into P satisfied the requirements for a tax-free liquidation under section 332 of the Code. The liquidation was not motivated by the evasion or avoidance of federal income tax.

LAW AND ANALYSIS

* * *

[U]nder section 338, in the case of any qualified stock purchase, rules are provided governing whether the transaction gives rise to purchase of target stock treatment or purchase of target asset treatment * * *.

A qualified stock purchase is generally the purchase by a corporation of at least 80 percent of a target's stock * * * within a 12–month period. Section 338(d)(3) * * *.

Stock purchase or asset purchase treatment generally turns on whether the purchasing corporation makes * * * a section 338 election. If the election is made * * *, asset purchase treatment results and section 338 of the Code generally treats all of the assets of the target as having been sold by the target at fair market value on the date of the qualified stock purchase and then repurchased by the target on the following day. The basis of the target's assets is adjusted to reflect the stock purchase price and other relevant items. If an election is not made * * *, stock purchase treatment generally results. In such a case, the basis of the target's assets is not adjusted to reflect the stock purchase price and other relevant items. * * *

In Situations 1 and 2, the step-transaction doctrine is properly applied to disregard the existence of S for federal income tax purposes. S had no significance apart from P's acquisition of the T stock. S was formed for the sole purpose of enabling P to acquire the T stock, and S did not conduct any activities that were not related to that acquisition. Accordingly, the transaction is treated as a qualified stock purchase of T stock by P.

In Situation 2, the step-transaction doctrine does not apply to treat the stock acquisition and liquidation as an asset purchase. * * * Under section 338, asset purchase treatment turns on whether a section 338 election is made * * * following a qualified stock purchase of target stock and not on whether the target's stock is acquired to obtain the assets through a prompt liquidation of the target. The acquiring corporation may receive stock purchase treatment or asset purchase treatment whether or not the target is subsequently liquidated. A qualified stock purchase of target stock is accorded independent significance from a subsequent liquidation of the target regardless of whether a section 338 election is made * * *. This treatment results even if the liquidation occurs to comply with state law. Accordingly, in Situation 2, the acquisition is treated as a qualified stock purchase by P of T stock followed by a tax-free liquidation of T into P.

HOLDING

(1) In Situations 1 and 2, P is treated as having acquired stock of T in a qualified stock purchase under section 338 of the Code.

(2) In Situation 2, P is treated as having acquired stock of T in a qualified stock purchase under section 338 followed by a liquidation of T into P, rather than having made an acquisition of assets * * *.

NOTES

1. *I.R.C. § 338.* Chapter 11 examined I.R.C. § 338, a provision that comes into play when a corporation purchases at least 80% of the stock of another corporation (a "qualified stock purchase"). When a qualified stock purchase occurs, the basis of the target corporation's assets is not affected, unless the purchasing corporation elects to treat the target as if it sold its assets, in which case gains (and losses) are recognized and the basis of each target asset is stepped-up (or down) roughly to market value. See pp. 495–501. Revenue Ruling 90–95 indicates that a reverse triangular merger that fails to qualify as a reorganization is treated as a purchase by the parent of target corporation stock when the subsidiary of parent serves merely as an acquisition vehicle. Thus, the transaction can represent a "qualified stock purchase," in which case the acquiring corporation may make a § 338 election to trigger the gains (and losses) in the target's assets.

2. *Taxable versus tax-free reverse triangular merger.* Is Situation 1 of Revenue Ruling 90–95 consistent with the earlier Revenue Rulings issued in connection with tax-free reverse triangular mergers? See Rev. Rul. 67–448 (p. 610), Rev. Rul. 74–564 (p. 612).

3. *Taxable forward triangular merger.* Would you expect a *forward* triangular cash merger also to be treated as a qualified stock purchase? If not, what impact does a forward triangular cash merger have on the target corporation's assets?

4. *Taxable reverse triangular merger followed by liquidation.* In Situation 2 of Revenue Ruling 90–95, the Internal Revenue Service refrained from applying the step-transaction doctrine. The reverse triangular merger and subsequent liquidation were not collapsed. Thus, the transactions were not treated as an asset acquisition. Instead, the taxable reverse triangular merger was regarded as separate and distinct from the subsequent liquidation. As such, the taxable reverse triangular merger was treated as a qualified stock purchase subject to I.R.C. § 338 and the subsequent liquidation was treated as a tax-free transaction governed by I.R.C. §§ 332 and 337. By contrast, in Rev. Rul. 67–274 (p. 562), the Internal Revenue Service applied the step-transaction doctrine to a stock-for-stock acquisition followed immediately by a liquidation of the target. There, the two steps were collapsed and the transaction was treated as an asset acquisition that qualified as a type C reorganization. Can these two rulings be reconciled? See Rev. Rul. 2001–46 which follows.

Revenue Ruling 2001–46

2001–42 I.R.B. 321.

ISSUE

Under the facts described below, what is the proper tax treatment if, pursuant to an integrated plan, a newly formed wholly-owned subsidiary of an acquiring corporation merges into a target corporation, followed by the merger of the target corporation into the acquiring corporation?

FACTS

[C]orporation X owns all the stock of Corporation Y, a newly formed wholly-owned subsidiary. Pursuant to an integrated plan, X acquires all of the stock of Corporation T, an unrelated corporation, in a statutory merger of Y into T (the "Acquisition Merger"), with T surviving. In the Acquisition Merger, the T shareholders exchange their T stock for consideration, 70 percent of which is X voting stock and 30 percent of which is cash. Following the Acquisition Merger and as part of the plan, T merges into X in a statutory merger (the "Upstream Merger"). Assume that, absent some prohibition against the application of the step-transaction doctrine, the step-transaction doctrine would apply to treat the Acquisition Merger and the Upstream Merger as a single integrated acquisition by X of all the assets of T. Also assume that the single integrated transaction would satisfy the nonstatutory requirements of a reorganization under § 368(a) of the Internal Revenue Code.

* * *

LAW

Section 338(a) provides that if a corporation makes a qualified stock purchase and makes an election under that section, then the target corporation (i) shall be treated as having sold all of its assets at the close of the acquisition date at fair market value and (ii) shall be treated as a new corporation which purchased all of its assets as of the beginning of the day after the acquisition date. * * *

Rev. Rul. 90–95, 1990–2 C.B. 67 (Situation 2), holds that the merger of a newly formed wholly-owned subsidiary into a target corporation with the target corporation shareholders receiving solely cash in exchange for their stock, immediately followed by the merger of the target corporation into the domestic parent of the merged subsidiary, will be treated as a qualified stock purchase of the target corporation followed by a § 332 liquidation of the target corporation. As a result, the parent's basis in the target corporation's assets will be the same as the basis of the assets in the target corporation's hands. The ruling explains that even though "the step-transaction doctrine is properly applied to disregard the existence of the [merged subsidiary]," so that the first step is treated as a stock purchase, the acquisition of the target corporation's stock is accorded independent significance from the subsequent liquidation of the target corporation and, therefore, is treated as a qualified stock purchase regardless of whether a § 338 election is made.

Section 1.338–3(d) of the Income Tax Regulations incorporates the approach of Rev. Rul. 90–95 into the regulations by requiring the purchasing corporation * * * to treat certain asset transfers following a qualified stock purchase (where no § 338 election is made) independently of the qualified stock purchase. * * *

Section 368(a)(1)(A) defines the term "reorganization" as a statutory merger or consolidation. Section 368(a)(2)(E) provides that a transaction otherwise qualifying under § 368(a)(1)(A) shall not be disqualified by reason of the fact that stock of a corporation (controlling corporation), which before the merger was in control of the merged corporation, is used in the transaction if (i) after the transaction, the corporation surviving the merger holds substantially all of its properties and the properties of the merged corporation, and (ii) in the transaction, former shareholders of the surviving corporation exchange, for an amount of voting stock of the controlling corporation, an amount of stock in the surviving corporation which constitutes control of such corporation.

In Rev. Rul. 67–274, 1967–2 C.B. 141 [p. 562], Corporation Y acquires all of the stock of Corporation X in exchange for some of the voting stock of Y and, thereafter, X completely liquidates into Y. The ruling holds that because the two steps are parts of a plan of reorganization, they cannot be considered independently of each other. Thus, the steps do not qualify as a reorganization under § 368(a)(1)(B) followed by a liquidation under § 332, but instead qualify as an acquisition of X's assets in a reorganization under § 368(a)(1)(C).

ANALYSIS

[B]ecause of the amount of cash consideration paid to the T shareholders, the Acquisition Merger could not qualify as a reorganization under § 368(a)(1)(A) and § 368(a)(2)(E). If the Acquisition Merger and the Upstream Merger * * * were treated as separate from each other, as were the steps in Situation (2) of Rev. Rul. 90–95, the Acquisition Merger would be treated as a stock acquisition that is a qualified stock purchase, because the stock is not acquired in a § 354 or § 356 exchange. The Upstream Merger would qualify as a liquidation under § 332.

However, if the approach reflected in Rev. Rul. 67–274 were applied * * *, the transaction would be treated as an integrated acquisition of T's assets by X in a single statutory merger (without a preliminary stock acquisition). Accordingly, unless the policies underlying § 338 dictate otherwise, the integrated asset acquisition * * * is properly treated as a statutory merger of T into X that qualifies as a reorganization under § 368(a)(1)(A). See King Enterprises, Inc. v. United States [p. 594] (in a case that predated § 338, the court applied the step-transaction doctrine to treat the acquisition of the stock of a target corporation followed by the merger of the target corporation into the acquiring corporation as a reorganization under § 368(a)(1)(A)); J.E. Seagram Corp. v. Commissioner [p. 583] (same). Therefore, it is necessary to determine whether the approach reflected in Rev. Rul. 90–95 applies where the step-transaction doctrine would otherwise apply to treat the transaction as an asset acquisition that qualifies as a reorganization under § 368(a).

Rev. Rul. 90–95 and Reg. § 1.338–3(d) reject the approach reflected in Rev. Rul. 67–274 where the application of that approach would treat the purchase of a target corporation's stock without a § 338 election followed by the liquidation or merger of the target corporation as the purchase of the target corporation's assets resulting in a cost basis in the assets under § 1012. The rejection of step integration in Rev. Rul. 90–95 and § 1.338–3(d) is based on Congressional intent that § 338 "replace any nonstatutory treatment of a stock purchase as an asset purchase under the Kimbell–Diamond doctrine." H.R. Rep. No. 760, 97th Cong., 2d Sess. 536 (1982), 1982–2 C.B. 600, 632. (In Kimbell–Diamond Milling Co. v. Commissioner [p. 493], the court held that the purchase of the stock of a target corporation for the purpose of obtaining its assets through a prompt liquidation should be treated by the purchaser as a purchase of the target corporation's assets with the purchaser receiving a cost basis in the assets.)

Rev. Rul. 90–95 and Reg. § 1.338–3(d) treat the acquisition of the stock of the target corporation as a qualified stock purchase followed by a separate carryover basis transaction in order to preclude any nonstatutory treatment of the steps as an integrated asset purchase. The policy underlying § 338 is not violated by treating [the transactions in this Ruling] as a single statutory merger of T into X because such treatment results in a transaction that qualifies as a reorganization under § 368(a)(1)(A) in which X acquires the assets of T with a carryover basis under § 362, and does not result in a cost basis for those assets under § 1012. Thus, * * * the step-transaction doctrine applies to treat the Acquisition Merger and the Upstream Merger not as a stock acquisition that is a qualified stock purchase followed by a § 332 liquidation, but instead as an acquisition of T's assets through a single statutory merger of T into X that qualifies as a reorganization under § 368(a)(1)(A). Accordingly, a § 338 election may not be made in such a situation.

     * * *

HOLDING

Under the facts presented, if, pursuant to an integrated plan, a newly formed wholly owned subsidiary of an acquiring corporation merges into a target corporation, followed by the merger of the target corporation into the acquiring corporation, the transaction is treated as a single statutory merger of the target corporation into the acquiring corporation that qualifies as a reorganization under § 368(a)(1)(A).

[T]he Service and the Treasury are considering whether to issue regulations that would reflect the general principles of this revenue ruling, but would allow taxpayers to make a valid election under § 338(h)(10) with respect to a step of a multi-step transaction that, viewed independently, is a qualified stock purchase * * *.

NOTES

1. *Tax consequences of alternative treatments.* What are the tax consequences of treating the Acquisition Merger and the Upstream Merger as separate and distinct transactions? What are the tax consequences of treating the two mergers as a single integrated transaction?

2. *Reconciliation with Revenue Ruling 90–95.* In Rev. Rul. 90–95, Situation 2, the reverse subsidiary merger and the liquidation were treated as separate and distinct steps. In Rev. Rul. 2001–46, the Acquisition Merger and the Upstream Merger were treated as a single unified transaction. Can the two rulings be reconciled?

3. *Reconciliation with Revenue Ruling 67–274.* In both Rev. Rul. 67–274 and Rev. Rul. 2001–46, the initial acquisition and subsequent liquidation were integrated and treated as an asset acquisition. What common feature justifies this treatment?

4. *Application of emerging principle.* Acquiring Corporation acquires 51% of the stock of Target Corporation for stock of Acquiring Corporation. Acquiring Corporation then acquires the remaining 49% of Target by executing the following steps: a) Acquiring forms Subsidiary Corporation, and b) Subsidiary merges into Target in a reverse triangular merger in which the 49% of Target stock not owned by Acquiring is converted into Acquiring stock (2/3) and cash (1/3). If the initial acquisition of 51% of Target stock and the subsequent acquisition of the remaining 49% of Target stock were treated as separate and distinct transactions, what would be the tax consequences of each transaction? If, instead, the two transactions were integrated into a single reverse triangular merger, what would be the tax consequences of that transaction? Based on the reasoning of Rev. Rul. 2001–46, what outcome would you expect? See Rev. Rul. 2001–26, 2001–23 I.R.B. 1297.

5. *Important assumption.* Rev. Rul. 2001–46 assumes that "the step-transaction doctrine would apply to treat the Acquisition Merger and the Upstream Merger as a single integrated acquisition by X of all the assets of T." How significant is this assumption to the holding of the ruling?

6. *Revitalization of King Enterprises.* Rev. Rul. 2001–46 cites King Enterprises [p. 594] in support of its decision to integrate the transactions. Both the ruling and the King Enterprises case led to outcomes that were favorable to the taxpayers. Will the application of King Enterprises lead to taxpayer favorable outcomes in all cases? For a critique of Rev. Rul. 2001–46's reliance on King Enterprises, see Jeffrey L. Kwall & Kristina Maynard, "Dethroning King Enterprises," 58 Tax Lawyer 1 (Fall, 2004).

7. *Section 338(h)(10) election.* In 2003, the Treasury promulgated regulations allowing taxpayers to make a § 338(h)(10) election for a target corporation in certain multi-step acquisitions. Specifically, if a purchasing corporation (P) acquires the stock of a target corporation (T) in a transaction which, viewed independently, is a qualified stock purchase and, after the stock acquisition, T is merged into P, a § 338(h)(10) may be made for T. The § 338(h)(10) election may be made regardless of whether the acquisition of the T stock and the merger of T into P would otherwise qualify as a reorganization. See Treas. Reg. §§ 1.338(h)(10)–1(c)(2), (e) Examples 11, 12.

Revenue Ruling 2008–25

2008–21 I.R.B. 986.

ISSUE

What is the proper Federal income tax treatment of the transaction described below?

FACTS

T is a corporation all of the stock of which is owned by individual A. T has 150x dollars worth of assets and 50x dollars of liabilities. P is a corporation that is unrelated to A and T. * * * P forms corporation X, a wholly owned subsidiary, for the sole purpose of acquiring all of the stock of T by causing X to merge into T in a statutory merger (the "Acquisition Merger"). In the Acquisition Merger, P acquires all of the stock of T, and A exchanges the T stock for 10x dollars in cash and P voting stock worth 90x dollars. Following the Acquisition Merger and as part of an integrated plan that included the Acquisition Merger, T completely liquidates into P (the "Liquidation"). In the Liquidation, T transfers all of its assets to P and P assumes all of T's liabilities. The Liquidation is not accomplished through a statutory merger. After the Liquidation, P continues to conduct the business previously conducted by T.

LAW

[S]ection 1.368–1(a) generally provides that in determining whether a transaction qualifies as a reorganization under § 368(a), the transaction must be evaluated under relevant provisions of law, including the step transaction doctrine.

Section 1.368–2(k) provides, in part, that a transaction otherwise qualifying as a reorganization under § 368(a) shall not be disqualified or recharacterized as a result of one or more distributions to shareholders if the requirements of § 1.368–1(d) are satisfied, the property distributed consists of assets of the surviving corporation, and the aggregate of such distributions does not consist of an amount of assets of the surviving corporation that would result in a liquidation of such corporation for Federal income tax purposes.

Rev. Rul. 67–274, 1967–2 C.B. 141, holds that an acquiring corporation's acquisition of all of the stock of a target corporation solely in exchange for voting stock of the acquiring corporation, followed by the liquidation of the target corporation as part of the same plan, will be treated as an acquisition by the acquiring corporation of substantially all of the target corporation's assets in a reorganization described in § 368 (a) (1) (C). The ruling explains that, under these circumstances, the stock acquisition and the liquidation are part of the overall plan of reorganization and the two steps may not be considered independently of each other for Federal income tax purposes.

Rev. Rul. 2001–46, 2001–2 C.B. 321, holds that, where a newly formed wholly owned subsidiary of an acquiring corporation merged into a target corporation, followed by the merger of the target corporation into the acquiring corporation, the step transaction doctrine is applied to integrate the steps and treat the transaction as a single statutory merger of the target corporation into the acquiring corporation. Noting that the rejection of step integration in Rev. Rul. 90–95, 1990–2 C.B. 67, and § 1.338–3 (d) is based on Congressional intent that § 338 replace any nonstatutory treatment of a stock purchase as an asset purchase under the Kimbell–Diamond doctrine, the Service found that the policy underlying § 338 is not violated by treating the steps as a single statutory merger of the target into the acquiring corporation because such treatment results in a transaction that qualifies as a reorganization in which the acquiring corporation acquires the assets of the target corporation with a carryover basis under § 362, rather than receiving a cost basis in those assets under § 1012. (In *Kimbell–Diamond Milling Co. v. Commissioner* [p. 493], the court held that the purchase of the stock of a target corporation for the purpose of obtaining its assets through a prompt liquidation should be treated by the purchaser as a purchase of the target corporation's assets with the purchaser receiving a cost basis in the assets.)

* * *

Section 338 was enacted in 1982 and was "intended to replace any nonstatutory treatment of a stock purchase as an asset purchase under the Kimbell–Diamond doctrine." H.R. Conf. Rep. No. 760, 97th Cong, 2d Sess. 536 (1982), 1982–2 C.B. 600, 632. Stock purchase or asset purchase treatment generally turns on whether the purchasing corporation makes or is deemed to make a § 338 election. If the election is made or deemed made, asset purchase treatment results and the basis of the target assets is adjusted to reflect the stock purchase price and other relevant items. If an election is not made or deemed made, the stock purchase treatment generally results. In such a case, the basis of the target assets is not adjusted to reflect the stock purchase price and other relevant items.

Rev. Rul. 90–95 (Situation 2), holds that the merger of a newly formed wholly owned domestic subsidiary into a target corporation with the target corporation shareholders receiving solely cash in exchange for their stock, immediately followed by the merger of the target corporation into the domestic parent of the merged subsidiary, will be treated as a qualified stock purchase of the target corporation followed by a § 332 liquidation of the target corporation. As a result, the parent's basis in the target corporation's assets will be the same as the basis of the assets in the target corporation's hands. The ruling explains that even though "the step-transaction doctrine is properly applied to disregard the existence of the [merged subsidiary]," so that the first step is treated as a stock purchase, the acquisition of the target corporation's stock is accorded independent significance from the subsequent liquidation of the target corporation and, therefore, is treated as a qualified stock purchase regardless of whether a § 338 election is made. Thus, in that case, the step transaction doctrine was not applied to treat the transaction as a direct acquisition by the domestic parent of the assets of the target corporation because such an application would have resulted in treating a stock purchase as an asset purchase, which would be inconsistent with the repeal of the Kimbell–Diamond doctrine and § 338.

Section 1.338–3(d) incorporates the approach of Rev. Rul. 90–95 into the regulations by requiring the purchasing corporation to treat certain asset transfers following a qualified stock purchase (where no § 338 election is made) independently of the qualified stock purchase. In the example in § 1.338–3(d)(5), the purchase for cash of 85 percent of the stock of a target corporation, followed by the merger of the target corporation into a wholly owned subsidiary of the purchasing corporation, is treated as a qualified stock purchase of the stock of the target corporation followed by a § 368 reorganization of the target corporation into the subsidiary. As a result, the subsidiary's basis in the target corporation's assets is the same as the basis of the assets in the target corporation's hands.

ANALYSIS

If the Acquisition Merger and the Liquidation were treated as separate from each other, the Acquisition Merger would be treated as a stock acquisition that qualifies as a reorganization under § 368(a)(1)(A) by reason of § 368(a)(2)(E), and the Liquidation would qualify under § 332. However, as provided in § 1.368–1(a), in determining whether a transaction qualifies as a reorganization under § 368(a), the transaction must be evaluated under relevant provisions of law, including the step transaction doctrine. In this case, because T was completely liquidated, the § 1.368–2(k) safe harbor exception from the application of the step transaction doctrine does not apply. Accordingly, the Acquisition Merger and the Liquidation may not be considered independently of each other for purposes of determining whether the transaction satisfies the statutory requirements of a reorganization described in § 368(a)(1)(A) by reason of § 368(a)(2)(E). As such, this transaction does not qualify as a reorganization described in § 368(a)(1)(A) by reason of § 368(a)(2)(E) because, after the transaction, T does not hold substantially all of its properties and the properties of the merged corporation.

In determining whether the transaction is a reorganization, the approach reflected in Rev. Rul. 67–274 and Rev. Rul. 2001–46 is applied to ignore P's acquisition of the T stock in the Acquisition Merger and to treat the transaction as a direct acquisition by P of T's assets in exchange for 10x dollars in cash, 90x dollars worth of P voting stock, and the assumption of T's liabilities.

However, unlike the transactions considered in Rev. Rul. 67–274 * * * and 2001–46, a direct acquisition by P of T's assets in this case does not qualify as a reorganization under § 368 (a). P's acquisition of T's assets is not a reorganization described in § 368(a)(1)(C) because the consideration exchanged is not solely P voting stock and the requirements of § 368(a)(2)(B) are not satisfied. Section 368(a)(2)(B) would treat P as acquiring 40 percent of T's assets for consideration other than P voting stock (liabilities assumed of 50x dollars, plus 10x dollars cash). P's acquisition of T's assets is not a reorganization described in § 368(a)(1)(D) because neither T nor A (nor a combination thereof) was in control of P (within the meaning of § 368(a)(2)(H)(i)) immediately after the transfer. Additionally, the transaction is not a reorganization under § 368(a)(1)(A) because T did not merge into P. Accordingly, the overall transaction is not a reorganization under § 368(a).

* * *

Rev. Rul. 90–95 and § 1.338–3(d) reject the step integration approach reflected in Rev. Rul. 67–274 where the application of that approach would treat the purchase of a target corporation's stock without a § 338 election followed by the liquidation or merger of the target corporation as the purchase of the target corporation's assets resulting in a cost basis in the assets under § 1012. Rev. Rul. 90–95 and § 1.338–3(d) treat the acquisition of the stock of the target corporation as a qualified stock purchase followed by a separate carryover basis transaction in order to preclude any nonstatutory treatment of the steps as an integrated asset purchase.

In this case, further application of the approach reflected in Rev. Rul. 67–274, integrating the acquisition of T stock with the liquidation of T, would result in treating the acquisition of T stock as a taxable purchase of T's assets. Such treatment would violate the policy underlying § 338 that a cost basis in acquired assets should not be obtained through the purchase of stock where no § 338 election is made. Accordingly, consistent with the analysis set forth in Rev. Rul. 90–95, the acquisition of the stock of T is treated as a qualified stock purchase by P followed by the liquidation of T into P under § 332.

HOLDING

The transaction is not a reorganization under § 368(a). The Acquisition Merger is a qualified stock purchase by P of the stock of T under § 338(d)(3). The Liquidation is a complete liquidation of a controlled subsidiary under § 332.

NOTES

1. *Tax consequences of alternative treatments.* What would the tax consequences have been if the Acquisition Merger and the Liquidation had been treated as separate and distinct transactions? What would the tax consequences have been if the two steps had been treated as a single integrated transaction?

2. *Rejection of integrated transaction treatment.* Why did the Internal Revenue Service reject treating the two steps as a single integrated transaction? Was the rejection of integrated transaction treatment consistent with Rev. Rul. 90–95?

3.   *Upstream merger versus liquidation.* Would the two steps in Rev. Rul. 2008–25 have been integrated into a single reorganization if the second step had entailed an upstream merger (like the second step in Rev. Rul. 2001–46), rather than the physical transfer of all of target's assets in a liquidation?

4.   *Failure of Acquisition Merger to qualify as a reorganization.* Why did the Acquisition Merger, by itself, fail to qualify as a reorganization? How were the shareholders of the target impacted by the Internal Revenue Service's treatment of the Acquisition Merger? Can the consequences to the target shareholders in Rev. Rul. 2008–25 and Rev. Rul. 90–95 be reconciled? Could any precautions have been taken by the target shareholders in Rev. Rul. 2008–25 to ensure that the Acquisition Merger would qualify as a reorganization?

G.   BANKRUPTCY REORGANIZATIONS

I.R.C. § 368(a)(1)(G)

Congress enacted I.R.C. § 368(a)(1)(G) as part of the Bankruptcy Tax Act of 1980. This new definition of corporate reorganization was intended to facilitate the rehabilitation of financially distressed businesses. The following excerpt from the Senate Finance Committee Report explains the provision.

Senate Finance Committee Report to the Bankruptcy Tax Act of 1980

S.Rep. No. 96–1035, 96th Cong., 2d Sess. (1980).

* * *

Definition of reorganization

In general. The bill adds a new category—"G" reorganizations—to the general Code definition of tax-free reorganizations (sec. 368(a)(1)). The new category includes certain transfers of assets pursuant to a court-approved reorganization plan in a bankruptcy case under new title 11 of the U.S. Code, or in a receivership, foreclosure, or similar proceeding in a Federal or State court.

In order to facilitate the rehabilitation of corporate debtors in bankruptcy, etc., [this provision is] designed to eliminate many requirements which have effectively precluded financially troubled companies from utilizing the generally applicable tax-free reorganization provisions of present law. To achieve this purpose, the new "G" reorganization provision does not require compliance with State merger laws (as in category "A" reorganizations), does not require that the financially distressed corporation receive solely stock of the acquiring corporation in exchange for its assets (category "C"), and does not require that the former shareholders of the financially distressed corporation control the corporation which receives the assets (category "D").

The "G" reorganization provision added by the bill requires the transfer of assets by a corporation in a bankruptcy or similar case, and the distribution (in pursuance of the court-approved reorganization plan) of stock or securities of the acquiring corporation in a transaction which qualifies under sections 354, 355, or 356 of the Code. This distribution requirement is designed to assure that either substantially all of the assets of the financially troubled corporation, or assets which consist of an active business under the tests of section 355, are transferred to the acquiring corporation.

"Substantially all" test. The "substantially all" test in the "G" reorganization provision is to be interpreted in light of the underlying intent in adding the new "G" category, namely, to facilitate the reorganization of companies in bankruptcy or similar cases for rehabilitative purposes. Accordingly, it is intended that facts and circumstances relevant to this intent, such as the insolvent corporation's need to pay off creditors or to sell assets or divisions to raise cash, are to be taken into account in determining whether a transaction qualifies as a "G" reorganization. For example, a transaction is not precluded from satisfying the "substantially all" test for purposes of the new "G" category merely because, prior to a transfer to the acquiring corporation, payments to creditors and asset sales were made in order to leave the debtor with more manageable operating assets to continue in business.

Relation to other provisions. * * * A transaction in a bankruptcy or similar case which does not satisfy the requirements of new category "G" is not * * * precluded from qualifying as a tax-free reorganization under one of the other categories of section 368(a)(1). For example, an acquisition of the stock of a company in bankruptcy, or a recapitalization of such a company, which transactions are not covered by the new "G" category, can qualify for nonrecognition treatment under sections 368(a)(1)(B) or (E), respectively.

Continuity of interest rules. The "continuity of interest" requirement which the courts and the Treasury have long imposed as a prerequisite for nonrecognition treatment for a corporate reorganization must be met in order to satisfy the requirements of new category "G". Only reorganizations—as distinguished from liquidations in bankruptcy and sales of property to either new or old interests supplying new capital and discharging the obligations of the debtor corporation—can qualify for tax-free treatment. It is expected that the courts and the Treasury will apply to "G" reorganizations continuity-of-interest rules which * * * [permit] shareholders or junior creditors, who might previously have been excluded, [to] retain an interest in the reorganized corporation.

For example, if an insolvent corporation's assets are transferred to a second corporation in a bankruptcy case, the most senior class of creditor to receive stock, together with all equal and junior classes (including share-holders who receive any consideration for their stock), should generally be considered the proprietors of the insolvent corporation for "continuity" purposes. However, if the shareholders receive consideration other than stock of the acquiring corporation, the transaction should be examined to determine if it represents a purchase rather than a reorganization.

Thus, short-term creditors who receive stock for their claims may be counted toward satisfying the continuity of interest rule, although any gain or loss realized by such creditors will be recognized for income tax purposes.

Triangular reorganizations. The bill permits a corporation to acquire a debtor corporation in a "G" reorganization in exchange for stock of the parent of the acquiring corporation rather than for its own stock. [See I.R.C. §§ 368(a)(2)(D), 368(b) (fourth sentence).]

In addition, the bill permits an acquisition in the form of a "reverse merger" of an insolvent corporation (i.e., where no former shareholder of the surviving corporation receives any consideration for his stock) in a bankruptcy or similar case if the former creditors of the surviving corporation exchange their claims for voting stock of the controlling corporation which has a value equal to at least 80 percent of the value of the debt of the surviving corporation. [See I.R.C. § 368(a)(3)(E).]

Transfer to controlled subsidiary. The bill permits a corporation which acquires substantially all the assets of a debtor corporation in a "G" reorganization to transfer the acquired assets to a controlled subsidiary without endangering the tax-free status of the reorganization. This provision places "G" reorganizations on a similar footing with other categories of reorganizations. [See I.R.C. §§ 368(a)(2)(C), 368(b) (third sentence).]

Carryover of tax attributes. Under the bill, the statutory rule generally governing carryover of tax attributes in corporate reorganizations (Code sec. 381) also applies in the case of a "G" reorganization * * *.

 * * *

Example. The reorganization provisions of the bill are illustrated in part by the following example.

Assume that Corporation A is in a bankruptcy case * * *. Immediately prior to a transfer under a plan of reorganization, A's assets have an adjusted basis of $75,000 and a fair market value of $100,000. A has a net operating loss carryover of $200,000. A has outstanding bonds of $100,000 * * * and trade debts of $100,000.

Under the plan of reorganization, A is to transfer all its assets to Corporation B in exchange for $100,000 of B stock. Corporation A will distribute the stock, one-half to the security holders and one-half to the trade creditors, in exchange for their claims against A. A's shareholders will receive nothing.

The transaction qualifies as a reorganization under new section 368(a)(1)(G) of the Code, since all the creditors are here treated as proprietors for continuity of interest purposes. Thus, A recognizes no gain or loss on the transfer of its assets to B (Code sec. 361). B's basis in the assets is $75,000 (sec. 362), and B succeeds to A's net operating loss carryover (sec. 381).

Under the bill, the pro-rata distribution of B stock to A's creditors does not result in income from discharge of indebtedness or require attribute reduction.

* * *

NOTES

1. *Minimum requirements.* What are the minimum requirements that must be satisfied for an acquisition to qualify as a G reorganization?

2. *G versus A or C reorganization.* Describe the specific features that generally make a G reorganization more attractive to the financially distressed corporation than an A reorganization or a C reorganization. What degree of financial distress must exist for a corporation to utilize the G reorganization?

H. CONTINGENT STOCK

Often, an acquiring corporation will issue contingent stock as part of the consideration in a corporate acquisition. Is contingent stock "boot" that could either spoil a reorganization or trigger partial gain recognition in a transaction that qualifies as a reorganization?

Carlberg v. United States

United States Court of Appeals, Eighth Circuit, 1960.
281 F.2d 507.

■ BLACKMUN, CIRCUIT JUDGE.

This case involves the federal income tax consequences of one aspect of the statutory merger, effected in November 1956, of The Long–Bell Lumber Corporation, a Maryland corporation, and The Long–Bell Lumber Company, a Missouri corporation, into International Paper Company, a New York corporation. These corporate entities will be referred to as "Maryland", "Missouri", and "International", respectively.

The government raises no question as to the bona fide business purposes of the merger. The sole issue is whether the "Certificates of Contingent Interest", received by shareholders of Maryland and Missouri upon the merger, qualify as "stock", within the meaning of I.R.C. § 354(a), or, instead, as "other property", within the meaning of I.R.C. § 356(a)(1).

[U]nder the plan of merger each stockholder of Maryland and each stockholder of Missouri received, in exchange for his shares in those corporations, a certificate for shares of common of International (the shares in the aggregate totaling 849,997) and "a contingent interest in certain reserved shares of such common stock" of International * * * represented by a "Certificate of Contingent Interest."

The Certificates of Contingent Interest came about in this manner: At the time of the merger Missouri possessed two unresolved but potentially substantial liabilities. One was its possible obligation for unsettled federal income taxes for certain past taxable years. The other was litigation pending against Missouri in federal court. International lacked complete knowledge concerning these matters in controversy and it was therefore agreed that under the plan of merger, in order to protect International, 49,997 shares of its common, which would otherwise then also have been issued to the shareholders of Maryland and Missouri, would be set aside as "Reserved Shares" pending the determination of these liabilities of Missouri and that Certificates of Contingent Interest would issue with respect to them. As the liabilities would become resolved and as expenses with respect to them would be incurred, the Reserved Shares were to be reduced monthly by charges computed according to a formula based upon quoted values of International common. After all deductions of this kind had been made any remaining Reserved Shares were to be distributed to the then holders of the Certificates.

* * *

This particular taxpayer at the time of the merger was the owner of 504 shares of Maryland and of 200 shares of Missouri. Upon the merger she received for these stock certificates 413 shares of International common and Certificates of Contingent Interest for 24.31416 units of contingent interest.

The then value of what the taxpayer received upon the merger exceeded her income tax basis in her Maryland and Missouri shares. The government concedes, however, that the merger was a "statutory merger" under I.R.C. § 368(a)(1)(A) and that the certificates for the 413 whole shares of International common were 'stock' which came to her under I.R.C. § 354(a)(1) without recognition of gain. This leaves in controversy only the Certificates of Contingent Interest and the treatment to be accorded them for income tax purposes.

The government's position is that the Certificates constitute a different kind of property than the International common; that they were, in effect, "boot"; that they do not qualify for the tax free treatment enjoyed by the stock under I.R.C. § 354(a)(1); and that they are to be treated, instead, under I.R.C. § 356(a) as dividends. The taxpayer contends that the Certificates represent and are nothing other than International common; that while the exact number of shares of that stock ultimately to be forthcoming to the taxpayer was not known in 1956 and could not then be known, because Missouri's potential liabilities were unresolved, that fact does not negative the Certificates' character as stock; and that like the shares, they were received under I.R.C. § 354(a)(1) without recognition of gain.

* * *

As the government in its brief states, apparently "the issue in this case has not previously been litigated in any previous case".

We observe, initially, that the Code does not define the term "stock" as it is used in the reorganization sections. Neither do the Regulations. In the absence of definitive help from these sources the term deserves only its ordinary meaning.

* * *

[W]e feel that the Certificates are properly interpreted and analyzed in the light of purpose, practicality, and substance. We turn to these in order.

1. Purpose. The purpose of the reorganization sections and the purpose of this merger are significant factors. Generally, under our income tax laws, the entire amount of gain realized on the sale or exchange of property is recognized and taxed. However, there are certain exceptions to this. Among these is I.R.C. § 354(a)'s provision with respect to corporate reorganizations. Treas. Reg. § 1.368–1(b) is entitled "Purpose". It states the general rule of taxability of gain upon exchange of property but then says,

> The purpose of the reorganization provisions of the Internal Revenue Code is to except from the general rule certain specifically described exchanges incident to such readjustments of corporate structures made in one of the particular ways specified in the Code, as are required by business exigencies and which effect only a readjustment of continuing interest in property under modified corporate forms.

[A]ssuming, as we must in the light of the government's concession, that the necessary "business exigency" and a "readjustment of continuing interest in property under a modified corporate form" are both present here with respect to the shares of International common, we fail to see why, in line with these expressed purposes, the same conclusion does not follow with respect to the Certificates of Contingent Interest. Certainly the Certificates here provide "continuity of interest" in the surviving corporation just as do the taxpayer's shares. The Certificates can produce nothing other than stock and nothing other than a continuity of interest. The Certificates therefore fit the expressed basic purpose of the tax free provisions of the reorganization sections.

2. Practicality. The practical and realistic aspects of the situation are also persuasive. The parties here were confronted with the problem of Missouri's potential liabilities. They were faced with the necessity of affording some protection to International with respect to those liabilities and, at the same time, of effecting the desired statutory merger with the consequent business benefits which it was felt would result therefrom. The concept of the Reserved Shares seems to have been an ideal and logical one to solve the problem of these contingent liabilities. While it protected International, at the same time it preserved for the stockholders of Maryland and Missouri the right to their respective portions of any additional shares of International to which they were entitled. Furthermore, it did this in a fair and precise manner by measuring that interest by the eventual outcome of the tax and litigation controversies. Had they chosen

to do so, the parties to the reorganization could have resolved the problem arbitrarily by distributing outright something less than the 49,997 Reserved Shares to the Maryland and Missouri stockholders in 1956 at the time of the merger and by letting International then take the benefit or the detriment of any ultimate difference. That the fairer and more exact method was chosen should not result in unfavorable tax consequences.

We emphasize also that, however one may choose to describe it, the Certificates of Contingent Interest represented only International common and nothing else. What the holder possessed was either stock or it was nothing. The number of shares to be forthcoming, it is true, was not determined with exactitude at the time of the merger but that fact does not change the character of the interest. And to argue that because it traded independently of International's whole shares proves that it is something apart from the stock is, we think, an unrealistic appraisal of the significance of market action.

* * *

[3.] Substance. It has often been said in tax arguments, and occasionally decided that substance must prevail over form. If this observation has any independent legal force or merit in the determination of tax causes, it compels a conclusion that the substance of the Certificates equates only with stock of International. The rule of substance over form, therefore, this time operates in the taxpayer's favor.

For these reasons of purpose, practicality and substance, we hold that the property interest represented by the Certificates of Contingent Interest in this reorganization is "stock" within the meaning of I.R.C. § 354(a)(1) rather than "other property" within the meaning of § 356(a)(1) or "boot" and that the Certificates' receipt by the taxpayer in 1956 did not result in recognized income to her.

NOTES

1. *Reorganization treatment.* Why did the Internal Revenue Service concede that the Carlberg transaction qualified as a reorganization even if the contingent stock constituted boot?

2. *Transferability of contingent interests.* Were the Certificates of Contingent Interest issued in the Carlberg transaction transferable? Why might transferability be relevant to whether the Certificates constitute boot?

Revenue Ruling 66–112

1966–1 Cum.Bull. 68.

Advice has been requested whether the transaction described below satisfies the "solely for voting stock" requirement of I.R.C. § 368(a)(1)(B).

The capital stock of M corporation was owned equally by X corporation and Y corporation. For good business reasons Y was interested in acquiring

X's one-half interest in M. Because M was closely held it was difficult to ascertain the fair market value of the M stock. Accordingly, X and Y entered into an agreement pursuant to which X transferred its one-half interest in M to Y in exchange for 40,000 shares of Y's voting stock. In addition, the agreement accorded X the right to receive additional shares of Y's voting stock in each of the succeeding 4 years following the date of the initial exchange in which M's net income exceeded a specified amount. If M's net income in the succeeding 4 years did not exceed the specified amount, no additional shares were to be received by X. The maximum number of additional shares of Y voting stock which could be received under the plan of reorganization was 20,000 shares. The right to receive such additional shares was not assignable and such right could give rise to the receipt of only additional voting stock.

Section 368 (a)(1)(B) of the Code provides that the term "reorganization" includes the acquisition by one corporation, in exchange solely for all or a part of its voting stock, of stock of another corporation if, immediately after the acquisition, the acquiring corporation has control of such other corporation (whether or not such acquiring corporation had control immediately before the acquisition).

The "control" requirement of section 368(a)(1)(B) of the Code is clearly satisfied since Y owns all of the stock of M immediately after the initial exchange. The only question remaining is whether the "solely for voting stock" requirement has been met. Whether this requirement has been met is dependent on the treatment to be accorded the contractual right of X to receive additional voting shares of Y based upon the net income of M. If such right is considered other property, the "solely for voting stock" requirement of section 368(a)(1)(B) of the Code will not have been satisfied nor will the requirements of section 354(a) of the Code have been met.

Under the facts of this case, the reorganization exchange has been fully consummated, except insofar as the contingent contractual right to receive additional voting stock of Y is concerned. This right is not assignable and it can give rise to only additional Y voting stock. Because of this and the fact that only voting stock has been and can be issued under the terms of the plan of reorganization, the initial receipt by X of 40,000 shares of Y voting stock and the later receipt by X of up to 20,000 additional shares of such stock that may be issued in the 4–year period following the initial exchange will satisfy the "solely for voting stock" requirement of section 368(a)(1)(B) of the Code.

* * *

In the present case the contingent contractual right to additional voting stock in the future is not assignable and can only ripen into additional voting stock. Accordingly, under the circumstances set forth above, the existence of this right will not be treated as violating the "solely for voting stock" requirement of section 368(a)(1)(B) of the Code. * * *

NOTES

1. *Consequences of boot.* What would the tax consequences to X have been if the right to receive additional shares had been treated as boot?

2. *Transferability of contingent interests.* Was the contingent right to additional shares in Rev. Rul. 66–112 transferable? Will the Internal Revenue Service rule that transferable contingent rights are not boot? See the Revenue Procedure that follows.

Revenue Procedure 84–42

1984–1 Cum.Bull. 521.

SECTION 1. BACKGROUND

.01 Rev. Proc. 77–37, 1977–2 C.B. 568, sets forth certain operating rules of the Internal Revenue Service pertaining to issuing ruling letters and in determining whether it should decline to issue ruling letters.

    * * *

SECTION 2. PROCEDURE

.01 Section 3.03 of Rev. Proc. 77–37 is amplified to read as follows:

In transactions under sections 368(a)(1)(A), 368(a)(1)(B), 368(a)(1)(C), 368(a)(1)(D), 368(a)(1)(E), and 351 of the Code, it is not necessary that all the stock which is to be issued in exchange for the requisite stock or property, be issued immediately provided: (1) that all the stock will be issued within 5 years from the date of transfer of assets or stock for reorganizations under sections 368(a)(1)(A), 368(a)(1)(C), 368(a)(1)(D), and 368(a)(1)(E), or within 5 years from the date of the initial distribution in the case of transactions under sections 368(a)(1)(B) and 351; (2) there is a valid business reason for not issuing all the stock immediately, such as difficulty in determining the value of one or both of the corporations involved in the transactions; (3) the maximum number of shares which may be issued in the exchange is stated; (4) at least 50 percent of the maximum number of shares of each class of stock which may be issued is issued in the initial distribution; (5) the agreement evidencing the right to receive stock in the future prohibits assignment (except by operation of law) or if the agreement does not prohibit assignment, the right must not be evidenced by negotiable certificates of any kind and must not be readily marketable; (6) such right can give rise to the receipt only of additional stock of the corporation making the underlying distribution; (7) such stock issuance will not be triggered by an event the occurrence or nonoccurrence of which is within the control of shareholders; (8) such stock issuance will not be triggered by the payment of additional tax or reduction in tax paid as a result of a Service audit of the shareholders or the corporation * * *; and (9) the mechanism for the calculation of the additional stock to be issued is objective and readily ascertainable. Stock issued as compensation, royalties or any other consideration other than in exchange for stock or assets will not be considered to have been received in the exchange. Until the final distribution of the total number of shares of stock to be issued in the exchange is made, the interim basis of the stock of the issuing corporation received in the exchange by the shareholders * * * will be determined, pursuant to section 358(a), as though the maximum number of shares to be issued * * * has been received by the shareholders.

In connection with item 3.03(8) above, the Service reserves the right to refuse to rule if, based on all the facts and circumstances of a case, it is determined that the principal purpose of the triggering mechanism is the reduction in federal income taxes.

* * *

NOTE

Justification for conditions. What justification exists for the nine conditions that must be met before the Internal Revenue Service will consider ruling that a contingent right to additional shares is not boot? To what extent can those conditions be reconciled with the Carlberg court's decision?

I. Proposal for Uniform Acquisition Scheme—Preview of the Future?

In 1985, the Staff of the Senate Finance Committee issued a Report that criticized the complex and inconsistent set of tax rules that apply to corporate acquisitions and proposed legislation that would tax all corporate acquisitions in a consistent and rational fashion. Although the proposed legislation has not been enacted, the Report serves as a useful tool for placing existing law into its proper perspective. The following excerpts should be examined with this goal in mind.

The Subchapter C Revision Act of 1985

A Final Report Prepared by the Staff of the Committee on Finance of the United States Senate (1985).

PART ONE: GENERAL EXPLANATION

I. INTRODUCTION

The "Subchapter C Revision Act of 1985," represents the culmination of a lengthy, comprehensive examination of the fundamental rules in the Internal Revenue Code relating to the Federal income taxation of corporations and their investors. Over the years, those rules have developed largely in a piecemeal fashion, as provisions have been added or modified to address specifically targeted problems or abuses. Taken together, however, the rules have often been criticized as inconsistent and unnecessarily complex, producing uncertain and, at times, capricious results in various transactions.

Despite these criticisms, over the last 50 years, Congress has not had occasion to provide a careful and thorough review of the rules as a whole, to determine whether a more cohesive, internally consistent set of rules could be developed in the area. This report, which proposes in bill form significant revisions to Subchapter C of Chapter 1 of the Internal Revenue Code, dealing generally with corporate distributions and adjustments, represents a first step towards providing that cohesive body of rules.

* * *

II. DESCRIPTION OF CURRENT LAW

[Omitted]

III. REASONS FOR CHANGE

A. General Reasons for Change

[T]he current law of Subchapter C is seriously flawed. The "law" consists of a series of rules, some statutory and others of judicial origin, which, when taken together, lack consistency, are unnecessarily complex, and are often subject to manipulation. By providing uncertain and often capricious tax consequences to business transactions, the law inadequately addresses the needs of businessmen, their corporations, and their investors. Moreover, by being inconsistent and subject to manipulation, the law is biased, at times encouraging tax-motivated transactions, and at times discouraging or making less efficient legitimate business dealings. It is far from clear whether the bias of current law serves any particular Congressional policy goal. Further, it is highly questionable, given the complexity and uncertainty of current law, whether any Congressional policy initiatives could effectively be implemented if the present structure of Subchapter C were retained.

The inadequacy of current law presents three interrelated principal reasons for change. First, current law needs to be made more rational and consistent, thereby providing greater certainty and less complexity in the area. For example, under current law, an "A" reorganization (statutory merger or consolidation) may involve a significant amount of cash consideration, a "B" reorganization (stock-for-stock acquisition) cannot have any cash consideration, and a "C" reorganization (stock-for-assets acquisition) may involve a small amount of cash consideration. No policy justification can be found for these and other distinctions. The bill would propose to eliminate artificial distinctions of that sort.

Second, current law should be made more neutral, providing less influence over, and less interference with, general business dealings. [I]n the right circumstances, a merger or an acquisition may be motivated, in whole or in part, by the favorable tax consequences to the target corporation in the transaction, or by the favorable tax attributes obtained by the acquiring corporation in the transaction. In addition, in many other cases, current law requires tax-*structured* deals (whether dictating the use of certain kinds of consideration, formation of holding companies, or other non-economic steps) which create unnecessary inefficiencies from a business standpoint. This bill would propose eliminating many of these biases and non-economic requirements.

Finally, current law needs to be reformed and made less subject to manipulation * * *.

B.   Detailed Reasons for Change

1. *Problems relating to the definition of "reorganization."* As outlined below, the different definitional requirements for a "reorganization" create much of the complexity in current law. Some of these requirements are based on statutory rules, and others are of judicial origin. There are persuasive arguments for standardizing and making uniform these rules, as well as the rules prescribing the various forms of taxable acquisitions.

a. Boot as consideration.—No consideration other than voting stock is permitted in a B reorganization. A C reorganization permits a limited amount of boot (up to 20 percent of the total consideration). No specific statutory rule limits the amount of boot in an A reorganization, although the continuity of interest doctrine imposes some limitation. In certain cases, the assumption of liabilities may be treated as boot and in certain other cases, it may not be. No policy justification can be found for maintaining these disparate rules in what are essentially economically equivalent transactions.

b. Voting stock as consideration.—The qualifying consideration in a B or C reorganization, or a reverse triangular merger, must be voting stock. No such limitation applies in an A reorganization or a forward triangular merger.

c. Stock of corporation in control of acquiring corporation as consideration.—If structured correctly, as many as three tiers of acquiring corporations may be involved in an acquisitive transaction without affecting reorganization status. It is unclear from the statute whether reorganization status can be preserved if the structuring is not proper and, for example, the acquiring corporation is in the third tier of corporations * * *. It is also questionable whether stock of a corporation involving more remote ownership may be used. This introduces unnecessary rigidity when a target corporation is acquired by one or more members of an affiliated group.

d. Subsidiary mergers.—Different rules apply depending upon the direction of a subsidiary merger under section 368(a)(2)(D) or 368(a)(2)(E). Further, the "substantially all" limitation (discussed below) applies to subsidiary mergers even though they are nominally classified as A reorganizations. Thus, the requirements for a subsidiary merger are closer to C reorganizations than A reorganizations. The different, inconsistent, and complex requirements applicable to an acquisition through a subsidiary have been described as impossible to justify.

e. "Substantially all" requirement.—As noted, C reorganizations and subsidiary mergers impose a "substantially all" limitation. Certain

D reorganizations have the same requirement. No such limitation is contained in an A reorganization. Thus, for example, a predisposition of assets prior to an acquisition may cause the transaction to fail as a C reorganization [Helvering v. Elkhorn Coal Co., p. 523], but [not] as an A reorganization [Commissioner v. Morris Trust, p. 738].

Furthermore, the exact meaning of "substantially all" is unclear. Ruling guidelines applicable to C reorganizations and subsidiary mergers establish a 70 percent of gross assets and 90 percent of net assets standard [Rev. Proc. 77–37, p. 529, Note 6]. Case law in the D reorganization area has permitted a much smaller percentage of assets to qualify as "substantially all" [Smothers v. United States, p. 788].

f. Predisposition of assets.—As described above, a predisposition of assets prior to an acquisition may affect qualification as a C reorganization or a subsidiary merger. No such problem generally occurs in an A or B reorganization.

g. Overlap issues.—With the exception of a transaction qualifying as both a C and D reorganization where D reorganization status is mandated [I.R.C. § 368(a)(2)(A)], the statute does not provide rules settling overlap questions between and among reorganization provisions. This creates substantial uncertainty where the tax consequences of the transaction depend upon the specific category of reorganization that is satisfied.

h. Continuity of interest requirement.—This judicial doctrine is of uncertain application. The portion of total consideration consisting of an equity interest must be a "material part" of the consideration for the transferred assets [Helvering v. Minnesota Tea Company, p. 517, Note 2]. However, where 38 percent of the consideration consisted of callable preferred stock, this requirement has been considered satisfied [John A. Nelson Company v. Helvering, p. 514].

Moreover, the assumption underlying the limitation is that preferred treatment should be provided to consideration in the form of stock because stock represents a continuing commitment by the shareholders of the target corporation in the risks of the target business after the acquisition. This policy goal may not be effectively implemented where, for example, preferred stock subject to early redemption is provided tax-free treatment whereas a long-term creditor interest is not. In that case, the preferred stock may represent much less of a continuing commitment in the business risks of the target corporation than the long-term creditor interest.

* * *

Finally, the existence of continuity of interest may depend upon the nature of the interest in the target corporation surrendered by the target investor. For example, in a merger of a stock savings and loan association into a mutual savings and loan association, where the former shareholders of the target corporation received passbook savings accounts and certificates of deposit in the acquiring entity (the only form of "equity" available in the acquiring entity), the Supreme Court held that the continuity of interest requirement was not satisfied [Paulsen v. Commissioner, p. 572]. In contrast, where interests in a mutual savings and loan association were exchanged for interests in an acquiring mutual savings and loan association, the IRS held that continuity of interest was satisfied.

i. Continuity of business enterprise and business purpose doctrines.—Two other non-statutory requirements for a corporate reorganization are the business purpose and continuity of business enterprise doctrines. The regulations provide that the trade or business of the target corporation must be continued, or a "significant portion" of the target company's historic business assets must be used in a trade or business following the acquisition, in order to satisfy the continuity of business enterprise requirement. Some uncertainty surrounds the exact parameters of these tests.

j. Linking of shareholder level consequences to corporate level consequences and to tax treatment of other shareholders.—Current law links the shareholder level consequences of a reorganization to the corporate level consequences and to the tax treatment of other shareholders in the transaction. This produces a number of anomalous results.

For example, a transaction that fails reorganization status at the corporate level (e.g., because a predisposition of assets causes failure of the "substantially all" requirement) will therefore be fully taxable at the shareholder level, even though the shareholders of the target corporation all receive stock in the acquiring corporation. This is contrary to the policy decision that stock in an acquiring corporation should entitle a target shareholder to tax-free treatment.

As another example, failure to satisfy a shareholder level requirement (e.g., continuity of interest) will make a transaction completely taxable at the corporate level. This recently occurred in the case of Paulsen v. Commissioner [p. 572] where, because of failure of continuity of interest, a merger of a stock savings and loan association into a mutual savings and loan association was a taxable transaction. A more rational system would permit the corporate merger to be tax-free so long as the acquiring entity obtained only a carryover basis in the assets transferred.

A final example is illustrated by May B. Kass v. Commissioner [p. 580]. In that case, a single minority target shareholder who received solely stock in the acquiring corporation in an acquisition, was required to treat the exchange as a taxable one because of failure of the overall transaction to satisfy continuity of interest. No apparent policy reason can be found to justify linking the tax consequences for one shareholder of a target corporation to the tax treatment of other such shareholders. Furthermore, * * * the well-advised may, in any event, be able to obtain nonrecognition treatment for the minority shareholder through the formation of a holding company.

k. Whipsaw.—[T]he complexity of the reorganization definition creates many whipsaw possibilities against the government or the taxpayer. The statutory scheme is replete with reasons for different taxpayers to characterize a transaction differently: taxable or tax-free treatment of stock received by such shareholders; taxable or tax-free treatment to the target corporation itself; carryover or cost basis treatment to the acquiring corporation; survival or termination of attributes of the target corporation. The risk of whipsaw has often led the IRS to decline to rule in a number of areas, producing additional uncertainty.

Explicit electivity of the tax result of a transaction, and separation of corporate and shareholder level tax consequences, would do much to minimize the whipsaw possibilities.

* * *

[2.] *Problems relating to treatment of investors in a reorganization.* In addition to the problems identified above, current law provides some special problems relating to the proper tax treatment of investors in a reorganization.

a. Treatment of securities.—Current law treats the fair market value of securities received in a reorganization as boot except to the extent the principal amount of securities received does not exceed the principal amount of securities surrendered. [T]he proper measure of boot is the excess of the issue price of securities received over the basis of securities surrendered.

* * *

[3.] *Discontinuities between stock and asset acquisitions.* An acquisition of the stock of a target corporation and an acquisition of its assets often have identical economic consequences. Under present law, however, the tax consequences of the two transactions may vary dramatically.

a. Acquisition of stock v. acquisition of assets.—An acquisition of stock may be taxable or tax-free to the target shareholders, depending upon whether the transaction qualifies as a reorganization. In either event, there is no immediate corporate level tax consequences in the transaction, no step-up in the basis of the corporate assets, and absent some limitation under section 382, corporate level attributes are preserved intact. An exception applies where the transaction is taxable at the shareholder level and a section 338 election is made.

In contrast, an asset acquisition triggers immediate tax consequences at the corporate level unless the transaction qualifies as a reorganization. If the transaction is not a reorganization, the acquiring corporation obtains a stepped-up basis in assets acquired, and corporate attributes are terminated. * * *

In short, current law permits taxpayers to structure economically equivalent transactions in a variety of ways, sometimes with dramatically disparate tax consequences. This flexibility operates to the benefit of the well-advised, but to the detriment of the ill-advised. No policy justification can be found for this outcome.

b.   Basis in stock in controlled subsidiaries.—The discontinuities under current law between stock acquisitions and asset acquisitions often result from the disparities between "outside" stock basis and "inside" asset basis of a controlled subsidiary. Yet, current law does not provide any uniform system for conforming the two.

For example, if P acquires the stock of T in a B reorganization, P's basis in the T stock is determined by the historical basis of the former shareholders of T in their stock. This may present significant practical problems. Further, the historical stock basis of the former shareholders may have no relation to the "inside" asset basis of T.

If, on the other hand, P acquires the assets of T and then drops the assets down to newly-formed S, P obtains a basis in S stock equal to the net basis of the T assets. * * *

IV. SUMMARY OF PROPOSALS

The principal proposals contained in the bill are described below * * *.

A.   *Definition of qualified acquisition (new section 364 of the Code)*. In general, the bill consolidates, simplifies, and makes uniform the rules classifying corporate mergers and acquisitions * * *.

New section 364 defines "qualified acquisition" as meaning any "qualified stock acquisition" or any "qualified asset acquisition." A qualified stock acquisition is defined as any transaction or series of transactions during the 12–month acquisition period in which one corporation acquires stock representing control of another corporation. A qualified asset acquisition means (1) any statutory merger or consolidation, or (2) any other transaction in which one corporation acquires at least 70 percent of the gross fair market value and at least 90 percent of the net fair market value of the assets of another corporation held immediately before the acquisition, and the transferor corporation distributes, within 12 months of the acquisition date, all of its assets (other than assets retained to meet claims) to its shareholders or creditors.

For these purposes, the definition of "control" is conformed to that contained in section 1504(a)(2) of the Code.

* * *

The common-law doctrines of continuity of interest, continuity of business enterprise, and business purpose would have no applicability in determining whether a transaction qualifies as a qualified acquisition.

The bill repeals section 368 acquisitive reorganizations ("A", "B" and "C" reorganizations and subsidiary mergers) under current law and would be replaced by the rules for qualified acquisitions. The "D" reorganization rules would be replaced by special rules * * * relating to acquisitions between related parties. Transactions qualifying under current law as an "E" reorganization * * * and an "F" reorganization * * * are conformed to the definition of qualified acquisition. Finally, the "G" reorganization rules (bankruptcy reorganizations), developed largely in response to continuity of interest problems * * *, are no longer needed and therefore are repealed.

B. *Elective tax treatment of qualified acquisitions (new section 365 of the Code).* The corporate level tax consequences of a qualified acquisition are explicitly made elective. Under new section 365, all qualified acquisitions are treated as "carryover basis acquisitions" unless an election to be treated as a "cost basis acquisition" is made.

In general, elections may be made on a corporation-by-corporation basis. Thus, for example, if an acquiring corporation makes a qualified stock acquisition of both a target corporation and a target subsidiary, a cost basis election may be made for the target corporation but, if desired, no such election need be made for the target subsidiary.

Within a single corporation, the same election must generally apply for all of the assets of the corporation. A consistency rule would provide that assets that are acquired which were held by a single corporation during the consistency period must be treated consistently, either as all cost basis or all carryover basis.

* * *

In general, no cost basis election may be made with respect to any qualified acquisition between related parties. These generally refer to transactions where, after application of the attribution rules, there is a 50 percent or greater common ownership between the target and acquiring corporations. * * * [A] mandatory cost basis election generally applies to a qualified asset acquisition where the acquiring corporation is a non-taxable entity (such as a tax-exempt entity, a regulated investment company, or a foreign corporation).

* * *

C. *Corporate level tax consequences of qualified acquisitions (sections 361, 362 and 381 of the Code).* The corporate level tax consequences of a qualified acquisition result directly from the election made at the corporate level. For example, in the case of a carryover basis acquisition, no gain or loss is recognized by the target corporation and the acquiring corporation obtains a carryover basis in any assets acquired. Attributes carry over under section 381.

In the case of a cost basis acquisition, the target corporation recognizes gain or loss and the acquiring corporation obtains a basis in any assets acquired determined under section 1012. Attributes do not carry over. Where the cost basis acquisition is a qualified stock acquisition, the target corporation is deemed to have sold all of its assets for fair market value at the close of the acquisition date in a transaction in which gain or loss is recognized, and then is treated as a new corporation which purchased all of such assets as of the beginning of the day after the acquisition date.

* * *

The basis of any property received by a target corporation in a qualified asset acquisition is the fair market value of such property on the acquisition date. * * *.

Under the bill, section * * * 338 of current law [is] repealed.

D. *Shareholder level tax consequences of qualified acquisitions (sections 354, 356, and 358 of the Code).* In general, shareholder level tax consequences of a qualified acquisition are determined independent of the corporate level tax consequences and independent of the election made at the corporate level. Thus, even if a transaction is treated as a cost basis acquisition at the corporate level, it may be wholly or partly tax free at the shareholder level. In addition, shareholder level consequences are generally determined shareholder-by-shareholder, and the consequences to one shareholder do not affect the tax treatment of other shareholders or investors of the target corporation.

As a general rule, nonrecognition treatment is provided to shareholders or security holders of the target corporation upon receipt of "qualifying consideration," i.e., stock or securities of the acquiring corporation * * *. The nonrecognition rule applies to the receipt of securities only to the extent the issue price of any securities received does not exceed the adjusted basis of any securities surrendered.

* * *

Receipt of "nonqualifying consideration" (i.e., any consideration other than qualifying consideration) generally results in recognition of gain to the shareholder or security holder.

* * *

In general, shareholders or security holders obtain an [exchanged] basis in any qualifying consideration received, and a fair market value basis in any nonqualifying consideration received. * * *.

* * *

NOTE

Other consistency schemes. Unfortunately, Congress has demonstrated little interest in recent years toward engaging in a systematic overhaul of the tax rules that apply to corporate dispositions and acquisitions. Commentators continue to explore alternative approaches to establishing consistency in this area. The Senate Finance Committee contemplated an elective scheme. Under this scheme, the transferor corporation and the acquiring corporation would elect whether the transaction should be treated as taxable to the transferor (with a corresponding step-up or step-down in asset basis to the acquiring corporation) or nontaxable to the transferor (with historical basis in the transferred business perpetuated for the acquiring corporation). As an alternative to an elective scheme, a mandatory scheme might be adopted. Two alternative mandatory schemes exist. On the one hand, all corporate dispositions could be taxed immediately regardless of the nature of the consideration provided by the acquiring corporation (with corresponding basis adjustments for the acquiring corporation). Alternatively, all corporate dispositions could be accorded tax free treatment and, correspondingly, historical asset basis would be perpetuated. For a thorough evaluation of the merits of a mandatory taxation scheme, see Glenn E. Coven, "Taxing Corporate Acquisitions: A Proposal for Mandatory Uniform Rules," 44 Tax Law Review 145 (1989).

*

CHAPTER 13

CARRYOVERS AND CARRYBACKS

Every corporation has certain unique tax qualities. For example, it has a basis in its assets. It may have a net operating loss carryover[1] or a capital loss carryover.[2] A variety of other tax attributes also exist. See I.R.C. §§ 381(c)(1)–(26).

When a business conducted by a corporation is transferred, the corporation's tax attributes may or may not accompany the transferred business. If a corporation sells its assets, the tax attributes of the selling corporation remain with the seller and simply disappear if the seller is liquidated. When a corporation transfers its assets in a nontaxable reorganization, however, the transferor's tax attributes gravitate to the acquiring corporation along with the transferred assets. For example, the acquiring corporation receives a transferred basis in assets acquired in a reorganization. See I.R.C. § 362(b). In addition to basis, the attributes identified in I.R.C. § 381(c) also gravitate to the acquiring corporation when assets are transferred in a reorganization (or in a subsidiary liquidation that satisfies I.R.C. § 332). See I.R.C. § 381(a). When the shareholders of a corporation sell their stock or transfer their stock in a reorganization, the target corporation and its tax attributes remain intact and ownership of the corporate entity shifts to the transferee.[3]

The tax attribute that has received the greatest attention from Congress and the courts in connection with the transfer of a corporate business is the net operating loss ("NOL"). When a C Corporation has deductions in excess of gross income, the resulting NOL may be carried back and applied against taxable income in the two tax years prior to the year in which the loss arose. If the entire NOL is not absorbed by taxable income in the two preceding years, the remaining amount may be carried forward and applied against taxable income for up to twenty years after the year in which the loss arose. See I.R.C. § 172; pp. 86–88. Both Congress and the courts have dramatically narrowed the opportunities that exist to apply tax losses of one enterprise against income generated by another enterprise. Much attention has been directed toward restricting the application of pre-acquisition losses to post-acquisition income (loss carryovers). Restrictions

---

1. See I.R.C. § 172; pp. 86–88.

2. See I.R.C. § 1212(a)(1).

3. If stock is sold and the buyer makes an election under I.R.C. § 338, however, the deemed asset sale extinguishes the target's historical attributes. See I.R.C. § 338(a)(1); pp. 86–88.

also exist on the application of post-acquisition losses to pre-acquisition income (loss carrybacks).

A. RESTRICTIONS ON LOSS CARRYOVERS

1. THE EVIL

Larry Low is the sole shareholder of Loser, Inc., a C Corporation. Over the years, Larry has contributed more than $1,000,000 to the corporation. The corporation's deductions exceeded its gross income during each of the past several years and the corporation currently has an NOL carryover of $1,000,000. The prospect of future profitability is bleak. Loser, Inc. has assets worth roughly $100,000 in which it has a basis of roughly $100,000.

Winner, Inc. is a C Corporation that has consistently generated taxable income of roughly $3,000,000 in each of the past several years and anticipates similar amounts of income in future years. Winner would like to acquire Loser's NOL carryover and use it to offset Winner's future taxable income.

If Winner acquires the assets of Loser for $100,000, Loser realizes no gain on the asset sale but Loser's NOL disappears if Loser is liquidated. In contrast, if Winner acquires the assets of Loser for stock in a transaction that qualifies as a reorganization, Winner receives Loser's NOL carryover. See I.R.C. § 381(a)(1). If the acquisition occurs on December 31, Year 4, and the tax law imposed no restrictions, Winner could offset its Year 5 taxable income by Loser's $1,000,000 NOL carryover. As a result, Winner's Year 5 tax liability would be reduced by roughly $340,000. The tax savings derived by Winner could be shared with Loser if, at the time of the acquisition, the parties negotiated a $170,000 increase in the purchase price (mostly in the form of stock to maintain reorganization treatment). In this event, the transfer of the NOL carryover would enable each taxpayer to gain $170,000 at the expense of the government.

Neither the courts nor Congress were receptive to the prospect of using one corporation's tax losses to offset future income of another corporation. The NOL rules were intended to permit one taxpayer to average income and losses over a period of years. See p. 87. They were not intended to permit a loss to offset income unrelated to the loss. The earliest attacks on this result, however, were waged with relatively unsophisticated weapons.

2. PRIMITIVE REMEDIES

Libson Shops, Inc. v. Koehler

Supreme Court of the United States, 1957.
353 U.S. 382, 77 S.Ct. 990.

■ MR. JUSTICE BURTON delivered the opinion of the Court.

The issue before us is whether * * * a corporation resulting from a merger of 17 separate incorporated businesses, which had filed separate income tax returns, may carry over and deduct the pre-merger net operating losses of three of its constituent corporations from the post-merger income attributable to the other businesses. We hold that such a carry-over and deduction is not permissible.

Petitioner, Libson Shops, Inc., was incorporated * * * to provide management services for corporations selling women's apparel at retail * * *. At about the same time, the same interests incorporated 16 separate corporations to sell women's apparel at retail at separate locations * * *. Each of these 16 sales corporations was operated separately and filed separate income tax returns. Petitioner's sole activity was to provide management services for them. The outstanding stock of all 17 corporations was owned * * * by the same individuals in the same proportions.

On August 1, 1949, the 16 sales corporations were merged into petitioner * * *. New shares of petitioner's stock were issued, pro rata, in exchange for the stock of the sales corporations * * *. Following the merger, petitioner conducted the entire business as a single enterprise. Thus, the effect of the merger was to convert 16 retail businesses and one managing agency, reporting their incomes separately, into a single enterprise filing one income tax return.

Prior to the merger, three of the sales corporations showed net operating losses [totaling $22,432.76] * * *. In the year following the merger, each of the retail units formerly operated by these three corporations continued to sustain a net operating loss.

In its income tax return for the first year after the merger, petitioner claimed a deduction of the above $22,432.76 as a carry-over of its pre-merger losses * * *. The Commissioner of Internal Revenue disallowed it and petitioner paid the resulting tax deficiency. In due course petitioner brought this suit for a refund * * *. [T]he * * * District Court * * * dismissed petitioner's complaint and the Court of Appeals affirmed. We granted certiorari * * *.

[The predecessor to I.R.C. § 172] provide[d] generally (1) that a "net operating loss" is the excess of the taxpayer's deductions over its gross income; (2) that, if the taxpayer has a net operating loss, the loss may be used as a "net operating loss carry-back" to the two prior years and, if not exhausted by that carry-back, the remainder may be used as a "net operating loss carry-over" to the three succeeding years; and (3) that the aggregate of the net operating loss carry-backs and carry-overs applicable to a given taxable year is the "net operating loss deduction * * *."

We are concerned here with a claim to carry over an operating loss to the immediately succeeding taxable year. The particular provision on which petitioner's case rests is as follows:

If for any taxable year beginning after December 31, 1947, and before January 1, 1950, the taxpayer has a net operating loss, such net operating loss shall be a net operating loss carry-over for each of the three succeeding taxable years * * *.

The controversy centers on the meaning of "the taxpayer." The contentions of the parties require us to decide whether it can be said that petitioner, a combination of 16 sales businesses, is "the taxpayer" having the pre-merger losses of three of those businesses.

In support of its denial of the carry-over, the Government argues that this statutory privilege is not available unless the corporation claiming it is the same taxable entity as that which sustained the loss * * *. Petitioner, on the other hand, argues that a corporation resulting from a statutory merger is treated as the same taxable entity as its constituents to whose legal attributes it has succeeded by operation of state law. However, we find it unnecessary to discuss this issue since an alternative argument made by the Government is dispositive of this case. The Government contends that the carry-over privilege is not available unless there is a continuity of business enterprise. It argues that the prior year's loss can be offset against the current year's income only to the extent that this income is derived from the operation of substantially the same business which produced the loss. Only to that extent is the same "taxpayer" involved.

The requirement of a continuity of business enterprise as applied to this case is in accord with the legislative history of the carry-over and carry-back provisions. Those provisions were enacted to ameliorate the unduly drastic consequences of taxing income strictly on an annual basis. They were designed to permit a taxpayer to set off its lean years against its lush years, and to strike something like an average taxable income computed over a period longer than one year. There is, however, no indication in their legislative history that these provisions were designed to permit the averaging of the pre-merger losses of one business with the post-merger income of some other business which had been operated and taxed separately before the merger. What history there is suggests that Congress primarily was concerned with the fluctuating income of a single business.

* * *

We do not imply that a question of tax evasion or avoidance is involved. [The predecessor to I.R.C. § 269] does contain provisions which may vitiate a tax deduction that was made possible by the acquisition of corporate property for the "principal purpose" of tax evasion or avoidance. And that section is inapplicable here since there was no finding that tax evasion or avoidance was the "principal purpose" of the merger. The fact that [the predecessor to I.R.C. § 269] is inapplicable does not mean that petitioner is automatically entitled to a carry-over. The availability of this privilege depends on the proper interpretation to be given to the carry-over provisions. We find nothing in those provisions which suggests that they should be construed to give a "windfall" to a taxpayer who happens to have merged with other corporations. The purpose of these provisions is not to give a merged taxpayer a tax advantage over others who have not merged. We conclude that petitioner is not entitled to a carry-over since the income against which the offset is claimed was not produced by substantially the same businesses which incurred the losses.

NOTES

1. *Prior law.* Prior to the Libson Shops decision, the courts focused on whether the corporate entity that existed after the acquisition was the entity that had incurred the loss. See, e.g., Alprosa Watch Corp. v. Commissioner, 11 T.C. 240, 1948 WL 37 (1948) (NOL carryover could be applied against the income of a newly created business conducted by the corporation that incurred the NOL, notwithstanding that the ownership of the stock of the corporation had changed and that the old business that generated the NOL was discontinued). This may explain why the Commissioner argued in the Libson Shops case that the loss should be disallowed because the taxpayer corporation was not the same entity that sustained the loss. See p. 648. That argument (which the Libson Shops court did not reach) could no longer be advanced with respect to transactions occurring after enactment of the 1954 Code because I.R.C. § 381 explicitly sanctions the transfer of an NOL carryover in a statutory merger that qualifies as a reorganization. See I.R.C. § 381(a)(2).

2. *Administering the Libson Shops doctrine.* Under the Libson Shops doctrine, NOL carryovers may only be used to offset income generated by "substantially the same business which produced the loss." While this approach may seem logical in theory, it is generally difficult to isolate the post-acquisition income and deductions of the constituent parts of a combined enterprise. Consequently, the Libson Shops doctrine is problematic from a practical standpoint.

3. *I.R.C. § 382.* In addition to I.R.C. § 381, the 1954 Code included the earliest version of § 382, a statutory restriction on the use of NOL carryovers after an acquisition. Disagreement existed among the courts as to whether the Libson Shops case operated as an independent judicial restriction on the use of NOL carryovers with respect to transactions that occurred after enactment of the 1954 Code. Compare Maxwell Hardware Co. v. Commissioner, 343 F.2d 713 (9th Cir.1965) (holding that Libson Shops did not apply to post–1954 Code transactions) with Rev. Rul. 63–40, 1963–1 C.B. 46, as modified by T.I.R. 773 (10/13/65) (suggesting Libson Shops still applied to post–1954 Code transactions).

4. *I.R.C. § 269.* Even prior to enactment of the 1954 Code, a broad, anti-tax avoidance provision (the predecessor to I.R.C. § 269) was sometimes invoked to deny the use of an NOL carryover after an acquisition. As the Libson Shops court suggests and the Stange case that follows illustrates, the effectiveness of I.R.C. § 269 is severely limited by the motive standard it employs.

Stange Company v. Commissioner

United States Tax Court, 1977.
36 T.C.M. 31.

■ SCOTT, JUDGE: * * *

FINDINGS OF FACT

     * * *

     Stange Company is * * * the successor * * * of * * * Media Graphics, Inc. (MGI). * * *

The controversy here principally involves transactions relating to * * * MGI and April Corporation (April). * * *

MGI's * * * business was commercial photography * * *. [I]n December of 1965 G.F. DeCoursin, Mack Duce, and Norris Adams each purchased substantial amounts of MGI stock, and by December of 1967 they had acquired 51 percent of the stock.

By December of 1965, MGI had accumulated a substantial earnings deficit. It was having difficulty meeting its current obligations to employees and suppliers and had incurred substantial debts. * * *

On April 13, 1966, [April Corporation] was organized. * * * Until the acquisition of MGI by April in May of 1968, April had outstanding 10,000 shares, owned equally by G.F. DeCoursin and Mack Duce.

April was formed to acquire the assets of a bankrupt corporation, Jem Foods, which had been in the business of blending doughnut and pancake mixes and other dried products principally for distribution in Texas. One of its customers was Kentucky Fried Chicken (KFC) for whom it blended fried chicken batter. Shortly after the acquisition of Jem's assets, April discontinued its unprofitable lines of business and eventually limited its activities solely to blending KFC's seasoned flour for national distribution. * * * It continued operations with KFC as its only customer until May of 1968, the date of the acquisition here in issue.

* * *

After its organization, April's management was concerned continuously about its relationship with KFC, its sole customer. KFC was engaged in rapid expansion, and the personnel with whom April's employees dealt were often changing. There were occasional complaints from KFC's franchisees about product quality and the use of April's pre-mixed flour, rather than using flour mixed themselves. April's management was also concerned with the financial security of KFC. Other franchise fried chicken restaurant chains had bankrupted, and some of KFC's diversification activities were regarded as questionable.

* * *

In early April of 1968, the management of April and MGI evidenced an interest in reorganizing and consolidating the businesses of the two corporations. * * * The accountants [initially] suggested that to preserve MGI's net operating loss carryovers of about $90,000 April should merge into MGI with April's shareholders exchanging their stock for MGI common stock. * * *

On April 19, 1968, * * * a tentative plan of reorganization and a schedule of action were prepared. The form of reorganization suggested by the accountants was the creation of a holding company (April) owning all the stock of an operating company (MGI) which would operate the businesses formerly owned by April and MGI separately. This configuration would be achieved by an exchange by [all the] MGI shareholders of [all the] MGI stock for April stock. April would then transfer its assets and liabilities to MGI, either as a capital contribution or in exchange for additional MGI stock. * * *

* * *

On May 13, 1968, the directors and shareholders of both April and MGI met and adopted the proposed reorganization plan. * * *

* * *

After the reorganization of April and MGI, administrative services of both corporations were consolidated and the administrative staff of twelve was cut by three or four persons.

* * *

In 1969, April formed a new subsidiary to acquire the assets of a company that manufactured refrigeration equipment for trucks. * * * In 1970, April formed another subsidiary * * * to operate in the chemical cleaning business. * * * The April management investigated several other diverse businesses as possibilities for acquisition during this period.

April Corporation had the following earnings history during the 3 years in which it was an operating company.

Period Ending	Earnings (Loss)
December 31, 1966	($13,884.89)
December 31, 1967	$47,111.94
December 31, 1968	$43,724.08

* * *

Media Graphics, Inc. reported the following earnings during the years prior to its consolidation with April:

Period Ending	Earnings (Loss)
August 31, 1964	($54,060.38)
August 31, 1965	($46,125.43)
August 31, 1966	$12,132.71
August 31, 1967	$2,948.85

Thus, MGI reported a net operating loss carryover to its fiscal year ending August 31, 1968, of $85,104.25. * * *

[O]n May 18, 1968, the assets and liabilities of April were transferred from April to MGI on their books, and thereafter accounting for the operations previously owned by April was made as a division of MGI. For simplicity, this division will hereafter be referred to as the flour division and MGI's prior operations will be referred to as the studio division.

MGI as a whole was continuously profitable after the reorganization. However, the studio division, the operations of which produced the losses here in issue, continued after the consolidation to produce losses in its normal operations for the remainder of MGI's fiscal year ending August 31, 1968, and for its fiscal year ending August 30, 1969. * * *

* * *

On its Federal income tax return for its fiscal year ending August 31, 1968, MGI reported a net operating loss carryover of $85,104.25 and deducted $4,646.18 of this net operating loss to offset taxable income in this amount reported before net operating loss deduction * * *.

On its Federal income tax return for its fiscal year ending August 31, 1969, MGI deducted from reported income of $274,985.62 prior to net operating loss deduction [the remaining] net operating loss carried over from prior years * * *.

Respondent in his notice of deficiency disallowed the above net operating loss deductions and increased taxable income by the amount of the studio division losses during both portions of the fiscal year ending August 31, 1968. * * * Respondent explained these adjustments as follows:

> It is determined that the principal purpose for April Corporation's acquisition of control of * * * Media Graphics, Inc. and the transfer of its business to [MGI], on May 18, 1968, was to gain the benefit of Media Graphics' net operating losses * * *, thus avoiding payment of federal income taxes.

OPINION

* * *

Respondent has disallowed to MGI certain deductions * * * pursuant to section 269(a) based on the acquisition of MGI stock by April and the acquisition of April's assets by MGI. * * *

Petitioner asserts that the acquisition of all MGI stock by April was not an acquisition described in section 269(a)(1) and that the receipt of April's assets by MGI was not an acquisition described in section 269(a)(2). These acquisitions are further argued by petitioner to have been made for a purpose other than that prohibited by section 269(a). Respondent disputes each of these contentions.

For the reasons discussed below, we find that the acquisitions of MGI stock by April and of April's assets by MGI did not have as their principal purpose the evasion or avoidance of Federal income tax, and we therefore hold for petitioner. In so holding, we do not reach the alternative arguments of petitioner that neither of these acquisitions meets the requirements of section 269(a)(1) or (2).

In our view the evidence is clear that the acquisition by April of control of MGI and the acquisition by MGI of April's assets were steps contemplated and taken as integral parts of a single plan of action adopted by the common owners of the two corporations. * * * Thus, while either acquisition might arguably satisfy the threshold requirements of section 269(a)(1) and (2), we may look to the purposes of the overall plan to determine the principal purpose for both acquisitions. If that purpose is not to evade or avoid Federal income tax, then section 269 does not authorize respondent's disallowance of deductions * * * in this case.

For tax evasion or avoidance to be the principal purpose for an acquisition under section 269, it must be the purpose that "outranks, or exceeds in importance, any other one purpose." S. Rept. No. 627, 78th Cong., 1st Sess. (1943), 1944 C.B. 973. The determination of the purposes of the acquisitions here in issue must be made by an examination of all events surrounding the transactions and all facts shown by the record.

Petitioner has asserted several purposes which it claims have motivated the acquisitions here. These asserted purposes predictably do not include tax avoidance. They include:

(1) supplying capital to MGI;

(2) providing economy in administration of the two business entities;

(3) providing diversity of investment; and

(4) creating a vehicle for future business acquisitions and diversification.

First, petitioner contends that MGI's need for capital required the combination of April and MGI assets in one corporate vehicle. The record shows that MGI was having difficulty obtaining cash to pay employees and suppliers. It had borrowed heavily, and its credit was poor. Furthermore, it needed additional funds to improve its physical plant. * * *

Our examination convinces us that MGI did in fact have a significant need for additional funds. Respondent, however, argues that this need could have been satisfied by intercorporate loans. While loans could have supplied cash for some period, the attendant obligation to repay reduces the desirability of this remedy. Certainly, choice of an arrangement providing a permanent infusion of capital to MGI is within the scope of sound business judgment. We find that petitioner's asserted purpose was a legitimate and significant purpose for the acquisitions. * * *

Petitioner also contends that economy was gained by consolidation of the administrative functions of the two corporations. The record shows that the bookkeeping and payroll functions were consolidated and that three or four employees were eliminated from a combined staff of twelve as a result of the reorganization. Respondent argues that this economy could have been approximated by intercorporate arrangements for sharing of employees and office space. While such an arrangement might lead to some economy, we are convinced that in this case the degree of savings was significantly greater in the wholly consolidated operation. * * *

As a third business purpose for the acquisitions, petitioner contends that the owners of April sought to diversify their investment. It notes that the continued success of April was dependent upon maintaining its KFC business and upon KFC's own financial health. Diversification is argued to have provided more security for April stockholders and a corporation more attractive to investors.

We do not doubt that the owners of April felt insecure in their total dependence upon KFC. However, we can discern no improvement in their condition after the reorganization. April's owners had been substantial stockholders in MGI since December of 1965 and at the time of the acquisitions here they controlled MGI. In this position their investment was as diversified as it could be after the acquisitions. The reorganization did not alter the risk April assumed in its relationship with KFC, nor did it provide any alternative use for April's assets if the KFC business were lost.

[F]or these reasons, we conclude that petitioner has failed to show that diversification of investment was a significant purpose of the questioned acquisitions.

Finally, petitioner argues that a major purpose of the acquisitions was to provide a corporate structure adaptable to future corporate acquisitions. The record shows that the original owners and managers of April planned, even before the formation of April, to acquire a number of businesses within a corporate structure and eventually to make a public offering of stock. From 1965 to 1970, they did in fact make four such acquisitions, beginning with April and MGI. Petitioner's witnesses testified that the reorganization of April and MGI into holding and operating companies, respectively, was intended to, and in fact did, facilitate the later acquisitions.

We find that this asserted purpose was a legitimate and significant purpose for the acquisitions in issue. * * *

Though petitioner argues otherwise, we also find that one other purpose of the acquisitions in the instant case was to obtain the Federal income tax benefit resulting from the use of MGI's net operating loss carryover * * * to reduce earnings of the flour division. It is apparent that these carryovers would have been of no benefit had income-producing assets not been aligned in some way with the loss-producing corporation. In initial discussions with their accountants, the April and MGI managers were informed of methods of reorganization that would preserve the carryovers. Both Mr. DeCoursin and Mr. Adams testified that they were aware of the tax benefits of the acquisitions, and each had some idea of the level of tax savings. These facts alone do not establish tax avoidance as the principal purpose of the acquisitions, however. It is well established that the consideration of tax consequences is to be expected of any prudent businessman and that such consideration does not mandatorily require application of section 269. However, the magnitude of the recognized tax saving does have a bearing on its importance. In this case, the evidence shows that the tax saving gained by the reorganization was approximately $50,000.

As discussed above, there were several purposes for the acquisition of MGI stock by April and for the acquisition of April's assets by MGI. We have carefully considered the relative importance of these purposes to the April and MGI directors and shareholders at the time of the acquisitions. Mr. DeCoursin and Mr. Adams testified that the tax benefits were of little significance in their decisions. Respondent argues that the magnitude of the tax saving involved dictates a different conclusion. From a consideration of the entire record, we find that tax avoidance, while one purpose, did not exceed in importance any one of the other purposes for which the acquisitions in question were made. Consequently, the acquisitions did not have as their principal purpose the evasion or avoidance of Federal income tax and therefore respondent erred in disallowing the questioned deductions * * * under section 269.

NOTES

1. *Tax consequences of transfers.* Did the transfer of the MGI stock to April and/or the transfer of April's assets to MGI satisfy the Internal Revenue Code's definition of a "reorganization"? See I.R.C. § 368(a)(1). What were the tax consequences of these transactions? See I.R.C. §§ 118(a), 351(a), 358(a), 362(a), (b).

2. *Impact of Libson Shops doctrine.* Could MGI have used its NOL carryover if the Stange court had applied the Libson Shops doctrine?

3. *Impact of I.R.C. § 269.* The Stange court did not reach the taxpayer's argument that the transactions were not within the scope of I.R.C. § 269(a). Were either of the transactions described by that provision?

4. *Scope of I.R.C. § 269.* I.R.C. § 269 is not confined to acquisitions involving businesses with NOL carryovers. The provision can apply to acquisitions involving, "current, past or prospective credits, deductions, net operating losses or other allowances." Treas. Reg. § 1.269–3(b)(1).

3.   EFFECTIVE STATUTORY RESPONSE

The Internal Revenue Code of 1954 marked the beginning of a thirty-two year struggle by Congress to develop a mechanical provision that would, in appropriate cases, restrict the use of an NOL carryover after an acquisition, irrespective of the taxpayer's motives. It was not until 1986 that Congress finally achieved this goal. At that time, the current version of I.R.C. § 382 was enacted.

The current version of I.R.C. § 382 identifies potentially abusive transactions by focusing principally on changes in the stock ownership of a corporation with an NOL carryover (a "loss corporation"). When more than half of the stock of a loss corporation is transferred to new owners, an "ownership change" occurs and a statutory limitation is activated. After an ownership change occurs, the amount of income that a pre-existing NOL carryover may absorb is limited to a conservative estimate of the income that the loss corporation might have earned from the assets it owned immediately before the ownership change. The statute effectively precludes NOLs incurred before the new owners acquired a majority interest from absorbing income generated from capital provided by the new owners. By restricting the amount of income to which an NOL carryover may be applied, the statute normally eliminates the incentive to acquire a loss corporation to gain access to its NOL carryover.

I.R.C. § 382 is a technically complex provision that can best be mastered by focusing on two questions. First, what events must occur to trigger an "ownership change"? Second, how much income can an NOL carryover be applied against after an ownership change occurs?

a.   THE TRIGGER

I.R.C. §§ 382(g), (i), (k), (*l*)(3)

Conditions for an Ownership Change. I.R.C. § 382 is triggered by an "ownership change" (I.R.C. § 382(g)) with respect to a "loss corporation" (I.R.C. § 382(k)(1)). An ownership change occurs when *both* of the following conditions are met:

(a) An "owner shift involving a 5% shareholder" or an "equity structure shift" occurs. See I.R.C. §§ 382(g)(1)–(3).

(b) Immediately after the owner shift or equity structure shift, the percentage of stock owned by one or more 5% shareholders has increased by more than 50 percentage points over the lowest percentage of stock of the loss corporation owned by such shareholders at any time during the "testing period" (the immediately preceding three years). I.R.C. §§ 382(g)(1), (i).

The first condition for an ownership change merely identifies the point in time to assess whether the second condition has been satisfied. The first condition is satisfied almost any time a share of stock in a loss corporation changes hands. An "owner shift involving a 5% shareholder" occurs when there is *any* change in the respective ownership of stock of a loss corporation and the change affects the percentage of stock owned by a 5% shareholder before or after the change. I.R.C. § 382(g)(2). Thus, if Alicia owns 100% of the outstanding stock of a loss corporation and she sells a single share to an unrelated party (or the corporation issues a single new share to a party unrelated to Alicia), an "owner shift involving a 5% shareholder" occurs because Alicia no longer owns 100% of the stock of the loss corporation. An "equity structure shift" encompasses most reorganizations, as well as certain taxable reorganization-type transactions, public offerings and similar transactions. I.R.C. § 382(g)(3). A single transaction may entail both an owner shift involving a 5% shareholder and an equity structure shift.

The second condition for an ownership change is the heart of the § 382 trigger. It is only after the aggregate increase in stock ownership by 5% shareholders over a three year period crosses the designated 50% threshold that a limit is imposed on the amount of future income to which an NOL carryover may be applied.

Example 13–A (Mechanics of testing for ownership change): Bobbi always owned all 100 of the outstanding shares of Medco, Inc., a corporation with an NOL carryover. Bobbi now sells 50 shares of Medco to an unrelated party, Cal. The sale of shares is an "owner shift involving a 5% shareholder." An "ownership change" does not occur, however, because the percentage of stock owned by Cal in Medco (the "loss corporation") has not increased by *more than* 50 percentage points over the lowest percentage of stock of Medco owned by Cal during the immediately preceding three years. Cal's interest in Medco increased by 50 percentage points (from zero to 50%), not *more than* 50 percentage points. Bobbi's interest in Medco decreased (from 100% to 50%) and she is ignored because the test focuses exclusively on those shareholders whose percentage interests have increased.

Problem 13–1 (Identifying an ownership change): With regard to Example 13–A, would an ownership change occur if *one* of the following events occurred sometime after Bobbi sold the 50 shares of Medco to Cal?

(a) Bobbi sold an additional share of Medco stock to Cal.

(b) Cal sold ten of the shares he purchased from Bobbi to Esther (an unrelated party).

Identifying the Loss Corporation. A "loss corporation" is a corporation entitled to use an NOL carryover (or having an NOL for the taxable year in which the ownership change occurs). I.R.C. § 382(k)(1). A corporation entitled to use an NOL carryover may or may not have incurred the NOL that gave rise to the carryover. When stock of a corporation that incurred an NOL is transferred, the corporation remains intact and retains its tax attributes, including any NOL carryover stemming from the NOL it incurred. By contrast, when assets of a corporation with an NOL carryover are acquired by a profitable corporation in a transaction to which I.R.C. § 381 applies, the profitable corporation becomes a "loss corporation" when it inherits the NOL carryover.[4] In these circumstances, the profitable corporation becomes a "loss corporation" notwithstanding that the profitable corporation did not incur the NOL that gave rise to the carryover.

Example 13–B (Loss corporation that did not incur NOL): Gregg has always owned all 4,000 of the outstanding shares of Nender Co., a corporation with an NOL carryover. Nender has a market value of $4,000,000. Harriet has always owned all 3,000 of the outstanding shares of Prender, Inc., a profitable corporation. Prender has a market value of $6,000,000. Nender transfers all of its assets to Prender in exchange for 2,000 newly issued Prender shares and distributes the Prender shares to Gregg in a transaction that qualifies as a C reorganization.

An "ownership change" has occurred because the C reorganization is an "equity structure shift" (I.R.C. § 382(g)(3)) and the percentage of stock of "the loss corporation" (Prender)[5] owned by Harriet (60%)[6] has increased by more than 50 percentage points over the lowest percent-

---

4. See I.R.C. § 381(c)(1).

5. Prender is a "loss corporation" after the equity structure shift because Prender is "entitled to use" Nender's NOL carryover. See I.R.C. §§ 381(c)(1), 382(k)(1).

6. Harriet owns 3,000 out of 5,000 outstanding shares of Prender after the acquisition.

age of stock of a "predecessor corporation" (Nender)[7] owned by Harriet during the immediately preceding three years (zero). Gregg's interest in a loss corporation decreased (from 100% to 40%) so he is ignored in testing for an ownership change.

Problem 13–2 (Relevance of reorganization): Would the ownership change in Example 13–B have been avoided if the acquisition failed to qualify as a reorganization?

Problem 13–3 (Impact of reversing acquisition): In Example 13–B, would an ownership change be avoided if the acquisition were reversed (i.e., if Prender transferred all of its assets to Nender in exchange for 6,000 newly issued shares of Nender which Prender distributed to Harriet in a transaction that qualified as a C reorganization)?

Identifying 5% Shareholders—Family Unit. A "5% shareholder" is any person holding 5% or more of the stock of the loss corporation during the testing period. I.R.C. § 382(k)(7). For purposes of I.R.C. § 382, an individual and all members of her family as defined in I.R.C. § 318(a)(1) are treated as one person. I.R.C. § 382(l)(3)(A)(i). Thus, transfers of shares of a loss corporation among family members do not contribute to an ownership change.

Garber Industries v. Commissioner

United States Court of Appeals, Fifth Circuit, 2006.
435 F.3d 555.

■ DAVIS, CIRCUIT JUDGE: * * *

I.

Garber Industries Holding Co., Inc. ("Garber Industries") was incorporated in December 1982. Charles M. Garber owned 3,492.85 shares (68%) of the stock and his brother Kenneth R. Garber owned 1,312 shares (26%). The remaining shares were owned by siblings, spouses or children of the two main shareholders. Garber Industries suffered operating losses from 1983 to 1989 and again in 1992. Under I.R.C. § 172 net operating losses ("NOLs") could be carried forward and deducted. At the end of 1997, the balance of NOL carryforwards was over twenty million dollars.

In July 1996, Garber Industries undertook a reorganization. As a result of the reorganization, Charles Garber's ownership interest decreased from 68% to 19% and Kenneth Garber's ownership interest increased from 26% to 65%. The remaining ownership of the company remained unchanged.

---

7. See I.R.C. § 382(g)(1)(B).

*

The critical transfer with respect to this case occurred in April 1998 when Kenneth Garber and his wife sold all of their shares of Garber Industries stock (65%) to Charles Garber. Charles Garber's ownership interest increased from 19% to 84%. No other Garber Industries' stock changed ownership in that year.

On its 1998 return, Garber Industries deducted a net operating loss carryover of $808,935. The IRS audited the taxpayer's 1997 and 1998 returns and determined that the company had undergone an ownership change under section 382 as a result of Kenneth's stock sale to Charles in 1998. Under the Internal Revenue Code, an ownership change limits the amount of NOL carryover that can be deducted. As applied to Garber Industries, an ownership change would limit the NOL deduction to $121,258. In June 2001, the Commissioner issued a Notice of Deficiency resulting from the reduction in the amount of allowable deduction of net operating loss.

Garber Industries challenged the deficiency in the Tax Court. The parties settled all issues except those relating to the 1998 stock sale. It was agreed that if Kenneth's sale did not constitute an ownership change, the 1998 NOL carryover would be allowed in full and the tax deficiency for 1998 would be $5,070. The parties also agreed that if the sale did constitute an ownership change, the tax deficiency for 1998 would be $311,188. The Tax Court ruled in favor of the Commissioner and held that the sale between the brothers did constitute an ownership change thus limiting the deductibility of the NOL carryforwards and creating a larger tax deficiency for Garber Industries. Garber Industries appeals.

II.

The sole issue in this case is whether an ownership change occurred in relation to Garber Industries, as a result of the 1998 stock sale from Kenneth to Charles Garber, which triggers a limitation in the deduction of NOL carryforwards by the corporation under § 382 of the Internal Revenue Code. Whether an ownership change occurred depends on whether ownership of Kenneth's and Charles' Garber Industries stock can be aggregated or attributed to each other under the ownership rules set forth in §§ 382 and 318. If the brothers' stock can be aggregated or its ownership attributed to each other, then a sale between them does not cause an ownership change.

The purpose of section 382 is to prevent trafficking in net operating loss carryovers, which in the absence of a limitation may ordinarily be carried forward for 20 years. The statute limits the use of NOL carryovers by the "new loss corporation"—the corporation possessing the losses after an ownership change. § 382(a). An ownership change occurs if, immediately after an "owner shift" or "equity structure shift," the percentage of stock owned by one or more shareholders owning 5% or more of the corporation ("5% shareholder") has increased by more than 50 percentage points over the lowest percentage of stock owned by such persons during the testing period. § 382(g)(1), (k)(7). The testing period is the three year period ending on the date of the owner shift or equity structure shift. § 382(i). An owner shift is any change in corporate ownership affecting the percentage of stock owned by a 5% shareholder. § 382(g)(2).

Both Kenneth and Charles Garber were 5% shareholders. In the absence of an exception or modification to the above rules, the 1998 stock sale from Kenneth to Charles clearly caused an ownership change because the sale caused the ownership of Charles Garber to increase by more than 50 percentage points (from 19% to 84%).

In some circumstances, § 382 allows stock owned by family members to be grouped together for purposes of determining whether an ownership change occurred. To determine ownership of stock under § 382, the statute refers to the constructive ownership rules of § 318, with certain modifications. Subsection (*l*)(3)(A) of section 382 states—

(*l*) Certain additional operating rules. For purposes of this section—

>   (3) Operating rules relating to ownership of stock.

>>   (A) Constructive ownership. Section 318 (relating to constructive ownership of stock) shall apply in determining ownership of stock, except that—

>>>   (i) paragraphs (1) and (5)(B) of section 318(a) shall not apply and an individual and all members of his family described in paragraph (1) of section 318(a) shall be treated as 1 individual for purposes of applying this section[.]

The plain language of the Code supports the Tax Court's decision that the Garber Industries stock owned by Kenneth cannot be attributed to his brother Charles, or vice versa. Section 382(*l*)(3)(A) states that "an individual and all members of his family described in paragraph (1) of section 318(a) shall be treated as 1 individual for purposes of applying this section." The family members listed in paragraph (1) of section 318(a) are a person's "spouse", "his children, grandchildren, and parents." This list does not include siblings, which is the relationship between Charles and Kenneth Garber. Accordingly, the stock owned by each brother is not treated as owned by the other and the transaction between them as 5% shareholders triggers an ownership change in the company. We see nothing in the statute or argument of Garber Industries that persuades us that this simple reading of section 382 is not the correct one.

* * *

Garber Industries suggests that § 382 can be read to allow ownership to be attributed to and from a parent without regard to whether the parent is also a shareholder of the loss corporation. If this were allowed, a family group could be formed to aggregate the stock of Kenneth and Charles Garber around their common parent. We agree with the Tax Court that the individual or individuals who form the basis for the ownership analysis must be shareholders of the loss corporation. The whole point of section 382 is to identify ownership changes relative to 5% shareholders; a change of ownership by such a shareholder is the only change the statute addresses. Sections 382(g)(1), (g)(2), (k)(7). An ownership change is defined in terms of owner shifts affecting 5% shareholders. Section 382(g). All stock owners who are less than 5% shareholders of the corporation are grouped and their stock is treated as owned by one 5% shareholder. Id. Accordingly, it follows that the "individual" referred to in the constructive ownership analysis provisions of § 382(*l*)(3)(A) must be a shareholder and that individual is the starting point for the formation of a family group consisting of that individual's spouse, parents, children and grandchildren.

III.

In summary, the Tax Court properly interpreted § 382 as applied to a sale of stock between two shareholder brothers, when no parent or grandparent was a shareholder of the loss corporation. Section 382, by incorporating the limited family description from § 318 (spouse, parents, children and grandchildren) limits the relatives of a shareholder whose stock can be aggregated with that of the shareholder in question and clearly does not include siblings. * * * The taxpayer's attempt to perform the aggregation analysis through a non-stockholder parent must fail. The Tax Court's use of a shareholder of the loss corporation as the starting point for stock aggregation is consistent with the nature of the analysis under § 382, which looks for ownership shifts affecting 5% shareholders. Applying these rules to the facts of this case, the stock of Kenneth and Charles Garber cannot be aggregated and the 1998 stock sale between them resulted in an ownership change affecting Garber Industries under § 382.

For the foregoing reasons, the judgment of the Tax Court is affirmed.

NOTE

Parent as a shareholder. Would the court have reached a different result if, when Kenneth sold all of his shares to Charles, a parent of the Garber brothers had been alive and that parent had been a shareholder of Garber Industries?

Identifying 5% Shareholders—Entity Attribution. In addition to treating all family members as one person, I.R.C. § 382 generally causes all shares owned by an entity to be attributed up to the individual owners of the entity and treats the shares as no longer being held by the entity from which attributed. See I.R.C. § 382(*l*)(3)(A)(ii). Thus, when an entity owns shares of a loss corporation, those shares are attributed up (and through any intervening entities) to the individual owners to measure ownership by 5% shareholders.[9]

Example 13–C (Attributing shares held by entity to individual owners of entity): Edna has always owned all 3,000 of the outstanding shares of

---

9. This rule does not apply to shares attributed to any individual who would own, actually and constructively, less than 5% of the stock of the loss corporation. See Treas. Reg. § 1.382–2T(j)(1). But see discussion of public groups, pp. 662–663.

Land, Inc., a corporation with an NOL carryover. Land has a market value of $3,000,000. Forest has always owned all 5,000 of the outstanding shares of Opaque Co., a profitable corporation. Opaque has a market value of $1,000,000. Edna now transfers all of her stock in Land to Opaque solely in exchange for 15,000 newly issued shares of Opaque in a transaction that qualifies as a B reorganization.

An ownership change has *not* occurred. Although the exchange of shares is an "equity structure shift," the percentage of stock in the loss corporation (Land) owned by 5% shareholders has not increased by more than 50 percentage points over the lowest percentage of stock owned by those shareholders during the testing period. After the equity structure shift, Opaque is the legal owner of all 3,000 shares of Land. For purposes of I.R.C. § 382, however, 25% of the Land shares are attributed to Forest[10] and 75% of the Land shares are attributed to Edna.[11] Before the equity structure shift, Forest owned no Land shares and Edna owned 100% of the Land shares. Thus, no ownership change occurred because the percentage of stock in the loss corporation owned by Forest increased by only 25 percentage points (from zero to 25%) and the percentage of stock in the loss corporation owned by Edna declined.

Problem 13–4 (Reversing the acquisition): In Example 13–C, would an ownership change occur if the acquisition were reversed (i.e., if Land acquired all of the stock of Opaque from Forest in exchange for 1,000 newly issued shares of Land in a B reorganization)?

Identifying 5% Shareholders—Public Groups. In determining whether an ownership change has occurred, all stock owned by persons who own less than 5% of the stock of a loss corporation is aggregated and treated as owned by a single 5% shareholder. I.R.C. § 382(g)(4)(A). This rule generally renders it unnecessary to keep track of day-to-day transfers of stock of a widely-held loss corporation.

Example 13–D (Aggregation of less than 5% shareholders): Ranco is a publicly traded corporation with an NOL carryover. Ranco has 100,000,000 outstanding shares of stock and no one person owns at least 5,000,000 shares. Shares of Ranco are traded every day among many individuals. Under I.R.C. § 382, all of Ranco's shares are aggregated and treated as owned by a single 5% shareholder. Regardless of how many of Ranco's outstanding shares are sold in the marketplace, an ownership change will not occur unless a person acquires more than 50% of the outstanding stock over a three year period (or more than

---

10. After the acquisition, Forest owns 5,000 of the 20,000 outstanding Opaque shares thereby causing 25% of the 3,000 Land shares owned by Opaque to be attributed to Forest. See I.R.C. §§ 382(*l*)(3)(A)(ii), 318(a)(2)(C).

11. After the acquisition, Edna owns 15,000 of the 20,000 outstanding Opaque shares thereby causing 75% of the 3,000 Land shares owned by Opaque to be attributed to Edna. See I.R.C. §§ 382(*l*)(3)(A)(ii), 318(a)(2)(C).

one person acquires at least 5% of the stock of Ranco and those persons, in the aggregate, acquire more than 50% of the outstanding stock over a three year period).

Unfortunately, the treatment of less than 5% shareholders is often far more complicated than Example 13–D suggests. For example, special rules segregate less than 5% shareholders into multiple groups when shares of a loss corporation are acquired or disposed of in certain identifiable transactions. When these "segregation rules" apply, an ownership change may occur even if no one person owns at least 5% of the stock of the loss corporation at any time during the testing period. Among the events that trigger the segregation rules are an equity structure shift, a redemption and a new issuance of shares. See I.R.C. §§ 382(g)(4)(B)(i), (C); Treas. Reg. § 1.382–2T(j)(2).

> *Example 13–E (Equity structure shift)*: Same facts as Example 13–B (p. 657), except that Nender and Prender each have many shareholders no one of whom owns at least 5% of the stock of either corporation before the acquisition. In the absence of the segregation rules, no ownership change occurs when Prender acquires Nender in a type C reorganization if none of the post-reorganization shareholders of Prender owns at least 5% of the stock of Prender. Under the segregation rules, however, the former Nender shareholders ("target shareholders") and the original Prender shareholders ("acquiring shareholders") are treated as separate 5% shareholders. An ownership change occurs, therefore, because the acquiring shareholders own a 60% interest in the loss corporation after the equity structure shift (3,000 out of 5,000 outstanding shares of Prender) and they owned no interest in the predecessor corporation (Nender).

> *Example 13–F (Redemption)*: Same facts as Example 13–D, but Ranco redeems 30,000,000 shares. No person owns as much as 5% of Ranco's outstanding stock before or after the redemption. In the absence of the segregation rules, no ownership change occurs. Under the segregation rules, however, the redeemed shareholders ("departing group") and the continuing shareholders ("continuing group") are treated as separate 5% shareholders. An ownership change still does not occur, however, because the percentage of stock owned by the continuing group in Ranco increased by only thirty percentage points, from 70% to 100%.

A new issuance of shares by a loss corporation also triggers the segregation rules. See Treas. Reg. § 1.382–2T(j)(2)(iii)(B)(ii). In the case of a new issuance of shares, however, the regulations create certain exceptions to the segregation rules that diminish the likelihood of an ownership change. See Treas. Reg. § 1.382–3(j). For example, when a corporation issues additional shares to the public for cash, the segregation rules do not apply to a portion of the newly issued shares and that portion of the newly issued shares is treated as acquired by pre-existing less than 5% shareholders. The portion of a new issuance to which the segregation rules do not apply is half the percentage of the corporation's stock owned by less than 5% shareholders immediately before the issuance. Thus, if 70% of the loss corporation's stock is owned by less than 5% shareholders before the issuance of additional shares for cash, 35% ($\frac{1}{2} \times 70\%$) of the newly issued shares are excepted from the segregation rules because those shares are treated as acquired by pre-existing less than 5% shareholders.

> *Example 13–G (New issuance)*: Same facts as Example 13–D (p. 662), but Ranco sells an additional 300,000,000 shares of stock to the public for cash. Even after the public offering, no person owns as much as 5% of Ranco's outstanding stock. In the absence of the segregation rules, no ownership change occurs since all of Ranco's stock is owned by less than 5% shareholders both before and after the public offering. Under the segregation rules, however, Ranco's original shareholders ("old group") and the new shareholders ("new group") are treated as separate 5% shareholders. Because 100% of Ranco's stock is owned by less than 5% shareholders before the issuance, however, the segregation rules do not apply to 50% of the new issuance (half of the 100% of Ranco owned by the old group immediately before the issuance). Thus, the new group is only treated as owning 150,000,000 shares of Ranco after the issuance (300,000,000 less the 50% treated as acquired by the old group). An ownership change does not occur because the percentage of stock in Ranco owned by the new group increases from zero to 37.5%.[12]

The regulations allow the loss corporation to treat an even greater amount of newly issued shares as acquired by pre-existing less than 5% shareholders if it has actual knowledge that a greater amount of the newly issued shares was in fact acquired by pre-existing less than 5% shareholders. In addition, the regulations create an exception from the segregation rules for certain small issuances of shares (roughly an amount equal to 10% of the corporation's previously outstanding shares). See Treas. Reg. § 1.382–3(j).

NOTE

Option attribution rules. I.R.C. § 382 invokes the option attribution rules of I.R.C. § 318(a)(4) and treats an option as exercised if exercise results in an ownership change. See I.R.C. § 382(*l*)(3)(A)(iv). In addition, the statute treats a wide range of interests like an option. See I.R.C. § 382(*l*)(3)(A) (final sentence). Normally, an option (or similar interest) is not treated as exercised, unless "a principal purpose of the issuance, transfer or structuring of the option is to avoid or ameliorate the impact of an ownership change" and certain other conditions are satisfied. See Treas. Reg. § 1.382–4(d).

---

12. After the offering, the new group is treated as owning 150,000,000 of the 400,000,000 outstanding shares of Ranco which equals 37.5%.

Problem 13–5 (Identifying an ownership change): Determine whether each of the following transactions results in an "ownership change."

(a) *Public offering.* Loss Co. is a corporation with 1,000,000 outstanding shares and an NOL carryover. Loss Co. makes a public offering of 9,000,000 new shares. No investor acquires more than 100,000 shares of Loss Co.'s stock in the public offering. Prior to the public offering, all of the stock of Loss Co. is owned by:

    1. one individual.

    2. many individuals each of whom owns less than 5%.

    3. the same individuals who buy the newly issued shares.

(b) *Equity structure shifts.* Loss Co. is a corporation with 600,000 outstanding shares and an NOL carryover. All of Loss Co.'s shares are owned by Jay. Profit Co. is a profitable corporation with 80,000 outstanding shares all of which are owned by Kaye. Jay and Kaye are not related.

    1. Loss Co. merges into Profit Co. in a transaction that qualifies as a reorganization under I.R.C. § 368(a)(1)(A) and Jay receives:

        i. 20,000 newly issued Profit Co. shares.

        ii. 120,000 newly issued Profit Co. shares.

    2. Would the answers to 1.i. and/or 1.ii. change if, instead of merging Loss Co. into Profit Co.,

        i. Loss Co. were merged into a newly formed subsidiary of Profit Co. in a transaction that satisfies I.R.C. § 368(a)(2)(D)?

        ii. A newly formed subsidiary of Profit Co. were merged into Loss Co. in a transaction that satisfies I.R.C. § 368(a)(2)(E)?

    3. Instead of merging Loss Co. into another entity, Profit Co. merges into Loss Co. in an A reorganization and Kaye receives:

        i. 2,400,000 newly issued Loss Co. shares.

        ii. 400,000 newly issued Loss Co. shares.

    4. Would any of the answers to 1., 2. and 3. change if Jay were Kaye's father?

(c) *Gratuitous transfers.* Loss Co. is a corporation with 1,000,000 outstanding shares and an NOL carryover. All of Loss Co.'s shares are owned by Lee. See I.R.C. § 382(*l*)(3)(B).

    1. Lee gives 600,000 of her Loss Co. shares to her friend Maria.

    2. Instead of transferring shares during her lifetime, Lee dies and her Loss Co. shares pass under her will; half to a niece and half to a nephew.

3. Instead of dying, Lee transfers 750,000 of her Loss Co. shares to her husband pursuant to their divorce.

b. THE LIMITATION

I.R.C. §§ 382(a)–(f), (k)

When an "ownership change" occurs, the loss corporation's NOL carryover is not affected. Instead, a limit is imposed on the annual amount of future taxable income against which the NOL carryover may be applied ("the section 382 limitation"). See I.R.C. § 382(b). Specifically, the amount of the taxable income of any "new loss corporation" (I.R.C. § 382(k)(3)) for any "post-change year" (I.R.C. § 382(d)(2)) which may be offset by "pre-change losses" (I.R.C. § 382(d)(1)) shall not exceed the "section 382 limitation" for such year. I.R.C. § 382(a).

The section 382 limitation represents a conservative estimate of the amount of income that the loss corporation can be expected to generate in future years based on its value immediately before the ownership change. The statute, in effect, looks to how much income would be generated if, immediately before the ownership change, the entire value of the loss corporation were invested in long-term tax-exempt bonds. Specifically, the maximum amount of annual income against which the NOL carryover may be applied after an ownership change occurs is the product of,

(a) the value of all the stock of the loss corporation immediately before the ownership change, and

(b) the long-term tax-exempt rate promulgated by the Internal Revenue Service that applies to the month in which the ownership change occurs.

See I.R.C. §§ 382(b), (e)(1), (f).

Example 13–H (Calculating the limitation): Loss Co. has an NOL carryover of $10,000,000. An ownership change occurs with respect to Loss Co. on December 31, Year 4. At that time, the value of Loss Co.'s stock is $4,000,000 and the long-term tax exempt rate is 5%. The "§ 382 limitation" is $200,000.[13] If, in Year 5, Loss Co. generates $1,000,000 of taxable income (before taking into account the NOL carryover), it may apply the NOL carryover against only $200,000 of that income leaving $800,000 of income on which it must pay tax.

Problem 13–6 (Taxable income below limitation): Same facts as Example 13–H. If, in Year 6, Loss Co. generates $150,000 of taxable income (before applying the NOL carryover), how much of Loss Co.'s income may be offset by the NOL carryover? If, in Year 7, Loss Co. generates $700,000 of taxable income (before applying the NOL carryover), how much of Loss Co.'s income may be offset by the NOL carryover? See I.R.C. § 382(b)(2).

---

13. $4,000,000 (value of loss corporation) × 5% (long-term tax exempt rate) = $200,000.

Problem 13–7 (Continuity of business and aging of carryovers): Target is a corporation with an NOL carryover of $1,000,000. Acquiring is a profitable corporation. Target is merged into Acquiring in an A reorganization that causes an ownership change on December 31, Year 20. At that time, the value of Target's stock is $3,000,000 and the long-term tax exempt rate is 7%. Acquiring (the surviving corporation in the merger) generates the following income (before taking into account the NOL carryover):

Year	Taxable Income (before NOL)
21	$100,000
22	$200,000
23	$430,000

How much of the NOL carryover may be utilized in Years 21, 22, and 23 if:

(a) Acquiring sells the assets it received from Target and uses the proceeds of sale to enter into a new business if the sale of the assets occurs in,

    1. Year 21?

    2. Year 22?

    3. Year 23? See I.R.C. § 382(c).

(b) Acquiring retains Target's assets, but Target incurred the NOL from which the carryover germinated in Year 2. See I.R.C. § 172(b)(1)(A)(ii).

NOTES

1. *Incentive to acquire loss corporation.* Does I.R.C. § 382 generally eliminate the incentive to acquire a loss corporation when the reason for the acquisition is to gain access to the loss corporation's NOL carryover? What circumstances must exist for this incentive to remain?

2. *Allocation of income in year of ownership change.* When an ownership change occurs, the I.R.C. § 382 limitation does not apply to taxable income allocable to that part of the tax year through the day on which the ownership change occurs (the "change date"). See I.R.C. §§ 382(b)(3), (j). As a general rule, taxable income is allocated ratably to each day in the year. Regulations permit the taxpayer to elect to compute the actual amount of taxable income generated before and after the change date. See Treas. Reg. § 1.382–6. Under what circumstances would a taxpayer wish to make this election?

3. *Built-in gains and losses of loss corporation (I.R.C. § 382(h)).* The § 382 limitation is often adjusted for the net unrealized appreciation or depreciation in the assets of a loss corporation at the time of an ownership change. See I.R.C. § 382(h). Assume that Loss Co., a corporation with a $2,000,000 NOL carryover, has assets with a value of $1,000,000 and a basis of $100,000 before an ownership change occurs. In the absence of the ownership change, the $900,000 gain recognized on a sale of Loss Co.'s. assets for $1,000,000 could be absorbed in its entirety by the NOL carryover. Since this potential income was built into Loss Co.'s assets before the ownership change occurred, the § 382 limitation is increased in any year after the ownership change in which part or all of the built-in gain is recognized. By contrast, if Loss Co. had a value of $100,000 and a basis of $1,000,000 in its assets at the time of the ownership change, a sale of the assets before the ownership change for $100,000 would have increased Loss Co.'s NOL carryover (or capital loss carryover). Consequently, if such loss is recognized after the ownership change, it must be restricted in the same fashion as a pre-change loss, rather than be treated as a post-change loss not subject to the § 382 limitation. A de minimis rule with fairly hefty thresholds must be satisfied before the rules of I.R.C. § 382(h) will apply. See I.R.C. § 382(h)(3)(B).

A loss corporation with a net unrealized built-in gain will wish to maximize that amount, whereas a loss corporation with a net unrealized built-in loss will wish to minimize that amount. Why? As might be expected, the statute is drafted in a manner that assumes that any gain recognized after an ownership change is *not* attributable to net unrealized built-in gain and that any loss recognized after an ownership change is attributable to net unrealized built-in loss. See I.R.C. § 382(h)(2). This is an instance where an appraisal is critical. Unless it is certain that § 382(h) does not apply to the loss corporation (due to the de minimis rule), the assets of the loss corporation should be appraised on an asset-by-asset basis as of the date of the ownership change.

4. *Impact of § 338 election.* Chapter 11 suggested that an election under I.R.C. § 338 might be desirable when the target corporation has sufficient net operating losses to absorb any gain realized on the deemed sale of its assets. See p. 501, Note 2. Does a "qualified stock purchase" under I.R.C. § 338 normally result in an "ownership change" under I.R.C. § 382? See I.R.C. §§ 338(d)(3), 382(g). If so, to what extent can the target's NOL carryover be utilized against the gain triggered by the deemed sale? See I.R.C. § 382(h).

5. *Impact of bankruptcy.* I.R.C. § 382 operates in a less stringent fashion when the loss corporation is in bankruptcy before the ownership change occurs. See I.R.C. § 382(*l*)(5).

6. *Relation to Libson Shops and I.R.C. § 269.* Unfortunately, ambiguities continue to exist with respect to the interplay between I.R.C. § 382, the Libson Shops doctrine and I.R.C. § 269. It appears that the Libson Shops doctrine does not apply once an ownership change under § 382 occurs. The Libson Shops doctrine may still have some vitality, however, with respect to transactions that do not cause an ownership change. I.R.C. § 269, on the other hand, can apparently apply along with I.R.C. § 382. See Treas. Reg. § 1.269–7. What tax consequences follow when both I.R.C. §§ 382 and 269 apply to a transaction?

7. *Other tax attributes.* An ownership change under § 382 triggers limitations on attributes other than an NOL carryover. In addition, restrictions are imposed on the utilization of capital loss carryovers and certain tax credits. See I.R.C. § 383.

8. *Built-in gains of profitable corporation (I.R.C. § 384).* I.R.C. § 384 prevents certain results regarded as undermining the repeal of the General Utilities rule. See pp. 29–33. As a general matter, I.R.C. § 384 precludes a corporation owning assets with an aggregate value in excess of basis ("built-in gain") that acquires or is acquired by a corporation with an NOL carryover (or with assets having an aggregate basis in excess of value) from utilizing the NOL carryover to offset any built-in gain recognized within five years after the acquisition. This is another instance where an appraisal is critical.

I.R.C. § 384 is triggered when one corporation acquires the assets of another in certain reorganizations or acquires 80% of the stock of another corporation and, in either case, one of the corporations has built-in gain (a "gain corporation"). In this event, I.R.C. § 384 prevents any built-in gain recognized within five years of the acquisition from being offset by pre-acquisition NOLs or built-in losses of the other corporation. The same de minimis rule that excludes certain corporations from the scope of I.R.C. § 382(h) (see p. 667, Note 3) applies to I.R.C. § 384. See I.R.C. §§ 382(h)(3)(B), 384(c)(8).

I.R.C. § 384 can apply to transactions that are not within the scope of I.R.C. § 382 as well as to some, but not all, transactions that involve a § 382 ownership change. When both provisions are activated by the same transaction, I.R.C. § 384 presumably takes priority with respect to the built-in gains income to which it applies.

9. *Additional restrictions on affiliated groups.* When the stock of a corporation with an NOL carryover is acquired by another corporation or when the assets of a corporation with an NOL carryover are acquired by a subsidiary of another corporation in a transaction to which I.R.C. § 381 applies, the corporation with the NOL carryover or its successor (in the case of an asset transfer) may become part of an "affiliated group." See I.R.C. § 1504(a). The members of an affiliated group may elect to file a single tax return that reflects the collective taxable income of the group (a "consolidated return"), in lieu of each corporation filing a separate tax return. See I.R.C. § 1501. This privilege may seem to create an opportunity to apply the NOL carryover of the acquired corporation (or the § 382 limitation amount in the event the acquisition triggered an ownership change) against post-acquisition income of other members of the affiliated group. The regulations governing consolidated returns, however, normally bar the application of one corporation's NOL carryover against the income of other members of the affiliated group when the carryover is attributable to an NOL generated before the corporation became a member of the affiliated group. Other restrictions apply when an affiliated group with its own NOL carryover acquires a profitable corporation. See generally Treas. Reg. § 1.1502–21.

B.   RESTRICTIONS ON LOSS CARRYBACKS

I.R.C. § 381(b)(3)

The Libson Shops doctrine and I.R.C. § 382 restrict the carrying *forward* of an NOL incurred *before* an acquisition occurs. When an NOL is incurred *after* an acquisition takes place, no restrictions are generally imposed on the carrying *forward* of the NOL.[14] In most cases, however, an NOL is carried back to the two preceding tax years before the remaining unabsorbed portion, if any, is carried to a subsequent year. See I.R.C. § 172(b). When an NOL generated after an asset acquisition to which I.R.C. § 381 applies is carried back, it generally may be applied only against pre-acquisition income of the *acquiring* corporation and not against the pre-acquisition income of the *transferor* corporation. See I.R.C. § 381(b)(3). As the following case indicates, however, the general rule might not be as rigid as it appears.

Bercy Industries, Inc. v. Commissioner

United States Court of Appeals, Ninth Circuit, 1981.
640 F.2d 1058.

■ Before TRASK and NELSON, CIRCUIT JUDGES, and SOLOMON, DISTRICT JUDGE.

TRASK, CIRCUIT JUDGE:

* * *

I

Bercy Industries was incorporated in 1965. In 1968, a corporation named Beverly Enterprises established a subsidiary shell corporation, Beverly Manor. Beverly Manor remained a shell until April 23, 1970, the date of the reorganization here at issue. On that date, Bercy Industries (Old Bercy) was acquired by Beverly Manor by means of a triangular merger. Old Bercy was merged into Beverly Manor, which then changed its name to Bercy Industries (New Bercy). All shareholders of Old Bercy exchanged their stock for shares of stock in Beverly Enterprises, the parent. The Old Bercy stock was then cancelled.

Although it had been anticipated that New Bercy would be as profitable as Old Bercy had been, New Bercy suffered a loss for the post-reorganization period April 23 to December 31, 1970. Relying on the carryover provisions of section 172 of the Code, New Bercy attempted to carry back this loss to offset net operating income of Old Bercy in its two preceding tax years. It is this carryback that the Commissioner disallowed, and which is the subject of this appeal.

---

14. Restrictions are imposed on carrying forward a post-change NOL if it is attributable to a "built-in" loss. See I.R.C. § 382(h); p. 667, Note 3.

Appellant raises [one] issue * * *: whether Congress, in enacting section 381, intended to prevent the subsidiary corporation in a triangular merger from carrying back post-merger losses to offset premerger income of the transferor corporation, where the subsidiary was a mere shell before the merger * * *.

II

Under I.R.C. § 172, a corporation which incurs a net operating loss in any tax year may carry this loss back [two] tax years, or forward [twenty] tax years, to offset net operating income earned during those years. Section 172 reflects congressional recognition that business income often fluctuates widely from year to year, and that, consequently, a carryover provision is necessary to mitigate the inequitable and excessive tax liabilities that would result from determination of income on a strictly annual basis.

In 1954, Congress enacted section 381 as part of a substantial revision of the entire Code. The Commissioner argues that Congress intended this provision to preempt and replace prior case law with reliable and consistent rules for carrying over pre-and post-reorganization income and loss. Conceding this to be the general purpose of section 381, appellant nevertheless argues that it is an oversimplified characterization of congressional intent with respect to subsection (b)(3). We agree.

* * *

With respect to the enactment of subsection (b)(3) of section 381, the legislative history shows that Congress was concerned with a complex accounting problem—deciding how a post-reorganization loss should be allocated between the acquiring corporation and the transferor corporations, and, therefore, how much of the loss should be carried back to offset each entity's income in the preceding [two] tax years. The Senate Finance Committee * * * stated, however, that,

> [i]n two important areas * * * *the problem of allocating the loss is not involved, and it is suggested that in such cases, at least, there should be no limit on carrybacks.* One is the case of a reincorporation of the same corporation in a different state, or upon expiration of its charter. Another instance is that of the wholly owned subsidiary which is liquidated into its parent, which parent suffers a net operating loss in the following year. (emphasis added)

This language strongly suggests that when a reorganization generates no complex problems of post-reorganization loss allocation, Congress intended that the surviving corporate taxpayer be able to carry back such losses without limitation.

Because Congress specifically identified two circumstances in which loss carrybacks should be permitted, the Commissioner argues that if Congress had also intended to permit carrybacks in a triangular merger involving a shell corporation, it would have specifically mentioned this circumstance as well. In 1954, however, the Code did not permit a corporation to use its parent's stock as consideration for the acquisition of another corporation's assets in a tax-free reorganization. This prevented the use of shells in effecting such reorganizations. Congress did not suggest that this type of tax-free reorganization be removed from the carryback restrictions of section 381(b)(3) because such a reorganization was not then tax-free. Such use of parent stock was sanctioned by amendments to the Code in 1968 and 1971. We find nothing in the text or legislative history of these amendments which would suggest that they were intended to expand the scope of section 381(b)(3) beyond the problem to which it was originally directed, i.e., allocation of post-reorganization loss.

* * *

Both legislative history and statutory structure support the conclusion that Congress was preoccupied with post-reorganization allocation problems when it enacted the loss carryback restriction. [T]he intent of Congress with respect to subsection (b)(3) of section 381 was to prohibit carryback of post-reorganization losses pursuant to section 172 only when such a carryback would entail complex problems of post-reorganization loss allocation.

III

The Commissioner states that section 381(b)(3) reflects a policy of not permitting loss carrybacks when the legal and economic identity of the corporation has been substantially altered. The Commissioner argues that Old Bercy was legally transformed by its merger into New Bercy and the subsequent cancellation of its stock. He further argues that the reorganization transformed Old Bercy economically by shifting control of that corporation from its own shareholders to those of Beverly Enterprises.

Even assuming that the Commissioner has correctly articulated the congressional policy underlying subsection (b)(3), we are not persuaded that a material change in identity resulted from the reorganization here at issue. The reorganization involved only one set of operating assets, one set of books, and one tax history. New Bercy is operating the same commercial business that Old Bercy operated. There is no problem of allocating a post-reorganization loss to different pre-reorganization businesses. Regardless of the formal technicalities of the transaction, the indisputable fact is that the same business generated both the income and the loss.[15] The legislative history of section 381 shows that Congress intended that a loss carryback be available in circumstances such as these.

---

15. The Commissioner makes much of the fact that because of the reorganization, the benefit of the loss carryback will accrue to a different set of shareholders than the one that owned Bercy at the time it earned the income to be offset. We fail to see why this should prevent a carryback. Sections 381 and 382 are grounded on two competing theories: (1) A loss carryover ought to be available only when the shareholders who were the "beneficial sufferers" of such loss retain an interest in its use, as the Commissioner argues; and (2) a loss carryover ought to be available only for use against profits from business activities which gave rise to the loss. These two theories conflict in large degree, so that any particular subsection of 381 or 382 may favor one theory over the other. As our discussion of congressional intent indicates, * * * theory (2), rather than theory (1), clearly animates subsection (b)(3). Moreover, we note that the former shareholders of Old Bercy are now minority holders of Beverly Enterprises, and have a continuing, albeit diminished, interest in carryback of the post-reorganization loss. Finally, the Commissioner himself concedes that a loss carryback would

IV

[W]e have discovered no tax policy, nor does the Commissioner articulate one, that would be promoted by denying a loss carryback in this instance. * * * To deny a loss carryback on the facts of this case would exalt form over substance. Accordingly, we hold that subsection (b)(3) of section 381 does not prevent Bercy from using the loss carryback provisions of section 172. * * *

NOTES

1. *Relevance of which corporation survives.* I.R.C. § 382 normally has the same impact on NOL carryovers when a loss corporation and a profitable corporation are combined in a reorganization regardless of which of the two corporations survives. See Problems 13–3, 13–4, 13–5(b)3. Does I.R.C. § 381(b) normally have the same effect on NOL carrybacks regardless of which corporation survives the acquisition?

2. *Alternative structure.* Bercy was fortunate that the court made an equitable decision that was contrary to the literal language of the statute. How might the transaction have been structured to avoid the entire issue? See I.R.C. § 368(a)(2)(E).

3. *Conflicting theories.* The footnote to the Bercy court's opinion acknowledges two competing theories on which the 1954 versions of I.R.C. §§ 381 and 382 were grounded. The Bercy court suggests that the two theories conflict and that I.R.C. § 381(b)(3) manifests the second theory. In contrast, the current version of I.R.C. § 382 principally reflects the first theory (in light of the ownership change standard), though remnants of the second theory also exist (see I.R.C. § 382(c)). Are the potential abuses surrounding the carrying forward of pre-acquisition NOLs and the carrying back of post-acquisition NOLs different? If so, is the difference sufficient to justify statutory responses that embrace different theories? Would it be more rational to adopt the same theory in responding to both sets of potential abuses?

4. *Impact of I.R.C. § 269.* Could I.R.C. § 269 be applied to disallow the carryback of a post-acquisition NOL? See Treas. Reg. § 1.269–3(b)(1).

5. *Corporate equity reduction transaction.* I.R.C. § 172(b)(1)(E) disallows the carry*back* of corporate NOLs created by interest deductions with respect to indebtedness incurred in a "corporate equity reduction transaction" ("CERT"). What is a CERT? See I.R.C. § 172(h)(3). The CERT restriction reflects concern by Congress about debt-financed acquisitions of businesses. Why should Congress care about the manner in which a business acquisition is financed? Is I.R.C. § 172(b)(1)(E) a reasonable way of responding to this concern? Why does I.R.C. § 172(b)(1)(E) not restrict the carry*over* of NOLs within its scope?

*

---

have been permitted had Bercy reorganized pursuant to a reverse triangular merger, yet such a reorganization would have resulted in the same change in shareholder ownership which the Commissioner now argues should prevent the carryback.

CHAPTER 14

TRANSFERS INVOLVING S CORPORATIONS

The fact that a business is conducted by an S Corporation, rather than a C Corporation, does not change the methods by which the business can be transferred. A transfer of an S Corporation's business can be effectuated through an asset transfer, a stock transfer or a statutory merger. Many of the same tax issues are raised regardless of whether the transferred business is conducted by an S Corporation or a C Corporation. Chapter 14 focuses on some of the unique issues presented by the interplay of Subchapters C and S when a business conducted by an S Corporation is transferred.

A. TAXABLE TRANSFERS

1. ASSET TRANSFER

IRS Letter Ruling 9218019

1/23/92.

[Dear] * * *:

We received your letter * * * requesting a ruling on behalf of A about the tax consequences to a shareholder on a sale by an S corporation of its assets followed by a liquidating distribution of the proceeds of the sale in the same taxable year as the sale. This letter is in reply to your request.

In 1969, X was incorporated under the laws of Z. X elected S corporation status * * *. Since 1969, X has owned, as its sole capital asset, a commercial building located in Z * * *.

At the time of death, B owned all of X corporation's stock. On B's death, B's estate, A, became the owner of all X corporation's stock. C, who is B's only beneficiary, does not wish to operate the commercial building that is the sole asset of X. Thus, the executors of A propose to sell the commercial building owned by X, and to distribute the cash proceeds to A in complete liquidation of X.

* * *

Based on the information submitted and * * * representations made by the taxpayer, we reach the following conclusions.

675

Under section 1014(a), A's basis in the stock of X will be stepped-up to the fair market value of the property as of the date of B's death. Under section 1001(a), X's gain from the sale of its commercial building will be measured by the difference between the amount realized on the sale of the building and X's adjusted basis in the building.

Section 1366 requires all items of an S corporation's income to pass-through to the S corporation shareholders. Thus, we conclude that the gain realized by X on the sale of its commercial building will pass-through to and be recognized by A, its sole shareholder. Further, we conclude that under section 1367(a)(1), A's stepped-up basis under section 1014(a) will be increased by the amount realized and passed-through to A on X's sale of its building.

Under section 336(a) of the Code, a liquidating corporation recognizes gain or loss on the distribution of property in complete liquidation. However, X is not a taxable entity under section 1363(a)(1), and any gain or loss recognized would be recognized by X's shareholder. In addition, X is distributing cash not appreciated assets. Thus, we conclude that section 336(a) does not require recognition of gain or loss on the distribution of cash in complete liquidation of X.

In addition, assuming the liquidation of X qualifies as a complete liquidation under section 331(a) of the Code, we conclude that the amounts received by A in the distribution in complete liquidation of X are treated as in full payment in exchange for A's stock in accordance with section 331(a). We further conclude that A's gain or loss, under section 1001, will be measured by the difference between the amount of cash received and A's adjusted basis in its X stock surrendered.

* * *

We direct this ruling only to the taxpayer requesting it. Under section 6110(j)(3) of the Code, this ruling may not be cited or used as precedent * * *.

NOTES

1. *Application.* If the building held by X had a market value of $1,000,000 on the date of B's death and X had a basis of $400,000 in the building at the time of sale, what are the tax consequences of the transactions described in the Private Letter Ruling? How would the analysis change if the asset held by X was inventory, rather than a capital asset? See I.R.C. § 1211(b).

2. *Sale and liquidation before death of shareholder.* Compare the tax consequences derived in Note 1 with the consequences that would result if X sold its building and liquidated *before* B died, assuming that B had little basis in the X stock. How would this analysis change if the asset held by X were inventory, rather than a capital asset?

3. *Corporate level tax.* Is a corporate level tax ever imposed when an S Corporation sells its assets at a gain and liquidates? See I.R.C. § 1374; pp. 135–138.

4. *Intangible assets and shareholder agreements.* When an S Corporation sells its assets, how are the shareholders of the selling S Corporation and the buyer affected by that part of the price allocated to,

> (a) goodwill? See pp. 482–484 and Example 11–C, p. 485.

> (b) a covenant not to compete entered into with a shareholder-employee of the selling corporation? See p. 478, Note 4, and Problem 11–5, p. 487.

> (c) an employment agreement entered into with a shareholder-employee of the selling corporation? See p. 478, Note 4, and Problem 11–6, p. 487.

2.   STOCK TRANSFER

When stock of an S Corporation is sold, any gain or loss recognized by the selling shareholders is normally characterized as capital gain. But see I.R.C. § 1244 (certain losses allowed on sale of stock in "small business corporation" characterized as ordinary loss, see p. 300, Note 2). The buyers of stock of an S Corporation take a cost basis in the purchased shares. See I.R.C. § 1012. If the buyers are eligible S Corporation shareholders, a pro rata share of the income or loss of the S Corporation for the entire year in which the sale occurs is allocated to both the selling shareholders and the buyers, unless a closing of the books election under I.R.C. § 1377(a)(2) is made. See I.R.C. §§ 1366(a), 1377(a), pp. 102–106. The pro rata share rule creates the potential for abuse in certain circumstances.

> *Example 14–A (Abuse of pro rata share rule)*: Gail owns all the stock of S Corporation until October 31, Year 6 (⅚ of the year), at which time she sells all of her stock to Howard. Howard owns all the stock of S Corporation for the remainder of Year 6 (⅙ of the year). Before December 31, Year 6, Howard contributes to S Corporation capital assets in which he has a basis of $1,000,000. S Corporation takes a transferred basis in the assets. See I.R.C. § 362(a). On December 31, Year 6, S Corporation sells the assets contributed by Howard for $7,000,000 and recognizes a $6,000,000 capital gain.

> In the absence of a closing of the books election under I.R.C. § 1377(a)(2), $5,000,000 (⅚) of the capital gain in the assets contributed by Howard is allocated to Gail. I.R.C. § 1377(a)(1). Five-sixths of the gain is allocated to Gail notwithstanding that her departure before the contribution and sale of Howard's assets deprives Gail of any right to any of the consideration received by the S Corporation from the buyer of Howard's assets. The overallocation of capital gain income to Gail is neutralized, however, by a corresponding increase in the basis of Gail's stock. See I.R.C. § 1367(a)(1). This increase in the basis of

Gail's stock reduces the capital gain she would otherwise recognize on the sale of her stock (or may even cause her to recognize a capital loss on the sale of her stock). Thus, Gail is not adversely affected by the overallocation of the S Corporation's capital gain income to her. Would the same be true if the assets Howard contributed generated an ordinary gain when they were sold?

In the absence of a closing of the books election, Howard is taxed on only $1,000,000 (⅙) of the gain, notwithstanding that the entire $6,000,000 gain recognized by S Corporation accrues to his benefit. Howard will not be taxed on the additional $5,000,000 until the proceeds from the sale of the contributed assets are distributed to Howard (see I.R.C. § 1368) or until Howard sells his stock (assuming the selling price will reflect the value in the corporation). Will Howard (or his successor) ever be taxed on the proceeds from the sale of the contributed assets if Howard dies while owning the stock and before the proceeds of sale are distributed? See I.R.C. § 1014.

What would be the tax consequences to Gail and Howard if a closing of the books election were made? See I.R.C. § 1377(a)(2); pp. 102–106.

If stock of an S Corporation is sold to a corporate buyer, the purchasing corporation is eligible to make an election under I.R.C. § 338 to step-up the basis of the target's assets to market value. See I.R.C. § 338(a); pp. 495–498. If a § 338 election is made, the target S Corporation is deemed to sell its assets at market value after the S election terminates and any gain recognized on the deemed sale is reported by the target as a C Corporation. See Treas. Reg. § 1.338–1(e)(3). Section 338 elections are rarely made because the cost of the current tax normally exceeds the present value of the tax savings derived from the increase in the basis of the corporation's assets.[1]

As an alternative to a § 338 election, the acquiring corporation and the shareholders of the target S Corporation ("target shareholders") may jointly make an election under I.R.C. § 338(h)(10) to step-up the basis of the target's assets to market value. See I.R.C. § 338(h)(10); Treas. Reg. § 1.338(h)(10)–1(c)(2), (d)(1)(iii); pp. 502–503. If a § 338(h)(10) election is made, the gain realized by the target shareholders on the sale of their stock is not recognized. Treas. Reg. § 1.338(h)(10)–1(e)(2)(iv). Instead, the S Corporation is deemed to sell its assets at market value while the target

---

1. If stock of an S Corporation is sold to a corporate buyer, the S election of the acquired corporation will terminate because no shares of an S Corporation may be held by another corporation. I.R.C. § 1361(b)(1)(B). If the buyer is an S Corporation, however, the buyer can elect to treat the acquired corporation as a "qualified subchapter S subsidiary." If the buyer makes that election, the separate corporate existence of the acquired corporation is ignored for Federal tax purposes and all assets, liabilities, and items of income and deduction of the acquired corporation are treated as assets, liabilities, and items of income and deduction of the buyer. See I.R.C. § 1361(b)(3). A purchasing S Corporation can make both a § 338 election and a qualified subchapter S subsidiary election with respect to the acquired corporation. See Treas. Reg. § 1.1361–4(b)(4).

shareholders still own the S Corporation. Treas. Reg. § 1.338(h)(10)–1(e)(1). Any gain that results from the fictional asset sale is taxed to the target shareholders and the basis in their shares is correspondingly increased. I.R.C. §§ 1366(a), 1367(a)(1). The S Corporation is then treated as liquidating while still owned by the target shareholders. Treas. Reg. § 1.338(h)(10)–1(e)(2)(ii). The fictional liquidation could trigger additional gains (or losses) to the target shareholders under I.R.C. § 331(a). In many cases, however, the amount, character, and timing of the target shareholders' gains will be the same regardless of whether a § 338(h)(10) election is made.[2] In these circumstances, a § 338(h)(10) election is desirable because it steps-up the basis in the target corporation's assets to market value at no additional tax cost to any of the parties to the transaction.

NOTE

Asset sale versus stock sale. From an income tax standpoint, is it generally preferable to structure the taxable transfer of a business conducted by an S Corporation as an asset sale or as a stock sale?

B.   NONTAXABLE TRANSFERS

When a corporate business is transferred in exchange for stock of another corporation, taxes may be deferred if the transaction qualifies as a reorganization. See Chapter 12. Regardless of whether C Corporations or S Corporations participate in the transaction, the reorganization rules apply in the same manner.

NOTE

Impact of non-taxable acquisition on corporate level taxes of acquiring S Corporation. When an S Corporation acquires the assets of a C Corporation in a nonrecognition transaction, the acquisition can create or augment exposure to the corporate level tax of I.R.C. § 1374. See I.R.C. § 1374(d)(8); pp. 135–138. When an S Corporation acquires the assets of a C Corporation in a transaction to which I.R.C. § 381 applies, the acquiring S Corporation inherits any earnings & profits of the C Corporation which can create or augment exposure to the corporate level tax of I.R.C. § 1375. See I.R.C. §§ 381(a)(1), (c)(2), 1375; pp. 138–141.

---

2. One instance in which a § 338(h)(10) election would increase the tax liability of the target shareholders is where the S Corporation owns assets which generate ordinary gains when they are deemed to be sold.

*

PART SIX

CORPORATE DIVISIONS AND REARRANGEMENTS

Part Five of this casebook examined the tax consequences that follow when two corporations are amalgamated. In contrast, Part Six focuses on transactions that involve a single corporation. Chapter 15 explores the tax consequences that follow when a single corporation conducting multiple businesses distributes a business to its shareholders or transfers a business to a subsidiary corporation and distributes the stock of the subsidiary to its shareholders. Chapter 16 examines the tax consequences of modifying the capital structure or the operating entity of a single corporation. Some of the transactions examined in Part Six can be structured as tax-free reorganizations and other transactions explored in Part Six qualify for tax-free or tax advantaged treatment under other provisions of the Internal Revenue Code.

*

CHAPTER 15

CORPORATE DIVISIONS

A corporate enterprise can be divided by causing the corporation to distribute a group of assets to its shareholders. Alternatively, the division can be accomplished by causing the corporation ("parent") to contribute that group of assets to a newly formed subsidiary in exchange for stock of the subsidiary and then to distribute the subsidiary stock to the parent's shareholders. Regardless of whether the corporation distributes assets or subsidiary stock, the transaction represents a "distribution" and could properly have been examined in Chapter 5. The tax consequences of dividing an enterprise are deferred to this point, however, because a distribution of subsidiary stock may qualify as a "reorganization".

A.   DISTRIBUTION OF ASSETS— TAXABLE PARTIAL LIQUIDATION

1.   SHAREHOLDER LEVEL CONSEQUENCES

I.R.C. §§ 302(b)(4), (e)

As a general rule, the distribution of a group of corporate assets is treated as a dividend to the recipient shareholders provided the value of the distributed assets does not exceed the earnings & profits of the distributing corporation. See I.R.C. §§ 301, 316; pp. 201–208. If the distribution is in "partial liquidation" of the distributing corporation, however, each recipient shareholder (who is not a corporation) is treated as receiving a payment in exchange for part of her stock. See I.R.C. §§ 302(a), (b)(4). How do the tax consequences of a payment in exchange for stock differ from the tax consequences of a dividend?

Commissioner v. Sullivan

United States Court of Appeals, Fifth Circuit, 1954.
210 F.2d 607.

■ HOLMES, CIRCUIT JUDGE.

* * *

The Texon Royalty Company * * * made a distribution in kind on April 1, 1943, to its two sole stockholders in cancellation of 2,000 shares, or two fifths, of its capital stock * * *. The question presented here is whether the redemption and cancellation of the stock was at such time and in such manner as to make the distribution essentially equivalent to a taxable dividend so as to be taxable to the recipients to the extent of Texon's accumulated earnings and profits, instead of being treated as payment in exchange for the stock and subject only to a capital gains tax * * *.

The Tax Court held that * * * the taxpayers' entire gain on the distribution was taxable as a long-term capital gain. This holding was based primarily upon findings of fact, in substance as follows: Texon held a great many producing oil leases outside of the Agua Dulce oil field, which was a high pressure field. A suit for damages from a blowout which occurred in prior operations in that field was pending against Texon at the time of the distribution. The leases transferred needed to be developed, and they were transferred because Texon did not want to take the risk of developing them and because it did not have authority under its charter to drill wells. The same reasons prompted the distribution of its drilling equipment. Another reason was that this equipment could be used in the development of the oil properties transferred. The gas payment and the notes were included in the distribution in order to furnish the distributors with additional capital or credit to aid them in the development of the properties transferred, which was undertaken soon after the distribution. The drilling equipment was transferred by the stockholders to a corporation in connection with the development. The avoidance of taxes was not one of the reasons for the distribution.

The petitioner argues that, if the redemption of stock is made pro rata, any business purpose for the redemption thereof will usually be outweighed by the net effect of the transaction. The respondents contend that the Tax Court has weighed the evidence in this case with regard to the net effect of the transaction as well as to the business purposes of the corporation, and has found that the distribution was dictated by the reasonable needs of the corporate business, not merely to benefit the stockholders by giving them a share of the earnings of the corporation.

The Tax Court's opinion expressly refers to its considering the net effect of the transaction; and we cannot say that it used the wrong test, or that there was any specific test for the issue before it. We agree that the pro rata redemption of stock will generally be considered as effecting a distribution essentially equivalent to a dividend distribution to the extent of the earnings and profits, but * * * the question depends upon the particular circumstances of each case.

    * * *

The distribution of the high-pressure leases and the drilling equipment constituted a contraction of Texon's business. When there is a contraction or shrinkage of corporate business, the need of a corporation for funds to carry on its former activities is largely eliminated. Following a contraction of its activities, and with surplus funds on hand, good business and accounting practices dictated a redemption of a portion of the corporation's capital stock * * *.

Strong as is the pro-rata factor in this case, it is not sufficient in itself to require or authorize us to set aside the findings of the Tax Court * * *.

The decisions of the Tax Court are affirmed.

Revenue Ruling 79–275

1979–2 Cum.Bull. 137.

ISSUE

Does the distribution by a corporation to its shareholders of appreciated securities in substitution of a note received upon the sale by the corporation of the assets of one of its businesses qualify as a distribution in partial liquidation within the meaning of [the predecessor to I.R.C. § 302(b)(4)]?

FACTS

X corporation has been in the poultry processing business since its incorporation in 1965. In 1968, X went into the chicken farming business as a separate and distinct operation. After several years of profitable operation, the chicken farming business began to lose money. Because of this, the management of X decided to completely terminate the chicken farming business. In June, 1978 all the chicken farm properties of X were sold for 100x dollars. Payment was represented by a note, secured by a mortgage, payable over a 10 year period. X continued to engage in the poultry processing business.

Following the termination of the chicken farming business X adopted a plan of partial liquidation on September 5, 1978. In lieu of distributing the note and mortgage that X had received from the sale of the farm properties, X distributed appreciated marketable securities the fair market value of which was equal to the fair market value of the note. These marketable securities had been used by X as working capital in the poultry processing business. The distribution was pro rata to the shareholders of X, was pursuant to the adopted plan of partial liquidation, and occurred within the taxable year in which the plan was adopted. Each shareholder turned in for cancellation and redemption a portion of his or her stock in the corporation equal in value to the value of the distribution received.

LAW AND ANALYSIS

* * *

If the distribution satisfies the safe harbor requirements of [the predecessor to I.R.C. § 302(e)(2),] then it would be considered not essentially equivalent to a dividend for purposes of [the predecessor to I.R.C. § 302(e)(1)(A)]. If it does not satisfy the requirements of [the predecessor to I.R.C. § 302(e)(2)], then a separate determination of nondividend equivalence must be made for purposes of [the predecessor to I.R.C. § 302(e)(1)(A)]. In either case, the distribution will qualify as being in partial liquidation within the meaning of [the predecessor to I.R.C.

§ 302(e)(1)] only if the other two requirements of that section are met—namely, the distribution is * * * pursuant to a plan and occurs within the taxable year in which the plan is adopted or within the succeeding taxable year.

The stock of X was redeemed pursuant to a plan of partial liquidation, the redemption occurred within the taxable year in which the plan was adopted, the sale of the chicken farming business for 100x dollars constituted the necessary contraction (termination) of the corporate business, and the value of the assets distributed was equal to the amount attributable to such contraction. Therefore, the issue to be resolved is whether the distribution of marketable securities in lieu of the note and mortgage can be treated for purposes of [the predecessor to I.R.C. § 302(e)(2)(A)] as being a distribution that is attributable to X's ceasing to conduct the chicken farming business and if not, does the distribution qualify as not essentially equivalent to a dividend within the meaning of [the predecessor to I.R.C. § 302(e)(1)(A)].

The term "attributable to" contained in [the predecessor to I.R.C. § 302(e)(2)(A)] is descriptive of the proceeds from the sale of the assets of the terminated business. In order to qualify under [the predecessor to I.R.C. § 302(e)(2)(A)], the distribution must include all of the assets of the terminated business or the proceeds of the sale of such assets. Furthermore, only the assets of the terminated trade or business, or the proceeds from the sale of such assets, or a combination thereof, can be distributed in a distribution qualifying as a partial liquidation under [the predecessor to I.R.C. § 302(e)(2)(A)]. Since the marketable securities were not the proceeds from the sale of the chicken farming business, but, instead, were distributed in lieu of the proceeds, their distribution was not "attributable to" X's having ceased the conduct of the chicken farming business. Accordingly, the entire distribution does not qualify under [the predecessor to I.R.C. § 302(e)(2)].

Thus, a determination must be made as to whether the distribution is not essentially equivalent to a dividend within the meaning of [the predecessor to I.R.C. § 302(e)(1)(A)]. In 1954 Congress * * * provided that ["partial liquidation"] included those distributions characterized by what happens solely at the corporate level by reason of the assets distributed. Congress also made it clear that a distribution resulting from the contraction of a corporate business would fall within the general language of [the predecessor to I.R.C. § 302(e)(1)(A)]. Therefore, it is the type of assets that are distributed that * * * [determines] a "partial liquidation". If the assets that are distributed are related to the contraction of the corporate business, then the distribution will be treated as a partial liquidation. On the other hand, if there is no nexus between the assets distributed and the corporate contraction, then the transaction * * * [is not a partial liquidation]. In order to distinguish between a distribution of assets that are related to the contraction and a distribution of assets that are not related to the contraction, the Internal Revenue Service has required a segregation of the proceeds of the sale of the assets, and has further required that the assets or the proceeds not be used in the remaining corporate business for any period of time.

When the chicken farming business was sold, it was sold for consideration represented by a note and mortgage. The note and mortgage are the proceeds attributable to X's ceasing to conduct the chicken farming business and are the only assets that may be distributed by X in partial liquidation under [the predecessor to I.R.C. § 302(e)(1)(A)], other than a portion of the working capital of X reasonably attributable to the terminated business activity and no longer required in the operation of the remaining business activities.

HOLDING

X's distribution of marketable securities to its shareholders, in substitution for a note received upon the sale by X of the assets of its terminated chicken farming business, will not qualify as a distribution in partial liquidation within the meaning of [the predecessor to I.R.C. § 302(b)(4)] because the distribution does not qualify under either [the predecessor to I.R.C. § 302(e)(2)] or as not essentially equivalent to a dividend within the meaning of [the predecessor to I.R.C. § 302(e)(1)(A)] * * *. Since the distribution of the marketable securities is a pro rata distribution to all of the shareholders of X, it [does not satisfy any of the tests in I.R.C. § 302(b) and, accordingly] does not qualify under section 302(a) as payment in exchange for the redeemed stock attributable thereto. Therefore, by virtue of section 302(d), the distribution is treated as a distribution of property to which section 301 applies.

Revenue Ruling 90–13

1990–1 Cum.Bull. 65.

ISSUE

Must shareholders surrender stock in the distributing corporation to qualify for partial liquidation treatment under section 302(b)(4) and (e) of the Internal Revenue Code, if the distribution is pro rata?

FACTS

Corporation X operated two divisions of equal size and had one class of stock outstanding, which was owned by individuals A and B * * *.

Pursuant to a plan of partial liquidation, X sold one of its divisions to an unrelated party for cash and distributed the cash proceeds of the sale to A and B pro rata, A and B did not surrender any stock in exchange for the cash distributed by X.

Except for the question as to whether there must be a surrender of stock by the shareholders, the transaction qualifies as a partial liquidation under section 302(b)(4) and (e) of the Code.

LAW AND ANALYSIS

* * *

Under section 302(b)(4)(A) and (B) of the Code, respectively, two requirements for partial liquidation treatment are that (1) stock be redeemed and (2) the redemption be in partial liquidation within the meaning of section 302(e). The second requirement can be satisfied (as the facts here indicate it has been satisfied) irrespective of an actual stock surrender because under section 302(b)(4)(B) and (e) this requirement is tested at the corporate level, not the shareholder level, and is not concerned with stock ownership.

However, the first requirement—that stock be redeemed—is tested at the shareholder level. Moreover, the reference to section 317(b) of the Code in section 302(a) raises the question whether an actual surrender of stock is required for a transaction to be treated as a partial liquidation under section 302(b)(4).

* * *

The [Tax Equity and Fiscal Responsibility Act of 1982 (TEFRA)] conference report, in explaining the treatment of partial liquidations, states:

> Under present law, a distribution in partial liquidation may take place without an actual surrender of stock by the shareholders. A constructive redemption of stock is deemed to occur in such transactions. The conferees intend that the treatment of partial liquidations under present law * * * is to continue for such transactions under new section 302(e).

Section 317(b) of the Code requires a corporation to acquire its stock in order for a transaction to be treated as a redemption under section 302. As indicated by the above-quoted committee report, a deemed surrender of stock in a pro rata distribution satisfies the redemption requirement of sections 302 and 317(b) in partial liquidation transactions * * *. In the situation presented by this revenue ruling, the requirement of sections 302 and 317(b) is met by a deemed surrender of stock.

HOLDING

The pro rata distribution by X to its shareholders, individuals A and B, qualifies as a distribution in redemption of stock held by A and B in partial liquidation of X under section 302(b)(4) and (e) of the Code, even though the shareholders did not surrender any of their stock.

NOTES

1. *Qualified trade or business.* The "safe harbor" of I.R.C. § 302(e)(2) requires the existence of two discrete "qualified trades or businesses." The assets distributed must represent (or be attributable to) a "qualified trade or business" and the distributing corporation must continue to conduct a "qualified trade or business." Can these requirements be reconciled with the factors considered in the Sullivan case (p. 683)?

Review the definition of a "qualified trade or business" in I.R.C. § 302(e)(3). A similar concept plays a critical role in determining whether favorable tax treatment will be accorded a corporate division effectuated by a distribution of subsidiary stock. See I.R.C. § 355(b), pp. 715–729.

2. *Substitution of property.* In Revenue Ruling 79–275 (p. 685), a partial liquidation would have occurred if the corporation had distributed the note and mortgage it received for the chicken farm properties, rather than distributing the marketable securities. What might the taxpayers have been hoping to accomplish by substituting the marketable securities for the note and mortgage?

3. *Amount of shareholder's income.* When a corporation makes a pro rata distribution in partial liquidation, does the value of the property received by each shareholder represent gross income? If not, how is the amount of each shareholder's income quantified? See Rev. Rul. 90–13.

4. *Corporate shareholders.* Distributions in partial liquidation received by corporate shareholders are not treated as received in exchange for stock. See I.R.C. § 302(b)(4)(A). Is the omission of corporate shareholders from the scope of I.R.C. § 302(b)(4) disadvantageous to most corporate shareholders that receive distributions in partial liquidation? See I.R.C. §§ 301, 243, 1059(e)(1)(A)(i). Does a corporate shareholder that is an S Corporation remain within the scope of I.R.C. § 302(b)(4)?

2.   CORPORATE LEVEL CONSEQUENCES

I.R.C. § 311

Prior to the repeal of the General Utilities rule (see pp. 29–33), neither gains nor losses were typically recognized by a corporation making a distribution in partial liquidation. Under current law, however, a corporation making a distribution in partial liquidation is governed by the general rules that apply to other non-liquidating distributions. Specifically, the corporation is treated as selling any of the distributed assets with a value in excess of the corporation's basis and must recognize the resulting gains. See I.R.C. § 311(b)(1). In contrast, the corporation may not recognize losses with respect to distributed assets in which the corporation has a basis in excess of value. See I.R.C. § 311(a).

The fact that a corporate level tax is now generally imposed on a partial liquidation has greatly dampened enthusiasm for this transaction. A partial liquidation may still be appealing, however, when a corporation conducting multiple businesses has a substantial net operating loss (NOL) carryover and the shareholders of the corporation have a market value basis in their stock. In these circumstances, a pro rata distribution of substantial assets might be made without triggering a tax liability at either the corporate level (gain offset by NOL carryover) or the shareholder level (amount realized offset by basis in stock). If the shareholders have a market value basis in their stock because they recently purchased the stock, might I.R.C. § 382 or § 269 impede the corporation from applying its NOL carryover against the corporate level gain that is triggered when the partial liquidation occurs? See I.R.C. § 382(h).

B. DISTRIBUTION OF STOCK— TAX-FREE SPIN-OFF/SPLIT-OFF

In lieu of distributing a specific group of assets to its shareholders, a corporation ("Distributing") can be divided by transferring that group of assets to a newly formed subsidiary ("Controlled") and then transferring the stock of Controlled to the shareholders of Distributing. After the transaction, none of the corporate assets are in the hands of the shareholders. Rather, the shareholders own the stock of two corporations: Distributing, which holds all the original assets other than those that were transferred to Controlled; and Controlled, which holds the remaining assets. A division accomplished by distributing stock of a subsidiary is often referred to as a "spin-off".

Historically, the tax issues presented by a spin-off were generally confined to the shareholder level. From the shareholder's perspective, a compelling case can be made that a spin-off represents a mere division of a single property into two pieces and, as such, is not an appropriate time to impose a tax. If tax-free treatment were accorded to every spin-off, however, a spin-off could easily be utilized to convert dividend income to capital gains.

Example 15–A (Potential for spin-off to convert dividend to capital gains): Mindy and Norman each own half the stock of Distributing Corporation. Distributing has $1,000,000 of earnings & profits. If Distributing distributes $200,000 to each of its shareholders, each shareholder receives $200,000 of dividend income. See I.R.C. § 301; pp. 201–208. If all spin-offs were tax-free, however, the shareholders could receive $200,000, yet avoid dividend income, if the following actions were taken:

> (a) Distributing transfers $400,000 to a newly formed subsidiary, Controlled Corporation, in exchange for all the stock of Controlled;

> (b) Distributing distributes half the Controlled stock to Mindy and the other half to Norman (the "spin-off"); and

> (c) Controlled liquidates by distributing $200,000 to each of Mindy and Norman (see I.R.C. § 331(a)) or Mindy and Norman each sell their Controlled stock for $200,000 (see I.R.C. § 1001(a)). In either case, the income of Mindy and Norman is characterized as capital gains.

Example 15–A demonstrates that a spin-off, by itself, does not convert dividend income to capital gains. Dividends are avoided only if the spin-off is followed by a disposition of the stock of Controlled (or a disposition of the stock of Distributing).[1] In these circumstances, the shareholders convert a part of their corporate investment to money without surrendering *any* proprietary interest in the retained corporation. This endpoint can ordinarily be reached only through a dividend distribution.

Unfortunately, the tax law cannot wait to see whether a subsequent disposition occurs before attaching tax consequences to a spin-off. Rather, a series of common law and statutory requirements are used to predict whether the spin-off will ultimately lead to the conversion of dividends to capital gains. The tax consequences of the spin-off are based on this prediction. If the spin-off fails to satisfy any of the common law or statutory requirements, the distribution of Controlled shares (step (b) in Example 15–A) is treated like any other "one-side distribution" of property (a dividend to the extent of earnings & profits), regardless of whether a subsequent disposition of the stock of either corporation ever occurs. If the spin-off satisfies all the common law and statutory requirements, it is treated as a tax-free division of property.

Now that dividends are taxed at capital gains rates, the potential shareholder level tax avoidance associated with a spin-off has diminished considerably. When a spin-off qualifies for tax-free treatment, however, a portion of the basis in each shareholder's stock of Distributing shifts to the stock of Controlled. See I.R.C. § 358(b); Treas. Reg. § 1.358–2(a)(2). Thus, if subsequent to a tax-free spin-off, a shareholder sells the Controlled stock, the shareholder's taxable gain will be less than it would have been if the distribution of the Controlled stock had been taxed in its entirety as a dividend (because the consideration received by the selling shareholder is offset by the basis allocated to the Controlled stock). Also, in the case of a shareholder with capital losses, the capital gain recognized on a sale of the Controlled stock after a tax-free spin-off could be offset by such capital losses. By contrast, a distribution of Controlled stock taxed as a dividend cannot be offset by capital losses. Finally, only dividends received through the end of 2012 are taxed at capital gains rates. Beginning in 2013, dividends will again be taxed as ordinary income unless Congress extends the tax break. Thus, although the shareholder level tax avoidance that § 355 was directed at has diminished considerably, some potential tax avoidance still exists.

Prior to the repeal of the General Utilities rule in 1986, a spin-off was not viewed as a means for achieving corporate level tax avoidance. At that time, a corporation generally could distribute appreciated assets without triggering a corporate level tax.[2] Under current law, however, a spin-off that satisfies both the common law and the statutory requirements remains

---

1. In Example 15–A, the shareholders segregated extraneous assets in Controlled and subsequently disposed of Controlled in a capital gains transaction. The same result could have been achieved by segregating the extraneous assets in Distributing (i.e., by having Distributing transfer all of its assets except for $400,000 to Controlled) and, after the spin-off of Controlled, disposing of Distributing in a capital gains transaction (i.e., by liquidating Distributing or having the shareholders sell their Distributing stock).

2. See pp. 29–33.

one of the few transactions that is still accorded tax-free treatment at the corporate level. Congress has responded to concerns that spin-offs now might serve as a means for circumventing the corporate level tax by creating additional statutory requirements that must be satisfied before a spin-off will be accorded tax-free treatment. These new requirements will be examined after the traditional rules are explored in greater detail.

1. SHAREHOLDER LEVEL CONSEQUENCES

I.R.C. §§ 355(a), (b)

a. THE EVIL

Gregory v. Helvering

Supreme Court of the United States, 1935.
293 U.S. 465, 55 S.Ct. 266.

■ MR. JUSTICE SUTHERLAND delivered the opinion of the Court.

Petitioner in 1928 was the owner of all the stock of United Mortgage Corporation. That corporation held among its assets 1,000 shares of the Monitor Securities Corporation. For the sole purpose of procuring a transfer of these shares to herself in order to sell them for her individual profit, and, at the same time, diminish the amount of income tax which would result from a direct transfer by way of dividend, she sought to bring about a "reorganization" * * *. To that end, * * * the Averill Corporation [was] organized * * * on September 18, 1928. Three days later, the United Mortgage Corporation transferred to the Averill Corporation the 1,000 shares of Monitor stock, for which all the shares of the Averill Corporation were issued to the petitioner. On September 24, the Averill Corporation was * * * liquidated by distributing all its assets, namely, the Monitor shares, to the petitioner. No other business was ever transacted, or intended to be transacted, by that company. Petitioner immediately sold the Monitor shares for $133,333.33. She returned for taxation as capital net gain the sum of $76,007.88, based upon an apportioned cost of $57,325.45 * * *.

The Commissioner of Internal Revenue, being of opinion that the reorganization attempted was without substance and must be disregarded, held that petitioner was liable for a tax as though the United [Mortgage] corporation had paid her a dividend consisting of the amount realized from the sale of the Monitor shares. [T]he Board of Tax Appeals * * * rejected the commissioner's view and upheld that of petitioner. [T]he circuit court of appeals sustained the commissioner and reversed the board, holding that there had been no "reorganization" within the meaning of the statute * * *.

Section 112 of the Revenue Act of 1928 [provided as follows]:

(g) Distribution of stock on reorganization.—If there is distributed, in pursuance of a plan of reorganization, to a shareholder in a corporation a party to the reorganization, stock or securities in such corporation or in another corporation a party to the reorganization, without the surrender by such shareholder of stock or securities in such a corporation, no gain to the distributee from the receipt of such stock or securities shall be recognized * * *.

* * *

(i) Definition of reorganization.—As used in this section

(1) The term "reorganization" means * * * (B) a transfer by a corporation of all or a part of its assets to another corporation if immediately after the transfer the transferor or its stockholders or both are in control of the corporation to which the assets are transferred * * *.

It is earnestly contended on behalf of the taxpayer that since every element required by the foregoing subdivision (B) is to be found in what was done, a statutory reorganization was effected; and that the motive of the taxpayer thereby to escape payment of a tax will not alter the result or make unlawful what the statute allows. It is quite true that if a reorganization in reality was effected within the meaning of subdivision (B), the ulterior purpose mentioned will be disregarded. The legal right of a taxpayer to decrease the amount of what otherwise would be his taxes, or altogether avoid them, by means which the law permits, cannot be doubted. But the question for determination is whether what was done, apart from the tax motive, was the thing which the statute intended * * *.

When subdivision (B) speaks of a transfer of assets by one corporation to another, it means a transfer made "in pursuance of a plan of reorganization" of corporate business; and not a transfer of assets by one corporation to another in pursuance of a plan having no relation to the business of either, as plainly is the case here. Putting aside, then, the question of motive in respect of taxation altogether, and fixing the character of the proceeding by what actually occurred, what do we find? Simply an operation having no business or corporate purpose—a mere device which put on the form of a corporate reorganization as a disguise for concealing its real character, and the sole object and accomplishment of which was the consummation of a preconceived plan, not to reorganize a business or any part of a business, but to transfer a parcel of corporate shares to the petitioner. No doubt, a new and valid corporation was created. But that corporation was nothing more than a contrivance to the end last described. It was brought into existence for no other purpose; it performed, as it was intended from the beginning it should perform, no other function. When that limited function had been exercised, it immediately was put to death.

In these circumstances, the facts speak for themselves and are susceptible of but one interpretation. The whole undertaking, though conducted according to the terms of subdivision (B), was in fact an elaborate and devious form of conveyance masquerading as a corporate reorganization, and nothing else. The rule which excludes from consideration the motive of tax avoidance is not pertinent to the situation, because the transaction upon its face lies outside the plain intent of the statute. To hold otherwise would be to exalt artifice above reality and to deprive the statutory provision in question of all serious purpose.

Judgment affirmed.

NOTES

1. *The four steps in Gregory.* The fact pattern of the Gregory case entailed the following steps:

> Step 1.   United Mortgage transferred Monitor shares to Averill in exchange for Averill stock.

> Step 2.   United Mortgage distributed the stock of Averill to Mrs. Gregory.

> Step 3.   Averill transferred the Monitor shares to Mrs. Gregory in liquidation.

> Step 4.   Mrs. Gregory sold the Monitor shares.

Although the facts indicate that Averill issued its shares directly to Mrs. Gregory (as part of Step 1), the Averill shares, in substance, represented consideration for the property United Mortgage transferred to Averill (the Monitor shares) and should be analyzed accordingly (see Steps 1 and 2).

2. *Step 1 (Drop-down).* Under the Revenue Act of 1928, Step 1 alone was sufficient for a "reorganization". See § 112(i)(1)(B) of the Revenue Act of 1928 (quoted in Gregory). Under current law, Step 1 alone will not qualify as a "reorganization". The transfer of *part* of a corporation's assets to a newly formed subsidiary can serve as an element of a reorganization under current law. A reorganization is accomplished, however, only if Step 1 is part of a plan that also entails a distribution of subsidiary stock that satisfies the requirements of I.R.C. § 355. See I.R.C. § 368(a)(1)(D). If the distribution satisfies I.R.C. § 355, the entire transaction may qualify as a "divisive" D reorganization. (Recall that the transfer of "substantially all" of a corporation's assets to a second corporation followed by a distribution of the second corporation's stock may qualify as a "nondivisive" D reorganization if the distribution satisfies I.R.C. § 354. See pp. 544–545).

Under current law, what are the tax consequences of Step 1, alone, to United Mortgage and Averill? See I.R.C. §§ 351(a), 358(a), 362(a), 1032(a).

3. *Step 2 (Distribution).* Under the Revenue Act of 1928, Mrs. Gregory could receive the Averill shares tax-free only if she received those shares in a "reorganization". See I.R.C. § 112(g) of the Revenue Act of 1928 (quoted in Gregory). Under current law, shareholders receiving a distribution of subsidiary stock are accorded tax-free treatment if the distribution satisfies the requirements of I.R.C. § 355. In contrast to earlier law, shareholder level tax consequences are not dependent upon whether the distribution is part of a "reorganization". I.R.C. § 355(a)(2)(C). Corporate level tax consequences are also generally not dependent upon whether the distribution is part of a "reorganization". See I.R.C. §§ 355(c), 361(c).

Mrs. Gregory claimed she was entitled to tax-free treatment by virtue of § 112(g) of the Revenue Act of 1928. Was that provision a nonrecognition provision or an exclusion? Did Mrs. Gregory need a nonrecognition provision or an exclusion? Under current law, I.R.C. § 355 is both a nonrecognition provision and an exclusion. See I.R.C. § 355(a)(1) (last two lines).

When subsidiary stock is distributed in a transaction that satisfies I.R.C. § 355, what is the basis of the recipient shareholders in that stock? See I.R.C. § 358(b); Treas. Reg. § 1.358–2(a)(2) ("If as the result of a * * * distribution under the terms of section * * * 355 * * * a shareholder who owned stock of only one class before the transaction owns stock of two or more classes after the transaction, then the basis of all the stock held before the transaction shall be allocated among the stock of all classes * * * held immediately after the transaction in proportion to the fair market values of the stock of each class.")

When subsidiary stock is distributed in a transaction that does not qualify under I.R.C. § 355, what is the basis of the recipient shareholders in that stock? See I.R.C. § 301(d).

When subsidiary stock is distributed in a transaction that satisfies I.R.C. § 355, earnings & profits of the distributing corporation are generally allocated between the distributing corporation and the controlled corporation in proportion to the market value of each corporation. See I.R.C. § 312(h); Treas. Reg. § 1.312–10.

4. *Step 3 (Liquidation).* The Gregory Court found that Steps 1 and 2 did not represent a reorganization but nevertheless respected the corporate existence of Averill. If Steps 1 and 2 had been treated as a reorganization, what shareholder level tax consequences would have followed from Step 3? See I.R.C. §§ 331, 334(a). In light of the Gregory Court's finding that no reorganization occurred but that the existence of Averill should be respected, what shareholder level tax consequences resulted from Step 3?

5. *Step 4 (Sale).* If Steps 1 and 2 had been treated as a reorganization and Step 3 was treated as a distribution in liquidation, what tax consequences would have followed from Step 4? In light of the Gregory Court's finding that no reorganization occurred, what tax consequences resulted from Step 4?

6. *Perceived evil.* Which of the four steps resulted in adverse tax consequences to Mrs. Gregory as a result of the Court's holding? Is the perceived evil actually manifested by that step? Describe the perceived evil of the Gregory transaction.

b.   THE DEFENSE

When a corporation ("Distributing") contributes a group of assets to a newly formed corporation ("Controlled") and Distributing then transfers the stock of Controlled to the shareholders of Distributing, the shareholders receive a distribution of "property" that normally is taxed as a dividend. See I.R.C. §§ 317(a), 301(c), 316(a). If, however, I.R.C. § 355(a)(1) and certain common law requirements are satisfied, the recipient shareholders may exclude the value of the stock received from income.

For a spin-off to be accorded tax-free treatment, all of the following requirements must be satisfied:

1. The transaction is carried out for one or more corporate business purposes. Treas. Reg. § 1.355–2(b).

2. The distributing corporation distributes solely stock or securities of the controlled corporation. I.R.C. § 355(a)(1)(A); Treas. Reg. § 1.355–2(a).

3. The transaction is not used principally as a "device" for the distribution of the earnings and profits of the distributing corporation, the controlled corporation or both corporations. I.R.C. § 355(a)(1)(B); Treas. Reg. § 1.355–2(d).

4. The distributing corporation and the controlled corporation are each engaged immediately after the distribution in the active conduct of a trade or business. I.R.C. §§ 355(a)(1)(C), (b); Treas. Reg. § 1.355–3.

5. The distributing corporation distributes all of its stock or securities in the controlled corporation or, in very limited circumstances, distributes only an amount of stock representing "control" (as defined in I.R.C. § 368(c)). I.R.C. § 355(a)(1)(D); Treas. Reg. § 1.355–2(e).

6. The historical shareholders of the distributing corporation own an amount of stock establishing a continuity of interest in both corporations after the distribution. Treas. Reg. § 1.355–2(c).

NOTES

1. *Concentration on controversial requirements.* Although all six of the above requirements must be satisfied before a spin-off qualifies for tax-free treatment, the second and fifth requirements are rarely controversial. The other four requirements will be explored in greater detail in the sections that follow.

2. *Focus of I.R.C. § 355.* I.R.C. § 355(a)(1), for the most part, represents Congress's response to the perceived evil in Gregory. At which Step in the Gregory transaction is I.R.C. § 355(a)(1) directed? See p. 694, Note 1.

3. *Scope of "property".* Only "property" distributions are potentially taxed as dividends. See I.R.C. § 301(a). "Property" for this purpose, does not include stock in the distributing corporation. I.R.C. § 317(a). Is stock distributed in a corporate division "property" that could be taxed as a dividend in the absence of I.R.C. § 355?

4. *Partial liquidation versus spin-off, shareholder level comparison.* Distinguish the shareholder level tax consequences of a corporate division accomplished by distributing a group of assets in a partial liquidation (see pp. 683–690) from the shareholder level tax consequences of a corporate division accomplished by distributing stock of a subsidiary containing the same group of assets in a tax-free spin-off. Can the difference be justified?

(1) BUSINESS PURPOSE FOR THE DISTRIBUTION

Treas. Reg. § 1.355–2(b)

The business purpose requirement that emerged from the Gregory case must still be satisfied for a spin-off to be accorded tax-free treatment. Though not in the statute, the business purpose requirement has long been applied by the courts.

Commissioner v. Wilson

United States Court of Appeals, Ninth Circuit, 1965.
353 F.2d 184.

■ MADDEN, JUDGE:

* * *

One William C. Wilson operated a furniture store business. He died in 1950. His * * * two sons, who are the taxpayers in this litigation, continued the business as a partnership. In 1955 Wilson's Furniture, Inc., hereinafter called Wilson's Inc., was formed. The assets of the partnership were transferred to the corporation, and all of the stock of the corporation was issued to the two sons * * *.

In 1958 Wilson's Inc. formed another corporation, Wil–Plan, and transferred to it the conditional sales contracts which Wilson's Inc. had on hand as a result of selling furniture on deferred payments. An automobile owned by Wilson's Inc. was also transferred to Wil–Plan in this transaction. All of the stock in Wil–Plan was distributed to the two taxpayers herein, who * * * were the sole stockholders in Wilson's Inc. The fair market value of the stock in Wil–Plan delivered to each of the two taxpayers was $69,020.07. The accumulated earnings and profits of Wilson's Inc., at the time of the incorporation of Wil–Plan, were $48,889.98.

The taxpayers did not, in their tax returns for 1958, include any income attributable to the stock in Wil–Plan which had been distributed to them in that year. The Commissioner of Internal Revenue mailed timely deficiency notices to each of them, asserting a deficiency against each of some $11,000. The taxpayers filed in the Tax Court timely petitions for redetermination of the deficiencies. [T]he Tax Court decided in favor of the taxpayers, and the Commissioner seeks, in this court, review and reversal of that decision.

Section 355 of the Internal Revenue Code of 1954 is difficult reading * * *. Its purpose and the purpose of its predecessors is to give to stockholders in a corporation controlled by them the privilege of separating or "spinning off" from their corporation a part of its assets and activities and lodging the separated part in another corporation which is controlled by the same stockholders. Since, after the spin-off, the real owners of the assets are the same persons who owned them before, Congress has * * * allowed [the owners], without penalty, to have their real ownership divided into smaller artificial entities than the single original corporation, if the real owners decide that such a division would be desirable. Congress early learned, however, that shareholders would select the part of the assets of an original corporation which could most readily be converted into cash or its equivalent, spin off those parts into the second corporation, distribute the stock in that corporation to themselves, and thus have available for sale and capital gains tax treatment the stock in that corporation, though in fact what they sold represented accumulated earnings of the original corporation, which earnings, if they had been paid directly to the shareholders of the original corporation, would have been fully taxable to them as dividend income.

Section 355 contains, as did its predecessors, a prohibition against the use of the spin-off as a "device for the distribution of the earnings and profits of the distributing corporation or the controlled corporation." § 355(a)(1)(B). The section also contained other requirements which had to be complied with in order to qualify a spin-off as a tax-free transaction. The Commissioner urges that some of these requirements were not complied with but, in view of the position which we take in this opinion, we find it unnecessary to resolve those problems.

* * *

[I]n addition to the requirements for tax-free spin-offs expressly written into section 355, the requirement stated for the Supreme Court of the United States by Mr. Justice Sutherland in the case of Gregory v. Helvering [p. 692] is and has been an essential part of the law. That requirement is, briefly stated, that a literal compliance with the provisions of the statute relating to tax-free corporate reorganizations is not enough; that there must be a valid business purpose for the reorganization. * * *

[B]oth parties recognize the business purpose requirement stated in Gregory v. Helvering. The taxpayers assert that they had three business purposes in separating the ownership and management of the conditional sales contracts acquired by Wilson's Inc. in the furniture store business and placing them in Wil–Plan. Here the taxpayer's difficulty is that the Tax Court expressly stated that none of the three business purposes asserted in the Tax Court litigation as the motive for the formation of Wil–Plan was, in fact, a bona fide motive. We can read no other meaning into the Tax Court's language than that these asserted reasons were nonexistent when Wil–Plan was created, but were afterthoughts presented in the litigation.

In view of the Tax Court's conclusion that the several business purposes asserted by the taxpayer were nonexistent, and the fact that the Tax Court did not find any other business purpose, the taxpayers, in view of their recognition of the necessity of satisfying the Gregory v. Helvering requirement, would have expected to lose their case in the Tax Court. But they won their case. The Tax Court found that they did not have a tax-avoidance purpose in creating Wil–Plan. The Commissioner argued that the tax advantage sought by the taxpayers in creating Wil–Plan was that it gave them the opportunity to sell the stock of Wil–Plan or to liquidate it at some future time and thereby receive a distribution of the earnings and profits of Wilson's Inc. as a capital gain. Answering this argument, the Tax Court wrote:

> The answer to that position is that in the present case we have found that there was no plan or intention to achieve any such result and no attempt to do so has in fact been made.

We seem to be confronted with what may be a unique situation, that of a corporation reorganization which had no business reason and which had no tax avoidance purpose, but which had the effect of removing from the risks and vicissitudes of a retail furniture business accumulated earnings in a form readily convertible by the shareholders into cash, by selling their stock in the spin-off corporation or by liquidating it and receiving and selling those easily liquidated assets. The shareholders have and will continue to have a tax advantage whenever they choose to make use of it, even though, as the Tax Court found, they never thought of the reorganization in terms of a tax advantage.

We think that, in this practical area of taxation, so much in the way of liability for taxes can hardly be allowed to depend solely upon what goes on in someone's mind. If the assets transferred to Wil–Plan had been United States or municipal or high grade corporate bonds, the purpose of the spin-off might well have been the removal of these assets from the risks of the retail furniture business, with the motive of creating security for old age or for their families and without any thought of tax consequences. Yet it would be unfair to shareholders who are fully taxed upon dividends received by them to give such an advantage to the beneficiaries of a spin-off without a business purpose. We suppose that is the reason for the Gregory v. Helvering doctrine. Congress, in enacting section 355 and its predecessors, was trying to give to business enterprisers leeway in readjusting their corporate arrangements to better suit their business purposes. If the rearrangement had that purpose, Congress was willing to concede them some possible tax advantages. If the rearrangement had no business purpose, let the taxes fall where they might.

As we have said, the taxpayers urge in this court, as they did in the Tax Court, that there were business reasons for the creation of Wil–Plan. But the Tax Court held that there were none, and that holding is well supported by the Tax Court's discussion of the evidence. The Commissioner urges in this court, as he did in the Tax Court, that there was a tax avoidance motive in creating Wil–Plan. But the Tax Court held that there was no such motive. Its holding was based upon the oral testimony of one of the taxpayers, which testimony the court said, "rang true." We cannot find that that holding is clearly erroneous.

We conclude, however, that even if there is no tax avoidance motive, a reorganization having no business reason does not result in the tax advantages which section 355 confers upon those who satisfy the legal requirements for its benefits.

The decision of the Tax Court is reversed * * *.

Revenue Ruling 2003–74

2003–29 I.R.B. 77.

ISSUE

Whether, in the situation described below, the distribution of the stock of a controlled corporation by a distributing corporation to enable the management of each corporation to concentrate on its own business satisfies the business purpose requirement of § 1.355–2(b) of the Income Tax Regulations.

FACTS

Distributing is a publicly traded corporation that conducts a software technology business. Controlled, a wholly owned subsidiary of Distributing, conducts a paper products business. One shareholder, who does not actively participate in the management or operations of Distributing or Controlled, owns eight percent of the outstanding Distributing stock.

The software business develops and markets software for various applications. It is a high-growth business [whose success depends] on innovation and acquisitions of related businesses. It is the business around which Distributing originally developed and remains the core operation. The paper products business manufactures and distributes paper products. It was acquired five years ago to support the software business and is significantly smaller than the software business. The paper products business grows at a slow to moderate rate largely through increased efficiencies in productivity.

Distributing's senior management devotes more of its time to the software business because it believes that business presents better opportunities for growth. Indeed, it would like to concentrate solely on the software business but is prevented from doing so by the need to service the paper products business. The management of the paper products business, on the other hand, believes that the disproportionate attention paid the software business deprives the paper products business of the management resources needed for its full development.

To enable Distributing's senior management to concentrate on the software business and the management of the paper products business to concentrate on its own operation, Distributing distributes the Controlled stock to Distributing's shareholders, pro rata. Because Distributing's senior management would have continued responsibility for the paper products business as long as Distributing owns a controlling interest in the stock of the corporation operating the paper products business, there is no other nontaxable transaction that would permit Distributing's senior management to concentrate on the software business and permit the paper products business to have a senior management that adequately serves that business. Distributing's directors and senior management expect that each business will benefit in a real and substantial way from the separation.

Following the distribution, no officer will serve both Distributing and Controlled. However, two of Distributing's eight directors will also serve on Controlled's six-person board. Director A will help with administrative aspects of the transition. His term will expire after two years, and he cannot seek reelection. Director B is recognized as an expert in corporate finance. His presence on the Controlled board is intended to reassure the financial markets by providing a sense of continuity. His term will expire after six years, at which time he may seek reelection. Both directors are officers of Distributing, but neither will be an officer or employee of Controlled.

Apart from the issue of whether the business purpose requirement of § 1.355–2(b) is satisfied, the distribution meets all of the requirements of § 355.

LAW

Section 355 provides that if certain requirements are met, a corporation may distribute stock and securities in a controlled corporation to its shareholders and security holders without causing the distributing corporation or the distributees to recognize gain or loss.

To qualify as a distribution described in § 355, a distribution must, in addition to satisfying the statutory requirements of § 355, satisfy certain requirements in the regulations, including the business purpose requirement. Section 1.355–2(b)(1) provides that a distribution must be motivated, in whole or substantial part, by one or more corporate business purposes. A corporate business purpose is a real and substantial non-Federal tax purpose germane to the business of the distributing corporation, the controlled corporation, or the affiliated group to which the distributing corporation belongs. Section 1.355–2(b)(2). The principal reason for the business purpose requirement is to provide nonrecognition treatment only to distributions that are incident to readjustments of corporate structures required by business exigencies and that effect only readjustments of continuing interests in property under modified corporate forms. Section 1.355–2(b)(1). If a corporate business purpose can be achieved through a nontaxable transaction that does not involve the distribution of stock of a controlled corporation and that is neither impractical nor unduly expensive, then the separation is not carried out for that corporate business purpose. Section 1.355–2(b)(3).

ANALYSIS

The distribution of Controlled stock by Distributing to Distributing's shareholders will enable Distributing's senior management to concentrate its efforts on the software business, which it believes presents better opportunities for growth, and allow the management of the paper products business to secure for that business the management resources needed for its full development. There is no other nontaxable transaction that would permit Distributing's senior management to concentrate on the software business and permit the paper products business to have a senior management that adequately serves that business, and it is expected that the separation of the two businesses will enhance the success of each business in a real and substantial way.

Although the continuing relationship between Distributing and Controlled evidenced by the two common directors appears inconsistent with the assertion that the software business and the paper products business require independent management teams, this relationship does not conflict with the business purpose for the separation. Director A will serve for only a short period and will further that purpose by aiding in the creation of two independently administered operations. Director B will assist the separation by calming market concerns that might otherwise adversely affect one or both businesses. Further, the two directors together constitute only a minority of each board.

Hence, the distribution of Controlled stock by Distributing to Distributing's shareholders is motivated in whole or substantial part by a real and substantial non-Federal tax purpose germane to the businesses of Distributing and Controlled and satisfies the corporate business purpose requirement of § 1.355–2(b).

HOLDING

In the situation described above, the distribution of the stock of a controlled corporation by a distributing corporation to enable the management of each corporation to concentrate on its own business satisfies the business purpose requirement of § 1.355–2(b).

Revenue Ruling 2003–75

2003–29 I.R.B. 79.

ISSUE

Whether, in the situation described below, the distribution of the stock of a controlled corporation to resolve a capital allocation problem between the distributing and controlled corporations satisfies the business purpose requirement of § 1.355–2(b) of the Income Tax Regulations.

FACTS

Distributing is a publicly traded corporation that conducts a pharmaceuticals business. Controlled, a wholly owned subsidiary of Distributing, conducts a cosmetics business. One shareholder, who does not actively participate in the management or operations of Distributing or Controlled, owns six percent of the outstanding Distributing stock.

The pharmaceuticals business develops, manufactures, and markets specialty drugs. It is a high-margin business that emphasizes rapid growth through innovation. The cosmetics business develops, manufactures, and markets cosmetics. It is a low-margin business that grows at a moderate rate by increasing its productivity and market share. Both businesses require substantial capital for reinvestment and research and development.

Distributing does all of the borrowing for both Distributing and Controlled and makes all decisions regarding the allocation of capital spending between the pharmaceuticals and cosmetics businesses. Because Distributing's capital spending in recent years for both the pharmaceuticals and cosmetics businesses has outpaced internally generated cash flow from the businesses, it has had to limit total expenditures to maintain its credit ratings. Although the decisions reached by Distributing's senior management regarding the allocation of capital spending usually favor the pharmaceuticals business due to its higher rate of growth and profit margin, the competition for capital prevents both businesses from consistently pursuing development strategies that the management of each business believes are appropriate.

To eliminate this competition for capital, Distributing distributes the Controlled stock to Distributing's shareholders, pro rata. Because the total capital available to the two businesses would continue to be limited as long as the two businesses remained within the same corporate group, there is no other nontaxable transaction that would solve the competition problem. It is expected that both businesses will benefit from the separation, and that the cosmetics business will benefit in a real and substantial way as a result of increased control over its capital spending and direct access to the capital markets.

To facilitate the separation, Distributing and Controlled will enter into transitional agreements that relate to information technology, benefits administration, and accounting and tax matters. Other than the tax matters agreement, each agreement will terminate after two years absent extraordinary circumstances, in which case the affected agreement may be extended on arm's-length terms for a limited period. Following the separation, there will be no cross-guarantee or cross-collateralization of debt between Distributing and Controlled, and an arm's-length loan from Distributing to Controlled for working capital will have a term of two years.

Apart from the issue of whether the business purpose requirement of § 1.355–2(b) is satisfied, the distribution meets all the requirements of § 355.

* * *

ANALYSIS

The operation of the pharmaceuticals business and the cosmetics business within the same corporate group causes capital allocation problems that prevent each business from pursuing the development strategies most appropriate to its operation. The separation of the two businesses is the only nontaxable transaction that will resolve these problems. It is expected that both businesses will benefit from the separation, and that the separation will enhance the success of the cosmetics business in a real and substantial way.

The limited continuing relationship between Distributing and Controlled evidenced by the various administrative agreements and the loan for working capital is not incompatible with the extent of separation contemplated by § 355. The administrative agreements, except for the tax matters agreement, and the loan are transitional and short-term, and all are designed to facilitate, rather than impede, the separation of the pharmaceuticals business from the cosmetics business.

Hence, the distribution of Controlled stock by Distributing to Distributing's shareholders is motivated in whole or substantial part by a real and substantial non-Federal tax purpose germane to the business of Controlled and satisfies the corporate business purpose requirement of § 1.355–2(b).

HOLDING

In the situation described above, the distribution of the stock of a controlled corporation to resolve a capital allocation problem between the distributing and controlled corporations satisfies the business purpose requirement of § 1.355–2(b).

NOTES

1. *Corporate business purpose defined.* Regulations promulgated under I.R.C. § 355 provide that tax-free treatment will only be achieved when a spin-off is motivated by one or more corporate business purposes. See Treas. Reg. § 1.355–2(b)(1). The regulations define a corporate business purpose as, "a real and substantial non Federal tax purpose germane to the business of the distributing corporation [or] the controlled corporation." Treas. Reg. § 1.355–2(b)(2). Will the corporate business purpose requirement be satisfied when a spin-off is motivated by the personal interests of the shareholders? See Treas. Reg. §§ 1.355–2(b)(2), (5) Example 2.

2. *Creation of subsidiary.* Unless a parent-subsidiary configuration already exists, a subsidiary must be created as a prerequisite to a spin-off (see Example 15–A, Step (a), p. 690). If the act of creating a subsidiary accomplishes the purported business purpose for the spin-off, will the subsequent spin-off be accorded tax-free treatment? See Treas. Reg. §§ 1.355–2(b)(3), (5) Examples 3–5.

3. *Spin-off without reorganization.* When a subsidiary is created as a prerequisite to a spin-off, a divisive D reorganization occurs if the spin-off satisfies the requirements of I.R.C. § 355. See I.R.C. § 368(a)(1)(D). Even in the absence of the § 355 regulations, the reorganization could not be achieved without satisfying the common law business purpose requirement. See Gregory, p. 692. When a parent-subsidiary configuration already exists, however, the mere distribution of subsidiary stock to shareholders can qualify for tax-free treatment under I.R.C. § 355, notwithstanding the absence of a corporate reorganization. See I.R.C. § 355(a)(2)(C). The § 355 regulations confirm that the business purpose requirement also applies to a spin-off that is not part of a reorganization. See Treas. Reg. § 1.355–2(b)(1).

4. *Change in circumstances.* Will the business purpose requirement be satisfied when a spin-off is motivated by a corporate business purpose that cannot be achieved due to an unexpected change in circumstances following the distribution? See Rev. Rul. 2003–55, 2003–22 I.R.B. 961 (ruling that the business purpose requirement is satisfied when a parent corporation distributes the stock of its subsidiary to facilitate a public offering of the subsidiary's shares notwithstanding that following the distribution but before the offering can be undertaken, market conditions unexpectedly deteriorate to such an extent that the offering is postponed and the subsidiary ultimately funds its capital needs by selling debentures).

5. *Private letter rulings.* The Internal Revenue Service has announced a pilot program whereby it will no longer determine whether a proposed or completed distribution of stock of a controlled corporation is being carried out for a corporate business purpose; rather, the taxpayer must now represent that a legitimate business purpose exists. See Rev. Proc. 2003–48, 2003–29 I.R.B. 86.

(2) Not a Device for the Distribution of Earnings and Profits

I.R.C. § 355(a)(1)(B)

Treas. Reg. § 1.355–2(d)

In addition to demonstrating that the spin-off was motivated by a corporate business purpose, the taxpayer must show that the spin-off was, "not used principally as a device for the distribution of the earnings and profits of the distributing corporation or the controlled corporation or both." I.R.C. § 355(a)(1)(B). This requirement has long wreaked havoc from a planning standpoint due to its subjective nature and the fact that it compels the taxpayer to prove a negative.

Pulliam v. Commissioner

United States Tax Court, 1997.
73 T.C.M. 3052, nonacq. 1998–2 Cum.Bull. 664.

■ DAWSON, JUDGE: * * *

FINDINGS OF FACT

* * *

Pulliam Funeral Homes, P.C. (Homes) is a corporation chartered in the State of Illinois * * *. Clark D. Pulliam (Mr. Pulliam) [is] the sole shareholder, director, and president of Homes. Mr. Pulliam is a licensed funeral director and embalmer in the State of Illinois. * * * Prior to January 1, 1992, Homes operated three funeral homes located in the rural eastern Illinois towns of Robinson, Oblong, and Hudsonville. * * *

Homes is a successful and profitable business. In 1991 Mr. Pulliam was paid a salary of $181,400. Prior to 1992, Homes had not paid any dividends, and it had unappropriated retained earnings of $1,112,445 on December 31, 1991.

* * *

Earl L. Deckard (Mr. Deckard), a licensed funeral director and embalmer in Illinois, was * * * the resident manager and embalmer at Oblong where he was in charge of day-to-day operations of the funeral home. He was the only full-time employee at the Oblong facility * * *. He was well connected in both the Oblong and Robinson communities. * * *

Prior to 1991, Mr. Deckard had spoken to Mr. Pulliam about acquiring a financial interest in the Oblong facility. * * * Mr. Deckard was not interested in any minority ownership in Homes. He later so indicated in writing that he "had absolutely no interest in a minority interest in Pulliam Funeral Home, P.C.". Also prior to 1991, Mr. Pulliam and Mr. Deckard had some disagreements regarding the operation of the Oblong facility. Consequently, in early 1991, Mr. Deckard purchased property adjacent to his residence on which he intended to construct and operate his own funeral home in Oblong.

Mr. Pulliam discovered that Mr. Deckard had purchased the property in Oblong and that he planned to construct and operate a funeral home in competition with Homes. This would have caused Homes to lose a key employee. Homes would also have lost business in the small market area of Oblong and vicinity, and it would have had an adverse impact on its profits.

* * *

A meeting was held in July 1991 [at which an] informal agreement was reached whereby Mr. Deckard would acquire an ownership interest in the Oblong facility * * *. The corporate minutes of Homes, dated July 2, 1991, stated as follows:

> The sole stockholder and director of Pulliam Funeral Homes, PC., conducted a special meeting of said Corporation * * * for the purpose of considering an offer from long-time employee Earl L. Deckard to purchase an interest in the business of Oblong, Illinois. After consideration, it was decided that Mr. Deckard could purchase up to 49% of the Oblong location, after a spin-off from Pulliam Funeral Homes, P.C., into Pulliam–Deckard Funeral Chapel, P.C., in which Clark D. Pulliam would be the sole stockholder, and from which up to 49% of the stock could be sold to Earl L. Deckard.

* * *

A Spin-off Agreement * * * provided, in pertinent part, as follows:

WHEREAS, PULLIAM FUNERAL HOMES, P.C. proposes to transfer to PULLIAM DECKARD FUNERAL CHAPEL, P.C. the real estate and improvements, and other assets set forth on Exhibit A attached, heretofore used by it in that portion of its business operation situated in Oblong, Illinois, in return for all the issued and outstanding shares of PULLIAM DECKARD FUNERAL CHAPEL, P.C. and to simultaneously transfer to CLARK D. PULLIAM, the sole shareholder of PULLIAM FUNERAL HOME, P.C. all of said outstanding and issued shares of PULLIAM DECKARD FUNERAL CHAPEL, P.C.

NOW, THEREFORE, in consideration of mutual covenants and undertakings of the respective parties hereto, it is agreed as follows:

1. PULLIAM FUNERAL HOMES, P.C. does hereby agree to transfer into PULLIAM DECKARD FUNERAL CHAPEL, P.C., effective January 1, 1992, all of those assets more particularly identified on Exhibit A which is attached hereto and incorporated herein by this reference.

2. Simultaneous with the transfer of the assets as provided for in paragraph 1 above, PULLIAM DECKARD FUNERAL CHAPEL, P.C. agrees to transfer to PULLIAM FUNERAL HOMES, P.C. all of the issued and outstanding shares of stock of PULLIAM DECKARD FUNERAL CHAPEL, P.C., which in turn will transfer said shares to its sole shareholder, CLARK D. PULLIAM.

3. It is the intention of all parties hereto that no gain or loss for income tax purposes will be recognized in that said transaction shall constitute a "spin-off" pursuant to Section 355 of the Internal Revenue Code * * *.

[A Stock Purchase Agreement], signed by Mr. Pulliam and Mr. Deckard, * * * provided, in pertinent part, as follows:

WHEREAS, PULLIAM owns 100 percent (1000 shares) of the common stock of PULLIAM DECKARD FUNERAL CHAPEL, P.C., an Illinois Corporation; and

WHEREAS, DECKARD desires to purchase from PULLIAM, and PULLIAM desires to sell to DECKARD 49 percent (490 shares) of the common stock of PULLIAM DECKARD FUNERAL CHAPEL, P.C., an Illinois Corporation.

NOW, THEREFORE, in consideration of the mutual covenants and undertakings of the respective parties hereto, it is agreed as follows:

1. DECKARD agrees to purchase from PULLIAM, and PULLIAM agrees to sell to DECKARD 49 percent (490 shares) of the common stock of PULLIAM DECKARD FUNERAL CHAPEL, P.C., an Illinois Corporation, for the sum of $789 per share, for a total of $386,610, payable by DECKARD to PULLIAM as follows:

    A. $40,000 upon execution of this Agreement, * * *.

    B. The remaining balance of $346,610, together with interest thereon at the rate of 10 percent per annum amortized over a period of 15 years, shall be paid by DECKARD to PULLIAM in equal annual installments of $45,570.13, which includes principal and interest, beginning March 15, 1993 * * *.

* * *

4. DECKARD agrees not to compete with PULLIAM or PULLIAM
    FUNERAL HOMES, P.C., under the same terms and conditions as
    are contained in * * * the EMPLOYMENT AGREEMENT at-
    tached hereto and incorporated herein by this reference * * *.

* * *

The $789 per share fair market value of Chapel's stock was based on
[an] appraisal report * * * dated January 9, 1992, which determined that
the total fair market value of the Oblong facility was $789,500. * * *

On January 1, 1992, a spin-off of Homes' assets and liabilities with
respect to the Oblong funeral home was consummated. * * * On March 6,
1992, Mr. Pulliam transferred a certificate [for 490 shares of Chapel] to the
First National Bank of Robinson as escrow agent pursuant to the Stock
Purchase Agreement between him and Mr. Deckard. Mr. Pulliam received
the initial $40,000 payment from Mr. Deckard in 1992 pursuant to the
Agreement.

By the terms of the Employment Agreement Mr. Deckard was to
provide management and other services as funeral director and assist in the
overall operation and supervision of the Oblong facility, and to preserve
and increase its goodwill. His compensation was $39,000 per year. It
contained, among other provisions, a covenant not to compete with Chapel
for a period of 3 years after the termination of his employment. It also
contained a non-solicitation clause and a covenant for the protection of
confidential information.

* * *

Mr. Deckard defaulted in 1994 on the installment sale. His employment by Chapel then ended. He demanded that Mr. Pulliam return the
payments he had made, but later settled for $5,000. After defaulting, Mr.
Deckard abided by his covenant not to compete with Chapel, which prevented him from working as a funeral director in Oblong. Mr. Pulliam
reacquired almost all of Chapel's common stock * * *.

In the notice of deficiency respondent determined that Mr. Pulliam
received dividends of $789,500 from Homes, which were not reported on
[his] Federal income tax return for 1992. Therefore, [his] taxable income
was increased [by] $789,500.

OPINION

* * *

* * * [Mr. Pulliam] contends that the spin-off by Homes of the Chapel
stock * * * qualifies as a tax-free distribution pursuant to section 355. [He
argues] that there were strong corporate business purposes for Homes to
create Chapel because it wanted to protect itself from any possible competition by Mr. Deckard in the funeral business in the Oblong area, and it
wanted to reemploy Mr. Deckard as a key employee to operate and manage
the Oblong facility. He also argues that Homes had to distribute Chapel's
stock to Mr. Pulliam because it was believed that Illinois law required

funeral homes to be professional service corporations having shareholders who are licensed by the State of Illinois as funeral directors and embalmers. Thus, petitioner maintains that both of these corporate business purposes are strong evidence of nondevice which overcomes the evidence that there was principally a device for the distribution of the earnings and profits of Homes or Chapel or both.

To the contrary, it is respondent's position that this transaction fails to qualify as a tax-free distribution of stock under section 355 * * *. Respondent argues that there was no corporate business purpose for the distribution by Homes of Chapel stock to Mr. Pulliam, and that there was no compelling reason to distribute Chapel's stock to Mr. Pulliam other than to distribute substantial earnings and profits of Homes to Mr. Pulliam without being subject to the dividend provisions of section 301. It is further argued that, when Homes distributed the Chapel stock, Illinois law relating to funeral homes did not require that Chapel's * * * shareholders be licensed funeral directors and embalmers * * *. Thus, respondent contends that various devices present here clearly show that the transaction was used principally as a device for the distribution of Homes' earnings and profits. In addition, respondent asserts that the business objectives of Homes could have been satisfied without a distribution to Mr. Pulliam either by having Mr. Deckard purchase 49 percent of the Chapel stock from Homes or by having Mr. Deckard purchase newly issued Chapel stock from Chapel.

Device and Nondevice

At the outset it is important to note that, after a spin-off, a shareholder can sell or exchange stock in either the spin-off corporation or the distributing corporation in a transaction qualifying for capital gains treatment. The shareholder will get this favorable capital gains treatment even though he continues to hold stock representing part of his investment. Therefore, under certain circumstances, a spin-off can be used to avoid the ordinary income tax treatment imposed on dividends to bail out corporate earnings. * * * Because of continuing Congressional concern that a spin-off might be used to avoid the tax on dividends, section 355(a)(1)(B) provides that a spin-off cannot qualify as tax-free if it is used principally as a "device" to distribute earnings and profits.

Whether the distribution in this case qualifies as tax-free under section 355 turns upon the answer to the narrow question of whether the device factors present in the transaction outweigh the nondevice factors. If the device factors are predominant, the spin-off cannot qualify as tax-free because it has been used principally as a device for the distribution of earnings and profits of the distributing corporation (Homes) or the controlled corporation (Chapel) or both. On the other hand, if the nondevice factors are strong enough to overcome the device factors, the spin-off will qualify as tax-free. Sec. 1.355–2(d)(2) and (3), Income Tax Regs. The determination must be based on all the facts and circumstances. Sec. 1.355–2(d)(1), Income Tax Regs.

Device Factors

A sale of stock after a spin-off is "evidence of device." Sec. 1.355–2(d)(2)(iii)(A), Income Tax Regs. A subsequent sale of stock pursuant to an arrangement negotiated or agreed upon before the distribution is "substantial evidence of device." Sec. 1.355–2(d)(2)(iii)(B), Income Tax Regs. In this case it was clearly prearranged that, after the spin-off of stock in Chapel to Mr. Pulliam, he would make an installment sale of 490 shares of that stock to Mr. Deckard. Thus, there is substantial evidence of device.

Generally, the greater the percentage of the stock sold after the distribution, the stronger the evidence of device. In addition, the shorter the period of time between the distribution and the sale, the stronger the evidence of device. Sec. 1.355–2(d)(2)(iii), Income Tax Regs. Here 49 percent of Chapel's stock was sold to Mr. Deckard, and the distribution and the sale of stock were both deemed to have taken effect as of January 1, 1992. * * *

Nondevice Factors

Among nondevice factors is a corporate business purpose. Sec. 1.355–2(d)(3)(ii), Income Tax Regs. Since any spin-off must have a corporate business purpose to qualify as tax-free, this nondevice factor will always be present to some extent in any qualifying spin-off. Under the balancing approach adopted in the regulations, the stronger the evidence of device, the stronger the corporate business purpose that is necessary to prevent a determination that the transaction was used principally as a device. Id. Factors that are relevant in weighing the strength of the business purpose include: (1) The importance of achieving the purpose to the success of the business; (2) the extent to which the transaction is prompted by a person not having a proprietary interest in either corporation, or by other outside factors beyond the control of the distributing corporation; and (3) the immediacy of the conditions prompting the transaction. Sec. 1.355–2(d)(3)(ii)(A), (B) and (C), Income Tax Regs. As reflected in our findings of fact, two strong corporate business purposes for the spin-off are present in this case. If Mr. Deckard had carried out his plans to build and operate a funeral home in Oblong in competition with Homes it would have divided the funeral business in that area, thus having an adverse impact on Homes' profits. In addition, the services of an experienced funeral director and key employee (Mr. Deckard) would have been lost to the Homes organization. These purposes were vitally important to the continued success of Homes' business. The transaction was prompted by the actions of Mr. Deckard, who had no proprietary interest in Homes at that time. The immediate possible threat of competition to Homes in Oblong prompted the transaction.

Independent Corporate Business Purposes

Section 1.355–2(b)(1), Income Tax Regs., provides an affirmative requirement that a spin-off have one or more corporate business purposes. This is independent of the device test. The requirement limits tax-free treatment under section 355 to spin-offs motivated by non-tax business reasons, and thus prevents tax avoidance opportunities from arising. Id. Section 1.355–2(b)(2), Income Tax Regs., defines a corporate business purpose as a real and substantial non-Federal tax purpose germane to the distributing corporation, the controlled corporation, or the affiliated group to which the distributing corporation belongs. * * *

In this case, as we have previously indicated, independent corporate business purposes existed for the transaction. The protection against competition and the retention of a key employee are both strong and compelling business purposes * * *.

Respondent stresses that there must be a business purpose not only for dividing the business into separate corporations, but also for direct ownership of the corporations by the shareholders. Petitioner asserts that he believed Illinois law required Chapel's shareholders to be individuals, who were licensed funeral directors and embalmers, rather than a corporation, and therefore it was necessary to create Chapel as a professional service corporation with Mr. Pulliam owning its stock before the installment sale of 490 shares to Mr. Deckard. Respondent disputes this assertion as being incorrect and misleading. It is argued that Illinois law did not require Homes to distribute Chapel's stock to Mr. Pulliam, but it could have held the stock in Chapel and sold 490 shares directly to Mr. Deckard. Thus, respondent argues, "the unnecessary use of a professional service corporation, coupled with the specious argument that a professional service corporation was required by Illinois law, demonstrates an obvious attempt to structure the transaction to avoid the provisions of section 355(a)(1)(B)."

We agree with petitioner. Mr. Pulliam's attorney and accountants reasonably believed that it was necessary to create Chapel as a professional service corporation, and in our judgment their belief was well founded. * * * Arguably under the Illinois corporate requirements, we think that initially only Mr. Pulliam (and later Mr. Deckard) could have held Chapel's stock. Homes could not have done so. Consequently, Homes' distribution of Chapel's stock to Mr. Pulliam had a definite business purpose.

Section 1.355–2(b)(3), Income Tax Regs., states that a distribution is not carried out for a valid corporate business purpose if the business purpose can be achieved through a nontaxable transaction that does not involve the distribution of stock of a controlled corporation and which is neither impractical nor unduly expensive. In the circumstances of this case we think the corporate business purpose of * * * providing Mr. Deckard with a minority interest in Chapel could not have been achieved without an installment sale because of Mr. Deckard's financial condition and the Illinois Professional Corporation Act requirement that licensed individuals be the stockholders of Chapel. Homes could not have owned the Chapel stock during the installment sale. Consequently, we reject respondent's arguments that the business objectives of Homes could have been achieved in a nontaxable transaction without a distribution of Chapel stock to Mr. Pulliam.

* * *

We also find Example (1) of section 1.355–2(d)(4), Income Tax Regs., to be distinguishable from the facts of the instant case. In Example (1) corporation X, whose stock was owned solely by individual A, distributed the stock of Y, a wholly owned subsidiary of X, to A, so that individual B, a key employee, could afford to purchase stock in X. After the distribution of the Y stock, A sold some of his X stock to B. Because X could have issued additional shares to give B an equivalent interest in X, the sale of X stock by A is deemed to be substantial evidence of device, and the transaction is considered to be used principally as a device. Here, by contrast, no additional stock could have been issued by Homes because Mr. Deckard did not want Homes' stock, Homes could not be a stockholder of Chapel under Illinois law, Mr. Pulliam and Homes would not sell Homes' stock to Mr. Deckard, and, in any event, Mr. Deckard could not afford to purchase any meaningful amount of Homes' stock. The entire distribution in Example (1) of section 1.355–2(d)(4), Income Tax Regs., was made so that the key employee could afford to buy stock in the distributing corporation, as opposed to the controlled corporation in this case. As a result, the fact pattern in Example (1) is different from the situation present in the instant case.

Based on all the facts and circumstances present in this record, we conclude, on balance, that the strong corporate business purposes and nondevice factors outweigh and overcome the device factors, so that the distribution by Homes of Chapel stock to Mr. Pulliam qualifies as tax-free under section 355. * * *

NOTES

1. *Post spin-off sale of stock to key-employee.* It is quite common for a high level, non-shareholder employee who is instrumental in the corporation's success (a "key-employee") to insist on acquiring stock in the enterprise. If the corporation conducts two businesses and the key-employee's activities are confined to one of these businesses, the key employee's desire to acquire an equity interest only in the business in which she is involved may serve as the business purpose for a spin-off. How strong must a key-employee's desire to purchase an equity interest be before that desire can serve as the business purpose for the spin-off? Two examples in the regulations state that a key-employee, "has indicated that he will seriously consider leaving the company if he is not given the opportunity to purchase a significant amount of stock." See Treas. Reg. §§ 1.355–2(b)(5), Example 8; –2(d)(4), Example 1. Private letter rulings issued under I.R.C. § 355 indicate that many other key-employees have made this same statement. Is this merely a coincidence? Does the key-employee derive any *tax* benefit from making this statement? Who counsels the key-employee to make this statement? What ethical issues does the counselor face in these circumstances?

The mere transfer of the business in which the key-employee is involved to a subsidiary corporation should be sufficient to satisfy the key-employee's desire to acquire an equity interest only in that business, unless an impediment exists to the key-employee acquiring stock in a subsidiary corporation. See Treas. Reg. § 1.355–2(b)(5), Example 8 (involving subsidiary barred by state law from issuing stock to key-employee). Even if no legal impediment exists to issuing subsidiary stock to a key-employee, the key-employee's desire to purchase stock can apparently still serve as the business purpose for a spin-off if the key-employee represents that she will not consider purchasing stock in a subsidiary corporation. See, e.g., IRS Letter Rulings 200422020 (2/9/04), 200227016 (3/29/02). Why might a key-employee object to owning stock in a subsidiary corporation? In the Pulliam case, why was it unnecessary for Mr. Deckard to object to owning stock in a subsidiary?

2. *Post spin-off stock sale as evidence of device.* A sale or exchange of stock of the Distributing Corporation or the Controlled Corporation after the distribution serves as evidence of a device. Treas. Reg. § 1.355–2(d)(2)(iii). When a spin-off is undertaken to enable a key-employee to purchase stock in a corporation conducting the business in which the key-employee is involved, the spin-off may be deemed a device if the key-employee purchases stock from a shareholder who participated in the spin-off. See Treas. Reg. § 1.355–2(d)(4), Example 1. Instead, the key-employee must purchase shares directly from the issuing corporation to avoid a device problem. If a key-employee desires to acquire a 10% interest in a corporation with a value of $900,000, it should cost the employee $90,000 to acquire such an interest from the shareholders of that corporation. If the key-employee must purchase the stock from the corporation, rather than from the shareholders, how much will it cost him to acquire a 10% interest?

The Pulliam court distinguished Treas. Reg. § 1.355–2(d)(4), Example 1 on the ground that Mr. Deckard purchased stock in the Controlled Corporation, rather than the Distributing Corporation. Is that distinction meaningful? Are the facts that Mr. Deckard ultimately defaulted on the installment obligation and Mr. Pulliam reacquired almost all of Chapel's common stock relevant to the outcome of the case?

3. *Uncertain role of the device requirement.* Now that dividends are taxed at capital gains rates, the role of the device requirement is uncertain. The device requirement was originally intended to guard against the conversion of dividends to capital gains. Because dividends are now taxed at capital gains rates, a shareholder is generally indifferent between the two, unless the shareholder has capital losses (which cannot be applied against dividends). The device requirement has also played a secondary role of impeding shareholders from reducing the amount of income resulting from a taxable distribution. See Treas. Reg. § 1.355–2(d)(1) (third sentence). By utilizing the basis allocated to the shares of the distributed corporation in a tax-free spin-off, the gain realized on the subsequent sale of those shares is reduced. Is it likely that the possibility of basis recovery was a significant factor in the Pulliam case? What if Pulliam had died shortly before the spin-off? See I.R.C. § 1014.

Although dividends are now taxed at capital gains rates, a spin-off can still be utilized as a vehicle for reducing the amount of a shareholder's income whenever a shareholder has significant basis in her shares. If the device requirement's primary concern is now to be basis recovery, however, many rules developed under prior law must be changed. Unless dividends revert to being taxed as ordinary income in 2013 (as currently scheduled) or Congress revisits section 355, the role of the device requirement will remain a mystery.

4. *Pro rata distribution as evidence of device; spin-off versus split-off.* When the Distributing Corporation distributes stock of the Controlled Corporation "pro rata", evidence of a device exists. See Treas. Reg. § 1.355–2(d)(2)(ii). A "pro rata" distribution means that the shares of Controlled are distributed to the shareholders of Distributing in proportion to each shareholder's relative interest in Distributing. For example, if Fran and Greg each own half of the stock of Distributing which owns all of the stock of Controlled, the distribution by Distributing of half of its Controlled stock to Fran and half of its Controlled stock to Greg is a pro rata distribution. Why did a pro rata distribution serve as evidence of a device when dividends were taxed as ordinary income? Now that dividends are taxed at capital gains rates, should a pro rata distribution still serve as evidence of a device?

In contrast to a pro rata distribution, if Fran and Greg wish to part company and both Distributing and Controlled are of roughly the same value, Distributing might distribute all of its Controlled stock to Fran *in exchange for* all of her Distributing stock. Non pro rata distributions of this type are commonly referred to as "split-offs". (The term "spin-off" technically only describes a pro rata distribution, though it is frequently used in a generic sense to identify both pro rata and non pro rata distributions.) After the split-off, Fran owns all of the stock of Controlled and Greg owns all of the stock of Distributing. A less extreme non pro rata split-off also is possible. For example, Distributing might distribute ⅓ of its Controlled stock to Fran and ⅔ to Greg *in exchange for* ⅓ of Fran's and ⅔ of Greg's Distributing stock. In the absence of I.R.C. § 355, what would be the tax consequences to a shareholder who participates in a split-off? See I.R.C. §§ 302, 317(b).

I.R.C. § 355 can apply to a split-off. See I.R.C. § 355(a)(2)(A). (A tax-free split-off is illustrated in the Coady case at p. 715.) Does a shareholder who receives Controlled stock in a split-off need a nonrecognition provision or an exclusion to avoid income? See I.R.C. § 302. Does a shareholder who receives Controlled stock in a spin-off need a nonrecognition provision or an exclusion to avoid income? Does I.R.C. § 355(a)(1) operate as a nonrecognition provision or as an exclusion?

Can a split-off that fails to satisfy I.R.C. § 355 qualify as a partial liquidation? See Morgenstern v. Commissioner, 56 T.C. 44 (1971) (distribution of stock of controlled corporation will not qualify as partial liquidation under predecessor to I.R.C. § 302(b)(4) even if distribution of assets held by controlled subsidiary would qualify as partial liquidation).

5. *Nature and use of assets as evidence of device.* If the Distributing Corporation or the Controlled Corporation owns assets not used in a trade or business or if either corporation holds a disproportionate amount of liquid assets, evidence of a device may exist. See Treas. Reg. §§ 1.355–2(d)(2)(iv), –2(d)(4) Examples 2–4. Why is the nature and use of each corporation's assets relevant to assessing whether a divisive transaction represents a device to distribute earnings & profits? Should the nature and use of a corporation's assets remain relevant now that dividends are taxed at capital gains rates?

6. *Evidence of non-device.* Why are each of the factors designated in Treas. Reg. § 1.355–2(d)(3) evidence of non-device? Should these factors still be regarded as evidence of non-device now that dividends are taxed at capital gains rates?

7. *Transactions ordinarily not considered a device.* Why are each of the transactions described in Treas. Reg. § 1.355–2(d)(5) "ordinarily not considered a device"? Now that dividends are taxed at capital gains rates, should these transactions still normally not be considered a device?

8. *Relationship between business purpose requirement and device restriction.* What relationship exists between the corporate business purpose requirement and the device restriction? See Treas. Reg. § 1.355–2(d)(3)(ii). Are both requirements desirable now that dividends are taxed at capital gains rates?

9. *Private letter rulings.* The Internal Revenue Service has announced a pilot program whereby it will no longer determine whether a proposed or completed distribution of stock of a controlled corporation is used principally as a device; rather, the taxpayer must now represent that the distribution is not used principally as a device. See Rev. Proc. 2003–48, 2003–29 I.R.B. 86.

(3) BOTH CORPORATIONS ENGAGED IN ACTIVE BUSINESS

I.R.C. §§ 355(a)(1)(C), (b)

Treas. Reg. § 1.355–3

In contrast to the somewhat amorphous business purpose requirement and device restriction, a highly technical requirement exists with respect to the content of each corporation emerging from a corporate division. For a stock distribution to satisfy I.R.C. § 355, both the Distributing Corporation and the Controlled Corporation normally must be engaged in the "active conduct of a trade or business" immediately after the distribution. See I.R.C. §§ 355(a)(1)(C), (b)(1)(A).

Coady v. Commissioner

Tax Court of the United States, 1960.
33 T.C. 771.

■ TIETJENS, JUDGE:

* * *

Edmund P. Coady [is] hereinafter referred to as the petitioner * * *.

Christopher Construction Co., an Ohio corporation, is now engaged, and for more than 5 years prior to November 15, 1954, was engaged, in the active conduct of a construction business primarily in and around Columbus, Ohio. In an average year the Christopher Company undertook approximately 6 construction contracts, no one of which lasted for more than 2 years. Its gross receipts varied between $1,500,000 and $2,000,000 per year.

At its central office, located at 16 East Broad Street in Columbus, the Christopher Company kept its books of account, paid its employees, prepared bids for its jobs, and, excepting minor amounts of tools and supplies, made its purchases. In addition, it maintained temporary field offices at each jobsite. It also maintained a central repair and storage depot for its equipment. Equipment in use on particular jobs was kept at the jobsite until work was terminated. Then, it would either be returned to the central depot or moved to another jobsite.

[T]he stock of the Christopher Company was owned by M. Christopher and the petitioner. * * * [E]ach owned 50 per cent of the company's stock.

Sometime prior to November 15, 1954, differences arose between the petitioner and Christopher. As a result, they entered into an agreement for the division of the Christopher Company into two separate enterprises. Pursuant to that agreement, the Christopher Company, on November 15, 1954, organized E. P. Coady and Co., to which it transferred the following assets, approximating one-half the Christopher Company's total assets:

A contract for the construction of a sewage disposal plant at Columbus, Ohio, dated June 1, 1954.

A part of its equipment.

A part of its cash, and certain other items.

In consideration for the receipt of these assets, E. P. Coady and Co. transferred all of its stock to the Christopher Company. The Christopher Company retained the following assets, which were of the same type as those transferred to E. P. Coady and Co.:

A contract for a sewage treatment plant in Charleston, West Virginia.

A part of its equipment.

A part of its cash.

Immediately thereafter, the Christopher Company distributed to the petitioner all of the stock of E. P. Coady and Co. held by it in exchange for all of the stock of the Christopher Company held by petitioner. The fair market value of the stock of E. P. Coady and Co. received by petitioner was $140,000. His basis in the Christopher Company stock surrendered was $72,500.

Since the distribution, both E. P. Coady and Co. and the Christopher Company have been actively engaged in the construction business.

On their 1954 Federal income tax return, petitioner * * * reported no gain or loss on the exchange of the Christopher Company stock for the stock of E. P. Coady and Co.

Respondent determined that petitioner realized a capital gain on that exchange in the amount of $67,500 * * *.

Petitioner contends that the distribution to him of the E. P. Coady and Co. stock qualified for tax-free treatment under the provisions of section 355 of the 1954 Code, arguing that it was received pursuant to a distribution of a controlled corporation's stock within the meaning of that section.

Respondent on the other hand maintains petitioner's receipt of the Coady stock did not fall within those distributions favored by section 355, inasmuch as the 5–year active business requirements of section 355(b) were not met. More particularly he argues that section 355 does not apply to the separation of a "single business"; and, inasmuch as the Christopher Company was engaged in only one trade or business (construction contracting), the gain realized by petitioner upon receipt of the Coady stock was taxable. As authority for his position respondent points to that portion of his regulations which expressly provides that section 355 does not apply to the division of a single business.

Conceding that the Christopher Company was engaged in a "single business" immediately prior to the instant transaction, petitioner contends that the regulations, insofar as they limit the applicability of section 355 to divisions of only those corporations which have conducted two or more separate and distinct businesses for a 5–year period, are without support in the law, are without justification, are unreasonable and arbitrary, and therefore are invalid.

Thus, the issue is narrowed to the question of whether the challenged portion of the regulations constitutes a valid construction of the statute, or whether it is unreasonable and plainly inconsistent therewith. * * *

Section 355 of the 1954 Code represents the latest of a series of legislative enactments designed to deal with the tax effect upon shareholders of various corporate separations. * * * A careful reading of section 355, as well as the Finance Committee report which accompanied its enactment, reveals no language, express or implied, denying tax-free treatment at the shareholder level to a transaction, otherwise qualifying under section 355, on the grounds that it represents the division or separation of a "single" trade or business.

　　* * *

The active business requirements of 355(b)(1) prohibit the tax-free separation of a corporation into active and inactive entities. * * * Neither 355(b)(1)(A) nor (B) concerns itself with the existence of a plurality of businesses per se; rather both speak in terms of a plurality of corporate entities engaged in the active conduct of a trade or business, a distinction we believe to be vital in light of provisions of 355(b)(2).

Section 355(b)(2) details the rules for determining whether a corporation is engaged in the active conduct of a trade or business * * *. Again we note the statute avoids the use of the plural when referring to "trade or business" * * *.

Respondent maintains that a reading of 355(b)(2)(B) in conjunction with the requirement of 355(b)(1) that both "the distributing corporation, *and* the controlled corporation * * *, [be] engaged immediately after the distribution in the active conduct of a trade or business" (emphasis supplied) indicates Congress intended the provisions of the statute to apply only where, immediately after the distribution, there exist two separate and distinct businesses, one operated by the distributing corporation and one operated by the controlled corporation, both of which were actively conducted for the 5–year period immediately preceding the distribution. In our judgment the statute does not support this construction.

As noted, the only reference to plurality appears in section 355(b)(1), and deals with corporate entities, not businesses. Recognizing the divisive nature of the transaction, subsection (b)(1) contemplates that where there was only one corporate entity prior to the various transfers, immediately subsequent thereto, there will be two or more corporations. In order to insure that a tax-free separation will involve the separation only of those assets attributable to the carrying on of an active trade or business, and further to prevent the tax-free division of an active corporation into active and inactive entities, (b)(1) further provides that each of the surviving corporations must be engaged in the active conduct of a trade or business.

A careful reading of the definition of the active conduct of a trade or business contained in subsection (b)(2) indicates that its function is also to prevent the tax-free separation of active and inactive assets into active and inactive corporate entities. This is apparent from the use of the adjective "such," meaning before-mentioned, to modify "trade or business" in subsection (b)(2)(B), thus providing that the trade or business, required by (b)(2)(B) to have had a 5–year active history prior to the distribution, is the same trade or business which (b)(2)(A) requires to be actively conducted immediately after the distribution. Nowhere in (b)(2) do we find, as respondent suggests we should, language denying the benefits of section 355 to the division of a single trade or business.

* * *

There being no language, either in the statute or committee report, which denies tax-free treatment under section 355 to a transaction solely on the grounds that it represents an attempt to divide a single trade or business, the Commissioner's regulations which impose such a restriction are invalid, and cannot be sustained.

* * *

Inasmuch as the parties treat the distribution as otherwise qualifying under section 355 for tax-free treatment, and inasmuch as we have found that portion of the regulations denying application of section 355 to the division of a single business to be invalid, we conclude that petitioner properly treated the distribution to him of the stock of E. P. Coady and Co. as a nontaxable transaction.

* * *

[Dissenting opinions omitted]

NOTES

1. *Vertical versus horizontal division.* Regulations promulgated under I.R.C. § 355 embrace the Coady holding by clarifying that the active business requirement may be satisfied by dividing a single business in two where both parts contain all the stages of the original business (a "vertical" division). See Treas. Reg. § 1.355–3(c) Examples 4–6. The regulations also acknowledge the possibility that a single business may be divided "horizontally" whereby certain functions of the original business are performed by each corporation after the division, but neither corporation contains all the stages of the original business. See Treas. Reg. § 1.355–3(c) Examples 9–11. In the case of a horizontal division, however, caution must be exercised to insure that each corporation engages in sufficient activity to constitute a trade or business (see Treas. Reg. § 1.355–3(b)(2)(ii)) and that such a division does not run afoul of the device restriction (see Treas. Reg. § 1.355–2(d)(2)(iv)(C)). Why are the regulations more stringent with respect to horizontal divisions than with respect to vertical divisions?

2. *Investment property and real estate.* The regulations provide for close scrutiny of certain separations of investment property and real estate. See Treas. Reg. §§ 1.355–3(b)(2)(iii),(iv), (c) Examples 1–3, 12, 13. Why are these transactions suspect?

3. *Consequences of taxable split-off.* The transaction effectuated in Coady was a "split-off", rather than a "spin-off". See p. 714, Note 4. What are the tax consequences when a split-off does not satisfy the requirements of I.R.C. § 355? See I.R.C. §§ 302, 317(b).

4. *Division of single business not a partial liquidation.* If, rather than contributing assets to a newly formed corporation, the Christopher Company had simply distributed those assets to Edmund Coady in exchange for all the stock of the Christopher Company owned by him, the transaction would apparently not qualify as a partial liquidation under the safe harbor of I.R.C. § 302(e). Rather, it appears that separate businesses must exist for a distribution to qualify as a partial liquidation. See, e.g., Kenton Meadows Co. v. Commissioner, 766 F.2d 142 (4th Cir.1985) (separate businesses required; a separate business must contribute a substantial part of the combined corporate income and operate under some form of separate supervision and control).

Revenue Ruling 2003–18

2003–7 I.R.B. 467.

ISSUE

Whether the acquisition by a dealer engaged in the sale and service of brand X automobiles of a franchise to sell and service brand Y automobiles and the assets to operate the franchise constitutes an expansion of the brand X business rather than the acquisition of a new or different business under § 1.355–3(b)(3)(ii) of the Income Tax Regulations.

FACTS

Corporation D has been engaged under a dealer franchise in the sale and service of brand X automobiles since Year 1. For over five years before Year 8, these operations had been carried on in two buildings (L and M) within the same city. In Year 8, D acquired a franchise for the sale and service of brand Y automobiles and purchased the inventories, equipment, and leasehold of a former brand Y automobile dealer who operated in a building adjoining D's building L. Shortly thereafter, D relocated the inventory of brand X automobiles from building L to building M. Thereafter, D used building M exclusively for the sale and service of brand X automobiles and used building L and the adjoining leasehold exclusively for the sale and service of brand Y automobiles.

In Year 10, D transferred all of the assets, including building M, and liabilities of the brand X automobile dealership to a new corporation, C, in exchange for the stock of C, and distributed the stock of C pro rata to its shareholders.

LAW AND ANALYSIS

Section 355(a) of the Internal Revenue Code provides that a corporation may distribute stock and securities in a controlled corporation to its shareholders and security holders in a transaction that will not cause the distributees to recognize gain or loss, provided that, among other requirements, (i) each of the distributing corporation and controlled corporation is engaged, immediately after the distribution, in the active conduct of a trade or business, (ii) each trade or business has been actively conducted throughout the five-year period ending on the date of the distribution, and (iii) neither trade or business has been acquired in a transaction in which gain or loss was recognized, in whole or in part, within the five-year period. Sections 355(b)(1)(A), 355(b)(2)(B), and 355(b)(2)(C).

In determining whether an active trade or business has been conducted by a corporation throughout the five-year period preceding the distribution, the fact that a trade or business underwent change during the five-year period (for example, by the addition of new or the dropping of old products, changes in production capacity, and the like) shall be disregarded, provided that the changes are not of such a character as to constitute the acquisition of a new or different business. Section 1.355–3(b)(3)(ii). In particular, if a corporation engaged in the active conduct of one trade or business during that five-year period purchased, created, or otherwise acquired another trade or business in the same line of business, then the acquisition of that other business is ordinarily treated as an expansion of the original business, all of which is treated as having been actively conducted during that five-year period, unless that purchase, creation, or other acquisition effects a change of such character as to constitute the acquisition of a new or different business. Id.

[In Example (7) of § 1.355–3(c), corporation X had owned and operated a department store in the downtown area of the City of G for six years before acquiring a parcel of land in a suburban area of G and constructing a new department store. Three years after the construction, X transferred the suburban store and related business assets to new subsidiary Y and distributed the Y stock to X's shareholders. Citing § 1.355–3(b)(3)(i) and (ii), the example concludes that X and Y both satisfy the requirements of § 355(b).]

In Example (8) of § 1.355–3(c), corporation X had owned and operated hardware stores in several states for four years before purchasing the assets of a hardware store in State M where X had not previously conducted business. Two years after the purchase, X transferred the State M store and related business assets to new subsidiary Y and distributed the Y stock to X's shareholders. Citing § 1.355–3(b)(3)(i) and (ii), the example concludes that X and Y both satisfy the requirements of section 355(b).

In this case, because (i) the product of the brand X automobile dealership is similar to the product of the brand Y automobile dealership, (ii) the business activities associated with the operation of the brand X automobile dealership (i.e., sales and service) are the same as the business activities associated with the operation of the brand Y automobile dealership, and (iii) the operation of the brand Y automobile dealership involves the use of the experience and know-how that D developed in the operation of the brand X automobile dealership, the brand Y automobile dealership is in the same line of business as the brand X dealership and its acquisition does not constitute the acquisition of a new or different business under § 1.355–3(b)(3)(ii). Instead, it constitutes an expansion of D's existing business. Accordingly, each of D and C is engaged in the active conduct of a five-year active trade or business immediately after the distribution. See § 1.355–3(c), Example (8).

HOLDING

The acquisition by D, a brand X automobile dealer, of the brand Y automobile dealership constitutes an expansion of the brand X business and does not constitute the acquisition of a new or different business under § 1.355–3(b)(3)(ii).

Revenue Ruling 2003–38

2003–17 I.R.B. 811.

ISSUE

Whether the creation by a corporation engaged in the retail shoe store business of an Internet web site on which the corporation will sell shoes at retail constitutes an expansion of the corporation's business rather than the acquisition of a new or different business under § 1.355–3(b)(3)(ii) of the Income Tax Regulations.

FACTS

Corporation D has operated a retail shoe store business, under the name "D," since Year 1 in a manner that meets the requirements of § 355(b) of the Internal Revenue Code. D's sales are made exclusively to customers who frequent its retail stores in shopping malls and other locations. D's business enjoys favorable name recognition, customer loyalty, and other elements of goodwill in the retail shoe market. In Year 8, D creates an Internet web site and begins selling shoes at retail on the web site. To a significant extent, the operation of the web site draws upon D's experience and know-how. The web site is named "D.com" to take advantage of the name recognition, customer loyalty, and other elements of goodwill associated with D and the D name and to enhance the web site's chances for success in its initial stages. In Year 10, D transfers all of the web site's assets and liabilities to corporation C, a newly formed, wholly owned subsidiary of D, and distributes the stock of C pro rata to D's shareholders. Apart from the issue of whether the web site is considered an expansion of D's business and therefore entitled to share the business's five-year history at the time of the distribution in Year 10, the distribution meets all the requirements of § 355.

LAW

[See discussion of law in Rev. Rul. 2003–18 at pp. 720–721.]

ANALYSIS

The product of the retail shoe store business and the product of the web site are the same (shoes), and the principal business activities of the retail shoe store business are the same as those of the web site (purchasing shoes at wholesale and reselling them at retail). Selling shoes on a web site requires some know-how not associated with operating a retail store, such as familiarity with different marketing approaches, distribution chains, and technical operations issues. Nevertheless, the web site's operation does draw to a significant extent on D's existing experience and know-how, and the web site's success will depend in large measure on the goodwill associated with D and the D name. Accordingly, the creation by D of the Internet web site does not constitute the acquisition of a new or different business under § 1.355–3(b)(3)(ii). Instead, it is an expansion of D's retail shoe store business. Therefore, each of D and C is engaged in the active conduct of a five-year active trade or business immediately after the distribution. See Rev. Rul. 2003–18 and § 1.355–3(c), Examples (7) and (8).

HOLDING

The creation by a corporation engaged in the retail shoe store business of an Internet web site that sells shoes at retail constitutes an expansion of the retail shoe store business rather than the acquisition of a new or different business under § 1.355–3(b)(3)(ii).

NOTES

1. *Statutory active business requirements.* Pursuant to I.R.C. § 355(b)(1)(A), both the Distributing Corporation and the Controlled Corporation must be engaged immediately after the distribution in the active conduct of a trade or business. The following four requirements must be satisfied for a corporation to be treated as engaged in the active conduct of a trade or business (see I.R.C. § 355(b)(2)):

(a) *Engaged in business.* The corporation must be engaged in the active conduct of a trade or business. I.R.C. § 355(b)(2)(A). In making this determination, however, the activities of certain related corporations can also be taken into account. See I.R.C. § 355(b)(3).

(b) *Five year history.* A qualifying business must have an operating history of at least five years. I.R.C. § 355(b)(2)(B).

(c) *No taxable asset acquisition.* A qualifying business need not be owned by (or controlled by) the Distributing Corporation or the Controlled Corporation during the entire five year period preceding the distribution, but it cannot be acquired during that period in a taxable asset acquisition. I.R.C. § 355(b)(2)(C) (but see Treas. Reg. §§ 1.355–3(b)(3), –3(c) Examples 7–8).

(d) *No taxable stock acquisition.* A qualifying business cannot be acquired during the five year period preceding the distribution in a taxable stock acquisition. I.R.C. § 355(b)(2)(D).[3] In effect, the restriction on acquiring the *assets* of a business in a taxable transaction within five years before a spin-off cannot be avoided by instead acquiring *stock* of a corporation containing those assets in a taxable transaction within five years before the spin-off.

2. *Purchase of stock of controlled corporation within five years of spin-off.* Read I.R.C. § 355(a)(3)(B). How does that provision relate to I.R.C. § 355(b)(2)(D)? See the Dunn case that follows.

The Edna Louise Dunn Trust v. Commissioner

United States Tax Court, 1986, acq. 1997–1 Cum.Bull. 1.
86 T.C. 745.

■ TANNENWALD, JUDGE: Respondent determined a deficiency of $29.64 in petitioner's Federal income taxes for the taxable year ended May 31, 1984.

---

3. To focus on the part of I.R.C. § 355(b)(2)(D) that relates to shareholder level consequences, assume (until instructed to the contrary) that I.R.C. § 355(b)(2)(D)(*i*) reads as follows:

"(i) * * * was not acquired by the distributing corporation directly (or through 1 or more corporations), within such period, or"

The omitted statutory language relates to corporate level consequences and is examined at pp. 731–735.

The issue for decision is whether a portion of the stock distributed to petitioner pursuant to a reorganization and divestiture plan constituted "other property" under section 355(a)(3)(B).

* * *

[P]etitioner owned 400 shares of common stock of American Telephone and Telegraph Company ("AT&T") * * *. Petitioner received, as of January 1, 1984, a distribution [from AT&T] * * * of 40 shares of stock of * * * Pacific Telesis Group ("PacTel Group") * * * ([one of] AT&T's seven regional holding Companies ("RHCs")). Petitioner did not include in its gross income * * * any amount on account of the receipt of these shares of the [PacTel Group].

Until January 1, 1984, AT&T was the common parent corporation of a group of corporations * * * whose principal business was the furnishing of communications services and equipment. The group included 22 Bell operating companies ("BOCs") which were * * * subsidiaries of AT&T * * *. The BOCs provided various communications services within their respective geographic operating areas * * *. In addition to its function as a holding company for the group, AT&T was itself directly and continuously engaged in an active trade or business since 1885. Such business * * * provided interstate and international telecommunications service.

[AT&T had long owned all of the outstanding stock of the BOCs, with the exception of roughly 15% of the stock of the Pacific Telephone and Telegraph Company ("Pacific"). On May 12, 1982, AT&T acquired the minority shares of Pacific in a taxable reverse triangular merger. For tax purposes, AT&T was treated as purchasing those minority shares in a taxable transaction.]

On August 24, 1982, a longstanding antitrust suit between AT&T and the United States Government was disposed of by a judicially-approved agreement between the parties. Under the terms of that decision * * *, certain "local exchange" functions of the BOCs were to be placed in the aforementioned seven RHCs and AT&T was to divest itself of its holdings therein.

* * *

[T]o accomplish the divestiture, the 22 BOCs would be grouped into seven regions. A separate, independent holding company structure was established for each region. [PacTel was the holding company established for the region in which Pacific operated.] This structure was subsequently incorporated in a Plan of Reorganization * * * approved by the court.

* * *

In accordance with the Plan of Reorganization, AT&T and its affiliates would transfer to each regional holding company, in exchange for the latter's voting stock, the stock of the appropriate BOCs and other assets * * *. [Pursuant to the Plan, AT&T would transfer all of the stock of Pacific (the 85% it had long owned and the 15% it purchased in 1982) to PacTel in exchange for the stock of PacTel.] [A]T&T would then distribute to its stockholders one share of [PacTel] stock * * * for every ten shares of AT&T stock owned by AT&T shareholders of record at the close of business on December 30, 1983 * * *.

* * *

[In response to a ruling request filed by AT&T,] the IRS ruled that no gain or loss would be recognized on the transfer of stock of [Pacific to PacTel] * * * in exchange for [PacTel] stock * * *. [With regard to the distribution by AT&T of the PacTel stock to the AT&T shareholders, however,] the IRS ruled that a portion of the PacTel Group stock was taxable to the AT&T shareholders. The IRS thereafter advised that this portion of the PacTel Group stock had a value at the time of distribution equal to $.39 per share of AT&T stock and the parties have accepted that value for the purposes of this case.

Section 355(a)(1) allows a corporation to make a tax-free distribution of the stock of a controlled corporation * * * provided [that, among other requirements,] the active business requirement of section 355(b) is met and the transaction is deemed not to be merely a "device" to distribute tax free, earnings and profits which otherwise would be taxable as a dividend. There is no dispute between the parties that these conditions have been satisfied. The issue upon which they have parted company is whether the limitations of section 355(a)(3)(B) apply. That section provides for the taxation of part of the distribution as follows—

(B) Stock Acquired In Taxable Transactions Within 5 Years Treated As Boot.—For purposes of this section * * * and so much of section 356 as relates to this section, stock of a controlled corporation acquired by the distributing corporation *by reason of any transaction*—

(i) which occurs within 5 years of the distribution of such stock, and

(ii) in which gain or loss was recognized in whole or in part,

shall not be treated as stock of such controlled corporation, but as other property. [Emphasis added.]

Section 356(b), in turn, provides that "the fair market value of such other property shall be treated as a distribution of property to which section 301 applies."

Petitioner concedes that, if AT&T had distributed the Pacific stock directly to its shareholders, the [roughly 15% of the] Pacific stock acquired in the merger would have been treated as "other property" under section 355(a)(3)(B), because the merger was a taxable transaction that took place within five years of the divestiture. Petitioner argues, however, that it was PacTel Group stock, not Pacific stock, which AT&T distributed to its shareholders. Since this stock was acquired in what respondent concedes was a tax-free exchange, petitioner argues that none of such stock can be categorized as "other property".

Respondent contends that petitioner's position is overly simplistic and that the language of section 355(a)(3)(B) is sufficiently broad to permit an interpretation which will be more accommodating to what he views as the legislative purpose behind the section's enactment, namely to preclude not only direct distributions of purchased interests in an active business but also indirect distributions of such interests emanating from a holding company structure. By way of amplification of his position, respondent argues that (1) we should treat a portion of the PacTel Group common stock as having been acquired via the prior taxable acquisition of Pacific stock with the result that the "by reason of any transaction" provision of section 355(a)(3)(B) is satisfied, or (2) in view of the overall statutory framework of section 355, Pacific, as part of the PacTel Group, falls within the ambit of the statutory phrase "controlled corporation" as that term is used in section 355(a)(3)(B). As a consequence, respondent concludes that such portion of PacTel stock as represents the fair market value of the Pacific stock (stipulated to be $.39 per share of AT&T stock) constitutes "other property" and is taxable as a dividend.

A literal reading of section 355(a)(3)(B) appears to support petitioner's position. On its face, the statutory language is directed to the distribution "of *stock of a controlled corporation*, acquired by the distributing corporation by reason of any [taxable] transaction [occurring] within 5 years of the *distribution of such stock.*" (Emphasis added.) As used in section 355(a)(1)(A) the term "controlled corporation" means a corporation which the distributing corporation "controls immediately before the distribution" within the meaning of section 368(c). Since AT&T did not own directly any stock of Pacific immediately before the distribution, and because the stock attribution rules of section 318 are not applicable to section 368(c), it follows that, from a literal standpoint, Pacific was not a "controlled corporation" of AT&T for purposes of section 355(a)(3)(B). On this basis, petitioner would prevail.

We think it appropriate, however, not simply to adhere to the literal meaning of section 355(a)(3)(B). It can be argued—as indeed respondent does herein—that the words of that section are sufficiently ambiguous to permit a resort to legislative history, an aspect of this case to which we now turn our attention.

[The legislative history does not support respondent's conclusion.] * * * [R]espondent [also argues] that the overall statutory framework of section 355 requires section 355(a)(3)(B) to be interpreted as focusing not merely on the stock of the controlled corporation being distributed, but on the actual operating subsidiary included in the spin-off. Respondent correctly points out that the statutory framework of section 355(b)(2)(A) "itself envisions situations where a holding company will be used as the distributing mechanism for an active subsidiary." It provides that a corporation will qualify as an "active business" if for the 5 year period ending on the date of distribution it has been—

> engaged in the active conduct of a trade or business, *or substantially all of its assets consist of stock and securities of a corporation controlled by it* (immediately after the distribution) which is so engaged, * * *. [Emphasis added.]

Thus, section 355(b)(2)(A) allows the distributing corporation to "look through" the controlled corporation to its underlying active subsidiary in order to satisfy the active business requirement. Similarly, to qualify as an active trade or business under section 355(b)(2)(D) during the 5 years prior to the distribution of stock, it must be established that—

> control of a corporation which (at the time of acquisition of control) was conducting such trade or business—
>
> (i) was not acquired [by the distributing corporation] directly (or through one or more corporations) * * * [within such period].

Therefore, much like section 355(b)(2)(A), this section cuts through the form of the spin-off and focuses directly on the underlying active subsidiary when considering whether or not a corporation qualifies as an active trade or business.

From this legislative framework, respondent concludes that, since it is the activity of the underlying subsidiary that qualifies the spin-off as a tax-free section 355 distribution to begin with, it is only logical and consistent that for section 355(a)(3)(B) purposes, we must also focus on the underlying active subsidiary. Unfortunately for respondent, * * * neither the words of section 355(a)(3)(B), nor its legislative history, support his conclusion. Furthermore, although respondent discusses at great length the Congressional purpose behind the passage of the "active business" provisions of section 355(b), his attempts to explain why we should interpret section 355(a)(3)(B) in a similar light, so that these two sections are read in "symmetry," with a focus on the active subsidiary, are far from convincing. Absent a clearer statement of legislative intent that we should look through the stock of the controlled corporation, we find it difficult to make the analytical jump respondent asks of us. In fact, in light of the clear and detailed statutory scheme of section 355(b), the conspicuous absence of similar language in section 355(a)(3)(B) suggests that Congress was not only aware of the claimed "inconsistency," but intended just such a result * * *.

However, our inquiry is not over. While it appears that both the plain meaning of section 355(a)(3)(B), as well as its legislative history, support petitioner's position, we also recognize that—"the courts have some leeway in interpreting a statute if the adoption of a literal or usual meaning of its words would lead to absurd results * * * or would thwart the obvious purpose of the statute."

[W]e are satisfied that our reliance on the wording of the statute involved herein would not have any such deleterious consequences either in terms of sections 355(a)(3)(B) specifically or section 355 generally.

* * *

[B]y spinning off PacTel Group stock, AT&T did not bail out earnings and profits and thus undermine the general statutory purpose of section 355, because the Pacific stock acquired from the minority shareholders pursuant to the merger has remained in corporate solution and has never passed into the hands of AT&T's shareholders * * *.

* * *

The long and the short of the matter is that we see no thwarting of legislative purpose by confining section 355(a)(3)(B) to the situations which Congress obviously had in mind at the time of its enactment. In so concluding, we are constrained to observe that, if respondent feels that a transaction of the type involved herein represents an obvious attempt to bail out earnings and profits in violation of the purpose behind section 355, he is not without his remedy. He can challenge such a transaction as a "device" under section 355(a)(1)(B). He has chosen not to do so in this case, because of the conceded business purpose * * * involved in implementing the antitrust decree * * *, and we are satisfied that he should not be permitted to avoid this channel of attack by means of an overly broad construction of section 355(a)(3)(B) * * *.

[E]ssentially respondent seeks to have us do what Congress might have done if the type of transaction involved herein had been brought to its attention. But it is not within the province of this Court thus to expand upon the handiwork of the legislature * * *.

NOTES

1. *Acquisition of control in a taxable transaction.* How would the tax consequences to Dunn have changed if AT&T had owned only 75% of the stock of Pacific (rather than the actual 85%) before AT&T acquired the remaining shares of Pacific? See I.R.C. § 355(b)(2)(D). If AT&T had owned only 75% of the stock of Pacific and, instead of purchasing the remaining Pacific shares, AT&T lent money to Pacific that Pacific used to redeem its minority shareholders, would the subsequent spin-off of Pacific have satisfied the active business requirement? See McLaulin v. Commissioner, 115 T.C. 255 (2000), aff'd. 276 F.3d 1269 (11th Cir.2001) (§ 355(b)(2)(D)(ii) is violated when one corporation (Distributing) that owns 50% of the stock of another corporation (Controlled) lends Controlled money to redeem its other 50% shareholder immediately before Distributing spins-off Controlled).

2. *Tax avoidance potential.* How great is the potential for tax avoidance created by the Dunn case?

3. *Corporate split-up.* In addition to the spin-off and the split-off (see p. 714, Note 4), I.R.C. § 355 also applies to a "split-up", the liquidation of a holding company (Distributing Corporation) that, before the distribution, owns *no assets* other than the stock of two or more subsidiaries (Controlled Corporations) each of which is engaged in the active conduct of a trade or business immediately after the distribution. I.R.C. § 355(b)(1)(B) enables a holding company that distributes the stock of *all* of its operating subsidiaries to satisfy the active business requirement. That transaction does not satisfy I.R.C. § 355(b)(1)(A) because the Distributing Corporation does not conduct a trade or business *after* the distribution.

4. *Relationship among active business requirement, business purpose requirement and device restriction.* To what extent does the active business requirement overlap with the business purpose requirement and the device restriction? Are all three requirements necessary to guard against the evil posed by the Gregory case? Of the three, which one is the most effective?

5. *Cash rich split-offs.* The active business requirement could historically be satisfied when a corporation's business represented a small part of its assets. Thus, the stock of a corporation with substantial liquid assets and a small active business might be distributed in a transaction satisfying the active business requirement. In the case of a pro-rata spin-off, such a distribution would normally run afoul of the device requirement. But a non pro-rata split-off that would otherwise qualify for sale treatment under § 302(a) might escape that limitation, too. In response to a proliferation of "cash rich split-offs," Congress enacted I.R.C. § 355(g) in 2006. That provision precludes § 355 from applying when: 1) either the distributing corporation or the controlled corporation is a "disqualified investment corporation," and 2) any person who did not hold at least 50% of the voting power or value of the stock of either corporation immediately before the distribution holds such an interest immediately after the distribution. A "disqualified investment corporation" exists when the fair market value of the corporation's investment assets is at least two-thirds of the fair market value of all of its assets.

(4) CONTINUITY OF PROPRIETARY INTEREST

Treas. Reg. § 1.355–2(c)

Even if all the statutory requirements of I.R.C. § 355(a)(1) are satisfied and a corporate business purpose exists for the transaction, a distribution of subsidiary stock will not qualify for tax-free treatment under I.R.C. § 355 unless it effects, "a readjustment of continuing interests in the property of the distributing and controlled corporations." Treas. Reg. § 1.355–2(c)(1). This continuity of proprietary interest requirement is satisfied when *any* of the historical shareholders of the distributing corporation own at least 50% of the stock of the distributing corporation and the controlled corporation after the division.

In a pro rata spin-off, the shareholders of the distributing corporation own 100% of the stock of both the distributing corporation and the controlled corporation after the spin-off. A pro rata spin-off, therefore, should normally satisfy the continuity of proprietary interest requirement. The requirement may not be satisfied, however, if more than 50% of the stock of the distributing corporation is acquired so close in proximity to the spin-off that the new owners are not regarded as the historical shareholders for continuity of proprietary interest purposes. See Kass v. Commissioner, p. 580.

A non pro rata split-off also normally satisfies the continuity of proprietary interest requirement because the same historical shareholders need not maintain a continuing interest in both corporations.

Example 15–B (Evaluating continuity of proprietary interest in a split-off): Ollie and Patrice each own 50 of the 100 outstanding shares of Distributing Corporation which, in turn, owns all the stock of Controlled Corporation. Distributing and Controlled have each been engaged in the active conduct of a trade or business for more than five years. The businesses are of roughly equal value. Due to irreconcilable differences between Ollie and Patrice, the businesses would operate far more efficiently if one business was owned solely by Ollie and the other business was owned solely by Patrice. To achieve this end, Distributing distributes all of the Controlled Stock to Patrice in exchange for all of her Distributing stock. After the exchange, Ollie owns all the stock of Distributing and Patrice owns all the stock of Controlled.

The continuity of proprietary interest requirement is satisfied because historical shareholders own at least 50% of both Distributing and Controlled after the split-off. The split-off satisfies the continuity of proprietary interest requirement, notwithstanding that different historical shareholders own stock in each corporation after the split-off. See Treas. Reg. § 1.355–2(c)(2) Example 1.

Problem 15–1 (Testing for continuity of proprietary interest): Same facts as in Example 15–B but shortly before the split-off, Quinn purchases 25 shares of Distributing from Ollie. After the split-off, therefore, Ollie and Quinn each own half the stock of Distributing and Patrice owns all the stock of Controlled.

(a) Does the split-off satisfy the continuity of proprietary interest requirement? See Treas. Reg. § 1.355–2(c)(2) Example 2.

(b) Would the split-off satisfy the continuity of proprietary interest requirement if Quinn had purchased 30 shares of Distributing from Ollie (rather than 25 shares)? See Treas. Reg. § 1.355–2(c)(2) Examples 3–4.

(c) Would the answer to (a) or (b) change if the Controlled stock were distributed to Ollie and Quinn in exchange for their Distributing shares with Patrice retaining all of her Distributing shares?

(d) Would the answer to (a) or (b) change if the Controlled shares were distributed pro rata to all of the Distributing shareholders and none of the Distributing shares were surrendered (a spin-off occurred, rather than a split-off)?

NOTES

1. *Continuity of business enterprise.* Treas. Reg. § 1.355–1(b) provides, in part, that "Section 355 contemplates the continued operation of the business or businesses existing prior to the separation." How does this requirement compare to the continuity of business enterprise requirement that applies to acquisitive reorganizations? See pp. 518–520. To what extent does the active business requirement already implement this mandate? See I.R.C. §§ 355(b)(1)(A), (2)(A).

2. *Alternative to I.R.C. § 355.* Does the evil that I.R.C. § 355 is designed to guard against only appear when a taxable disposition of the stock of the controlled corporation or the distributing corporation occurs after the spin-off (or split-off)? If so, might Congress have developed a mechanism that attacked the tax consequences of the subsequent taxable disposition, in light of the uncertainty that exists at the time of the distribution as to whether the evil will, in fact, occur? Consider this possibility when I.R.C. § 306 is examined in Chapter 16. Now that dividends are taxed at capital gains rates, can a stronger case be made for enacting a provision that attacks an actual post-distribution taxable disposition of stock?

2. CORPORATE LEVEL CONSEQUENCES

Prior to the repeal of the General Utilities rule in 1986 (see pp. 29–33), little attention was directed to the corporate level tax issues raised by a spin-off. Since that time, however, much attention has been focused on the abuses that may stem from according nonrecognition treatment to the distributing corporation when it distributes stock of a subsidiary in a transaction that satisfies I.R.C. § 355. See I.R.C. §§ 355(c), 361(c).

a. SPIN–OFF AFTER TAXABLE STOCK TRANSFER

I.R.C. § 355(b)(2)(D)(i)

In 1987, Congress amended I.R.C. § 355 to curtail tax-free treatment when a spin-off follows a taxable acquisition of the stock of the distributing corporation. That amendment is now encompassed by the following statutory language at the beginning of I.R.C. § 355(b)(2)(D)(i):

> "(i) was not acquired by any distributee corporation directly (or through 1 or more corporations, whether through the distributing corporation or otherwise) within the period described in subparagraph (B) * * *."[4]

The amendment was directed, in part, at the situation described in Revenue Ruling 74–5.

Revenue Ruling 74–5

1974–1 Cum.Bull. 82.

Advice has been requested whether the transaction * * * described below satisf[ies] the active trade or business requirements of section 355(b) of the Internal Revenue Code of 1954.

---

4. This is the statutory language omitted from the earlier discussion of I.R.C. § 355(b)(2)(D)(i). See p. 723, footnote 3.

All the outstanding stock of P corporation is owned by individual shareholders. In 1969, P acquired for cash all the outstanding stock of X corporation from T corporation, an unrelated party, in a transaction in which gain or loss was recognized to T. The assets of X include all the outstanding stock of Y corporation. X has owned all the Y stock since 1965. In 1971, X distributed all the Y stock to P * * *. P, X, and Y have each conducted an active trade or business since 1960.

Section 355 of the Code provides for the distribution without recognition of gain or loss to the shareholders of the stock of a corporation controlled by the distributing corporation. For such treatment, section 355(b)(1)(A) requires that both the distributing corporation and the controlled corporation be engaged immediately after the distribution in the active conduct of a trade or business. Section 355(b)(2)(A), in defining an active trade or business, requires that the distributing corporation and the controlled corporation each be engaged in the active conduct of a trade or business * * *. Section 355(b)(2)(B) provides that such trade or business must have been actively conducted throughout the five-year period ending on the date of the distribution. Section 355(b)(2)(C) provides that the trade or business must not have been acquired within the period described in section 355(b)(2)(B) in a transaction in which gain or loss was recognized in whole or in part.

Section 355(b)(2)(D) of the Code provides further that control of a corporation, which at the time of acquisition of control was conducting an active trade or business, must not have been acquired * * * [by the distributing corporation] within the five-year period described in section 355(b)(2)(B) * * *.

The purpose of section 355(b)(2)(D) of the Code is to prevent a distributing corporation from accumulating excess funds to purchase the stock of a corporation having an active business and immediately distributing such stock to its shareholders. Thus, where control is acquired by the distributing corporation in a transaction in which gain or loss is recognized, the distributing corporation cannot distribute the stock of the controlled corporation within the five-year period and qualify under section 355.

The requirements of sections 355(b)(2)(A), (B), and (C) of the Code are met with regard to * * * the distribution by X of the Y stock to P * * *. The question presented is whether the requirements of section 355(b)(2)(D) have been met with regard to * * * the distribution * * * since P acquired control of X directly and Y indirectly within the five-year period prior to the distributions in a transaction in which gain or loss was recognized.

The distribution by X of the Y stock to P satisfies the requirements of section 355(b)(2)(D) of the Code even though P * * * acquired control of X directly and Y indirectly within the five-year period prior to distribution in a transaction in which gain or loss was recognized. The purchase of the X stock by P within the five-year period is not the type of transaction to which section 355(b)(2)(D) is directed since P is merely the shareholder receiving the distributions and not the distributing or controlled corporation. In the distribution of the Y stock to P, it is impossible for P to pass accumulated excess funds through another corporation to P shareholders. Thus, in this transaction, the abuse that section 355(b)(2)(D) was designed to prevent is not present and the section has no application to the acquisition of control of X, and indirectly of Y, by P.

* * *

Problem 15–2 (Avoidance of corporate level gain after repeal of General Utilities rule): This Problem illustrates how the transaction described in Revenue Ruling 74–5 (p. 731) might have been utilized to avoid a corporate level tax. Distributing Corporation ("Distributing") fabricates steel and manufactures sweaters. Distributing has owned both of these businesses for more than five years. The steel business consists of assets with a value of $4,000,000 in which Distributing has a basis of $1,000,000. The sweater business consists of assets with a value of $6,000,000. XYZ Corporation ("XYZ") recently purchased the stock of Distributing for $10,000,000. XYZ would like to sell the steel business for $4,000,000 without triggering any taxable gain. Consider whether this goal is achieved by any of the following alternative transactions.

(a) *Sale of assets.* Distributing sells the assets of the steel business for $4,000,000. See I.R.C. § 1001.

(b) *Distribution of assets.* Distributing distributes the assets of the steel business to XYZ which then sells those assets for $4,000,000. See I.R.C. § 311(b).

(c) *Transfer of assets to subsidiary followed by sale of subsidiary stock.* Distributing transfers the assets of the steel business to Controlled Corporation ("Controlled"), a newly formed subsidiary, and sells the stock of Controlled for $4,000,000. See I.R.C. §§ 351(a), 358(a), 1001.

(d) *Transfer of assets to subsidiary followed by spin-off and sale of stock of unwanted corporation.*

    (i) Prior to the 1987 amendment to I.R.C. § 355(b)(2)(D)(i), Distributing transfers the assets of the steel business to Controlled Corporation ("Controlled"), a newly formed subsidiary, and then distributes the stock of Controlled to XYZ. See Rev. Rul. 74–5 (p. 731); I.R.C. § 358(b) and Treas. Reg. § 1.358–2(a)(2). XYZ then sells the stock of Controlled for $4,000,000.

    (ii) The transaction described in (i) is executed today. See I.R.C. § 355(b)(2)(D)(i), as amended; Rev. Rul. 89–37 which follows.

Revenue Ruling 89–37

1989–1 Cum.Bull. 107.

PURPOSE

    This revenue ruling [renders] Rev. Rul. 74–5, 1974–1 C.B. 82, [obsolete] in light of the amendment of section 355(b)(2)(D) of the Internal Revenue Code by * * * the Revenue Act of 1987, ("Act") and * * * the Technical and Miscellaneous Revenue Act of 1988, ("TMRA").

LAW AND ANALYSIS

Rev. Rul. 74–5 involved a distribution of the stock of a controlled corporation, Y, by a distributing corporation, X, to X's parent corporation, P, 2 years after P acquired the stock of X for cash in a transaction in which gain or loss was recognized * * *. At the time of the * * * distribution, X had owned the stock of Y for more than 5 years * * *. Rev. Rul. 74–5 considered whether the requirements of section 355(b)(2)(D) of the Code were met with regard to * * * the distribution * * *.

Section 355(b)(2)(D) of the Code, prior to its amendment by the Act and TMRA, provided that control of a corporation that, at the time of acquisition of control, was conducting an active trade or business, must not have been acquired * * * [by the distributing corporation] within the 5–year period described in section 355(b)(2)(B) * * *.

Rev. Rul. 74–5 concluded that the * * * distribution was not the type of transaction to which section 355(b)(2)(D) of the Code was directed because P was merely the shareholder receiving the distribution and not the distributing corporation or the controlled corporation and, therefore, the ruling held that section 355(b)(2)(D) was inapplicable to the * * * distribution * * *.

[T]he Act and * * * TMRA amended section 355(b)(2)(D) of the Code to provide that a corporation is engaged in the active conduct of a trade or business only if control of a corporation which (at the time of acquisition of control) was conducting such trade or business (i) was not acquired by any distributee corporation directly (or through one or more corporations, whether through the distributing corporation or otherwise) within the 5–year period ending on the date of the distribution, and was not acquired by the distributing corporation directly (or through one or more corporations) within such period, or (ii) was so acquired by any such corporation within such period, but, in each case in which such control was so acquired, it was so acquired only by reason of transactions in which gain or loss was not recognized in whole or in part, or only by reason of such transactions combined with acquisitions before the beginning of such period.

Under section 355(b)(2)(D) of the Code, as amended * * *, the * * * distribution described in Rev. Rul. 74–5 is now a transaction described in section 355(b)(2)(D). Therefore, because Y was acquired by a distributee corporation within the meaning of section 355(b)(2)(D) in a transaction in which gain or loss was recognized within the 5–year period prior to the distribution, the * * * distribution fails to meet the active trade or business requirement of section 355(b)(2)(D).

      * * *

NOTE

Shareholder level tax consequences. The 1987 amendment to I.R.C. § 355(b)(2)(D)(i) was intended to respond to corporate level tax avoidance. What impact does that amendment have on shareholder level tax consequences? See I.R.C. §§ 355(a)(1)(C), 301. Of what relevance is the fact that the amendment applies only to a "corporate distributee" that acquires "control"? See I.R.C. § 243.

b. SPLIT–OFF AFTER TAXABLE STOCK TRANSFER

I.R.C. § 355(d)

The 1987 amendment to I.R.C. § 355(b)(2)(D)(i) eliminated the potential for corporate tax avoidance when a spin-off followed a taxable acquisition of the stock of the distributing corporation. However, Congress still perceived opportunities for corporate tax avoidance in certain split-off transactions. For example, in lieu of the alternatives delineated in Problem 15–2 (p. 733), suppose that shortly after purchasing the stock of Distributing for $10,000,000, XYZ sells 40% of the Distributing stock to Buyer Corporation ("Buyer") for $4,000,000. Thereafter, Distributing transfers the assets of the steel business to a newly formed subsidiary ("Controlled"), and then distributes the stock of Controlled to Buyer *in exchange for* Buyer's Distributing stock. In this situation, I.R.C. § 355(b)(2)(D)(i) is satisfied because Buyer acquired only 40% of the stock of Distributing (i.e., Buyer is not a distributee corporation that acquired "control" of Distributing). Hence, if no other remedy existed, Distributing would not recognize gain with respect to the distribution of the Controlled stock (see I.R.C. § 361(c)) and the steel business would have been sold without triggering a corporate level gain. In response to this perceived abuse, Congress enacted I.R.C. § 355(d) in 1990. The Committee Reports that follow explain the purpose and effect of § 355(d).

Divisive Transactions in Connection with Changes in Ownership (New Section 355(d))

H.Rep. No. 5835, 104th Cong., 1st Sess. (1990).

* * *

Reasons for Change

Some corporate taxpayers may attempt, under present-law rules governing divisive transactions, to dispose of subsidiaries in transactions that resemble sales, or to obtain a fair market value stepped-up basis for any future dispositions, without incurring corporate level tax. The avoidance of corporate level tax is inconsistent with the repeal of the *General Utilities* doctrine as part of the Tax Reform Act of 1986.

Under the present-law rules, individual purchasers, or corporate purchasers of less than 80 percent, of the stock of a parent corporation may attempt to utilize section 355 to acquire a subsidiary from the parent without the parent incurring any corporate-level tax. The purchaser may acquire stock of the parent equal in value to the value of the desired subsidiary or division, and later surrender that stock for stock of the subsidiary, in a transaction intended to qualify as a non-pro-rata tax-free divisive transaction. Alternatively, the transaction might be structured as a surrender of the parent stock by all shareholders other than the acquiring corporation, in exchange for a distribution (intended to be tax-free) of all subsidiaries or activities other than those the acquiring corporation desires.

In addition, a non-corporate purchaser, or a corporate purchaser of less than 80 percent of the stock of another corporation, may attempt to utilize section 355 to obtain a stepped up fair market value basis in a subsidiary of an acquired corporation, enabling a subsequent disposition of that subsidiary without a corporate-level tax.

The provisions for tax-free divisive transactions under section 355 were a limited exception to the repeal of the *General Utilities* doctrine, intended to permit historic shareholders to continue to carry on their historic corporate businesses in separate corporations. It is believed that the benefit of tax-free treatment should not apply where the divisive transaction, combined with a stock purchase resulting in a change of ownership, in effect results in the disposition of a significant part of the historic shareholders' interests in one or more of the divided corporations.

The present-law provisions granting tax-free treatment at the corporate level are particularly troublesome because they may offer taxpayers an opportunity to avoid the general rule that corporate-level gain is recognized when an asset (including stock of a subsidiary) is disposed of. There is special concern about the possibility for the distributing corporation to avoid corporate-level tax on the transfer of a subsidiary. Therefore, although the provision does not affect shareholder treatment if section 355 is otherwise available, it does impose tax at the corporate level, in light of the potential avoidance of corporate tax on what is in effect a sale of a subsidiary.

* * *

Explanation of Provision

In general.—The conference agreement generally requires recognition of corporate-level gain (but does not require recognition by the distributee shareholders) on a distribution of subsidiary stock or securities qualifying under section 355 (whether or not part of a reorganization otherwise described in section 361(c)(2)) if, immediately after the distribution, a shareholder holds a 50–percent or greater interest in the distributing corporation or a distributed subsidiary that is attributable to stock or securities that were acquired by purchase within the preceding 5–year period. Thus, for example, under the provision, the distributing corporation will recognize gain on the distribution of subsidiary stock and securities if a person purchases distributing corporation stock or securities, and within 5 years, 50 percent or more of the subsidiary stock is distributed to that person in exchange for the purchased stock or securities. The distributing corporation will recognize gain as if it had sold the distributed subsidiary stock and securities to the distributee at fair market value.

* * *

Disqualified distribution.—A disqualified distribution is any section 355 distribution if, immediately after the distribution, any person holds disqualified stock in either the distributing corporation or any distributed controlled corporation constituting a 50–percent or greater interest in such corporation.

Disqualified stock.—The conference agreement defines disqualified stock to include any stock in the distributing corporation or any controlled corporation acquired by purchase during the 5–year period ending on the date of distribution. In addition, disqualified stock includes stock in any controlled corporation received in the distribution, to the extent attributable to distributions on stock or securities in the distributing corporation acquired by purchase during the 5–year period ending on the date of the distribution.

Example 1.—Assume that individual A acquires by purchase a 20–percent interest in the stock of corporation P and a 10–percent interest in the stock of its subsidiary, S, and 40 percent or more of the stock of S is distributed to A within 5 years in exchange for his 20–percent interest in P. (The remainder of the S stock distributed in the section 355 distribution is distributed to other shareholders.) Under the provision P must recognize gain with respect to the distributed stock of S because all 50 percent of the stock of S held by A is disqualified stock.

Example 2.—Assume that individual A acquires by purchase a 20–percent interest in corporation P and P redeems stock of other shareholders so that A's interest in P increases to a 30 percent interest. Within 5 years of A's purchase, P distributes 50 percent of the stock of its subsidiary, S, to A in exchange for his 30 percent interest in P (the remainder of the stock of S distributed in the section 355 transaction is distributed to other shareholders). P recognizes gain on the distribution of the stock of S because all 50 percent of the stock of S held by A is disqualified stock.

Problem 15–3 (Impact of § 355(d)): Same facts as Problem 15–2 (p. 733), but assume that XYZ sells 40% of the Distributing stock to Buyer for $4,000,000 shortly after XYZ purchased all the stock of Distributing. What are the tax consequences to Distributing under current law if shortly after XYZ's sale of Distributing stock to Buyer, Distributing transfers the assets of the steel business to Controlled and distributes the Controlled stock to Buyer in exchange for Buyer's Distributing stock? See I.R.C. §§ 355(d)(1)–(3), 361(c). Do the tax consequences to Distributing change if XYZ holds all the Distributing stock for five years before XYZ sells 40% of the Distributing stock to Buyer and the split-off is effectuated? Does I.R.C. § 355(d) impact on shareholder level tax consequences (in this case, the tax consequences to Buyer)? See I.R.C. §§ 355(d)(1), 355(a).

c.   SPIN–OFF BEFORE TAX–FREE REORGANIZATION

I.R.C. § 355(e)

The enactment of I.R.C. §§ 355(b)(2)(D)(i) and 355(d) pretty much eliminated the potential for corporate tax avoidance when a spin-off or split-off followed a taxable acquisition of the stock of the distributing corporation. Opportunities to avoid the corporate tax were still perceived to exist, however, when a spin-off preceded a nontaxable disposition of the distributing corporation or the controlled corporation. In 1997, Congress enacted I.R.C. § 355(e) to remedy these corporate tax avoidance opportunities. The Morris Trust case that follows illustrates the type of transaction that attracted the attention of Congress.

Commissioner v. Mary Archer W. Morris Trust

United States Court of Appeals, Fourth Circuit, 1966.
367 F.2d 794.

■ HAYNSWORTH, CHIEF JUDGE. * * *

In 1960, a merger agreement was negotiated by the directors of American Commercial Bank and Security National Bank of Greensboro, a national bank. [T]hough American was slightly larger than Security, it was found desirable to operate the merged institutions under Security's national charter, after changing the name to North Carolina National Bank. * * *.

For many years, American had operated an insurance department. This was a substantial impediment to the accomplishment of the merger, for a national bank is prohibited from operating an insurance department * * *. To avoid a violation of the national banking laws, therefore, and to accomplish the merger under Security's national charter, it was prerequisite that American rid itself of its insurance business.

The required step to make it nubile was accomplished by American's organization of a new corporation, American Commercial Agency, Inc., to which American transferred its insurance business assets in exchange for Agency's stock which was immediately distributed to American's stockholders. * * * [American was then merged into Security and the name of the combined enterprise was changed to NCNB.]

Though American's spin-off of its insurance business was a "D" reorganization, as defined in § 368(a)(1), provided the distribution of Agency's stock qualified for non-recognition of gain under § 355, the Commissioner contended that the active business requirements of § 355(b)(1)(A) were not met, since American's banking business was not continued in unaltered corporate form. He also finds an inherent incompatibility in substantially simultaneous divisive and amalgamating reorganizations.

Section 355(b)(1)(A) requires that both the distributing corporation and the controlled corporation be "engaged immediately after the distribution in the active conduct of a trade or business." There was literal compliance with that requirement, for the spin-off, including the distribution of Agency's stock to American's stockholders, preceded the merger. The Commissioner asks that we look at both steps together, contending that North Carolina National Bank was not the distributing corporation and that its subsequent conduct of American's banking business does not satisfy the requirement.

* * *

Section 355(b) requires that the distributing corporation be engaged in the active conduct of a trade or business "immediately after the distribution." This is * * * in marked contrast to § 355(b)'s highly particularized requirements respecting the duration of the active business prior to the reorganization and the methods by which it was acquired. This contrast suggests a literal reading of the post-reorganization requirement and a holding that the Congress intended to restrict it to the situation existing "immediately after the distribution."

Such a reading is quite consistent with the prior history. It quite adequately meets the problem posed by the Gregory v. Helvering [p. 692] situation in which, immediately after the distribution, one of the corporations held only liquid or investment assets. It sufficiently serves the requirements of permanence and of continuity, for as long as an active business is being conducted immediately after the distribution, there is no substantial opportunity for the stockholders to sever their interest in the business except through a separable, taxable transaction. If the corporation proceeds to withdraw assets from the conduct of the active business and to abandon it, the Commissioner has recourse to the back-up provisions of § 355(a)(1)(B) and to the limitations of the underlying principles. At the same time, the limitation, so construed, will not inhibit continued stockholder conduct of the active business through altered corporate form and with further changes in corporate structure, the very thing the reorganization sections were intended to facilitate.

Applied to this case, there is no violation of any of the underlying limiting principles. There was no empty formalism, no utilization of empty corporate structures, no attempt to recast a taxable transaction in nontaxable form and no withdrawal of liquid assets. There is no question but that American's insurance and banking businesses met all of the active business requirements of § 355(b)(2). It was intended that both businesses be continued indefinitely, and each has been. American's merger with Security, in no sense, was a discontinuance of American's banking business, which opened the day after the merger with the same employees, the same depositors and customers. There was clearly the requisite continuity of stockholder interest, for American's former stockholders remained in 100% control of the insurance company, while, in the merger, they received 54.385% of the common stock of North Carolina National Bank, the remainder going to Security's former stockholders. There was a strong business purpose for both the spin-off and the merger, and tax avoidance by American's stockholders was neither a predominant nor a subordinate purpose. In short, though both of the transactions be viewed together, there were none of the evils or misuses which the limiting principles and the statutory limitations were designed to exclude.

We are thus led to the conclusion that this carefully drawn statute should not be read more broadly than it was written to deny nonrecognition of gain to reorganizations of real businesses of the type which Congress clearly intended to facilitate by according to them nonrecognition of present gain.

The Commissioner, indeed, concedes that American's stockholders would have realized no gain had American not been merged into Security after, but substantially contemporaneously with, Agency's spin-off. Insofar as it is contended that § 355(b)(1)(A) requires the distributing corporation to continue the conduct of an active business, recognition of gain to American's stockholders on their receipt of Agency's stock would depend upon the economically irrelevant technicality of the identity of the surviving corporation in the merger. Had American been the survivor, it would in every literal and substantive sense have continued the conduct of its banking business.

Surely, the Congress which drafted these comprehensive provisions did not intend the incidence of taxation to turn upon so insubstantial a technicality. Its differentiation on the basis of the economic substance of transactions is too evident to permit such a conclusion.

This, too, the Commissioner seems to recognize, at least conditionally, for he says that gain to the stockholders would have been recognized even if American had been the surviving corporation. This would necessitate our reading into § 355(b)(1)(A) an implicit requirement that the distributing corporation, without undergoing any reorganization whatever, whether or not it resulted in a change in its corporate identity, continue the conduct of its active business.

We cannot read this broader limitation into the statute for the same reasons we cannot read into it the narrower one of maintenance of the same corporate identity. The congressional limitation of the post-distribution active business requirement to the situation existing "immediately after the distribution" was deliberate. Consistent with the general statutory scheme, it is quite inconsistent with the Commissioner's contention.

The requirement of § 368(a)(1)(D) that the transferor or its stockholders be in control of the spun-off corporation immediately after the transfer is of no assistance to the Commissioner. It is directed solely to control of the transferee, and was fully met here. It contains no requirement of continuing control of the transferor. Though a subsequent sale of the transferor's stock, under some circumstances, might form the basis of a contention that the transaction was the equivalent of a dividend within the meaning of § 355(a)(1)(B) and the underlying principles, the control requirements imply no limitation upon subsequent reorganizations of the transferor.

There is no distinction in the statute between subsequent amalgamating reorganizations in which the stockholders of the spin-off transferor would own 80% or more of the relevant classes of stock of the reorganized transferor, and those in which they would not. The statute draws no line between major and minor amalgamations in prospect at the time of the spin-off. Nothing of the sort is suggested by the detailed control-active business requirements in the five-year predistribution period, for there the distinction is between taxable and nontaxable acquisitions, and a tax free exchange within the five-year period does not violate the active business-control requirement whether it was a major or a minor acquisition. Reorganizations in which no gain or loss is recognized, sanctioned by the statute's control provision when occurring in the five years preceding the spin-off, are not prohibited in the post-distribution period.

As we have noticed above, the merger cannot by any stretch of imagination be said to have affected the continuity of interest of American's stockholders or to have constituted a violation of the principle underlying the statutory control requirement. The view is the same whether it be directed to each of the successive steps severally or to the whole.

Nor can we find elsewhere in the Code any support for the Commissioner's suggestion of incompatibility between substantially contemporaneous divisive and amalgamating reorganizations. The 1954 Code contains no inkling of it; nor does its immediate legislative history. * * *

For the reasons which we have canvassed, we think the Tax Court * * * correctly decided that American's stockholders realized no recognizable taxable gain upon their receipt in the "D" reorganization of the stock of Agency.

NOTES

1. *Treatment of shareholders.* In the Morris Trust case, the Internal Revenue Service endeavored to tax the distributee-shareholders. Does I.R.C. § 355(e) impose adverse tax consequences at the shareholder level?

2. *Impact of § 355(e) on Morris Trust case.* If the events in Morris Trust transpired after the enactment of § 355(e), would that provision impact on the tax consequences?

3. *Spin-off before tax-free asset transfer.* I.R.C. § 355(e) applies to a spin-off that precedes a tax-free transfer of the *stock* of the Distributing Corporation or the Controlled Corporation. Can I.R.C. § 355(e) be circumvented by following a spin-off with a tax-free transfer of the *assets* of the Distributing Corporation or the Controlled Corporation? See I.R.C. § 355(e)(3)(B).

4. *Spin-off after tax-free reorganization.* Although the transactions at which I.R.C. § 355(e) was directed generally involve a spin-off *preceding* a tax-free reorganization, the provision is drafted broadly enough to apply to a spin-off *following* a tax-free reorganization. Section 355(e) applies to a spin-off that is "part of a plan" to shift a 50% or greater interest in the Distributing Corporation or the Controlled Corporation. I.R.C. § 355(e)(2)(A). Such a plan is presumed to exist if the shift in ownership occurs within two years *before or after* the spin-off. I.R.C. § 355(e)(2)(B).

Revenue Ruling 2005–65

IRB 2005–41.

ISSUE

Under the facts described below, is a distribution of a controlled corporation by a distributing corporation part of a plan pursuant to which one or more persons acquire stock in the distributing corporation under § 355(e) of the Internal Revenue Code and § 1.355–7 of the Income Tax Regulations?

FACTS

Distributing is a publicly traded corporation that conducts a pharmaceuticals business. Controlled, a wholly owned subsidiary of Distributing, conducts a cosmetics business. Distributing does all of the borrowing for both Distributing and Controlled and makes all decisions regarding the allocation of capital spending between the pharmaceuticals and cosmetics businesses. Because Distributing's capital spending in recent years for both the pharmaceuticals and cosmetics businesses has outpaced internally generated cash flow from the businesses, it has had to limit total expenditures to maintain its credit ratings. Although the decisions reached by Distributing's senior management regarding the allocation of capital spending usually favor the pharmaceuticals business due to its higher rate of growth and profit margin, the competition for capital prevents both businesses from consistently pursuing development strategies that the management of each business believes are appropriate.

To eliminate this competition for capital, and in light of the unavailability of nontaxable alternatives, Distributing decides and publicly announces that it intends to distribute all the stock of Controlled pro rata to Distributing's shareholders. It is expected that both businesses will benefit in a real and substantial way from the distribution. This business purpose is a corporate business purpose (within the meaning of § 1.355–2(b)). The distribution is substantially motivated by this business purpose, and not by a business purpose to facilitate an acquisition.

After the announcement but before the distribution, X, a widely held corporation that is engaged in the pharmaceuticals business, and Distributing begin discussions regarding an acquisition. There were no discussions between Distributing or Controlled and X or its shareholders regarding an acquisition or a distribution before the announcement. In addition, Distributing would have been able to continue the successful operation of its pharmaceuticals business without combining with X. During its negotiations with Distributing, X indicates that it favors the distribution. X merges into Distributing before the distribution but nothing in the merger agreement requires the distribution.

As a result of the merger, X's former shareholders receive 55 percent of Distributing's stock. In addition, X's chairman of the board and chief executive officer become the chairman of the board and chief executive officer, respectively, of Distributing. Six months after the merger, Distributing distributes the stock of Controlled pro rata in a distribution to which § 355 applies and to which § 355(d) does not apply. At the time of the distribution, the distribution continues to be substantially motivated by the business purpose of eliminating the competition for capital between the pharmaceuticals and cosmetics businesses.

LAW

Section 355(c) generally provides that no gain or loss is recognized to the distributing corporation on a distribution of stock in a controlled corporation to which § 355 applies and which is not in pursuance of a plan of reorganization. Section 355(e) generally denies nonrecognition treatment under § 355(c) if the distribution is part of a plan (or series of related transactions) (a plan) pursuant to which one or more persons acquire directly or indirectly stock representing a 50–percent or greater interest in the distributing corporation or any controlled corporation.

Section 1.355–7(b)(1) provides that whether a distribution and an acquisition are part of a plan is determined based on all the facts and circumstances, including those set forth in § 1.355–7(b)(3) (plan factors) and (4) (non-plan factors). The weight to be given each of the facts and circumstances depends on the particular case. The determination does not depend on the relative number of plan factors compared to the number of non-plan factors that are present.

Section 1.355–7(b)(3)(iii) provides that, in the case of an acquisition before a distribution, if at some time during the two-year period ending on the date of the acquisition there were discussions by Distributing or Controlled with the acquirer regarding a distribution, such discussions tend to show that the distribution and the acquisition are part of a plan. The weight to be accorded this fact depends on the nature, extent, and timing of the discussions. In addition, the fact that the acquirer intends to cause a distribution and, immediately after the acquisition, can meaningfully participate in the decision regarding whether to make a distribution, tends to show that the distribution and the acquisition are part of a plan.

Section 1.355–7(b)(4)(iii) provides that, in the case of an acquisition before a distribution, the absence of discussions by Distributing or Controlled with the acquirer regarding a distribution during the two-year period ending on the date of the earlier to occur of the acquisition or the first public announcement regarding the distribution tends to show that the distribution and the acquisition are not part of a plan. However, this factor does not apply to an acquisition where the acquirer intends to cause a distribution and, immediately after the acquisition, can meaningfully participate in the decision regarding whether to make a distribution.

Section 1.355–7(b)(4)(v) provides that the fact that the distribution was motivated in whole or substantial part by a corporate business purpose (within the meaning of § 1.355–2(b)) other than a business purpose to facilitate the acquisition or a similar acquisition tends to show that the distribution and the acquisition are not part of a plan.

Section 1.355–7(b)(4)(vi) provides that the fact that the distribution would have occurred at approximately the same time and in similar form regardless of the acquisition or a similar acquisition tends to show that the distribution and the acquisition are not part of a plan.

ANALYSIS

Whether the X shareholders' acquisition of Distributing stock and Distributing's distribution of Controlled are part of a plan depends on all the facts and circumstances, including those described in § 1.355–7(b). The fact that Distributing discussed the distribution with X during the two-year period ending on the date of the acquisition tends to show that the distribution and the acquisition are part of a plan. See § 1.355–7(b)(3)(iii). In addition, X's shareholders may constitute acquirers who intend to cause a distribution and who, immediately after the acquisition, can meaningfully participate (through X's chairman of the board and chief executive officer who become D's chairman of the board and chief executive officer) in the decision regarding whether to distribute Controlled. However, the fact that Distributing publicly announced the distribution before discussions with X regarding both an acquisition and a distribution began suggests that the plan factor in § 1.355–7(b)(3)(iii) should be accorded less weight than it would have been accorded had there been such discussions before the public announcement.

With respect to those factors that tend to show that the distribution and the acquisition are not part of a plan, the absence of discussions by Distributing or Controlled with X or its shareholders during the two-year period ending on the date of the public announcement regarding the distribution would tend to show that the distribution and the acquisition are not part of a plan only if X's shareholders are not acquirers who intend to cause a distribution and who, immediately after the acquisition, can meaningfully participate in the decision regarding whether to distribute Controlled. See § 1.355–7(b)(4)(iii). Because X's chairman of the board and chief executive officer become the chairman and chief executive officer, respectively, of Distributing, X's shareholders may have the ability to meaningfully participate in the decision whether to distribute Controlled. Therefore, the absence of discussions by Distributing or Controlled with X or its shareholders during the two-year period ending on the date of the public announcement regarding the distribution may not tend to show that the distribution and the acquisition are not part of a plan.

Nonetheless, the fact that the distribution was substantially motivated by a corporate business purpose (within the meaning of § 1.355–2(b)) other than a business purpose to facilitate the acquisition or a similar acquisition, and the fact that the distribution would have occurred at approximately the same time and in similar form regardless of the acquisition or a similar acquisition, tend to show that the distribution and the acquisition are not part of a plan. See § 1.355–7(b)(4)(v), (vi). The fact that the public announcement of the distribution preceded discussions by Distributing or Controlled with X or its shareholders, and the fact that Distributing's business would have continued to operate successfully even if the merger had not occurred, evidence that the distribution originally was not substantially motivated by a business purpose to facilitate the acquisition or a similar acquisition. Moreover, after the merger, Distributing continued to be substantially motivated by the same corporate business purpose (within the meaning of § 1.355–2(b)) other than a business purpose to facilitate the acquisition or a similar acquisition (§ 1.355–7(b)(4)(v)). In addition, the fact that Distributing decided to distribute Controlled and announced that decision before it began discussions with X regarding the combination suggests that the distribution would have occurred at approximately the same time and in similar form regardless of Distributing's combination with X and the corresponding acquisition of Distributing stock by the X shareholders.

Considering all the facts and circumstances, particularly the fact that the distribution was motivated by a corporate business purpose (within the meaning of § 1.355–2(b)) other than a business purpose to facilitate the acquisition or a similar acquisition, and the fact that the distribution would have occurred at approximately the same time and in similar form regardless of the acquisition or a similar acquisition, the acquisition and distribution are not part of a plan under § 355(e) and § 1.355–7(b).

HOLDING

Under the facts described above, the acquisition and the distribution are not part of a plan under § 355(e) and § 1.355–7(b).

NOTES

1. *No requirement of tax-free reorganization.* Does § 355(e) provide that the requisite shift of a 50% or greater interest in the Distributing Corporation or the Controlled Corporation must occur as the result of a tax-free reorganization? See I.R.C. § 355(e)(2)(A). Would § 355(e) apply if, after a spin-off, more than 50% of the stock of the Distributing Corporation or the Controlled Corporation were sold by the shareholders? See I.R.C. § 355(a)(1)(B). Would § 355(e) apply if, after a spin-off, the Distributing Corporation or the Controlled Corporation sold newly issued stock to the public representing more than a 50% ownership interest?

2. *Impact of § 355(e) on split-off.* Can § 355(e) apply to a split-off? See I.R.C. § 355(e)(3)(A)(ii).

3. *Private letter rulings.* The Internal Revenue Service has announced a pilot program whereby it will no longer determine whether a proposed or completed distribution of stock of a controlled corporation and an acquisition are part of a plan under I.R.C. § 355(e). Rather, the taxpayer must now represent that the distribution is not part of a plan described in I.R.C. § 355(e)(2)(A)(ii). See Rev. Proc. 2003–48, 2003–29 I.R.B. 86.

4. *Relaxed control requirement for purposes of drop-down.* Assume that Distributing Corporation transfers a business to newly-formed Controlled Corporation and then distributes the stock of Controlled in a transaction that satisfies I.R.C. § 355(a). Also assume that the distribution is part of a plan that involves the disposition of *30%* of the stock of Controlled. I.R.C. § 355(e) would not trigger any gain to Distributing because less than 50% of the Controlled stock is transferred. However, Distributing still must satisfy I.R.C. §§ 351(a) or 361(a) to avoid recognizing any gain on the initial drop-down of assets to Controlled. For § 351(a) to apply, Distributing must be in "control" of Controlled, i.e., own at least 80% of Controlled. See I.R.C. § 368(c). For § 361(a) to apply, the drop-down and distribution must qualify as a divisive D reorganization which also requires Distributing to be in "control" and, therefore, to own at least 80% of Controlled. See I.R.C. §§ 368(a)(1)(D), (c). Could Distributing's plan to transfer 30% of Controlled cause Distributing to be treated as owning only 70% of Controlled after the drop-down, thereby violating the 80% ownership requirement that must be satisfied for either nonrecognition rule (§ 351(a) or § 361(a)) to apply to the drop-down? See I.R.C. §§ 351(c)(2), 368(a)(2)(H)(ii).

> *Problem 15–4 (Impact of § 355(e)):* Distributing Corporation ("Distributing") manufactures sweaters. Distributing's sweater business consists of assets with a value of $6,000,000. Distributing also owns all the stock of Controlled Corporation ("Controlled") which manufactures steel. The stock of Controlled has a value of $4,000,000 and a basis of $1,000,000. Distributing and Controlled have owned their respective businesses for more than five years. In addition, Distributing has owned Controlled for more than five years. What are the tax consequences of each of the following alternatives?
>
> (a) Distributing distributes the stock of Controlled in a transaction that satisfies the requirements of I.R.C. § 355(a). One year after the spin-off, the shareholders of Controlled transfer the stock of Controlled in exchange for shares of Acquiring Corporation with a value of $4,000,000 in a transaction that qualifies as a reorganization. After the reorganization, the former shareholders of Controlled own 40% of the stock of Acquiring.
>
> (b) Same as (a) but after the reorganization, the former shareholders of Controlled own 60% of the stock of Acquiring.
>
> (c) Same as (a) but the reorganization occurs three years after the spin-off.
>
> (d) Distributing distributes the stock of Controlled in a transaction that satisfies the requirements of I.R.C. § 355(a). One year after the spin-off, the shareholders of Distributing transfer the stock of Distributing in exchange for shares of Acquiring Corporation with a value of $6,000,000 in a transaction that qualifies as a reorganization. After the reorganization, the former shareholders of Distributing own 40% of the stock of Acquiring.
>
> (e) Distributing merges into Acquiring Corporation in a transaction that qualifies as a reorganization. As a result of the merger, the former shareholders of Distributing own 40% of the stock of Acquiring. One year after the merger, Acquiring distributes the stock of Controlled in a transaction that satisfies the requirements of I.R.C. § 355(a).
>
> (f) Distributing distributes the stock of Controlled in a transaction that satisfies the requirements of I.R.C. § 355(a). One year after the spin-off, Distributing sells newly issued stock to the public that represents a 60% interest in Distributing.
>
> (g) Same as (f) but the stock Distributing sells to the public represents a 40% interest in Distributing.

CHAPTER 16

CORPORATE REARRANGEMENTS

Chapter 16 explores transactions that change the capital structure or the operating entity of a single corporate enterprise. For the most part, these transactions are viewed as mere changes in form and are either governed by specific statutory exclusions (see I.R.C. §§ 305, 306) or are treated as reorganizations (E, F or nondivisive D reorganizations).

A. CHANGE IN CAPITAL STRUCTURE

The capital structure of a corporation changes when the corporation issues additional shares of its own stock to existing shareholders. The tax consequences to the recipients of these shares vary depending upon whether common stock or preferred stock is issued and whether previously outstanding stock is surrendered in exchange for the new shares.

1. DISTRIBUTION OF COMMON STOCK

I.R.C. §§ 305, 307

Treas. Reg. §§ 1.305–1(a), (b), –2, –3(a), (b)(1)–(4), –7(a), 1.307–1(a)

a. THE GENERAL RULE

Towne v. Eisner

Supreme Court of the United States, 1918.
245 U.S. 418, 38 S.Ct. 158.

■ MR. JUSTICE HOLMES delivered the opinion of the Court.

This is a suit to recover the amount of a tax paid [by a shareholder] under duress in respect of a stock dividend alleged by the Government to be income * * *. The facts alleged are that the corporation voted * * * to transfer $1,500,000 [of retained earnings] * * * to its capital account, and to issue fifteen thousand shares of stock representing the same to its stockholders * * * and that the plaintiff received as his due proportion [4,174–½] shares. The defendant compelled the plaintiff to pay an income tax upon this stock as equivalent to $417,450 income in cash. The District Court held that the stock was income within the meaning of the Income Tax [Act] of October 3, 1913 * * *.

* * *

[N]otwithstanding the thoughtful discussion that the case received below we cannot doubt that the dividend was capital * * * for the purposes of the Income Tax Law * * *.

> A stock dividend really takes nothing from the property of the corporation, and adds nothing to the interests of the shareholders. Its property is not diminished, and their interests are not increased * * *. The proportional interest of each shareholder remains the same. The only change is in the evidence which represents that interest, the new shares and the original shares together representing the same proportional interest that the original shares represented before the issue of the new ones.

Gibbons v. Mahon, 136 U.S. 549, 559. In short, the corporation is no poorer and the stockholder is no richer than they were before. If the plaintiff gained any small advantage by the change, it certainly was not an advantage of $417,450, the sum upon which he was taxed. It is alleged and admitted that he receives no more in the way of dividends and that his old and new certificates together are worth only what the old ones were worth before. If the sum had been carried from surplus to capital account without a corresponding issue of stock certificates, * * * we do not suppose that anyone would contend that the plaintiff had received an accession to his income. Presumably his certificate would have the same value as before. Again, if certificates for $1,000 par were split up into ten certificates each, for $100, we presume that no one would call the new certificates income. What has happened is that the plaintiff's old certificates have been split up in effect and have diminished in value to the extent of the value of the new.

Judgment reversed.

NOTES

1. *Constitutionality of taxing stock dividends.* In Eisner v. Macomber, 252 U.S. 189, 40 S.Ct. 189 (1920), the Supreme Court concluded that the Sixteenth Amendment to the Constitution bars Congress from taxing shareholders on the receipt of a common stock dividend. Most legal scholars no longer believe that a constitutional impediment exists to taxing stock dividends.

2. *Enrichment as prerequisite for taxation.* The Towne court justifies its conclusion that stock dividends are not taxable by asserting that "the corporation is no poorer and the shareholder is no richer than they were before" the stock dividend. Is enrichment always a prerequisite to taxation under current law? See I.R.C. § 61(a)(3). Is the potential shareholder income created by a stock dividend described in I.R.C. § 61(a)(3) or I.R.C. § 61(a)(7)?

3. *Codification of Towne.* The Towne court's holding was influenced by the fact that the proportional interest of each shareholder remained the same both before and after the issuance of the stock dividend. This proportional interest test serves as the foundation for the taxation of stock dividends under current law. As a general rule, stock dividends are excluded from each recipient shareholder's gross income. I.R.C. § 305(a). Several exceptions to this rule exist. See I.R.C. §§ 305(b), (c). Most of these exceptions involve transactions that actually or potentially effectuate a change in the proportional interest of one or more shareholders of the corporation.

4. *Issuance of stock to shareholder-employee.* Is the issuance of additional shares of stock of the distributing corporation to an employee who is also a shareholder excluded from the recipient's gross income? Does it matter whether additional shares are also issued to the other shareholders of the corporation? See I.R.C. §§ 61(a)(1), 305(a).

5. *Stock dividend versus stock split.* Towne involved a "stock dividend" but the last two sentences of the Court's opinion analogize the transaction to a "stock split". The two transactions are economically similar, but normally are undertaken for different reasons and have different financial effects.

A "stock dividend" normally entails the distribution of a relatively small number of new shares of stock with respect to already outstanding shares. As compared to a cash distribution, a stock dividend enables the corporation to conserve assets. A "stock split" entails the division of already outstanding shares into a multiple number of shares. Publicly-traded corporations often engage in stock splits to lower the price of their shares hoping to increase the attractiveness of their shares to investors. Neither transaction, however, normally changes the total value of each shareholder's investment in the corporation. Why not?

From a financial standpoint, a stock dividend entails a bookkeeping transfer of retained earnings to the corporation's capital account which may impact on the legal capacity of the corporation to pay future dividends. A stock split simply increases the number of outstanding shares; it does not change the book equity accounts.[1]

Do the shareholder level tax consequences of stock dividends and stock splits differ? See I.R.C. §§ 305(a), 307(a), 1036; Treas. Reg. § 1.307–1(a). What are the corporate level tax consequences of each transaction? See I.R.C. § 1032. How does each transaction impact on the corporation's earnings & profits? See I.R.C. § 312(d)(1); Treas. Reg. § 1.312–1(d).

Example 16–A: Ariel and Boris each purchased 50 of the 100 outstanding common shares of ZZZ, Inc. for $55,000.

(a) *Stock dividend.* If ZZZ, Inc. issues a 10% common stock dividend, five additional shares are issued to each shareholder. After the stock dividend, each shareholder still owns 50% of the stock of ZZZ (55 of 110 shares). Each shareholder may exclude the value of the five shares from income. I.R.C. § 305(a). Before the stock dividend, each share-

---

1. For additional discussion of stock dividends and stock splits, see Harry G. Henn & John R. Alexander, *Laws of Corporations* §§ 329–330 (3d ed. 1983 & Supp. 1986).

holder has a basis of $1,100 in each share of ZZZ stock.[2] After the stock dividend, each shareholder has a basis of $1,000 in each share of ZZZ stock.[3]

(b) *Stock split.* If ZZZ effectuates a "2–for–1" stock split (in lieu of issuing a common stock dividend), 50 additional shares are issued to each shareholder. After the stock split, each shareholder still owns 50% of the stock of ZZZ (100 of 200 shares). The stock split does not create any income to the shareholders. After the stock split, each shareholder has a basis of $550 in each share of ZZZ stock.[4]

b. EXCEPTIONS TO TAX–FREE TREATMENT

Revenue Ruling 76–53

1976–1 Cum.Bull. 87.

* * *

X, a widely held corporation that regularly distributes its earnings and profits, adopted a plan permitting the shareholders of X to choose to have all of the cash dividends otherwise payable on the common shares owned by the shareholder automatically invested to purchase additional shares of X common stock. The shareholders who elect to participate in the plan acquire X stock at a price equal to 95 percent of the fair market value of such stock on the dividend payment date * * *.

* * *

There is no requirement to participate in the plan and shareholders who do not participate receive their cash dividend payments in full * * *.

Prior to the dividend payment date, no cash dividend is available to either X's participating or nonparticipating shareholders * * *.

A participant may withdraw from the plan at any time, and certificates for whole shares credited to the participant's account are issued to the participant * * *.

* * *

Section 305(a) of the Internal Revenue Code of 1954 provides that, with certain exceptions, gross income does not include the amount of any distribution of the stock of a corporation made by such corporation to its shareholders with respect to its stock * * *.

Section 305(b)(1) of the Code provides that section 305(a) will not apply, and the distribution will be treated as a distribution to which section 301 applies, if the distribution is, at the election of any shareholder * * *, payable either in the stock of the distributing corporation or in property.

---

2. $55,000 ÷ 50 shares = $1,100.

3. $55,000 ÷ 55 shares = $1,000. See Treas. Reg. § 1.307–1(a).

4. $55,000 ÷ 100 shares = $550.

Section 1.305–2(a) of the Income Tax Regulations provides that if any shareholder has the right to an election or option with respect to whether a distribution shall be made either in money or any other property, or in stock or rights to acquire stock of the distributing corporation, then, with respect to all shareholders, the distribution of stock or rights to acquire stock is treated as a distribution of property to which section 301 of the Code applies regardless of (1) whether the distribution is actually made in whole or in part in stock or in stock rights; (2) whether the election or option is exercised or exercisable before or after the declaration of the distribution; (3) whether the declaration of the distribution provides that the distribution will be made in one medium unless the shareholder specifically requests payment in another; (4) * * *; or (5) whether all or part of the shareholders have the election.

Section 1.305–1(b)(1) of the regulations provides that where a distribution of stock or rights to acquire stock of a corporation is treated as a distribution of property to which section 301 of the Code applies by reason of section 305(b), the amount of the distribution, in accordance with section 301(b) and section 1.301–1 is the fair market value of such stock or rights on the date of the distribution.

* * *

Applying these rules to the facts of the instant case, the distributions made by X while the plan is in effect are properly treated as payable either in X's stock or in cash at the election of X's common shareholders within the meaning of section 305(b)(1) of the Code and the regulations thereunder * * *.

Accordingly, under the circumstances described above, it is held as follows:

1. A shareholder of X who participates in the plan will be treated as having received a distribution to which section 301 of the Code applies by reason of the application of section 305(b)(1). Pursuant to section 1.305–1(b) of the regulations, the amount of the distribution to the participating shareholders * * * will be the fair market value of the X stock received on the date of the distribution. The amount of the distribution to the nonparticipating shareholders under section 301 will be the amount of the cash received by such shareholders. Section 1.305–2(b), Example (1).

2. The basis of the shares credited to the account of a participating shareholder pursuant to the dividend reinvestment aspect of the plan will equal the amount of the distribution measured by the fair market value of the stock as of the date of the distribution * * *.

NOTES

1. *Receipt of stock by some shareholders and property by others.* I.R.C. § 305(b)(1) applies if the distribution is, at the election of *any* shareholder, payable in stock or property. Not surprisingly, a shareholder who opts to receive property in these circumstances will be taxed on the value of the property as a dividend, assuming the corporation has sufficient earnings & profits. See I.R.C. §§ 301, 316. Any shareholder who receives stock is likewise taxed on the value of the stock received, regardless of whether that shareholder could have elected to receive property instead of stock. See Treas. Reg. § 1.305–1(b)(1). The justification for this result is that the shareholder who receives stock increases her proportional ownership interest in the corporation.

> *Example 16–B (Impact on proportional interest)*: Some time ago, Ariel and Boris each purchased 50 of the 100 outstanding common shares of ZZZ, Inc. for $55,000. ZZZ now offers to distribute $10,000 or five additional ZZZ shares to each of Ariel and Boris. Ariel chooses the $10,000 and Boris chooses the five additional shares. (Assume that the five shares issued to Boris have a value of $2,000 per share.) The distribution causes Boris's ownership interest to increase from 50% to 52.4%.[5] Each of Ariel and Boris have $10,000 of dividend income, assuming ZZZ has sufficient earnings & profits. See I.R.C. §§ 301(a)–(c), 305(b)(1); Treas. Reg. § 1.305–1(b)(1). Boris takes a basis of $2,000 in each of the five ZZZ shares distributed to him. I.R.C. § 301(d). The transaction does not affect the basis of Ariel and Boris in the 50 ZZZ shares originally purchased by each of them.

2. *Receipt of stock by all shareholders.* Section 305(b)(1) is even more far reaching than Note 1 reveals. Even if all shareholders, in fact, receive stock so that each shareholder's proportional interest remains the same, the distribution is taxable to *all* shareholders if *any* shareholder could have elected to receive property instead of stock.

> *Problem 16–1 (Impact on proportional interest and tax consequences)*: The Wabash Corporation has 400 shares of one class of common stock outstanding, 300 of which are owned by Ellen and 100 of which are owned by Frank. The value of the Wabash Corporation is $4,000,000. Wabash plans to issue 25 additional shares to Frank and has offered Ellen the choice of receiving 75 additional shares or $600,000. If Ellen opts to take the 75 additional shares, will the distribution of shares to Ellen and Frank change their proportional interests in Wabash? What are the tax consequences to Ellen and Frank if Ellen opts to take,
>
> (a) the 75 additional shares?
>
> (b) the $600,000?

3. *Impact of redemption on proportional interest of non-participating shareholders.* When a corporation redeems stock from one or more of its shareholders, the proportional interest of the shareholders who are not redeemed increases. For example, assume that Jerry, Kara and Larry each own 100 of the 300 outstanding shares of the Begat Corporation. If Begat redeems all of Jerry's shares, each of Kara and Larry's proportional interest increases from 33–⅓% to 50%. Although Kara and Larry still own

---

5. 55 ÷ 105 = 52.4%.

the same number of shares, their proportional interests increase because fewer shares of Begat are outstanding after Jerry's shares are redeemed. Might this increase in proportional interest trigger income to Kara and Larry? See I.R.C. §§ 305(b)(2), (c) (first sentence); Rev. Rul. 78–60, which follows.

Revenue Ruling 78–60

1978–1 Cum.Bull. 81.

Advice has been requested whether under section 302(a) of the Internal Revenue Code of 1954 the stock redemptions described below qualified for exchange treatment, and whether under section 305(b)(2) and (c) the shareholders who experienced increases in their proportional interests in the redeeming corporation as a result of the stock redemptions will be treated as having received distributions of property to which section 301 applies.

Corporation Z has only one class of stock outstanding. The Z common stock is held by 24 shareholders, all of whom are descendants, or spouses of descendants, of the founder of Z.

In 1975, when Z had 6,000 shares of common stock outstanding, the board of directors of Z adopted a plan of annual redemption to provide a means for its shareholders to sell their stock. The plan provides that Z will annually redeem up to 40 shares of its outstanding stock at a price established annually by the Z board of directors. Each shareholder of Z is entitled to cause Z to redeem two-thirds of one percent of the shareholder's stock each year. If some shareholders choose not to participate fully in the plan during any year, the other shareholders can cause Z to redeem more than two-thirds of one percent of their stock, up to the maximum of 40 shares.

Pursuant to the plan of annual redemption, Z redeemed 40 shares of its stock in 1976. Eight shareholders participated in the redemptions * * *.

* * *

[N]one of the 1976 redemptions qualified for exchange treatment under section 302(a) of the Code. All of the redemptions are to be treated as distributions of property to which section 301 applies.

* * *

Section 305(b)(2) of the Code provides that section 301 will apply to a distribution by a corporation of its stock if the distribution * * * has the result of the receipt of property by some shareholders, and increases the proportional interests of other shareholders in the assets or earnings and profits of the corporation.

Section 305(c) of the Code authorizes regulations under which a redemption treated as a section 301 distribution will be treated as a section 301 distribution to any shareholder whose proportional interest in the earnings and profits or assets of the corporation is increased by the redemption.

Section 1.305–7(a) of the Income Tax Regulations provides that a redemption treated as a section 301 distribution will generally be treated as a distribution to which sections 305(b)(2) and 301 of the Code apply if the proportional interest of any shareholder in the earnings and profits or assets of the corporation deemed to have made the stock distribution is increased by the redemption, and the distribution has the result described in section 305(b)(2). The distribution is to be deemed made to any shareholder whose interest in the earnings and profits or assets of the distributing corporation is increased by the redemption.

Section 1.305–3(b)(3) of the regulations provides that for a distribution of property to meet the requirements of section 305(b)(2) of the Code, the distribution must be made to a shareholder in the capacity as a shareholder and must be a distribution to which section 301 * * * applies. A distribution of property incident to an isolated redemption will not cause section 305(b)(2) to apply even though the redemption distribution is treated as a section 301 distribution.

Section 305 of the Code does not make the constructive stock ownership rules of section 318(a) applicable to its provisions.

The 16 shareholders of Z who did not tender any stock for redemption in 1976 experienced increases in their proportional interests of the earnings and profits and assets of Z (without taking into account constructive stock ownership under section 318 of the Code) as a result of the redemptions * * *. The 1976 redemptions were not isolated but were undertaken pursuant to an ongoing plan of annual stock redemptions. Finally, the 1976 redemptions are to be treated as distributions of property to which section 301 of the Code applies.

Accordingly, * * * the 16 shareholders of Z who did not participate in the 1976 redemptions are deemed to have received stock distributions to which sections 305(b)(2) and 301 of the Code apply. See examples (8) and (9) of section 1.305–3(e) of the regulations for a method of computing the amounts of the deemed distributions.

NOTES

1. *Identifying value received by non-redeeming shareholders.* In Rev. Rul. 78–60, what did the shareholders who did not participate in the redemptions receive? On what are they being taxed? See Treas. Reg. § 1.305–3(e) Example 8.

2. *Redemption treated as I.R.C. § 301 distribution, isolated redemption exception.* For a redemption to trigger adverse tax consequences to non-participating shareholders, the redemption must be treated as an I.R.C. § 301 distribution. See I.R.C. § 305(c); Treas. Reg. § 1.305–3(b)(3). Even if a redemption is treated as an I.R.C. § 301 distribution, an "isolated" redemption will not trigger income to the non participating shareholders.

See Treas. Reg. §§ 1.305–3(b)(3) (last sentence), –3(e) Examples 10–11, –7(a). Why is a redemption that is treated as an I.R.C. § 301 distribution viewed differently under I.R.C. § 305 from a redemption that qualifies for sale treatment under I.R.C. § 302(a)?

3. *I.R.C. § 305(b)(2) and Towne.* Can I.R.C. § 305(b)(2) be reconciled with the analysis of the Supreme Court in Towne (p. 747)?

Revenue Ruling 90–11

1990–1 Cum.Bull. 10.

ISSUE

What are the federal income tax consequences, if any, of a corporation's adoption of a plan as described below, commonly referred to as a "poison pill" plan, which provides the corporation's shareholders with the right to purchase additional shares of stock upon the occurrence of certain events?

FACTS

X is a publicly held domestic corporation. X's board of directors adopted a plan (the "Plan") that provides the common shareholders of X with "poison pill" rights (the "Rights"). The adoption of the Plan constituted the distribution of a dividend under state law. The principal purpose of the adoption of the Plan was to establish a mechanism by which the corporation could, in the future, provide shareholders with rights to purchase stock at substantially less than fair market value as a means of responding to unsolicited offers to acquire X.

The Rights are rights to purchase a fraction of a share of "preferred stock" for each share of common stock held upon the occurrence of a "triggering event," subject to the restrictions described below. The fractional share of preferred stock has voting, dividend, and liquidation rights that make it the economic equivalent of one common share. Until the issuance of the Rights certificates, as described below, the Rights are not exercisable or separately tradable, nor are they represented by any certificate other than the common stock certificate itself. If no triggering event occurs, the Rights expire a years after their creation.

A triggering event is the earlier of the tender offer for, or actual acquisition of, at least b percent of X's common stock by an investor or investor group. If X does not redeem the Rights, as described below, by the end of the c-day period following a triggering event, it must issue Rights certificates to all persons that held X common stock on the date of the triggering event, including the investor or investor group that caused the triggering event. Once issued, the Rights certificates are tradable separately from the common stock. At any time until d days after the actual acquisition by an investor or investor group of at least b percent of X's common stock, X can redeem the Rights without shareholder approval * * * for e cents per Right, which is a nominal amount in relation to the current market value of the share of X common stock.

Upon the issuance of the Rights certificates, the Rights can be exercised but, until [an acquisition of *f* percent of X's stock by an investor or investor group or a business combination involving X], the exercise price is several times the trading price of a share of common stock at the time X adopted the Plan. * * * The occurrence of [an acquisition of *f* percent of X's stock by an investor or investor group or a business combination involving X] gives the holder of each Right, other than the investor or investor group, the right to buy, for *g* dollars, stock of X [or the surviving corporation] that has a value substantially greater than *g* dollars.

At the time X's board of directors adopted the Plan, the likelihood that the Rights would, at any time, be exercised was both remote and speculative.

HOLDING

The adoption of the Plan by X's board of directors does not constitute the distribution of stock or property by X to its shareholders, an exchange of property or stock (either taxable or nontaxable), or any other event giving rise to the realization of gross income by any taxpayer. This revenue ruling does not address the federal income tax consequences of any redemption of Rights, or of any transaction involving Rights subsequent to a triggering event.

* * *

NOTES

1. *Impact of I.R.C. § 305 when plan adopted.* Could I.R.C. § 305 have triggered adverse tax consequences to the shareholders of X upon the adoption of the poison pill plan? See I.R.C. § 305(d)(1). Why do you think the Internal Revenue Service ruled that the adoption of the plan did not constitute the distribution of stock to X's shareholders?

2. *Impact of I.R.C. § 305 at time of later event.* What are the tax consequences to the shareholders of X if,

(a) X issues Rights certificates? See I.R.C. § 305(b)(2).

(b) after the issuance of Rights certificates by X, an investor or investor group acquires *f* percent of X's stock or a business combination involving X occurs? See I.R.C. §§ 305(b)(2), (c).

2.   Distribution of Preferred Stock

I.R.C. §§ 305, 306

Treas. Reg. §§ 1.305–4, –5(a), –6(a); 1.306–1, –2, –3(a)–(e)

Chamberlin v. Commissioner

United States Court of Appeals, Sixth Circuit, 1953.
207 F.2d 462.

■ Miller, Circuit Judge.

The Metal Moulding Corporation, hereinafter referred to as the Corporation, is * * * engaged in the business of manufacturing metal moldings and bright work trim used in the manufacture of automobiles. It was incorporated on December 2, 1924 with an authorized common capital stock of * * * $150,000, represented by 1,500 shares of $100 par value voting common stock. [U]ntil December 20, 1946, the issued and outstanding common stock totaled 1,002–½ shares, of which [petitioner,] Chamberlin and his wife together owned 83.8% * * *.

The business of the Corporation prospered * * *.

On December 16, 1946, the Corporation's authorized capital stock was increased * * * to $650,000, represented by 6,500 shares of $100 par value common stock. On December 20, 1946, a stock dividend was declared and distributed of five shares of common for each share of common outstanding, and the Corporation's accounts were adjusted by transferring $501,250 from earned surplus to capital account.

On December 26, 1946, the articles of incorporation were amended so as to authorize, in addition to the 6,500 shares of common stock, 8,020 shares of 4–½% cumulative $100 par value preferred stock. On December 28, 1946, a stock dividend was declared of 1–⅛ shares of the newly authorized preferred stock for each share of common stock outstanding, to be issued pro rata to the holders of common stock as of December 27, 1946, and the Company's accounts were adjusted by transferring $802,000 from earned surplus to capital account * * *.

On December 30, 1946, as the result of prior negotiations hereinafter referred to, all of the holders of the preferred stock * * * signed a "Purchase Agreement," with The Northwestern Mutual Life Insurance Company and The Lincoln National Life Insurance Company * * *. Under the "Purchase Agreement" 4,000 shares of the preferred stock [were] sold to each of the two insurance companies at a cash price of $100 per share * * *.

* * *

In the latter part of 1945, the Corporation's attorney and Chamberlin discussed with an investment firm in Chicago the possibility of selling an issue of preferred stock similar to the stock subsequently issued. The Corporation had such a large accumulated earned surplus it was fearful of being subjected to the [accumulated earnings tax] but at the same time Chamberlin, the majority stockholder, was not willing to have the Corporation distribute any substantial portion of its earned surplus as ordinary dividends because his individual income was taxable at high surtax rates. It was proposed that the issuance of a stock dividend to the stockholders and the sale of it by the stockholders would enable the stockholders to obtain accumulated earnings of the Corporation in the form of capital gains rather than as taxable dividends. The investment counselor contacted The Lincoln National Life Insurance Company of Fort Wayne, Indiana, and * * * on November 20, 1946, The Lincoln National Life Insurance Company's finance committee approved the proposed issue and the purchase of one-half [of the preferred stock to be issued]. The Northwestern Mutual Life Insurance Company was contacted for the purpose of participating in the purchase of the preferred stock. [A]bout two weeks before December 30, 1946, its committee on investments approved the purchase of 4,000 shares of the preferred stock to be issued * * *.

The preferred stock contained the following provisions among others: the holders were entitled to cumulative cash dividends * * * payable quarterly * * *; the stock was subject to redemption on any quarterly dividend date * * * at par * * *; it was subject to mandatory retirement in amounts not exceeding 2,000 shares on May 1, 1948 and 1,000 on May 1 of each succeeding year * * * until fully retired on May 1, 1954 * * *. These provisions had been discussed with the Lincoln National Life Insurance Company and some of them * * * were included * * * to satisfy the investment requirements of the two insurance companies.

No agreement of purchase and sale was entered into between any of the petitioners and either of the two insurance companies prior to the "Purchase Agreement" executed on December 30, 1946, but the stockholders and directors of the Corporation took the necessary actions to put the negotiated plan into effect, as hereinabove set out, only after the insurance companies certified their willingness to participate in the purchase, if, as, and when the preferred stock was issued on the terms and conditions prescribed by them * * *.

In reporting this sale of the preferred stock in their 1946 tax returns, each of the stockholders reported his proportion of the proceeds from the sale as a net long-term capital gain * * *.

The Respondent ruled that the preferred stock constituted a dividend taxable as ordinary income * * *.

Before considering the ruling of the Tax Court it is well to briefly review some of the Supreme Court decisions involving the taxability of stock dividends * * *. In Towne v. Eisner, 245 U.S. 418, and Eisner v. Macomber, 252 U.S. 189, the Court held that a stock dividend of common stock to the holders of the common stock was not income to the stockholder taxable by Congress under the Sixteenth Amendment, in that it did not alter the preexisting proportional interest of any stockholder or increase the intrinsic value of his holding or of the aggregate holdings of the other stockholders as they stood before * * *. In Koshland v. Helvering, 298 U.S. 441, the Court held that a stock dividend of common stock to the holders of preferred stock was taxable income because it gave the preferred stockholder an interest different from that which his former stockholdings represented * * *. In Helvering v. Sprouse, 318 U.S. 604, and in Strassburger v. Commissioner of Internal Revenue, 318 U.S. 604, the Court restated the rule that in order to render a stock dividend taxable as income, there must be a change brought about by the issue of shares as a dividend whereby the proportional interest of the stockholder after the distribution was essentially different from his former interest. The rule was applied to the facts in the Strassburger case where preferred stock was created and distributed as a stock dividend to a stockholder who owned the entire outstanding common stock, the Court holding that the preferred stock dividend did not constitute taxable income.

The Commissioner supported his assessment on the ground that although the preferred stock was issued as a non-taxable dividend, a concerted plan to sell the dividend shares was formulated prior to the distribution of such shares, which, coupled with actual sale immediately after receipt and the payment of the proceeds of sale direct to the stockholders constituted a taxable dividend to the extent of available earnings. He also took the position that the plan and the immediate sale resulted in a change in the proportional interest of the stockholders which was sufficient to exclude it from the rulings in the Supreme Court cases above referred to.

* * *

The Tax Court held that the issue of whether the stock dividend constituted income to the stockholders should be determined from a consideration of all the facts and circumstances surrounding the issuance of the dividend * * *; that each case involving a stock dividend must be decided upon its own facts and circumstances * * *; that * * * considering the real substance of the transaction * * * the stock dividend was not in good faith for any bona fide corporate business purpose, and that the attending circumstances * * * made it the equivalent of a cash dividend distribution out of available earnings, thus constituting ordinary taxable income in the amount of the value of the preferred shares received. The court also said that the real purpose of the issuance of the preferred shares was concurrently to place them in the hands of others not then stockholders of the Corporation, thereby substantially altering the common stockholders' preexisting proportional interests in the Corporation's net assets * * *.

In our opinion, the declaration and distribution of the preferred stock dividend, considered by itself, falls clearly within the principles established in Towne v. Eisner and Eisner v. Macomber and is controlled by the ruling in the Strassburger case. Accordingly, as a preliminary matter, we do not agree with the Tax Court's statement that the stock dividend is taxable because as a result of the dividend and immediate sale thereafter it substantially altered the common stockholders' preexisting proportional interests in the Corporation's net assets. The sale to the insurance companies of course resulted in such a change, but the legal effect of the dividend with respect to rights in the corporate assets is determined at the time of its distribution, not by what the stockholders do with it after its receipt * * *. It seems clear to us that if taxability exists, it is not because of the change in pre-existing proportional interests caused by a later sale, but by reason of the other ground relied upon by the Tax Court, namely, that viewed in all its aspects it was a distribution of cash rather than a distribution of stock * * *.

The general principle is well settled that a taxpayer has the legal right to decrease the amount of what otherwise would be his taxes, or altogether avoid them, by means which the law permits; and that the taxpayer's motive to avoid taxation will not establish liability if the transaction does not do so without it.

It is equally well settled that this principle does not prevent the Government from going behind the form which the transaction takes and ascertaining the reality and genuineness of the component parts of the transaction in order to determine whether the transaction is really what it purports to be or is merely a formality without substance which for tax purposes can and should be disregarded * * *.

The question accordingly presented is not whether the overall transaction, admittedly carried out for the purpose of avoiding taxes, actually avoided taxes which would have been incurred if the transaction had taken a different form, but whether the stock dividend was a stock dividend in substance as well as in form.

No question is raised about the legality of the declaration of the dividend. Respondent does not contend that proper corporate procedure was not used in creating the preferred stock and in distributing it to the stockholders in the form of a dividend. If the transaction had stopped there we think it is clear that the dividend would not have been taxable in the hands of the stockholders. Whether the declaration of the dividend was in furtherance of any corporate business purpose or was the result of correct judgment and proper business policy on the part of the management, we believe is immaterial [to] this phase of the case. The Supreme Court cases in no way suggest that the taxability of a stock dividend depends on the purpose of its issuance or the good or bad judgment of the directors in capitalizing earnings instead of distributing them. The decisions are based squarely upon the proportional interest doctrine * * *.

Nor is there any question about the genuineness and unconditional character of the sale of the preferred stock by the stockholders who received it to the two insurance companies. The facts show conclusively that title passed irrevocably from the stockholders to the insurance companies, and that the sellers received in cash without restriction a full consideration, the adequacy of which respondent does not question. But respondent contends that the sale of the stock following immediately upon its receipt resulted in the stockholder acquiring cash instead of stock, thus making it a taxable dividend * * *. There are two answers to this contention.

A non-taxable stock dividend does not become a taxable cash dividend upon its sale by the recipient. On the contrary, it is a sale of a capital asset * * *.

* * *

The other answer to the contention is that although the stockholder acquired money in the final analysis, he did not receive either money or property from the Corporation. [T]he money he received was received from the insurance companies. It was not a "distribution" by the corporation declaring the dividend * * *.

We come then to what in our opinion is the dominant and decisive issue in the case, namely, whether the stock dividend, which, by reason of its redemption feature, enabled the Corporation to ultimately distribute its earnings to its stockholders on a taxable basis materially lower than would have been the case by declaring and paying the usual cash dividend, was a bona fide one, in substance as well as in form * * *.

In our opinion, the stock dividend in this case * * * was an issue of stock in substance as well as in form. According to its terms, and in the absence of a finding that it was immediately or shortly thereafter redeemed at a premium, we assume that a large portion of it has remained outstanding over a period of years with some of it still unredeemed after nearly seven years. It has been in the hands of the investing public, free of any control by the Corporation or its owners, whose enforceable rights with respect to operations of the corporation would not be waived or neglected. Substantial sums have been paid in dividends. The insurance companies bought it in the regular course of their business and have held it as approved investments. For the court to now tell them that they have been holding a sham issue of stock would be most startling and disturbing news.

It also seems clear that the insurance companies were not purchasers in form only without acquiring any real interest in the property conveyed. The character of the transaction as a bona fide investment on the part of the insurance companies is not challenged by the respondent. The element of a formal conduit without any business interest is entirely lacking.

* * *

Each case necessarily depends upon its own facts. The facts in this case show tax avoidance, and it is so conceded by petitioner. But they also show a series of legal transactions, no one of which is fictitious or so lacking in substance as to be anything different from what it purports to be. Unless we are to adopt the broad policy of holding taxable any series of transactions, the purpose and result of which is the avoidance of taxes which would otherwise accrue if handled in a different way, regardless of the legality and realities of the component parts, the tax assessed by the Commissioner was successfully avoided in the present case. We do not construe the controlling decisions as having adopted that view.

In deciding this case it must be kept in mind that it does not involve a ruling that the profit derived from the sale of the stock dividend is or is not taxable income. Such profit is conceded to be taxable. The issue is whether it is taxable as income from a cash dividend or as income resulting from a long-term capital gain * * *. Congress has adopted the policy of taxing long-term capital gains differently from ordinary income. [I]t has specifically excluded certain transactions with respect to stock dividends from the classification of a capital gain. The present transaction is not within the exclusion. If the profit from a transaction like the one here involved is to be taxed at the same rate as ordinary income, it should be done by appropriate legislation, not court decision.

The judgment is reversed * * *.

NOTES

1. *Impact of I.R.C. § 305 on Chamberlin and Koshland.* What impact does I.R.C. § 305 have on a distribution of preferred stock with respect to common stock (the fact pattern in Chamberlin)? See I.R.C. § 305(a). What impact does I.R.C. § 305 have on a distribution of common stock with respect to preferred (the fact pattern in Koshland that was noted in the Chamberlin opinion)? See I.R.C. § 305(b)(4); Treas. Reg. § 1.305–5(a). Can the different treatment of these two transactions be reconciled? Can the tax consequences of these transactions be reconciled with the tax consequences of the transaction described in I.R.C. § 305(b)(3)? See I.R.C. § 305(b)(3); Treas. Reg. § 1.305–4.

2. *Distribution of convertible preferred stock.* I.R.C. § 305(b)(5) addresses the distribution of a type of preferred stock that allows the recipients to exchange the preferred stock for a specified amount of common stock within a designated time period. If all the recipients exchange this preferred stock for common stock, the distribution has the same effect as a tax-free common stock dividend. In contrast, if only some of this preferred stock is converted into common, tax-free treatment is not merited because the shareholders who convert will increase their proportional interest in the assets and earnings of the corporation, while those who do not convert will retain the preferred stock. See I.R.C. §§ 305(b)(2), (3). The statute suggests that convertible preferred stock may be excluded from income only if the taxpayer establishes that the distribution will not have the result described in I.R.C. § 305(b)(2). See I.R.C. § 305(b)(5). The regulations lighten this burden of proving a negative, however, by granting tax-free treatment if no basis exists for predicting when and how much of the preferred stock will be converted to common stock. See Treas. Reg. § 1.305–6(a), (b) Example 1 (Section 301 does not apply to a distribution of preferred stock that is convertible to common for a period of twenty years where dividend rates were "normal").

3. *Impact of preferred stock dividend on earnings & profits.* The Chamberlin court suggests that the preferred stock dividend was motivated at least in part by the corporation's fear of being subjected to the accumulated earnings tax. The accumulated earnings tax is normally imposed when a corporation accumulates earnings & profits in excess of reasonable business needs. See I.R.C. §§ 531–37; pp. 66–78. Does the issuance of a preferred stock dividend reduce the earnings & profits of the issuing corporation? See I.R.C. §§ 305(a), 312(d); Treas. Reg. § 1.312–1(d).

4. *Legislative response to Chamberlin—I.R.C. § 306.* I.R.C. § 306 was enacted shortly after the Chamberlin decision. The provision endeavors to bar a preferred stock dividend from enabling shareholders to convert potential dividend income to capital gains without surrendering any proportional interest in the earnings or assets of the corporation. Even after the enactment of § 306, a preferred stock dividend still may be excluded from the recipient's gross income. See I.R.C. § 305(a). The preferred stock, however, is tainted and labeled "section 306 stock." See I.R.C. § 306(c). The taint has no adverse effect until a disposition of the stock occurs. When section 306 stock is sold or redeemed, at least a part of the consideration received is normally taxed as dividend income. In addition, the basis in the section 306 stock normally cannot be applied against the consideration received when computing taxable income. Now that dividends are taxed at capital gains rates, the characterization aspect of section 306 will not have significant implications unless the shareholder disposing of the section 306 stock has capital losses from other transactions. However, section 306 can still have significant implications when quantifying the amount of income that results from a disposition. The Senate Finance Committee Report that follows elaborates on the provision.

Section 306. Dispositions of Certain Stock

S.Rep. No. 1622, 83d Congress, 2d Sess. (1954).

Section 306 of your committee's bill represents an * * * approach to the problem of the so-called preferred stock bail-out * * *. Under your committee's approach, * * * the original recipient of the dividend stock is, in general, taxed on its disposition as if there had been a cash, rather than a stock, distribution to him in the first instance.

Your committee introduces a new term into the tax law, "section 306 stock." In general, section 306 stock is preferred stock issued as a stock dividend, whether in connection with a corporate reorganization or otherwise, at a time when the issuing corporation has earnings and profits.

Subsection (a) of section 306 prescribes the general rules as to the tax treatment of the disposition or redemption of section 306 stock. Paragraph (1) relates to dispositions of such stock other than by redemption. The term disposition includes sales * * *. If the section 306 stock is sold the amount realized is treated as gain from the sale of property which is not a capital asset to the extent of the stock's ratable share of earnings and profits of the issuing corporation at the time of its distribution. Thus, assume that a shareholder owns 1,000 shares of the common stock of a corporation and that they are the only shares of its stock outstanding. Assume also that the shareholder acquires 1,000 shares of preferred stock with a fair market value for each share of $100 issued to him as a dividend on his common stock at a time when the corporation has $100,000 in accumulated earnings. There is no tax to the shareholder at the time of receipt of the stock but it is characterized as section 306 stock. If it is sold for $100,000 the shareholder will be taxed on the entire sale proceeds at the rates applicable to ordinary income.

The determination of the section 306 stock's ratable share of earnings at the time of its distribution is to be made in accordance with its fair market value at such time. It should also be noted that it would be immaterial that $100,000 were distributed to the stockholder as a dividend on his common stock subsequent to the distribution of the stock dividend. The stock dividend is nevertheless section 306 stock because of the corporate earnings in existence at the time of its distribution.

Subparagraph (B) of paragraph (1) provides that if the amount received from the sale of section 306 stock exceeds the amount treated as ordinary income, such excess, shall, to the extent of gain, be accorded capital-gain treatment. Thus, if in the preceding example the stock had been sold for $110,000 (instead of $100,000) the $10,000 would be taxed at the rates applicable to capital gain. Subparagraph (C) of paragraph (1) provides that in no event is any loss to be allowed with respect to the sale of section 306 stock.

Paragraph (2) of subsection (a) provides that if the section 306 stock is redeemed, the amount realized is to be treated as a distribution of property to which section 301 applies. Thus, if the section 306 stock was distributed at a time when there was an amount of corporate earnings attributable to it equal to its full fair market value at that time, but if there are no corporate earnings, accumulated or current, at the time of redemption, the amount received on redemption of section 306 stock would be treated under section 301 as a return of capital. No loss would be allowed in such a case under section 301.

It should be noted that where section 306 stock is redeemed the rules of section 302(a) and (b), relating to cases where amounts received in redemption of stock will be taxed at capital gain rates, are not applicable. Section 306 operates independently of section 302 and contains its own rules concerning instances where your committee does not consider it appropriate to tax proceeds received with respect to section 306 stock at the rates applicable to ordinary income.

Subsection (b) of section 306 sets forth the cases excepted from your committee's general treatment of section 306 stock. Paragraph (1)(A) provides that if a shareholder sells his entire stock interest in the corporation (to a person other than one through whom the ownership of the stock would, under section 318, be attributed back to him) the sale shall be treated as a sale or exchange of property; that is, a capital asset, or noncapital asset, depending on the manner in which it is held (as inventory or otherwise) by the seller.

Subparagraph (B) provides that if the complete termination is effected by means of the redemption route, rather than sale, then the redemption is treated as one to which section 302(b)(3) applies. Thus, the rules of constructive ownership of stock among members of a family are waived to the same extent provided in section 302(c)(2). Accordingly, if a shareholder redeems all his section 306 stock, together with the stock with respect to which it was distributed, the tax consequences of such a redemption (or subsequent reacquisition of an interest) are to be governed by section 302(b)(3), as supplemented by section 302(c)(2).

Paragraph (2) of subsection (b) excepts from the general rules of this section, redemptions of section 306 stock pursuant to a partial or complete liquidation * * *. [Editor's note: The exception for partial liquidations now appears in I.R.C. § 306(b)(1)(B).] In the case of a partial liquidation your committee contemplates a contraction of the corporate business so that it is immaterial that the distribution in partial liquidation is with respect to section 306 stock. A bona fide contraction of the corporate business is not considered a means of distributing corporate earnings to shareholders at capital gains rates.

Paragraph (3) of subsection (b) excepts from the general rules of this section, transactions with respect to which gain or loss is not recognized. In addition to the receipt of stock in exchange for section 306 stock pursuant to a reorganization, your committee intends to include exchanges to which section 1036 * * * applies. However, in the case of a reorganization, unless the stock received in exchange for the section 306 stock is common stock, it will also be characterized as section 306 stock by reason of section 306(c)(1)(B). This last provision will also characterize as section 306 stock, stock received in an exchange to which section 1036 relating to certain exchanges of stock for stock applies where the exchanged stock was section 306 stock.

Paragraph (4) of subsection (b) excepts from the general rule of subsection (a) those transactions not in avoidance of this section where it is established to the satisfaction of the Secretary that the transaction was not in pursuance of a plan having as one of its principal purposes the avoidance of Federal income tax. Subparagraph (A) of this paragraph applies to cases where the distribution itself, coupled with the disposition or redemption was not in pursuance of such a plan. This subparagraph is intended to apply to the case of dividends and isolated dispositions of section 306 stock by minority shareholders who do not in the aggregate have control of the distributing corporation. In such a case it would seem to your committee to be inappropriate to impute to such shareholders an intention to remove corporate earnings at the tax rates applicable only to capital gains.

Subparagraph (B) of subsection (b)(4) applies to a case where the shareholder has made a prior or simultaneous disposition (or redemption) of the underlying stock with respect to which the section 306 stock was issued. Thus if a shareholder received a distribution of 100 shares of section 306 stock on his holdings of 100 shares of voting common stock in a corporation and sells his voting common stock before he disposes of his section 306 stock, the subsequent disposition of his section 306 stock would not ordinarily be considered a tax avoidance disposition since he has previously parted with the stock which allows him to participate in the ownership of the business.

Section 306(c) sets forth the definition of section 306 stock. Paragraph (1)(A) of subsection (c) provides that section 306 stock is any stock (other than common stock issued with respect to common stock) distributed to the seller thereof, if by reason of section 305(a) any part of such distribution was not includible in the gross income of the shareholder. Thus, a stock dividend (other than a dividend in common stock issued with respect to common stock) is considered section 306 stock.

Subparagraph (B) of paragraph (1) of subsection (c) provides that stock received in connection with a plan of reorganization within the meaning of section 368(a), or in a disposition or exchange to which section 355 applies, is section 306 stock, if the effect of the transaction was substantially the same as the receipt of a stock dividend. The subparagraph also makes it clear that section 306 stock exchanged for section 306 stock shall retain its characteristics. This subparagraph provides that common stock received as a result of a corporate reorganization or separation shall not be considered section 306 stock in any event. Thus, the shareholder is always permitted an opportunity to downgrade preferred stock characterized as section 306 stock in his hands by causing a recapitalization and exchange of such stock for common stock.

Subparagraph (C) provides that section 306 stock includes stock the basis of which in the hands of the shareholder selling or otherwise disposing of such stock is determined by reference to the basis of section 306 stock. Subparagraph (C), however, is limited to cases other than those to which subparagraph (B) is applicable, that is, the reorganization type of case which would otherwise be within this subparagraph. Under this subparagraph common stock could be section 306 stock. Thus, if a person owning section 306 stock transfers it to a corporation controlled by him in exchange for common stock, the common stock received would be section 306 stock in his hands and subject to the rules of subsection (a) on its disposition. Subparagraph (C) also would remove from the category of section 306 stock, stock owned by a decedent at death since such stock takes a new basis under section 1014.

Paragraph (2) of subsection (c) excepts from the definition of section 306 stock any stock no part of the distribution of which would have been a dividend at the time of distribution if money had been distributed in lieu of the stock. Thus, preferred stock received at the time of original incorporation would not be section 306 stock. Also, stock issued at the time an existing corporation had no earnings and profits would not be section 306 stock.

* * *

NOTE

Impact of I.R.C. § 306 on Chamberlin. How does I.R.C. § 306 change the tax consequences of the Chamberlin fact pattern?

> *Problem 16–2 (Sale/redemption of § 306 stock):* Chuck and Mickie each own half the common stock of Diamond, Inc. At the end of Year 3, Diamond, Inc. distributes 200 shares of preferred stock with a market value of $200,000 pro rata with respect to its common stock. At the time of the distribution, Diamond, Inc. had earnings & profits of $300,000. The 100 shares of preferred stock distributed to Chuck had a value of $100,000 and an allocated basis of $70,000. See I.R.C. § 307(a); Treas. Reg. § 1.307–1. What are the tax consequences to Chuck if, at the end of Year 5, when Diamond, Inc. has earnings & profits of $500,000,
>
> (a) Chuck sells the preferred stock for $100,000? See I.R.C. § 306(a)(1); Treas. Reg. § 1.306–1(b). What if Chuck sells the preferred stock for $400,000?
>
> (b) Diamond, Inc. redeems Chuck's preferred shares for $400,000? See I.R.C. § 306(a)(2); Treas. Reg. §§ 1.306–1(c), 1.312–1(e).

What happens to the basis in Chuck's preferred stock in each case? See Treas. Reg. § 1.306–1(b).

What impact does each transaction have on the earnings & profits of Diamond, Inc.? See I.R.C. §§ 306(a), 312(a); Treas. Reg. § 1.306–1(b)(1).

3.   RECAPITALIZATION

I.R.C. § 368(a)(1)(E)

Treas. Reg. § 1.368–2(e)

Bazley v. Commissioner

Supreme Court of the United States, 1947.
331 U.S. 737, 67 S.Ct. 1489.

■ MR. JUSTICE FRANKFURTER delivered the opinion of the Court.

[T]he Commissioner of Internal Revenue assessed an income tax deficiency against the taxpayer for the year 1939. Its validity depends on the legal significance of the recapitalization in that year of a family corporation in which the taxpayer [owned 798] and his wife owned [201] * * * of the Company's one thousand shares. These had a par value of $100. Under the plan of reorganization the taxpayer, his wife, and the holder of the additional share were to turn in their old shares and receive in exchange for each old share five new shares [with] a stated value of $60, and new debenture bonds, having a total face value of $400,000, payable in ten years but callable at any time. Accordingly, the taxpayer received 3,990 shares of the new stock for the 798 shares of his old holding and debentures in the amount of $319,200. At the time of these transactions the earned surplus of the corporation was $855,783.82.

The Commissioner charged to the taxpayer as income the full value of the debentures. The Tax Court affirmed the Commissioner's determination, against the taxpayer's contention that as a "recapitalization" the transaction was a tax-free "reorganization" and that the debentures were "securities in a corporation a party to a reorganization," "exchanged solely for stock or securities in such corporation" "in pursuance of the plan of reorganization," and as such no gain is recognized for income tax purposes. The Tax Court found that the recapitalization had "no legitimate corporate business purpose" and was therefore not a "reorganization" within the statute. The distribution of debentures, it concluded, was a disguised dividend * * *. The Circuit Court of Appeals for the Third Circuit, sitting en banc, affirmed, two judges dissenting.

While § 112(g) [the predecessor to I.R.C. § 368(a)(1)] informs us that "reorganization" means, among other things, "a recapitalization," it does not inform us what "recapitalization" means. "Recapitalization" in connection with the income tax has been part of the revenue laws since 1921. Congress has never defined it and the Treasury Regulations shed only limited light. One thing is certain. Congress did not incorporate some technical concept, whether that of accountants or of other specialists, into § 112(g), assuming that there is agreement among specialists as to the meaning of recapitalization. And so, recapitalization as used in § 112(g) must draw its meaning from its function in that section. It is one of the forms of reorganization which obtains the privileges afforded by § 112(g). Therefore, "recapitalization" must be construed with reference to the presuppositions and purpose of § 112(g). It was not the purpose of the reorganization provision to exempt from payment of a tax what as a practical matter is realized gain. Normally, a distribution by a corporation, whatever form it takes, is a definite and rather unambiguous event. It furnishes the proper occasion for the determination and taxation of gain. But there are circumstances where a formal distribution, directly or through exchange of securities, represents merely a new form of the previous participation in an enterprise, involving no change of substance in the rights and relations of the interested parties one to another or to the corporate assets. As to these, Congress has said that they are not to be deemed significant occasions for determining taxable gain.

These considerations underlie § 112(g) and they should dominate the scope to be given to the various sections, all of which converge toward a common purpose. Application of the language of such a revenue provision is not an exercise in framing abstract definitions. In a series of cases this Court has withheld the benefits of the reorganization provision in situations which might have satisfied provisions of the section treated as inert language, because they were not reorganizations of the kind with which § 112, in its purpose and particulars, concerns itself.

Congress has not attempted a definition of what is recapitalization and we shall follow its example. The search for relevant meaning is often satisfied not by a futile attempt at abstract definition but by pricking a line through concrete applications. Meaning frequently is built up by assured recognition of what does not come within a concept the content of which is in controversy. Since a recapitalization within the scope of § 112 is an aspect of reorganization, nothing can be a recapitalization for this purpose unless it partakes of those characteristics of a reorganization which underlie the purpose of Congress in postponing the tax liability.

No doubt there was a recapitalization of the Bazley corporation in the sense that the symbols that represented its capital were changed, so that the fiscal basis of its operations would appear very differently on its books. But the form of a transaction as reflected by correct corporate accounting opens questions as to the proper application of a taxing statute; it does not close them. Corporate accounting may represent that correspondence between change in the form of capital structure and essential identity in fact which is of the essence of a transaction relieved from taxation as a reorganization. What is controlling is that a new arrangement intrinsically partake of the elements of reorganization which underlie the Congressional exemption and not merely give the appearance of it to accomplish a distribution of earnings. In the case of a corporation which has undistributed earnings, the creation of new corporate obligations which are transferred to stockholders in relation to their former holdings, so as to produce, for all practical purposes, the same result as a distribution of cash earnings of equivalent value, cannot obtain tax immunity because cast in the form of a recapitalization-reorganization. The governing legal rule can hardly be stated more narrowly. To attempt to do so would only challenge astuteness in evading it. And so it is hard to escape the conclusion that whether in a particular case a paper recapitalization is no more than an admissible attempt to avoid the consequences of an outright distribution of earnings turns on details of corporate affairs, judgment on which must be left to the Tax Court.

What have we here? No doubt, if the Bazley corporation had issued the debentures to Bazley and his wife without any recapitalization, it would have made a taxable distribution. Instead, these debentures were issued as part of a family arrangement, the only additional ingredient being an unrelated modification of the capital account. The debentures were found to be worth at least their principal amount, and they were virtually cash because they were callable at the will of the corporation which in this case was the will of the taxpayer. One does not have to pursue the motives behind actions, even in the more ascertainable forms of purpose, to find, as did the Tax Court, that the whole arrangement took this form instead of an outright distribution of cash or debentures, because the latter would undoubtedly have been taxable income whereas what was done could, with a show of reason, claim the shelter of the immunity of a recapitalization-reorganization.

The Commissioner, the Tax Court and the Circuit Court of Appeals agree that nothing was accomplished that would not have been accomplished by an outright debenture dividend. And since we find no misconception of law on the part of the Tax Court and the Circuit Court of Appeals, whatever may have been their choice of phrasing, their application of the law to the facts of this case must stand. A "reorganization" which is merely a vehicle, however elaborate or elegant, for conveying earnings from accumulations to the stockholders is not a reorganization under § 112. This disposes of the case as a matter of law, since the facts as found by the Tax Court bring them within it * * *.

■ Mr. Justice Douglas and Mr. Justice Burton dissent * * * for the reasons stated in the joint dissent of Judges Maris and Goodrich in the court below.

[Editor's note: The appeals court dissenting opinion follows.]

The critical question in this case is, we think, one of law and one upon which this Court has an obligation to exercise its own judgment when the decision of the Tax Court is brought here for review. That question is whether a corporate reorganization, in order to be tax free, must be one conducted for a "corporate business purpose" of the corporation as distinguished from serving a proper business interest of the shareholders.

That this question is squarely presented there can be no doubt. The Tax Court's findings of fact with regard to the reasons for the transaction here in question are as follows: "Reasons for adopting the transaction hereinafter described, involving the issuance of additional common stock and of debenture bonds, were that the original shareholders, by obtaining debenture bonds for their stockholdings, would receive a security which was much less fluctuating and more readily marketable, particularly in case it was necessary for a deceased shareholder's estate to liquidate his investment in the corporation in order to meet inheritance taxes or for other purposes, and that if it became necessary to sell some portion of their investment in the corporation the debenture bonds could be sold without reducing the Bazley family stock control of the corporation; that the contemplated entry into the hazardous road building business made it desirable to put the original stockholders in possession of bonds which would place them in a position of sharing alike with creditors to the extent of the debentures instead of ranking after creditors if the business did not succeed * * *."

An additional finding of fact is made as to the relation of the purpose and the corporate business. It reads as follows: "There was no legitimate purpose of the corporate business of J. Robert Bazley, Inc., in the issuance and distribution to the stockholders of $400,000 in debenture bonds."

The significance of these findings of fact is pointed up by the discussion of the Tax Court when it says: "Such objectives as to create a security more desirable for the stockholders as being less fluctuating in value, more regular and certain in its income, easier to market for inheritance tax payments, and furnishing greater safety against claims of corporate creditors are easily understandable from the standpoint of the stockholders. They furnish persuasive reasons why the stockholders wanted to change the form of their investment. But, as we have said, a desire to encompass such an exchange without occasioning the tax consequences usually attendant upon those transactions would not supply the necessary purpose as a business or corporate object."

We accept the Tax Court's findings of fact. We also, now that we understand we are so to do, accept its conclusion when it applies its facts to a correct rule of law regardless of whether we, in a particular instance, would have reached the same conclusion or not. But if we believe the legal criterion used by the Tax Court is incorrect, it is our duty so to say and to send the case back for appropriate proceedings under the application of what we deem the correct criterion.

We think that the criterion here making a distinction between "corporate" and "shareholder" purpose is incorrect. The foundation for it is supposed to be Gregory v. Helvering [see p. 692]. That case involved the formation of a dummy corporation which did no business other than to participate in a transfer which the taxpayer was seeking to effect without tax liability. What we had was a sale masquerading as a reorganization. The court struck through the sham.

To expand that decision into a rule of law such as is now contended for is to push it beyond anything which we think the court could have had in mind. Nor do we think the expansion is one which a reasonable growth beyond Gregory v. Helvering would call for. We have long since passed the place in our thinking where we view the corporation as "an artificial being, invisible, intangible and existing only in contemplation of law." We think of it as a device that shareholders use to carry on their business as a group. A corporation does not have purposes apart from its shareholders. Shareholders, of course, may have conflicting interests among themselves with regard to the conduct of their common enterprise. They may fight with each other, perhaps, in order to elect A instead of B to the directorship of their company. And, of course, aside from their interest in the common enterprise, called their corporation, they have interests as varied as the hopes and desires of human beings. But when we talk about the interest of shareholders in connection with the business enterprise and have a finding of fact that such and such a thing was done and that it was to the shareholders' business advantage, speaking of them as a group, we do not find substance in a distinction between the business advantages of the shareholders with respect to the corporation or the business advantages of the corporation itself.

* * *

We think the distinction attempted coming, as it does, quite a number of years after Gregory v. Helvering, is one not established by that decision, the statute, nor the regulations. If reorganization provisions contain too many avenues of escape for taxes which ought to be collected the Congress can close those avenues by appropriate legislation which can be so framed and defined as to leave the way clear to what it deems are business transactions in which no gain or loss should be recognized. We do not think it should be by judicial decision which establishes the exceedingly vague criterion as to whether a given transaction was to the interest of the shareholder as distinguished from the interest of the corporation in which he holds shares of stock.

* * *

NOTES

1. *Distribution of stock and debentures.* If the corporation in Bazley had simply distributed the new stock and the debentures without causing the shareholders to surrender their old shares, what would be the tax consequences to the shareholders under current law? See I.R.C. §§ 301, 305, 317(a).

2. *Treatment of securities in a reorganization.* The Bazley case was decided before the enactment of I.R.C. § 354(a)(2) and § 356. If the transaction in Bazley qualified as a reorganization and the debentures were treated as "securities", what would the tax consequences to the shareholders be under current law? See I.R.C. §§ 354(a)(2)(A), 356(a), (d). Do these consequences change if the debentures are not treated as securities?

3. *Nonqualified preferred stock in a recapitalization.* When "nonqualified preferred stock" is received in a transaction that qualifies as a reorganization, the nonqualified preferred stock is normally treated as boot. I.R.C.

§§ 354(a)(2)(C)(i), 356(e). An exception to boot treatment exists, however, for nonqualified preferred stock received in connection with the recapitalization of a "family-owned" corporation. I.R.C. § 354(a)(2)(C)(ii).

4. *Shareholder versus corporate purpose.* Whether a shareholder business purpose will satisfy the common law business purpose requirement for a reorganization remains ambiguous under current law. Compare Treas. Reg. §§ 1.368–1(b), (c) (mandating corporate purpose) with Lewis v. Commissioner, 176 F.2d 646 (1st Cir.1949) and Estate of Parshelsky v. Commissioner, 303 F.2d 14 (2d Cir.1962) (both cases accepting a shareholder purpose other than tax avoidance).

5. *Continuity of proprietary interest and continuity of business enterprise.* For a transaction to qualify as a reorganization, it is generally necessary to satisfy both statutory and common law requirements. See pp. 513–522. As indicated by Bazley, a recapitalization must satisfy the common law business purpose requirement to qualify as a reorganization. A recapitalization, however, is not subject to the continuity of proprietary interest requirement and the continuity of business enterprise requirement. See Treas. Reg. § 1.368–1(b).

Revenue Ruling 86–25

1986–1 Cum.Bull. 202.

ISSUE

Is the transaction described below a reorganization as defined in section 368(a)(1)(E) of the Internal Revenue Code or is it a distribution of property to which section 301 applies by reason of the application of section 305(b)(3)?

FACTS

X, a closely held domestic corporation, had 3,000 shares of $100 par value voting common stock ("old common") outstanding. For valid business reasons, a plan of reorganization was adopted pursuant to which X authorized the issuance of a new class A no par value voting common stock, a new class B no par value nonvoting common stock, and a new class C $100 par value nonvoting, nonparticipating, nonconvertible preferred stock. The only difference between the class A and class B common stock was the voting rights of the class A stock, and the only difference between the class A common stock and the old common stock was the par values * * *.

The plan of reorganization provided that each outstanding share of old common stock could be exchanged either for one share of class A common stock plus 99 shares of class B common stock, or for one share of class A common stock plus six shares of class C preferred stock. Pursuant to the plan of reorganization, one group of X shareholders surrendered 2,500 shares of X old common stock in exchange for 2,500 shares of class A common stock and 15,000 shares of class C preferred stock. A second group of shareholders surrendered 500 shares of old common stock in exchange for 500 shares of class A common stock and 49,500 shares of class B common stock. The value of the stock received by each shareholder of X was equal to the value of the stock surrendered by such shareholder in the exchange. The exchange of stock was an isolated transaction and not part of a plan to increase periodically the proportionate interest of any shareholder in the assets or earnings and profits of X.

LAW AND ANALYSIS

Section 368(a)(1)(E) of the code provides that the term "reorganization" includes a recapitalization * * *.

* * *

Section 305(a) of the Code contains the general rule that gross income does not include the amount of any distribution of the stock of a corporation made by such corporation to its shareholders with respect to its stock.

Section 305(b)(3) of the Code provides that section 305(a) shall not apply to a distribution by a corporation of its stock, and the distribution shall be treated as a distribution of property to which section 301 applies if the distribution * * * has the result of the receipt of preferred stock by some common shareholders and the receipt of common stock by other common shareholders.

Section 305(c) of the Code provides that a change in redemption price, a difference between redemption price and issue price, a redemption which is treated as a distribution to which section 301 applies, or any transaction (including a recapitalization) having a similar effect on the interest of any shareholder may be treated as a distribution with respect to any shareholder whose proportionate interest in the earnings and profits or assets of the corporation is increased by such change, difference, redemption, or similar transaction.

Section 1.305–7(c)(1) of the Income Tax Regulations provides that a recapitalization (whether or not an isolated transaction) will be deemed to result in a distribution to which section 305(c) of the Code applies if it is pursuant to a plan to periodically increase a shareholder's proportionate interest in the assets or earnings and profits of the corporation.

* * *

In the instant case, had X made an outright distribution of the new preferred stock and new class B common stock on the old common stock, the distribution would have been taxable as a distribution of property under section 301 of the Code by reason of the application of section 305(b)(3).

Nevertheless, a transaction that effects a reshuffling of a corporation's capital structure will be respected as a recapitalization exchange to which section 305(b)(3) of the Code does not apply so long as it has a bona fide business purpose and is an isolated transaction and not part of a plan to increase periodically the proportionate interest of any shareholder in the assets or earnings and profits of a corporation. Compare Bazley v. Commissioner, 331 U.S. 737 (1947), 1947–2 C.B. 79, (the exchange lacked a bona fide business purpose and was therefore not a reorganization) and section 1.301–1(1) of the regulations (a distribution occurring at the same time as a recapitalization is taxable as a dividend if, in substance, it is not part of the recapitalization).

HOLDING

Under the circumstances set forth above, the exchange of old voting common stock for either class A voting common stock plus class C nonvoting preferred stock or class A voting common stock plus class B nonvoting common stock, will qualify as a tax-free recapitalization under section 368(a)(1)(E) and 354(a) of the Code, and will not be treated as distributions of property to which section 301 applies by reason of the application of section 305(b)(3).

Revenue Ruling 83–119

1983–2 Cum.Bull. 57.

ISSUE

In a recapitalization where a corporation issues preferred stock that must be redeemed on the holder's death at a price in excess of one hundred and ten percent of the issue price, is the amount of the excess redemption premium treated, by reason of section 305(c) of the Internal Revenue Code, as a distribution with respect to preferred stock within the meaning of section 305(b)(4)?[6] If so, when is this distribution deemed to be received?

FACTS

A domestic corporation, X, had outstanding 100 shares of common stock. A owned 80 shares of the X common stock and B, A's child, owned the other 20 shares. A was actively engaged in X's business as its president, and B was a key employee. A retired from the business and resigned as a director, officer, and employee of X with no intention to take part in the future activities of X. Pursuant to a plan of recapitalization for the purpose of transferring control and ownership of the common stock to B in conjunction with A's retirement, a single class of nonvoting, dividend paying preferred stock was authorized. [O]n the death of a shareholder of the preferred stock, X is required to redeem the preferred stock from the shareholder's estate or beneficiaries at its par value of 1,000x dollars per share. On January 1, 1981, A had a life expectancy of 24 years determined by using the actuarial tables provided in section 1.72–9 of the regulations.

---

6. Editor's note. I.R.C. § 305(c) treats the recipients of certain preferred stock that may be redeemed at a future time for a price in excess of the issue price as constructively receiving additional distributions on preferred stock. These additional distributions are generally taxed as dividends to the recipients. I.R.C. §§ 305(b)(4), 301. Constructive distributions are deemed to occur, however, only to the extent that the difference between the redemption price and the issue price exceeds a "reasonable premium". See Treas. Reg. §§ 1.305–5(b), (d) Examples 4, 5, 7.

On January 1, 1981, A exchanged 80 shares of common stock for 80 shares of preferred stock. Following this exchange, A held all of the preferred stock, and B held all of the common stock that X then had outstanding.

On the date of the exchange the X common stock surrendered had a fair market value of 1,000x dollars per share, and the X preferred stock had a par value of 1,000x dollars per share. The one-for-one exchange ratio resulted because the par value of the preferred stock was presumed to represent its fair market value. However, the fair market value of the preferred stock was only 600x dollars per share. Thus, A surrendered X common stock with a fair market value of 80,000x dollars (80 × 1,000x dollars) in exchange for X preferred stock with a fair market value of 48,000x dollars (80 × 600x dollars).

The exchange of all of A's X common stock for X preferred stock is a recapitalization within the meaning of section 368(a)(1)(E) of the Code. Under section 354, no gain or loss will be recognized to A with regard to the receipt of the preferred stock to the extent of its 48,000x dollars fair market value. However, the 32,000x dollars excess in the fair market value of the X common stock surrendered by A as compared to the fair market value of the preferred stock A received will be treated as having been used to make a gift, pay compensation, satisfy obligations of any kind, or for whatever purposes the facts indicate.

LAW AND ANALYSIS

Section 305(a) of the Code provides generally that gross income does not include the amount of any distribution of the stock of a corporation made by such corporation to its shareholders with respect to its stock, except as otherwise provided in section 305(b) or (c).

Section 305(b)(4) of the Code provides, in part, that section 305(a) will not apply to a distribution by a corporation of its stock, and the distribution will be treated as a distribution of property to which section 301 applies, if the distribution is with respect to preferred stock.

Section 305(c) of the Code provides, in part, that the Secretary shall prescribe regulations under which a difference between issue price and redemption price will be treated as a distribution with respect to any shareholder whose proportionate interest in the earnings and profits or assets of the corporation is increased by the transaction. Section 1.305–7(a) of the regulations provides, under the authority of section 305(c), that an unreasonable redemption premium on preferred stock will be treated in accordance with section 1.305–5.

Section 1.305–5(b)(1) of the regulations provides that if a corporation issues preferred stock which may be redeemed after a specific period of time at a price higher than the issue price, the difference will be considered under the authority of section 305(c) of the Code to be a distribution of additional stock on preferred stock (section 305(b)(4)) constructively received by the shareholder over the period of time during which the preferred stock cannot be called for redemption. However, section 1.305–

5(b)(2) states that section 1.305–5(b)(1) will not apply to the extent that the difference between issue price and redemption price is a reasonable redemption premium * * *. Section 1.305–5(b)(2) also states that a redemption premium not in excess of 10 percent of the issue price on stock which is not redeemable for five years from the date of issuance shall be considered reasonable.

* * *

One element which is necessary to taxability under sections 305(b) and (c) is that there must be a distribution. Regarding this requirement, section 305(b) deals with actual distributions, and section 305(c) deems certain transactions which are not actual distributions to be distributions for section 305 purposes. Certain recapitalizations, even if isolated, are treated as distributions under [the] regulations. That is, an actual exchange of stock, even though clearly isolated, can be treated as a distribution if the exchange is pursuant to a larger plan to periodically increase a shareholder's proportionate interest * * *.

Although an exchange of stock in an isolated recapitalization would not in itself result in section 305(b) and (c) applicability, the terms of the preferred stock used in the exchange may result in this applicability. The difference between issue price and redemption price and the fact that the stock cannot be called for redemption for a specific period of time are the factors which combine to produce a deemed distribution. The imposition of tax results from the deemed distribution of additional preferred stock over the period the stock cannot be called or presented for redemption.

* * *

In the present situation, X common stock was exchanged by A for X preferred stock. Since the exchange was not part of a plan to periodically increase a shareholder's proportionate interest, the recapitalization itself did not result in a deemed distribution. However, the preferred stock will be redeemed by X on the death of a shareholder at a price of $1,000x dollars per share. Since the preferred stock had a fair market value of 600x dollars per share on the date of issuance, the preferred stock has a redemption premium of 400x dollars per share. There is no evidence that a call premium in excess of 60x dollars was reasonable. Because (1) the X stock is closely held, (2) no public offerings are planned, (3) the X stock is held by members of a family group within the meaning of section 318(a), and (4) the stock is not readily marketable, it is presumed that, at the time of the exchange, the shareholders intended that A would not transfer the preferred stock, and, therefore, redemption would occur upon A's death * * *. Because A has a life expectancy of 24 years, the 400x dollar redemption premium on the X preferred stock has substantially the same effect as a 400x dollar redemption premium payable at the end of a fixed term of 24 years.

HOLDING

The recapitalization in which X issues X preferred stock that must be redeemed on the shareholder's death at a price (1,000x dollars) which exceeds the issue price (600x dollars) results in the recipient, A, being deemed to receive a distribution of additional stock with respect to preferred stock, within the meaning of section 305(b)(4) of the Code, by reason of section 305(c), in the amount of 340x dollars (400x dollars less a deemed reasonable redemption premium of 60x dollars) on each share of preferred stock. This amount will be constructively received ratably (14.16x dollars per share per year) over A' s life expectancy of 24 years, and will be treated as a distribution to which section 301 applies. If A should die earlier, any part of the 340x dollars per share not yet constructively received by A would be deemed received at the time of A's death.

NOTES

1. *Time value of money and economic accrual principles.* I.R.C. § 305(c) authorizes the Treasury to promulgate regulations,

> (a) incorporating time value of money principles to gauge the reasonableness of a redemption premium (I.R.C. § 305(c)(1)), and

> (b) utilizing economic accrual principles to control the timing of the income resulting from an unreasonable redemption premium (I.R.C. § 305(c)(3)), rather than allowing that income to be reported in the straight-line manner illustrated in Revenue Ruling 83–119.

See Treas. Reg. § 1.305–5(b).

2. *I.R.C. § 1036.* I.R.C. § 1036 permits certain stock exchanges to qualify for nonrecognition treatment regardless of whether the transaction qualifies as a reorganization. Could I.R.C. § 1036 apply to the transaction in,

> (a) Bazley (p. 767)?

> (b) Rev. Rul. 86–25 (p. 772)?

> (c) Rev. Rul. 83–119 (p. 774)?

B.   CHANGE IN OPERATING ENTITY

In contrast to a change in capital structure, the assets of an existing corporate entity may be transferred to a new corporate entity owned by the same shareholders. Although the transfer of assets from one corporate entity to another normally entails at least one realization event, transactions of this type are often treated as reorganizations and thereby accorded nonrecognition treatment.

1.   F REORGANIZATION

I.R.C. § 368(a)(1)(F)

Revenue Ruling 57–276

1957–1 Cum.Bull. 126.

Advice has been requested regarding the requirements for filing Federal income tax returns in cases involving corporate reorganizations which qualify under section 368(a)(1)(F) of the Internal Revenue Code of 1954, and which also qualify as reorganizations under subparagraph (A), (C), or (D) of section 368(a)(1) of the Code.

The instant situation involves [an] existing corporation which reincorporated under the laws of a state other than that of original incorporation. [The] corporation organized a new corporation in the other state, and * * * then merged into its newly organized corporation under applicable merger statutes of the states concerned * * *. [The] merger qualified as a reorganization under both section 368(a)(1)(A) and section 368(a)(1)(F) of the Code.

Section 381(b) of the Code, relating to carryovers in certain corporate acquisitions, provides, in part, as follows:

> (b) OPERATING RULES.—Except in the case of an acquisition in connection with a reorganization described in subparagraph (F) of section 368(a)(1)—
>
> > (1) The taxable year of the distributor or transferor corporation shall end on the date of distribution or transfer.

Section 368(a)(1)(F) of the Code provides that the term "reorganization" means:

> (F) a mere change in identity, form or place of organization, however effected.
>
> * * *

Often a reorganization under section 368(a)(1)(F) of the Code will meet the requirements of subparagraphs (A),(C), or (D) of section 368(a)(1). It * * * was not the intention of Congress in enacting section 368(a)(1) of the Code to hold that just because a reorganization meets some other provision of section 368(a)(1) the provisions of subparagraph (F) of that section are not complied with even though the transaction also qualifies under subparagraph (F). Taking a contrary view * * * would, for all practical purposes, defeat the provisions of section 381(b) of the Code, since many section 368(a)(1)(F) reorganizations meet some other provisions of section 368(a)(1).

Accordingly, it is held that where a corporate reorganization comes within the provisions of section 368(a)(1)(F) of the Code, pursuant to the provisions of section 381(b) of the Code, that part of the taxable year before the reorganization and that part of the taxable year after the reorganization constitute a single taxable year of the acquiring corporation, notwithstanding the fact that such reorganization also qualifies under another provision of section 368(a)(1) of the Code. An income tax return for the full taxable year is required to be filed by the acquiring corporation. The transferor corporation is not required to file an income tax return for any portion of such year * * *.

Revenue Ruling 66–284

1966–2 Cum.Bull. 115.

In determining the applicability of Revenue Ruling 57–276 [p. 777], * * * advice has been requested whether the statutory merger described below qualifies as a reorganization within the meaning of section 368(a)(1)(F) of the Code.

For a valid business purpose, X Corporation, a publicly held State A Corporation, desired to reincorporate in State B. Accordingly, X organized a new X Corporation in State B and then merged itself into new X pursuant to the laws of States A and B.

Shareholders owning less than one percent of the outstanding shares of old X voted against the plan of merger. These dissenting shareholders elected to have their shares appraised under State law and they received payment representing the fair value of their shares. All other shareholders participated in the merger and received one share of new X stock for each share of old X stock surrendered.

Pursuant to the plan of merger, new X received the assets and assumed the liabilities of old X and continued the same business without interruption.

Section 368(a)(1)(F) of the Code provides, in part, that a mere change in place of organization is a reorganization. Revenue Ruling 58–422 states, in part, that section 368(a)(1)(F) of the Code is applicable to all reorganizations where there is no change in existing shareholders or in the assets of the corporation involved. A question has been raised whether the instant transaction, which qualifies as a reorganization described in section 368(a)(1)(A) of the Code, also qualifies as a reorganization described in section 368(a)(1)(F) of the Code in view of the action taken by the dissenting shareholders.

Where, as in the instant case, a plan of merger is designed only to effect a change in the corporation's place of organization, the Internal Revenue Service considers the failure of dissenting shareholders owning a total of less than 1 percent of the outstanding shares to participate in the plan of merger to be such a de minimis change in the corporation's shareholders and its assets as not to disqualify the merger as a reorganization under section 368(a)(1)(F) of the Code. Accordingly, pursuant to the provisions of section 381(b) of the Code, * * * that portion of the taxable year prior to the effective date of the reorganization and that portion of the taxable year after such effective date constitute a single taxable year for new X Corporation.

NOTES

1. *Alternatives to merger.* In each revenue ruling, a corporation's state of incorporation was changed by utilizing a merger. What other transaction(s) might have been utilized to change the state of incorporation? Describe the realization events that occur in each of these transactions.

2. *Impact on tax year.* As the revenue rulings indicate, the taxable year of a corporation does not end when it is transferred in an F reorganization. See I.R.C. § 381(b)(1). Can you think of any circumstances in which this result might be significant? See I.R.C. §§ 381(c)(1), (3), 172(b)(1),

1212(a)(1)(B). Why is an F reorganization treated differently from other reorganizations in this respect?

3. *Common law continuity requirements.* An F reorganization is not subject to the continuity of proprietary interest requirement or the continuity of business enterprise requirement. See Treas. Reg. § 1.368–1(b).

2. LIQUIDATION–REINCORPORATION

Berghash v. Commissioner

Tax Court of the United States, 1965.
43 T.C. 743, aff'd 361 F.2d 257 (2d Cir.1966).

■ WITHEY, JUDGE:

FINDINGS OF FACT

Petitioner Hyman H. * * * Berghash * * * [owned all 200 outstanding shares of common stock of] petitioner Delavan–Bailey Drug Co., Inc. (sometimes hereinafter referred to as the old corporation or the predecessor corporation), a dissolved corporation that originally was incorporated under the laws of the State of New York * * *. [D]elavan-Bailey Drug Co., Inc., owned and operated a retail drugstore located in Buffalo, N.Y.

* * *

[S]idney Lettman * * * was employed as a pharmacist by Delavan–Bailey on August 3, 1953. Early in 1954, Lettman became the manager of the Delavan–Bailey drugstore and was continuously employed as its manager until the discontinuance of business by that corporation in 1957.

* * *

In December 1956, Lettman told Berghash that he had made up his mind to strike out on his own * * * and * * * that unless [Berghash] would sell him 50 percent of Delavan–Bailey, he would leave its employ as manager.

Subsequently Berghash told Lettman that he was willing to sell him a 50–percent interest in the business of Delavan–Bailey. Thereafter the parties reached agreement as to the worth of the Delavan–Bailey assets and the amount Lettman would pay for a 50–percent interest.

* * *

The amount of investment by Lettman for a 50–percent interest in the business agreed upon between Berghash and Lettman was $25,000. This amount was the maximum amount Lettman felt he was able to raise from savings and borrowings.

* * *

After the parties had reached an agreement Berghash consulted his accountants and lawyer who formulated the method for carrying out the agreement and prepared a written contract * * *.

[Berghash and Lettman formed a New York corporation known as Dorn's Drugs, Inc. (sometimes hereinafter referred to as Dorn's or the survivor or successor corporation).]

On December 30, 1956, the stockholders of Delavan–Bailey adopted a plan of complete liquidation * * *.

On January 29, 1957, Berghash and Lettman entered into a written contract which provided that Delavan–Bailey should forthwith sell to Dorn's its inventory, goodwill, and fixtures. Dorn's was to pay $30,518.59 for the fixtures, $20,000 for the goodwill, and * * * the actual wholesale cost [of the] * * * inventory * * *. Lettman agreed to purchase 100 shares of the common stock of Dorn's and to pay to that corporation $25,000 therefor in cash. Delavan–Bailey agreed to purchase the remaining 100 shares of the common stock of Dorn's for $25,000, the payment to be made by deducting that amount from the price of the assets purchased by Dorn's. Dorn's was to execute a negotiable promissory note for the balance of the purchase price of the assets * * *. It was further agreed that Lettman should be employed by Dorn's as manager of its pharmacy at a stated salary and that Berghash should be employed to conduct its bookkeeping and other records at a stated salary. The agreement also provided that if Berghash should become dissatisfied for any reason with the services of Lettman as manager or with his continuance as a stockholder, officer, or director, Berghash would have the right to purchase the stock of Lettman in Dorn's for a price to be determined according to a formula specified in the contract.

Pursuant to the contract executed January 29, 1957, Lettman paid to Dorn's $25,000 cash on January 30, 1957, in payment for 100 shares of the common stock of Dorn's, which thereafter issued the shares to him.

The balance sheet of Delavan–Bailey Drug Co., Inc., as of January 29, 1957 * * *:

Assets

Cash on hand and on deposit	$ 58,831.89
Accounts receivable	3,149.22
Inventories	70,583.05
Supplies	463.48
Deposits	1,150.00
Fixtures (net after depreciation)	4,300.35
Auto (net after depreciation)	1,481.88
	$139,959.87

Liabilities and capital

Federal income taxes payable	$ 13,097.47
Franchise taxes payable	2,053.19
Capital stock	2,211.46
Earned surplus	122,597.75
	$139,959.87

On January 29, 1957, Delavan–Bailey sold its fixtures to Dorn's for $30,518.59, its goodwill for $20,000, and its inventory for $70,583.05.

Dorn's paid Delavan–Bailey * * * by delivering its negotiable promissory note dated January 29, 1957, payable to the old corporation in the principal amount of $96,101.64 and by thereafter issuing to Delavan–Bailey 100 shares of its common stock for $25,000 registered in the name of Berghash. The note issued by Dorn's was payable at the rate of $1,000 per month and bore interest at the rate of 6 percent on the unpaid balance * * *.

* * *

Between January 29, 1957, and May 5, 1957, Delavan–Bailey * * * distributed in liquidation to Berghash * * * the 100 shares of the common stock of the corporation known as Dorn's, its promissory note in the principal amount of $96,101.64, and cash in the total amount of $49,313.17. The adjusted basis of the petitioner in the capital stock of Delavan–Bailey on the date of its liquidation was $2,211.46. The accumulated earnings and profits of Delavan–Bailey at the date of its liquidation * * * were $122,050.11.

Delavan–Bailey was dissolved by the filing of a certificate of dissolution with the Secretary of State of New York on April 23, 1957.

[T]he corporate name of Dorn's was [subsequently] changed to Delavan–Bailey Drug Co., Inc., and this has since continued to be its corporate name.

* * *

On * * * [his] income tax return for 1957, * * * Berghash reported the gain on the liquidation of Delavan–Bailey as long-term capital gain with gross proceeds of $170,414.81, a cost basis of $2,211.46, and capital gain of $168,203.35.

In his notice of deficiency the respondent determined that as a result of the withdrawal of corporate assets from Delavan–Bailey, * * * Berghash realized dividend income in the amount of $122,050.11, plus long-term capital gain of $48,364.70.[7]

Delavan–Bailey Drug Co., Inc., on its income tax return for the taxable period beginning January 1, 1957, and ending February 28, 1957, reported a long-term capital gain on the sale of its fixtures and goodwill totaling $46,218.24 but claimed that such gain was not recognized because of the applicability of [former] section 337 of the Internal Revenue Code of 1954 * * *.[8]

In his deficiency notice the respondent determined that long-term capital gain in the amount of $46,218.24 must be included in petitioner's income * * *.

---

7. Editor's note. It does not appear that the Internal Revenue Service gave the taxpayer credit in the notice of deficiency for his $2,211.46 basis in the stock of Delavan–Bailey.

8. Editor's note. Prior to the repeal of the General Utilities rule in 1986 (see pp. 29–33), former I.R.C. § 337 provided that a corporation that sold its assets after adopting a plan of liquidation and liquidated within one year of adopting the plan generally did not recognize any gains or losses on the asset sale. Former I.R.C. § 337 was repealed in 1986, and the current version of I.R.C. § 337 bears no relationship to the former version.

OPINION

The respondent's principal contention is that the net result of the transaction in question is the distribution of dividend income by the Delavan–Bailey Drug Co., Inc., to the extent of its * * * earnings and profits in the amount of $122,050.11 as a dividend to Hyman Berghash. The respondent has determined that the balance of the distribution, less the basis of Berghash in the stock of Delavan–Bailey, constitutes long-term capital gain.

The respondent claims, in the alternative, that * * * the liquidating distributions made by Delavan–Bailey Drug Co., Inc., between January 29, 1957, and May 5, 1957, did not constitute a bona fide liquidation * * * within the meaning of [former] section 337 of the Code.

The petitioners contend that the series of steps heretofore described in our Findings of Fact amounted to a complete liquidation of the old corporation within the meaning of [former] section 337 of the 1954 Code and that the distributions by Delavan–Bailey on January 29, 1957, are taxable to Hyman and Rose Berghash as long-term capital gain under section * * * 331(a).

In support of his principal contention that the distribution to Hyman Berghash constituted a dividend distribution, the respondent argues (1) that the transaction was totally lacking in economic substance, and (2), in the alternative, that the consummation of the contract executed by Lettman and Berghash resulted in a nontaxable reorganization within the meaning of section 368(a)(1) of the Code.

* * *

We are convinced from the record that the transaction here under attack was bona fide in every respect, was motivated by business considerations, and that any purpose to minimize income tax liability, if present at all, played only a minor role * * *. Berghash valued Lettman's ability as manager of the Delavan–Bailey store and * * * agreed to sell him a one-half interest in that corporation in order to retain his services.

Lettman and Berghash agreed on the value of the Delavan–Bailey Drug Co., Inc., which on January 29, 1957, had * * * a balance sheet net worth of $124,809.21. Lettman informed Berghash that the very maximum he would be able to afford to invest in a drugstore was $25,000. With such a limited amount of capital, Lettman would have been able to purchase not more than one-fifth of the outstanding stock of the Delavan–Bailey Drug Co., Inc., from Hyman Berghash. Because of the disparity between Lettman's capital of $25,000 and the value of one-half the balance sheet net worth of Delavan–Bailey Drug Co., Inc., which was approximately $62,400, the parties decided to [incorporate] Dorn's Drugs, Inc. * * *.

* * *

Because of the fact that the initial discussions in 1956 related to the possibility of a purchase by Lettman of one-half the stock of Delavan–Bailey, the respondent claims that the real effect of the transaction in question was a sale by Berghash of one-half of his stock in the old corporation to Lettman, and that the transfer of assets by the predecessor corporation to Dorn's Drugs, Inc., should be disregarded as a sham sale. However, because of Lettman's limited capital, it would have been impossible, as pointed out above, for the parties to have carried out their purpose of investing in the store on a 50–50 basis through a sale by Berghash of half the outstanding stock of Delavan–Bailey. Although it may have been possible to have arranged the same result by causing the old corporation to redeem a portion of Berghash's stock, followed by the issuance of additional shares of Delavan–Bailey to Lettman, this is not what the parties actually did. So long as the transaction was genuine, petitioners had every right to select any method they preferred of achieving a desired result regardless of the tax consequences flowing therefrom * * *.

* * *

It accordingly appears to us that there were excellent business reasons underlying the arrangement agreed upon by Berghash and Lettman, and we are convinced by the record that each of the steps involved possessed economic substance and that no part of the transaction or the net result thereof properly can be viewed as a sham.

The respondent next contends that the transaction in question amounted to a nontaxable reorganization under section 368(a)(1) of the Code. If the transaction can be fitted into one of the definitions of a tax-deferred reorganization specified in section 368(a)(1), section 356(a)(2) could be brought into operation in the event the distributions to Hyman Berghash were found to be equivalent to a dividend.

The respondent first asserts that the arrangement in question amounted to a nontaxable reorganization under section 368(a)(1)(F) of the Code * * *.

Although the exact function and scope of the (F) reorganization in the scheme of tax-deferred transactions described in section 368(a)(1) have never been clearly defined, it is apparent from the language of subparagraph (F) that it is distinguishable from the five preceding types of reorganizations as encompassing only the simplest and least significant of corporate changes. The (F)-type reorganization presumes that the surviving corporation is the same corporation as the predecessor in every respect, except for minor or technical differences. For instance, the (F) reorganization typically has been understood to comprehend only such insignificant modifications as the reincorporation of the same corporate business with the same assets and the same stockholders surviving under a new charter either in the same or in a different State * * *.

The decisions involving subparagraph (F) or its counterpart in prior revenue acts consistently have imposed at least one major limitation on transactions that have been claimed to qualify thereunder: if a change in stock ownership or a shift in proprietary interest occurs, the transaction will fail to qualify as an (F) reorganization.

* * *

In the instant case there occurred a drastic shift in the proprietary interest of the owner of the predecessor corporation. Hyman Berghash, who had owned all of the stock * * * of the old Delavan–Bailey Drug Co., Inc., wound up as the owner of only 50 percent of the stock of the successor corporation * * *. Despite the fact that all of the operating assets were carried over to the successor corporation, which continued exactly the same business, in the same location, as had been conducted by the predecessor, the radical shift in stock ownership which occurred precludes us from holding that the transaction amounted to no more than "a mere change in identity, form, or place of organization" within the meaning of section 368(a)(1)(F).

[T]he respondent claims that if we do not find that the transaction in question constitutes an (F) reorganization, then it must qualify as a (D) reorganization.

The requirements of a (D)-type reorganization as pertaining to corporate amalgamations * * * are set forth in two sections of the Code which Congress has explicitly linked together—section 368(a)(1)(D) and section 354(b)(1). In order to qualify as a reorganization under those sections:

(1) There must be a transfer by a corporation of "substantially all" of its assets to another corporation;

(2) Immediately after the transfer the transferor corporation, or one or more of its shareholders, or any combination thereof, must be in control of the transferee; and

(3) All of the remaining property of the transferor as well as all of the stock, securities, and other property acquired by it pursuant to the exchange must be distributed to its shareholders under the plan of reorganization, i.e., there must be a complete liquidation of the transferor.

It is true, as the respondent points out, that the liquidation of a predecessor corporation such as occurred here may represent merely a step incidental to a statutory reorganization.

In the situation here presented it is impossible to view the result as a (D) reorganization because of the conspicuous failure of the transaction to qualify under the "control" requirements of subparagraph (D) and section 368(c). Hyman Berghash, who owned * * * [all the] outstanding shares of the old corporation * * *, acquired only 50 percent of the outstanding common stock of Dorn's Drugs, Inc., Sidney Lettman owning the balance thereof. Berghash's proportionate share of the voting stock of the successor corporation thus falls far short of the 80 percent necessary to satisfy the "control" requirement of section 368(c) and precludes compliance with the statutory tests set forth under subparagraph (D).

* * *

The respondent seeks to have us find that the requisite control existed in Hyman Berghash by totally disregarding Lettman's purchase of 100 shares of Dorn's common stock as being an unrelated step in achieving the end result. If Lettman's purchase of 100 shares of common stock of Dorn's could be ignored, Berghash could be regarded as owning 100 percent of the stock of that corporation. But since the obvious purpose of the entire arrangement was to enable Lettman to acquire a one-half interest in the business of Delavan–Bailey and inasmuch as the parties have stipulated that Lettman actually paid Dorn's $25,000 in cash for the issuance of 100 shares of its common stock, it would be impossible on the record before us to disregard as an unrelated step what appears to be the most critical fact and the paramount purpose of the entire transaction.

The second argument advanced by respondent in support of his position that Hyman Berghash actually acquired control of Dorn's Drugs, Inc., within the meaning of section 368(a)(1)(D) and (c), is that the provision in the agreement executed by the parties on January 29, 1957, under which Berghash had a right to purchase the stock of Lettman in the event he should become dissatisfied with his services as manager or his position as a stockholder or an officer in Dorn's, amounted to the beneficial ownership of Lettman's stock. The respondent thus concludes that we should view Berghash as having effective control of 100 percent of the stock of Dorn's.

If Berghash is to be viewed as the beneficial or constructive owner of the stock of Lettman for purposes of determining control under section 368, it is first essential, assuming the provision in question constitutes an option, to determine whether, under some provision of the 1954 Code, the stock of an optionor is attributable to the option holder. Section 318(a)(3) contains a provision requiring in certain situations the attribution of stock ownership to the holder of an option to acquire such stock. However, section 318(a) expressly provides that that section shall apply only "For purposes of those provisions of this subchapter to which the rules contained in this section are expressly made applicable—".

Section 318 is not expressly made applicable to * * * section 368 * * *. Consequently, the stock attribution rule of section 318(a)(3) * * * is not applicable [in this situation] * * *.

    * * *

In view of the foregoing, * * * we hold that the liquidating distributions of [Delavan–Bailey] * * * are thus taxable to [Berghash] as long-term capital gain under the provisions of section 331(a).

In the absence of a nontaxable reorganization under section 368(a)(1), it is the respondent's final contention that for purposes of determining the applicability of [former] section 337 of the Code there was no complete liquidation of the predecessor corporation within the meaning thereof. He contends that this is so because of the fact that the successor corporation continued to operate exactly the same drugstore, under the same name, and in the same location as previously had been conducted by the old corporation. The respondent claims, without the citation of any authority, that [former] section 337 can apply only where a bona fide termination of the business of the liquidating corporation has occurred.

    * * *

On December 30, 1956, Delavan–Bailey Drug Co., Inc., adopted a plan of complete liquidation * * *. [A]ll of the liquidating sales and distributions took place within the 12–month period beginning on the date of the adoption of the plan of complete liquidation and the transactions complied with the requirements of [former] section 337. We therefore hold that no gain or loss is recognizable to Delavan–Bailey Drug Co., Inc., as a result of the sale in question.

NOTES

1. *Change in stock ownership inconsistent with F reorganization.* It is well established that the F reorganization does not accommodate a transaction that entails a shift in the ownership of a corporation's stock. See Helvering v. Southwest Consol. Corp., 315 U.S. 194, 62 S.Ct. 546 (1942) (transaction involving change in stock ownership is not a "mere change in identity, form or place of organization").

2. *Tax consequences of reorganization.* If the transaction in Berghash had been treated as a reorganization, how would that treatment have impacted on:

(a) the amount of Berghash's income? See I.R.C. § 356(a)(1).

(b) the character of Berghash's income? See I.R.C. § 356(a)(2).

(c) the amount of Delavan–Bailey's income? See I.R.C. § 361(a).

3. *"Control" for nondivisive D reorganization.* Long after the Berghash decision, Congress enacted I.R.C. § 368(a)(2)(H)(i). Under current law, would the transaction in Berghash qualify as a nondivisive D reorganization? See pp. 544–545.

4. *Impact of attribution rules on characterization of boot gain in reorganization.* Long after the Berghash decision, Congress amended I.R.C. § 356(a)(2) by adding the parenthetical language "determined with the application of section 318(a)". What impact, if any, does that amendment have on the tax consequences of a transaction like that executed in the Berghash case? See I.R.C. § 318(a)(4).

5. *Leveraged buyout.* The Berghash case illustrates a relatively primitive "leveraged buyout", an acquisition financed by borrowing against the assets of the acquired business. Leveraged buyouts became quite popular in the late 1900's when the buyers of a business often financed the bulk of the purchase price by borrowing against the assets of the business. These buyers expected to be able to generate sufficient income from the acquired assets to service the substantial indebtedness incurred to fund the acquisition. If sufficient income was generated, the buyers acquired ownership of a substantial business by investing a relatively small amount of their own capital. If the business faltered under the weight of its debts, the buyers only lost the relatively small amount of capital invested.

Smothers v. United States

United States Court of Appeals, Fifth Circuit, 1981.
642 F.2d 894.

■ Before WISDOM, GARZA and REAVLEY, CIRCUIT JUDGES.

WISDOM, CIRCUIT JUDGE:

* * *

I.

[J].E. and Doris Smothers * * * organized Texas Industrial Laundries of San Antonio, Inc. (TIL) [and] owned all of its outstanding stock * * *. TIL engaged in the business of renting industrial uniforms and other industrial cleaning equipment * * *. It owned its own laundry equipment as well.

Shortly after the incorporation of TIL, the taxpayers organized another corporation, Industrial Uniform Services, Inc. (IUS), specifically to oppose a particular competitor in the San Antonio industrial laundry market. The taxpayers owned all of the stock of IUS * * *. Unlike TIL, IUS did not own laundry equipment; it had to contract with an unrelated company to launder the uniforms it rented to customers. J.E. Smothers personally managed IUS, as well as TIL, but chose not to pay himself a salary from IUS in any of the years of its existence.

IUS evidently succeeded in drawing business away from competing firms, for TIL purchased its main competitor in 1965. IUS continued in business, however, until 1969. On the advice of their accountant, the taxpayers then decided to dissolve IUS and sell all of its non-liquid assets to TIL. On November 1, 1969, IUS adopted a plan of liquidation in compliance with [former] I.R.C. § 337,[9] and on November 30, it sold the following assets to TIL for cash at their fair market value (stipulated to be the same as their book value):

Assets	Amount
Noncompetitive covenant	$ 3,894.60
Fixed assets	491.25
Rental property	18,000.00
Prepaid insurance	240.21
Water deposit	7.50
Total	$22,637.56

* * *

After this sale, IUS promptly distributed its remaining assets to its shareholders, the taxpayers, and then dissolved under Texas law:

---

9. Editor's note. Prior to the repeal of the General Utilities rule in 1986 (see pp. 29–33), former I.R.C. § 337 provided that a corporation that sold its assets after adopting a plan of liquidation and liquidated within one year of adopting the plan generally did not recognize any gains or losses on the asset sale. Former I.R.C. § 337 was repealed in 1986, and the current version of I.R.C. § 337 bears no relationship to the former version.

Assets	Amount
Cash (received from TIL)	$ 22,637.56
Cash (of IUS)	2,003.05
Notes receivable	138,000.00
Accrued interest receivable	35.42
Claim against the State of Texas	889.67
Liabilities assumed	(14,403.35)
Total	$149,162.35

TIL hired all three of IUS's employees immediately after the dissolution, and TIL continued to serve most of IUS's customers.

In computing their federal income tax liability for 1969, the taxpayers treated this distribution by IUS as a distribution in complete liquidation within § 331(a). Accordingly, they reported the difference between the value of the assets they received in that distribution, $149,162.35, and the basis of their IUS stock, $1,000, as long-term capital gain. Upon audit, the IRS recharacterized the transaction between TIL and IUS as a reorganization within § 368(a)(1)(D), and therefore treated the distribution to the taxpayers as equivalent to a dividend under § 356(a)(2). Because IUS had sufficient earnings and profits to cover that distribution, the entire distribution was therefore taxable to the Smothers' at ordinary income rates * * *.

The district court held that the transaction constituted a reorganization and rendered judgment for the IRS.

II.

Subchapter C of the Internal Revenue Code broadly contemplates that the retained earnings of a continuing business carried on in corporate form can be placed in the hands of its shareholders only after they pay a tax on those earnings at ordinary income rates. That general rule is, of course, primarily a consequence of § 301, which taxes dividend distributions as ordinary income. The Code provides for capital gain treatment of corporate distributions in a few limited circumstances, but only when there is either a significant change in relative ownership of the corporation, as in certain redemption transactions, or when the shareholders no longer conduct the business themselves in corporate form, as in true liquidation transactions. The history of Subchapter C in large part has been the story of how Congress, the courts, and the IRS have been called upon to foil attempts by taxpayers to abuse these exceptional provisions. Ingenious taxpayers have repeatedly devised transactions which formally come within these provisions, yet which have the effect of permitting shareholders to withdraw profits at capital gain rates while carrying on a continuing business enterprise in corporate form without substantial change in ownership. This is just such a case.

The transaction in issue here is of the genus known as liquidation-reincorporation, or reincorporation. The common denominator of such transactions is their use of the liquidation provisions of the Code, which permit liquidating distributions to be received at capital gain rates, as a device through which the dividend provisions may be circumvented. Reincorporations come in two basic patterns. In one, the corporation is dissolved and its assets are distributed to its shareholders in liquidation. The shareholders then promptly reincorporate all the assets necessary to the operation of the business, while retaining accumulated cash or other surplus assets. The transaction in this case is of the alternate form. In it, the corporation transfers the assets necessary to its business to another corporation owned by the same shareholders in exchange for securities or, as here, for cash, and then liquidates. If the minimal technical requirements of [former] § 337 are met, as they indisputably were here, the exchange at the corporate level will not result in the recognition of gain by the transferor corporation. If formal compliance with the liquidation provisions were the only necessity, both patterns would enable shareholders to withdraw profits from a continuing corporate business enterprise at capital gain rates by paper shuffling. Unchecked, these reincorporation techniques would eviscerate the dividend provisions of the Code.

That result can be avoided by recharacterizing such transactions, in accordance with their true nature, as reorganizations. A reorganization is, in essence, a transaction between corporations that results merely in "a continuance of the proprietary interests in the continuing enterprise under modified corporate form"—a phrase that precisely describes the effect of a reincorporation. Congress specifically recognized that the throw-off of surplus assets to shareholders in the course of a reorganization can be equivalent to a dividend, and if so, should be taxed as such. §§ 356(a)(1)–(2). The reincorporation transactions described above result in a dividend payment to the shareholders in every meaningful financial sense. The assets retained by the shareholders therefore should be taxed as dividends as long as the transaction can be fitted within the technical requirements of one of the * * * classes of reorganizations recognized by § 368(a)(1).

In general, reincorporation transactions are most easily assimilated into § 368(a)(1)(D) ("D reorganization"), as the IRS attempted to do in this case. A transaction qualifies as a D reorganization only if it meets six statutory requirements:

(1) There must be a transfer by a corporation (§ 368(a)(1)(D));

(2) of substantially all of its assets (§ 354(b)(1)(A));

(3) to a corporation controlled by the shareholders of the transferor corporation, or by the transferor corporation itself (§ 368(a)(1)(D));

(4) in exchange for stock or securities of the transferee corporation (§ 354(a)(1));

(5) followed by a distribution of the stock or securities of the transferee corporation to the transferor's shareholders (§ 354(b)(1)(B));

(6) pursuant to a plan of reorganization (§ 368(a)(1)(D)).

On this appeal, the taxpayers concede that the transaction in issue meets every technical prerequisite for characterization as a D reorganization, except for one. They argue that since the assets sold by IUS to TIL amounted to only 15% of IUS's net worth, TIL did not acquire "substantially all of the assets" of IUS within the meaning of § 354(b)(1)(A).

We hold to the contrary. The words "substantially all assets" are not self-defining. What proportion of a corporation's assets is "substantially all" in this context, and less obviously, what "assets" are to be counted in making this determination, cannot be answered without reference to the structure of Subchapter C. To maintain the integrity of the dividend provisions of the Code, "substantially all assets" in this context must be interpreted as an inartistic way of expressing the concept of "transfer of a continuing business". [I]t is in a sense simply a limited codification of the general nonstatutory "continuity of business enterprise" requirement applicable to all reorganizations.

This interpretation finds support in the history of § 368(a)(1)(D) and § 354(b)(1)(A) * * *. The "substantially all assets" requirement of § 354(b)(1)(A) and the amendment of § 368(a)(1)(D) incorporating that requirement were added * * * [in] 1954 * * * as part of a package of amendments aimed at plugging a different loophole—the bail-out of corporate earnings and profits at capital gains rates through divisive reorganizations. There is no indication that Congress wished to relax the application of the reorganization provisions to reincorporation transactions. Indeed, the committee reports indicate the contrary * * *.

Courts have * * * interpreted the * * * technical conditions for a D reorganization in ways that accomplish the Congressional intent to reach reincorporation transactions. For example, the literal language of § 368(a)(1)(D) and §§ 354(a), 354(b)(1)(B) requires that the transferee corporation "exchange" some of its "stock or securities" for the assets of the transferor, and that those items be "distributed" to the shareholders of the transferor, before a D reorganization can be found. Yet both of those requirements have uniformly been ignored as "meaningless gestures" in the reincorporation context, in which the same shareholders own all the stock of both corporations. Smothers does not even challenge the applicability of that principle here.

Properly interpreted, therefore, the assets looked to when making the "substantially all assets" determination should be * * * only the assets necessary to operate the corporate business—whether or not those assets would appear on a corporate balance sheet * * *. Two errors in particular should be avoided. Inclusion of assets unnecessary to the operation of the business in the "substantially all assets" assessment would open the way for the shareholders of any enterprise to turn dividends into capital gain at will. For example, if we assume that "substantially all" means greater than 90%, then a corporation need only cease declaring dividends and accumulate surplus liquid assets until their value exceeds 10% of the total value of all corporate assets. The shareholders could then transfer the assets actively used in the business to a second corporation owned by them and liquidate the old corporation. Such a liquidating distribution would be a dividend in any meaningful sense, but an interpretation of "substantially all assets" that took surplus assets into account would permit the shareholders to treat it as capital gain * * *. Courts therefore have invariably ignored all surplus assets and have focused on the operating assets of the business—the tangible assets actively used in the business—when making the "substantially all assets" assessment.

Second, exclusion of assets not shown on a balance sheet * * * from the "substantially all assets" assessment would offer an unjustified windfall to the owners of service businesses conducted in corporate form. The most important assets of such a business may be its reputation and the availability of skilled management and trained employees, none of which show up on a standard balance sheet. Other courts have correctly recognized that in appropriate cases those intangible assets alone may constitute substantially all of the corporate assets. Otherwise, for example, a sole legal practitioner who owns nothing but a desk and chair could incorporate himself, accumulate earnings, and then set up a new corporation and liquidate the old at capital gain rates—as long as he is careful to buy a new desk and chair for the new corporation, rather than transferring the old.

When these principles are applied to this case, it is plain that "substantially all of the assets" of IUS were transferred to TIL, and that the transaction as a whole constituted a reorganization. TIL and IUS were both managed and wholly owned by Smothers. By the nature of its business, IUS was wholly a service enterprise * * *. IUS's most important assets—its reputation, sales staff, and the managerial services of Smothers—were all transferred to TIL. TIL rehired all three of IUS's employees immediately after IUS's liquidation, and continued to serve IUS's old customers. The same business enterprise was conducted by the same people under the same ownership, and the only assets removed from corporate solution were accumulated liquid assets unnecessary to the operation of the business. To treat this transaction as other than a reorganization would deny economic reality; to permit Smothers to extract the retained earnings of IUS at capital gain rates would make a mockery of the dividend provisions of the Internal Revenue Code.

We do not perceive ordinary income treatment here to be particularly harsh, or a "tax trap for the unwary". It places the Smothers' only in the position they would have been in if they had extracted the retained earnings of IUS as the Code contemplates they should have—by periodically declaring dividends.

■ GARZA, CIRCUIT JUDGE, dissenting:

After carefully reading the majority's opinion, I find that I must respectfully dissent. Unlike my Brothers, who apparently feel that it is their duty to "plug loopholes", I would remain content in applying the tax law as it reads leaving the United States Congress to deal with the consequences of the tax law as it has been drafted. The only issue before this court on appeal is whether or not IUS transferred "substantially all of its assets" to TIL. Instead of dealing with this straightforward question, the majority has made a case of evil against liquidation-reincorporation abuses and, in an attempt to remedy every such perceived abuse, they have relieved the Congress of its burden to change the law [governing] * * * the "D reorganization" requirements. Essentially, the majority has changed the definition of "substantially all assets" to mean only "necessary operating assets." I believe if Congress had meant "necessary operating assets" it would have said so * * *. In my mind "substantially all" plainly means all of the assets except for an insubstantial amount. Under such a definition, the sale of 15% of IUS's assets to TIL could hardly be defined as "substantially all" of IUS's assets.

However, even after having redefined "substantially all" to mean "necessary operating assets", the IUS liquidation still falls short of the "D reorganization" requirements because the stipulated facts are that absolutely none of the assets sold from IUS to TIL were necessary operating assets for either corporation. Faced with an absence of a proper factual setting, the majority goes on to define necessary operating assets as including a corporation's intangible assets. Now while a sale of intangible assets might be an appropriate consideration in determining whether or not "substantially all" assets of a corporation have been transferred, such a consideration simply has no bearing in this case. All of the assets transferred to TIL were depreciated tangible objects sold at book value after which IUS completely ceased all business operations. There simply was no other transfer of IUS's intangible assets as a continuing business.

The majority has placed great emphasis on the fact that three of IUS's route salesmen were subsequently employed by TIL and that Mr. Smothers' managerial services were available to TIL. Regardless of whether or not these facts enhanced TIL's business, the fact remains that neither the route salesmen or Mr. Smothers' services were transferred as assets from one corporation to another. After IUS ceased business its route salesmen were free to seek any employment they desired. Likewise, Mr. Smothers was never obligated to perform services for TIL. From these facts I cannot agree that there was a transfer of a continuing business. The majority imputes adverse tax consequences to IUS's stockholders simply because TIL offered new employment to the route salesmen who were unemployed upon cessation of IUS's business operations. The majority places future stockholders, in Mr. Smothers' position, of choosing between unfavorable tax consequences and helping secure future employment to loyal and deserving employees whom otherwise would be unemployed.

Although the Internal Revenue Service has never questioned the bona fides of IUS's liquidation, the majority has gone beyond the stipulated facts by characterizing the liquidation as a tax avoidance scam. I simply cannot agree. After starting from scratch, Mr. Smothers worked for over a dozen years refraining from drawing salary in order that IUS could pay its taxes, employees and other operating expenses and in order for IUS to become a successful self-sustaining business enterprise. Mr. Smothers was successful but, now that he no longer could devote his service to IUS, his years of labor are now labeled by the majority as a mere "paper shuffle." I do not share the majority's attitude.

* * *

[I] do not believe that taxpayers or the tax laws are served by upholding an IRS deficiency for the sole purpose of "plugging loopholes."

NOTES

1. *F reorganization.* The appeal in Smothers does not indicate whether the IRS endeavored to treat the transaction as an F reorganization. Would the Smothers court have rejected F reorganization treatment for the same reason it was rejected by the Berghash court? Subsequent to the Smothers decision, Congress amended I.R.C. § 368(a)(1)(F) by adding the language "of one corporation" to the definition of an F reorganization. Under current law, could the statutory definition of an F reorganization be satisfied by the transaction,

    (a) in Smothers?

    (b) in Berghash?

2. *Tax consequences of sale/liquidation versus reorganization.* Under current law, what would be the tax consequences to Smothers and to IUS if the transaction in the Smothers case were treated as,

    (a) a sale of assets followed by a liquidation of IUS?

    (b) a D reorganization?

3. *Taxpayer's preference under current law.* Under current law, would taxpayers normally prefer to have a sale of assets followed by a liquidation taxed as a reorganization or not? See I.R.C. §§ 336, 361. When taxpayers desire reorganization treatment under these circumstances, can the statutory amendments and judicial decisions that enabled the government to treat purported liquidations as D reorganizations be used against the government? See the case that follows.

Warsaw Photographic Associates, Inc. v. Commissioner

United States Tax Court, 1985.
84 T.C. 21.

■ CHABOT, JUDGE:

FINDINGS OF FACT

    * * *

From 1935 or earlier, Warsaw Studios, Inc. (hereinafter sometimes referred to as "Studios"), and its predecessors were engaged actively in the commercial photography business. Studios was so engaged until July 2, 1973 * * *.

A certificate of incorporation for Studios was filed with the New York Department of State on June 30, 1964 * * *. By * * * amendment filed June 30, 1965, Studios increased the number of its authorized shares by 5,250 shares, making the aggregate number of authorized shares 15,500. This amendment further provides that 15,000 of these shares are common shares with $1 par value. The remaining 500 shares are cumulative preferred with $1,000 par value. The cumulative dividends are at the rate of 3% annually * * *.

As of July 1, 1965, Studios had 325 outstanding shares of preferred stock, which had a total par value of $325,000. Warsaw & Co., Inc., a corporation owned solely by J. J. Warsaw, was the record owner of all of Studios' preferred stock.

[On June 29, 1973,] Studios' common stock was owned as set forth in Table 1.

Table 1

Owner	Number of Common Shares
Warsaw & Co., Inc.	7,549
William J. Zad	375
Stephen Neil	250
Gilbert S. Shawn	250
Donald Riley	200
John Basilion	162
James V. Oliver	142
Joseph G. Lewandowski	134
David Martin	128
Richard Dennis	175
Winfield S. Sinn, Jr.	92

* * *

[All the individual] Studios' shareholders [sometimes referred to collectively as "the 10 shareholders"] were also employees of Studios * * *.

Studios leased office space at two locations in Manhattan, New York. One of these locations was in a building known as * * * 40 East 34th Street * * * (hereinafter sometimes referred to as "the 34th Street lease") * * *.

* * *

The other office space location was in a building known as 36 East 31st Street * * * (hereinafter sometimes referred to as "the 31st Street lease") * * *.

* * *

[The 10 shareholders] thought that Studios could be made profitable if it could get out of the 34th Street lease which [they] considered "debilitating" and if the number of employees could be reduced. [They] obtained legal advice on how to do this.

Acting on legal advice, the 10 shareholders decided to organize a new corporation. On June 29, 1973, a corporation was incorporated under New York law under the name of Pegasus Studio, Ltd. Three days later, on July 2, 1973, the directors and shareholders of this corporation met and unanimously approved a resolution to amend the certificate of incorporation to change the corporation's name to Warsaw Photographic Associates, Inc. (This corporation is the petitioner in the instant case.) * * * Each of the 10 shareholders subscribed to and paid for 100 shares of common stock * * * $100 per share, or a total price of $10,000 * * *. The total number of shares issued on petitioner's incorporation was 1,000 shares (hereinafter sometimes referred to as "the 1,000 shares"), for a total capital of $100,000.

* * *

[P]etitioner adopted a plan whereby Studios was to transfer all of its operating assets to petitioner. In connection with this plan, the 10 shareholders, who were also shareholders of Studios, were to each receive directly ten additional shares of petitioner's common stock.

On June 27, 1973, Studios' board of directors held a special meeting at which they adopted a plan of reorganization. Studios' directors understood the reorganization to involve a transfer of substantially all of its assets to petitioner and the issuance by petitioner of 100 shares of its stock (hereinafter sometimes referred to as "the 100 shares") directly to the 10 shareholders. Studios' understanding of "substantially all of its assets" is the same as petitioner's understanding of all of Studios' operating assets. As part of this plan, the 10 shareholders were to surrender their stock in Studios for cancellation.

On July 2, 1973, Studios and petitioner entered into a written agreement of "REORGANIZATION, SALE and PURCHASE" * * *.

* * *

Studios transferred to petitioner the assets to fully equip ten photography studios, as well as assets used in Studios' bookkeeping office, fitting rooms, carpentry shop, storage center, and shipping room * * *.

The value of the assets to be transferred by Studios was discussed among and negotiated by the executive employees of Studios, some of whom were also shareholders of petitioner. [The] president of both Studios and petitioner wrote a letter, dated July 2, 1973, to Studios' counsel confirming that in his opinion $20,000 for all of Studios' equipment was fair to both parties * * *.

* * *

Studios contracted with petitioner to also transfer its goodwill. In the negotiations leading to the transaction between petitioner and Studios, the focus was not on the goodwill or going-concern value of Studios' business. Studios' creditors could not have forced Studios' employees to continue to work for Studios. Seventy-five of Studios' 126 employees were hired by petitioner when Studios transferred the assets to petitioner.

Studios assigned all its right, title, and interest in the 31st Street leases but did not assign its right, title, and interest in the 34th Street lease.

Petitioner agreed to complete Studios' work in progress and assume Studios' liabilities to customers in connection with this work * * *. Studios kept its computer and telephones, as well as cash and accounts receivable to be used to pay its creditors.

On or about July 17, 1973, the lessor under the 34th Street lease sued on account of Studios' nonpayment of the July 1973 rent under this lease.

On July 23, 1973, Studios made a general assignment for the benefit of creditors. The assignee, Stanley S. Horvath (hereinafter sometimes referred to as "Horvath"), did not try to set aside Studios' transfer of assets to petitioner, because Horvath believed that petitioner had paid fair consideration for these assets. Horvath has not made any payments to Studios' creditors or to Warsaw & Company, Inc., the owner of all the outstanding preferred stock and 7,549 shares of the outstanding common stock.

On or about March 20, 1975, Studios filed its Federal corporate income tax return for its taxable year ending June 30, 1973. On this tax return, Studios claimed a net operating loss of $262,727. On or about March 20, 1975, Studios filed its tax return for the short period July 1 through July 24, 1973. On this tax return, Studios claimed a net operating loss of $101,221 which, when added to the previous year's loss made a total of $363,948. On or about March 17, 1975, petitioner filed its tax return for its taxable year 1974, on which it deducted this $363,948.

* * *

OPINION

* * *

Ordinarily, a corporation is a separate entity for Federal income tax purposes; its tax attributes are not combined with those of its shareholders or other corporations. One of the major exceptions to this normal rule is part of the complex of provisions relating to corporate reorganizations, in particular that part of the complex that allows a corporation to use for income tax purposes certain parts of the income tax history of another corporation.

Corporate reorganizations * * * qualify for special treatment for Federal income tax purposes under certain rules. The dispute in the instant case is as to whether petitioner is entitled to the special treatment provided under two of these rules. One of these rules gives a transferee corporation a carryover basis (subject to certain adjustments) in the assets acquired from the transferor corporation. Section 362(b). The other of these rules allows the transferee corporation to "succeed to and take into account" certain tax attributes of the transferor, including net operating loss carryovers (the tax attribute in issue in the instant case). Sections 381(a) and 381(c).

Of the various definitions of corporate reorganization, the parties have apparently limited the controversy to whether the transaction qualifies as a nondivisive D reorganization. Section 368(a)(1)(D) * * *.

In order to qualify as a nondivisive D reorganization (and thus, permit petitioner to (1) use Studios' bases for calculating depreciation and (2) under sections 368(a)(1)(D) and 354, deduct Studios' net operating losses), the transaction in the instant case must satisfy a series of statutory requirements and also a series of judicial requirements.

Respondent contends that the transfer from Studios to petitioner does not qualify as a nondivisive D reorganization because it does not satisfy certain of the statutory and judicial requirements. Instead, respondent contends, the transfer of assets from Studios to petitioner is a sale. Respondent maintains that the transaction does not satisfy the statutory requirement that stock of the transferee corporation (i.e., petitioner) be issued and distributed in the purported reorganization. Respondent also maintains that the transaction does not satisfy the judicial requirement of continuity of interest. Specifically, respondent asserts that the continuity of interest requirement is not satisfied because either (1) "the preferred shareholder [Warsaw & Co., Inc.] had the proprietary interest in [Studios]" and did not continue an interest in petitioner, or (2) the minority shareholders who did continue an interest "had too small a proprietary interest in [Studios]."

Petitioner contends that the transaction between Studios and petitioner qualifies as a nondivisive D reorganization because it satisfies all the statutory and judicial requirements. In particular, petitioner contends that the 100 shares were given as consideration for Studios' assets and that the 100 shares were worth at least $42,727, far more than the $21,000 of cash and other property transferred by petitioner to Studios. Petitioner further contends that the fact that the 100 shares were issued directly to the 10 shareholders, rather than first to Studios and then distributed from Studios to the 10 shareholders, does not mean that petitioner's stock was not distributed within the meaning of section 354(b)(1)(B). Petitioner also asserts that the continuity of interest requirement is satisfied. In making this assertion, petitioner further contends that the proper test for applying the continuity of interest test is whether the stock of the transferee corporation (petitioner) represents a substantial part of the consideration given in the transaction and not whether a certain percentage of historic shareholders of the transferor continue as shareholders of the transferee.

We agree with respondent that the transaction is not a D reorganization because of the failure to satisfy the statutory requirement that petitioner's stock be distributed in a transaction which qualifies under section 354.

In order for a transaction to be a D reorganization, the transaction must be one "which qualifies under section 354 * * *." (Sec. 368(a)(1)(D)). In order for petitioner to succeed to Studios' net operating losses under a D reorganization, Studios must have received stock of petitioner and Studios must have distributed the stock it thus received (Secs. 354(a)(1) and 354(a)(1)(B)). The July 2, 1973, agreement between petitioner and Studios provides * * * that, as part of the consideration flowing from petitioner to Studios, "The Buyer is hereby issuing 10 shares of Common Stock * * * of the Buyer to each of the shareholders of the Seller other than Warsaw & Co., Inc. who are the only shareholders of the buyer." There was not literally a transfer of petitioner's stock from petitioner to Studios and a distribution of this stock by Studios to Studios' shareholders. Accordingly, we conclude that the statute's formal requirements have not been met in this regard.

It is true that we have repeatedly held that, when the stock ownership of transferor and transferee is identical, the actual distribution would be a mere formality and the statute [section 368(a)(1)(D)] may be satisfied without it. However, in the instant case, the stock ownerships of petitioner and Studios were not identical. Warsaw & Co., Inc., which owned about 80 percent of Studios' common stock and all of Studios' preferred stock, was not a shareholder in petitioner. The 10 shareholders, each holding 10 percent of petitioner's shares, had differing holdings in Studios * * *. Indeed, apart from Shawn and Neil (each holding 250 shares) none of the 10 shareholders held the same number of Studios' shares as any of the others among the 10 shareholders (see Table 1 * * * supra), even though all were equal shareholders in petitioner.

Thus, the instant case does not qualify for the one exception that the courts have created regarding the stock transfer and distribution rule. Compliance with this rule is essential for the net operating loss carryover benefit sought by petitioner (secs. 381(a)(2) and 354(b)(1)(B)) and the carryover basis benefit sought by petitioner (secs. 362(b), 368(a)(1)(D), and 354(b)(1)(B)). Accordingly, we conclude that petitioner is entitled to use neither of the tax benefits it seeks to carry over from Studios.

On brief, petitioner makes the following contention regarding the stock transfer and distribution requirement:

> Code section 354(b)(1)(B) requires that all properties of the transferor corporation must be distributed in pursuance of the plan of reorganization. This provision is satisfied whenever, pursuant to the plan of reorganization, the shareholders of the transferor receive shares of the transferee sufficient to satisfy the control requirements of Code section 368(a)(1)(D). A direct issuance of shares of the transferee corporation to shareholders of the transferor corporation will suffice. An actual exchange of the transferor corporation's assets for shares of the transferee corporation, followed by a distribution of those shares to the transferor corporation's shareholders is not required. Where as in the case at bar the acquiring corporation issues stock directly to the shareholders of the transferor corporation in consideration of the assets received from the transferor corporation, the transfer is treated as if the shares were first issued to the transferor corporation and then distributed in redemption of the outstanding shares of the transferor corporation.

[The court discusses the cases relied on by petitioner in which the requirements of an actual stock transfer and distribution were ignored.]

All of [the] authorities on which petitioner relies are distinguishable from the instant case in that the transferors and transferees in those instances had identical ownership, while in the instant case the ownership interests in petitioner and Studios differed widely. Further, in each of the cases in which a court has held that the requirement of an actual stock transfer and distribution may be ignored, it was respondent who urged on the court that the realities of the situation belied the form chosen by the taxpayer. In those situations where the courts have departed from the literal language of the statute, it was to counter a perceived abuse by the taxpayer, these courts having concluded that the taxpayer should not be permitted to shape the form of the transaction so as to secure an unwarranted benefit. We have not found, and petitioner has not cited * * * any case in this area in which the court has acceded to a taxpayer's urging that the taxpayer be permitted to obtain a D reorganization tax benefit even though the form of the transaction which the taxpayer shaped did not meet the literal requirements of the statute.

Petitioner contends that the "transaction in form and in substance qualified as a reorganization described in Code section 368(a)(1)(D)". Petitioner states that the transaction, and Studios' subsequent assignment for benefit of creditors, were designed as a convenient way to shed a burdensome obligation (i.e., the 34th Street lease) * * *.

We have already concluded that the transaction failed to satisfy one of the formal statutory requirements of section 368(a)(1)(D) * * *.

When we examine the substance of what was done, we conclude that it points toward "sale" at least as much as toward "reorganization". Ten people put up an aggregate of $100,000 to acquire and bankroll a going business. The business had suffered substantial losses. The 10 shareholders trimmed the work force and avoided the burdens of an unfavorable lease, and apparently succeeded in reviving the business. The 10 shareholders had owned about 20 percent of the old corporation's common stock and none of its preferred. If they had purchased the remaining common stock or a controlling interest, then * * * the corporation's tax characteristics would not be affected by the substance of the change in ownership and control. Apparently for a legitimate business reason (escaping from the burdens of the 34th Street lease), the 10 shareholders specifically turned down an opportunity to buy the old corporation, thus turning down the simple route toward retention of the old corporation's tax attributes.

If the 10 shareholders (or petitioner, their new corporation) had merely purchased Studios' assets, then the transaction would be a sale, the normal tax rules would apply (i.e., petitioner would not be entitled to use Studios' tax attributes) even though petitioner carried on the business that Studios had carried on and did so with essentially the same work force at the "same old stand".

What, in these circumstances, is the matter of substance that distinguishes the transaction from a sale? Petitioner contends that the issuance of the 100 shares is an element of substance that (1) enables the transaction to satisfy the statutory requirement of stock distribution [and] (2) enables the transaction to satisfy the judicial requirement that its stock be a substantial part of the consideration given by it * * *.

After examining the transaction with care in light of petitioner's contentions, we note the following:

Firstly, the 100 shares effected no change, not even a subtle one, in the positions of the 10 shareholders. Each of the 10 shareholders merely had one extra piece of paper. No one involved in the transaction—not petitioner, Studios, the 10 shareholders, Warsaw & Co., Inc., or J. J. Warsaw—were any richer or any poorer on account of the issuance of the 100 shares, than they would have been if no shares were issued or if 1,000,000 shares were issued.

Secondly, care was taken to be sure that the 100 shares were not held by Studios at any time. This element is of some significance because Studios made a general assignment for the benefit of creditors only 3 weeks after the transaction in dispute, and the assignee was not able to find assets to make any payments to the creditors.

Thirdly, although the 100 shares were supposed to be issued to the 10 shareholders in their capacities as Studios' shareholders, they were issued in proportion to the 10 shareholders' ownership of petitioner and not in proportion to the 10 shareholders' ownership of Studios.

* * *

On answering brief, petitioner tells us that "[t]axation is a practical art; labels will not replace or substitute for judgment as to the roles played by the parties and whether or not those roles were acted out in such a way as to effect a reorganization described by the Internal Revenue Code". We agree. We conclude that, as a practical matter, the appearance of the 100 shares in the transaction provides only a smell of reorganization. We will not speculate as to why the July 2, 1973, agreement provided for the issuance of the 100 shares in such a manner that their issuance satisfies neither the form nor the substance of section 368(a)(1)(D). We conclude that the 100 shares did not constitute any part of petitioner's consideration for the assets, tangible or intangible, that petitioner received from Studios * * *.

NOTES

1. *Transfer of tax attributes in reorganization.* Why did the taxpayers want the transaction in the Warsaw case to qualify as a reorganization? See I.R.C. §§ 362(b), 381(a), (c)(1). Recall that even when an acquisition is within the scope of I.R.C. § 381, the ability of an acquiring corporation to utilize the target's net operating losses may be restricted by various other provisions of the Code. See, e.g., I.R.C. §§ 269, 382; pp. 646–669.

2. *F reorganization.* Could the transaction in Warsaw qualify as an F reorganization under current law?

3. *Deference to precedent.* Would the transaction in Warsaw have qualified as a D reorganization if the Warsaw court had deferred to the precedent established when the government was asserting D reorganization treatment? Is the Warsaw court's position that precedent should be accorded a different degree of deference depending on whether the government or the taxpayer is asserting reorganization treatment defensible? Is this merely a manifestation of the rule that the taxpayer must accept the consequences of a chosen form?

4. *Taxpayer motivation.* Now that dividends are taxed at capital gains rates, would you expect taxpayers to be more or less motivated to exploit the liquidation/reincorporation jurisprudence resulting from the government's past efforts to expand the doctrine?

3. Conversion to Limited Liability Company

IRS Letter Ruling 9701029

10/2/96.

[X is a Delaware corporation.] X's outstanding stock is owned by five domestic corporations (collectively, the Owners). The Owners will form LLC, a limited liability company under Delaware's Limited Liability Company Act (the Act), by contributing an aggregate of b dollars to LLC in exchange for interests in LLC's profits and losses. The Owners' contributions to and interests in LLC will be proportionate to their relative interests in X.

Shortly after LLC's formation, X and LLC will enter into an Agreement of Merger under the Act, merging X into LLC, with LLC surviving. As a result of the merger, LLC will succeed to all of X's property, assets, and liabilities.

[LLC will be treated as a partnership for federal income tax purposes under § 7701(a)(2).]

Based solely upon the information submitted and the representations made, we conclude that:

(1) For federal income tax purposes, X's statutory merger into LLC pursuant to Delaware law will be treated as (i) a transfer by X of its assets to LLC in exchange for LLC's assumption of X's liabilities and X's receipt of Ownership Interests, followed by (ii) a distribution of the Ownership Interests to the Owners in complete liquidation of X within the meaning of § 331.

(2) Pursuant to § 722, X's basis in the Ownership Interests received pursuant to the merger shall equal the adjusted basis of X's assets at the time of contribution.

(3) No gain or loss will result to X or LLC upon X's contribution of its assets to LLC in exchange for Ownership Interests under § 721.

(4) X will recognize gain or loss on the distribution of the Ownership Interests to the Owners in complete liquidation as if X had sold the distributed Ownership Interests to the Owners at their fair market value at the time of the distribution [pursuant to § 336(a)].

(5) The property distributed by X to each Owner in complete liquidation will be treated as full payment in exchange for the Owner's X stock within the meaning of § 331(a). Gain or loss will be recognized

by each Owner equal to the difference between (i) the fair market value of the Ownership Interest received by each Owner in exchange for the Owner's X stock and (ii) the Owner's adjusted basis in the X stock.

(6) The basis of the Ownership Interest received by each Owner upon X's complete liquidation will be the Ownership Interest's fair market value determined at the time of the distribution [pursuant to § 334(a)].

* * *

NOTES

1. *Mitigating double tax on conversion of corporation to limited liability company.* It is often extremely expensive to convert a C Corporation to a limited liability company taxed as a partnership due to the double tax triggered by the conversion. Under what circumstances might the corporate tax resulting from such a conversion be insignificant? See I.R.C. §§ 172, 1212(a). Under what circumstances might the shareholder tax resulting from such a conversion be insignificant? See I.R.C. §§ 1014, 1212(b).

2. *State merger laws can apply to limited liability companies.* Historically, state merger laws applied only to corporations. In recent years, however, many states have expanded the scope of their merger laws to encompass limited liability companies. As a result, the transaction described in IRS Letter Ruling 9701029 qualified as a merger under state law. Why did the transaction fail to qualify as a "reorganization" for Federal income tax purposes? See Treas. Reg. § 1.368–2(b)(1).

3. *Election to tax limited liability company as a corporation.* An unincorporated enterprise with at least two owners is generally taxed as a partnership unless the enterprise elects to be taxed as a corporation. Treas. Reg. § 301.7701–3. If the limited liability company in IRS Letter Ruling 9701029 had elected to be taxed as a corporation, could the transaction have qualified as a "reorganization" for Federal income tax purposes? Why is it generally disadvantageous for a limited liability company to elect to be taxed as a corporation?

4. *Merger of corporation into limited liability company with single corporate member.* An unincorporated entity with a single owner is generally disregarded as an entity separate from its owner. Treas. Reg. § 301.7701–3. If a corporation is merged into a limited liability company whose sole member is another corporation, can the merger qualify as a "reorganization" for Federal income tax purposes? See the private letter ruling that follows.

IRS Letter Ruling 200236005

5/23/02.

This letter responds to your authorized representative's letter dated December 4, 2001, in which you requested rulings under section 368 of the Internal Revenue Code.

Acquiring [is] a State X corporation. Acquiring has outstanding a single class of common stock which is publicly traded. Acquiring is engaged in Business Y.

Disregarded Entity is a newly formed, State X limited liability company that is wholly-owned by Acquiring. Disregarded Entity is treated as a disregarded entity for Federal tax purposes. Disregarded Entity has been organized for the sole purpose of effecting the proposed transaction.

Target [is] a State X corporation. Target has outstanding a single class of common stock which is publicly traded on Market. Target is engaged in Business Z.

For what are represented as valid business reasons, Acquiring and Target have proposed the following transaction: Under State X General Corporation Law and the State X Limited Liability Company Act, Target will be merged with and into Disregarded Entity, with Disregarded Entity surviving (the "Merger"). Disregarded Entity will acquire all of the assets and assume all of the liabilities of Target. Target shareholders will be entitled to receive a% of a share of Acquiring common stock in exchange for each share of Target common stock.

The following representations have been made in connection with the proposed transactions.

a. The fair market value of Acquiring stock and other consideration, if any, received by each Target shareholder will be approximately equal to the fair market value of the shares of Target stock surrendered in the exchange.

b. At least 50% of the proprietary interest in Target will be exchanged for stock of Acquiring and will have been preserved within the meaning of Treas. Reg. section 1.368–1(e).

c. In connection with the potential reorganization, neither Acquiring, nor any person related to Acquiring (within the meaning of Treas. Reg. section 1.368–1(e)(3)) has any plan or intention to reacquire any Acquiring stock issued in the transaction in exchange for any consideration other than Acquiring stock.

d. Acquiring does not have any plan or intention to sell or otherwise dispose of any of the assets of Target acquired in the transaction, except for dispositions made in the ordinary course of business or transfers described in section 368(a)(2)(C) of the Code or described in Treas. Reg. section 1.368–2(k).

e. The liabilities of Target assumed by Acquiring and the liabilities to which the transferred assets of Target are subject were incurred by Target in the ordinary course of its business.

f. Following the transaction, Acquiring will continue the historic business of Target or use a significant portion of Target's historic business assets in its business.

g. Acquiring, Target, and the shareholders of Target will pay their respective expenses, if any, incurred in connection with the transaction.

* * *

[h.] Disregarded Entity is a domestic single member limited liability company which is a "disregarded entity" within the meaning of proposed regulation section 1.368–2(b)(1)(i)(A).

Based solely on the information submitted and the representations made, we hold that:

(1) Provided that the merger of Target into Disregarded Entity qualifies as a statutory merger in accordance with applicable state law, the proposed merger of Target into Disregarded Entity will qualify as a statutory merger as that term is used in section 368(a)(1)(A) of the Code, and the transaction will constitute a reorganization within the meaning of section 368(a)(1)(A).

* * *

This ruling is directed only to the taxpayer(s) requesting it. Section 6110(k)(3) of the Code provides that it may not be used or cited as precedent.

NOTE

Merger of corporation into single-member limited liability company and vice versa. Subsequent to the issuance of the letter ruling, regulations were promulgated confirming that the merger of Target into a single-member LLC owned by Acquiring can qualify as a reorganization. See Treas. Reg. §§ 1.368–2(b)(1)(ii), (iii) Example 2. Rather than merging the Target into a single-member LLC owned by Acquiring, could the merger of a single-member LLC of the Target into Acquiring qualify as a reorganization? See Treas. Reg. §§ 1.368–2(b)(1)(ii), (iii) Example 6. Why do the outcomes of these two cases differ?

INDEX

807

†